ANESTHESIOLOGY
REVIEW
A COMPREHENSIVE Q&A GUIDE

FIRST EDITION

Authors:

Ivan Keser, MD[1]
Admir Hadzic, MD, PhD[2,3]

Contributors:

Jirka Cops, MSc, PhD[4] | Darren Jacobs, MSc[4]
Jill Vanhaeren, MSc[4] | Stien Beyens, MSc[4]
Catherine Vandepitte, MD, PhD[3] | Leander Mancel, MD[3]
Laurens Peene, MD[3] | Angela Lucia Balocco, MD[5]
Ana Lopez Gutiérrez, MD, PhD[3] | Imré Van Herreweghe, MD[3]
Walter Staelens, MD[3] | Sarah Shiba, MD[3] | William Aerts, MD[3]

[1] Specialist in anesthesiology and resuscitation
General Hospital Dr. Abdulah Nakaš, Sarajevo, B&H
[2] Ex-professor Columbia University, New York, USA
[3] Anesthesiology, Ziekenhuis Oost-Limburg, Genk, Belgium
[4] NYSORA, New York, Belgium
[5] Anesthesiology, University Hospital Leuven, Belgium

NYSORA© PRESS

Publishing Division of NYSORA, Inc
2585 Broadway, suite 183, New York, NY10025
info@nysora.com, www.nysora.com

Anesthesiology Review: A Comprehensive Q&A Guide

The Anesthesiology Review features an unparalleled collection of more than 1,800 questions, meticulously crafted from 312 specific topics that span the entire spectrum of anesthesiology practice. Each question challenges and expands the reader's understanding, ensuring a solid grasp of both fundamental concepts and advanced techniques. The questions cover the entire field of Anesthesiology, providing a 360-degree view of the field.

What sets this guide apart is its adherence to the latest published information, ensuring that readers are not only preparing with comprehensive content but are also up to date with the most current standards and practices in anesthesiology.

Each question has been written and reviewed by NYSORA's team of International experts and passionate educators, guaranteeing an unmatched level of precision and expertise. A rationale for the best answer with every question enhances the learning experience, allowing readers to understand not just the 'what,' but the 'why' behind each answer, fostering deeper learning and retention.

"Anesthesiology Review" is not just another question book; it is the most comprehensive text available for the review of anesthesia, tailored for both oral and written board examinations. The international contributors of this volume assure that the content is globally applicable, no matter where in the world you study or practice anesthesiology.

The creation of this guide was driven by a clear recognition of the void in anesthesiology education - a need for a resource that is not only exhaustive and authoritative but also engaging and accessible. "Anesthesiology Review" fills this void, offering a single, reliable source for comprehensive review and learning.

In summary, "Anesthesiology Review: A Comprehensive Q&A Guide" by NYSORA is more than just a book; it is a pivotal educational tool that promises to transform how anesthesiology is learned and practiced. It stands as a testament to NYSORA's commitment to advancing the field of anesthesiology through education, ensuring that both current and future generations of anesthesiologists are equipped with the knowledge and skills to excel in their practice.

Dedication

This book is dedicated to the students and practitioners of anesthesiology, whose unwavering commitment to patient care inspires us every day.

Foreword

In modern medicine, anesthesiology stands as a testament to the incredible advancements and nuanced understanding of human physiology and pharmacology. It is a field that demands not only a deep reservoir of knowledge but also the ability to apply this knowledge with precision and care. Recognizing the critical role anesthesiologists play in patient care, we saw the need for a resource that could both challenge and support these dedicated professionals at every stage of their careers.

"Anesthesiology Review: A Comprehensive Q&A Guide" is the culmination of years of NYSORA's dedication to education. Crafted by the esteemed international team at NYSORA, this guide is designed to be an indispensable tool for both the aspiring student and the seasoned practitioner of anesthesiology. Our goal was to create a resource that not only prepares individuals for the rigors of board examinations but also updates and enriches their understanding and practice of anesthesiology.

The journey through the pages of this book is one of discovery, challenge, and, ultimately, mastery. Each question and answer has been carefully selected to reflect the core principles and the cutting-edge advancements in the field. The depth and breadth of content presented here will inspire a new generation of anesthesiologists to strive for excellence.

As you embark on this journey, remember that the path to mastery is a lifelong pursuit. It is our hope that "Anesthesiology Review" will be a trusted companion along the way, providing clarity, insight, and the joy of discovery. To all who seek to deepen their knowledge and enhance their practice of anesthesiology, this book is for you. It is the most up-to-date review available!

Let the journey begin.

With warm regards,
Drs. Keser and Hadzic.

Acknowledgments

As we reflect on the journey that led to the creation of "Anesthesiology Review: A Comprehensive Q&A Guide," we are filled with gratitude for the many individuals and teams whose dedication, expertise, and support made this book possible. First and foremost, we extend our heartfelt thanks to the NYSORA fellows, whose commitment to excellence and innovation in anesthesiology has been a constant source of inspiration. Your contributions have been invaluable, and this book is a testament to your hard work and dedication.

We also wish to acknowledge the tireless efforts of NYSORA's scientific and educational teams. Your passion for advancing the field of anesthesiology through rigorous research and high-quality education has been the backbone of this project. Your insights and expertise have shaped this guide into a resource that will benefit countless learners and practitioners.

A special note of appreciation goes to NYSORA's design office, led by Nenad Markovic. Your creativity and attention to detail have brought the pages of this book to life, making complex concepts accessible and engaging. Your work has not only enhanced the aesthetic appeal of this guide but has also significantly contributed to its educational value.

We are also grateful to the entire NYSORA and VisionExpo teams for your unwavering support and collaboration. Finally, many thanks to NYSORA huge community whose feedback on many aspects of the Anesthesia Review shaped this project into one of the most comprehensive updates in anesthesiology in this format, up-to-date.

Our families deserve a special acknowledgment. Your understanding, patience, and support have been our foundation throughout the countless hours spent away from you, grinding away on this book. Your sacrifices have not gone unnoticed, and we are eternally grateful for your love and encouragement.

Lastly, NYSORA thanks and recognizes Dr. Ivan Kesser, MD, for his emerging leadership in the field of anesthesiology and pain medicine education. In closing, we offer our sincere thanks to everyone who has supported this project, directly or indirectly. Your collective efforts have made this monumental undertaking possible.

The NYSORA TEAM.

Notice / Disclaimer

The practice of medicine is continuously changing. The authors and the publisher of this work have checked with sources believed to be reliable in their efforts to provide information that is in line with the available standards at the time of publication. However, in view of the possibility of human error or changes in medical practice, neither the authors, the publisher, nor any other party who has been involved in the preparation or publication of this work warrants that the information contained herein is accurate or complete. Likewise, they disclaim all responsibility for any errors omissions, or results obtained from the use of the information contained in this work. Users of the work are encouraged to corroborate the information contained herein with other sources. Readers are also advised to check the current product information for the equipment used for anesthesia to be certain that the information contained in this work is accurate. Furthermore, medical practitioners must adhere to the protocols and guidelines established in their respective practices or hospitals, as these may vary and take precedence over general recommendations. The authors advise the readers to fact-check the accuracy of the information and use their own.

Library of Congress Identification

Authors:
Ivan Keser, MD
Prof. Admir Hadzic, MD, PhD

Contributors:
Jirka Cops, MSc, PhD
Darren Jacobs, MSc
Jill Vanhaeren, MSc
Stien Beyens, MSc
Catherine Vandepitte, MD, PhD
Leander Mancel, MD
Laurens Peene, MD
Angela Lucia Balocco, MD
Ana Lopez Gutiérrez, MD, PhD
Imré Van Herreweghe, MD
Walter Staelens, MD
Sarah Shiba, MD
William Aerts, MD

Title: **Anesthesiology Review: A Comprehensive Q&A Guide**
First Edition, 2024.

Identifiers:
Library of Congress Control Number: 2024906952
ISBN 979-8-9899218-1-2

Table of Contents

Introduction

Welcome to "Anesthesiology Review: A Comprehensive Q&A Guide", an educational resource meticulously designed to support and challenge both students and practitioners in the field of anesthesiology. This book represents a unique collaboration among some of the brightest minds in anesthesiology under the auspices of the NYSORA's Educational and Scientific teams. Our aim is to provide a comprehensive, engaging, and up-to-date tool that will not only prepare you for board examinations but also deepen your understanding and enhance your practice in this critical medical specialty.

Anesthesiology is a field that requires a profound understanding of physiology, pharmacology, and patient safety, alongside the ability to make rapid, informed decisions. Recognizing the complexity and breadth of knowledge required, we have compiled over 1,800 questions covering 312 specific topics that span the entire spectrum of anesthesiology. Each question is accompanied by a detailed rationale for the best answer, encouraging not just memorization, but a deeper understanding of the concepts and their applications.

"Anesthesiology Review" is more than just a question-and-answer book; it is a comprehensive guide designed for a diverse audience. Whether you are a medical student embarking on your journey, a resident honing your skills, or a seasoned practitioner staying abreast of the latest developments, this guide is tailored to meet your needs. Furthermore, recognizing the varied learning preferences and busy schedules of our readers, we have made this guide available in both print and e-book formats, allowing you to learn and review whenever and wherever you choose.

As you commit to reading this book, we encourage you to engage with the material actively, challenge yourself with the questions, and reflect on the rationales provided. Our hope is that "Anesthesiology Review" will not only aid in your immediate educational goals but also inspire a lifelong pursuit of excellence and continuous learning in the field of anesthesiology.

We are honored to accompany you on this journey of discovery and mastery in anesthesiology. Let this book be your guide and companion as you navigate the complexities and rewards of this essential medical specialty.

Welcome to "Anesthesiology Review". Let the journey begin.

AIRWAY ISSUES

AIRWAY ABSCESS & INFECTION

01
CHAPTER

Questions:

1. Signs and symptoms of retropharyngeal abscess are?
- A. Difficulty breathing
- B. Severe headache
- C. Stiff neck
- D. All of the above

2. Complications of a retropharyngeal abscess are?
- A. Aspiration pneumonia
- B. Swelling and inflammation in the abdomen
- C. Meningitis
- D. Bloating and nausea

3. Management of patients with retropharyngeal abscesses can consist of?
- A. Investigating the airway using an X-ray or CT-scan
- B. Performing preoxygenation
- C. Treating retropharyngeal abscess with broadspectrum IV antibiotics
- D. All of the above

4. Upper ear infections can lead to retropharyngeal abscess formation (collection of pus in the retropharyngeal space)?
- A. True
- B. False

5. Patients with HIV have a higher risk of developing a retropharyngeal abscess.
- A. True
- B. False

6. A 45-year-old man with a previous ear infection and a history of HIV presents to the emergency department complaining of severe sore throat, swollen lymph nodes, difficulty speaking, noisy breathing, coughing, and fever. On arrival at the emergency department, his respiratory rate is 20/minute with a SpO2 of 96%. Which of the following should be performed next?
- A. Investigate the airway using an X-ray or CT scan, labs (including complete blood count, blood cultures), and careful airway monitoring
- B. Induce general anesthesia followed by bag-mask ventilation (BVM) with cricoid pressure with subsequent orotracheal intubation
- C. Induce general anesthesia followed by rapid sequence orotracheal intubation
- D. Noninvasive positive pressure ventilation to maintain SpO2 above 95%

Answers:

1. Answer D (All of the above)

Early retropharyngeal abscess presents as an upper airway infection with cough, runny nose, sneezing, throat pain, and fever. As this infection progresses, symptoms related to the upper airway, like severe sore throat, swollen lymph nodes, stiff neck, coughing, severe headache, and fever, become more prominent and typically progress over days. The following are red flags in a patient's history that should be concerning for upper airway obstruction: difficulty breathing, difficulty speaking, noisy breathing, inability to tolerate oral secretions.

2. Answer A (Aspiration pneumonia)

The oropharynx of a patient with a suspected retropharyngeal abscess should only be thoroughly examined with palpation or probing by clinicians who are experienced in emergent airway management. Abscess rupture can occur during the examination of the posterior pharynx, leading to aspiration and potential asphyxiation or pneumonia, extension to a mediastinal abscess, Lemierre's syndrome, and vascular complications (e.g., thrombophlebitis of the internal jugular vein). It has been suggested that this exam should be performed with patients in the Trendelenburg position to prevent aspiration in case of abscess rupture, and suction equipment should be readily available.

3. Answer D (All of the above)

CT of the neck with intravenous contrast is the most definitive imaging modality to evaluate patients with a retropharyngeal abscess. If there is a concern for airway compromise in these patients, a clinician who is trained in emergency airway management should be present while the CT scan is being obtained. Patients may require an emergent surgical airway if upper airway obstruction occurs. All patients presenting with a confirmed diagnosis of retropharyngeal infection require hospital admission, intravenous antibiotics, and otolaryngology consultation. Antibiotic therapy should cover upper respiratory organisms, including anaerobic organisms. Surgical drainage is needed when there are large abscesses, complications, or a poor response to medical management. Securing the airway in patients undergoing surgical intervention to control retropharyngeal abscesses is challenging for anesthesiologists. Awake fiberoptic intubation has been recommended as the first choice to control the airway in adults with retropharyngeal abscess for managing difficult airways, and that emergent surgical airway is recommended if fiberoptic intubation is not available or has failed.

4. Answer A (True)

The retropharyngeal space contains chains of lymph nodes that drain the nasopharynx, adenoids, posterior paranasal sinuses, and middle ear. In children, an antecedent upper respiratory tract infection can result in suppurative adenitis of these retropharyngeal lymph nodes and eventual abscess formation. As these retropharyngeal lymph nodes atrophy and involute during normal development, antecedent upper respiratory tract infection resulting in retropharyngeal abscess becomes less likely. In older children and adults, trauma to the posterior pharynx resulting in retropharyngeal infection is the more likely mechanism through which retropharyngeal abscess originates.

5. Answer A (True)

Retropharyngeal abscess occurs most frequently in children younger than six years old due to retropharyngeal space lymph node degeneration after adolescence. In adults, cases have been reported in patients with immunodeficiency, such as diabetes mellitus, HIV infection, patients undergoing hemodialysis, or related to trauma and foreign bodies.

6. Answer A (Investigate the airway using an X-ray or CT scan, Labs (including complete blood count, blood cultures), careful airway monitoring)

In a patient without a compromised airway, if the retropharyngeal abscess is suspected only after a CT scan and laboratory tests, we can make an accurate diagnosis, of course, with careful monitoring of the airway during the whole process. Induction of general anesthesia, cricoid pressure, positive pressure ventilation, and intubation with direct laryngoscopy can lead to complete airway closure, abscess rupture, and pus aspiration during the procedure. It is critical to assess the risk of a potentially difficult airway and prepare the most appropriate airway management method.

Recommended literature

1. Apfelbaum JL, Hagberg CA, Connis RT, et al. 2022 American Society of Anesthesiologists Practice Guidelines for Management of the Difficult Airway. Anesthesiology. 2022;136(1):31-81.
2. Cho SY, Woo JH, Kim YJ, et al. Airway management in patients with deep neck infections: A retrospective analysis [published correction appears in Medicine (Baltimore). 2016 Oct 21;95(42):e36c2]. Medicine (Baltimore). 2016;95(27):e4125.
3. Straker, Tracey, Shobana Rajan, and Mazen A. Maktabi (eds), ' Anesthetic Management of the Patient with Retropharyngeal Abscess with Emphasis on Perioperative and Airway Management', in Tracey Straker, Shobana Rajan, and Magdalena Anitescu (eds), Anesthesiology: A Problem-Based Learning Approach, Anesthesiology A Problem Based Learning (New York, 2018; online edn, Oxford Academic, 1 Nov. 2018).
4. Jain H, Knorr TL, Sinha V. Retropharyngeal Abscess. [Updated 2022 Nov 8]. In: StatPearls [Internet]. Treasure Island (FL): StatPearls Publishing; 2023 Jan-. Available from: https://www.ncbi.nlm.nih.gov/books/NBK441873/

Airway issues
AIRWAY TRAUMA

01
CHAPTER

Questions:

1. **Maxillofacial airway trauma can be associated with?**
   A. Increased intracranial pressure
   B. Neurological deficit
   C. Neurogenic shock
   D. All of the above

2. **Signs and symptoms of airway trauma are?**
   A. Laryngeal dyspnea
   B. Stridor
   C. Cyanosis
   D. All of the above

3. **During airway management in patients with airway trauma to prevent further damage, the most reasonable course of action would be to?**
   A. Avoid cricoid pressure
   B. Avoid bronchoscopy
   C. Avoid Trendelenburg position
   D. Avoid awake fiber intubation

4. **When treating patients with airway trauma, consider the Trendelenburg position to?**
   A. Achieve a better view for intubation
   B. Reduce intracranial pressure
   C. Minimize the risk of air embolism
   D. Decrease blood pressure

5. **Intravenous induction and neuromuscular blockade should be avoided in cooperative patients with airway trauma.**
   A. True
   B. False

6. **A young male patient is admitted to the emergency department following a fall from a ladder. He was placed in a cervical collar, extricated, and brought to the ED on a backboard. His initial ED vitals signs revealed BP 130/70 mm Hg, a pulse of 100 bpm, a temperature of 37.2°C, and SpO2 of 96% on room air. His GCS score was 15. Upon removal of the cervical collar, he was noted to have ecchymosis with mild edema of his anterior neck, as well as subcutaneous emphysema that extended down to his nipple line on the right. His trachea was midline but seemed tender to palpation.**
   Which of the following is the best course of action to take?
   A. Manage trauma with ALS, preoxygenation with 100% O2, bronchoscopy
   B. Manage trauma with ALS, IV induction, neuromuscular blockade, intubation with video laryngoscope
   C. Manage trauma with ALS, ventilate the patient with positive pressure, intubate with a rigid laryngoscope
   D. Manage trauma with ALS, preoxygenation with 100% O2, intubate using intubating stylets

Answers:

1. Answer D (All of the above)

Maxillofacial trauma is the most common type of blunt trauma to the airway and can involve the maxillary/mandibular or central facial region and spread intracranially. Trauma in this anatomical area can be associated with traumatic brain injury and skull base fracture, cervical spine fracture, ophthalmic injury, vascular injury, aspiration of blood, and debris. A red flag should be raised if symptoms such as signs of increased intracranial pressure, neurological deficit, neurogenic shock, significant bleeding due to fracture displacement, or airway obstruction appear.

2. Answer D (All of the above)

The symptoms and signs of airway injury depend on the site and the severity of the injury. Subcutaneous emphysema is the most common finding in airway injury, occurring in up to 87% of the patients. Laceration of the mediastinal pleura and bronchial injuries may allow air to enter the pleural cavity; pneumothorax occurs in 17-70% of these patients. The air can also be trapped in the mediastinum and a crackling rumor concurrent with the heartbeat may be heard on the auscultation over the precordium (Hamman's sign). Dyspnea, tachypnea, and respiratory distress are found in 59-100% of the patients, while hemoptysis can be seen in up to 74% of the cases. Voice changes varying from hoarseness to aphonia may result from laryngeal fractures, laryngotracheal separation, vocal cord tears, and recurrent laryngeal nerve injury.

3. Answer A (Avoid cricoid pressure)

Although rapid sequence endotracheal intubation is frequent in trauma patients in those with airway injuries may result disastrously. The pressure over a fractured cricoid may dislocate it enough to completely distort the upper airway, change the view of the physician performing the intubation, or even lead to complete airway transection and obstruction. Attempts to blindly overpass an upper airway injury may worsen the laceration and/or create a false passage of the tube.

4. Answer C (Minimizing the risk of air embolism)

Patients who are physiologically unstable or have signs of uncontrolled bleeding, rapidly expanding neck hematomas, or hypovolemic shock not responsive to resuscitation should be suspected of having a large vessel injury and urgently transferred to the operating room, as surgical exploration is indicated. If a large vessel has been injured, a supine or Trendelenburg position will minimize the risk of air embolism. Trendelenburg's position prevents the gas embolism from occluding the outflow tract by placing the right ventricular cavity in a more superior position.

5. Answer A (True)

Intravenous induction and neuromuscular blockade in cooperative patients with airway trauma should be avoided since apnea and the loss of smooth muscle tone may lead to the complete collapse of an already traumatized and distorted airway kept functional by the surrounding musculature. Therefore, spontaneous breathing of the patient should be preferred until a safe airway has been achieved.

6. Answer A (Manage trauma with ALS, preoxygenation with 100% O2, bronchoscopy)

Bronchoscopy and chest CT represent the procedures of choice for the definitive diagnosis of an airway injury. Bronchoscopy allows the site of the rupture to be located, its extension and depth and ensures that the tube cuff is inflated beyond the site of injury. Endotracheal intubation via a flexible bronchoscope is the preferred method for airway management and for the definitive diagnosis of an airway injury.

Recommended literature

1. Shilston J, Evans DL, Simons A, Evans DA. Initial management of blunt and penetrating neck trauma. BJA Educ. 2021;21(9):329-335.
2. Mercer SJ, Jones CP, Bridge M, Clitheroe E, Morton B, Groom P. Systematic review of the anaesthetic management of non-iatrogenic acute adult airway trauma. Br J Anaesth. 2016;117 Suppl 1:i49-i59.
3. Jain U, McCunn M, Smith CE, Pittet JF. Management of the Traumatized Airway. Anesthesiology. 2016;124(1):199-206.
4. Prokakis C, Koletsis EN, Dedeilias P, Fligou F, Filos K, Dougenis D. Airway trauma: a review on epidemiology, mechanisms of injury, diagnosis and treatment. J Cardiothorac Surg. 2014;9:117.
5. Abernathy JH, Reeves ST: Airway catastrophes. Curr Opin Anaesthesiol. 2010, 23: 41-46.
6. Hurford WE, Peralta R: Management of tracheal trauma. Can J Anesth. 2003, 50 (suppl): R1-R6.

DIFFICULT AIRWAY MANAGEMENT

Questions:

1. If the initial intubation attempt is unsuccessful and face mask ventilation is not adequate, which of the following would be the best next step?
   A. Cricothyroidotomy
   B. Fiberoptic intubation
   C. Supraglottic airway device placement
   D. Wake the patient up

2. Predictors of difficult mask ventilation include?
   A. Obesity
   B. Large tongue
   C. Beard
   D. All of the above

3. Which complication contributes to difficult airway management?
   A. Obstructive sleep apnea
   B. Chronic obstructive pulmonary disease
   C. Aortic stenosis
   D. Hyperthyroidism

4. Which of the following conditions contributes to difficult airway management?
   A. Diabetes mellitus
   B. Hypertension
   C. Renal failure
   D. Liver failure

5. With proper preoxygenation, apnea time can be extended to 8 minutes.
   A. True
   B. False

6. You are called for assistance following two unsuccessful attempts at tracheal intubation. A 39-year-old man presented for elective cholecystectomy. After preoxygenation, general anesthesia was induced with propofol and rocuronium. The first two attempts at intubation were difficult, leading to the decision to secure the airway with a laryngeal mask airway (LMA). What is the next appropriate step in managing this patient?
   A. Wake the patient up and perform an awake fibreoptic intubation
   B. Fiberoptic intubation through a LMA
   C. Remove the LMA and attempt a video laryngoscopy
   D. Replace the LMA with the ProSeal laryngeal mask to facilitate positive pressure ventilation

Answers:

1. **Answer C (Supraglottic airway device placement)**

   Planning for failed intubation should form part of the preinduction briefing, particularly for urgent surgery. Emphasis is placed on assessment, preparation, positioning, preoxygenation, maintenance of oxygenation, and minimizing trauma from airway interventions. It is recommended that the number of airway interventions be limited, and blind techniques using a bougie or through supraglottic airway devices have been superseded by video or fiber optically guided intubation. If tracheal intubation fails, supraglottic airway devices are recommended to provide a route for oxygenation while reviewing how to proceed. Second-generation devices have advantages and are recommended.

2. **Answer D (All of the above)**

   Difficult mask ventilation is defined as the inability of an unassisted anesthesiologist to maintain the measured oxygen saturation as measured by pulse oximetry > 92% or to prevent or reverse signs of inadequate ventilation during positive pressure mask ventilation under general anesthesia. Risk factors identified as potential for difficult mask ventilation are higher body mass index, older age, macroglossia, beard, lack of teeth, history of snoring, increased Mallampati grade, lower thyromental distance, and distorted facial anatomy.

3. **Answer A (Obstructive sleep apnea)**

   Obstructive sleep apnea is associated with a number of anatomical changes in the upper airway, including oropharyngeal crowding, upper airway narrowing, macroglossia, retrognathia, thick neck, reduced mandibular length, inferiorly positioned hyoid bone and retro position of the maxilla, all of which are risk factors for difficult intubation/ventilation. Every patient diagnosed with obstructive sleep apnea or with clinical suspicion of obstructive sleep apnea should be considered to have a difficult airway until proven otherwise.

4. **Answer A (Diabetes mellitus)**

   Diabetes mellitus is a condition that can contribute to difficult airway management. This is due to various factors, including potential anatomical changes in the airway associated with long-standing diabetes, such as obesity and soft tissue changes. Additionally, diabetic patients are prone to limited joint mobility syndrome. The atlanto occipital joint involvement limits adequate extension of the head and neck during laryngoscopy making intubation difficult. Diabetic stiff joint syndrome, also known as limited joint mobility syndrome, is a disease process by which microvascular disease leads to abnormal cross-linkage of collagen by non-enzymatic glycosylation in connective tissue as a result of chronic hyperglycemia. Hypertension, renal failure, and liver failure are not typically directly associated with difficulty in airway management. While these conditions can have systemic effects that may impact the overall health of the patient and their response to anesthesia, they do not directly affect the anatomical or functional aspects of the airway in the same way as diabetes mellitus.

5. **Answer A (True)**

   Preoxygenation increases the oxygen reserve, delays the onset of hypoxia, and allows more time for laryngoscopy and tracheal intubation or to airway rescue if intubation fails. In healthy adults, the duration of apnea without desaturation (defined as the interval between the onset of apnea and the time peripheral capillary oxygen saturation reaches a value of ≤ 90%) is limited to 1–2 min whilst breathing room air but can be extended to 8 min with preoxygenation with 100% O2.

6. **Answer B (Fiberoptic intubation through a LMA)**

   Intubation through an intubating laryngeal mask airway has been part of the practice guidelines for the management of difficult airways since 2004. Intubation through an LMA is only appropriate if the clinical situation is stable, oxygenation is possible via the LMA, and the anesthetist is trained in the technique. Limiting the number of airway interventions is a core principle of safe airway management; repeated attempts at intubation through an LMA are inappropriate.

Recommended literature

1. Apfelbaum JL, Hagberg CA, Connis RT, et al. 2022 American Society of Anesthesiologists Practice Guidelines for Management of the Difficult Airway. Anesthesiology. 2022;136(1):31-81.
2. Frerk C, Mitchell VS, McNarry AF, et al. Difficult Airway Society 2015 guidelines for management of unanticipated difficult intubation in adults. Br J Anaesth. 2015;115(6):827-848.
3. Olivier Langeron, Eva Masso, Catherine Huraux, Michel Guggiari, André Bianchi, Pierre Coriat, Bruno Riou; Prediction of Difficult Mask Ventilation. Anesthesiology 2000; 92:1229–1236 doi: https://doi.org/10.1097/00000542-200005000-00009.
4. Hashim K, Thomas M. Sensitivity of palm print sign in prediction of difficult laryngoscopy in diabetes: A comparison with other airway indices. Indian J Anaesth. 2014 May;58(3):298-302. doi: 10.4103/0019-5049.135042. PMID: 25024473; PMCID: PMC4090996.
5. Leong SM, Tiwari A, Chung F, Wong DT. Obstructive sleep apnea as a risk factor associated with difficult airway management - A narrative review. J Clin Anesth. 2018 Mar;45:63-68. doi: 10.1016/j.jclinane.2017.12.024. Epub 2018 Jan 4. PMID: 29291467.

EXPANDING NECK HEMATOMA

01
CHAPTER

Questions:

1. **Hematoma of the neck can manifest as?**
   A. Esophageal compression
   B. Tracheal compression
   C. Tracheal displacement
   D. All of the above

2. **Signs and symptoms of neck hematoma are?**
   A. Neck tightness
   B. Neck swelling
   C. Change in voice quality
   D. All of the above

3. **A patient who underwent total thyroidectomy for toxic nodular goiter developed sudden respiratory distress two hours after surgery, followed by dyspnea hypoxia, tachypnea stridor, and tracheal deviation. The most appropriate immediate measure should be?**
   A. CT scan
   B. Blood tests
   C. Intubation
   D. Non-invasive positive pressure ventilation

4. **What is the most common presentation of post-thyroidectomy neck hematoma?**
   A. Hypotension
   B. Respiratory distress
   C. Neck pain
   D. Hoarseness

5. **In the absence of compromised airway or hemodynamic instability, neck hematoma can be successfully treated conservatively.**
   A. True
   B. False

6. **A 28-year-old male presents to the emergency department with neck swelling and difficulty breathing. The patient reports that he was involved in a motor vehicle accident earlier today and struck his neck against the steering wheel. On physical examination, the patient has a large, tender, and expanding hematoma in his neck. He is also dyspneic and tachypneic. Vital signs reveal a heart rate of 130 beats per minute, blood pressure of 90/50 mmHg, and oxygen saturation of 90% on room air. Which of the following is the most appropriate initial management for this patient?**
   A. Administer intravenous antibiotics
   B. Begin immediate anticoagulation therapy
   C. Perform a surgical airway
   D. Provide supplemental oxygen and prepare for intubation

Answers:

1. Answer D (All of the above)

Hematoma of the neck can manifest as esophageal compression, tracheal compression, and tracheal displacement, as well as successive emergence of subcutaneous ecchymosis. The hematoma can result in compression of nearby structures, which can lead to airway compromise and difficulty swallowing. The subcutaneous ecchymosis can occur as a result of bleeding from the hematoma.

2. Answer D (All of the above)

Neck hematoma can cause a range of signs and symptoms depending on the location and size of the hematoma, and the structures it compresses. Here are some of the common signs and symptoms of neck hematoma: neck tightness or pressure, neck swelling or enlargement, pain or tenderness in the neck, change in voice quality (such as hoarseness or difficulty speaking), difficulty breathing, shortness of breath, wheezing, stridor, dizziness, weakness, fainting, sweating or feeling anxious. These signs and symptoms may develop gradually or rapidly and can be life-threatening if not treated promptly.

3. Answer C (Intubation)

The patient's sudden respiratory distress, dyspnea, hypoxia, tachypnea, stridor, and tracheal deviation suggest the possibility of an expanding neck hematoma, which is a medical emergency that can rapidly progress to airway compromise and cardiovascular collapse. Intubation is the most appropriate immediate measure in this situation to secure the airway, ensure adequate oxygenation and ventilation, and prevent further deterioration. CT scans and blood tests may be necessary to confirm the diagnosis and identify the source of bleeding, but they should not delay or replace the immediate management of airway compromise. Non-invasive positive pressure ventilation (NIPPV) and IV fluid bolus may be helpful in some cases of respiratory distress, but they are not the first-line treatment for an expanding neck hematoma with airway compromise.

4. Answer B (Respiratory distress)

Most patients with post-thyroidectomy neck hematoma present with respiratory distress. This is thought to be due to mechanical compression of the trachea or mucosal edema of the supraglottic larynx and pharynx caused by the expanding hematoma. While hypotension can occur in some cases, respiratory distress is the more common presentation. Neck pain and hoarseness can also occur but are less common than respiratory distress in this context.

5. Answer A (True)

In the absence of compromised airway or hemodynamic instability, cases have been successfully treated conservatively, but observation and close monitoring may be appropriate. If the patient's condition deteriorates or if there is any indication of airway compromise or hemodynamic instability, prompt intervention is necessary, which may include surgical intervention. Therefore, the decision to pursue conservative management should be made on a case-by-case basis, taking into account the patient's clinical status and underlying condition.

6. Answer D (Provide supplemental oxygen and prepare for intubation)

The patient's presentation concerns an expanding neck hematoma, which is a medical emergency that requires prompt management. The hematoma likely resulted from the blunt neck trauma sustained during the motor vehicle accident. The patient is also dyspneic and tachypneic, indicating airway compromise. The most appropriate initial management for this patient is to provide supplemental oxygen and prepare for intubation. This will help to maintain oxygenation and secure the airway, which is essential in preventing further deterioration of the patient's condition. Administering intravenous antibiotics, beginning immediate anticoagulation therapy, or obtaining a CT scan of the neck are not the most appropriate initial management steps for this patient. A surgical airway may be required in the case of failed intubation, but it should not be the initial management step.

Recommended literature

1. Alfraidy, D, Helmi, H, Alamodi Alghamdi, M, Bokhari, A, Alsaif, A. Rare cause of acute neck hematoma. Clin Case Rep. 2019; 7: 1378– 1381.
2. Shuker ST. Expanding Hematoma's Life-Threatening Neck and Face Emergency Management of Ballistic Injuries. J Craniofac Surg. 2 016;27(5):1282-1285.
3. Shakespeare WA, Lanier WL, Perkins WJ, Pasternak JJ. Airway management in patients who develop neck hematomas after carotid endarterectomy. Anesth Analg. 2010;110(2):588-593.
4. Barash PG, Cahalan MK, Cullen BF, Stock C, Stoelting RK, Ortega R, Sharar SR, Holt H. Clinical anesthesia. 2017. Eight edition. Wolters Kluwer.
5. de Carvalho AY, Gomes CC, Chulam TC, Vartanian JG, Carvalho GB, Lira RB, Kohler HF, Kowalski LP. Risk Factors and Outcomes of Postoperative Neck Hematomas: An Analysis of 5,900 Thyroidectomies Performed at a Cancer Center. Int Arch Otorhinolaryngol. 2021 Jul;25(3):e421-e427. doi: 10.1055/s-0040-1714129. Epub 2020 Sep 30. PMID: 34377179; PMCID: PMC8321642.
6. Chaffanjon PC, Chavanis N, Chabre O, Brichon PY. Extracapsular hematoma of the parathyroid glands. World J Surg. 2003 Jan;27(1):14-7. doi: 10.1007/s00268-002-6429-y. PMID: 12557032.

LUNG PROTECTIVE VENTILATION

01

CHAPTER

Questions:

1. **Lung protective ventilation is recommended as the default ventilation strategy for which group of patients?**

   A. Those with chronic obstructive pulmonary disease (COPD)

   B. Those undergoing cardiac surgery

   C. All mechanically ventilated patients

   D. Those with pulmonary fibrosis

2. **Which of the following ventilatory parameters are associated with intraoperative lung protective ventilation?**

   A. A tidal volume of 6-8 mL/kg predicted body weight

   B. A tidal volume of 8-12 mL/kg predicted body weight

   C. PEEP 3 cm H_2O

   D. Median plateau pressure $\geq$ 16 cm H_2O

3. **Ventilator-induced lung injury (VILI) occurs via?**

   A. Volutrauma (high tidal volumes)

   B. Atelectotrauma (repetitive and rapid opening of the alveoli)

   C. Biotrauma (Inflammatory damage, apoptotic/fibroproliferative processes, the translocation of bacteria and pro-inflammatory mediators)

   D. All of the above

4. **An elderly man is brought to the ICU intubated for respiratory failure of unknown etiology, bilateral lung infiltrates on chest radiography of a non-cardiac origin, and a PaO/FiO ratio of less than 300 mmHg. His predicted body weight is 80 kg. What would be your initial settings on volume control ventilation? Choose all that apply.**

   A. Tidal volume 480 mL

   B. Peak inspiratory pressure 35 cm H_2O

   C. PEEP 3 cm H_2O

   D. I:E 2:1

5. **Ventilator-induced lung injury (VILI) shares common pathophysiological features with acute respiratory distress syndrome (ARDS).**

   A. True

   B. False

6. **A 64-year-old female patient with a predicted body weight of 60 kg with acute respiratory distress syndrome (ARDS) due to aspiration pneumonia is being mechanically ventilated in the ICU. The ventilation settings are as follows: volume control, tidal volume 480 mL, respiratory rate 18 breaths per minute, PEEP (positive end-expiratory pressure) 10 cm H_2O, FiO$_2$ 60%, plateau pressure 30 cm H_2O, and peak inspiratory pressure 38 cm H_2O. In the arterial blood gas test, pH 7.35, PaO$_2$ 75 mmHg, PaCO$_2$ 50 mmHg. What change should you make to the ventilator settings?**

   A. No change

   B. Increase PEEP

   C. Decrease tidal volume

   D. Increase FiO$_2$

Answers:

1. Answer C (All mechanically ventilated patients)

Lung protective ventilation (LPV) is recommended as the default ventilation strategy for all mechanically ventilated patients, regardless of the underlying condition. LPV aims to reduce the risk of ventilator-induced lung injury (VILI) by using lower tidal volumes, limiting plateau pressures, and utilizing positive end-expiratory pressure (PEEP) to maintain alveolar recruitment and reduce atelectasis. While patients with specific lung conditions like COPD or pulmonary fibrosis may benefit from LPV, it is recommended for all mechanically ventilated patients to minimize the risk of pulmonary complications.

2. Answer A (A tidal volume of 6-8 mL/kg predicted body weight)

Ventilatory parameters that have been associated with intraoperative lung protection ventilation include a tidal volume of 6-8 mL/kg predicted body weight to reduce the risk of volutrauma, a PEEP of at least 5 cm H_2O to prevent alveolar collapse and maintain functional residual capacity, and a median plateau pressure of less than or equal to 16 cm H_2O to reduce the risk of barotrauma.

3. Answer D (All of the above)

Ventilator-induced lung injury (VILI) is caused by a combination of different factors, which include volutrauma (injury caused by high tidal volumes), barotrauma (injury caused by high inspiratory pressures), atelectotrauma (injury caused by repetitive and rapid opening of the alveoli), and biotrauma (injury caused by inflammatory damage, apoptotic/fibroproliferative processes, and the translocation of bacteria and pro-inflammatory mediators). These factors can lead to lung inflammation, edema, and impaired gas exchange. Therefore, lung protective ventilation strategies aim to minimize these factors and prevent VILI.

4. Answer A (Tidal volume 480 mL)

The ventilator should initially be set to a tidal volume of 6-8 mL/predicted body weight and positive end-expiratory pressure (PEEP) of 5 cm H_2O. PEEP should be individualized after that. The appropriate initial settings on volume control ventilation for this patient would be a tidal volume of 480 mL: To follow the lung protective ventilation strategy, the tidal volume should be 6 mL/kg predicted body weight. In this case, the predicted body weight is 80 kg, so the tidal volume should be 480 mL. Plateau pressure 15 cm H_2O: To prevent barotrauma and minimize the risk of VILI, the plateau pressure should be kept below 30 cm H_2O. Aim to keep it below 15 cm H_2O if possible. Respiratory rate 16 breaths per minute: The respiratory rate should be adjusted to maintain an appropriate minute ventilation based on the patient's arterial blood gas results and clinical condition. I:E 1:2: The I:E ratio can be adjusted based on the patient's clinical condition and response to ventilation. An I:E ratio of 1:2 is a reasonable starting point. Start positive end-expiratory pressure (PEEP) at 5 cm H_2O. The peak inspiratory pressure should be adjusted to maintain appropriate tidal volume and minute ventilation while keeping the plateau pressure below 30 cm H_2O. A peak inspiratory pressure of 35 cm H_2O is high and may increase the risk of barotrauma and VILI.

5. Answer A (True)

VILI occurs most often in patients with predisposing factors for ARDS. The pathophysiology of VILI and ARDS involves similar mechanisms, such as mechanical stress and strain on the lung tissue, disruption of the alveolar-capillary membrane, and release of pro-inflammatory mediators.

6. Answer C (Decrease tidal volume)

The best option for this patient would be to decrease the tidal volume to prevent volutrauma and decrease peak inspiratory and plateau pressure. A tidal volume of 6 mL/kg predicted body weight is recommended for patients with ARDS. Therefore, the tidal volume for this patient should be reduced to approximately 360 mL.

Recommended literature

1. Young CC, Harris EM, Vacchiano C, et al. Lung-protective ventilation for the surgical patient: international expert panel-based consensus recommendations. Br J Anaesth. 2019;123(6):898-913.
2. O'Gara B, Talmor D. Perioperative lung protective ventilation. BMJ. 2018;362:k3030. Published 2018 Sep 10. doi:10.1136/bmj.k3030.
3. Beitler JR, Malhotra A, Thompson BT. Ventilator-induced Lung Injury. Clin Chest Med. 2016;37(4):633-646.
4. Petrucci N, De Feo C. Lung protective ventilation strategy for the acute respiratory distress syndrome. Cochrane Database Syst Rev. 2013;2013(2):CD003844. Published 2013 Feb 28.

Airway issues
MICROLARYNGOSCOPY AND AIRWAY LASER

Questions:

1. **The common ventilatory strategies for laser airway surgery include?**
   A. Conventional endotracheal intubation
   B. Jet ventilation
   C. Intermittent apnea technique
   D. All of the above

2. **What are the advantages of airway laser surgery?**
   A. Reduction of tissue reaction
   B. Preservation of normal tissue
   C. Complete sterility
   D. All of the above

3. **What is the main cause of airway obstruction during micro-laryngoscopy and airway laser surgery?**
   A. Laryngospasm
   B. Airway fire
   C. Barotrauma
   D. Obstructing tumor

4. **Which of the following statements regarding laser airway surgery and endotracheal tubes is correct?**
   A. Laser-resistant endotracheal tubes are not necessary for laser airway surgery
   B. Laser-resistant endotracheal tubes are required only for nasal intubation during laser airway surgery
   C. Laser-resistant endotracheal tubes are recommended for intubation during laser airway surgery to prevent tube combustion
   D. Laser-resistant endotracheal tubes are only used for pediatric patients during laser airway surgery

5. **The guidelines of the American Society of Anesthesiologists recommend the use of double-cuffed tubes filled with saline solution with the addition of methylene blue for laser airway surgery.**
   A. True
   B. False

6. **A 55-year-old female patient is undergoing laser excision of a vocal cord polyp. The airway is secured with a "laser-resistant/non-combustible" endotracheal tube. During the procedure, the surgeon inadvertently causes the tube cuff to burst, resulting in a small flame of fire in the surgical field. What is the most appropriate immediate measure?**
   A. Increasing the inspired oxygen concentration
   B. Continuing with laser resection to complete the procedure as soon as possible
   C. Flooding the field with normal saline
   D. Increasing the nitrous oxide concentration to reduce the inspired oxygen concentration

Answers:

1. Answer D (All of the above)

During laser airway surgery, all of the above ventilatory strategies may be employed depending on the patient's condition and the nature of the surgical procedure.

2. Answer D (All of the above)

Laser surgery offers several advantages to the surgeon and patient, i.e., microscopic precision, a bloodless operative field, reduction of tissue reaction, preservation of normal tissue, and complete sterility. One of the major advantages is the microscopic precision that can be achieved with the laser beam. The surgeon can precisely target the tissue being operated on, minimizing the risk of damage to surrounding tissues. The laser beam can cauterize blood vessels as it cuts, reducing bleeding during surgery. Laser surgery also offers a reduction in tissue reaction. A focused laser beam leads to less tissue damage and, thus, less inflammation and scarring. Preservation of normal tissue is another advantage of laser surgery. The laser beam can precisely target the area of tissue that needs to be removed or modified, leaving surrounding healthy tissue largely unaffected. Finally, laser surgery can provide a completely sterile operative field. Unlike traditional surgical instruments, the laser beam does not come into contact with the tissue being operated on, reducing the risk of infection. This can be especially important in surgeries where the risk of infection is high or where the patient's immune system may be compromised.

3. Answer D (Obstructing tumor)

The main cause of airway obstruction during micro-laryngoscopy and airway laser surgery is usually due to obstructing tumor or tissue swelling, rather than laryngospasm, airway fire, or barotrauma.

4. Answer C (Laser-resistant endotracheal tubes are recommended for intubation during laser airway surgery to prevent tube combustion)

Laser airway surgery involves the use of a high-intensity laser to cut or vaporize tissues in the airway. During this procedure, there is a risk of the endotracheal tube becoming damaged or combusting due to the high-energy laser beam. Laser-resistant endotracheal tubes are specially designed to withstand the thermal effects of the laser and reduce the risk of tube combustion. These tubes are made of materials that are less likely to ignite or melt when exposed to the laser beam, providing a higher level of safety for the patient. It's important to note that while laser-resistant tubes are recommended for laser airway surgery, they may not be necessary for all types of airway surgeries. The decision to use a laser-resistant tube should be based on the specific requirements of the procedure and the equipment available.

5. Answer A (True)

The guidelines of the American Society of Anesthesiologists recommend during laser airway surgery the use of laser-resistant/non-combustible endotracheal tubes, laser-resistant tubes are typically double-cuffed to provide a secure seal and prevent the laser from damaging the airway or the tube itself. Additionally, the cuff of the endotracheal tube can be filled with saline solution with the addition of a dye such as methylene blue to provide a visual alert if the balloon is inadvertently popped.

6. Answer C (Flooding the field with normal saline)

The most appropriate immediate measure would be to stop the laser and flood the surgical field with saline to extinguish the fire. The next step would be to immediately exchange the endotracheal tube if it sustained any damage.

Recommended literature

1. Pearson, K., Mcguire, B., 2017. Anaesthesia for laryngo-tracheal surgery, including tubeless field techniques. BJA Education 17, 242–248.
2. Hemantkumar, Indrani. (2017). Anesthesia for Laser Surgery of the Airway. An International Journal Otorhinolaryngology Clinics. 9. 1-5. 10.5005/jp-journals-10003-1250.

Airway issues
PENETRATING NECK INJURIES

01
CHAPTER

Questions:

1. **Which of the following is a potential complication of a penetrating neck injury?**
   A. Massive hemothorax
   B. Esophageal tear
   C. Vertebral artery dissection
   D. All of the above

2. **What is the recommended technique for securing the airway in a patient with a penetrating neck injury who cannot be intubated?**
   A. Cricothyrotomy
   B. Fiberoptic intubation
   C. Laryngeal mask airway insertion
   D. Non-invasive positive pressure ventilation

3. **What is the first step in the management of a patient with a penetrating neck injury?**
   A. Administer analgesia
   B. Secure the airway
   C. Control the bleeding
   D. Perform a CT scan

4. **What is the main goal in managing a patient with a penetrating neck injury?**
   A. Control bleeding and prevent shock
   B. Secure the airway and maintain oxygenation
   C. Assess for complications and provide appropriate interventions
   D. All of the above

5. **Bag-mask positive pressure ventilation in patients with penetrating neck injury increases bleeding and airway obstruction.**
   A. True
   B. False

6. **A 28-year-old male was brought to the emergency department after a knife attack to the neck. On examination, he was tachycardic, hypotensive, and pale. A pulsatile bleeding was noted in the neck, and there was a subcutaneous emphysema on palpation. What would be the initial management of the patient?**
   A. Immediate surgical exploration
   B. Hemodynamic stabilization and airway management
   C. Administration of antibiotics
   D. Imaging studies, such as CTA or MRI

Answers:

1. **Answer D (All of the above)**

   A penetrating neck injury can cause damage to major blood vessels, including the carotid artery and jugular vein, leading to massive bleeding. It can also result in damage to the esophagus, trachea, and other structures in the neck. Additionally, a penetrating neck injury can cause damage to the vertebral artery, leading to vertebral artery dissection and damage to the spinal cord or nerves.

2. **Answer A (Cricothyrotomy)**

   The recommended technique for securing the airway in a patient with a penetrating neck injury who cannot be intubated is cricothyrotomy. Cricothyrotomy is an emergency procedure that involves making a small incision through the skin and cricothyroid membrane to establish an airway. It is the preferred technique in cases where intubation is not possible due to the nature of the injury or the patient's condition. Fiberoptic intubation, laryngeal mask airway insertion, and non-invasive positive pressure ventilation are not recommended in cases of penetrating neck injury. These techniques may worsen the injury or cause further damage to the airway or neck structures.

3. **Answer B (Secure the airway)**

   In cases of penetrating neck injury, there is a risk of airway obstruction, which can lead to respiratory distress and hypoxemia. Therefore, the priority in managing such patients is to secure the airway to ensure adequate ventilation and oxygenation. After securing the airway, the next step is to control the bleeding to prevent further blood loss, followed by administration of analgesia to relieve pain and performing imaging studies such as a CT scan to evaluate the extent of injury.

4. **Answer D (All of the above)**

   The main goal in managing a patient with a penetrating neck injury is to control bleeding and prevent shock, secure the airway and maintain oxygenation, assess for complications, and provide appropriate interventions. Penetrating neck injuries can be life-threatening, and the main goal of management is to stabilize the patient and prevent further harm. This includes controlling bleeding to prevent shock and ensuring adequate oxygenation by securing the airway. Once these initial steps are taken, the healthcare provider should continue to monitor the patient for signs of complications such as infection, nerve damage, or other injuries to surrounding structures and provide appropriate interventions as needed.

5. **Answer A (True)**

   Positive pressure ventilation in patients with penetrating neck injuries can increase bleeding and airway obstruction. Therefore, in cases of penetrating neck injuries, it is generally recommended to avoid positive pressure ventilation until the airway is secured and bleeding is controlled.

6. **Answer B (Hemodynamic stabilization and airway management)**

   The patient is presenting with signs of shock, which indicates significant blood loss. The pulsatile bleeding in the neck suggests an arterial injury, which can lead to exsanguination if not managed promptly. The subcutaneous emphysema suggests the presence of an air leak, which can worsen the patient's condition. Therefore, the first priority in managing this patient is to stabilize their hemodynamics and secure their airway.

Recommended literature

1. McCann C, Watson A, Barnes D. Major burns: Part 1. Epidemiology, pathophysiology and initial management. BJA Educ. 2022;22(3):94-103.
2. Nowicki JL, Stew B, Ooi E. Penetrating neck injuries: a guide to evaluation and management. Ann R Coll Surg Engl. 2018;100(1):6-11.
3. Huh H, Han JH, Chung JY, et al. Anesthetic management of penetrating neck injury patient with embedded knife -A case report-. Korean J Anesthesiol. 2012;62(2):172-174.

PULMONARY ASPIRATION

01
CHAPTER

Questions:

1. **What are the risk factors for pulmonary aspiration due to delayed gastric emptying?**
   A. Recent trauma
   B. Systemic diseases, including diabetes mellitus and chronic kidney disease
   C. Opioids
   D. All of the above

2. **Which of the following can cause delayed gastric emptying and increase the risk of pulmonary aspiration?**
   A. Antibiotics
   B. Heart failure
   C. Diabetes mellitus
   D. All of the above

3. **What are the three possible outcomes that can result from pulmonary aspiration?**
   A. Viral pneumonia, bacterial pneumonia, and acute respiratory distress syndrome
   B. Chemical pneumonitis, bacterial pneumonia, and acute respiratory distress syndrome
   C. Asthma, emphysema, and chronic obstructive pulmonary disease
   D. Congestive heart failure, pulmonary edema, and pleural effusion

4. **What is the most important factor in managing pulmonary aspiration?**
   A. Rapid administration of antibiotics
   B. Securing a safe airway
   C. Reducing gastric volume
   D. Increasing the pH of gastric contents

5. **Steroid administration enhances the prognosis of pulmonary aspiration.**
   A. True
   B. False

6. **A 62-year-old male with a history of chronic obstructive pulmonary disease (COPD) and hypertension was admitted to the emergency department with shortness of breath and fever. He was diagnosed with community-acquired pneumonia and required intubation for respiratory distress. During the intubation process, the patient aspirated gastric contents. His oxygen saturation decreased, and he developed acute respiratory distress syndrome (ARDS). What is the immediate management for a patient who aspirates during intubation?**
   A. Administer antibiotics
   B. Administer steroids
   C. Perform a bronchoscopy
   D. Suction the airway and provide oxygen support

Answers:

1. Answer D (all of the above)

Pulmonary aspiration is the inhalation of material, such as food or gastric contents, into the lungs. This can lead to pneumonia and other serious complications. The risk factors for pulmonary aspiration due to delayed gastric emptying include systemic disease (including diabetes mellitus and chronic kidney disease), recent trauma to the head, neck, or chest, opioids and other sedatives, increased intracranial pressure, previous gastrointestinal surgery and pregnancy (including active labor).

2. Answer C (Diabetes mellitus)

Diabetes mellitus is a risk factor for pulmonary aspiration due to delayed gastric emptying. This condition, known as diabetic gastroparesis, is a potential complication that occurs in the setting of poorly controlled diabetes, resulting from dysfunction in the coordination and function of the autonomic nervous system, neurons, and specialized pacemaker cells of the stomach and intestine, and the smooth muscle cells of the gastrointestinal tract.

3. Answer B (Chemical pneumonitis, bacterial pneumonia, and acute respiratory distress syndrome)

Chemical pneumonitis, bacterial pneumonia, and acute respiratory distress syndrome are three potential conditions that can result from pulmonary aspiration. When material is aspirated into the lungs, it can cause inflammation and damage to the lung tissue. This can lead to chemical pneumonitis, which is an inflammation of the lung tissue caused by the chemical irritation of aspirated material. Bacterial pneumonia can also occur as a result of aspiration. Acute respiratory distress syndrome (ARDS) is a severe lung condition that can also develop as a result of aspiration, as the inflammation and damage to the lung tissue impair gas exchange.

4. Answer B (Securing a safe airway)

Securing a safe airway is the most important factor in managing pulmonary aspiration. When the material is aspirated into the lungs, it can obstruct the airway and potentially lead to respiratory distress or failure. Therefore, the priority in managing pulmonary aspiration is to secure a safe airway to ensure adequate gas exchange.

5. Answer B (False)

There is no evidence to support the routine use of steroids in the treatment of pulmonary aspiration. The main controversies surrounding treatment decisions involve the decision to use antibiotics and steroids. Antibiotics should only be used if pneumonia develops, as early antibiotics may lead to the selection of virulent bacteria, including pseudomonas. There is no evidence that the use of steroids reduces mortality or improves outcomes. Therefore the routine use of steroids in the treatment of pulmonary aspiration should be avoided, and treatment should be individualized on a case-by-case basis.

6. Answer D (Suction the airway and provide oxygen support)

Aspiration during intubation can occur when gastric contents reflux up into the throat and are then drawn into the lungs. This can lead to obstruction of the airway and potentially cause respiratory distress or failure. Therefore, the priority in managing this situation is to clear the airway, the trachea should be suctioned after securing a safe airway, ideally before positive pressure ventilation to prevent the distal displacement of aspirated material. The immediate management for a patient who aspirates during intubation is to suction the airway and provide oxygen support.

Recommended literature

1. Michael Robinson, MB ChB FRCA, Andrew Davidson, MA MBBS FRCA FFICM, Aspiration under anaesthesia: risk assessment and decision-making, Continuing Education in Anaesthesia Critical Care & Pain, Volume 14, Issue 4, August 2014, Pages 171–175.
2. Asai T. Editorial II: Who is at increased risk of pulmonary aspiration?. Br J Anaesth. 2004;93(4):497–500.
3. Muscedere J, Dodek P, Keenan S, Fowler R, Cook D, Heyland D. Comprehensive evidence-based clinical practice guidelines for ventilator-associated pneumonia: prevention. J Crit Care, 2008, vol. 23 (pg. 126-37).

RIGID BRONCHOSCOPY

01
CHAPTER

Questions:

1. **What is the primary indication for rigid bronchoscopy?**
   A. Diagnosis of respiratory infections
   B. Treatment of airway cancers
   C. Assessment of lung function
   D. Management of asthma

2. **Which of the following is NOT a potential complication of rigid bronchoscopy?**
   A. Hemorrhage
   B. Systemic gas embolism
   C. Allergic reaction to anesthesia
   D. Dissemination of post-obstructive pneumonia

3. **What are the possible mechanical complications of rigid bronchoscopy?**
   A. Trauma to the teeth, oropharynx, vocal cords, or other glottic structures
   B. Laryngospasm
   C. Pneumothorax
   D. All of the above

4. **What type of anesthesia is typically used for rigid bronchoscopy?**
   A. Regional anesthesia
   B. Conscious sedation
   C. General anesthesia
   D. Local anesthesia

5. **Patients with baseline hypercarbia and hemodynamic instability are at increased risk for complications during rigid bronchoscopy.**
   A. True
   B. False

6. **A 60-year-old female patient is recovering in the PACU after an uneventful rigid bronchoscopy when she begins to complain of pleuritic chest pain. Which of the following is the best next step in the evaluation of this patient?**
   A. Administration of an albuterol nebulizer
   B. Chest X-ray or point-of-care lung ultrasound
   C. Electrocardiogram and cardiac enzymes
   D. Transthoracic echocardiogram

Answers:

1. **Answer B (Treatment of airway cancers)**

   Rigid bronchoscopy is often used for the treatment of airway cancers, such as the removal of tumors or stenosis. While it can also be used for the diagnosis of respiratory infections, it is not the primary indication.

2. **Answer C (Allergic reaction to anesthesia)**

   While allergic reactions to anesthesia can occur with any medical procedure involving anesthesia, it is not a specific complication of rigid bronchoscopy.

3. **Answer D (All of the above)**

   The possible mechanical complications of rigid bronchoscopy include trauma to the teeth, oropharynx, vocal cords, and other glottic structures, laryngospasm, pneumothorax, and hemorrhage. These complications may occur due to the use of a non-flexible metal rod and may require immediate intervention to prevent further damage. Other potential complications include airway trauma, perforation, fire, systemic gas embolism, and dissemination of post-obstructive pneumonia.

4. **Answer C (General anesthesia)**

   Rigid bronchoscopy typically requires general anesthesia to ensure patient safety and comfort during the procedure.

5. **Answer A (True)**

   Patients with baseline hypercarbia and hemodynamic instability are at increased risk for complications during rigid bronchoscopy due to the potential effects of the procedure on respiratory and cardiovascular function. The use of anesthesia and the introduction of instruments into the airway can cause changes in oxygenation, ventilation, and hemodynamics, which can be particularly challenging for patients with preexisting respiratory and cardiovascular issues. Careful preoperative evaluation and management are necessary to minimize these risks and ensure the safety of the patient during the procedure.

6. **Answer B (Chest X-ray)**

   The next best step in the evaluation of a patient with pleuritic chest pain post-rigid bronchoscopy is a chest X-ray or point-of-care lung ultrasound. This can help evaluate for complications such as pneumothorax or hemothorax. Administration of an albuterol nebulizer would be indicated if the patient had bronchospasm, but it would not be the first step in evaluating pleuritic chest pain. An electrocardiogram and cardiac enzymes would be indicated if the patient had suspected cardiac chest pain, but again, this is not the most likely cause of chest pain in this scenario. A transthoracic echocardiogram would not be the first step in the evaluation of chest pain post-rigid bronchoscopy, and it would not be indicated unless there was suspicion of cardiac complications such as pericardial effusion.

Recommended literature

1. Galway U, Zura A, Khanna S, Wang M, Turan A, Ruetzler K. Anesthetic considerations for bronchoscopic procedures: a narrative review based on the Cleveland Clinic experience. J Thorac Dis. 2019;11(7):3156-3170.
2. Kabadayi, Selin & Bellamy, Mark. (2016). Bronchoscopy in critical care. BJA Education. 17. mkw040. 10.1093/bjaed/mkw040.
3. Pathak V, Welsby I, Mahmood K, Wahidi M, MacIntyre N, Shofer S. Ventilation and anesthetic approaches for rigid bronchoscopy. Ann Am Thorac Soc. 2014;11(4):628-634.

TRACHEOSTOMY

Questions:

1. **What is the primary indication for performing a tracheostomy in the ICU?**
    A. Aspiration risk
    B. Upper airway obstruction
    C. Prolonged mechanical ventilation
    D. Chronic lung disease

2. **What is a potential complication of a tracheostomy?**
    A. Infection
    B. Hemorrhage
    C. Tracheomalacia
    D. All of the above

3. **What is a potential long-term complication of a tracheostomy?**
    A. Hemorrhage
    B. Pneumothorax
    C. Tracheomalacia
    D. Failure of procedure

4. **How is the correct position and size of a tracheostomy tube typically assessed?**
    A. By auscultation of breath sounds
    B. By measuring arterial blood gases
    C. By combining capnography, endoscopy, and cuff pressure
    D. By observing chest X-rays

5. **Tracheostomy for intubated and long term ventilated patients is commonly performed under local anesthesia in the operating room.**
    A. True
    B. False

6. **A 60-year-old male with a history of laryngeal cancer underwent a total laryngectomy with a permanent tracheostomy stoma 6 months ago. He was recently admitted to the ICU with respiratory distress and a high fever. In the ICU, his tracheostomy tube becomes totally occluded and cannot be cleared with suctioning. The most appropriate course of action while waiting for the ENT surgeon would be?**
    A. Bag mask or laryngeal mask airway until help arrives
    B. Attempt to intubate with GlideScope or direct laryngoscopy
    C. Oral or nasal fiberoptic intubation
    D. Remove the tracheostomy tube and intubate the laryngectomy stoma with an endotracheal tube

Answers:

1. **Answer C (Prolonged mechanical ventilation)**

   Prolonged mechanical ventilation is the main indication for a tracheostomy, as it allows for long-term access to the airway for mechanical ventilation.

2. **Answer D (All of the above)**

   Complications of a tracheostomy can include infection, hemorrhage, tracheomalacia, aspiration, tube displacement, tracheal stenosis, pneumothorax, tracheocutaneous fistula, failure of procedure, surgical emphysema, infection, tracheal necrosis, tracheo-arterial fistula. It is important to monitor patients closely for any signs of complications and to provide appropriate management as needed.

3. **Answer C (Tracheomalacia)**

   Tracheomalacia is a potential long-term complication of a tracheostomy. It is characterized by weakness of the tracheal walls and supporting cartilage. It results in dynamic compression of the airway, where the cross-sectional area of the trachea is reduced by expiratory compression. Acquired tracheomalacia results from complications associated with the use of endotracheal or tracheostomy tubes.

4. **Answer C (By combining capnography, endoscopy, and cuff pressure)**

   Capnography, endoscopy, and cuff pressure are typically used in combination to assess the position and size of a tracheostomy tube, as this provides more accurate information about the location of the tube and the adequacy of ventilation.

5. **Answer B (False)**

   Tracheostomy for intubated and long term ventilated patient is commonly performed under general anesthesia in the operating room. This approach ensures that the patient is unconscious and unable to feel pain during the procedure. General anesthesia also allows for better control of the airway and ventilation, which is particularly important during a tracheostomy, where access to the airway is being established or modified. Additionally, general anesthesia provides optimal conditions for the surgical team to perform the procedure safely and effectively.

6. **Answer D (Remove the tracheostomy tube and intubate the laryngectomy stoma with an endotracheal tube)**

   In this scenario, the patient has a history of laryngectomy, and the tracheostomy tube has become totally occluded and cannot be cleared with suctioning. Therefore, the most appropriate course of action would be to remove the tracheostomy tube and intubate the laryngectomy stoma with an endotracheal tube or another tracheostomy tube placed via the only opening to the airway, allowing for adequate oxygenation and ventilation until the ENT surgeon arrives to address the issue. When placing the ETT, care should be taken not to place it too far because the distance from the stoma to the carina is small, and the ETT can easily pass past the carina and enter the bronchus.

Recommended literature

1. Rosero EB, Corbett J, Mau T, Joshi GP. Intraoperative Airway Management Considerations for Adult Patients Presenting With Tracheostomy: A Narrative Review. Anesth Analg. 2021;132(4):1003-1011.
2. Lewith H, Athanassoglou V. Update on management of tracheostomy. BJA Educ. 2019;19(11):370-376.
3. Jaffe: Anesthesiologist's Manual of Surgical Procedures, ed 5, pp 203–207; Miller: Miller's Anesthesia, ed 8, pp 2542–2543).

CARDIAC DISEASES

ADULT CONGENITAL HEART DISEASE (ACHD)

Questions:

1. **Which of the following is NOT a common symptom of congenital heart disease in adults?**
   A. Shortness of breath
   B. Blue skin, lips, and fingernails
   C. Muscle weakness
   D. Irregular heart rhythms

2. **Which of the following is classified as a severe complexity ACHD lesion?**
   A. Isolated mitral valve disease
   B. Repaired sinus venosus atrial septal defect
   C. Double-outlet ventricle
   D. Moderate pulmonary stenosis

3. **Which of the following is classified as a simple ACHD lesion?**
   A. Tetralogy of Fallot
   B. Eisenmenger syndrome
   C. Patent foramen ovale
   D. Aorta to left ventricular fistula

4. **Which of the following is a common comorbidity associated with ACHD?**
   A. Diabetes mellitus type
   B. Inflammatory bowel disease
   C. Pulmonary hypertension
   D. Cerebrovascular accident

5. **A high BMI > 35 is a risk factor for ACHD.**
   A. True
   B. False

6. **A 35-year-old female with a history of repaired tetralogy of Fallot (TOF) presented for elective laparoscopic cholecystectomy. She had undergone total surgical correction of her TOF at the age of 4 and had been asymptomatic since then. During the anesthetic induction, the patient became hypotensive, and her oxygen saturation decreased to 85%. The surgical team was notified, and the surgery was immediately aborted. The patient was placed on 100% oxygen and given intravenous fluids and inotropic support. Her blood pressure and oxygen saturation improved, and she was transferred to the intensive care unit for further monitoring. What is the likely cause of the patient's hypotension and desaturation during anesthetic induction?**
   A. Undiagnosed pulmonary hypertension
   B. Hypovolemia
   C. Anesthesia overdose
   D. Allergic reaction

Answers:

1. **Answer C (Muscle weakness)**

   Muscle weakness is not a common symptom of congenital heart disease in adults. Common symptoms of congenital heart disease in adults include irregular heart rhythms (arrhythmias), blue skin, lips, and fingernails (cyanosis), shortness of breath, feeling tired very quickly with activity, and swelling of body tissue or organs (edema). Muscle weakness is more commonly associated with other conditions, such as neuromuscular disorders or metabolic diseases.

2. **Answer C (Double-outlet ventricle)**

   Severe complexity ACHD lesions are those that result in significant functional limitation and often require complex surgical interventions. The double-outlet ventricle is classified as a severe complexity ACHD lesion. This anomaly occurs when both the aorta and the pulmonary artery arise from the same ventricle, leading to the mixing of oxygenated and deoxygenated blood. Other examples of severe complexity ACHD lesions include all types of cyanotic heart disease, Eisenmenger syndrome, Fontan procedure or total cavopulmonary connection, mitral, tricuspid, or pulmonary atresia, pulmonary hypertension, any single-ventricle circulation, transposition of the great vessels, truncus arteriosus, and very rare complex anomalies like criss-cross heart, isomerism, ventricular inversion, and heterotaxy syndromes. These lesions are associated with significant morbidity and mortality and require specialized care and management.

3. **Answer C (Patent foramen ovale)**

   A patent foramen ovale (PFO) is classified as a simple ACHD lesion. Simple ACHD lesions are those that confer no functional limitations or have undergone curative surgery. A PFO is a common congenital heart defect where a small opening between the two atria of the heart fails to close properly after birth. Other examples of simple ACHD lesions include isolated aortic valve disease, isolated mitral valve disease (excluding certain complex forms), isolated patent foramen ovale, small atrial septal defect, ventricular septal defect, and mild pulmonary stenosis. These defects are typically straightforward to manage and do not significantly impact a person's health or quality of life.

4. **Answer C (Pulmonary hypertension)**

   Pulmonary hypertension is a common comorbidity associated with ACHD. Many individuals with ACHD have pulmonary hypertension because the structural abnormalities in their hearts cause increased pressure in the pulmonary arteries. This leads to decreased blood flow to the lungs and reduced oxygen levels in the body.

5. **Answer B (False)**

   Obesity, specifically with a BMI greater than 35, is a comorbidity associated with ACHD, not a risk factor. While obesity itself may not directly cause ACHD, it significantly increases the risk of developing heart disease and can worsen outcomes in individuals with preexisting heart conditions.

6. **Answer A (Undiagnosed pulmonary hypertension)**

   The patient's history of repaired TOF puts her at risk for developing pulmonary hypertension. During anesthetic induction, the patient's pulmonary vascular resistance may have increased, leading to a decrease in cardiac output and oxygen saturation. The immediate response to provide oxygen, fluids, and inotropic support suggests that the anesthesia team suspected a cardiovascular event. Further investigation may be needed to confirm a diagnosis of pulmonary hypertension and to plan for future anesthetics.

Recommended literature

1. Agarwal S, Kendall J, Quarterman C. Perioperative management of thoracic and thoracoabdominal aneurysms. BJA Educ. 2019;19(4):119-125.
2. Gregory SH, Yalamuri SM, Bishawi M, Swaminathan M. The Perioperative Management of Ascending Aortic Dissection. Anesth Analg. 2018;127(6):1302-1313.
3. Nienaber CA, Clough RE. Management of acute aortic dissection. Lancet. 2015;385(9970):800-811. doi:10.1016/S0140-6736(14)61005-9

AORTIC DISSECTION

Questions:

1. Which of the following is a risk factor for aortic dissection?
    A. Long-term arterial hypotension
    B. Smoking
    C. Low LDL cholesterol
    D. Hereditary anemia

2. Which medication is commonly used to control heart rate and blood pressure in aortic dissection?
    A. Digoxin
    B. Calcium channel blockers
    C. Beta-blockers
    D. ACE inhibitors

3. What is the imaging modality of choice for acute aortic dissection in unstable patients?
    A. CT
    B. TTE
    C. TEE
    D. MRI

4. What is the target heart rate for patients with aortic dissection who are receiving beta-blockers?
    A. 55-65 bpm
    B. 65-75 bpm
    C. 75-85 bpm
    D. 85-95 bpm

5. A combination of a parenteral β blocker and a vasodilator is the preferred therapy for acute hypertension in patients with aortic dissection.
    A. True
    B. False

6. A 56-year-old male with a history of hypertension presented to the emergency department with sudden-onset chest pain radiating to his back. A computed tomography (CT) scan revealed a type A aortic dissection involving the ascending aorta and aortic arch. Given the life-threatening nature of aortic dissection, the patient was taken for emergent surgical repair. General anesthesia with endotracheal intubation was administered with careful attention to hemodynamic stability. Which of the following is the most appropriate hemodynamic goal for anesthesia management in aortic dissection surgery?
    A. MAP of 100-120 mmHg
    B. MAP of 80-100 mmHg
    C. MAP of 60-80 mmHg
    D. MAP of 40-60 mmHg

Answers:

1. Answer B (Smoking)

Smoking is a risk factor for aortic dissection. The nicotine in tobacco products causes an increase in blood pressure and heart rate, which can lead to an aortic dissection. Long-term arterial hypertension, not hypotension, is also a risk factor for aortic dissection. Low LDL cholesterol and hereditary anemia are not associated with an increased risk of aortic dissection.

2. Answer C (Beta-blockers)

One of the main goals of treatment is to control blood pressure and heart rate to reduce the risk of further tearing or rupture of the aorta. Beta-blockers reduce heart rate and blood pressure, decreasing the amount of force on the weakened aortic wall. While calcium channel blockers and ACE inhibitors can also be used to control blood pressure in aortic dissection, beta-blockers are the first-line therapy because they have been shown to reduce mortality and the risk of further complications in patients with aortic dissection.

3. Answer C (TEE)

In unstable patients with acute aortic dissection, transesophageal echocardiography (TEE) is the imaging modality of choice. TEE, when combined with bedside transthoracic echocardiography (TTE), has the priority in this setting to exclude new-onset aortic regurgitation, pericardial effusion, or to visualize proximal dissection. TEE evaluation, added to the transthoracic suprasternal view, has good accuracy to diagnose acute aortic dissection (type A), even intraoperatively, with near 100% sensitivity and specificity. Color-Doppler is often able to assess entry sites and/or false lumen flow to confirm a proximal dissection. While CT remains the initial diagnostic imaging technique in stable patients with suspected acute aortic dissection, TEE is preferred in unstable patients. MRI is rarely used in the acute emergency setting of symptomatic patients and is more useful in follow-up evaluations.

4. Answer A (50-60 bpm)

The target heart rate for patients with aortic dissection who are receiving beta-blockers is typically around 55 to 65 beats per minute (bpm). This range is selected because reducing the heart rate helps decrease the shear forces acting on the aortic wall, which can reduce the risk of further propagation of the dissection. Lowering the heart rate also reduces the force of left ventricular contraction, which is important because the velocity of this contraction can impact the progression of the dissection. Therefore, maintaining a heart rate within this range is considered optimal for managing aortic dissection.

5. Answer A (True)

In aortic dissection and aortic aneurysm, the propagation of aortic dissection depends not only on the absolute blood pressure but also on the velocity of left ventricular contraction. A vasodilator alone, instead of decreasing the heart rate, may even cause reflex tachycardia, thus causing the propagation of the dissection. Therefore, the optimum treatment involves a combination of a parenteral β blocker and a vasodilator, with the heart rate targeted around 55 to 65 beats/minute. The β blocker of choice in this situation is generally esmolol and, alternatively, labetalol or metoprolol.

6. Answer C (MAP of 60-80 mmHg)

In anesthesia management of aortic dissection surgery, the goal is to maintain adequate tissue perfusion while avoiding excessive blood pressure, which can lead to propagation of the dissection or rupture of the aorta. The recommended hemodynamic goals include a MAP of 60-80 mmHg and a heart rate of 60-80 beats per minute. This can be achieved with the use of intravenous medications such as beta-blockers, vasodilators, and inotropes, as well as careful fluid management.

Recommended literature

1. Agarwal S, Kendall J, Quarterman C. Perioperative management of thoracic and thoracoabdominal aneurysms. BJA Educ. 2019;19(4):119-125.
2. Gregory SH, Yalamuri SM, Bishawi M, Swaminathan M. The Perioperative Management of Ascending Aortic Dissection. Anesth Analg. 2018;127(6):1302-1313.
3. Nienaber CA, Clough RE. Management of acute aortic dissection. Lancet. 2015;385(9970):800-811. doi:10.1016/S0140-6736(14)61005-9.

AORTIC REGURGITATION

Questions:

1. **Which of the following is the most common cause of chronic aortic regurgitation?**
   A. Infective endocarditis
   B. Atherosclerotic degeneration of the valve
   C. Traumatic injury
   D. Dissection of the aorta

2. **What is the most common cause of acute aortic regurgitation?**
   A. Aortic dissection
   B. Infective endocarditis
   C. Traumatic injury
   D. All of the above

3. **Which of the following is a sign of severe aortic regurgitation?**
   A. Collapsing pulse and wide pulse pressure
   B. Bradycardia
   C. Narrow pulse pressure
   D. Hypotension

4. **Immediate treatment of acute severe aortic regurgitation includes?**
   A. Beta-blockers
   B. Nitroprusside
   C. Intra-aortic balloon pump
   D. All of the above

5. **Patients with chronic aortic regurgitation can remain asymptomatic for years.**
   A. True
   B. False

6. **A 60-year-old man comes to the clinic with complaints of shortness of breath on exertion and fatigue. He states that he had rheumatic fever as a child and that he has had these symptoms for the past few months. On physical examination, the patient has a blood pressure of 150/60 mmHg, a heart rate of 120 beats per minute, with a loud, blowing diastolic murmur best heard at the left sternal border, with a palpable carotid pulsation and head nodding with each pulse. Based on the history and examination findings, what is the likely diagnosis?**
   A. Aortic stenosis
   B. Aortic regurgitation
   C. Mitral stenosis
   D. Mitral regurgitation

Answers:

1. Answer B (Atherosclerotic degeneration of the valve)

Aortic regurgitation is a condition characterized by diastolic reversal of blood flow from the aorta to the left ventricle. Chronic aortic regurgitation is the most common form of the disease and can be caused by a number of factors. It is most often caused by atherosclerotic valve degeneration and/or congenital bicuspid aortic valve.

2. Answer D (All of the above)

Acute aortic regurgitation is characterized by a sudden increase in the end-diastolic volume of the left ventricle. In severe cases, patients often have pulmonary edema and even cardiogenic shock. Acute aortic regurgitation can develop from valvular abnormalities (most commonly infective endocarditis) and aortic abnormalities (mainly aortic dissection). Iatrogenic causes, such as traumatic injuries or during transcutaneous procedures on the aortic valve, can also lead to acute aortic regurgitation.

3. Answer A (Collapsing pulse and wide pulse pressure)

A collapsing pulse and wide pulse pressure are characteristic signs of severe aortic regurgitation. The collapsing pulse is caused by the backflow of blood into the left ventricle during diastole, which leads to a rapid rise and fall of the arterial pulse. The wide pulse pressure is due to the difference between the systolic and diastolic blood pressure, which is increased in severe aortic regurgitation.

4. Answer B (Nitroprusside)

The immediate treatment of acute severe aortic regurgitation involves afterload reduction with intravenous nitroprusside. Nitroprusside reduces systemic vascular resistance, which subsequently decreases afterload on the heart. This helps to improve forward cardiac output and reduce regurgitant volume. Beta-blockers are not indicated in acute severe aortic regurgitation as they can block the compensatory tachycardia and worsen the cardiac output. Intra-aortic balloon pump is contraindicated in acute severe aortic regurgitation as it can worsen aortic regurgitation by increasing diastolic pressure and aortic root diameter.

5. Answer A (True)

Compensatory mechanisms allow patients to remain stable and asymptomatic for many years, even in the presence of severe aortic regurgitation. When symptoms do occur, they are due to left heart failure, including increasing intolerance to physical exertion, chest pain, increasing exercise intolerance, dyspnea, paroxysmal nocturnal dyspnea or orthopnea.

6. Answer B (Aortic regurgitation)

The patient's history of rheumatic fever suggests a potential etiology for aortic regurgitation. A loud, blowing diastolic murmur best heard at the left sternal border, along with a collapsing pulse, wide pulse pressure, De Musset's sign (head nods with each pulse), Corrigan's sign (visible carotid pulsation) are classic signs of aortic regurgitation. To confirm the diagnosis, it is necessary to carry out further diagnostics such as an echocardiogram.

Recommended literature

1. Flint N, Wunderlich NC, Shmueli H, Ben-Zekry S, Siegel RJ, Beigel R. Aortic Regurgitation. Curr Cardiol Rep. 2019;21(7):65.
2. Pollard BJ, Kitchen, G. Handbook of Clinical Anaesthesia. Fourth Edition. CRC Press. 2018. 978-1-4987-6289-2.
3. Hines, R. L. (2017). Stoelting's anesthesia and co-existing disease (7th ed.). Elsevier – Health Sciences Division
4. Nishimura RA, Otto CM, Bonow RO, et al. 2014 AHA/ACC Guideline for the Management of Patients With Valvular Heart Disease: executive summary: a report of the American College of Cardiology/American Heart Association Task Force on Practice Guidelines [published correction appears in Circulation. 2014 Jun 10;129(23):e650]. Circulation. 2014;129(23):2440-2492.

AORTIC STENOSIS

Questions:

1. **Which of the following is not a causative mechanism of aortic stenosis (AS)?**
   A. Degenerative calcified aortic stenosis
   B. Congenital bicuspid aortic valve
   C. Rheumatic aortic stenosis
   D. Atrial fibrillation

2. **What parameter is used to assess the severity of aortic stenosis?**
   A. Left ventricular ejection fraction
   B. Right ventricular ejection fraction
   C. Aortic valve area
   D. Pulmonary artery pressure

3. **Which drug is the agent of choice for the treatment of hypotension in AS patients?**
   A. Dobutamine
   B. Milrinone
   C. Epinephrine
   D. Phenylephrine

4. **Which of the following is a principle of anesthetic management for aortic stenosis?**
   A. Optimization of preload, afterload, and contractility
   B. Avoidance of bradycardia, tachycardia, and sinus rhythm disturbances
   C. Monitoring of vital signs, including blood pressure, heart rate, and respiratory rate
   D. All of the above

5. **The mean gradient (mmHg) of the pressure across the valve above 40 mmHg is a sign of mild aortic stenosis.**
   A. True
   B. False

6. **An 85-year-old man with a history of high blood pressure and type 2 diabetes mellitus is scheduled for hip replacement surgery. During the preoperative assessment, a systolic murmur is detected on auscultation. Further evaluation with an echocardiogram reveals moderate aortic stenosis. The patient is otherwise stable and asymptomatic from the aortic stenosis. What statement is true about aortic stenosis (AS) and anesthesia?**
   A. General anesthesia with endotracheal intubation is the only option for this patient
   B. Low-dose spinal anesthesia may provide more stable hemodynamics than general anesthesia
   C. Neuraxial anesthesia has been contraindicated in patients with aortic stenosis
   D. Local anesthesia with conscious sedation is a good alternative

Answers:

1. Answer D (Atrial fibrillation)

Atrial fibrillation is a cardiac arrhythmia that is not directly related to the development of aortic stenosis. Some of the possible causes of the development of aortic stenosis are degenerative calcified aortic stenosis, congenital bicuspid aortic valve, and rheumatic aortic stenosis. Degenerative calcified aortic stenosis is the most common cause and occurs due to progressive fibrosis and calcification of the leaflets of the aortic valves over time. The congenitally bicuspid aortic valve is a structural abnormality in which the valve has two leaflets instead of three and can lead to fibrosis and calcification over time. Rheumatic aortic stenosis is a long-term consequence of acute rheumatic fever, which can cause inflammation and scarring of the valve leaflets.

2. Answer C (Aortic valve area)

The parameter used to assess the severity of aortic stenosis is the aortic valve area (AVA). Echocardiographic parameters, including peak velocity, mean gradient, AVA, indexed AVA, and velocity ratio, are used in conjunction to determine the severity of aortic stenosis. In adults with normal aortic valves, the valve area is approximately 3.0 to 4.0 cm². As aortic stenosis (AS) develops, the minimal pressure gradient is present until the orifice area becomes less than half of normal. The pressure gradient across a stenotic valve is directly related to the valve orifice area and the transvalvular flow.

3. Answer D (Phenylephrine)

Phenylephrine is the agent of choice for the treatment of hypotension in patients with aortic stenosis. Phenylephrine acts predominantly on alpha receptors, leading to vasoconstriction and an increase in systemic vascular resistance. This increase in vascular resistance helps to maintain coronary perfusion pressure (CPP) without significantly increasing chronotropy or heart rate, which is beneficial in patients with aortic stenosis who are at risk of worsening the obstruction across the aortic valve with agents that increase heart rate or contractility. Therefore, phenylephrine is preferred for managing hypotension in these patients, as it can help maintain adequate perfusion pressure without exacerbating the underlying pathology of aortic stenosis.

4. Answer D (All of the above)

The anesthetic management for aortic stenosis aims to optimize preload, afterload, and contractility while avoiding bradycardia, tachycardia, and sinus rhythm disturbances. This involves ensuring adequate preload for optimal cardiac output without fluid overload, reducing afterload to ease the workload on the hypertrophied left ventricle, and managing contractility to prevent worsening of obstruction or myocardial ischemia. Vital signs, including blood pressure, heart rate, and respiratory rate, must be closely monitored to promptly detect any changes indicating stenosis progression or anesthesia-related complications. The overarching goal is to maintain hemodynamic stability, minimizing the risk of myocardial ischemia or compromised cardiac output during anesthesia in patients with aortic stenosis.

5. Answer B (False)

A mean gradient (mmHg) of the pressure across the valve exceeding 40 mmHg is indicative of severe, not mild, aortic stenosis. In the presence of symptoms and/or reduced ejection fraction (EF), severe AS is defined by a mean gradient ≥ 40 mmHg, aortic peak velocity ≥ 4 m/s, and AVA ≤ 1 cm² (or an indexed AVA ≤ 0.6 cm²/m²), warranting surgical or percutaneous treatment for improved outcomes. Moderate AS, on the other hand, is defined by an AVA > 1 and < 1.5 cm² and an average gradient > 20 but < 40 mmHg. Mild AS typically has an AVA > 1.5 cm² and a mean gradient < 20 mmHg.

6. Answer B (Low dose spinal may provide more stable hemodynamics than general anesthesia)

Traditionally, spinal anesthesia has been considered contraindicated in patients with aortic stenosis due to the risk of sympathetic nervous system block and resultant hypotension, which could lead to myocardial ischemia. However, recent research has shown that low-dose isobaric spinal anesthesia can be safely used in patients with aortic stenosis undergoing lower limb surgery. This approach has been associated with stable hemodynamics and excellent perioperative outcomes. Therefore, in patients with multiple comorbidities where avoiding general anesthesia is beneficial, low-dose spinal anesthesia may be a suitable alternative and may provide more stable hemodynamics compared to general anesthesia, which often causes hypotension.

Recommended literature

1. Schneider AC. A review of aortic stenosis: an anesthetic perspective. J Anesth Crit Care Open Access. 2018;10(6):262-264.
2. Baumgartner H Chair, Hung J Co-Chair, Bermejo J, et al. Recommendations on the echocardiographic assessment of aortic valve stenosis: a focused update from the European Association of Cardiovascular Imaging and the American Society of Echocardiography. Eur Heart J Cardiovasc Imaging. 2017;18(3):254-275.
3. Brown J, Morgan-Hughes NJ. Aortic stenosis and non-cardiac surgery. Continuing Education in Anaesthesia Critical Care & Pain. 2005;5(1):1-4.

ATRIAL FIBRILLATION (AF)

02
CHAPTER

Questions:

1. **Which of the following is the most common sustained arrhythmia?**
   A. Ventricular tachycardia
   B. Supraventricular tachycardia
   C. Atrial fibrillation
   D. Sinus bradycardia

2. **What is the recommended therapy for rate control in patients with perioperative atrial fibrillation?**
   A. Amiodaron
   B. Beta-blockers
   C. Calcium channel blockers
   D. All of the above

3. **When is cardioversion indicated in patients with perioperative atrial fibrillation?**
   A. In all patients with atrial fibrillation
   B. In stable patients with atrial fibrillation that has recently appeared
   C. In unstable patients with atrial fibrillation that has recently appeared
   D. Cardioversion is contraindicated in perioperative atrial fibrillation

4. **Which of the following should be avoided in patients with perioperative atrial fibrillation?**
   A. Hypotension
   B. Hypoxia
   C. Hypercarbia
   D. All of the above

5. **Hypoglycemia is a potential arrhythmogenic factor in patients with perioperative atrial fibrillation.**
   A. True
   B. False

6. **A 68-year-old patient with a history of hypertension and atrial fibrillation underwent hip replacement surgery. In the operating room, before anesthesia and surgery begin, the patient's heart rate suddenly increases to 170 beats per minute, BP 140/80 mmHg, SpO2 98%. The anesthesiologist administers Amiodarone 150 mg IV, but the heart rate remains high. What is the next course of action?**
   A. Stop the procedure
   B. Continue the procedure
   C. Administer additional doses of amiodarone and wait
   D. Order cardioversion

Answers:

1. **Answer C (Atrial fibrillation)**

   Atrial fibrillation is the most common sustained arrhythmia, increases with age, and presents with a wide spectrum of symptoms and severity. Paroxysmal, persistent, and permanent forms require very individualized approaches to management.

2. **Answer D (All of the above)**

   Rate control is an important management strategy in patients with perioperative atrial fibrillation to prevent complications such as congestive heart failure and embolic events. Amiodarone, beta-blockers, and calcium channel blockers are effective rate-control agents in these patients. The choice will depend on the individual factors of the patient and the presence of comorbidities. In some cases, combination therapy with two or more agents may also be necessary.

3. **Answer B (In stable patients with atrial fibrillation that has recently appeared)**

   Cardioversion is the re-establishment of normal sinus rhythm by the application of electric shocks or the administration of antiarrhythmics. It may be considered in stable patients with new-onset atrial fibrillation who have not responded to pharmacological rate control or anticoagulant therapy. However, cardioversion is contraindicated in unstable patients with new-onset atrial fibrillation who have hemodynamic instability or severe pulmonary edema, as it may lead to further deterioration of their condition.

4. **Answer D (All of the above)**

   Patients with perioperative atrial fibrillation are at increased risk of complications such as congestive heart failure, embolic events, and stroke. Therefore, it is important to avoid factors that can aggravate these complications. Hypotension, hypoxia, and hypercarbia can lead to reduced cardiac output and oxygen delivery, which can increase the risk of side effects. Close monitoring and prompt treatment of these factors are crucial in patients with perioperative atrial fibrillation.

5. **Answer A (True)**

   Electrolyte disturbances, primarily hypokalemia and hypomagnesemia, as well as hypoglycemia, are potential arrhythmogenic factors in patients with perioperative atrial fibrillation. It is important to monitor and manage these factors to reduce the risk of adverse events.

6. **Answer C (Administer additional doses of amiodarone and wait)**

   If the initial dose of amiodarone does not effectively control the heart rate, additional doses can be administered while closely monitoring the patient. The recommended regimen for amiodarone IV is usually an initial loading dose of 150 mg over 10 minutes may be repeated after 10 minutes as necessary, followed by a maintenance infusion of 1 mg/min for 6 hours, then 0.5 mg/min for the next 18 hours, for a total of 24 hours of therapy. However, dosing may vary depending on the patient's condition and the physician's preference. Stopping the procedure may not be necessary unless the patient's condition worsens or becomes unstable, and cardioversion is typically reserved for cases of prolonged atrial fibrillation.

Recommended literature

1. Karamchandani K, Khanna AK, Bose S, Fernando RJ, Walkey AJ. Atrial Fibrillation: Current Evidence and Management Strategies During the Perioperative Period. Anesthesia & Analgesia. 2020;130(1).
2. Wijesurendra RS, Casadei B. Mechanisms of atrial fibrillation. Heart. 2019;105(24):1860-1867.

Cardiac diseases
ATRIAL SEPTAL DEFECT (ASD)

Questions:

1. **What is the most common type of congenital heart defect?**
    A. Ventricular septal defect
    B. Coronary sinus defect
    C. Atrial septal defect
    D. Truncus arteriosus

2. **What is the main diagnostic tool used to confirm the diagnosis of ASD?**
    A. Echocardiogram
    B. Electrocardiogram (ECG)
    C. Magnetic resonance imaging (MRI)
    D. X-ray of the chest

3. **Which of the following is not a risk factor for ASD?**
    A. Down syndrome
    B. Rubella
    C. Alcohol
    D. Congenital tricuspid atresia

4. **What is the consequence of chronic volume overload in patients with ASD?**
    A. Increased pulmonary vascular resistance
    B. Increased systemic vascular resistance
    C. Decreased cardiac output
    D. None of the above

5. **Maternal alcohol exposure is a risk factor for ASD.**
    A. True
    B. False

6. **A 35-year-old patient is scheduled to have an ASD closed. She had a history of recurrent respiratory infections and dyspnea on exertion. Transthoracic echocardiography revealed a moderate-sized ASD with a left-to-right shunt and an enlarged right atrium and ventricle. She had no other medical history of interest or comorbidities. Which of the following measures should be taken into account during the patient's anesthetic management?**
    A. Avoidance of air bubbles
    B. Maintenance of preload and sinus rhythm
    C. Control of heart rate and contractility
    D. All of the above

Answers:

1. **Answer C (Atrial septal defect)**

   Atrial septal defect (ASD) is one of the most common types of congenital heart defects, occurring in about 25% of children.

2. **Answer A (Echocardiogram)**

   An echocardiogram is the primary diagnostic tool used to confirm the diagnosis of ASD.

3. **Answer D (Congenital tricuspid atresia)**

   Maternal alcohol consumption during pregnancy, Down syndrome, and rubella infection during pregnancy are known risk factors for ASD. Tricuspid atresia is a birth defect of the heart where the valve that controls blood flow from the right upper chamber of the heart to the right lower chamber of the heart doesn't form at all. This defect is distinct from ASD and is not considered a risk factor for it.

4. **Answer A (Increased pulmonary vascular resistance)**

   In patients with ASD, blood flows from the left atrium to the right atrium, creating a left-right shunt. This leads to chronic volume overload of the right heart, which causes an increase in pulmonary vascular resistance. Over time, increased pulmonary vascular resistance leads to pulmonary hypertension.

5. **Answer A (True)**

   Maternal alcohol exposure is a known risk factor for the development of certain congenital heart defects, including ASD. Fetal alcohol syndrome is a condition that occurs when a mother drinks alcohol during pregnancy, and it can cause a range of physical, behavioral, and intellectual disabilities in the child. One of the potential effects of fetal alcohol syndrome (FAS) is the development of heart defects, including ASD.

6. **Answer D (All of the above)**

   Anesthetic management of patients with ASD includes avoiding air bubbles, maintaining preload and sinus rhythm, and controlling heart rate and contractility. Air bubbles should be avoided as they may cause paradoxical embolization and lead to stroke or systemic embolization in ASD patients. It is important to maintain preload in patients with ASD because they have a left-to-right shunt that can lead to volume overload on the right side of the heart. Control of heart rate and contractility is important for maintaining cardiac output and preventing arrhythmias.

Recommended literature

1. Menillo AM, Lee LS, Pearson-Shaver AL. Atrial Septal Defect. [Updated 2022 Aug 8]. In: StatPearls [Internet]. Treasure Island (FL): StatPearls Publishing; 2022 Jan-. Available from: https://www.ncbi.nlm.nih.gov/books/NBK535440/
2. Yen P. ASD and VSD Flow Dynamics and Anesthetic Management. Anesth Prog. 2015;62(3):125-130.
3. Calvert PA, Klein AA. Anaesthesia for percutaneous closure of atrial septal defects. Continuing Education in Anaesthesia Critical Care & Pain. 2008;8(1):16-20.

BRUGADA SYNDROME (BRS)

02
CHAPTER

Questions:

1. In what percentage of Brugada syndrome cases is the causative genetic mutation not identified?
   A. Up to 10%
   B. Up to 40%
   C. Up to 60%
   D. Up to 80%

2. Which ECG finding is potentially diagnostic for Brugada syndrome?
   A. Prolonged QT interval
   B. PR interval prolongation
   C. Coved ST-segment elevation > 2mm in > 1 of V1-V3 followed by a negative T wave
   D. QRS complex widening

3. What genetic mutations are associated with Brugada syndrome?
   A. Mutations encoding sodium channels
   B. Mutations encoding calcium channels
   C. Mutations encoding potassium channels
   D. All of the above

4. Which of the following conditions can reproduce a Brugada type 1 ECG?
   A. Early repolarization
   B. Athletic heart
   C. Pulmonary embolism
   D. All of the above

5. Brugada syndrome is believed to be responsible for 40% of cases of sudden cardiac death in structurally normal hearts.
   A. True
   B. False

6. A 45-year-old man with no significant medical history presented to the emergency department with complaints of syncope. He reported feeling dizzy and light-headed for several days before the syncopal episode. On subsequent questioning, he reported a family history of his father's sudden cardiac death at a young age. The physical examination was normal, and the initial laboratory findings were within normal limits. An ECG was performed, which revealed Brugada type 1. What is the most common symptomatic presentation of Brugada syndrome?
   A. Palpitations
   B. Chest discomfort
   C. Syncope and nocturnal agonal respiration
   D. All of the above

Answers:

1. **Answer D (Up to 80%)**

   Up to 80% of patients with Brugada syndrome do not have an identifiable causative gene mutation.

2. **Answer C (Coved ST-segment elevation > 2mm in > 1 of V1-V3 followed by a negative T wave)**

   Coved ST-segment elevation > 2mm in > 1 of V1-V3 followed by a negative T wave is the only ECG abnormality that is potentially diagnostic for Brugada syndrome. It is often referred to as the Brugada sign.

3. **Answer D (All of the above)**

   Brugada syndrome is a cardiac ion channel abnormality associated with 19 genetic mutations encoding sodium, calcium, or potassium channels. These mutations result in increased or decreased activity of these channels, which can affect the heart's normal electrical activity.

4. **Answer D (All of the above)**

   Brugada type 1 ECG morphology is characterized by an ST-segment elevation (with T-wave inversion) of at least 2 mm in leads V1 and/or V2 when placed in the standard or superior position, either spontaneously or after application of Na-channel blockers such as ajmaline or flecainide. However, the differential diagnosis of Brugada syndrome is complicated by the fact that this EKG pattern can mimic several other conditions. These conditions include early repolarization, which is a common variant and often benign finding in young people, athlete's heart, which is a physiological adaptation to regular physical training, and pulmonary embolism, which can cause right ventricular strain and ST-segment elevation in V1-V4. Other conditions that can cause a Brugada type 1 ECG include acute coronary events, electrolyte disturbances, pericarditis, myocarditis, dissecting aortic aneurysm, arrhythmogenic right ventricular cardiomyopathy, etc.

5. **Answer A (True)**

   Brugada syndrome is estimated to be responsible for up to 40% of cases of sudden cardiac death in people with structurally normal hearts.

6. **Answer D (All of the above)**

   The most common symptomatic presentation of Brugada syndrome may include syncope, palpitations, chest discomfort, nocturnal agonal respiration, and sudden cardiac death. The presence of a Brugada type 1 ECG pattern is an important diagnostic feature of the syndrome.

Recommended literature

1. Levy D, Bigham C, Tomlinson D. Anaesthesia for patients with hereditary arrhythmias part I: Brugada syndrome. BJA Educ. 2018;18(6):159-165.

Cardiac diseases
CARDIAC CONTUSION

02
CHAPTER

Questions:

1. Which of the following is the most common cause of heart contusion?
    A. Atherosclerosis
    B. Myocardial infarction
    C. Blunt thoracic trauma
    D. Coronary artery disease

2. Which of the following signs and symptoms is most commonly associated with cardiac contusion?
    A. Chest pain
    B. Difficulty breathing
    C. Arrhythmias
    D. Syncope

3. Which of the following is a potential complication of heart contusion?
    A. Cardiac tamponade
    B. Pulmonary embolism
    C. Aortic dissection
    D. Ischemic stroke

4. Which of the following diagnostic tools is most commonly used to diagnose cardiac contusion?
    A. EKG
    B. Measurement of cardiac biomarkers (troponin T, troponin I, CK-MB)
    C. Echocardiography
    D. All of the above

5. Patients with suspected cardiac contusion may not show symptoms immediately after trauma, but severe arrhythmia or cardiac arrest may occur within 72 hours.
    A. True
    B. False

6. A 40-year-old man who was involved in a traffic accident. He was wearing a seat belt, but his chest hit the steering wheel. He was brought to the emergency room complaining of chest pains and palpitations. On examination, he has bruising over his chest, chest X-ray shows no signs of fracture or pneumothorax, but EKG shows irregular heartbeat. What is the most appropriate initial treatment strategy for a patient with suspected cardiac contusion?
    A. Immediate discharge home
    B. Observation in the emergency department
    C. Admission to the general hospital ward
    D. Admission to the ICU

Answers:

1. Answer C (Blunt thoracic trauma)

Contusion of the heart is most often caused by blunt trauma to the chest, which exerts a decelerating force on the front of the chest. The force leads to hematomas or microscopic bleeding of the heart muscle.

2. Answer C (Arrhythmias)

Arrhythmias, including premature ventricular complexes, atrial fibrillation, and ventricular fibrillation, are the most common signs and symptoms associated with cardiac contusion and may occur within 24 hours of trauma.

3. Answer A (Cardiac tamponade)

Cardiac contusion can cause mechanical injury to the heart muscle, such as atrial or chordal rupture, which can lead to cardiac tamponade. Cardiac tamponade occurs when there is an accumulation of blood, in the pericardial sac that surrounds the heart, pressing on the heart and impairing its function.

4. Answer D (All of the above)

The diagnosis of cardiac contusion remains controversial, and the use of different diagnostic tools is recommended to increase diagnostic accuracy. ECG, echocardiography (ultrasound), and measurement of cardiac biomarkers such as troponin T, troponin I, and CK-MB are commonly used to diagnose cardiac contusion. However, none of these diagnostic tools alone can confirm the diagnosis and a combination of tools should be used to increase diagnostic accuracy.

5. Answer A (True)

Patients with cardiac contusion may not show symptoms immediately after thoracic trauma but may experience severe arrhythmia or even cardiac arrest within 72 hours. Therefore, it is important to closely monitor these patients and consider admission to the ICU for follow-up.

6. Answer D (Admission to the ICU)

Patients suspected of having cardiac contusion should be admitted to the ICU for close monitoring of their condition. Once admitted, diagnostic tests such as ECG, echocardiography, and measurement of cardiac biomarkers (troponin T, troponin I, CK-MB) can be used to determine the extent of the trauma and assess cardiac function and intracardiac volume. Treatment for cardiac contusion typically involves managing any associated complications, such as arrhythmias or cardiogenic shock, using approaches such as invasive angiography, revascularization, inotropes/vasopressors, fluid resuscitation, ventilation, and mechanical support. The appropriate treatment approach will depend on the severity of the patient's condition and the specific complications they are experiencing.

Recommended literature

1. Van Lieshout EMM, Verhofstad MHJ, Van Silfhout DJT, Dubois EA. Diagnostic approach for myocardial contusion: a retrospective evaluation of patient data and review of the literature. Eur J Trauma Emerg Surg. 2021;47(4):1259-1272.
2. Thiele H, Ohman EM, Desch S, Eitel I, de Waha S. Management of cardiogenic shock. European Heart Journal. 2015;36(20):1223-30.

Cardiac diseases

CARDIAC IMPLANTABLE ELECTRONIC DEVICES (CIEDS)

02
CHAPTER

Questions:

1. **What is the purpose of preoperative testing with implantable electronic devices (CIED)?**
   A. Identify the CIED manufacturer
   B. To assess the patient's dependence on the pacing
   C. To temporarily deactivate the CIED
   D. Increase the energy level for monopolar electrosurgery

2. **Which of the following imaging tests requires a temporary suspension of the anti-tachycardia function of the implantable cardioverter-defibrillator (ICD) prior to scanning?**
   A. Computed tomography (CT)
   B. Magnetic resonance imaging (MRI)
   C. X-ray
   D. Positron emission tomography (PET)

3. **What is the recommended approach during electrosurgery to minimize interference with a CIED?**
   A. Increase the output power of the electrosurgical unit
   B. Place the electrosurgical electrode away from the CIED generator or leads
   C. Place the CIED in standby mode for stimulation
   D. Perform the grounding of the CIED lines

4. **What is the recommended treatment approach for a patient with CIED undergoing electroconvulsive therapy (ECT)?**
   A. Stop the anti-tachycardia function of the CIED
   B. Increase the pacing rate of the pacemaker
   C. Give antiarrhythmic drugs before ECT
   D. Change the pacing function to asynchronous mode

5. **During lithotripsy, is it recommended to direct the lithotripsy beam near the CIED generator to minimize potential damage to the CIED.**
   A. True
   B. False

6. **A 60-year-old patient with a history of complete heart block and a permanent pacemaker implanted for cardiac pacing is scheduled for a dental procedure. Which of the following is a recommended precaution during a dental procedure for a patient with a permanent pacemaker?**
   A. Administration of general anesthesia
   B. Avoiding the use of dental X-rays
   C. Placing the dental chair in an upright position
   D. Use of bipolar electrosurgery

Answers:

1. **Answer B (Assess the patient's dependence on the pacing)**

   Preoperative Cardiac Implantable Electronic Device (CIED) testing is used to assess the patient's dependence on stimulation. This includes assessing the patient's reliance on the CIED as an appropriate pacemaker.

2. **Answer B (Magnetic resonance imaging (MRI))**

   Prior to MRI, the anti-tachycardia function of the implantable cardioverter defibrillator (ICD) must be temporarily suspended. MRI uses strong magnetic fields and radio frequency pulses that can potentially interfere with the normal operation of the ICD. To avoid unwanted shocks or inappropriate device behavior during scanning, the anti-tachycardia function of the ICD must be temporarily suspended.

3. **Answer B (Place the electrosurgical electrode away from the CIED generator or electrodes)**

   The recommended approach during electrosurgery to reduce interference with a CIED is to place the electrosurgical lead away from the CIED generator or leads. By keeping the electrosurgical current path away from the CIED generator and electrodes, the likelihood of EMI affecting device function is minimized.

4. **Answer D (Change the pacing function to asynchronous mode)**

   The recommended approach for managing a patient with a CIED undergoing electroconvulsive therapy (ECT) is to change the pacing function to an asynchronous mode. ECT involves the administration of an electrical stimulus to induce a controlled seizure for therapeutic purposes. To prevent potential interference with the CIED or interruptions in pacing during the procedure, it is necessary to change the pacing function to asynchronous mode.

5. **Answer B (False)**

   It is not recommended to direct the lithotripsy beam near the CIED generator during lithotripsy. The CIED generator and leads should be kept as far away as possible from the lithotripsy beam to reduce the risk of electromagnetic interference and potential malfunction of the CIED. Directing the lithotripsy beam towards the CIED generator can increase the likelihood of electromagnetic interference and may pose a risk to the functioning of the device.

6. **Answer D (Use of bipolar electrosurgery)**

   One of the recommended precautions during most procedures for patients with a permanent pacemaker is to use bipolar electrosurgery if possible. Bipolar electrosurgery, compared to monopolar electrosurgery, carries a lower risk of interference with the pacemaker. During bipolar electrosurgery, the electric current flows between the two tips of the instrument and does not pass through the patient's body. This reduces the risk of electromagnetic interference (EMI) affecting the pacemaker, which could potentially disrupt its proper functioning.

Recommended literature

1. Practice advisory for the perioperative management of patients with cardiac implantable electronic devices: pacemakers and implantable cardioverter-defibrillators 2020. Apfelbaum JL, Schulman PM, Mahajan A, Connis RT, Agarkar M. Anesthesiology. 2020;132:225–252.
2. Stone ME, Salter B, Fischer A. Perioperative management of patients with cardiac implantable electronic devices. British Journal of Anaesthesia. 2011;107:i16–i26.

CARDIAC TAMPONADE

Questions:

1. Which of the following is NOT a common cause of cardiac tamponade?

    A. Pericarditis

    B. Tuberculosis

    C. Hypertension

    D. Trauma

2. Which of the following is NOT a sign of cardiac tamponade?

    A. Paradoxical pulse

    B. Dilated neck veins

    C. Bradycardia

    D. Low mean arterial pressure

3. What term is used to describe an excessive drop in systemic arterial pressure during inspiration?

    A. Paradoxical pulse

    B. Alternating pulse

    C. Buffered pulse

    D. Bigeminal pulse

4. How does cardiac tamponade affect cardiac output?

    A. It increases the cardiac output

    B. It has no effect on the cardiac output

    C. Decreases cardiac output

    D. Causes arrhythmias

5. Gradually developing pericardial effusions are largely asymptomatic.

    A. True

    B. False

6. A 60-year-old male with a history of lung cancer presents to the emergency department with acute-onset dyspnea, chest discomfort, and hypotension. On physical examination, his blood pressure is 80/50 mmHg, heart rate is 130 beats per minute, and jugular venous distension is present. Auscultation reveals distant heart sounds and pulsus paradoxus. An ECG shows low-voltage QRS complexes. Chest X-ray reveals an enlarged cardiac silhouette. Transthoracic echocardiography shows a large pericardial effusion with a collapse of the right atrium and ventricle during diastole. What is the most likely diagnosis for this patient?

    A. Cardiac tamponade

    B. Acute myocardial infarction

    C. Pulmonary embolism

    D. Tension pneumothorax

Answers:

1. **Answer C (Hypertension)**

   Common causes of cardiac tamponade include pericarditis, tuberculosis, trauma, malignancy, and iatrogenic causes.

2. **Answer C (Bradycardia)**

   Bradycardia is not a typical sign of cardiac tamponade. Instead, tachycardia is more commonly seen due to sympathetic stimulation.

3. **Answer A (Pulsus paradoxus)**

   Pulsus paradoxus refers to an excessive drop in systemic arterial pressure during inspiration and is a characteristic finding in cardiac tamponade.

4. **Answer C (Decreases cardiac output)**

   Cardiac tamponade leads to compression of the heart chambers, which increases intrapericardial pressure and alters ventricular filling. This ultimately reduces cardiac output.

5. **Answer A (True)**

   Gradually developing pericardial effusions are often largely asymptomatic. This is because the pericardium has the ability to stretch and accommodate the increasing fluid volume over time. As a result, there may be a gradual increase in intrapericardial pressure without causing significant compression of the heart chambers or impairment of cardiac function.

6. **Answer A (Cardiac tamponade)**

   The clinical presentation in this case, including acute-onset dyspnea, chest discomfort, hypotension, jugular venous distension, distant heart sounds, pulsus paradoxus, low voltage QRS complexes on ECG, enlarged cardiac silhouette on chest X-ray, and a large pericardial effusion with collapse of the right atrium and ventricle during diastole on echocardiography, is highly suggestive of cardiac tamponade. Cardiac tamponade occurs when the heart chambers are compressed due to the accumulation of fluid in the pericardial space. This leads to decreased cardiac output and the characteristic signs and symptoms seen in this patient.

Recommended literature

1. Madhivathanan PR, Corredor C, Smith A. Perioperative implications of pericardial effusions and cardiac tamponade. BJA Educ. 2020;20(7):226-234.
2. Clinical Anesthesiology: 5th Edition, Morgan, GE, Mikhail, MS, Murray, MJ. Anesthesia for Cardiac Surgery: Cardiac Tamponade. 474-76.
3. Essence of Anesthesia Practice: 4th Edition, Fleisher, LA, Roizen, Michael, F, Roizen. Cardiac Tamponade. 76.

CARDIOMYOPATHIES

Questions:

1. **What is the leading cause of heart failure and arrhythmia in young adults?**
   A. Dilated cardiomyopathy
   B. Hypertrophic cardiomyopathy
   C. Restrictive cardiomyopathy
   D. Arrhythmogenic cardiomyopathy of the right ventricle

2. **Which cardiomyopathy is characterized by hypertrophy of the left ventricle in the absence of other structural abnormalities?**
   A. Dilated cardiomyopathy
   B. Hypertrophic cardiomyopathy
   C. Restrictive cardiomyopathy
   D. Arrhythmogenic right ventricular cardiomyopathy

3. **What is the first-line medication for treating rhythm disturbances in arrhythmogenic right ventricular cardiomyopathy?**
   A. Amiodarone
   B. Lidocaine
   C. Beta-blockers
   D. Calcium channel blockers

4. **Which monitoring modality can provide real-time assessment of left ventricular outflow tract obstruction in hypertrophic cardiomyopathy?**
   A. Echocardiography
   B. Electrocardiography
   C. MRI of the heart
   D. Transesophageal echocardiography

5. **Restrictive cardiomyopathy is associated with impaired ventricular diastolic function due to fibrotic or infiltrative changes in the myocardium.**
   A. True
   B. False

6. **A 45-year-old male presents to the emergency department with complaints of exertional dyspnea, fatigue, and peripheral edema. He has a past medical history of hypertension and diabetes. On physical examination, there is elevated jugular venous pressure, bilateral crackles on lung auscultation, and pitting edema in the lower extremities. An electrocardiogram shows left ventricular hypertrophy. Echocardiography reveals impaired diastolic function with normal systolic function of the left ventricle. Based on the findings, the patient is diagnosed with a specific type of cardiomyopathy. What is the most likely diagnosis?**
   A. Dilated cardiomyopathy
   B. Hypertrophic cardiomyopathy
   C. Restrictive cardiomyopathy
   D. Arrhythmogenic right ventricular cardiomyopathy

Answers:

1. Answer A (Dilated cardiomyopathy)

Dilated cardiomyopathy is the leading cause of heart failure and arrhythmia in young adults. It is characterized by the dilatation of the left and right ventricles and impaired systolic function. Dilated cardiomyopathy can be idiopathic or associated with various factors such as familial predisposition, post-viral infection, ischemic heart disease, hypertension, diabetes, malformation syndrome, alcohol excess, neuromuscular disorders, inborn errors of metabolism, and exposure to cardiotoxic agents. These structural and functional abnormalities of the heart muscle can lead to the development of heart failure and arrhythmias in young adults.

2. Answer B (Hypertrophic cardiomyopathy)

Hypertrophic cardiomyopathy is characterized by hypertrophy of the left ventricle in the absence of other structural abnormalities. It is an inherited disease of the myocardium. The hypertrophy can occur in various patterns, such as asymmetrical, concentric, midventricular, and apical, and it can also involve the right ventricle. This hypertrophy leads to diastolic impairment of the left ventricle, and in the end stages, it can cause biventricular systolic dysfunction due to myocardial fibrosis.

3. Answer A (Amiodarone)

The first-line medication for treating rhythm disturbances in arrhythmogenic right ventricular cardiomyopathy is Amiodarone. Arrhythmogenic right ventricular cardiomyopathy is a complex genetic condition that involves structural abnormalities and cardiac dysfunction of the right ventricle, which can also extend to the left ventricle. This condition is associated with arrhythmias, including supraventricular and ventricular arrhythmias, which can pose a significant risk to patients.

4. Answer D (Transesophageal echocardiography)

Transesophageal echocardiography is a monitoring modality that can provide real-time assessment of left ventricular outflow tract obstruction in hypertrophic cardiomyopathy. It allows real-time dynamic assessment of the presence and severity of outflow tract obstruction and guides management and treatment accordingly.

5. Answer A (True)

Restrictive cardiomyopathy is associated with impaired ventricular diastolic function due to fibrotic or infiltrative changes in the myocardium. In this condition, the myocardium becomes stiff and less compliant, which impairs the filling of the ventricles during diastole. The fibrotic or infiltrative changes can be primary (idiopathic) or secondary to conditions such as amyloidosis, sarcoidosis, hemochromatosis, ischemic heart disease, hypertension, and valvular disease.

6. Answer C (Restrictive cardiomyopathy)

The patient's clinical presentation, including exertional dyspnea, fatigue, peripheral edema, elevated jugular venous pressure, lung crackles, and pitting edema, along with an electrocardiogram showing left ventricular hypertrophy and echocardiography demonstrating impaired diastolic function with normal systolic function, is consistent with restrictive cardiomyopathy. In restrictive cardiomyopathy, there is impaired ventricular diastolic function due to fibrotic or infiltrative changes in the myocardium, leading to stiffness and reduced compliance of the ventricles. This results in impaired filling during diastole and subsequent symptoms of heart failure. The patient's history of hypertension and diabetes may be contributing factors to the development of restrictive cardiomyopathy.

Recommended literature

1.   Ibrahim IR, Sharma V. Cardiomyopathy and anaesthesia. BJA Education. 2017;17(11):363-9.

CORONARY ARTERY DISEASE

02
CHAPTER

Questions:

1. **Which of the following is the most common cause of coronary artery disease (CAD)?**

   A. Hypertension

   B. Smoking

   C. Diabetes mellitus

   D. Atheromatous disease

2. **Which of the following risk factors for CAD is non-modifiable?**

   A. Hypertension

   B. Obesity

   C. Advancing age

   D. Sedentary lifestyle

3. **What is the primary consequence of coronary artery disease?**

   A. Myocardial infarction

   B. Dysrhythmias

   C. Heart failure

   D. All of the above

4. **Which statement about NSAIDs and CAD is true?**

   A. Avoid using all NSAIDs in patients with established cardiovascular disease

   B. NSAIDs are Cox 2 inhibitors and are the recommended form of analgesia for patients with coronary artery disease (CAD)

   C. NSAIDs are primarily used for their antipyretic effects in patients with CAD

   D. NSAIDs have no significant interactions with medications commonly used in the management of CAD

5. **Beta-blockers should be continued in the perioperative period for patients with CAD.**

   A. True

   B. False

6. **A 60-year-old male patient with a history of CAD and well-controlled hypertension presents for preoperative assessment before elective hernia repair surgery. He is currently on atenolol for his CAD and amlodipine for his hypertension. He reports occasional exertional chest pain, which resolves with rest. On physical examination, his blood pressure is 140/90 mmHg, his heart rate is 72 bpm, and he has no signs of heart failure. ECG shows no acute changes. What is the most appropriate next step in the preoperative assessment of this patient with CAD and hypertension before hernia repair surgery?**

   A. Perform a stress test to evaluate cardiac ischemia

   B. Initiate additional antihypertensive therapy

   C. Obtain an echocardiogram to assess left ventricular function

   D. Continue with the planned surgery and optimize medical management

Answers:

1. Answer D (Atheromatous disease)

Atheromatous disease, characterized by the formation of fatty deposits within the walls of the coronary arteries, remains the most common cause of coronary artery disease (CAD). These plaques can narrow the arteries, leading to reduced blood flow to the heart muscle, which can result in myocardial ischemia and other complications associated with CAD. While hypertension, smoking, and diabetes mellitus are risk factors for CAD, atheromatous disease is the primary underlying cause.

2. Answer C (Advancing age)

Advancing age is a non-modifiable risk factor for CAD. While factors such as hypertension, obesity, and a sedentary lifestyle can be modified through interventions and lifestyle changes, age itself cannot be changed or modified.

3. Answer D (All of the above)

CAD can have various consequences on the heart. These consequences include myocardial infarction, dysrhythmias, and heart failure. CAD can lead to the development of atherosclerotic plaques within the coronary arteries, which can cause partial or complete blockage of blood flow to the heart muscle. This restriction of blood flow can result in a heart attack; in addition to myocardial infarction, CAD can also disrupt the normal electrical signals within the heart, leading to dysrhythmias. Furthermore, CAD can weaken the heart muscle over time, leading to heart failure.

4. Answer A (Avoid using all NSAIDs in patients with established cardiovascular disease)

NSAIDs are not recommended for routine use in patients with established cardiovascular disease due to their potential to increase the risk of cardiovascular events. This risk is thought to be related to the inhibition of prostaglandins, which can lead to vasoconstriction, sodium and water retention, and increased blood pressure. Additionally, NSAIDs may increase the risk of thrombosis by affecting platelet function. Therefore, alternative analgesic options should be considered for patients with cardiovascular disease to minimize the risk of adverse cardiovascular events.

5. Answer A (True)

Beta-blockers should generally be continued during the perioperative period for patients with CAD or other cardiovascular conditions. Abrupt discontinuation of beta blockers can lead to rebound hypertension, increased heart rate, and potential cardiovascular complications during and after surgery.

6. Answer A (Perform a stress test to evaluate cardiac ischemia)

In this case of a patient with CAD and hypertension scheduled for hernia repair surgery, the most appropriate next step in the preoperative assessment is to perform a stress test to evaluate cardiac ischemia. The patient's history of exertional chest pain raises concerns about potential cardiac ischemia during times of increased stress, such as during surgery.

Recommended literature

1. Pollard BJ, Kitchen, G. Handbook of Clinical Anaesthesia. Fourth Edition. CRC Press. 2018. 978-1-4987-6289-2

Cardiac diseases
INFECTIVE ENDOCARDITIS: PROPHYLAXIS

Questions:

1. **What is the preferred antibiotic regimen for a high-risk patient without a penicillin allergy?**
   A. Cephalexin 2 g orally
   B. Clindamycin 600 mg orally
   C. Ciprofloxacin 500 mg orally
   D. Amoxicillin 2 g orally

2. **Which of the following patients would require antibiotic prophylaxis for infective endocarditis?**
   A. A patient with a prosthetic heart valve
   B. A patient with a history of IE
   C. A patient with congenital heart disease (CHD)
   D. All of the above

3. **How soon before a procedure should antibiotics be administered for infective endocarditis prophylaxis?**
   A. Immediately before the procedure
   B. 1 hour before the procedure
   C. 4 hours before the procedure
   D. 24 hours before the procedure

4. **What is the potential risk associated with antibiotic use for infective endocarditis prophylaxis?**
   A. Increased risk of anaphylaxis
   B. Increased risk of bacterial resistance
   C. Increased risk of heart failure
   D. Increased risk of ischemic cerebrovascular accident

5. **A patient with a prosthetic heart valve undergoing a routine dental cleaning requires antibiotic prophylaxis for infective endocarditis.**
   A. True
   B. False

6. **A 60-year-old man with a history of hypertension, diabetes, and a prosthetic heart valve is scheduled to undergo hernia repair surgery. Which of the following is the most appropriate recommendation regarding antibiotic prophylaxis?**
   A. He should receive antibiotic prophylaxis for hernia repair surgery
   B. He does not need antibiotic prophylaxis for hernia repair surgery
   C. He should receive antibiotic prophylaxis only if he has a known penicillin allergy
   D. He should receive antibiotic prophylaxis if the hernia repair operation lasts less than 1 hour

Answers:

1. Answer D (Amoxicillin 2 g orally)

Amoxicillin is the antibiotic of choice for high-risk patients without a penicillin allergy for infective endocarditis prophylaxis. Other antibiotics listed in the options, such as cephalexin, clindamycin, and ciprofloxacin, may have alternative uses but are not the preferred choices for infective endocarditis prophylaxis in high-risk patients without a penicillin allergy.

2. Answer D (All of the above)

All of the mentioned patients would require antibiotic prophylaxis for infective endocarditis. Patients with a prosthetic heart valve, a history of infective endocarditis (IE), or certain types of congenital heart disease (CHD) are considered high-risk patients. High-risk patients undergoing high-risk procedures, such as dental or surgical procedures with manipulation of the gingiva, are recommended to receive antibiotic prophylaxis for infective endocarditis.

3. Answer B (1 hour before the procedure)

Antibiotics for infective endocarditis prophylaxis should be administered 30-60 minutes (1 hour) before the procedure. This allows sufficient time for the antibiotics to reach effective levels in the bloodstream and provide protection during the procedure. Administering the antibiotics immediately before the procedure or several hours before may not provide the optimal concentration needed for prophylaxis. Therefore, the recommended timeframe is 1 hour before the procedure to ensure adequate antibiotic levels are achieved.

4. Answer B (Increased risk of bacterial resistance)

The potential risk associated with antibiotic use for infective endocarditis prophylaxis is an increased risk of bacterial resistance. This means that the bacteria targeted by the antibiotics may become resistant to their effects, reducing the effectiveness of the antibiotics in future infections.

5. Answer B (False)

A patient with a prosthetic heart valve undergoing a routine dental cleaning does not require antibiotic prophylaxis for infective endocarditis. Antibiotic prophylaxis is recommended for certain high-risk patients with prosthetic heart valves but is not necessary for routine dental cleanings. The need for antibiotic prophylaxis in dental procedures is usually reserved for those involving manipulation of the gingiva or periapical region of teeth, such as root canal treatments or extractions.

6. Answer A (He should receive antibiotic prophylaxis for hernia repair surgery)

Patients with a history of infective endocarditis are considered high-risk patients for subsequent infections. Surgical procedures that involve the insertion of prosthetic material, such as hernia repair, are also considered high-risk procedures. Therefore, it is recommended that the patient, in this case, receives antibiotic prophylaxis to reduce the risk of infective endocarditis during hernia repair surgery.

Recommended literature

1. Habib G, Lancellotti P, Antunes MJ, et al. 2015 ESC Guidelines for the management of infective endocarditis: The Task Force for the Management of Infective Endocarditis of the European Society of Cardiology (ESC). Endorsed by: European Association for Cardio-Thoracic Surgery (EACTS), the European Association of Nuclear Medicine (EANM). Eur Heart J. 2015;36(44):3075-3128.

INTRAOPERATIVE ARRHYTHMIAS

02
CHAPTER

Questions:

1. Which of the following is a risk factor for developing intraoperative arrhythmias?
   A. Smoking
   B. Hypertension
   C. Thyroid disease
   D. All of the above

2. Which of the following is a surgical risk factor for intraoperative arrhythmias?
   A. Inadequate anesthesia
   B. Electrolyte disorders
   C. Valvular heart disease
   D. Beta-agonist medications

3. What is the recommended treatment for stable supraventricular tachycardia during surgery?
   A. Defibrillation
   B. Cardioversion
   C. Amiodarone
   D. Adenosine

4. The treatment for hemodynamically unstable ventricular tachycardia during surgery may include?
   A. Atropine
   B. Pacing
   C. Adenosine
   D. Defibrillation

5. Laryngoscopy during airway management can lead to bradycardia.
   A. True
   B. False

6. A 60-year-old male patient with a history of hypertension and coronary artery disease is scheduled for coronary artery bypass graft surgery. The patient has been brought into the operating room and anesthesia induction has been initiated. As the surgery begins, the patient's heart rate suddenly increases, and a wide-complex ventricular rhythm is observed on the electrocardiogram (ECG) monitor. Which medication would be most appropriate for the management of the observed wide-complex ventricular rhythm in this case?
   A. Atropine
   B. Adenosine
   C. Amiodarone
   D. Epinephrine

Answers:

1. **Answer D (All of the above)**

   Various patient factors can influence intraoperative arrhythmias. Smoking is known to increase the risk of developing arrhythmias due to its detrimental effects on the cardiovascular system. Hypertension, or high blood pressure, is a risk factor for arrhythmias as it can lead to structural and electrical abnormalities in the heart. Thyroid disease, including both hypothyroidism and hyperthyroidism, can disrupt the thyroid hormone's normal function, which can directly affect the heart's electrical conduction system and increase the risk of arrhythmias.

2. **Answer A (Inadequate anesthesia)**

   Various surgical factors can influence intraoperative arrhythmias. Inadequate anesthesia, which refers to a suboptimal depth of anesthesia, is a known surgical risk factor for the development of arrhythmias. It can lead to hemodynamic instability, which may trigger arrhythmias during surgery. Electrolyte disorders, valvular heart disease, and beta-agonist medications are more of a patient-related risk factor.

3. **Answer D (Adenosine)**

   Adenosine is the recommended treatment for stable supraventricular tachycardia (SVT) during surgery. Adenosine is a medication that works by temporarily blocking the electrical conduction in the atrioventricular (AV) node, which can interrupt the reentry circuit responsible for SVT. It is typically administered as a rapid intravenous bolus.

4. **Answer D (Defibrillation)**

   Hemodynamically unstable ventricular tachycardia (VT) during surgery requires immediate intervention to restore normal cardiac rhythm and circulation. In this context, defibrillation is the recommended treatment. Defibrillation involves delivering a high-energy electric shock to the heart to terminate the arrhythmia and allow the heart to resume a normal rhythm.

5. **Answer A (True)**

   Laryngoscopy, which involves the manipulation of the airway during intubation, can stimulate the trigeminovagal reflex and lead to bradycardia.

6. **Answer C (Amiodarone)**

   In this case, the wide-complex ventricular rhythm observed on the ECG monitor suggests the presence of VT, a potentially life-threatening arrhythmia. Amiodarone (Class III antiarrhythmic with potassium, calcium, and sodium channel-blocking properties) is the primary antiarrhythmic agent for wide-complex tachycardia.

Recommended literature

1. Noor ZM. Md. Life-Threatening Cardiac Arrhythmias during Anesthesia and Surgery. Cardiac Arrhythmias – Translational Approach from Pathophysiology to Advanced Care. 2021. doi: 10.5772/intechopen.101371.
2. Pollard BJ, Kitchen G. Handbook of Clinical Anaesthesia. 4th ed. Taylor & Francis group; 2018. Chapter 30 Management problems, Shelton C.

Cardiac diseases
MITRAL REGURGITATION

Questions:

1. **What is the primary cause of mitral regurgitation?**
   A. Left ventricular dysfunction
   B. Atrial fibrillation
   C. Pathology of the mitral valve preventing normal closure
   D. Pulmonary circulation overload

2. **Which type of mitral regurgitation is caused by left ventricle dysfunction?**
   A. Primary mitral regurgitation
   B. Secondary mitral regurgitation
   C. Acute mitral regurgitation
   D. Chronic mitral regurgitation

3. **What is the recommended treatment for acute mitral regurgitation?**
   A. β-blockers and diuretics
   B. Vasodilators and nitrates
   C. Valve repair surgery
   D. ACE inhibitors and nitrates

4. **Which parameter is used to define the severity of mitral regurgitation based on transoesophageal echocardiography?**
   A. Regurgitant fraction
   B. Regurgitant orifice area
   C. Regurgitant volume
   D. Left ventricular ejection fraction

5. **In symptomatic patients with severe left ventricle failure and secondary mitral regurgitation, surgery is the definitive therapy.**
   A. True
   B. False

6. **A 70-year-old female patient with a known history of chronic mitral regurgitation presents for elective hip replacement surgery due to severe osteoarthritis. She experiences occasional shortness of breath on exertion and mild fatigue. Physical examination reveals a holosystolic murmur at the apex, consistent with chronic mitral regurgitation. The patient's echocardiogram shows moderate-to-severe chronic mitral regurgitation. Considering the patient's chronic mitral regurgitation and the planned hip surgery, which of the following goals is most critical in the anesthetic management of MR?**
   A. Maintenance of normal SVR with a slow heart rate in order to maintain a favorable myocardial oxygen demand–supply ratio
   B. Use of an inhalational anesthetic in preference to intravenous agents in order to achieve pulmonary vasodilation
   C. Maintenance of normal SVR using an I.V. infusion of metaraminol if required
   D. Maintenance of a normal to high heart rate avoiding sudden bradycardia, and maintenance of a normal to low SVR

Answers:

1. **Answer C (Pathology of the mitral valve preventing normal closure)**

   Mitral regurgitation occurs when there is abnormal leakage of blood from the left ventricle back into the left atrium during systole. The primary cause of mitral regurgitation is pathology affecting the mitral valve itself, which prevents its normal closure. This can include various factors such as degenerative changes, infective endocarditis leading to vegetation on the valve leaflets, rupture of chordae tendineae, or papillary muscle rupture. These pathologies disrupt the proper functioning of the mitral valve, resulting in the backflow of blood and regurgitation into the left atrium.

2. **Answer B (Secondary mitral regurgitation)**

   Secondary mitral regurgitation is caused by dysfunction of the left ventricle, which impairs the closing mechanism of the mitral valve. This dysfunction of the left ventricle can be due to conditions such as ischemic heart disease, dilated cardiomyopathy, or left ventricular remodeling after myocardial infarction. When the left ventricle is unable to contract properly or becomes enlarged, it affects the normal closing of the mitral valve, leading to regurgitation of blood back into the left atrium during systole. In contrast, primary mitral regurgitation is caused by pathology of the mitral valve itself, such as degenerative changes or infective endocarditis. Acute and chronic refer to the timing and duration of the mitral regurgitation rather than the underlying cause.

3. **Answer B (Vasodilators and nitrates)**

   The recommended treatment for acute mitral regurgitation involves reducing filling pressures with nitrates and decreasing afterload with vasodilators. Filling pressure reduction with nitrates and afterload reduction with vasodilators can help alleviate symptoms and mitigate the impact of acute regurgitation. Therefore, the administration of vasodilators and nitrates is the recommended treatment for acute mitral regurgitation. The other options, including β-blockers, ACE inhibitors, and valve repair surgery, may be utilized in the management of chronic mitral regurgitation or in specific situations, but they are not the recommended first-line treatment for acute cases.

4. **Answer A (Regurgitant fraction)**

   Transoesophageal echocardiography is considered the gold standard for assessing the severity of mitral regurgitation. Several parameters are used to define the severity of mitral regurgitation, including regurgitant fraction, regurgitant orifice area, and regurgitant volume. Among these parameters, the regurgitant fraction is specifically used to assess the severity based on transoesophageal echocardiography. Regurgitant fraction refers to the proportion of the left ventricular stroke volume that regurgitates back into the left atrium during systole. It is expressed as a percentage and provides a quantitative measure of the severity of regurgitation.

5. **Answer B (False)**

   In symptomatic patients with severe left ventricular failure and secondary mitral regurgitation, the benefits of surgery are controversial unless the underlying condition causing the secondary regurgitation can be reversed. In these situations, the primary focus of management is typically on optimizing medical treatment for heart failure.

6. **Answer D (Maintenance of a normal to high heart rate avoiding sudden bradycardia, and maintenance of a normal to low SVR)**

   In the anesthetic management of a patient with chronic mitral regurgitation (MR) undergoing hip surgery, the most critical goal is to maintain a normal to high heart rate while avoiding sudden bradycardia and maintaining a normal to low systemic vascular resistance (SVR). Maintaining a normal to high heart rate helps preserve the forward flow and cardiac output, reducing the symptoms associated with MR. Sudden bradycardia should be avoided as it can further decrease forward flow and exacerbate symptoms. Additionally, maintaining a normal to low SVR is crucial in the management of MR. By reducing SVR, the resistance against which the left ventricle must pump is decreased, improving forward flow and reducing regurgitant volume.

Recommended literature

1. Holmes K, Gibbison B, Vohra HA. Mitral valve and mitral valve disease. BJA Education. 2017;17(1):1-9.

Cardiac diseases
MITRAL STENOSIS

Questions:

1. Which compensatory mechanism helps to maintain normal pulmonary venous pressures in mitral stenosis?
   A. Left ventricular hypertrophy
   B. Left atrial dilation
   C. Increased cardiac output
   D. Pulmonary artery vasoconstriction

2. What is the most common cause of mitral stenosis?
   A. Rheumatic fever
   B. Degenerative calcification
   C. Endocarditis
   D. Infiltrating diseases

3. Which of the following parameters is used to assess the severity of mitral stenosis?
   A. Mean pressure decrease
   B. Pressure half-time
   C. Valve area
   D. All of the above

4. What is the valve area range for severe mitral stenosis?
   A. 1.6–2.0 cm^2
   B. 1.5–1.0 cm^2
   C. < 1.0 cm^2
   D. > 2.0 cm^2

5. Nitrous oxide is the gas of choice in patients with mitral stenosis during anesthesia.
   A. True
   B. False

6. A 28-year-old pregnant woman, in the 38th week of gestation, with a known history of mitral stenosis comes to the delivery department in active labor. She is in regular labor and has moderate pain. The patient's medical history reveals that her mitral stenosis is well managed with medication, and she has had regular follow-ups with her cardiologist throughout her pregnancy. What would be the analgesia of choice for this patient?
   A. No analgesia
   B. Nitrous oxide
   C. Epidural analgesia
   D. Remifentanil

Answers:

1. **Answer B (Left atrial dilation)**

   In mitral stenosis, the narrowing of the mitral valve restricts the flow of blood from the left atrium to the left ventricle during diastole. To compensate for this obstruction, the left atrium undergoes dilation as a compensatory mechanism.

2. **Answer A (Rheumatic fever)**

   The most common cause of mitral stenosis is rheumatic fever. Uncommon causes of mitral stenosis are calcification of the mitral valve leaflets and congenital heart disease. Other causes of mitral stenosis include infective endocarditis, mitral annular calcification, endomyocardial fibroelastosis, malignant carcinoid syndrome, systemic lupus erythematosus, Whipple disease, Fabry disease, and rheumatoid arthritis.

3. **Answer D (All of the above)**

   The severity of mitral stenosis can be assessed using multiple parameters. All three parameters mentioned above are utilized to assess the severity of mitral stenosis. Each parameter provides valuable information about the degree of obstruction in the mitral valve and helps guide treatment decisions. When evaluating a patient with mitral stenosis, clinicians often consider these parameters collectively to determine the severity of the condition and plan appropriate management strategies.

4. **Answer C (< 1.0 cm²)**

   A valve area of less than 1.0 cm² is considered indicative of severe stenosis and represents a critical level of obstruction to blood flow. As the valve area decreases, the severity of mitral stenosis increases, leading to elevated pressures in the left atrium and pulmonary circulation.

5. **Answer B (False)**

   Nitrous oxide is not the gas of choice in patients with mitral stenosis during anesthesia. The use of nitrous oxide in patients with mitral stenosis should be approached with caution. Nitrous oxide can cause pulmonary vasoconstriction, which can further increase pulmonary artery pressures in patients with mitral stenosis. This can potentially worsen the patient's condition by exacerbating pulmonary hypertension.

6. **Answer C (Epidural analgesia)**

   Epidural analgesia provides effective pain control while minimizing the risk of cardiovascular complications. In patients with mitral stenosis, the hemodynamic changes associated with labor, such as increased sympathetic activity and pain-induced tachycardia, can pose risks to cardiovascular stability. Epidural analgesia helps mitigate these risks by reducing pain and sympathetic response, maintaining hemodynamic stability, and preventing tachycardia. Therefore, epidural analgesia is a safer option with better control over pain relief and fewer risks in this patient population.

Recommended literature

1. Holmes K, Gibbison B, Vohra HA. Mitral valve and mitral valve disease. BJA Education. 2017;17(1):1-9.
2. Nishimura RA, Otto CM, Bonow RO, et al. 2014 AHA/ACC guideline for the management of patients with valvular heart disease: a report of the American College of Cardiology/American Heart Association Task Force on Practice Guidelines. J Am Coll Cardiol 2014; 63:e57.
3. Shah SN, Sharma S. Mitral Stenosis. [Updated 2022 Aug 8]. In: StatPearls [Internet]. Treasure Island (FL): StatPearls Publishing; 2023 Jan-. Available from: https://www.ncbi.nlm.nih.gov/books/NBK430742/

PULMONARY HYPERTENSION (PH)

Questions:

1. **Post-capillary pulmonary hypertension is primarily caused by?**
   A. Left-sided heart diseases
   B. Chronic thromboembolism
   C. Lung diseases
   D. Multisystemic disorders

2. **Chronic thromboembolic pulmonary hypertension (CTEPH) is best treated with?**
   A. Pulmonary vasodilator therapy
   B. Lung transplantation
   C. Pulmonary endarterectomy
   D. Immunosuppressive therapy

3. **Which medication class is primarily indicated for the treatment of Idiopathic pulmonary hypertension, HIV, and drug/toxin-induced pulmonary hypertension?**
   A. Beta-blockers
   B. Angiotensin-converting enzyme (ACE) inhibitors
   C. Pulmonary vasodilators
   D. Anticoagulants

4. **Which of the following hemodynamic parameters should be monitored in the management of pulmonary hypertension?**
   A. Central venous pressure
   B. Pulmonary vascular resistance
   C. Systemic arterial pressure
   D. All of the above

5. **Viagra is a phosphodiesterase-5 inhibitor commonly used in the treatment of pulmonary arterial hypertension (PAH).**
   A. True
   B. False

6. **A 68-year-old patient with chronic obstructive pulmonary disease (COPD) and pulmonary hypertension comes for a planned total hip replacement surgery. During the past few months, the patient experienced worsening shortness of breath and intolerance of physical activity. What anesthetic technique might be preferred in this patient?**
   A. General anesthesia with high doses of opioids
   B. Monitored anesthesia care (MAC)
   C. Regional anesthesia
   D. Total intravenous anesthesia (TIVA)

Answers:

1. **Answer A (Left-sided heart disease)**

   Post-capillary pulmonary hypertension is primarily caused by left-sided heart diseases. These conditions, such as systolic or diastolic heart failure or valvular heart diseases, lead to increased pressure in the pulmonary veins and capillaries, resulting in elevated pulmonary capillary wedge pressure and subsequent post-capillary pulmonary hypertension.

2. **Answer C (Pulmonary endarterectomy)**

   Chronic thromboembolic pulmonary hypertension (CTEPH) is best treated with pulmonary endarterectomy. This surgical procedure involves removing chronic blood clots from the pulmonary arteries, addressing the underlying cause of CTEPH, and improving pulmonary blood flow. Pulmonary endarterectomy is considered the treatment of choice for eligible patients with CTEPH, offering the potential for significant improvement in pulmonary hypertension and symptoms.

3. **Answer C (Pulmonary vasodilators)**

   The medication class primarily indicated for the treatment of idiopathic pulmonary hypertension, HIV-induced pulmonary hypertension, and drug/toxin-induced pulmonary hypertension is pulmonary vasodilators. These medications dilate the pulmonary arteries, reduce pulmonary vascular resistance, and improve blood flow in the pulmonary circulation.

4. **Answer D (All of the above)**

   During the intraoperative treatment of pulmonary hypertension, it is important to monitor multiple hemodynamic parameters to assess and optimize the patient's condition. The central venous pressure (CVP) provides information about right ventricular preload and helps guide fluid management. Pulmonary vascular resistance (PVR) reflects the resistance to blood flow in the pulmonary circulation and can help assess the effectiveness of pulmonary vasodilator therapy. Systemic arterial pressure (SAP) provides information about systemic perfusion and helps ensure adequate organ perfusion. Monitoring all of these parameters allows for a comprehensive evaluation of the patient's hemodynamic status and response to treatment, guiding appropriate interventions to optimize pulmonary and systemic circulation.

5. **Answer A (True)**

   Viagra, also known by its generic name sildenafil, is a phosphodiesterase-5 (PDE-5) inhibitor that is commonly used in the treatment of pulmonary arterial hypertension (PAH). By inhibiting the PDE-5 enzyme, sildenafil helps to relax and dilate the pulmonary arteries, reducing pulmonary vascular resistance and improving blood flow in the pulmonary circulation.

6. **Answer C (Regional anesthesia)**

   In these patients with COPD and pulmonary hypertension, regional anesthesia may be desirable to optimize pain control while reducing systemic opioid requirements. The stress, pain, acidosis, and hypoxemia often encountered during surgery can increase pulmonary hypertension and precipitate right ventricular decompensation. Regional anesthetic techniques, such as neuraxial anesthesia (spinal or epidural anesthesia) or peripheral nerve blocks, can provide effective anesthesia but with careful titration to maintain hemodynamic stability and avoid excessive sympathetic stimulation.

Recommended literature

1. Price L, Brame A, Martinez G, Mukerjee B, Harries C, Kempny A, et al. Perioperative management of patients with Pulmonary Hypertension undergoing Non-Cardiac Surgery: A Systemic Review and UK Consensus Statement. European Respiratory Journal. 2020;56(suppl 64):1467.
2. Elliot CA, Kiely DG. Pulmonary hypertension. Continuing Education in Anaesthesia Critical Care & Pain. 2006;6(1):17-22.

Cardiac diseases
QT PROLONGATION

Questions:

1. **Which of the following cardiac arrhythmias is associated with QT prolongation?**
   A. Atrial fibrillation
   B. Supraventricular tachycardia
   C. Wolff-Parkinson-White Syndrome
   D. Torsade de pointes

2. **Anesthesia and surgery can provoke Torsade de pointes in patients with QT prolongation due to?**
   A. Increased parasympathetic activity
   B. Altered neuroendocrine response
   C. Dysfunction of the autonomic nervous system
   D. Increased sympathetic stimulation

3. **Which electrolytes play a crucial role in the management of QT prolongation?**
   A. Sodium and calcium
   B. Calcium and potassium
   C. Potassium and magnesium
   D. Magnesium and sodium

4. **Which of the following medications is known to prolong the QT interval?**
   A. Dexmedetomidine
   B. Droperidol
   C. Fluoroquinolones
   D. All of above

5. **What is an acquired condition that can cause Torsade de pointes?**
   A. Hypomagnesemia
   B. Cirrhosis
   C. Hypothyroidism
   D. All of the above

6. **A 40-year-old patient underwent a total hip replacement under spinal anesthesia. He has a history of addiction and has been on methadone for the past 3 years. Halfway thorough the procedure, he complains of chest discomfort, and ECG shows irregular, wide complexes (Torsade de pointes). Her blood pressure is 110/60 mmHg. Which of the listed antiarrhythmics should be used in this patient?**
   A. Intravenous amiodarone 150 mg
   B. Intravenous lidocaine 100 mg
   C. Intravenous beta-blocker (e.g., propranolol) 10 mg
   D. Intravenous magnesium 2 g

Answers:

1. Answer D (Torsade de pointes)

Torsade de pointes is the specific type of cardiac arrhythmia associated with QT prolongation. QT prolongation predisposes individuals to develop torsade de pointes, which is an uncommon and distinctive form of polymorphic ventricular tachycardia (VT) characterized by a gradual change in the amplitude and twisting of the QRS complexes around the isoelectric line.

2. Answer D (Increased sympathetic stimulation)

The increase in sympathetic tone associated with anesthesia and surgery can provoke torsade de pointes in patients with QT prolongation due to increased sympathetic stimulation. Sympathetic stimulation can further disrupt the already impaired ventricular repolarization and contribute to the development of arrhythmias. It is important to carefully manage and control sympathetic stimulation during the perioperative period in patients with QT prolongation to reduce the risk of torsade de pointes.

3. Answer C (Potassium and magnesium)

Potassium and magnesium levels are crucial considerations in the management of QT prolongation. Hypokalemia and hypomagnesemia can further prolong the QT interval and increase the risk of arrhythmias, including torsade de pointes. Potassium is essential for maintaining normal cardiac electrical activity, including repolarization. Magnesium is involved in various cardiac ion channels, including those responsible for repolarization. Monitoring and correcting potassium and magnesium levels, when necessary, are essential in managing patients with QT prolongation to reduce the risk of life-threatening arrhythmias.

4. Answer D (All of the above)

All of the listed medications, including dexmedetomidine, droperidol, and fluoroquinolones, have the potential to prolong the QT interval. These medications have been associated with an increased risk of QT prolongation and Torsade de Pointes.

5. Answer D (All of the above)

All of these conditions, including hypomagnesemia, cirrhosis, and hypothyroidism, can predispose individuals to develop Torsade de Pointes. These acquired conditions can disrupt the heart's normal electrical activity and increase the risk of QT prolongation, which in turn predisposes to Torsade de Pointes.

6. Answer D (Intravenous magnesium 2g)

Magnesium sulfate is the recommended treatment for Torsade de Pointes associated with QT prolongation. It stabilizes the membranes of cardiac cells and helps restore normal repolarization. In this case, the patient's chest discomfort and the presence of irregular, wide complexes on the EKG combined with methadone therapy suggest Torsade de Pointes. Methadone is independently associated with a prolonged QT interval and progression to torsade de pointes. Administration of intravenous magnesium sulfate at a dose of 2 g would be an appropriate treatment choice to suppress the arrhythmia and correct the underlying electrolyte imbalance. All other antiarrhythmics can be used for certain types of ventricular arrhythmias but are not the primary treatment for Torsade de Pointes.

Recommended literature

1. Cohagan B, Brandis D. Torsade de Pointes. [Updated 2022 Aug 8]. In: StatPearls [Internet]. Treasure Island (FL): StatPearls Publishing; 2022 Jan-. Available from: https://www.ncbi.nlm.nih.gov/books/NBK459388/
2. O'Hare M, Maldonado Y, Munro J, Ackerman MJ, Ramakrishna H, Sorajja D. Perioperative management of patients with congenital or acquired disorders of the QT interval. Br J Anaesth. 2018;120(4):629-644.
3. Hunter JD, Sharma P, Rathi S. Long QT syndrome. Continuing Education in Anaesthesia Critical Care & Pain. 2008;8(2):67-70.
4. Kies SJ, Pabelick CM, Hurley HA, White RD, Ackerman MJ. Anesthesia for patients with congenital long QT syndrome. Anesthesiology. 2005;102(1):204-210.

RIGHT HEART FAILURE

Questions:

1. Which of the following is NOT a sign or symptom of right heart failure (RHF)?
   A. Elevated jugular venous pressure
   B. Peripheral edema
   C. Left ventricular hypertrophy
   D. Ascites

2. Which of the following can be seen in RHF on a chest x-ray?
   A. Enlarged left ventricle
   B. Pneumothorax
   C. Pleural effusion
   D. Dilated ascending aorta

3. What is the consequence of elevated filling pressures on the right side of the heart?
   A. Forward failure and pulmonary congestion
   B. Backward failure and systemic venous congestion
   C. Left ventricular hypertrophy and reduced cardiac output
   D. Increased stroke volume and improved tissue perfusion

4. Which is not a sign and symptom of right heart failure?
   A. Loss of breath
   B. Increased jugular venous pressure/jugular venous distension
   C. Hepatosplenomegaly/liver pulsation
   D. Cyanosis

5. Diuretics are commonly used in the management of acute right heart failure.
   A. True
   B. False

6. A 65-year-old patient with a history of chronic obstructive pulmonary disease (COPD) and pulmonary hypertension comes to the emergency department with worsening dyspnea and peripheral edema. He reports severe sinusitis that lasts for several days and worsens. He is hypotensive and tachypneic, and his auscultatory breath sounds are weakened. Its oxygen saturation is 88% in room air. Which drug would be contraindicated in treatment?
   A. Decongestants
   B. Diuretics
   C. Dobutamine
   D. Nitroglycerin

Answers:

1. Answer C (Left ventricular hypertrophy)

Left ventricular hypertrophy is not a direct sign or symptom of right heart failure. It refers to the thickening of the left ventricular wall, which is typically associated with chronic left heart pathology rather than right heart failure. Elevated jugular venous pressure, peripheral edema, and ascites are commonly observed signs and symptoms of right heart failure due to impaired venous return and fluid retention.

2. Answer C (Pleural effusion)

In heart failure, pleural effusion is the result of increased interstitial fluid in the lungs due to increased pulmonary capillary pressure. Pleural effusions usually occur in patients with left heart failure. However, patients with pulmonary hypertension and isolated right heart failure often also have a pleural effusion.

3. Answer B (Backward failure and systemic venous congestion)

The consequence of elevated filling pressures on the right side of the heart is backward failure and systemic venous congestion. This results in elevated pressures within the right atrium and systemic venous system, leading to congestion of the systemic veins. This congestion can manifest as peripheral edema, hepatomegaly, ascites, and other signs of venous congestion throughout the body.

4. Answer D (Cyanosis)

Cyanosis is not usually associated with right heart failure; it is more often associated with left heart failure. In left heart failure, impaired left ventricular function can result in inadequate blood oxygenation, leading to systemic hypoxia and cyanosis. On the other hand, right heart failure primarily affects the right side of the heart, leading to venous congestion and symptoms such as increased jugular venous pressure, hepatosplenomegaly, and peripheral edema. While individuals with right heart failure may have an underlying left heart failure, the cyanosis itself is not a direct sign of right heart failure but is related to left heart dysfunction.

5. Answer A (True)

Diuretics are commonly used in the management of acute right heart failure, as it is a condition often characterized by fluid overload and venous congestion, and diuretics help promote diuresis and reduce fluid retention in the body. By increasing the excretion of water and sodium in the urine, diuretics can help alleviate symptoms such as peripheral edema, ascites, and pulmonary congestion.

6. Answer A (Decongestants)

Decongestants, such as pseudoephedrine or phenylephrine, are commonly used to relieve nasal congestion. They act by constricting blood vessels, including the pulmonary vessels, which can lead to increased pulmonary vascular resistance and worsen the patient's pulmonary hypertension and acute right heart failure.

Recommended literature

1. Houston BA, Brittain EL, Tedford RJ. Right, Ventricular Failure. N Engl J Med. 2023;388(12):1111-1125.
2. Price LC, Martinez G, Brame A, et al. Perioperative management of patients with pulmonary hypertension undergoing non-cardiothoracic, non-obstetric surgery: a systematic review and expert consensus statement. Br J Anaesth. 2021;126(4):774-790.
3. Murphy, E., Shelley, B., 2019. Clinical presentation and management of right ventricular dysfunction. BJA Education 19, 183–190.
4. Cops J, Mullens W, Verbrugge FH, et al. Selective abdominal venous congestion induces adverse renal and hepatic morphological and functional alterations despite a preserved cardiac function. Sci Rep. 2018;8(1):17757.
5. Cops J, Mullens W, Verbrugge FH, et al. Selective abdominal venous congestion to investigate cardiorenal interactions in a rat model. PLoS One. 2018;13(5):e0197687. Published 2018 May 29.
6. Konstam MA, Kiernan MS, Bernstein D, et al. Evaluation and Management of Right-Sided Heart Failure: A Scientific Statement From the American Heart Association. Circulation. 2018;137(20):e578-e622.
7. Murphy, E., Shelley, B., 2018. The right ventricle—structural and functional importance for anaesthesia and intensive care. BJA Education 18, 239–245.
8. Gorter TM, van Veldhuisen DJ, Bauersachs J, et al. Right heart dysfunction and failure in heart failure with preserved ejection fraction: mechanisms and management. Position statement on behalf of the Heart Failure Association of the European Society of Cardiology. Eur J Heart Fail. 2018;20(1):16-37.
9. Kevin LG. 2007. Right ventricular failure. Continuing Education in Anaesthesia Critical Care & Pain. 7;3:89-94.

TRANSPLANTED HEART

Questions:

1. **Which of the following is true regarding the innervation of a transplanted heart?**
   A. It retains sympathetic innervation but loses parasympathetic innervation
   B. It lacks both sympathetic and parasympathetic innervation
   C. It retains parasympathetic innervation but loses sympathetic innervation
   D. It retains both sympathetic and parasympathetic innervation

2. **What is the typical resting heart rate in a patient with a transplanted heart?**
   A. 60-80 bpm
   B. 80-100 bpm
   C. 90-110 bpm
   D. 110-120 bpm

3. **How does a transplanted heart respond to hypovolemia?**
   A. By increasing heart rate
   B. By increasing contractility
   C. It is dependent on venous return
   D. By decreasing systemic vascular resistance

4. **What is the mechanism of action of neostigmine in managing a transplanted heart patient?**
   A. Neostigmine increases sympathetic activity in the heart
   B. Neostigmine decreases parasympathetic activity in the heart
   C. Neostigmine stimulates cholinergic receptors in the peripheral cardiac parasympathetic pathway
   D. Neostigmine indirectly blocks both nicotinic and muscarinic receptors

5. **80% of recipients of a transplanted heart demonstrate two p-waves on ECG.**
   A. True
   B. False

6. **A 40-year-old man with a history significant for non-ischemic cardiomyopathy underwent an orthotopic heart transplant (OHT). His medical history also includes type II diabetes mellitus, hypertension, chronic kidney disease stage III, and chronic anemia. One month following the transplantation, the patient remains in the intensive care unit (ICU) and is experiencing bradycardia. Which drug is NOT appropriate management for bradycardia in a patient with a transplanted heart?**
   A. Isoprenaline
   B. Atropine
   C. Norepinephrine
   D. Epinephrine

Answers:

1. Answer B (It lacks both sympathetic and parasympathetic innervation)

A transplanted heart lacks sensory, sympathetic, and parasympathetic innervation. This means that the transplanted heart does not receive signals from the autonomic nervous system, which controls the sympathetic and parasympathetic functions of the heart. As a result, the transplanted heart does not respond to normal neural inputs that regulate heart rate, contractility, and other functions. This absence of innervation has implications for the management of patients with transplanted hearts, as the heart may not respond appropriately to changes in physiological conditions such as hypovolemia or stress.

2. Answer C (90-110 bpm)

A transplanted heart lacks sensory, sympathetic, and parasympathetic innervation. Without parasympathetic innervation, vagal tone is lost, leading to a higher resting heart rate of 90-110 bpm. This higher resting heart rate is a result of the absence of the normal inhibitory influence of the parasympathetic nervous system on the heart. It's important to note that over time, both sympathetic and parasympathetic reinnervation can occur in a transplanted heart, but the degree of reinnervation is incomplete, nonuniform, variable between patients, and heterogeneous within the same patient.

3. Answer C (It is dependent on venous return)

In the case of hypovolemia, a normal heart can increase its cardiac output by stimulating neurohormonal pathways, resulting in increased heart rate and contractility. However, a transplanted heart lacks this ability due to the absence of sympathetic and parasympathetic innervation. Instead, a transplanted heart is "preload dependent," meaning that cardiac output becomes dependent on venous return. This is because the transplanted heart cannot increase heart rate or contractility in response to hypovolemia, and therefore, its ability to maintain cardiac output relies on the amount of blood returning to the heart from the venous system.

4. Answer C (Neostigmine stimulates cholinergic receptors in the peripheral cardiac parasympathetic pathway)

Neostigmine produces a dose-dependent, atropine-sensitive reduction in heart rate in cardiac transplant patients by directly stimulating cholinergic receptors in the peripheral cardiac parasympathetic pathway. This stimulation leads to an increase in parasympathetic activity in the heart, which can result in bradycardia. It is important to exercise caution when administering neostigmine to cardiac transplant patients to avoid potentially catastrophic bradycardic responses.

5. Answer A (True)

In 80% of recipients of a transplanted heart, the ECG will demonstrate two p-waves. This is due to the retention of the posterior portion of the atrial walls from the original heart. This unique ECG finding is a result of the surgical technique used during heart transplantation, where the posterior portion of the recipient's atrial walls is left intact to facilitate the anastomosis of the donor heart's atria. This results in the appearance of two distinct p-waves on the ECG in the majority of recipients.

6. Answer B (Atropine)

During the heart transplant surgery, the connections that allow the heart to respond to parasympathetic stimulation are severed, leading to a loss of this pathway. Atropine acts by blocking the action of acetylcholine at parasympathetic sites, which would normally increase heart rate by blocking the vagus nerve's inhibitory effects. However, in a transplanted heart, this mechanism is ineffective because the heart does not receive parasympathetic innervation. Instead of atropine, other agents such as isoproterenol, glucagon, epinephrine, or norepinephrine, which have a direct effect on the heart and do not rely on intact parasympathetic pathways, should be considered for managing bradycardia in patients with transplanted hearts.

Recommended literature

1. Pollard BJ, Kitchen, G. Handbook of Clinical Anaesthesia. Fourth Edition. CRC Press. 2018. 978-1-4987-6289-2.

TRICUSPID REGURGITATION (TR)

Questions:

1. **Which statement about tricuspid regurgitation (TR) is true?**
   A. TR is primarily a result of left-sided valvular heart disease
   B. TR is often associated with right-sided valvular heart disease
   C. TR is commonly caused by isolated tricuspid valve abnormalities
   D. TR is exclusively caused by congenital heart defects

2. **Tricuspid regurgitation can also develop as a result of?**
   A. Infection, such as infective endocarditis or rheumatic fever
   B. Congenital heart disease, such as Ebstein anomaly
   C. Marfan syndrome
   D. All of the above

3. **Which is NOT a symptom of tricuspid regurgitation?**
   A. Fatigue
   B. Swelling
   C. Abnormal heart rhythms
   D. Sweating

4. **What is the management approach for tricuspid regurgitation?**
   A. Repair or replacement of the tricuspid valve
   B. Medication to manage symptoms
   C. Treatment of primary causes and comorbidities
   D. All of the above

5. **Upper abdominal pain is one of the signs of tricuspid regurgitation.**
   A. True
   B. False

6. **A 58-year-old male presents to the cardiology clinic with complaints of fatigue and shortness of breath. He has a history of rheumatic fever in childhood but has not experienced any cardiac symptoms until recently. On examination, his blood pressure is 130/80 mmHg, heart rate is 90 bpm, and jugular venous pressure is elevated with prominent systolic pulsations. On auscultation, a holosystolic murmur is heard at the lower left sternal border that increases with inspiration. An echocardiogram is performed, revealing severe TR with a central jet and an enlarged right atrium. Which of the following is the most likely cause of tricuspid regurgitation in this patient?**
   A. Rheumatic heart disease
   B. Congenital heart disease
   C. Pulmonary hypertension
   D. Atrial fibrillation

Answers:

1. Answer B (TR is often associated with right-sided valvular heart disease)

Tricuspid regurgitation (TR) is often associated with right-sided valvular heart disease, such as pulmonary hypertension or tricuspid valve abnormalities. While left-sided valvular heart disease can contribute to TR indirectly by causing pulmonary hypertension and right heart strain, it is not the primary cause of TR.

2. Answer D (All of the above)

All of the above options are correct as they represent different etiologies that can contribute to the development of tricuspid regurgitation. TR can develop as a result of various factors, including heart failure, pulmonary hypertension, cardiomyopathy, infection, congenital heart disease, and certain genetic conditions.

3. Answer D (Sweating)

Sweating is not typically a symptom directly associated with TR. TR primarily affects the heart and circulatory system, leading to symptoms that reflect the impact on cardiac function and blood flow. Sweating can be associated with other cardiovascular conditions or general factors such as anxiety, exercise, or hormonal changes, but it is not a specific symptom of TR.

4. Answer D (All of the above)

The management approach for TR involves a comprehensive approach that includes multiple strategies. These strategies include repairing or replacing the tricuspid valve, medication to manage symptoms, and addressing the primary causes and comorbidities associated with TR. Repair or replacement of the tricuspid valve may be considered in cases where the severity of TR warrants intervention. The decision between repair or replacement depends on factors such as the extent of valve damage and the overall condition of the patient. Medication is often used to manage symptoms associated with TR, such as heart failure symptoms. Medications may include diuretics to reduce fluid overload, beta-blockers or ACE inhibitors to improve ventricular function, and medications to control arrhythmias if present. Treatment of primary causes and comorbidities is an important aspect of TR management. Identifying and addressing any underlying conditions or diseases that contribute to TR is crucial. For example, if TR is secondary to left-sided valvular heart disease, treatment of the primary left-sided valvular abnormality may help alleviate TR.

5. Answer A (True)

Upper abdominal pain can be one of the signs of TR, particularly in more advanced cases. While TR primarily affects the heart and circulatory system, the elevated pressure and congestion in the right side of the heart can result in liver enlargement and congestion, leading to hepatomegaly. This can cause upper abdominal pain or discomfort. Additionally, the accumulation of fluid in the abdominal cavity (ascites) that can occur in severe TR can also contribute to upper abdominal discomfort or pain. It's important to note that upper abdominal pain is not a specific or exclusive symptom of TR, and it can be present in various other conditions affecting the liver, gastrointestinal tract, or other organs. Therefore, a comprehensive evaluation is necessary to determine the exact cause of upper abdominal pain and differentiate it from other potential causes.

6. Answer A (Rheumatic heart disease)

In this case, the most likely cause of TR in the patient is rheumatic heart disease. The patient's history of rheumatic fever in childhood, along with the presence of a holosystolic murmur at the lower left sternal border, suggests that rheumatic heart disease has led to the development of TR. The presence of an enlarged right atrium on the echocardiogram is consistent with chronic volume overload due to severe TR. The elevated jugular venous pressure and prominent systolic pulsations further support the diagnosis of significant tricuspid regurgitation. While congenital heart disease, pulmonary hypertension, and atrial fibrillation can also contribute to the development of TR, the patient's history of rheumatic fever and the characteristic findings on examination and echocardiogram make rheumatic heart disease the most likely cause in this case.

Recommended literature

1. Antunes MJ, Rodríguez-Palomares J, Prendergast B, De Bonis M, Rosenhek R, Al-Attar N, et al. Management of tricuspid valve regurgitation: Position statement of the European Society of Cardiology Working Groups of Cardiovascular Surgery and Valvular Heart Disease. European Journal of Cardio-Thoracic Surgery. 2017;52(6):1022-30.

Cardiac diseases
WOLFF-PARKINSON-WHITE SYNDROME

Questions:

1. **What is the underlying mechanism of Wolff-Parkinson-White (WPW) syndrome?**
   A. Atherosclerosis of coronary arteries
   B. Impaired functioning of the sinoatrial node
   C. Abnormal accessory pathways between the atria and ventricles
   D. Atrioventricular (AV) node obstruction

2. **Which of the following electrocardiographic findings is characteristic of WPW syndrome?**
   A. Prolonged QT interval
   B. Narrow QRS complex
   C. Delta wave
   D. Absence of P wave

3. **What is the first-line treatment for stable WPW-associated tachycardias?**
   A. Vagal maneuvers
   B. Administration of adenosine
   C. Electrical cardioversion
   D. Catheter ablation

4. **Which of the following medications should generally be avoided in patients with WPW syndrome?**
   A. Beta-blockers
   B. Diuretics
   C. Antiplatelet agents
   D. Anticoagulants

5. **Ketamine should be used with caution in patients with WPW syndrome.**
   A. True
   B. False

6. **A 50-year-old female with a known history of WPW syndrome is scheduled for elective laparoscopic hysterectomy under general anesthesia. The patient has been experiencing occasional episodes of palpitations and lightheadedness but has not had any recent episodes. She takes no medication at this moment, and preoperative evaluation reveals no other significant medical history. The patient is otherwise healthy, and all preoperative investigations, including electrocardiogram (ECG), are within normal limits. During the surgery, a sudden development of an unstable arrhythmia occurs. The patient's heart rate increases to 180 beats per minute, and her blood pressure drops to 60/40 mmHg; the ECG shows a rapid supraventricular tachycardia (SVT) with a wide QRS complex, consistent with a tachyarrhythmia associated with WPW syndrome.**
   What is the most appropriate immediate intervention?
   A. Administration of intravenous adenosine
   B. Initiation of synchronized electrical cardioversion
   C. Administration of intravenous beta-blocker
   D. Adjustment of inhaled anesthetic concentration

Answers:

1. **Answer C (Abnormal accessory pathways between atria and ventricles)**

   The underlying mechanism of Wolff-Parkinson-White syndrome is abnormal accessory pathways that provide an additional electrical connection between the atria and ventricles. These accessory pathways, known as Kent's bundle, bypass the normal electrical conduction system, specifically the atrioventricular (AV) node, and allow electrical impulses to bypass the AV node and directly stimulate the ventricles, resulting in premature depolarization.

2. **Answer C (Delta wave)**

   The presence of a delta wave on the electrocardiogram (ECG) is a characteristic finding in WPW syndrome. It represents the initial indistinct upstroke of the QRS complex. Abnormal accessory pathways provide additional electrical coupling between the atria and ventricles, resulting in premature depolarization. This premature depolarization is responsible for the characteristic electrocardiographic findings seen in WPW syndrome, such as a shortened PR interval, a prolonged QRS complex, and an indistinct upstroke of the QRS complex known as the delta wave.

3. **Answer A (Vagal maneuvers)**

   First-line treatment for stable tachycardias associated with WPW is usually vagal maneuvers, such as carotid massage or the Valsalva maneuver. These maneuvers work by stimulating the vagus nerve, which helps regulate the heart's electrical activity.

4. **Answer A (Beta-blockers)**

   AV node blockers should be avoided in atrial fibrillation and atrial flutter with Wolff-Parkinson-White syndrome (WPW). In particular, avoid adenosine, diltiazem, verapamil, and other calcium channel blockers and beta-blockers. They can exacerbate the syndrome by blocking the heart's normal electrical pathway and facilitating antegrade conduction via the accessory pathway.

5. **Answer A (True)**

   Ketamine is a dissociative anesthetic that is commonly used in various clinical settings. However, it can also have adverse effects on the cardiovascular system, including increasing heart rate, blood pressure, and cardiac output. These effects can be particularly concerning in patients with WPW syndrome, who are at risk of developing rapid, potentially life-threatening arrhythmias. The use of ketamine in patients with WPW syndrome should be approached with caution, and proper monitoring of the patient's cardiovascular status is necessary. The drug should be used at the lowest effective dose and titrated carefully to avoid excessive increases in heart rate and blood pressure.

6. **Answer B (Initiation of synchronized electrical cardioversion)**

   In the event of a sudden development of an unstable arrhythmia during surgery, the priority is to address the compromised hemodynamic status and restore normal rhythm promptly. In patients with WPW syndrome, the accessory pathway can conduct electrical impulses rapidly, potentially leading to ventricular fibrillation or other life-threatening arrhythmias. In this scenario, synchronized electrical cardioversion is the most appropriate immediate intervention. Overall, prompt recognition of the unstable arrhythmia and the initiation of synchronized electrical cardioversion is crucial to restore normal cardiac rhythm and stabilize the patient's hemodynamic status, ensuring the best possible outcome.

Recommended literature

1. Bengali R, Wellens HJ, Jiang Y. Perioperative management of the Wolff-Parkinson-White syndrome. J Cardiothorac Vasc Anesth. 2014;28(5):1375-1386.

CRITICAL CARE

ABDOMINAL COMPARTMENT SYNDROME

Questions:

1. What is the normal range for intra-abdominal pressure (IAP) in healthy individuals?
   A. 0-2 mmHg
   B. 2-5 mmHg
   C. 5-7 mmHg
   D. 7-10 mmHg

2. Abdominal compartment syndrome (ACS) is characterized by?
   A. IAP > 5 mmHg
   B. IAP ≥ 12 mmHg
   C. IAP > 20 mmHg
   D. IAP ≥ 30 mmHg

3. What is the calculation for abdominal perfusion pressure (APP)?
   A. Mean arterial pressure (MAP) + Intra-abdominal pressure (IAP)
   B. Mean arterial pressure (MAP) - Intra-abdominal pressure (IAP)
   C. Intra-abdominal pressure (IAP) - Mean arterial pressure (MAP)
   D. Mean arterial pressure (MAP) + Intracranial pressure (ICP)

4. What are the potential consequences of decompression in abdominal compartment syndrome ACS?
   A. Increase in cardiac output and systemic vascular resistance
   B. Decrease in oxygenation and ventilation-perfusion mismatch
   C. Risk of systemic acidosis and hyperkalemia
   D. All of the above

5. Performing abdominal compartment decompression is a management strategy to lower intra-abdominal pressure in abdominal compartment syndrome ACS?
   A. True
   B. False

6. A 55-year-old male patient with a history of chronic liver disease and ascites presents to the emergency department with worsening abdominal pain and distention. On examination, his abdomen is tense and distended. He appears lethargic and has decreased urine output. His vital signs are as follows: blood pressure 100/70 mmHg, heart rate 110 bpm, respiratory rate 22 breaths per minute, and oxygen saturation 92% on room air. Laboratory tests reveal metabolic acidosis with a pH of 7.25 and elevated serum potassium levels. An abdominal ultrasound confirms the presence of significant ascites. What is the most appropriate initial management for this patient?
   A. Administration of diuretics to reduce fluid overload
   B. Placement of an intragastric catheter to measure intra-abdominal pressure (IAP)
   C. Immediate decompression of the abdomen with paracentesis
   D. Initiation of broad-spectrum antibiotics for suspected infection

Answers:

1. Answer B (2-5 mmHg)

The normal range for intra-abdominal pressure (IAP) in healthy individuals is between 2-5 mmHg.

2. Answer C (IAP > 20 mmHg)

Abdominal compartment syndrome (ACS) is defined as IAP rising above 20 mmHg, leading to new organ dysfunction.

3. Answer B (Mean arterial pressure (MAP) - Intra-abdominal pressure (IAP))

The abdominal blood flow pressure is known as the abdominal perfusion pressure (APP) and can be calculated as the difference between mean arterial pressure (MAP) and IAP. Therefore, the changes in APP are strongly dependent on changes in MAP and IAP.

4. Answer D (All of the above)

Decompression in ACS can lead to an increase in cardiac output and systemic vascular resistance, a decrease in oxygenation and ventilation-perfusion mismatch, and carry the risk of systemic acidosis and hyperkalemia. Decompression of the abdomen leads to a sudden decrease in IAP. This sudden reduction in pressure can cause a rapid increase in cardiac output and systemic vascular resistance. It occurs because the release of pressure allows improved venous return and cardiac preload. Decompression of the abdomen can result in a sudden change in respiratory compliance, leading to alterations in oxygenation and ventilation-perfusion mismatch. It is important to avoid overventilation and carefully manage respiratory parameters during decompression. Decompression in ACS can cause reperfusion of previously compromised organs and tissues. This reperfusion can lead to the release of metabolites and toxins, which may contribute to systemic acidosis. Additionally, the sudden release of potassium (hyperkalemia) from the ischemic tissues can occur, potentially leading to cardiac arrhythmias and other complications.

5. Answer A (True)

Abdominal compartment decompression, such as opening the abdominal wound and performing temporary closure with mesh or a plastic bag, is a management strategy to lower intra-abdominal pressure in ACS.

6. Answer C (Immediate decompression of the abdomen with paracentesis)

Based on the patient's presentation, including worsening abdominal pain, tense distension, lethargy, decreased urine output, and laboratory findings of metabolic acidosis and elevated serum potassium levels, the most appropriate initial management is immediate decompression of the abdomen with paracentesis. The patient's symptoms and physical findings suggest the development of ACS due to the significant ascites, leading to increased IAP. Immediate decompression through paracentesis helps relieve the elevated IAP and prevent further organ dysfunction.

Recommended literature

1. Neil Berry, Simon Fletcher, Abdominal compartment syndrome, Continuing Education in Anaesthesia Critical Care & Pain, Volume 12, Issue 3, June 2012, Pages 110–117.
2. Mullens W, Abrahams Z, Skouri HN, et al. Elevated intra-abdominal pressure in acute decompensated heart failure: a potential contributor to worsening renal function? J Am Coll Cardiol. 2008;51(3):300-306.

Critical care

ACUTE RESPIRATORY DISTRESS SYNDROME

03
CHAPTER

Questions:

1. **What is the main feature of acute respiratory distress syndrome (ARDS)?**
   A. Hypoxemia
   B. Damage to endothelial cells
   C. Alveolar edema
   D. All of the above

2. **Which of the following is NOT a risk factor for ARDS?**
   A. Pneumonia
   B. Pulmonary contusion
   C. Cardiogenic shock
   D. Nonpulmonary sepsis

3. **According to the Berlin definition, which criteria are required for the diagnosis of ARDS?**
   A. PaO/FiO ratio of less than 300 mmHg and bilateral opacities on chest imaging
   B. Acute onset of respiratory failure and tachycardia
   C. Elevated C-reactive protein and leukocytosis
   D. Pulmonary fibrosis and decreased lung compliance

4. **Which medication has been shown to improve oxygenation in some cases of ARDS?**
   A. Antibiotics
   B. Steroids
   C. Anticoagulants
   D. Bronchodilators

5. **Prone positioning in ARDS helps to improve oxygenation and better overall lung function.**
   A. True
   B. False

6. **A 60-year-old patient underwent urgent surgery due to a perforated peptic ulcer. The patient has a history of gastroesophageal reflux disease (GERD) and is currently on proton pump inhibitor (PPI) therapy. Upon assessment, the patient appears agitated and in severe distress, with labored breathing and oxygen saturation of 88% on room air. Auscultation of the chest reveals bibasilar rales. Arterial blood gas analysis reveals hypoxemia and respiratory acidosis. What is the most appropriate anesthetic management for this patient?**
   A. Rapid sequence induction (RSI) with cricoid pressure and endotracheal intubation
   B. Inhalation induction with sevoflurane and subsequent endotracheal intubation
   C. Awake fiberoptic intubation
   D. Noninvasive positive pressure ventilation (NIPPV) with bilevel positive airway pressure (BiPAP)

Answers:

1. **Answer D (All of the above)**

   Acute respiratory distress syndrome (ARDS) is characterized by a combination of features, including hypoxemia, stiff lungs, alveolar edema, endothelial cell damage, and neutrophil infiltration.

2. **Answer C (Cardiogenic shock)**

   Cardiogenic shock is not a direct risk factor for the development of ARDS. While heart failure can result in respiratory symptoms, it does not typically lead to the characteristic lung injury seen in ARDS.

3. **Answer A (PaO/FiO ratio of less than 300 mmHg and bilateral opacities on chest imaging)**

   According to the Berlin definition of ARDS, which is widely used for diagnosing ARDS, the criteria required for the diagnosis include acute onset, bilateral lung infiltrates on chest radiography of a non-cardiac origin, exclusion of cardiac failure or fluid overload as the primary cause, and a PaO/FiO ratio of less than 300 mmHg.

4. **Answer B (Steroids)**

   In some cases of ARDS, the administration of steroids, such as methylprednisolone, has been found to improve oxygenation. The mechanism of action is believed to involve reducing inflammation and modulating the immune response. However, the use of steroids in ARDS remains a topic of debate and should be individualized based on the patient's condition and underlying cause.

5. **Answer A (True)**

   The benefits of prone positioning in ARDS include improved oxygenation, better ventilation-perfusion matching, and enhanced lung mechanics. Prone positioning is often recommended as part of the management strategy for patients with moderate to severe ARDS.

6. **Answer A (Rapid sequence induction (RSI) with cricoid pressure and endotracheal intubation)**

   Based on the patient's history and clinical presentation, aspiration pneumonitis is suspected as a possible cause of her respiratory distress. Prompt intervention is essential to support the patient's respiratory function, initiate appropriate treatment, and prevent progression to ARDS. In this case, the most appropriate anesthetic management for this patient would be rapid sequence induction (RSI) with cricoid pressure and endotracheal intubation.

Recommended literature

1. Battaglini D, Robba C, Rocco PRM, De Abreu MG, Pelosi P, Ball L. Perioperative anaesthetic management of patients with or at risk of acute distress respiratory syndrome undergoing emergency surgery. BMC Anesthesiol. 2019;19(1):153.
2. DiSilvio B, Young M, Gordon A, Malik K, Singh A, Cheema T. Complications and Outcomes of Acute Respiratory Distress Syndrome. Crit Care Nurs Q. 2019;42(4):349-361.
3. Robert Wise, David Bishop, Gavin Joynt & Reitze Rodseth (2018) Perioperative ARDS and lung injury: for anaesthesia and beyond, Southern African Journal of Anaesthesia and Analgesia, 24:2, 32-39.
4. Fanelli V, Vlachou A, Ghannadian S, Simonetti U, Slutsky AS, Zhang H. Acute respiratory distress syndrome: new definition, current and future therapeutic options. J Thorac Dis. 2013;5(3):326-334.

BURNS

Questions:

1. **Which of the following is a key consideration for the anesthetist during surgery for major burns?**
   A. Hypertension
   B. Hypothermia
   C. Hypernatremia
   D. Hyperglycemia

2. **Which of the following is a potential effect of burn injuries on the cardiovascular system?**
   A. Hypervolemia
   B. Hypertension
   C. Myocardial depression
   D. Increased cardiac output

3. **What is the primary challenge associated with airway management in burn patients?**
   A. Airway edema
   B. Bronchospasm
   C. Tracheal stenosis
   D. Alveolar collapse

4. **Which of the following is a potential systemic effect of major burns?**
   A. Hypothyroidism
   B. Hyperglycemia
   C. Hypotension
   D. Hypokalemia

5. **Enteral nutrition should be started as early as possible after a burn injury.**
   A. True
   B. False

6. **A 50-year-old male patient with major burn injuries is admitted to the burn unit. He sustained deep partial-thickness burns over 40% of his total body surface area (TBSA) due to a fire accident. The patient is experiencing severe pain and exhibits blistering and mottled skin. His vital signs show tachycardia, hypotension, and decreased urine output. Which of the following is an appropriate calculation for fluid resuscitation in this patient, based on the extent of his burn injuries?**
   A. Modified Brooke formula
   B. Ringer's lactate solution
   C. Parkland formula
   D. Crystalloid bolus

Answers:

1. **Answer B (Hypothermia)**

   During surgery for major burns, one of the key considerations for the anesthetist is hypothermia. The loss of skin integrity in burn patients impairs their ability to regulate body temperature, making them prone to significant heat loss. Maintaining a warm environment and addressing hypothermia is crucial during the perioperative period to prevent complications and optimize patient outcomes.

2. **Answer C (Myocardial depression)**

   Burn injuries can have various effects on the cardiovascular system, and one of the potential effects is myocardial depression. Burn patients may experience decreased cardiac output due to the impairment of myocardial function. This can result in a decreased ability of the heart to pump blood effectively, leading to reduced systemic perfusion.

3. **Answer A (Airway edema)**

   The primary challenge associated with airway management in burn patients is airway edema. Burn injuries can lead to inflammation and swelling of the airway tissues, including the pharynx, larynx, and trachea. This edema can cause narrowing or obstruction of the airway, leading to respiratory distress and potentially compromising the patient's ability to breathe adequately. Prompt recognition and appropriate management of airway edema are essential in burn patients to ensure adequate oxygenation and ventilation.

4. **Answer B (Hyperglycemia)**

   Major burns can have systemic effects on the body, and one of the potential systemic effects is hyperglycemia. Burn injuries can trigger a hypermetabolic response characterized by increased levels of stress hormones, such as catecholamines, cortisol, and glucagon. These hormonal changes can lead to increased blood glucose levels, resulting in hyperglycemia. It is important to closely monitor and manage glucose levels in burn patients to prevent complications associated with elevated blood sugar.

5. **Answer A (True)**

   Starting enteral nutrition early (4-6 hours) after a large burn injury (> 20% TBSA) is thought to blunt the metabolic response to burn injury and lead to improved outcomes. Early nutritional support is an essential component of burn care to prevent ileus, stress ulceration, and the effects of hypermetabolism. Enteral nutrition may be oral; however, many burn patients will require an oral or nasoenteric feeding tube placement.

6. **Answer C (Parkland formula)**

   The Parkland formula is an appropriate calculation for fluid resuscitation in patients with major burn injuries. It is commonly used to estimate the initial fluid requirements in the first 24 hours after a burn. The formula calculates the total volume of fluid needed by considering the patient's weight and the percentage of the total body surface area (TBSA) that is burned. The standard Parkland formula is 2-4 mL x kg x %TBSA burned, with half of the calculated fluid given in the first 8 hours and the remaining half administered over the subsequent 16 hours.

Recommended literature

1. McCann C, Watson A, Barnes D. Major burns: Part 1. Epidemiology, pathophysiology and initial management. BJA Educ. 2022;22(3):94-103.
2. McGovern C, Puxty K, Paton L. Major burns: part 2. Anaesthesia, intensive care and pain management. BJA Educ. 2022;22(4):138-145.

Critical care
CRUSH INJURIES

Questions:

1. **What is the primary electrolyte imbalance associated with rhabdomyolysis?**
   A. Hyperkalemia
   B. Hyponatremia
   C. Hypocalcemia
   D. Hypophosphatemia

2. **Which of the following is a management approach for crush injuries?**
   A. Administering antibiotics
   B. Monitoring blood glucose levels
   C. Providing 100% oxygen supplementation
   D. Applying heat packs to affected areas

3. **Which of the following organs is most affected by crush injuries and rhabdomyolysis?**
   A. Liver
   B. Kidneys
   C. Lungs
   D. Heart

4. **Which of the following is a potential cardiovascular complication of crush injuries?**
   A. Hypertension
   B. Bradycardia
   C. Cardiac arrhythmias
   D. Peripheral edema

5. **In case of crush injury and consequent hyperkalemia, K over 6.6 mmol/l, prescribe insulin 10 IU in 50 mL of 50% dextrose over 15 minutes.**
   A. True
   B. False

6. **A 42-year-old woman was involved in a severe traffic accident where her lower extremities became trapped under the wreckage of her vehicle. After being rescued, she was immediately rushed to the emergency room due to severe pain and pronounced swelling in her legs. Upon examination, her lower limbs are noticeably cold to the touch, and she experiences diminished sensation below the site of the injury. Her blood pressure is measured at 110/60 mmHg, and her heart rate is elevated at 110 beats per minute. In order to monitor her renal function, a urinary catheter is placed, and approximately 100 mL of urine is extracted, which appears "cola" colored. Which of the following complications is commonly associated with crush injuries and rhabdomyolysis in this patient?**
   A. Hyperglycemia
   B. Hypertension
   C. Acute respiratory distress syndrome (ARDS)
   D. Acute kidney injury (AKI)

Answers:

1. Answer A (Hyperkalemia)

Rhabdomyolysis is the breakdown of skeletal muscle tissue, which leads to the release of various substances into the bloodstream, including potassium (K+). The damaged muscle cells release intracellular potassium, resulting in increased levels of potassium in the blood, a condition known as hyperkalemia. Hyperkalemia can have serious implications on cardiac function and can lead to cardiac arrhythmias or even cardiac arrest if not properly managed. Therefore, monitoring and managing potassium levels are crucial in the management of rhabdomyolysis.

2. Answer C (Providing 100% oxygen supplementation)

Crush injuries can result in tissue damage, compromised blood flow, and potential ischemia-reperfusion injury. By providing 100% oxygen, the goal is to improve tissue oxygenation and minimize further damage. Oxygen supplementation helps in supporting cellular metabolism, promoting wound healing, and preventing complications associated with inadequate oxygen supply.

3. Answer B (Kidneys)

Crush injuries and rhabdomyolysis can lead to acute kidney injury (AKI) due to the release of myoglobin and other substances from damaged muscle tissue. The release of myoglobin into the bloodstream can overwhelm the kidneys' filtration capacity, leading to myoglobinuria and potentially causing tubular obstruction, intrarenal vasoconstriction, and renal dysfunction. The accumulation of myoglobin and other substances can result in acute tubular necrosis and impairment of renal function.

4. Answer C (Cardiac arrhythmias)

Crush injuries can lead to various cardiovascular complications, and one of the potential complications is cardiac arrhythmias. Crush injuries, particularly severe ones, can result in the release of substances like myoglobin into the bloodstream. These substances, along with the associated electrolyte imbalances and tissue damage, can disrupt the normal electrical conduction system of the heart, leading to abnormal heart rhythms or cardiac arrhythmias. Additionally, the release of potassium from damaged muscle cells in crush injuries can cause hyperkalemia, which further increases the risk of cardiac arrhythmias. Hyperkalemia can affect the normal depolarization and repolarization of cardiac cells, potentially leading to irregular heart rhythms.

5. Answer A (True)

Short-acting insulin, usually given with dextrose to prevent hypoglycemia, rapidly redistributes potassium into the cells and is considered the first-line treatment for severe hyperkalemia. The standard dose of insulin used for the treatment of hyperkalemia is 10 units. It can be administered either intravenously or intramuscularly. Insulin 10 units is estimated to lower serum potassium by 0.6–1.2 mmol/L within 15 minutes of administration, with effects lasting 4–6 hours. Dextrose is administered along with insulin to prevent hypoglycemia since insulin can lower blood glucose levels. The typical concentration used is 50% dextrose solution. The insulin and dextrose mixture is typically administered over 15 minutes to 1 hour to prevent rapid shifts in blood glucose levels.

6. Answer D (Acute kidney injury (AKI))

In this case, the patient presents with several key features suggestive of crush injuries and rhabdomyolysis. The prolonged compression and subsequent release of the lower extremities, as well as the severe pain, swelling, and diminished sensation, are consistent with crush injuries. Furthermore, the presence of "cola" colored urine indicates the release of myoglobin, a breakdown product of muscle tissue, into the urinary system. Myoglobinuria is a characteristic finding in rhabdomyolysis, a condition where muscle breakdown occurs and myoglobin is released into the bloodstream. One of the most significant complications associated with crush injuries and rhabdomyolysis is AKI. The myoglobin released from damaged muscle cells can cause tubular obstruction, intrarenal vasoconstriction, and direct tubular injury, leading to impaired kidney function and acute kidney injury. The "cola" colored urine observed in this case is indicative of myoglobinuria, further supporting the diagnosis of rhabdomyolysis and the associated risk of AKI.

Recommended literature

1. Pollard BJ, Kitchen, G. Handbook of Clinical Anaesthesia. Fourth Edition. CRC Press. 2018. 978-1-4987-6289-2.
2. James Williams, MBBCh FRCA FFICM, Chris Thorpe, MBBS FRCA FFICM, Rhabdomyolysis, Continuing Education in Anaesthesia Critical Care & Pain, Volume 14, Issue 4, August 2014, Pages 163–166.
3. Rajagopalan S. Crush Injuries and the Crush Syndrome. Med J Armed Forces India. 2010;66(4):317-320.

Critical care
DROWNING

Questions:

1. **Leading unintentional injury causes of death include?**
   A. Motor vehicle accidents
   B. Poisoning
   C. Drowning
   D. All of the above

2. **Which factor is the strongest predictor of outcome in drowning cases?**
   A. Age of the victim
   B. Type of liquid involved
   C. Submersion time
   D. Presence of witnesses

3. **Which factor is associated with a high mortality rate in drowning-related cardiac arrest?**
   A. Submersion exceeding 25 minutes
   B. Absence of pulse upon arrival at the emergency room
   C. Unconscious state upon arrival at the emergency department
   D. All of the above

4. **Which of the following are mechanisms of injury associated with drowning?**
   A. Hypoxia
   B. Hypothermia
   C. Coagulopathy
   D. All of the above

5. **Survival after cardiac arrest from drowning-related asphyxia is rare.**
   A. True
   B. False

6. **A 45-year-old male was found unconscious in a cold lake after a suspected drowning incident. Bystanders immediately pulled him out of the water and called emergency services. On arrival, the patient is unresponsive, not breathing, and does not have a palpable pulse. Basic life support (BLS) is initiated with chest compressions and rescue breaths. As the emergency medical team arrives, they continue resuscitation efforts and prepare for advanced life support. When managing a drowning patient with hypothermia, which of the following interventions should be avoided until the body temperature is over 30°C?**
   A. Hypothermia induction
   B. Administration of epinephrine
   C. Initiation of chest compressions
   D. Application of an automated external defibrillator (AED)

Answers:

1. **Answer D (All of the above)**

   Leading unintentional injury causes of death include motor vehicle accidents, poisoning, and drowning. These three factors contribute significantly to the global burden of unintentional injuries resulting in death.

2. **Answer C (Submersion time)**

   Submersion time is the strongest predictor of outcome in drowning cases. The duration that a person remains submerged significantly impacts their chances of survival and the extent of potential complications. Prolonged submersion time leads to a higher risk of severe injury or death.

3. **Answer D (All of the above)**

   All three factors listed, submersion exceeding 25 minutes, absence of pulse upon arrival at the emergency room, and unconscious state upon arrival at the emergency department, are associated with a high mortality rate in drowning-related cardiac arrest. Submersion exceeding 25 minutes indicates a prolonged period without oxygen, significantly increasing the risk of severe injury or death. The longer a person remains submerged, the higher the likelihood of irreversible damage to vital organs, including the brain. The absence of a pulse upon arrival at the emergency room suggests a failed resuscitation attempt or an extremely critical condition. Being unconscious upon arrival at the emergency department indicates a severe neurological state, potentially resulting from the lack of oxygen during the drowning incident. Unconsciousness is often associated with significant brain injury, and the prognosis may be poor.

4. **Answer D (All of the above)**

   Drowning can lead to various mechanisms of injury. Hypoxia occurs due to the inhalation of fluid in the lungs, which interferes with oxygen exchange and can potentially cause cardiac arrest. Hypothermia is another consequence of drowning, as immersion in cold water lowers body temperature, leading to physiological changes and potentially worsening outcomes. Coagulopathy, or abnormal blood clotting, can also occur as a result of drowning.

5. **Answer A (True)**

   Unfortunately, the outcome for individuals who experience cardiac arrest due to drowning-related asphyxia is generally poor. The prolonged submersion time, delayed initiation of resuscitation, and potential complications associated with drowning contribute to the low survival rate.

6. **Answer B (Administration of epinephrine)**

   In a drowning patient with hypothermia, it is important to avoid administering epinephrine until the body temperature is over 30°C. Administering epinephrine during hypothermia can lead to adverse effects such as peripheral vasoconstriction and potentially worsening cardiac arrest. The management of hypothermic drowning patients should focus on initiating and maintaining effective CPR, providing appropriate ventilation, and optimizing rewarming techniques to raise the body temperature. Epinephrine administration is generally delayed until the body temperature reaches a more favorable level above 30°C.

Recommended literature

1. Lott C, Truhlář A, Alfonzo A, et al. European Resuscitation Council Guidelines 2021: Cardiac arrest in special circumstances. Resuscitation. 2021;161:152-219.

INHALATION INJURY

03
CHAPTER

Questions:

1. **Which of the following is a common cause of upper airway injury in inhalation injury?**
   A. Chemical exposure
   B. Hot air
   C. Carbon monoxide poisoning
   D. Tracheobronchial injury

2. **Which of the following is a sign or symptom of inhalation injury?**
   A. Abdominal pain
   B. Joint stiffness
   C. Hoarseness
   D. Blurred vision

3. **What is the primary management approach for inhalation injury?**
   A. Antibiotic therapy
   B. Surgical intervention
   C. 100% oxygen administration
   D. Fluid resuscitation

4. **What is the most common cause of systemic toxicity in inhalation injury?**
   A. Hydrogen cyanide exposure
   B. Chlorine inhalation
   C. Acid aspiration
   D. Carbon monoxide poisoning

5. **Inhalation of noxious gases (e.g. chlorine) can lead to tracheobronchial injury, causing bronchospasm, bronchiolar plugging, and atelectasis.**
   A. True
   B. False

6. **A 35-year-old male presents to the emergency department after being involved in a house fire. He was trapped inside the burning building for several minutes before being rescued. On examination, the patient is conscious but in significant distress. He has singed facial hair, carbonaceous sputum, and hoarseness of voice. His vital signs show tachycardia and tachypnea. Pulse oximetry reveals an oxygen saturation of 88% on room air. The patient is immediately placed on 100% oxygen via a non-rebreather mask. What is the most appropriate initial management approach for this patient's respiratory distress?**
   A. Nebulized bronchodilators
   B. Endotracheal intubation
   C. Nasal cannula
   D. Noninvasive positive pressure ventilation (NIPPV)

Answers:

1. **Answer B (Hot air)**

   A common cause of upper airway injury in inhalation injury is the inhalation of hot air. When hot air is inhaled, it can cause damage to the upper airway, resulting in laryngeal obstruction, mucosal slough, and other injuries specific to the upper respiratory tract. Chemical exposure can cause tracheobronchial injury rather than upper airway injury. Carbon monoxide poisoning and tracheobronchial injury are not directly associated with upper airway injury.

2. **Answer C (Hoarseness)**

   Hoarseness is a common sign of inhalation injury. Other symptoms may include voice changes, stridor, cough, respiratory distress, decreased level of consciousness, and nausea.

3. **Answer C (100% oxygen administration)**

   The primary management approach for inhalation injury is 100% oxygen administration. Inhalation injury often results in impaired oxygenation due to damage to the respiratory tract or lung tissue. Administering 100% oxygen helps to improve oxygenation and alleviate hypoxemia, which is crucial for the well-being of the patient.

4. **Answer D (Carbon monoxide poisoning)**

   Carbon monoxide (CO) poisoning is the most common cause of systemic toxicity in inhalation injury. When a person inhales smoke or other combustion byproducts, such as those produced in fires, carbon monoxide can be present. Carbon monoxide binds to hemoglobin in red blood cells with a higher affinity than oxygen, resulting in reduced oxygen-carrying capacity in the blood. This can lead to tissue hypoxia and systemic toxicity.

5. **Answer A (True)**

   Chlorine is a highly reactive gas that can irritate and damage the respiratory tract upon inhalation. It can cause inflammation, swelling, and constriction of the airways, leading to bronchospasm and increased mucus production. Additionally, chlorine gas can directly damage the lining of the bronchioles, leading to bronchiolar plugging and obstruction; this can result in impaired airflow and atelectasis.

6. **Answer B (Endotracheal intubation)**

   Based on the patient's presentation with significant distress, hoarseness, carbonaceous sputum, and low oxygen saturation, there is a high suspicion of inhalation injury and airway compromise. Endotracheal intubation is the most appropriate initial management approach in this case to secure the patient's airway, protect it from further injury or obstruction, and ensure adequate oxygenation and ventilation. It allows for control of the airway and the delivery of high levels of oxygen.

Recommended literature

1. Preea Gill, FRCA, Rebecca V Martin, FRCA FFICM, Smoke inhalation injury, BJA Education, Volume 15, Issue 3, June 2015, Pages 143–148.
2. Bittner EA, Shank E, Woodson L, Martyn JA. Acute and perioperative care of the burn-injured patient. Anesthesiology. 2015;122(2):448-464.

ORGAN DONATION

Questions:

1. **Which criteria are used to diagnose brain death?**
    A. Somatic and circulatory criteria
    B. Neurological criteria
    C. Cardiopulmonary criteria
    D. Renal function criteria

2. **What is the minimum time that must elapse after cardiac death is declared before organ procurement can begin?**
    A. 1 minute
    B. 5 minutes
    C. 15 minutes
    D. 30 minutes

3. **Which of the following is NOT a parameter targeted for the active management of potential organ donors?**
    A. Heart rate
    B. Urine output
    C. Pulmonary capillary wedge pressure
    D. Body temperature

4. **What is the primary aim of lung protective ventilatory strategies in potential organ donors?**
    A. Maintaining adequate oxygenation
    B. Preventing atelectasis and lung injury
    C. Increasing tidal volume
    D. Reducing pulmonary capillary wedge pressure

5. **In the management of a potential organ donor with a diagnosis of brain death, if the patient presents with a large volume of dilute urine and increased serum sodium levels, treatment with vasopressin is indicated.**
    A. True
    B. False

6. **You are an anesthesiologist involved in the management of a potential organ donor. The patient is a 42-year-old female who experienced a devastating subarachnoid hemorrhage resulting in brain death. The diagnosis of brain death has been confirmed based on comprehensive neurological criteria. As part of the active management of the potential organ donor, you are closely monitoring the patient's vital signs and physiological parameters to optimize organ quality for transplantation. During your assessment, you notice that the patient's arterial pressure remains persistently low despite fluid resuscitation. You decide to initiate vasopressor therapy to improve blood pressure and maintain organ perfusion. Which vasopressor would be the first-line choice in managing the low arterial pressure in this potential organ donor?**
    A. Norepinephrine
    B. Epinephrine
    C. Dopamine
    D. Vasopressin

Answers:

1. **Answer B (Neurological criteria)**

   Brain death is diagnosed based on neurological criteria, which involve the determination of complete and irreversible loss of brain function. These criteria typically include assessments of coma, absence of brainstem reflexes, and apnea testing. Somatic and circulatory criteria, cardiopulmonary criteria, and renal function criteria are not used to diagnose brain death.

2. **Answer B (5 minutes)**

   After cardiac death is declared, a minimum of 5 minutes must elapse before organ procurement can begin. This waiting period ensures that irreversible cessation of circulation has occurred. It allows time for medical professionals to confirm that the cardiac arrest is not reversible and that there is no chance of spontaneous return of circulation. The waiting period helps ensure that the organs intended for transplantation have truly ceased functioning before the procurement process begins.

3. **Answer C (Pulmonary capillary wedge pressure)**

   The parameters targeted for the active management of potential organ donors include heart rate, urine output, and body temperature. These parameters are important indicators of the donor's physiological status and organ perfusion. Heart rate reflects cardiovascular function; urine output reflects renal perfusion and body temperature reflects overall metabolic status and homeostasis. However, pulmonary capillary wedge pressure is not specifically targeted for active management in potential organ donors. It may be monitored to assess cardiac function, but it is not part of the active management parameters.

4. **Answer B (Preventing atelectasis and lung injury)**

   The primary aim of lung protective ventilatory strategies in potential organ donors is to prevent atelectasis and lung injury. These strategies involve using lower tidal volumes, limiting plateau pressures, and optimizing positive end-expiratory pressure (PEEP) to minimize the risk of ventilator-associated lung injury. By protecting the lungs from damage, these strategies aim to maintain the viability and function of the donated lungs for transplantation. While maintaining adequate oxygenation is important, the main goal of lung portective ventilatory strategies is to prevent lung injury rather than focusing solely on oxygenation. Increasing tidal volume or reducing pulmonary capillary wedge pressure are not the primary aims of lung protective ventilatory strategies.

5. **Answer A (True)**

   In the context of brain death and organ donor management, if a potential organ donor with a diagnosis of brain death exhibits a large volume of dilute urine and increased serum sodium levels, it suggests the possibility of diabetes insipidus. Diabetes insipidus can occur as a result of the disruption of vasopressin production or action due to brain death. The primary goal in the management of organ donors with diabetes insipidus is to maintain adequate fluid balance and prevent dehydration. Vasopressin or its synthetic analog, desmopressin, is commonly used to replace the deficient vasopressin hormone and manage the excessive urine output seen in diabetes insipidus.

6. **Answer D (Vasopressin)**

   In managing low arterial pressure in a potential organ donor, vasopressin is considered a first-line vasopressor. Vasopressin is a potent vasoconstrictor that acts on vascular smooth muscle receptors to increase systemic vascular resistance and raise blood pressure. It is particularly useful in cases of refractory hypotension. The recommended dose of vasopressin in this setting is 0.01-0.04 IU/min. This dosage can help restore and maintain blood pressure while optimizing organ perfusion. Vasopressin is often preferred in potential organ donors due to its beneficial effects on maintaining stable blood pressure and minimizing adverse effects on cardiac function.

Recommended literature

1. Balogh J. Srikar J, Diaz G, Williams GW, Moguilevitch M. The role of anesthisiologists in organ donation. Transplantation reports. 2022;7(4).
2. Corbett S, Trainor D, Gaffney A. Perioperative management of the organ donor after diagnosis of death using neurological criteria. BJA Educ. 2021;21(5):194-200.
3. McKeown DW, Bonser RS, Kellum JA. Management of the heartbeating brain-dead organ donor. Br J Anaesth. 2012 Jan;108 Suppl 1:i96-107.

Critical care
PREGNANT TRAUMA PATIENTS

Questions:

1. **What is the most common cause of fetal death in pregnant trauma patients?**
   A. Fetal hemorrhage
   B. Placental abruption
   C. Uterine rupture
   D. Preterm labor

2. **What is the recommended approach to managing pregnant trauma patients?**
   A. Follow the ABCDE approach
   B. Focus only on stabilizing the mother
   C. Urgently deliver the fetus in all cases
   D. Perform immediate caesarean delivery

3. **What is the primary goal of managing trauma during pregnancy?**
   A. Preserve maternal life
   B. Preserve fetal life
   C. Prevent placental abruption
   D. Prevent preterm labor

4. **What are the discharge criteria for pregnant trauma patients?**
   A. Resolution of contractions
   B. No vaginal bleeding
   C. A reassuring fetal heart tracing
   D. All of the above

5. **In pregnant trauma patients with spinal immobilization, nasal intubation is the method of choice for airway management.**
   A. True
   B. False

6. **A 28-year-old pregnant woman, currently at 34 weeks gestation, presents to the emergency department following a car crash. She complains of severe left-sided chest pain and shortness of breath. On examination, she appears anxious and experiences difficulty breathing. Her blood pressure is 90/60 mmHg, her respiratory rate is 32 breaths per minute, and her oxygen saturation is 92%. Auscultation of the chest reveals an absence of breath sounds on the left side. Fetal heart rate monitoring shows a baseline of 150 bpm with good variability. The patient's initial laboratory tests are within normal limits. Bedside ultrasound examination shows the absence of lung sliding and the presence of a lung point, indicating a pneumothorax. Given the clinical presentation and ultrasound findings, the recommended site for the insertion of a chest drain in the anterior or mid-axillary line is the?**
   A. 2th–3rd intercostal space
   B. 3rd–4th intercostal space
   C. 4th–5th intercostal space
   D. 5th–6th intercostal space

Answers:

1. Answer B (Placental abruption)

Placental abruption refers to the separation of the placenta from the uterine wall before delivery. It is the most common cause of fetal death in pregnant trauma patients. Placental abruption can occur as a result of trauma, and the sudden separation of the placenta can lead to compromised blood flow to the fetus, depriving it of oxygen and nutrients. This can result in fetal distress and, in severe cases, fetal death. Prompt recognition and management of placental abruption are essential to minimize the potential for adverse outcomes in both the mother and the fetus.

2. Answer A (Follow the ABCDE approach)

The recommended approach to managing pregnant trauma patients is to follow the ABCDE approach, which stands for airway, breathing, circulation, disability, and exposure. This approach is a systematic and comprehensive way to assess and manage trauma patients, including pregnant women.

3. Answer A (Preserve maternal life)

The primary goal of managing trauma during pregnancy is to preserve maternal life. While the well-being of the fetus is also important and must be considered, the immediate priority is ensuring the survival and stabilization of the mother. Maternal survival is essential to provide the best possible outcome for both the mother and the fetus. Managing trauma in pregnancy requires a comprehensive and multidisciplinary approach that takes into account the unique anatomical and physiological changes in pregnancy. Prompt assessment, resuscitation, and treatment of any life-threatening injuries in the mother are crucial to preserving her life. Simultaneously, efforts should be made to monitor and optimize the well-being of the fetus.

4. Answer D (All of the above)

The discharge criteria for pregnant trauma patients include multiple factors that need to be considered to ensure the well-being of both the mother and the fetus. These criteria include the resolution of contractions, no vaginal bleeding, reassuring fetal heart tracing, intact membranes, and no uterine tenderness. All of these factors are important indicators of stability and the absence of ongoing complications that could require further medical intervention. By meeting all of these criteria, it provides assurance that the patient is in a condition suitable for discharge from the healthcare facility.

5. Answer B (False)

Nasal intubation is not the method of choice for airway management in pregnant trauma patients with spinal immobilization. Pregnancy leads to friable mucosa with capillary engorgement. For this reason, nasal airways should be avoided in these patients to minimize the risk of bleeding. It is important to note that the specific approach to airway management should be determined based on the individual patient's condition, the severity of the trauma, and the expertise of the healthcare providers involved in the management.

6. Answer B (3rd–4th intercostal space)

In the management of pneumothorax, the primary goal is to relieve the pressure on the lung and restore lung function. The placement of the chest drain allows for the removal of air or fluid from the pleural space, re-expanding the collapsed lung and relieving respiratory distress. The diaphragm is positioned higher during pregnancy in the third trimester and so it should be avoided placing chest tubes below the fourth intercostal space in these patients. Placing chest drains higher, in the 3rd or 4th intercostal space, in pregnant patients accounts for the elevated diaphragm and provides a balance between effective drainage and fetal protection.

Recommended literature

1. Irving, T., Menon, R., Ciantar, E., 2021. Trauma during pregnancy. BJA Education 21, 10–19.
2. Huls CK, Detlefs C. Trauma in pregnancy. Semin Perinatol. 2018;42(1):13–20.
3. Jain V, Chari R, Maslovitz S, et al. Guidelines for the Management of a Pregnant Trauma Patient. J Obstet Gynaecol Can. 2015;37(6):553–574.

Critical care
SEPSIS

03
CHAPTER

Questions:

1. **Which of the following best defines sepsis?**
   A. An infection localized to a specific organ
   B. An uncontrolled systemic response to infection causing organ dysfunction
   C. An infection limited to the bloodstream
   D. An infection caused by bacteria only

2. **Which of the following is NOT one of the quick Sequential Organ Failure Assessment (qSOFA) criteria for sepsis?**
   A. Altered mental status
   B. Systolic blood pressure < 100 mmHg
   C. Respiratory rate > 22 breaths per minute
   D. Diastolic blood pressure > 90 mmHg

3. **Septic shock is a life-threatening condition characterized by?**
   A. Severe infection without organ dysfunction
   B. Low blood pressure due to sepsis that does not improve with fluid replacement
   C. Dysregulated immune response to infection
   D. Infection caused only by fungi

4. **What is the purpose of lactate monitoring in sepsis?**
   A. To assess kidney function
   B. To measure oxygen saturation
   C. To evaluate liver function
   D. To assess tissue perfusion

5. **Low platelet count, high CRP, and elevated levels of serum lactate, along with the need for invasive mechanical ventilation, were found to be independent predictors of mortality in severely septic patients.**
   A. True
   B. False

6. **A 65-year-old male patient with a history of diabetes and obesity is admitted to the hospital with fever, altered mental status, and hypotension. On physical examination, his respiratory rate is 26 breaths per minute, heart rate is 110 beats per minute, blood pressure is 90/60 mmHg, and he appears confused. Laboratory tests reveal an elevated white blood cell count, hyperglycemia, and elevated serum lactate levels. The patient is diagnosed with severe sepsis. Which of the following is the most appropriate INITIAL management for this patient with severe sepsis?**
   A. Administration of broad-spectrum antibiotics
   B. Initiation of intravenous fluid resuscitation
   C. Placement of an arterial line for blood pressure monitoring
   D. Initiation of vasopressor therapy

Answers:

1. Answer B (An uncontrolled systemic response to infection causing organ dysfunction)

Sepsis is a serious clinical condition characterized by damage to the immune system as a result of an uncontrolled response to infection. Septic patients show complications such as fever, cardiovascular shock, and/or systemic organ failure.

2. Answer D (Diastolic blood pressure > 90 mmHg)

The quick Sequential Organ Failure Assessment (qSOFA) criteria are used as a screening tool for sepsis. They consist of three clinical signs: altered mental status, systolic blood pressure < 100 mmHg, and respiratory rate > 22 breaths per minute. These criteria help identify patients with an increased risk of poor outcomes related to suspected infection. Diastolic blood pressure is not included as one of the qSOFA criteria.

3. Answer B (Low blood pressure due to sepsis that does not improve with fluid replacement)

Septic shock is a life-threatening condition characterized by low blood pressure that does not improve with fluid replacement, despite adequate fluid resuscitation. It is a severe form of sepsis where the body's response to infection leads to widespread inflammation and significant cardiovascular dysfunction.

4. Answer D (To assess tissue perfusion)

The purpose of lactate monitoring in sepsis is to assess tissue perfusion. Lactate is produced as a byproduct of anaerobic metabolism, which occurs when there is insufficient oxygen supply to meet the metabolic demands of the tissues. In sepsis, inadequate tissue perfusion can occur due to impaired blood flow and oxygen delivery. Elevated lactate levels in sepsis indicate tissue hypoperfusion and can indicate the severity of the condition. Therefore, monitoring lactate levels helps clinicians evaluate the adequacy of tissue perfusion and guide the management of sepsis.

5. Answer A (True)

Low platelet count, elevated levels of C-reactive protein (CRP), elevated levels of serum lactate, and the need for invasive mechanical ventilation have been identified as independent predictors of mortality in severely septic patients. These factors, in combination, contribute to the overall severity and prognosis of severe sepsis and can help predict mortality in these patients.

6. Answer B (Initiation of intravenous fluid resuscitation)

In the management of severe sepsis, early and aggressive fluid resuscitation is a crucial step to optimize tissue perfusion and improve patient outcomes. Hypotension and signs of inadequate organ perfusion are common in severe sepsis, and fluid resuscitation is essential to restore intravascular volume and maintain blood pressure. Therefore, the most appropriate initial management for this patient would be to initiate intravenous fluid resuscitation. The administration of broad-spectrum antibiotics is an important step in the management of sepsis, but fluid resuscitation should be prioritized as it addresses immediate hemodynamic instability. The placement of an arterial line for blood pressure monitoring can be considered but is not the most urgent intervention in this scenario. Initiation of vasopressor therapy may be necessary if fluid resuscitation alone does not restore blood pressure, but it is not the initial step and should be considered after fluid resuscitation.

Recommended literature

1. Ammar, M.A., Ammar, A.A., Wieruszewski, P.M. et al. Timing of vasoactive agents and corticosteroid initiation in septic shock. Ann. Intensive Care 12, 47 (2022).
2. Charlton, M., Thompson, J.P., 2019. Pharmacokinetics in sepsis. BJA Education 19, 7–13.
3. Gyawali B, Ramakrishna K, Dhamoon AS. Sepsis: The evolution in definition, pathophysiology, and management. SAGE Open Med. 2019;7:2050312119835043.
4. Keeley A, Hine P, Nsutebu EThe recognition and management of sepsis and septic shock: a guide for non-intensivistsPostgraduate Medical Journal 2017;93:626-634.
5. Nunnally, M.E., 2016. Sepsis for the anaesthetist. British Journal of Anaesthesia 117, 44–51.
6. Eissa D, Carton EG, Buggy DJ. Anaesthetic management of patients with severe sepsis. Br J Anaesth. 2010;105(6):734-743.

Critical care

TRANSFUSION OF BLOOD PRODUCTS

03
CHAPTER

Questions:

1. What is the recommended ratio of red blood cells (RBCs), fresh frozen plasma (FFP), and platelets for the transfusion of blood products in case of massive hemorrhage?

   A. 2-1-1

   B. 1-1-1

   C. 1-2-1

   D. 1-1-2

2. What is the recommended hemoglobin cutoff for transfusion of red blood cells (RBCs) in hemodynamically stable patients?

   A. 6 g/dL

   B. 7 g/dL

   C. 8 g/dL

   D. 9 g/dL

3. How much does one unit of platelets raise the platelet count?

   A. 10,000-20,000/µL

   B. 20,000-30,000/µL

   C. 30,000-50,000/µL

   D. 50,000-100,000/µL

4. What is the standard dose of FFP per kilogram of body weight?

   A. 5-10 mL/kg

   B. 10-15 mL/kg

   C. 15-20 mL/kg

   D. 20-25 mL/kg

5. Prophylactic platelet transfusion for elective placement of a central venous catheter (CVC) should be prescribed with a platelet count < 50,000/µL.

   A. True

   B. False

6. A 60-year-old male patient with a history of hypertension and recently diagnosed tibial fracture is scheduled to undergo urgent surgical repair under anesthesia. The patient's preoperative platelet count is 55,000/µL. What is the appropriate management regarding platelet transfusion in this case?

   A. Platelet transfusion is not indicated in this patient

   B. Platelet transfusion should be considered to raise the platelet count

   C. Platelet transfusion is mandatory to prevent bleeding during surgery

   D. Platelet transfusion is recommended only if the platelet count falls below 30,000/µL

Answers:

1. Answer B (1-1-1)

In cases of massive hemorrhage, the recommended ratio for transfusion of blood products is 1-1-1, which means giving one unit of red blood cells (RBCs), one unit of fresh frozen plasma (FFP), and one unit of platelets. This balanced ratio helps to maintain adequate oxygen-carrying capacity, replace coagulation factors, and restore platelet function, respectively, in order to manage the massive hemorrhage effectively.

2. Answer B (7 g/dL)

The recommended hemoglobin cutoff for transfusion of red blood cells (RBCs) in hemodynamically stable patients is 7 g/dL. This means that transfusion of RBCs should generally be considered when the patient's hemoglobin level falls below 7 g/dL, provided that the patient is stable from a cardiovascular standpoint. The decision to transfuse RBCs should also take into account the patient's clinical condition, symptoms, and individual factors. It's important to note that transfusion thresholds may vary based on specific clinical scenarios or patient characteristics, so clinical judgement should be exercised in determining the need for transfusion in individual cases.

3. Answer C (30,000-50,000/μL)

One unit of platelets typically raises the platelet count by approximately 30,000-50,000/μL. Platelet transfusions are given to increase the platelet count and improve hemostasis in individuals with thrombocytopenia or active bleeding. The specific range of platelet count increase may vary depending on the individual and other factors, but a general approximation is within the range of 30,000-50,000/μL per unit of platelets transfused.

4. Answer C (15-20 mL/kg)

The standard dose of FFP per kilogram of body weight is 15-20 mL/kg. When FFP is administered, this dosage range is generally used to calculate the amount needed based on the patient's weight. The purpose of FFP transfusion is to provide coagulation factors and other components found in plasma to patients with specific clinical indications. It's important to note that the actual dose may be adjusted based on the patient's specific needs, the underlying condition, and the clinical judgement.

5. Answer B (False)

The statement is false. Prophylactic platelet transfusion for elective placement of a central venous catheter (CVC) should be prescribed with a platelet count < 20,000/μL. When a patient's platelet count falls below this threshold, it is recommended to administer a platelet transfusion before CVC placement to minimize the risk of bleeding.

6. Answer A (Platelet transfusion is not indicated in this patient)

In patients undergoing surgery, platelet transfusion is generally not indicated solely based on the platelet count of 55,000/μL. The decision to transfuse platelets should be based on the patient's clinical condition, bleeding risk, and other factors beyond the platelet count. A platelet count of 55,000/μL is not significantly low and may be adequate for most surgical procedures, especially in the absence of active bleeding or specific indications. The anesthesia team should closely monitor the patient during surgery and manage any bleeding or coagulation issues accordingly, without routine platelet transfusion.

Recommended literature

1. Storch EK, Custer BS, Jacobs MR, Menitove JE, Mintz PD. Review of current transfusion therapy and blood banking practices. Blood Rev. 2019;38:100593.
2. Carson JL, Guyatt G, Heddle NM, et al. Clinical Practice Guidelines From the AABB: Red Blood Cell Transfusion Thresholds and Storage. JAMA. 2016;316(19):2025-2035.
3. Holcomb JB, Tilley BC, Baraniuk S, et al. Transfusion of plasma, platelets, and red blood cells in a 1:1:1 vs a 1:1:2 ratio and mortality in patients with severe trauma: the PROPPR randomized clinical trial. JAMA. 2015;313(5):471-482.

TRAUMA

Questions:

1. **Which scoring system is commonly used to assess the severity of trauma?**
   A. Glasgow Coma Scale (GCS)
   B. Abbreviated Injury Scale (AIS)
   C. Injury Severity Score (ISS)
   D. Trauma Injury Severity Score (TISS)

2. **Which of the following is an immediately life-threatening injury in trauma?**
   A. Airway obstruction
   B. Traumatic diaphragmatic tear
   C. Tension pneumothorax
   D. All of the above

3. **What is the purpose of permissive hypotension in trauma management?**
   A. Maintain high blood pressure
   B. Reduce blood loss
   C. Prevent infection
   D. Increase oxygen delivery

4. **What is the recommended approach for thromboprophylaxis in trauma patients?**
   A. Early mobilization
   B. Pneumatic compression devices
   C. Pharmacological prophylaxis
   D. All of the above

5. **The use of cervical collars in trauma patients may increase secondary neurological injury and intracranial pressure.**
   A. True
   B. False

6. **A 45-year-old male patient presents to the emergency department with a dislocated shoulder. The patient reports severe pain and limited range of motion in his left shoulder following a fall while playing sports. Physical examination reveals an obvious deformity of the left shoulder joint with loss of normal contour. The neurovascular examination is intact. Radiographic imaging confirms the diagnosis of an anterior dislocation of the shoulder. Which anesthesia management technique is typically used for reducing a dislocated shoulder?**
   A. General anesthesia with endotracheal intubation
   B. Monitored anesthesia care (MAC)
   C. Regional anesthesia with an interscalene nerve block
   D. Local anesthesia with intravenous sedation

Answers:

1. Answer C (Injury Severity Score (ISS))

The commonly used scoring system to assess the severity of trauma is the Injury Severity Score (ISS). The ISS evaluates the severity of injuries in different body regions and provides an overall score. It uses the Abbreviated Injury Scale (AIS) to assign scores to specific injuries. The AIS scores range from 1 to 6, with 1 being a minor injury and 6 indicating an unsurvivable injury. To calculate the ISS, the three most severely injured body regions are identified, and their AIS scores are squared and summed. This provides an overall score that helps categorize the trauma's severity. The ISS score ranges from 1 to 75, with higher scores indicating more severe injuries.

2. Answer C (All of the above)

The Deadly Dozen comprises major thoracic injuries, categorized into the Lethal Six and the Hidden Six. The Lethal Six (airway obstruction, tension pneumothorax, cardiac tamponade, open pneumothorax, massive hemothorax, and flail chest) are immediate, life-threatening injuries requiring urgent evaluation and treatment during the primary survey. In contrast, the Hidden Six (thoracic aortic disruption, tracheobronchial disruption, myocardial contusion, traumatic diaphragmatic tear, esophageal disruption, and pulmonary contusion) are potentially life-threatening injuries that should be identified during the secondary survey. These injuries may manifest as either immediately life-threatening or potentially life-threatening events, highlighting the critical importance of systematic evaluation and management in trauma care.

3. Answer B (Reduce blood loss)

The purpose of permissive hypotension in trauma management is to reduce blood loss. Permissive hypotension involves intentionally maintaining lower blood pressure levels than normal to minimize bleeding in trauma patients. By keeping the blood pressure lower, it helps to limit the flow of blood from injured blood vessels and reduce hemorrhage. The rationale behind permissive hypotension is to avoid excessive fluid administration, which can increase blood pressure and potentially worsen bleeding from damaged blood vessels. By keeping blood pressure slightly lower, it helps to preserve clot formation and reduce ongoing bleeding, particularly in cases of uncontrolled hemorrhage. It is important to note that permissive hypotension should be carefully balanced, as maintaining excessively low blood pressure can compromise tissue perfusion and oxygen delivery. The goal is to strike a balance between reducing blood loss and maintaining adequate organ perfusion.

4. Answer D (All of the above)

A multimodal approach consisting of early mobilization, pneumatic compression devices, and pharmacological prophylaxis is recommended for thromboprophylaxis in trauma patients. These strategies work together to reduce the risk of venous thromboembolism (VTE) and its associated complications.

5. Answer A (True)

The use of cervical collars in trauma patients has the potential to increase secondary neurological injury and intracranial pressure. Cervical collars are often employed as a precautionary measure to immobilize the cervical spine and protect against potential spinal cord injury. However, they can also exert unintended effects. Improperly fitted or overly tight cervical collars may impede venous return from the brain, resulting in increased intracranial pressure. Additionally, the rigid immobilization provided by the collar can hinder neck movement and interfere with proper alignment of the cervical spine, potentially exacerbating spinal cord injury or neurological damage. The collar should be properly fitted and periodically reassessed to ensure it is not causing undue pressure or compromising neurological function.

6. Answer B (Monitored anesthesia care (MAC))

The anesthesia management technique typically used for reducing a dislocated shoulder is monitored anesthesia care (MAC). The purposes of MAC are to provide patients with safe sedation, comfort, pain control, and satisfaction. Reducing a dislocated shoulder often requires the application of manual traction and manipulation to realign the joint. Sedation and analgesia are utilized to ensure patient comfort and cooperation during the reduction procedure. Medications used during MAC include midazolam (Versed); fentanyl; propofol (Diprivan) to achieve the desired level of sedation and pain control. General anesthesia with endotracheal intubation is typically not necessary for shoulder reduction procedures unless there are specific indications, such as patient intolerance to conscious sedation or the need for muscle relaxation. Regional anesthesia with an interscalene nerve block can provide excellent analgesia for shoulder surgery, but it is not typically used solely for reducing a dislocated shoulder. Local anesthesia with intravenous sedation may provide some pain control but may not be sufficient for patient comfort during the reduction procedure.

Recommended literature

1. Pollard BJ, Kitchen, G. Handbook of Clinical Anaesthesia. Fourth Edition. CRC Press. 2018. 978-1-4987-6289-2.
2. Tobin JM, Barras WP, Bree S, et al. Anesthesia for Trauma Patients. Mil Med. 2018;183(suppl_2):32-35.
3. Uday Jain, Maureen McCunn, Charles E. Smith, Jean-Francois Pittet; Management of the Traumatized Airway. Anesthesiology 2016; 124:199-206.

EMERGENCIES

Emergencies
ADVANCED LIFE SUPPORT

04
CHAPTER

Questions:

1. Which of the following is a potential cause of perioperative cardiac arrest related to anesthesia?

    A. Increased sympathetic tone

    B. Malignant hyperthermia

    C. Hyperventilation-induced alkalosis

    D. Administration of steroids

2. What is the recommended compression-to-ventilation ratio during CPR in adults?

    A. 5:1

    B. 15:2

    C. 30:2

    D. 100:1

3. How does therapeutic hypothermia show promise in post-resuscitation care?

    A. Stabilize blood pressure

    B. Reduce metabolic demand

    C. Minimize neurological damage

    D. Prevent arrhythmias

4. What is the recommended initial dose of epinephrine (adrenaline) during cardiac arrest management?

    A. 10 mg

    B. 1 mg

    C. 0.1 mg

    D. 0.01 mg

5. Defibrillation is only effective if the rhythm is asystole.

    A. True

    B. False

6. A 75-year-old male patient with a history of cardiomyopathy and coronary artery disease is undergoing laparoscopic cholecystectomy surgery under general anesthesia. Upon sevoflurane induction, the patient suddenly converts from normal sinus rhythm to pulseless ventricular tachycardia. What is the next appropriate course of action for managing the pulseless ventricular tachycardia in this patient?

    A. Administer a precordial thump

    B. Perform immediate defibrillation

    C. Administer intravenous epinephrine

    D. Initiate chest compressions

Answers:

1. Answer B (Malignant hyperthermia)

Perioperative cardiac arrest related to anesthesia can have various causes, but one potential cause is malignant hyperthermia. Malignant hyperthermia is a rare but potentially life-threatening reaction to certain medications used during anesthesia, particularly volatile inhalation anesthetics and succinylcholine. Signs and symptoms of malignant hyperthermia include tachycardia, tachypnea, hypoxemia, hypercarbia, metabolic and respiratory acidosis, hyperkalemia, cardiac dysrhythmias, hypotension, skeletal muscle rigidity, and hyperthermia. It is usually triggered by specific genetic mutations and can occur in susceptible individuals. It is crucial for healthcare providers to be aware of the signs and symptoms of malignant hyperthermia and promptly manage it if suspected to prevent further complications, including cardiac arrest.

2. Answer C (30:2)

The recommended compression-to-ventilation ratio during CPR in adults is 30 compressions to 2 ventilations. High-quality chest compressions are crucial for maintaining circulation during cardiac arrest. Maintaining an appropriate compression-to-ventilation ratio is important for effective CPR and maximizing the chances of successful resuscitation during cardiac arrest. It helps ensure adequate blood flow and oxygenation to the body's tissues while minimizing interruptions in chest compression.

3. Answer C (Minimize neurological damage)

Therapeutic hypothermia, or targeted temperature management (TTM), is utilized in post-resuscitation care to reduce the body's core temperature and minimize neurological damage following cardiac arrest. Evidence suggests TTM is safe with few adverse effects, allowing its use alongside post-resuscitation procedures like angiography and extracorporeal life support. While studies in adults haven't found significant differences compared to normothermia, TTM may benefit certain patient subgroups. In pediatric patients, TTM hasn't shown significant effectiveness differences, but some studies suggest positive effects on survival and neurological status. More research, including larger RCTs and meta-analyses, is needed. Out-of-hospital TTM's impact is controversial due to associated pulmonary edema with intravenous cold saline, but intranasal devices may offer a safer approach. Overall, while TTM holds promise for minimizing neurological damage, further research is needed to clarify its effectiveness and refine its application.

4. Answer B (1 mg)

Epinephrine is a medication commonly used in advanced cardiac life support (ACLS) protocols to improve perfusion during cardiac arrest. The recommended dose of epinephrine hydrochloride is 1.0 mg (10 mL of a 1:10000 solution) administered IV every 3 to 5 minutes during resuscitation. Each dose given by peripheral injection should be followed by a 20 mL flush of IV fluid to ensure delivery of the drug into the central compartment.

5. Answer B (False)

Defibrillation is not effective for asystole, which is the absence of any electrical activity in the heart. Asystole is considered a non-shockable rhythm. Defibrillation is primarily effective for shockable rhythms, such as ventricular fibrillation (VF) and pulseless ventricular tachycardia (VT). These rhythms involve abnormal and rapid electrical activity in the ventricles of the heart. By delivering a well-timed electrical shock, defibrillation aims to restore a normal and coordinated electrical rhythm to the heart. For asystole, other interventions are necessary, such as high-quality cardiopulmonary resuscitation (CPR), administering appropriate medications, and identifying and treating reversible causes.

6. Answer B (Perform immediate defibrillation)

In the case of pulseless ventricular tachycardia (VT), the immediate course of action should be to perform immediate defibrillation. Ventricular tachycardia is a life-threatening arrhythmia characterized by rapid, abnormal electrical impulses in the ventricles, resulting in an ineffective contraction and a lack of sufficient blood flow to the vital organs. Pulseless VT requires prompt defibrillation to restore a normal cardiac rhythm. Prompt recognition of the rhythm and appropriate intervention are vital for successful resuscitation and the restoration of normal cardiac function.

Recommended literature

1. Soar J, Böttiger BW, Carli P, et al. European Resuscitation Council Guidelines 2021: Adult advanced life support [published correction appears in Resuscitation. 2021 Oct;167:105-106]. Resuscitation. 2021;161:115-151.
2. Moitra VK, Einav S, Thies KC, et al. Cardiac Arrest in the Operating Room: Resuscitation and Management for the Anesthesiologist: Part 1. Anesth Analg. 2018;126(3):876-888.
3. Pollard BJ, Kitchen, G. Handbook of Clinical Anaesthesia. Fourth Edition. CRC Press. 2018. 978-1-4987-6289-2.
4. McEvoy MD, Thies KC, Einav S, et al. Cardiac Arrest in the Operating Room: Part 2-Special Situations in the Perioperative Period [published correction appears in Anesth Analg. 2018 May;126(5):1797]. Anesth Analg. 2018;126(3):889-903.
5. Moitra VK, Gabrielli A, Maccioli GA, O'Connor MF. Anesthesia advanced circulatory life support. Can J Anaesth. 2012 Jun;59(6):586-603. doi: 10.1007/s12630-012-9699-3.

Emergencies
AIRWAY FIRE

Questions:

1. **What are the three components required for an airway fire, known as the "fire triad"?**
   A. Oxygen, carbon dioxide, and ignition source
   B. Oxygen, nitrous oxide, and fuel
   C. Nitrous oxide, carbon dioxide, and ignition source
   D. Oxygen, fuel, and ignition source

2. **Which of the following is NOT a recommended preventive measure for airway fires?**
   A. Minimizing oxygen concentration
   B. Keep sponges and gauzes dry near ignition sources
   C. Avoiding the use of ignition sources near oxidizer-enriched environments
   D. Using laser-resistant cuffed tracheal tubes for airway laser procedures

3. **Which of the following supplies should be immediately available in the operating room for managing an airway fire?**
   A. Replacement tracheal tubes, guides, facemasks
   B. Multiple containers of sterile saline
   C. A CO_2 fire extinguisher
   D. All of the above

4. **What is the recommended action if an airway fire cannot be quickly extinguished and the patient's safety is compromised?**
   A. Continue the surgical procedure and monitor the fire closely
   B. Evacuate the patient from the operating room while securing the airway and providing ventilation
   C. Immediately call for a code blue and initiate CPR
   D. Activate the fire alarm and wait for the fire department to arrive

5. **During procedures that are high-risk for an airway fire the drapes should be configured to avoid oxidizer pooling or accumulation.**
   A. True
   B. False

6. **The patient is a 60-year-old male undergoing laser treatment for tracheal stenosis. Despite all the preventive measures, an airway fire occurs during the procedure. The fire is quickly identified, and the team initiates the appropriate response. The tracheal tube is exchanged, and the fire is extinguished by pouring saline into the airway. The patient's safety is now ensured, but there is a concern about potential airway injury. What is the next appropriate step in this situation?**
   A. Administer systemic corticosteroids to reduce airway inflammation
   B. Transfer the patient to the intensive care unit for close monitoring
   C. Continue the surgical procedure while monitoring the patient's vital signs
   D. Perform a bronchoscopy to assess for airway injury

Answers:

1. **Answer D (Oxygen, fuel, and ignition source)**

   The three components required for an airway fire, often referred to as the "fire triad," are oxygen, fuel, and an ignition source. Oxygen acts as an oxidizer, supporting the combustion process. It is commonly used during anesthesia and surgery to maintain the oxygenation of the patient. Fuel refers to any flammable material that can support a fire. In the context of airway fire, potential sources of fuel can include tracheal tubes, sponges, drapes, gauzes, alcohol-containing solutions, oxygen masks, nasal cannulae, the patient's hair, dressings, gowns, gloves, or packaging materials. An ignition source is the element that initiates the fire. Examples of common ignition sources in the operating room include electrosurgical devices, lasers, heated probes, burrs and drills, fiberoptic scopes, and defibrillator paddles or pads.

2. **Answer B (Keep sponges and gauzes dry near ignition sources)**

   Keeping sponges and gauze dry near ignition sources is not a recommended preventive measure for airway fires. Moistening sponges and gauze near ignition sources is actually a recommended preventive measure to reduce their flammability. The moisture acts as a barrier to combustion, helping to prevent rapid ignition and mitigate the spread of fire. The other options are valid preventive measures for airway fires.

3. **Answer D (All of the above)**

   All the supplies mentioned in the options should be immediately available in the operating room for managing an airway fire. Having replacement tracheal tubes, guides, and facemasks readily available is crucial during an airway fire incident. These supplies may be needed to secure the patient's airway and provide adequate ventilation if the primary airway equipment is compromised or damaged. Sterile saline is an essential component for managing an airway fire. It can be used to irrigate and cool the airway and surrounding tissues in case of a fire. The availability of multiple containers ensures an adequate supply for immediate use. A CO_2 fire extinguisher is specifically designed for managing fires involving flammable liquids and electrical equipment, making it suitable for use in an operating room environment. It can be used to extinguish the fire quickly and effectively, minimizing potential harm to the patient and surgical team. Having all of these supplies readily available ensures preparedness and enables prompt action during an airway fire incident. It allows for immediate airway management, cooling of the affected area, and extinguishing of the fire, reducing the potential for further complications and ensuring the safety of the patient and healthcare providers.

4. **Answer B (Evacuate the patient from the operating room while securing the airway and providing ventilation)**

   If an airway fire cannot be quickly extinguished and the patient's safety is compromised, the recommended action is to prioritize the patient's well-being and evacuate them from the operating room. This involves the following steps: Ensure the patient's airway is secured to maintain ventilation and oxygenation. Once the airway is secured, provide manual ventilation or utilize a mechanical ventilator to deliver oxygen to the patient and maintain adequate oxygenation. Safely transport the patient out of the operating room to an area where they can receive further care and evaluation. The other options are not the recommended actions in this situation.

5. **Answer A (True)**

   During procedures that are considered high-risk for an airway fire, it is important to configure the drapes to avoid oxidizer pooling or accumulation. This preventive measure aims to minimize the concentration of oxidizers, such as oxygen or nitrous oxide, in the immediate vicinity of potential fuel sources. By ensuring proper drape configuration, the risk of creating a localized environment with a high concentration of oxidizers is reduced, thereby lowering the potential for an airway fire.

6. **Answer D (Perform a bronchoscopy to assess for airway injury)**

   Although the immediate priority was to extinguish the fire and ensure the patient's safety by exchanging the tracheal tube and pouring saline into the airway, there is still a need to assess for potential airway injury caused by the fire. A bronchoscopy is a diagnostic procedure that allows direct visualization of the airway, and it can provide valuable information about any injury or damage caused by the fire, such as thermal injury, tissue necrosis, or airway obstruction. By performing a bronchoscopy, the extent of the airway injury can be evaluated, and appropriate management can be initiated to ensure optimal patient care.

Recommended literature

1. Cowles CE Jr, Culp WC Jr. Prevention of and response to surgical fires. BJA Educ. 2019;19(8):261-266.
2. Akhtar N, Ansar F, Baig MS, Abbas A. Airway fires during surgery: Management and prevention. J Anaesthesiol Clin Pharmacol. 2016;Jan-Mar;32(1):109-11.
3. Apfelbaum JL, Caplan RA, Barker SJ, et al. Practice advisory for the prevention and management of operating room fires: an updated report by the American Society of Anesthesiologists Task Force on Operating Room Fires. Anesthesiology. 2013;118(2):271-290.

Emergencies
ANAPHYLAXIS

Questions:

1. **What are the most common triggers of anaphylactic reactions?**
   A. Insect stings
   B. Latex
   C. Foods
   D. All of the above

2. **What is the most common cause of anaphylaxis in the operating room (OR)?**
   A. Neuromuscular blockers
   B. Latex
   C. Antibiotics
   D. Propofol

3. **Which of the following is not a sign or symptom of anaphylaxis?**
   A. Sweating
   B. Rash/hives
   C. Fever
   D. Wheezing/shortness of breath

4. **What is the first-line treatment for anaphylaxis?**
   A. Antihistamines
   B. Steroids
   C. Intravenous fluids
   D. Epinephrine

5. **Avocados can trigger a latex allergy.**
   A. True
   B. False

6. **A 45-year-old woman with no known drug allergies was scheduled for a hysterectomy under general anesthesia. After induction of anesthesia with propofol, followed by succinylcholine for muscle relaxation, fentanyl for analgesia, and cefazolin as prophylactic antibiotic coverage, the patient develops sudden-onset symptoms, including wheezing, facial swelling, hypotension, and generalized urticaria. Which drug is the most likely cause of true anaphylaxis in a patient under anesthesia?**
   A. Propofol
   B. Succinylcholine
   C. Fentanyl
   D. Cefazolin

Answers:

1. **Answer D (All of the above)**

Anaphylactic reactions can be triggered by various substances. While the most common triggers of anaphylaxis are foods, other triggers include insect stings, medications, and latex. It's important to note that anaphylaxis can also be triggered by other substances, but the provided options cover the most prevalent triggers.

2. **Answer A (Neuromuscular blockers)**

Anaphylaxis can occur in the operating room (OR) due to various factors, but one of the most common causes is the administration of neuromuscular blockers. Latex allergy is another significant concern in the OR, but it is not the most common cause of anaphylaxis. Antibiotics and propofol can also rarely trigger anaphylaxis, but they are not as commonly associated with anaphylactic reactions in the OR as neuromuscular blockers.

3. **Answer C (Fever)**

Anaphylaxis is a severe allergic reaction that can affect multiple systems in the body. It typically presents with a variety of signs and symptoms. However, fever is not considered a characteristic sign or symptom of anaphylaxis. The most common signs and symptoms of anaphylaxis include sweating, rash/hives, wheezing/shortness of breath, along with other respiratory, cardiovascular, gastrointestinal, or skin-related symptoms.

4. **Answer D (Epinephrine)**

Epinephrine is considered the first-line treatment for anaphylaxis. It is a medication that acts quickly to counteract the severe allergic reaction and stabilize the body. Epinephrine works by constricting blood vessels, relaxing smooth muscles in the airways, and reducing the release of inflammatory substances. These actions help improve breathing, increase blood pressure, and alleviate symptoms during an anaphylactic reaction. Administer epinephrine IV as a bolus of 10-100 µg, depending on the severity of the symptoms, and repeat bolus administration as necessary; if the patient requires continued bolus administration of epinephrine, consider infusion of epinephrine 1-10 µg/min. It's important to note that epinephrine should be administered promptly and without delay in cases of suspected anaphylaxis, as it is the most effective medication for reversing the potentially life-threatening effects of anaphylaxis.

5. **Answer A (True)**

Avocado can trigger a latex allergy in some individuals. This phenomenon is known as latex-fruit syndrome. Avocado contains proteins that are structurally similar to those found in natural latex from rubber trees. Therefore, people allergic to latex may experience cross-reactivity when consuming avocado, leading to allergic symptoms such as oral itching, swelling, hives, or even anaphylaxis in severe cases.

6. **Answer B (succinylcholine)**

In this case, the patient develops sudden symptoms and is highly suggestive of an anaphylactic reaction. Neuromuscular blocking agents (NMBAs) have been shown to be the most common cause of true anaphylaxis in anesthetized patients, followed by latex and antibiotics. Among the drugs administered in this case, succinylcholine (NMBA) is the most likely cause of the patient's symptoms. It is important to recognize and treat anaphylaxis immediately to prevent further complications and ensure patient safety. Treatment includes discontinuation of the triggering agent if known, administration of epinephrine, intravenous fluids, and other supportive measures.

Recommended literature

1. Garvey LH, Dewachter P, Hepner DL, et al. Management of suspected immediate perioperative allergic reactions: an international overview and consensus recommendations. Br J Anaesth. 2019;123(1):e50-e64.
2. Dewachter P, Mouton-Faivre C, Emala CW. Anaphylaxis and anesthesia: controversies and new insights. Anesthesiology. 2009;111(5):1141-1150.

Emergencies
BRONCHOSPASM

Questions:

1. **What is the primary cause of bronchospasm?**
   A. Release of histamine from mast cells
   B. Infection of the upper respiratory tract
   C. Exposure to cold air
   D. Tracheal intubation

2. **Which of the following is NOT a common symptom of bronchospasm?**
   A. Wheezing
   B. Prolonged expiration
   C. Increased tidal volume
   D. Decreased oxygen saturation

3. **Which of the following is a preventive measure for bronchospasm during the perioperative period?**
   A. Inhaled β2-agonist administration before surgery
   B. Induction of anesthesia with propofol
   C. Administration of intravenous steroids
   D. Monitoring end-tidal CO_2 levels

4. **What is the role of propofol in preventing bronchospasm?**
   A. It acts as a bronchodilator
   B. It reduces the release of histamine
   C. It promotes relaxation of bronchial smooth muscles
   D. It improves oxygen saturation

5. **An adequate depth of anesthesia before airway instrumentation can help prevent bronchospasm.**
   A. True
   B. False

6. **A 50-year-old woman with a history of mild asthma is undergoing hysteroscopy with a laryngeal mask airway. Ten minutes after induction, airway pressures increase significantly, and bilateral wheezes are appreciated. The anesthesiologist suspects bronchospasm. What immediate action should be taken?**
   A. Administer bolus propofol to deepen the anesthesia
   B. Administer intravenous nitroglycerin
   C. Increase the concentration of inhaled sevoflurane
   D. Switch the patient to a volume-controlled mode of ventilation

Answers:

1. **Answer A (Release of histamine from mast cells)**

   The primary cause of bronchospasm is the release of histamine from mast cells. Bronchospasm occurs when the smooth muscles in the bronchioles of the lungs contract, leading to the narrowing of the airways. This constriction is triggered by the release of substances, including histamine, from mast cells or basophils. Histamine is released in response to various stimuli, such as anaphylatoxins, cold air, smoking, upper respiratory tract infections, or inhaled irritants. When histamine binds to its receptors in the bronchial smooth muscles, it causes their contraction and subsequent bronchospasm.

2. **Answer C (Increased tidal volume)**

   Bronchospasm is characterized by symptoms such as wheezing, prolonged expiration, decreased tidal volume, and decreased oxygen saturation. An increase in tidal volume is not typically observed in bronchospasm.

3. **Answer A (Inhaled β2-agonist administration before surgery)**

   Preventive measures for bronchospasm during the perioperative period aim to reduce the risk of bronchospasm and maintain optimal respiratory function during surgery. Inhaled β2-agonists, such as salbutamol, are bronchodilators that relax the smooth muscles of the airways, leading to improved airflow and decreased bronchospasm. By administering an inhaled β2-agonist before surgery, the bronchial smooth muscles can be relaxed, reducing the likelihood of bronchospasm occurring during or after the procedure.

4. **Answer C (It promotes relaxation of bronchial smooth muscles)**

   Propofol, an intravenous anesthetic agent, plays a role in preventing bronchospasm by promoting the relaxation of bronchial smooth muscles. During the induction of anesthesia, the administration of propofol leads to a decrease in sympathetic outflow and a subsequent reduction in the tone of bronchial smooth muscles. While propofol itself is not a bronchodilator in the traditional sense, its action on the central nervous system and the subsequent reduction in sympathetic activity result in the relaxation of bronchial smooth muscles. This relaxation helps to prevent or minimize bronchospasm during airway instrumentation, such as intubation.

5. **Answer A (True)**

   An adequate depth of anesthesia before airway instrumentation can help prevent bronchospasm. When a patient is properly anesthetized, it leads to the relaxation of the bronchial smooth muscles, reducing the likelihood of bronchospasm during airway interventions such as intubation or airway manipulation.

6. **Answer A (Administer bolus propofol to deepen the anesthetic)**

   In a patient with mild reactive airway disease experiencing bronchospasm under anesthesia, the most likely cause is light anesthesia. Deepening the plane of anesthesia by administering a bolus of propofol is an appropriate next step to treat bronchospasm. Increasing the depth of anesthesia helps to relax the bronchial smooth muscles and alleviate bronchoconstriction. Inhaled agents may not be as effective in this scenario due to impaired gas flow caused by bronchospasm. The laryngeal mask airway may limit the amount of positive pressure that can be delivered, further compromising ventilation while the bronchospasm persists. Therefore, an intravenous agent, such as propofol, is more appropriate to deepen the anesthesia and address the bronchospasm.

Recommended literature

1. Pollard BJ, Kitchen, G. Handbook of Clinical Anaesthesia. Fourth Edition. CRC Press. 2018. 978-1-4987-6289-2.
2. Vojdani S. Bronchospasm During Induction of Anesthesia: A Case Report and Literature Review. Galen Med J. 2018 May 19;7:e846.
3. Pascale Dewachter, Claudie Mouton-Faivre, Charles W. Emala, Sadek Beloucif, Bruno Riou; Case Scenario: Bronchospasm during Anesthetic Induction. Anesthesiology 2011; 114:1200.
4. Westhorpe RN, Ludbrook GL, Helps SC. Crisis management during anaesthesia: bronchospasm. Qual Saf Health Care. 2005;14(3):e7.

Emergencies
COMPARTMENT SYNDROME

04
CHAPTER

Questions:

1. **Which of the following is NOT a potential cause of acute compartment syndrome?**
   A. Closed tibial shaft fracture
   B. Soft tissue crush injuries
   C. Prolonged limb compression
   D. Open forearm fractures

2. **What is the normal range for compartment pressure?**
   A. 12-18 mmHg
   B. 18-24 mmHg
   C. 24-30 mmHg
   D. 30-36 mmHg

3. **What is the recommended management for compartment syndrome?**
   A. Immediate administration of antibiotics
   B. Application of ice packs to the affected area
   C. Administration of hyperbaric oxygen therapy
   D. Fasciotomy to relieve pressure

4. **How can compartment syndrome be tested?**
   A. Measurement of compartment pressure
   B. Magnetic resonance imaging (MRI)
   C. Blood tests for creatine kinase levels
   D. Ultrasound examination of the affected area

5. **In cases where compartment syndrome is suspected, regional analgesia is the method of choice for providing pain relief.**
   A. True
   B. False

6. **A 35-year-old man was scheduled for surgery for tibial shaft fractures. The patient has a history of opioid sensitivity and wants effective pain management after surgery. What is the most appropriate analgesic technique for this patient?**
   A. Multimodal analgesia with an additional femoral block with 20 mL of 0.25% bupivacaine
   B. Multimodal analgesia with an additional femoral block with 20 mL of 0.5% bupivacaine
   C. Multimodal analgesia "PRN" with morphine
   D. Multimodal analgesia with intravenous infusion of morphine

Answers:

1. **Answer D (Open forearm fractures)**

   Acute compartment syndrome can be caused by various factors that lead to increased pressure within a compartment, such as closed tibial shaft fractures, soft tissue crush injuries, and prolonged limb compression. Open fractures, which have an open wound communicating with the fracture site, are less likely to result in compartment syndrome because the communication with the external environment allows for some decompression of the compartment pressure. On the other hand, closed fractures, where the skin remains intact, pose a higher risk as the pressure within the compartment can increase without any means of decompression.

2. **Answer A (12-18 mmHg)**

   The normal range for compartment pressure is generally considered to be within 12-18 mmHg. In a healthy individual, the pressure within the compartments of the body should fall within this range. Pressures below this range may indicate inadequate perfusion, while pressures above this range are considered abnormal and may indicate the presence of compartment syndrome. It is important to monitor compartment pressures in suspected cases of compartment syndrome to determine if they exceed the normal range and require prompt intervention.

3. **Answer D (Fasciotomy to relieve pressure)**

   The recommended management for compartment syndrome is fasciotomy to relieve the increased pressure within the affected compartment. Fasciotomy allows decompression of the compartment, reducing the risk of tissue damage and potential complications associated with compartment syndrome.

4. **Answer A (Measurement of compartment pressure)**

   Compartment syndrome can be diagnosed primarily through the measurement of compartment pressure. This is typically done using a device called a compartment pressure monitor or a handheld manometer. The pressure is measured within the affected compartment to determine if it exceeds the normal range, which is typically considered to be 12-18 mmHg. Pressure readings above this range suggest compartment syndrome and may indicate the need for immediate intervention. MRI can provide detailed images of the affected tissues and help evaluate muscle viability. Blood tests for creatine kinase levels can indicate muscle damage and ultrasound examinations can help assess fluid collection or evaluate blood flow in the affected area. However, direct measurement of compartment pressure is the gold standard for diagnosing compartment syndrome.

5. **Answer B (False)**

   Regional analgesia is not the method of choice for providing pain relief in cases where compartment syndrome is suspected. Regional analgesias, such as nerve blocks or epidural anesthesia, may be contraindicated in the presence of compartment syndrome as it can mask the signs and symptoms, potentially delaying the diagnosis and appropriate surgical management. Adequate pain control is important, but it is achieved through systemic analgesics rather than regional anesthesia in cases of suspected compartment syndrome.

6. **Answer A (Multimodal analgesia with an additional femoral block using 20 ml 0.25% bupivacaine)**

   Given the patient's history of opioid sensitivity and the need for effective postoperative pain management, a multimodal analgesic approach with an additional femoral block using 20 ml of 0.25% bupivacaine is the method of choice. Applying a reduced concentration of bupivacaine (0.25%) minimizes the risk of masking signs of compartment syndrome. Single or continuous peripheral nerve blocks using lower concentrations of local anesthetics without adjuncts are considered safe because they are not associated with a delay in the diagnosis of compartment syndrome.

Recommended literature

1. Nathanson, M.H., Harrop-Griffiths, W., Aldington, D.J., Forward, D., Mannion, S., Kinnear-Mellor, R.G.M., Miller, K.L., Ratnayake, B., Wiles, M.D., Wolmarans, M.R., 2021. Regional analgesia for lower leg trauma and the risk of acute compartment syndrome. Anaesthesia 76, 1518–1525.
2. Farrow C, Bodenham A, Troxler M. 2011. Acute limb compartment syndromes. Continuing Education in Anaesthesia Critical Care & Pain. 11;1:24-28.
3. https://www.nysora.com/topics/sub-specialties/acute-compartment-syndrome-limb-implications-regional-anesthesia/

Emergencies
DELAYED EMERGENCE

Questions:

1. Which of the following is NOT a risk factor associated with an increased risk of delayed emergence?

   A. Older age

   B. Psychological disorders

   C. Chronic kidney disease

   D. Gender

2. Which metabolic alteration can contribute to delayed emergence?

   A. Hyperglycemia

   B. Metabolic alkalosis

   C. Hypoglycemia

   D. Hypernatremia

3. What is the recommended management for benzodiazepine reversal in delayed emergence?

   A. Naloxone

   B. Sugammadex

   C. Neostigmine

   D. Flumazenil

4. Which infection can contribute to delayed emergence?

   A. Encephalitis

   B. Meningitis

   C. Sepsis

   D. All of the above

5. St. John's wort tea is recommended to be consumed the night before surgery due to its calming effect and benefits on anesthesia.

   A. True

   B. False

6. A 45-year-old patient underwent abdominal surgery under general anesthesia. After the procedure, the patient's emergence from anesthesia was unexpectedly delayed. The patient is hemodynamically stable but remains unresponsive. She shows no signs of spontaneous breathing, and her pupils are pinpoint in size. TOF yields 4 twitches. What is the appropriate treatment for this patient?

   A. Administer naloxone

   B. Administer sugammadex

   C. Administer neostigmine

   D. Administer flumazenil

Answers:

1. Answer D (Gender)

Among the options listed, gender is not considered a significant risk factor associated with an increased risk of delayed emergence. Factors such as older age, psychological disorders, and chronic kidney disease have been identified as potential risk factors for delayed emergence from general anesthesia. However, gender itself does not have a direct correlation with the likelihood of experiencing delayed emergence.

2. Answer C (Hypoglycemia)

Hypoglycemia is a metabolic alteration that can contribute to delayed emergence. Glucose is the primary energy source for the brain, and when blood glucose levels are too low, it can impair brain function, including the recovery of consciousness after anesthesia. Hypoglycemia can occur due to various factors, such as prolonged fasting, excessive insulin administration, or certain medical conditions affecting glucose regulation.

3. Answer D (Flumazenil)

The recommended management for benzodiazepine reversal in cases of delayed emergence is the administration of flumazenil. Flumazenil is a specific antagonist for benzodiazepines and can rapidly reverse their sedative effects. It competitively binds to the same receptors in the brain that benzodiazepines target, displacing them and reversing their effects. By blocking the action of benzodiazepines, flumazenil can help restore consciousness and alertness in patients experiencing delayed emergence due to the effects of these medications. It is important to note that flumazenil has a short half-life, so the patient's condition should be closely monitored after its administration.

4. Answer D (All of the above)

All of the listed infections, including encephalitis, meningitis, and sepsis, can contribute to delayed emergence from anesthesia. In the presence of these infections, the inflammatory response and direct effects on the brain can disrupt the normal processes of regaining consciousness after anesthesia, resulting in delayed emergence. Proper identification and management of the underlying infection are essential for facilitating the recovery of consciousness in such cases.

5. Answer B (False)

Consuming St. John's wort tea the night before surgery is not recommended. St. John's wort is an herbal supplement known for its potential interactions with various medications, including anesthetics. Taking St. John's wort tea before surgery can lead to unpredictable effects on anesthesia, potentially prolonging the recovery process and increasing the risk of complications.

6. Answer A (Give naloxone)

The correct answer is to give naloxone. The patient's delayed onset, along with pinpoint pupils, unresponsiveness, and respiratory depression, suggest opioid-related effects. Naloxone is a specific opioid receptor antagonist used to reverse the effects of opioid overdose or toxicity. Administration of naloxone can rapidly reverse respiratory depression, improve ventilation, and restore consciousness. Monitoring vital signs is important, but addressing the underlying cause, which in this case is opioid-related, is critical to the patient's well-being.

Recommended literature

1. Cascella M, Bimonte S, Di Napoli R. Delayed Emergence from Anesthesia: What We Know and How We Act. Local Reg Anesth. 2020 Nov 5;13:195-206.
2. Thomas E, Martin F, Pollard B. Delayed recovery of consciousness after general anaesthesia. BJA Educ. 2020 May;20(5):173-179.
3. Rafizadeh S, Kerry-Gnazzo AR, DeWalt K. An Unresponsive Patient in Postanesthesia Care Unit: A Case Report of an Unusual Diagnosis for a Common Problem. A A Pract. 2020 Aug;14(10):e01293.
4. Yonekura H, Murayama N, Yamazaki H, Sobue K. A Case of Delayed Emergence After Propofol Anesthesia: Genetic Analysis. A A Case Rep. 2016 Dec 1;7(11):243-246.

DENTAL LUXATION, FRACTURE OR AVULSION

04

CHAPTER

Questions:

1. **What is the immediate treatment required for an avulsed tooth?**
   A. Cleaning the tooth with soap and water
   B. Placing the tooth in a glass of water
   C. Replanting the tooth into its socket
   D. Leaving the tooth outside to dry

2. **What is the appropriate course of action if an avulsed tooth cannot be replanted immediately?**
   A. Wrap the tooth in a tissue and leave it on the counter
   B. Rinse the tooth with water and store it in a plastic bag
   C. Place the tooth in a glass of water and seek dental care
   D. Store the tooth in a container with milk or saline solution

3. **Which medium is suitable for storing an avulsed tooth temporarily?**
   A. Saliva
   B. HBSS
   C. Milk
   D. All of the above

4. **What is the recommended handling method for an avulsed tooth?**
   A. Hold the tooth by the root
   B. Scrub the tooth with toothpaste
   C. Rinse the tooth with soap
   D. Hold the tooth by the crown

5. **Avulsed teeth are dental emergencies and require immediate treatment.**
   A. True
   B. False

6. **A 40-year-old woman was scheduled for a surgical procedure that required general anesthesia. During the intubation process, the anesthesiologist encountered difficulty and performed multiple attempts at laryngoscopy. After the procedure, the patient complained of pain and swelling in her lower jaw. Upon examination, it was discovered that one of her lower premolar teeth was mobile. What is the most likely dental injury that occurred during the intubation process?**
   A. Dental avulsion
   B. Dental fracture
   C. Dental luxation
   D. All of the above

Answers:

1. **Answer C (Replanting the tooth into its socket)**

   The immediate treatment for an avulsed tooth is to replant it into its socket if possible. Replantation should be done carefully, holding the tooth by the crown and avoiding touching the root surface.

2. **Answer D (Store the tooth in a container with milk or saline solution)**

   If an avulsed tooth cannot be replanted immediately, it should be stored in an appropriate medium to prevent drying out. A container with milk or saline solution provides a suitable environment to preserve the tooth until professional dental care can be obtained.

3. **Answer D (All of the above)**

   All of the options mentioned – saliva, HBSS (Hank's Balanced Salt Solution), and milk – are suitable mediums for temporarily storing an avulsed tooth. These mediums help to keep the tooth's cells hydrated and provide a favorable environment for preserving the tooth until dental care is sought.

4. **Answer D (Hold the tooth by the crown)**

   When handling an avulsed tooth, it is important to hold it carefully by the crown (top part) and avoid touching the root surface to minimize damage.

5. **Answer A (True)**

   Avulsed teeth refer to teeth that have been completely dislodged or knocked out from their sockets. Due to the risk of permanent tooth loss, avulsed teeth are considered dental emergencies that require immediate treatment. Prompt action increases the chances of saving the tooth.

6. **Answer C (Dental luxation)**

   Dental luxation occurs when trauma disrupts the tissues, ligaments, and bone that hold the tooth in place. Laryngoscopy can exert forces on the teeth and surrounding structures, potentially causing dental injuries. The patient's complaint of pain and swelling, along with the mobility of the lower premolar tooth, suggests dental luxation as the most likely dental injury. Dental avulsion refers to complete tooth dislodgement, which is not indicated in this case. Dental fracture typically involves a break in the tooth structure.

Recommended literature

1. Bourguignon C, Cohenca N, Lauridsen E, et al. International Association of Dental Traumatology guidelines for the management of traumatic dental injuries: 1. Fractures and luxations. Dent Traumatol. 2020;36(4):314–330.
2. Fouad AF, Abbott PV, Tsilingaridis G, Cohenca N, Lauridsen E, Bourguignon C, et al. International Association of Dental Traumatology guidelines for the management of traumatic dental injuries: 2. Avulsion of permanent teeth. Dent Traumatol. 2020;36(4):331-42.

EXTRAVASATION INJURIES

Questions:

1. **Which of the following is NOT a risk factor associated with extravasation injuries?**
   A. Fragile veins
   B. Preexisting cutaneous pathophysiology
   C. Increased vigilance of the healthcare provider
   D. Toxicity of the drug

2. **Which category of anesthetic/ICU agents is more likely to cause extravasation injury?**
   A. Hyperosmolar agents
   B. Acids/alkalis
   C. Vasoactive agents
   D. All of the above

3. **Propofol, ondansetron, rocuronium, and cyclizine can cause?**
   A. Tissue necrosis
   B. Discomfort or pain on injection
   C. Venous spasms
   D. Allergic reactions

4. **Which intervention is NOT recommended for the management of extravasation injuries?**
   A. Aspiration of extravasated fluid
   B. Elevation of the limb
   C. Applying warm compresses
   D. Immediate removal of the catheter

5. **Phentolamine mesylate 10 mg may be added to each liter of solution containing norepinephrine to counteract its vasopressor effects.**
   A. True
   B. False

6. **A 65-year-old patient with a history of atrial fibrillation is scheduled for hip surgery. The patient's heart rate was elevated at 130 beats per minute during the preoperative assessment. In order to control the heart rate, the anesthesiologist decides to administer amiodarone intravenously. The medication is administered through a peripheral intravenous line in the patient's hand. However, shortly after the injection, the patient experiences severe pain at the injection site, accompanied by swelling and redness. What is the most likely cause of the patient's symptoms?**
   A. Extravasation of amiodarone
   B. Allergic reaction to amiodarone
   C. Infection at the catheter insertion site
   D. Phlebitis due to amiodarone infusion

Answers:

1. Answer C (Increased vigilance of the healthcare provider)

The risk factors associated with extravasation injuries preexisting cutaneous, vascular, or lymphatic pathophysiology, fragile or mobile veins, site of injection, toxicity of the drug, amount of agent extravasated, duration of tissue exposure, and decreased vigilance of doctor or patient. Increased vigilance is not associated with extravasation injuries.

2. Answer D (All of the above)

These agents can contribute to extravasation injuries due to their properties, such as solution cytotoxicity, osmolality, vasoconstrictor properties, and infusion pressure. All the options, hyperosmolar agents, acids/alkalis, and vasoactive agents are likely to cause extravasation injuries.

3. Answer B (Discomfort or pain on injection)

Propofol, ondansetron, rocuronium, and cyclizine are known to cause discomfort or pain at the injection site. These medications can lead to localized symptoms of discomfort or pain when administered. However, tissue necrosis, venous spasms, or allergic reactions as side effects are not associated with these medications.

4. Answer D (Immediate removal of the catheter)

In the early management of extravasation injuries, it is generally recommended to leave the catheter inserted. While removing the catheter may eventually be necessary, it is not the initial step in managing extravasation injuries. The primary focus initially is on addressing the extravasated fluid and providing supportive measures to minimize tissue damage and promote healing. This may involve interventions such as aspirating the extravasated fluid, elevating the limb, applying warm compresses, and other appropriate measures.

5. Answer A (True)

Prevention and treatment of dermal necrosis and sloughing following intravenous administration or extravasation of norepinephrine can be accomplished with 10 mg of phentolamine mesylate added to each liter of noradrenaline-containing solution. It is important to note that the addition of phentolamine mesylate in this preventive measure does not affect the pressor effect of norepinephrine. The recommended treatment for norepinephrine extravasation involves injecting 5 to 10 mg of phentolamine mesylate in 10 mL of saline into the area of extravasation within 12 hours. This treatment helps counteract the vasoconstrictive effects of norepinephrine and minimize tissue damage.

6. Answer A (Extravasation of amiodarone)

The most likely cause of the patient's symptoms is extravasation of amiodarone. Extravasation is the unintended leakage of intravenous fluid or medication into the surrounding tissue during administration. In this case, the severe pain, swelling, and redness at the injection site indicate local tissue damage caused by the extravasation of amiodarone. Amiodarone is known to be an irritant to the tissues, and its extravasation can cause local tissue damage, resulting in pain and inflammation.

Recommended literature

1. Al-Benna S, O'Boyle C, Holley J. Extravasation injuries in adults. ISRN Dermatol. 2013 May 8;2013:856541.
2. Lake C, Beecroft CL. Extravasation injuries and accidental intra-arterial injection, Continuing Education in Anaesthesia Critical Care & Pain, Volume 10, Issue 4, August 2010, Pages 109-113.
3. Schummer W, Schummer C, Bayer O, Müller A, Bredle D, Karzai W. Extravasation Injury in the Perioperative Setting. Anesthesia & Analgesia: March 2005 – Volume 100 – Issue 3 – p 722-727.

Emergencies
FAT EMBOLISM SYNDROME

Questions:

1. **What is the mortality rate associated with Fat Embolism Syndrome (FES)?**
   A. 1-5%
   B. 5-10%
   C. 10-20%
   D. 20-30%

2. **Which of the following conditions is NOT considered a cause of FES?**
   A. Liposuction
   B. Bone marrow transplant
   C. Acute pancreatitis
   D. Acute myocardial infarction

3. **What is the suggested treatment for FES-related respiratory distress?**
   A. Corticosteroids
   B. Heparin
   C. Albumin
   D. Intubation/ventilation

4. **Which of the following statements about the use of heparin in FES is true?**
   A. Heparin is routinely recommended for the treatment of FES.
   B. Heparin helps in the clearance of fat globules from the bloodstream.
   C. Heparin is primarily used to prevent cardiovascular complications in FES.
   D. The use of heparin in FES is not supported by strong evidence.

5. **Increased hematocrit is a laboratory finding associated with FES.**
   A. True
   B. False

6. **A 32-year-old male presents to the emergency department with a history of a motor vehicle accident. He sustained a closed fracture of his left femur and complains of increasing pain, swelling, and difficulty moving his leg. Upon examination, you notice a petechial rash on his chest and upper extremities. His respiratory rate is 28 breaths/min, and oxygen saturation is 88% on room air. X-rays confirm a displaced femoral shaft fracture. What is the recommended approach for fracture management in this patient with suspected FES?**
   A. Operative correction
   B. Traction alone
   C. Application of external fixators
   D. Conservative management with immobilization

Answers:

1. Answer C (10-20%)

The mortality rate for FES is estimated to be 10-20%. FES is a serious condition that can lead to significant morbidity and mortality. It is important to recognize the signs and symptoms of FES promptly and initiate appropriate management to minimize complications and improve outcomes.

2. Answer D (Acute myocardial infarction)

FES is a condition characterized by the presence of fat globules within the lung parenchyma or peripheral microcirculation, leading to tissue damage and systemic inflammatory response. While several conditions can predispose individuals to FES, acute myocardial infarction is not typically associated with fat embolism.

3. Answer D (Intubation/ventilation)

In cases of severe respiratory distress associated with Fat Embolism Syndrome (FES), respiratory support in the form of intubation and mechanical ventilation is often necessary. FES can cause significant lung injury, leading to respiratory insufficiency, hypoxemia, and acute respiratory distress syndrome (ARDS). Intubation and mechanical ventilation help provide adequate oxygenation and ventilation to support the patient's respiratory function. While corticosteroids, heparin, and albumin have the potential as treatments for FES, their role in managing FES-related respiratory distress is not well-established. Corticosteroids may have a role in reducing the risk of fat embolism in patients with long bone fractures, but their effectiveness in treating established FES is uncertain. Heparin and albumin, on the other hand, do not have strong evidence supporting their use in FES-related respiratory distress.

4. Answer D (The use of heparin in FES is not supported by strong evidence)

Explanation: The use of heparin in FES is controversial, and its routine use is not currently recommended. There is limited evidence to support its effectiveness in reducing pulmonary complications in FES. Heparin stimulates lipase activity and, therefore, may accelerate the clearance of lipids from circulation, but the resultant increase in free fatty acids could exacerbate the underlying proinflammatory physiology. Furthermore, anticoagulation in the setting of trauma and preexisting hematologic abnormalities may prove harmful. No randomized, controlled trials or extensive retrospective data exist to support the routine use of heparin or other anticoagulants in FES.

5. Answer B (False)

Increased hematocrit is not typically associated with FES. FES can often lead to a decrease in hematocrit due to factors such as ongoing bleeding, hemodilution, and the associated inflammatory response. The decrease in hematocrit can be seen as a result of the anemia caused by FES and other related factors.

6. Answer A (Operative correction)

In a patient with suspected FES, operative correction is the recommended approach for fracture management. FES is associated with the release of fat globules into the circulation, which can lead to systemic complications. Operative correction involves surgical stabilization of the fracture, which can minimize the risk of fat embolism and its associated complications. In this case, given the suspected FES and the severity of the fracture, operative correction should be considered as the primary treatment approach. This will not only address the fracture but also minimize the risk of further fat embolization and associated complications.

Recommended literature

1. Luff D, Hewson DW. Fat embolism syndrome. BJA Educ. 2021;21(9):322-328.
2. Pollard BJ, Kitchen, G. Handbook of Clinical Anaesthesia. Fourth Edition. CRC Press. 2018. 978-1-4987-6289-2.

Emergencies
FULL STOMACH

Questions:

1. **What is the recommended fasting time before surgery to consider the stomach "empty"?**
   A. 1 hour after a meal
   B. 6 hours after food and milky drinks
   C. 12 hours after any type of fluid intake
   D. No fasting time is necessary

2. **Which of the following factors can delay gastric emptying?**
   A. Electrolyte imbalance
   B. Fear and anxiety
   C. Mechanical obstruction of the gastrointestinal tract
   D. All of the above

3. **Which position can help minimize the risk of gastric regurgitation and aspiration during surgery?**
   A. Supine position
   B. Head-up position
   C. Prone position
   D. Trendelenburg position

4. **Which medication may be used to promote gastric emptying in patients with a full stomach?**
   A. Erythromycin
   B. Domperidone
   C. Metoclopramide
   D. All of the above

5. **Rapid sequence induction is commonly used to induce anesthesia and secure the airway in patients with a full stomach.**
   A. True
   B. False

6. **A 29-year-old pregnant woman at 39 weeks of gestation is scheduled for an elective caesarean section. She has a history of a previous caesarean section and is otherwise healthy. She has been fasting as per the hospital's guidelines, but she mentions that she had drunk 200 mL of apple juice approximately 2 hours ago. What should be the next step in managing this patient?**
   A. Proceed with the elective caesarean section as planned
   B. Delay the surgery and monitor the patient's blood glucose levels
   C. Delay the surgery and administer antacids
   D. Delay the surgery and wait for a longer fasting period

Answers:

1. **Answer B (6 hours after food and milky drinks)**

   The recommended fasting time before surgery to consider the stomach "empty" is typically 6 hours after food and milky drinks, 4 hours breast milk, and 2 hours clear liquids (excluding alcohol). This means that patients should refrain from eating any solid food or consuming milky drinks for at least 6 hours prior to their scheduled surgery. This fasting period allows enough time for the stomach to be partially empty, reducing the risk of regurgitation and aspiration of gastric contents during anesthesia. It's important to follow these fasting guidelines to minimize the potential complications associated with a full stomach during surgery.

2. **Answer D (All of the above)**

   All of the factors listed in the options can contribute to delayed gastric emptying. Mechanical obstruction of the gastrointestinal tract, such as from tumors, strictures, or hernias, can physically impede the movement of food through the digestive system. Ileus, which is a temporary paralysis of the intestine, can also delay gastric emptying. After surgical manipulation of the bowel, there can be a temporary slowdown in gastric motility. Recent trauma, electrolyte imbalances, peritonitis (inflammation of the abdominal cavity), pain, fear, and anxiety, the third trimester of pregnancy, and certain drugs can all affect the normal functioning of the gastrointestinal system and lead to delayed gastric emptying.

3. **Answer B (Head-up position)**

   The head-up position can help minimize the risk of gastric regurgitation and aspiration during surgery. Elevating the patient's head during surgery helps to promote the natural downward flow of gastric contents and prevents the reflux of stomach contents into the esophagus and airway. This position helps to maintain a clear airway and reduces the likelihood of regurgitation and subsequent aspiration of gastric contents. The supine position (lying flat on the back), prone position (lying face down), and Trendelenburg position (head down, feet elevated) do not offer the same benefits in terms of minimizing the risk of gastric regurgitation and aspiration.

4. **Answer D (All of the above)**

   All three medications mentioned in the options can be used to promote gastric emptying in patients with a full stomach. These medications work by different mechanisms but ultimately aid in promoting gastric emptying. Erythromycin, an antibiotic, has an interesting side effect of stimulating gastric motility. It can be used off-label to facilitate gastric emptying in certain cases. Domperidone is a medication that acts as a dopamine antagonist and promotes gastric motility. It is commonly used to treat gastrointestinal symptoms such as delayed gastric emptying, nausea, and vomiting. Metoclopramide is another medication that enhances gastric emptying by increasing the contraction of the stomach and improving gastrointestinal motility. It is frequently utilized to address delayed gastric emptying and symptoms like nausea and vomiting.

5. **Answer A (True)**

   Rapid sequence induction (RSI) is a commonly employed technique in patients with a full stomach to rapidly induce anesthesia and secure the airway. It is used when there is an increased risk of regurgitation and aspiration of gastric contents during induction of anesthesia. RSI involves the prompt administration of a rapid-acting induction agent followed by a neuromuscular blocking agent. The goal is to minimize the time between the induction of anesthesia and the placement of a cuffed endotracheal tube to secure the airway. This technique helps reduce the risk of gastric contents being regurgitated into the lungs, which can lead to serious respiratory complications.

6. **Answer A (Proceed with the elective caesarean section as planned)**

   In this case, it is appropriate to proceed with the elective caesarean section as planned, considering the 2-hour interval since the patient consumed the clear fluid (apple juice). Currently, the international guidelines for selective surgical fasting are 6 h of solid food and 2 h of clear fluids. Enhanced recovery after surgery (ERAS) protocols for patients undergoing caesarean delivery encourage drinking fluids, preferably carbohydrate-containing drinks, up to 2 h before surgery. Limiting the duration of fasting may enhance recovery after surgery and decrease the length of stay. It is important to evaluate each patient individually, taking into account their overall health and specific circumstances.

Recommended literature

1. Pollard BJ, Kitchen G. Handbook of Clinical Anaesthesia. 4th ed. Taylor & Francis group; 2018. Chapter 4 Gastrointestinal tract, Jackson MJ.

Emergencies
HIGH OR TOTAL SPINAL ANESTHESIA

Questions:

1. **What is the definition of high spinal anesthesia?**
   A. Spread of local anesthetic affecting the spinal nerves below T4
   B. Spread of local anesthetic affecting the spinal nerves above T4
   C. Intracranial spread of local anesthetic resulting in loss of consciousness
   D. Unrecognized dural puncture and intrathecal injection

2. **Which of the following factors can contribute to high spinal anesthesia?**
   A. Local anesthetic dose
   B. Patient position
   C. Pre-existing epidural block
   D. All of the above

3. **Which area is affected when high spinal anesthesia reaches the C6-C8 spinal level?**
   A. Cardiac sympathetic fibers
   B. Hands and arms
   C. Diaphragm and shoulders
   D. Brain stem

4. **What are the symptoms of intracranial spread in high spinal anesthesia?**
   A. Hypotension and bradycardia
   B. Slurred speech and sedation
   C. Paresthesia and weakness in the hands and arms
   D. Loss of consciousness and respiratory arrest

5. **The use of the Oxford wedge is recommended to prevent the cephalad spread of local anesthetic.**
   A. True
   B. False

6. **A 32-year-old woman underwent an emergency caesarean section under spinal anesthesia. Shortly after the administration of spinal anesthesia, the patient experiences a sudden drop in blood pressure. The blood pressure reading shows a significant decrease from baseline. The patient complains of paresthesia and numbness with weakness in the hands and arms. In addition, the patient also shows signs of shortness of breath, with difficulty in deep breathing, but still able to speak. What is the most appropriate treatment for this patient?**
   A. Give intravenous fluids and start vasopressor therapy
   B. Administer oxygen via face mask and start positive pressure ventilation
   C. Place the patient in the Trendelenburg position and raise the legs
   D. Perform endotracheal intubation and initiate positive pressure ventilation

Answers:

1. Answer B (Spread of local anesthetic affecting the spinal nerves above T4)

High spinal anesthesia is defined as a spread of local anesthetic that affects the spinal nerves above the T4 level. This means that the anesthetic reaches spinal nerves higher than T4, leading to variable severity of symptoms, including cardiovascular and/or respiratory compromise.

2. Answer D (All of the above)

Multiple factors can contribute to the occurrence of high spinal anesthesia. These factors include local anesthetic dose, positioning of the patient, pre-existing epidural block, unrecognized dural puncture with intrathecal injection, and accidental subdural block.

3. Answer B (Hands and arms)

When high spinal anesthesia reaches the C6-C8 spinal level, the areas that are primarily affected are the hands and arms. This can result in symptoms such as paresthesia or numbness in the hands and arms, as well as weakness of the hands and arms. The spread of anesthesia to this level can compromise the sensory and motor function of the upper extremities. It's important to monitor the patient closely for these symptoms and manage high spinal anesthesia promptly to prevent further complications.

4. Answer B (Slurred speech and sedation)

When high spinal anesthesia results in intracranial spread, the symptoms can include slurred speech and sedation. The intracranial spread refers to the local anesthetic extending beyond the spinal nerves and affecting the brain stem. This can lead to central nervous system depression, resulting in speech difficulties characterized by slurred speech and sedation.

5. Answer A (True)

The use of the Oxford wedge is recommended to prevent the cephalad spread of local anesthetic during epidural and spinal anesthesia. The position in which patients are made to lie down in the left lateral position with three pillows under the head and two pillows under the shoulder is called as Oxford position. Oxford position was described to prevent problems of aortocaval compression and unpredictable spread of spinal block.

6. Answer A (Give intravenous fluids and start vasopressor therapy)

In this case, the most appropriate treatment for a patient who has hypotension, paresthesia or numbness in the hands/arms, hand/arm weakness, and shortness of breath is to administer intravenous fluids and initiate vasopressor therapy. A sudden drop in blood pressure after spinal anesthesia is a common complication known as spinal-induced hypotension. It is caused by sympathetic blockade that results in vasodilation and reduced systemic vascular resistance. This can lead to a significant drop in blood pressure, which affects tissue perfusion. Administration of intravenous fluids helps increase the patient's intravascular volume, thereby improving cardiac output and blood pressure. In addition, vasopressor therapy should be initiated to restore peripheral vascular resistance and further increase blood pressure. Commonly used vasopressors in this scenario include phenylephrine or ephedrine. Administration of oxygen via face mask or even endotracheal intubation and initiation of positive pressure ventilation may be necessary if the patient develops severe respiratory distress or respiratory arrest. However, in this case, the patient is still able to speak, indicating that the respiratory compromise is not severe enough to require immediate positive pressure ventilation.

Recommended literature

1. Sivanandan S., Surendran A. (2019) Management of total spinal block in obstetrics. Update in Anaesthesia, 34: 22-25.
2. Reeve J. (2017) NHS Foundation trust clinical guideline: High Regional Block (including Total Spinal Anaesthesia).

HYPERTENSION

Questions:

1. Intraoperative hypertension can lead to which of the following complications?

   A. Myocardial infarction

   B. Cerebral edema

   C. Renal failure

   D. All of the above

2. Which of the following is NOT a potential cause of intraoperative hypertension?

   A. Pain

   B. Hypoxia

   C. Hyperthermia

   D. Surgical stimulation

3. The initial management approach for intraoperative hypertension includes?

   A. Stopping the surgical stimuli

   B. Administering vasodilators

   C. Deepening the anesthetic

   D. All of the above

4. Which of the following medications is an arterial and venous dilator commonly used to treat intraoperative hypertension?

   A. Hydralazine

   B. Nitroglycerin

   C. Labetalol

   D. Atenolol

5. Phentolamine is an alpha-blocker that relaxes vascular tone by blocking alpha-adrenergic receptors.

   A. True

   B. False

6. A 58-year-old patient with a history of hypertension and diabetes is undergoing a laparoscopic cholecystectomy procedure. During the surgery, the patient's blood pressure begins to rise, reaching 170/100 mmHg. The patient is stable, and there are no signs of end-organ damage. What is the most appropriate initial management approach for the patient's intraoperative hypertension?

   A. Administering nitroglycerin

   B. Increasing the depth of anesthesia

   C. Discontinuing the surgery

   D. Treating with an alpha-blocker

Answers:

1. Answer D (All of the above)

Intraoperative hypertension can lead to various complications, including myocardial infarction, renal failure, hemorrhage from the operation site, rupture of an existing aneurysm, encephalopathy, cerebral edema, or cerebral hemorrhage. These complications arise due to the increased stress on the cardiovascular system and blood vessels caused by elevated blood pressure. Inadequate blood flow and oxygen supply to vital organs can result in tissue damage, ischemia, and organ dysfunction, leading to the mentioned complications.

2. Answer C (Hyperthermia)

Intraoperative hypertension can be caused by several factors, including pain, hypoxia, and surgical stimulation. Pain can stimulate the sympathetic nervous system, leading to increased catecholamine release and subsequent vasoconstriction, which can raise blood pressure. Hypoxia can trigger a similar response, as the body tries to compensate for decreased oxygen delivery to tissues. Surgical stimulation, such as tissue manipulation or incision, can also lead to a sympathetic response and increased blood pressure. However, hyperthermia typically causes vasodilation and is more likely to lead to hypotension rather than hypertension. Therefore, hyperthermia is not a typical cause of intraoperative hypertension.

3. Answer D (All of the above)

Explanation: The initial management approach for intraoperative hypertension involves informing the surgeon and considering halting the surgical procedure if possible, administering vasodilators, and deepening the anesthetic. These steps aim to stabilize the patient's blood pressure. It is important to tailor the management approach to the individual patient's condition and consider the potential risks and benefits of each intervention.

4. Answer B (Nitroglycerin)

Nitroglycerin is a medication commonly used to treat intraoperative hypertension. It acts primarily as a venous dilator, meaning it relaxes and widens the veins. By dilating the veins, nitroglycerin reduces venous return and preload, which subsequently decreases cardiac output and lowers blood pressure. Although it has minimal direct arterial dilatory effects, the reduction in preload indirectly leads to arterial dilation. Nitroglycerin is typically administered intravenously and can be titrated to achieve the desired effect on blood pressure. The recommended starting infusion rate is often around 10 mcg/min, with subsequent adjustments based on the patient's response.

5. Answer A (True)

Phentolamine is an alpha-blocker that acts by blocking alpha-adrenergic receptors. Alpha-adrenergic receptors are found on the smooth muscle lining blood vessels, and their activation leads to vasoconstriction and increased vascular tone. By blocking these receptors, phentolamine promotes vasodilation and relaxation of vascular smooth muscle, resulting in a decrease in vascular tone.

6. Answer B (Increasing the depth of anesthesia)

In this case, the most appropriate initial management approach for the patient's intraoperative hypertension would be to increase the depth of anesthesia. The patient's elevated blood pressure is likely a result of increased sympathetic activity, possibly due to surgical stimulation or pain. By increasing the depth of anesthesia, the patient's sympathetic response can be blunted, leading to a reduction in blood pressure. Therefore, the priority in managing the patient's intraoperative hypertension is to increase the depth of anesthesia to achieve better hemodynamic control. This can be accomplished by adjusting the level of anesthetic agents or administering additional medications as necessary under the supervision of the anesthesiologist. Close monitoring of the patient's blood pressure and vital signs should continue throughout the procedure to ensure appropriate management and prevent further complications.

Recommended literature

1. Tait A, Howell SJ. Preoperative hypertension: perioperative implications and management. BJA Educ. 2021;21(11):426-432.
2. Yancey R. Anesthetic Management of the Hypertensive Patient: Part I. Anesth Prog. 2018;65(2):131-138.
3. Yancey R. Anesthetic Management of the Hypertensive Patient: Part II. Anesth Prog. 2018;65(3):206-213.
4. Pollard BJ, Kitchen, G. Handbook of Clinical Anaesthesia. Fourth Edition. CRC Press. 2018. 978-1-4987-6289-2.

HYPOGLYCEMIA

Questions:

1. **Which of the following is a neuroglycopenic symptom of hypoglycemia?**

   A. Tachycardia

   B. Diaphoresis

   C. Blurred vision

   D. Nausea

2. **Which of the following is an adrenergic symptom of hypoglycemia?**

   A. Dizziness

   B. Confusion

   C. Headache

   D. Diaphoresis

3. **What is the recommended blood sugar level cutoff for diagnosing hypoglycemia?**

   A. Below 100 mg/dL

   B. Below 80 mg/dL

   C. Below 70 mg/dL

   D. Below 60 mg/dL

4. **Which hormone is commonly used to raise blood sugar levels during refractory hypoglycemic episodes?**

   A. Insulin

   B. Glucagon

   C. Cortisol

   D. Epinephrine

5. **Hypoglycemia during general anesthesia is a common occurrence.**

   A. True

   B. False

6. **A 45-year-old male patient with a history of well-controlled type 2 diabetes mellitus is scheduled for laparoscopic cholecystectomy. The patient has been taking oral antidiabetic medications and has no other significant medical conditions. During the procedure, the anesthesiologist notices that the patient's heart rate is elevated (tachycardia) despite adequate depth of anesthesia and analgesia. The patient is also observed to be sweating excessively. Concerned about the possibility of hypoglycemia, the anesthesiologist decides to measure the patient's blood sugar level, which shows a reading of 60 mg/dL (2.9 mmol/L). What is the most appropriate initial intervention for managing the patient's hypoglycemia?**

   A. Administer IV dextrose (D50W 50 mL)

   B. Administer glucagon 1-2 mg IM

   C. Administer a bolus of intravenous insulin 10 IU

   D. Administer oral glucose gel 15 g

Answers:

1. **Answer C (Blurred vision)**

   Neuroglycopenic symptoms of hypoglycemia are related to the brain's inadequate glucose supply. These symptoms occur when the brain doesn't receive enough glucose to function properly. Blurred vision is one of the neuroglycopenic symptoms commonly associated with hypoglycemia. In addition to blurred vision, other neuroglycopenic symptoms of hypoglycemia include dizziness, headache, unusual behavior, confusion, altered mental status (like being drunk), seizures, loss of consciousness, and coma.

2. **Answer D (Diaphoresis)**

   Adrenergic symptoms of hypoglycemia are related to the body's response to low blood sugar levels. Diaphoresis, or excessive sweating, is an adrenergic symptom commonly observed in hypoglycemic individuals. In addition to diaphoresis, other adrenergic symptoms commonly observed in hypoglycemic individuals include tachycardia, palpitations, diaphoresis, clamminess, feeling shaky or trembling, hunger, nausea, tingling sensation, pale skin color, easily irritated, tearful, anxious, or moody.

3. **Answer C (Below 70 mg/dL)**

   Hypoglycemia is blood sugar levels below 70 mg/dL (or 3.9 mmol/L). This widely accepted cutoff value indicates a significant decrease in blood glucose levels. It is important to note that individual variations and specific clinical contexts may exist where different thresholds could be considered, but generally, a blood sugar level below 70 mg/dL is recognized as the cutoff for diagnosing hypoglycemia.

4. **Answer B (Glucagon)**

   Glucagon is a hormone that plays a vital role in glucose homeostasis. It is produced by the alpha cells of the pancreas and acts in opposition to insulin. When blood sugar levels drop too low, such as during severe hypoglycemic episodes, administering glucagon can help raise blood sugar levels. Glucagon works by stimulating the liver to convert stored glycogen into glucose through a process called glycogenolysis. This glucose is then released into the bloodstream, increasing blood sugar levels and restoring them to a more normal range.

5. **Answer B (False)**

   Hypoglycemia during general anesthesia is not a common occurrence. In fact, it is rarely reported in the general population. While some patients may have preexisting conditions or factors that increase their risk of experiencing hypoglycemia during anesthesia, such as diabetes or certain medications, the overall incidence of hypoglycemia in the general population undergoing anesthesia is low.

6. **Answer A (Administer IV dextrose (D5W 50 ml))**

   The most appropriate initial intervention for managing the patient's hypoglycemia is to administer IV dextrose (D50W 50 mL). Administering IV dextrose allows for the rapid and direct delivery of glucose into the patient's bloodstream, raising their blood sugar levels and correcting the hypoglycemic state. Severe hypoglycemia is generally defined as a blood glucose level below 54 mg/dL (3 mmol/L). Concentrated IV dextrose 50% (D50W) is most appropriate for severe hypoglycemia, providing 25 g of dextrose in a standard 50-mL bag. It is recommended to administer 10 to 25 g (20-50 mL) over 1 to 3 minutes. It's important to administer D50W slowly via peripheral or central sites, as rapid or excessive administration can induce hyperosmolar syndrome, and prolonged use (especially when insulin levels are high) can lead to hypokalemia. After D50W treatment, IV dextrose 5% or 10% in water is used to maintain blood glucose levels above 100 mg/dL.

Recommended literature

1. Pollard BJ, Kitchen, G. Handbook of Clinical Anaesthesia. Fourth Edition. CRC Press. 2018. 978-1-4987-6289-2.
2. Kalra S, Bajwa SJ, Baruah M, Sehgal V. Hypoglycaemia in anesthesiology practice: Diagnostic, preventive, and management strategies. Saudi J Anaesth. 2013;7(4):447-452.
3. Ackland, Gareth L. PhD, FRCA; Smith, Megan MBBS; McGlennan, Alan P. FRCA. Acute, Severe Hypoglycemia Occurring During General Anesthesia in a Nondiabetic Adult. Anesthesia & Analgesia: August 2007 – Volume 105 – Issue 2 – p 553-554.

Emergencies
HYPOTENSION

Questions:

1. **What is a possible sign of hypotension in the perioperative setting?**
   A. Low ETCO$_2$
   B. Bradycardia
   C. Weak pulse
   D. All of the above

2. **Which of the following is NOT a potential cause of hypotension in the perioperative period?**
   A. Excessive vasodilation
   B. Intravascular hypovolemia
   C. Hyperactive sympathetic nervous system
   D. Anesthetic agent overdose

3. **Which of the following factors is NOT considered a risk factor for perioperative hypotension?**
   A. Older age
   B. High ASA class
   C. Female sex
   D. Combination of general and regional anesthesia

4. **Which of the following is a recommended initial step in the management of hypotension during surgery?**
   A. Administering a bolus of vasopressor medication
   B. Administering a bolus of crystalloid solution
   C. Placing the patient in the Trendelenburg position
   D. Increasing the depth of anesthesia

5. **Delirium is a potential postoperative complication of hypotension.**
   A. True
   B. False

6. **A 68-year-old male patient with a history of hypertension and diabetes is scheduled for an elective cholecystectomy. The patient weighs 90 kg and has a baseline systolic arterial pressure (SAP) of 140 mmHg and a heart rate (HR) of 60 beats per minute. During the induction of anesthesia, the patient receives 160 mg of propofol, 2 mcg/kg fentanyl, and atracurium 50 mg. Preloading with 500 ml of saline is done, and anesthesia is maintained using sevoflurane with a minimum alveolar concentration (MAC) of 0.7. Ten minutes after the induction of anesthesia and after creating pneumoperitoneum with a pressure of 12 mmHg, the patient's SAP decreases to 90 mmHg, while the HR remains stable. What is the most appropriate next step in managing the patient's hypotension?**
   A. Reduce the MAC of sevoflurane
   B. Administer a bolus of 500 mL saline
   C. Administer norepinephrine 5 mcg
   D. Administer atropine 0.5 mg

Answers:

1. **Answer C (All of the above)**

   In the perioperative setting, a combination of low $ETCO_2$ (end-tidal carbon dioxide), bradycardia, and a weak pulse can indicate hypotension. Low $ETCO_2$ is often seen in volume-related hypotensive states with reduced cardiac output, while bradycardia is a physiological response to decreased arterial blood pressure and cardiac output. Bradycardia or asystole in the face of acute severe hypotension may serve as a mechanism to minimize further blood loss, prevent myocardial damage, and increase ventricular filling. An increase in ventricular filling causes an increase in stroke volume, leading to a greater increase in systolic pressure. Additionally, a weak pulse may suggest decreased perfusion pressure.

2. **Answer C (Hyperactive sympathetic nervous system)**

   In the perioperative period, hypotension can be caused by various factors. However, a hyperactive sympathetic nervous system would typically lead to vasoconstriction and increased blood pressure rather than hypotension.

3. **Answer C (Female sex)**

   Identified risk factors for perioperative hypotension include older age, high ASA class, male sex, lower pre-induction SAP, general anesthesia with propofol, the combination of general and regional anesthesia, duration of surgery, emergency surgery, and the use of certain antihypertensive medications. The female sex is not identified as a specific risk factor for perioperative hypotension.

4. **Answer B (Administering a bolus of crystalloid solution)**

   The recommended initial step in the management of hypotension during surgery is to administer a bolus of crystalloid solution. This is particularly indicated when hypotension is due to intravascular hypovolemia. Crystalloid solutions help to restore circulating blood volume and improve blood pressure. Administering a bolus of vasopressor medication and placing the patient in the Trendelenburg position may be considered as subsequent steps or interventions depending on the underlying cause of hypotension, but the initial step is administering a bolus of crystalloid solution.

5. **Answer A (True)**

   Delirium is indeed a potential postoperative complication associated with hypotension. Delirium refers to a state of acute confusion and changes in mental status that can occur following surgery. Hypotension, particularly when accompanied by decreased cerebral perfusion, can contribute to the development of delirium. It is important to monitor patients for signs of delirium postoperatively and address any underlying causes, such as hypotension, to minimize the risk and manage this complication effectively.

6. **Answer C (Administer norepinephrine 5 mcg)**

   In this case, the most appropriate next step in the management of the patient's hypotension would be to administer norepinephrine 5 mcg. The patient has received a preload with saline and is being maintained on sevoflurane anesthesia with a stable heart rate. However, the decrease in systolic arterial pressure (SAP) after pneumoperitoneum suggests a potential drop in systemic vascular resistance, requiring vasopressor support. Norepinephrine is a potent vasopressor that acts on alpha-adrenergic receptors, causing vasoconstriction and increasing systemic vascular resistance, which helps raise blood pressure.

Recommended literature

1. Weinberg L, Li SY, Louis M, et al. Reported definitions of intraoperative hypotension in adults undergoing non-cardiac surgery under general anaesthesia: a review. BMC Anesthesiol. 2022;22(1):69.
2. Guarracino, F., Bertini, P. Perioperative hypotension: causes and remedies. J Anesth Analg Crit Care 2, 17 (2022).
3. Kouz K, Hoppe P, Briesenick L, Saugel B. Intraoperative hypotension: Pathophysiology, clinical relevance, and therapeutic approaches. Indian J Anaesth. 2020;64(2):90-96.
4. Lonjaret L, Lairez O, Minville V, Geeraerts T. Optimal perioperative management of arterial blood pressure. Integr Blood Press Control. 2014;7:49-59.

Emergencies
HYPOVOLEMIA

04
CHAPTER

Questions:

1. What is the hallmark symptom of hypovolemic shock?
   A. Hypertension
   B. Bradycardia
   C. Pale and cool skin
   D. Excessive sweating

2. Which of the following is NOT a symptom of hypovolemia?
   A. Thirst
   B. Fatigue
   C. Muscle cramps
   D. Increased urine output

3. Which of the following is a crystalloid solution commonly used in hypovolemia treatment?
   A. Human serum albumin
   B. Dextran
   C. Hydroxyethyl starch
   D. Lactated Ringer's solution

4. How should fluid responsiveness be assessed in hemodynamically unstable adults?
   A. Pulmonary artery catheter insertion
   B. Passive leg raising followed by measurement of blood pressure or stroke volume
   C. Central venous pressure monitoring
   D. Arterial blood gas analysis

5. Hypovolemia and dehydration are interchangeable terms.
   A. True
   B. False

6. A 35-year-old female patient is undergoing a gynecological operation due to bleeding from the ovaries. On arrival, she was pale and significantly distressed. Her Glasgow Coma Scale score is 14, her respiratory rate is 18 breaths/min, her heart rate is 99 bpm, and her blood pressure is 90/60 mmHg. The pre-operative hemoglobin (Hb) level is 7.6 g/dL. The most appropriate fluid replacement for this patient's condition is:
   A. Blood transfusion
   B. Crystalloid solution (lactated Ringer's solution)
   C. Fibrinogen concentrate or cryoprecipitate
   D. All of the above

Answers:

1. **Answer C (Pale and cool skin)**

   The hallmark symptom of hypovolemic shock is pale and cool skin. Hypovolemic shock occurs when there is a significant loss of blood or fluid, leading to inadequate tissue perfusion. In response to reduced blood volume, the body constricts blood vessels in an attempt to maintain blood pressure and redirect blood flow to vital organs. This vasoconstriction causes the skin to appear pale as blood flow to the periphery is reduced. Additionally, the coolness of the skin is a result of decreased blood perfusion and reduced heat distribution to the skin surface.

2. **Answer D (Increased urine output)**

   Hypovolemia refers to a decrease in extracellular fluid volume, which can lead to various symptoms and signs related to inadequate fluid balance and tissue perfusion. Increased urine output, however, is not typically associated with hypovolemia. In hypovolemic states, the body conserves fluid by reducing urine production in order to maintain fluid volume and prevent further fluid loss. Increased urine output may be more indicative of conditions such as diabetes or diuretic use, where there is excessive fluid loss or increased urine production.

3. **Answer D (Lactated Ringer's solution)**

   Lactated Ringer's solution is a commonly used crystalloid solution in the treatment of hypovolemia. It closely resembles the electrolyte composition of plasma and is composed of sodium chloride, potassium chloride, calcium chloride, and sodium lactate in sterile water. It is often preferred for fluid resuscitation and maintenance in various clinical settings, including hypovolemia, due to its balanced electrolyte composition and compatibility with the body's needs. While all of the options mentioned can be used in fluid therapy, lactated Ringer's solution is a crystalloid solution commonly chosen for hypovolemia treatment due to its balanced electrolyte composition and compatibility with various clinical conditions.

4. **Answer B (Passive leg raising followed by measurement of blood pressure or stroke volume)**

   Assessing fluid responsiveness is important in the management of hemodynamically unstable adults. It helps determine whether additional fluid administration is beneficial or if other interventions are required. Passive leg raising followed by the measurement of blood pressure or stroke volume is a reliable method to assess fluid responsiveness. This involves raising the patient's legs passively to an angle of 45 degrees or higher while monitoring changes in blood pressure or stroke volume. An increase in stroke volume or blood pressure indicates fluid responsiveness, suggesting that the patient will likely benefit from additional fluid administration.

5. **Answer B (False)**

   Hypovolemia and dehydration are not interchangeable terms. While both conditions involve a decrease in fluid volume, they have different underlying causes and can have distinct clinical manifestations. Hypovolemia refers specifically to a reduction in extracellular fluid volume, which can be caused by various factors such as bleeding, excessive fluid loss, or decreased fluid intake. It is characterized by a decrease in both blood volume and interstitial fluid volume. Dehydration, on the other hand, refers to a state of insufficient body water content, which can result from inadequate fluid intake, excessive fluid loss, or a combination of both. Dehydration can occur without significant loss of blood volume and can affect both intracellular and extracellular fluid compartments. While hypovolemia can lead to dehydration if fluid losses are not adequately replenished, dehydration does not necessarily imply hypovolemia. It is important to differentiate between these terms when assessing and managing patients to ensure appropriate treatment strategies are employed.

6. **Answer D (All of the above)**

   The patient's presentation with a pale appearance, signs of distress, low blood pressure, and low Hb level indicates significant blood loss and hypovolemia. In this case, a combination of interventions is necessary to address the underlying problem and optimize the patient's condition. The patient's low Hb level of 7.6 g/dL indicates anemia, likely due to the bleeding. Blood transfusion is necessary to replenish the lost red blood cells, improve oxygen-carrying capacity, and correct anemia. Crystalloid solutions, such as lactated Ringer's solution, are isotonic fluids that help restore intravascular volume. They are commonly used for fluid resuscitation in cases of hypovolemia. Additionally, fibrinogen concentrate or cryoprecipitate may be required to address coagulopathy and improve hemostasis, especially in cases of significant bleeding. In addition, a high platelet/red blood cell (pRBC) ratio is suggested to support hemostasis and clot formation.

Recommended literature

1. Joshi, G. 2022. Intraoperative fluid management. Up to date. https://www.uptodate.com/contents/intraoperative-fluid-management#H254311346
2. Jha, A., Zilahi, G., Rhodes, A., 2021. Vasoactive therapy in shock. BJA Education 21, 270–277.
3. Timothy E. Miller, Paul S. Myles; Perioperative Fluid Therapy for Major Surgery. Anesthesiology 2019; 130:825–832.
4. Noel-Morgan J, Muir WW. Anesthesia-Associated Relative Hypovolemia: Mechanisms, Monitoring, and Treatment Considerations. Front Vet Sci. 2018;5:53.
5. Al-Khafaji, A., Webb, A. 2004. Fluid resuscitation. Continuing Education in Anaesthesia Critical Care & Pain. 4;4:127-131.

Emergencies
HYPOXEMIA

Questions:

1. **Which of the following criteria best defines acute hypoxemic respiratory failure?**
   A. Severe hypoxemia (PaO_2 < 60 mmHg) with hypercapnia
   B. Severe hypoxemia (PaO_2 < 60 mmHg) without hypercapnia
   C. Severe hypercapnia ($PaCO_2$ > 60 mmHg) in the presence of respiratory acidosis
   D. Acute onset of dyspnea with no clear etiology

2. **Which of the following is a sign or symptom of hypoxemia?**
   A. Headache
   B. Cyanosis
   C. Use of chest and abdominal muscles to breathe
   D. All of the above

3. **Acute hypoxemia will eventually cause circulatory arrest due to myocardial hypoxia with?**
   A. Irreversible cardiac damage
   B. Loss of consciousness within 10 seconds
   C. Irreversible brain damage within 4-5 minutes
   D. All of the above

4. **Which of the following measures should be adjusted to optimize oxygenation in a hypoxemic patient during anesthesia after intubation?**
   A. Additional neuromuscular blockade
   B. Recruitment maneuver
   C. Increase FiO_2
   D. All of the above

5. **Hypoxia and hypoxemia are interchangeable terms.**
   A. True
   B. False

6. **A 55-year-old patient with a history of hypertension and anxiety is scheduled for eye surgery under anesthesia. The anesthesia went without any problems. The patient received droperidol 5 mg intravenously for sedation and prevention of postoperative nausea and vomiting (PONV). During the surgical procedure, towards the end, the anesthesiologist notices that the patient's oxygen saturation has dropped to 88%. The patient also exhibits tachycardia, elevated blood pressure, sweating, and muscle stiffness. What is the most likely cause of the patient's hypoxemia?**
   A. Pleural effusion
   B. Pneumothorax
   C. Decreased cardiac output
   D. Neuroleptic malignant syndrome

Answers:

1. Answer B (Severe hypoxemia (PaO$_2$ < 60 mmHg) without hypercapnia)

Acute hypoxemic respiratory failure is defined as severe hypoxemia (PaO$_2$ < 60 mmHg) without hypercapnia. It is caused by intrapulmonary shunting of blood resulting in ventilation-perfusion (V/Q) mismatch due to airspace filling or collapse (e.g., cardiogenic or non-cardiogenic pulmonary edema, pneumonia, pulmonary hemorrhage) or possibly airway disease (e.g., sometimes asthma, COPD); or by intracardiac shunting of blood from the right- to the left-sided circulation. Findings include dyspnea and tachypnea. Diagnosis is by arterial blood gas measurement and chest X-ray. Treatment usually requires mechanical ventilation.

2. Answer C (All of the above)

Hypoxemia refers to low oxygen levels in the blood, which can lead to various signs and symptoms. Shortness of breath, increased breathing rate, headache, coughing, and tachycardia are all common signs of hypoxemia. Cyanosis is also a sign of hypoxemia. Additionally, the use of chest and abdominal muscles to breathe can indicate the body's effort to compensate for low oxygen levels.

3. Answer D (All of the above)

Acute hypoxemia, which refers to a sudden decrease in the partial pressure of oxygen in the blood, can have severe consequences on various organs in the body, including the heart and brain. Prolonged hypoxemia can lead to insufficient oxygen supply to the heart muscle, resulting in myocardial hypoxia. If left untreated, this can eventually cause irreversible cardiac damage, potentially leading to heart failure or other cardiac complications. When the brain does not receive an adequate supply of oxygen, it can quickly lead to loss of consciousness. The brain is highly sensitive to oxygen deprivation, and within a matter of seconds, a person can lose consciousness due to acute hypoxemia. Prolonged hypoxemia can cause severe and irreversible damage to brain tissues. The brain relies heavily on oxygen for proper functioning, and without sufficient oxygen supply, brain cells can suffer irreparable damage. Studies indicate that significant brain damage can occur within 4-5 minutes of sustained hypoxemia.

4. Answer D (All of the above)

To optimize oxygenation in a hypoxemic patient during anesthesia after intubation, multiple measures can be adjusted. Additional neuromuscular blockade may not directly impact oxygenation but can facilitate mechanical ventilation and patient-ventilator synchrony, which are important for effective gas exchange. A recruitment maneuver is a technique used to open collapsed or poorly ventilated areas of the lungs. It involves briefly increasing the airway pressure to re-expand collapsed lung units, improving ventilation and oxygenation. FiO$_2$ (Fraction of Inspired Oxygen) refers to the concentration or percentage of oxygen in the gas mixture delivered to the patient during mechanical ventilation. Increasing the FiO$_2$ can raise the oxygen content and improve oxygenation in hypoxemic patients. Combining all of these measures can effectively optimize oxygenation in a hypoxemic patient during anesthesia after intubation.

5. Answer B (False)

Hypoxia and hypoxemia are not interchangeable terms. Hypoxemia specifically refers to low oxygen levels in arterial blood, typically caused by issues related to breathing or circulation. Hypoxia, on the other hand, refers to a state in which tissues in the body are not receiving an adequate supply of oxygen, and it can occur with or without hypoxemia. While severe hypoxemia suggests the presence of hypoxia, hypoxemia and hypoxia are not always synonymous. Hypoxia cannot be directly measured, but hypoxemia can be diagnosed through tests such as pulse oximetry and arterial blood gas testing. Hypoxia may not be present in certain cases of hypoxemia if there is compensation by the heart. For instance, while exercising, blood oxygen levels decrease due to the exertion from the muscles, but the heart rate increases in response to sustain oxygen delivery to the muscles in use. On the other hand, hypoxia can be present without hypoxemia if the tissues cannot use oxygen provided by the blood, which occurs in cyanide poisoning cases.

6. Answer D (Neuroleptic malignant syndrome)

The patient's symptoms, including decreased oxygen saturation, tachycardia, elevated blood pressure, sweating, and muscle stiffness, are suggestive of neuroleptic malignant syndrome (NMS), which can be a severe side effect of droperidol or other neuroleptics. Neuroleptic malignant syndrome is a rare but potentially life-threatening condition that can occur as a complication of certain medications, including droperidol. A neuroleptic malignant syndrome is characterized by a hypermetabolic state and can lead to severe muscle rigidity, autonomic dysregulation, altered mental status, and even multiple organ failure. The decrease in oxygen saturation and other symptoms observed in this case is consistent with the manifestations of NMS.

Recommended literature

1. Pollard BJ, Kitchen, G. Handbook of Clinical Anaesthesia. Fourth Edition. CRC Press. 2018. 978-1-4987-6289-2.
2. Rozé H, Lafargue M, Ouattara A. Case scenario: Management of intraoperative hypoxemia during one-lung ventilation. Anesthesiology. 2011;114(1):167-174.

INCREASED AIRWAY PRESSURE

Questions:

1. Which of the following is NOT a potential cause of increased airway pressure in a mechanically ventilated patient?
   A. Pulmonary edema
   B. Kinked breathing circuit
   C. Ascites
   D. Inspiratory concentration of sevoflurane above 2.0 VV%

2. Airway pressure typically ≥ 30 cm H_2O plateau pressure exceeding safe limits can lead to?
   A. Barotrauma
   B. Bronchospasm
   C. Pulmonary edema
   D. Atelectasis

3. Which of the following are signs and symptoms of increased airway pressure in a mechanically ventilated patient?
   A. High plateau and peak airway pressures
   B. Distorted capnography
   C. Hemodynamic instability
   D. All of the above

4. Which factors can contribute to increased airway pressure in a mechanically ventilated patient?
   A. Pulmonary edema
   B. Obesity
   C. Inadequate depth of anesthesia
   D. All of the above

5. Patients with kyphoscoliosis are at risk of increased airway pressure primarily due to decreased pulmonary compliance.
   A. True
   B. False

6. A 55-year-old male patient with a history of asthma is scheduled for elective abdominal surgery under general anesthesia. After preoxygenation, induction of general anesthesia is initiated with intravenous medication, and endotracheal intubation is performed. During the surgical procedure, the patient's airway pressures are consistently elevated, and wheezing and diminished breath sounds are appreciated on auscultation. Which of the following immediate intervention is appropriate?
   A. Consider magnesium sulfate
   B. IV salbutamol 100-200 mcg IV
   C. Increased concentration of a volatile anesthetic (sevoflurane)
   D. All of the above

Answers:

1. Answer D (Inspiratory concentration of sevoflurane above 2.0 VV%)

The inspiratory concentration of sevoflurane above 2.0 VV% is not a potential cause of increased airway pressure in mechanically ventilated patients. Sevoflurane is a volatile anesthetic commonly used during general anesthesia. While high concentrations of sevoflurane may cause respiratory depression and affect the depth of anesthesia, they do not directly lead to increased airway pressure. On the other hand, the other options listed are potential causes of increased airway pressure.

2. Answer A (Barotrauma)

When airway pressure exceeds the safe limits, typically greater than or equal to 30 cm H_2O plateau pressure, it can lead to barotrauma. Barotrauma refers to tissue damage or injury caused by excessive pressure within the respiratory system. Excessive airway pressure can cause damage to the lung tissues, leading to complications such as pneumothorax, subcutaneous emphysema, or pneumomediastinum. These conditions are classified as forms of barotrauma.

3. Answer D (All of the above)

Signs and symptoms of increased airway pressure in a mechanically ventilated patient include high plateau and peak airway pressures, distorted capnography, inadequate tidal volumes, and hemodynamic instability. Therefore, the correct answer is all of the above.

4. Answer D (All of the above)

All of the mentioned factors can contribute to increased airway pressure in mechanically ventilated patients. Pulmonary edema refers to fluid accumulation in the lungs, which can decrease lung compliance and increase airway pressure. Obesity can lead to reduced chest wall compliance, making it more difficult for the patient to ventilate and resulting in increased airway pressure. Inadequate depth of anesthesia can trigger bronchospasm, leading to increased airway resistance and subsequent increase in airway pressure.

5. Answer A (True)

Patients with kyphoscoliosis are at risk of increased airway pressure primarily due to decreased pulmonary compliance. The abnormal spinal curvature in kyphoscoliosis restricts lung expansion and can result in reduced lung volumes and increased stiffness. As a result, it requires higher airway pressures to ventilate the patient, leading to increased airway pressure adequately.

6. Answer D (All of the above)

The patient's clinical presentation with elevated airway pressures, wheezing, and diminished breath sounds suggests bronchospasm, a common complication in patients with asthma undergoing surgery. Prompt interventions are necessary to manage bronchospasm and alleviate elevated airway pressures. Administering magnesium sulfate is a recommended intervention as it acts as a bronchodilator and helps relax the smooth muscles in the airways, improving airflow and decreasing airway resistance. The suggested dose is typically 1-2 g intravenously. IV salbutamol is also an appropriate intervention as it is a selective beta-2 adrenergic agonist that acts as a bronchodilator. It can be given in a dose of 100-200 mcg intravenously to provide rapid relief of bronchospasm. Increasing the concentration of a volatile anesthetic, such as sevoflurane, can help achieve bronchodilation and reduce airway pressures. However, this intervention may not be as immediate or targeted as the administration of bronchodilators. These interventions aim to relieve bronchospasm, improve ventilation, and prevent complications associated with elevated airway pressures.

Recommended literature

1. Gouel-Cheron A, Neukirch C, Kantor E, et al. Clinical reasoning in anaphylactic shock: addressing the challenges faced by anaesthesiologists in real time: A clinical review and management algorithms. Eur J Anaesthesiol. 2021;38(11):1158-1167.
2. Woods BD, Sladen RN. Perioperative considerations for the patient with asthma and bronchospasm. Br J Anaesth. 2009;103 Suppl 1:i57-i65.

Emergencies
INCREASED INTRACRANIAL PRESSURE

Questions:

1. What is the most frequent cause of morbidity and mortality in patients with traumatic brain injury and subarachnoid hemorrhage?
   A. Brain tumors
   B. Increased ICP
   C. Hydrocephalus
   D. Infection

2. What is the recommended head position to help promote venous outflow and reduce ICP?
   A. Head flat
   B. Head elevated to 90 degrees
   C. Head declined to 30 degrees
   D. Head elevated to 30 degrees

3. Which medication can be used to reduce brain edema and lower ICP by drawing fluid out of the brain tissue?
   A. Propofol
   B. Nitroglycerin
   C. Mannitol
   D. Topiramate

4. Which trigger can cause spikes in ICP during awake craniotomy?
   A. Hyperventilation
   B. Shivering
   C. Coughing
   D. Hypotension

5. In patients with intracranial hypertension, inhalation anesthetics should be avoided.
   A. True
   B. False

6. A 55-year-old male patient with a known history of glioblastoma presents for awake craniotomy and tumor resection. The patient has been experiencing progressively worsening headaches, nausea, and focal neurological deficits over the past few weeks. On examination, the patient has papilledema and exhibits signs of increased intracranial pressure (ICP). The neurosurgeon decides to proceed with the operation to relieve the mass effect and reduce ICP. Upon surgical manipulation and brain retraction, the medical team notices certain signs indicative of increased ICP. Which of the following signs is consistent with increased intracranial pressure during the operation?
   A. Widened pulse pressure
   B. Irregular respirations
   C. Bradycardia
   D. All of the above

Answers:

1. **Answer B (Increased ICP)**

   While all the options listed can have implications in these conditions, increased intracranial pressure (ICP) is the primary concern. When ICP rises, it can impair cerebral perfusion pressure, cerebral blood flow, and cerebral oxygenation, leading to ischemia, edema, and further increases in ICP. These effects can cause significant damage to the brain and contribute to morbidity and mortality in patients with traumatic brain injury and subarachnoid hemorrhage. Therefore, increased ICP is the most frequent cause of morbidity and mortality in these patients.

2. **Answer D (Head elevated to 30 degrees)**

   When managing ICP, elevating the head of the bed to 30 degrees is recommended to help promote venous outflow and reduce ICP. This position allows for improved drainage of blood from the brain and helps to minimize congestion in the cerebral veins. By promoting venous outflow, the elevated head position can help alleviate the pressure inside the skull and reduce ICP. It is important to note that the specific degree of head elevation may vary depending on the patient's condition and clinical judgement, but a 30-degree elevation is generally considered optimal in most cases.

3. **Answer C (Mannitol)**

   Mannitol is a medication that can be used to reduce brain edema and lower ICP by drawing fluid out of the brain tissue. Mannitol is a hyperosmolar agent, which means it has the ability to create an osmotic gradient across the blood-brain barrier. When administered intravenously, mannitol increases the osmolarity of the blood, causing water to be drawn out from brain cells and into the bloodstream. This reduction in brain tissue volume helps to alleviate brain edema and subsequently lowers ICP.

4. **Answer C (Coughing)**

   During awake craniotomy, various activities or triggers can potentially lead to spikes in ICP. Coughing involves a forceful expulsion of air from the lungs, which can lead to increased intrathoracic pressure and subsequent increases in ICP. This temporary rise in ICP during coughing can be of concern, especially in patients with pre-existing elevated ICP or compromised intracranial compliance. Therefore, it is essential to manage and minimize coughing episodes during awake craniotomy to prevent adverse effects on ICP and cerebral perfusion.

5. **Answer A (True)**

   Inhalation anesthetics can potentially ICP and should be avoided in patients with intracranial hypertension. Inhalation anesthetics, such as volatile agents like isoflurane or sevoflurane, can cause cerebral vasodilation, leading to increased cerebral blood flow and subsequently elevated ICP. Therefore, it is generally recommended to choose intravenous anesthetics, such as propofol or barbiturates, in patients with intracranial hypertension to minimize the risk of further increasing ICP and its associated complications.

6. **Answer D (All of the above)**

   The signs indicative of increased ICP observed during the operation include widened pulse pressure, irregular respirations, and bradycardia. These three signs together are known as Cushing's triad, which is a classic manifestation of increased ICP. Management strategies for increased ICP during the operation may include adjusting anesthesia depth, maintaining controlled ventilation to ensure normocapnia or mild hypocapnia, avoiding extreme fluctuations in blood pressure, and optimizing cerebral perfusion pressure. Surgical interventions such as releasing cerebrospinal fluid or performing a decompressive craniectomy may also be considered. The specific approach depends on the patient's condition, the surgical procedure, and the clinical judgement of the surgical and anesthesia teams.

Recommended literature

1. Desai VR, Sadrameli SS, Hoppe S, Lee JJ, Jenson A, Steele WJ, et al. Contemporary Management of Increased Intraoperative Intracranial Pressure: Evidence-Based Anesthetic and Surgical Review. World Neurosurgery. 2019;129:120-9.
2. Ragland J, Lee K. Critical Care Management and Monitoring of Intracranial Pressure. J Neurocrit Care. 2016;9(2):105-12.
3. Tameem A, Krovvidi H. Cerebral physiology. Continuing Education in Anaesthesia Critical Care & Pain. 2013;13(4):113-8.

LARYNGOSPASM

Questions:

1. **Which of the following signs are associated with laryngospasm?**
   A. Respiratory stridor
   B. Rapidly decreasing oxygen saturation
   C. Suprasternal and supraclavicular retractions
   D. All of the above

2. **Which of the following procedures are considered risk factors for laryngospasm?**
   A. Appendectomy
   B. Skin transplant
   C. Tonsillectomy and adenoidectomy
   D. All of the above

3. **What is a recommended pharmacological prevention strategy for laryngospasm?**
   A. Administration of magnesium intraoperatively
   B. Administration of aminophylline intraoperatively
   C. Administration of dexamethasone intraoperatively
   D. Administration of morphine intraoperatively

4. **Which of the following maneuvers can be used to relieve laryngospasm?**
   A. Larson maneuver
   B. Heimlich maneuver
   C. Trendelenburg position
   D. Abdominal thrust maneuver

5. **Ketamine induction is considered to have a higher risk for laryngospasm.**
   A. True
   B. False

6. **A 21-year-old female patient presents to the gynecology clinic for a dilation and curettage procedure. The patient has upper airway infections and is scheduled for sedation during the procedure. In consideration of the patient's medical history, which of the following drugs should be avoided for sedation?**
   A. Propofol
   B. Thiopental
   C. Midazolam
   D. Fentanyl

Answers:

1. **Answer D (All of the above)**

Laryngospasm is characterized by the sustained closure of the vocal cords, leading to partial or complete obstruction of the airway. Several signs can be observed during an episode of laryngospasm, such as respiratory stridor, paradoxical respiratory movements, suprasternal and supraclavicular retractions, rapidly decreasing oxygen saturation, excessive chest movements without reservoir bag movement or capnogram reading, bradycardia, negative pressure pulmonary edema, cardiac arrest, pulmonary aspiration, and arrhythmias.

2. **Answer D (All of the above)**

Laryngospasm can occur as a complication during various procedures, and all of the listed options are recognized as risk factors for laryngospasm. While the incidence of laryngospasm is generally low (around 1%), certain procedures have been associated with higher rates of laryngospasm. Tonsillectomy and adenoidectomy, in particular, have a higher incidence, reaching up to 25%. Appendectomy and skin transplant surgeries can also contribute to the risk of laryngospasm.

3. **Answer A (Administration of magnesium intraoperatively)**

A recommended pharmacological prevention strategy for laryngospasm is the intraoperative administration of magnesium. Magnesium, when administered intravenously at a dose of 15 mg/kg during surgery, has been suggested as a preventive measure for laryngospasm. Magnesium is believed to have muscle relaxant properties and may help reduce the likelihood of laryngospasm occurring during the procedure.

4. **Answer A (Larson maneuver)**

The Larson maneuver is a technique used to relieve laryngospasm. It consists of bilateral pressure application on the mastoid processes at the level of styloid processes, between the posterior branch of the mandible and the anterior mastoid process. This results in laryngospasm cessation by provoking pain and relaxing the vocal cords.

5. **Answer A (True)**

Laryngospasm is a potential complication that can occur during the induction of anesthesia. Certain induction agents have been associated with an increased risk of laryngospasm, including ketamine and thiopental. These medications can induce muscle rigidity and increase the sensitivity of the airway, making the occurrence of laryngospasm more likely.

6. **Answer B (Thiopental)**

Given the patient's history of upper airway infections, the drug that should be avoided for sedation is thiopental. Thiopental is a barbiturate anesthetic that can induce muscle rigidity and increase airway sensitivity, potentially exacerbating laryngeal spasms or airway obstruction. In patients with compromised airways, such as those with a history of upper airway infections, using a different sedative agent would be a safer choice.

Recommended literature

1. Gavel G, Walker RWM. Laryngospasm in anaesthesia. Continuing Education in Anaesthesia Critical Care & Pain. 2014;14(2):47-51.
2. Silva CR, Pereira T, Henriques D, Lanca F. Comprehensive review of laryngospasm. WFSA Resource Library. https://resources.wfsahq.org/uia/volume-35/comprehensive-review-of-laryngospasm/. Published July 8, 2020. Accessed February 2, 2023.
3. Visvanathan T, Kluger MT, Webb RK, Westhorpe RN. Crisis management during anaesthesia: laryngospasm. Qual Saf Health Care. 2005;14(3):e3.

Emergencies
LOCAL ANESTHETIC SYSTEMIC TOXICITY (LAST)

04
CHAPTER

Questions:

1. What is one of the prodromal symptoms of local anesthetic systemic toxicity (LAST)?
   A. Seizures
   B. Perioral numbness
   C. Tinnitus
   D. Loss of consciousness

2. Which of the following is a characteristic feature of early-onset ECG changes in LAST?
   A. Increased PR and QTc intervals
   B. QRS abnormalities (bundle branch blocks)
   C. Increased ST intervals with/without refractory brady-/tachyarrhythmias
   D. All of the above

3. For how long should monitoring be continued for patients after the injection of large volumes or toxic doses of local anesthetics (LAs)?
   A. 5-10 minutes after injection
   B. 30-45 minutes after injection
   C. 1-2 hours after injection
   D. 6-8 hours after injection

4. What is the recommended treatment for cardiovascular toxicity associated with LAST?
   A. High-flow oxygen therapy
   B. Intravenous lipid emulsion therapy
   C. Antiepileptic agents
   D. Endotracheal intubation

5. Aspiration before the injection is a preventive measure to avoid accidental intravascular injection and reduce the risk of LAST.
   A. True
   B. False

6. A 55-year-old patient presents to the orthopedic clinic for a rotator cuff repair surgery. The anesthesiologist decides to perform an interscalene brachial plexus block using a local anesthetic solution containing ropivacaine and lidocaine for regional anesthesia. The patient's vital signs are stable immediately after the administration of anesthesia, and his mental status is assessed as normal through verbal communication. However, approximately 25 minutes into the surgery, the patient exhibits concerning symptoms. The patient suddenly develops perioral numbness and a metallic taste in the mouth. Subsequently, the patient experiences seizures, but no cardiovascular symptoms are observed. What is the recommended initial treatment for seizures associated with LAST in this case?
   A. Intravenous lipid emulsion therapy
   B. Benzodiazepines
   C. Phenytoin
   D. Administer epinephrine

Answers:

1. **Answer B (Perioral numbness)**

   One of the prodromal symptoms of local anesthetic systemic toxicity (LAST) is perioral numbness. This refers to a loss of sensation or numbness around the mouth or lips. It is important to note that prodromal symptoms are early warning signs that may precede the onset of more severe symptoms or complications. Other prodromal symptoms that can occur with LAST include metallic taste, tinnitus, agitation, dysarthria, and confusion. These may be followed by more severe central nervous system (CNS) derangements such as seizures and coma. These symptoms can serve as indicators that the local anesthetic may have entered the systemic circulation and that systemic toxicity may be developing. Recognizing these prodromal symptoms is crucial for early identification and intervention to prevent further complications.

2. **Answer D (All of the above)**

   Early-onset ECG changes in LAST can manifest in multiple ways. These changes can include increased PR and QTc intervals on the ECG, QRS abnormalities such as bundle branch blocks, and increased ST intervals with or without refractory brady- or tachyarrhythmias. These ECG alterations are important indicators of cardiac involvement and should be recognized as potential signs of LAST. Monitoring the ECG is essential in identifying these changes and initiating appropriate interventions to manage the cardiovascular effects of LAST. Therefore, option "all of the above" is the correct answer as it encompasses the various characteristic ECG changes associated with early-onset LAST.

3. **Answer B (30-45 minutes after injection)**

   Monitoring of patients after the injection of large volumes or toxic doses of local anesthetics is crucial to detect any signs or symptoms of LAST and ensure prompt intervention. Monitoring should be continued for at least 30-45 minutes after injection. This duration allows for the observation of any delayed systemic absorption or the manifestation of LAST symptoms that may occur within that time frame. It is important to note that LAST can occur immediately at the time of injection or up to an hour after it due to delayed tissue absorption.

4. **Answer B (Intravenous lipid emulsion therapy)**

   Intravenous lipid emulsion therapy is the recommended treatment for cardiovascular toxicity associated with LAST. This therapy involves the administration of a lipid emulsion intravenously to counteract the toxic effects of local anesthetics on the cardiovascular system. Local anesthetics, especially lipophilic ones like bupivacaine, can cause cardiac toxicity by impairing cardiac conduction, decreasing cardiac contractility, and disrupting vascular control. Intravenous lipid emulsion therapy works by creating a lipid sink that sequesters the lipophilic local anesthetic molecules, reducing their concentration and toxic effects in the tissues.

5. **Answer A (True)**

   Aspiration before injection is a preventive measure to avoid accidental intravascular injection and reduce the risk of LAST. Aspiration involves pulling back on the syringe plunger after needle insertion but before injection to check for any signs of blood return. If blood is aspirated, it indicates that the needle tip is within a blood vessel, and injecting the local anesthetic at that point could result in intravascular administration. It is important to note that aspiration is not foolproof and may not always detect intravascular needle placement. Therefore, in addition to aspiration, other safety measures such as careful technique, appropriate dose calculation, and continuous patient monitoring are also essential to minimize the risk of LAST.

6. **Answer B (Benzodiazepines)**

   In this case, the patient develops symptoms consistent with LAST after the interscalene brachial plexus block. The prodromal symptoms of perioral numbness and metallic taste indicate the potential systemic absorption of the local anesthetic. Subsequently, the patient experiences seizures, a manifestation of central nervous system toxicity. The recommended initial treatment for seizures associated with LAST is the administration of benzodiazepines. Benzodiazepines, such as midazolam or diazepam, are effective in controlling seizures and stabilizing the patient. They work by enhancing the inhibitory action of gamma-aminobutyric acid (GABA), an inhibitory neurotransmitter in the central nervous system. Intravenous lipid emulsion therapy is a rescue therapy for cardiovascular toxicity associated with LAST, but it is not the initial treatment for seizures. Phenytoin is an antiepileptic agent, but benzodiazepines are preferred for initial seizure control in LAST. Administering epinephrine is not indicated as it can potentially worsen the cardiovascular effects of LAST. Therefore, in this case, the most appropriate initial treatment for seizures associated with LAST is the administration of benzodiazepines.

Recommended literature

1. Kim JY, Park BI, Heo MH, Kim KW, Lee SI, Kim KT, Choe WJ, Park JS, Kim JH. Two cases of late-onset cardiovascular toxicities after a single injection of local anesthetics during supraclavicular brachial plexus block - A report of two cases. Anesth Pain Med (Seoul). 2022 Apr;17(2):228-234. doi: 10.17085/apm.21093. Epub 2021 Dec 28. PMID: 34974644; PMCID: PMC9091664.
2. Liu Y, Zhang J, Yu P, Niu J, Yu S. Mechanisms and Efficacy of Intravenous Lipid Emulsion Treatment for Systemic Toxicity From Local Anesthetics. Front Med (Lausanne). 2021 Nov 8;8:756866. doi: 10.3389/fmed.2021.756866. PMID: 34820396; PMCID: PMC8606423.
3. Ok SH, Hong JM, Lee SH, Sohn JT. Lipid Emulsion for Treating Local Anesthetic Systemic Toxicity. Int J Med Sci. 2018 May 14;15(7):713-722. doi: 10.7150/ijms.22643. PMID: 29910676; PMCID: PMC6001420.

MALIGNANT HYPERTHERMIA

04
CHAPTER

Questions:

1. **What is the primary genetic defect associated with malignant hyperthermia?**
   A. CACNA1S
   B. STAC3
   C. RYR1
   D. DHPR

2. **Which of the following is a risk factor for malignant hyperthermia?**
   A. Patients with idiopathic hyperCKemia
   B. Patients with Duchenne muscular dystrophy
   C. Family history of MH
   D. All of the above

3. **Which of the following should be avoided in patients at risk for malignant hyperthermia?**
   A. Non-depolarizing muscle relaxants
   B. Intravenous opioids
   C. Propofol
   D. Depolarizing muscle relaxants

4. **Which medication is considered the specific antidote for malignant hyperthermia?**
   A. Flumazenil
   B. Naloxone
   C. Dantrolene
   D. Intralipid

5. **Calcium channel blockers are the recommended management for arrhythmias in malignant hyperthermia.**
   A. True
   B. False

6. **A 3-year-old male child is scheduled for tonsillectomy under general anesthesia. The child has no significant medical history, but there is a possible genetic predisposition for malignant hyperthermia (MH). The child's uncle has a confirmed diagnosis of malignant hyperthermia (MH) and has experienced an MH crisis during a previous surgical procedure. Which of the following drugs should be used with special caution in this case?**
   A. Propofol
   B. Sevoflurane
   C. Rocuronium
   D. Succinylcholine

Answers:

1. **Answer C (RYR1)**

The primary genetic defect associated with malignant hyperthermia is found in the RYR1 gene. Malignant hyperthermia is most commonly caused by mutations in the RYR1 gene, which codes for the ryanodine receptor type 1. This receptor plays a crucial role in regulating calcium release from the sarcoplasmic reticulum in skeletal muscle cells.

2. **Answer D (All of the above)**

All of the listed options, including patients with idiopathic hyperCKemia, patients with Duchenne muscular dystrophy, and a family history of MH, are risk factors for malignant hyperthermia (MH). Patients with idiopathic hyperCKemia, a condition characterized by persistently elevated levels of creatine kinase (CK) without a known cause, have been associated with an increased risk of MH. The underlying mechanisms linking idiopathic hyperCKemia and MH are not fully understood, but there is evidence to suggest a potential genetic predisposition. Duchenne muscular dystrophy (DMD), an inherited muscle disorder, is also considered a risk factor for MH. Individuals with DMD have a higher susceptibility to MH when exposed to triggering agents such as certain anesthetics. The presence of DMD indicates a predisposition to develop MH. Having a family history of MH is a well-known risk factor. If an individual has a close relative with confirmed susceptibility to MH, it suggests a genetic predisposition within the family. In such cases, there is an increased risk for the individual to develop MH if exposed to triggering agents.

3. **Answer D (Depolarizing muscle relaxants)**

Patients at risk for malignant hyperthermia should avoid depolarizing muscle relaxants. Depolarizing muscle relaxants, such as succinylcholine, are known triggers of MH. When administered to susceptible individuals, depolarizing muscle relaxants can lead to a rapid and uncontrolled release of intracellular calcium, resulting in muscle rigidity, hypermetabolism, and other signs of MH.

4. **Answer C (Dantrolene)**

Dantrolene is considered the specific antidote for malignant hyperthermia. It is a medication that acts by inhibiting calcium release from the sarcoplasmic reticulum in muscle cells. By reducing intracellular calcium levels, dantrolene helps counteract the hypermetabolic state and muscle rigidity associated with malignant hyperthermia. During an episode of malignant hyperthermia, an uncontrolled release of intracellular calcium occurs, leading to sustained muscle contraction, increased metabolism, and elevated body temperature. Dantrolene, when administered promptly, helps reverse these effects and is the primary pharmacological intervention for managing malignant hyperthermia.

5. **Answer B (False)**

The use of calcium channel blockers is contraindicated in the management of arrhythmias during a malignant hyperthermia (MH) crisis. In the context of MH, calcium channel blockers such as verapamil or diltiazem should be avoided. These medications can potentially exacerbate the MH crisis by worsening hyperkalemia, myocardial depression, and hypotension when co-administered with dantrolene. Dantrolene is the primary medication for managing MH as it specifically targets the underlying mechanism of excessive calcium release from the sarcoplasmic reticulum. Therefore, it is crucial not to withhold dantrolene treatment for MH, even in patients who are receiving preoperative maintenance therapy with calcium channel blockers.

6. **Answer D (Succinylcholine)**

In male children of this age, the use of succinylcholine should be approached with special caution. Succinylcholine is a depolarizing muscle relaxant that is commonly used during anesthesia to facilitate endotracheal intubation. However, it carries certain risks and considerations, especially in pediatric patients. Succinylcholine has been associated with an increased risk of complications, including MH; while MH is relatively rare, it is more common in children and individuals with a genetic predisposition. It is essential to realize that succinylcholine carries the risk of serious side effects, especially in young children, males, and individuals with unknown medical histories. Therefore, it is prudent to exercise caution and consider alternative muscle relaxants, such as non-depolarizing agents like rocuronium, in male children of this age to minimize the potential risk of MH.

Recommended literature

1. Hopkins PM, Girard T, Dalay S, et al. Malignant hyperthermia 2020: Guideline from the Association of Anaesthetists. Anaesthesia. 2021;76(5):655-664.
2. Gupta, Pawan K, and Philip M Hopkins. "Diagnosis and Management of Malignant Hyperthermia." BJA Education, vol. 17, no. 7, July 2017, pp. 249–254, 10.1093/bjaed/mkw079.

PERIOPERATIVE BLEEDING

Questions:

1. What is the primary factor responsible for converting fibrinogen into fibrin during clot formation?
   A. Factor XIII
   B. Thrombomodulin
   C. Factor VIIa
   D. Thrombin

2. Which factor is deficient in hemophilia A?
   A. Factor II
   B. Factor VIII
   C. Factor IX
   D. Factor XIII

3. Which of the following is an antifibrinolytic agent commonly used in the management of perioperative bleeding?
   A. Tranexamic acid (TXA)
   B. Desmopressin (DDAVP)
   C. Prothrombin complex concentrate (PCC)
   D. Recombinant activated factor VII (rFVIIa)

4. What is the recommended fibrinogen level during bleeding to promote clot formation?
   A. < 1 g/L
   B. 1.5-2 g/L
   C. 3-4 g/L
   D. > 5 g/L

5. International normalized ratio (INR) is a laboratory test commonly used to monitor the effectiveness of low molecular weight heparin (LMWH) in perioperative bleeding management.
   A. True
   B. False

6. A 30-year-old pregnant woman at 34 weeks gestation presents to the labor and delivery unit for an urgent caesarean section due to fetal distress. She has a history of gestational hypertension and is currently taking labetalol for blood pressure control. Additionally, the patient has been receiving prophylactic low molecular weight heparin (LMWH) at a dose of 40 mg daily for thromboprophylaxis. It is a plan to perform spinal anesthesia for the caesarean section. What is the appropriate time interval between the last dose of LMWH and performing spinal anesthesia in this patient?
   A. 6 hours
   B. 12 hours
   C. 24 hours
   D. 48 hours

Answers:

1. Answer D (Thrombin)

Thrombin is the primary factor responsible for converting fibrinogen into fibrin during clot formation. Thrombin is a key enzyme in the coagulation cascade and is generated through the activation of factors Xa and Va. Thrombin acts on fibrinogen, a soluble plasma protein, and cleaves it into fibrin monomers. These fibrin monomers then undergo polymerization and cross-linking, resulting in the formation of a stable fibrin clot. Thrombin not only converts fibrinogen into fibrin but also plays a crucial role in the amplification of coagulation by activating other factors in the cascade and promoting further thrombin generation. Additionally, thrombin has pro-inflammatory properties and can activate platelets, leading to platelet aggregation and clot stabilization.

2. Answer B (Factor VIII)

Hemophilia A, also known as classical hemophilia, is a genetic bleeding disorder characterized by a deficiency or dysfunction of clotting factor VIII. Factor VIII is an essential component of the intrinsic pathway of the coagulation cascade. It plays a crucial role in the formation of blood clots by aiding in the activation of factor X to factor Xa, which is necessary for the conversion of prothrombin to thrombin. In individuals with hemophilia A, the reduced or absent activity of factor VIII impairs the normal clotting process, leading to prolonged bleeding episodes and difficulty in achieving hemostasis. This condition is inherited in an X-linked recessive manner, meaning it primarily affects males, while females are typically carriers of the gene mutation.

3. Answer A (Tranexamic acid (TXA))

Tranexamic acid (TXA) is an antifibrinolytic agent commonly used in the management of perioperative bleeding. It works by inhibiting the breakdown of blood clots and reducing excessive bleeding. TXA functions by binding to plasminogen and preventing its conversion to plasmin, which is responsible for the degradation of fibrin clots. TXA is particularly useful in surgical procedures associated with significant blood loss, such as orthopedic surgery, cardiovascular surgery, and trauma cases. It can be administered orally, intravenously, or topically, depending on the specific situation and the severity of the bleeding.

4. Answer B (1.5-2 g/L)

Fibrinogen is a critical component of clot formation. It is converted into insoluble fibrin by the action of thrombin and cross-linked by factor XIII, resulting in the formation of a stable clot. During bleeding, maintaining an appropriate fibrinogen level is crucial to promote effective clot formation and control bleeding. The recommended fibrinogen level during bleeding is typically 1.5-2 g/L. This range ensures an adequate concentration of fibrinogen in the blood to support clot formation and stability. If the fibrinogen level falls below this range, it may impair the ability of the blood to form a stable clot, leading to continued bleeding.

5. Answer B (False)

The International Normalized Ratio (INR) is not typically used to monitor the effectiveness of Low Molecular Weight Heparin (LMWH) in perioperative bleeding management. The INR is primarily used to monitor the effectiveness of oral anticoagulants, such as warfarin, which act by inhibiting vitamin K-dependent clotting factors. LMWH, on the other hand, is a different type of anticoagulant that works by inhibiting factor Xa and has a more predictable anticoagulant effect compared to oral anticoagulants. Anti-Xa activity is a specific laboratory test used to monitor the anticoagulant effect of LMWH in perioperative bleeding management.

6. Answer B (12 hours)

When managing patients receiving LMWH who require neuraxial anesthesia, it is crucial to balance the need for anticoagulation with the risk of bleeding complications. The timing of spinal anesthesia in relation to the last dose of LMWH is an important consideration. In patients receiving prophylactic LMWH, the appropriate time interval between the last dose of LMWH and performing spinal anesthesia for a caesarean section is 12 hours. This interval allows for adequate clearance of LMWH from the system, minimizing the risk of spinal hematoma formation and associated bleeding complications.

Recommended literature

1. Kietaibl S, Ahmed A, Afshari A, Albaladejo P, Aldecoa C, Barauskas G, et al. Management of severe peri-operative bleeding: Guidelines from the European Society of Anaesthesiology and Intensive Care: Second update 2022. European Journal of Anaesthesiology I EJA. 2023;40(4).
2. Ghadimi K, Levy JH, Welsby IJ. Perioperative management of the bleeding patient. Br J Anaesth. 2016;117(suppl 3):iii18-iii30.

Emergencies
PERIOPERATIVE MYOCARDIAL INFARCTION/INJURY (PMI)

Questions:

1. **What is the definition of perioperative myocardial infarction/injury (PMI)?**
   A. Myocardial infarction occurring during surgery
   B. Troponin increase due to ischemia within 7 days after surgery
   C. Increase in troponin caused by ischemia within 30 days after surgery
   D. Ischemic ECG changes during surgery

2. **Which of the following is NOT a patient-specific risk factor for PMI?**
   A. Renal failure
   B. Male sex
   C. Diabetes
   D. Peripheral artery disease

3. **Which intraoperative factor is associated with an increased risk of PMI?**
   A. Short surgery duration
   B. Laparoscopic surgery
   C. Intraoperative tachycardia
   D. Minimal intraoperative fluid administration

4. **What is a recommended prophylactic treatment for high-risk patients to prevent PMI?**
   A. Antiarrhythmic medications
   B. Anticoagulants
   C. β-adrenergic blockers
   D. Vasodilators

5. **PMI is primarily attributed to acute coronary artery occlusion resulting from plaque rupture and thrombosis.**
   A. True
   B. False

6. **A 72-year-old female with a medical history significant for renal failure, diabetes, peripheral artery disease, and heavy smoking underwent hip replacement surgery under spinal anesthesia. Within 30 minutes intraoperatively, hypotensive and tachycardic developed diaphoresis, pallor, and nausea. An electrocardiogram (ECG) on the monitor revealed nonspecific ST-T changes in the inferior leads and multiple premature ventricular contractions (PVCs). Immediate 12-lead ECG shows ST-segment depression, and cardiac troponin (cTn) and creatine kinase-MB biomarkers are significantly elevated. PMI is suspected. Which statement regarding coronary intervention in the management of PMI is true?**
   A. It is the first-line treatment for all cases of PMI
   B. It should be considered in all patients with elevated troponin levels
   C. It is rarely indicated as the first-line treatment
   D. It is indicated only in patients with ST-segment elevation

Answers:

1. **Answer C (Increase in troponin caused by ischemia within 30 days after surgery)**

   Perioperative myocardial injury/infarction (PMI) is defined as the increase of cardiac troponin caused by perioperative ischemia, which mostly occurs during or within 30 days after the operation. This increase in troponin levels can increase the risk of short-term and long-term death. It is recommended to screen troponin in elderly patients during the perioperative period to identify patients with postoperative myocardial injury promptly and provide appropriate treatment to improve prognosis.

2. **Answer B (Male sex)**

   Patient-specific risk factors for PMI include previous coronary artery disease, age over 70 years, female sex, renal failure, diabetes, peripheral artery disease, emergency or redo surgery, and severe left ventricular dysfunction (LVEF < 35%) or cardiogenic shock. While male sex is a known risk factor for cardiovascular disease, it is not specifically listed as a patient-specific risk factor for PMI in this context.

3. **Answer C (Intraoperative tachycardia)**

   The intraoperative factor associated with an increased risk of PMI is intraoperative tachycardia. This is supported by studies showing that prolonged intraoperative time with hypotension, intraoperative heart rate exceeding 110 or dropping below 55 beats per minute, and receiving perioperative vasopressors are also significant risk factors for PMI. Intraoperative hypotension, particularly if prolonged (Mean Arterial Pressure < 55 mmHg), is notably associated with a higher risk of PMI. These findings underscore the importance of careful intraoperative monitoring and management to minimize the risk of PMI.

4. **Answer C (β-adrenergic blockers)**

   The recommended prophylactic treatment for high-risk patients to prevent PMI is β-adrenergic blockers. These medications are effective in reducing the incidence of PMI by decreasing myocardial oxygen demand and improving myocardial oxygen supply-demand balance. Other prophylactic measures include calcium channel blockers, α2 agonists, statins, aspirin, and coronary revascularization, although further investigation is required. It's important to note that while cardiovascular drugs like antiplatelet agents, β-blockers, statins, and angiotensin-converting enzyme inhibitors can be beneficial in reducing postoperative myocardial ischemia, their use should be carefully considered due to the risk of perioperative bleeding.

5. **Answer B (False)**

   While acute coronary artery occlusion resulting from plaque rupture and thrombosis can contribute to PMI, the primary pathophysiological mechanism of PMI involves an imbalance between myocardial oxygen supply and demand. This imbalance can be exacerbated by preoperative and postoperative risk factors, leading to a mismatch in oxygen supply and demand. Treatment strategies for PMI should focus on controlling these risk factors and using drugs recommended in treatment guidelines.

6. **Answer C (It is rarely indicated as the first-line treatment)**

   In the management of PMI suspected in this patient, coronary intervention is not the first-line treatment. The most important goals in managing PMI are confirming the diagnosis, relieving ischemia, assessing hemodynamic status, and initiating reperfusion if necessary. Critical actions in the intraoperative period include ensuring adequate oxygenation, monitoring and managing hemodynamic stability, and correcting any abnormalities present. Pharmacological management, such as correcting arrhythmias and minimizing myocardial work and oxygen demand, is also crucial. Communication with the surgical team, operating room (OR) staff, and cardiology consultation are essential for optimal management and prognosis.

Recommended literature

1. Gao L, Chen L, He J, et al. Perioperative Myocardial Injury/Infarction After Non-cardiac Surgery in Elderly Patients. Front Cardiovasc Med. 2022;9:910879.
2. Landesberg G, Beattie WS, Mosseri M, Jaffe AS, Alpert JS. Perioperative myocardial infarction. Circulation. 2009;119(22):2936-2944.
3. Nashef S., Roques F., Michel P., et al. European system for cardiac operative risk evaluation. Eur J Cardiothorac Surg 1999; 16:9-13

POSTOPERATIVE VISUAL LOSS (POVL)

04
CHAPTER

Questions:

1. Which of the following surgeries is associated with the highest risk of postoperative visual loss (POVL)?
   A. Cardiac surgery
   B. Spine surgery
   C. Head and neck surgery
   D. Ophthalmic surgery

2. Which of the following is NOT a common cause of long-term or permanent POVL?
   A. Central retinal artery occlusion (CRAO)
   B. Ischemic optic neuropathy (ION)
   C. Corneal abrasion
   D. Branch retinal artery occlusion (BRAO)

3. Which of the following risk factors is NOT associated with POVL?
   A. Atherosclerosis
   B. Smoking
   C. Hypercoagulability
   D. Hyperkalemia

4. Which of the following is a risk factor for POVL?
   A. Obesity
   B. Use of the Wilson frame
   C. Prone positioning
   D. All of the above

5. Intraoperative hyperventilation is a recommended preventive measure for POVL.
   A. True
   B. False

6. A 70-year-old male patient with a history of benign prostatic hyperplasia (BPH) and hypertension undergoes a transurethral resection of the prostate (TURP) procedure. The surgery is uneventful, and the patient is recovering well in the postoperative period. However, approximately 12 hours after the operation, the patient starts experiencing restlessness, headache, tachypnea, and a burning sensation in the face and hands. Furthermore, he suddenly complains of complete loss of vision in both eyes. What is the most likely cause of the patient's sudden visual loss?
   A. Retinal artery occlusion (RAO)
   B. Ischemic optic neuropathy (ION)
   C. Cortical blindness
   D. TURP glycine toxicity

Answers:

1. Answer B (Spine surgery)

Spine surgery is associated with the highest risk of postoperative visual loss (POVL). While complications can occur in any surgery, including cardiac surgery, head and neck surgery, and ophthalmic surgery, the risk of POVL is particularly prominent in spinal procedures. This is likely due to factors such as the intricate anatomy and proximity of the spinal cord and associated blood supply, as well as the potential for intraoperative positioning-related pressure on the eyes and optic nerves.

2. Answer C (Corneal abrasion)

While corneal abrasion can cause discomfort and temporary visual disturbances, it does not typically lead to long-term or permanent visual loss. On the other hand, both retinal artery occlusion and ischemic optic neuropathy (ION) are known causes of POVL. Retinal artery occlusion involves the blockage of blood flow to the retina, leading to visual impairment. ION refers to the damage or ischemia of the optic nerve, resulting in visual loss.

3. Answer D (Hyperkalemia)

Hyperkalemia is not a risk factor associated with POVL. Atherosclerosis, smoking, and hypercoagulability are recognized risk factors for POVL, hyperkalemia, an elevated level of potassium in the blood, is not directly associated with POVL.

4. Answer D (All of the above)

All of the listed options are recognized risk factors for POVL. Obesity, due to its association with cardiovascular diseases and impaired blood flow, increases the risk of ocular complications during surgery. The use of the Wilson frame, a surgical positioning device, can contribute to the improper distribution of pressure on the eyes and optic nerves, potentially leading to visual loss. Prone positioning, commonly used in surgeries such as spinal procedures, can also cause pressure-related ocular complications.

5. Answer B (False)

Intraoperative hyperventilation is not a recommended preventive measure for POVL. In fact, it is advised to avoid hyperventilation during surgery to minimize the risk of POVL. Hyperventilation can lead to a decrease in carbon dioxide levels in the blood, causing vasoconstriction and potentially compromising blood flow to the optic nerves and retinal arteries.

6. Answer D (TURP glycine toxicity)

The most likely cause of the patient's sudden visual loss is TURP glycine toxicity. During TURP procedures, glycine is commonly used as an irrigating solution to ensure a clear surgical field. However, excessive absorption of glycine into the bloodstream can lead to systemic toxicity, resulting in electrolyte imbalances and fluid overload. This can manifest as symptoms such as restlessness, headache, tachypnea, and a burning sensation in the face and hands. In severe cases, TURP glycine toxicity can cause optic nerve edema and lead to sudden vision loss.

Recommended literature

1. Mac Grory B, Schrag M, Biousse V, et al. Management of Central Retinal Artery Occlusion: A Scientific Statement From the American Heart Association [published correction appears in Stroke. 2021 Jun;52(6):e309]. Stroke. 2021;52(6):e282-e294.
2. Brunk AJ, Ehrhardt KP, Green JB, Mothersele SM, Kaye AD. Postoperative Visual Loss: Anatomy, Pathogenesis, and Anesthesia Considerations. In: Fox IIICJ, Cornett EM, Ghali GE, editors. Catastrophic Perioperative Complications and Management: A Comprehensive Textbook. Cham: Springer International Publishing; 2019. p. 19-29.
3. Fleisher, L.A. and Rosenbaum, S.H. (2018) Complications in Anesthesia. Philadelphia, PA: Elsevier.
4. Kitaba A, Martin DP, Gopalakrishnan S, Tobias JD. Perioperative visual loss after nonocular surgery. J Anesth. 2013;27(6):919-926.
5. Lee LA. Perioperative visual loss and anesthetic management. Curr Opin Anaesthesiol. 2013;26(3):375-381.
6. Frost EA. Visual loss after anesthesia different causes: different solutions–a review. Middle East J Anaesthesiol. 2010;20(5):639-648.
7. Roth S. Perioperative visual loss: what do we know, what can we do? British Journal of Anaesthesia. 2009;103:i31-i40.

Emergencies
SEIZURES

Questions:

1. **What is the definition of a seizure?**
   A. Sudden loss of consciousness
   B. Uncontrolled burst of electrical activity in the brain
   C. Temporary confusion and disorientation
   D. Focal jerking movements involving the arms and legs

2. **Which type of seizure involves shaking movements involving only part of the body with variable levels of consciousness?**
   A. Tonic-clonic seizure
   B. Absence seizure
   C. Myoclonic seizure
   D. Focal seizure

3. **Which of the following is NOT a potential cause of seizures?**
   A. Dehydration
   B. Dialysis disequilibrium syndrome
   C. Delirium tremens
   D. All of the above

4. **What is the recommended management approach for an individual experiencing a seizure?**
   A. Perform CPR immediately
   B. Administer high-flow oxygen
   C. Maintain airway, breathing, and circulation
   D. Apply cold compresses to the head

5. **Approximately 8–10% of people will experience an epileptic seizure during their lifetime.**
   A. True
   B. False

6. **A 30-year-old man is scheduled for an elective cholecystectomy under general anesthesia. He has no significant medical history. During the surgical procedure, the patient experiences a sudden and uncontrolled burst of electrical activity in his brain, resulting in a seizure. The seizure involves shaking movements of his entire body. What is the recommended immediate therapy for managing the first episode of a seizure during anesthesia?**
   A. Administer Midazolam 2 mg
   B. Administer Carbamazepine 200 mg
   C. Administer Sodium valproate 500 mg
   D. Administer Gabapentin 300 mg

Answers:

1. Answer B (Uncontrolled burst of electrical activity in the brain)

A seizure is defined as an uncontrolled burst of electrical activity in the brain. This electrical activity disrupts the normal functioning of the brain, leading to various changes in behavior, movements, feelings, and levels of consciousness. Seizures can manifest in different ways, depending on the specific type of seizure and the areas of the brain involved.

2. Answer D (Focal seizure)

Focal seizures, also known as partial seizures, are characterized by abnormal electrical activity in a specific part of the brain. These seizures can cause a variety of symptoms, including shaking movements involving only part of the body and variable levels of consciousness. Focal seizures can be further classified as either simple or complex, depending on whether or not there is an impairment of consciousness during the seizure. The shaking movements in a focal seizure are typically limited to a specific region of the body, such as an arm or a leg, rather than involving the entire body, as seen in tonic-clonic seizures. Absence seizures are characterized by brief periods of staring and temporary loss of awareness, while myoclonic seizures involve sudden, brief muscle jerks.

3. Answer D (All of the above)

All of the options provided (dehydration, dialysis disequilibrium syndrome, and delirium tremens) are potential causes of seizures. Dehydration can disrupt the balance of electrolytes in the body, leading to abnormal brain activity. Dialysis disequilibrium syndrome can occur in individuals undergoing dialysis treatment and is characterized by rapid changes in electrolyte and fluid levels, which can trigger seizures. Delirium tremens is a severe form of alcohol withdrawal syndrome and can manifest with symptoms including seizures.

4. Answer C (Maintain airway, breathing, and circulation)

The recommended management approach for an individual experiencing a seizure is maintaining their airway, breathing, and circulation. This involves ensuring their safety during the seizure and taking measures to prevent any harm or injury. It is important to clear the area around the person of any objects that could pose a risk, such as sharp or hard objects. Placing the person in the recovery position can help maintain an open airway and prevent obstruction. This position also helps prevent aspiration if there is any saliva or vomit present. It is crucial to closely monitor the person's breathing and circulation during and after the seizure.

5. Answer A (True)

Approximately 8–10% of people will experience an epileptic seizure during their lifetime. Epileptic seizures are not uncommon and can occur in individuals of different ages and backgrounds. It is important to note that experiencing a single seizure does not necessarily mean that a person has epilepsy. Epilepsy is typically diagnosed when a person experiences recurrent seizures, usually two or more, that are not caused by a known and reversible medical condition.

6. Answer A (Administer Midazolam 2 mg)

The recommended immediate therapy for managing the first episode of a seizure during anesthesia is to administer Midazolam 2 mg intravenously. Midazolam is a short-acting benzodiazepine that is commonly used to treat seizures. It works by enhancing the inhibitory effects of the neurotransmitter GABA in the brain, helping to suppress abnormal electrical activity and terminate the seizure. Carbamazepine, Sodium valproate, and Gabapentin are antiepileptic medications used for long-term management and prevention of seizures. They are not typically administered as immediate therapy during an acute seizure episode.

Recommended literature

1. Carter, E.L., Adapa, R.M., 2015. Adult epilepsy and anaesthesia. BJA Education 15, 111–117.
2. DE WAELE, LIESBETH, Paul Boon, Berten Ceulemans, Bernard Dan, Anna Jansen, Benjamin Legros, Patricia Leroy, Francoise Delmelle, Michel Ossemann, Sylvie De Raedt, Katrien Smets, Patrick Van de Voorde, Helene Verhelst, and Lieven Lagae. 2013. First Line Management of Prolonged Convulsive Seizures in Children and Adults: Good Practice Points. Acta Neurologica Belgica. 113 (4): 375–380.
3. Gratrix A, Enright S. 2005. Epilepsy in anaesthesia and intensive care. Continuing Education in Anaesthesia Critical Care & Pain. 5;4:118-121.

STATUS EPILEPTICUS

Questions:

1. **Which of the following best defines status epilepticus?**
   - A. A single seizure lasting for more than 3 minutes
   - B. Two or more sequential seizures with full recovery of consciousness between seizures
   - C. Continuous seizure activity lasting for more than 30 minutes
   - D. Prolonged seizure activity with associated convulsions

2. **Which medication is the first-line treatment for status epilepticus?**
   - A. Fosphenytoin
   - B. Sodium valproate
   - C. Benzodiazepines
   - D. Levetiracetam

3. **What are the complications of untreated status epilepticus?**
   - A. Hypotension and bradycardia
   - B. Cerebral damage and multi-organ failure
   - C. Respiratory depression and hyponatremia
   - D. Consumptive coagulopathy and rhabdomyolysis

4. **What is the potential risk associated with IV diazepam in the management of status epilepticus?**
   - A. Risk of respiratory depression
   - B. Higher risk of hypotension
   - C. Shorter duration of action
   - D. Low efficacy in terminating seizures

5. **Epilepsy can occur at any age but is commonly diagnosed in those aged below 5 or over 80 years.**
   - A. True
   - B. False

6. **A 35-year-old woman presents to the emergency department with an episode of prolonged seizure activity. She experienced continuous convulsive movements for the past 45 minutes without any recovery of consciousness in between. This is her first seizure episode, and her family members called emergency services for immediate help. Upon arrival, the medical team assesses the patient's vital signs and provides appropriate supportive measures, including ensuring a patent airway and establishing intravenous access. The seizure activity is still ongoing. Which of the intravenous (IV) drugs below is LEAST useful in the treatment of status epilepticus?**
   - A. Propofol
   - B. Midazolam
   - C. Thiopental
   - D. Dexmedetomidine

Answers:

1. Answer C (Continuous seizure activity lasting for more than 30 minutes)

Status epilepticus is defined as continuous seizure activity that lasts for more than 30 minutes or the occurrence of two or more sequential seizures without full recovery of consciousness between seizures. It is a medical emergency that requires immediate intervention. This continuous seizure activity can be convulsive or non-convulsive, and it poses a risk of cerebral damage if not treated promptly. The duration of 30 minutes is used as a guideline to distinguish status epilepticus from a single seizure or clustered seizures with full recovery in between.

2. Answer C (Benzodiazepines)

Benzodiazepines are considered the first-line treatment for status epilepticus. They are rapid-acting anticonvulsant medications that can quickly terminate seizure activity. Commonly used benzodiazepines for this purpose include lorazepam, diazepam, and midazolam. Benzodiazepines are preferred as the initial treatment because they act quickly and have a high success rate in stopping seizures. They can be administered intravenously, intramuscularly, or rectally, depending on the available route of administration and the patient's clinical condition. Fosphenytoin, sodium valproate, and levetiracetam are also commonly used in the treatment of status epilepticus, but they are typically considered second-line or adjunctive therapies if the initial benzodiazepine treatment is ineffective. These medications may be used to provide additional seizure control and prevent seizure recurrence.

3. Answer B (Cerebral damage and multi-organ failure)

Untreated status epilepticus can lead to serious complications, including cerebral damage and multi-organ failure. The prolonged and uncontrolled seizure activity in status epilepticus puts significant stress on the brain and other organs, leading to potential injury and dysfunction. Cerebral damage is a major concern in untreated status epilepticus. The prolonged seizure activity can cause neuronal injury, hypoxia, increased intracranial pressure, and cerebral edema. These factors contribute to the risk of brain damage and can have long-lasting neurological consequences. Multi-organ failure is another potential complication. The prolonged seizure activity and the associated physiological changes can disrupt the normal functioning of various organ systems. It can lead to systemic complications such as cardiovascular instability, metabolic imbalances, respiratory depression, and electrolyte disturbances. If left untreated, these can progress to multi-organ failure.

4. Answer A (Risk of respiratory depression)

Diazepam, a benzodiazepine medication, can cause respiratory depression as a side effect. It can depress the central nervous system, leading to decreased respiratory drive and potentially resulting in respiratory depression or even respiratory arrest in some cases. This risk is more pronounced with IV administration of diazepam or during the management of status epilepticus, where rapid control of seizures is critical but must be balanced with the potential for adverse effects. Monitoring of respiratory status is therefore essential when using IV diazepam for this purpose.

5. Answer B (False)

Epilepsy can occur at any age but is commonly diagnosed in those aged below 20 or over 65 years. While epilepsy can affect individuals of all age groups, certain age ranges are more commonly associated with epilepsy diagnosis.

6. Answer D (Dexmedetomidine)

Dexmedetomidine is a selective alpha-2 adrenergic agonist that has sedative properties. It is commonly used for its sedative and analgesic effects in critically ill patients. However, it lacks direct antiepileptic activity and does not have the same seizure-suppressing properties as the other options listed. On the other hand, propofol, midazolam, and thiopental are all commonly used IV drugs in the treatment of status epilepticus. They have potent antiepileptic properties and can effectively terminate ongoing seizure activity.

Recommended literature

1. Glauser T, Shinnar S, Gloss D, et al. Evidence-Based Guideline: Treatment of Convulsive Status Epilepticus in Children and Adults: Report of the Guideline Committee of the American Epilepsy Society. Epilepsy Curr. 2016;16(1):48-61.
2. Betjemann JP, Lowenstein DH. Status epilepticus in adults. Lancet Neurol. 2015;14(6):615-624.
3. Perks A, Cheema S, Mohanraj R. Anaesthesia and epilepsy. BJA: British Journal of Anaesthesia. 2012;108(4):562-71.

Emergencies
TENSION PNEUMOTHORAX

Questions:

1. **What is the primary mechanism of tension pneumothorax?**
   A. Air leakage from the lung into the pleural space
   B. Accumulation of air in the pleural space
   C. Inadequate lung expansion during inspiration
   D. Compression of the lung by fluid in the pleural space

2. **Which clinical finding is characteristic of tension pneumothorax?**
   A. Increased breath sounds on the affected side
   B. Hyper-resonant percussion sounds on the affected side
   C. Equal expansion of both lungs on auscultation
   D. Normal jugular vein distension

3. **What is the immediate management of a hemodynamically unstable patient with tension pneumothorax?**
   A. Chest X-ray
   B. Perform needle decompression
   C. Insert a chest tube
   D. Initiate positive pressure ventilation

4. **What procedure is recommended if needle decompression and chest tube placement fails or is not feasible?**
   A. Video-assisted thoracoscopic surgery (VATS)
   B. Initiate positive pressure ventilation
   C. One lung ventilation
   D. Bronchoscopy

5. **Cardiac tamponade can present with signs and symptoms similar to tension pneumothorax.**
   A. True
   B. False

6. **A 28-year-old male is brought to the emergency department after sustaining a penetrating chest wound during a physical altercation. He is in significant distress, complaining of severe chest pain and difficulty breathing. On examination, there is a visible entry wound in the left anterior chest wall with subcutaneous emphysema. Breath sounds are absent on the left side, and there is a tracheal deviation to the right. The patient appears pale and diaphoretic. What is the most appropriate initial treatment for this patient?**
   A. Administer supplemental oxygen
   B. Perform needle decompression
   C. Insert a chest tube
   D. Apply an airtight occlusive bandage and clean plastic sheeting

157

Answers:

1. **Answer B (Accumulation of air in the pleural space)**

   Tension pneumothorax occurs when air accumulates in the pleural space. This can happen due to a one-way valve mechanism, where air enters the pleural space during inspiration but cannot escape during expiration. As a result, the trapped air progressively increases the pressure within the pleural space, leading to lung collapse and compression of mediastinal structures. This condition is considered life-threatening and requires immediate intervention to relieve the pressure and restore lung function.

2. **Answer B (Hyper-resonant percussion sounds on the affected side)**

   Tension pneumothorax is characterized by hyper-resonant percussion sounds on the affected side of the chest. This is due to the increased air accumulation in the pleural space, resulting in a hollow or booming sound upon percussion. In contrast, normal lung tissue produces a dull or resonant sound during percussion. The hyper-resonance in tension pneumothorax is caused by the presence of air and the absence of lung tissue in the affected area. Other clinical findings associated with tension pneumothorax may include decreased or absent breath sounds, reduced tactile fremitus, asymmetrical lung expansion upon auscultation, and signs of hemodynamic instability such as jugular vein distension and decreased blood pressure.

3. **Answer B (Perform needle decompression)**

   In a hemodynamically unstable patient with tension pneumothorax, immediate management involves performing needle decompression. This procedure is performed at the bedside and involves inserting a large-bore needle into the affected pleural space to relieve the pressure caused by the trapped air. Needle decompression helps to rapidly decompress the tension pneumothorax, alleviate symptoms, and improve hemodynamic stability. It is a life-saving procedure that should be performed as soon as possible in a patient with signs of cardiovascular compromise.

4. **Answer A (Video-assisted thoracoscopic surgery (VATS))**

   If needle decompression and chest tube placement fails or is not feasible in the management of tension pneumothorax, more invasive procedures, such as VATS, may be necessary. VATS is a minimally invasive surgical procedure that uses a small camera and surgical instruments inserted through small incisions in the chest wall. It allows for visualization of the pleural space and the ability to perform various surgical interventions, including drainage of the pneumothorax and repair of any underlying lung or pleural pathology.

5. **Answer A (True)**

   Cardiac tamponade can present with signs and symptoms similar to tension pneumothorax, leading to potential confusion in clinical presentation. Both conditions can cause hemodynamic instability, leading to hypotension, jugular vein distension, and impaired cardiac function. In both cases, the compromised cardiac output can result in similar clinical features such as tachycardia, dyspnea, and cyanosis. The key distinguishing factor between tension pneumothorax and cardiac tamponade is the underlying cause. Tension pneumothorax is caused by the accumulation of air in the pleural space, leading to lung compression and subsequent cardiovascular compromise. On the other hand, cardiac tamponade is caused by the accumulation of fluid (typically blood) in the pericardial sac, which leads to impaired cardiac filling and function. To differentiate between tension pneumothorax and cardiac tamponade, further evaluation and diagnostic procedures are necessary, such as imaging studies (e.g., chest X-ray, echocardiogram), physical examination findings (e.g., muffled heart sounds in cardiac tamponade), and clinical context. Prompt recognition and appropriate management of these conditions are crucial as they require different treatment approaches.

6. **Answer D (Apply an airtight occlusive bandage and clean plastic sheeting)**

   The patient's clinical presentation with a penetrating chest wound, absent breath sounds on the left side, tracheal deviation, and signs of hemodynamic instability is highly concerning for tension pneumothorax. Tension pneumothorax requires immediate intervention to relieve the pressure and prevent further compromise of the patient's respiratory and cardiovascular status. The most appropriate initial treatment is to apply an airtight occlusive bandage and clean plastic sheeting over the penetrating chest wound. This technique, known as an "occlusive dressing," helps to prevent the entry of air into the pleural space and limits the progression of tension pneumothorax. The bandage should be airtight to create a seal and the clean plastic sheeting should be placed over the wound to further prevent air ingress.

Recommended literature

1. Jalota Sahota R, Sayad E. Tension Pneumothorax. [Updated 2022 Nov 28]. In: StatPearls [Internet]. Treasure Island (FL): StatPearls Publishing; 2022 Jan-. Available from: https://www.ncbi.nlm.nih.gov/books/NBK559090/.
2. MacDuff A, Arnold A, Harvey J. Management of spontaneous pneumothorax: British Thoracic Society pleural disease guideline 2010. Thorax. 2010;65(Suppl 2):ii18.
3. Paramasivam E, Bodenham A. Air leaks, pneumothorax, and chest drains. Continuing Education in Anaesthesia Critical Care & Pain. 2008;8(6):204-9.

Emergencies
TRANSFUSION REACTIONS

04
CHAPTER

Questions:

1. Which type of transfusion reaction is characterized by the destruction of red blood cells due to ABO incompatibility?
    A. Allergic/anaphylactic reaction
    B. Delayed hemolytic reaction
    C. Febrile non-hemolytic reaction
    D. Acute hemolytic reaction

2. Transfusion-related acute lung injury (TRALI) is characterized by?
    A. Sudden drop in blood pressure during or after a transfusion
    B. Mild fever and unexplained drop in hemoglobin levels
    C. Destruction of red blood cells due to ABO incompatibility
    D. Sudden onset of respiratory distress and non-cardiogenic pulmonary edema

3. Which type of transfusion reaction can occur when the volume of transfused blood exceeds the recipient's circulatory capacity?
    A. Acute hemolytic reaction
    B. Transfusion-associated circulatory overload
    C. Transfusion-related acute lung injury
    D. Febrile non-hemolytic reaction

4. Which preventive measure can help reduce the risk of transfusion reactions?
    A. Close adherence to blood handling and administration policies
    B. Laboratory testing
    C. Prospective monitoring and planning of transfusions
    D. All of the above

5. Cross-matching is a laboratory test that is essential to determine compatibility between the donor and recipient blood types, helping to minimize the risk of adverse transfusion reactions.
    A. True
    B. False

6. A 65-year-old male patient with a history of chronic kidney disease and end-stage renal disease presents to the emergency department with severe anemia due to gastrointestinal bleeding. He requires an urgent blood transfusion. Blood samples are collected for typing and cross-matching, and a compatible unit of packed red blood cells (PRBCs) is selected. The patient's blood type is B positive (B+), and the selected PRBC unit is also B positive (B+). The transfusion is initiated, and 15 minutes into the infusion, the patient develops sudden onset chills, rigors, fever, and hypotension. What is the most likely transfusion reaction occurring in this patient?
    A. Acute hemolytic reaction
    B. Febrile non-hemolytic reaction
    C. Allergic/anaphylactic reaction
    D. Transfusion-associated circulatory overload (TACO)

Answers:

1. **Answer D (Acute hemolytic reaction)**

   Acute hemolytic reactions occur when there is ABO incompatibility between the donor and recipient blood types, leading to the destruction of transfused red blood cells. ABO incompatibility means that the donor's blood type (A, B, AB, or O) is incompatible with the recipient's blood type. For example, if a patient with blood type A receives blood type B, their immune system will recognize the transfused red blood cells as foreign and mount an immune response, resulting in the destruction of the red blood cells. The symptoms of an acute hemolytic reaction can include fever, chills, rigors, hypotension, nausea, vomiting, and hemoglobinuria. It is a potentially life-threatening reaction and requires immediate recognition and management.

2. **Answer D (Sudden onset of respiratory distress and non-cardiogenic pulmonary edema)**

   Transfusion-related acute lung injury (TRALI) is a severe reaction that occurs after a blood transfusion. It is characterized by the sudden onset of respiratory distress and non-cardiogenic pulmonary edema. TRALI is often associated with donor antibodies against the recipient's white blood cells, and it is not directly related to ABO incompatibility or the destruction of red blood cells. The symptoms of TRALI include rapid onset of shortness of breath, difficulty breathing, coughing, and low oxygen levels. It is a serious condition that requires immediate medical attention and supportive care, including oxygen therapy and respiratory support. The underlying cause of TRALI is believed to be an immune reaction triggered by specific antibodies present in the transfused blood product, leading to lung injury.

3. **Answer B (Transfusion-associated circulatory overload)**

   Transfusion-associated circulatory overload (TACO) is a type of transfusion reaction that occurs when the volume of transfused blood exceeds the recipient's circulatory capacity. This can happen when a large volume of blood is transfused too quickly. TACO is characterized by symptoms related to fluid overload, such as dyspnea, tachypnea, cough, pulmonary edema, and elevated blood pressure. In TACO, the excess fluid can lead to an increased workload on the heart and compromised oxygenation. Patients with pre-existing cardiac or renal conditions are particularly susceptible to this type of reaction. Preventive measures such as careful monitoring of the transfusion rate and volume, as well as assessing the recipient's circulatory status, are essential to minimize the risk of TACO.

4. **Answer D (All of the above)**

   All of the mentioned preventive measures can help reduce the risk of transfusion reactions. Close adherence to blood handling and administration policies ensures safe practices. Laboratory testing helps identify compatibility issues, while prospective monitoring and planning allow for proactive management. Also, comprehensive training of staff ensures they are knowledgeable about proper procedures, and adopting a restrictive transfusion strategy helps avoid unnecessary transfusions, reducing the overall risk of adverse reactions.

5. **Answer A (True)**

   Cross-matching is a crucial laboratory test performed to determine the compatibility between the donor and recipient blood types before a blood transfusion. It involves mixing a sample of the recipient's blood with the donor's blood to check for any agglutination or other reactions, indicating an incompatible match. By ensuring a compatible match through cross-matching, the risk of adverse transfusion reactions, such as acute hemolytic reactions, can be significantly minimized. Therefore, cross-matching plays an essential role in promoting safe and successful blood transfusions.

6. **Answer B (Febrile non-hemolytic reaction)**

   Febrile non-hemolytic reactions are characterized by fever, chills, rigors, and occasionally hypotension without evidence of hemolysis. These reactions are typically caused by the recipient's antibodies reacting against donor white blood cells or platelets. They are more common in patients who have previously been transfused or have received multiple transfusions. In this case, the patient developed sudden onset chills, rigors, fever, and hypotension after the transfusion was initiated. These symptoms are consistent with a febrile non-hemolytic reaction. The absence of signs such as hemoglobinuria or evidence of ABO incompatibility suggests that acute hemolytic reaction is less likely. The management of febrile non-hemolytic reactions involves supportive care and symptomatic treatment. Blood pressure monitoring and supportive care are important to ensure the patient's stability and well-being during the reaction. In febrile, nonhemolytic reactions, fever usually resolves in 15-30 minutes without specific treatment. If fever causes discomfort, oral acetaminophen (325-500 mg) may be administered. Avoid aspirin because of its prolonged adverse effect on platelet function.

Recommended literature

1. Delaney M, Wendel S, Bercovitz RS, et al. Transfusion reactions: prevention, diagnosis, and treatment. Lancet. 2016;388(10061):2825-2836.

VENOUS AIR EMBOLISM (VAE)

Questions:

1. **What is the most common iatrogenic cause of venous air embolism (VAE)?**

   A. Cardiac surgery

   B. Central/peripheral venous access

   C. Endoscopy

   D. All of the above

2. **Which of the following is NOT a sign or symptom of venous air embolism?**

   A. Tachycardia

   B. Hypertension

   C. Hypoxia

   D. Altered mental status

3. **What is the recommended patient positioning during the insertion of central venous catheters to prevent venous air embolism?**

   A. Sitting position

   B. Trendelenburg position

   C. Supine position

   D. Left lateral decubitus position

4. **Which gas is commonly used during surgery but should be avoided in patients at high risk of venous air embolism?**

   A. Oxygen

   B. Nitrous oxide

   C. Sevoflurane

   D. Isoflurane

5. **The left lateral decubitus position is recommended for patients suspected of having venous air embolism to prevent further air entrainment and promote air elimination from the right atrium.**

   A. True

   B. False

6. **A 65-year-old male patient with end-stage renal disease is admitted for hemodialysis. During the placement of the central venous catheter (CVC), the patient becomes hypotensive and experiences a sudden onset of dyspnea. The healthcare team suspects VAE as a potential complication. What is the characteristic cardiac auscultation finding associated with venous air embolism?**

   A. S3 gallop

   B. S4 gallop

   C. Mill wheel murmur

   D. Pericardial friction rub

Answers:

1. **Answer D (All of the above)**

   Venous air embolism (VAE) is an iatrogenic complication that can occur in various clinical scenarios. In addition to cardiac surgery, central/peripheral venous access, and endoscopy, other factors such as trauma, barotrauma, various surgical procedures (including vascular and neurosurgery), angiography, tissue biopsy, thoracocentesis, and hemodialysis can also contribute to the occurrence of VAE.

2. **Answer B (Hypertension)**

   While tachycardia, hypoxia, and altered mental status are commonly observed signs and symptoms of venous air embolism, hypertension is not typically associated with this condition. In fact, hypotension is more commonly observed due to the obstruction of blood flow caused by air embolism.

3. **Answer B (Trendelenburg position)**

   In the case of internal jugular and subclavian access for central venous catheter placement, a 15-degree Trendelenburg position can be obtained if feasible according to the clinical situation. This position helps to reduce the risk of venous air embolism during the procedure. Furthermore, it is advisable to avoid the placement of venous catheters during inspiration when negative intra-thoracic pressure is at its maximum. This precaution helps to minimize the potential for air entry into the vasculature during catheter insertion.

4. **Answer B (Nitrous oxide)**

   Nitrous oxide should be avoided to minimize the risk of venous air embolism. Nitrous oxide is a gas commonly used in anesthesia, but it can potentially expand gas pockets and increase the risk of air entrainment and embolism. Therefore, it is recommended to avoid the use of nitrous oxide in patients at high risk for venous air embolism or during procedures where air embolism is a concern.

5. **Answer A (True)**

   In cases of venous air embolism, Durant's maneuver is performed by placing the patient in the left lateral decubitus and Trendelenburg position. This serves to encourage the air bubble to move out of the right ventricular outflow tract and into the right atrium, thereby relieving the "air-lock" effect responsible for the potentially catastrophic cardiopulmonary collapse. It is important to note that, in the case of arterial air embolism, patients should be kept in the flat supine position as the head-down position may worsen cerebral edema.

6. **Answer C (Mill wheel murmur)**

   The characteristic cardiac auscultation finding associated with venous air embolism is a "mill wheel" murmur. This murmur is caused by air bubbles within the cardiac chambers, particularly the right side of the heart. The turbulent flow of blood passing through the air bubbles produces a unique sound resembling the turning of a mill wheel. Detection of this murmur on cardiac auscultation can raise suspicion for venous air embolism.

Recommended literature

1. Chuang DY, Sundararajan S, Sundararajan VA, Feldman DI, Xiong W. Accidental Air Embolism. Stroke. 2019;50(7):e183-e186.
2. McCarthy CJ, Behravesh S, Naidu SG, Oklu R. Air Embolism: Diagnosis, Clinical Management and Outcomes. Diagnostics (Basel). 2017;7(1):5. Published 2017 Jan 17.
3. Mirski MA, Lele AV, Fitzsimmons L, Toung TJ. Diagnosis and treatment of vascular air embolism. Anesthesiology. 2007;106(1):164-177.
4. Webber S, Andrzejowski J, Francis G. Gas embolism in anaesthesia. BJA CEPD Reviews. 2002;2(2):53-7.

VENOUS THROMBOEMBOLISM

04

CHAPTER

Questions:

1. **Which of the following is a risk factor for venous thromboembolism (VTE)?**

   A. Previous VTE

   B. Obesity

   C. Twin gestation

   D. All of the above

2. **What is the recommended duration of anticoagulation treatment for VTE secondary to transient risk factors?**

   A. 1-3 months

   B. 3-6 months

   C. 6-12 months

   D. > 12 months

3. **What is the primary treatment option for deep vein thrombosis (DVT)?**

   A. Thrombolytics

   B. Aspirin

   C. Thrombectomy/embolectomy

   D. Low molecular weight heparins (LMWH)

4. **Which of the following is a diagnostic test for pulmonary embolism (PE)?**

   A. Computed tomographic pulmonary angiography (CTPA)

   B. Ventilation-perfusion scan

   C. Pulmonary angiography

   D. All of the above

5. **An inferior vena cava filter is the first option for managing PE in patients with DVT.**

   A. True

   B. False

6. **A 28-year-old pregnant woman, G1P0 (gravida 1, para 0), with a history of thrombophilia, is scheduled for an elective caesarean section. Besides thrombophilia, she has no significant medical history or other known risk factors for VTE. Which of the following measures is the most appropriate for postoperative prevention of VTE in this patient?**

   A. Use of sequential compression devices (SCDs)

   B. Administration of low molecular weight heparin (LMWH)

   C. Early ambulation post-surgery

   D. All of the above

Answers:

1. Answer D (All of the above)

All of the listed options are recognized risk factors for venous thromboembolism (VTE). A history of previous VTE increases the risk of developing another episode in the future. Obesity, defined as a high body mass index (BMI), is associated with a prothrombotic state, leading to an increased risk of VTE. Pregnancy, especially with multiple gestations like twins, is a well-known risk factor for VTE due to the hormonal and physiological changes that occur during pregnancy.

2. Answer B (3-6 months)

Anticoagulation treatment is generally maintained for 3-6 months for VTE secondary to transient risk factors. The ASH guidelines stratify patients by whether the patient's prior VTE was in the setting of a transient risk factor, recommending 3 to 6 months in duration of anticoagulation if the prior VTE was provoked by a transient risk factor and indefinite anticoagulation if the prior VTE was without a transient risk factor.

3. Answer D (Low molecular weight heparins (LMWH))

The primary treatment option for deep vein thrombosis (DVT) is the administration of anticoagulant medications, with low molecular weight heparins (LMWH) being the preferred choice. LMWHs, such as enoxaparin and dalteparin, are effective in preventing the extension of existing blood clots and the formation of new clots. These medications inhibit the clotting factors in the blood, reducing the risk of further thrombus formation and allowing the body's natural fibrinolysis process to gradually dissolve the existing clot.

4. Answer D (All of the above)

Computed tomographic pulmonary angiography (CTPA), ventilation-perfusion scan (V/Q scan), and pulmonary angiography are all diagnostic tests used for the evaluation and diagnosis of pulmonary embolism (PE). CTPA is the preferred imaging modality, while V/Q scan and pulmonary angiography may be used in specific situations or when other imaging modalities are inconclusive.

5. Answer B (False)

The primary treatment option for managing PE in patients with DVT is anticoagulation therapy with medications such as LMWH or direct oral anticoagulants (DOACs). The use of an inferior vena cava (IVC) filter is not the first-line treatment but may be considered when anticoagulation is contraindicated or has failed or in specific situations where there is a high risk of recurrent PE. The IVC filter is a device placed in the inferior vena cava to catch blood clots and prevent them from reaching the lungs. However, it is typically reserved for cases where other treatment options are not suitable or effective.

6. Answer D (All of the above)

Thrombophilia is a significant risk factor for developing VTE, especially in the context of surgery and pregnancy. To effectively prevent VTE in this high-risk patient, a multimodal approach combining multiple preventive measures is recommended. This includes the use of sequential compression devices (SCDs) to prevent blood stasis, administration of LMWH for pharmacological thromboprophylaxis, and early ambulation post-surgery to promote blood flow and reduce the risk of clot formation. By combining these measures, the patient's risk of developing VTE can be effectively reduced.

Recommended literature

1. Gordon RJ, Lombard FW. Perioperative Venous Thromboembolism: A Review. Anesthesia & Analgesia. 2017;125(2).
2. Barker RC, Marval P. Venous thromboembolism: risks and prevention. Continuing Education in Anaesthesia Critical Care & Pain. 2011;11(1):18-23.
3. National Clinical Guideline Centre – Acute and Chronic Conditions (UK). Venous Thromboembolism: Reducing the Risk of Venous Thromboembolism (Deep Vein Thrombosis and Pulmonary Embolism) in Patients Admitted to Hospital. London: Royal College of Physicians (UK); 2010. (NICE Clinical Guidelines, No. 92.) 2, Summary of recommendations. Available from: https://www.ncbi.nlm.nih.gov/books/NBK116536/
4. Joyce E, Haymart B, Kong X, Ali MA, Carrigan M, Kaatz S, Shah V, Kline-Rogers E, Kozlowski J, Froehlich JB, Barnes GD. Length of Anticoagulation in Provoked Venous Thromboembolism: A Multicenter Study of How Real-World Practice Mirrors Guideline Recommendations. J Am Heart Assoc. 2022 Nov;11(21):e025471. doi: 10.1161/JAHA.122.025471. Epub 2022 Oct 26. PMID: 36285782; PMCID: PMC9673630.

ENDOCRINOLOGY

Endocrinology
ACROMEGALY

05
CHAPTER

Questions:

1. **Acromegaly is caused by an excess of growth hormone (GH) secretion due to?**
   A. Pituitary adenoma
   B. Thyroid adenoma
   C. Adrenal adenoma
   D. Renal adenoma

2. **Which of the following is NOT a sign or symptom of acromegaly?**
   A. Enlarged lower jaw
   B. Thickened vocal cords
   C. Carpal tunnel syndrome
   D. Exophthalmos

3. **The preferred treatment for acromegaly is?**
   A. Radiation therapy
   B. Somatostatin analogs
   C. Dopamine agonists
   D. Surgery to remove the pituitary tumor

4. **The medications used to reduce GH production in acromegaly are called?**
   A. Somatostatin analogs
   B. Dopamine agonists
   C. GH receptor antagonists
   D. Insulin sensitizers

5. **Cardiomyopathy is a common complication associated with acromegaly.**
   A. True
   B. False

6. **A 42-year-old female with a known diagnosis of acromegaly is scheduled for surgical removal of a pituitary adenoma. On physical examination, she has enlarged hands and feet, macroglossia, and a protruding lower jaw. The airway examination reveals a Mallampati class III view with limited mouth opening due to reduced temporomandibular joint mobility. Her previous medical history is significant for hypertension and diabetes mellitus. Preoperative transthoracic echocardiography shows mild left ventricular hypertrophy. Considering the patient's acromegaly diagnosis and airway findings, which of the following is the most appropriate anesthesia management for this patient?**
   A. Awake fiberoptic intubation
   B. Direct laryngoscopy and tracheal intubation with caution
   C. Nasal intubation with a smaller endotracheal tube
   D. Supraglottic airway

Answers:

1. **Answer A (Pituitary adenoma)**

   Acromegaly is primarily caused by the presence of a pituitary adenoma, which is a noncancerous tumor of the pituitary gland. This adenoma leads to the excessive secretion of growth hormone (GH) and subsequently results in the clinical manifestations of acromegaly.

2. **Answer D (Exophthalmos)**

   Exophthalmos refers to bulging or protrusion of the eyes, which is commonly associated with conditions like Graves' disease and thyroid-related orbitopathy, but it is not a typical sign or symptom of acromegaly. The enlarged lower jaw, thickened vocal cords, and carpal tunnel syndrome are signs and symptoms commonly seen in acromegaly.

3. **Answer D (Surgery to remove the pituitary tumor)**

   The preferred treatment for acromegaly is surgery to remove the pituitary tumor, causing the excess production of GH. This surgical procedure is known as transsphenoidal adenomectomy. By removing the tumor, the source of excessive GH secretion is eliminated, which helps in normalizing hormone levels and alleviating the symptoms of acromegaly. While radiation therapy, somatostatin analogs, and dopamine agonists may be used as adjunctive treatments, surgery is generally considered the primary and preferred approach for the long-term management of acromegaly.

4. **Answer A (Somatostatin analogs)**

   In the treatment of acromegaly, somatostatin analogs are commonly used agents to reduce the production and secretion of GH. Somatostatin analogs, such as octreotide and lanreotide, mimic the action of somatostatin, a natural hormone that inhibits the release of GH. By binding to somatostatin receptors on pituitary tumor cells, these analogs help regulate and lower GH levels in individuals with acromegaly.

5. **Answer A (True)**

   Cardiomyopathy is a common finding in people with acromegaly. The excessive secretion of GH in acromegaly can lead to structural and functional changes in the heart, including left ventricular hypertrophy and impaired left ventricular function. These cardiac changes can ultimately result in cardiomyopathy and contribute to cardiovascular complications associated with acromegaly.

6. **Answer A (Awake fiberoptic intubation)**

   Given the patient's diagnosis of acromegaly and the associated airway findings of macroglossia, Mallampati class III view, and limited mouth opening, awake fiberoptic intubation is the preferred technique. Awake fiberoptic intubation allows for a controlled and guided placement of the endotracheal tube under direct visualization, ensuring a secure airway while maintaining spontaneous breathing. This technique is particularly beneficial in cases where direct laryngoscopy and tracheal intubation may be challenging due to limited mouth opening and potential difficulty visualizing the glottic opening. Direct laryngoscopy and tracheal intubation can be more challenging in patients with difficult airways, such as those with acromegaly. Nasal intubation may be complicated by nasal turbinate enlargement. Supraglottic airway devices are not typically recommended in patients with severe airway obstruction, such as those with macroglossia, as they may not provide adequate ventilation and can increase the risk of airway obstruction.

Recommended literature

1. Menon R, Murphy PG, Lindley AM. Anaesthesia and pituitary disease. Continuing Education in Anaesthesia Critical Care & Pain. 2011;11(4):133-137.
2. Smith M, Hirsch NP. Pituitary disease and anaesthesia. Br J Anaesth. 2000;85(1):3-14.
3. Seidman PA, Kofke WA, Policare R, Young M. Anaesthetic complications of acromegaly. Br J Anaesth. 2000;84(2):179-182.

ADRENOCORTICAL INSUFFICIENCY

Questions:

1. **Which of the following hormones is deficient in primary adrenal insufficiency?**

   A. Glucocorticoids

   B. Mineralocorticoids

   C. Androgens

   D. All of the above

2. **Secondary adrenal insufficiency is caused by?**

   A. Deficient corticotropin-releasing hormone (CRH) secretion

   B. Deficient adrenocorticotropin hormone (ACTH) secretion

   C. Directly affected adrenal glands

   D. Excessive glucocorticoid production

3. **Addisonian crisis is characterized by?**

   A. Hypertension, hyperglycemia, and hyperkalemia

   B. Hypotension, hypoglycemia, and hyperkalemia

   C. Abdominal pain, vomiting, and hypokalemia

   D. Increased pigmentation, muscle pain, hypernatremia

4. **The treatment for acute adrenal crisis includes?**

   A. Intravenous fluids and glucocorticoids

   B. Diuretics and mineralocorticoids

   C. Surgical intervention

   D. D5W and Insulin

5. **An Addisonian crisis can be triggered by anesthesia.**

   A. True

   B. False

6. **A 62-year-old female with a known history of primary adrenal insufficiency (Addison's disease) presents to the hospital for an elective hysterectomy. She has been on chronic oral glucocorticoid (prednisolone 10 mg) and mineralocorticoid (fludrocortisone 0.1 mg) replacement therapy. The patient reports recent fatigue, anorexia, and weight loss. Her vital signs show postural hypotension. Laboratory tests reveal hyponatremia and hyperkalemia. What is the appropriate perioperative management for this patient with primary adrenal insufficiency undergoing elective surgery?**

   A. Continue the patient's usual glucocorticoid and mineralocorticoid replacement therapy

   B. Temporarily withhold the patient's glucocorticoid and mineralocorticoid replacement therapy

   C. Administer stress-dose glucocorticoids during the perioperative period

   D. Increase the patient's mineralocorticoid replacement therapy

Answers:

1. Answer D (All of the above)

In primary adrenal insufficiency, also known as Addison's disease, there is deficient secretion of glucocorticoids, mineralocorticoids, and androgens by the adrenal glands. The adrenal glands, which are directly affected in this condition, fail to produce adequate levels of these hormones. As a result, not only is the production of glucocorticoids (such as cortisol) reduced but also the production of mineralocorticoids (such as aldosterone) and androgens.

2. Answer B (Deficient adrenocorticotropin hormone (ACTH) secretion)

Secondary adrenal insufficiency occurs when there is deficient secretion of adrenocorticotropin hormone (ACTH) by the pituitary gland. ACTH is responsible for stimulating the adrenal glands to produce cortisol and other adrenal hormones. In secondary adrenal insufficiency, the adrenal glands themselves are not directly affected, but rather there is a problem with the production or release of ACTH from the pituitary gland. This can result from various causes, such as pituitary gland dysfunction, hypothalamic dysfunction, or the use of exogenous glucocorticoids that suppress the production of ACTH. As a result of the deficient ACTH secretion, the adrenal glands do not receive the necessary stimulation to produce adequate levels of cortisol, leading to secondary adrenal insufficiency.

3. Answer B (Hypotension, hypoglycemia, and hyperkalemia)

An Addisonian crisis is characterized by hypotension, hypoglycemia, and hyperkalemia. These symptoms occur due to the severe deficiency of glucocorticoids and mineralocorticoids in individuals with adrenal insufficiency. An Addisonian crisis refers to a life-threatening situation that occurs in individuals with adrenal insufficiency, particularly in cases of undiagnosed or untreated Addison's disease, combined with sudden stress on the body. During an Addisonian crisis, there is a severe deficiency of glucocorticoids and mineralocorticoids, which are essential for maintaining blood pressure, electrolyte balance, and glucose metabolism.

4. Answer A (Intravenous fluids and glucocorticoids)

The treatment for an acute adrenal crisis involves the administration of intravenous fluids and glucocorticoids. Acute adrenal crisis is a life-threatening condition characterized by severe adrenal insufficiency, often triggered by sudden stress or trauma. Intravenous fluids are given to address dehydration and help stabilize blood pressure. Glucocorticoids, such as hydrocortisone, are administered to replace the deficient cortisol and provide the necessary hormonal support. These medications are crucial in restoring hormonal balance and preventing further complications.

5. Answer A (True)

An Addisonian crisis can be triggered by anesthesia. Anesthesia and surgical procedures impose significant stress on the body, which can lead to decompensation of adrenocortical insufficiency, particularly in individuals with undiagnosed or untreated Addison's disease. The stress response during anesthesia can place additional demands on the adrenal glands to produce adequate levels of cortisol and other hormones. However, in individuals with compromised adrenal function, the adrenal glands may not be able to meet these increased demands, leading to an acute adrenal crisis. Therefore, it is crucial to identify and appropriately manage patients with adrenocortical insufficiency before undergoing anesthesia to prevent the occurrence of an Addisonian crisis.

6. Answer C (Administer stress-dose glucocorticoids during the perioperative period)

In patients with primary adrenal insufficiency (Addison's disease) undergoing surgery, it is crucial to provide appropriate perioperative management to prevent an adrenal crisis. These patients have a reduced ability to mount a stress response due to deficient cortisol production, making them vulnerable to hypotension, hypoglycemia, and electrolyte imbalances during surgery and the immediate postoperative period. Administering stress-dose glucocorticoids during the perioperative period is the appropriate management approach. The patient should receive intravenous hydrocortisone, a synthetic glucocorticoid, to mimic the physiological stress response. The typical stress-dose regimen is 100 mg of intravenous hydrocortisone given preoperatively, followed by 50-100 mg every 6-8 hours intraoperatively and for the first 24 hours postoperatively. The dose can then be gradually tapered back to the patient's usual maintenance dose of oral glucocorticoid therapy.

Recommended literature

1. Pollard BJ, Kitchen G. Handbook of Clinical Anaesthesia. 4th ed. Taylor & Francis group; 2018. Chapter 6 Endocrine system.
2. Davies MJ, Hardman JG. Anaesthesia and adrenocortical disease. Continuing Education in Anaesthesia. Critical Care & Pain. 2005;5(4):122-126.

Endocrinology

ALCOHOL WITHDRAWAL SYNDROME

05
CHAPTER

Questions:

1. What is the first-line treatment for alcohol withdrawal syndrome (AWS) and delirium tremens?

    A. Clomethiazole

    B. Haloperidol

    C. Benzodiazepines

    D. Clonidine

2. Which medication is not advised for the treatment of AWS and delirium tremens in critically ill patients due to an elevated risk of pneumonia?

    A. Clomethiazole

    B. Diazepam

    C. Lorazepam

    D. Chlordiazepoxide

3. Which medical disorder is associated with chronic alcoholism and involves a thiamine deficiency?

    A. Wernicke-Korsakoff syndrome

    B. Peripheral neuropathy

    C. Cardiomyopathy

    D. Pancreatitis

4. What is the recommended tool for monitoring the effectiveness of prophylactic or fixed-schedule treatment regimens for alcohol withdrawal?

    A. CIWA-Ar scale

    B. Glasgow Coma Scale

    C. Ramsay Sedation Scale

    D. Hamilton Anxiety Rating Scale

5. The mortality rate of delirium tremens is approximately 10%.

    A. True

    B. False

6. A 55-year-old male with a history of chronic alcohol abuse is scheduled for elective abdominal surgery. He has been consuming alcohol excessively for the past several years and reports no attempts to quit or decrease his alcohol intake before the surgery. The surgical procedure is performed successfully under general anesthesia. On the second postoperative day, the patient becomes agitated and restless and experiences tremors. He is diaphoretic, tachycardic, and hypertensive. The initial diagnosis of alcohol withdrawal syndrome is made. The patient is promptly started on benzodiazepines and haloperidol, but his symptoms persist despite adequate doses. In severe cases of alcohol withdrawal, where initial treatment is unresponsive, what intervention may be necessary?

    A. Intravenous fluid administration

    B. Propofol infusion

    C. Clomethiazole administration

    D. Carbamazepine therapy

Answers:

1. Answer C (Benzodiazepines)

The first-line treatment for alcohol withdrawal syndrome (AWS) and delirium tremens is benzodiazepines. Benzodiazepines are a class of medications that have sedative, anxiolytic, and anticonvulsant properties. They work by enhancing the inhibitory effects of the neurotransmitter GABA (gamma-aminobutyric acid) in the brain, which helps to reduce the excitability and hyperactivity seen during alcohol withdrawal. Benzodiazepines are effective in managing the symptoms of AWS, such as tremors, anxiety, agitation, and seizures. They help to alleviate withdrawal symptoms, prevent complications, and provide relief to individuals undergoing alcohol detoxification. Commonly used benzodiazepines for AWS and delirium tremens include chlordiazepoxide, diazepam, and lorazepam.

2. Answer A (Clomethiazole)

Clomethiazole is not advised for the treatment of AWS and delirium tremens in critically ill patients due to an elevated risk of pneumonia. Clomethiazole can increase bronchial secretions, potentially leading to respiratory complications, including an increased susceptibility to pneumonia.

3. Answer A (Wernicke-Korsakoff syndrome)

Wernicke-Korsakoff syndrome is a medical disorder associated with chronic alcoholism and involves a thiamine (vitamin B1) deficiency. Thiamine plays a crucial role in energy metabolism and the proper functioning of the nervous system. Chronic alcohol consumption can lead to poor dietary intake, impaired absorption, and increased thiamine excretion, resulting in thiamine deficiency. It is characterized by neurological symptoms such as confusion, ataxia, oculomotor abnormalities in the acute phase (Wernicke's encephalopathy), and severe memory loss, confabulation, and cognitive impairments in the chronic phase (Korsakoff syndrome). Thiamine supplementation is a crucial component of the treatment for this condition.

4. Answer A (CIWA-Ar scale)

The recommended tool for monitoring the effectiveness of prophylactic or fixed-schedule treatment regimens for alcohol withdrawal is the CIWA-Ar (Clinical Institute Withdrawal Assessment for Alcohol-Revised) scale. This scale is specifically designed to assess and quantify the severity of alcohol withdrawal symptoms. The CIWA-Ar scale evaluates various symptoms, including tremors, sweating, anxiety, agitation, nausea, and headache, among others. By assessing the severity of these symptoms, healthcare professionals can determine the appropriate treatment approach, including the need for medication and its dosage. Using the CIWA-Ar scale allows for a systematic and standardized assessment of alcohol withdrawal symptoms, ensuring that treatment is tailored to the individual's needs. It helps to guide the administration of medications in both prophylactic and symptom-triggered treatment regimens, optimizing patient care during the withdrawal process.

5. Answer A (True)

The mortality rate of delirium tremens is approximately 10%. Delirium tremens is a severe form of alcohol withdrawal characterized by rapid onset confusion, hallucinations, agitation, and autonomic hyperactivity. It can lead to serious medical complications such as hypotension, dysrhythmias, or seizures, which contribute to the mortality rate. Prompt recognition, appropriate management, and medical intervention are crucial in reducing the risk of mortality associated with delirium tremens.

6. Answer B (Propofol infusion)

In severe cases of alcohol withdrawal that are unresponsive to initial treatment, propofol infusion may be necessary. Propofol is a short-acting sedative-hypnotic agent commonly used for induction and maintenance of anesthesia. In the context of alcohol withdrawal, it can be used to provide deep sedation to patients who are severely agitated and not responding to standard treatment. In this case, the patient's symptoms of agitation, restlessness, tremors, diaphoresis, tachycardia, and hypertension are indicative of severe alcohol withdrawal. Despite the administration of benzodiazepines and haloperidol, his symptoms persist, suggesting an inadequate response to the initial treatment. In such cases, propofol infusion can be initiated to achieve deep sedation, which helps to alleviate severe agitation and provide a calming effect. It's important to closely monitor the patient during the propofol infusion, ensuring appropriate titration to maintain the desired level of sedation. The use of propofol in this scenario requires careful consideration of potential respiratory depression and hemodynamic effects.

Recommended literature

1. Ungur A, L, Neumann T, Borchers F, Spies C: Perioperative Management of Alcohol Withdrawal Syndrome. Visc Med 2020;36:160-166.
2. Chapman, Richard & Plaat, Felicity. (2009). Alcohol and anaesthesia. Continuing Education in Anaesthesia, Critical Care & Pain. 9. 10-13.

Endocrinology
ANOREXIA NERVOSA

Questions:

1. Anorexia nervosa can lead to metabolic alkalosis due to?
   A. Excessive fluid intake
   B. Increased bicarbonate production
   C. Vomiting
   D. Decreased lung compliance

2. Anorexia nervosa is associated with reduced levels of which hormone?
   A. Luteinizing hormone (LH)
   B. Adrenocorticotropic hormone (ACTH)
   C. Growth hormone (GH)
   D. Cortisol

3. Which of the following cardiovascular changes is associated with anorexia nervosa?
   A. Hypertension
   B. Tachycardia
   C. Mitral valve stenosis
   D. Bradycardia

4. Which of the following is a dermatological sign associated with anorexia nervosa?
   A. Alopecia areata
   B. Vitiligo
   C. Psoriasis
   D. Lanugo hair

5. Russell's sign can be associated with anorexia nervosa.
   A. True
   B. False

6. A 30-year-old woman is scheduled for an emergency appendectomy due to acute appendicitis. She has a history of anorexia nervosa and has recently relapsed, resulting in a significantly low body weight. Which of the following precautions should be considered regarding anesthesia in a patient with a history of anorexia nervosa?
   A. Perform rapid sequence induction (RSI)
   B. Avoid hypothermia
   C. Avoid hyperventilation
   D. All of the above

Answers:

1. Answer C (Vomiting)

Anorexia nervosa can lead to metabolic alkalosis through the behavior of vomiting. These actions result in the loss of stomach acid or bicarbonate from the body. When an individual with anorexia nervosa induces vomiting as part of their disordered eating behaviors, it can cause the loss of hydrochloric acid (HCl) from the stomach. Hydrochloric acid is an acidic component that aids in the digestion of food in the stomach. With the loss of stomach acid, the body's acid-base balance is disrupted, leading to an alkaline shift in the blood pH.

2. Answer A (Luteinizing hormone (LH))

Anorexia nervosa can result in hormonal imbalances, including reduced levels of LH. LH is a hormone produced by the pituitary gland that plays a crucial role in regulating the menstrual cycle and reproductive function in both males and females. LH will be correspondingly diminished in anorexia nervosa because the changes in gonadotropins are due to central hypothalamic hypogonadism secondary to starvation rather than increasing, as would be expected with a failing gonad.

3. Answer B (Bradycardia)

Bradycardia (pulse < 60) and hypotension are commonly observed in patients with anorexia nervosa, with bradycardia present in up to 95% of patients. The underlying mechanism of bradycardia in anorexia nervosa is believed to involve physiological adaptations to increased vagal tone and decreased energy metabolism due to low caloric intake. Structural changes in the heart, such as decreased left ventricular muscle mass secondary to malnutrition, may contribute to bradycardia. It has been proposed that bradycardia acts as a compensatory mechanism to prevent heart failure in individuals with atrophic hearts.

4. Answer D (Lanugo hair)

Lanugo hair is a dermatological sign associated with anorexia nervosa. Lanugo refers to fine, soft, and downy hair that grows on the body, typically in areas where terminal hair is not normally present. In individuals with anorexia nervosa, the body may respond to low body weight and nutritional deficiencies by growing lanugo hair. This hair growth is considered a compensatory mechanism aimed at preserving body heat and providing additional insulation in response to the lack of subcutaneous fat and reduced body temperature regulation commonly seen in individuals with anorexia nervosa.

5. Answer A (True)

Russell's sign is associated with anorexia nervosa. Russell's sign refers to calluses or scars on the knuckles or back of the hand caused by self-induced vomiting. In individuals with anorexia nervosa, self-induced vomiting is a common behavior used to control weight or eliminate food. The repeated act of inserting fingers into the mouth and throat to induce vomiting can lead to trauma and damage to the skin on the knuckles or hand, resulting in the development of calluses or scars.

6. Answer D (All of the above)

All of the above precautions should be considered regarding anesthesia in a patient with a history of anorexia nervosa. RSI is a technique used to secure the patient's airway quickly and minimize the risk of aspiration during intubation. Individuals with anorexia nervosa may have a higher likelihood of gastroesophageal reflux and aspiration due to delayed gastric emptying. Anorexia nervosa can lead to a decreased ability to regulate body temperature, making patients more susceptible to hypothermia during anesthesia. Maintaining normothermia is essential to prevent adverse effects on cardiovascular function, wound healing, and coagulation. Hyperventilation can lead to respiratory alkalosis, which is characterized by low levels of carbon dioxide in the blood. Individuals with anorexia nervosa may already have altered acid-base balance due to metabolic disturbances (Metabolic alkalosis). Hyperventilation can further disrupt this balance and lead to complications.

Recommended literature

1. Denner AM, Townley SA. Anorexia nervosa: perioperative implications. Continuing Education in Anaesthesia Critical Care & Pain. 2009;9(2):61-4.

CARCINOID

Questions:

1. **What is one of the primary symptoms of carcinoid syndrome?**
   A. Skin rash
   B. Muscle weakness
   C. Joint pain
   D. Skin flushing

2. **Which of the following hormones is frequently secreted by carcinoid tumors?**
   A. Insulin
   B. Glucagon
   C. Serotonin
   D. Thyroxine

3. **Which organ is commonly affected by metastases from carcinoid tumors?**
   A. Liver
   B. Kidneys
   C. Brain
   D. Pancreas

4. **Which medication is commonly used to block excess hormone secretion in patients with carcinoid tumors?**
   A. Octreotide
   B. Ozempic
   C. Metformin
   D. Prednisone

5. **Hypothermia is one of the potential triggers for perioperative carcinoid crises.**
   A. True
   B. False

6. **A 55-year-old female patient with a known diagnosis of midgut carcinoid tumor presents for a scheduled exploratory laparotomy and tumor resection. Preoperative investigations have revealed liver metastases, and the tumor has been deemed unresectable. The patient is scheduled for palliative surgery to alleviate symptoms and improve quality of life. During anesthesia induction, the patient receives a combination of propofol, fentanyl, and rocuronium. Throughout the procedure, close monitoring of hemodynamics, oxygen saturation, and end-tidal carbon dioxide levels is maintained. The surgical team performs meticulous tumor manipulation, taking care to avoid excessive handling to minimize the risk of carcinoid crisis. Despite all measures, the patient experiences a sudden onset of bronchospasm, with wheezing and difficulty breathing. What medication can be administered to manage bronchospasms in patients with carcinoid tumors?**
   A. β2 adrenergic agonists
   B. Epinephrine
   C. Ipratropium
   D. Theophylline

Answers:

1. Answer D (Skin flushing)

One of the primary symptoms of carcinoid syndrome is skin flushing. Carcinoid tumors can release vasoactive substances such as serotonin and histamine into the bloodstream, leading to dilation of blood vessels and resulting in episodes of skin flushing. Flushing can occur in different patterns and may vary in duration and intensity depending on the location and type of the carcinoid tumor. It is a characteristic feature of carcinoid syndrome and is often accompanied by other symptoms such as diarrhea, abdominal pain, and bronchospasm.

2. Answer C (Serotonin)

Carcinoid tumors are benign or malignant growths that sometimes produce excessive amounts of hormone-like substances (such as serotonin), resulting in carcinoid syndrome. Serotonin is a vasoactive substance that can be released into the bloodstream by carcinoid tumors derived from neuroendocrine cells. The excessive production and release of serotonin by carcinoid tumors can contribute to the characteristic symptoms associated with carcinoid syndrome, such as skin flushing, diarrhea, and bronchoconstriction. Other hormones and vasoactive substances, such as histamine, prostaglandins, and substance P, may also be secreted by carcinoid tumors, but serotonin is one of the most commonly produced and recognized hormones in the context of carcinoid tumors.

3. Answer A (Liver)

Carcinoid tumors have a high tendency to metastasize to the liver. The presence of liver metastases can contribute to the development of carcinoid syndrome, as the tumor cells release vasoactive substances into the systemic circulation. Carcinoid syndrome occurs when the tumor produces excessive amounts of serotonin in an individual with liver metastases. In patients who have no spread to the liver, the serotonin released by an intestinal tumor will be broken down to an inactive substance; thus, carcinoid syndrome does not occur.

4. Answer A (Octreotide)

Octreotide is a medication commonly used to block excess hormone secretion in patients with carcinoid tumors. Octreotide is a synthetic somatostatin analog that acts by binding to somatostatin receptors on the tumor cells, inhibiting the release of various hormones and vasoactive substances, including serotonin, gastrin, and others. By reducing the secretion of these substances, octreotide helps alleviate the symptoms associated with carcinoid syndrome, such as flushing, diarrhea, and bronchospasm. It is administered as an injection and is an important component of the medical management of patients with carcinoid tumors.

5. Answer A (True)

Hypothermia is one of the potential triggers for perioperative carcinoid crises. This can lead to an acute and severe systemic response, known as a carcinoid crisis, characterized by sudden onset of flushing, hypotension, tachycardia, bronchospasm, and other symptoms associated with carcinoid syndrome. Other triggers include histamine-releasing drugs, vasoactive drugs, succinylcholine, and tumor manipulation, as well as hypovolemia, hypoxia, and hypercarbia.

6. Answer C (Ipratropium)

Ipratropium is the appropriate medication for managing bronchospasms in patients with carcinoid tumors. It is an anticholinergic bronchodilator that helps alleviate bronchospasm by blocking the muscarinic receptors in the airways. This leads to bronchodilation and improves the symptoms of wheezing and difficulty breathing. It is considered a safe choice for managing bronchospasms in patients with carcinoid tumors, unlike conventional drugs such as β2 adrenergic agonists, epinephrine, and theophylline, which can potentially stimulate the release of tumor mediators and worsen symptoms. Additionally, other measures like administering octreotide, corticosteroids, and antihistamines may also be used to effectively manage bronchospasms during a carcinoid crisis.

Recommended literature

1. Kaltsas G, Caplin M, Davies P, et al. ENETS Consensus Guidelines for the Standards of Care in Neuroendocrine Tumors: Pre- and Perioperative Therapy in Patients with Neuroendocrine Tumors. Neuroendocrinology. 2017;105(3):245-254.
2. Powell B, Al Mukhtar A, Mills GH. Carcinoid: the disease and its implications for anaesthesia. Continuing Education in Anaesthesia Critical Care & Pain. 2011;11(1):9-13.
3. Mancuso K, Kaye AD, Boudreaux JP, et al. Carcinoid syndrome and perioperative anesthetic considerations. J Clin Anesth. 2011;23(4):329-341.

Endocrinology
CUSHING'S SYNDROME

05
CHAPTER

Questions:

1. What is the primary hormone involved in the development of Cushing's syndrome?

   A. Insulin

   B. Glucagon

   C. Cortisol

   D. Thyroid hormone

2. Which of the following is NOT a common symptom of Cushing's syndrome?

   A. Moon face

   B. Buffalo hump

   C. Purple striae

   D. Thickened skin

3. What is the characteristic appearance of patients with Cushing's syndrome?

   A. Generalized obesity

   B. Apple-shaped obesity

   C. Central obesity with thin extremities

   D. Peripheral obesity with a thin central body

4. Which medication can be used to inhibit the release and synthesis of glucocorticoids in the management of Cushing's syndrome?

   A. Insulin

   B. Metformin

   C. Ketoconazole

   D. Aspirin

5. Perioperative hyperglycemia in patients with Cushing's syndrome is often managed with insulin infusion.

   A. True

   B. False

6. A 62-year-old female patient with a known history of Cushing's syndrome secondary to an adrenal adenoma underwent successful surgical removal of the adenoma. The patient presents with central obesity, moon face, and thin extremities. She is now scheduled for an elective laparoscopic cholecystectomy. The patient is currently on long-term cortisol substitution therapy. The patient's blood pressure is well-controlled with antihypertensive medication. Which of the following anesthetic considerations should be made for this patient?

   A. Possible difficult airway

   B. Hypokalemic metabolic alkalosis

   C. Perioperative steroid replacement

   D. All of the above

Answers:

1. **Answer C (Cortisol)**

   Cortisol is the primary hormone involved in the development of Cushing's syndrome. Cushing's syndrome is characterized by prolonged exposure to high levels of glucocorticoids, particularly cortisol. Cortisol is a steroid hormone produced by the adrenal glands and plays a crucial role in regulating various processes in the body, including metabolism, immune response, and stress response. In Cushing's syndrome, there is an excess production of cortisol, either due to excessive secretion of adrenocorticotropic hormone (ACTH) by the pituitary gland (Cushing's disease) or due to tumors in the adrenal glands themselves (adrenal Cushing's) or other parts of the body (ectopic Cushing's). The excess cortisol leads to the signs and symptoms associated with Cushing's syndrome.

2. **Answer D (Thickened skin)**

   Thickened skin is not a common symptom of Cushing's syndrome. In fact, individuals with Cushing's syndrome often have thin, fragile skin that bruises easily. Individuals with Cushing's syndrome typically present with symptoms such as moon face, buffalo hump, and purple striae.

3. **Answer C (Central obesity with thin extremities)**

   Patients with Cushing's syndrome typically exhibit a characteristic appearance of central obesity with thin extremities. This refers to the accumulation of fat in the central body regions, such as the abdomen and trunk, while the arms and legs may appear relatively thin. This pattern of fat distribution is often referred to as "central obesity with thin extremities" or "truncal obesity." It is a result of the metabolic effects of excess cortisol, which can lead to fat accumulation in the abdominal area while causing muscle wasting in the extremities.

4. **Answer C (Ketoconazole)**

   Ketoconazole is primarily known as an antifungal agent but has also been found to inhibit steroid synthesis, including the production of cortisol. It is used as an adrenal enzyme inhibitor in the management of Cushing's syndrome. By blocking the enzyme cytochrome P450 11B1, which is involved in cortisol production, ketoconazole helps reduce cortisol levels in the body and control the symptoms of Cushing's syndrome. Additionally, other adrenal enzyme inhibitors like metyrapone, mitotane, and aminoglutethimide can be utilized for similar purposes in the management of Cushing's syndrome.

5. **Answer A (True)**

   Perioperative hyperglycemia in patients with Cushing's syndrome is often managed with insulin infusion. Maintaining optimal glycemic control is important to prevent complications associated with hyperglycemia, such as impaired wound healing and increased risk of infection. Insulin infusion helps regulate blood glucose levels and allows for tight glycemic control during the perioperative period. Regular monitoring of blood glucose levels and adjustment of insulin infusion rates are performed to maintain glucose within recommended ranges for optimal patient outcomes.

6. **Answer D (All of the above)**

   When considering the anesthetic management of a patient with Cushing's syndrome, multiple considerations should be taken into account. Patients with Cushing's syndrome may have characteristic physical features such as a moon face, fat deposition in the neck area, and reduced neck mobility, which can make intubation challenging. Assessing the airway before anesthesia induction and having appropriate airway management plans are crucial. Cushing's syndrome can lead to excessive cortisol levels, which can cause electrolyte imbalances, including hypokalemia and metabolic alkalosis. These imbalances should be identified and managed appropriately during the perioperative period. Patients on long-term cortisol substitution therapy will require perioperative adjustments in their steroid replacement regimen. In such cases, perioperative steroid replacement may be necessary to prevent adrenal insufficiency and maintain physiological cortisol levels during surgery and the immediate postoperative period.

Recommended literature

1. Melanie Davies, FRCA, Jonathan Hardman, DM FRCA, Anaesthesia and adrenocortical disease, Continuing Education in Anaesthesia Critical Care & Pain, Volume 5, Issue 4, August 2005, Pages 122–126, https://doi.org/10.1093/bjaceaccp/mki033.
2. Domi R, Sula H, Kaci M, Paparisto S, Bodeci A, Xhemali A. Anesthetic considerations on adrenal gland surgery. J Clin Med Res. 2015;7(1):1-7.

DIABETES INSIPIDUS

Questions:

1. **Which of the following statements about Diabetes insipidus (DI) is true?**
   A. DI is a common perioperative complication
   B. DI is associated with decreased release of antidiuretic hormone
   C. DI can be effectively managed with fluid restriction
   D. DI is primarily caused by surgical manipulation

2. **What is the cause of nephrogenic diabetes?**
   A. Familial or genetic causes
   B. Use of Lithium
   C. High blood sugar
   D. All of the above

3. **What is the main treatment for central DI?**
   A. Thiazide diuretics
   B. Desmopressin
   C. Fluid restriction
   D. Aspirin

4. **What is the recommended treatment for nephrogenic DI?**
   A. Desmopressin (DDAVP)
   B. Thiazide diuretics
   C. Fluid restriction
   D. Spironolactone

5. **Polyuria and polydipsia are the most common symptoms of DI.**
   A. True
   B. False

6. **A 65-year-old male is admitted to the ICU after undergoing extensive cardiac bypass surgery. He is intubated, mechanically ventilated, and sedated, with stable hemodynamics. Over the past four hours, the nursing staff has observed a polyuria of 500 ml per hour, despite signs of hypovolemia. Laboratory evaluation reveals a urine specific gravity of less than 1.010 and a urine osmolality of less than 100 mOsm/kg. Additionally, the patient's serum sodium and plasma osmolality are elevated. What anesthetic medication is the associated agent in the majority of case reports of transient DI or polyuria?**
   A. Dexmedetomidine
   B. Propofol
   C. Rocuronium
   D. Midazolam

Answers:

1. Answer B (DI is associated with decreased release of antidiuretic hormone)

Diabetes insipidus (DI) is a disorder characterized by the inability to concentrate urine due to either a lack of antidiuretic hormone (ADH) production (central DI) or the kidneys' insensitivity to ADH (nephrogenic DI). Central DI is the most common form and is caused by a decrease in the production or release of ADH from the hypothalamus or pituitary gland. This results in polyuria and polydipsia as the body tries to compensate for the loss of water. Treatment typically involves replacing ADH or addressing the underlying cause, depending on the type of DI.

2. Answer D (All of the above)

Nephrogenic DI can be caused by familial or genetic factors, specifically mutations in the AQP2 gene that codes for the aquaporin-2 protein, leading to a lack of response to ADH. It can also be caused by metabolic issues such as high blood sugar, high blood calcium, and low potassium levels. Additionally, the use of certain drugs like lithium, often used to treat bipolar disorder, can decrease the expression of aquaporin-2, contributing to nephrogenic DI. Various diseases affecting the kidneys, such as amyloidosis, obstructive uropathy, chronic kidney disease, and polycystic kidney disease, can also lead to nephrogenic DI.

3. Answer B (Desmopressin)

The main treatment for central DI is desmopressin (DDAVP). Desmopressin is a synthetic form of ADH that helps reduce urine output and relieve thirst in individuals with central DI. It works by increasing water reabsorption in the kidneys, thus reducing the amount of urine produced.

4. Answer B (Thiazide diuretics)

The recommended treatment for nephrogenic DI includes thiazide diuretics, which help reduce urine volume by increasing sodium and water reabsorption in the kidneys. Thiazides are often used in combination with amiloride to reduce the risk of hypokalemia associated with thiazide use. Additionally, fluid replacement and reduced solute load are part of the management strategy for nephrogenic DI. DDAVP, which is used to treat central DI, is not effective in nephrogenic DI because the kidneys are unable to respond to ADH. Spironolactone, a potassium-sparing diuretic, is not typically used in the treatment of DI.

5. Answer A (True)

Polyuria (excessive urination) and polydipsia (excessive thirst) are indeed the most common symptoms of DI. These symptoms occur due to the inability of the kidneys to concentrate urine, leading to the excretion of large amounts of dilute urine, which then triggers the sensation of thirst. Other symptoms can include nocturia (frequent urination at night), craving for ice water, fatigue, and dehydration. It's important to note that while polyuria and polydipsia are common in DI, they are not exclusive to this condition and can occur in other disorders as well.

6. Answer A (Dexmedetomidine)

DI is a rare but potential complication of anesthesia or sedation, which may be overlooked, and therefore diagnosis and appropriate treatment may be delayed. Dexmedetomidine has been identified as the associated agent in the majority of case reports when transient DI or polyuria is present. Various mechanisms have been proposed for how dexmedetomidine and other anesthetic agents can lead to DI. Dexmedetomidine, a highly selective, short-acting alpha-2 agonist, has been shown in animal studies to decrease both central arginine vasopressin (AVP) release and peripheral nephrogenic response to AVP, resulting in a diuretic response. While this polyuric response has not been definitively demonstrated in human studies, a growing number of case reports suggest a link between dexmedetomidine use and DI. These reports include both continuous infusions for several hours and single-loading doses. Other anesthetic agents, such as sevoflurane, ketamine, and propofol, have also been implicated in causing DI, although they are less frequently reported compared to dexmedetomidine. These agents may affect AVP release or renal function through different mechanisms.

Recommended literature

1. Mutter CM, Smith T, Menze O, Zakharia M, Nguyen H. Diabetes Insipidus: Pathogenesis, Diagnosis, and Clinical Management. Cureus. 2021;13(2):e13523.
2. Dharshan AC, Kohli-Seth R. Chapter 117. Diabetes Insipidus. In: Atchabahian A, Gupta R. eds. The Anesthesia Guide. McGraw Hill; 2013. Accessed January 17, 2023.

Endocrinology
DIABETIC KETOACIDOSIS

Questions:

1. **What is the primary mechanism of diabetic ketoacidosis (DKA) leading to metabolic acidosis?**
   A. Decreased gluconeogenesis
   B. Increased insulin secretion
   C. Enhanced lipolysis
   D. Decreased ketone production

2. **Which statement about DKA is true?**
   A. It is more common in patients with type 2 diabetes
   B. It is characterized by hypoglycemia
   C. It does not lead to metabolic acidosis
   D. It is triggered by an insulin deficiency

3. **Which of the following is a potential trigger for DKA?**
   A. Hypothyroidism
   B. Appendicitis
   C. Hypocalcemia
   D. Vitamin B12 deficiency

4. **Which electrolyte should be closely monitored and replaced in patients with DKA?**
   A. Sodium
   B. Calcium
   C. Potassium
   D. Magnesium

5. **Bicarbonate administration should be considered if the pH is < 7.15.**
   A. True
   B. False

6. **A 16-year-old female patient presents to the emergency department with a history of type 1 diabetes mellitus for seven years. She complains of nausea, vomiting, and shortness of breath over the past two days. On examination, her vital signs include a respiratory rate of 26 breaths per minute and a pulse rate of 112 beats per minute. She appears dehydrated, with sunken eyes and a dry mouth. Laboratory investigations reveal markedly elevated blood glucose levels at 500 mg/dL (27.8 mmol/l) and arterial blood gas analysis showing a pH of 7.250, pCO_2 of 35.3 mm Hg, base deficit of -14, and HCO_3 of 14.9. Urine ketones are measured at 3+, consistent with metabolic acidosis in DKA. All other laboratory investigations are within normal limits. There are no signs of infection on systemic examination. The patient was diagnosed with DKA, and she was promptly initiated on IV fluids, insulin therapy, and electrolyte replacement by established DKA management protocols. What is the initial recommended fluid bolus for a patient with DKA who is clinically hypovolemic?**
   A. 250 mL of 0.9% saline
   B. 500 mL of 0.9% saline
   C. 750 mL of 0.9% saline
   D. 1500 mL of 0.9% saline

Answers:

1. **Answer C (Enhanced lipolysis)**

Diabetic ketoacidosis (DKA) is a potentially life-threatening complication of diabetes mellitus. It results from a relative or absolute insulin deficiency with an excess of hyperglycemic hormones (i.e., glucagon, catecholamines, cortisol, and growth hormone) leading to hyperglycemia because of increased gluconeogenesis, accelerated glycogenolysis, and impaired glucose use by peripheral tissues. In the absence of sufficient insulin, cells cannot take up glucose, so the body begins breaking down fat for energy, leading to lipolysis and the synthesis of ketoacids. These ketoacids, such as acetoacetate and beta-hydroxybutyrate, accumulate in the blood, leading to metabolic acidosis.

2. **Answer D (It is triggered by an insulin deficiency)**

DKA is more common in patients with type 1 diabetes, although it can occur in patients with type 2 diabetes under certain circumstances. It is characterized by hyperglycemia, not hypoglycemia, and it leads to metabolic acidosis due to the accumulation of ketoacids. DKA is triggered by an insulin deficiency, often due to missed insulin doses in patients with diabetes.

3. **Answer B (Appendicitis)**

DKA can be triggered by various factors, including infection or inflammation, such as appendicitis, pneumonia, urinary tract infection (UTI), or foot ulcer. Other triggers include inadequate insulin administration, myocardial infarction, stroke, certain medications (e.g., steroids, cocaine), pregnancy, and trauma. These triggers can lead to an increase in counterregulatory hormones (e.g., glucagon, cortisol, catecholamines) and a subsequent decrease in insulin, leading to hyperglycemia and ketoacidosis in individuals with diabetes.

4. **Answer C (Potassium)**

In patients with DKA, potassium should be closely monitored and replaced as needed. Insulin therapy can lead to an intracellular shift of potassium, potentially causing hypokalemia if left uncorrected. The goal is to maintain a potassium level of 4–5 mEq/L, irrespective of the initial level. Potassium replacement typically involves administering 10-15 mEq/h for at least the first 4 hours. Additionally, magnesium and phosphate levels should also be monitored and replaced as necessary.

5. **Answer B (False)**

Bicarbonate administration should generally not be considered for the management of DKA, even if the pH is < 7.15. Acidosis in DKA typically corrects itself with insulin treatment. Bicarbonate administration is only recommended in severe cases of acidosis (pH < 7.0) or in the presence of hemodynamic instability, which is rare. The decision to use bicarbonate should be made cautiously, as it can lead to complications such as paradoxical cerebrospinal fluid acidosis and hypokalemia.

6. **Answer D (1500 mL of 0.9% saline)**

Patients with DKA are consistently dehydrated, with an average free water deficit of about 100 mL/kg of body weight. Intravenous (IV) fluid therapy in DKA helps expand intravascular volume, improve renal perfusion, and reduce peripheral insulin resistance by lowering levels of counter-regulatory hormones, ultimately leading to a reduction in blood glucose levels. The initial recommended fluid replacement in DKA is 0.9% sodium chloride (normal saline) at a rate of 15–20 ml/kg (approximately 1000–1500 mL) over the first hour. Subsequent fluid management is based on an ongoing assessment of the patient's clinical condition. For patients with mild or moderate hypovolemia, 0.9% sodium chloride is given at a rate of 500 ml/h for 4 hours, followed by 250–500 ml/h, depending on the clinical condition. Once hypovolemia is corrected, the type of IV fluids is determined by the level of corrected serum sodium. If the level is low (< 135 mmol/L), 0.9% sodium chloride is continued; if normal or high (≥ 135 mmol/L), IV fluids should be changed to 0.45% sodium chloride. Once blood glucose reaches ≤ 11.1 mmol/L (200 mg/dL), 5% dextrose should be added along with 0.45% sodium chloride at a rate of 150–250 ml/h to maintain blood glucose concentration at 8.3–11.1 mmol/L (150–200 mg/dL).

Recommended literature

1. Levy N, Penfold NW, Dhatariya K. Perioperative management of the patient with diabetes requiring emergency surgery. BJA Education. 2017;17(4):129-136.
2. Hallet A, Modi A, Levy N. Developments in the management of diabetic ketoacidosis in adults: implications for anaesthetists. BJA Education. 2016;16(1):8-14.
3. Patel K, Kohli-Seth R. Chapter 210. Diabetic Ketoacidosis. In: Atchabahian A, Gupta R. eds. The Anesthesia Guide. McGraw Hill; 2013. Accessed January 17, 2023.

DIABETES MELLITUS TYPE 2

Questions:

1. Which of the following is a characteristic of diabetes mellitus type 2?
    A. Increased insulin secretion by pancreatic β-cells
    B. Ketosis-prone condition
    C. Onset typically occurs during childhood
    D. Preservation of insulin sensitivity

2. Which of the following medications should be used with caution in patients with diabetes mellitus type 2 due to its potential to exacerbate insulin resistance?
    A. Sulphonylureas
    B. Biguanides
    C. Thiazolidinediones
    D. Dexamethasone

3. Which of the following complications is NOT commonly associated with diabetes mellitus type 2?
    A. Diabetic retinopathy
    B. Diabetic neuropathy
    C. Diabetic ketoacidosis
    D. Diabetic nephropathy

4. What is the effect of carbohydrate loading before surgery?
    A. Increased insulin resistance
    B. Decreased blood glucose levels
    C. Improved wound healing
    D. Counteraction of insulin resistance

5. Anesthesia influences glucose response during surgery.
    A. True
    B. False

6. A 62-year-old woman with a history of type 2 diabetes is scheduled for total knee replacement surgery due to severe osteoarthritis. The patient has been taking a combination of metformin and sulfonylurea for her diabetes management. Preoperative laboratory investigations reveal a fasting glucose level of 150 mg/dL (8.3 mmol/L) and an HbA1c of 7.2%. The patient is scheduled to receive general anesthesia for the procedure. On the morning of the surgery, the patient's blood glucose level is 200 mg/dL (11.1 mmol/L). What is the most appropriate course of action regarding the patient's antidiabetic medications on the morning of the surgery?
    A. Continue the usual dose of metformin
    B. Continue the usual dose of sulfonylurea
    C. Continue the usual doses of both metformin and sulfonylurea
    D. Initiate insulin therapy according to a sliding scale

Answers:

1. **Answer D (Preservation of insulin sensitivity)**

   Diabetes mellitus type 2 is characterized by the preservation of insulin secretion by pancreatic β-cells but a reduced response of target tissues (such as muscle, liver, and adipose tissue) to insulin, known as insulin resistance. Insulin resistance results in impaired glucose uptake and utilization, leading to elevated blood glucose levels. In contrast to diabetes mellitus type 1, which is characterized by autoimmune destruction of pancreatic β-cells and absolute insulin deficiency, type 2 diabetes involves a combination of insulin resistance and relative insulin deficiency. Although the pancreatic β-cells continue to produce insulin, the body's tissues become less responsive to its effects.

2. **Answer D (Dexamethasone)**

   Dexamethasone, a corticosteroid medication, should be used with caution in patients with diabetes mellitus type 2 due to its potential to exacerbate insulin resistance. Corticosteroids can impair glucose metabolism and increase insulin resistance, leading to elevated blood glucose levels. This can worsen glycemic control in individuals with diabetes and potentially require adjustments to their diabetes management plan. Therefore, careful monitoring of blood glucose levels and potential adjustments to diabetes medications or insulin dosages may be necessary when using dexamethasone in patients with diabetes mellitus type 2.

3. **Answer C (Diabetic ketoacidosis)**

   Diabetic ketoacidosis (DKA) is less common in type 2 diabetics compared to type 1 diabetics because these patients are thought to be insulin resistant rather than insulin deficient. In type 2 diabetes, there is usually some level of endogenous insulin production, which helps prevent the development of DKA.

4. **Answer D (Counteraction of insulin resistance)**

   Carbohydrate loading before surgery has been shown to counteract insulin resistance. The stress of surgery and anesthesia can lead to impaired insulin action, resulting in elevated blood glucose levels and increased insulin resistance. By providing a high carbohydrate load before surgery, the body's glycogen stores are replenished, leading to improved insulin sensitivity and glucose utilization. Carbohydrate loading before surgery helps to provide a readily available energy source and reduces the need for the body to rely on protein breakdown for energy. This can help preserve muscle mass and prevent catabolism during the perioperative period. By counteracting insulin resistance, carbohydrate loading can contribute to better glycemic control and reduce the risk of perioperative hyperglycemia.

5. **Answer A (True)**

   Anesthesia does influence glucose response during surgery. The stress of surgery and anesthesia can lead to physiological changes, including elevated blood glucose levels and impaired insulin action. Anesthesia can affect glucose metabolism through various mechanisms, such as increasing the release of stress hormones like epinephrine and cortisol, which can lead to insulin resistance and elevated blood glucose levels. Additionally, certain anesthetic agents and techniques, such as the use of certain inhalation agents or intravenous medications, can directly affect glucose metabolism. These agents can either increase or decrease blood glucose levels, depending on their specific effects on insulin secretion, insulin sensitivity, or hepatic glucose production.

6. **Answer D (Initiate insulin therapy according to a sliding scale)**

   The most appropriate course of action, in this case, is to initiate insulin therapy according to a sliding scale. In this case, the patient's fasting blood glucose level on the morning of the surgery is elevated, indicating suboptimal glycemic control. Given the need for surgery and the potential stress response during the procedure, it is crucial to achieve tight glycemic control to minimize perioperative complications. Continuing the usual doses of both metformin and/or sulfonylurea poses a risk of both lactic acidosis and hypoglycemia. Hence, it is not recommended during the perioperative period. Initiating insulin therapy according to a sliding scale allows for precise control of blood glucose levels during the perioperative period. Insulin therapy can be adjusted based on frequent blood glucose monitoring to maintain glycemic targets and prevent hyperglycemia and hypoglycemia.

Recommended literature

1. Pollard BJ, Kitchen, G. Handbook of Clinical Anaesthesia. Fourth Edition. CRC Press. 2018. 978-1-4987-6289-2.
2. Pontes JPJ, Mendes FF, Vasconcelos MM, Batista NR. Avaliação e manejo perioperatório de pacientes com diabetes melito. Um desafio para o anestesiologista [Evaluation and perioperative management of patients with diabetes mellitus. A challenge for the anesthesiologist]. Braz J Anesthesiol. 2018;68(1):75-86.
3. Cornelius BW. Patients With Type 2 Diabetes: Anesthetic Management in the Ambulatory Setting: Part 2: Pharmacology and Guidelines for Perioperative Management. Anesth Prog. 2017;64(1):39-44.
4. Stubbs, D.J., Levy, N., Dhatariya, K., 2017. Diabetes medication pharmacology. BJA Education 17, 198–207.
5. Nicholson G, Hall GM. 2011. Diabetes and adult surgical inpatients. Continuing Education in Anaesthesia Critical CAre & Pain. 11;6:234-238.
6. Robertshaw HJ, Hall GM. Diabetes mellitus: anaesthetic management [published correction appears in Anaesthesia. 2007 Jan;62(1):100]. Anaesthesia. 2006;61(12):1187-1190.
7. McAnulty GR, Robertshaw HJ, Hall GM. Anaesthetic management of patients with diabetes mellitus. Br J Anaesth. 2000;85(1):80-90.

Endocrinology
EUGLYCEMIC DIABETIC KETOACIDOSIS

Questions:

1. Which of the following is a characteristic feature of euglycemic diabetic ketoacidosis (EDKA)?

   A. Hyperglycemia

   B. Hypoglycemia

   C. Euglycemia

   D. All of the above

2. Which of the following hormones plays a significant role in the pathophysiology of EDKA?

   A. Insulin

   B. Glucagon

   C. Growth hormone

   D. Aldosterone

3. What is the primary cause of the increased ketone bodies seen in EDKA?

   A. Excessive dietary fat intake

   B. Impaired renal function

   C. Insulin deficiency

   D. Decreased glucagon secretion

4. Which of the following is NOT a common etiology of EDKA?

   A. Alcohol use

   B. Glycogen storage disorders

   C. Hyperglycemia

   D. Pregnancy

5. Sodium-glucose cotransporter 2 (SGLT2) inhibitors are a class of medications associated with an increased risk of EDKA.

   A. True

   B. False

6. A 44-year-old man with type 2 diabetes presented to the emergency department with malaise, fatigue, heartburn, and decreased exercise capacity. He had been taking sitagliptin, empagliflozin, and metformin for 2 years. Symptoms began 4 days earlier, coinciding with a switch to a ketogenic diet. On examination, he appeared lethargic and dehydrated. Laboratory tests showed sodium 132 mmol/L, potassium 5.5 mmol/L, serum bicarbonate 9 mmol/L, anion gap 24 mmol/L, serum glucose 150 mg/dL, and β-hydroxybutyrate 8.89 mmol/L. Urine tests revealed ketones 150 mg/dL and urine glucose 1,000 mg/dL. Arterial blood gas showed a pH of 7.11, pCO_2 < 19 mmHg, pO_2 105 mmHg, and bicarbonate 8.2 mmol/L. Admitted with suspected EDKA, he received D5/0.45% sodium chloride with 20 mEq potassium chloride at 250 mL/hour. What is the next step in the management of EDKA?

   A. Fluid restriction

   B. Insulin therapy

   C. Potassium supplementation

   D. Serum albumin therapy

Answers:

1. Answer C (Euglycemia)

Diabetic ketoacidosis (DKA) is traditionally defined by the triad of hyperglycemia (> 250 mg/dL or > 13.9 mmol/L), anion-gap acidosis, and increased plasma ketones. Euglycemic DKA (EDKA) is defined as DKA without marked hyperglycemia, which means blood glucose levels are within the normal range up to no significant hyperglycemia (less than 250 mg/dL or 13.9 mmol/L). This is in contrast to typical DKA, where hyperglycemia is a hallmark feature. Despite normal blood glucose levels, patients with EDKA exhibit severe metabolic acidosis (arterial pH less than 7.3, serum bicarbonate less than 18 mEq/L) and ketonemia. EDKA is a severe and life-threatening complication of diabetes mellitus that can occur in various conditions.

2. Answer B (Glucagon)

A relative deficiency of insulin and excess of counter-regulatory hormones such as glucagon characterizes EDKA. The increased glucagon/insulin ratio leads to increased lipolysis, free fatty acids, and ketoacidosis. Other hormones, such as epinephrine and cortisol, also contribute to the pathophysiology of EDKA, but glucagon plays a significant role in promoting ketogenesis in this condition.

3. Answer C (Insulin deficiency)

The primary cause of the increased ketone bodies seen in EDKA is insulin deficiency. In EDKA, there is a relative deficiency of insulin, which leads to increased lipolysis and subsequent production of ketone bodies. This is in contrast to typical DKA, where absolute or severe insulin deficiency leads to hyperglycemia and ketosis. In EDKA, despite normal blood glucose levels, insufficient insulin results in ketosis and metabolic acidosis.

4. Answer C (Hyperglycemia)

Hyperglycemia is not a common etiology of EDKA, as the hallmark of EDKA is euglycemia (blood glucose levels within the normal range). EDKA can occur in various conditions such as starvation, alcohol use, glycogen storage disorders, pregnancy, and the use of certain medications like sodium-glucose cotransporter 2 (SGLT2) inhibitors. Despite normal or slightly elevated blood glucose levels, patients with EDKA exhibit severe metabolic acidosis and ketonemia.

5. Answer A (True)

SGLT2 inhibitors are a class of medications associated with an increased risk of EDKA. SGLT2 inhibitors work by inhibiting glucose reabsorption in the proximal renal tubules, leading to glycosuria. This glycosuria results in diminished insulin production and elevated plasma glucagon concentrations, which can contribute to the development of EDKA. It is important to monitor patients on SGLT2 inhibitors for signs and symptoms of EDKA, even in the absence of marked hyperglycemia.

6. Answer B (Insulin therapy)

The next step in the management of EDKA is insulin therapy. Insulin helps to reverse ketosis by promoting glucose uptake and inhibiting lipolysis and ketogenesis. In this case, the patient was started on insulin therapy along with intravenous fluids containing dextrose to avoid hypoglycemia. The initial standard regular insulin dosage of the drip was decreased based on glycemia. No additional potassium supplementation was required based on his admission potassium level. The main difference in therapy for euglycemic DKA versus ordinary DKA is the type of IV fluids provided and the insulin dosage administered. Patients with EDKA are typically started on D5/0.45% sodium chloride with potassium chloride to avoid hypoglycemia and hasten the clearance of ketosis. Insulin infusion should be started at a rate contingent on glycemia levels and carefully monitored along with fluid and electrolyte status.

Recommended literature

1. Nasa P, Chaudhary S, Shrivastava PK, Singh A. Euglycemic diabetic ketoacidosis: A missed diagnosis. World J Diabetes. 2021;12(5):514-523.
2. Thiruvenkatarajan, V., Meyer, E.J., Nanjappa, N., Van Wijk, R.M., Jesudason, D., 2019. Perioperative diabetic ketoacidosis associated with sodium-glucose co-transporter-2 inhibitors: a systematic review. British Journal of Anaesthesia 123, 27–36.
3. Rawla, P., Vellipuram, A.R., Bandaru, S.S., Pradeep Raj, J., 2017. Euglycemic diabetic ketoacidosis: a diagnostic and therapeutic dilemma. Endocrinology, Diabetes & Metabolism Case Reports 2017.
4. Modi A, Agrawal A, Morgan F. Euglycemic Diabetic Ketoacidosis: A Review. Curr Diabetes Rev. 2017;13(3):315-321.

Endocrinology
HYPERALDOSTERONISM

05
CHAPTER

Questions:

1. **Which of the following hormones is overproduced in hyperaldosteronism?**

   A. Cortisol

   B. Insulin

   C. Aldosterone

   D. Thyroxine

2. **What is the primary cause of secondary hyperaldosteronism?**

   A. Overactive renin-angiotensin-aldosterone system (RAAS)

   B. Congestive heart failure

   C. Adrenal gland tumor

   D. Renal artery stenosis

3. **Which of the following is not a symptom of hyperaldosteronism?**

   A. Hypertension

   B. Muscle weakness

   C. Hyperkalemia

   D. Polyuria

4. **Which diuretic is commonly used as an aldosterone antagonist in the treatment of hyperaldosteronism?**

   A. Furosemide

   B. Hydrochlorothiazide

   C. Spironolactone

   D. Acetazolamide

5. **Atrial fibrillation and left ventricular hypertrophy are complications seen in hyperaldosteronism.**

   A. True

   B. False

6. **A 60-year-old man presents to the clinic with uncontrolled hypertension and muscle weakness. He states that he feels tired and has noticed increased thirst and frequent urination. On physical examination, his blood pressure is elevated, and he appears dehydrated. Laboratory tests reveal hypokalemia (low potassium levels) and metabolic alkalosis (imbalance in blood pH). The patient's medical history is unremarkable. Upon further inquiry, his wife mentions that lately, he has been consuming more licorice sweets. The most likely cause of symptoms in this patient is?**

   A. Adrenal gland tumor

   B. Renal artery stenosis

   C. Overactive renin-angiotensin-aldosterone system (RAAS)

   D. Excessive intake of licorice

Answers:

1. Answer C (Aldosterone)

Hyperaldosteronism is characterized by the overproduction of aldosterone, a hormone the adrenal glands produce. Aldosterone plays a crucial role in regulating blood pressure by controlling the levels of sodium and potassium in the blood. Excessive production of aldosterone leads to increased sodium reabsorption and potassium excretion, resulting in hypertension and hypokalemia.

2. Answer A (Overactive renin-angiotensin-aldosterone system (RAAS))

Secondary hyperaldosteronism is characterized by the overproduction of aldosterone due to an overactive renin-angiotensin-aldosterone system (RAAS). The RAAS is a complex hormonal system regulating blood pressure and fluid balance. Various conditions can lead to an overactive RAAS, such as renal artery stenosis, congestive heart failure, cirrhosis of the liver, or kidney diseases. These conditions result in decreased blood flow to the kidneys or other mechanisms that stimulate the release of renin, initiating the RAAS cascade and subsequent aldosterone production. Therefore, the primary cause of secondary hyperaldosteronism is an overactive renin-angiotensin-aldosterone system.

3. Answer C (Hyperkalemia)

Hyperkalemia is not a symptom of hyperaldosteronism. In hyperaldosteronism, the excessive production of aldosterone causes increased excretion of potassium in the urine, leading to hypokalemia. The symptoms associated with hyperaldosteronism include hypertension, headache, dizziness, vision changes, difficulty breathing, fluid and electrolyte imbalances (such as hypokalemia), muscle weakness, muscle spasm, tingling and numbness, fatigue, polydipsia, polyuria, hypernatremia, hypermagnesemia, metabolic alkalosis, and volume depletion.

4. Answer C (Spironolactone)

Spironolactone is a diuretic commonly used as an aldosterone antagonist in treating hyperaldosteronism. It belongs to the class of medications known as potassium-sparing diuretics. Spironolactone works by blocking the receptors to which aldosterone normally binds, preventing its effects. By acting as an aldosterone antagonist, spironolactone helps to counteract the excessive effects of aldosterone, such as sodium retention and potassium excretion, which can contribute to hypertension and electrolyte imbalances seen in hyperaldosteronism.

5. Answer A (True)

The most common complications associated with hyperaldosteronism are primarily caused by hypertension, which is a characteristic feature of the condition. These complications include atrial fibrillation, left ventricular hypertrophy, heart attack, and stroke. These cardiovascular complications highlight the importance of managing and controlling blood pressure in individuals with hyperaldosteronism to prevent potential adverse outcomes.

6. Answer D (Excessive intake of licorice)

In this case, the patient's symptoms of uncontrolled hypertension, muscle weakness, fatigue, increased thirst, and frequent urination, along with the laboratory findings of hypokalemia and metabolic alkalosis, suggest a condition resembling primary hyperaldosteronism. However, the patient's medical history is unremarkable, making an adrenal gland tumor or renal artery stenosis less likely. The key clue, in this case, is the information provided by the patient's wife regarding his recent excessive intake of licorice sweets. Licorice contains a compound called glycyrrhizin, which inhibits the enzyme responsible for breaking down cortisol, resulting in increased cortisol levels. Elevated cortisol levels can mimic the effects of aldosterone, causing sodium retention and potassium excretion, leading to hypertension, hypokalemia, and metabolic alkalosis. Therefore, in this patient, the most likely cause of the symptoms resembling primary hyperaldosteronism is the excessive intake of licorice. It is important to consider dietary factors and medication history to identify potential causes of secondary hyperaldosteronism-like symptoms and provide appropriate management for the patient.

Recommended literature

1. Domi R, Sula H, Kaci M, Paparisto S, Bodeci A, Xhemali A. Anesthetic considerations on adrenal gland surgery. J Clin Med Res. 2015;7(1):1-7.
2. Jano A, Domi R, Berdica L, et al. Anaesthetic considerations of Conn syndrome: a case presentation and mini-review the anaesthesiologist and Conn syndrome. Clin Med Res 2014;3(5):132-135.
3. Davies M, Hardman J. Anaesthesia and adrenocortical disease. Continuing Education in Anaesthesia, Critical Care & Pain. 2005;5(4):122-126.

Endocrinology
HYPERCAPNIA

Questions:

1. Which underlying pathology is NOT associated with hypercapnia?
   A. Chronic obstructive pulmonary disease (COPD)
   B. Asthma exacerbation
   C. Diabetic ketoacidosis
   D. Hyperventilation syndrome

2. Which of the following conditions is NOT a potential cause of hypercapnia?
   A. Obesity-hypoventilation syndrome
   B. Myxedema
   C. Polyneuropathy
   D. Pneumothorax

3. Which of the following conditions can lead to increased metabolic CO_2 production?
   A. Hypothyroidism
   B. Exercise
   C. Hypothermia
   D. Decreased catabolism in sepsis

4. What is the primary treatment for hypercapnia in patients with acute exacerbation of chronic obstructive pulmonary disease (COPD)?
   A. Sodium bicarbonate administration
   B. Anticoagulants
   C. Non-invasive ventilation
   D. Antibiotic therapy

5. Prone position ventilation in critically ill ventilated patients decreases hypercapnia.
   A. True
   B. False

6. A 60-year-old female patient with no significant medical history is undergoing laparoscopic cholecystectomy. The patient weighs 60 kg, and the ventilator settings include volume-controlled ventilation with a tidal volume (TV) of 400 mL and a respiratory rate of 14 breaths per minute. Positive end-expiratory pressure (PEEP) is set at 5 cmH_2O, and the plateau pressure is measured as 16 cmH_2O. The patient's oxygen saturation (SpO_2) is 100%, and vital signs remain stable throughout the procedure. However, the capnography monitor shows an end-tidal carbon dioxide ($ETCO_2$) level of 52 mmHg and an inspired CO_2 of 10 mmHg. Based on the capnography findings, what should be done next?
   A. Administer bronchodilators
   B. Increase the respiratory rate
   C. Reduce the intra-abdominal pressure
   D. Replace the soda lime absorbent

Answers:

1. Answer D (Hyperventilation syndrome)

Hyperventilation syndrome is not associated with hypercapnia. Hyperventilation syndrome leads to hypocapnia due to the excessive elimination of carbon dioxide. However, chronic obstructive pulmonary disease (COPD), asthma exacerbation, and diabetic ketoacidosis are associated with hypercapnia due to their effects on respiration and gas exchange.

2. Answer D (Pneumothorax)

Pneumothorax primarily impacts gas exchange, often leading to hypoxemia and respiratory distress. While it can trigger compensatory hyperventilation and result in hypocapnia, it does not directly cause hypercapnia. Hypocapnia can occur in various pulmonary diseases such as pneumonia, asthma, pneumothorax, pulmonary edema, and pulmonary embolism, as these conditions can cause hypoxemia, leading to compensatory hyperventilation and subsequent hypocapnia.

3. Answer B (Exercise)

The condition that can lead to increased metabolic CO_2 production is exercise. During exercise, increased physical activity raises metabolism and results in higher carbon dioxide production as a byproduct of increased cellular respiration. Hypothyroidism, hypothermia, and decreased catabolism in sepsis are not associated with increased metabolic CO_2 production.

4. Answer C (Non-invasive ventilation)

The primary treatment for hypercapnia caused by an acute exacerbation of COPD is non-invasive ventilation. Non-invasive ventilation, such as BiPAP or CPAP, can provide support to the respiratory system, improve ventilation, and assist in removing excess carbon dioxide. These interventions help to relieve respiratory distress, enhance gas exchange, and decrease carbon dioxide levels. While sodium bicarbonate administration, anticoagulants, and antibiotic therapy may have roles in certain aspects of COPD management (e.g., treating metabolic acidosis, preventing thromboembolic events, and managing infections), they are not the primary treatment for hypercapnia itself.

5. Answer A (True)

Prone position ventilation is a therapeutic approach used in critically ill ventilated patients to improve oxygenation and gas exchange. While its primary goal is to enhance oxygenation, it can also contribute to the reduction of hypercapnia. Prone position ventilation helps to redistribute ventilation and perfusion within the lungs, leading to improved matching of airflow and blood flow. This can enhance carbon dioxide elimination, thus decreasing hypercapnia. Additionally, the prone position can also improve lung mechanics and reduce the severity of ventilation-perfusion mismatch, further aiding in the reduction of hypercapnia.

6. Answer D (Replace the soda lime absorbent)

The capnography findings of an elevated end-tidal carbon dioxide (ETCO2) level of 50 mmHg and an elevated inspired carbon dioxide (ICO2) level of 10 mmHg suggest inadequate carbon dioxide elimination and potential rebreathing of carbon dioxide. In this case, the most appropriate action is to replace the soda lime absorbent. Soda lime is a commonly used absorbent in anesthesia machines that removes carbon dioxide from exhaled gases. Over time, the soda lime becomes exhausted and can fail to effectively remove carbon dioxide, leading to elevated ETCO2 levels. Replacing the soda lime absorbent ensures proper functioning and adequate removal of carbon dioxide during the procedure.

Recommended literature

1. Rawat D, Modi P, Sharma S. Hypercapnea. [Updated 2022 Jul 25]. In: StatPearls [Internet]. Treasure Island (FL): StatPearls Publishing; 2022 Jan-. Available from: https://www.ncbi.nlm.nih.gov/books/NBK500012/.
2. Tiruvoipati R, Gupta S, Pilcher D, Bailey M. Management of hypercapnia in critically ill mechanically ventilated patients-A narrative review of literature. J Intensive Care Soc. 2020;21(4):327-333.

HYPERGLYCEMIA

05
CHAPTER

Questions:

1. Which of the following is a symptom of hyperglycemia?

   A. Polyphagia

   B. Polydipsia

   C. Polyuria

   D. All of the above

2. What is the typical fasting blood glucose level indicative of hyperglycemia?

   A. Above 100 mg/dL (5,6 mmol/L)

   B. Above 125 mg/dL (6,9 mmol/L)

   C. Above 150 mg/dL (8,3 mmol/L)

   D. Above 200 mg/dL (11,1 mmol/L)

3. Which of the following medical conditions can cause hyperglycemia?

   A. Acromegaly

   B. Hypothyroidism

   C. Hypoparathyroidism

   D. Addison's disease

4. Which of the following medications is known to potentially cause hyperglycemia?

   A. Thiazide diuretics

   B. Alpha blockers

   C. ACE inhibitors

   D. Potassium-sparing diuretics

5. Untreated hyperglycemia can lead to ketoacidosis.

   A. True

   B. False

6. A 21-year-old male with a known history of type 1 diabetes presents to the emergency department with complaints of dry mouth, abdominal pain, nausea, vomiting, and shortness of breath. He reports feeling progressively unwell over the past 24 hours. On physical examination, his blood pressure is 130/80 mmHg, heart rate is 110 bpm, and respiratory rate is 30 breaths per minute. Laboratory tests reveal a blood glucose level of 400 mg/dL (22.2 mmol/L), the presence of ketones in the urine, and metabolic acidosis. What are the appropriate management strategies for this patient?

   A. Intravenous fluid resuscitation

   B. Insulin therapy

   C. Electrolyte replacement

   D. All of the above

Answers:

1. **Answer D (All of the above)**

   All of the listed options are symptoms of hyperglycemia. Polyphagia refers to increased hunger or excessive appetite, which can be a result of the body's inability to utilize glucose properly and meet its energy needs. Polydipsia refers to increased thirst, as high blood glucose levels can cause dehydration and trigger a greater need for fluid intake. Polyuria refers to increased urination, which occurs as the kidneys attempt to eliminate the excess glucose from the body through urine.

2. **Answer B (125 mg/dL (6.9 mmol/L))**

   A typical fasting blood glucose level above 125 mg/dL (6.9 mmol/L) is considered indicative of hyperglycemia. Fasting blood glucose refers to the measurement of blood glucose after an overnight fast and is an important diagnostic criterion for diabetes. A fasting blood glucose level of 125 mg/dL (6.9 mmol/L) or higher on two separate occasions is commonly used to diagnose diabetes.

3. **Answer A (Acromegaly)**

   Acromegaly is a medical condition caused by excessive growth hormone production, usually due to a benign tumor in the pituitary gland. Excess growth hormone (GH) in acromegaly stimulates gluconeogenesis and lipolysis, leading to hyperglycemia and elevated free fatty acid levels. GH also causes both hepatic and peripheral insulin resistance, resulting in compensatory hyperinsulinemia. These mechanisms contribute to the development of hyperglycemia in acromegaly.

4. **Answer A (Thiazide diuretics)**

   Thiazide diuretics, commonly prescribed for hypertension and fluid retention, can have an adverse effect on blood glucose levels and potentially lead to hyperglycemia. They may reduce insulin sensitivity and impair glucose tolerance, contributing to elevated blood glucose levels. It is important for individuals taking thiazide diuretics to monitor their blood glucose levels regularly, especially if they have diabetes or are at risk for developing it.

5. **Answer A (True)**

   Diabetic ketoacidosis (DKA) is a life-threatening condition that can occur as a result of untreated or poorly managed hyperglycemia. DKA typically develops in individuals with diabetes, especially those with type 1 diabetes, and is characterized by high blood glucose levels, a buildup of ketones in the blood, and metabolic acidosis. It is important to promptly treat hyperglycemia to prevent the progression to DKA, as it can lead to serious complications and requires immediate medical attention.

6. **Answer D (All of the above)**

   The patient's symptoms, laboratory findings, and history of type 1 diabetes are consistent with DKA. The management of DKA involves a comprehensive approach that includes intravenous fluid resuscitation, insulin therapy, and electrolyte replacement. Intravenous fluid resuscitation is essential to address the dehydration and electrolyte imbalances caused by excessive urination and vomiting. Fluids, typically isotonic saline, are administered to restore circulating volume and correct dehydration. Insulin therapy is crucial to lower blood glucose levels and halt ketone production. Regular insulin is usually administered intravenously as a continuous infusion. This helps promote glucose uptake by cells and inhibits ketone formation. Electrolyte replacement is necessary to restore imbalances caused by fluid losses and metabolic derangements. Commonly affected electrolytes include potassium, which may be initially elevated and subsequently depleted during treatment, and bicarbonate, which may be reduced due to metabolic acidosis.

Recommended literature

1. Duggan EW, Carlson K, Umpierrez GE. Perioperative Hyperglycemia Management: an update. Anesthesiology. 2017;126(3):547-560.
2. Stubbs, D.J., Levy, N., Dhatariya, K., 2017. The rationale and the strategies to achieve perioperative glycaemic control. BJA Education 17, 185-193.

HYPERKALEMIA

05

CHAPTER

Questions:

1. **Which of the following is a symptom of hyperkalemia?**
   A. Nausea
   B. Muscle fasciculations
   C. Peaked T wave
   D. All of the above

2. **Which medication can contribute to hyperkalemia?**
   A. Proton pump inhibitors (PPIs)
   B. Anticoagulants
   C. Beta-blockers
   D. Antihistamines

3. **What is the first step in managing hyperkalemia?**
   A. Administer calcium chloride
   B. Check for pseudohyperkalemia
   C. Start insulin and glucose infusion
   D. Initiate dialysis

4. **Which of the following is a cardiac manifestation commonly associated with hyperkalemia?**
   A. Inverted T waves
   B. ST-segment elevation
   C. U wave
   D. Peaked T waves

5. **Rhabdomyolysis can lead to the release of potassium into the bloodstream and contribute to hyperkalemia.**
   A. True
   B. False

6. **A 45-year-old male patient is scheduled for an emergency appendectomy under general anesthesia. During the induction of anesthesia, succinylcholine is administered for neuromuscular blockade. Shortly after the administration of succinylcholine, the patient's electrocardiogram (ECG) shows tall, peaked, and tented T waves, widened and flattened P waves, widening of the QRS complex, and bradycardia. The anesthesiologist suspects hyperkalemia as the cause of these ECG changes. What is the appropriate therapy for the suspected hyperkalemia in this case?**
   A. Intravenous calcium chloride 10% - 10 mL
   B. Intravenous insulin regular - 10 units
   C. Intravenous sodium bicarbonate 8.4% - 50 mEq
   D. Intravenous sodium polystyrene sulfonate (Kayexalate) - 15 g

Answers:

1. **Answer D (All of the above)**

   All the listed symptoms are potential manifestations of hyperkalemia. Hyperkalemia can present with various signs and symptoms affecting different body systems. Gastrointestinal symptoms may include nausea, vomiting, and diarrhea. Neuromuscular manifestations can include paresthesias, muscle fasciculations, and ascending paralysis of the extremities, which may lead to quadriplegia. Cardiac symptoms may include dyspnea, and progressive electrocardiogram (ECG) changes with increasing severity of hyperkalemia, such as peaked T waves, wide PR interval, wide QRS duration, loss of P wave, and the characteristic sinusoidal wave pattern.

2. **Answer C (Beta-blockers)**

   Beta-blockers can induce hyperkalemia, particularly in patients with comorbidities such as renal dysfunction or insulin insufficiency. Beta-blockers can affect potassium regulation through multiple mechanisms. The suppression of aldosterone secretion from the adrenal cortex reduces the excretion of potassium by the kidneys, leading to an increase in potassium levels. Additionally, beta-blockers can decrease cellular uptake of potassium by blocking beta-receptors, which in turn reduces the activity of the voltage-gated sodium-potassium adenosine triphosphate (ATP) pump responsible for transporting potassium into cells.

3. **Answer B (Check for pseudohyperkalemia)**

   The first step in managing hyperkalemia is to check for pseudohyperkalemia. Pseudohyperkalemia is a condition in which there is a falsely elevated level of potassium in the blood sample, which may occur due to factors such as poor blood sample storage or handling. Before initiating treatment for hyperkalemia, it is crucial to ensure that the laboratory result is accurate and reflects the true potassium level in the patient's bloodstream.

4. **Answer D (Peaked T waves)**

   Hyperkalemia can cause specific ECG alterations, including tall, peaked, and tented T waves, widened and flattened P waves, widening of the QRS complex, AV blocks, sine wave rhythms, and asystole. Peaked T waves are considered a hallmark ECG finding associated with hyperkalemia, reflecting the abnormal repolarization of the ventricles due to elevated potassium levels.

5. **Answer A (True)**

   Rhabdomyolysis, which is the breakdown of muscle tissue, can lead to the release of potassium into the bloodstream and contribute to hyperkalemia. During rhabdomyolysis, the destruction of muscle cells releases their intracellular contents, including potassium, into the bloodstream. The elevated levels of potassium can then lead to hyperkalemia.

6. **Answer A (Intravenous calcium chloride 10% - 10 mL)**

   The ECG changes observed in this patient, including tall, peaked, and tented T waves, widened and flattened P waves, widening of the QRS complex, and bradycardia, are indicative of hyperkalemia. Hyperkalemia can be a potential complication of succinylcholine administration, particularly in patients with underlying risk factors. The appropriate therapy for hyperkalemia, especially when ECG changes and cardiac symptoms are present, involves the administration of calcium gluconate. Calcium gluconate works by stabilizing the cardiac cell membrane and counteracting the cardiac effects of elevated potassium levels. It is important to administer calcium gluconate slowly over a few minutes and closely monitor the patient's ECG and vital signs during administration.

Recommended literature

1. Lott C, Truhlář A, Alfonzo A, et al. European Resuscitation Council Guidelines 2021: Cardiac arrest in special circumstances [published correction appears in Resuscitation. 2021 Oct;167:91-92]. Resuscitation. 2021;161:152-219.
2. Palmer BF, Carrero JJ, Clegg DJ, et al. Clinical Management of Hyperkalemia. Mayo Clin Proc. 2021;96(3):744-762.
3. Palmer BF, Clegg DJ. Diagnosis and treatment of hyperkalemia. Cleve Clin J Med. 2017;84(12):934-942. doi:10.3949/ccjm.84a.17056.

HYPERNATREMIA

Questions:

1. Which of the following is a symptom of mild hypernatremia?
   A. Muscle weakness
   B. Headache
   C. Restlessness
   D. All of the above

2. Which of the following conditions can cause primary hypodipsia?
   A. Increased sodium intake
   B. Destruction of the hypothalamic thirst center
   C. Hyperglycemia
   D. Diabetes insipidus

3. Which of the following is the first-line choice for fluid replacement in hypernatremia?
   A. Hypotonic IV solutions
   B. Isotonic IV solutions
   C. Oral free water
   D. Hypertonic IV solutions

4. What is the risk associated with rapid correction or overcorrection of hypernatremia?
   A. Hypovolemia
   B. Hypervolemia
   C. Cerebral edema
   D. Renal failure

5. A combination of inadequate fluid intake and increased free water loss is the most common cause of hypernatremia in the elderly.
   A. True
   B. False

6. A 75-year-old woman is admitted to the hospital with confusion and lethargy. Her medical history includes hypertension and heart failure. She is living alone and probably has difficulties obtaining adequate fluid volumes. Laboratory tests reveal a serum sodium level of 160 mmol/L. The patient's volume status is assessed as euvolemic. To correct the hypernatremia, it is a plan that correction should be done with hypotonic fluids orally or via intravenous (IV) route. What is the recommended rate of correction for hypernatremia in this case?
   A. 0.5 mmol/L per hour
   B. 1 mmol/L per hour
   C. 2 mmol/L per hour
   D. 5 mmol/L per hour

Answers:

1. Answer D (All of the above)

Symptoms of mild hypernatremia can vary but commonly include anorexia, muscle weakness, restlessness, headache, and confusion. Nausea can also be present, although it is not as commonly associated with mild hypernatremia. It's important to note that symptoms can worsen as the condition progresses to more severe levels.

2. Answer B (Destruction of the hypothalamic thirst center)

Primary hypodipsia, which is a lack of thirst, is typically caused by the destruction of the hypothalamic thirst center. This destruction can be a result of various conditions such as tumors, granulomatous disease, vascular disease, or trauma.

3. Answer C (Oral free water)

The first-line choice for fluid replacement in hypernatremia is oral free water. Oral intake of water allows for the correction of the water deficit and helps restore the balance of fluids in the body. This approach is preferred when the patient is able to tolerate oral intake and has no contraindications. Hypotonic IV solutions may be considered in severe cases or when oral intake is not feasible, but they should be administered with caution to prevent rapid correction and the risk of cerebral edema.

4. Answer C (Cerebral edema)

Rapid correction or overcorrection of hypernatremia can increase the risk of cerebral edema. When the serum sodium levels are rapidly decreased, water moves into brain cells, causing them to swell. This swelling can lead to cerebral edema, which can result in severe neurological symptoms and complications.

5. Answer A (True)

Inadequate fluid intake and increased free water loss, often due to age-related changes in thirst sensation and renal function, are the most common causes of hypernatremia in the elderly population. As people age, the thirst mechanism can weaken, leading to reduced fluid intake. Additionally, renal function may decline, resulting in impaired concentration and conservation of urine. These factors contribute to a higher risk of developing hypernatremia in older individuals, particularly those who are frail, living alone, or have difficulties obtaining adequate fluid volumes.

6. Answer A (0.5 mmol/L per hour)

Based on the patient's euvolemic status, comorbidities, and questionable fluid intake, it is more likely that we are dealing with chronic hypernatremia in this case. Chronic hypernatremia refers to a sustained elevation in serum sodium levels over a longer period, typically lasting more than 48 hours. For chronic hypernatremia, the recommended correction rate is 0.5 mmol/L per hour. This gradual correction allows for a controlled decrease in serum sodium levels, reducing the risk of complications such as cerebral edema. In euvolemic patients, oral-free water is the preferred first-line choice for fluid replacement. If the patient is unable to tolerate oral intake or requires more rapid correction, hypotonic IV solutions such as 0.45% saline or 5% dextrose in water may be administered. The infusion rate should be adjusted to achieve the recommended correction rate of 0.5 mmol/L per hour.

Recommended literature

1. Braun MM, Barstow CH, Pyzocha NJ. Diagnosis and management of sodium disorders: hyponatremia and hypernatremia. Am Fam Physician. 2015;91(5):299-307.

Endocrinology
HYPERPARATHYROIDISM

05
CHAPTER

Questions:

1. **What is NOT the main effector site of parathyroid hormone (PTH)?**
   A. Kidneys
   B. Intestines
   C. Bone
   D. Liver

2. **Which of the following is NOT a symptom of hyperparathyroidism?**
   A. Muscle weakness
   B. Pancreatitis
   C. Osteopetrosis
   D. Renal stones

3. **Which of the following is a characteristic ECG finding in hyperparathyroidism-induced hypercalcemia?**
   A. Shortened QT interval
   B. Shortened PR interval
   C. Tall T waves
   D. Low QRS voltage

4. **What is the treatment of choice for primary hyperparathyroidism (HPT)?**
   A. Calcium supplementation
   B. Parathyroidectomy
   C. Vitamin D therapy
   D. Bisphosphonates

5. **Multiple endocrine neoplasia syndromes (MEN) is a genetic condition associated with an increased risk of hyperparathyroidism.**
   A. True
   B. False

6. **A 40-year-old woman presented with a week-long history of nausea and vomiting and complained of mental status alteration, including confusion and agitation, in the 24 hours before her admission. She denied any history of past illness. Laboratory tests showed a severe hypercalcemia crisis with a serum calcium level of 5.21 mmol/L and a serum intact parathyroid hormone level of > 5000 pg/mL. Which of the following is NOT a recommended management option for hyperparathyroidism-induced hypercalcemia?**
   A. Rehydration
   B. Vitamin A
   C. Loop diuretics
   D. Calcitonin

Answers:

1. Answer D (Liver)

The main effector sites responding directly or indirectly to parathyroid hormone (PTH) are the intestines, kidneys, and bone. PTH acts on the intestines to increase calcium absorption, on the kidneys to increase calcium reabsorption and activate vitamin D, and on the bone to stimulate the release of calcium from the bone matrix. The liver is not a primary effector site of PTH.

2. Answer C (Osteopetrosis)

The symptoms of hyperparathyroidism (HPT) are primarily caused by hypercalcemia. These include cardiovascular manifestations such as hypertension and ECG changes, neurological symptoms like mental status changes and weakness, respiratory issues including potential muscle weakness, symptoms such as osteoporosis and pathological fractures, gastrointestinal symptoms like abdominal pain and pancreatitis, renal symptoms including polyuria and renal stones, and hematopoietic symptoms like anemia. Osteopetrosis, characterized by abnormally dense bones due to defective osteoclast function, is not a typical symptom of hyperparathyroidism.

3. Answer A (Shortened QT interval)

The main ECG abnormality seen with hypercalcemia is a shortening of the QT interval. In severe hypercalcemia, Osborn waves (J waves) may be seen, and ventricular irritability and ventricular fibrillation arrest have been reported with extreme hypercalcemia. ECG changes in hypercalcemia can mimic myocardial ischemia or infarction. Short QT interval is the most common finding, often contributed by shortening the ST segment. The ST segment may be completely absent and replaced by an inverted small T-wave directly after the R-wave. Other ECG changes associated with hypercalcemia include decreased T-wave amplitude, T-wave notching, J-point elevation mimicking ST-segment elevation, transient ST segment elevation, bradycardia, sinus arrest, premature ectopic beats, PR prolongation, and increased QRS complex amplitude.

4. Answer B (Parathyroidectomy)

The treatment of choice for primary HPT is parathyroidectomy. Primary HPT is characterized by hyperfunction of the parathyroid glands, leading to the overproduction of PTH. While a single parathyroid adenoma causes most cases of primary HPT, other causes include double adenomas, multi-gland hyperplasia, and parathyroid cancer. The diagnosis of primary HPT is typically made biochemically, and the only curative treatment is surgical removal of the affected parathyroid tissue.

5. Answer A (True)

Multiple endocrine neoplasia syndromes (MEN) are genetic conditions that are associated with an increased risk of hyperparathyroidism. MEN syndromes are characterized by developing tumors in multiple endocrine glands, including the parathyroid glands. There are several types of MEN syndromes, including MEN1 and MEN2, which are inherited in an autosomal dominant pattern. Individuals with MEN syndromes have an increased risk of developing hyperparathyroidism, along with other endocrine tumors such as those affecting the pituitary gland, pancreas, and adrenal glands.

6. Answer B (Vitamin A)

Vitamin A is not a recommended management option for hyperparathyroidism-induced hypercalcemia. Vitamin A toxicity can lead to hypercalcemia and should be avoided in the treatment of hypercalcemia. Vitamin A toxicity is often overlooked in the diagnostic evaluation of hypercalcemia. The diagnostic evaluation of hypercalcemia should start with establishing the role of PTH in its pathogenesis. An elevated PTH level may indicate primary hyperparathyroidism, tertiary hyperparathyroidism, or familial hypocalciuric hypercalcemia. A low PTH should trigger an evaluation for hypercalcemia induced by PTH-related peptide (PTHrP). Vitamin A toxicity should be considered in the diagnostic workup along with malignancy, bone metastasis, vitamin D or calcium toxicity, increased 1,25-hydroxyvitamin D production (e.g., from granulomatous disorders and lymphomas), hyperthyroidism, monoclonal gammopathy, and immobility. In the management of hyperparathyroidism-induced hypercalcemia, aggressive intravenous fluid resuscitation, loop diuretic treatment, vitamin D, intravenous bisphosphonates, and calcitonin therapy are recommended options to help lower serum calcium levels.

Recommended literature

1. Malhotra S, Sodhi V. Anaesthesia for thyroid and parathyroid surgery. Continuing Education in Anaesthesia Critical Care & Pain. 2007;7(2):55-58.

Endocrinology
HYPERTHYROIDISM/THYROID STORM

05
CHAPTER

Questions:

1. **What is the most common cause of hyperthyroidism in a younger population?**
   A. Graves' disease
   B. Toxic multinodular goiter
   C. Hashimoto's disease
   D. Thyroid adenoma

2. **Which of the following is not a symptom of hyperthyroidism?**
   A. Weight loss
   B. Fatigue
   C. Diarrhea
   D. Cold intolerance

3. **What is the primary goal of treatment for thyroid storm?**
   A. Lower thyroid hormone levels
   B. Control hyperthermia
   C. Stabilize hemodynamics
   D. Address complications

4. **Which medication is used to inhibit the synthesis of thyroid hormones in the treatment of hyperthyroidism?**
   A. Thionamide
   B. Beta-blocker
   C. Calcium channel blocker
   D. Thyroid receptor antibody

5. **Amiodarone is indicated for the treatment of atrial fibrillation in a patient with a thyroid storm.**
   A. True
   B. False

6. **A 25-year-old male with known hyperthyroidism presents to the emergency department with severe abdominal pain localized in the right lower quadrant. The patient also exhibits symptoms of palpitations, weight loss, and heat intolerance. On examination, an enlarged thyroid gland is observed. Preoperative laboratory tests reveal elevated levels of free T3 and T4. The patient has been receiving beta-blockers to control his heart rate. Urgent appendectomy is initiated due to the patient's condition. During the operation, the heart rate is 110 beats per minute, and blood pressure is elevated. Boluses of Esmolol 0.5 mg/kg have been administered. What is the next step in the management of this patient during the appendectomy procedure?**
   A. Administer Amiodarone 150 mg bolus
   B. Consider plasmapheresis
   C. Administer PTU (propylthiouracil) 200-400 mg
   D. Administer Dantrolene 2.5 mg/kg

Answers:

1. **Answer A (Graves' disease)**

   Graves' disease is the most common cause of hyperthyroidism in a younger population. It is an autoimmune disorder in which the body produces thyroid-stimulating antibodies that bind to the thyroid gland's TSH receptors, leading to excessive production of thyroid hormones. This condition is more prevalent in women and is often associated with other autoimmune disorders. The disease is classically characterized by the triad of goiter, exophthalmos, and pretibial myxedema.

2. **Answer D (Cold intolerance)**

   Cold intolerance is not a symptom commonly associated with hyperthyroidism. Hyperthyroidism is characterized by an overactive thyroid gland that produces excessive thyroid hormones, which can lead to symptoms such as weight loss despite increased appetite, fatigue, diarrhea, increased gastrointestinal motility, heat intolerance, and excessive sweating. Cold intolerance, on the other hand, is typically associated with hypothyroidism, a condition characterized by an underactive thyroid gland and decreased production of thyroid hormones.

3. **Answer C (Stabilize hemodynamics)**

   The primary goal of treatment for thyroid storm is to stabilize hemodynamics. A thyroid storm is a severe and life-threatening complication of hyperthyroidism characterized by a sudden and exaggerated release of thyroid hormones into the bloodstream. This excessive thyroid hormone release can lead to various cardiovascular manifestations, including tachycardia, hypertension, arrhythmias, and cardiac dysfunction. To achieve hemodynamic stabilization, treatment measures focus on controlling heart rate, blood pressure, and other cardiovascular parameters. Medications such as beta-blockers, such as esmolol or propranolol, are often used to lower heart rate and blood pressure. In addition to hemodynamic stabilization, other aspects of management include reducing thyroid hormone levels, controlling hyperthermia, and addressing complications such as electrolyte abnormalities and organ dysfunction. However, the primary focus initially is on stabilizing the patient's hemodynamics to prevent further deterioration and improve outcomes.

4. **Answer A (Thionamide)**

   Thionamide medications are used to inhibit the synthesis of thyroid hormones in the treatment of hyperthyroidism. Thionamides, such as carbimazole or propylthiouracil (PTU), work by blocking the enzyme thyroid peroxidase, which is involved in the production of thyroid hormones. By inhibiting this enzyme, thionamides help reduce the synthesis of triiodothyronine (T3) and thyroxine (T4) in the thyroid gland. Thionamides are commonly used as a first-line treatment for hyperthyroidism, especially in cases of Graves' disease. They can effectively control the excessive production of thyroid hormones and help alleviate the symptoms associated with hyperthyroidism. It's important to note that thionamides may take several weeks to achieve their full effect, and close monitoring of thyroid hormone levels is necessary during treatment.

5. **Answer B (False)**

   Amiodarone is not the medication of choice for treating atrial fibrillation in thyroid storm. While amiodarone is commonly used to treat atrial fibrillation in other contexts, it is generally avoided in the treatment of atrial fibrillation specifically associated with thyroid storm. Amiodarone contains high levels of iodine, which can exacerbate the hyperthyroid state in the thyroid storm. The excess iodine can further increase thyroid hormone production and worsen the symptoms of thyroid storm. Therefore, amiodarone should be avoided in this scenario. In the management of atrial fibrillation in the context of a thyroid storm, alternative medications such as beta-blockers or calcium channel blockers are often preferred.

6. **Answer C (Administer PTU (propylthiouracil) 200-400 mg)**

   In the management of a patient with known hyperthyroidism, it is important to control the underlying hyperthyroid state during the surgical procedure to minimize potential complications. The patient's heart rate of 110 beats per minute and elevated blood pressure indicate ongoing hyperthyroid manifestations despite receiving beta-blockers. Propylthiouracil (PTU) is an antithyroid medication that inhibits the conversion of thyroxine (T4) to triiodothyronine (T3) and reduces the production of thyroid hormones. Administering PTU at a dose of 200-400 mg helps further suppress thyroid hormone synthesis and control the hyperthyroid state during the surgical procedure.

Recommended literature

1. Pokhrel B, Aiman W, Bhusal K. Thyroid Storm. [Updated 2022 Oct 6]. In: StatPearls [Internet]. Treasure Island (FL): StatPearls Publishing; 2022 Jan-. Available from: https://www.ncbi.nlm.nih.gov/books/NBK448095/.
2. Mathew P, Rawla P. Hyperthyroidism. [Updated 2022 Jul 23]. In: StatPearls [Internet]. Treasure Island (FL): StatPearls Publishing; 2022 Jan-. Available from: https://www.ncbi.nlm.nih.gov/books/NBK537053/.
3. Carroll R, Matfin G. Endocrine and metabolic emergencies: thyroid storm. Ther Adv Endocrinol Metab. 2010;1(3):139-145.
4. Farling PA. Thyroid disease. BJA: British Journal of Anaesthesia. 2000;85(1):15-28.

HYPOKALEMIA

Questions:

1. **What is the typical serum potassium level used to define hypokalemia?**

    A. < 2.0 mmol/L

    B. < 2.5 mmol/L

    C. < 3.0 mmol/L

    D. < 3.5 mmol/L

2. **Which of the following is not a gastrointestinal symptom associated with hypokalemia?**

    A. Nausea

    B. Constipation

    C. Diarrhea

    D. Gastrointestinal paralysis

3. **Which medication is not commonly associated with inducing hypokalemia?**

    A. Thiazide diuretics

    B. Beta-2-agonists

    C. Calcium channel blockers

    D. Loop diuretics

4. **Which of the following rare syndromes does NOT cause hypokalemia?**

    A. Gitelman syndrome

    B. Bartter syndrome

    C. Liddle syndrome

    D. Gordon's syndrome

5. **Hypomagnesemia can cause hypokalemia.**

    A. True

    B. False

6. **A 60-year-old male with a history of heart failure presents to the emergency department with worsening shortness of breath and lower extremity edema. He has been receiving treatment with both a thiazide diuretic and a loop diuretic. On examination, he has elevated jugular venous pressure, bilateral crackles on lung auscultation, and significant pitting edema. Laboratory tests reveal a serum potassium level of 2.0 mmol/L (normal range: 3.5-5.0 mmol/L). How should the patient's hypokalemia be managed?**

    A. KCL 20 mEq PO qDay

    B. KCL 40 mEq PO qDay

    C. KCL 20 mEq/hr IV

    D. KCL 40 mEq/hr IV

Answers:

1. **Answer D (< 3.5 mmol/L)**

   The typical serum potassium level used to define hypokalemia is a concentration of less than 3.5 mmol/L. Hypokalemia is diagnosed when the blood potassium level falls below this threshold. It is important to note that the normal range for serum potassium can vary slightly between different laboratories and reference ranges, but generally, a level below 3.5 mmol/L is considered indicative of hypokalemia.

2. **Answer C (Diarrhea)**

   Diarrhea is not typically considered a gastrointestinal symptom associated with hypokalemia. Hypokalemia can affect gastrointestinal function, leading to symptoms such as nausea, constipation, and gastrointestinal paralysis. While chronic diarrhea can cause gastrointestinal potassium loss, it is not a symptom of hypokalemia itself.

3. **Answer C (Calcium channel blockers)**

   Calcium channel blockers are not commonly associated with inducing hypokalemia. Thiazide diuretics, loop diuretics, and beta-2-agonists, on the other hand, are known to cause potassium loss and can contribute to the development of hypokalemia.

4. **Answer D (Gordon's syndrome)**

   Gordon's syndrome (also known as pseudohypoaldosteronism type 2) does not cause hypokalemia. Gordon's syndrome is a rare genetic disorder characterized by mutations in specific genes involved in sodium and potassium transport in the kidneys. These mutations result in increased renal sodium reabsorption and potassium excretion, leading to hypertension and hyperkalemia rather than hypokalemia. On the other hand, Gitelman syndrome, Bartter syndrome, and Liddle syndrome are all associated with hypokalemia.

5. **Answer A (True)**

   Magnesium plays a crucial role in regulating potassium balance in the body. Low levels of magnesium can impair the reabsorption of potassium in the kidneys, leading to increased urinary excretion of potassium and subsequent hypokalemia. Therefore, hypomagnesemia is known to be associated with and can contribute to the development of hypokalemia.

6. **Answer D (KCL 40 mEq/hr IV)**

   In this case, the patient has severe hypokalemia with a serum potassium level of 2.0 mmol/L. Immediate intravenous potassium replacement is necessary for prompt correction of the potassium imbalance. The dose and rate of administration are dependent upon the specific condition of each patient. If the serum potassium level is greater than 2.5 mEq/liter, potassium can be given at a rate not to exceed 10 mEq/hour in a concentration of up to 40 mEq/liter. The 24-hour total dose should not exceed 200 mEq. If urgent treatment is indicated (serum potassium level less than 2.0 mEq/liter with electrocardiographic changes and/or muscle paralysis), potassium chloride may be infused very cautiously at a rate of up to 40 mEq/hour. In such cases, continuous cardiac monitoring is essential. As much as 400 mEq may be administered in a 24-hour period. In critical conditions, potassium chloride may be administered in saline (unless contraindicated) rather than in dextrose-containing fluids, as dextrose may lower serum potassium levels.

Recommended literature

1. Kardalas E, Paschou SA, Anagnostis P, Muscogiuri G, Siasos G, Vryonidou A. Hypokalemia: a clinical update. Endocr Connect. 2018;7(4):R135-R146.
2. Viera AJ, Wouk N. Potassium Disorders: Hypokalemia and Hyperkalemia. Am Fam Physician. 2015;92(6):487-495.

HYPONATREMIA

Questions:

1. What is the serum sodium concentration range for defining moderate hyponatremia?
   A. 125-129 mmol/L
   B. 130-135 mmol/L
   C. < 125 mmol/L
   D. > 135 mmol/L

2. Which of the following symptoms is associated with hyponatremia?
   A. Confusion
   B. Headache
   C. Vomiting
   D. All of the above

3. What is the primary treatment for mild hyponatremia?
   A. Fluid restriction
   B. Hypertonic saline
   C. Diuretics
   D. Intravenous fluids

4. Which of the following medical conditions is NOT associated with hyponatremia?
   A. SIADH
   B. Heart failure
   C. Hypothyroidism
   D. Diabetes insipidus

5. Liver cirrhosis can cause hyponatremia.
   A. True
   B. False

6. A 50-year-old female presents to the hospital with complaints of nausea, confusion, and weakness. She has a history of chronic liver cirrhosis due to alcohol abuse and has been experiencing abdominal swelling for the past few months. Her vital signs include a blood pressure of 120/80 mmHg, heart rate of 90 bpm, and temperature of 37.2°C. Laboratory tests reveal a serum sodium level of 124 mmol/L. What is the most appropriate initial treatment for severe hyponatremia?
   A. Fluid restriction
   B. Intravenous 3% NaCl 150 mL
   C. Oral sodium supplements
   D. Diuretics

Answers:

1. **Answer A (125-129 mmol/L)**

   Moderate hyponatremia is defined by a serum sodium concentration between 125-129 mmol/L. This means that when the level of sodium in the blood falls within this range, it indicates a moderate case of hyponatremia. Mild hyponatremia is characterized by a serum sodium concentration between 130-135 mmol/L, while severe hyponatremia is indicated by a serum sodium concentration below 125 mmol/L.

2. **Answer D (All of the above)**

   All of the listed symptoms can be associated with hyponatremia. When the body's sodium levels are low, it can lead to various neurological and gastrointestinal symptoms, such as confusion, headache (moderate symptoms), and vomiting (severe symptoms). These symptoms can occur depending on the severity of hyponatremia and its impact on the body's water and electrolyte balance.

3. **Answer A (Fluid restriction)**

   For mild hyponatremia, the primary treatment approach is fluid restriction. By limiting the intake of fluids, the goal is to prevent further dilution of sodium levels in the blood and promote a gradual increase in serum sodium concentration. In mild cases, fluid restriction alone can be sufficient to correct the hyponatremia and restore the body's electrolyte balance. It is essential for healthcare professionals to closely monitor the patient's condition during fluid restriction to ensure that sodium levels do not drop further and to address any underlying causes of hyponatremia if present.

4. **Answer D (Diabetes insipidus)**

   Diabetes insipidus is a condition that is NOT associated with hyponatremia. In fact, it is a condition characterized by excessive urination and thirst due to the kidneys' inability to concentrate urine properly, leading to the excretion of large amounts of diluted urine. As a result, it can cause dehydration and hypernatremia rather than hyponatremia.

5. **Answer A (True)**

   Liver cirrhosis can cause hyponatremia. Liver cirrhosis is a condition in which the liver becomes scarred and loses its normal function due to chronic liver disease. Patients with cirrhosis may develop hyponatremia due to either hypovolemia (loss of extracellular fluid due to diuretics) or hypervolemia (expanded extracellular fluid volume due to the inability of the kidneys to excrete solute-free water proportionate to the amount of free water ingested).

6. **Answer B (Intravenous 3% NaCl 150 mL)**

   The most appropriate initial treatment for severe hyponatremia is intravenous 3% NaCl at a rate of 150 mL over 20 minutes. In severe hyponatremia with neurological symptoms, rapid correction is necessary but should be performed cautiously to prevent complications like osmotic demyelination syndrome. The aim of treatment in this case is to correct hyponatremia at a rate of 5 mmol/L per 24 hours, with a maximum correction limit of 10 mmol/L in the first 24 hours and 8 mmol/L in the subsequent 24 hours. The administration of 3% NaCl solution at the specified rate ensures that the correction is carried out within safe limits to prevent potential neurological complications associated with rapid sodium level changes.

Recommended literature

1. Spasovski G, Vanholder R, Allolio B, et al. Clinical practice guideline on diagnosis and treatment of hyponatraemia [published correction appears in Nephrol Dial Transplant. 2014 Jun;40(6):924]. Nephrol Dial Transplant. 2014;29 Suppl 2:i1-i39.
2. Hoorn EJ, Zietse R. Diagnosis and Treatment of Hyponatremia: Compilation of the Guidelines. J Am Soc Nephrol. 2017;28(5):1340-1349.
3. John S, Thuluvath PJ. Hyponatremia in cirrhosis: pathophysiology and management. World J Gastroenterol. 2015 Mar 21;21(11):3197-205. doi: 10.3748/wjg.v21. i11.3197. PMID: 25805925; PMCID: PMC4363748.

HYPOPARATHYROIDISM

Questions:

1. What is the primary cause of symptoms in patients with hypoparathyroidism?
   - A. Hypercalcemia
   - B. Hyperphosphatemia
   - C. Hypocalcemia
   - D. Hypophosphatemia

2. Which of the following signs is used to assess neuromuscular irritability in patients with hypoparathyroidism?
   - A. Chvostek sign
   - B. Brudzinski's sign
   - C. Babinski sign
   - D. Kernig sign

3. Which complication is NOT associated with hypoparathyroidism?
   - A. Seizures
   - B. Clouded vision due to cataracts
   - C. Hypertension
   - D. QT prolongation and arrhythmias

4. What is the main effector site responding directly or indirectly to parathyroid hormone (PTH)?
   - A. Lungs
   - B. Liver
   - C. Kidneys
   - D. Heart

5. Hyperventilation should be avoided in patients with hyperparathyroidism.
   - A. True
   - B. False

6. A 42-year-old male presents to the clinic complaining of muscle cramps, tingling sensation around his mouth, and frequent spasms in his hands and feet. He mentions feeling fatigued and has noticed that these symptoms have been progressively worsening over the past few weeks. He has a medical history of undergoing a thyroidectomy six months ago due to thyroid cancer. What is the most appropriate therapy for this condition?
   - A. Intravenous infusion of calcium
   - B. High-dose vitamin D supplementation
   - C. Magnesium replacement therapy
   - D. Oral calcium and vitamin D supplements

Answers:

1. Answer C (Hypocalcemia)

The primary cause of symptoms in patients with hypoparathyroidism is hypocalcemia. Hypoparathyroidism is a condition in which the parathyroid glands do not produce enough parathyroid hormone (PTH). Parathyroid hormone plays a crucial role in maintaining normal calcium homeostasis in the body. When there is insufficient production of PTH, the levels of calcium in the blood decrease, leading to hypocalcemia. Calcium is essential for various physiological processes, including muscle and nerve function, blood clotting, and bone health. Therefore, the symptoms experienced by individuals with hypoparathyroidism are primarily a result of the low levels of calcium in the bloodstream.

2. Answer A (Chvostek sign)

The Chvostek sign is used to assess neuromuscular irritability in patients with hypoparathyroidism, specifically those who are experiencing hypocalcemia. The sign is named after the Czech physician František Chvostek. The Chvostek sign is elicited by tapping or lightly striking the facial nerve, which is located just in front of the ear and below the temple. When the facial nerve is tapped, it causes facial muscles to contract, resulting in twitching or spasms of the ipsilateral facial muscles. The most common muscle affected is the orbicularis oris, which is the circular muscle around the mouth.

3. Answer C (Hypertension)

Hypertension is NOT a complication associated with hypoparathyroidism. The complications of hypoparathyroidism include seizures, hypotension, QT prolongation and arrhythmias, congestive heart failure, bronchospasm, laryngospasm, problems with kidney function, bone changes, delayed mental development in children, and clouded vision due to cataracts.

4. Answer C (Kidneys)

The main effector site responding directly or indirectly to PTH is the kidneys. When calcium levels in the blood are low, the parathyroid glands secrete PTH, which acts on various target tissues to increase blood calcium levels. The primary target organ for PTH is the kidneys, where it exerts its effects to enhance calcium reabsorption in the renal tubules, leading to decreased calcium excretion in the urine. This action helps to conserve calcium in the body and raise blood calcium levels. Additionally, PTH indirectly affects the intestines and bones. In the intestines, PTH stimulates the conversion of vitamin D to its active form, which enhances the absorption of calcium from the diet. In bones, PTH promotes the release of calcium from the bone tissue, further contributing to increased calcium levels in the blood.

5. Answer A (True)

Avoiding hyperventilation in a patient with hypoparathyroidism is crucial. Hyperventilation can exacerbate the symptoms of hypocalcemia in these patients and may lead to a further decrease in ionized calcium levels. Hyperventilation causes respiratory alkalosis, which shifts the acid-base balance in the body towards alkalinity. This alkalotic state can decrease the binding of calcium to albumin, leading to an increase in the levels of ionized (free) calcium in the blood. As a result, there is a transient drop in blood calcium levels, worsening the hypocalcemia-related symptoms, such as neuromuscular irritability, tetany, and spasms.

6. Answer D (Oral calcium and vitamin D supplements)

Given the patient's medical history of thyroidectomy and presenting symptoms, the most appropriate therapy for his condition is oral calcium and vitamin D supplements. Thyroidectomy is the surgical removal of the thyroid gland, and in some cases, it may also involve the removal of the parathyroid glands, which are located near the thyroid. Accidental removal or damage to the parathyroid glands can result in hypoparathyroidism, with insufficient PTH production. This leads to low levels of calcium in the blood, causing symptoms such as muscle cramps, a tingling sensation around the mouth, and spasms in the hands and feet. The most appropriate and effective treatment for managing hypocalcemia in this patient is through oral calcium and vitamin D supplements. Calcium supplements provide an external source of calcium to raise blood calcium levels, while vitamin D helps enhance calcium absorption in the intestines. This combination of therapy helps maintain adequate calcium levels in the blood, alleviating the patient's symptoms of hypocalcemia.

Recommended literature

1. Hypoparathyroidism. In: Bissonnette B, Luginbuehl I, Marciniak B, Dalens BJ. eds. Syndromes: Rapid Recognition and Perioperative Implications. McGraw Hill; 2006. Accessed March 06, 2023. https://accessanesthesiology.mhmedical.com/content.aspx?bookid=852&sectionid=49517707.

HYPOTHYROIDISM

Questions:

1. **What is the possible cause of primary hypothyroidism?**
   A. Iodine deficiency
   B. Postpartum thyroiditis
   C. Autoimmune thyroid disease
   D. All of the above

2. **Which of the following hormones is primarily responsible for stimulating the thyroid gland to produce thyroid hormones?**
   A. Thyroid-stimulating hormone (TSH)
   B. Triiodothyronine (T3)
   C. Thyroxine (T4)
   D. Thyrotropin-releasing hormone (TRH)

3. **Which symptom is NOT commonly associated with hypothyroidism?**
   A. Weight gain
   B. Increased sweating
   C. Cold intolerance
   D. Fatigue

4. **Which of the following laboratory findings is commonly seen in hypothyroidism?**
   A. Elevated TSH and elevated free T4
   B. Elevated TSH and decreased free T4
   C. Decreased TSH and elevated free T4
   D. Decreased TSH and decreased free T4

5. **Sheehan syndrome is one of the possible causes of hypothyroidism in younger men.**
   A. True
   B. False

6. **A 55-year-old female patient with a history of hypothyroidism due to Hashimoto's thyroiditis is scheduled for elective surgery to repair a hernia. She has been taking levothyroxine medication to manage her hypothyroidism for the past 3 years. The patient reports no recent changes in her symptoms, and her thyroid function tests have been stable on her current dose of levothyroxine. The surgery is planned to be performed under general anesthesia. What is the most appropriate perioperative management?**
   A. Discontinue levothyroxine medication before surgery
   B. Administer higher doses of anesthesia due to decreased drug metabolism
   C. Continue levothyroxine and ensure euthyroid state before surgery
   D. Avoid intravenous fluids to prevent fluid retention

Answers:

1. **Answer D (All of the above)**

   A possible cause of primary hypothyroidism includes a number of factors that can cause the thyroid gland to not produce adequate amounts of thyroid hormone. These causes include iodine deficiency, autoimmune thyroid disease (Hashimoto's thyroiditis), certain medications, radioactive iodine thyroid therapy, thyroid surgery, radiation therapy to the head or neck, subacute granulomatous thyroiditis, and postpartum thyroiditis. All of these factors can contribute to primary hypothyroidism by affecting thyroid function and its ability to produce thyroid hormone.

2. **Answer A (Thyroid-stimulating hormone (TSH))**

   Thyroid-stimulating hormone (TSH) is primarily responsible for stimulating the thyroid gland to produce thyroid hormones. TSH is produced and released by the pituitary gland in response to low levels of thyroid hormones (T3 and T4) in the blood. When TSH binds to specific receptors on the thyroid gland, it stimulates the production and release of thyroid hormones into the bloodstream.

3. **Answer B (Increased sweating)**

   Increased sweating is NOT commonly associated with hypothyroidism. In fact, hypothyroidism often leads to decreased sweating due to the reduced metabolic rate and heat production in the body. Hypothyroidism is associated with a wide range of symptoms, including cold intolerance, weight gain, dry skin, hair loss, constipation, fatigue, and menstrual cycle abnormalities. Other common manifestations include depression, cognitive impairments, muscle cramps, and prolonged QT interval. Bradycardia, dull facial expressions, and pericardial effusion are also seen in some cases.

4. **Answer B (Elevated TSH and decreased free T4)**

   Hypothyroidism is characterized by decreased production of T3 and T4 by the thyroid gland. In response to the low levels of thyroid hormones, the pituitary gland increases the secretion of TSH to stimulate the thyroid gland to produce more thyroid hormones. Therefore, in hypothyroidism, TSH levels are typically elevated (elevated TSH). However, due to the thyroid gland's reduced function, the levels of free thyroxine (T4) are decreased, leading to low levels of circulating T4 (decreased free T4). This combination of elevated TSH and decreased free T4 is a common laboratory finding in patients with hypothyroidism and helps in the diagnosis of the condition.

5. **Answer B (False)**

   Sheehan syndrome is not a common cause of hypothyroidism in younger men. Sheehan syndrome typically occurs in women, especially following severe postpartum bleeding. It is characterized by damage to the pituitary gland, leading to hormone deficiencies. While Sheehan syndrome can cause hypothyroidism in women, it is extremely rare in younger men. Hypothyroidism in men is more commonly associated with other causes, such as autoimmune thyroid disorders (e.g., Hashimoto's thyroiditis) or medications that affect thyroid function.

6. **Answer C (Continue levothyroxine and ensure euthyroid state before surgery)**

   In patients with hypothyroidism who are scheduled for elective surgery, it is crucial to maintain a euthyroid state perioperatively. Abruptly discontinuing levothyroxine medication can lead to hypothyroidism exacerbation, causing adverse effects on various body systems, including the cardiovascular and respiratory systems. Therefore, it is generally recommended to continue the patient's levothyroxine and ensure that the thyroid function is stable and well-controlled before the surgery. This approach helps minimize perioperative complications and ensures optimal patient outcomes.

Recommended literature

1. Patil N, Rehman A, Jialal I. Hypothyroidism. [Updated 2022 Aug 8]. In: StatPearls [Internet]. Treasure Island (FL): StatPearls Publishing; 2022 Jan-. Available from: https://www.ncbi.nlm.nih.gov/books/NBK519536/.
2. Farling PA. Thyroid disease. BJA: British Journal of Anaesthesia. 2000;85(1):15-28.
3. Palace MR. Perioperative Management of Thyroid Dysfunction. Health Serv Insights. 2017;10:1178632916689677. Published 2017 Feb 20.

Endocrinology
MALNUTRITION

Questions:

1. Malnutrition involves a deficiency, excess, or imbalance of food and nutrients that can lead to which of the following diseases resulting from excessive or inadequate intake of essential nutrients?

    A. Kwashiorkor

    B. Keshan disease

    C. Pellagra

    D. All of the above

2. Malnutrition can cause vitamin A insufficiency, which can lead to which condition?

    A. Blindness

    B. Osteoporosis

    C. Anemia

    D. Pneumothorax

3. Malnourished patients may have reduced drug dosing requirements due to?

    A. Enhanced drug metabolism

    B. Increased drug absorption

    C. Altered drug binding

    D. Reduced drug elimination

4. Malnutrition can cause a reduction in cardiac output and increased risk of arrhythmias due to disturbances in which two components?

    A. Vitamin A and calcium

    B. Iron and ferritin

    C. Potassium and magnesium

    D. Protein and glucose

5. Pseudocholinesterase deficiency is affected by malnutrition.

    A. True

    B. False

6. A 65-year-old man was admitted to the hospital for emergency surgery to repair a hip fracture caused by a fall at home. He has a history of chronic obstructive pulmonary disease (COPD) and a recent diagnosis of malnutrition due to poor food intake and unintentional weight loss over the past few months. On admission, his BMI is 17.5 kg/m², indicating severe malnutrition. During the preoperative assessment, the anesthesiologist assesses the patient's nutritional status and its potential impact on anesthesia and surgical outcomes. The anesthesiologist notes that malnutrition can lead to a decrease in muscle mass, impaired respiratory function, changes in drug metabolism, and increased susceptibility to perioperative complications. Given the patient's malnutrition and underlying COPD, what type of anesthesia would you choose in this case?

    A. Intravenous anesthesia

    B. General anesthesia

    C. Spinal anesthesia

    D. All of the above

Answers:

1. **Answer D (All of the above)**

   Malnutrition encompasses various conditions that arise from deficiencies, excesses, or imbalances in food and nutrient intake. Each option Kwashiorkor, Keshan disease, and Pellagra represents a specific disease resulting from inadequate intake of essential nutrients. Kwashiorkor is caused by a deficiency of protein, Keshan disease results from a deficiency of selenium, and Pellagra is triggered by a deficiency of niacin (vitamin B3).

2. **Answer A (Blindness)**

   Malnutrition can cause vitamin A insufficiency, leading to a condition called xerophthalmia. Xerophthalmia is characterized by dryness, inflammation, and ulceration of the cornea, which can ultimately result in blindness. Vitamin A is essential for maintaining healthy vision and preventing eye-related disorders. Inadequate intake of vitamin A due to malnutrition can result in xerophthalmia, making blindness the correct answer. This condition is particularly concerning in children and is a leading cause of childhood blindness in developing countries where malnutrition is prevalent.

3. **Answer C (Altered drug binding)**

   Malnourished patients may have reduced drug dosing requirements due to altered drug binding. Malnutrition can lead to decreased levels of serum proteins, particularly albumin, which are responsible for binding and transporting many drugs in the bloodstream. With reduced albumin levels, there is an increased proportion of free, unbound drugs in circulation. Since it is the free, unbound fraction of a drug that is pharmacologically active, the effective drug concentration in the body may be higher in malnourished patients even with lower total drug doses. As a result of altered drug binding, the pharmacokinetics of certain drugs may be significantly affected in malnourished individuals. This can lead to increased drug potency and a higher risk of drug toxicity.

4. **Answer C (Potassium and magnesium)**

   Malnutrition can lead to disturbances in potassium and magnesium levels, which are critical electrolytes for maintaining normal cardiac function. Imbalances in these electrolytes can disrupt the electrical signaling in the heart, leading to arrhythmias and reduced cardiac output. Proper nutrition and maintaining adequate levels of potassium and magnesium are essential to support normal cardiac function and reduce the risk of cardiac complications associated with malnutrition.

5. **Answer A (True)**

   Pseudocholinesteras is an enzyme that plays a role in breaking down certain drugs, including certain muscle relaxants used during anesthesia. Malnutrition, particularly severe protein malnutrition, can lead to reduced levels of serum proteins, including pseudocholinesterase. Therefore, malnutrition can affect the activity and levels of pseudocholinesterase, potentially resulting in a deficiency. Pseudocholinesterase deficiency can have clinical implications during anesthesia, especially when using certain non-depolarizing muscle relaxants, as these drugs rely on pseudocholinesterase for their metabolism and elimination from the body. In patients with pseudocholinesterase deficiency, the duration of action of these muscle relaxants may be prolonged, leading to delayed recovery of muscle function.

6. **Answer C (Spinal anesthesia)**

   Given the patient's malnutrition and underlying COPD, spinal anesthesia is the most suitable type of anesthesia in this case. Spinal anesthesia provides effective pain relief without the potential respiratory risks associated with general anesthesia or intravenous anesthesia, making it a safer option for the patient. This approach is particularly beneficial in malnourished patients, as it can help minimize potential cardiovascular and respiratory challenges associated with general anesthesia.

Recommended literature

1. Pollard BJ, Kitchen G. Handbook of Clinical Anaesthesia. 4th ed. Taylor & Francis group; 2018. Chapter 4 Gastrointestinal tract, Jackson MJ.
2. Edwards S. Anaesthetising the malnourished patient. Update in Anaesthesia. 2016;31:31-37.

METABOLIC ACIDOSIS

Questions:

1. **What is the primary mechanism responsible for anion gap metabolic acidosis?**
   A. Excessive bicarbonate loss
   B. Accumulation of lactic acid
   C. Impaired glucose tolerance
   D. Alkali ingestion

2. **What is the primary mechanism responsible for non-anion gap metabolic acidosis?**
   A. Alkali ingestion
   B. Increased lactate production
   C. Accumulation of ketoacids
   D. Excessive bicarbonate loss

3. **Which of the following conditions can cause a non-anion gap metabolic acidosis associated with low serum potassium?**
   A. Salicylate intoxication
   B. Diabetic ketoacidosis
   C. Proximal renal tubular acidosis
   D. Toxic alcohol intoxication

4. **What is the expected compensation mechanism in metabolic acidosis involving the respiratory system?**
   A. Decreased respiratory rate
   B. Increased respiratory rate
   C. No change in respiratory rate
   D. All of above

5. **Metabolic acidosis can lead to a loss of bone in the body.**
   A. True
   B. False

6. **A 65-year-old woman is undergoing hip surgery under spinal anesthesia. During the operation, she was tachycardic and hypotensive. The anesthesiologist administers intravenous fluids for resuscitation, using 0.9% normal saline. Intraoperative laboratory findings: blood pH: 7.20; Serum bicarbonate (HCO3-): 20 mEq/L; Serum chloride: 115 mEq/L; Serum sodium: 138 mEq/L. What is the most likely diagnosis of the patient's condition based on the presented case and intraoperative laboratory findings?**
   A. Diabetic ketoacidosis (DKA)
   B. Respiratory acidosis
   C. Hyperchloremic metabolic acidosis
   D. Metabolic alkalosis

Answers:

1. **Answer B (Accumulation of lactic acid)**

Anion gap metabolic acidosis occurs when there is an accumulation of acids, particularly lactic acid, in the bloodstream. This accumulation leads to an increase in the concentration of hydrogen ions (H+) in the blood, resulting in a decrease in serum bicarbonate (HCO3-) levels. Lactic acid is produced through anaerobic metabolism, which occurs when tissues are deprived of sufficient oxygen. In situations such as intense exercise, shock, severe sepsis, or inadequate tissue perfusion, the body switches to anaerobic metabolism, and glucose is metabolized into lactic acid instead of being fully oxidized to carbon dioxide and water. The liver can normally metabolize and clear lactic acid from the bloodstream efficiently. However, in conditions where there is an excessive production of lactic acid, such as in severe hypoperfusion or tissue hypoxia, the liver's capacity to clear it is overwhelmed, leading to an increase in the anion gap and anion gap metabolic acidosis.

2. **Answer D (Excessive bicarbonate loss)**

Non-anion gap metabolic acidosis occurs when there is a net loss of HCO3- from the body, leading to a decrease in serum bicarbonate levels. Bicarbonate is an important buffer in the blood that helps maintain the body's acid-base balance. It acts as a base and neutralizes excess H+ to prevent the blood from becoming too acidic. When there is excessive loss of bicarbonate from the body, either through the kidneys (renal bicarbonate wasting) or the gastrointestinal tract (e.g., diarrhea), the body's ability to buffer acids is compromised, resulting in a decrease in the serum bicarbonate concentration.

3. **Answer C (Proximal renal tubular acidosis)**

Proximal renal tubular acidosis (RTA) is a condition that can cause a non-anion gap metabolic acidosis associated with low serum potassium. In proximal RTA, there is a defect in the proximal tubules of the kidneys, leading to impaired reabsorption of bicarbonate. As a result, there is a loss of bicarbonate in the urine, which contributes to the development of metabolic acidosis. The acidosis in proximal RTA is characterized by a normal anion gap, as there is no significant accumulation of unmeasured anions in the blood. Hypokalemia is common due to osmotic diuresis because of decreased HCO3 reabsorption causing increased flow rate to distal tubule and causing increased potassium excretion.

4. **Answer B (Increased respiratory rate)**

The expected compensation mechanism in metabolic acidosis involving the respiratory system is hyperventilation. In metabolic acidosis, there is an accumulation of acid (e.g., lactic acid or ketoacids), which leads to a decrease in blood pH and a decrease in serum HCO3-. To compensate for the acidic environment, the body's respiratory system responds by increasing the respiratory rate. Hyperventilation helps to blow off excess carbon dioxide (CO2) from the body. CO2 is acidic when it reacts with water in the blood, forming carbonic acid (H2CO3). By increasing the rate of breathing, more CO2 is expelled through the lungs, which reduces the carbonic acid concentration in the blood. As a result, the overall acidity in the blood decreases, and the pH level begins to rise, partially compensating for the metabolic acidosis. This respiratory compensation is a rapid response mechanism that occurs within minutes to hours to help restore the acid-base balance in the body.

5. **Answer A (True)**

Metabolic acidosis can lead to a loss of bone in the body. When the blood becomes acidic due to metabolic acidosis, the body tries to buffer the excess H+ by releasing calcium carbonate from bone tissue into the bloodstream. The released calcium acts as a base and helps neutralize the excess acidity in the blood. However, this process can result in a net loss of calcium from the bones over time, leading to demineralization and weakening of the bones. Chronic metabolic acidosis, if left untreated or poorly controlled, can have adverse effects on bone health and may contribute to conditions such as osteoporosis or an increased risk of fractures.

6. **Answer C (Hyperchloremic metabolic acidosis)**

Based on the case presentation and intraoperative laboratory findings, the most likely diagnosis of the patient's condition is hyperchloremic metabolic acidosis due to fluid resuscitation. During hip surgery under spinal anesthesia, the patient is hypotensive, a common side effect of spinal anesthesia. To resolve hypotension and restore intravascular volume, the anesthesiologist administers intravenous fluids for resuscitation. One of the common resuscitation fluids is 0.9% saline (NS). Iatrogenic hyperchloremic metabolic acidosis is a condition that can occur as a result of excessive administration of chloride over sodium, usually seen with the use of 0.9% saline. The high chloride content of NS can lead to an increase in serum chloride, resulting in hyperchloremia. An excess of chloride ions can disrupt the body's acid-base balance, leading to metabolic acidosis.

Recommended literature

1. Burger MK, Schaller DJ. Metabolic Acidosis. [Updated 2022 Jul 19]. In: StatPearls [Internet]. Treasure Island (FL): StatPearls Publishing; 2022 Jan-. Available from: https://www.ncbi.nlm.nih.gov/books/NBK482146/.
2. Fleisher, Lee A., and Stanley H. Rosenbaum. Complications in Anesthesia. Elsevier, 2018.
3. Kraut, J., Madias, N. Metabolic acidosis: pathophysiology, diagnosis and management. Nat Rev Nephrol 6, 274–285 (2010).

Endocrinology
METABOLIC ALKALOSIS

05
CHAPTER

Questions:

1. **Which of the following is a characteristic feature of metabolic alkalosis?**
   A. Decreased serum pH levels
   B. Decreased serum bicarbonate (HCO_3-) levels
   C. Decreased serum Chloride (Cl-) levels
   D. Increased serum Potassium (K+) levels

2. **Which of the following is a compensatory mechanism for metabolic alkalosis?**
   A. Hyperventilation and increased CO_2 elimination
   B. Hypoventilation and decreased CO_2 elimination
   C. Increase in hydrogen ion excretion in the kidneys
   D. Increase in potassium and magnesium retention in the kidneys

3. **Which of the following is an adverse effect of metabolic alkalosis?**
   A. Increased myocardial contractility
   B. Decreased cerebral blood flow
   C. Increase of peripheral oxygen unloading
   D. Decreased neuromuscular excitability

4. **Which of the following mechanisms can lead to metabolic alkalosis?**
   A. Decreased hydrogen ion excretion in the kidneys
   B. Hyperventilation and CO_2 retention
   C. Decreased bicarbonate retention in the kidneys
   D. Excessive intake of sodium bicarbonate

5. **Gitelman syndrome is a condition that is commonly associated with metabolic alkalosis.**
   A. True
   B. False

6. **A 58-year-old male is admitted to the ICU following abdominal surgery for the management of a complicated bowel obstruction. The patient underwent a laparotomy with resection of a segment of the small intestine due to a strangulated hernia creating a high ileostomy. On the second postoperative day patients laboratory tests reveal the following results: Arterial blood gas (ABG): pH 7.52, $PaCO_2$ 40 mmHg, HCO_3- 32 mmol/L; Serum electrolytes: Sodium (Na+) 138 mEq/L, Potassium (K+) 2.8 mEq/L, Chloride (Cl-) 80 mEq/L; Complete blood count (CBC): Normal. What is the likely mechanism responsible for the metabolic alkalosis in this ICU post-surgery patient?**
   A. Excessive intake of alkaline substances
   B. Impaired renal excretion of bicarbonate
   C. GI hydrogen loss due to vomiting
   D. High-volume ileostomy output

Answers:

1. **Answer C (Decreased serum Chloride (Cl-) levels)**

   In metabolic alkalosis, the ion that is typically decreased in the blood is chloride (Cl-). Metabolic alkalosis is often associated with hypochloremia, which is a relative decrease in serum chloride levels. Metabolic alkalosis can occur due to various causes, such as excessive vomiting, diuretic use, or excessive intake of alkaline substances like bicarbonates. In these conditions, there can be a loss of Cl- along with hydrogen ions (H+), leading to a decrease in serum chloride levels. It is important to note that while chloride levels are typically decreased in metabolic alkalosis, other ions like sodium (Na+), potassium (K+), and calcium (Ca2+) may be affected differently based on the underlying cause and compensatory mechanisms. For example, metabolic alkalosis is often associated with hypokalemia due to the loss of potassium ions along with hydrogen ions in the kidneys.

2. **Answer B (Hypoventilation and decreased CO_2 elimination)**

   In metabolic alkalosis, there is an excessive accumulation of bicarbonate (HCO_3^-) in the blood, leading to an increase in pH and an alkaline environment. To compensate for this alkalosis and attempt to restore the acid-base balance, the body responds by retaining carbon dioxide (CO_2). When a person hypoventilates, they retain more CO_2 in the body, leading to an increase in arterial carbon dioxide pressure ($PaCO_2$). This increase in $PaCO_2$ is known as respiratory compensation for metabolic alkalosis. The higher $PaCO_2$ helps to counteract the alkalosis by forming carbonic acid (H_2CO_3) when it reacts with water, which can then dissociate into H+ and HCO_3^-. This process helps lower the pH and partially offset the alkalosis caused by the increased bicarbonate levels.

3. **Answer B (Decreased cerebral blood flow)**

   In metabolic alkalosis, there is an excessive accumulation of HCO_3^- in the blood, leading to an increase in pH and alkalosis. This alkalotic state can cause vasoconstriction in the cerebral blood vessels, leading to a reduction in cerebral blood flow, which may cause symptoms like dizziness, confusion, and impaired mental status or lead to neurological symptoms like seizures or loss of consciousness.

4. **Answer D (Excessive intake of sodium bicarbonate)**

   Metabolic alkalosis occurs when there is an excessive accumulation of HCO_3^- in the blood, leading to an increase in pH and an alkalotic state. One way this can happen is through the excessive ingestion of exogenous sources of bicarbonate, such as sodium bicarbonate ($NaHCO_3$) or other alkaline substances. When sodium bicarbonate or alkaline substances are ingested, they are absorbed into the bloodstream, increasing the concentration of bicarbonate ions. As a result, the ratio of bicarbonate to hydrogen ions in the blood shifts towards alkalosis, leading to an increase in pH.

5. **Answer A (True)**

   Gitelman syndrome is a rare genetic disorder that affects the kidneys' ability to reabsorb certain electrolytes, including sodium, chloride, magnesium, and potassium. The primary defect in Gitelman syndrome is a mutation in the SLC12A3 gene, which encodes for a sodium-chloride cotransporter in the distal convoluted tubules of the kidneys. Due to the impaired function of this cotransporter, there is increased renal excretion of sodium, chloride, and magnesium, leading to their loss in the urine. The loss of chloride ions results in a relative increase in HCO_3^- levels in the blood, causing metabolic alkalosis. The key features of Gitelman syndrome include hypokalemia, metabolic alkalosis, hypomagnesemia, and hypocalciuria.

6. **Answer D (High-volume ileostomy output)**

   After abdominal surgery with ileostomy creation, the patient experiences a high output of fluid and electrolytes through the stoma. Metabolic alkalosis can occur due to the excessive loss of gastric acid and potassium through the ileostomy, leading to an increase in serum pH and HCO_3^- levels. Appropriate management involves replacing fluid and electrolyte losses, addressing the underlying cause of the high-output ileostomy, and restoring acid-base balance to improve the patient's condition.

Recommended literature

1. Brinkman JE, Sharma S. Physiology, Metabolic Alkalosis. [Updated 2022 Jul 18]. In: StatPearls [Internet]. Treasure Island (FL): StatPearls Publishing; 2022 Jan-. Available from: https://www.ncbi.nlm.nih.gov/books/NBK482291/.
2. Tinawi M. Pathophysiology, Evaluation, and Management of Metabolic Alkalosis. Cureus. 2021;13(1):e12841. Published 2021 Jan 21.

MULTIPLE ENDOCRINE NEOPLASIA SYNDROMES

Questions:

1. Which of the following is a genetic polyglandular cancer syndrome associated with an increased risk of medullary thyroid carcinoma, pheochromocytoma, and hyperparathyroidism?

   A. MEN Type 1

   B. MEN Type 2

   C. Gastrinoma

   D. Prolactinoma

2. A patient with MEN Type 1 presents with symptoms of hypercalcemia. Which of the following endocrine glands is most likely affected?

   A. Parathyroid glands

   B. Thyroid gland

   C. Pancreatic islets

   D. Adrenal glands

3. A patient with MEN Type 2 presents with symptoms of excessive sweating, hypertension, and tachycardia. Which tumor is most likely responsible for these symptoms?

   A. Gastrinoma

   B. Insulinoma

   C. Pheochromocytoma

   D. Medullary thyroid carcinoma

4. In MEN Type 1, which endocrine gland is affected when a patient presents with symptoms related to high levels of prolactin?

   A. Parathyroid glands

   B. Adrenal glands

   C. Pancreatic islets

   D. Pituitary gland

5. Patients with insulinomas are prone to recurrent hypoglycemia due to excessive insulin secretion.

   A. True

   B. False

6. A 30-year-old female patient presents to her gynecologist with complaints of irregular menstrual cycles and difficulty getting pregnant. She also mentions experiencing milky discharge from her nipples occasionally, even though she is not pregnant or breastfeeding. Her father had a history of hyperparathyroidism, and her sister was diagnosed with a pituitary tumor. What is the most likely diagnosis for the patient's symptoms and examination findings?

   A. Hyperthyroidism

   B. Hyperparathyroidism

   C. Prolactinoma

   D. Polycystic ovary syndrome (PCOS)

Answers:

1. Answer B (MEN Type 2)

MEN Type 2 is a genetic polyglandular cancer syndrome that is associated with an increased risk of developing medullary thyroid carcinoma, pheochromocytoma, and hyperparathyroidism. In MEN Type 2, all patients develop medullary thyroid carcinoma, a cancer of the thyroid gland, and they also have an increased risk of developing pheochromocytoma, a tumor of the adrenal glands, and hyperparathyroidism, which involves overactivity of the parathyroid glands. The condition is caused by oncogenic point mutations of the RET gene located on chromosome 10cen-10q11.2. This syndrome requires careful monitoring and management due to the potential for multiple tumors affecting different endocrine glands and the risk of malignancy.

2. Answer A (Parathyroid glands)

In a patient with MEN Type 1 presenting with symptoms of hypercalcemia, the most likely affected endocrine glands are the parathyroid glands. Hypercalcemia is a condition characterized by elevated levels of calcium in the blood, and it is commonly associated with hyperparathyroidism. In MEN Type 1, parathyroid tumors or hyperplasia of the parathyroid glands can lead to the overproduction of parathyroid hormone (PTH), which, in turn, causes the release of calcium from bones and increases its absorption from the intestines, leading to elevated calcium levels in the blood.

3. Answer C (Pheochromocytoma)

In a patient with MEN Type 2 presenting with symptoms of excessive sweating, hypertension, and tachycardia, the most likely responsible tumor is a pheochromocytoma. Pheochromocytoma is a tumor of the adrenal medulla, which is a part of the adrenal glands. These tumors produce excessive amounts of catecholamines, such as epinephrine and norepinephrine, which can lead to the classic symptoms of excessive sweating, hypertension, and tachycardia.

4. Answer D (Pituitary gland)

In MEN Type 1, when a patient presents with symptoms related to high levels of prolactin, the affected endocrine gland is the pituitary gland. MEN Type 1 can lead to the development of pituitary adenomas, specifically prolactinomas, which are tumors that secrete excessive amounts of prolactin. Prolactinomas can cause various symptoms, depending on the sex of the affected individual. In women, high levels of prolactin can lead to changes in menstruation, such as irregular menstruation or amenorrhea, infertility, and galactorrhea. In men, prolactinomas can cause decreased libido, erectile dysfunction, and infertility. In both men and women, large prolactinomas can compress surrounding structures, leading to symptoms like headaches and vision changes.

5. Answer A (True)

Insulinomas are tumors of the pancreas that produce excess insulin. As a result, patients with insulinomas experience recurrent hypoglycemia. Hypoglycemia can lead to various symptoms, including confusion, dizziness, shakiness, sweating, weakness, and even loss of consciousness if severe. The excessive insulin secretion from the insulinoma causes a drop in blood sugar levels, leading to hypoglycemic episodes. The condition requires careful monitoring and management to prevent severe hypoglycemia and its associated complications. Treatment often involves surgical removal of the insulinoma to resolve the issue of excessive insulin production and restore normal blood sugar levels.

6. Answer C (Prolactinoma)

The patient's clinical presentation of irregular menstrual cycles, difficulty getting pregnant, galactorrhea, and family history of hyperparathyroidism and pituitary tumor strongly suggests a diagnosis of prolactinoma. Prolactinoma is a type of pituitary adenoma that causes excessive secretion of prolactin, a hormone responsible for milk production in breastfeeding mothers. In non-pregnant and non-breastfeeding individuals, elevated levels of prolactin can lead to irregular menstrual cycles and difficulty getting pregnant. The milky discharge from the nipples is a result of prolactin's effect on the breast tissue.

Recommended literature

1. Multiple Endocrine Neoplasia (MEN). In: Bissonnette B, Luginbuehl I, Marciniak B, Dalens BJ. eds. Syndromes: Rapid Recognition and Perioperative Implications. McGraw Hill; 2006. Accessed March 07, 2023. https://accessanesthesiology.mhmedical.com/content.aspx?bookid=852&sectionid=49517985.
2. Grant F. Anesthetic considerations in the multiple endocrine neoplasia syndromes. Curr Opin Anaesthesiol. 2005;18(3):345-352.

Endocrinology
OBESITY

Questions:

1. Which of the following is the WHO-defined BMI threshold for obesity?
   A. BMI ≥ 25 kg/m2
   B. BMI ≥ 30 kg/m2
   C. BMI ≥ 35 kg/m2
   D. BMI ≥ 40 kg/m2

2. Which condition is a complication of obesity?
   A. Osteoarthritis
   B. Obstructive sleep apnea (OSA)
   C. Depression
   D. All of the above

3. Which anesthesia maintenance technique is recommended for obese patients to reduce the risk of laryngospasm and postoperative nausea and vomiting?
   A. Total Intravenous Anesthesia (TIVA)
   B. Inhalational anesthesia with isoflurane
   C. Inhalational anesthesia with desflurane
   D. Inhalational anesthesia with sevoflurane

4. Which obesity-related comorbidity can affect the bioavailability of oral medications due to alterations in the small bowel?
   A. Previous sleeve gastrectomy
   B. Previous adjustable gastric banding
   C. Previous vertical Sleeve Gastrectomy
   D. Previous Roux-en-Y gastric bypass surgery

5. RSI is required in obese patients without specific risk factors for aspiration.
   A. True
   B. False

6. A 50-year-old female with severe obesity (BMI over 40 kg/m2) is scheduled for an elective laparoscopic gastric bypass surgery. She also has a history of type 2 diabetes mellitus, hypertension, and obstructive sleep apnea. What is the recommended patient position during induction of anesthesia for obese patients to reduce dyspnea and improve laryngoscopy?
   A. Supine position
   B. Trendelenburg position
   C. Reverse Trendelenburg position
   D. Semi-upright position

Answers:

1. Answer B (BMI $\geq$ 30 kg/m2)

Overweight and obesity are defined as abnormal or excessive fat accumulation that presents a risk to health. A body mass index (BMI) over 25 is considered overweight, and the World Health Organization (WHO) defines obesity as having a BMI greater than or equal to 30 kg/m2.

2. Answer D (All of the above)

Obesity is associated with a multitude of complications, ranging from musculoskeletal issues like osteoarthritis due to added strain on weight-bearing joints to sleep-related problems such as obstructive sleep apnea (OSA) caused by upper airway collapse during sleep. Psychological aspects also play a role, with obesity being linked to depression influenced by body image and social stigma. Furthermore, obesity is closely connected to various vascular diseases, including hypertension, cardiovascular diseases, and an elevated risk of stroke due to the metabolic changes associated with increased fat accumulation. Additionally, obesity is a major risk factor for type 2 diabetes mellitus and metabolic syndrome. Moreover, obesity is linked to an increased risk of various cancers, affecting organs like the uterus, cervix, endometrium, ovary, breast, colon, rectum, esophagus, liver, gallbladder, pancreas, kidney, and prostate. Digestive problems can also occur in obese individuals, and obesity hypoventilation syndrome (OHS) is a respiratory condition that can further exacerbate respiratory health issues in these patients. Overall, obesity has far-reaching implications on health and is associated with a wide array of complications affecting various body systems.

3. Answer A (Total Intravenous Anesthesia (TIVA))

Total Intravenous Anesthesia (TIVA) is recommended for obese patients to reduce the risk of laryngospasm and postoperative nausea and vomiting (PONV). Laryngospasm is a spasm of the vocal cords that can occur during or after anesthesia induction, and obese patients may be at higher risk due to airway challenges. TIVA provides a smoother anesthetic depth, which can help minimize the risk of laryngospasm during airway manipulation. Additionally, TIVA is associated with a lower incidence of PONV compared to inhalational anesthesia, which can be particularly beneficial for obese patients who are already at an increased risk of PONV due to factors such as delayed gastric emptying.

4. Answer D (Previous Roux-en-Y gastric bypass surgery)

Roux-en-Y gastric bypass is a common bariatric surgery that involves creating a small pouch from the stomach and attaching it to the small intestine, bypassing a significant portion of the stomach and duodenum. This alteration in the anatomy can impact the absorption of certain oral medications, as they may not come into contact with the usual surface area of the stomach and proximal small intestine. As a result, the bioavailability of these medications may be affected, potentially leading to changes in their therapeutic effectiveness and dosing requirements.

5. Answer B (False)

Rapid sequence intubation (RSI) is not routinely required in obese patients without specific risk factors for aspiration. RSI is a technique used to secure the airway rapidly in patients at high risk of aspiration, such as those with full stomachs or certain conditions that increase the risk of regurgitation and aspiration during induction of anesthesia. Obese patients, in general, do not have an increased risk of aspiration solely due to their obesity. However, RSI may be considered if an obese patient has additional risk factors for aspiration. In the absence of specific risk factors for aspiration, a standard induction of anesthesia can be performed without the need for RSI.

6. Answer D (Semi-upright position)

The semi-upright position with elevation of the upper body until the ear tragus and sternal notch are aligned horizontally is recommended during induction of anesthesia for obese patients. This position offers advantages such as reducing dyspnea and improving laryngoscopy, which is particularly important in obese patients who may experience respiratory challenges. The semi-upright position optimizes airway management and enhances overall patient comfort during anesthesia induction and throughout the surgical procedure.

Recommended literature

1. Seyni-Boureima R, Zhang Z, Antoine MM, Antoine-Frank CD. A review on the anesthetic management of obese patients undergoing surgery. BMC Anesthesiol. 2022; 22(98).
2. Wynn-Hebden A, Bouch DC. Anaesthesia for the obese patient. BJA Education. 2020;20(11):388-395.
3. Dority J, Hassan ZU, Chau D. Anesthetic implications of obesity in the surgical patient. Clin Colon Rectal Surg. 2011;24(4):222-228.

PANHYPOPITUITARISM

Questions:

1. **What is panhypopituitarism characterized by?**
   - A. Excessive production of pituitary hormones
   - B. Deficiency in all pituitary hormones
   - C. Deficiency in some pituitary hormones
   - D. Excessive production of growth hormone

2. **Which of the following hormones is NOT produced by the anterior lobe of the pituitary gland?**
   - A. Adrenocorticotropic hormone (ACTH)
   - B. Follicle-stimulating hormone (FSH)
   - C. Antidiuretic hormone (ADH)
   - D. Growth hormone (GH)

3. **Which of the following is NOT a common symptom of panhypopituitarism?**
   - A. Growth problems (in children)
   - B. Excessive thirst and urination
   - C. Obesity
   - D. Hyperglycemia

4. **Which of the following complications is commonly associated with panhypopituitarism?**
   - A. Obesity
   - B. Increased cholesterol
   - C. Estradiol deficiency
   - D. All of the above

5. **Deficiency of antidiuretic hormone (ADH) can indeed lead to hyponatremia.**
   - A. True
   - B. False

6. **A 42-year-old male patient with a history of pituitary adenoma presents for surgical resection of the tumor. The patient has been diagnosed with panhypopituitarism due to the tumor's compression on the pituitary gland, resulting in deficiencies of all pituitary hormones. He is currently on hormone replacement therapy to manage his hormonal deficiencies. The anesthesiologist takes into consideration the patient's panhypopituitarism and the need for perioperative stress dose steroids. Which of the following is the primary purpose of perioperative stress dose steroids in patients with panhypopituitarism undergoing surgery?**
   - A. To prevent hypertension
   - B. To prevent an adrenal crisis
   - C. To stimulate growth hormone production
   - D. To manage hyperglycemia

Answers:

1. **Answer B (Deficiency in all pituitary hormones)**

   Panhypopituitarism is characterized by a deficiency in all of the hormones produced by the pituitary gland, also known as the "master gland" of the body. The affected hormones include adrenocorticotropic hormone (ACTH), follicle-stimulating hormone (FSH), luteinizing hormone (LH), growth hormone (GH), prolactin (PRL), thyroid-stimulating hormone (TSH), antidiuretic hormone (ADH) or vasopressin, and oxytocin. This deficiency can lead to a wide range of symptoms and health issues depending on the specific hormones affected. To manage the condition effectively, individuals with panhypopituitarism require hormone replacement therapy to replace the deficient hormones. If left untreated, panhypopituitarism can have serious consequences for the overall health and well-being of the affected individual.

2. **Answer C (Antidiuretic hormone (ADH))**

   The anterior lobe of the pituitary gland produces ACTH, FSH, GH, LH, PRL, and TSH. The posterior lobe produces ADH and oxytocin.

3. **Answer D (Hyperglycemia)**

   Panhypopituitarism is characterized by a deficiency in all hormones produced by the pituitary gland, and the symptoms experienced by individuals depend on which specific hormone is deficient. Common signs and symptoms include growth problems in children, obesity, hair loss, bradycardia, hypoglycemia, hypotension, fatigue, nausea or dizziness, depression and/or anxiety, frequent infections, sensitivity to cold, unusually dry skin, unexplained weight loss or weight gain, dyslipidemia, and tachycardia. Excessive thirst and urination can occur due to ADH deficiency. Female and male infertility may also be present. In infants, children, or adolescents, additional symptoms can include prolonged jaundice in newborns, micropenis, slowed growth, and delayed puberty. However, hyperglycemia is NOT a common symptom of panhypopituitarism. Instead, panhypopituitarism can lead to hypoglycemia due to deficiencies in certain hormones like growth hormone and ACTH.

4. **Answer D (All of the above)**

   Panhypopituitarism, a condition characterized by a deficiency in all pituitary hormones, can lead to various complications. These complications can include obesity due to the lack of GH and other hormonal imbalances affecting metabolism. Additionally, hormonal deficiencies in panhypopituitarism can result in increased cholesterol levels, contributing to dyslipidemia and metabolic disturbances. Furthermore, estradiol deficiency can occur in females, potentially leading to osteoporosis and other related consequences.

5. **Answer A (True)**

   ADH plays a crucial role in regulating water balance in the body by promoting water reabsorption in the kidneys. When ADH levels are low or insufficient, the kidneys are unable to properly conserve water, leading to increased urine volume and excessive water loss. As a result, the sodium concentration in the blood becomes diluted, causing hyponatremia.

6. **Answer B (To prevent an adrenal crisis)**

   In patients with panhypopituitarism, there is a deficiency in ACTH, leading to reduced cortisol production in the adrenal glands. During surgery or other significant stressors, the body requires higher levels of cortisol to respond effectively. Without adequate cortisol, the patient is at risk of experiencing an adrenal crisis characterized by symptoms like weakness, hypotension, hypoglycemia, and other life-threatening complications. To prevent this, perioperative stress dose steroids, such as hydrocortisone, are administered to mimic the body's natural response and provide sufficient cortisol levels during the perioperative period. This practice is crucial in ensuring the patient's stability and well-being during surgery and minimizing the risk of adrenal insufficiency-related complications.

Recommended literature

1. Raut MS, Kar S, Maheshwari A, Shivnani G, Dubey S. Perioperative management in a patient with panhypopituitarism – evidence based approach: a case report. Eur Heart J Case Rep. 2019;3(3):ytz145. Published 2019 Sep 18.
2. Malhotra, Surender & Jangra, Kiran & Saini, Vikas. (2013). Pituitary Surgery and Anesthetic Management: An Update. World Journal of Endocrine Surgery. 5. 1-5. 10.5005/jp-journals-10002-1114.
3. Menon R, Murphy PG, Lidnley AM. 2011. Anaesthesia and pituitary disease. Continuing Education in Anaesthesia Critical Care & Pain. 11;4:133-137.

PARATHYROIDECTOMY

Questions:

1. What is the primary indication for a parathyroidectomy?

   A. Hypocalcemia

   B. Hypercalcemia

   C. Hypoparathyroidism

   D. Hyperparathyroidism

2. Secondary hyperparathyroidism is typically associated with which of the following conditions?

   A. Adenoma of the parathyroid glands

   B. Vitamin D deficiency

   C. Carcinoma of the parathyroid glands

   D. Ectopic hyperparathyroidism

3. Which of the following is NOT a symptom of hyperparathyroidism?

   A. Skeletal muscle weakness

   B. Bone pain

   C. Polyuria

   D. Tetany

4. Which nerve is at risk of damage during a parathyroidectomy?

   A. Phrenic nerve

   B. Vagus nerve

   C. Recurrent laryngeal nerve

   D. Accessory nerve

5. Parathyroidectomy is frequently performed alongside thyroidectomy.

   A. True

   B. False

6. A 56-year-old male patient presents to the hospital for an operation to remove the enlarged parathyroid glands responsible for the excessive production of parathyroid hormone (PTH), causing hypercalcemia. He complained of recurrent kidney stones, generalized bone pain, and fatigue. His medical history reveals chronic kidney disease (CKD) stage 3 and longstanding hyperparathyroidism due to secondary hyperparathyroidism from vitamin D deficiency. Given the patient's chronic kidney disease, anesthesia for parathyroidectomy should be managed with caution. Preoperative optimization is crucial to correct any electrolyte imbalances. Intravenous hydration is initiated to ensure adequate fluid status, and loop diuretics may be used to enhance urinary calcium excretion. What is the primary reason for administering bisphosphonates to the patient before a parathyroidectomy?

   A. Enhance urinary calcium excretion

   B. Induce anesthesia

   C. Correct hypocalcemia

   D. Lower serum calcium levels

Answers:

1. **Answer D (Hyperparathyroidism)**

The primary indication for a parathyroidectomy is hyperparathyroidism. Hyperparathyroidism is a medical condition characterized by overactivity of one or more of the parathyroid glands, leading to excessive production of parathyroid hormone (PTH). This, in turn, causes an increase in the levels of calcium in the blood. During a parathyroidectomy, one or more of the affected parathyroid glands are surgically removed to normalize PTH secretion and calcium levels in the body.

2. **Answer B (Vitamin D deficiency)**

Secondary hyperparathyroidism is typically associated with vitamin D deficiency. When there is a lack of sufficient vitamin D in the body, it affects the absorption of calcium from the intestines, leading to hypocalcemia. In response to the low calcium levels, the parathyroid glands become overactive and produce more PTH. The increased PTH secretion helps to mobilize calcium from bones and increase its reabsorption in the kidneys, which can lead to secondary hyperparathyroidism. Secondary hyperparathyroidism is often seen in conditions where there is chronic kidney disease or other disorders that interfere with the body's ability to activate or utilize vitamin D properly.

3. **Answer D (Tetany)**

Tetany is not a symptom of hyperparathyroidism; it is actually a symptom of hypoparathyroidism. Hyperparathyroidism is characterized by overactivity of the parathyroid glands, leading to excessive production of PTH and elevated levels of calcium in the blood. The symptoms of hyperparathyroidism include skeletal muscle weakness, bone pain, and polyuria. On the other hand, tetany is a symptom of hypoparathyroidism, a condition characterized by underactivity of the parathyroid glands and reduced levels of PTH, leading to hypocalcemia and neuromuscular irritability.

4. **Answer C (Recurrent laryngeal nerve)**

During a parathyroidectomy, the recurrent laryngeal nerve is at risk of damage. The recurrent laryngeal nerves are branches of the vagus nerve that supply motor innervation to the muscles of the larynx and are responsible for controlling vocal cord movement during speech and swallowing. The parathyroid glands are located close to the recurrent laryngeal nerves in the neck. When performing a parathyroidectomy, there is a possibility of inadvertent injury to these nerves. If the recurrent laryngeal nerves are damaged during the surgery, it can lead to vocal cord paralysis and voice changes, such as hoarseness or difficulty speaking.

5. **Answer A (True)**

Parathyroidectomy is frequently performed alongside thyroidectomy. The parathyroid glands are small, pea-sized glands located near or attached to the thyroid gland in the neck. Since the parathyroid glands are intimately associated with the thyroid gland, thyroidectomy may require special attention to preserve and protect the parathyroid glands and their blood supply. If a patient has both thyroid issues and parathyroid gland issues, the surgeon may perform both procedures during the same operation. This simultaneous approach ensures appropriate management of both the thyroid and parathyroid conditions while minimizing additional surgeries and complications.

6. **Answer: D (Lower serum calcium levels)**

Bisphosphonates are administered to lower serum calcium levels in patients with hypercalcemia, such as in this case of secondary hyperparathyroidism due to vitamin D deficiency. These medications inhibit bone resorption and help reduce calcium release from bones into the bloodstream, effectively lowering serum calcium levels. By doing so, bisphosphonates aim to mitigate the risk of hypercalcemia during the parathyroidectomy procedure and its associated complications.

Recommended literature

1. Pollard BJ, Kitchen G. Handbook of Clinical Anaesthesia. 4th ed. Taylor & Francis group; 2018. Chapter 20 Head and neck surgery, Macnab R and Bexon K.
2. Malhotra S, Sodhi V. Anaesthesia for thyroid and parathyroid surgery. Continuing Education in Anaesthesia Critical Care & Pain. 2007;7(2):55-58.

PERIOPERATIVE STEROIDS

Questions:

1. Which of the following conditions is NOT commonly treated with chronic steroid therapy?
   A. Inflammatory bowel disease
   B. Rheumatoid arthritis
   C. Asthma
   D. Diabetes mellitus

2. What is the primary mechanism behind the development of secondary adrenal insufficiency in patients on chronic steroid therapy?
   A. Direct toxicity to the adrenal glands
   B. Hypothalamic-pituitary-adrenal (HPA) axis suppression
   C. Increased production of cortisol
   D. Inhibition of the renin-angiotensin-aldosterone system

3. Which of the following is NOT a role of cortisol in the body?
   A. Stimulate gluconeogenesis
   B. Activate anti-stress and anti-inflammatory pathways
   C. Inhibit catecholamine production
   D. Maintain cardiac output and contractility

4. How might an adrenal crisis present in the anesthetized patient?
   A. Seizures
   B. Tachycardia
   C. Hypertension
   D. Severe hypotension

5. Insulin administration is typically part of the treatment for a perioperative adrenal crisis.
   A. True
   B. False

6. A 60-year-old female with a history of rheumatoid arthritis (RA), hypertension, and diabetes mellitus (DM), is scheduled for hip replacement surgery due to severe hip joint damage. She has been managed with a moderate dose of corticosteroid therapy for the last 3 months to control her RA symptoms. The patient has no known allergies, and her other medications include lisinopril 20 mg daily for hypertension and metformin 1000 mg twice daily for DM. She denies any recent illnesses or changes in her health status. How should perioperative stress-dose steroids be dosed for this patient?
   A. Hydrocortisone 25 mg i.v. q8h x 3 doses
   B. Hydrocortisone 50 mg i.v. q8h x 3 doses
   C. Hydrocortisone 75 mg i.v. q8h x 3 doses
   D. Hydrocortisone 100 mg i.v. q8h x 3 doses

Answers:

1. **Answer D (Diabetes mellitus)**

Chronic steroid therapy is not commonly used to treat diabetes mellitus. Instead, it is used in the treatment of many other conditions such as inflammatory bowel disease, rheumatologic disease, asthma, chronic obstructive pulmonary disease, and as immunosuppression for transplant recipients. Chronic steroid therapy in these conditions helps to reduce inflammation and suppress the immune response, but it can also lead to adverse effects such as HPA axis suppression and secondary adrenal insufficiency.

2. **Answer B (Hypothalamic-pituitary-adrenal (HPA) axis suppression)**

Patients on chronic steroid therapy may develop secondary adrenal insufficiency due to HPA axis suppression. Chronic administration of exogenous glucocorticoids can lead to low levels of corticotropin-releasing hormone (CRH) and adrenocorticotropic hormone (ACTH), which are responsible for stimulating cortisol production. This can result in atrophy of the adrenal zona fasciculata and a decrease in cortisol production, leading to secondary adrenal insufficiency. Unlike primary adrenal insufficiency, where there is direct adrenal gland dysfunction, in secondary adrenal insufficiency, the adrenal glands are structurally intact but functionally suppressed. The renin-angiotensin-aldosterone system remains intact in secondary adrenal insufficiency, so patients do not develop mineralocorticoid deficiency. However, inadequate cortisol levels may predispose patients to vasodilation and hypotension. In the perioperative period, secondary adrenal insufficiency can manifest as an adrenal crisis, necessitating prompt recognition and treatment.

3. **Answer C (Inhibit catecholamine production)**

Cortisol does not directly inhibit catecholamine production; instead, it modulates the effects of catecholamines. Cortisol plays several key roles in the body, including stimulating gluconeogenesis, activating anti-stress and anti-inflammatory pathways, maintaining cardiac output and contractility via modulation of β-receptor synthesis and function, and enhancing vascular tone by increasing sensitivity to catecholamines.

4. **Answer D (Severe hypotension)**

An adrenal crisis in an anesthetized patient may present as severe hypotension. Unlike in awake patients, the typical signs and symptoms of an adrenal crisis, such as altered mental status, abdominal pain, nausea, vomiting, and weakness, may not be evident. Instead, the primary manifestation in the anesthetized patient is often severe, persistent hypotension that is poorly responsive to fluid and vasopressor therapy. Tachycardia and hypertension are less likely in this context, and seizures are not typically associated with adrenal crisis.

5. **Answer B (False)**

Insulin administration is not typically part of the treatment for a perioperative adrenal crisis. Perioperative adrenal crisis is primarily treated with stress-dose steroids to replace deficient cortisol levels and stabilize the patient. Supportive care with fluids and vasopressors may also be necessary to manage hemodynamic instability. Insulin therapy is not a standard treatment for adrenal crisis unless there is a specific indication, such as concurrent diabetes management.

6. **Answer B (Hydrocortisone 50 mg i.v. q8h x 3 doses)**

For a 60-year-old female with rheumatoid arthritis, hypertension, and diabetes mellitus scheduled for hip replacement surgery and managed with corticosteroids, the appropriate perioperative stress-dose steroid regimen is hydrocortisone 50 mg i.v. q8h x 3 doses. This patient falls into the intermediate-risk category for HPA axis suppression, warranting the use of stress-dose steroids to prevent adrenal crisis. Perioperative stress-dose steroids are indicated for patients at risk of adrenal insufficiency due to chronic glucocorticoid therapy. This includes those with a history of adrenal suppression from long-term corticosteroid use (> 20 mg/day of prednisone or equivalent for > 3 weeks) or clinical features of Cushing syndrome. Patients on moderate-dose corticosteroids (> 5 mg but < 20 mg/day of prednisone) fall into an intermediate-risk category and may require stress-dose steroids based on surgical stress and their perioperative condition. Hydrocortisone 50 mg i.v. q8h x 3 doses is typically used for moderate-risk surgeries. Close monitoring postoperatively is essential for signs of adrenal insufficiency, especially if hemodynamic instability occurs. Adjustments to the steroid regimen should be made based on the patient's perioperative course and the need for continued therapy.

Recommended literature

1. Liu MM, Reidy AB, Saatee S, Collard CD. Perioperative Steroid Management: Approaches Based on Current Evidence. Anesthesiology. 2017;127:166-172.

PHEOCHROMOCYTOMA

Questions:

1. **Which of the following neuroendocrine tumors arises from chromaffin cells in the adrenal medulla?**
   A. Paraganglioma
   B. Neurofibroma
   C. Pheochromocytoma
   D. Ganglioneuroma

2. **Which genetic syndrome is associated with pheochromocytoma?**
   A. Multiple Endocrine Neoplasia type 2 (MEN 2)
   B. Neurofibromatosis type 1
   C. Von Hippel-Lindau disease
   D. All of the above

3. **The primary treatment for pheochromocytoma is:**
   A. Chemotherapy
   B. Radiation therapy
   C. Hormone replacement therapy
   D. Surgical removal of the tumor

4. **Which medication is used to control heart rate in patients with pheochromocytoma?**
   A. Atenolol
   B. Phentolamine
   C. Sodium nitroprusside
   D. Magnesium sulfate

5. **Phenoxybenzamine is an essential initial treatment in patients with pheochromocytoma during surgery.**
   A. True
   B. False

6. **A 38-year-old woman presents with a history of recurrent episodes of severe headaches, palpitations, and sweating. Further investigation reveals an adrenal mass consistent with a pheochromocytoma. The tumor is located in her left adrenal gland, and surgical resection is planned to alleviate her symptoms and prevent potential complications. What medications should be avoided due to the potential risk of exacerbating hemodynamic instability caused by excessive catecholamine release?**
   A. Atracurium
   B. Succinylcholine
   C. Pancuronium
   D. All of the above

Answers:

1. Answer C (Pheochromocytoma)

Pheochromocytoma is a neuroendocrine tumor that arises from chromaffin cells in the adrenal medulla. Chromaffin cells are specialized cells in the adrenal medulla that produce and release catecholamines, including adrenaline and noradrenaline. When a pheochromocytoma develops, it results in the overproduction of these catecholamines. This excess secretion of adrenaline and noradrenaline can lead to various symptoms, including hypertension, tachycardia, headaches, sweating, and other signs associated with increased sympathetic nervous system activity.

2. Answer D (All of the above)

Adrenal pheochromocytoma is associated with several familial syndromic disorders, including von Hippel-Lindau (VHL) syndrome, multiple endocrine neoplasia type 2 (MEN2), and, to a lesser extent, neurofibromatosis type 1 (NF1). All of these disorders have an autosomal dominant inheritance pattern. VHL syndrome is characterized by tumors and cysts in multiple organs, including the adrenal glands. MEN2 is associated with tumors in various endocrine glands, and pheochromocytoma is a key feature, particularly in the MEN2A subtype. NF1, caused by mutations in the NF1 gene, can also lead to adrenal pheochromocytoma, although it is less commonly observed compared to VHL and MEN2.

3. Answer D (Surgical removal of the tumor)

The primary treatment for pheochromocytoma is surgical removal of the tumor. This curative approach aims to stop excessive catecholamine secretion and prevent further complications related to elevated adrenaline and noradrenaline levels. Preoperative management may involve the use of alpha-blockers and beta-blockers to stabilize blood pressure and heart rate. Chemotherapy and radiation therapy are not the main treatments for pheochromocytoma, as these tumors are typically not responsive to these modalities. Hormone replacement therapy is not the primary approach either, and close postoperative monitoring is essential to assess catecholamine levels and monitor for any recurrence of the tumor.

4. Answer A (Atenolol)

In patients with pheochromocytoma, excessive secretion of catecholamines can lead to tachycardia and tachydysrhythmias. Beta-blockers are commonly used to control the heart rate and manage these cardiovascular effects. Atenolol is one such beta-blocker that is frequently employed in patients with pheochromocytoma to reduce the heart rate and the force of heart contractions. By blocking beta-adrenergic receptors, atenolol inhibits the effects of circulating catecholamines on the heart, helping to maintain a more stable heart rate during surgery or other interventions.

5. Answer A (True)

Phenoxybenzamine is an alpha-blocker and is considered an initial treatment in patients with pheochromocytoma during surgery. It is used to achieve adequate alpha-blockade before surgical removal of the tumor. Alpha-blockers like phenoxybenzamine work by blocking the alpha-adrenergic receptors, reducing vascular resistance, and preventing hypertensive crises caused by the sudden release of catecholamines during tumor manipulation. By blocking alpha-adrenergic receptors, phenoxybenzamine reduces vascular resistance and allows for controlled blood pressure before the surgical procedure. This step is crucial to ensure safer anesthesia induction and successful surgical management of pheochromocytoma.

6. Answer D (All of the above)

In a patient with pheochromocytoma, it is crucial to avoid medications that can exacerbate hemodynamic instability caused by excessive catecholamine release during surgery. During induction, succinylcholine should be avoided as it produces sympathetic activation and can lead to a surge in catecholamines due to abdominal muscle contraction transmitted to the tumor mass. Tubocurarine, atracurium, and mivacurium should be avoided as they can induce histamine release, which may worsen hypertensive episodes. Pancuronium is also not preferred due to its indirect sympathetic stimulation profile, which can further contribute to cardiovascular instability. Vecuronium is preferred as a muscle relaxant due to its cardiovascular stability and lack of histamine release. Choosing the appropriate muscle relaxant, such as vecuronium, is vital in patients with pheochromocytoma to ensure a safer perioperative course and minimize the risk of hemodynamic complications related to catecholamine release.

Recommended literature

1. Connor D, Boumphrey S. Perioperative care of phaeochromocytoma. BJA Education. 2016;16(5):153-158.
2. Domi R, Sula H. Pheochromocytoma, the Challenge to Anesthesiologists. Journal Of Endocrinology And Metabolism. 2011;1(3):97-100.

PORPHYRIA

Questions:

1. Which of the following is a characteristic feature of acute porphyria crisis?
   A. Recurrent chest pain with fever
   B. Severe abdominal pain associated with tachycardia
   C. Progressive muscle weakness with a rash
   D. Persistent headaches with visual disturbances

2. What is a trigger for an acute crisis in porphyria?
   A. Smoking
   B. Alcohol consumption
   C. Dehydration
   D. All of the above

3. Which of the following drugs should be avoided in patients with porphyria undergoing anesthesia?
   A. Propofol
   B. Bupivacaine
   C. Thiopental
   D. Ondansetron

4. Which of the following is a non-acute porphyria?
   A. Acute Intermittent Porphyria (AIP)
   B. Variegate Porphyria (VP)
   C. Hereditary Coproporphyria (HCP)
   D. Porphyria Cutanea Tarda (PCT)

5. The first-line treatment for an acute porphyria crisis involves injections of hemin.
   A. True
   B. False

6. A 36-year-old female with a history of Acute Intermittent Porphyria (AIP) presents for an emergency laparoscopic cholecystectomy due to acute cholecystitis. Given the patient's medical history of AIP, meticulous anesthesia management is essential to avoid triggering or exacerbating the acute crisis during the perioperative period. The anesthesiologist reviews the patient's medical records and consults with a porphyria specialist to plan the safest anesthesia approach. Which electrolyte disturbance is commonly seen in acute porphyria crises?
   A. Low serum sodium
   B. Low serum potassium
   C. Low serum calcium
   D. High serum magnesium

Answers:

1. Answer B (Severe abdominal pain associated with tachycardia)

A characteristic feature of an acute porphyria crisis is severe abdominal pain that is poorly localized and is usually associated with symptoms like nausea, vomiting, and tachycardia. This abdominal pain is often described as colicky and can be intense. The pain may be so severe that it can mimic other conditions like endometriosis, pelvic inflammatory disease, or irritable bowel syndrome. Patients experiencing an acute porphyria crisis may also present with other symptoms, but severe abdominal pain with tachycardia is a key hallmark of this condition.

2. Answer D (All of the above)

An acute crisis in porphyria can be triggered by various factors, including smoking, alcohol consumption, dehydration, fasting, infection, certain drugs, endogenous hormones, and stress. These triggers can interfere with the heme biosynthesis pathway, leading to the accumulation of porphyrins and causing severe symptoms such as abdominal pain, nausea, constipation, palpitations, confusion, neurological manifestations, tachycardia, and hypertension.

3. Answer C (Thiopental)

Thiopental is a barbiturate anesthetic agent and is considered unsafe in porphyria due to its potential to induce porphyria attacks. Barbiturates can stimulate the heme biosynthesis pathway, leading to the accumulation of porphyrins and exacerbating the condition. Propofol and bupivacaine are safe choices for anesthesia in porphyria patients, and ondansetron can be used as an antiemetic without significant concerns for triggering an acute crisis.

4. Answer D (Porphyria Cutanea Tarda (PCT))

Porphyria Cutanea Tarda (PCT) is a non-acute porphyria. Unlike acute porphyrias such as Acute Intermittent Porphyria (AIP), Variegate Porphyria (VP), and Hereditary Coproporphyria (HCP), non-acute porphyrias do not typically lead to acute neurovisceral crises. Instead, they primarily manifest with cutaneous symptoms. PCT is characterized by photosensitivity and the development of skin lesions, such as vesicles and bullae, when the skin is exposed to sunlight. While non-acute porphyrias are important to be aware of, they are less relevant for anesthesiologists as they do not present the same acute medical management challenges as acute porphyrias. Other non-acute porphyrias include Congenital Erythropoietic Porphyria and Erythropoietic Protoporphyria.

5. Answer A (True)

The first-line treatment for an acute porphyria crisis involves injections of hemin. Hemin is a form of heme that is administered intravenously to patients experiencing an acute attack of porphyria. Hemin helps to suppress the overproduction of porphyrins and alleviates symptoms by providing an exogenous source of heme. By doing so, hemin can help reduce the accumulation of toxic porphyrin intermediates and prevent further exacerbation of the crisis. Prompt administration of hemin is crucial to managing an acute porphyria crisis effectively and preventing complications. Other supportive measures may also be employed, but hemin remains the primary and most effective treatment for acute attacks in porphyria.

6. Answer A (Low serum sodium)

Acute porphyria crises commonly present with hyponatremia. Hyponatremia occurs due to several factors during acute attacks. One contributing factor is the syndrome of inappropriate antidiuretic hormone secretion (SIADH), which can lead to excessive water retention and dilution of sodium levels in the blood. Additionally, gastrointestinal symptoms such as vomiting and diarrhea during a crisis can result in fluid losses, further exacerbating hyponatremia. Another factor is the administration of high volumes of dextrose solutions intravenously during resuscitation, which can cause a dilutional effect on serum sodium. Hyponatremia is a significant concern in acute porphyria, as it may lead to neurological manifestations such as seizures. Therefore, it is crucial to monitor and correct serum sodium levels promptly during an acute porphyria crisis to prevent complications and manage the condition effectively. During the patient's anesthesia, careful monitoring of serum sodium levels and appropriate fluid management will be essential to ensure her safety and well-being during the surgical procedure.

Recommended literature

1. Findley H, Philips A, Cole D, Nair A. Porphyrias: implications for anaesthesia, critical care, and pain medicine. Continuing Education in Anaesthesia Critical Care & Pain. 2012;12(3):128-133.

Endocrinology
SIADH

05
CHAPTER

Questions:

1. **What is the primary cause of symptoms associated with SIADH?**
   A. Excessive release of aldosterone
   B. Excessive release of antidiuretic hormone (ADH)
   C. Reduced release of vasopressin
   D. Increased release of thyroid-stimulating hormone (TSH)

2. **Which of the following laboratory findings is characteristic of SIADH?**
   A. Hypernatremia
   B. Hypokalemia
   C. Hyperkalemia
   D. Hyponatremia

3. **What is the primary treatment for SIADH-induced hyponatremia?**
   A. Fluid overload
   B. Water restriction
   C. Intravenous administration of hypotonic saline
   D. Dialysis

4. **Which medication can be used to reduce fluid retention in patients with SIADH?**
   A. Insulin
   B. Loop diuretics
   C. Glucagon
   D. Beta-blockers

5. **SIADH is associated with polyuria.**
   A. True
   B. False

6. **A 55-year-old male is admitted to the hospital complaining of nausea, vomiting, and generalized weakness. He has a past medical history of small cell lung cancer (SCLC) diagnosed three months ago, and has been undergoing chemotherapy. On examination, he appears lethargic and disoriented. Laboratory tests reveal hyponatremia and elevated urine osmolality. What is the most likely cause of the hyponatremia in this patient?**
   A. Excessive sodium intake
   B. Reduced water retention in the kidneys
   C. Elevated antidiuretic hormone (ADH) levels leading to water retention
   D. Impaired aldosterone production

Answers:

1. Answer B (Excessive release of antidiuretic hormone (ADH))

The primary cause of symptoms associated with SIADH (Syndrome of Inappropriate Antidiuretic Hormone Secretion) is the excessive release of antidiuretic hormone (ADH), also known as vasopressin. This abnormal and increased release of ADH leads to water retention in the kidneys and dilution of sodium in the bloodstream, causing hyponatremia. Hyponatremia is responsible for the various neurological and non-neurological symptoms observed in SIADH, ranging from mild manifestations like headache and lethargy to more severe symptoms such as confusion, seizures, and coma.

2. Answer D (Hyponatremia)

The characteristic laboratory finding associated with SIADH is hyponatremia. In SIADH, there is an excessive release of ADH, which leads to increased water retention in the kidneys and dilution of sodium in the bloodstream. This causes the sodium levels to decrease below the normal range, resulting in hyponatremia. Hyponatremia is the hallmark of SIADH and is responsible for the various signs and symptoms observed in this condition.

3. Answer B (Water restriction)

The primary treatment for SIADH-induced hyponatremia is water restriction. SIADH is characterized by excessive release of ADH, leading to increased water retention in the kidneys and dilution of sodium in the bloodstream, which causes hyponatremia. By restricting water intake, the body's water balance can be restored, and the diluted sodium levels can be corrected. Reducing water intake helps to limit further water retention and allows the body to excrete excess water, gradually increasing the serum sodium concentration to a more normal range.

4. Answer B (Loop diuretics)

Loop diuretics, such as furosemide, can reduce fluid retention in patients with SIADH. Loop diuretics act on the kidneys to increase the excretion of water and sodium, promoting diuresis and reducing fluid retention. By increasing urine output, loop diuretics help to eliminate excess water from the body and can be effective in managing fluid overload associated with SIADH-induced hyponatremia.

5. Answer B (False)

SIADH is not associated with polyuria. In fact, SIADH is characterized by impaired water excretion from the kidneys, leading to water retention and reduced urine output (oliguria or even anuria in severe cases). The primary abnormality in SIADH is the excessive release of ADH or vasopressin, which increases water reabsorption in the kidneys and causes the body to retain water. As a result, the urine becomes more concentrated, and the patient may have decreased urine output.

6. Answer C (Elevated ADH levels leading to water retention)

The most likely cause of hyponatremia in this patient with small cell lung cancer (SCLC) is the elevated levels of ADH associated with the SIADH. In SIADH, there is an abnormal and excessive release of ADH from the posterior pituitary gland or an abnormal non-pituitary source. This excessive release of ADH leads to increased water reabsorption in the kidneys, resulting in water retention and dilution of sodium in the bloodstream, causing hyponatremia. In this patient, the hyponatremia is likely a consequence of the ectopic production of ADH by the SCLC tumor cells. Certain tumors, including SCLC, can produce and release hormones, including ADH, inappropriately, leading to SIADH.

Recommended literature

1. Gross P. Clinical management of SIADH. Therapeutic advances in endocrinology and metabolism. 2012;3(2):61-73.
2. SIADH. In: Bissonnette B, Luginbuehl I, Marciniak B, Dalens BJ. eds. Syndromes: Rapid Recognition and Perioperative Implications. McGraw Hill; 2006. Accessed January 20, 2023.

THYROIDECTOMY

Questions:

1. **What is the main indication for a total thyroidectomy?**
   A. Symptomatic benign thyroid goiter
   B. Thyroid carcinoma
   C. Refractory hyperthyroidism
   D. All of the above

2. **In a near-total thyroidectomy, what is preserved to minimize the risk of postoperative hypoparathyroidism?**
   A. Thyroid isthmus
   B. Recurrent laryngeal nerve
   C. Superior parathyroid gland
   D. Thyroid nodule

3. **Which of the following thyroid cancer types is more likely to produce calcitonin?**
   A. Papillary
   B. Follicular
   C. Medullary
   D. Anaplastic

4. **Which of the following complications is associated with recurrent laryngeal nerve palsy after thyroidectomy?**
   A. Hypothyroidism
   B. Hoarseness
   C. Hypoparathyroidism
   D. Chyle leaks

5. **Chyle leak is NOT a complication associated with thyroidectomy.**
   A. True
   B. False

6. **A 45-year-old female patient has just undergone a near-total thyroidectomy for thyroid cancer. The surgery was uneventful, and the patient is now in the immediate postoperative period in the recovery room. Their vital signs are stable, and she is being closely monitored for any signs of complications. What is the main concern during the immediate postoperative period after thyroidectomy?**
   A. Hematoma
   B. Recurrent laryngeal nerve palsy
   C. Superior laryngeal nerve injury
   D. Parathyroid insufficiency

Answers:

1. **Answer D (All of the above)**

   Thyroidectomy is a surgical procedure performed for various benign and malignant conditions affecting the thyroid gland. Indications for thyroidectomy include thyroid nodules, hyperthyroidism, obstructive or substernal goiter, differentiated (papillary or follicular) thyroid cancer, medullary thyroid cancer (MTC), anaplastic thyroid cancer, primary thyroid lymphoma (surgery is limited to obtaining tissue biopsy), and metastases to the thyroid from extrathyroidal primary cancer (most commonly renal cell and lung cancer). The decision to perform thyroidectomy is based on the patient's specific condition and treatment plan, with the aim of addressing the underlying thyroid disorder effectively.

2. **Answer C (Superior parathyroid gland)**

   In a near-total thyroidectomy, most of the thyroid gland is removed, leaving a small amount of thyroid tissue on one or both sides, typically in the vicinity of the recurrent laryngeal nerve and the superior parathyroid gland. The primary reason for preserving the superior parathyroid gland is to minimize the risk of postoperative hypoparathyroidism. The parathyroid glands are small, hormone-secreting glands located near or embedded within the thyroid gland. They play a crucial role in calcium regulation in the body. Preserving the superior parathyroid gland during a near-total thyroidectomy helps to maintain adequate parathyroid function and prevent postoperative complications related to low levels of parathyroid hormone (PTH), which can lead to hypocalcemia and subsequent hypoparathyroidism.

3. **Answer C (Medullary)**

   MTC is the thyroid cancer type that is more likely to produce calcitonin. MTC originates from the parafollicular or C-cells of the thyroid gland, which normally produces calcitonin, a hormone involved in regulating calcium levels in the body. Therefore, in cases of MTC, the tumor cells themselves often produce calcitonin, leading to elevated levels of this hormone in the blood.

4. **Answer B (Hoarseness)**

   Recurrent laryngeal nerve palsy is a known complication associated with thyroidectomy. The recurrent laryngeal nerves are crucial nerves that supply the vocal cords, and they pass close to the thyroid gland. During thyroidectomy, there is a risk of accidental injury or damage to these nerves, leading to temporary or permanent hoarseness of the voice.

5. **Answer B (False)**

   Chyle leak is a potential complication associated with thyroidectomy. A chyle leak occurs when lymphatic fluid called chyle leaks from the thoracic duct or its tributaries in the neck. During thyroidectomy, especially when extensive dissection is involved, the lymphatic vessels can be damaged, leading to chyle leakage into the surrounding tissues. Chyle leaks can cause swelling and discomfort in the neck, and the leaked fluid may also drain externally through a wound or surgical drain. Chyle leaks are considered rare complications after thyroid surgery, but they can occur and require appropriate management and care.

6. **Answer A (Hematoma)**

   Hematoma formation at the surgical site is a critical issue that can lead to airway compromise and asphyxiation if left unrecognized or rapidly expanding. While the overall incidence of bleeding after thyroid surgery is relatively low, its potentially life-threatening consequences make it a primary concern for postoperative management. In addition to hematoma formation, thyroidectomy carries the possibility of severe postoperative complications, such as recurrent laryngeal nerve palsy, superior laryngeal nerve injury, and parathyroid insufficiency, all of which can significantly impact the patient's quality of life. However, bleeding stands out as a genuinely life-threatening complication that necessitates immediate surgical intervention. Reoperation due to bleeding can lead to further complications, underscoring the critical importance of close monitoring and timely intervention to ensure patient safety and prevent adverse outcomes, including death.

Recommended literature

1. Pollard BJ, Kitchen G. Handbook of Clinical Anaesthesia. 4th ed. Taylor & Francis group; 2018. Chapter 20 Head and neck surgery, Macnab R and Bexon K.

HEMATOLOGY

ACUTE LEUKEMIA

06
CHAPTER

Questions:

1. **What is acute leukemia characterized by?**
   A. Proliferation of mature white blood cells
   B. A rapid increase in the number of platelets
   C. Proliferation of immature white blood cells
   D. Low hemoglobin and high platelet count

2. **Which of the following is a symptom of acute leukemia?**
   A. Bone and joint pain
   B. Swollen lymph nodes
   C. Abdominal pain
   D. All of the above

3. **Which of the following risk factors is NOT associated with acute leukemia?**
   A. Radiation exposure
   B. Smoking
   C. Down syndrome
   D. Alcoholism

4. **Which of the following is not typically considered a potential consideration for anesthesia in patients with acute leukemia during the perioperative period?**
   A. Impaired immunity
   B. Thrombocytopenia
   C. Hyperleukocytosis
   D. Liver cirrhosis

5. **Chemotherapy is the first line of treatment for Acute lymphoblastic leukemia (ALL) and Acute myelogenous leukemia (AML).**
   A. True
   B. False

6. **The patient, a 45-year-old male, has undergone a bone marrow transplantation and is currently in the recovery room. The patient's blood test results reveal that he has a hemoglobin level of 80 g/L, and a platelet count of 50,000/μL. Considering the patient's blood test results after the bone marrow transplantation, which of the following postoperative analgesia medications should be avoided?**
   A. NSAID
   B. Tramadol
   C. Morphine
   D. Paracetamol

Answers:

1. Answer C (Proliferation of immature white blood cells)

Acute leukemia is characterized by the proliferation of immature white blood cells, also known as blasts, in the bone marrow or peripheral blood. These immature cells do not fully develop into functional white blood cells and accumulate rapidly, leading to an imbalance in the normal blood cell population. As a result, the bone marrow is unable to produce sufficient healthy blood cells, including red blood cells and platelets, leading to low hemoglobin levels and low platelet counts.

2. Answer D (All of the above)

Acute leukemia is characterized by the proliferation of immature white blood cells, which can lead to a variety of symptoms such as bone and joint pain, swollen lymph nodes, abdominal pain caused by a swollen liver or spleen, unintentional weight loss, pale skin, fatigue, frequent infections, bleeding issues like nosebleeds and bruising, high temperature/fever, night sweats, skin rashes, and a feeling of fullness or discomfort in the abdomen. Both Acute Lymphoblastic Leukemia (ALL) and Acute Myelogenous Leukemia (AML) can manifest these symptoms due to the rapid accumulation of abnormal cells in the bone marrow and peripheral blood.

3. Answer D (Alcoholism)

Acute leukemia is linked to various risk factors, such as radiation and benzene exposure, smoking, chemotherapy, certain blood disorders like myelodysplasia, myelofibrosis, and polycythemia, as well as specific genetic disorders like Down syndrome and Fanconi's anemia. Notably, alcoholism is not associated with an increased likelihood of developing acute leukemia. However, it is crucial to understand that drinking during acute leukemia treatment can significantly impact overall health and recovery.

4. Answer D (Liver cirrhosis)

Patients with acute leukemia require meticulous attention and special considerations during anesthesia due to their unique medical condition. While liver cirrhosis is not typically associated with acute leukemia and is not relevant to the perioperative management of these patients, anesthesia care should focus on addressing the specific considerations related to acute leukemia and its treatment. These considerations include the heightened risk of infection due to impaired immunity, thrombocytopenia, which increases the likelihood of bleeding and hemorrhage, and hyperleukocytosis, which may lead to complications like leukostasis. Additionally, disseminated intravascular coagulopathy (DIC) with potential bleeding and clotting issues, as well as tumor lysis syndrome (TLS) causing metabolic imbalances and acute renal failure, should be carefully managed. Moreover, neurologic and pulmonary complications arising from leukemic infiltrates or infections, and potential chemotherapy-related complications such as end-organ dysfunction or cardiomyopathy, should be taken into account. Furthermore, the risk of graft-versus-host disease following bone marrow transplantation, susceptibility to opportunistic infections like viral, bacterial, and fungal pathogens, and the heightened risk of sepsis due to compromised immune function should also be considered as vital aspects of anesthesia care for patients with acute leukemia.

5. Answer A (True)

Chemotherapy is the first-line treatment for both ALL and AML. These two types of acute leukemia are the most common among adults and children, and chemotherapy forms the cornerstone of their initial treatment. For ALL, a combination of different chemotherapy drugs is used to target and eliminate the rapidly dividing leukemia cells. Similarly, AML is also treated with a combination of chemotherapy drugs, with the specific regimen tailored to the subtype and the patient's individual factors. While additional therapies like targeted treatments or stem cell transplantation may be considered based on the patient's response and specific risk factors, chemotherapy remains the primary and essential first-line treatment for both ALL and AML.

6. Answer A (NSAID)

The patient's post-transplant blood test results indicate anemia and thrombocytopenia. These conditions put the patient at a significant risk of bleeding, as platelets play a crucial role in blood clotting. Non-steroidal anti-inflammatory drugs (NSAIDs), such as aspirin or ibuprofen, have antiplatelet effects and can further increase the risk of bleeding in patients with thrombocytopenia. Therefore, NSAIDs should be avoided as postoperative analgesia in this patient to reduce the risk of bleeding complications. Instead, pain management options such as tramadol or paracetamol can be considered, as they have minimal impact on platelet function and do not pose an increased risk of bleeding.

Recommended literature

1. Groenewold MD, Olthof CG, Bosch DJ. Anaesthesia after neoadjuvant chemotherapy, immunotherapy or radiotherapy. BJA Educ. 2022;22(1):12-19.
2. Louise Oduro-Dominah L, Brennan LH, Anaesthetic management of the child with haematological malignancy, Continuing Education in Anaesthesia Critical Care & Pain, Volume 13, Issue 5, October 2013, Pages 158–164.
3. Allan N, Siller C, Breen A. Anaesthetic implications of chemotherapy, Continuing Education in Anaesthesia Critical Care & Pain, Volume 12, Issue 2, April 2012, Pages 52–56.

Hematology
ANTIPHOSPHOLIPID ANTIBODY SYNDROME

Questions:

1. **What is the main mechanism of antiphospholipid antibody syndrome (APS)?**
   A. Excessive production of red blood cells
   B. Autoantibodies attack tissues in the body by mistake
   C. Overactive immune response to viral infections
   D. Deficiency of platelets in the blood

2. **Which of the following is a common symptom of APS?**
   A. Abdominal pain
   B. Joint swelling
   C. Cognitive dysfunction
   D. Elevated blood sugar levels

3. **Which type of APS is associated with another underlying autoimmune disease?**
   A. Primary APS
   B. Secondary APS
   C. Hereditary APS
   D. Catastrophic APS

4. **Which of the following is NOT a risk factor for APS?**
   A. Radiation exposure
   B. Pregnancy
   C. Smoking
   D. High cholesterol levels

5. **Low-dose aspirin is the primary thromboprophylaxis for patients diagnosed with APS who have no previous history of vascular thrombosis and/or obstetric events.**
   A. True
   B. False

6. **A 28-year-old pregnant woman has been diagnosed with APS during her current pregnancy. She has no prior history of vascular thrombosis or obstetric events. What should be the thromboprophylaxis for this pregnant woman with APS?**
   A. Low-dose aspirin and oral anticoagulants
   B. Low-dose aspirin and LMWH (Low-Molecular-Weight Heparin)
   C. Low-dose aspirin and corticosteroids
   D. High-dose aspirin and intravenous immunoglobulin

241

Answers:

1. Answer B (Autoantibodies attacking tissues in the body by mistake)

The main mechanism of antiphospholipid antibody syndrome (APS) is the production of autoantibodies that attack phospholipids. These autoantibodies, known as antiphospholipid antibodies, target phospholipids and associated proteins, leading to abnormal clotting and an increased risk of blood clots forming in arteries and veins. This attack on phospholipids can cause various complications, such as deep vein thrombosis (DVT), pulmonary embolism, stroke, and other thrombotic events. Additionally, APS can also cause pregnancy-related complications, such as miscarriages, stillbirths, and other obstetric complications, due to interference with normal blood flow in the placenta.

2. Answer C (Cognitive dysfunction)

APS is a complex autoimmune disorder that can present with a wide range of symptoms affecting various organs and systems. Among these manifestations, cognitive dysfunction is a common neurological symptom observed in APS patients. The syndrome can also cause vascular thrombosis, leading to arterial and venous thrombosis, obstetric morbidity such as fetal death and recurrent spontaneous abortions, cardiac issues like valvular heart disease and cardiomyopathies, as well as dermatologic, renal, and hematologic manifestations.

3. Answer B (Secondary APS)

Secondary APS is the type of APS that is associated with another underlying autoimmune disease. In this case, APS coexists with another autoimmune disorder, most commonly systemic lupus erythematosus (SLE). When APS occurs alongside another autoimmune disease, it is referred to as secondary APS.

4. Answer A (Radiation exposure)

Radiation exposure is not a recognized risk factor for APS. APS is primarily an autoimmune disorder characterized by the production of autoantibodies that attack phospholipids in the blood, leading to an increased risk of blood clot formation. The risk factors for APS include pregnancy, immobility, surgery, smoking, use of oral contraceptives or estrogen therapy for menopause, high cholesterol and triglyceride levels, and the presence of systemic autoimmune diseases such as lupus.

5. Answer A (True)

Low-dose aspirin (usually 75-100 mg per day) is often used as primary thromboprophylaxis for patients with APS who have no prior history of vascular thrombosis and/or obstetric events. Aspirin is an antiplatelet medication that helps to prevent platelets from aggregating and forming blood clots. By using low-dose aspirin in APS patients without a history of thrombotic events, the aim is to reduce the risk of future clot formation and its associated complications.

6. Answer B (Low-dose aspirin and LMWH (Low-Molecular-Weight Heparin))

Thromboprophylaxis in pregnant women with APS typically involves a combination of low-dose aspirin and LMWH (Low-Molecular-Weight Heparin). Low-dose aspirin helps reduce platelet aggregation and blood clot formation, while LMWH is an anticoagulant that can prevent the formation of blood clots. This combination has been shown to be effective in reducing the risk of pregnancy complications, such as miscarriages, stillbirths, and other obstetric issues, in women with APS.

Recommended literature

1. Kim JW, Kim TW, Ryu KH, Park SG, Jeong CY, Park DH. Anaesthetic considerations for patients with antiphospholipid syndrome undergoing non-cardiac surgery. J Int Med Res. 2020;48(1):300060519896889.

Hematology
COAGULOPATHY

Questions:

1. **What is the definition of coagulopathy?**
   A. A condition characterized by excessive clot formation
   B. A condition in which the blood's ability to form clots is impaired
   C. A genetic disorder causing abnormal platelet function
   D. A rare autoimmune disease affecting blood coagulation

2. **Which of the following is NOT a potential cause of coagulopathy?**
   A. Hemophilia
   B. Liver disease
   C. Von Willebrand disease
   D. Antiphospholipid syndrome

3. **What is the target hemoglobin level for red blood cell transfusions in patients with coagulopathy?**
   A. 10-12 g/dL
   B. 8-10 g/dL
   C. 7-9 g/dL
   D. 6-8 g/dL

4. **Which statement about hypothermia is incorrect?**
   A. Hypothermia impairs thrombin generation
   B. Hypothermia inhibits fibrinogen synthesis
   C. Hypothermia contributes to platelet dysfunction
   D. Hypothermia promotes coagulation enzymes

5. **ROTEM (Rotational Thromboelastometry) is a near-patient testing technique that provides real-time information about a patient's clotting function.**
   A. True
   B. False

6. **You are an anesthesiologist in the preoperative evaluation clinic, and a 12-year-old boy is scheduled for dental surgery. During the preoperative assessment, the boy's mother informs you that her brother has been diagnosed with hemophilia A. Which test below would be the best screening test for hemophilia A?**
   A. Activated Partial Thromboplastin Time (APTT or PTT)
   B. Prothrombin Time (PT)
   C. Complete Blood Count (CBC)
   D. Bleeding time

Answers:

1. **Answer B (A condition in which the blood's ability to form clots is impaired)**

   Coagulopathy is a medical condition characterized by impaired blood coagulation, leading to a reduced ability to form blood clots. This condition can result in a tendency toward prolonged or excessive bleeding, either spontaneously or following an injury. It can be caused by various factors, including genetic disorders, acquired factors such as liver disease, the use of certain medications like anticoagulants, and other conditions like disseminated intravascular coagulation (DIC). The impaired coagulation can be due to deficiencies or dysfunction of clotting factors, platelets, or other components involved in the clotting process.

2. **Answer D (Antiphospholipid Syndrome)**

   Antiphospholipid Syndrome is not a potential cause of coagulopathy. It is an autoimmune disorder characterized by the presence of antiphospholipid antibodies that can cause blood clots in both veins and arteries. However, coagulopathy specifically refers to a condition where the blood's ability to form clots is impaired, leading to a tendency toward prolonged or excessive bleeding. The causes of coagulopathy include genetic conditions such as hemophilia and Von Willebrand disease, as well as acquired factors like anticoagulant medications (e.g., warfarin), the continued use of antibiotics, liver disease, or disseminated intravascular coagulation (DIC). In coagulopathy, activation of coagulation can lead to the consumption of clotting factors, particularly factor V and fibrinogen, resulting in a consumptive coagulopathy.

3. **Answer C (7-9 g/dL)**

   The target hemoglobin level for red blood cell transfusions in patients with coagulopathy is between 7-9 g/dL. The transfusion threshold of 7 g/dL for red blood cells is based on evidence from clinical trials and guidelines. It is important to note that the optimal transfusion threshold may vary depending on the patient's specific clinical condition, age, comorbidities, and other factors. The threshold of 7 g/dL is commonly used in various clinical scenarios, especially in patients with coagulopathy, but it is not a one-size-fits-all approach.

4. **Answer D (Hypothermia promotes coagulation enzymes)**

   This statement is incorrect because hypothermia actually impairs coagulation rather than promoting it. Hypothermia is associated with various adverse effects on the blood clotting process. It slows down thrombin generation, which is a key enzyme involved in clot formation. Additionally, hypothermia inhibits fibrinogen synthesis, leading to a reduced ability to form stable fibrin clots. Furthermore, it contributes to platelet dysfunction, impairing their ability to aggregate and participate in clot formation. In summary, hypothermia has a significant negative impact on the coagulation cascade, making patients more susceptible to bleeding complications.

5. **Answer A (True)**

   ROTEM (Rotational Thromboelastometry) is a near-patient testing technique used to assess a patient's clotting function in real-time. It is a valuable tool in managing coagulation disorders and guiding appropriate treatment during surgery, trauma, or other clinical situations where rapid assessment of clotting function is crucial. ROTEM measures the viscoelastic properties of the blood clot as it forms, providing information about clot formation, strength, stability, and fibrinolysis. This real-time data allows clinicians to tailor specific interventions, such as blood component transfusions or administration of clotting agents like tranexamic acid, to optimize patient outcomes.

6. **Answer A (Activated Partial Thromboplastin Time (APTT or PTT))**

   The best screening test for hemophilia A Activated Partial Thromboplastin Time (APTT or PTT). Hemophilia A is characterized by a deficiency of factor VIII, a clotting factor involved in the intrinsic pathway of coagulation. APTT assesses the function of the intrinsic pathway and can help detect abnormalities related to factors II, VIII, IX, X, XI, and XII and fibrinogen. It is widely used as an initial screening test for hemophilia A, as it evaluates the time it takes for a blood clot to form in response to specific activators. If the APTT is prolonged, further testing can be done to confirm the diagnosis and identify the specific clotting factor deficiency. Option B, Prothrombin Time (PT), primarily assesses the extrinsic pathway of coagulation and is not sensitive to detecting factor VIII deficiency seen in hemophilia A. Option C, Complete Blood Count (CBC), provides information about the number of blood cells but does not directly assess clotting function. Option D, Bleeding time, measures the time it takes for a small skin incision to stop bleeding and is not specific enough to diagnose hemophilia A.

Recommended literature

1. Hofer S, Schlimp CJ, Casu S, Grouzi E. Management of Coagulopathy in Bleeding Patients. J Clin Med. 2021;11(1):1.
2. Pollard BJ, Kitchen, G. Handbook of Clinical Anaesthesia. Fourth Edition. CRC Press. 2018. 978-1-4987-6289-2.
3. Simmons J, Powel M. 2016. Acute traumatic coagulopathy: pathophysiology and resuscitation. BJA: British journal of anaesthesia. 17;3:31-43.
4. Gaunt, C., Woolley, T., 2014. Management of haemorrhage in major trauma. Continuing Education in Anaesthesia Critical Care & Pain 14, 251-255.
5. Daniel Bolliger, Klaus Görlinger, Kenichi A. Tanaka, David S. Warner; Pathophysiology and Treatment of Coagulopathy in Massive Hemorrhage and Hemodilution. Anesthesiology 2010; 113:1205-1219.

DISSEMINATED INTRAVASCULAR COAGULATION (DIC)

Questions:

1. Which of the following best describes Disseminated Intravascular Coagulation (DIC)?
   A. A condition characterized by localized blood clot formation
   B. A disorder with simultaneous thrombotic and bleeding problems
   C. A disease caused exclusively by sepsis
   D. A condition that primarily affects the respiratory system

2. What is the main underlying mechanism responsible for DIC's development?
   A. Impaired production of clotting factors by the liver
   B. Excessive immune reactions in the body
   C. Systemic activation of blood coagulation
   D. Toxin release from cancer cells

3. Which of the following is NOT a common sign or symptom of DIC?
   A. Bleeding from wound sites
   B. Confusion and memory loss
   C. Unexplained fever
   D. Excessive blood clotting in the veins

4. Which condition is a known cause of DIC?
   A. Major surgery
   B. Cirrhosis
   C. Snake venom
   D. All of the above

5. The kidneys are the primary organs responsible for the production of clotting factors in the body.
   A. True
   B. False

6. A 32-year-old woman presents with severe bleeding during or after delivery. She has a history of placental separation during childbirth. Clinical examination reveals bleeding from the wound site, gums, and mouth, along with easy bruising. Laboratory tests show a critically low fibrinogen level (< 1 g/L). Based on the signs and symptoms, DIC is suspected. What is the mainstay treatment for DIC-induced severe bleeding with low fibrinogen levels?
   A. Cryoprecipitate
   B. Fresh frozen plasma (FFP)
   C. Platelet transfusion
   D. Vitamin K administration

Answers:

1. Answer B (A disorder with simultaneous thrombotic and bleeding problems)

Disseminated Intravascular Coagulation (DIC) is a serious medical condition characterized by the widespread activation of the body's blood clotting system, leading to the formation of microvascular thrombi throughout the body. These thrombi can block blood flow to vital organs, resulting in multiple organ dysfunction syndrome (MODS). At the same time, DIC can also cause the consumption of clotting factors and platelets, leading to an increased risk of life-threatening bleeding.

2. Answer C (Systemic activation of blood coagulation)

DIC is characterized by the systemic activation of the body's blood coagulation system. This means that the clotting process is activated throughout the entire circulatory system, leading to the formation of small blood clots in various organs and tissues. The widespread activation of blood coagulation is the main underlying mechanism responsible for the development of DIC. While other options may contribute to clotting abnormalities in specific conditions, they are not the primary mechanism that drives DIC. In DIC, the balance between pro-coagulant and anti-coagulant factors is disrupted, leading to excessive clot formation and consumption of clotting factors, which results in both thrombotic and bleeding problems.

3. Answer D (Excessive blood clotting in the veins)

DIC is primarily characterized by the widespread activation of the body's blood clotting system, leading to the formation of small blood clots throughout the microvasculature. While bleeding from wound sites or from the nose, gums, or mouth, confusion, memory loss, change of behavior, and unexplained fever are common signs and symptoms of DIC, excessive blood clotting in the veins is not a typical feature of the condition.

4. Answer D (All of the above)

DIC is a serious medical condition characterized by the systemic activation of the body's blood coagulation system, which leads to the formation of small blood clots throughout the microvasculature. The conditions, such as sepsis, major organ damage, cirrhosis, pancreatitis, severe injury, burns, major surgery, severe immune reactions, exposure to toxins like snake venom, serious pregnancy-related problems, certain types of cancer, and COVID-19, can all trigger DIC through different pathways, but the common feature among them is the activation of the clotting system.

5. Answer B (False)

The kidneys are not the primary organs responsible for the production of clotting factors in the body. The liver is the main organ responsible for the synthesis of clotting factors, including factors involved in the coagulation cascade. The liver plays a central role in producing and releasing these clotting factors into the bloodstream, where they participate in the clotting process. In contrast, the kidneys are not directly involved in the production of clotting factors and do not play a significant role in the coagulation process.

6. Answer A (Cryoprecipitate)

The mainstay treatment for DIC-induced severe bleeding with low fibrinogen levels is cryoprecipitate administration. As fibrinogen is a critical coagulation factor in the hemostatic process, its depletion in DIC leads to the observed bleeding manifestations. Cryoprecipitate, being rich in fibrinogen, along with factors VIII and XIII and von Willebrand factor, helps replenish the depleted fibrinogen levels and supports clot formation, thereby controlling the bleeding. It is important to administer fibrinogen replacement, such as cryoprecipitate, before fresh frozen plasma (FFP), as FFP may not provide sufficient fibrinogen content. Additionally, other therapies may also be considered, depending on the severity and underlying cause of DIC. FFP can be administered to correct coagulation deficiencies, including factors II, V, VII, IX, and X. Platelet transfusion may be necessary in cases of significant thrombocytopenia. Furthermore, the use of specific treatments targeting the underlying cause of DIC, such as treating the infection in sepsis-associated DIC or addressing the placental separation in the postpartum setting, is essential for effective management.

Recommended literature

1. Thachil J. Disseminated Intravascular Coagulation: A Practical Approach. Anesthesiology. 2016;125(1):230-236.
2. Ridley, S., Taylor, B., Gunning, K., 2007. Medical management of bleeding in critically ill patients. Continuing Education in Anaesthesia Critical Care & Pain 7, 116–121.

FACTOR V LEIDEN

Questions:

1. **What is Factor V Leiden?**
   A. A deficiency of factor V in the blood
   B. An autosomal recessive disorder affecting the F5 gene
   C. An inherited mutation of the F5 gene leads to increased resistance to activated protein C
   D. A disorder caused by an excess of activated protein C in the blood

2. **What is the most common inherited blood clotting disorder?**
   A. Hemophilia A
   B. Von Willebrand disease
   C. Factor V Leiden
   D. Hemophilia B

3. **Which of the following is NOT a risk factor for developing blood clots in individuals with Factor V Leiden?**
   A. Immobility
   B. Estrogen-based therapies
   C. Non-O blood type
   D. High intake of vitamin K-rich foods

4. **Which of the following clotting factors is a natural anticoagulant protein in the blood?**
   A. Factor V
   B. Factor VIII
   C. Factor X
   D. Activated protein C

5. **Patients with the Factor V Leiden mutation require lifelong thromboprophylaxis therapy.**
   A. True
   B. False

6. **A 42-year-old patient is scheduled for elective knee surgery due to persistent joint pain. He has a medical history of Factor V Leiden. What is the significance of Factor V Leiden during perioperative periods?**
   A. Increased risk of bleeding
   B. Increased risk of clotting events
   C. No impact on perioperative outcomes
   D. Increased risk of infection

Answers:

1. **Answer C (An inherited mutation of the F5 gene leading to increased resistance to activated protein C)**

   Factor V Leiden is an autosomal dominant inherited mutation of the F5 gene, which controls the production of factor V, one of the clotting factors in the blood. This mutation leads to increased resistance to activated protein C, which is a natural anticoagulant protein in the blood. As a result, the regulation of blood clotting is disrupted, and affected individuals have an increased risk of blood clot formation, particularly deep vein thrombosis (DVT) and pulmonary embolism (PE). It is important to note that Factor V Leiden is not a deficiency of factor V or a disorder caused by an excess of activated protein C, but rather it is a specific inherited genetic mutation affecting factor V regulation in the clotting process.

2. **Answer C (Factor V Leiden)**

   Factor V Leiden is the most common inherited blood clotting disorder. It is an autosomal dominant inherited mutation of the F5 gene, which controls factor V production, leading to increased resistance to activated protein C and an increased risk of blood clot formation. Heterozygosity of the mutation is prevalent in approximately 1% to 5% of the unselected white population and in roughly 10% to 20% of individuals with venous thromboembolism (VTE). Heterozygosity increases the lifetime risk of thrombosis by about 7-fold, while homozygosity (which is rare) increases the risk by approximately 20-fold. Despite the elevated risk of VTE, there is no clinical evidence that heterozygosity of factor V Leiden increases overall mortality.

3. **Answer D (High intake of vitamin K-rich foods)**

   While immobility, intake of estrogen-based therapies, surgeries or injuries, and having a non-O blood type are considered risk factors for developing blood clots in individuals with Factor V Leiden, high intake of vitamin K-rich foods is not associated with an increased risk of clotting in this context. Vitamin K is essential for blood clotting regulation, but its consumption from dietary sources typically does not lead to a significant impact on clotting risk in individuals with Factor V Leiden.

4. **Answer D (Activated protein C)**

   Activated protein C is a natural anticoagulant protein in the blood. It plays a vital role in regulating the blood clotting process by inhibiting the activity of factors Va and VIIIa, which are essential for clot formation. Activated protein C helps prevent excessive clotting and maintains the balance between clot formation and clot dissolution. In the context of Factor V Leiden, a mutation that causes increased resistance to activated protein C, the anticoagulant function of activated protein C is compromised, leading to an increased risk of blood clot formation.

5. **Answer B (False)**

   Only patients with a history of VTE require treatment. Asymptomatic individuals with the Factor V Leiden mutation do not routinely receive long-term prophylactic anticoagulation. Instead, the decision to initiate prophylactic anticoagulation in asymptomatic heterozygotes is based on circumstantial risk factors. These factors may include situations where the individual is at higher risk for blood clot formation, such as during extended periods of immobility (e.g., after surgery or prolonged bed rest). In such cases, a short course of prophylactic anticoagulation may be considered to prevent initial thrombosis.

6. **Answer B (Increased risk of clotting events)**

   During perioperative periods, individuals with Factor V Leiden are at an increased risk of clotting events. The genetic mutation causes a higher tendency for blood clot formation, especially in situations with increased clotting risk, such as surgery. Proper perioperative management, including prophylactic anticoagulant therapy, when appropriate, is essential to mitigate the risk of thrombotic events and ensure a successful surgical outcome.

Recommended literature

1. Shah UJ, Madan Narayanan M, J Graham Smith JH. 2015. Anaesthetic considerations in patients with inherited disorders of coagulation. Continuing Education in Anaesthesia Critical Care & Pain. 15;1 26-31.
2. Albagoush SA, Koya S, Chakraborty RK, et al. Factor V Leiden Mutation. [Updated 2023 Apr 8]. In: StatPearls [Internet]. Treasure Island (FL): StatPearls Publishing; 2023 Jan-. Available from: https://www.ncbi.nlm.nih.gov/books/NBK534802/

Hematology
G6PD DEFICIENCY

Questions:

1. **What is the most common mode of inheritance of G6PD deficiency?**
   A. Autosomal dominant
   B. Autosomal recessive
   C. X-linked dominant
   D. X-linked recessive

2. **What role does G6PD play in red blood cells?**
   A. It synthesizes hemoglobin
   B. It protects against viral infections
   C. It produces energy in the form of ATP
   D. It protects against oxidative stress

3. **Which of the following foods should individuals with G6PD deficiency avoid?**
   A. Apples
   B. Fava beans
   C. Chicken
   D. Rice

4. **What can be seen in the red blood cells of individuals with G6PD deficiency under certain conditions?**
   A. Nuclei
   B. Heinz bodies
   C. Mitochondria
   D. Ribosomes

5. **Individuals carrying G6PD variants may experience partial protection against malaria.**
   A. True
   B. False

6. **A 35-year-old male patient has been diagnosed with glucose-6-phosphate dehydrogenase (G6PD) deficiency. He is scheduled to undergo surgery for a hernia repair under general anesthesia. The anesthesiologist and surgical team must be aware of his condition to prevent triggers that could lead to hemolysis. Common medications that can trigger hemolysis in G6PD-deficient patients should be avoided or used with caution. Which of the following medications can trigger hemolysis in individuals with G6PD deficiency?**
   A. Propofol
   B. Fentanyl
   C. Aspirin
   D. Dexamethason

Answers:

1. Answer D (X-linked recessive)

G6PD deficiency is primarily inherited in an X-linked recessive manner. This means that the gene responsible for G6PD deficiency is located on the X chromosome. Since males have only one X chromosome (XY), a mutation on that single X chromosome can lead to the expression of the disorder. Females, on the other hand, have two X chromosomes (XX) and typically need to inherit the mutated gene from both parents to express the disorder. As a result, males are more commonly affected by G6PD deficiency, as they have a higher chance of inheriting a single mutated X chromosome. This pattern of inheritance is a key characteristic of X-linked recessive disorders.

2. Answer D (It protects against oxidative stress)

Glucose-6-phosphate dehydrogenase (G6PD) is an enzyme that plays a crucial role in protecting red blood cells against oxidative stress, which occurs when reactive oxygen species (ROS) accumulate within cells. ROS are highly reactive molecules that can damage cellular components like proteins, lipids, and DNA, leading to cell dysfunction and even cell death. In the context of red blood cells, G6PD is particularly important because these cells are highly susceptible to oxidative stress due to their exposure to oxygen and other reactive molecules while transporting oxygen throughout the body. Individuals with G6PD deficiency lack the protective mechanism provided by adequate levels of the enzyme, making their red blood cells more vulnerable to oxidative damage and hemolysis when exposed to oxidative stressors.

3. Answer B (Fava beans)

Individuals with G6PD deficiency should avoid consuming fava beans (also known as broad beans). Fava beans contain certain compounds, such as vicine and convicine, that can trigger hemolysis in people with G6PD deficiency. These compounds can induce oxidative stress in red blood cells, leading to their breakdown.

4. Answer B (Heinz bodies)

Heinz bodies are abnormal structures that can be seen in the red blood cells of individuals with G6PD deficiency under certain conditions. Heinz bodies are formed when denatured or oxidized hemoglobin within the red blood cells clumps together, creating inclusion bodies that are not normally present. In G6PD deficiency, red blood cells lack sufficient protection against oxidative stress, making them more prone to the formation of Heinz bodies when exposed to oxidative agents. These Heinz bodies can compromise the structural integrity of the red blood cells and increase their susceptibility to hemolysis. The presence of Heinz bodies is an important diagnostic feature in G6PD deficiency and can be observed microscopically in stained blood smears, helping clinicians identify individuals with the condition and evaluate the severity of their red blood cell damage.

5. Answer A (True)

It is true that individuals with certain variants of G6PD deficiency may be partially protected against malaria, which is an infectious disease transmitted by certain species of mosquitoes. This protection is believed to result from the fact that the parasite causing malaria (Plasmodium) relies on the oxidative stress response of red blood cells to survive and replicate within the cells. In individuals with G6PD deficiency, red blood cells are already more susceptible to oxidative stress due to the lack of the G6PD enzyme. This increased susceptibility can create an environment within the red blood cells that is less conducive to the growth and survival of the malaria parasite. As a result, individuals with G6PD deficiency variants may have a reduced risk of developing severe forms of malaria. However, it's important to note that this protection is not absolute, and the relationship between G6PD deficiency and malaria is complex and can vary depending on the specific G6PD variant, the population, and other factors.

6. Answer C (Aspirin)

Aspirin is one of the medications that can trigger hemolysis in individuals with G6PD deficiency. Other common medications that should be avoided or used with caution in G6PD-deficient patients include acetaminophen, chloroquine, primaquine, sulfonamides, and certain antibiotics. These medications can induce oxidative stress and damage red blood cells in individuals with G6PD deficiency.

Recommended literature

1. Cicvarić, A., Glavaš Tahtler, J., Vukoja Vukušić, T., Bekavac, I., Kvolik, S., 2022. Management of Anesthesia and Perioperative Procedures in a Child with Glucose-6-Phosphate Dehydrogenase Deficiency. Journal of Clinical Medicine 11, 6476.
2. Goi T, Shionoya Y, Sunada K, Nakamura K. General Anesthesia in a Glucose-6-Phosphate Dehydrogenase Deficiency Child: A Case Report. Anesth Prog. 2019;66(2):94-96.
3. Pollard BJ, Kitchen, G. Handbook of Clinical Anaesthesia. Fourth Edition. CRC Press. 2018. 978-1-4987-6289-2.
4. Valiaveedan S, Mahajan C, Rath GP, Bindra A, Marda MK. Anaesthetic management in patients with glucose-6-phosphate dehydrogenase deficiency undergoing neurosurgical procedures. Indian J Anaesth. 2011;55(1):68-70.

Hematology
HEMOPHILIA

Questions:

1. **What is the main underlying cause of hemophilia?**
   A. Autoimmune disorders
   B. Deficiency of clotting factors
   C. Elevated levels of fibrinogen
   D. Excessive platelet aggregation

2. **Which type of hemophilia is caused by a lack or decrease of clotting factor VIII?**
   A. Hemophilia A
   B. Hemophilia B
   C. Hemophilia C
   D. Hemophilia D

3. **What is the main difference between mild and severe hemophilia in terms of factor activity levels?**
   A. Mild hemophilia has lower factor activity levels than severe hemophilia
   B. Severe hemophilia has lower factor activity levels than mild hemophilia
   C. Mild and severe hemophilia have the same factor activity levels
   D. Factor activity levels are not related to the severity of hemophilia

4. **What is the primary treatment for hemophilia?**
   A. Antibiotics
   B. Steroids
   C. Replacement therapy with clotting factors
   D. Antiviral medications

5. **Christmas Disease is caused by a deficiency of clotting factor VIII.**
   A. True
   B. False

6. **A 30-year-old woman has been managing her mild hemophilia A since she was a child. She has successfully navigated the challenges of her condition and maintained an active lifestyle. Recently, she learned that she needs to undergo a planned abdominal surgery due to a non-life-threatening medical issue. Her factor VIII levels are around 30% (IU/mL), indicative of her mild hemophilia A. The hematologist discusses the importance of optimizing her factor VIII levels before the surgery to minimize bleeding risks. They also explore the option of using desmopressin as part of her preoperative management. What role does desmopressin play in the patient's preoperative management of her moderate hemophilia A?**
   A. It replaces deficient clotting factors
   B. It stimulates platelet production
   C. It enhances fibrinogen levels
   D. It can temporarily increase factor VIII levels

Answers:

1. Answer B (Deficiency of clotting factors)

The main underlying cause of hemophilia is a deficiency or reduced activity of specific clotting factors. Hemophilia is a genetic disorder, often inherited as an X-linked recessive trait. This means that the genes responsible for producing the deficient clotting factors are located on the X chromosome. When these genes are mutated or absent, the production of the respective clotting factor is impaired, leading to a reduced ability of the blood to clot properly. As a result, individuals with hemophilia are at risk of prolonged bleeding after injuries, surgeries, or other forms of trauma. This deficiency in clotting factors is what distinguishes hemophilia from other bleeding disorders, and it is the primary cause of the disorder's characteristic symptoms and complications.

2. Answer A (Hemophilia A)

Hemophilia A is the type of hemophilia that is caused by a lack or decrease of clotting factor VIII. Factor VIII is an essential protein involved in the blood clotting cascade. In individuals with hemophilia A, there is a genetic mutation that leads to reduced levels or functional impairment of factor VIII. As a result, these individuals experience difficulties in forming stable blood clots, leading to prolonged bleeding times and an increased risk of bleeding episodes, both spontaneously and after injuries or surgeries. Hemophilia A is the most common type of hemophilia and is often classified by the severity of factor VIII deficiency into mild, moderate, or severe cases.

3. Answer B (Severe hemophilia has lower factor activity levels than mild hemophilia)

The main difference between mild and severe hemophilia lies in the factor activity levels. Factor activity levels refer to the amount of the deficient clotting factor in the blood. In severe hemophilia, the factor activity levels are very low, generally less than 1% of normal levels. This significant deficiency in clotting factors results in a higher risk of bleeding episodes and more severe bleeding symptoms. On the other hand, in mild hemophilia, the factor activity levels are higher, typically ranging from 5% to 40% of normal levels. Individuals with mild hemophilia may experience milder bleeding symptoms and may not have spontaneous bleeding but are still at an increased risk of bleeding after injuries or surgeries. The severity of hemophilia is closely related to the factor activity levels, with a more severe deficiency leading to more frequent and severe bleeding episodes.

4. Answer C (Replacement therapy with clotting factors)

The primary treatment for hemophilia involves replacement therapy with clotting factors. Hemophilia is characterized by a deficiency or reduced activity of specific clotting factors (factor VIII in hemophilia A and factor IX in hemophilia B). Replacement therapy aims to provide the missing or deficient clotting factor by infusing it into the patient's bloodstream. This helps restore the ability of the blood to clot properly, reducing the risk of bleeding and managing bleeding episodes more effectively.

5. Answer B (False)

Christmas Disease, also known as hemophilia B, is not caused by a deficiency of clotting factor VIII. Rather, it is caused by a deficiency of clotting factor IX. Hemophilia B is a genetic bleeding disorder where individuals lack sufficient factor IX, which is required for effective blood clotting. This deficiency leads to prolonged bleeding times and an increased susceptibility to bleeding episodes, especially after injuries or surgeries. Clotting factor VIII deficiency is associated with hemophilia A, not Christmas Disease (hemophilia B).

6. Answer D (It can temporarily increase factor VIII levels)

Desmopressin can be a valuable tool in the preoperative management of individuals with mild to moderate hemophilia A. By stimulating the release of stored factor VIII; it can lead to a temporary increase in factor VIII levels, thereby enhancing blood clotting ability and reducing bleeding risks during and after surgery. However, its effectiveness may vary among individuals, and it's important to consider the individual's specific case and hemophilia severity. In the context of mild hemophilia A, desmopressin can be employed to strengthen clotting mechanisms before surgery.

Recommended literature

1. Shah UJ, Madan Narayanan M, J Graham Smith JH. Anaesthetic considerations in patients with inherited disorders of coagulation, Continuing Education in Anaesthesia Critical Care & Pain, Volume 15, Issue 1, February 2015, Pages 26–31.

HEPARIN-INDUCED THROMBOCYTOPENIA (HIT)

06
CHAPTER

Questions:

1. **What is the primary mechanism behind the development of Heparin-induced thrombocytopenia (HIT)?**
   A. Platelet activation by heparin
   B. Formation of immune complexes between heparin and platelet factor 4 (PF4)
   C. Direct inhibition of platelet aggregation
   D. Suppression of immune response

2. **What is the time frame during which HIT Type II (immune-mediated) typically occurs after initiating heparin therapy?**
   A. 1-4 days
   B. 5-14 days
   C. 15-30 days
   D. 30-60 days

3. **Which type of heparin is associated with a higher risk of HIT?**
   A. Low-molecular-weight heparin (LMWH)
   B. Unfractionated heparin (UFH)
   C. Heparinoids
   D. Fondaparinux

4. **What does the 4Ts Probability Scale assess in the context of HIT?**
   A. Platelet count fluctuations
   B. Thrombosis and bleeding risks
   C. Likelihood of HIT diagnosis
   D. Anesthesia-related complications

5. **HIT Type I occurs within 1 to 4 days of starting heparin therapy, causing a mild decrease in platelet count that usually resolves spontaneously.**
   A. True
   B. False

6. **A 65-year-old patient with chronic hypertension and atrial fibrillation (AF) was scheduled for gallbladder removal surgery. As part of the preoperative evaluation, the patient's cardiologist five days earlier had adjusted her anticoagulation therapy from warfarin to enoxaparin (1.0 mg/kg twice daily) as a bridge therapy for AF. The day before the surgery, during the final assessment, a significant decline in platelet count (more than 50% from baseline) was observed, and the anesthesiologist suspected HIT. What is the primary treatment approach for a patient suspected of having HIT before undergoing anesthesia?**
   A. Administering platelet transfusions
   B. Continuing heparin therapy
   C. Switching to unfractionated heparin
   D. Discontinuing heparin therapy

Answers:

1. **Answer B (Formation of immune complexes between heparin and platelet factor 4 (PF4))**

The primary mechanism behind the development of heparin-induced thrombocytopenia (HIT) is the formation of immune complexes between heparin and platelet factor 4 (PF4). When heparin is administered, it can bind to platelet factor 4 (PF4), a protein that is released by platelets. This heparin-PF4 complex triggers an immune response in certain individuals, leading to the production of antibodies against this complex. These antibodies cause platelet activation and aggregation, which promotes clotting and the formation of blood clots. This hyperactivation of platelets and the clotting process results in a paradoxical prothrombotic state, where new blood clots can form instead of preventing them. This immune-mediated reaction is the hallmark of HIT and is responsible for thrombocytopenia and the increased risk of thrombosis seen in HIT patients.

2. **Answer B (5-14 days)**

The onset of HIT Type II occurs around 5 to 14 days after starting heparin therapy. This delayed onset is due to the time required for the immune system to produce antibodies against the heparin-PF4 complex. It's during this period that the immune-mediated platelet activation and clotting cascade are triggered, leading to severe thrombocytopenia and the increased risk of thrombotic events that characterize HIT Type II.

3. **Answer B (Unfractionated heparin (UFH))**

HIT is more commonly associated with unfractionated heparin (UFH) than with low-molecular-weight heparin (LMWH) or other types of anticoagulants. This increased risk is likely due to the higher content of long chains of polysaccharides in UFH, which can enhance the formation of the heparin-PF4 immune complexes that trigger the immune response leading to HIT. However, it's important to note that while LMWH and other alternatives carry a lower risk, they are not entirely risk-free, and HIT can still occur in certain cases.

4. **Answer C (Likelihood of HIT diagnosis)**

The 4Ts Probability Scale assesses the likelihood of HIT diagnosis by evaluating four key clinical factors: Timing of thrombocytopenia onset, thrombocytopenia severity (> 50% decrease in platelet count to a nadir of $\geq 20 \times 10^9$ /L), presence of thrombosis or other sequelae of HIT, and exclusion of other causes of thrombocytopenia. The cumulative score derived from these factors helps estimate the probability of HIT.

5. **Answer A (True)**

HIT Type I is characterized by its occurrence within 1 to 4 days of initiating heparin therapy. This type typically results in a mild decrease in platelet count, often referred to as thrombocytopenia, which is usually transient and resolves on its own without the need for specific treatment. HIT Type I is considered a nonimmune response and is generally less concerning than HIT Type II (immune-mediated), which occurs later and involves more severe thrombocytopenia and an immune-mediated mechanism leading to an increased risk of thrombosis.

6. **Answer D (Discontinuing heparin therapy)**

Discontinuing heparin therapy, including enoxaparin, is crucial to halt the immune response and reduce the risk of complications in suspected HIT cases. Alternative anticoagulation strategies should be considered for perioperative care. Given the HIT suspicion and potential thrombotic risk, postponing the surgery is advisable to allow time for the immune response to subside. Alternative thromboprophylaxis options such as direct thrombin inhibitors (e.g., argatroban, bivalirudin) should be considered in consultation with the cardiology and surgical teams to manage the patient's anticoagulation needs while minimizing the risk of bleeding during surgery. The coordinated effort among the teams ensures patient safety and optimal management of the HIT suspicion before proceeding with the surgery.

Recommended literature

1. Andreas Koster, Michael Nagler, Gabor Erdoes, Jerrold H. Levy; Heparin-induced Thrombocytopenia: Perioperative Diagnosis and Management. Anesthesiology 2022; 136:336–344.
2. Linkins LA. Heparin induced thrombocytopenia. BMJ. 2015;350:g7566. Published 2015 Jan 8.
3. Ahmed I, Majeed A, Powell R. Heparin induced thrombocytopenia: diagnosis and management update. Postgrad Med J. 2007;83(983):575-582.
4. Baroletti, S.A., Goldhaber, S.Z., 2006. Heparin-Induced Thrombocytopenia. Circulation 114, e355–e356.

IDIOPATHIC THROMBOCYTOPENIC PURPURA (ITP)

06
CHAPTER

Questions:

1. Which of the following is a characteristic feature of idiopathic thrombocytopenic purpura (ITP)?
   A. Elevated platelet count
   B. Hyperpigmented skin lesions
   C. Excessive clotting and thrombosis
   D. Easy bruising and purpura

2. What is the primary mechanism underlying ITP?
   A. Overproduction of platelets by the bone marrow
   B. Autoimmune destruction of platelets
   C. Impaired clotting factor synthesis
   D. Excessive platelet aggregation

3. Which type of ITP primarily affects young children and often follows a viral infection?
   A. Acute thrombocytopenic purpura
   B. Chronic thrombocytopenic purpura
   C. Secondary thrombocytopenic purpura
   D. Hereditary thrombocytopenic purpura

4. Which of the following is NOT a potential cause of ITP?
   A. Medication-induced immune reaction
   B. Bacterial infections
   C. Pregnancy
   D. Genetic inheritance

5. Splenectomy is generally considered as a first-line therapy in ITP patients.
   A. True
   B. False

6. A 37-year-old patient arrives at the emergency department (ED) with significant vaginal bleeding and reports easy bruising. A confirmed diagnosis of ITP is on record, and the platelet count measures at 35,000 platelets/µL (normal range: 150,000 - 450,000 platelets/µL). Considering the confirmed diagnosis of ITP, the low platelet count, and the ongoing vaginal bleeding, which of the following treatment options is NOT considered a first-line approach for managing acute bleeding in ITP patients?
   A. Platelet transfusions
   B. Steroids
   C. Intravenous immunoglobulin (IVIG)
   D. Immunosuppressants

Answers:

1. Answer D (Easy bruising and purpura)

Idiopathic Thrombocytopenic Purpura (ITP) is characterized by a low platelet count, leading to easy bruising and the development of purpura. Purpura refers to the purple or red discolorations on the skin or mucous membranes caused by bleeding underneath. Due to the low levels of platelets, the blood's ability to clot is compromised, resulting in a higher susceptibility to bleeding and easy bruising.

2. Answer B (Autoimmune destruction of platelets)

The primary mechanism underlying ITP is the autoimmune destruction of platelets. In ITP, the immune system mistakenly produces antibodies that target and destroy platelets. This immune response leads to a decreased platelet count in the blood, which can result in easy bruising, bleeding, and the characteristic purpura.

3. Answer A (Acute thrombocytopenic purpura)

Acute thrombocytopenic purpura primarily affects young children and often follows a viral infection. It is a type of ITP that occurs suddenly and is usually self-limiting. It is characterized by a rapid onset of low platelet counts, leading to easy bruising, bleeding, and purpura. In many cases, acute thrombocytopenic purpura resolves within a few weeks to months without specific treatment.

4. Answer D (Genetic inheritance)

Genetic inheritance is not considered a common cause of ITP. ITP is primarily an autoimmune disorder, and while genetics may play a role in predisposition to certain immune-related conditions, genetic inheritance is not a well-established cause of ITP. Thrombocytopenic Purpura primarily results from autoimmune processes triggered by factors such as medication-induced immune reactions, infections like those caused by chickenpox, hepatitis C, or AIDS, immune disorders such as rheumatoid arthritis and lupus, and certain cancers like low-grade lymphomas and leukemia. Additionally, pregnancy can lead to immune changes that contribute to ITP.

5. Answer B (False)

Splenectomy is not considered a first-line therapy in ITP patients. Instead, it is generally considered a second-line therapy in refractory ITP patients and in those who have relapsed after an initial response to medical treatment. Approximately 80% of patients respond well to splenectomy, with a significant proportion experiencing long-term remission without requiring further treatment. However, due to the potential risks and the availability of other treatment options, splenectomy is typically reserved for cases where other treatments have not been successful.

6. Answer D (Immunosuppressants)

In the context of acute bleeding in a patient with confirmed ITP, the use of immunosuppressants such as azathioprine, cyclosporine, diphenylsulfone, sirolimus, and mycophenolate mofetil is NOT considered a first-line treatment. Instead, if a patient with suspected ITP presents to the ED with a critical hemorrhage, the emergency physician should initiate treatment with a platelet transfusion, corticosteroids, and intravenous immune globulin (IVIG) as soon as possible. Immunosuppressants are typically considered as second or third-line treatments for ITP, to be utilized when other treatment approaches have proven ineffective.

Recommended literature

1. Toyomasu Y, Shimabukuro R, Moriyama H, et al. Successful perioperative management of a patient with idiopathic thrombocytopenic purpura undergoing emergent appendectomy: Report of a case. Int J Surg Case Rep. 2013;4(10):898-900.
2. Ramalingam, G., Jones, N., Besser, M., 2016. Platelets for anaesthetists—part 1: physiology and pathology. BJA Education 16, 134-139.
3. Warrier R, Chauhan A. Management of immune thrombocytopenic purpura: an update. Ochsner J. 2012;12(3):221-227.
4. Guidelines for the investigation and management of idiopathic thrombocytopenic purpura in adults, children and in pregnancy. 2003. British Journal of Haematology 120, 574-596.

JEHOVAH'S WITNESS PATIENTS

Questions:

1. What is the primary reason Jehovah's Witnesses refuse blood transfusions?

    A. Fear of infections

    B. Medical complications

    C. Religious beliefs

    D. Financial concerns

2. Which of the following blood products align with the religious beliefs of Jehovah's Witness patients, making them potentially acceptable for medical procedures?

    A. Platelets

    B. Plasma

    C. Autologous predonation

    D. Packed red cells

3. Which of the following procedures is generally considered acceptable for Jehovah's Witness patients?

    A. Plasma transfusion

    B. Autologous predonation

    C. Recombinant erythropoietin

    D. Whole blood transfusion

4. Which medical procedure might be acceptable for a Jehovah's Witness patient undergoing surgery?

    A. Acute hypervolemic hemodilution

    B. Packed red cell transfusion

    C. Plasma exchange

    D. Platelet transfusion

5. Cryoprecipitate might be considered an acceptable option for medical treatment among Jehovah's Witness patients.

    A. True

    B. False

6. A 45-year-old devout Jehovah's Witness is scheduled for elective abdominal surgery due to a non-malignant condition. She has steadfastly expressed her religious beliefs, which prohibit the acceptance of blood transfusions. As her anesthetic team, you are tasked with devising an anesthetic plan that minimizes blood loss while respecting her religious convictions. Which of the following anesthetic techniques might be preferred to minimize blood loss during surgery?

    A. Hypotensive anesthesia

    B. High-dose opioid anesthesia

    C. Inhalational anesthesia

    D. Intravenous anesthesia

Answers:

1. Answer C (Religious beliefs)

The primary reason Jehovah's Witnesses refuse blood transfusions is based on their deeply ingrained religious beliefs. According to their interpretation of biblical scriptures, Jehovah's Witnesses believe that consuming or receiving another creature's blood, even through transfusions, is prohibited. They perceive no distinction between ingesting blood and receiving it intravenously. This religious conviction is so strong that Jehovah's Witnesses often opt to decline blood transfusions for themselves and their children, as they consider the procedure to carry the risk of jeopardizing their eternal salvation. This stance is reinforced legally, as they assert that blood transfusions violate their right to privacy and impede their freedom to practice their religious faith. Consequently, the decision to refuse blood transfusions is primarily rooted in the profound religious principles upheld by Jehovah's Witnesses.

2. Answer A (Platelets)

Among the blood products considered by Jehovah's Witness patients, platelets, clotting factors, albumin, immunoglobulins, epidural blood patch, and the use of a cell saver may be potentially acceptable for medical procedures, aligning with their religious beliefs. However, whole blood, packed red cells, plasma, and autologous predonation are generally considered unacceptable due to their prohibition on these components, reflecting the Jehovah's Witness stance on blood transfusions and preservation.

3. Answer C (Recombinant erythropoietin)

Recombinant erythropoietin is generally considered acceptable for Jehovah's Witness patients. Recombinant erythropoietin is a synthetic form of a hormone that stimulates the production of red blood cells by the bone marrow. This approach aligns with Jehovah's Witness beliefs because it does not involve the direct transfusion of whole blood or its components. Instead, it aids the patient's body in producing more red blood cells, which can help manage anemia without violating their religious principles. In contrast, plasma transfusion, autologous predonation, and whole blood transfusion are typically not accepted by Jehovah's Witness patients due to their religious stance against blood transfusions.

4. Answer A (Acute hypervolemic hemodilution)

Acute hypervolemic hemodilution involves diluting a patient's blood with non-blood fluids before surgery, with the intention of reducing the concentration of red blood cells. This can help minimize the need for blood transfusions during and after the surgical procedure, which aligns with the blood conservation principles important to Jehovah's Witness patients.

5. Answer A (True)

Cryoprecipitate is a blood product that contains high levels of clotting factors and fibrinogen. For certain medical situations, such as severe bleeding or clotting disorders, cryoprecipitate might be considered acceptable for Jehovah's Witness patients. While Jehovah's Witnesses typically avoid whole blood and major blood components, the use of specific blood products like cryoprecipitate, which can help address clotting issues without directly conflicting with their beliefs, may be deemed suitable under certain circumstances.

6. Answer A (Hypotensive anesthesia)

In this case, hypotensive anesthesia might be preferred to minimize blood loss during surgery. Deliberate hypotension, achieved by carefully reducing blood pressure, can help reduce intraoperative bleeding and subsequent transfusion requirements, aligning with the patient's religious beliefs. However, the usage of deliberate hypotension and other blood conservation strategies should be approached with caution, especially in patients with significant cardiovascular, cerebrovascular, renal, or hepatic disease. While deliberate hypotension and hypothermia have been shown to effectively reduce transfusion requirements in Jehovah's Witness patients, careful consideration of the patient's medical history is crucial to ensure the chosen technique is safe and appropriate for her individual circumstances.

Recommended literature

1. Lawson, T., Ralph, C., 2015. Perioperative Jehovah's Witnesses: a review. British Journal of Anaesthesia 115, 676–687.
2. Milligan LC, Bellamy MC. Anaesthesia and critical care of Jehovah's Witnesses. Continuing Education in Anaesthesia Critical Care & Pain. 2004/ 4;(2); 35–39.

PERIOPERATIVE ANEMIA

Questions:

1. **During anesthesia, what potential impact can anemia have on oxygen delivery to tissues?**
   A. Anemia increases oxygen delivery to tissues.
   B. Anemia has no effect on oxygen delivery.
   C. Anemia decreases oxygen delivery to tissues.
   D. Anemia enhances blood clot formation.

2. **Which of the following is considered a hallmark of chronic anemia?**
   A. Resting tachycardia
   B. Pale skin
   C. Fatigue
   D. None of the above

3. **Which classification of anemia is characterized by a mean corpuscular volume (MCV) less than 80 fL?**
   A. Microcytic
   B. Normocytic
   C. Macrocytic
   D. Hypochromic

4. **Which type of anemia is characterized by a deficiency in erythropoietin (EPO)?**
   A. Iron deficiency anemia
   B. Hypoproliferative anemias
   C. Hemolytic anemia
   D. Sideroblastic anemia

5. **Rheumatoid arthritis can contribute to anemia of inflammation.**
   A. True
   B. False

6. **A 45-year-old patient presents with persistent fatigue, weakness, and occasional dizziness. The patient has a history of chronic gastritis. To further assess the patient's symptoms, a comprehensive evaluation was performed, including laboratory tests. The results revealed a hemoglobin level of 90 g/dL (normal range: 12.1 - 15.1 g/dL for women). In addition to the low hemoglobin, the MCV was elevated at 110 fL (normal range: 80 - 100 fL). Considering the patient's medical history and laboratory findings, what is the most likely cause of the anemia?**
   A. Iron deficiency
   B. Vitamin B12 deficiency
   C. Thalassemia
   D. Hemolytic anemia

Answers:

1. Answer C (Anemia decreases oxygen delivery to tissues)

Anemia is characterized by a decreased number of red blood cells or a lower-than-normal hemoglobin concentration, both of which are responsible for carrying oxygen from the lungs to tissues and organs. With reduced hemoglobin levels, there is a diminished capacity to bind and transport oxygen. This results in less oxygen being available for delivery to the body's tissues during anesthesia. Therefore, anemia leads to a decrease in oxygen-carrying capacity and subsequently reduces oxygen delivery to tissues.

2. Answer D (None of the above)

While all the listed options are potential signs and symptoms of anemia, none of them can be considered an exclusive hallmark of chronic anemia. It's important to note that people with long-existing anemia might exhibit these symptoms, but their presence alone cannot definitively diagnose chronic anemia, as they can also be present in other medical conditions. Anemia, whether acute or chronic, can manifest with various symptoms, and its diagnosis should be based on a combination of clinical evaluation, laboratory tests, and consideration of the individual's medical history.

3. Answer A (Microcytic)

Microcytic anemia is characterized by a mean corpuscular volume (MCV) of less than 80 fL. The MCV is a measurement that indicates the average size of red blood cells. In microcytic anemia, the red blood cells are smaller than normal, which can be observed in conditions like iron deficiency anemia and thalassemia. An MCV value under 80 fL signifies that the red blood cells are smaller than the typical range (80 to 100 fL) and supports the diagnosis of microcytic anemia. This distinction is important because different types of anemia have specific underlying causes, and the MCV value is a valuable parameter for determining the classification of anemia and guiding further diagnostic investigations.

4. Answer B (Hypoproliferative anemias)

Hypoproliferative anemias are a group of anemias characterized by a reduced production of red blood cells in the bone marrow. Erythropoietin (EPO) is a hormone produced by the kidneys that plays a crucial role in stimulating the production of red blood cells. In hypoproliferative anemias, there is a deficiency in EPO production or response, leading to a decreased production of red blood cells. Hypoproliferative anemia is also a prominent feature of hematologic diseases that are described as bone marrow failure states; these include aplastic anemia, myelodysplastic syndrome (MDS), pure RBC aplasia (PRCA), and myelophthisis.

5. Answer A (True)

Rheumatoid arthritis can contribute to anemia of inflammation, also known as anemia of chronic disease. Anemia of inflammation is a type of anemia that commonly occurs in individuals with chronic inflammatory conditions, including autoimmune disorders like rheumatoid arthritis. Inflammation, such as that seen in rheumatoid arthritis, can affect the body's iron metabolism and utilization. Chronic inflammation can lead to changes in iron storage and transport, resulting in reduced availability of iron for red blood cell production. This disruption in iron homeostasis can lead to anemia. Furthermore, inflammatory cytokines produced during chronic inflammation can interfere with the production and lifespan of red blood cells. These cytokines can suppress the production of EPO, a hormone that stimulates red blood cell production and can also accelerate the breakdown of red blood cells in the bloodstream. As a result of these mechanisms, individuals with rheumatoid arthritis may develop anemia of inflammation, which is characterized by lower hemoglobin levels and decreased red blood cell counts.

6. Answer B (Vitamin B12 deficiency)

Chronic gastritis, a condition characterized by inflammation of the stomach lining, can impair the absorption of essential nutrients, including vitamin B12, due to reduced production of intrinsic factor, a protein necessary for vitamin B12 absorption. This malabsorption can lead to a deficiency in vitamin B12, also known as cobalamin. Vitamin B12 is essential for DNA synthesis and proper maturation of red blood cells in the bone marrow. Inadequate levels of vitamin B12 can result in a type of anemia called megaloblastic anemia, which is characterized by enlarged and immature red blood cells. The hemoglobin level of 90 g/dL, combined with the elevated MCV of 110 fL, indicates macrocytic anemia, a hallmark of megaloblastic anemia. To confirm the diagnosis, it's crucial to measure serum vitamin B12 levels and perform other relevant tests, such as assessing serum folate levels and performing intrinsic factor antibodies testing.

Recommended literature

1. Hare GMT, Mazer CD. Anemia: Perioperative Risk and Treatment Opportunity. Anesthesiology. 2021;135(3):520-530.
2. Cascio MJ, DeLoughery TG. Anemia: Evaluation and Diagnostic Tests. Med Clin North Am. 2017;101(2):263-284.
3. Chernecky CC et al. Laboratory Tests and Diagnostic Procedures. 6th ed. Philadelphia, PA: Elsevier; 2013:621-623.

POLYCYTHEMIA (ERYTHROCYTOSIS)

06
CHAPTER

Questions:

1. **What is the underlying cause of primary polycythemia (polycythemia vera)?**
   A. Chronic obstructive pulmonary disease (COPD)
   B. Idiopathic origin
   C. Genetic mutation of JAK2 gene
   D. Excessive alcohol intake

2. **Apparent polycythemia is characterized by?**
   A. Increased red cell mass
   B. Elevated levels of erythropoietin (EPO)
   C. Reduced plasma volume
   D. Presence of JAK2 mutation

3. **Which clinical manifestation is NOT commonly associated with polycythemia?**
   A. Splenomegaly
   B. Hypotension
   C. Pruritus
   D. Episodic blurred vision

4. **What is the primary goal of treatment in secondary polycythemia?**
   A. Phlebotomy
   B. Correction of genetic mutation
   C. Management of underlying condition
   D. Cytoreductive therapy

5. **Therapeutic phlebotomy has long been considered the treatment of choice in most patients with polycythemia.**
   A. True
   B. False

6. **A 45-year-old man is presented for emergency surgery for intramedullary nailing of a right femur fracture following a road traffic accident. He has no significant medical or surgical history except for occasional mild headaches. Routine hematologic investigations reveal elevated hemoglobin (19 g/dL) and hematocrit (57%) levels, along with a platelet count of 600 × 10^9/L. Despite the absence of symptoms suggestive of polycythemia vera, the diagnosis is confirmed. Which component is NOT a keystone in the anesthetic management of patients with polycythemia vera?**
   A. Avoid hypoxia during anesthetic management
   B. Ensure low-dose aspirin is continued in PV
   C. Avoid regional anesthesia techniques to reduce the risk of thromboembolic episodes
   D. Ensure hydration with strict monitoring for adequate urine output

Answers:

1. Answer C (Genetic mutation of JAK2 gene)

Primary polycythemia, also known as polycythemia vera (PV), is a myeloproliferative disorder characterized by the clonal proliferation of myeloid cells. The underlying cause of primary polycythemia is a genetic mutation in the JAK2 (Janus kinase 2) gene. This mutation leads to the overactivation of JAK-STAT signaling pathways, resulting in the excessive production of red blood cells, platelets, and white blood cells. It's important to note that the JAK2 mutation is not specific to PV alone. This mutation is also found in patients with other myeloproliferative disorders, such as primary thrombocytosis and primary myelofibrosis.

2. Answer C (Reduced plasma volume)

Apparent polycythemia, also known as relative polycythemia or stress polycythemia, is characterized by an increase in hematocrit (Hct) and hemoglobin (Hb) levels on laboratory tests but without an actual increase in red blood cell mass. The increase in Hct and Hb is primarily due to a reduction in plasma volume rather than an overproduction of red blood cells. It can be associated with conditions such as obesity, hypertension, smoking, excessive alcohol intake, and diuretic use.

3. Answer B (Hypotension)

The clinical manifestation NOT commonly associated with polycythemia is hypotension. Polycythemia, characterized by elevated red blood cell mass, is often accompanied by symptoms such as splenomegaly, pruritus, episodic blurred vision, fatigue, headaches, dizziness, red skin, peripheral tingling, itching, hypertension, mucosal cyanosis, bruising, petechiae, unusual bleeding, nosebleeds, and enlarged spleen or liver. The increase in red blood cell mass typically leads to increased blood viscosity and hypertension, making hypotension an uncommon presentation in polycythemia.

4. Answer C (Management of underlying condition)

The primary goal of treatment in secondary polycythemia is the management of the underlying condition that is leading to the increased production of red blood cells. Secondary polycythemia occurs as a compensatory mechanism in response to chronic tissue hypoxia or inappropriate production of erythropoietin (EPO) by the kidneys. The increased EPO production stimulates the bone marrow to produce more red blood cells, resulting in an elevated red cell mass. Causes of secondary polycythemia include conditions such as chronic obstructive pulmonary disease (COPD), obstructive sleep apnea (OSA), cyanotic heart disease, altitude exposure, renal artery stenosis, renal tumors, and transplanted kidneys.

5. Answer A (True)

Therapeutic phlebotomy is commonly considered the treatment of choice in many patients with polycythemia. This procedure involves removing a specific volume of blood to reduce the excessive red blood cell mass, thereby alleviating symptoms related to increased blood viscosity and reducing the risk of thrombotic complications. The frequency and volume of phlebotomies may vary based on individual patient factors and disease severity, and the decision to initiate treatment should involve consultation with a healthcare provider to ensure optimal management.

6. Answer C (Avoid regional anesthesia techniques to reduce the risk of thromboembolic episodes)

The component that is NOT a keystone in the anesthetic management of patients with PV is the suggestion to avoid regional anesthesia techniques to reduce the risk of thromboembolic episodes. Contrary to this option, current consensus opinion suggests that neuraxial anesthesia in patients with polycythemia vera is considered safe. This is attributed to a lower risk of thrombotic events and hypoxemia compared to general anesthesia. It is important to note that neuraxial anesthesia is likely safe, provided that the patient's platelet and neutrophil counts are adequate and they are not currently receiving anticoagulation.

Recommended literature

1. Pollard BJ, Kitchen G. Handbook of Clinical Anaesthesia. 4th ed. Taylor & Francis group; 2018. Chapter 7 The blood, Duncan A.

Hematology
SICKLE CELL DISEASE

Questions:

1. What is the primary underlying cause of tissue infarction and pain episodes in sickle cell disease?
    - A. Excessive red blood cell production
    - B. Rigid and aggregated sickle cells occluding blood vessels
    - C. Elevated levels of white blood cells
    - D. Decreased oxygen affinity of hemoglobin

2. Which hemoglobin variant is responsible for the characteristic sickling of red blood cells in sickle cell disease?
    - A. Hemoglobin A (HbA)
    - B. Hemoglobin F (HbF)
    - C. Hemoglobin C (HbC)
    - D. Hemoglobin S (HbS)

3. Which of the following symptoms is NOT commonly associated with sickle cell disease?
    - A. Episodes of pain
    - B. Delayed growth or puberty
    - C. High blood sugar levels
    - D. Swelling of hands and feet

4. What is the most common reason for hospitalization in sickle cell patients?
    - A. Acute pain crisis
    - B. Stroke
    - C. Aplastic crisis
    - D. Acute chest syndrome (ACS)

5. Hypertension is typically considered a direct precipitant of vaso-occlusive crises in sickle cell disease.
    - A. True
    - B. False

6. A 30-year-old female patient with sickle cell disease is admitted for surgical repair of an ankle fracture following a fall. She has a history of recurrent pain crises, and acute chest syndrome, and has been managed with hydroxyurea therapy. Her preoperative hemoglobin level is 10.2 g/dL, and she reports occasional shortness of breath with strenuous activity. The surgeon plans to use a tourniquet during the surgery. What is the correct statement regarding tourniquet use in this patient population?
    - A. Tourniquet use in this patient population is not associated with increased complications
    - B. The tourniquet will be placed at the proximal part of the limb at the greatest circumference of the limb
    - C. Tourniquet use of longer than 30 minutes increases the risk of compression neurapraxia
    - D. Avoid limb tourniquets or apply them as distal as possible

Answers:

1. Answer B (Rigid and aggregated sickle cells occluding blood vessels)

The primary underlying cause of tissue infarction and pain episodes in sickle cell disease is the formation of rigid and aggregated sickle cells that occlude small blood vessels. In individuals with sickle cell disease, the shape of the red blood cells becomes deformed due to the presence of abnormal hemoglobin S (HbS). These deformed sickle cells are less flexible than normal red blood cells and tend to clump together, leading to occlusions in the small blood vessels. As a result of these occlusions, blood flow to various tissues and organs becomes compromised, leading to tissue damage and infarction. This lack of blood flow can cause severe pain, known as sickle cell "crises," as well as more serious complications like organ damage and strokes.

2. Answer D (Hemoglobin S (HbS))

Hemoglobin S (HbS) is the hemoglobin variant responsible for the characteristic sickling of red blood cells in sickle cell disease. In individuals with sickle cell disease, a mutation in the HBB gene causes the production of abnormal hemoglobin molecules, specifically hemoglobin S. Hemoglobin S has a unique property in which, under certain conditions, it forms long, rigid structures within the red blood cells. This leads to the distorted and "sickle" shape of the cells. When these sickled red blood cells travel through the bloodstream, they can become stuck in small blood vessels, obstructing blood flow and causing tissue damage. This vaso-occlusive process contributes to the hallmark complications of sickle cell disease, including pain episodes, tissue infarction, and organ damage.

3. Answer C (High blood sugar levels)

High blood sugar levels (hyperglycemia) are not commonly associated with sickle cell disease. The characteristic symptoms of sickle cell disease primarily involve the altered structure and function of red blood cells due to hemoglobin S (HbS). These symptoms include chronic anemia, recurrent episodes of pain known as sickle cell crises, swelling of hands and feet due to vaso-occlusion, susceptibility to infections, delayed growth or puberty, and vision problems. While individuals with sickle cell disease might have a slightly increased risk of developing diabetes, high blood sugar levels are not a typical or prominent feature of the disease.

4. Answer A (Acute pain crisis)

The most common reason for hospitalization in sickle cell patients is often related to acute pain crises. These episodes of severe and intense pain occur due to the vaso-occlusion of blood vessels by sickled red blood cells, leading to tissue ischemia and pain. Acute pain crises can affect various regions of the body, causing significant discomfort and requiring medical attention for pain management, hydration, and other supportive measures. These painful episodes are a hallmark of sickle cell disease and a major factor in the healthcare management of affected individuals. While complications like stroke, aplastic crisis, and acute chest syndrome are also important reasons for hospitalization, acute pain crises are the most frequent cause of hospital admissions in sickle cell patients.

5. Answer B (False)

Hypertension is not typically considered a direct precipitant of vaso-occlusive crises in sickle cell disease. The hallmark of vaso-occlusive crises is the occlusion of small blood vessels by rigid, aggregated sickle cells, resulting in tissue ischemia and pain. Conditions such as hypoxia, vascular stasis, hypothermia, hypovolemia/hypotension, and acidosis are more commonly acknowledged as triggers for sickle cell crises. These factors can contribute to the formation of clumps of sickle cells, escalating the risk of vaso-occlusion.

6. Answer D (Avoid limb tourniquets or apply them as distal as possible)

In patients with sickle cell disease, particularly those with a history of vaso-occlusive crises and complications, it is recommended to avoid the use of limb tourniquets whenever possible or to apply them as distal as possible. This approach aims to minimize the risk of vaso-occlusive events and complications related to prolonged tourniquet use. While tourniquets can be beneficial during surgery to reduce blood loss and improve visualization, their use can potentially lead to complications, including vaso-occlusion and compression neurapraxia. Given the patient's history of sickle cell disease and associated complications, careful consideration should be given to tourniquet use and its potential impact on her condition.

Recommended literature

1. Pollard BJ, Kitchen, G. Handbook of Clinical Anaesthesia. Fourth Edition. CRC Press. 2018. 978-1-4987-6289-2.
2. Wilson, M., Forsyth, P., Whiteside, J.. Haemoglobinopathy and sickle cell disease. Continuing Education in Anaesthesia Critical Care & Pain. 2010. 10, 24–28.

THALASSEMIA

Questions:

1. **Thalassemia is characterized by?**
    A. Increased hemoglobin production
    B. Deficient synthesis of alpha or beta globin chains
    C. Excess production of both alpha and beta chains
    D. Abnormal white blood cell count

2. **What is the term for the genetic disorder that results from the interaction of α0 and α+ determinants in alpha thalassemia?**
    A. Hemoglobin H disease
    B. Thalassemia intermedia
    C. Cooley anemia
    D. Hemoglobin S disease

3. **Beta thalassemia minor is characterized by?**
    A. Profound anemia requiring lifelong blood transfusions
    B. Hemoglobin H disease
    C. Loss of both beta globin alleles
    D. Asymptomatic carriers or mild anemia

4. **Which clinical manifestation is associated with thalassemia?**
    A. Osteopetrosis
    B. Encephalopathy
    C. Liver cirrhosis
    D. Gastric ulcers

5. **Cooley anemia results in profound anemia requiring lifelong blood transfusions.**
    A. True
    B. False

6. **A 45-year-old woman of Southeast Asian descent presents to her primary care physician with complaints of persistent fatigue, shortness of breath, and weakness. She mentions that she has been experiencing these symptoms for several months and has noticed that her skin appears paler than usual. A physical examination reveals mild splenomegaly. Her blood test results show a hemoglobin level of 9.2 g/dL (normal range: 12.0 - 15.5 g/dL) and microcytic hypochromic red blood cells. How can the suspected diagnosis of thalassemia be confirmed in this case?**
    A. Complete blood count
    B. Metzer index
    C. Hemoglobin electrophoresis
    D. Iron studies

Answers:

1. **Answer B (Deficient synthesis of alpha or beta globin chains)**

   A thalassemia is an inherited group of hematological disorders characterized by a deficiency in the synthesis of either alpha or beta globin chains, which are essential components of hemoglobin. In thalassemia, due to the deficient synthesis of either alpha or beta globin chains, there is a decreased production of normal hemoglobin. This results in a disruption of the normal structure and function of red blood cells, leading to anemia, which is a condition characterized by a reduced ability of the blood to carry oxygen. Anemia in thalassemia can cause fatigue, weakness, and other related symptoms.

2. **Answer A (Hemoglobin H disease)**

   Hemoglobin H disease is the term used to describe the genetic disorder that results from the interaction of α0 and α+ determinants in alpha thalassemia. This condition occurs when there is a loss of three alpha-globin genes, leading to a deficiency in alpha-globin chains. The remaining alpha globin chains form abnormal hemoglobin, known as hemoglobin H (HbH). In Hemoglobin H disease, the reduced production of alpha globin chains leads to an imbalance in the alpha-to-beta globin chain ratio in hemoglobin molecules. This imbalance can cause instability and increased destruction of red blood cells, leading to chronic hemolytic anemia. Patients with Hemoglobin H disease typically have hemoglobin levels of 8–10 g/dL and may require medical management and monitoring.

3. **Answer D (Asymptomatic carriers or mild anemia)**

   Beta thalassemia minor, also known as beta thalassemia trait, is characterized by asymptomatic carriers or individuals with mild anemia. In beta thalassemia minor, there is a mutation or deficiency in one of the two beta globin alleles, leading to reduced production of beta-globin chains. However, the remaining normal beta globin allele is usually sufficient to produce enough functional hemoglobin for normal physiological function. People with beta thalassemia minor typically do not require lifelong blood transfusions or experience profound anemia. Their hemoglobin levels are slightly below normal, typically around 2-3 g/dL lower than the reference range, but they generally lead normal lives without significant symptoms. It's important to note that beta thalassemia minor carriers may pass on the gene mutation to their offspring.

4. **Answer C (Liver cirrhosis)**

   Thalassemia is associated with various clinical manifestations, including liver cirrhosis due to iron overload, which can lead to liver dysfunction and fibrosis. Additionally, thalassemia-related complications encompass cardiomyopathy, cardiac hypertrophy, myocarditis, and pericarditis, often linked to excess iron deposition affecting the heart. Renal tubular dysfunction and endocrinopathies such as diabetes, hypothyroidism, hypoparathyroidism, and adrenal insufficiency may arise from iron-induced damage to kidneys and hormonal systems. Furthermore, thalassemia-related immunosuppression increases the risk of infections, underscoring the need for vigilant monitoring and management to mitigate these potential sequelae.

5. **Answer A (True)**

   Cooley's anemia, also known as beta-thalassemia major, results in profound anemia that typically requires lifelong and regular blood transfusions. In individuals with beta-thalassemia major, both beta globin alleles are affected, leading to a severe deficiency in the production of functional beta globin chains. This deficiency results in a significant reduction in hemoglobin levels, causing severe anemia. Lifelong blood transfusions are necessary to provide the patient with functional red blood cells and to maintain adequate oxygen-carrying capacity in the bloodstream. Without regular blood transfusions, individuals with beta-thalassemia major would be at high risk of complications and life-threatening consequences due to severe anemia.

6. **Answer C (Hemoglobin electrophoresis)**

   The presented symptoms, including persistent fatigue, shortness of breath, weakness, paler skin, and mild splenomegaly, along with the blood test results showing a low hemoglobin level and microcytic hypochromic red blood cells, raise suspicion of thalassemia. Hemoglobin electrophoresis is a crucial diagnostic test that identifies the types of hemoglobin present in the blood. In thalassemia, abnormal hemoglobin variants and imbalances in the production of alpha and beta globin chains can be detected through this test, providing a definitive diagnosis. While a complete blood count (CBC), iron studies, and other tests like the Metzer index contribute to the diagnostic process, hemoglobin electrophoresis is specifically tailored to detect hemoglobinopathies like thalassemia. Thorough clinical assessment and laboratory testing, including genetic testing for alpha thalassemia, are essential to confirm the diagnosis of thalassemia.

Recommended literature

1. Pollard BJ, Kitchen, G. Handbook of Clinical Anaesthesia. Fourth Edition. CRC Press. 2018. 978-1-4987-6289-2.
2. Thomas, C., Lumb, A.B., 2012. Physiology of haemoglobin. Continuing Education in Anaesthesia Critical Care & Pain 12, 251–256.
3. Wilson, M., Forsyth, P., Whiteside, J., 2010. Haemoglobinopathy and sickle cell disease. Continuing Education in Anaesthesia Critical Care & Pain 10, 24–28.

TUMOR LYSIS SYNDROME

Questions:

1. **What is tumor lysis syndrome (TLS)?**
    A. A condition caused by excess calcium in the blood
    B. A disorder characterized by abnormal blood clotting
    C. An electrolyte imbalance resulting from rapid cancer cell death
    D. A type of anemia caused by iron deficiency

2. **Which of the following cancers is most commonly associated with tumor lysis syndrome?**
    A. Breast cancer
    B. Lung cancer
    C. Non-Hodgkin lymphoma
    D. Colorectal cancer

3. **Which electrolyte imbalance is typically observed in tumor lysis syndrome?**
    A. Hypernatremia
    B. Hypermagnesemia
    C. Hyperkalemia
    D. Hypercalcemia

4. **What is the primary mechanism behind tumor lysis syndrome?**
    A. The cancer spreads from where it started to a distant part of the body
    B. Rapid cancer cell death and release of intracellular contents
    C. The endocrine tumor arises from cells that produce hormones
    D. Immune system reaction to a cancerous tumor

5. **TLS is analogous to rhabdomyolysis.**
    A. True
    B. False

6. **A 32-year-old man with non-Hodgkin lymphoma is scheduled for surgery to remove a large tumor mass. The medical team is closely monitoring for potential TLS during and after the surgical procedure. Which electrolyte imbalance is NOT of particular concern in managing anesthesia for this patient due to potential tumor lysis syndrome?**
    A. Hyperkalemia
    B. Hyperphosphatemia
    C. Hypocalcemia
    D. Hyponatremia

Answers:

1. **Answer C (An electrolyte imbalance resulting from rapid cancer cell death)**

   Tumor lysis syndrome (TLS) is a medical condition characterized by an electrolyte imbalance that occurs as a result of the rapid breakdown of cancer cells. When a large number of cancer cells die within a short period, their contents, including potassium, phosphate, and uric acid, are released into the bloodstream. This can overwhelm the body's ability to process and eliminate these substances, leading to imbalances in electrolytes such as potassium, phosphate, and calcium.

2. **Answer C (Non-Hodgkin lymphoma)**

   TLS is most commonly associated with non-Hodgkin lymphoma, particularly high-risk subtypes such as Burkitt's lymphoma and other aggressive Non-Hodgkin lymphomas. Additionally, acute lymphoblastic leukemia and acute myeloid leukemia are also frequently linked to TLS. These cancers are characterized by high cell turnover rates, rapid growth, and large tumor burdens, which can lead to a significant release of intracellular contents into the bloodstream upon treatment or spontaneously.

3. **Answer C (Hyperkalemia)**

   In TLS, hyperkalemia is a common electrolyte imbalance that is typically observed. This occurs when cancer cells rapidly die and release their contents into the bloodstream, including intracellular potassium. As a result, the balance between potassium inside and outside the cells is disrupted, leading to an increase in blood potassium levels. Hyperkalemia can have serious consequences, particularly affecting the heart's electrical activity and potentially leading to cardiac arrhythmias or other cardiac complications. Managing hyperkalemia is an important aspect of treating and preventing complications associated with TLS.

4. **Answer B (Rapid cancer cell death and release of intracellular contents)**

   TLS is characterized by the rapid death (necrosis) of a significant number of cancer cells. This process leads to the release of intracellular contents, which include substances like uric acid, electrolytes (potassium and phosphate), and other cellular components, into the bloodstream. As a result, several physiological imbalances occur, including acute hyperuricemia and electrolyte abnormalities such as hyperkalemia, hyperphosphatemia, and hypocalcemia. These disruptions in electrolyte and metabolite levels can contribute to complications like acute kidney injury (AKI) and other adverse effects.

5. **Answer A (True)**

   TLS and rhabdomyolysis share some similarities in their underlying mechanisms. Both conditions involve the rapid breakdown of cells, leading to the release of intracellular contents into the bloodstream. In TLS, large numbers of tumor cells undergo necrosis, releasing substances such as uric acid and electrolytes into the circulation. In rhabdomyolysis, muscle cells break down due to various causes, releasing myoglobin and other cellular components into the bloodstream. The release of intracellular contents in both TLS and rhabdomyolysis can lead to similar complications, including electrolyte imbalances, AKI, and other systemic effects.

6. **Answer D (Hyponatremia)**

   TLS primarily involves notable electrolyte imbalances such as hyperkalemia, hyperphosphatemia, and hypocalcemia, while hyponatremia is not a distinctive hallmark of TLS. During anesthesia management, the primary focus should be on effectively addressing the core electrolyte imbalances seen in TLS, namely hyperkalemia, hyperphosphatemia, and hypocalcemia, due to their substantial impact on the patient's perioperative course, including cardiac stability, muscle function, and overall surgical outcomes.

Recommended literature

1. Puri I, Sharma D, Gunturu KS, Ahmed AA. Diagnosis and management of tumor lysis syndrome. J Community Hosp Intern Med Perspect. 2020;10(3):269-272.
2. Gupta, A., Moore, J.A., 2018. Tumor Lysis Syndrome. JAMA Oncology 4, 895.
3. Oduro-Dominah L, Brennan LJ. Anaesthetic management of the child with haematological malignancy. Continuing Education in Anaesthesia Critical Care & Pain. 2013. 13;(5);158-164.
4. Behl D, Hendrickson AW, Moynihan TJ. Oncologic emergencies. Crit Care Clin. 2010;26(1):181-205.
5. Beed M, Levitt M, Bokhari SW. Intensive care management of patients with haematological malignancy. Continuing Education in Anaesthesia Critical Care & Pain. 2010.10;(6);167-171.

Hematology

VON WILLEBRAND'S DISEASE (VWD)

Questions:

1. What is the most common inherited bleeding disorder?
   A. Hemophilia A
   B. Von Willebrand's Disease (VWD)
   C. Hemophilia B
   D. Thrombocytopenia

2. Which type of VWD is characterized by a complete absence of von Willebrand factor (vWF) synthesis?
   A. Type 1
   B. Type 2A
   C. Type 2B
   D. Type 3

3. Which type of VWD is associated with an increased risk of thrombosis due to increased platelet agglutination?
   A. Type 2A
   B. Type 2B
   C. Type 2M
   D. Type 2N

4. Which treatment option stimulates the release of stored vWF and FVIII?
   A. Tranexamic acid
   B. Factor VIII concentrates
   C. Desmopressin (DDAVP)
   D. vWF plasma-derived concentrates

5. On average, the levels of vWF and FVIII are lower in humans with type O blood.
   A. True
   B. False

6. A 42-year-old patient is being prepared for surgery to address chronic joint pain. The patient has been experiencing several symptoms that have raised concerns about a possible bleeding disorder. Over the years, the patient has noticed easy bruising, even from minor bumps, recurrent nosebleeds without any apparent cause, and bleeding gums after brushing teeth. Given the patient's bleeding tendencies, the medical team suspects VWD, a hereditary bleeding disorder. The patient's vWF activity level is tested, and the result shows a Von Willebrand Ristocetin Cofactor (vWF:RCo) level of 15 IU/dL. What is the primary function of the vWF?
   A. Inhibiting platelet activation
   B. Promoting fibrinolysis
   C. Stabilizing circulating factor IX
   D. Facilitating platelet adhesion and aggregation

Answers:

1. Answer B (Von Willebrand's Disease (VWD))

The most common inherited bleeding disorder is von Willebrand disease (VWD), affecting as many as 1 in 100 people. This disorder stems from a deficiency or dysfunction in a vital blood protein known as von Willebrand factor (VWF), which is responsible for regulating bleeding. Individuals with VWD exhibit either insufficient quantities of VWF or impaired functionality of the protein, causing delays in blood clotting and prolonged bleeding episodes. VWD is categorized into three primary types (1, 2, and 3), with each type manifesting in varying degrees of severity, ranging from mild to moderate to severe.

2. Answer D (Type 3)

Among the various types of VWD, Type 3 is characterized by a complete absence of vWF synthesis. vWF is a critical protein that plays a pivotal role in blood clotting and platelet function. In Type 3 VWD, there is a total lack of vWF production, leading to a significant reduction in the stabilization of circulating factor VIII (FVIII), another essential factor for blood clotting. Consequently, individuals with Type 3 VWD experience severe bleeding tendencies, which can manifest as prolonged bleeding following even minor injuries, joint bleeding, and other significant bleeding complications. Type 3 VWD represents the most severe form of the disorder, and those affected often require comprehensive and targeted treatment, including the administration of vWF and FVIII concentrates to manage and prevent bleeding episodes. Given the absence of vWF, the levels of plasma factor VIII are decreased despite normal synthesis, underscoring the essential role vWF plays in stabilizing FVIII and supporting efficient blood clotting.

3. Answer B (Type 2B)

Among the subtypes of Type 2 VWD, Type 2B is associated with an increased risk of thrombosis due to heightened platelet agglutination. In Type 2B VWD, the vWF exhibits abnormal characteristics that cause it to bind excessively to platelets, resulting in their agglutination or clumping. While this heightened platelet response can contribute to abnormal blood clot formation, paradoxically, it can also lead to an increased risk of thrombosis or the formation of blood clots within blood vessels. The unique platelet-binding properties of vWF in Type 2B VWD can result in a complex interplay between bleeding and clotting tendencies. While increased platelet agglutination heightens the risk of thrombosis, it can also lead to platelet depletion and thus contribute to bleeding symptoms.

4. Answer C (Desmopressin (DDAVP))

Desmopressin (DDAVP) is a treatment option that stimulates the release of stored vWF and factor VIII (FVIII) from endothelial cells and platelets. DDAVP is a synthetic analog of the antidiuretic hormone vasopressin, and when administered, it promotes the secretion of vWF and FVIII into the bloodstream. This action is particularly beneficial for individuals with certain types of VWD and mild hemophilia A, as it can enhance their blood clotting ability and help manage bleeding tendencies.

5. Answer A (True)

ABO histo-blood group plays a significant role in determining the plasma levels of factor VIII (FVIII) and vWF, two essential components involved in blood clotting. It has been observed that individuals with blood group O typically have lower plasma levels of FVIII and vWF compared to individuals with blood types A, B, or AB. Specifically, blood group O individuals have approximately 25% lower plasma levels of both FVIII and vWF. Both vWF and FVIII are important components of the blood clotting process, and their levels can vary based on blood type genetics.

6. Answer D (Facilitating platelet adhesion and aggregation)

vWF plays a critical role in blood clotting by facilitating platelet adhesion and aggregation. When a blood vessel is injured, vWF helps platelets adhere to the exposed subendothelial cells at the injury site. This initial adhesion is essential for the formation of a stable blood clot. Additionally, vWF forms bridges between platelets and helps aggregate them, leading to the formation of a hemostatic plug that prevents further bleeding. It's noteworthy that the reference range for vWF:RCo is typically around 50-150 IU/dL. Importantly, vWF levels can vary due to factors such as acute stress, as seen in situations like pregnancy. Guidelines define diagnostic thresholds for VWD based on vWF levels. A level of < 30 IU/dL (30% of normal) for either VWF antigen or vWF:RCo is considered diagnostic for VWD, irrespective of bleeding symptoms. Furthermore, a level of < 50 IU/dL, along with abnormal bleeding, confirms the diagnosis of VWD. In the scenario described, the patient's vWF:RCo level of 15 IU/dL falls below the diagnostic threshold for VWD, aligning with the patient's symptoms of easy bruising, recurrent nosebleeds, prolonged postoperative bleeding, and bleeding gums. This indicates impaired platelet adhesion and aggregation, in turn explaining the patient's bleeding tendencies.

Recommended literature

1. Uptodate: von Willebrand disease (vWD):Treatment of major bleeding and major surgery, Paula James, MD, FRCPC, literature review current Nov 2022, last updated Sep 12, 2022.
2. Shah UJ, Madan Narayanan M, J Graham Smith JH. Anaesthetic considerations in patients with inherited disorders of coagulation. Continuing Education in Anaesthesia Critical Care & Pain, Volume 15, Issue 1, February 2015, Pages 26–31.
3. Training in anaesthesia: the essential curriculum; Oxford Specialty Training, Chapter 15 pp392–393; ISBN: 978-0-19-922726-6.

HEPATIC DISEASES

END STAGE LIVER DISEASE (ESLD)

07
CHAPTER

Questions:

1. What is the NOT primary cause of end-stage liver disease (ESLD)?
   A. Alcohol consumption
   B. Viruses
   C. Chronic cholecystitis with gallstone
   D. Autoimmune diseases

2. Which of the following is NOT a common symptom of end-stage liver disease?
   A. Weakness
   B. Fever
   C. Jaundice
   D. Fatigue

3. Which of the following is a common complication of end-stage liver disease?
   A. Ascites
   B. Pancreatitis
   C. Peritonitis
   D. Pneumothorax

4. What is the most effective and definitive treatment for end-stage liver disease when conservative management is no longer effective?
   A. Dialysis
   B. Blood Transfusion
   C. Liver Transplantation
   D. Chemotherapy

5. The end-stage liver disease is characterized by altered mental status and cognitive dysfunction.
   A. True
   B. False

6. A patient with end-stage liver disease is scheduled for laparoscopic surgery to address chronic cholecystitis and a perforated gallbladder. After the successful induction of anesthesia and the commencement of the laparoscopic procedure, the surgeon requests the anesthesiologist to insert a nasogastric tube. What is the life-threatening complication that the anesthesiologist should be aware of when inserting the nasogastric tube for a patient with end-stage liver disease undergoing laparoscopic surgery?
   A. Aspiration
   B. Epistaxis
   C. Esophageal Perforation
   D. Varices Perforation

Answers:

1. Answer C (Chronic cholecystitis with gallstone)

While chronic cholecystitis with gallstones can lead to complications such as inflammation of the gallbladder and bile ducts, it is not considered a primary cause of end-stage liver disease (ESLD). The primary causes of ESLD typically involve factors that lead to chronic liver damage, such as alcohol consumption, viral infections (like hepatitis B and C), and autoimmune diseases (like autoimmune hepatitis). These factors can result in cirrhosis, which is a major precursor to ESLD. While gallstones can cause problems in the gallbladder and bile ducts, they are not directly responsible for the progression to end-stage liver disease.

2. Answer B (Fever)

The symptom "Fever" is not a common manifestation of ESLD. However, ESLD is associated with a range of symptoms, including weakness, fatigue, loss of appetite, nausea, vomiting, weight loss, abdominal pain and bloating, itching, bleeding varices, ascites, encephalopathy, and jaundice. These symptoms are primarily a result of impaired liver function, metabolic changes, and complications arising from advanced liver disease, such as cirrhosis and its associated consequences.

3. Answer A (Ascites)

Ascites is a particularly prevalent and clinically significant complication of ESLD. Ascites refers to the abnormal accumulation of fluid within the abdominal cavity, a consequence of both impaired liver function and increased pressure within the portal vein, a condition known as portal hypertension. This fluid retention can lead to abdominal distension and discomfort, further complicating the patient's condition. Other complications associated with ESLD include bleeding varices, jaundice, hepatocellular carcinoma, hepatic encephalopathy, splenomegaly, and sensitivity to medications, among others. While gallstones, pancreatitis, peritonitis, and pneumothorax can occur in various contexts, they are not primary complications directly attributed to ESLD.

4. Answer C (Liver Transplantation)

When conservative management measures prove insufficient in addressing the advanced stages of ESLD, liver transplantation stands out as the most effective and definitive treatment option. Liver transplantation involves surgically replacing the diseased liver with a healthy donor liver, offering the chance for a patient to regain proper liver function and quality of life. This procedure is particularly valuable when the liver's capabilities have been severely compromised, and it addresses the underlying cause of ESLD.

5. Answer A (True)

ESLD can lead to a neurological complication known as hepatic encephalopathy. Hepatic encephalopathy is characterized by altered mental status and cognitive dysfunction, ranging from mild confusion to severe disorientation, personality changes, and even coma. The condition is a result of the liver's reduced ability to detoxify ammonia and other toxins, which accumulate in the bloodstream and affect brain function. Therefore, altered mental status and cognitive dysfunction are important clinical features of hepatic encephalopathy, which commonly occurs in the advanced stages of ESLD.

6. Answer D (Varices Perforation)

In patients with end-stage liver disease, particularly those undergoing surgery, the presence of esophageal varices is a critical concern. Esophageal varices are dilated and fragile blood vessels in the esophagus that result from portal hypertension, a common consequence of advanced liver disease. Inserting a nasogastric tube in a patient with esophageal varices can potentially lead to variceal rupture and life-threatening hemorrhage. The anesthesiologist must exercise caution during nasogastric tube insertion to avoid trauma to these varices, and in the presence of suspected or known esophageal varices, alternate methods of managing gastric decompression might be considered to prevent this serious complication.

Recommended literature

1. Abbas N, Makker J, Abbas H, Balar B. Perioperative Care of Patients With Liver Cirrhosis: A Review. Health Serv Insights. 2017;10:1178632917691270. Published 2017 Feb 24.
2. Rakesh Vaja, BSc MBChB FRCA, Larry McNicol, MBBS (Hons) FRCA FANZCA, Imogen Sisley, MBChB MRCP FRCA, Anaesthesia for patients with liver disease, Continuing Education in Anaesthesia Critical Care & Pain, Volume 10, Issue 1, February 2010, Pages 15-19.

Hepatic diseases
JAUNDICE

Questions:

1. What is the primary underlying mechanism that leads to the yellowish discoloration of the skin and sclera in jaundice?
   A. Elevated urobilinogen levels
   B. Elevated biliverdin levels
   C. Elevated bilirubin levels
   D. Elevated stercobilinogen levels

2. What is the possible cause of jaundice in adults?
   A. Alcoholic liver disease
   B. Cholestasis of pregnancy
   C. Gilbert syndrome
   D. All of the above

3. Which symptom is NOT commonly associated with jaundice?
   A. Yellowish discoloration of sclera
   B. Pale stool
   C. Pale yellow urine
   D. Itchiness

4. Which condition is NOT associated with the prehepatic cause of jaundice?
   A. Sickle-cell anemia
   B. Chronic hepatitis
   C. Pyruvate kinase deficiency
   D. Microangiopathic hemolytic anemia

5. Gilbert syndrome is a medical condition that requires emergency medical intervention.
   A. True
   B. False

6. A 45-year-old patient presents with a constellation of symptoms that include yellowish discoloration of the skin, mucous membranes, and sclera, accompanied by itchiness, pale stools, dark urine, abdominal pain, fatigue, weight loss, vomiting, and fever. Laboratory tests reveal a serum bilirubin level of 6.5 mg/dL, with a conjugated bilirubin level of 3.2 mg/dL. Which type of jaundice is the probable cause of this patient's condition?
   A. Prehepatic jaundice
   B. Hepatic jaundice
   C. Posthepatic jaundice
   D. Hemolytic jaundice

Answers:

1. Answer C (Elevated bilirubin levels)

The primary underlying mechanism that leads to the yellowish discoloration of the skin and sclera in jaundice is the accumulation of elevated levels of bilirubin in the bloodstream. Bilirubin is a yellow pigment that results from the breakdown of hemoglobin in red blood cells. Normally, bilirubin is processed by the liver, conjugated, and excreted in bile. However, in cases of liver dysfunction or other factors affecting bilirubin metabolism, bilirubin can accumulate in the body tissues, leading to the characteristic yellow coloration seen in jaundice. This yellow pigment is responsible for the yellowing of the skin, mucous membranes, and sclera in jaundice.

2. Answer D (All of the above)

Jaundice in adults has diverse underlying causes involving disorders and factors that impact bilirubin metabolism, liver function, or the biliary system. These encompass conditions such as hepatitis, cirrhosis, biliary tract obstructions, drug-induced liver injury, pancreatic disorders, hemolytic anemias, autoimmune diseases, as well as primary sclerosing cholangitis. Each cause presents its distinctive characteristics, ranging from liver inflammation and dysfunction to bile flow obstruction, all culminating in the common manifestation of jaundice.

3. Answer C (Pale yellow urine)

Pale yellow urine is not commonly associated with jaundice. Jaundice is characterized by the yellowish discoloration of the skin, mucous membranes, and sclera due to elevated bilirubin levels in the bloodstream. The yellow coloration is a result of hyperbilirubinemia (serum bilirubin ≥ 3 mg/dL) and is visible in various tissues and fluids, such as the skin and eyes. Pale stool is a common symptom of jaundice due to the impaired flow of bile into the intestine, resulting in reduced bilirubin excretion in the stool. Itchiness can also occur as a symptom of jaundice, and dark urine is a result of the presence of bilirubin in the urine. Other symptoms like abdominal pain, fatigue, weight loss, vomiting, and fever can be associated with jaundice depending on the underlying cause and its effects on the body.

4. Answer B (Chronic hepatitis)

The prehepatic cause of jaundice encompasses conditions characterized by increased breakdown of red blood cells before liver metabolism, resulting in elevated unconjugated serum bilirubin levels. Sickle-cell anemia, spherocytosis, thalassemia, pyruvate kinase deficiency, glucose-6-phosphate dehydrogenase deficiency, microangiopathic hemolytic anemia, hemolytic-uremic syndrome, and severe malaria all fit this category as they involve various forms of hemolysis leading to the release of unconjugated bilirubin. Chronic hepatitis, on the other hand, primarily affects liver cells due to viral infections or other factors, resulting in liver inflammation and dysfunction, but it does not directly contribute to increased erythrocyte breakdown and unconjugated bilirubin accumulation, which are characteristic of the prehepatic jaundice category.

5. Answer B (False)

Gilbert syndrome is a benign and relatively mild genetic disorder that does not typically require emergency medical intervention. It is characterized by intermittent episodes of mild jaundice, often triggered by factors like stress, illness, or fasting. The condition does not usually cause severe symptoms or complications that would necessitate immediate medical attention. However, individuals with Gilbert syndrome should still be under medical care for proper management and monitoring, especially if they experience significant jaundice or other related symptoms.

6. Answer C (Posthepatic jaundice)

The symptoms presented by the patient, including yellowish discoloration of the skin, itchiness, pale stools, dark urine, abdominal pain, fatigue, weight loss, vomiting, and fever, along with elevated serum bilirubin levels (particularly conjugated bilirubin), suggest a likely diagnosis of posthepatic jaundice. Posthepatic jaundice, also known as obstructive jaundice, occurs when there is a blockage in the bile ducts, preventing the proper flow of bile from the liver to the intestines. The elevated conjugated bilirubin levels indicate that the blockage is occurring after the conjugation of bilirubin in the liver. The symptoms and laboratory results align with the common causes of posthepatic jaundice, such as bile duct obstruction due to gallstones or tumors, leading to the accumulation of bilirubin in the bloodstream and resulting in the classic manifestations of jaundice.

Recommended literature

1. Pollard BJ, Kitchen G. Handbook of Clinical Anaesthesia. 4th ed. Taylor & Francis group; 2018. Chapter 4 Gastrointestinal tract, Jackson MJ.
2. Wang L, Yu W. Obstructive jaundice and perioperative management. Acta Anaesthesiol Taiwan. 2014;52(1):22-29.

LIVER RESECTION

Questions:

1. **What is the primary mechanism through which the liver regenerates functional tissue after resection?**
   A. Metaplasia of the remaining tissue
   B. Hyperplasia of the remaining tissue
   C. Hypertrophy of the remaining tissue
   D. Dysplasia of the remaining tissue

2. **Which blood vessels primarily supply the liver with blood?**
   A. Inferior vena cava and hepatic artery
   B. Aorta and hepatic veins
   C. Portal vein and hepatic artery
   D. Portal vein and hepatic veins

3. **Which of the following is a potential complication of liver resection?**
   A. Pleural effusion
   B. Bile leakage
   C. Deep vein thrombosis
   D. All of the above

4. **Which type of liver resection involves removing a segment or a part of a segment with a tumor?**
   A. Right lateral segmentectomy
   B. Left lateral segmentectomy
   C. Minor liver resection
   D. Major liver resection

5. **Administration of N-acetylcysteine could reduce post-hepatectomy liver failure.**
   A. True
   B. False

6. **A 52-year-old male patient has been diagnosed with hepatocellular carcinoma (HCC) located on the right lobe of the liver. To address the malignancy, a major liver resection is scheduled to remove the right lobe. As the medical teams prepare for the surgery, various considerations related to anesthesia management are being addressed to ensure a successful and safe procedure. Which statement is incorrect about anesthesia management for liver resection?**
   A. General anesthesia with controlled ventilation is the commonly employed technique
   B. Atracurium/cisatracurium are preferred as they are unaffected by liver dysfunction
   C. Adequate IV fluid administration in the pre-resection phase (at least 5 mL/kg)
   D. TIVA is the preferred technique for anesthesia maintenance

Answers:

1. **Answer B (Hyperplasia of the remaining tissue)**

   After liver resection, the remaining liver tissue has the remarkable ability to regenerate and restore its function. This process primarily occurs through hyperplasia, which is the increase in the number of cells within the remaining liver tissue. Unlike hypertrophy, which involves the enlargement of individual cells, hyperplasia results in the growth of new liver cells. This hyperplastic response is a key mechanism that enables the liver to compensate for the loss of tissue and maintain its vital functions. As new cells are generated and the tissue proliferates, the liver gradually regains its functional capacity. This regenerative ability is a distinctive characteristic of the liver and plays a significant role in its recovery following surgical resection or injury.

2. **Answer C (Portal vein and hepatic artery)**

   The liver is a highly vascular organ that receives its blood supply from two main sources the portal vein and the hepatic artery. About 80% of the liver's blood supply comes from the portal vein. The portal vein carries nutrient-rich blood from the intestines, stomach, and spleen to the liver. This blood contains digested nutrients, as well as substances absorbed from the gastrointestinal tract. The liver plays a crucial role in processing and detoxifying these substances. The remaining 20% of the liver's blood supply comes from the hepatic artery. The hepatic artery carries oxygenated blood from the heart to the liver. The combination of these two blood sources, the portal vein and the hepatic artery, ensures that the liver performs its various functions, including metabolism, detoxification, and synthesis of essential proteins.

3. **Answer D (All of the above)**

   Liver resection is a complex surgical procedure that carries the potential for various complications. These include infection, bleeding, bile leakage from damage to bile ducts, pleural effusion involving fluid accumulation in the pleural cavity, ascites with fluid buildup in the abdominal cavity due to disrupted fluid balance, as well as the risk of deep vein thrombosis due to surgery-related immobility. Additionally, kidney failure and liver failure can arise from factors such as decreased blood flow or inadequate tissue compensation.

4. **Answer C (Minor liver resection)**

   A minor liver resection, also known as a segmental or wedge resection, involves the removal of a segment or a part of a segment of the liver that includes a tumor. This surgical approach is used when the tumor is located within a specific segment of the liver, and it allows for the removal of the affected portion while preserving as much healthy liver tissue as possible.

5. **Answer A (True)**

   N-acetylcysteine (NAC) is an antioxidant and precursor to glutathione, a natural antioxidant produced by the body. Glutathione plays a vital role in counteracting oxidative stress and inflammation. In the context of liver surgery, including liver resection, the administration of NAC has been studied for its potential benefits in reducing postoperative complications, including liver failure. Given that oxidative stress and inflammation play roles in hepatic ischemia-reperfusion injury, NAC's ability to enhance endogenous antioxidants and mitigate oxidative stress can be beneficial. By blocking oxidative stress and reducing inflammation, NAC may contribute to protecting liver tissue from damage, thereby potentially reducing the risk of post-hepatectomy liver failure.

6. **Answer C (Adequate IV fluid administration in pre-resection phase (at least 5 mL/kg))**

   The statement that adequate intravenous (IV) fluid administration should be at least 5 mL/kg in the pre-resection phase is incorrect. Anesthesia management during major liver resection involves minimizing pre-resection IV fluids to a maximum rate of 1 mL/kg/hr. The objective is to maintain a low central venous pressure (CVP) during the dissection and transection phases to reduce venous bleeding. Post resection, judicious fluid intervention is carried out to restore euvolemia. Fluid administration strategies are tailored to optimize cardiac preload while minimizing blood loss and maintaining hemodynamic stability.

Recommended literature

1. Pollard BJ, Kitchen, G. Handbook of Clinical Anaesthesia. Fourth Edition. CRC Press. 2018. 978-1-4987-6289-2.
2. Page AJ, Kooby DA. Perioperative management of hepatic resection. J Gastrointest Oncol. 2012;3(1):19-27.
3. Harto A, Mills G. 2009. Anaesthesia for hepatic resection surgery. Continuing Education in Anaesthesia Critical Care & Pain9;1:1-5.

PATIENT WITH A LIVER TRANSPLANT

07
CHAPTER

Questions:

1. **What is the most common technique used for liver transplantation?**
   A. Heterotopic liver transplantation
   B. Isograft liver transplantation
   C. Orthotopic liver transplantation
   D. Allograft liver transplantation

2. **Which medication used for immunosuppression after liver transplantation is associated with nephrotoxicity?**
   A. Azathioprine
   B. Corticosteroids
   C. Cyclosporine
   D. All of the above

3. **Which of the subsequent options is NOT counted among the long-term complications that patients may encounter following a liver transplant?**
   A. Arterial hypertension
   B. Renal failure
   C. Bone complications
   D. Chronic obstructive pulmonary disease

4. **Which of the following anesthetic medications is more likely to exhibit adverse effects due to an increase in liver function impairment and should consequently be avoided in liver transplant surgery?**
   A. Propofol
   B. Sevoflurane
   C. Ketamine
   D. Midazolam

5. **Fentanyl is a safe option for pain management during liver transplant surgery in the presence of deranged liver function.**
   A. True
   B. False

6. **A 50-year-old patient who has undergone a successful liver transplant procedure to address end-stage liver disease secondary to nonalcoholic steatohepatitis is presently in the postoperative phase, receiving attentive monitoring within the Intensive Care Unit (ICU). In this critical stage of recovery, it's crucial to ensure the patient's comfort and well-being. Which of the following is NOT a recommended postoperative pain management strategy after a liver transplant?**
   A. Ibuprofen and Acetaminophen
   B. Epidural analgesia
   C. Opioid IV patient-controlled analgesia (PCA)
   D. Single-shot neuraxial opioids administration

Answers:

1. **Answer C (Orthotopic liver transplantation)**

The most common technique used for liver transplantation is orthotopic liver transplantation. In this procedure, the diseased native liver is replaced with a healthy liver, or a portion of it, obtained from a deceased or living donor. The donor's liver is positioned in the same anatomical location as the original liver. This technique allows for the restoration of normal liver function and is the standard approach for treating end-stage liver disease and acute liver failure. It ensures that the new liver has proper vascular and biliary connections, enabling it to function effectively within the recipient's body.

2. **Answer C (Cyclosporine)**

Cyclosporine, a potent immunosuppressive agent commonly employed in conjunction with solid organ transplantation, including liver transplants, effectively curtails the immune response against the transplanted organ. However, it is associated with the potential to cause nephrotoxicity, which manifests in the renal vasculature, glomeruli, and tubular function, potentially giving rise to various clinical syndromes that compromise kidney function. Consequently, diligent monitoring and management of kidney function become paramount imperatives in patients undergoing cyclosporine treatment.

3. **Answer D (Chronic obstructive pulmonary disease)**

The array of enduring complications that could emerge after a liver transplant includes chronic rejection, renal failure, arterial hypertension, diabetes mellitus, dyslipidemia, obesity, bone complications, neurological complications, and malignancy. Chronic obstructive pulmonary disease (COPD) primarily affects the respiratory system and isn't typically linked to liver transplantation.

4. **Answer D (Midazolam)**

Midazolam is extensively metabolized by the liver, and its inactive metabolites are excreted in the urine. In cases of worsening liver function, the clearance of drugs like midazolam can be compromised, leading to prolonged and potentially excessive sedation. Patients with severe liver disease are more susceptible to adverse effects from medications, particularly those with sedative properties such as benzodiazepines, opioids, antihistamines, and antiemetics. As a result, midazolam administration might need to be adjusted or avoided in liver transplant surgery to prevent excessive sedation and its potential complications.

5. **Answer A (True)**

Fentanyl is considered one of the safer options for pain management in liver transplant surgery when liver function is deranged. It is a potent opioid analgesic that is less affected by liver dysfunction compared to some other opioids. Fentanyl is known to be heavily protein-bound and is thought to be unaffected by cirrhosis. Additionally, fentanyl has no toxic metabolites, making it potentially better tolerated in cirrhotic patients. However, even though it's considered safer, the administration and dosing of any medication, including fentanyl, should be carefully monitored in patients with liver disease. Other opioids like hydromorphone may also be considered due to their better tolerance and adjustability in patients with advanced liver disease.

6. **Answer A (Ibuprofen and Acetaminophen)**

While ibuprofen and acetaminophen are often used for pain management, their use after liver transplant surgery should be approached with caution. Acetaminophen (paracetamol) is metabolized by the liver and can become hepatotoxic when glutathione stores are rapidly depleted, a concern in post-liver transplant patients. Additionally, non-steroidal anti-inflammatory agents (NSAIDs) like ibuprofen are not recommended after liver transplantation due to potential liver injury, drug interactions, and serious side effects. Considering the vulnerable state of liver transplant recipients, alternative pain management options such as epidural analgesia, opioid IV patient-controlled analgesia (PCA), or single-shot neuraxial opioid administration are more suitable choices to ensure patient comfort and minimize risks.

Recommended literature

1. Pollard BJ, Kitchen G. Handbook of Clinical Anaesthesia. 4th ed. Taylor & Francis group; 2018. Chapter 4 Gastrointestinal tract, Jackson MJ.

MISCELLANEOUS

AWARENESS DURING ANESTHESIA

Questions:

1. Which of the following statements about the incidence of intraoperative awareness is NOT accurate?
   A. Intraoperative awareness is a significant clinical problem
   B. The estimated overall incidence of intraoperative awareness is approximately 0.1%
   C. Intraoperative awareness is consistently high in abdominal surgical cases
   D. The incidence of intraoperative awareness can vary based on specific circumstances

2. Which of the following risk factors is NOT associated with an increased likelihood of experiencing awareness during anesthesia?
   A. Male gender
   B. Pregnancy
   C. Obesity
   D. Ketamine use

3. Which type of anesthesia is associated with a higher risk of awareness during surgery?
   A. Inhalational anesthesia
   B. MAC anesthesia
   C. Regional anesthesia
   D. Total intravenous anesthesia (TIVA)

4. Which psychological condition occurs within 3 days to 1 month after a traumatic event and may include symptoms like flashbacks and avoidance of distressing memories?
   A. Major Depressive Disorder
   B. Post-Traumatic Stress Disorder (PTSD)
   C. Acute Stress Disorder (ASD)
   D. Generalized Anxiety Disorder

5. Benzodiazepines should be used prophylactically to reduce the risk of intraoperative awareness.
   A. True
   B. False

6. A patient is scheduled for emergency surgery due to a tibial fracture resulting from trauma. The patient is obese and requires general anesthesia using total intravenous anesthesia. During the preoperative assessment, the patient mentioned a previous experience with awareness during a caesarean section procedure performed two years ago. The patient is concerned about the possibility of experiencing awareness again during the upcoming surgery. Which technique is NOT a recommended action for reducing the risk of intraoperative awareness for this patient?
   A. Preoperative administration of opioids
   B. Brain function monitors
   C. Monitoring blood pressure and heart rate
   D. Checking the anesthesia delivery system before induction

Answers:

1. Answer C (Intraoperative awareness is consistently high in abdominal surgical cases)

The incidence of intraoperative awareness is not uniformly elevated in abdominal surgical cases; instead, it exhibits variability contingent upon distinct circumstances and risk factors. These encompass procedures such as cardiac surgery, caesarean section, trauma surgery, and emergency surgery. Significantly, intraoperative awareness constitutes a noteworthy clinical concern, with an estimated overall incidence of around 0.1%.

2. Answer A (Male gender)

Among the listed risk factors for experiencing awareness during anesthesia, the male gender is not associated with an increased likelihood. However, several other factors, such as pregnancy, obesity, and ketamine use, have been linked to an increased risk of intraoperative awareness. Other risk factors include neuromuscular blocking, female gender, total intravenous anesthesia (TIVA), cardiothoracic patients, trauma & emergency surgery, difficult intubation, history of AAGA (accidental awareness during general anesthesia), chronic drug use, and lack of monitoring.

3. Answer D (Total intravenous anesthesia (TIVA))

Total intravenous anesthesia is associated with a higher risk of awareness during surgery. TIVA lacks real-time monitoring of blood anesthetic concentration, which increases the risk of awareness. Studies have shown that TIVA is associated with a greater risk of awareness compared to end-tidal anesthetic agent concentration-based inhalational anesthesia.

4. Answer C (Acute Stress Disorder (ASD))

Acute Stress Disorder (ASD) is a psychological condition that occurs shortly after a traumatic event, typically within 3 days to 1 month. It is characterized by symptoms such as recurring distressing memories, nightmares, flashbacks, intense psychological or physical distress upon reminders of the event, avoidance of distressing memories, altered sense of reality, memory loss for the traumatic event, disturbed sleep, irritability, hypervigilance, concentration difficulties, and exaggerated startle response. This condition is different from Post-Traumatic Stress Disorder (PTSD), which involves similar symptoms but persists for more than a month after the traumatic event.

5. Answer B (False)

The use of benzodiazepines as a component of anesthesia to reduce the risk of intraoperative awareness should be decided on a case-by-case basis. While benzodiazepines may be administered prophylactically for selected patients (such as those with increased risk of intraoperative awareness), the decision should be made carefully due to potential drawbacks. Benzodiazepines can lead to delayed emergence, and therefore, their prophylactic use should be approached cautiously, taking individual patient factors into account.

6. Answer A (Preoperative administration of opioids)

Preoperative administration of opioids is NOT a recommended action for reducing the risk of intraoperative awareness. While opioids can provide pain relief and sedation, they are not specifically targeted at preventing awareness during anesthesia. In this case, the patient's history of previous awareness during a caesarean section indicates a need for careful consideration of anesthesia techniques to minimize the risk of recurrence. Techniques such as using brain function monitors, monitoring blood pressure and heart rate, checking the anesthesia delivery system before induction, ensuring proper equipment and medication, prophylactic preoperative administration of benzodiazepines, monitoring neuromuscular block if necessary, and using target-controlled infusion for total IV anesthesia are more relevant strategies for reducing the risk of intraoperative awareness and ensuring patient safety during the emergency surgery. These techniques aim to maintain appropriate anesthesia depth and patient monitoring to prevent awareness and ensure a successful surgery outcome.

Recommended literature

1. Kim MC, Fricchione GL, Akeju O. Accidental awareness under general anaesthesia: Incidence, risk factors, and psychological management. BJA Education. 2021;21(4):154-61.
2. Mashour GA, Avidan MS. Intraoperative awareness: controversies and non-controversies. Br J Anaesth. 2015;115 Suppl 1:i20-i26.
3. Tasbihgou SR, Vogels MF, Absalom AR. Accidental awareness during general anaesthesia – a narrative review. Anaesthesia. 2018;73(1):112-22.
4. Mashour GA, Orser BA, Avidan MS, Warner DS. Intraoperative Awareness: From Neurobiology to Clinical Practice. Anesthesiology. 2011;114(5):1218-33.

BARIATRIC SURGERY

Questions:

1. Which type of bariatric surgery involves the placement of an inflatable tube made of soft silicone around the upper portion of the stomach?
   A. Gastric bypass surgery
   B. Sleeve gastrectomy
   C. Adjustable gastric band
   D. Intragastric balloon

2. What is the primary mechanism of action for gastric sleeve surgery?
   A. Decreasing nutrient absorption
   B. Altering hunger hormones
   C. Reducing stomach size
   D. Rearranging the small intestine

3. Among the listed complications, which one is NOT typically associated with bariatric surgery?
   A. Diabetes mellitus
   B. Blood clots
   C. Malnutrition
   D. Gallstones

4. Which hormones undergo reduction after specific types of bariatric surgery, resulting in an impact on hunger regulation?
   A. Gastrin
   B. Cholecystokinin
   C. Glucagon
   D. Ghrelin

5. Epidural analgesia is the cornerstone of pain management after bariatric surgery.
   A. True
   B. False

6. A 38-year-old female patient with a history of prolonged obesity is facing significant health challenges due to her weight-related issues. She presents with a body mass index (BMI) of 42 kg/m². Her medical history reveals diagnoses of type 2 diabetes, hypertension, hypothyroidism, and severe joint pain. Considering her complex health condition, her healthcare professional has recommended gastric bypass surgery as a potentially transformative intervention to enhance her overall health and well-being. Which of the following is an obesity-related condition that can potentially improve after bariatric surgery?
   A. Osteoarthritis
   B. Cardiovascular disease
   C. Hypothireosis
   D. All of the above

Answers:

1. **Answer C (Adjustable gastric band)**

   Adjustable gastric band surgery involves the placement of an inflatable tube made of soft silicone around the upper portion of the stomach. This creates a small pouch above the band and a larger pouch below the band. The band can be adjusted by inflating or deflating it with saline to control the size of the upper pouch, which restricts the amount of food the patient can comfortably eat. This procedure primarily works through the mechanism of restricting food intake, allowing the individual to feel full after consuming smaller meals.

2. **Answer C (Reducing stomach size)**

   Gastric sleeve surgery, also known as sleeve gastrectomy, involves the surgical removal of a large portion of the stomach along the greater curvature, resulting in a significant reduction in stomach size. This procedure primarily works by restricting the amount of food the patient can consume in one sitting. The smaller stomach size limits the amount of food that can be held, leading to early satiety and reduced food intake. This restriction helps patients feel full faster and consume fewer calories, contributing to weight loss. While the surgery may also have secondary effects on hormones that regulate hunger and satiety, such as ghrelin, the primary mechanism of action is the physical reduction in stomach size.

3. **Answer A (Diabetes mellitus)**

   Diabetes mellitus is not a typical complication of bariatric surgery; in fact, bariatric surgery is often performed to improve or even resolve conditions like diabetes mellitus type 2. Bariatric surgery can lead to significant weight loss and positive metabolic changes that help manage or alleviate diabetes. Blood clots (deep vein thrombosis or pulmonary embolism), malabsorption and malnutrition, and gallstones are known risks that patients undergoing bariatric surgery might face. These complications can arise due to changes in anatomy, dietary modifications, or other factors related to the surgical procedure.

4. **Answer D (Ghrelin)**

   Following certain forms of bariatric surgery, such as sleeve gastrectomy, there is a decrease in the hormone ghrelin. Ghrelin, often recognized as the "hunger hormone," is responsible for stimulating appetite and the sensation of hunger. Bariatric procedures that involve altering the stomach's size, such as sleeve gastrectomy, lead to reduced production of ghrelin. This reduction in ghrelin levels contributes to diminished feelings of hunger and increased feelings of fullness, facilitating weight loss. While the other hormones mentioned play roles in digestion and metabolic processes, they are not the primary drivers of hunger modulation as affected by bariatric surgery.

5. **Answer B (False)**

   Epidural analgesia for postoperative pain is effective but is not required in laparoscopic bariatric surgery. While epidural analgesia can be highly effective for postoperative pain management, especially in open surgeries, it is not considered a mandatory component for laparoscopic bariatric surgery. Multimodal analgesia, involving a combination of tramadol, acetaminophen, and NSAID, can offer better postoperative pain relief, shorter PACU (Post-Anesthesia Care Unit) duration, reduced opioid requirement, earlier ambulation, shorter hospital stay, and less postoperative hypopnoea.

6. **Answer D (All of the above)**

   All of the listed conditions can potentially improve after bariatric surgery. Bariatric surgery often leads to significant weight loss, which in turn can have positive effects on various obesity-related health problems. This improvement is attributed to the reduction in excess body weight and the associated metabolic changes. Conditions like high blood pressure, diabetes, sleep apnea, asthma, arthritis, thyroid dysfunction, and cholesterol levels are among the many obesity-related health problems that may see improvement or even resolution following successful bariatric surgery.

Recommended literature

1. Pollard BJ, Kitchen G. Handbook of Clinical Anaesthesia. 4th ed. Taylor & Francis group; 2018. Chapter 10 Abdominal surgery.

BEACH CHAIR POSITION

Questions:

1. What is the NOT primary advantage of placing patients in the beach chair position during shoulder surgery?
   A. Reduced risk of brachial plexus injury
   B. Increased cerebral perfusion
   C. Improved access to the surgical site
   D. Decreased risk of bleeding

2. Which of the following is a potential risk associated with the beach chair position?
   A. Brachial plexus injury
   B. Enhanced venous return to the heart
   C. Reduced functional residual capacity (FRC)
   D. Decrease in cerebral perfusion

3. What is NOT a potential consequence of excessive neck flexion in the beach chair position?
   A. Vascular obstruction in the neck
   B. Obstruction of ETT/SGD
   C. Tongue/oropharyngeal swelling
   D. Paradoxical air embolism

4. Which potential complication can arise due to the operative site being positioned above the level of the heart in the beach chair position, exposing non-collapsible veins to atmospheric pressure?
   A. Decrease in cerebral perfusion
   B. Stroke
   C. Bradycardia or cardiac arrest
   D. Venous air embolism

5. The use of nitrous oxide in the gas mixture during fossa craniotomy helps minimize the risk of pneumocephalus.
   A. True
   B. False

6. A 45-year-old male patient presented at the hospital with a history of diabetes and a persistent right rotator cuff injury. His condition required surgical intervention, specifically shoulder joint surgery, to address the issue. The surgical plan involved performing the procedure with the patient in the sitting position under an interscalene block. During the surgical procedure, approximately fifteen minutes after the commencement of the surgery, the patient experienced a sudden and alarming sequence of events. He developed apnea, bradycardia, and hypotension These combined symptoms pointed to a cardiovascular collapse. The patient's medical history of diabetes, coupled with the unique surgical approach of performing the procedure in the sitting position under an interscalene block, potentially contributed to the occurrence of this critical event. Which reflex is likely to be associated with the symptoms observed during this case?
   A. Fight-or-flight reflex
   B. Bezold-Jarisch reflex
   C. Tonic-clonic reflex
   D. Reflex sympathetic dystrophy

Answers:

1. Answer B (Increased cerebral perfusion)

While increased cerebral perfusion is a concern in the beach chair position, it is not the primary advantage. The upright posture can potentially lead to reduced cerebral perfusion due to changes in blood flow dynamics. Preventing cerebral hypoperfusion becomes a priority during procedures in this position, underscoring the necessity of vigilant monitoring and intervention to maintain cerebral blood flow. The primary advantages of the beach chair position are improved surgical access, reduced risk of brachial plexus injury, improved access to the surgical site, and decreased risk of bleeding due to the effect of gravity on blood flow.

2. Answer D (Decrease in cerebral perfusion)

The potential risk associated with the beach chair position is a decrease in cerebral perfusion. Placing patients in a semi-sitting position can alter blood flow dynamics, potentially leading to reduced blood flow to the brain and compromised cerebral perfusion. Alongside this risk, other notable risks related to the beach chair position include hypotension due to decreased venous return, the potential for venous and paradoxical air embolism, excessive neck flexion, bradycardia or cardiac arrest from vagal stimulation, upper airway obstruction, and risks like pneumocephalus, subdural hematoma, quadriplegia, and stroke due to altered blood flow or positioning-related factors. Careful monitoring and management are crucial to ensure patient safety during procedures in the beach chair position.

3. Answer D (Paradoxical air embolism)

Excessive neck flexion in the beach chair position can lead to a range of potential consequences. These include vascular obstruction in the neck, which can impede blood flow to crucial structures; the obstruction of airway devices like endotracheal tubes or supraglottic devices, hampering proper ventilation and oxygenation; and the risk of tongue and oropharyngeal swelling due to sustained pressure on these tissues. However, paradoxical air embolism, a condition where the gas bubbles are able to traverse a right to left shunt, gaining access to the systemic arterial circulation causing ischemic symptoms in end organs, is not a direct outcome of excessive neck flexion.

4. Answer D (Venous air embolism)

In the beach chair position, where the operative site is elevated above the heart, non-collapsible veins are exposed to atmospheric pressure. This situation can potentially create a pressure gradient that allows air to enter the veins and travel to the heart, causing venous air embolism. Air embolism occurs when air bubbles obstruct blood vessels and compromise circulation, which can have serious consequences. While other complications, such as a decrease in cerebral perfusion, stroke, and bradycardia or cardiac arrest, are possible in specific circumstances, the scenario described in the question primarily highlights the risk of venous air embolism due to the exposed non-collapsible veins in the elevated operative site.

5. Answer B (False)

While nitrous oxide (N2O) is commonly used as an inhaled anesthetic, its association with the development of tension pneumocephalus has been discussed in the medical literature. Notably, using nitrous oxide during neurosurgical procedures, such as fossa craniotomy, can potentially increase the risk of tension pneumocephalus, particularly when there is preexisting pneumocephalus. This complication can manifest as the Cushing response, and immediate decompression is crucial for the patient's survival. Given the potential risk, the use of nitrous oxide in neurosurgical procedures, especially when preexisting pneumocephalus is present, should be approached cautiously. Proper consideration of the potential complications and alternative anesthetic options is vital to ensuring patient safety during such procedures.

6. Answer B (Bezold-Jarisch reflex)

The sudden occurrence of bradycardia and hypotension during the surgical procedure is likely associated with the Bezold-Jarisch reflex (BJR). This reflex is known for its triad of responses, including apnea, bradycardia, and hypotension. It is characterized by a combination of vasodilation, bradycardia, and hypotension and can be triggered by various factors, including orthostasis, hypovolemia, hemorrhage, and certain medical procedures such as interscalene block for shoulder surgery in the sitting position. In this case, the patient's history of diabetes and the use of interscalene block in the sitting position for the surgery could have contributed to the activation of the BJR, leading to the cardiovascular collapse observed. To manage the situation, anticholinergics and vasopressors were administered intravenously, and the patient's position was promptly changed to the supine position, resulting in a rapid normalization of vital signs.

Recommended literature

1. Murphy GS, Greenberg SB, Szokol JW. Safety of Beach Chair Position Shoulder Surgery: A Review of the Current Literature. Anesth Analg. 2019;129(1):101-118.
2. Hewson DW, Oldman M, Bedforth NM. Regional anaesthesia for shoulder surgery. BJA Education. 2019;19(4):98-104.
3. Rozet I, Vavilala MS. Risks and benefits of patient positioning during neurosurgical care. Anesthesiol Clin. 2007;25(3):631-x.

BLEOMYCIN EXPOSURE

08
CHAPTER

Questions:

1. **What is the primary mechanism of action of bleomycin in treating cancer?**
   A. Inhibition of DNA synthesis
   B. Direct cytotoxic effect on cancer cells
   C. Binding to metal ions and oxidative DNA damage
   D. Induction of apoptosis

2. **Which tissue is particularly sensitive to bleomycin-induced damage due to low concentrations of bleomycin hydrolase?**
   A. Liver
   B. Heart
   C. Lung
   D. Kidney

3. **What is the most common symptom of bleomycin-induced toxicity?**
   A. Nausea
   B. Heart palpitations
   C. Dry cough
   D. Headache

4. **What enzyme inactivates bleomycin?**
   A. Bleomycin polymerase
   B. Bleomycin kinase
   C. Bleomycin hydrolase
   D. Bleomycin polymerase

5. **Oxygen therapy is the primary treatment for dyspnea in patients who have undergone bleomycin therapy.**
   A. True
   B. False

6. **A 28-year-old patient presents for a cholecystectomy procedure. The patient was diagnosed with Hodgkin's disease 2 years ago and underwent bleomycin therapy as part of the treatment protocol. Considering the patient's history of Hodgkin's disease and previous bleomycin therapy, the anesthesiologist needs to be mindful of the potential pulmonary toxicity associated with oxygen therapy. What is the recommended oxygen saturation range for patients who have received bleomycin therapy?**
   A. 95-100%
   B. 90-94%
   C. 88-92%
   D. 85-89%

Answers:

1. Answer C (Binding to metal ions and oxidative DNA damage)

Bleomycin is an antitumor antibiotic that primarily exerts its effects through binding to metal ions, particularly iron, and causing oxidative damage to DNA. This oxidative damage results in DNA strand breaks and lesions within cancer cells. These damaged DNA strands disrupt the normal cell division and growth processes, ultimately leading to cell death. The drug does not directly inhibit DNA synthesis or induce apoptosis. While it does have a direct cytotoxic effect on cancer cells, this effect is primarily achieved through its ability to cause oxidative DNA damage rather than a generalized cytotoxic action.

2. Answer C (Lung)

Lung tissue is particularly sensitive to bleomycin-induced damage due to low concentrations of bleomycin hydrolase. Bleomycin hydrolase is an enzyme responsible for breaking down and inactivating bleomycin. In tissues with higher levels of bleomycin hydrolase, the drug can be more effectively neutralized, reducing its potentially damaging effects. However, lung tissue has relatively low levels of bleomycin hydrolase, making it susceptible to the toxic effects of bleomycin. This sensitivity to bleomycin-induced damage in the lung is a significant concern, as it can lead to pulmonary toxicity, which may manifest as subacute pulmonary damage and potentially progress to life-threatening pulmonary fibrosis.

3. Answer C (Dry cough)

The most common symptom of bleomycin-induced toxicity is a dry cough. This cough often serves as an early indicator of pulmonary involvement and can be a presenting symptom of bleomycin-induced lung injury. Alongside the dry cough, other pulmonary symptoms such as dyspnea, tachypnea, and fine rales may also be observed during physical examination. These symptoms are reflective of the adverse effects of bleomycin on lung tissue. Bleomycin is known to have significant toxic effects on the lungs and skin, with pulmonary toxicity being one of the most serious adverse reactions.

4. Answer C (Bleomycin hydrolase)

Bleomycin is inactivated by the enzyme bleomycin hydrolase. This enzyme plays a crucial role in breaking down and neutralizing bleomycin, which helps mitigate its potential toxic effects on tissues and cells. Bleomycin hydrolase catalyzes the hydrolysis of bleomycin, leading to its inactivation and clearance from the body. This process is essential for regulating the levels of active bleomycin and preventing excessive damage to tissues, particularly those that are sensitive to bleomycin-induced toxicity, such as the lungs and skin. It's worth noting that the relatively low concentrations of bleomycin hydrolase in lung tissue contribute to the heightened sensitivity of the lungs to bleomycin-induced damage. This can lead to pulmonary toxicity, a significant adverse effect associated with bleomycin therapy.

5. Answer B (False)

Oxygen therapy is not the primary treatment for dyspnea in patients who have undergone bleomycin therapy. In fact, due to the potential risk of exacerbating pulmonary toxicity, oxygen therapy should be used with caution in such patients. While oxygen therapy might be necessary in cases of severe hypoxemia, it is not the mainstay treatment for dyspnea in this context. Patients who have received bleomycin therapy are at an increased risk of developing pulmonary toxicity, which can be life-threatening. Exposure to high levels of inspired oxygen (FiO2) can further contribute to the progression of lung damage.

6. Answer C (88-92%)

The recommended oxygen saturation range for patients who have received bleomycin therapy is 88-92%. This range is crucial to balance oxygen supplementation while minimizing the potential harm caused by high levels of FiO2. The lungs of patients treated with bleomycin are at a higher risk of developing pulmonary toxicity, and exposure to excessive oxygen concentrations can further contribute to this risk. Choosing an oxygen saturation range between 88% and 92% allows adequate oxygen delivery to the tissues while avoiding the potential detrimental effects of high FiO2 on lung function. This cautious approach is essential to prevent the progression of pulmonary damage and fibrosis associated with bleomycin therapy.

Recommended literature

1. Groenewold MD, Olthof CG, Bosch DJ. Anaesthesia after neoadjuvant chemotherapy, immunotherapy or radiotherapy. BJA Educ. 2022;22(1):12-19.
2. Brandt JP, Gerriets V. Bleomycin. [Updated 2022 Aug 29]. In: StatPearls [Internet]. Treasure Island (FL): StatPearls Publishing; 2022 Jan-. Available from: https://www.ncbi.nlm.nih.gov/books/NBK555895/.
3. Della Latta V, Cecchettini A, Del Ry S, Morales MA. Bleomycin in the setting of lung fibrosis induction: From biological mechanisms to counteractions. Pharmacological Research. 2015;97:122-30.
4. Allan N, Siller C, Breen A. Anaesthetic implications of chemotherapy. Continuing Education in Anaesthesia Critical Care & Pain. 2012;12(2):52-6.

CANNABIS USE

Questions:

1. Which of the following psychoactive compounds in marijuana is responsible for its euphoric effects as well as anxiety, sedation, relaxation, and altered perception?
   - A. THC (delta-9-tetrahydrocannabinol)
   - B. CBD (Cannabidiol)
   - C. CB1 receptors
   - D. CB2 receptors

2. What is the primary mechanism of action of CBD on the endocannabinoid system?
   - A. Antagonist of CB1 receptor
   - B. Antagonist of CB2 receptor
   - C. Negative allosteric modulator of CB1 receptor
   - D. Positive allosteric modulator of CB2 receptor

3. What is the primary acute cardiovascular effect of marijuana use?
   - A. Bradycardia
   - B. Vasodilation
   - C. Hypotension
   - D. Heart Failure

4. What is NOT accurate for patients with recent marijuana use undergoing anesthesia?
   - A. Elevated intra-op BIS (Bispectral Index)
   - B. Reduced volatile anesthetic requirements
   - C. Increased induction dose requirements
   - D. Greater post-operative pain requirements

5. Patients with coronary heart disease (CAD) have an increased risk of MI within 1 hour after marijuana use.
   - A. True
   - B. False

6. A 45-year-old patient is scheduled for an elective cholecystectomy due to symptomatic gallstones. During the preoperative assessment, there is suspicion that the patient may have used marijuana recently. The anesthesiologist needs to address this potential marijuana use and be prepared to adapt the anesthesia plan or possibly delay the procedure as needed. What is the NOT recommended approach for patients who are suspected to have used marijuana shortly before elective surgery?
   - A. Assessing the history of use
   - B. Conducting a toxicology screen
   - C. Assessing the use of other drugs
   - D. Ruling out acute intoxication

Answers:

1. Answer A (THC (delta-9-tetrahydrocannabinol))

THC, or delta-9-tetrahydrocannabinol, is the psychoactive compound in marijuana that is primarily responsible for its euphoric effects as well as other acute effects like anxiety, sedation, relaxation, and altered spatial/temporal perception. It binds to CB1 receptors in the central nervous system, leading to these various psychoactive responses. This interaction with CB1 receptors results in a wide range of psychological and physiological effects associated with the consumption of marijuana. On the other hand, CBD (Cannabidiol) is not primarily responsible for the euphoric effects and altered perception; instead, it has a more complex pharmacological profile, including acting as a negative allosteric modulator of CB1 receptors. CB1 and CB2 receptors are the targets of THC and CBD, respectively, and are part of the endocannabinoid system that regulates various physiological processes in the body.

2. Answer C (Negative allosteric modulator of CB1 receptor)

The primary mechanism of action of CBD on the endocannabinoid system is as a negative allosteric modulator of the CB1 receptor. The endocannabinoid system comprises cannabinoid receptors located in various areas of the body, including the peripheral and central nervous systems, as well as the brain. This system plays a pivotal role in regulating numerous physiological responses such as pain, memory, appetite, and mood. This negative allosteric modulation by CBD on CB1 receptors has significant therapeutic implications. It allows for a more refined approach compared to direct agonists, which can lead to psychomimetic effects, and direct antagonists, which may cause depressant effects. It is worth noting that CBD is prescribed for certain conditions like epilepsy and is being studied for its potential benefits in various domains, including mood disorders, chronic pain management, inflammatory diseases, and neurodegenerative disorders such as Alzheimer's and Parkinson's disease. However, at present, FDA approval for CBD oil treatment in these contexts is still pending as further research and clinical trials are ongoing.

3. Answer B (Vasodilation)

The primary acute cardiovascular effect associated with marijuana use is vasodilation, a mechanism characterized by the relaxation and dilation of blood vessels, encompassing both arteries and veins. This vasodilation is thought to initiate a reflex tachycardia in response to the vascular relaxation induced by marijuana. This elevated heart rate can extend for a duration of approximately 2-3 hours subsequent to marijuana consumption. Coinciding with this heightened HR, there frequently exists a concomitant minor increase in supine blood pressure. It's important to note that while vasodilation may contribute to the sense of relaxation, increased heart rate and altered blood pressure can have implications for cardiovascular health, particularly in individuals with preexisting heart conditions.

4. Answer B (Reduced volatile anesthetic requirements)

When considering patients who have recently used marijuana and are undergoing anesthesia, it's crucial to assess the potential effects on anesthesia management. While options A, C, and D are valid concerns influenced by marijuana use, the assertion that these patients would necessitate reduced volatile anesthetic requirements is NOT accurate. Contrarily, individuals who have consumed marijuana may actually require larger volatile anesthetic requirements due to the interaction between cannabis compounds, particularly THC, and anesthetic agents.

5. Answer A (True)

Individuals with coronary artery disease (CAD) face an increased risk of myocardial infarction (MI) within 1 hour after marijuana use. The interaction between marijuana and the cardiovascular system can lead to certain adverse effects, particularly in individuals with preexisting heart conditions like CAD. The elevation in heart rate, potential for vasodilation, and changes in blood pressure associated with marijuana consumption can collectively create conditions that elevate the risk of MI in susceptible patients. As a precautionary measure, it is advisable to delay elective surgery for at least 1 hour after acute marijuana use. This allows time for the acute effects of marijuana on the cardiovascular system to subside before subjecting the patient to the stresses of surgery and anesthesia.

6. Answer B (Conducting a toxicology screen)

Marijuana's lipophilic nature and prolonged elimination half-life can result in its detection in urine for a prolonged period, even weeks to months after usage has ceased. Therefore, a toxicology screen may not accurately reflect recent marijuana use. Instead, focusing on assessing the history of use, considering the use of other drugs, and ruling out acute intoxication are more appropriate strategies to ascertain the patient's condition and suitability for elective surgery. In light of the patient's suspected recent marijuana use, the anesthesiologist must be prepared to potentially modify the anesthesia plan or delay the elective cholecystectomy if deemed necessary. This proactive approach is essential to ensure patient safety and optimize anesthesia management, taking into account potential cardiovascular effects and interactions of marijuana with anesthetic agents.

Recommended literature

1. UNODC World Drug Report 2022 highlights trends on cannabis post-legalization, environmental impacts of illicit drugs, and drug use among women and Youth. United Nations: Office on Drugs and Crime. https://www.unodc.org/unodc/en/press/releases/2022/June/unodc-world-drug-report-2022-highlights-trends-on-cannabis-post-legalization-environmental-impacts-of-illicit-drugs-and-drug-use-among-women-and-youth.html. Published June 27, 2022. Accessed February 3, 2023.
2. Ladha KS, McLaren-Blades A, Goel A, Buys MJ, Farquhar-Smith P, Haroutounian S, et al. Perioperative Pain and Addiction Interdisciplinary Network (PAIN): consensus recommendations for perioperative management of cannabis and cannabinoid-based medicine users by a modified Delphi process. British Journal of Anaesthesia. 2021;126(1):304-18.
3. Alexander JC, Joshi GP. A review of the anesthetic implications of marijuana use. Proc (Bayl Univ Med Cent). 2019;32(3):364-371. Published 2019 May 21.

CORNEAL ABRASION

Questions:

1. **What is the most common ophthalmologic complication in patients undergoing general anesthesia for nonocular surgery?**
   A. Retinal detachment
   B. Glaucoma
   C. Corneal abrasion
   D. Cataract

2. **Which of the following factors can contribute to the development of corneal abrasion during surgery?**
   A. Increased tear production
   B. Contact with cleaning solutions retained on the anesthetic mask
   C. Active contraction of the orbicularis oculi muscle
   D. Presence of Bell's phenomenon during anesthesia

3. **Which positioning during surgery is associated with an increased risk of corneal exposure and dryness?**
   A. Supine position
   B. Fowler's position
   C. Prone position
   D. Sitting position

4. **What is the primary function of Bell's phenomenon in protecting the cornea?**
   A. Lubricating the cornea
   B. Promoting tear production
   C. Rotating the eyeball downward
   D. Rotating the eyeball upward

5. **Corneal abrasion often occurs under general anesthesia.**
   A. True
   B. False

6. **A patient with Graves' disease, which presents with thyroid dysfunction and exophthalmos, was scheduled for a surgical procedure under general anesthesia. Given the risk of corneal abrasion due to the exophthalmos, the anesthesiologist took special precautions to prevent potential complications during the surgery. What is the preferred method for preventing corneal abrasion in high-risk patients during general anesthesia?**
   A. Fat-based ocular lubricants
   B. Hydrogel dressings
   C. Eyelid taping
   D. Ophthalmic corticosteroids

Answers:

1. Answer C (Corneal abrasion)

Corneal abrasion is the most common ophthalmologic complication in patients undergoing general anesthesia for nonocular surgery. A corneal abrasion refers to the scraping or injury of the corneal surface, which can lead to discomfort, pain, and potential complications if not managed appropriately. It occurs due to various factors such as mechanical injury, inadvertent pressure on the eyeball, exposure keratopathy, and reduced tear production during anesthesia.

2. Answer B (Contact with cleaning solutions retained on the anesthetic mask)

Contact with cleaning solutions retained on the anesthetic mask can contribute to the development of corneal abrasion during surgery. Chemical injury, including contact with cleaning solutions, can cause corneal abrasion. Spillage of antimicrobial solutions into the eyes during skin preparation or contact with cleaning solutions on the anesthetic mask can lead to irritation and injury of the corneal surface. This emphasizes the importance of proper cleaning practices and avoiding contact of such solutions with the eyes during surgical procedures.

3. Answer C (Prone position)

The prone position is associated with an increased risk of corneal exposure and dryness, leading to an elevated risk of corneal abrasion. In the prone position, the patient is lying face-down, which can result in incomplete eyelid closure and inadequate protection of the cornea. This lack of protection can lead to corneal exposure and dryness, increasing the likelihood of corneal abrasion.

4. Answer D (Rotating the eyeball upward)

The primary function of Bell's phenomenon is to rotate the eyeball upward. This protective mechanism is absent during anesthesia. During periods of sleep, when a person's eyes are closed, the upward rotation of the eyeball ensures that the cornea doesn't come into direct contact with surfaces, thereby preventing potential abrasion or injury. During anesthesia, the absence of Bell's phenomenon contributes to the risk of corneal abrasion, as the eye's natural protective mechanism is compromised.

5. Answer B (False)

Corneal abrasion under anesthesia is relatively rare. However, when it does occur, it can lead to foreign body sensation in the eye and cause substantial pain and discomfort. If not managed properly, this condition can even escalate to ocular infection and potential loss of vision. It's crucial to acknowledge the potential severity of corneal abrasion and ensure appropriate measures are taken to prevent and manage it, despite its infrequent occurrence during anesthesia.

6. Answer C (Eyelid taping)

Eyelid taping is the preferred method for preventing corneal abrasion during general anesthesia, offering substantial protection by ensuring complete eye closure. Clinical evidence suggests that taping alone is effective and no additional benefit arises from combining it with ointment or viscous eye drops. Proper technique is crucial to avoid eyelash inversion into the conjunctiva. This approach is particularly valuable for high-risk patients undergoing anesthesia care, like those with exophthalmos related to Graves' disease. For optimal coverage, the tape should span the entire lid line, placed after the loss of the lid reflex post-induction and before securing the airway (unless rapid sequence intubation is performed), with periodic checks during longer procedures to maintain closed eyes, ensuring comprehensive protection against corneal abrasion.

Recommended literature

1. Hewson DW, Hardman JG. Physical injuries during anaesthesia. BJA Educ. 2018;18(10):310-316.
2. Malafa MM, Coleman JE, Bowman RW, Rohrich RJ. Perioperative Corneal Abrasion: Updated Guidelines for Prevention and Management. Plast Reconstr Surg. 2016 May;137(5):790e-798e.
3. Lichter JR, Marr LB, Schilling DE, et al. A Department-of-Anesthesiology-based management protocol for perioperative corneal abrasions. Clin Ophthalmol. 2015;9:1689-1695. Published 2015 Sep 11.
4. Grixti A, Sadri M, Watts MT. Corneal protection during general anesthesia for nonocular surgery. Ocul Surf. 2013;11(2):109-118.

FLUID AND ELECTROLYTE BALANCE

Questions:

1. **Which of the following is a major cation in the intracellular compartment?**
   A. Sodium (Na⁺)
   B. Potassium (K⁺)
   C. Calcium (Ca²⁺)
   D. Magnesium (Mg²⁺)

2. **Which of the following electrolytes is primarily distributed intracellularly?**
   A. Chloride (Cl⁻)
   B. Bicarbonate (HCO₃⁻)
   C. Phosphate (HPO₄²⁻)
   D. Sulfate (SO₄²⁻)

3. **Which age group has the highest percentage of total body water (% TBW)?**
   A. Neonate
   B. Infant
   C. Adult male
   D. Adult female

4. **Which approach to perioperative fluid therapy is supported by the most evidence?**
   A. Liberal strategy
   B. Goal-directed therapy
   C. Restrictive fluid management
   D. A case-based approach

5. **The use of carbohydrate drinks up until 2 h prior to surgery has multiple benefits, but increases the risk of aspiration.**
   A. True
   B. False

6. **A patient is recovering from gastric sleeve surgery, a procedure used for weight loss. The patient is in the postoperative period and is being closely monitored by the medical team. As part of the recovery process, the medical team is focusing on proper fluid management to ensure optimal healing and prevent complications. What is NOT a correct statement regarding postoperative fluid management for the patient recovering from surgery?**
   A. It is recommended that patients receive 25–35 mL/kg of water per day in the recovery period
   B. Early transition to oral hydration postoperatively improves conditions for healing and recovery from surgery
   C. Anuria can be a normal and expected occurrence as a result of judicious fluid management in the perioperative period
   D. Excessive i.v. fluid administration generally leads to increased fluid in the intravascular space that eventually cannot be contained

Answers:

1. Answer B (Potassium (K⁺))

Potassium (K^+) is a major cation primarily found in the intracellular compartment. Its concentration inside cells is significantly higher, around 140 mmol/L, compared to the extracellular fluid, where it is present at approximately 4 mmol/L. This concentration gradient is maintained by the sodium-potassium pump (Na^+/K^+ pump), which is crucial for maintaining proper cell membrane potential and functions such as nerve conduction and muscle contraction. Imbalances in intracellular and extracellular potassium levels can lead to serious physiological disruptions, making potassium regulation essential for overall cellular and physiological health.

2. Answer C (Phosphate (HPO_4^{2-}))

Electrolyte distribution within the body's fluid compartments is essential for maintaining various physiological processes. Chloride, bicarbonate, and phosphate are key anions that contribute to these mechanisms. Chloride is pivotal for proper hydration, cation balance, and maintaining the electrical neutrality of extracellular fluid. Bicarbonate plays a crucial role in the body's acid-base balance by participating in a buffer system that regulates pH. While both chloride and bicarbonate have a significant presence in extracellular fluid, it's phosphate that stands out in terms of intracellular distribution. Phosphate, in the form of HPO_4^{2-}, is predominantly found within the intracellular fluid compartment. It plays a vital role as a major constituent of this compartment and is integral to regulating metabolic processes and serving as a buffering agent within animal cells.

3. Answer A (Neonate)

Among the provided age groups, neonates have the highest percentage of total body water (% TBW) at 75% of their body weight, followed by infants at 70% TBW, adult males at 60% TBW, and adult females at 55% TBW. These variations in % TBW among different age groups reflect the dynamic changes in body composition and hydration status across the lifespan. These differences have significant implications for fluid balance, electrolyte distribution, and medical interventions in various clinical settings.

4. Answer B (Goal-directed therapy)

Currently, there is no consensus about the optimum intraoperative fluid therapy strategy. However, a growing body of evidence supports the beneficial effects of adopting "Goal-directed therapy" (GDT) over either the "liberal" or "restrictive" fluid therapy strategies. Management of intraoperative fluids has undergone significant evolution, from initially providing minimal fluids due to concerns about postoperative complications to the realization that inadequate fluid administration had negative effects on postoperative outcomes. The liberal administration of fluids during surgery, once considered standard practice, has been associated with complications such as pulmonary congestion, decreased tissue oxygenation, and delayed recovery. In contrast, GDT emphasizes treating fluids as medications and titrating their administration based on specific goals, similar to other perioperative medications. GDT aims to optimize fluid administration during surgery to achieve desired clinical effects and has shown promise in improving patient outcomes by preventing both fluid overload and inadequate perfusion. As such, evidence suggests that adopting a goal-directed therapy approach for perioperative fluid management is a more effective strategy.

5. Answer B (False)

The use of carbohydrate drinks up until 2 hours prior to surgery has multiple benefits without increasing the risk of aspiration. Preoperative hydration with carbohydrate drinks offers several advantages without posing an increased risk of aspiration. These benefits include improving the patient's metabolic status, reducing insulin resistance, decreasing anxiety, and alleviating postoperative nausea and vomiting (PONV). Contrary to the belief that oral intake before surgery might increase the risk of aspiration, current evidence suggests that clear carbohydrate drinks can be safely consumed up to 2 hours before surgery without compromising patient safety.

6. Answer C (Anuria can be a normal and expected occurrence as a result of judicious fluid management in the perioperative period)

Anuria is not considered a normal or expected occurrence as a result of judicious fluid management in the perioperative period. Anuria typically indicates a severe problem related to kidney function or other underlying health issues and requires immediate medical attention. On the other hand, oliguria, the reduced production of urine, may occur in response to surgery-related stress but does not necessarily indicate abnormal fluid management. Recent studies suggest that an oliguria threshold of 0.3 ml kg-1 h-1 may be associated with an increased risk of acute kidney injury, highlighting the importance of careful fluid management to prevent kidney-related complications. It is crucial to differentiate between anuria and oliguria, with the former being abnormal and requiring prompt intervention.

Recommended literature

1. Pollard BJ, Kitchen, G. Handbook of Clinical Anaesthesia. Fourth Edition. CRC Press. 2018. 978-1-4987-6289-2.
2. Rassam SS, Counsell DJ. Perioperative electrolyte and fluid balance. Continuing Education in Anaesthesia Critical Care & Pain. 2005;5(5):157-60.

GASTROESOPHAGEAL REFLUX DISEASE

Questions:

1. GERD patients are at an increased risk of aspiration during anesthesia due to?
    A. Overactive lower esophageal sphincter (LES)
    B. Impaired esophageal motility
    C. Increased stomach emptying
    D. Inadequate closure of the LES

2. Which of the following is NOT a symptom of gastroesophageal reflux disease (GERD)?
    A. Chronic cough
    B. Dental corrosion
    C. Sinusitis
    D. Strawberry tongue

3. Which of the following foods is generally NOT associated with exacerbating acid reflux?
    A. Chocolate
    B. Mint
    C. Coffee
    D. Apple cider vinegar

4. In patients with GERD, which factor among the following increases the risk of aspiration?
    A. Prognathic mandible
    B. TIVA
    C. Lithotomy position
    D. Prokinetics

5. Scleroderma, a type of connective tissue disorder, increases the risk of aspiration.
    A. True
    B. False

6. A 45-year-old patient is scheduled for laparoscopic hernia repair. The patient's medical history includes GERD, obesity, and a history of delayed stomach emptying. Given these factors, the anesthesia team is carefully planning the patient's intraoperative management to mitigate the risk of aspiration. What is NOT a recommended intraoperative management approach for high-risk patients with GERD and multiple risk factors for aspiration?
    A. Insert large-bore nasogastric tube and aspirate
    B. Position the patient head-down to reduce the risk of aspiration in case of regurgitation
    C. Rapid Sequence Induction (RSI) with cricoid pressure
    D. Place the patient in the lateral position for the emergence

Answers:

1. **Answer D (Inadequate closure of the LES)**

   GERD patients are at an increased risk of aspiration during anesthesia due to the inadequate closure of the lower esophageal sphincter (LES). The lower esophageal sphincter is a muscular ring that normally functions to prevent the backflow of stomach contents into the esophagus. In patients with GERD, this sphincter may be weakened or dysfunctional, allowing stomach acid and other contents to reflux back into the esophagus and potentially into the respiratory tract during anesthesia. This can lead to aspiration, where these acidic or irritant contents are inhaled into the lungs, causing inflammation, infection, or other pulmonary complications.

2. **Answer D (Strawberry tongue)**

   Strawberry tongue is not a symptom of gastroesophageal reflux disease (GERD). GERD symptoms encompass heartburn, regurgitation, taste of acid, upper abdominal or non-cardiac chest pain, globus, swallowing difficulties, bad breath, and bloating, as well as extraesophageal symptoms like chronic cough, sore throat, dental corrosion, sinusitis, bronchitis, pulmonary fibrosis, recurrent aspiration pneumonia, hoarseness, hiccups, laryngitis, hypersalivation, and new or worsening asthma. Strawberry tongue, characterized by a red and swollen tongue with a bumpy texture, is associated with conditions like scarlet fever or Kawasaki disease rather than GERD.

3. **Answer D (Apple cider vinegar)**

   Apple cider vinegar is generally not associated with exacerbating acid reflux. While chocolate, mint, and coffee are known to potentially trigger or worsen acid reflux due to their effects on relaxing the LES or stimulating stomach acid production, apple cider vinegar does not typically fall into this category. In fact, some individuals believe that diluted apple cider vinegar might have neutral or even beneficial effects on acid reflux symptoms, although scientific evidence supporting this is limited, and individual responses vary. Factors that can exacerbate acid reflux include smoking, consuming large meals or eating late at night, eating fatty or fried foods, drinking alcohol and coffee, and taking certain medications such as aspirin, benzodiazepines, calcium channel blockers, tricyclic antidepressants, NSAIDs, and certain asthma medicines. These factors can contribute to the relaxation of the LES or increase stomach acid production, thereby increasing the risk of acid reflux symptoms.

4. **Answer C (Lithotomy position)**

   Among the factors that increase the risk of aspiration in patients with GERD, Lithotomy position is a significant contributor. The lithotomy position can potentially contribute to regurgitation and aspiration of gastric contents due to the effects of gravity on the LES and the potential for increased abdominal pressure. Other factors that increase the risk of aspiration include the urgency of surgery, airway problems, inadequate depth of anesthesia, gastrointestinal problems, depressed consciousness, increased severity of illness, and obesity.

5. **Answer A (True)**

   Patients with scleroderma commonly encounter a spectrum of complications, notably including challenges related to difficult airway management and an elevated risk of aspiration. Moreover, the gastrointestinal (GI) system, a frequently affected domain in systemic sclerosis (SSc), manifests abnormalities in over 90% of patients. Within this context, conditions such as gastro-oesophageal reflux and dysmotility are prevalent, substantiating a heightened susceptibility to aspiration during anesthesia.

6. **Answer B (Position patient head-down to reduce risk of aspiration in case of regurgitation)**

   Positioning the patient head down to reduce aspiration in case of regurgitation is NOT a recommended intraoperative management approach for high-risk patients with GERD and multiple risk factors for aspiration. Placing the patient in a head-down position can actually increase the risk of regurgitation and aspiration by allowing gastric contents to flow more easily into the upper airway. This position is counterproductive in minimizing aspiration risk. Inserting a large-bore nasogastric tube and aspirating may help decompress the stomach and reduce the risk of regurgitation during surgery. Rapid Sequence Induction with cricoid pressure is a standard approach to prevent regurgitation during induction of anesthesia. Placing the patient in the lateral position for emergence is beneficial as it can facilitate better airway management and minimize the risk of aspiration during emergence from anesthesia.

Recommended literature

1. Jolliffe DM. Practical gastric physiology. Continuing Education in Anaesthesia Critical Care & Pain. 2009;9(6):173-177.

GERIATRIC PATIENTS

Questions:

1. **Which of the following physiological changes commonly occurs in geriatric patients?**
    A. Increased cardiac output
    B. Decreased systemic vascular resistance
    C. Decreased preload and afterload
    D. Left ventricular hypertrophy

2. **Which physiological change is NOT associated with aging?**
    A. Decreased chest wall compliance
    B. Decreased inspiratory capacity
    C. Decreased pulmonary elasticity
    D. Decreased closing capacity

3. **Which surgery is NOT commonly performed in geriatric patients?**
    A. Cataract surgery
    B. Cholecystectomy
    C. Appendectomy
    D. TURP

4. **What is a major concern when managing geriatric patients with cognitive impairment undergoing surgery?**
    A. Allomnesia
    B. Cognitive decline
    C. Delirium
    D. Dementia

5. **The minimum alveolar concentration (MAC) of inhaled anesthetics increases with age.**
    A. True
    B. False

6. **A 95-year-old patient is admitted to the hospital for hip fracture surgery following a fall at home. The patient has a complex medical history, including hypertension, type 2 diabetes, and mild cognitive impairment. The anesthesiologist is considering the appropriate anesthesia management for this patient, taking into account their age and comorbidities. Which of the following statements is NOT true regarding anesthesia management in elderly patients with multiple comorbidities undergoing anesthesia and surgery?**
    A. Propofol requires only 50 to 70 percent dosing relative to that of a younger patient to achieve the same effect.
    B. Opioids are significantly more potent due to decreased clearance and increased neurologic sensitivity.
    C. Neuromuscular blocking agents eliminated by ester hydrolysis or Hoffmann degradation should be avoided or used sparingly, as these agents can prolong paralysis in geriatric patients.
    D. Moderate administration of crystalloids or colloids to maintain euvolemia and avoid CHF exacerbation, pulmonary edema, and dilutional coagulopathies is appropriate for most patients.

Answers:

1. **Answer D (Left ventricular hypertrophy)**

Aging brings about various changes in the cardiovascular system, and left ventricular hypertrophy is one of these changes. Left ventricular hypertrophy refers to the thickening of the muscular wall of the left ventricle of the heart. This condition often develops as a response to increased workload on the heart, such as when the heart has to pump against elevated systemic vascular resistance. In geriatric patients, due to factors such as increased systemic vascular stiffness and higher systolic arterial pressures caused by arterial wall thickening and reduced vessel elasticity, the heart may need to work harder to overcome the increased resistance in the blood vessels. This increased workload can lead to the development of left ventricular hypertrophy over time.

2. **Answer D (Decreased closing capacity)**

Decreased closing capacity is NOT typically associated with aging. Closing capacity refers to the lung volume at which small airways start to close during expiration. It increases with age and can lead to airway obstruction during normal tidal breathing. In contrast, decreased inspiratory capacity, decreased pulmonary elasticity, and decreased chest wall compliance are all important pulmonary changes associated with aging. These changes, along with the increase in closing capacity, can predispose elderly patients to ventilation-perfusion mismatch, airway collapse, and respiratory failure.

3. **Answer C (Appendectomy)**

The surgery that is NOT commonly performed in geriatric patients is Appendectomy. Common surgeries in the elderly include procedures such as cataract surgery, trans-urethral resection of the prostate (TURP), hip fracture surgery, knee arthroplasty, cholecystectomy, pacemaker implantation, and colorectal excision. Appendectomy, while not exclusive to any age group, is generally less common among geriatric patients compared to conditions and surgeries more prevalent in this population due to age-related health considerations.

4. **Answer C (Delirium)**

The major concern when managing geriatric patients with cognitive impairment undergoing surgery is Delirium. Delirium is an acute and fluctuating disturbance in attention, awareness, and cognitive function that often occurs in older adults, especially those with preexisting cognitive impairment. Surgery and hospitalization can trigger or exacerbate delirium due to factors like anesthesia, medications, unfamiliar environment, and stress. Delirium can lead to complications, increased length of hospital stay, and poorer outcomes.

5. **Answer B (False)**

The minimum alveolar concentration (MAC) of inhaled anesthetics actually decreases with age. MAC is a measure of the potency of an inhaled anesthetic, representing the concentration at which 50% of patients do not respond to a surgical incision. MAC is known to peak at around 6 months of age and then decrease by about 6% per decade throughout adulthood, regardless of the specific volatile anesthetic used. This age-dependent decrease in MAC is an important consideration in adjusting anesthesia dosages for older patients.

6. **Answer C (Neuromuscular blocking agents eliminated by ester hydrolysis or Hoffmann degradation should be avoided or used sparingly, as these agents can prolong paralysis in geriatric patients)**

Neuromuscular blocking agents (NMBAs) play a crucial role in facilitating intubation and providing muscle relaxation during surgery. However, in elderly patients with altered pharmacokinetics and increased sensitivity to medications, the choice and dosing of NMBAs require careful consideration. Unlike other NMBAs, agents eliminated by ester hydrolysis or Hoffmann degradation, such as atracurium, cisatracurium, and mivacurium, are less likely to cause prolonged paralysis in geriatric patients due to their unique elimination pathways that are not dependent on hepatic metabolism and clearance. These agents offer a safer option for maintaining appropriate muscle relaxation without risking prolonged paralysis in the elderly population with multiple comorbidities. Proper selection of NMBAs is essential to ensure the patient's safety and optimal surgical outcomes.

Recommended literature

1. Staheli B, Rondeau B. Anesthetic Considerations In The Geriatric Population. [Updated 2022 Jun 5]. In: StatPearls [Internet]. Treasure Island (FL): StatPearls Publishing; 2022 Jan-. Available from: https://www.ncbi.nlm.nih.gov/books/NBK572137/.
2. Murray D, Dodds C. Perioperative care of the elderly. Continuing Education in Anaesthesia Critical Care & Pain. 2004;4(6):193-6.

INFLAMMATORY BOWEL DISEASE

08
CHAPTER

Questions:

1. **What is the primary underlying cause of inflammatory bowel disease (IBD)?**
   A. Bacterial infection
   B. Genetic mutation
   C. Environmental factors
   D. Autoimmune responses

2. **Which layer(s) of the bowel wall inside the gastrointestinal tract can be affected in Crohn's disease?**
   A. Mucosa only
   B. Mucosa and submucosa
   C. Mucosa, submucosa, and muscular layer
   D. Mucosa, submucosa, muscular layer, and serosa

3. **Which of the following statements about ulcerative colitis is accurate?**
   A. It primarily affects the small intestine
   B. Damaged areas appear in patches next to areas of healthy tissue
   C. Inflammation can lead to transmural abscesses
   D. It is limited to the colon and rectum

4. **What is a potential complication of both Crohn's disease and ulcerative colitis?**
   A. Skin and eye inflammation
   B. Anemia due to vitamin C deficiency
   C. Lung infections
   D. Tireoiditis

5. **Most people are diagnosed with IBD before the age of 30.**
   A. True
   B. False

6. **A 32-year-old patient with a history of Crohn's disease is scheduled for surgery for bowel resection due to complications related to the disease. The patient's ongoing therapy includes Mesalamine (800 mg 3 x1), Azathioprine (2 mg/kg/day), Methotrexate (15 mg/week), and Prednisone (20 mg/day). This is his third operation of bowel resection, and the patient has a history of poor wound healing and postoperative infections during the previous operation. What statement regarding patients' medication regimens during the perioperative period is correct?**
   A. Continue Mesalamine, Azathioprine, Methotrexate, and Prednisone
   B. Stop all medications the day before surgery
   C. Stop all medications on the day of surgery and supplement glucocorticoid
   D. Continue Prednisone only; stop all other medications

Answers:

1. **Answer D (Autoimmune responses)**

   Inflammatory bowel disease (IBD) is primarily caused by autoimmune responses. While multiple factors contribute to the development of IBD, including genetic predisposition and environmental triggers, the main mechanism behind the condition is an abnormal immune response. In individuals with IBD, the immune system mistakenly identifies components of the gastrointestinal tract as foreign or harmful, leading to chronic inflammation and tissue damage. This autoimmune response results in the characteristic symptoms and complications associated with Crohn's disease and ulcerative colitis, the two main types of IBD.

2. **Answer D (Mucosa, submucosa, muscular layer, and serosa)**

   Crohn's disease is characterized by transmural inflammation, which means that the inflammation extends through the entire thickness of the gastrointestinal (GI) tract wall. This inflammation can affect all layers of the bowel wall, from the innermost mucosa to the outermost serosa. The layers of the GI tract wall include the mucosa (inner layer), submucosa, muscular layer (muscularis propria), and serosa (outer layer). The comprehensive involvement of these layers contributes to the complexity of Crohn's disease and its associated complications, such as strictures, fistulas, and abscesses.

3. **Answer D (It is limited to the colon and rectum)**

   Ulcerative colitis is characterized by inflammation that is confined to the colon and rectum. Unlike Crohn's disease, which can affect various parts of the gastrointestinal tract, ulcerative colitis is restricted to the innermost lining of the colon and rectum. The inflammation is continuous and typically begins at the rectum, extending upwards into the colon. This distinct pattern differentiates ulcerative colitis from Crohn's disease.

4. **Answer A (Skin and eye inflammation)**

   Both Crohn's disease and ulcerative colitis can lead to various extraintestinal manifestations beyond the gastrointestinal tract. One common complication shared by both conditions is inflammation affecting the skin and eyes. This can manifest as conditions such as erythema nodosum and iritis/uveitis. These manifestations are due to the systemic nature of inflammatory bowel diseases, where the inflammation can affect other parts of the body besides the intestines.

5. **Answer A (True)**

   IBD, which includes conditions like Crohn's disease and ulcerative colitis, typically manifests and is diagnosed before the age of 30. While the exact age of diagnosis can vary, the majority of cases are identified during a person's earlier years, which can have significant implications for long-term management and quality of life.

6. **Answer C (Stop all medications on the day of surgery and supplement glucocorticoid)**

   In this case, the patient with a history of Crohn's disease and complications related to the disease is undergoing his third operation for bowel resection; the appropriate perioperative medication management involves stopping all medications, including Mesalamine, Azathioprine, Methotrexate, and Prednisone, on the day of surgery. To address potential adrenal insufficiency related to chronic steroid use, it's recommended to provide glucocorticoid supplementation. To address potential adrenal insufficiency related to chronic steroid use, and considering the major surgical stress with the patient having taken Prednisone at a dose of 20 mg/d for more than 3 weeks, it's recommended to provide glucocorticoid supplementation. Specifically, administer Hydrocortisone 100 mg IV for induction, followed by Hydrocortisone 50 mg IV every 8 hours for the first 24 hours, and then 25 mg IV every 8 hours for the next 24 to 48 hours during the maintenance phase. This approach balances the need to minimize immunosuppression and optimize wound healing while ensuring the patient's stress response is appropriately managed during surgery.

Recommended literature

1. Nickerson TP, Merchea A. Perioperative Considerations in Crohn Disease and Ulcerative Colitis. Clin Colon Rectal Surg. 2016;29(2):80-84.
2. Kumar A, Auron M, Aneja A, Mohr F, Jain A, Shen B. Inflammatory bowel disease: perioperative pharmacological considerations. Mayo Clin Proc. 2011;86(8):748-757.

LAPAROSCOPIC SURGERY

08
CHAPTER

Questions:

1. Which of the following is NOT a benefit of laparoscopic surgery?

   A. Reduced wound infection

   B. Faster recovery

   C. Effective tactile feedback

   D. Reduced postoperative pain

2. What is NOT a risk associated with laparoscopic surgery?

   A. Acute kidney injury

   B. Pulmonary atelectasis

   C. Venous air embolism

   D. Heart attack

3. Which of the following is a characteristic complication of laparoscopic surgery that manifests as a bulge with a crackling sensation upon palpation or pressure?

   A. Gas embolism

   B. Capnothorax

   C. Subcutaneous emphysema

   D. Capnopericardium

4. What is the primary role of lung protective ventilation in the management of laparoscopic surgery?

   A. Preventing gas embolism

   B. Reducing the risk of atelectasis

   C. Reducing the risk of subcutaneous emphysema

   D. Preventing ventilation/perfusion (V/Q) mismatch

5. Compartment syndrome is a common complication of laparoscopic surgery.

   A. True

   B. False

6. A 30-year-old female patient at 18 weeks gestation presents with severe lower abdominal pain and is diagnosed with acute appendicitis. The surgical team plans for a laparoscopic appendectomy to remove her inflamed appendix promptly. The anesthesiologist in charge is considering the possible consequences of laparoscopic surgery. What statement is NOT true regarding laparoscopic surgery in this case?

   A. Postoperative nausea and vomiting (PONV) is a predicted complication of laparoscopic surgery

   B. Pregnancy is an absolute contraindication for laparoscopic surgery

   C. Lower pressure pneumoperitoneum (10–12 mmHg) with proper hydration of the patient can prevent the consequences of preload and afterload on cardiac function

   D. The choice of anesthetic technique for abdominal laparoscopic surgery is general anesthesia

Answers:

1. Answer C (Effective tactile feedback)

Laparoscopic surgery is known for its benefits, including reduced wound infection, faster recovery, reduced morbidity, and reduced postoperative pain. However, one of its disadvantages is that it limits the surgeon's ability to feel and manipulate tissue due to the absence of direct tactile feedback, making it challenging to assess the necessary force to apply during the procedure and accurately judge the tissue's properties.

2. Answer D (Heart attack)

While laparoscopic surgery is associated with risks such as acute kidney injury (AKI), pulmonary atelectasis, and venous air embolism (VAE), a heart attack is not typically listed as a direct risk specifically associated with laparoscopic surgery. While surgical procedures can put stress on the cardiovascular system, a heart attack is a complex medical event that may occur during various medical conditions but is not a commonly mentioned risk specific to laparoscopic surgery.

3. Answer C (Subcutaneous emphysema)

Subcutaneous emphysema is a condition that can occur as a complication of laparoscopic surgery. It is characterized by the presence of air or gas in the subcutaneous tissue layers beneath the skin. When palpated or pressed, it often produces a distinctive crackling or crepitus sensation due to the trapped air. This condition typically resolves on its own but may require monitoring in some cases. It is important to differentiate subcutaneous emphysema from other complications, such as gas embolism or intrathoracic issues like capnothorax or capnopericardium, as they have different clinical implications.

4. Answer B (Reducing the risk of atelectasis)

The primary role of lung protective ventilation in laparoscopic surgery is to reduce the risk of atelectasis. Atelectasis is the partial or complete collapse of lung tissue, which can occur when there is reduced lung volume or improper aeration of lung segments. During laparoscopic surgery, the pneumoperitoneum can affect normal diaphragmatic movement and lung function, potentially leading to atelectasis. Lung protective ventilation strategies aim to maintain adequate lung volume, minimize atelectasis, and optimize gas exchange. While preventing gas embolism and maintaining appropriate ventilation/perfusion (V/Q) matching are essential considerations during laparoscopic surgery, their primary role is not lung protection but rather ensuring overall patient safety and oxygenation.

5. Answer B (False)

Compartment syndrome is not a common complication of laparoscopic surgery. Instead, laparoscopic surgery is associated with different complications such as occult hemorrhage, vascular or solid organ injury, gas embolism, subcutaneous emphysema, capnothorax, capnomediastinum, capnopericardium, and complications related to patient positioning. These complications are more relevant to the abdominal and thoracic areas involved in laparoscopic procedures, but compartment syndrome typically is not associated with this type of surgery.

6. Answer B (Pregnancy is an absolute contraindication for laparoscopic surgery)

Pregnancy is not an absolute contraindication for laparoscopic surgery. In cases where surgery is necessary during pregnancy, it should ideally be scheduled after the first trimester, and the patient should be under the proper care of an obstetrician. Uterine relaxant drugs can be used to minimize the risk of uterine contractions during surgery. Special precautions, such as careful port placement and maintaining appropriate levels of end-tidal CO2 (et-CO2) to prevent fetal acidosis, should be taken. However, pregnancy is not an absolute contraindication for laparoscopic surgery, and the decision should be made based on the patient's clinical condition and gestational age, as discussed in the provided explanation.

Recommended literature

1. Bajwa SJ, Kulshrestha A. Anaesthesia for laparoscopic surgery: General vs regional anesthesia. J Minim Access Surg. 2016;12(1):4-9.
2. Hayden P, Sarah Cowman S. Continuing Education in Anaesthesia Critical Care & Pain, Volume 11, Issue 5, October 2011, Pages 177-180.

METHEMOGLOBINEMIA

Questions:

1. **What is the primary underlying mechanism of methemoglobinemia?**
   A. Reduction of hemoglobin iron to (Fe^{2+})
   B. Oxidation of hemoglobin iron to (Fe^{3+})
   C. Reduction of hemoglobin iron to (Fe^{3+})
   D. Oxidation of hemoglobin iron to (Fe^{2+})

2. **What is the normal range for methemoglobin levels in the blood?**
   A. 0-1%
   B. 1-2%
   C. 2-3%
   D. 3-4%

3. **Which of the following is NOT a common causative agent of acquired methemoglobinemia?**
   A. Benzocaine
   B. Nitroglycerin
   C. Prilocaine
   D. Aminoglycosides

4. **What does a "saturation gap" in the context of methemoglobinemia indicate?**
   A. A gap between arterial and venous oxygen saturation
   B. A gap between SpO2 and SaO2 measurements
   C. A gap between oxygen transport
   D. A gap between oxygen and hemoglobin-facilitated diffusion

5. **Vitamin C is the preferred treatment for methemoglobinemia in patients with G6PD deficiency.**
   A. True
   B. False

6. **A 56-year-old male presents to the emergency department with cyanosis and shortness of breath. His vital signs are stable, but his SpO2 reading on pulse oximetry shows 85%, even though his arterial oxygen levels (PaO2) are within the normal range. Upon physical examination, the patient's blood is drawn for laboratory analysis, revealing a chocolate brown color. Further tests confirm a methemoglobin (MetHb) level of 40%. Given the clinical presentation and laboratory findings, methemoglobinemia is suspected. What is the initial therapy for this patient's methemoglobinemia?**
   A. Methylene blue
   B. Hyperbaric oxygen therapy
   C. Vitamin C
   D. Red blood cell transfusion

Answers:

1. Answer B (Oxidation of hemoglobin iron to (Fe^3+))

Methemoglobinemia primarily occurs due to the oxidation of hemoglobin iron, converting it to the ferric (Fe^{3+}) state. This oxidized form of hemoglobin, known as methemoglobin, cannot effectively bind and transport oxygen, leading to impaired oxygen delivery to tissues. In methemoglobin, iron has been oxidized to Fe^{3+} from its normal ferrous (Fe^{2+}) state, which is essential for oxygen binding. This change in iron's oxidation state is the central mechanism underlying methemoglobinemia.

2. Answer B (1-2%)

The normal range for methemoglobin (MetHb) levels in the blood typically falls between 1% and 2%. However, the clinical significance of MetHb levels depends on the total hemoglobin concentration in the blood. For instance, a patient with a lower total hemoglobin level (e.g., 10 g/dL) and 10% methemoglobin will have a lower total methemoglobin concentration (1 g/dL) and is unlikely to exhibit symptoms. In contrast, a patient with a higher total hemoglobin level (e.g., 18 g/dL) and the same 10% methemoglobin will have a higher total methemoglobin concentration (1.8 g/dL) and may display signs of cyanosis due to the increased absolute amount of methemoglobin. When the total MetHb level exceeds 1.5 g/dL, it can lead to cyanosis. Notably, patients with abnormal MetHb levels are typically asymptomatic until the MetHb levels exceed 20% of the total hemoglobin. In cases where MetHb levels range between 20% and 50% of total hemoglobin, patients may experience mild to moderate symptoms of hypoxemia, while levels between 50% and 70% of total hemoglobin can result in severe symptoms.

3. Answer D (Aminoglycosides)

Aminoglycosides are not typically associated with causing acquired methemoglobinemia. Several drugs and substances are listed as potential causative agents of methemoglobinemia. Prilocaine, for instance, is metabolized by the liver to o-toluidine, which can oxidize hemoglobin and cause dose-dependent methemoglobinemia. Benzocaine, found in topical local anesthetic sprays, can also induce methemoglobinemia in a dose-independent manner. Lidocaine, tetracaine, nitrates, sulfonamides, dapsone, phenytoin, metoclopramide, aniline dye, and certain antimalarials like chloroquine or primaquine are known to be common causes of methemoglobinemia.

4. Answer B (A gap between SpO2 and SaO2 measurements)

In the context of methemoglobinemia, a "saturation gap" refers to the difference between two measurements: SpO2 (peripheral oxygen saturation) and SaO2 (arterial oxygen saturation). SpO2 is commonly measured non-invasively using pulse oximetry, while SaO2 represents the oxygen saturation in arterial blood and is usually measured through arterial blood gas analysis. This gap can suggest the presence of abnormal hemoglobin forms, such as methemoglobin, which does not bind oxygen as efficiently as normal hemoglobin, leading to a difference in the oxygen saturation measurements. The saturation gap greater than 5% is a significant finding and strongly indicates the presence of abnormal forms of hemoglobin.

5. Answer A (True)

The administration of methylene blue, which is commonly used to treat methemoglobinemia, can lead to hemolysis in patients with glucose-6-phosphate dehydrogenase (G6PD) deficiency. As a result, in G6PD-deficient individuals with methemoglobinemia, the preferred treatment is vitamin C at a dose of 2 mg/kg intravenously. In severe cases, an exchange transfusion may also be necessary to remove excess methemoglobin from the bloodstream.

6. Answer A (Methylene blue)

The treatment for methemoglobinemia should be initiated in symptomatic patients or when the MetHb level is greater than 30%. In this case, the patient is symptomatic with cyanosis and a MetHb level of 40%, making treatment necessary. The definitive treatment for methemoglobinemia is the administration of methylene blue at a dose of 1-2 mg/kg intravenously over 5 minutes. This dose can be repeated in an hour after the initial dose. Methylene blue acts as an electron donor, effectively reducing oxidized hemoglobin (MetHb) back to its normal, functional form. In individuals with G6PD deficiency, the administration of methylene blue can lead to hemolysis. In refractory cases or when methylene blue is contraindicated, alternative treatments such as hyperbaric oxygen therapy or red blood cell transfusion may be considered.

Recommended literature

1. Ludlow JT, Wilkerson RG, Nappe TM. Methemoglobinemia. [Updated 2022 Aug 29]. In: StatPearls [Internet]. Treasure Island (FL): StatPearls Publishing; 2022 Jan-. Available from: https://www.ncbi.nlm.nih.gov/books/NBK537317/.
2. Guay J. Methemoglobinemia related to local anesthetics: a summary of 242 episodes. Anesth Analg. 2009;108(3):837-845.

NON-OPERATING ROOM ANESTHESIA (NORA)

Questions:

1. **What does NORA stand for in the context of anesthesia practice?**
   A. Normal Operating Room Anesthesia
   B. Non-Operative Room Anesthesia
   C. New Operating Room Arrangement
   D. Non-Operating Room Anesthesia

2. **What is a challenge faced by anesthesia providers in NORA settings?**
   A. A greater proportion of ASA status III-V patients
   B. Lack of familiarity with equipment
   C. Exposure to radiation
   D. All of the above

3. **Which of the following procedures is often performed in an interventional radiology suite and may require NORA?**
   A. Shoulder arthroscopy
   B. Pilonidal cyst removal
   C. Phrenic nerve block
   D. Eye cataract surgery

4. **What is the primary reason for the use of anesthesia during Magnetic Resonance Imaging (MRI) for some patients?**
   A. To speed up the imaging process
   B. To reduce radiation exposure
   C. To eliminate the need for contrast agents
   D. To alleviate patient anxiety

5. **Retrieval of oocytes during the IVF procedure can be done only under general anesthesia.**
   A. True
   B. False

6. **A 56-year-old male patient is scheduled for an endoscopic retrograde cholangiopancreatography (ERCP) procedure to investigate and treat a suspected bile duct obstruction. The patient has a history of chronic obstructive pulmonary disease (COPD) and is currently on bronchodilators. He is also a former smoker. The patient is anxious about the procedure and prefers sedation to minimize discomfort. What would be the most suitable sedation choice for this patient considering his COPD history, former smoking habit, and preference for minimizing discomfort during the ERCP procedure?**
   A. Intravenous sedation with midazolam and fentanyl
   B. Topical lidocaine anesthesia alone
   C. Propofol sedation
   D. General anesthesia with endotracheal intubation

Answers:

1. **Answer D (Non-Operating Room Anesthesia)**

In the context of anesthesia practice, NORA stands for "Non-Operating Room Anesthesia." NORA represents the administration of anesthesia outside the traditional operating room environment, encompassing various medical procedures and interventions conducted in settings other than the OR. NORA has its unique challenges and considerations, which anesthesia providers must be familiar with to deliver high-quality care in these non-operating room settings.

2. **Answer D (All of the above)**

Anesthesia providers in NORA settings face numerous challenges, including a higher proportion of ASA status III-V patients, constraints of the room itself, potential lack of essential equipment, navigating unfamiliar environments, varying levels of familiarity with anesthesia procedures among staff, exposure to radiation in certain settings, the imperative to maintain high standards for anesthetic procedures and monitoring, and the need to address ad hoc requests, scheduling inconsistencies, and potential communication issues. These multifaceted challenges necessitate anesthesia providers to be adaptable, well-prepared, and committed to maintaining patient safety standards, regardless of the unique demands posed by NORA settings.

3. **Answer C (Phrenic nerve block)**

Phrenic nerve blocks, which are often performed in an interventional radiology suite, may require NORA. These blocks involve the administration of local anesthesia to the phrenic nerve to provide pain relief or diagnostic information for certain conditions. While procedures like shoulder arthroscopy, pilonidal cyst removal, and eye cataract surgery are typically performed in different settings and do not usually require NORA, phrenic nerve blocks fall within the realm of interventional radiology and may necessitate anesthesia in that environment. Other procedures such as endoscopies, interventional pulmonology, interventional cardiology, interventional radiology, radiological imaging (Magnetic Resonance Imaging), pediatric procedures, and in vitro fertilization (IVF) retrieval can also be performed in NORA settings depending on the clinical context and patient needs.

4. **Answer D (To alleviate patient anxiety)**

MRI scans can be intimidating and cause anxiety, especially in patients who may have claustrophobia or find the loud noises produced by the machine distressing. Anesthesia or sedation is employed to help these patients remain calm and comfortable during the procedure.

5. **Answer B (False)**

Retrieval of oocytes during an IVF procedure can be done under various anesthesia techniques, including paracervical block, epidural, spinal, general anesthesia, as well as IV sedation. The choice of anesthesia method depends on the patient's preferences, medical condition, and the clinician's judgment. General anesthesia is one option but not the only one.

6. **Answer C (Propofol sedation)**

Given the patient's history of COPD and former smoking habit, minimizing respiratory depression and ensuring rapid recovery is crucial. Propofol is an excellent choice for sedation during ERCP as it provides a smooth induction and maintenance with a short recovery time. It also has a low incidence of post-procedure nausea. While intravenous sedation with midazolam and fentanyl is a common choice, it may carry a slightly higher risk of respiratory depression in patients with COPD. Topical lidocaine anesthesia alone is inadequate for maintaining patient comfort during an ERCP procedure. General anesthesia with endotracheal intubation is typically reserved for patients with more complex airway management needs and is not the first-line choice for routine ERCP sedation. Propofol provides the desired level of sedation while minimizing the risk of respiratory compromise in this patient.

Recommended literature

1. Wong T, Georgiadis PL, Urman RD, Tsai MH. Non-Operating Room Anesthesia: Patient Selection and Special Considerations. Local Reg Anesth. 2020;13:1-9. Published 2020 Jan 8. doi:10.2147/LRA.S181458.
2. Chung M, Vazquez R. Non-Operating Room Anesthesia. In: Gropper MA, editor. Miller's Anesthesia, Ninth Edition, 2020. Elsevier, Philadelphia. p. 2284-2312.

PERIOPERATIVE HYPOTHERMIA

08
CHAPTER

Questions:

1. **What is the definition of perioperative hypothermia?**
   A. Core body temperature < 34.0°C
   B. Core body temperature < 35.0°C
   C. Core body temperature < 36.0°C
   D. Core body temperature < 37.0°C

2. **Which of the following phases of perioperative hypothermia is characterized by maximal vasoconstriction to balance heat loss and production?**
   A. Redistribution phase
   B. Heat loss phase
   C. Plateau phase
   D. Recovery phase

3. **Which factor is NOT a source of heat loss during surgery and anesthesia leading to perioperative hypothermia?**
   A. Radiation
   B. Conduction
   C. Insulation
   D. Convection

4. **Which patient condition is NOT a risk factor for perioperative hypothermia?**
   A. Low BMI
   B. Diabetic neuropathy
   C. Hyperthyroidism
   D. Paraplegia

5. **Shivering is a common consequence of perioperative hypothermia and can lead to increased surgical complications.**
   A. True
   B. False

6. **A 55-year-old patient with a BMI of 18.2 is scheduled for elective spine surgery. The patient has a medical history of type 1 diabetes and diabetic neuropathy. In this case, the anesthesiologist needs to keep in mind the increased risk of perioperative hypothermia due to the patient's low BMI, diabetes, and neuropathy. Patients with diabetes, especially those with neuropathy, are more susceptible to temperature regulation issues. Additionally, the patient's low BMI can contribute to reduced insulation and heat retention. What is one of the consequences of perioperative hypothermia related to drug metabolism?**
   A. Increased drug metabolism
   B. Decreased drug metabolism
   C. No effect on drug metabolism
   D. Faster drug absorption

Answers:

1. **Answer C (Core body temperature < 36.0°C)**

   Perioperative hypothermia is defined as a core body temperature that falls below 36.0°C during the perioperative period. This condition occurs when the body's ability to regulate its temperature is compromised during surgery and anesthesia, leading to a drop in core body temperature. Maintaining normal body temperature is crucial during surgery to prevent complications associated with hypothermia, such as increased risk of infection, impaired coagulation, increased blood loss, and other adverse effects.

2. **Answer C (Plateau phase)**

   Perioperative hypothermia progresses through three distinct phases. The first phase is the redistribution phase, characterized by vasodilation leading to warm blood moving to the peripheries and cool blood entering the core, causing a rapid temperature drop. Following this, the heat loss phase occurs, where heat loss exceeds metabolic heat production due to the effects of general anesthesia, resulting in a linear decline in temperature. Various sources of heat loss, including radiation, convection, evaporation, and conduction, contribute to this phase. Finally, the plateau phase is marked by maximal vasoconstriction, which balances heat loss and production, ultimately stabilizing the core body temperature.

3. **Answer C (Insulation)**

   During surgery and anesthesia leading to perioperative hypothermia, various sources of heat loss are at play. These include radiation, where the body emits heat in the form of electromagnetic waves; convection, where the heat dissipates through the movement of air or fluids; evaporation, as moisture on the skin or respiratory tract evaporates and takes away heat; and conduction, which involves the transfer of heat from the body to cooler surfaces or objects in direct contact. Insulation, on the other hand, is not a source of heat loss but a means to combat it. Insulating materials such as blankets and clothing are utilized to reduce heat loss and maintain the patient's body temperature during surgery, effectively preventing perioperative hypothermia.

4. **Answer C (Hyperthyroidism)**

   Hyperthyroidism is NOT a recognized risk factor for perioperative hypothermia. Perioperative hypothermia is associated with various patient-related factors, including ASA grade 2-5 (higher grade indicating a greater risk), preoperative temperature below 36.0°C, combined general and regional anesthesia, major or intermediate surgery, being at risk of cardiovascular complications, low BMI, diabetic neuropathy, paraplegia, and severe hypothyroidism. Hyperthyroidism, on the other hand, typically results in an increased metabolic rate and may actually lead to higher body temperature rather than hypothermia.

5. **Answer A (True)**

   Shivering is a common consequence of perioperative hypothermia. When a patient's core body temperature drops below the normal range due to perioperative hypothermia, the body may respond by initiating shivering as a natural mechanism to generate heat and raise the temperature. While shivering is a physiological response aimed at maintaining body temperature, it can have adverse consequences in the surgical setting. Shivering can lead to increased oxygen consumption, which may result in reduced oxygen availability for other vital organs. It can also lead to increased surgical complications, such as wound pain, increased blood pressure, and a higher risk of cardiac events. Therefore, it is essential to prevent and manage perioperative hypothermia to minimize the occurrence of shivering and its associated complications.

6. **Answer B (Decreased drug metabolism)**

   Perioperative hypothermia can lead to decreased drug metabolism. Hypothermia slows down metabolic processes within the body, including the metabolism of drugs. This can result in altered pharmacokinetics, potentially causing drug accumulation and prolonged effects. Anesthesiologists and healthcare providers must consider this when administering medications to hypothermic patients during surgery to ensure proper drug dosing and management.

Recommended literature

1. Rauch S, Miller C, Bräuer A, Wallner B, Bock M, Paal P. Perioperative Hypothermia-A Narrative Review. Int J Environ Res Public Health. 2021;18(16):8749. Published 2021 Aug 19.
2. Riley C, Andrzejowski J. Inadvertent perioperative hypothermia. BJA Educ. 2018;18(8):227-233.

PERIOPERATIVE MALNUTRITION

Questions:

1. **Which of the following is NOT a primary consequence of perioperative malnutrition?**
   A. Poor wound healing
   B. Increased intrapulmonary shunt V/Q mismatching
   C. Muscle protein depletion
   D. Systemic inflammation

2. **Which of the following is NOT a potential cause of perioperative malnutrition?**
   A. Surgery-related fasting
   B. Reduced food intake due to illness
   C. Enhanced recovery protocols
   D. Increased nutrient demands

3. **Which of the following statements is NOT indicative of severe malnutrition?**
   A. Weight loss > 10–15% within the past 6 months
   B. Subjective global assessment
   C. Serum albumin > 3 g L–1
   D. Body mass index < 18.5

4. **Which of the following is NOT a recommended approach to preoperative management of perioperative malnutrition?**
   A. Implementing a full-liquid diet
   B. Considering immunonutrition in all postoperative major abdominal surgical patients
   C. Initiating a high-protein diet on the day of surgery, with exceptions for bowel obstruction, ischemia, and patients with non-continuous bowel
   D. Prioritizing overall protein intake over total calorie intake in the postoperative period

5. **Perioperative malnutrition is a known independent predictor of poor postoperative outcomes.**
   A. True
   B. False

6. **A 65-year-old male patient is scheduled to undergo a major abdominal surgery to treat a gastrointestinal disorder. During the preoperative assessment, it was noted that the patient had unintentionally lost 15% of his body weight over the past six months. He reports decreased appetite, fatigue, and muscle weakness. His laboratory results reveal a serum albumin level of 2.8 g/L (below the normal range), and he has a BMI of 18.0. The patient has no known hepatic or renal dysfunction. Which statement regarding perioperative management in malnourished patients is NOT true?**
   A. Adequate rehydration prior to induction is essential to avoid cardiovascular collapse
   B. Malnourished patients are at increased risk of aspiration due to gastric distension and delayed gastric emptying
   C. Hyperventilate patients to reduce intracranial pressure (ICP) or relax a tense brain
   D. Malnourished patients are at high risk of intraoperative hypothermia

Answers:

1. Answer B (Increased intrapulmonary shunt V/Q mismatching)

Among the consequences of perioperative malnutrition, such as increased morbidity, mortality, extended hospital stays, and heightened healthcare expenses, patients are also at risk of experiencing cancer cachexia, muscle protein depletion, poor wound healing, and systemic inflammation. However, "increased intrapulmonary shunt V/Q mismatching" is not considered a primary consequence of perioperative malnutrition.

2. Answer C (Enhanced recovery protocols)

The potential causes of perioperative malnutrition include surgery-related fasting, reduced food intake due to illness, and increased nutrient demands. These factors can lead to inadequate nutrition before and after surgery, contributing to perioperative malnutrition. However, enhanced recovery protocols are designed to optimize perioperative care by minimizing fasting periods and providing early postoperative nutrition to improve patient outcomes and reduce complications. Therefore, enhanced recovery protocols are not a potential cause of perioperative malnutrition; instead, they aim to mitigate the risk of malnutrition during the perioperative period.

3. Answer C (Serum albumin > 3 g L−1)

Severe malnutrition is often characterized by significant weight loss (> 10–15% within the past 6 months), a low body mass index (BMI < 18.5), and clinical assessments such as subjective global assessments that evaluate various aspects of a patient's nutritional status. In contrast, a serum albumin level lower than 3 g L−1 (in the absence of hepatic or renal dysfunction) suggests that severe undernutrition may be present, as lower levels are more commonly observed in malnourished individuals.

4. Answer A (Implementing a full-liquid diet)

A full liquid diet is generally not recommended for preoperative management of malnutrition because it may lack essential nutrients, adequate calories, and protein needed to improve the nutritional status of patients before surgery. Other options, which involve considering immunonutrition, initiating a high-protein diet (with some exceptions), and prioritizing overall protein intake in the postoperative period, are more suitable strategies for addressing perioperative malnutrition.

5. Answer A (True)

Perioperative malnutrition is a known independent predictor of poor postoperative outcomes. Malnourished patients are at a higher risk of complications, longer hospital stays, increased mortality, and higher healthcare costs following surgery. Proper nutrition optimization before and after surgery is crucial to improve outcomes and reduce these risks.

6. Answer C (Hyperventilate patients to reduce intracranial pressure (ICP) or relax a tense brain)

Hyperventilation should be avoided as this can further lower potassium levels, lowering the threshold for life-threatening arrhythmias. Adequate rehydration prior to induction is essential to avoid cardiovascular collapse. Be wary of IV hydration in oedematous children. Malnourished patients are at increased risk of aspiration due to gastric distension and delayed gastric emptying, so consider inserting a nasogastric tube prior to intubation and have a low threshold for rapid sequence induction with cricoid pressure. Consider an antacid and a prokinetic prior to induction. Intraoperatively, malnourished patients are at high risk of intraoperative hypothermia, so make efforts to keep the patient warm with warmed IV fluids, patient warmer, and careful monitoring of perioperative core temperature.

Recommended literature

1. Matthews, L.S., Wootton, S.A., Davies, S.J., Levett, D.Z.H., 2021. Screening, assessment and management of perioperative malnutrition: a survey of UK practice. Perioperative Medicine 10.
2. Schonborn, J.L., Anderson, H., 2019. Perioperative medicine: a changing model of care. BJA Education 19, 27–33.
3. Williams, D.G.A., Molinger, J., Wischmeyer, P.E., 2019. The malnourished surgery patient. Current Opinion in Anaesthesiology 32, 405–411.
4. Wischmeyer, P.E., Carli, F., Evans, D.C., Guilbert, S., Kozar, R., Pryor, A., Thiele, R.H., Everett, S., Grocott, M., Gan, T.J., Shaw, A.D., Thacker, J.K.M., Miller, T.E., Hedrick, T.L., Mcevoy, M.D., Mythen, M.G., Bergamaschi, R., Gupta, R., Holubar, S.D., Senagore, A.J., Abola, R.E., Bennett-Guerrero, E., Kent, M.L., Feldman, L.S., Fiore, J.F., 2018. American Society for Enhanced Recovery and Perioperative Quality Initiative Joint Consensus Statement on Nutrition Screening and Therapy Within a Surgical Enhanced Recovery Pathway. Anesthesia & Analgesia 126, 1883–1895.

PERIOPERATIVE STROKE

08
CHAPTER

Questions:

1. **Which statement is true about perioperative stroke?**
    A. Perioperative stroke is an ischemic or hemorrhagic brain infarction that occurs during surgery or within 30 days of surgery
    B. Intraoperative brain infarction is usually caused by hypotension
    C. Ischemic brain infarction is often associated with patients who didn't receive thromboprophylaxis
    D. Most perioperative strokes occurred, on average, during the surgery

2. **Which of the following is NOT a patient-related risk factor for perioperative stroke?**
    A. Male sex
    B. Increasing age
    C. Hypertension
    D. Smoker or COPD

3. **Which surgical factor is associated with a higher risk of perioperative stroke?**
    A. Endocrine surgery
    B. Otolaryngology surgery
    C. Laparoscopic surgery
    D. Obstetric surgery

4. **What statement about emergency treatment in perioperative stroke is NOT true?**
    A. Rapid transfer to an acute stroke unit is a crucial step in optimizing care
    B. Intravenous thrombolysis is the primary recommended treatment and should start as soon as possible
    C. Mechanical thrombectomy is typically performed between 6 and 24 hours after symptom onset
    D. Aspirin can be used when deemed safe

5. **The incidence of perioperative stroke ranges from 0.1% to 1.9%.**
    A. True
    B. False

6. **A 75-year-old patient with a history of hypertension and a recent ischemic stroke (2 months ago) is presented with a broken femur due to a fall. The patient has been taking warfarin for stroke prevention following the recent stroke, and their INR (International Normalized Ratio) is within the therapeutic range. Considering the patient's recent stroke, therapy with warfarin, and the femur fracture, which management approach is most appropriate for this patient?**
    A. Don't delay surgery
    B. Delay surgery for 6 to 9 months
    C. Bridge warfarin for 5-7 days with enoxaparin
    D. The patient is a candidate for conservative treatment

Answers:

1. Answer A (Perioperative stroke is an ischemic or hemorrhagic brain infarction that occurs during surgery or within 30 days of surgery)

Perioperative stroke is defined as an ischemic or hemorrhagic brain infarction that occurs during surgery or within 30 days of surgery. While hypotension can be a risk factor for intraoperative brain infarction, it is not the sole cause. The relationship between thromboprophylaxis and perioperative stroke is not the primary characteristic of this condition. Moreover, the timing of perioperative strokes can vary, with some occurring during surgery, as seen in high-risk procedures like cardiovascular or neurosurgery, but many occur, on average, around seven days post-surgery for general surgical cases.

2. Answer A (Male sex)

Male sex is not typically considered a patient-related risk factor for perioperative stroke. Perioperative stroke risk factors often include medical conditions or characteristics that increase the likelihood of vascular events, such as hypertension, increasing age, and a history of smoking or chronic obstructive pulmonary disease (COPD). While stroke risk can vary among individuals, and gender-specific factors may play a role in certain cases, being male is not a consistently identified patient-related risk factor for perioperative stroke. It's worth noting that being female has also been recognized as a risk factor for perioperative stroke in both cardiovascular and non-cardiovascular surgeries. The reasons for sex differences in perioperative stroke are not completely understood but may involve factors such as the accelerated progression of atherosclerosis in elderly female patients after menopause and a history of stroke or transient ischemic attack, which elevates the risk for perioperative stroke.

3. Answer A (Endocrine surgery)

Surgical factors can significantly influence the risk of perioperative stroke, and among the options provided, endocrine surgery is associated with a higher risk. While the majority of general surgeries, including otolaryngology and laparoscopic procedures, generally pose a low risk of perioperative stroke, certain types of surgery, especially those involving vascular, thoracic, or transplantation procedures, carry a higher risk among general surgeries. Endocrine surgery (e.g., thyroid or parathyroid surgery) is considered high risk, particularly due to the vascular anatomy in the neck region. In contrast, obstetric surgery typically falls within the category of surgeries with lower perioperative stroke risk.

4. Answer B (Intravenous thrombolysis is the primary recommended treatment and should start as soon as possible)

While intravenous thrombolysis can be a treatment option for perioperative stroke, it is not necessarily the primary recommended treatment, and its use depends on various factors, including the type and timing of the stroke. Rapid transfer to an acute stroke unit is a crucial step in optimizing care for perioperative stroke patients. Mechanical thrombectomy is typically performed in certain cases, but the timing is specific (between 6 and 24 hours after symptom onset). Aspirin can be used when deemed safe but is not the primary treatment within the first hour of symptom onset.

5. Answer A (True)

The incidence of perioperative stroke is generally not high and can vary depending on the type of surgery and patient characteristics. In non-cardiac, non-neurologic, and non-major surgery, the incidence typically falls within the range of approximately 0.1% to 1.9%. However, it's important to note that in specific high-risk surgical scenarios, such as cardiac or brain surgery, the incidence of perioperative stroke can be significantly higher, affecting up to 10% of patients undergoing these procedures.

6. Answer A (Don't delay surgery)

There is also no evidence to suggest that delaying hip fracture repair is beneficial in patients receiving any type of anticoagulation. Because of this, deciding on the timing of surgery is often made through the collaboration of surgery, anesthesiology, and internal medicine and is often based on prior personal experience or institutional habits. Preoperatively, prompt warfarin reversal together with adequate investigation and optimization of the patient, should ensure timely, safe surgery. Early involvement of the anesthesia team should ensure an appropriate level of postoperative care for these patients.

Recommended literature

1. Ng JLW, Chan MTV, Gelb Adrian W, Warner David S. Perioperative Stroke in Noncardiac, Nonneurosurgical Surgery. Anesthesiology. 2011;115(4):879-90.
2. Lindberg AP, Flexman AM. Perioperative stroke after non-cardiac, non-neurological surgery. BJA Educ. 2021;21(2):59-65.
3. Benesch C, Glance LG, Derdeyn CP, Fleisher LA, Holloway RG, Messé SR, et al. Perioperative Neurological Evaluation and Management to Lower the Risk of Acute Stroke in Patients Undergoing Noncardiac, Nonneurological Surgery: A Scientific Statement From the American Heart Association/American Stroke Association. Circulation. 2021;143(19):e923-e46.

POSTOPERATIVE DELIRIUM (POD)

Questions:

1. **What is the primary characteristic of hyperactive postoperative delirium (POD)?**
   A. Lethargy and sedation
   B. Restlessness and agitation
   C. Slow response to questioning
   D. Minimal spontaneous movement

2. **Which of the following is NOT a predisposing factor for POD?**
   A. Sight loss
   B. Low serum albumin levels
   C. Female sex
   D. Frailty

3. **Which type of anesthesia is recommended as an alternative to reduce the risk of POD based on research findings?**
   A. Inhalation anesthesia (IA)
   B. Intravenous anesthesia (Total Intravenous Anesthesia - TIVA)
   C. Opioid-free anesthesia
   D. Opioid anesthesia

4. **Which of the following preventative measures is NOT a promising treatment of postoperative delirium?**
   A. Steroids
   B. Melatonin
   C. Dexmedetomidine
   D. Deeper sedation

5. **Ondansetron is a serotonin antagonist, which could represent a therapeutic or preventive option in POD.**
   A. True
   B. False

6. **A 68-year-old male patient is admitted to the Intensive Care Unit (ICU) following cardiac surgery. He has a history of multimorbidity, including hypertension and diabetes. Additionally, the patient has prior cognitive impairment, which has been noted in his medical records. Currently, he is experiencing a hypoactive form of delirium, characterized by lethargy and sedation, slow responses to questioning, and minimal spontaneous movement. What is not a suitable pharmacological treatment for managing the patient's hypoactive delirium in the ICU postoperatively?**
   A. IV paracetamol
   B. IV dexmedetomidine
   C. IV benzodiazepines
   D. IV haloperidol

Answers:

1. Answer B (Restlessness and agitation)

Hyperactive postoperative delirium (POD) is marked by a heightened state of restlessness and agitation in patients. They may also exhibit hypervigilance, often accompanied by hallucinations and delusions. This subtype of delirium is characterized by an overactive and hyper-aroused mental state, where patients may be excessively alert and agitated and may experience sensory disturbances, contributing to the presence of hallucinations and delusions.

2. Answer C (Female sex)

The female sex is not typically considered a predisposing factor for POD. While advanced age, male sex, low body mass index, sight or hearing loss, social isolation, multimorbidity, prior cognitive impairment, malnutrition, low serum albumin levels, and frailty are all recognized predisposing factors for POD, there isn't a well-established link between being female and a significantly increased risk of developing POD. However, it's important to note that individual patient characteristics and surgical contexts can vary, so healthcare providers should assess each patient's unique risk factors for delirium.

3. Answer B (Intravenous anesthesia (Total Intravenous Anesthesia - TIVA)

Total Intravenous Anesthesia (TIVA), particularly when using agents like propofol, may offer advantages in reducing the risk of POD compared to inhalation anesthesia (IA). For instance, studies have shown that TIVA is associated with a slightly decreased incidence of POD and morbidity. In older patients undergoing major cancer surgery, delirium was found to be one-third less common after propofol-based anesthesia compared to sevoflurane. Moreover, TIVA has been demonstrated to provide better hemodynamic stability in specific surgical procedures. Therefore, TIVA is recommended to reduce the risk of POD, especially in patients at a higher risk of developing postoperative delirium.

4. Answer D (Deeper sedation)

Deeper sedation is NOT considered a promising treatment for POD. In fact, deeper sedation may increase the risk of POD rather than prevent it. Excessive sedation can contribute to cognitive impairment, prolonged recovery, and a higher likelihood of delirium in postoperative patients. On the other hand, while TIVA, lighter sedation, dexmedetomidine, melatonin, and steroids have been considered as potential measures for preventing POD, it's important to note that they all require further investigation to establish their efficacy conclusively.

5. Answer A (True)

Ondansetron is a serotonin antagonist that represents a potential therapeutic or preventive option in POD. Serotonin has been suggested to play a role in delirium, and observational studies have shown higher levels of serotonin in delirious patients. Additionally, delirium is a major manifestation of serotonin syndrome. Ondansetron specifically targets the 5-HT3 receptor, and it is commonly used post-operatively to prevent nausea and vomiting. Furthermore, it has a better safety profile compared to haloperidol, which is the most commonly used agent for treating and preventing POD. However, it's important to note that while Ondansetron may be effective for POD, the evidence is limited, and more large randomized controlled trials (RCTs) are needed to establish its effectiveness conclusively.

6. Answer C (IV benzodiazepines)

In the case of this patient's hypoactive delirium in the ICU, IV benzodiazepines are not a suitable pharmacological treatment option. Recent evidence from the Cochrane Database of Systematic Reviews indicates that benzodiazepines should not be recommended for the treatment of postoperative delirium, as they can exacerbate hypoactive delirium conditions. This choice can lead to increased sedation and further cognitive impairment in patients who are already experiencing a hypoactive state. In contrast, IV paracetamol, IV dexmedetomidine, and IV haloperidol have been considered as treatment options, with varying degrees of evidence supporting their use in managing different aspects of delirium.

Recommended literature

1. Hoogma, Danny Feike; Milisen, Koen; Rex, Steffen; Al tmimi, Layth. Postoperative delirium: identifying the patient at risk and altering the course: A narrative review. European Journal of Anaesthesiology and Intensive Care 2(3):p e0022, June 2023.
2. Mossie A, Regasa T, Neme D, Awoke Z, Zemedkun A, Hailu S. Evidence-Based Guideline on Management of Postoperative Delirium in Older People for Low Resource Setting: Systematic Review Article. Int J Gen Med. 2022;15:4053-4065.
3. Swarbrick CJ, Partridge JSL. Evidence-based strategies to reduce the incidence of postoperative delirium: a narrative review. Anaesthesia. 2022;77 Suppl 1:92-101.
4. Subramaniam B, Shankar P, Shaefi S, et al. Effect of Intravenous Acetaminophen vs Placebo Combined With Propofol or Dexmedetomidine on Postoperative Delirium Among Older Patients Following Cardiac Surgery: The DEXACET Randomized Clinical Trial [published correction appears in JAMA. 2019 Jul 16;322(3):276]. JAMA. 2019;321(7):686-696.
5. Haque N, Naqvi RM, Dasgupta M. Efficacy of Ondansetron in the Prevention or Treatment of Post-operative Delirium-a Systematic Review. Can Geriatr J. 2019;22(1):1-6. Published 2019 Mar 30.
6. Khan BA, Perkins AJ, Gao S, et al. The Confusion Assessment Method for the ICU-7 Delirium Severity Scale: A Novel Delirium Severity Instrument for Use in the ICU. Crit Care Med. 2017;45(5):851-857.
7. Chan MT, Cheng BC, Lee TM, Gin T; CODA Trial Group. BIS-guided anesthesia decreases postoperative delirium and cognitive decline. J Neurosurg Anesthesiol. 2013;25(1):33-42.
8. Fong TG, Tulebaev SR, Inouye SK. Delirium in elderly adults: diagnosis, prevention and treatment. Nat Rev Neurol. 2009;5(4):210-220.
9. Robinson TN, Eiseman B. Postoperative delirium in the elderly: diagnosis and management. Clin Interv Aging. 2008;3(2):351-355.

POSTOPERATIVE NAUSEA AND VOMITING (PONV)

08
CHAPTER

Questions:

1. **What is the most common postoperative complication after pain?**
   A. Surgical site infection
   B. Postoperative nausea and vomiting (PONV)
   C. Deep vein thrombosis
   D. Hypoxia

2. **Which of the following is NOT a risk factor for PONV according to the Apfel simplified risk score?**
   A. Female gender
   B. Non-smoker
   C. History of PONV and/or motion sickness
   D. Age greater than 60 years

3. **In children, which of the following surgeries is considered a high-risk surgery for PONV?**
   A. Appendectomy
   B. Circumcision
   C. Strabismus surgery
   D. Dental extraction

4. **What are the antiemetics of choice in children with no risk factors for PONV?**
   A. Ondansetron
   B. Metoclopramide
   C. Dexamethasone and 5HT3 antagonist
   D. No prophylaxis required

5. **Patients who experience severe PONV often describe it as a more distressing experience than the pain.**
   A. True
   B. False

6. **A 45-year-old non-smoking patient with a history of migraines is scheduled for an elective hysteroscopy. The patient also has a medical history of PONV and/or motion sickness. What is NOT the most appropriate prophylactic treatment for preventing PONV in this patient based on their risk factors and the anesthesia technique used?**
   A. Prophylactic medications
   B. Regional anesthesia techniques
   C. Use volatile anesthetics
   D. Minimizing opioid use

Answers:

1. **Answer B (Postoperative nausea and vomiting (PONV))**

   Postoperative nausea and vomiting (PONV) is the second most common postoperative complication after pain. While pain is a common issue following surgery, PONV can also be a significant concern for patients. PONV can lead to discomfort, decreased patient satisfaction, dehydration, and other complications if not effectively managed.

2. **Answer D (Age greater than 60 years)**

   The Apfel simplified risk score is a scoring system used to assess the risk of PONV based on specific risk factors, including female gender, non-smoker, history of PONV and/or motion sickness, and the use of postoperative opioids. Each risk factor is assigned a point, and the total score can help healthcare providers determine the likelihood of PONV in a given patient.

3. **Answer C (Strabismus surgery)**

   In children, certain surgeries are considered high-risk for PONV, including strabismus surgery, adenotonsillectomy, and otoplasty. Among the options provided, strabismus surgery is considered a high-risk surgery for PONV. Strabismus surgery involves the correction of eye misalignment (crossed or wandering eyes) and can be associated with a higher incidence of PONV in pediatric patients compared to some other surgical procedures. The specific characteristics of strabismus surgery, along with individual patient factors, contribute to this increased risk.

4. **Answer D (No prophylaxis required)**

   Patients who present for surgery with none or one risk factor should receive no prophylactic antiemetics. In these cases, it is recommended not to administer preventive antiemetic medications because the risk of PONV is considered low. Instead, treatment for PONV should be initiated only if it occurs. Prophylactic antiemetics, such as ondansetron, dexamethasone, or droperidol, are typically reserved for children with two or more risk factors for PONV, as outlined in the scoring system.

5. **Answer A (True)**

   PONV can indeed be a profoundly distressing experience for patients. While pain is a well-known and significant concern after surgery, PONV can be particularly uncomfortable and distressing due to the persistent feeling of nausea and the act of vomiting. Patients may describe PONV as worse because it can lead to a sense of helplessness and a feeling of being unable to control the situation. This is why effective prevention and management of PONV are crucial components of perioperative care, as it can significantly impact the patient's overall surgical experience and satisfaction.

6. **Answer C (Use volatile anesthetics)**

   In the case of a 45-year-old patient with a history of migraines, a history of PONV, and scheduled for an elective hysteroscopy, the least appropriate prophylactic treatment for preventing PONV based on their risk factors and anesthesia technique used would be using volatile anesthetics. Volatile anesthetics are not typically employed as a primary prophylactic measure to prevent PONV and may, in some instances, even increase the risk of nausea and vomiting. Instead, in patients with known PONV risk factors like this individual, more effective strategies may include administering prophylactic antiemetic medications, minimizing opioid use for post-surgery pain management, or considering regional anesthesia techniques when appropriate.

Recommended literature

1. Gan TJ, Belani KG, Bergese S, et al. Fourth Consensus Guidelines for the Management of Postoperative Nausea and Vomiting [published correction appears in Anesth Analg. 2020 Nov;131(5):e241]. Anesth Analg. 2020;131(2):411-448.

POSTOPERATIVE NERVE INJURIES

08
CHAPTER

Questions:

1. **What is the NOT common mechanism of postoperative nerve injuries?**
   A. Ischemia
   B. Diabetic neuropathy
   C. Local anesthetic toxicity
   D. Double crush syndrome

2. **Which patient-specific factor is NOT listed as a risk factor for postoperative nerve injuries?**
   A. Obesity
   B. Hypertension
   C. Smoking
   D. Alcoholism

3. **Which surgical specialty is associated with a higher risk of postoperative nerve injuries?**
   A. Dermatology
   B. Ophthalmology
   C. Neurosurgery
   D. Gynecology

4. **What is the cause of ischemic nerve damage in the context of postoperative nerve injuries?**
   A. Hypotension
   B. Tourniquets
   C. Smoking
   D. LA toxicity

5. **High concentrations of local anesthetic increase the risk of developing perioperative peripheral nerve injuries.**
   A. True
   B. False

6. **A 60-year-old male patient, a smoker with a history of hypertension and diabetes mellitus, underwent elective transurethral resection of the prostate. He had previously undergone an open appendectomy for acute perforated appendicitis ten years ago. During the procedure, successful neuraxial anesthesia was administered, and the patient was placed in the lithotomy position. The surgery proceeded without complications. However, on the first postoperative day, the patient complained of paresthesia and a burning sensation in the right lateral thigh. What is the possible cause of the patient's complaints of paresthesia and burning pain in the right lateral thigh?**
   A. Lateral femoral cutaneous neuropathy
   B. Femoral neuropathy
   C. Ischiadic neuropathy
   D. Obturatorius neuropathy

Answers:

1. Answer B (Diabetic neuropathy)

Diabetic neuropathy is not a common mechanism of postoperative nerve injuries. Postoperative nerve injuries can occur due to various mechanisms, including direct nerve damage from surgery or needle trauma, stretch and compression of nerves, ischemia caused by factors like tourniquets or prolonged immobility, double crush syndrome, and local anesthetic toxicity. Another potential mechanism is the development of postoperative nerve injuries in patients with pre-existing peripheral neuropathies, which may include diabetic neuropathy. However, diabetic neuropathy is typically a chronic complication of diabetes and not a direct cause of postoperative nerve injuries.

2. Answer A (Obesity)

Obesity is not listed as one of the patient-specific risk factors for postoperative nerve injuries. Instead, other patient-specific factors that may increase the risk of developing postoperative nerve injuries encompass hypertension, diabetes mellitus, smoking, double crush syndrome, preexisting peripheral neuropathy, and anatomical abnormalities.

3. Answer C (Neurosurgery)

Neurosurgery is associated with a higher risk of postoperative nerve injuries. Other surgical procedures like cardiac surgery, gastrointestinal surgery, and orthopedic surgery are also associated with an increased risk of postoperative nerve injuries.

4. Answer B (Tourniquets)

The cause of ischemic nerve damage in the context of postoperative nerve injuries is primarily tourniquets. Tourniquets, when applied during surgery, can temporarily stop blood flow to a limb, leading to ischemia, which is a lack of blood supply to the affected area. Ischemia can damage nerves and is considered one of the mechanisms of postoperative nerve injuries. Additional factors such as prolonged immobility, the presence of a hematoma around a nerve, and exposure to local anesthetic agents can also contribute to ischemia and increase the risk of postoperative nerve injuries.

5. Answer A (True)

High concentrations of local anesthetics can increase the risk of developing perioperative peripheral nerve injuries. This risk arises due to the potential for cytotoxic axonal damage when local anesthetic solutions are injected intrafascicularly. Additionally, prolonged exposure to highly concentrated solutions further predisposes individuals to nerve injury.

6. Answer A (Lateral femoral cutaneous neuropathy)

The patient's complaints, including paresthesia and burning pain in the right lateral thigh, are indicative of lateral femoral cutaneous neuropathy. The lithotomy position, together with the patient's previous surgical history (open appendectomy), which may have resulted in the formation of scar tissue in the area, may have impinged the lateral femoral cutaneous nerve. This specific nerve supplies sensation to the lateral thigh, and injury or compression can lead to symptoms in this region. Positioning the patient for surgical procedures, such as the lithotomy position in this case, is a shared responsibility among the surgical team, including the surgeon, anesthesiologist, and nurses. While it provides optimal access for surgery, it's essential to consider each patient's individual medical history and potential risk factors to minimize the risk of complications like nerve injuries.

Recommended literature

1. Hewson DW, Bedforth NM, Hardman JG. Peripheral nerve injury arising in anaesthesia practice. Anaesthesia. 2018;73(S1):51-60.
2. Chui J, Murkin JM, Posner KL, Domino KB. Perioperative Peripheral Nerve Injury After General Anesthesia: A Qualitative Systematic Review. Anesth Analg. 2018;127(1):134-143.
3. Practice Advisory for the Prevention of Perioperative Peripheral Neuropathies 2018: An Updated Report by the American Society of Anesthesiologists Task Force on Prevention of Perioperative Peripheral Neuropathies*. Anesthesiology. 2018;128(1):11-26.
4. Lalkhen AG, Bhatia K. Perioperative peripheral nerve injuries. Continuing Education in Anaesthesia Critical Care & Pain. 2012;12(1):38-42.

Miscellaneous
POSTOPERATIVE NEUROCOGNITIVE DISORDER

08
CHAPTER

Questions:

1. Which of the following is NOT a cognitive domain evaluated for postoperative neurocognitive disorder (pNCD) diagnosis?
    A. Learning and memory
    B. Motor skills
    C. Social cognition
    D. Executive function

2. What is the primary risk factor for developing pNCD, as mentioned in the text?
    A. Young age
    B. Lower educational status
    C. The short duration of anesthesia
    D. Preoperative fasting

3. Which grade of pNCD is characterized by a noticeable decline in cognitive function that extends beyond normal aging changes?
    A. Mild Neurocognitive Disorder
    B. Major Neurocognitive Disorder
    C. Transient Cognitive Dysfunction
    D. Perioperative Delirium

4. Which cognitive test is widely used for Alzheimer's Disease detection but has low sensitivity for mild and medium cognitive dysfunction?
    A. MiniCog
    B. IQ-CODE
    C. MMSE (Mini-Mental State Examination)
    D. MoCA (Montreal Cognitive Assessment)

5. Postoperative neurocognitive disorder pNCD can be detected from the first day after surgery.
    A. True
    B. False

6. A 72-year-old patient with a history of hypertension and a previous stroke resulting in mild residual motor deficits is scheduled for total hip replacement surgery. Given his medical history, he is at risk for pNCD. In preparing for surgery, the medical team should consider strategies to minimize this risk. What action is NOT recommended as a prevention strategy for the development of pNCD in this patient?
    A. Avoid unnecessary postponement of surgery
    B. Avoid routine benzodiazepine administration
    C. Avoid deep sedation
    D. Avoid perioperative sensory orientation

Answers:

1. **Answer B (Motor skills)**

   Motor skills are not a cognitive domain evaluated for the diagnosis of postoperative neurocognitive disorder (pNCD). The assessment of pNCD primarily focuses on cognitive functions, and these cognitive domains include perceptual-motor function, language, learning and memory, social cognition, complex attention, and executive function. Motor skills, which pertain to physical coordination and movement, are distinct from cognitive functions and are not typically considered within the scope of cognitive assessment for pNCD diagnosis.

2. **Answer B (Lower educational status)**

   One of the risk factors for developing pNCD is lower educational status. This suggests that individuals with less formal education may be at a higher risk of experiencing cognitive decline following surgery. Other possible risks for developing pNCD include advanced age, disabilities, frailty, major surgery, history of alcohol abuse, history of stroke, longer duration of anesthesia, postoperative infection, respiratory complications, use of anticholinergic medication, and sevoflurane use for anesthesia.

3. **Answer A (Mild Neurocognitive Disorder)**

   Mild Neurocognitive Disorder refers to a condition in which an individual experiences a noticeable decline in cognitive function that extends beyond the typical changes associated with aging. This means that their cognitive abilities, such as memory, attention, and problem-solving skills, have deteriorated to a degree that is more significant than what one would expect due to natural aging processes. While the individual may still be able to perform daily activities, they may require adjustments or accommodations to maintain their independence. It represents a milder form of cognitive impairment compared to Major Neurocognitive Disorder, where the cognitive decline is more severe and significantly impacts a person's ability to carry out daily tasks and activities of living.

4. **Answer C (MMSE (Mini-Mental State Examination))**

   The Mini-Mental State Examination (MMSE) is a widely known and used cognitive test, particularly for detecting Alzheimer's Disease. However, it is known to have lower sensitivity when it comes to detecting mild and medium cognitive dysfunction. This means that while it may effectively identify severe cognitive impairment associated with conditions like Alzheimer's Disease, it may not be as effective in detecting more subtle cognitive changes or mild impairments, which can be important in the assessment of conditions like pNCD where milder cognitive changes are of concern. Other tests like the Montreal Cognitive Assessment (MoCA) are often preferred for their greater sensitivity in detecting milder cognitive deficits.

5. **Answer B (False)**

   pNCD is typically not detected immediately or from the first day after surgery. It usually takes some time for cognitive changes associated with pNCD to become noticeable and measurable. Usually, pNCD can be detected from 7 days after surgery. This means that cognitive assessment and diagnosis for pNCD are generally not conducted immediately after surgery but are performed after a period of time, allowing for the assessment of cognitive changes that persist beyond the immediate postoperative period.

6. **Answer D (Avoid perioperative sensory orientation)**

   In the context of preventing pNCD in high-risk patients like this 72-year-old patient with a history of hypertension and a previous stroke resulting in mild residual motor deficits, it is NOT recommended to avoid perioperative sensory orientation. Perioperative sensory orientation encourages patients to wear their glasses, hearing aids, and dentures until anesthesia induction, which helps maintain sensory input and orientation during the perioperative period. This strategy is important for cognitive well-being and should be encouraged. The other listed strategies, such as avoiding unnecessary postponement of surgery, avoiding routine benzodiazepine administration, and avoiding deep sedation, are all recommended preventive measures to minimize the risk of pNCD in high-risk patients.

Recommended literature

1. Brodier EA, Cibelli M. Postoperative cognitive dysfunction in clinical practice. BJA Educ. 2021;21(2):75-82.
2. Olotu C. Postoperative neurocognitive disorders. Curr Opin Anaesthesiol. 2020;33(1):101-108.
3. Shoair OA, Grasso Ii MP, Lahaye LA, Daniel R, Biddle CJ, Slattum PW. Incidence and risk factors for postoperative cognitive dysfunction in older adults undergoing major noncardiac surgery: A prospective study. J Anaesthesiol Clin Pharmacol. 2015;31(1):30-36.

POSTOPERATIVE PAIN MANAGEMENT

08
CHAPTER

Questions:

1. **What is the primary physiological consequence of uncontrolled postoperative pain?**
   A. Hypotension
   B. Hyperglycemia
   C. Hypoxia
   D. Bradycardia

2. **Which respiratory complication can result from pain following abdominal or thoracic surgery?**
   A. Metabolic acidosis
   B. Respiratory alkalosis
   C. Respiratory acidosis
   D. Metabolic alkalosis

3. **Which scale is often used to assess pain in cognitively impaired patients or children?**
   A. Numeric rating scale
   B. Verbal descriptor scale
   C. FLACC scale
   D. McGill Pain Questionnaire

4. **What is pre-emptive analgesia in the context of postoperative pain management?**
   A. Administering pain medication before surgery
   B. Administering pain medication only after pain onset
   C. Administering pain medication during surgery
   D. Administering regional anesthesia during surgery

5. **Multimodal approaches are the preferred approach to postoperative pain management in contemporary healthcare practice.**
   A. True
   B. False

6. **A 68-year-old patient with hypertension and type 2 diabetes is scheduled for total knee replacement surgery in spinal anesthesia. What is the most appropriate example of analgesia for this patient who is scheduled for total knee replacement surgery?**
   A. Continuous epidural analgesia
   B. Adductor canal block, Local Infiltration Analgesia (LIA), Dexamethasone, Acetaminophen, NSAID, Opioid for rescue
   C. Patient-controlled analgesia (PCA)
   D. Spinal anesthesia with no additional pain medications

Answers:

1. **Answer B (Hyperglycemia)**

   Uncontrolled postoperative pain leads to a cascade of physiological responses due to increased sympathetic activity and stress response. This stress response can result in several multisystem consequences, one of which is hyperglycemia. The increased release of stress hormones, such as cortisol and catecholamines, can elevate blood glucose levels. Hyperglycemia in the postoperative period can have negative effects on wound healing, immune function, and the overall recovery process.

2. **Answer C (Respiratory acidosis)**

   Pain following abdominal or thoracic surgery can lead to a respiratory complication known as respiratory acidosis. This occurs due to the reduced ability of the patient to take deep breaths and effectively ventilate their lungs. The pain leads to splinting of the diaphragm and chest wall, which results in decreased lung volumes. This reduction in lung capacity can lead to atelectasis, poor cough strength, retention of sputum, and an increased risk of respiratory infections. Additionally, inadequate ventilation can lead to a buildup of carbon dioxide (CO_2) in the bloodstream, causing respiratory acidosis. This condition is characterized by an elevated level of CO_2, leading to a decrease in blood pH. It is important to effectively manage postoperative pain to prevent these respiratory complications and ensure optimal lung function during the recovery period.

3. **Answer C (FLACC scale)**

   The FLACC scale is often used to assess pain in cognitively impaired patients or children. The FLACC scale stands for "Face, Legs, Activity, Cry, and Consolability." It is a behavioral pain assessment tool that evaluates specific indicators related to pain, such as facial expressions, leg movement, activity level, crying, and the ability to be consoled. This scale is particularly useful when patients cannot communicate their pain verbally or when assessing pain in pediatric populations who may not have developed the ability to express their pain in words effectively. By observing and scoring these behavioral indicators, healthcare providers can assess the presence and severity of pain in patients who may have difficulty expressing their discomfort verbally.

4. **Answer A (Administering pain medication before surgery)**

   Pre-emptive analgesia is a pain management strategy in the context of postoperative care that involves administering pain medication before surgery begins. The primary goal of pre-emptive analgesia is to reduce the sensitization of the nociceptive (pain) system that can occur during surgery. By providing analgesic medication prior to the surgical procedure, the aim is to "pre-empt" or prevent the establishment of heightened pain sensitivity. This approach is based on the idea that pain sensitivity can increase during and after surgery due to various factors, including inflammation and neural changes. Pre-emptive analgesia aims to protect the nociceptive system from these sensitizing effects. It is theorized that initiating pain management before surgery can be more effective in reducing immediate postoperative pain and potentially preventing the development of chronic pain.

5. **Answer (True)**

   These approaches involve combining various analgesic agents and techniques to target pain through different mechanisms. This approach is favored because it can provide effective pain relief while minimizing the risks associated with the overreliance on opioids. Multimodal pain management strategies are designed to enhance patient comfort, promote faster recovery, and reduce the potential for opioid-related side effects and complications, making them the preferred choice for postoperative pain management in modern healthcare.

6. **Answer B (Adductor canal block, Local Infiltration Analgesia (LIA), Dexamethasone, Acetaminophen, NSAID, Opioid for rescue)**

   For a 68-year-old patient with hypertension and type 2 diabetes scheduled for total knee replacement surgery under spinal anesthesia, the most appropriate analgesia approach is a perfect example of multimodal analgesia, as described in option B. This approach includes the utilization of an adductor canal block, LIA, dexamethasone, acetaminophen, a non-steroidal anti-inflammatory drug (NSAID), and an opioid for rescue. These components collectively provide targeted pain relief, minimize postoperative discomfort, and reduce the reliance on systemic opioids. This balanced approach to pain management is particularly suitable for patients with comorbidities like hypertension and type 2 diabetes, aiming to enhance postoperative recovery while managing pain effectively.

Recommended literature

1. Horn R, Kramer J. Postoperative Pain Control. [Updated 2022 Sep 19]. In: StatPearls [Internet]. Treasure Island (FL): StatPearls Publishing; 2022 Jan-. Available from: https://www.ncbi.nlm.nih.gov/books/NBK544298/.
2. Pollard BJ, Kitchen, G. Handbook of Clinical Anaesthesia. Fourth Edition. CRC Press. 2018. 978-1-4987-6289-2.
3. Tharakan L, Faber P. Pain management in day-case surgery. BJA Education. 2015;15(4):180-3.

PRONE POSITION

Questions:

1. **What is the primary physiological effect of prone positioning on arterial oxygen pressure?**
   A. Decreased arterial oxygen pressure
   B. Unchanged arterial oxygen pressure
   C. Slight increase in arterial oxygen pressure
   D. Marked increase in arterial oxygen pressure

2. **In prone surgery, what cardiovascular change occurs?**
   A. Increased stroke volume
   B. Decreased peripheral vascular resistance
   C. Reduced stroke volume
   D. Increased cardiac output

3. **What can prone positioning potentially cause in terms of cerebral blood flow?**
   A. Increased cerebral blood flow
   B. Reduced cerebral blood flow
   C. No change in cerebral blood flow
   D. Vessel constriction in the brain

4. **Which of the following is a direct pressure injury associated with prone positioning?**
   A. Macroglossia
   B. Mediastinal compression
   C. Skin necrosis
   D. Peripheral vessel occlusion

5. **Peripheral nerve injuries are usually present in the recovery room.**
   A. True
   B. False

6. **During a spinal surgery, the patient is positioned prone. Unexpectedly, the endotracheal tube becomes dislodged, and the anesthesia team needs to manage the situation effectively to ensure the patient's safety. What is a correct statement and a part of the algorithm for managing the airway in patients in the prone position following unexpected extubation?**
   A. Maintain the patient in the prone position to minimize the risk of neck injury during rotation
   B. Utilize a supraglottic device
   C. Dont use apneic oxygenation, as it can potentially lead to respiratory acidosis
   D. Prioritize direct laryngoscopy over video laryngoscopy to enhance the likelihood of a successful first attempt

Answers:

1. Answer C (Slight increase in arterial oxygen pressure)

Prone positioning during surgery can lead to a slight increase in arterial oxygen pressure. This occurs because the redistribution of blood flow and changes in lung mechanics when a patient is in the prone position can improve ventilation-perfusion matching in the lungs, resulting in better oxygenation of the blood. While other physiological changes occur during prone positioning, such as reduced stroke volume and increased sympathetic activity, these changes can affect cardiac function and blood pressure but typically do not lead to a significant decrease in arterial oxygen pressure.

2. Answer C (Reduced stroke volume)

Prone positioning during surgery often leads to a reduction in stroke volume. When a patient is in the prone position, the pressure on the chest and abdomen can compress the thoracic cavity, which can impede the filling of the heart and reduce the volume of blood ejected with each heartbeat. This reduction in stroke volume triggers compensatory mechanisms, such as sympathetic nervous system activation, which increases heart rate and peripheral vascular resistance to help maintain blood pressure and cardiac output. These changes aim to compensate for the reduced stroke volume caused by the prone position.

3. Answer B (Reduced cerebral blood flow)

Prone positioning in surgery has been associated with a reduction in cerebral blood flow. When a patient is placed in the prone position, there may be increased pressure on the chest and abdomen, which can lead to changes in blood flow dynamics. This can result in a reduction in cerebral blood flow, which means that less blood is reaching the brain. Additionally, prone positioning may also lead to an increase in intracranial pressure, which can further affect cerebral blood flow.

4. Answer C (Skin necrosis)

Skin necrosis is a direct pressure injury commonly associated with prone positioning during surgery. When a patient is in the prone position, there is pressure exerted on various parts of the body, including the chest, abdomen, and pelvis. Prolonged pressure on the skin in these areas can lead to reduced blood flow to the skin tissues, which can result in skin necrosis or tissue death. Other direct pressure injuries include contact dermatitis, tracheal compression, salivary gland swelling, breast injury, injury to the genitalia, compression of the pinna, and compression of the femoral neurovascular bundle. It's worth noting that there are also indirect pressure injuries associated with prone positioning, such as macroglossia and oropharyngeal swelling, mediastinal compression, visceral ischemia, avascular necrosis of the femoral head, peripheral vessel occlusion, limb compartment syndrome, and rhabdomyolysis. These injuries are a result of the altered physiological conditions and pressure distribution caused by the prone position.

5. Answer B (False)

Peripheral nerve injuries that occur due to prone positioning during surgery typically do not present immediately in the recovery room. Instead, they often manifest after a period of time following the surgery. These injuries can take some time to become clinically evident, and in many cases, patients may not experience symptoms until several days after the procedure. In fact, peripheral nerve injuries from prone positioning during surgery typically become evident in 90% of cases within 7 days after the procedure. This delay in presentation underscores the importance of ongoing monitoring and follow-up care for patients who have undergone surgery in the prone position to detect and address any potential nerve injuries.

6. Answer B (Utilize a supraglottic device)

In the algorithm for managing the airway in patients in the prone position following unexpected extubation, one of the steps is to utilize a supraglottic device. Supraglottic devices, such as laryngeal mask airways (LMAs), play a crucial role in maintaining ventilation and oxygenation in situations where endotracheal intubation is compromised. They can quickly restore proper oxygenation while the anesthesia team assesses the situation and determines the best course of action. Supraglottic devices are particularly useful in scenarios like this, as they can be inserted without the need for direct visualization of the vocal cords, which can be challenging in the prone position.

Recommended literature

1. Kwee MM, Ho YH, Rozen WM. The prone position during surgery and its complications: a systematic review and evidence-based guidelines. Int Surg. 2015;100(2):292-303.
2. Feix B, Sturgess J. Anaesthesia in the prone position. Continuing Education in Anaesthesia Critical Care & Pain. 2014;14(6):291-7.
3. Edgcombe H, Carter K, Yarrow S. Anaesthesia in the prone position. BJA: British Journal of Anaesthesia. 2008;100(2):165-83.

SUCCINYLCHOLINE MYALGIAS

Questions:

1. **What is the primary mechanism of action of succinylcholine?**
   A. Inhibition of acetylcholinesterase
   B. Activation of acetylcholine (ACh) receptors
   C. Competitive acetylcholine antagonists
   D. Inhibition of muscle contraction

2. **Which of the following is NOT an adverse effect of succinylcholine?**
   A. Excessive salivation
   B. Malignant hyperthermia
   C. Muscle fasciculation
   D. Decreased intraocular pressure

3. **What is a potentially life-threatening complication associated with succinylcholine use related to mineral levels?**
   A. Hyperphosphatemia
   B. Hypernatremia
   C. Hyperkalemia
   D. Hypercalcemia

4. **What is the NOT recommended postoperative management strategy for succinylcholine-induced myalgias?**
   A. Muscle stretching exercises
   B. Vitamin C
   C. Lidocaine
   D. Neostigmine

5. **Succinylcholine myalgias may be severe and interfere with the return to normal activities of daily living.**
   A. True
   B. False

6. **A 62-year-old patient is scheduled to undergo a laparoscopic cholecystectomy under general anesthesia. The patient's medical history includes a diagnosis of gastroesophageal reflux disease (GERD) attributed to a hiatus hernia. Given the surgical procedure's requirements, the anesthesiologist plans to implement a Rapid Sequence Induction (RSI) technique. It's important to note that the patient has previously undergone surgical procedures where succinylcholine was utilized. On those occasions, the patient reported experiencing severe post-operative myalgias that significantly disrupted their ability to resume normal activities of daily living (ADLs). Which of the following is NOT a suggested method for preventing succinylcholine-induced myalgias?**
   A. Avoid the use of succinylcholine
   B. Using low-dose non-depolarizing muscle relaxants before sux
   C. Use a lower succinylcholine dose
   D. Administering vitamin C

Answers:

1. Answer B (Activation of acetylcholine receptors)

The primary mechanism of action of succinylcholine is the activation of acetylcholine receptors. Succinylcholine is a depolarizing neuromuscular blocking agent that acts as an acetylcholine receptor agonist. When it binds to the acetylcholine receptors on the motor endplate of muscle fibers, it causes depolarization and muscle contraction. However, succinylcholine is not metabolized by acetylcholinesterase, leading to persistent depolarization of the muscle fibers. This persistent depolarization eventually desensitizes the motor endplate to acetylcholine, resulting in paralysis rather than continued muscle contraction.

2. Answer D (Decreased intraocular pressure)

Decreased intraocular pressure is not among the recognized adverse effects of succinylcholine; instead, succinylcholine is known to potentially raise intraocular pressure, particularly concerning individuals with eye conditions. Succinylcholine, classified as a depolarizing neuromuscular blocking agent, is associated with an array of side effects, including excessive salivation, muscle fasciculation, jaw rigidity, and elevated intraocular pressure. Furthermore, it can give rise to more severe complications such as malignant hyperthermia, a life-threatening condition marked by a rapid increase in body temperature. It also encompasses autonomic symptoms like hypotension, flushing, tachycardia, and bradycardia, alongside potential occurrences of myoglobinuria/myoglobinemia, hypersensitivity reactions, and the frequently encountered myalgia side effect, which can persist for several days and result in substantial discomfort.

3. Answer C (Hyperkalemia)

A potentially life-threatening complication associated with succinylcholine use is hyperkalemia. Succinylcholine can trigger the release of intracellular potassium into the bloodstream, leading to elevated serum potassium levels. Hyperkalemia can have severe cardiac effects, potentially causing dangerous arrhythmias, cardiac arrest, and other life-threatening complications. Therefore, monitoring potassium levels and being prepared to manage hyperkalemia is crucial when using succinylcholine in clinical practice.

4. Answer D (Neostigmine)

The NOT recommended postoperative management strategy for succinylcholine-induced myalgias is Neostigmine. Neostigmine is primarily used for reversing the effects of non-depolarizing muscle relaxants by increasing acetylcholine levels at the neuromuscular junction. It is ineffective in preventing or managing the specific myalgias associated with succinylcholine use. In contrast, post-operative muscle stretching exercises, high-dose vitamin C, and lidocaine are potential strategies for addressing succinylcholine-induced myalgias.

5. Answer A (True)

Succinylcholine-induced myalgias can be severe and significantly interfere with a person's ability to resume normal activities of daily living. These myalgias are characterized by muscle pain and discomfort that may persist for several days after succinylcholine administration. This pain can be severe enough to impede a person's mobility, making it challenging to perform routine tasks and activities.

6. Answer C (Use lower succinylcholine dose)

The method that is NOT suggested for preventing succinylcholine-induced myalgias is using a lower succinylcholine dose. There are a range of effective strategies for myalgia prevention, including using low-dose non-depolarizing muscle relaxants before succinylcholine, lidocaine, and nonsteroidal anti-inflammatory drugs (NSAIDs). Additionally, a higher succinylcholine dose (1.5 mg/kg) has been proposed as it may reduce the occurrence of myalgias compared to a lower dose. Other methods, like muscle stretching exercises and vitamin C supplementation, have been reported to be effective. Pre-treatment with medications that interfere with intracellular calcium release, such as dantrolene, has shown promise in reducing myalgias. Furthermore, pre-treatment with calcium gluconate, which stabilizes cell membranes, has been protective. Comparative studies have suggested that induction of anesthesia with propofol may result in a decreased association of myalgias compared to thiopental. However, considering the various options, avoiding the use of succinylcholine and opting for alternative relaxants like rocuronium for Rapid Sequence Induction (RSI) may be the most favorable choice for preventing myalgias associated with succinylcholine use.

Recommended literature

1. Gulenay M, Mathai JK. Depolarizing Neuromuscular Blocking Drugs. [Updated 2022 Nov 17]. In: StatPearls [Internet]. Treasure Island (FL): StatPearls Publishing; 2022 Jan-. Available from: https://www.ncbi.nlm.nih.gov/books/NBK532996/.
2. Schreiber JU, Lysakowski C, Fuchs-Buder T, Tramèr MR. Prevention of succinylcholine-induced fasciculation and myalgia: a meta-analysis of randomized trials. Anesthesiology. 2005;103(4):877-884.

NEUROANESTHESIA

ACUTE SPINAL CORD INJURY

09
CHAPTER

Questions:

1. Which of the following is a sign commonly associated with acute Spinal Cord Injury (SCI)?

    A. Hypertension
    B. Tachycardia
    C. Bradycardia
    D. Hyperreflexia

2. What classification system is commonly used to assess the severity of SCI based on motor and sensory function preservation?

    A. Glasgow Coma Scale (GCS)
    B. American Spinal Injury (ASIA) impairment scale
    C. Modified Rankin Scale (MRS)
    D. Barthel Index

3. A patient with acute spinal cord injury exhibits an erection that is persistent and painful. What is this condition called?

    A. Priapism
    B. Progeria
    C. Prune-Belly Syndrome
    D. Prader-Willi syndrome

4. What should be the goal mean arterial pressure (MAP) to prevent secondary spinal cord injury in acute SCI patients?

    A. > 60
    B. > 70
    C. > 80
    D. > 90

5. Neurogenic shock is a potential complication of acute spinal cord injury characterized by hypotension and bradycardia.

    A. True
    B. False

6. A 38-year-old male was involved in a motor vehicle accident and sustained a traumatic injury to his cervical spine, resulting in acute spinal cord injury. He presents with flaccid paralysis of the lower limbs, loss of sensation below the level of injury, and diaphragmatic breathing. Upon assessment, his blood pressure is significantly reduced, and he exhibits bradycardia. The patient is immediately stabilized and transported to a specialized spinal cord injury center for further evaluation and treatment. In the management of this patient with acute spinal cord injury, which of the following is NOT a goal to prevent secondary complications?

    A. Hypoxemia
    B. Hypotension
    C. Hypoglycemia
    D. Hyperthermia

Answers:

1. Answer C (Bradycardia)

The sign commonly associated with acute Spinal Cord Injury (SCI) among the options provided is bradycardia. In SCI, there is often a loss of sympathetic tone, which normally helps maintain heart rate and blood pressure, leading to bradycardia and hypotension. This autonomic dysfunction is a result of the disruption of autonomic pathways in the spinal cord. Additionally, other signs such as diaphragmatic breathing, hypotension without an obvious cause, priapism, flaccid areflexia, and loss of pain response below a level can also be associated with SCI, reflecting various aspects of motor, sensory, and autonomic dysfunction that occur in individuals with spinal cord injuries.

2. Answer B (American Spinal Injury (ASIA) impairment scale)

The classification system commonly used to assess the severity of SCI based on motor and sensory function preservation is the American Spinal Injury (ASIA) impairment scale. This scale categorizes SCI into different grades ranging from A to E, each of which describes the extent of motor and sensory impairment. Grade A represents complete injury with no motor or sensory function preserved in the sacral segments S4-5, while Grade E indicates normal sensation and motor function in all segments. The ASIA impairment scale is widely utilized in clinical practice and research to standardize the assessment of SCI severity and guide treatment decisions.

3. Answer A (Priapism)

A patient with acute SCI exhibiting a persistent and painful erection is experiencing priapism. Priapism is a condition characterized by a prolonged and often painful erection that is unrelated to sexual arousal or stimulation. In the context of acute spinal cord injury, priapism can occur due to disruption of the autonomic nervous system, which controls sexual function, among other bodily functions. It is important to address priapism promptly to prevent potential complications.

4. Answer D (> 90)

The goal mean arterial pressure (MAP) to prevent secondary spinal cord injury in acute SCI patients is typically set at > 90 mm Hg. This elevated MAP is necessary to ensure adequate perfusion and oxygenation of the spinal cord, especially in the early stages following SCI. Maintaining a MAP above this threshold helps mitigate the risk of ischemia and further damage to the injured spinal cord. It's essential to monitor and manage blood pressure closely to achieve this goal, as inadequate perfusion can contribute to secondary injury in SCI patients.

5. Answer A (True)

Neurogenic shock is a potential complication of acute SCI characterized by both hypotension and bradycardia. This type of shock occurs due to the disruption of autonomic pathways in the spinal cord, specifically the sympathetic nervous system. When the sympathetic tone is lost, it results in vasodilation and decreased heart rate, leading to hypotension and bradycardia. Neurogenic shock is a significant concern in SCI patients and requires prompt medical attention and management to stabilize blood pressure and heart rate.

6. Answer C (Hypoglycemia)

The goal in the treatment of acute SCI is to prevent secondary complications that could exacerbate the injury or lead to additional problems. This includes preventing hypoxemia, hypotension, and hyperthermia, as these can all negatively impact the patient's condition. Additionally, maintaining normal blood glucose levels and preventing hyperglycemia is a crucial goal to prevent further complications in acute spinal cord injury management. Hyperglycemia can have adverse effects on the injured spinal cord and should be closely monitored and managed to optimize patient outcomes. Hypoglycemia can be harmful and should be avoided, but it is not a primary focus in preventing secondary complications in this context.

Recommended literature

1. Bonner S, Smith C. Initial management of acute spinal cord injury. Continuing Education in Anaesthesia Critical Care & Pain. 2013;13(6):224-31.
2. Dooney N, Dagal A. Anesthetic considerations in acute spinal cord trauma. Int J Crit Illn Inj Sci. 2011;1(1):36-43.

Neuroanesthesia
ANEURYSM COILING

09
CHAPTER

Questions:

1. **Which of the following is NOT a risk factor for developing intracranial aneurysms?**

   A. Smoking

   B. Hypertension

   C. Diabetes

   D. Marfan syndrome

2. **What is the typical initial symptom of subarachnoid hemorrhage due to aneurysm rupture?**

   A. Blurred vision

   B. Sudden onset of severe headache

   C. Muscle weakness

   D. Chest pain

3. **Which volatile anesthetic agent is preferred for neurovascular procedures due to its low potential for increasing cerebral blood flow and rapid offset?**

   A. Isoflurane

   B. Sevoflurane

   C. Desflurane

   D. Halothane

4. **What is the primary medical treatment for cerebral vasospasm following aneurysmal subarachnoid hemorrhage (SAH)?**

   A. Nimodipine

   B. Verapamil

   C. Lidocaine

   D. Heparin

5. **Most spontaneous (nontraumatic) subarachnoid hemorrhages are caused by a ruptured fusiform aneurysm.**

   A. True

   B. False

6. **A 58-year-old female patient presents to the hospital with a sudden, severe headache described as the "worst headache of her life." She has a history of hypertension and is a smoker. After a thorough evaluation, she was diagnosed with a subarachnoid hemorrhage (SAH) due to the rupture of an intracranial aneurysm. The decision is made to perform endovascular coiling to treat the aneurysm. The patient is scheduled for the procedure, and you, as the anesthesiologist, are responsible for providing appropriate anesthesia management. What is NOT appropriate anesthetic management for this patient undergoing endovascular coiling for an intracranial aneurysm?**

   A. Ventilation aims for mild hypocapnia to normocapnia

   B. Controlled hypertension is used in cases of iatrogenic vascular occlusion and acute thromboembolic stroke

   C. Propofol, remifentanil, and sevoflurane are a combination of choice

   D. Mild hypothermia has been shown to improve neurological outcome

Answers:

1. Answer C (Diabetes)

Intracranial aneurysms are associated with several risk factors, including smoking, hypertension, connective tissue disorders (such as Marfan syndrome and Ehlers–Danlos syndrome type IV), autosomal dominant polycystic kidney disease, neurofibromatosis type 1, coarctation of the aorta, and genetic predisposition. However, diabetes is not typically considered a risk factor for the development of intracranial aneurysms, so it is the correct choice as the option that is NOT a risk factor.

2. Answer B (Sudden onset of severe headache)

The typical initial symptom of subarachnoid hemorrhage (SAH) due to an aneurysm rupture is the sudden onset of severe headache. This headache is often described as the "worst headache of life" and is a key clinical feature of SAH. Other associated symptoms may include loss of consciousness, nausea and/or vomiting, nuchal rigidity, photophobia, and, in some cases, seizures. However, severe headache is the hallmark symptom that should raise suspicion of aneurysmal SAH.

3. Answer B (Sevoflurane)

Sevoflurane is the preferred choice for maintaining anesthesia during neurovascular procedures due to its low potential for increasing cerebral blood flow and rapid offset. All volatile agents have the potential to increase cerebral blood flow, cerebral blood volume, and intracranial pressure. However, sevoflurane is the preferred choice because it has a low potential for increasing cerebral blood flow and is associated with faster recovery and postoperative neurological assessment compared to other volatile agents.

4. Answer A (Nimodipine)

The primary medical treatment for cerebral vasospasm following aneurysmal SAH is nimodipine. Nimodipine is given orally and helps to prevent or treat cerebral vasospasm, which is a serious complication that can occur after SAH. It is a calcium channel blocker that specifically targets the blood vessels in the brain, helping to relax them and improve blood flow. This medication is considered a standard treatment in the management of SAH to reduce the risk of vasospasm-related complications.

5. Answer B (False)

Most spontaneous (nontraumatic) subarachnoid hemorrhages are not caused by ruptured fusiform aneurysms. In fact, most nontraumatic subarachnoid hemorrhages are caused by ruptured saccular aneurysms, also known as berry aneurysms. These saccular aneurysms are the most common cause of subarachnoid hemorrhage. Fusiform aneurysms, on the other hand, are characterized by a spindle-like shape and are less common than saccular aneurysms as a cause of subarachnoid hemorrhage.

6. Answer D (Mild hypothermia has been shown to improve neurological outcome)

Mild hypothermia is not considered appropriate anesthetic management for a patient undergoing endovascular coiling for an intracranial aneurysm. While hypothermia may be used in some surgical procedures to protect the brain and reduce metabolic demand, it is not typically employed during endovascular coiling. The goal of this procedure is to maintain normothermia to minimize the risk of complications.

Recommended literature

1. Deepak Sharma; Perioperative Management of Aneurysmal Subarachnoid Hemorrhage: A Narrative Review. Anesthesiology 2020; 133:1283–1305.
2. Campos JK, Lien BV, Wang AS, Lin LM. Advances in endovascular aneurysm management: coiling and adjunctive devices. Stroke Vasc Neurol. 2020;5(1):14-21. Published 2020 Mar 15.
3. Abd-Elsayed AA, Wehby AS, Farag E. Anesthetic management of patients with intracranial aneurysms. Ochsner J. 2014;14(3):418-425.

AUTONOMIC DYSREFLEXIA

09

CHAPTER

Questions:

1. Which of the following is a characteristic feature of autonomic dysreflexia (AD)?

   A. Tachycardia

   B. Hypertension

   C. Hyperthermia

   D. Vasodilation

2. In a patient with a spinal cord injury above T6, which of the following stimuli is most likely to trigger autonomic dysreflexia AD?

   A. Hyperglycemia

   B. Bright light

   C. Bladder distension

   D. Emotional stress

3. Which of the following interventions is NOT recommended for managing autonomic dysreflexia?

   A. Removing the noxious stimulus

   B. Administering nitroglycerin

   C. Elevating the head of the bed

   D. Initiating IV fluid bolus

4. Which of the following is a potentially life-threatening complication of autonomic dysreflexia?

   A. Hypotension

   B. Hypoglycemia

   C. Seizures

   D. Stroke

5. Supine with legs elevated is the recommended position for a patient experiencing autonomic dysreflexia.

   A. True

   B. False

6. A 45-year-old male with a history of spinal cord injury above the T6 level presents to the emergency department with a severe headache, hypertension, and bradycardia. The patient reports a sudden onset of symptoms while at home. On examination, the patient is alert and oriented. His blood pressure is 180/110 mmHg, heart rate is 50 beats per minute, and respiratory rate is 16 breaths per minute. Piloerection is noted above the level of injury, and the patient complains of a severe headache. There are no signs of trauma or infection at the site of injury. The patient is immediately placed in a seated position with the head elevated to 45 degrees. A Foley catheter is inserted to empty the bladder, which was found to be distended. The patient's symptoms improved slightly with these interventions, but his blood pressure remains elevated. Which of the following medications is a first-line treatment for autonomic dysreflexia in this patient?

   A. Phenylephrine

   B. Nitroglycerin

   C. Hydralazine

   D. Furosemide

Answers:

1. **Answer B (Hypertension)**

   Hypertension is a characteristic feature of autonomic dysreflexia (AD), a condition seen in individuals with spinal cord injuries at or above the T6 level. AD is triggered by noxious stimuli below the level of injury, such as bladder or bowel distension, leading to an uncoordinated sympathetic response. While tachycardia can also occur, bradycardia may be present due to simultaneous sympathetic and parasympathetic activation. Hyperthermia is not typical, and patients may exhibit cold skin due to peripheral vasoconstriction. Vasodilation is not a feature, as AD is marked by hypertension. Other signs and symptoms of AD include severe headache, piloerection above the level of injury, facial flushing, pallor, sweating in the lower body, visual disturbances, constricted pupils, nasal stuffiness, anxiety, nausea, vomiting, and dizziness.

2. **Answer C (Bladder distension)**

   In patients with spinal cord injuries above the T6 level, AD is most commonly triggered by noxious stimuli below the level of injury, such as bladder or bowel distension. These stimuli lead to an uncontrolled sympathetic response, resulting in hypertension, bradycardia, and other characteristic symptoms of AD. While loud noise, bright light, and emotional stress can trigger sympathetic responses, they are not typically associated with the development of AD in patients with spinal cord injuries. It is important to promptly identify and manage the triggering stimuli to prevent complications associated with AD.

3. **Answer D (Initiating IV fluid bolus)**

   Initiating IV fluid boluses is not recommended for managing AD because it can worsen hypertension. AD is characterized by an uncontrolled sympathetic response leading to hypertension, and giving IV fluids can exacerbate this condition. Instead, the primary goal of managing AD is to identify and remove the noxious stimulus, which is usually bladder or bowel distension. Administering vasodilators like nitroglycerin and elevating the head of the bed are appropriate interventions to help lower blood pressure in patients with AD. Therefore, while the other options are recommended interventions for AD, initiating IV fluid boluses should be avoided.

4. **Answer D (Stroke)**

   A potentially life-threatening complication of AD is stroke. Untreated AD can lead to severe hypertension, increasing the risk of complications such as intracranial hemorrhage. The higher the injury level, the greater the severity of the cardiovascular dysfunction, and there is a significantly increased risk of stroke by 300% to 400% in patients with AD. Hypotension, hypoglycemia, and seizures are not typical complications of AD. AD is characterized by uncontrolled sympathetic response leading to hypertension, bradycardia, and other symptoms.

5. **Answer B (False)**

   The recommended position for a patient experiencing AD is sitting upright with the legs dependent (dangling) to help reduce blood pressure. Elevating the head of the bed to 45 degrees can also help reduce blood pressure in a patient with AD. A supine position with legs elevated is not recommended for managing AD as it can potentially exacerbate hypertension. Any paraplegic or quadriplegic who complains of a severe headache should immediately be checked for possible autonomic dysreflexia by checking their blood pressure. If elevated, the patient should be moved to a sitting position with their legs dangling, and any constricting clothing or binders should be loosened or removed.

6. **Answer B (Nitroglycerin)**

   Nitroglycerin is the recommended initial emergency treatment for severe hypertension in patients with autonomic dysreflexia. One to two inches of nitroglycerin 2% paste should be placed on the skin above the level of the spinal cord injury. Nitroglycerin is a vasodilator that can help reduce blood pressure in patients with autonomic dysreflexia. Other acceptable antihypertensive treatments include nifedipine, sublingual captopril, sublingual clonidine, intravenous hydralazine, intravenous labetalol, phentolamine, sodium nitroprusside, diazoxide, prazosin, terazosin, among others. It is important to monitor the patient closely for signs of improvement and to avoid rapid decreases in blood pressure, which can lead to rebound hypotension. Repeated doses may be necessary, and the patient should be monitored for several hours after the initial episode to ensure stability.

Recommended literature

1. Allen KJ, Leslie SW. Autonomic Dysreflexia. [Updated 2022 Nov 28]. In: StatPearls [Internet]. Treasure Island (FL): StatPearls Publishing; 2022 Jan-. Available from: https://www.ncbi.nlm.nih.gov/books/NBK482434/
2. Petsas A, Drake J. Perioperative management for patients with a chronic spinal cord injury. BJA Education. 2015;15(3):123-30.

CHIARI MALFORMATION

Questions:

1. **Which anatomical structures are primarily affected by Arnold-Chiari malformation?**
   A. Frontal lobes
   B. Cerebellum
   C. Occipital lobes
   D. Temporal lobes

2. **What is the main diagnostic test used to evaluate patients with suspected Chiari malformation?**
   A. X-ray
   B. Ultrasound
   C. CT scan
   D. MRI

3. **What is the most common type of Chiari malformation?**
   A. Type 1 (CM-I)
   B. Type 2 (CM-II)
   C. Type 3 (CM-III)
   D. Type 4 (CM-IV)

4. **Patients with Chiari malformations are notoriously the group with the highest prevalence of allergy to?**
   A. Muscle relaxants
   B. Latex
   C. Chlorhexidine
   D. Antibiotics

5. **Hydrocephalus is a congenital condition that can lead to Chiari malformation.**
   A. True
   B. False

6. **A 38-year-old male patient with Arnold-Chiari malformation type 1,5 (ACM-1,5) presented for hip prosthesis implantation. He had previously undergone a general anesthesia procedure, during which difficult airway management and complications during awakening were encountered. Given these considerations, what type of anesthesia is preferable for this patient?**
   A. General anesthesia
   B. Spinal anesthesia
   C. Epidural anesthesia
   D. MAC anesthesia

Answers:

1. Answer B (Cerebellum)

Arnold-Chiari malformation primarily affects the anatomical structures of the cerebellum, brainstem, and craniocervical junction. In this condition, the cerebellar tonsil herniates down through the skull and into the spinal canal, leading to the obstruction of the normal flow of cerebrospinal fluid (CSF). This displacement of the cerebellar tonsil and associated anatomical anomalies involving the cerebellum and brainstem are characteristic features of Arnold-Chiari malformation.

2. Answer D (MRI (Magnetic Resonance Imaging))

Magnetic Resonance Imaging (MRI) is the primary and most effective diagnostic tool for evaluating Chiari malformation. MRI provides detailed and high-resolution images of the brain, spinal cord, and cranial anatomy, allowing healthcare professionals to visualize the exact location and extent of the cerebellar tonsillar herniation, as well as any associated structural abnormalities. Unlike X-rays or CT scans, which primarily provide information on bone structures, an MRI can capture soft tissues and CSF flow dynamics, making it the preferred choice for diagnosing Chiari malformation.

3. Answer A (Type 1 (CM-I))

Chiari malformation type 1 (CM-I) is the most frequently encountered form of this condition. In CM-I, the lower part of the cerebellum, known as the cerebellar tonsils, protrudes downward through the foramen magnum, which is the opening at the base of the skull. This type is often discovered incidentally during medical examinations or imaging studies for unrelated conditions. Many individuals with CM-I may have no noticeable symptoms or only mild symptoms, and it is not typically considered life-threatening. In contrast, the other types of Chiari malformation (CM-II, CM-III, and CM-IV) are less common and often associated with more severe neurological and developmental issues. CM-II, for example, is almost always accompanied by myelomeningocele, a form of spina bifida, and is generally more serious than CM-I. CM-III and CM-IV also involve complex structural abnormalities and are associated with severe neurological defects.

4. Answer B (Latex)

Latex allergy is a significant concern for patients with Chiari malformations. This group has the highest prevalence of latex allergy due to immunological mechanisms, including Type I and Type IV hypersensitivity reactions. Clinical manifestations of latex allergy can vary and may include symptoms such as angioedema, rhinitis, conjunctivitis, asthma, and even severe reactions like anaphylaxis. Moreover, individuals with latex allergy may also experience cross-reactions with allergens found in certain fruits, a condition known as latex-fruit syndrome. Common fruits associated with these cross-reactions include banana, avocado, kiwi, papaya, passion fruit, melon, pineapple, peach, chestnut, and others.

5. Answer A (True)

Hydrocephalus can be a congenital condition that may lead to Chiari malformation. Hydrocephalus is characterized by the accumulation of excess CSF within the brain's ventricles. When there is an increased volume of CSF, it can create pressure within the skull, leading to various structural changes and abnormalities in the brain. One possible consequence of hydrocephalus is the displacement of brain tissues, including the cerebellar tonsils, downward through the foramen magnum. This downward displacement is a defining characteristic of Chiari malformation, particularly Chiari malformation type 1 (CM-I). Therefore, individuals born with congenital hydrocephalus are at an increased risk of developing Chiari malformation as a result of the associated changes in brain anatomy caused by the excess CSF. However, it's important to note that not all cases of hydrocephalus lead to Chiari malformation, and the relationship between these conditions can vary.

6. Answer C (Epidural anesthesia)

In this case, epidural anesthesia was chosen as the preferred approach. This decision was based on several factors. Firstly, it aimed to ensure stable intracranial pressure (ICP) and hemodynamics throughout the procedure. Additionally, this approach helped avoid the respiratory complications experienced in the previous general anesthesia (GA) session. Patients with ACM malformation can develop obstructive apnea and central apnea during GA. To mitigate this risk, an awake fiberoptic intubation was considered, but given the patient's history, an extradural approach was favored. This approach provided stability in hemodynamics, minimized fluctuations in ICP, and allowed the patient to remain awake and cooperative. Furthermore, the risk of respiratory depression was reduced, as opioids were not administered. While spinal anesthesia (SA) was an alternative, it posed greater hemodynamic impact and was less controllable compared to epidural anesthesia. Accidental dural puncture was a potential concern, but the expert anesthesiologist minimized this risk during catheter placement.

Recommended literature

1. Coviello A, Golino L, Posillipo C, Marra A, Tognù A, Servillo G. Anesthetic management in a patient with Arnold-Chiari malformation type 1,5: A case report. Clin Case Rep. 2022;10(2):e05194.
2. Anesthetic management of a patient with Arnold-Chiari malformation type I with associated syringomyelia: A case report Anesth Pain Med. 2012;7(2):166-169.

CRANIOTOMY

Questions:

1. **Which condition is NOT an indication for craniotomy?**

   A. Brain aneurysm

   B. Pituitary adenomas

   C. Cervical spine fracture

   D. Brain abscess

2. **What is one of the contraindications for craniotomy mentioned in the text?**

   A. Young age

   B. Hypertension

   C. Advanced age

   D. Mild bleeding disorders

3. **What is the primary purpose of cortical stimulation and motor mapping during craniotomy?**

   A. To assess the patient's cognitive function

   B. To locate the eloquent motor areas with millimeter accuracy

   C. To monitor the patient's blood pressure

   D. To facilitate rapid emergence from anesthesia

4. **In which surgical position is there an increased risk of venous air embolism during a craniotomy?**

   A. Supine

   B. Prone

   C. Lateral decubitus

   D. Sitting

5. **Pressure-controlled ventilation is the preferred mode of ventilation during craniotomy procedures.**

   A. True

   B. False

6. **You are an anesthesiologist in charge of a patient undergoing a craniotomy to remove a brain tumor. The surgery has gone well, and now it's time to focus on the emergence phase to ensure a smooth transition from anesthesia to wakefulness while maintaining the patient's safety and neurological assessment. Key objectives during this critical phase include early neurological assessment, minimizing factors that could lead to intracranial pressure (ICP) spikes, providing adequate analgesia, and preventing postoperative nausea and vomiting (PONV) that may lead to increased ICP. As the surgery nears its conclusion, you start considering the crucial steps for a successful emergence from anesthesia, especially when dealing with craniotomy patients. What is NOT a good strategy for a smooth emergence from craniotomy surgery?**

   A. Continuing dexmetomitidin infusion after extubation

   B. Continuing midazolam infusion after extubation

   C. Continuing remifentanil infusion after extubation

   D. Exchanging the endotracheal tube for an LMA prior to extubation

Answers:

1. Answer C (Cervical spine fracture)

A craniotomy is a surgical procedure involving the removal of a part of the skull to access and treat intracranial conditions. The list of indications includes various conditions that can necessitate craniotomy. However, a cervical spine fracture is a condition involving damage to the vertebrae in the neck, and it does not typically require a craniotomy. Treatment for cervical spine fractures typically involves orthopedic or neurosurgical interventions specific to the spine and neck rather than intracranial surgery.

2. Answer C (Advanced age)

Advanced age is one of the contraindications for craniotomy. In the case of advanced age, it implies that older individuals may face increased surgical risks associated with craniotomy, and therefore, careful consideration is needed when determining the appropriateness of this procedure in such patients. Other contraindications listed in the text include poor functional status, severe cardiopulmonary disease, severe systemic collapse, pathologies that can be addressed by a single burr hole, altered preoperative coagulation parameters, and bleeding disorders.

3. Answer B (To locate the eloquent motor areas with millimeter accuracy)

Cortical stimulation and motor mapping are surgical techniques used to precisely identify the eloquent motor areas of the brain during craniotomy procedures. These techniques help the surgical team locate critical motor functions with high precision, often down to millimeter accuracy. This is crucial for minimizing damage to healthy brain tissue while removing tumors or addressing other intracranial pathologies.

4. Answer D (Sitting)

During a sitting craniotomy, the patient is positioned in a seated posture, with the head typically elevated above the level of the right atrium. This position creates a situation where the surgical site is often at or above the level of the right atrium, making it more susceptible to venous air embolism. Venous air embolism can occur when air enters the venous system, potentially leading to complications such as reduced end-tidal carbon dioxide, arrhythmias, right heart failure, and cardiovascular collapse.

5. Answer A (True)

Pressure-controlled ventilation is preferred over other ventilation modes in craniotomy. This preference is primarily due to its ability to avoid elevated intrathoracic pressure, which can increase intracranial pressure (ICP) in patients undergoing craniotomy. By using pressure-controlled ventilation, the anesthesiologist can maintain more precise control over the patient's ventilation and avoid potentially harmful increases in ICP, which is crucial for the safety and success of the surgery.

6. Answer B (Continuing Midazolam infusion after extubation)

In the context of craniotomy surgery, it is not advisable to continue a midazolam infusion after extubation as this long-acting sedative can lead to prolonged postoperative sedation, impairing the patient's ability to awaken promptly and assess their neurological status accurately. Conversely, strategies like continuing a dexmetomitidin infusion post-extubation, continuing a remifentanil infusion, and exchanging the endotracheal tube for an LMA are more suitable. Dexmetomitidin and remifentanil are short-acting agents that allow for a smoother emergence without causing prolonged sedation, and the use of an LMA can facilitate a comfortable transition from mechanical ventilation to spontaneous breathing. Minimizing the use of long-acting sedatives is essential for a quicker and smoother emergence, ensuring an accurate postoperative neurological assessment in craniotomy patients.

Recommended literature

1. Fernández-de Thomas RJ, De Jesus O. Craniotomy. [Updated 2022 Apr 9]. In: StatPearls [Internet]. Treasure Island (FL): StatPearls Publishing; 2022 Jan-. Available from: https://www.ncbi.nlm.nih.gov/books/NBK560922/
2. Keown, T., Bhangu, S. and Solanki3, S. (2022) Anaesthesia for craniotomy and brain tumour resection, WFSA. Available at: https://resources.wfsahq.org/atotw/anaesthesia-for-craniotomy-and-brain-tumour-resection/ (Accessed: January 18, 2023).
3. Dinsmore J. Anaesthesia for elective neurosurgery. BJA: British Journal of Anaesthesia. 2007;99(1):68-74.

EPILEPSY

Questions:

1. **What is the definition of epilepsy?**
   A. A single unprovoked seizure
   B. Two or more unprovoked seizures
   C. A seizure triggered by an external factor
   D. A seizure with loss of consciousness

2. **Which of the following is NOT a common symptom of epilepsy?**
   A. Staring spell
   B. Uncontrollable jerking movements
   C. Persistent headache
   D. Temporary confusion

3. **Which of the following can usually NOT increase seizure frequency in people with epilepsy?**
   A. High alcohol consumption
   B. Daily caffeine intake
   C. Tobacco smoking more than 20 cigarettes daily
   D. Sleep deprivation

4. **Which antiepileptic agent is associated with gingival hypertrophy and excess hair growth as side effects?**
   A. Phenytoin
   B. Sodium valproate
   C. Carbamazepine
   D. Lamotrigine

5. **Tonic seizures are characterized by sudden, brief muscle contractions and jerks.**
   A. True
   B. False

6. **A 35-year-old patient with a known history of epilepsy is scheduled for elective surgery to address a non-emergent medical condition. The patient has been on antiepileptic drug therapy and has experienced controlled seizures for several years. The surgical procedure is planned to be conducted under general anesthesia. Which factor is NOT known to precipitate seizures in patients with epilepsy?**
   A. Hypoxia
   B. Hyponatremia
   C. Hyperglycemia
   D. Uremia

Answers:

1. Answer B (Two or more unprovoked seizures)

Epilepsy is defined as a neurological disorder characterized by the occurrence of two or more unprovoked seizures. It is important to emphasize the term "unprovoked," which means that these seizures are not triggered by specific external factors, such as fever, trauma, or metabolic disturbances. While a single unprovoked seizure may be a concern, epilepsy is typically diagnosed when an individual experiences recurrent seizures, indicating an ongoing and chronic neurological condition. Seizures in epilepsy can manifest in various ways, including loss of consciousness, muscle jerking, staring spells, and other unusual behaviors, depending on the specific type of seizure.

2. Answer C (Persistent headache)

Persistent headache is not a common symptom of epilepsy. Epilepsy is primarily characterized by recurrent seizures, which can manifest in various forms such as staring spells, uncontrollable jerking movements, temporary confusion, loss of consciousness, stiff muscles, and psychological symptoms like fear or déjà vu. While some individuals with epilepsy may experience headaches, they are not considered a primary or defining symptom of the condition. It's important to differentiate between headaches and seizures, as they arise from different neurological mechanisms. Seizures result from abnormal electrical activity in the brain, whereas headaches can stem from various causes, including tension, migraines, or other medical conditions unrelated to epilepsy.

3. Answer B (Daily caffeine intake)

While high alcohol consumption, smoking more than 20 cigarettes daily, and sleep deprivation are known factors that can potentially increase seizure frequency in people with epilepsy, daily caffeine intake is typically not considered a significant risk factor for worsening seizures. Caffeine is a stimulant commonly found in coffee, tea, and some soft drinks. While excessive caffeine intake can lead to jitteriness, nervousness, or other side effects, it is generally not associated with a substantial increase in seizure frequency in most individuals with epilepsy. However, as with any substance, individual responses to caffeine may vary, and some people may be more sensitive to its effects.

4. Answer A (Phenytoin)

Gingival hypertrophy and excess hair growth are side effects commonly associated with the use of phenytoin, which is an antiepileptic agent. These side effects can occur as a result of long-term phenytoin therapy and may affect some individuals taking the medication.

5. Answer B (False)

Tonic seizures are not characterized by sudden, brief muscle contractions and jerks. In fact, tonic seizures are quite different in nature. Tonic seizures involve sudden and sustained muscle stiffness or contractions, and they are typically not associated with rapid jerking movements. These seizures can lead to a person's body becoming rigid, often causing them to fall if they are standing when the seizure occurs. On the other hand, seizures characterized by sudden, brief muscle contractions and jerks are typically referred to as myoclonic seizures. Myoclonic seizures involve rapid, involuntary muscle jerks, which can affect various parts of the body. These jerks can be quite brief and may occur singly or in a series.

6. Answer C (Hyperglycemia)

Seizures in individuals with epilepsy can be provoked by various factors, including hypoglycemia, hypoxemia, hypercarbia, hyponatremia, hypocalcemia, hypomagnesemia, exposure to toxins such as those associated with uremic or hepatic encephalopathy, the dialysis disequilibrium syndrome, and porphyria. These factors can lower the seizure threshold, making seizures more likely to occur. While extreme blood sugar fluctuations can have neurological effects, seizures due to hyperglycemia are not a common manifestation in individuals with epilepsy.

Recommended literature

1. Pollard BJ, Kitchen, G. Handbook of Clinical Anaesthesia. Fourth Edition. CRC Press. 2018. 978-1-4987-6289-2.
2. Carter, E.L., Adapa, R.M., 2015. Adult epilepsy and anaesthesia. BJA Education 15, 111–117.

Neuroanesthesia
HYDROCEPHALUS

Questions:

1. **What is the primary mechanism underlying hydrocephalus?**
   - A. Excessive blood circulation in the brain
   - B. Accumulation of cerebrospinal fluid
   - C. Swelling of brain tissues
   - D. Infection in the meninges

2. **What is NOT a type of hydrocephalus?**
   - A. Communicating hydrocephalus
   - B. Obstructive hydrocephalus
   - C. Normal pressure hydrocephalus
   - D. Low-pressure hydrocephalus

3. **What is NOT the symptom often observed in young and middle-aged adults with hydrocephalus?**
   - A. Urinary incontinence
   - B. Headache
   - C. Lethargy
   - D. Unusually large head

4. **What is the long-term treatment option for hydrocephalus involving placement of a ventricular catheter?**
   - A. External ventricular drain
   - B. Ventriculoperitoneal shunt
   - C. Ventriculopleural shunt
   - D. Ventriculoatrial shunt

5. **Infants and older adults are more commonly affected by hydrocephalus.**
   - A. True
   - B. False

6. **You are the anesthesiologist in charge of a pregnant patient who has a ventriculoperitoneal (VP) shunt due to hydrocephalus resulting from trauma. The patient's intracranial pressure (ICP) is currently within the normal range due to the shunt. The patient is scheduled for a caesarean section, and you need to determine the most appropriate anesthesia approach. What statement is true about spinal anesthesia in this case?**
   - A. Spinal anesthesia is not an absolute contraindication
   - B. Spinal anesthesia is a contraindication
   - C. Spinal anesthesia is an option only if the mother signs a special informed consent
   - D. Spinal analgesia is an option if you use meticulous antibiotic prophylaxis

347

Answers:

1. **Answer B (Accumulation of cerebrospinal fluid)**

   The primary mechanism underlying hydrocephalus is the accumulation of cerebrospinal fluid (CSF) in the ventricular system of the brain. Hydrocephalus occurs when there is an imbalance between the production of CSF in the brain's ventricles and the absorption or drainage of CSF. This imbalance leads to an excess of CSF, which accumulates within the brain, causing increased intracranial pressure (ICP). The increased pressure can compress brain tissues and structures, potentially leading to various neurological symptoms and complications associated with hydrocephalus.

2. **Answer D (Low-pressure hydrocephalus)**

   The four main types of hydrocephalus are obstructive hydrocephalus, communicating hydrocephalus, normal pressure hydrocephalus (NPH), and hypersecretory hydrocephalus. Obstructive hydrocephalus is characterized by a physical obstruction in the flow of CSF, often caused by tumors or other blockages. Communicating hydrocephalus involves issues with the absorption or circulation of CSF in the subarachnoid space, not necessarily within the ventricles themselves. NPH is a specific subtype of communicating hydrocephalus characterized by ventricular enlargement with relatively normal intracranial pressure and a triad of symptoms, including gait disturbance, urinary incontinence, and cognitive decline. While "low-pressure hydrocephalus" may be encountered as a descriptive term in some contexts, it is not a formal type of hydrocephalus classification, and hydrocephalus is more commonly categorized into the aforementioned types based on the underlying mechanisms of CSF flow disruption and clinical features.

3. **Answer D (Unusually large head)**

   An unusually large head (macrocephaly) is not a symptom commonly observed in young and middle-aged adults with hydrocephalus. Hydrocephalus typically presents with a variety of neurological symptoms such as headache, lethargy, loss of coordination or balance, loss of bladder control or frequent urination, vision problems, and decline in memory, concentration, and other thinking skills. In contrast, macrocephaly is more commonly associated with hydrocephalus in infants and young children, where the rapid accumulation of cerebrospinal fluid can cause the head to enlarge.

4. **Answer B (Ventriculoperitoneal shunt)**

   The long-term treatment option for hydrocephalus involving the placement of a ventricular catheter is a ventriculoperitoneal (VP) shunt. In this surgical procedure, a catheter is inserted into the cerebral ventricles to bypass any obstruction or malfunctioning arachnoid villi that may be preventing the normal drainage of CSF. The excess CSF is then drained into the peritoneal cavity, where it can be absorbed and reabsorbed by the body. This helps to alleviate the increased intracranial pressure associated with hydrocephalus and allows for the continuous drainage of excess CSF to prevent further buildup. While other shunt options, such as ventriculoatrial and ventriculopleural shunts, are available, the ventriculoperitoneal shunt is a common choice for the long-term management of hydrocephalus.

5. **Answer A (True)**

   Hydrocephalus can indeed occur at any age, but it is more commonly observed in infants and older adults, with a higher prevalence in individuals over the age of 60. Infants may develop hydrocephalus due to congenital factors or complications of premature birth, while older adults are at risk of acquired hydrocephalus, which may result from various underlying causes.

6. **Answer A (Spinal anesthesia is not an absolute contraindication)**

   In patients with CSF shunts, such as VP shunts, spinal anesthesia is not an absolute contraindication, although it is often approached cautiously due to concerns about the potential for shunt contamination or CNS infection. Importantly, there is no conclusive evidence to suggest that dural puncture during a spinal anesthetic compromises the function of the shunt. Obtaining informed consent from the patient is a fundamental requirement for any medical procedure, including spinal anesthesia, irrespective of the presence of a shunt. Additionally, antibiotic prophylaxis is commonly prescribed before such procedures. While antibiotics are typically administered to reduce the risk of wound infection, their effectiveness in preventing infection within the CSF pathways is limited due to the restricted penetration of many antibiotics into the cerebrospinal fluid.

Recommended literature

1. Krovvidi H, Flint G, Williams AV. Perioperative management of hydrocephalus. BJA Educ. 2018;18(5):140-146.
2. Pollard BJ, Kitchen G. Handbook of Clinical Anaesthesia. 4th ed. Taylor & Francis group; 2018. Chapter 14 Neurosurgery, Chapman E.

MÉNIÈRE'S DISEASE

09
CHAPTER

Questions:

1. Which of the following is NOT a common symptom of Ménière's disease?
   A. Fluctuating hearing loss
   B. Tinnitus
   C. Blurred vision
   D. Aural fullness

2. How long can a single episode of vertigo during Ménière's disease last?
   A. Less than 5 minutes
   B. Up to 30 minutes
   C. Several days
   D. 20 minutes to 24 hours

3. Which of the following is NOT a diagnostic criteria essential for confirming Ménière's disease?
   A. Hearing loss in the affected ear
   B. Fluctuating aural symptoms
   C. Two episodes of vertigo
   D. Family history of balance problems

4. What dietary modification is often recommended as a part of Ménière's disease management?
   A. Potassium restriction
   B. Sodium restriction
   C. Low sugar diet
   D. Low-fat diet

5. Thiazide diuretics are a commonly used treatment option for some patients with Ménière's disease.
   A. True
   B. False

6. A 45-year-old woman presents to the clinic with a history of recurrent episodes of vertigo, tinnitus, and fluctuating hearing loss in her right ear. She reports experiencing at least two spontaneous attacks of vertigo, each lasting between 20 minutes to 12 hours. On one occasion, an audiogram confirmed sensorineural hearing loss in her right ear during an episode of vertigo. Additionally, she has been experiencing fluctuating aural symptoms, including hearing loss, tinnitus, and a feeling of fullness in her right ear. Other potential causes of her symptoms, such as infections or structural abnormalities, have been ruled out by various diagnostic tests. Based on these findings, the patient is diagnosed with Ménière's disease. What type of medication should patients with Ménière's disease generally avoid?
   A. Betahistine
   B. Dramamine
   C. Hydrochlorothiazide
   D. Alka-Seltzer

Answers:

1. **Answer C (Blurred vision)**

   Blurred vision is not a common symptom of Ménière's disease. This inner ear disorder is primarily characterized by intermittent vertigo, tinnitus, fluctuating sensorineural hearing loss, and aural fullness. While Ménière's disease can have a substantial impact on balance and hearing, it does not typically manifest as blurred vision, which may be indicative of other medical conditions or unrelated eye issues.

2. **Answer D (20 minutes to 24 hours)**

   A single episode of vertigo during Ménière's disease can last from 20 minutes to 24 hours. This vertigo is characterized by sudden and severe spinning dizziness and is one of the hallmark symptoms of Ménière's disease. It typically has a relatively extended duration compared to other causes of vertigo, making it a distinctive condition feature.

3. **Answer D (Family history of balance problems)**

   The diagnosis of Ménière's disease relies on specific criteria that include experiencing two or more spontaneous attacks of vertigo, each lasting between 20 minutes to 12 hours, along with documented fluctuating low- to medium-frequency sensorineural hearing loss in the affected ear on at least one occasion before, during, or after one of these vertigo episodes, and the presence of fluctuating aural symptoms (such as hearing loss, tinnitus, or fullness) in the affected ear. Additionally, it is crucial to exclude other potential causes of these symptoms through various diagnostic tests. While family medical history can be relevant in understanding a patient's overall health, it is not among the primary diagnostic criteria for Ménière's disease.

4. **Answer B (Sodium restriction)**

   Dietary modification is an important aspect of Ménière's disease management. Sodium restriction is often recommended as part of the management plan for individuals with Ménière's disease. Reducing sodium intake can help regulate fluid balance in the body, potentially reducing the fluid buildup in the inner ear, which is believed to contribute to the symptoms of Ménière's disease. Additionally, caffeine restriction or elimination may also be advised, as caffeine can be a trigger for some individuals with Ménière's disease. These dietary modifications can help in symptom management and improve the overall quality of life for Ménière's disease patients.

5. **Answer A (True)**

   Thiazide diuretics can be considered a treatment option for individuals with Ménière's disease, particularly if fluid buildup in the inner ear is believed to contribute to their symptoms. However, the choice of treatment should be individualized based on the patient's specific symptoms, medical history, and response to other treatment options. It's important to note that while thiazide diuretics may be effective for some patients, they may not be the treatment of choice for everyone with Ménière's disease.

6. **Answer D (Alka-Seltzer)**

   Patients with Ménière's disease should avoid medications that can potentially exacerbate their symptoms. Alka-Seltzer is an antacid that contains sodium, which can lead to water retention. Water retention can interfere with the regulation of inner ear fluid, which is believed to be a factor in Ménière's disease. Therefore, Alka-Seltzer, as well as other medications and substances high in sodium, should be avoided by individuals with Ménière's disease to help manage their condition and minimize symptoms.

Recommended literature

1. Koenen L, Andaloro C. Meniere Disease. [Updated 2022 Sep 30]. In: StatPearls [Internet]. Treasure Island (FL): StatPearls Publishing; 2022 Jan-. Available from: https://www.ncbi.nlm.nih.gov/books/NBK536955/.
2. Kersbergen CJ, Ward BK. A Historical Perspective on Surgical Manipulation of the Membranous Labyrinth for Treatment of Meniere's Disease. Frontiers in Neurology. 2021;12.
3. Basura GJ, Adams ME, Monfared A, Schwartz SR, Antonelli PJ, Burkard R, et al. Clinical Practice Guideline: Ménière's Disease. Otolaryngology-Head and Neck Surgery. 2020;162(2_suppl):S1-S55.

Neuroanesthesia
PITUITARY SURGERY

Questions:

1. **What is the primary indication for surgical resection in patients with functioning pituitary adenomas?**
   - A. Visual loss
   - B. Hypertension
   - C. Hormone excess
   - D. Hypopituitarism

2. **What is the recommended position for the patient during transsphenoidal pituitary surgery, and why is it chosen?**
   - A. Supine position to minimize blood loss
   - B. Trendelenburg position to prevent venous air embolism
   - C. Head-up position to facilitate drainage but increase the risk of venous air embolism
   - D. Left lateral decubitus position to aid in tumor visualization

3. **Which anesthesia technique is favored for rapid recovery and neurologic examination after transsphenoidal pituitary surgery?**
   - A. Inhalation anesthesia with isoflurane
   - B. Propofol infusion without opioids
   - C. Remifentanil with propofol or a volatile agent
   - D. Dexmedetomidine infusion

4. **Which complication is more likely to occur in patients in the postoperative phase after pituitary surgery?**
   - A. Diabetes insipidus
   - B. Panhypopituitarism
   - C. Cushing's disease
   - D. Visual disturbances

5. **Ketorolac is an analgesic of choice for postoperative analgesia in patients undergoing transsphenoidal pituitary surgery.**
   - A. True
   - B. False

6. **During the transsphenoidal pituitary surgery in which a 45-year-old female with acromegaly was positioned in a head-up orientation for improved surgical access and reduced bleeding, a lumbar drain was placed after anesthesia induction. Anesthesia was maintained using remifentanil and sevoflurane to ensure hemodynamic stability and rapid emergence. Mid-surgery, the surgeon requested the anesthesiologist to inject sterile preservative-free saline into the lumbar drain. What is the logic behind this request?**
   - A. To induce hypothermia
   - B. To flush out the spinal drain
   - C. To move the pituitary toward the surgeon
   - D. To check for cerebrospinal fluid leaks

Answers:

1. Answer C (Hormone excess)

The primary indication for surgical resection in patients with symptomatic pituitary adenomas is hormone excess. Pituitary adenomas can be classified as functioning or nonfunctioning based on whether they secrete hormones. Functioning adenomas produce excessive amounts of hormones, leading to various clinical symptoms related to hormone excess. Surgical resection aims to remove or reduce the hormone-secreting tumor, thereby alleviating the symptoms associated with hormone excess.

2. Answer C (Head-up position to facilitate drainage but increase the risk of venous air embolism)

The recommended position for the patient during transsphenoidal pituitary surgery is the head-up position. This position involves elevating the head and upper body above the level of the heart. The primary reason for using the head-up position is to facilitate drainage and minimize blood flow to the surgical field, which helps to reduce bleeding during the procedure. However, it's important to note that the head-up position does come with an increased risk of venous air embolism (VAE). VAE occurs when air enters the venous system and can be a potentially serious complication. Elevating the head can create a situation where air can be drawn into venous vessels, especially if there is a breach in the surgical field or if the patient is in a sitting position. Therefore, while the head-up position helps with drainage and visualization, it must be managed carefully to prevent VAE.

3. Answer C (Remifentanil with propofol or a volatile agent)

The anesthesia technique favored for rapid recovery and neurologic examination after transsphenoidal pituitary surgery typically involves using remifentanil in combination with propofol or a volatile agent. Remifentanil is an ultra-short-acting opioid analgesic, and when used in combination with propofol or a volatile agent, it allows for rapid emergence from anesthesia. This combination provides excellent hemodynamic stability, rapid recovery, and the ability to conduct neurologic assessments shortly after the surgery. It is particularly advantageous for procedures like pituitary surgery, where it's essential to assess neurologic function and cognitive status promptly after the procedure.

4. Answer A (Diabetes insipidus)

Diabetes insipidus (DI) is more likely to occur in the post-operative phase after pituitary surgery. Transient DI is almost always present after surgery due to surgical manipulation of the pituitary stalk. However, this DI is expected to be transient and usually resolves or transitions to a milder form over the first-week post-surgery. Therefore, patients may experience DI in the immediate post-operative phase.

5. Answer B (False)

Ketorolac is not typically the analgesic of choice for postoperative analgesia in patients undergoing transsphenoidal pituitary surgery. While ketorolac is a nonsteroidal anti-inflammatory drug (NSAID) that can provide pain relief, it carries a theoretical risk of bleeding due to its antiplatelet effects. In the postoperative period after pituitary surgery, it's important to manage pain effectively while minimizing the risk of bleeding and other complications. Therefore, opioids are often used for postoperative pain control in these patients, and the choice of analgesic should be made considering the individual patient's condition and any contraindications.

6. Answer C (To move the pituitary toward the surgeon)

The logic behind the surgeon's request to inject sterile preservative-free saline into the lumbar drain during the transsphenoidal pituitary surgery in a head-up position is to move the pituitary toward the surgeon. Injecting sterile saline into the lumbar drain can temporarily change the cerebrospinal fluid (CSF) pressure and volume dynamics. This maneuver is often used to manipulate the position of the pituitary gland within the surgical field, allowing for better visualization and access during the procedure. It can help the surgeon by moving the pituitary gland closer to its working area, facilitating the resection of the pituitary adenoma while minimizing the risk of injury to surrounding structures.

Recommended literature

1. Dunn LK, Nemergut EC. Anesthesia for transsphenoidal pituitary surgery. Curr Opin Anaesthesiol. 2013;26(5):549-554.
2. Griffiths S, Perks A. The Hypothalamic Pituitary Axis Part 2: Anaesthesia For Pituitary Surgery. WFSA. Published July 26, 2010. Accessed January 19, 2023. https://resources.wfsahq.org/atotw/the-hypothalamic-pituitary-axis-part-2-anaesthesia-for-pituitary-surgery/

Neuroanesthesia

POSTERIOR FOSSA SURGERY

Questions:

1. **What structures surround the posterior fossa inferiorly and posteriorly?**
   A. The petrosal and mastoid components of the temporal bone
   B. The dorsum sellae and basilar portion of the occipital bone (clivus)
   C. The dural layer (tentorium cerebelli)
   D. The occipital bone

2. **Which tumor is most commonly found in the posterior fossa?**
   A. Cerebellar astrocytoma
   B. Brainstem glioma
   C. Medulloblastoma
   D. Hemangioblastoma

3. **What can an obstruction in the cerebral aqueduct lead to?**
   A. Epidermoid cyst
   B. Trigeminal neuralgia
   C. Hydrocephalus and increased intracranial pressure
   D. Quadriplegia

4. **What is the primary purpose of SSEP monitoring during posterior fossa surgery?**
   A. Evaluating cerebellar function
   B. Assessing cerebral perfusion pressure
   C. Monitoring cerebral function
   D. Evaluating motor function

5. **Intraoperative, neuromuscular blocking agents should be used to minimize surrounding interference with SSEP monitoring.**
   A. True
   B. False

6. **A 24-year-old man recently underwent posterior fossa surgery while in a prone position for resection of a vermian tumor. You are reviewing potential complications and their management with the medical team. Which of the following is NOT a common possible complication of this type of surgery?**
   A. Macroglossia
   B. Quadriplegia
   C. Pneumocephalus
   D. Exophthalmos

Answers:

1. **Answer D (The occipital bone)**

   The structures that surround the posterior fossa inferiorly and posteriorly are primarily composed of the occipital bone. This bony structure forms both the lower (inferior) and back (posterior) boundaries of the posterior fossa, providing vital structural support and protection for the contained structures, which include the brainstem, cerebellum, and lower cranial nerves. Additionally, the posterior fossa is further bordered by the dorsum sellae and basilar portion of the occipital bone anteriorly, the petrosal and mastoid components of the temporal bone laterally, and the dural layer known as the tentorium cerebelli superiorly, collectively creating its distinct anatomical confines.

2. **Answer C (Medulloblastoma)**

   Medulloblastoma is the most commonly found tumor in the posterior fossa. This malignancy primarily affects the cerebellum, which is located in the posterior fossa. Medulloblastomas are highly aggressive and are one of the most common malignant brain tumors in children. They typically require surgical intervention and may be part of a multimodal treatment approach that includes surgery, radiation therapy, and chemotherapy. While other tumors listed, such as cerebellar astrocytoma, brainstem glioma, and hemangioblastoma, can also occur in the posterior fossa, medulloblastoma is the most frequent in this specific location.

3. **Answer C (Hydrocephalus and increased intracranial pressure)**

   An obstruction in the cerebral aqueduct can lead to hydrocephalus, which is the accumulation of cerebrospinal fluid (CSF) within the brain's ventricles. This obstruction hinders the normal flow and drainage of CSF, resulting in an increased volume of CSF within the brain's ventricles. As a consequence, there is elevated intracranial pressure (ICP) due to the excess fluid, which can compress and damage brain tissue. Hydrocephalus, if left untreated, can lead to neurological symptoms and complications. It is a condition that often requires medical intervention, such as surgical placement of a shunt to divert excess CSF away from the brain to another part of the body, thereby relieving the increased pressure.

4. **Answer C (Monitoring cerebral function)**

   SSEP (Somatosensory Evoked Potential) monitoring during posterior fossa surgery primarily serves the purpose of monitoring cerebral function. SSEP measures the electrical activity of the brain's sensory pathways in response to sensory stimuli, such as electrical stimulation of peripheral nerves. During surgery in the posterior fossa, it is essential to ensure that the brain's sensory pathways and overall cerebral function are preserved. SSEP monitoring allows continuous assessment of the integrity of these pathways, helping to detect any potential damage or compromise to the brain's sensory functions.

5. **Answer B (False)**

   Intraoperatively, neuromuscular blocking agents should not be used to minimize interference with SSEP (Somatosensory Evoked Potential) monitoring. The use of neuromuscular blocking agents can interfere with SSEP monitoring because these agents paralyze the muscles, including those involved in generating the sensory evoked potentials. SSEP monitoring relies on the electrical responses generated by the sensory pathways in response to specific stimuli, typically involving sensory nerve stimulation. If neuromuscular blocking agents are administered, the patient's muscle activity is suppressed, and this can obscure or distort the SSEP signals, making it difficult or impossible to accurately monitor the patient's neurological function. To ensure the accuracy of SSEP monitoring, it is crucial to avoid the use of neuromuscular blocking agents during procedures where SSEP monitoring is employed. Instead, anesthetics should be carefully titrated to allow for monitoring while maintaining the patient's muscle function.

6. **Answer D (Exophthalmos)**

   Exophthalmos is NOT a common possible complication of posterior fossa surgery in the prone position for resection of a vermian tumor. This symptom is typically associated with conditions unrelated to the surgical procedure or positioning during posterior fossa surgery, such as Graves' disease or certain orbital pathologies. Conversely, complications such as macroglossia, quadriplegia, and pneumocephalus may be associated with this type of surgery, emphasizing the importance of careful positioning, airway management, and vigilance for intracranial air accumulation. While exophthalmos is not a typical concern, other potential complications, such as cardiovascular instability and venous air embolism, should also be considered.

Recommended literature

1. Sandhu K, Gupta N. Chapter 14 – Anesthesia for Posterior Fossa Surgery. In: Prabhakar H, editor. Essentials of Neuroanesthesia: Academic Press; 2017. p. 255-76.
2. Jagannathan S, Krovvidi H. Anaesthetic considerations for posterior fossa surgery. Continuing Education in Anaesthesia Critical Care & Pain. 2014;14(5):202-6.

Neuroanesthesia
SPINA BIFIDA

Questions:

1. **What is the most common type of spina bifida?**
   A. Meningocele
   B. Myelomeningocele
   C. Spina bifida occulta
   D. Tethered cord syndrome

2. **Which type of spina bifida is associated with herniation of the meninges but not the spinal cord itself?**
   A. Myelomeningocele
   B. Tethered cord syndrome
   C. Spina bifida occulta
   D. Meningocele

3. **What is the primary risk factor for the development of spina bifida?**
   A. Drug abuse during pregnancy
   B. Lack of folic acid intake
   C. Maternal age over 35 years
   D. Smoking during pregnancy

4. **Which condition is often associated with myelomeningocele and may require the placement of a shunt for management?**
   A. Scoliosis
   B. Hydrocephalus
   C. Lymphedema
   D. Tethered cord syndrome

5. **Patients with spina bifida may have an increased risk of latex allergy.**
   A. True
   B. False

6. **A 28-year-old pregnant woman with a known history of spina bifida occulta, presents to the obstetrics clinic for prenatal care. She is currently at 24 weeks of gestation with her first pregnancy. Her prenatal care has been progressing well, but she has concerns related to her spina bifida. The medical team wants to ensure her safety and address her questions regarding pregnancy and childbirth with spina bifida. What is NOT true about spina bifida occulta?**
   A. Neuraxial is generally safe
   B. Recommend to insert the needle remote from the site of malformation seen on imaging
   C. Patients are at a higher risk of post-dural puncture headache
   D. A bigger epidural space is easily identified

Answers:

1. Answer C (Spina bifida occulta)

Spina bifida occulta is the mildest and most common type of spina bifida. It involves a midline defect of the spinal column without protrusion of the spinal cord or meninges. In this type, the overlying skin is typically intact, and most affected individuals are asymptomatic. Spina bifida occulta is often discovered incidentally on radiographic examination and does not usually result in the same level of neurological deficits as the other forms of spina bifida, such as myelomeningocele.

2. Answer D (Meningocele)

Meningocele is a form of spina bifida in which the meninges herniate between the vertebrae, forming a cerebrospinal fluid-filled sac covered by a thin layer of skin. In this condition, the spinal cord remains in a normal position within the spinal canal. Unlike myelomeningocele, where both the spinal cord and meninges protrude through the defect, meningocele primarily involves the meninges without spinal cord involvement.

3. Answer B (Lack of folic acid intake during early pregnancy)

One of the primary risk factors for the development of spina bifida is a deficiency in folic acid intake, especially during the early stages of pregnancy. Folate is a B vitamin that plays a crucial role in neural tube development in the developing fetus. Insufficient folate intake can lead to neural tube defects, including spina bifida. This is why it's recommended that women who are planning to become pregnant or who are already pregnant take folic acid supplements to reduce the risk of neural tube defects.

4. Answer B (Hydrocephalus)

Myelomeningocele is the most severe form of spina bifida, and it is often associated with hydrocephalus. The presence of a myelomeningocele can disrupt the normal flow of CSF in the central nervous system, leading to hydrocephalus. To manage hydrocephalus and relieve the increased intracranial pressure associated with it, a ventriculoperitoneal (VP) shunt is often surgically implanted. The VP shunt helps drain excess CSF from the brain's ventricles to the abdominal cavity, where it can be reabsorbed by the body, thereby reducing pressure within the brain. Scoliosis, lymphedema, and tethered cord syndrome can also occur in individuals with myelomeningocele but are not typically managed with shunt placement.

5. Answer A (True)

All individuals with spina bifida should be considered at high risk for having an allergic reaction to rubber, particularly latex-containing products, and should avoid contact with rubber products, especially during medical or surgical procedures. This heightened risk for latex allergies is primarily due to overexposure as a consequence of repeated surgical procedures.

6. Answer D (A bigger epidural space is easily identified)

Spina bifida occulta is characterized by a midline defect in the spinal column without the herniation of the meninges or protrusion of the spinal cord. While it is generally considered safe to administer neuraxial anesthesia, such as an epidural, to individuals with spina bifida occulta, the condition may lead to anatomical variations in the spine. These variations can sometimes make it more challenging to identify the epidural space accurately. Therefore, it is not true that a bigger epidural space is easily identified in individuals with spina bifida occulta, as the anatomy may be altered due to the condition. This underscores the importance of caution and precision when performing neuraxial procedures in such cases.

Recommended literature

1. Sacco, A., Ushakov, F., Thompson, D., Peebles, D., Pandya, P., De Coppi, P., Wimalasundera, R., Attilakos, G., David, A.L., Deprest, J., 2019. Fetal surgery for open spina bifida. The Obstetrician & Gynaecologist 21, 271–282.
2. O'Neal MA. A Pregnant Woman with Spina Bifida: Need for a Multidisciplinary Labor Plan. Front Med (Lausanne). 2017;4:172.
3. Griffiths, S., Durbridge, J.A., 2011. Anaesthetic implications of neurological disease in pregnancy. Continuing Education in Anaesthesia Critical Care & Pain 11, 157–161.
4. Spina Bifida. In: Bissonnette B, Luginbuehl I, Marciniak B, Dalens BJ. eds. Syndromes: Rapid Recognition and Perioperative Implications. McGraw Hill; 2006.

SPINE SURGERY

Questions:

1. **What is the most common position for performing spinal procedures?**

   A. Supine

   B. Trendelenburg

   C. Prone

   D. Lithotomy

2. **Which of the following is NOT a common complication associated with the prone position during spine surgery?**

   A. Accidental extubation

   B. Corneal abrasions

   C. Peripheral nerve injury at the lumbar plexus

   D. Skin necrosis

3. **Which pathology is NOT commonly seen in patients undergoing spine surgery?**

   A. Trauma

   B. Infection

   C. Musculoskeletal disease

   D. Degenerative conditions

4. **To minimize the risk of ischemic optic neuropathy (ION) during spinal surgery, what position should the patient's head be in?**

   A. Lower than the heart

   B. Extend head fully

   C. At the same level as the heart

   D. Tilted to the left

5. **Somatosensory evoked potentials (SSEPs) monitoring is necessary during procedures where the spinal cord is at risk.**

   A. True

   B. False

6. **The 62-year-old patient has a history of severe cervical myelopathy due to degenerative disc disease and spinal stenosis. The surgical team has planned a posterior cervical decompression and fusion (PCDF) procedure to relieve spinal cord compression and alleviate neurological symptoms. Given the nature of the surgery and the need for continuous monitoring of motor evoked potentials (MEPs) to assess spinal cord integrity, the appropriate anesthetic technique is essential. Which anesthetic technique is the preferred choice for assessing MEPs?**

   A. Inhalational anaesthesia

   B. Total intravenous anaesthesia (TIVA)

   C. Opioid-free anaesthesia

   D. Neurolept anesthesia

Answers:

1. Answer C (Prone)

The most common position for performing spinal procedures is the prone position, where the patient is positioned face-down on the operating table. This positioning is preferred for spinal surgeries due to several advantages it offers. Firstly, it provides excellent access to the posterior aspect of the spine, which is often the target area for procedures like laminectomies, discectomies, and spinal fusions. Moreover, prone positioning aligns the spine naturally, facilitating surgical access without the need for frequent repositioning during the procedure. This position is also conducive to spinal cord monitoring, allowing for the use of intraoperative techniques like somatosensory evoked potentials (SSEPs) and motor evoked potentials (MEPs).

2. Answer C (Peripheral nerve injury at the lumbar plexus)

Complications of the prone position during spine surgery can be diverse and pose significant challenges. Accidental extubation is a potential issue due to the positioning of the patient; ophthalmic complications, such as corneal abrasions and postoperative visual loss, are associated with the prone position but affect the eyes and visual function. Skin necrosis is a concern, primarily related to pressure injuries. Peripheral nerve injuries, like ulnar nerve injury at the elbow or brachial plexus injury, are possible complications associated with the prone position, but injury to the lumbar plexus in this context is less common. Therefore, the correct answer is C. Peripheral nerve injury at the lumbar plexus. While nerve injuries are possible, they are more frequently seen in other nerve regions of the body during prone positioning for spinal surgery.

3. Answer C (Musculoskeletal disease)

Patients undergoing spine surgery typically present with one of five common pathologies: trauma (often unstable vertebral fractures), infection (such as epidural abscess), malignancy (either primary or metastatic), congenital conditions like scoliosis, and degenerative conditions. Musculoskeletal diseases, while certainly relevant to spine health, are not typically a primary indication for spine surgery. Instead, spine surgery is more commonly performed to address the other pathologies mentioned, which are more directly related to spinal stability, neurological issues, or life-threatening conditions.

4. Answer C (At the same level as the heart)

To minimize the risk of ischaemic optic neuropathy (ION) during spinal surgery, it is crucial to position the patient's head at or above the level of the heart. This helps avoid the head-down position, which can contribute to venous stasis and increase the risk of ION. Additionally, positioning the head in a forward position without excessive flexion, extension, lateral flexion, or rotation further reduces the risk of this complication. Maintaining proper head positioning is a critical aspect of patient safety during spinal surgery.

5. Answer A (True)

SSEPs monitoring is necessary during procedures where the spinal cord is at risk. SSEPs are used to assess the integrity and function of the spinal cord during surgery. These small amplitude potentials are measured over the sensory cortex or via epidural electrodes in response to stimuli applied to peripheral nerves. By monitoring SSEPs, medical professionals can detect any changes in spinal cord function promptly, allowing for immediate intervention if necessary. SSEP monitoring is a valuable tool to help ensure the safety of patients undergoing spinal procedures where spinal cord function may be compromised.

6. Answer B (Total intravenous anaesthesia (TIVA))

Total intravenous anesthesia (TIVA) is the preferred choice when assessing MEPs during spinal surgery. MEPs are used to monitor spinal cord function during procedures where the spinal cord is at risk, such as spinal deformity correction surgeries. TIVA allows for precise control of the depth of anesthesia while minimizing the use of inhalational anesthetics, which can interfere with MEP monitoring. TIVA typically involves the administration of intravenous agents like propofol and remifentanil, which can be titrated to maintain an appropriate level of anesthesia without affecting MEPs. This technique ensures that the neurophysiological monitoring of MEPs remains accurate and reliable throughout the surgery, reducing the risk of spinal cord injury.

Recommended literature

1. Pollard BJ, Kitchen, G. Handbook of Clinical Anaesthesia. Fourth Edition. CRC Press. 2018. 978-1-4987-6289-2.
2. Nowicki R. 2014. Anaesthesia for major spinal surgery. Continuing Education in Anaesthesia Critical Care & Pain. 14;4:147-152.

SUBARACHNOID HEMORRHAGE

Questions:

1. **What is the most common cause of subarachnoid hemorrhage (SAH)?**

   A. Trauma

   B. Arteriovenous malformations

   C. Intracranial aneurysm

   D. Moyamoya disease

2. **Which of the following is NOT a risk factor for SAH?**

   A. Hypertension

   B. Atherosclerosis

   C. Diabetes mellitus

   D. Smoking

3. **What is the classic clinical presentation of SAH?**

   A. Gradual onset of headache

   B. Sudden onset of the "worst headache of life"

   C. Headache that gets worse with physical activity, lights, sounds, or smells

   D. One side headache

4. **Which clinical grading scale is NOT commonly used to assess the severity of SAH?**

   A. Modified Rankin Scale

   B. Glasgow Coma Scale

   C. Hunt and Hess Scale

   D. Fisher Scale

5. **Intraventricular bleeding can cause acute ventricular dilatation and hydrocephalus.**

   A. True

   B. False

6. **A 47-year-old male patient is rushed to the emergency department after experiencing a sudden and severe headache at work. The pain, described as "the worst headache of my life," started abruptly and has been relentless. He also complains of nausea and photophobia. The patient has a history of hypertension for which he is taking medication. On physical examination, he appears distressed, exhibits nuchal rigidity, and has a blood pressure of 170/95 mmHg. Given the clinical presentation, the medical team suspects SAH and initiates immediate interventions. The patient undergoes a non-contrast cranial CT scan, which confirms the presence of SAH. Treatment is promptly initiated; which of the following is NOT a component of acute SAH management for this patient?**

   A. Hyperventilation

   B. External ventricular drain

   C. Seizure prophylaxis

   D. Anticoagulants

Answers:

1. Answer C (Intracranial aneurysm)

The etiology of subarachnoid hemorrhage (SAH) can vary, but in approximately 85% of cases, it is attributed to the rupture of intracranial aneurysms. These aneurysms are weak points in the walls of blood vessels in the brain, and their rupture leads to the sudden release of blood into the subarachnoid space, causing SAH. While arteriovenous malformations, trauma, and Moyamoya disease can also cause SAH, intracranial aneurysms are the most common and prevalent underlying cause of this condition.

2. Answer C (Diabetes mellitus)

Among the provided risk factors for SAH, diabetes mellitus is not typically considered a primary risk factor. While hypertension, atherosclerosis, cocaine use, alcohol abuse, smoking, connective tissue disorders, coarctation of the aorta, and certain congenital conditions are associated with an increased risk of SAH, diabetes mellitus is not commonly identified as a direct risk factor for SAH in the same way as the other listed factors.

3. Answer B (Sudden onset of the "worst headache of life")

The classic clinical presentation of SAH is the sudden onset of the "worst headache of life." This type of headache is often described by patients as extremely severe and abrupt in its onset. It is typically different from usual headaches, and patients often use this description to convey the intensity of the pain. This severe headache is a hallmark symptom of SAH and should raise suspicion of this condition, prompting further evaluation and diagnostic tests.

4. Answer A (Modified Rankin Scale)

The Modified Rankin Scale is not commonly used to assess the severity of SAH. Instead, the Glasgow Coma Scale (GCS), Hunt and Hess Scale, and Fisher Scale are more frequently employed in the assessment and grading of SAH. The GCS evaluates a patient's level of consciousness and neurological status, the Hunt and Hess Scale grades SAH patients based on clinical symptoms and neurological deficits, and the Fisher Scale classifies SAH based on the radiological appearance of blood on a CT scan. These scales play essential roles in the evaluation and management of SAH patients, whereas the Modified Rankin Scale is primarily focused on measuring functional outcomes following neurological events.

5. Answer A (True)

Intraventricular bleeding can cause acute ventricular dilatation and hydrocephalus. When blood accumulates within the ventricles of the brain as a result of intraventricular hemorrhage (IVH), it can obstruct the normal flow of cerebrospinal fluid (CSF). This obstruction can lead to an increase in intracranial pressure and ventricular enlargement, a condition known as acute hydrocephalus. Acute hydrocephalus can be a serious complication of intraventricular bleeding, requiring medical intervention such as external ventricular drainage to relieve the pressure and maintain proper CSF circulation.

6. Answer D (Anticoagulants)

In the acute management of SAH for this patient, anticoagulants are not typically a component of the management plan. The primary objectives in SAH management are to prevent re-bleeding, manage elevated intracranial pressure, and provide appropriate medical support. Anticoagulants, which can increase the risk of bleeding, are generally avoided in this context. Instead, life-saving treatment and symptom management measures include life support, placing a draining tube in the brain to relieve pressure, protecting the airway, medications to reduce intracranial swelling and manage blood pressure, prevention of artery spasms, pain relief, anti-anxiety medications, and seizure prevention or treatment, as appropriate. Surgical intervention may also be required to remove blood collections, relieve pressure, or repair aneurysms if they are the underlying cause of the SAH.

Recommended literature

1. Deepak Sharma; Perioperative Management of Aneurysmal Subarachnoid Hemorrhage: A Narrative Review. Anesthesiology 2020; 133:1283–1305.
2. Kundra S, Mahendru V, Gupta V, Choudhary AK. Principles of neuroanesthesia in aneurysmal subarachnoid hemorrhage. J Anaesthesiol Clin Pharmacol. 2014;30(3):328-337.
3. Luoma A, Reddy U. Acute management of aneurysmal subarachnoid haemorrhage. Continuing Education in Anaesthesia Critical Care & Pain. 2013;13(2):52-8.

TRAUMATIC BRAIN INJURY

09
CHAPTER

Questions:

1. **What is the leading cause of death and disability in young adults in the developed world?**

    A. Stroke

    B. Traumatic brain injury

    C. Cancer

    D. Heart disease

2. **Which classification system is commonly used to assess the severity of traumatic brain injury (TBI) based on the patient's neurological status?**

    A. Edinburgh Coma Scale

    B. Glasgow Coma Scale

    C. Abbreviated Injury Scale

    D. Canadian Neurological Scale

3. **When should tracheal intubation be considered in TBI patients?**

    A. If GCS ≤ 8

    B. In cases of severe TBI

    C. If there is evidence of cerebral ischemia

    D. After assessing ICP

4. **What type of solution should be avoided for volume replacement in TBI patients due to the risk of worsening cerebral edema?**

    A. Ringer's solution

    B. Normal saline

    C. D5W

    D. Colloid

5. **Steroids improve outcomes and lower ICP**

    A. True

    B. False

6. **A 45-year-old patient weighing 80 kg is admitted to the emergency department after a severe TBI. Due to the severity of the injury, the patient is intubated and mechanically ventilated. The ventilator settings are adjusted to deliver a tidal volume (TV) of 560 mL at a respiratory rate of 20 breaths per minute. The goal is to achieve mild hypocapnia, targeting a partial pressure of arterial carbon dioxide ($PaCO_2$) between 4.0 and 4.5 kPa. What is the primary goal of hyperventilation ($PaCO_2$ 4.0 – 4.5 kPa) in TBI patients?**

    A. To increase cerebral perfusion

    B. To decrease intracranial pressure

    C. To reduce cerebral blood flow

    D. To correct acidosis

Answers:

1. Answer B (Traumatic Brain Injury)

Traumatic Brain Injury (TBI) is the leading cause of death and disability in young adults in the developed world. TBI results from head trauma and can have a wide range of consequences, from mild concussions to severe brain damage, making it a significant public health concern. Stroke, cancer, and heart disease, while also serious health conditions, do not collectively account for as many deaths and disabilities in young adults as TBI does in the developed world.

2. Answer B (Glasgow Coma Scale)

The Glasgow Coma Scale (GCS) is commonly used to assess the severity of TBI based on the patient's neurological status. This widely recognized and validated tool evaluates three critical components of neurological function: eye-opening, verbal response, and motor response. Each component is assigned a score, and the sum of these scores provides an overall measure of consciousness and neurological impairment. TBI severity is often categorized using GCS scores, with scores of 13-15 indicating mild TBI, scores of 9-12 indicating moderate TBI, and scores less than 8 signifying severe TBI. The GCS serves as an essential clinical tool to quickly and objectively assess and classify TBI severity, guiding treatment decisions and prognosis assessment.

3. Answer A (If GCS ≤ 8)

Tracheal intubation should be considered in TBI patients if their GCS score is ≤ 8. The GCS is a critical tool for assessing the neurological status of TBI patients, and a GCS score of 8 or lower typically indicates a significant impairment in consciousness and airway protection. Intubation, in these cases, is essential to secure the airway and ensure adequate oxygenation and ventilation. It is performed to prevent further complications related to airway compromise and to maintain oxygen levels within the optimal range. Therefore, the decision to perform tracheal intubation in TBI patients is primarily based on their GCS score, with a score of 8 or less serving as a key threshold for intervention.

4. Answer C (D5W)

In TBI patients, D5W (Dextrose 5% in water) should be avoided for volume replacement due to the risk of worsening cerebral edema. D5W is a hypotonic solution, meaning it has a lower osmolarity compared to the body's fluids. When hypotonic solutions like D5W are administered intravenously, they can cause water to move into the brain cells, potentially increasing cerebral edema and intracranial pressure (ICP). To prevent this risk, isotonic crystalloid solutions like normal saline (0.9% sodium chloride) or Ringer's solution are preferred for volume replacement in TBI patients. Isotonic solutions have an osmolarity close to that of the body's fluids, reducing the risk of shifting water into brain cells and exacerbating cerebral edema.

5. Answer B (False)

Steroids, specifically glucocorticoids like dexamethasone, have been used in the past to manage TBI and other brain-related conditions. However, the statement that "Steroids improve outcomes and lower ICP" is false based on current medical knowledge and evidence. In fact, the use of steroids in TBI management is controversial, and their routine use is not recommended. Studies have shown that steroids do not consistently improve outcomes in TBI patients, and their administration can have potential side effects, including immunosuppression and hyperglycemia. Moreover, steroids do not have a proven role in lowering ICP in TBI patients. The primary focus in TBI management is on strategies such as maintaining adequate oxygenation, controlling ICP, preventing secondary brain injury, and optimizing cerebral perfusion pressure (CPP). Steroids are not considered a first-line treatment option for TBI and should be used sparingly and based on specific clinical indications under strict guidance.

6. Answer B (To decrease intracranial pressure)

Hyperventilation with the goal of achieving mild hypocapnia is primarily employed in TBI patients to decrease ICP. When carbon dioxide levels in the blood decrease due to hyperventilation, it leads to vasoconstriction of cerebral blood vessels, which, in turn, reduces cerebral blood flow and helps lower ICP. This effect is particularly useful in the acute phase of severe TBI to prevent or manage increased ICP, which can be detrimental to brain perfusion and recovery.

Recommended literature

1. Dinsmore J. Traumatic brain injury: an evidence-based review of management. Continuing Education in Anaesthesia Critical Care & Pain. 2013;13(6):189-95.
2. Curry P, Viernes D, Sharma D. Perioperative management of traumatic brain injury. Int J Crit Illn Inj Sci. 2011;1(1):27-35.
3. Moppett IK. Traumatic brain injury: assessment, resuscitation and early management. Br J Anaesth. 2007;99(1):18-31.

NEUROMUSCULAR DISEASES

AMYOTROPHIC LATERAL SCLEROSIS (ALS)

10
CHAPTER

Questions:

1. **What is the primary cause of death for patients with amyotrophic lateral sclerosis (ALS)?**
   A. Heart failure
   B. Stroke
   C. Respiratory failure
   D. Kidney failure

2. **Which of the following is NOT a common sign or symptom of ALS?**
   A. Muscle cramps and twitching (fasciculations)
   B. Weakness in the legs, feet, or ankles
   C. Visual disturbances
   D. Slurred speech

3. **What is the role of Riluzole (Rilutek) in ALS treatment?**
   A. Cure the disease
   B. Relieve pain and discomfort
   C. Slow down the progression of the disease
   D. Improve motor function

4. **Which environmental toxin exposure is NOT associated with an increased risk of ALS?**
   A. Lead
   B. DDT
   C. Selenium
   D. Asbestos

5. **The patient age group 30-40 years old is most commonly affected by ALS.**
   A. True
   B. False

6. **A 45-year-old male with ALS has been brought in for the surgical repair of a humerus fracture. He was diagnosed the ALS diagnosis four years ago when he experienced a gradual onset of progressive, asymmetric weakness in his upper and lower limbs, which was accompanied by difficulties in walking. Notably, he is a non-smoker with no other underlying medical conditions. Neurologically, the patient exhibits spasticity in both upper and lower limbs, along with exaggerated tendon reflexes. Additionally, he displays bradykinesia and resting tremors in all extremities. Crucially, there is no indication of bulbar dysfunction or truncal weakness. The consideration here is the use of a supraclavicular regional block for anesthesia.**
   A. Regional anesthesia can cause neuromyotonia-like contractions.
   B. Regional anesthesia can exacerbate ALS symptoms.
   C. Regional anesthesia can lead to hyperkalemia.
   D. Regional anesthesia is less effective in ALS patients.

Answers:

1. **Answer C (Respiratory failure)**

Amyotrophic lateral sclerosis (ALS) is a progressive neurodegenerative disease that primarily affects motor neurons in the brain and spinal cord. As the disease progresses, it leads to the degeneration of these motor neurons, ultimately affecting the muscles controlled by these neurons. The muscles required for breathing are also affected, and respiratory muscles gradually weaken. Respiratory failure occurs when these muscles become too weak to support effective breathing, leading to insufficient oxygenation of the body. As a result, patients with ALS often succumb to respiratory failure, making it the primary cause of death in ALS patients.

2. **Answer C (Visual disturbances)**

Visual disturbances are NOT a common sign or symptom of ALS. ALS primarily affects the motor neurons in the brain and spinal cord, leading to muscle weakness, atrophy, and motor dysfunction. The hallmark symptoms of ALS include muscle cramps, twitching, limb weakness, and slurred speech. Visual disturbances, such as problems with vision, are not typically associated with the disease, as ALS primarily targets the motor system, and sensory functions like vision are usually unaffected in the early stages of the condition.

3. **Answer C (Slow down the progression of the disease)**

Riluzole (marketed under the brand name Rilutek) is a medication used in the treatment of ALS. It is not a cure for the disease, nor does it directly relieve pain and discomfort or improve motor function. Instead, Riluzole is known to slow down the progression of ALS to some extent. It works by reducing the release of glutamate, a neurotransmitter that can be harmful to motor neurons when present in excessive amounts. By doing so, Riluzole may help preserve motor neurons and delay the worsening of symptoms, ultimately extending the time before respiratory failure and other severe complications occur. While it doesn't reverse the disease, it can provide some benefit by offering more time for patients to maintain their motor function and quality of life.

4. **Answer C (Selenium)**

Although selenium was found to be associated with ALS according to earlier epidemiologic studies, current evidence based on the population of European ancestry does not support the causal effect of selenium on ALS risk. While other environmental toxins like lead, DDT, and asbestos have shown stronger and more consistent associations with an increased risk of ALS, the link between selenium exposure and the disease remains less clear and is not widely supported by recent research.

5. **Answer B (False)**

ALS is most commonly diagnosed in the age group of 40-70 years old, and it is relatively rare in individuals younger than 30 or older than 70. While cases can occur outside of this age range, the peak incidence of ALS typically occurs in the 40-70 age group.

6. **Answer B (Regional anesthesia can exacerbate ALS symptoms)**

In the context of ALS, it's essential to consider that regional anesthesia can potentially exacerbate the patient's ALS symptoms. ALS is characterized by the degeneration of motor neurons, leading to muscle weakness and. Regional anesthesia can further compromise respiratory function and potentially worsen respiratory muscle weakness, including the risk of phrenic nerve palsy. Therefore, the use of regional anesthesia should be approached with caution, and the potential risks and benefits, including the risk of phrenic nerve palsy, should be carefully evaluated to ensure the safest and most appropriate anesthesia management for this patient.

Recommended literature

1. Gaik C, Wiesmann T. 2021Anaesthesia recommendations for Amyotrophic lateral sclerosis. Orphananesthesia.https://www.orphananesthesia.eu/en/rare-diseases/published-guidelines/amyotrophic-lateral-sclerosis/1684-amyotrophic-lateral-sclerosis-2/file.html
2. Sarna R, Gupta A, Arora G. Amyotrophic lateral sclerosis and anaesthetic challenges: Perioperative lignocaine infusion-an aid. Indian J Anaesth. 2020;64(5):448-449.
3. Thampi SM, David D, Chandy TT, Nandhakumar A. Anesthetic management of a patient with amyotrophic lateral sclerosis for transurethral resection of bladder tumor. Indian J Anaesth. 2013;57(2):197-199.
4. Marsh, S., Pittard, A., 2011. Neuromuscular disorders and anaesthesia. Part 2: specific neuromuscular disorders. Continuing Education in Anaesthesia Critical Care & Pain 11, 119-123.

Neuromuscular diseases
GUILLAIN-BARRÉ SYNDROME

10
CHAPTER

Questions:

1. **What is the most common cause of acute, flaccid, neuromuscular paralysis in the world?**

    A. Stroke

    B. Multiple sclerosis

    C. Guillain-Barré syndrome

    D. Myasthenia gravis

2. **Which age group tends to be more affected by Guillain-Barré syndrome?**

    A. Children

    B. Adolescents

    C. Young adults

    D. Elderly

3. **Which of the following pathogens is NOT commonly associated with Guillain-Barré syndrome?**

    A. Campylobacter jejuni

    B. Epstein Barr virus

    C. Influenza virus

    D. Mycoplasma pneumonia

4. **Which of the following symptoms is NOT commonly associated with Guillain-Barré syndrome?**

    A. Progressive motor weakness

    B. Sensory symptoms

    C. Confusion and delirium

    D. Facial palsy

5. **Guillain-Barré syndrome typically presents with rapidly progressive limb weakness, often starting in the legs and ascending.**

    A. True

    B. False

6. **A 45-year-old male presents to the emergency department with rapidly progressive muscle weakness and tingling sensations in his legs. He reports that these symptoms began a few days ago and have been steadily worsening. He also mentions a recent respiratory infection that resolved just before the onset of these symptoms. On examination, the patient is found to have bilateral lower limb weakness, loss of reflexes, and mild facial weakness. Given the clinical presentation and recent infection, the healthcare team suspects Guillain-Barré syndrome (GBS) and confirmed diagnosis with laboratory tests, electrophysiological studies, and the patient's cerebrospinal fluid (CSF) exam. What is the primary treatment of choice for Guillain-Barré syndrome?**

    A. Antibiotics

    B. Corticosteroids

    C. Immunoglobulins

    D. Antiviral medications

Answers:

1. Answer C (Guillain-Barré syndrome)

Guillain-Barré syndrome (GBS) is the most common cause of acute, flaccid, neuromuscular paralysis in the United States. GBS is an autoimmune disorder that affects the peripheral nervous system, leading to muscle weakness and paralysis. It typically presents with rapidly progressive muscle weakness, often starting in the legs and ascending upwards. GBS is often triggered by preceding infections, making it a significant cause of neuromuscular paralysis in the context of acute onset. While strokes, multiple sclerosis, and myasthenia gravis are neurological conditions that can cause various symptoms, they are not typically associated with the acute, flaccid, neuromuscular paralysis characteristic of GBS.

2. Answer C (Young adults)

Guillain-Barré syndrome can affect individuals of all ages, but it tends to be slightly more prevalent in young adults and the elderly. While GBS can occur in children and adolescents, it is often observed with higher incidence in individuals who are in their late teens to early adulthood or those who are elderly. The reasons for this age distribution are not entirely understood but may be related to various factors, including differences in immune responses and susceptibility to infections, which can trigger GBS.

3. Answer C (Influenza virus)

GBS is often associated with various infectious agents, including Campylobacter jejuni, Epstein Barr virus, Mycoplasma pneumonia, and Cytomegalovirus. These pathogens are commonly linked to GBS, and their infections can trigger the autoimmune response leading to GBS. However, it is less commonly associated with influenza virus compared to the other pathogens listed.

4. Answer C (Confusion and delirium)

Confusion and delirium are not commonly associated symptoms with GBS. GBS primarily presents with a distinctive set of symptoms, including progressive motor weakness, areflexia, facial palsy, ophthalmoplegia, sensory symptoms, severe pain, respiratory muscle weakness, and autonomic dysfunction, which can manifest as arrhythmias, blood pressure and pulse fluctuations, urinary retention, ileus, and excessive sweating. While GBS affects the peripheral nervous system, it does not typically involve cognitive impairment or delirium. Instead, it predominantly affects motor and sensory functions and can lead to muscle weakness and paralysis.

5. Answer A (True)

GBS typically presents with rapidly progressive limb weakness, often starting in the legs and ascending. This characteristic pattern of muscle weakness is one of the hallmark features of GBS. As the condition progresses, the weakness can ascend to involve the arms and even lead to respiratory muscle weakness in severe cases. The ascending nature of the weakness is a distinguishing feature of GBS and is commonly observed in patients with this condition.

6. Answer C (Immunoglobulins)

The primary treatment of choice for Guillain-Barré syndrome is intravenous immunoglobulins (IVIG). IVIG therapy is administered to suppress the autoimmune response believed to be responsible for the demyelination and nerve damage seen in GBS. It has been shown to be effective in reducing the severity and duration of symptoms and is considered the standard of care for GBS. While antibiotics, corticosteroids, and antiviral medications may be used in the treatment of other conditions, they are not the primary treatments for GBS and do not directly address the underlying autoimmune process involved in this syndrome. Early initiation of IVIG therapy is crucial to achieve the best outcomes for patients with GBS.

Recommended literature

1. Nguyen TP, Taylor RS. Guillain Barre Syndrome. [Updated 2022 Jul 4]. In: StatPearls [Internet]. Treasure Island (FL): StatPearls Publishing; 2022 Jan-. Available from: https://www.ncbi.nlm.nih.gov/books/NBK532254/
2. Pollard BJ, Kitchen, G. Handbook of Clinical Anaesthesia. Fourth Edition. CRC Press. 2018. 978-1-4987-6289-2.
3. Richards KJC, Cohen AT. Guillain-Barré syndrome. BJA CEPD Reviews. 2003;3(2):46-9.

LAMBERT-EATON MYASTHENIC SYNDROME (LEMS)

10
CHAPTER

Questions:

1. **What is the primary mechanism of dysfunction in Lambert-Eaton Myasthenic Syndrome (LEMS)?**
   A. Destruction of neuromuscular junctions
   B. Antibodies attacking calcium channels
   C. Decreased acetylcholine production
   D. Antibodies attacking postsynaptic acetylcholine receptors

2. **What symptom typically distinguishes LEMS from myasthenia gravis?**
   A. Unexpected tightening of one or more muscles
   B. Repetitive painful spasm of a muscle
   C. Muscle weakness improvement with exercise
   D. Weakness worsens with exercise

3. **Which type of LEMS is often associated with small-cell lung cancer?**
   A. Non-paraneoplastic LEMS
   B. Hypothyroidism-related LEMS
   C. Genetic LEMS
   D. Paraneoplastic LEMS

4. **Which medication is used to improve muscle strength by enhancing acetylcholine release in LEMS?**
   A. Prednisolone
   B. Guanidine
   C. Rituximab
   D. Pyridostigmine

5. **Patients with LEMS feel more proximal than distal weakness.**
   A. True
   B. False

6. **A 25-year-old patient with a known diagnosis of LEMS presents to the emergency department with acute appendicitis. The patient complains of worsening abdominal pain, nausea, and a low-grade fever. Clinical examination reveals tenderness and guarding in the right lower quadrant of the abdomen. The surgical team plans an urgent laparoscopic appendectomy, and antibiotic prophylaxis is also planned. What is the appropriate antibiotic regimen to prescribe for surgical prophylaxis in this patient with LEMS who presents with acute appendicitis?**
   A. Amikacin plus metronidazole
   B. Ciprofloxacin plus metronidazole
   C. Erythromycin plus metronidazole
   D. Ceftriaxone plus metronidazole

369

Answers:

1. **Answer B (Antibodies attacking calcium channels)**

   The primary mechanism of dysfunction in Lambert-Eaton Myasthenic Syndrome (LEMS) is the presence of antibodies that attack voltage-gated calcium channels in the presynaptic neuronal cell membrane. These calcium channels play a crucial role in the release of acetylcholine, a neurotransmitter, from the nerve terminals. When these calcium channels are attacked and disrupted by antibodies, it leads to a reduction in the release of acetylcholine at the neuromuscular junction. As a result, the communication between nerve cells and muscle cells is impaired, causing muscle weakness and other symptoms characteristic of LEMS. This attack on calcium channels is the hallmark of LEMS and distinguishes it from other neuromuscular disorders like myasthenia gravis, where the primary target is often postsynaptic acetylcholine receptors.

2. **Answer C (Muscle weakness improvement with exercise)**

   The symptom that typically distinguishes LEMS from myasthenia gravis is that muscle weakness in LEMS often improves with exercise. In LEMS, muscle strength tends to temporarily increase with repeated muscle use or exercise due to the gradual increase in the release of acetylcholine at the neuromuscular junction over time. This phenomenon is known as the "warm-up" effect. In contrast, in myasthenia gravis, muscle weakness typically worsens with exercise or repetitive use of muscles. This is due to the depletion of acetylcholine at the neuromuscular junction during sustained muscle activity.

3. **Answer D (Paraneoplastic LEMS)**

   Paraneoplastic LEMS is often associated with small-cell lung cancer. In approximately 50-60% of cases of paraneoplastic LEMS, there is an underlying small-cell lung cancer. This form of LEMS occurs as a result of the immune system's accidental attack on normal tissues while attempting to fight cancer. Paraneoplastic LEMS typically presents in older individuals, with an average age of onset around 60 years. The association between small-cell lung cancer and paraneoplastic LEMS is significant, and addressing the underlying cancer is an important part of the treatment, as improvement in LEMS symptoms can often be observed after treating the cancer.

4. **Answer B (Guanidine)**

   Guanidine is a medication used to improve muscle strength in LEMS by enhancing acetylcholine release at the neuromuscular junction. In LEMS, the autoimmune attack on voltage-gated calcium channels in the presynaptic neuronal cell membrane reduces the release of acetylcholine, which impairs the communication between nerve cells and muscle cells. Guanidine helps counteract this by increasing acetylcholine release, thereby improving muscle function and strength.

5. **Answer A (True)**

   In LEMS, patients often experience more proximal weakness than distal weakness. This is consistent with the typical pattern of muscle involvement in LEMS, where upper leg muscle strength is often affected first, followed by weakness in shoulder muscles, muscles of the hands and feet, and eventually, muscles affecting speech, swallowing, and eye muscles. The characteristic pattern of muscle weakness starting proximally and progressing distally is a hallmark of LEMS and can help differentiate it from other neuromuscular disorders.

6. **Answer D (Ceftriaxone plus metronidazole)**

   Some antibiotics can worsen LEMS symptoms because they have neuromuscular blocking effects. Exacerbation of weakness has been described after administration of aminoglycosides, fluoroquinolones, and erythromycin. Therefore, in a patient with known LEMS, it is essential to select antibiotics that do not exacerbate neuromuscular weakness. Ceftriaxone plus metronidazole is an appropriate choice for surgical prophylaxis in this case as it provides broad-spectrum coverage while minimizing the risk of worsening LEMS symptoms.

Recommended literature

1. Kesner VG, Oh SJ, Dimachkie MM, Barohn RJ. Lambert-Eaton Myasthenic Syndrome. Neurol Clin. 2018;36(2):379-394.
2. Weingarten TN, Araka CN, Mogensen ME, Sorenson JP, Marienau ME, Watson JC, Sprung J. 2014. Lambert-Eaton myasthenic syndrome during anesthesia: a report of 37 patients. Journal of Clinical anesthesia. 26;8:648-653.
3. Marsh, S., Pittard, A., 2011. Neuromuscular disorders and anaesthesia. Part 2: specific neuromuscular disorders. Continuing Education in Anaesthesia Critical Care & Pain 11, 119-123.

Neuromuscular diseases
MULTIPLE SCLEROSIS

Questions:

1. **What is the primary pathological feature of multiple sclerosis (MS)?**
   A. Neuroinflammation
   B. Axonal degeneration
   C. Demyelination
   D. Autoimmune response

2. **Which type of MS typically involves a gradual worsening of symptoms from the onset without distinct relapses and remissions?**
   A. Primary-progressive MS
   B. Relapsing-remitting MS
   C. Secondary-progressive MS
   D. Chronic progressive MS

3. **What is the primary goal of immunomodulatory therapy in MS management?**
   A. Treating chronic symptoms
   B. Preventing exacerbations
   C. Managing spasticity
   D. Improving cognitive function

4. **Which of the following is NOT a potential trigger for perioperative exacerbation of MS symptoms?**
   A. Hyperthermia
   B. Stress
   C. Neuraxial techniques
   D. Nitrous oxide exposure

5. **Optic neuritis is a common visual symptom of MS.**
   A. True
   B. False

6. **A 32-year-old pregnant woman, currently at 39 weeks of gestation, is scheduled for a caesarean section. She has a medical history of MS but has been in remission for several years. The patient has not experienced any recent exacerbations of her MS symptoms and has been on a stable medication regimen. In pregnant patients with MS, which neuraxial technique is considered acceptable?**
   A. Neither epidural nor spinal
   B. Spinal only
   C. Epidural only
   D. Both epidural and spinal

Answers:

1. Answer C (Demyelination)

Multiple sclerosis (MS) is characterized by the demyelination of nerve fibers in the central nervous system (CNS). Demyelination involves the loss of the protective myelin sheath that surrounds nerve fibers, leading to disruptions in nerve signal transmission. While neuroinflammation, axonal degeneration, and autoimmune responses are also associated with MS, demyelination is the primary pathological feature that distinguishes the disease. The loss of myelin results in a wide range of neurological symptoms and impairments, making it a hallmark of MS pathology.

2. Answer A (Primary-progressive MS)

The type of MS that typically involves a gradual worsening of symptoms from the onset without distinct relapses and remissions is known as primary-progressive MS (PPMS). In PPMS, individuals experience a continuous and steady progression of neurological symptoms without the episodic relapses and remissions characteristic of other forms of MS. This progressive course sets PPMS apart from relapsing-remitting MS (RRMS), which features periodic flare-ups followed by symptom improvement and secondary-progressive MS (SPMS), which starts as RRMS but eventually becomes more steadily progressive.

3. Answer B (Preventing exacerbations)

Immunomodulatory therapy, such as medications like interferon beta and glatiramer acetate, is primarily aimed at preventing exacerbations or relapses in individuals with MS. These medications work by modulating the immune system and reducing the frequency and severity of MS relapses, which are characterized by the sudden worsening of symptoms. While immunomodulatory therapy can help manage the disease's course and reduce the risk of exacerbations, it may not directly treat chronic symptoms, spasticity, or cognitive impairments associated with MS. These aspects of MS management often require additional treatments and interventions.

4. Answer D (Nitrous oxide exposure)

Nitrous oxide exposure is not typically considered a potential trigger for perioperative exacerbation of MS symptoms. On the other hand, factors like hyperthermia, stress, and the use of neuraxial techniques can potentially contribute to worsening MS symptoms during the perioperative period.

5. Answer A (True)

Optic neuritis is a common visual symptom of MS. It is characterized by inflammation of the optic nerve, which can result in vision problems such as blurred vision, pain with eye movement, and even temporary vision loss. Optic neuritis often occurs as an early symptom of MS and can affect one or both eyes. It is considered one of the neurological manifestations of the disease and is frequently seen in individuals with MS.

6. Answer D (Both epidural and spinal)

In pregnant patients with MS, both epidural and spinal neuraxial techniques are considered acceptable, depending on the individual patient's clinical condition and the preferences of the anesthesia and obstetric teams. It's crucial to assess the patient's neurological status, recent disease activity, and other relevant factors in consultation with the patient's neurologist to determine the most suitable approach for pain management during childbirth. The choice between epidural and spinal anesthesia will be based on the patient's specific circumstances and the recommendations of the medical team to ensure the safest and most effective delivery and pain management.

Recommended literature

1. Makris A, Piperopoulos A, Karmaniolou I. Multiple sclerosis: basic knowledge and new insights in perioperative management. J Anesth. 2014;28(2):267-278.
2. A.R. Doratta and A. Schubert. Multiple sclerosis and anesthetic implications. 2002 Curr Opin Anesthesiol 15:365-370.

MYASTHENIA GRAVIS

Questions:

1. **What is the primary mechanism responsible for muscle weakness in Myasthenia Gravis (MG)?**
    A. Increased muscle inflammation
    B. Decreased acetylcholine production
    C. Autoantibodies to AchR causing receptor blockade
    D. Overactivation of motor neurons

2. **Which of the following is NOT a common symptom of MG?**
    A. Dysphagia
    B. Diplopia
    C. Muscle twitching
    D. Ptosis

3. **What is a myasthenic crisis?**
    A. A severe autoimmune attack on muscle tissue
    B. A sudden increase in the number of acetylcholine receptors
    C. Respiratory failure due to severe muscle weakness
    D. An acute phase of MG remission

4. **Which of the following is NOT a common precipitant of myasthenic crisis?**
    A. Infection
    B. Surgery
    C. Hyperthermia
    D. Corticosteroid therapy

5. **A myasthenic crisis and a cholinergic crisis have the same symptoms.**
    A. True
    B. False

6. **A 28-year-old female patient is scheduled for elective breast augmentation surgery. The patient has a known medical history of MG. Her MG has been managed for several years with medication and routine follow-up care, with only occasional mild symptoms. Which class of drugs can exacerbate MG symptoms and should be avoided in MG patients during surgery?**
    A. Succinylcholine
    B. Pyridostigmine
    C. Rocuronium
    D. Diphenhydramine

Answers:

1. Answer C (Autoantibodies to AchR causing receptor blockade)

Myasthenia Gravis (MG) is an autoimmune disease that primarily affects the neuromuscular junction. The main mechanism responsible for muscle weakness in MG is the presence of autoantibodies directed against acetylcholine receptors (AchR) at the neuromuscular junction. These autoantibodies disrupt the function of AchR by binding to them, causing receptor blockade. This blockade leads to a decrease in the ability of acetylcholine, the neurotransmitter responsible for muscle contraction, to bind to and activate AchR. As a result, the transmission of signals from motor neurons to muscle fibers is impaired, resulting in muscle weakness and fatigue, especially during repetitive use of muscles.

2. Answer C (Muscle twitching)

Muscle twitching is not a common symptom of MG, which primarily manifests as muscle weakness and fatigue in various muscle groups. Common MG symptoms include ptosis, diplopia, dysarthria, dysphagia, dysphonia, and generalized muscle weakness, often more pronounced in proximal muscles. Respiratory muscle weakness can lead to dyspnea and is a potentially life-threatening feature of MG. While MG symptoms can vary throughout the day and from day to day, muscle twitching is not a typical characteristic of the condition.

3. Answer C (Respiratory failure due to severe muscle weakness)

A myasthenic crisis is a medical emergency characterized by respiratory failure due to severe muscle weakness in individuals with MG. Myasthenic crises typically occur when the weakness of respiratory muscles reaches a critical point, impairing the individual's ability to breathe adequately. Precipitating factors such as infections, surgery, stress, or medication changes can trigger or exacerbate a myasthenic crisis. Immediate medical attention and respiratory support, such as mechanical ventilation, are essential to manage this life-threatening condition and stabilize the patient's breathing.

4. Answer D (Corticosteroid therapy)

Corticosteroid therapy is not a common precipitant of a myasthenic crisis. Myasthenic crises are typically triggered by factors such as infection, surgery, and hyperthermia. Infections, particularly respiratory infections, can exacerbate MG symptoms and weaken respiratory muscles. Surgical procedures can be physically stressful and may lead to worsening MG symptoms, especially in the postoperative phase. Hyperthermia can also contribute to increased muscle weakness in MG patients. Corticosteroid therapy, when administered and monitored appropriately, is more likely to be a therapeutic agent for managing MG symptoms rather than a precipitant of myasthenic crises. However, abrupt changes in corticosteroid doses or their misuse without proper immunosuppressive therapy adjustment can potentially lead to MG exacerbations.

5. Answer B (False)

A myasthenic crisis and a cholinergic crisis do not have the same symptoms. While both crises can involve muscle weakness and respiratory distress, they have distinct underlying causes and responses to treatment. A myasthenic crisis is characterized by worsening muscle weakness in MG patients, typically triggered by factors like infections or surgery, leading to severe respiratory muscle weakness and respiratory failure. In contrast, a cholinergic crisis results from excessive cholinergic stimulation due to overmedication with acetylcholinesterase inhibitors, leading to symptoms such as muscle fasciculations, cramps, excessive salivation, diarrhea, and bradycardia.

6. Answer A (Succinylcholine)

In patients with MG, certain medications and anesthetic agents should be used with caution or avoided due to their potential to exacerbate MG symptoms. Succinylcholine, a depolarizing neuromuscular-blocking agent, should be avoided in MG patients during surgery. Succinylcholine can lead to prolonged muscle paralysis in individuals with MG, making it unsuitable for use in this patient population. Instead, non-depolarizing neuromuscular-blocking agents (NMBAs) like rocuronium and vecuronium are preferred choices for inducing muscle relaxation during surgery. Pyridostigmine is an acetylcholinesterase inhibitor used to manage MG symptoms and is generally continued in MG patients perioperatively to maintain neuromuscular transmission. Diphenhydramine is an antihistamine and is not typically associated with exacerbating MG symptoms during surgery.

Recommended literature

1. P. Daum, J. Smelt and I.R. Ibrahim. Perioperative management of myasthenia gravis. 2021, BJA Education, 21(11): 414-429.
2. Dhallu MS, Baiomi A, Biyyam M, Chilimuri S. Perioperative Management of Neurological Conditions. Health Serv Insights. 2017;10:1178632917711942.
3. Dillon FX. Anesthesia issues in the perioperative management of myasthenia gravis. Semin Neurol. 2004;24(1):83-94.

MYOTONIC DYSTROPHY

10
CHAPTER

Questions:

1. **What is the most common muscular dystrophy in the European population?**
   A. Duchenne muscular dystrophy
   B. Limb-girdle muscular dystrophy
   C. Myotonic dystrophy
   D. Becker muscular dystrophy

2. **What is the primary genetic cause of myotonic dystrophy type I (DM1)?**
   A. Expansion of a CCTG repeat
   B. Expansion of a CTG repeat
   C. Deletion of the DM1 protein kinase gene
   D. Inversion of the CCHC-type zinc finger nucleic acid-binding protein gene

3. **Which type of myotonic dystrophy is characterized by an onset during the second, third, or fourth decade of life, with myotonia as the primary initial symptom?**
   A. Congenital myotonic dystrophy
   B. Mild myotonic dystrophy
   C. Classic myotonic dystrophy
   D. Myotonic dystrophy type II (DM2)

4. **Which of the following is a common cardiac complication associated with myotonic dystrophy?**
   A. Hypertension
   B. Atrial fibrillation
   C. Coronary artery disease
   D. Peripheral artery disease

5. **Benzodiazepines are used to reduce sustained myotonia in myotonic dystrophy patients.**
   A. True
   B. False

6. **A 45-year-old female patient was admitted for total abdominal hysterectomy. She had been diagnosed with myotonic dystrophy type 1 (DM1) five years previously and had been experiencing weakness in the distal muscles. Electrophysiological tests confirmed the diagnosis, and her serum creatine phosphokinase (CPK) level was elevated at 2921 U/L (normal range, 43–272 U/L). Preoperative tests did not reveal any further abnormal findings. Which statement is NOT true about induction and maintenance of anesthesia for myotonic dystrophy patients?**
   A. Avoid regional anesthesia
   B. Muscle relaxants should be avoided as much as possible
   C. Patients are very sensitive to opiates and anesthetic agents
   D. Avoid the use of anticholinesterases for reversal

Answers:

1. Answer C (Myotonic dystrophy)

Myotonic dystrophy is the most common muscular dystrophy in the European population. It is an autosomal dominant genetic disorder characterized by muscle dystrophy, myotonia, and a range of multisystemic symptoms affecting various organs. While Duchenne muscular dystrophy is a well-known muscular dystrophy, it is less common than myotonic dystrophy, especially in the European population. Limb-girdle muscular dystrophy and Becker muscular dystrophy are also different types of muscular dystrophy, but they are not as common as myotonic dystrophy in this specific population.

2. Answer B (Expansion of a CTG repeat)

Myotonic dystrophy type I (DM1) is primarily caused by the expansion of a CTG repeat in the 3'-untranslated region of the DM1 protein kinase gene. This expansion of CTG repeats is a key genetic characteristic of DM1 and results in an RNA gain of function mutation, leading to the clinical features of the disease.

3. Answer C (Classic myotonic dystrophy)

Classic myotonic dystrophy is characterized by an onset during the second, third, or fourth decade of life, with myotonia as the primary initial symptom. This form of myotonic dystrophy typically presents in adulthood, and myotonia, which is prolonged muscle contractions, is one of the hallmark features. It often affects various muscles, leading to symptoms such as muscle weakness, myotonia, and other systemic issues.

4. Answer B (Atrial fibrillation)

A common cardiac complication associated with myotonic dystrophy is atrial fibrillation. Atrial fibrillation is an irregular and often rapid heart rate that can lead to various cardiac issues. Myotonic dystrophy can affect the heart's conduction system, leading to atrial arrhythmias, conduction system abnormalities, and ventricular arrhythmias.

5. Answer A (True)

Benzodiazepines are used to reduce sustained myotonia in myotonic dystrophy patients. Myotonia is a hallmark feature of myotonic dystrophy, characterized by prolonged muscle contractions. Benzodiazepines, a class of medications, can help alleviate myotonia by relaxing muscles and reducing muscle stiffness and contraction duration. These drugs can be effective in improving muscle function and overall comfort for individuals with myotonic dystrophy.

6. Answer A (Avoid regional anesthesia)

In the case of a patient with DM1, it is not true that regional anesthesia should be avoided. In fact, regional anesthesia can be a suitable choice for these patients, as it minimizes the need for systemic muscle relaxants and provides effective anesthesia and postoperative pain control. Spinal and epidural anesthesia have been reported as successful options for anesthesia in myotonic dystrophy patients, either as sole anesthetics or as part of postoperative analgesia. Regional anesthesia can help mitigate the risks associated with systemic muscle relaxants, which should indeed be avoided or used sparingly in this patient population due to the potential for worsening muscle weakness and myotonia.

Recommended literature

1. Vydra DG, Rayi A. Myotonic Dystrophy. [Updated 2022 Jun 27]. In: StatPearls [Internet]. Treasure Island (FL): StatPearls Publishing; 2022 Jan-. Available from: https://www.ncbi.nlm.nih.gov/books/NBK557446/
2. Pollard BJ, Kitchen, G. Handbook of Clinical Anaesthesia. Fourth Edition. CRC Press. 2018. 978-1-4987-6289-2.
3. Marsh S, Pittard A. Neuromuscular disorders and anaesthesia. Part 2: specific neuromuscular disorders. Continuing Education in Anaesthesia Critical Care & Pain. 2011;11(4):119-23.

Neuromuscular diseases
PARKINSON'S DISEASE

Questions:

1. **What is NOT a hallmark symptom of Parkinson's disease?**
   A. Muscle rigidity
   B. Resting tremor
   C. Bradykinesia
   D. Muscle tingling

2. **What is the most consistent risk factor for developing Parkinson's disease?**
   A. Environmental toxins
   B. Young age
   C. Genetic mutations
   D. Increasing age

3. **Which medication class is commonly used as monotherapy in early Parkinson's disease or as an adjunct to levodopa therapy?**
   A. Antidepressants
   B. Antisialogogues
   C. Dopamine agonists
   D. Anticholinergics

4. **What is the characteristic symptom that distinguishes dopamine agonist withdrawal syndrome (DAWS)?**
   A. Muscle rigidity
   B. Anxiety
   C. Sleep disturbances
   D. Dysphagia

5. **Depression is a feature of Parkinson's disease that may precede the formal diagnosis.**
   A. True
   B. False

6. **A 45-year-old woman with Parkinson's disease is suffering from severe postoperative nausea and vomiting following a robotic-assisted laparoscopic hysterectomy under general anesthesia. She takes Levodopa 500 mg x3 as a dopamine replacement agent for the treatment of Parkinson's disease. The most suitable choice of antiemetic from this list for this patient would be?**
   A. IV metoclopramide 10mg
   B. IV ondansetron 4mg
   C. IV prochlorperazine 12.5mg
   D. IV droperidol 2.5mg

Answers:

1. **Answer D (Muscle tingling)**

   Muscle tingling or paresthesia is not a hallmark symptom of Parkinson's disease. Parkinson's disease is primarily characterized by the hallmark symptoms of muscle rigidity, resting tremor, and bradykinesia, which play pivotal roles in its diagnosis. Muscle rigidity involves increased muscle tone and stiffness, resting tremor manifests as involuntary shaking of a limb at rest, and bradykinesia refers to slowness of movement.

2. **Answer D (Increasing age)**

   The most consistent and well-established risk factor for developing Parkinson's disease (PD) is increasing age. While the exact etiology of PD remains unknown, it is widely recognized that advancing age is a significant risk factor. PD is more commonly diagnosed in older individuals, and the prevalence of the disease increases with age, especially in populations over the age of 65. While genetic mutations and environmental factors may also contribute to the development of PD, increasing age is consistently identified as the primary risk factor associated with the onset of the disease.

3. **Answer C (Dopamine agonists)**

   Dopamine agonists, such as Pramipexole and Ropinirole, are commonly used as monotherapy in the treatment of early Parkinson's disease. These medications mimic the action of dopamine, a neurotransmitter that is deficient in Parkinson's disease. By stimulating dopamine receptors in the brain, dopamine agonists help alleviate the motor symptoms associated with the disease, including resting tremor, muscle rigidity, and bradykinesia. They are often prescribed early in the disease course to manage symptoms and may be used alone before the introduction of other medications like levodopa-carbidopa.

4. **Answer B (Anxiety)**

   Dopamine agonist withdrawal syndrome (DAWS) is characterized by a range of symptoms that can occur upon the withdrawal of dopamine agonist medications, such as Pramipexole or Ropinirole, which are commonly used in the treatment of Parkinson's disease. While several symptoms can be associated with DAWS, anxiety is a particularly distinctive and prominent feature. Other symptoms of DAWS include panic attacks, dysphoria, depression, agitation, irritability, suicidal ideation, fatigue, orthostatic hypotension, nausea, vomiting, diaphoresis, generalized pain, and drug cravings.

5. **Answer A (True)**

   Many individuals with Parkinson's disease experience symptoms of depression before the motor symptoms become pronounced or before they receive a formal diagnosis. Depression can be an early non-motor symptom of Parkinson's disease and is often considered a prodromal or preclinical sign.

6. **Answer B (IV ondansetron 4mg)**

   In this case, it's crucial to consider the patient's underlying condition, Parkinson's disease, and her medication regimen, which includes Levodopa, a dopamine replacement agent. The main concern with antiemetics in Parkinson's disease patients is the potential for extrapyramidal side effects, which can worsen Parkinson's symptoms. Metoclopramide, prochlorperazine, and droperidol all have dopamine-blocking properties and can lead to extrapyramidal side effects, making them less suitable choices for this patient. Ondansetron, on the other hand, does not have a significant impact on dopamine receptors and is generally considered a safer option for antiemesis in Parkinson's disease patients.

Recommended literature

1. Pollard BJ, Kitchen, G. Handbook of Clinical Anaesthesia. Fourth Edition. CRC Press. 2018. 978-1-4987-6289-2.
2. Chambers DJ, Sebastian J, Ahearn DJ. Parkinson's disease. BJA Education. 2017;17(4):145-9.

Neuromuscular diseases
POLYMYOSITIS AND DERMATOMYOSITIS

10
CHAPTER

Questions:

1. **What are polymyositis and dermatomyositis?**
   A. Viral infections affecting muscles
   B. Autoimmune myopathies
   C. Neurological disorders causing muscle weakness
   D. Joint diseases leading to skin inflammation

2. **Which of the following is NOT a common symptom of polymyositis and dermatomyositis?**
   A. Fever
   B. Weight loss
   C. Shortness of breath
   D. Skin rash

3. **Which of the following serum enzymes is NOT typically elevated in both polymyositis and dermatomyositis?**
   A. Aminotransferases
   B. Creatine phosphokinase
   C. Lactate dehydrogenase
   D. Alkaline phosphatase

4. **What is the first-line treatment for polymyositis and dermatomyositis?**
   A. Immunoglobulin therapy
   B. Immunosuppressive drugs
   C. Corticosteroids
   D. Exercise therapy

5. **Raynaud's phenomenon can be associated with polymyositis and dermatomyositis.**
   A. True
   B. False

6. **A patient with a known history of both polymyositis and dermatomyositis is presented for surgical management of a trimalleolar fracture. The patient is experiencing symptoms related to the fracture, which necessitates surgical intervention. Several primary concerns need to be addressed in the perioperative management of this case, but which one of the concerns listed below is NOT a primary concern for this type of patient?**
   A. Difficult airway
   B. Muscle relaxants
   C. Aspiration risk
   D. Neurological injury related to regional anesthesia

Answers:

1. Answer B (Autoimmune myopathies)

Polymyositis and dermatomyositis are autoimmune myopathies characterized by muscle inflammation and weakness, primarily affecting proximal skeletal muscles. They are not viral infections but rather conditions where the immune system mistakenly attacks muscle tissue. While they can result in muscle weakness, they are not neurological disorders and do not primarily involve joint diseases or skin inflammation. The key feature that distinguishes them is that dermatomyositis, in addition to muscle involvement, is associated with characteristic skin manifestations, setting it apart from polymyositis.

2. Answer D (Skin rash)

All of the symptoms listed in the question are common symptoms of polymyositis and dermatomyositis, except for a skin rash. Both conditions typically manifest with muscle weakness, contraction of the arms and legs, shortness of breath, difficulty swallowing, muscle tenderness or pain, Raynaud's phenomenon, fever, feeling tired, and weight loss. A distinguishing feature of dermatomyositis is the presence of a skin rash.

3. Answer D (Alkaline phosphatase)

In both polymyositis and dermatomyositis, serum enzymes derived from muscle are typically elevated due to muscle inflammation and damage. Elevations in serum creatine kinase (CK), lactate dehydrogenase (LDH), aldolase, and aminotransferases (which include enzymes like alanine aminotransferase or ALT and aspartate aminotransferase or AST) are commonly seen in these conditions. However, alkaline phosphatase is not one of the enzymes typically elevated in the context of muscle inflammation and myositis. Alkaline phosphatase is an enzyme that is more closely associated with liver and bone health. Elevated levels of alkaline phosphatase are often indicative of liver disease or bone-related conditions but are not a characteristic marker of polymyositis or dermatomyositis.

4. Answer C (Corticosteroids)

The first-line treatment for both polymyositis and dermatomyositis is typically corticosteroids, such as prednisone. Corticosteroids help reduce muscle inflammation and suppress the immune response responsible for damaging muscle tissue. They are often used as the initial treatment to control symptoms and halt the progression of these autoimmune myopathies. While immunosuppressive drugs are also an important part of the treatment plan and may be used in conjunction with corticosteroids, corticosteroids are usually the first-line therapy. Immunoglobulin therapy may be considered in some cases, especially when other treatments are ineffective or poorly tolerated. Exercise therapy is important in the management of these conditions, but it is not typically considered the first-line treatment. Exercise is utilized to reduce muscle swelling and build or restore muscle strength as part of the overall management plan.

5. Answer A (True)

Raynaud's phenomenon can be associated with both polymyositis and dermatomyositis. Raynaud's phenomenon is characterized by fingers and toes becoming cold and discolored in response to cold or stress. It is not specific to these conditions but can be one of the symptoms or manifestations seen in individuals with polymyositis and dermatomyositis due to their autoimmune nature and effects on the circulatory system.

6. Answer D (Neurological injury related to regional anesthesia)

In the perioperative management of a patient with known Polymyositis and Dermatomyositis undergoing surgery, the primary concerns are typically centered around ensuring a secure airway due to potential difficulties related to muscle contractures, carefully titrating muscle relaxants to avoid overdosing, and mitigating the risk of aspiration, particularly in the presence of reflux disease While regional anesthesia is preferred whenever possible, the primary concerns, in this case, are related to airway and muscle relaxant use. Neurological injury related to regional anesthesia is not a primary concern for this patient, although positioning for regional anesthesia may be challenging due to deformities and muscle contractures.

Recommended literature

1. Christopher-Stine L, Vleugels An Amato AA. 2022 Clinical manifestations of dermatomyositis and polymyositis in adults. Up To Date.
2. Pollard BJ, Kitchen, G. Handbook of Clinical Anaesthesia. Fourth Edition. CRC Press. 2018. 978-1-4987-6289-2.
3. Raychaudhuri SP, Mitra A. Polymyositis and dermatomyositis: Disease spectrum and classification. Indian J Dermatol. 2012;57(5):366-370.
4. Dalakas MC, Hohlfeld R. Polymyositis and dermatomyositis. Lancet. 2003;362(9388):971-982.

OBSTETRICS

Obstetrics
AMNIOTIC FLUID EMBOLISM

11
CHAPTER

Questions:

1. **What is the primary mechanism behind amniotic fluid embolism (AFE)?**
   A. Mechanical respiratory obstruction
   B. Humoral effect causing anaphylactoid reactions
   C. Fetal distress
   D. Placental abnormalities

2. **Which of the following is NOT a common sign or symptom of AFE?**
   A. Acute dyspnea
   B. Sudden chills and shivering
   C. Bradycardia in the mother
   D. Altered mental status

3. **Which phase of AFE involves acute renal failure and acute respiratory distress syndrome (ARDS)?**
   A. Phase 1
   B. Phase 2
   C. Phase 3
   D. Phase 4

4. **Which condition should NOT be considered in the differential diagnosis of AFE, especially if there is sudden chest pain and shortness of breath?**
   A. Anaphylaxis
   B. Transfusion reaction
   C. Pancreatitis
   D. Aortic dissection

5. **ECG changes in amniotic fluid embolism include the S1Q3T3 pattern with a prominent S wave in lead I and prominent Q and T waves in lead III.**
   A. True
   B. False

6. **A 33-year-old gravida 3, para 1 parturient presents for an emergency caesarean section. After emergence from general anesthesia, the endotracheal tube is removed, and the patient becomes cyanotic. Oxygen is administered by positive-pressure bag and mask ventilation. High airway pressures are necessary to ventilate the patient, and wheezing is noted over both lung fields, along with hypoxemia. The patient's blood pressure falls from 130/80 to 80/60 mmHg, and her heart rate increases from 100 to 150 beats per minute. AFE is suspected. Which diagnostic criteria must be met to confirm AFE?**
   A. Hypotension, hypoxia, coagulopathy
   B. Hypertension, hypoglycemia, tachycardia
   C. Hyperthermia, hematuria, hypertension
   D. Bradycardia, bronchospasm, anemia

Answers:

1. **Answer B (Humoral effect causing anaphylactoid reactions)**

   Amniotic fluid embolism (AFE) is primarily caused by a humoral effect that leads to anaphylactoid reactions or complement activation. It occurs when amniotic fluid, fetal cells, hair, or other debris enter the maternal pulmonary circulation, triggering an immune response and a cascade of reactions in the body. While mechanical respiratory obstruction can occur as a consequence of AFE, it is not the primary mechanism. The primary mechanism involves the release of vasoactive substances and other factors from the amniotic fluid into the maternal circulation, leading to cardiovascular collapse, respiratory distress, and coagulopathy.

2. **Answer C (Bradycardia in the mother)**

   Bradycardia in the mother is not a common sign or symptom of AFE. AFE primarily affects the maternal respiratory and circulatory systems, leading to symptoms such as acute dyspnea, sudden chills and shivering, altered mental status, cough, anxiety, labored breathing, and tachypnea. Fetal bradycardia can occur in cases of fetal distress, but it is a sign of distress in the fetus rather than a symptom experienced by the mother. Maternal bradycardia is not typically associated with AFE. Instead, AFE is characterized by maternal tachycardia due to the acute physiological changes and stress it induces.

3. **Answer C (Phase 3)**

   AFE progresses through several phases, with each phase representing distinct clinical manifestations and challenges. Phase 1 is characterized by respiratory and circulatory disorders in the mother, such as acute dyspnea, altered mental status, and cardiovascular instability. In phase 2, coagulation disturbances become prominent, leading to significant bleeding and clotting abnormalities. Phase 3 is marked by acute renal failure and acute respiratory distress syndrome (ARDS), representing a critical and life-threatening stage with multi-organ dysfunction. Finally, phase 4, if reached, represents the recovery phase, where stabilization and recuperation occur.

4. **Answer C (Pancreatitis)**

   Pancreatitis is not typically considered in the differential diagnosis of AFE, especially if there is sudden chest pain and shortness of breath. AFE primarily presents with respiratory and circulatory distress symptoms, such as acute dyspnea, sudden chills, altered mental status, and cardiovascular instability. Conditions like anaphylaxis, aortic dissection, cholesterol embolism, myocardial infarction, pulmonary embolism, septic shock, air embolism, and transfusion reaction are more relevant in the differential diagnosis of AFE because they share overlapping clinical features and can be associated with chest pain and shortness of breath. Pancreatitis is a condition involving inflammation of the pancreas and is not typically associated with these specific symptoms and clinical presentation in the context of AFE.

5. **Answer B (False)**

   The ECG changes described in the statement, specifically the "S1Q3T3 pattern" with a prominent S wave in lead I and prominent Q and T waves in lead III, are not typically associated with AFE. These specific ECG changes are often seen in the context of pulmonary embolism (PE), which can have overlapping clinical features with AFE due to the involvement of the pulmonary circulation. In AFE, ECG changes may occur but are not consistently characterized by the S1Q3T3 pattern. ECG findings in AFE can be variable and may include tachycardia, arrhythmias, ST-segment changes, and other non-specific abnormalities.

6. **Answer A (Hypotension, hypoxia, coagulopathy)**

   To confirm a diagnosis of AFE, specific diagnostic criteria must be met. These criteria include acute hypotension, acute hypoxia, and coagulopathy or severe hemorrhage. In this case, the patient's presentation aligns with these diagnostic criteria, further raising suspicion of AFE.

Recommended literature

1. Pollard BJ, Kitchen, G. Handbook of Clinical Anaesthesia. Fourth Edition. CRC Press. 2018. 978-1-4987-6289-2.
2. Kaur K, Bhardwaj M, Kumar P, Singhal S, Singh T, Hooda S. Amniotic fluid embolism. J Anaesthesiol Clin Pharmacol. 2016;32(2):153-159.

ANTEPARTUM BLEEDING

Questions:

1. **What is the definition of antepartum bleeding (APB)?**
   A. Bleeding after conception
   B. Bleeding after the birth of the baby
   C. Bleeding after 12 weeks of gestation
   D. Bleeding after 24 weeks of gestation

2. **Which of the following is NOT a degree of APB?**
   A. Bruising
   B. Spotting
   C. Minor hemorrhage
   D. Massive hemorrhage

3. **What is NOT a common cause of antepartum bleeding?**
   A. Breech position
   B. Vasa previa
   C. Uterine rupture
   D. Cervicitis

4. **Which of the following is NOT considered a fetal complication associated with antepartum bleeding?**
   A. Fetal hypoxia
   B. Fetal neural tube defect
   C. Prematurity
   D. Fetal death

5. **APB is occurring in 5% to 6% of pregnant women.**
   A. True
   B. False

6. **A 32-year-old woman, currently at 32 weeks of pregnancy, presents to the obstetrics clinic with signs of unexplained minor hemorrhage. She reports experiencing minimal spotting over the past few hours. Maternal monitoring, including vital signs, remains within the normal range, and fetal monitoring indicates that the baby is stable. Blood test results are also within normal limits. However, the healthcare team is concerned about the risk of premature delivery. What should be the preferred intervention in this case?**
   A. Emergency caesarean delivery
   B. Induce labor
   C. Corticosteroids
   D. Antibiotics

Answers:

1. Answer D (Bleeding after 24 weeks of gestation)

Antepartum bleeding (APB) is defined as bleeding from the genital tract that occurs after 24 weeks of gestation and before the birth of the baby. This definition distinguishes APB from bleeding that might occur earlier in pregnancy, such as during the first trimester, which is often referred to as "early pregnancy bleeding" and is considered separately from antepartum bleeding. APB is a significant concern in pregnancy, and this definition helps healthcare providers differentiate it from other types of bleeding during pregnancy.

2. Answer A (Bruising)

APB consists of four degrees: Spotting, characterized by minimal stains or spotting of blood; Minor hemorrhage, involving less than 50 mL of blood loss; Major hemorrhage, with blood loss ranging from 50 to 1000 mL and typically without signs of circulatory shock; and Massive hemorrhage, where blood loss exceeds 1000 mL, with or without accompanying circulatory shock. However, "Bruising" is not a degree of APB. These degrees of APB are defined by different levels of blood loss and related symptoms, but bruising typically results from contusions or trauma and is not a specific degree of antepartum bleeding.

3. Answer A (Breech position)

Breech position, where the baby's buttocks or feet are positioned to be delivered first instead of the head, is not a common cause of antepartum bleeding. The other options, including vasa previa, uterine rupture, cervicitis, placenta abnormalities, and amniotic fluid embolism, are associated with antepartum bleeding. Breech presentation relates to the fetal position for delivery and does not directly lead to antepartum bleeding.

4. Answer B (Fetal Neural Tube Defect)

Fetal neural tube defects, such as spina bifida, are typically congenital structural abnormalities in the central nervous system, and they are not directly associated with antepartum bleeding. The other options, including fetal hypoxia, prematurity (both iatrogenic and spontaneous), and fetal death, are considered fetal complications associated with antepartum bleeding. Fetal neural tube defects are generally considered birth defects that result from a failure of neural tube closure during early embryonic development and are not directly related to antepartum bleeding.

5. Answer A (True)

Antepartum bleeding occurs in approximately 5% to 6% of pregnant women, making it a relatively frequent issue during pregnancy. It is a significant concern due to its potential impact on both maternal and fetal health.

6. Answer C (Corticosteroids)

In cases of preterm birth associated with APB and the presence of signs suggestive of premature delivery, the preferred intervention is to administer corticosteroids. Corticosteroids, such as betamethasone or dexamethasone, are commonly used in such situations. These medications are given to the mother to promote fetal lung maturation, reduce the risk of respiratory distress syndrome in premature infants, and improve neonatal outcomes. Corticosteroids do not necessarily stop labor but prepare the fetal lungs to function better in the event of preterm birth. Emergency caesarean sections are typically performed when there is an immediate threat to the mother's or the fetus's life or well-being. Inducing labor or using antibiotics may be considered in specific situations but are not the primary choice when the primary concern is prematurity associated with APB.

Recommended literature

1. Walfish, M., Neuman, A., Wlody, D., 2009. Maternal haemorrhage. British Journal of Anaesthesia 103, i47–i56.
2. Mercier FJ, Van de Velde M. Major obstetric hemorrhage. Anesthesiol Clin. 2008;26(1):53-vi.
3. Antepartum haemorrhage Green-top Guideline No. 63 November 2011 royal College of obstreticans and gynaecologists. https://www.rcog.org.uk/media/pwdi1tef/gtg_63.pdf

BREASTFEEDING PATIENT

11

CHAPTER

Questions:

1. What is the Relative Infant Dose (RID) value that is generally considered safe for medications in breast milk?
   A. Less than 5%
   B. Less than 10%
   C. Less than 25%
   D. Less than 50%

2. Which opioid is not recommended for breastfeeding mothers due to the risk of neonatal opioid overdose?
   A. Morphine
   B. Codeine
   C. Oxycodone
   D. Hydromorphone

3. When can a breastfeeding mother typically resume nursing her infant after undergoing anesthesia?
   A. Immediately after surgery
   B. After 6 hours
   C. As soon as she is alert and stable
   D. The next day

4. Which analgesic is generally considered safe for breastfeeding mothers?
   A. Ibuprofen
   B. Diclofenac
   C. Naproxen
   D. Dexketoprofen

5. Aspirin in analgesic doses is generally safe for use in breastfeeding mothers.
   A. True
   B. False

6. A 25-year-old woman is scheduled for laparoscopic cholecystectomy and is also breastfeeding, with a strong desire to continue nursing her infant as soon as possible after the surgery. The anesthetic management must take into account the safety of both the mother and the infant. What anesthetic should be used with caution in these patients?
   A. Propofol
   B. Etomidate
   C. Thiopental
   D. Ketamine

Answers:

1. **Answer B (Less than 10%)**

   The Relative Infant Dose (RID) is a measure that indicates the percentage of a drug transferred from the mother's milk to the nursing infant relative to the mother's dose. An RID value of less than 10% is generally considered safe for medications in breast milk. This means that if the RID is less than 10%, it is unlikely that the medication in the breast milk will have a significant effect on the nursing infant, and it is considered safe for breastfeeding. RID values greater than 10% may raise concerns about potential risks to the infant, so medications with higher RID values may not be recommended for breastfeeding mothers to ensure the infant's safety.

2. **Answer B (Codeine)**

   Codeine is not recommended for breastfeeding mothers due to the risk of neonatal opioid overdose. Codeine is metabolized in the body to its active form (morphine) by the liver enzyme CYP2D6. However, there is a wide variability in how individuals metabolize codeine, and some mothers may be "ultra-metabolizers" of codeine, leading to high levels of morphine in their breast milk. If an "ultra-metabolizer" mother breastfeeds a "slow metabolizer" neonate, the infant may be exposed to excessive levels of morphine, which can lead to symptoms of opioid overdose in the newborn, including sedation, respiratory depression and other serious side effects. Therefore, due to this risk, codeine is generally not recommended for breastfeeding mothers, and alternative pain management options should be considered.

3. **Answer C (As soon as she is alert and stable)**

   Typically, a breastfeeding mother can resume nursing her infant as soon as she is alert and stable after undergoing anesthesia and surgery. This means that as soon as the mother has recovered from the effects of anesthesia, is awake, and can provide proper care for the baby, she can safely breastfeed. The key consideration is the mother's ability to care for the infant and the absence of lingering effects of anesthesia that might affect her alertness and coordination. There is generally no need to delay breastfeeding until the next day or for an extended period unless there are specific medical reasons or instructions from the healthcare provider to do so.

4. **Answer A (Ibuprofen)**

   Ibuprofen is generally considered safe for breastfeeding mothers. It belongs to the class of non-steroidal anti-inflammatory drugs (NSAIDs) and is commonly used for pain relief, including postoperative pain. Ibuprofen has a relatively low transfer to breast milk, and when taken as directed, it is usually considered safe for nursing infants. It is a preferred choice for pain management in breastfeeding mothers because of its safety profile.

5. **Answer B (False)**

   Aspirin (acetylsalicylic acid) is generally not considered safe for breastfeeding mothers, especially in analgesic doses. Aspirin is an NSAID that can pass into breast milk and potentially harm the nursing infant. The use of aspirin in breastfeeding mothers can be associated with a risk of Reye's syndrome in the infant, a rare but serious condition that can affect the liver and brain. Due to the potential risks associated with aspirin, it is advisable for breastfeeding mothers to avoid its use for pain relief. Instead, healthcare providers typically recommend other pain relievers, such as acetaminophen or ibuprofen, which have a better safety profile for use during breastfeeding.

6. **Answer D (Ketamine)**

   Ketamine is an anesthetic agent that should be used with caution in breastfeeding patients. While ketamine is generally considered safe for use during anesthesia, it is known to transfer into breast milk, albeit in relatively low amounts. Ketamine's safety during breastfeeding is a matter of some concern because it can potentially lead to neonatal sedation or behavioral changes in the nursing infant. The effects on the infant are typically short-lived, as ketamine is rapidly metabolized and excreted from the mother's body. In this case, since the breastfeeding mother wishes to continue breastfeeding as soon as possible after surgery, it is advisable to use anesthetic agents with lower RID values that are less likely to have a significant impact on the infant, like propofol, etomidate, or thiopental.

Recommended literature

1. Mitchell, J., Jones, W., Winkley, E., Kinsella, S.M., 2020. Guideline on anaesthesia and sedation in breastfeeding women 2020. Anaesthesia 75, 1482–1493.
2. Wanderer JP, Rathmell JP. 2017. Anesthesia & breastfeeding: more often than not, they are compatible. 127;4.
3. General principles for anesthesia and perioperative management for a patient who is breastfeeding. Uptodate.com
4. Statement on resuming breastfeeding after anesthesia. 2019. American Society of Anesthesiologists.

BREECH PRESENTATION

Questions:

1. **What is the primary characteristic that defines breech presentation?**

   A. Transverse fetal lie

   B. Fetal head enters the pelvis first

   C. Fetal buttocks or lower extremity entering the pelvis first

   D. Fetal spine positioned along the maternal spine

2. **Which type of breech presentation involves the fetus having flexion of both hips and straight legs with the feet near the fetal face?**

   A. Complete breech

   B. Frank breech

   C. Incomplete breech

   D. Footling breech

3. **Which factor is NOT associated with an increased risk of breech presentation?**

   A. Prematurity

   B. Uterine leiomyoma

   C. Multiple gestations

   D. Primiparity

4. **What is the primary concern that makes vaginal delivery unsafe for a breech baby?**

   A. Increased maternal discomfort

   B. Risk of maternal infection

   C. Risk of fetal injury and umbilical cord problems

   D. Longer labor duration

5. **Breech presentation occurs in approximately 3-4% of all term pregnancies.**

   A. True

   B. False

6. **A 23-year-old pregnant woman, at 40 weeks of gestation, presents to the labor and delivery unit in active labor. Her baby is in a breech presentation. As labor progresses, a critical situation arises where the fetal head becomes entrapped, necessitating immediate medical intervention. This scenario requires rapid decision-making and action to address the emergency and safely deliver the baby. What is NOT the appropriate course of action for this obstetric emergency?**

   A. Nitroglycerin IV 100-400 mcg

   B. General anesthesia with RSI

   C. Maintenance of anesthesia with 2-3 MAC of volatile agents

   D. Subarachnoidal block

Answers:

1. Answer C (Fetal buttocks or lower extremity entering the pelvis first)

Breech presentation is defined by the primary characteristic of the fetus having its buttocks or lower extremity entering the mother's pelvis first rather than the fetal head. This is the distinguishing feature that categorizes a presentation as breech. The other options do not define breech presentation.

2. Answer B (Frank breech)

The type of breech presentation that involves the fetus having flexion of both hips and straight legs with the feet near the fetal face is referred to as "Frank breech". In Frank breech, the baby's buttocks are the presenting part, and the legs are extended upward in a pike position, with the feet positioned close to the fetal face. It's important to distinguish Frank breech from the other types of breech presentations: "Complete breech" is characterized by both hips being flexed and both legs tucked in a tuck position; "Incomplete breech" includes various combinations of hip and leg positions, and it can encompass "footling breech", where one leg is extended and the foot or feet present, but not both legs in the extended position typical of Frank breech.

3. Answer D (Primiparity)

The factor that is NOT associated with an increased risk of breech presentation is primiparity or first-time pregnancy. While prematurity, uterine leiomyoma, and multiple gestations are known risk factors for breech presentation, first-time pregnancy does not increase the likelihood of breech presentation. Premature babies may not have rotated to a head-down position, uterine fibroids can interfere with fetal positioning, and multiple gestations can lead to breech presentations due to limited uterine space.

4. Answer C (Risk of fetal injury and umbilical cord problems)

The primary concern that makes vaginal delivery unsafe for a breech baby is the risk of fetal injury and umbilical cord problems. Breech presentation during vaginal delivery carries a higher risk of potential fetal injury, such as dislocated or broken bones, and umbilical cord issues, including cord compression, flattening, or twisting. These risks make a vaginal breech delivery less safe compared to a caesarean delivery.

5. Answer A (True)

Breech presentation is relatively common in pregnancies, occurring in approximately 3-4% of all term pregnancies. This means that for a significant portion of pregnancies, the baby is positioned with the buttocks or lower extremities entering the pelvis first instead of the head.

6. Answer D (Subarachnoidal block)

In this critical obstetric emergency scenario involving a 23-year-old pregnant woman in active labor at 40 weeks with a breech presentation and fetal head entrapment, the inappropriate course of action is placing a subarachnoidal block. The primary goal is to relax the uterus and liberate the entrapped fetal head. Various measures may be employed, including the use of nitroglycerin IV 100-400 mcg or nitroglycerin SL 400-800 mcg to achieve uterine relaxation. If these measures do not succeed, general anesthesia with RSI (propofol/succinylcholine) is necessary. Concurrently, "2-3 MAC of volatile agents" may be used to further relax the uterus. The primary focus remains on addressing the fetal head entrapment through obstetric maneuvers and, if required, the safe delivery of the baby through emergency caesarean section, all aimed at ensuring the well-being of both the mother and the infant.

Recommended literature

1. Gray CJ, Shanahan MM. 2022. Breech presentation. StatPearls.
2. Hofmeyer GD. 2022. Overview of breech presentation. Up to date.
3. 2017. Management of Breech Presentation. BJOG: An International Journal of Obstetrics & Gynaecology 124, e151-e177.
4. Stitely ML, Gherman RB. Labor with abnormal presentation and position. Obstet Gynecol Clin North Am. 2005;32(2):165-179.
5. Pratt SD. Anesthesia for breech presentation and multiple gestation. Clin Obstet Gynecol. 2003;46(3):711-729.
6. Pollack KL, Chestnut DH. 1990. Anesthesia for complicated vaginal deliveries. Anesthesiology clinics of North America. 8;1:115-129.

CAESAREAN DELIVERY

Questions:

1. Which anesthesia technique is commonly used for scheduled caesarean deliveries?
   A. General anesthesia
   B. Epidural anesthesia
   C. Combined spinal-epidural (CSE)
   D. Single-shot spinal anesthesia

2. What is the recommended time frame for the decision-to-delivery interval in cases of emergency caesarean sections?
   A. Immediately
   B. ≤ 10 minutes
   C. ≤ 30 minutes
   D. ≤ 60 minutes

3. What maternal condition is an absolute contraindication for using regional anesthesia in caesarean delivery?
   A. Multiples
   B. Preeclampsia
   C. Maternal high blood pressure
   D. Abnormalities of clotting

4. What is the primary reason for the shift from general anesthesia to neuraxial anesthesia for caesarean delivery?
   A. Reduced maternal mortality
   B. Reduced neonatal morbidity
   C. Faster onset of action
   D. Satisfactory anesthesia

5. Approximately 36 weeks gestation is not the recommended timing for elective caesarean delivery to optimize neonatal outcomes.
   A. True
   B. False

6. A 34-year-old woman is scheduled for an elective caesarean section under spinal anesthesia. The procedure goes smoothly, with adequate sensory and motor block achieved. The baby is delivered, and the cord is clamped. Following cord clamping, it is essential to administer a uterotonic drug to prevent and treat uterine atony and postpartum hemorrhage. Which uterotonic drug is considered the first-line choice to prevent and treat uterine atony and postpartum hemorrhage?
   A. Methylergonovine
   B. Oxytocin
   C. Misoprostol
   D. Ergometrine

Answers:

1. **Answer D (Single-shot spinal anesthesia)**

   Single-shot spinal anesthesia is frequently used for scheduled caesarean deliveries due to its advantages, including reliability and the ability to provide adequate pain relief during the procedure. Regional anesthesia, especially spinal anesthesia, has also been favored as the best choice for elective uncomplicated caesarean delivery, as it avoids airway-related risks, reduces the chances of aspiration of gastric content, and is relatively easy to perform. It is a preferred choice for elective procedures because of its effectiveness and rapid onset of action.

2. **Answer C (≤ 30 minutes)**

   In cases of emergency caesarean sections, the goal is to minimize the time between the decision to proceed with the surgery and the actual delivery of the baby to ensure the safety of both the mother and the fetus. The recommended time frame for the decision-to-delivery interval is typically within 30 minutes. This rapid response helps to address critical situations promptly and prevent complications that may arise during emergencies. It allows healthcare providers to prepare and perform the surgery efficiently to safeguard the well-being of the mother and the baby.

3. **Answer D (Abnormalities of clotting)**

   Abnormalities of clotting, such as coagulation disorders or bleeding disorders, are an absolute contraindication for regional anesthesia, including spinal or epidural anesthesia, during caesarean delivery. This contraindication extends to patients on anticoagulation therapy because anticoagulants can impair the blood's ability to clot, increasing the risk of bleeding and hematoma formation during regional anesthesia. When a patient is on anticoagulation therapy or has clotting abnormalities, there is a heightened risk of spinal or epidural hematoma formation, which can compress the spinal cord and lead to serious neurological complications. Therefore, in such cases, general anesthesia may be the preferred option for anesthesia during caesarean delivery to ensure the safety of the mother and baby, as it avoids the risk associated with regional anesthesia.

4. **Answer A (Reduced maternal mortality)**

   The shift from general anesthesia (GA) to neuraxial anesthesia (NA), which includes spinal or epidural anesthesia, for caesarean delivery has been primarily driven by the goal of reducing maternal mortality. Historical data indicated higher maternal mortality rates associated with general anesthesia. The use of general anesthesia during caesarean sections was linked to an increased risk of airway complications, aspiration of gastric contents, and difficulties in airway management, all of which could result in adverse maternal outcomes. Neuraxial anesthesia, on the other hand, avoids the potential complications associated with general anesthesia. It provides effective pain relief, ensures a maintained patent airway, and allows for better maternal respiratory function. This results in a significant reduction in maternal mortality rates during caesarean deliveries, making it the preferred choice for anesthesia in elective and non-emergent cases.

5. **Answer B (False)**

   The ideal timing for an elective caesarean delivery is typically around 39 weeks gestation. This allows for adequate fetal lung maturation, reducing the risk of neonatal respiratory distress syndrome and related complications. Elective caesarean deliveries at 36 weeks may increase the risk of neonatal health issues due to the baby's lungs and other vital organs not being fully developed.

6. **Answer B (Oxytocin)**

   Oxytocin is the preferred uterotonic agent in this situation because it helps the uterus contract, reducing the risk of excessive bleeding after delivery. It is effective, safe, and has minimal side effects when administered appropriately. Oxytocin can be given as a bolus dose immediately after delivery (e.g., 1 IU for an elective caesarean section), followed by a titrated intravenous infusion (e.g., starting at 2.5 IU/h). This helps the uterus to contract and minimizes the risk of postpartum hemorrhage. While other uterotonic drugs like methylergonovine, misoprostol, and ergometrine have their roles in managing postpartum hemorrhage, oxytocin is generally the first choice due to its safety profile and effectiveness in promoting uterine contractions.

Recommended literature

1. Neall G, Bampoe S, Sultan P. 2022. Analgesia for Caesarean section. BJA Education. 22;5:197-203.
2. Delgado C, Ring L, Mushambi MC. 2020. General anesthesia in obstetrics. BJA Education. 20;6:201-207.
3. Adshead, D., Wrench, I., Woolnough, M., 2020. Enhanced recovery for elective Caesarean section. BJA Education 20, 354–357.
4. Pollard BJ, Kitchen, G. Handbook of Clinical Anaesthesia. Fourth Edition. CRC Press. 2018. 978-1-4987-6289-2.
5. McGlennan A, Mustafa A. 2009. General anaesthesia for Caesarean section. Continuing Education in Anaesthesa Critical Care & Pain. 9;5:148-151.

CERVICAL CERCLAGE

Questions:

1. **What is the primary objective of cervical cerclage?**
   - A. To alleviate cervical infections
   - B. To prevent uterine contractions
   - C. To extend the duration of pregnancy in women at risk of preterm delivery due to cervical insufficiency
   - D. To expedite labor in high-risk pregnancies

2. **Which of the following is NOT a risk factor for cervical insufficiency requiring cerclage?**
   - A. Prior cervical procedures or trauma
   - B. Maternal connective tissue diseases
   - C. Multiple gestations
   - D. Maternal exposure to diethylstilbestrol in utero

3. **When might a history-indicated cervical cerclage be performed?**
   - A. Any time during pregnancy
   - B. Only during the first trimester
   - C. After experiencing a third-trimester loss
   - D. After one or more second-trimester pregnancy losses related to painless cervical dilation

4. **Which technique involves suturing anterior-posterior and posterior-anterior after an incision of the mucosa of the anterior cervix during cervical cerclage?**
   - A. McDonald method
   - B. Transabdominal cerclage
   - C. Shirodkar method
   - D. Transvaginal cerclage

5. **Rupture of fetal membranes is the risk associated with cervical cerclage.**
   - A. True
   - B. False

6. **A 23-week pregnant patient with a history of one second-trimester pregnancy loss related to painless cervical dilation is scheduled for a Shirodkar method of cervical cerclage. An ultrasound has confirmed that the cervical length in the current singleton pregnancy is less than 25 mm, indicating the need for the procedure. What is not a good statement regarding anesthesia technique for this patient?**
   - A. Induce spinal anesthesia in the sitting position
   - B. Epidural anesthesia should cover T10 - L1 as well as S2 - S4
   - C. Avoid NSAIDs
   - D. General anesthesia with volatile anesthetics and opioids

Answers:

1. **Answer C (To extend the duration of pregnancy in women at risk of preterm delivery due to cervical insufficiency)**

   The primary objective of cervical cerclage is to extend the duration of pregnancy in women who are at risk of preterm delivery due to cervical insufficiency. Cervical cerclage is a surgical procedure that involves suturing the cervix to reinforce it and prevent it from dilating prematurely. This helps in reducing the risk of preterm birth, which is a common complication associated with cervical insufficiency.

2. **Answer C (Multiple gestations)**

   Multiple gestations are NOT considered a typical risk factor for cervical insufficiency requiring cerclage. The risk factors for cervical insufficiency are prior cervical procedures or trauma, maternal connective tissue diseases or abnormalities, maternal exposure to diethylstilbestrol in utero, and other factors that can contribute to cervical insufficiency.

3. **Answer: D (After one or more second-trimester pregnancy losses related to painless cervical dilation)**

   A history-indicated cervical cerclage may be performed after experiencing one or more second-trimester pregnancy losses related to painless cervical dilation. This type of cerclage is indicated for women who have a history of such losses, and it is not limited to a specific trimester within pregnancy. It is aimed at preventing recurrent preterm births due to cervical insufficiency, which is evident from the history of second-trimester losses related to cervical dilation.

4. **Answer C (Shirodkar method)**

   The technique that involves suturing anterior-posterior and posterior-anterior after an incision of the mucosa of the anterior cervix during cervical cerclage is the Shirodkar method. In this method, the cervix is sutured both anteriorly and posteriorly after an incision is made in the mucosa of the anterior cervix. This procedure helps to reinforce and provide additional support to the cervix to prevent premature cervical dilation, reducing the risk of preterm birth.

5. **Answer A (True)**

   Rupture of fetal membranes is one of the potential risks associated with cervical cerclage, as indicated in the provided information. Cervical cerclage involves suturing the cervix to prevent it from dilating prematurely, but there is a risk that the fetal membranes may rupture during or after the procedure, which can lead to complications in the pregnancy.

6. **Answer A (Induce spinal anesthesia in the sitting position)**

   Inducing spinal anesthesia in the sitting position is not the best choice for this patient. The sitting position carries a risk of lumbar spine flexion, which can lead to bulging of the fetal membranes, their rupture, and subsequent fetal death. During a Shirodkar cerclage procedure, spinal or epidural anesthesia is often preferred because it provides effective regional anesthesia without the risks associated with general anesthesia. It is generally recommended to induce spinal or epidural anesthesia with the patient in a lateral or lying position to minimize position-related risks.

Recommended literature

1. Bieber KB, Olson SM. Cervical Cerclage. [Updated 2022 Aug 1]. In: StatPearls [Internet]. Treasure Island (FL): StatPearls Publishing; 2022 Jan-. Available from: https://www.ncbi.nlm.nih.gov/books/NBK560523/
2. Shennan, A, Story, L, Jacobsson, B, Grobman, WA; the FIGO Working Group for Preterm Birth. FIGO good practice recommendations on cervical cerclage for prevention of preterm birth. Int J Gynecol Obstet. 2021; 155: 19– 22.

CHALLENGES IN OBSTETRIC ANESTHESIOLOGY

11
CHAPTER

Questions:

1. Which type of pain is primarily experienced during the latter part of the first stage and into the second stage of labor?

   A. Visceral pain

   B. Somatic pain

   C. Neuropathic pain

   D. Referred pain

2. Which medication class does not cross the uteroplacental barrier?

   A. Propofol

   B. Benzodiazepines

   C. Neuromuscular blocking agents

   D. Opioids

3. What is the primary purpose of cricoid pressure during obstetric general anesthesia induction?

   A. To facilitate intubation

   B. To prevent gastric aspiration

   C. To monitor maternal heart rate

   D. To monitor fetal heart rate

4. What is the preferred approach for pain relief during the first and early second stages of labor?

   A. Intravenous opioids

   B. Epidural analgesia

   C. General anesthesia

   D. Spinal anesthesia

5. Use of Entonox during labor results in a low Apgar score at birth.

   A. True

   B. False

6. A 32-year-old pregnant patient, currently in labor, has a history of thrombophilia and is on a therapeutic dose of enoxaparin (40 mg) which she administered two hours before arriving at the hospital. She is experiencing significant pain during labor and is requesting pain relief. Given her medical history, what would be the most appropriate choice for pain relief in this case?

   A. Single shot spinal anesthesia

   B. Epidural anesthesia

   C. No Anesthesia

   D. PCA (Patient-Controlled Analgesia) with remifentanil

Answers:

1. **Answer B (Somatic pain)**

   During the latter part of the first stage and into the second stage of labor, somatic pain is primarily experienced. Somatic pain is mediated via spinal segments T12-L1 and S2-4, and it is located in the vagina, rectum, and perineum. This type of pain is different from the visceral pain experienced during the first and early second stages of labor, which is mediated by spinal segments T10 to L1 and is felt in the abdomen, sacrum, and back.

2. **Answer C (Neuromuscular blocking agents)**

   Neuromuscular blocking agents, such as vecuronium, rocuronium, and succinylcholine, do not cross the uteroplacental barrier. This means that they do not pass from the mother's bloodstream to the fetal bloodstream. In contrast, other medication classes like intravenous agents, benzodiazepines, and opioids are capable of crossing the uteroplacental barrier and can affect the fetus.

3. **Answer B (To prevent gastric aspiration)**

   The primary purpose of cricoid pressure during obstetric general anesthesia induction is to prevent gastric aspiration. It is a safety measure to reduce the risk of regurgitation and aspiration of stomach contents, which can be especially concerning during general anesthesia induction when patients are not conscious to protect their airways. Cricoid pressure is applied to the cricoid cartilage area in the neck to occlude the esophagus, thereby preventing the contents of the stomach from flowing back into the throat and potentially entering the respiratory system.

4. **Answer B (Epidural analgesia)**

   The preferred approach for pain relief during the first and early second stages of labor is epidural analgesia. Epidural analgesia involves the administration of local anesthetics and sometimes opioids into the epidural space to provide pain relief while allowing the mother to remain alert and participate in the birthing process.

5. **Answer B (False)**

   The use of Entonox (nitrous oxide and oxygen gas mixture) during labor is generally considered safe for both the mother and the fetus. It is commonly used as a form of inhaled analgesia to provide pain relief during labor and does not typically result in a low Apgar score at birth. The Apgar score is a quick assessment of a newborn's overall health and well-being at one minute and five minutes after birth, which assesses factors such as heart rate, respiratory effort, muscle tone, reflex irritability, and skin color. The administration of Entonox during labor is not associated with the factors that would lead to a low Apgar score.

6. **Answer D (PCA (Patient-Controlled Analgesia) with remifentanil)**

   In this scenario, with the patient having received enoxaparin two hours before labor and the contraindication for regional anesthesia due to the anticoagulant effects, PCA (Patient-Controlled Analgesia) with remifentanil is the most appropriate choice for pain relief during labor. While it may be considered less effective than epidural anesthesia, PCA with remifentanil is a safe and viable alternative when regional anesthesia is contraindicated. This method allows the patient to have control over their pain management, offering relief while minimizing the risk associated with recent anticoagulant administration. It is essential to monitor and adjust the PCA regimen as needed to ensure the patient's comfort and safety during labor.

Recommended literature

1. Delgado, C., Ring, L., Mushambi, M.C., 2020. General anaesthesia in obstetrics. BJA Education 20, 201–207.
2. Pollard BJ, Kitchen, G. Handbook of Clinical Anaesthesia. Fourth Edition. CRC Press. 2018. 978-1-4987-6289-2.

DYSPNEA DURING PREGNANCY

11
CHAPTER

Questions:

1. **Which trimester is associated with the typical onset of pathological dyspnea during pregnancy?**
   A. First trimester
   B. Second trimester
   C. Third trimester
   D. It can occur in any trimester

2. **What is the likely cause of physiological dyspnea during pregnancy?**
   A. Decrease in tidal volume
   B. Progesterone-induced hyperventilation
   C. Polycythemia
   D. Decreased pulmonary blood flow

3. **What is the primary treatment for venous thromboembolism in pregnant women?**
   A. Oral anticoagulants
   B. Injectable heparins
   C. Antiplatelet agents
   D. Thrombolytics

4. **Which of the following is NOT a potential cause of pathological dyspnea during pregnancy?**
   A. Pericarditis
   B. Pulmonary embolism
   C. Preeclampsia/eclampsia
   D. Hyperthyroidism

5. **60 – 70% of pregnant women experience some form of dyspnea during the gestation period.**
   A. True
   B. False

6. **The 23-year-old patient presented to ED with acute dyspnea that began in the second trimester of pregnancy. She is unable to tolerate the supine position and is experiencing difficulty in performing daily activities. A heart murmur is auscultated during the physical examination. A cardiac echocardiogram indicates findings suggestive of Cardiomyopathy with mitral regurgitation. Which drug class is contraindicated in the treatment of cardiac dysfunction during pregnancy?**
   A. Diuretics
   B. Beta-blockers
   C. ACE inhibitors
   D. Calcium channel blockers

Answers:

1. **Answer B (Second trimester)**

   Pathological dyspnea during pregnancy usually starts in the second trimester. While dyspnea can occur at any point during pregnancy, the second trimester is when it is more commonly observed in pathological cases. This is an important clinical consideration for healthcare providers when evaluating pregnant individuals with respiratory symptoms, as the timing of onset can provide valuable diagnostic information.

2. **Answer B (Progesterone-induced hyperventilation)**

   The likely cause of physiological dyspnea during pregnancy is progesterone-induced hyperventilation. This hormone, which increases during pregnancy, stimulates the respiratory center in the brain, leading to heightened ventilation. In addition to progesterone-induced hyperventilation, several factors, such as body habitus, anemia, and increased pulmonary blood flow, play a role in facilitating the increase in tidal volume required to meet the heightened oxygen consumption during pregnancy. These changes are normal adaptations to the physiological demands of pregnancy and help ensure adequate oxygen supply to both the mother and the developing fetus.

3. **Answer B (Injectable heparins)**

   The primary treatment for venous thromboembolism (VTE) in pregnant women is injectable heparins (such as low molecular weight heparin or unfractionated heparin) because they are considered safe for both the mother and the fetus. Oral anticoagulants and thrombolytics are generally avoided during pregnancy due to potential fetal risks, and antiplatelet agents are typically used for arterial rather than venous thromboembolic conditions.

4. **Answer D (Hyperthyroidism)**

   In the context of the listed potential causes for pathological dyspnea during pregnancy, hyperthyroidism is not typically associated with this symptom. While hyperthyroidism can cause various symptoms and complications, it is not a common cause of pathological dyspnea during pregnancy. The other options are known potential causes of pathological dyspnea during pregnancy.

5. **Answer A (True)**

   Dyspnea is a common symptom during pregnancy, and it is estimated that a significant percentage of pregnant women, approximately 60% to 70%, experience some form of dyspnea at various stages of their gestation period. This is often due to the physiological changes in the respiratory and cardiovascular systems that occur during pregnancy, as well as the increased oxygen demand associated with the growing fetus. It is important for healthcare providers to be aware of this common symptom and differentiate between physiological pregnancy-related dyspnea and pathological dyspnea to provide appropriate care.

6. **Answer C (ACE inhibitors)**

   In the context of this patient's cardiac dysfunction during pregnancy, ACE inhibitors (Angiotensin-Converting Enzyme inhibitors) are contraindicated. ACE inhibitors, such as enalapril or lisinopril, are known to pose a risk to the developing fetus, particularly during the second and third trimesters of pregnancy. They can lead to fetal renal impairment, oligohydramnios, and neonatal hypotension. Therefore, ACE inhibitors should not be used for the treatment of cardiac dysfunction during pregnancy. Instead, other medications or interventions may be considered, and the treatment plan should be developed in consultation with a specialist experienced in managing cardiac issues in pregnant individuals.

Recommended literature

1. Mehta N, Chen K, Hardy E, Powrie R. Respiratory disease in pregnancy. Best Pract Res Clin Obstet Gynaecol. 2015;29(5):598-611.
2. Hegewald MJ, Crapo RO. Respiratory physiology in pregnancy. Clin Chest Med.

Obstetrics
EXTERNAL CEPHALIC VERSION

11
CHAPTER

Questions:

1. What is the primary purpose of using tocolytic agents during an external cephalic version (ECV) procedure?
   A. To reduce maternal anxiety
   B. To induce labor contractions
   C. To relax the uterine muscles
   D. To stimulate fetal movement

2. Which presentation is most conducive to a successful ECV?
   A. Incomplete breech
   B. Footling breech
   C. Frank breech
   D. Complete breech

3. What is NOT a contraindication for performing an ECV?
   A. Diabetes mellitus
   B. Maternal hypertension
   C. Maternal hypotension
   D. Multiples

4. Which of the following factors may increase the success of ECV?
   A. Nulliparity
   B. Anterior placenta
   C. Decreased amniotic fluid
   D. Multiparity

5. The external cephalic version is typically most successful when performed around 34 weeks of pregnancy.
   A. True
   B. False

6. A 37-week pregnant patient is referred to the anesthesiology department for assistance with an ECV procedure. The gynecologist is seeking support in managing analgesia/anesthesia during the maneuver. The patient is positioned for ECV, and the medical team is ready to proceed. The anesthesiologist must decide on the appropriate technique for analgesia/anesthesia during ECV. What anesthesiologist technique increases the likelihood of successful ECV?
   A. Neuraxial anesthesia
   B. Intravenous sedation
   C. General anesthesia
   D. No analgesia

Answers:

1. Answer C (To relax the uterine muscles)

Tocolytic agents are used during an External Cephalic Version (ECV) procedure primarily to relax the uterine muscles. Their purpose is to inhibit or reduce uterine contractions, as uterine contractions can make the procedure more challenging and less successful. By relaxing the uterine muscles, tocolytic agents create a more favorable environment for the healthcare provider to attempt to turn the fetus from a non-vertex (breech or other non-head-first) position to a vertex (head-down) position.

2. Answer D (Complete breech)

A complete breech presentation is the most conducive to a successful ECV. In a complete breech presentation, the baby's legs are flexed at the hips and knees, with the feet close to the buttocks. This flexed position provides a relatively compact and stable fetal presentation, making it easier for healthcare providers to perform the ECV successfully. In contrast, other breech presentations, such as the frank breech presentation (where the baby's legs are extended alongside its body) or a footling breech presentation (where one or both of the baby's feet are positioned to come out first), can be more challenging for ECV because of the extended or less stable fetal positioning.

3. Answer C (Maternal hypotension)

Maternal hypotension is NOT a contraindication for performing an ECV. Contraindications are specific factors or conditions that would make the procedure too risky or unsuitable. Contraindications for ECV include conditions such as reduced amniotic fluid, vaginal bleeding, multiple pregnancies, abnormal fetal monitoring, ruptured membranes, placenta previa, vasa previa, irregularly shaped uterus, maternal hypertension, pre-eclampsia, diabetes mellitus, prior caesarean section, oligohydramnios, hyperextended fetal head, significant fetal or uterine anomalies, and fetal growth restriction.

4. Answer D (Multiparity)

Multiparous women, especially those who have had previous vaginal deliveries, may have a more accommodating uterine environment, making it easier to perform ECV successfully. In contrast, nulliparity is associated with a decreased success rate for ECV because the uterine muscles may be less relaxed, and the maternal pelvis may be less accustomed to childbirth.

5. Answer B (False)

The statement is false. The ECV is typically most successful when performed around 37 weeks of pregnancy, not 34 weeks. Most babies that are breech will naturally turn by about 36 to 37 weeks of gestation. ECV is often performed in the later stages of pregnancy, close to the term, to maximize the chances of success. At 34 weeks, the baby may not yet be in the optimal position for ECV, and performing it at that early stage may not be as effective. Therefore, it's usually recommended to wait until around 37 weeks for ECV when attempting to change the fetal presentation from breech to vertex.

6. Answer A (Neuraxial anesthesia)

Neuraxial anesthesia increases the likelihood of successful ECV, compared with intravenous or no analgesia. Neuraxial anesthesia provides pain relief and muscle relaxation, facilitating the ECV procedure. It allows the patient to remain awake while effectively managing pain and discomfort. When neuraxial analgesia/anesthesia is used, it is suggested to employ techniques such as Combined spinal epidural (CSE) rather than single-shot spinal anesthesia. This allows for the extension of the anesthetic if emergency caesarean birth becomes necessary.

Recommended literature

1. Weiniger, C.F., Rabkin, V., 2020. Neuraxial block and success of external cephalic version. BJA Education 20, 296-297.
2. Weiniger CF. Analgesia/anesthesia for external cephalic version. Curr Opin Anaesthesiol. 2013;26(3):278-287.
3. Rosman AN, Guijt A, Vlemmix F, Rijnders M, Mol BW, Kok M. Contraindications for external cephalic version in breech position at term: a systematic review. Acta Obstet Gynecol Scand. 2013;92(2):137-142.

FETAL DISTRESS

Questions:

1. **What is the normal range for fetal heart rate?**
   A. 80-120 beats per minute
   B. 110-160 beats per minute
   C. 120-180 beats per minute
   D. 140-200 beats per minute

2. **What is the primary cause of fetal anoxia?**
   A. Placental abruption
   B. Fetal tachycardia
   C. Maternal hypotension
   D. Aortocaval compression

3. **Late decelerations in fetal heart rate are typically associated with?**
   A. Fever
   B. Hypoxia
   C. Uterine contractions
   D. Fetal tachycardia

4. **What is the preferred anesthetic technique for Category 1 emergency CS?**
   A. General anesthesia
   B. Spinal anesthesia
   C. Epidural anesthesia
   D. CSE anesthesia

5. **Herpes simplex is a relative contraindication for fetal scalp blood pH sampling.**
   A. True
   B. False

6. **A 39-week pregnant woman is undergoing cardiotocography (CTG) monitoring to assess the fetal heart rate during labor. The CTG shows late decelerations. What is NOT a possible cause of this condition?**
   A. Placental abruption
   B. Cord compression
   C. Maternal hypertension
   D. Uterine contractions

Answers:

1. **Answer B (110-160 beats per minute)**

   The typical range for a normal fetal heart rate is approximately 110 to 160 beats per minute. Fetal heart rate can vary within this range, and it is an important parameter monitored during pregnancy and labor to assess the well-being of the fetus. Deviations from this range, such as persistent bradycardia (below 100 bpm) or tachycardia (above 160 bpm), can be indicative of fetal distress and may require medical attention and further evaluation.

2. **Answer A (Placental abruption)**

   Fetal anoxia, which is the complete cessation of gas exchange and a severe form of fetal distress, is most commonly caused by conditions like placental abruption. Placental abruption occurs when the placenta detaches prematurely from the uterine wall, leading to a sudden disruption in the oxygen supply to the fetus. This can result in a critical reduction in oxygen levels and, if not promptly managed, can have serious consequences for the well-being of the fetus. Fetal tachycardia, maternal hypotension, and aortocaval compression can also contribute to fetal distress, but placental abruption is a direct and significant cause of fetal anoxia.

3. **Answer B (Hypoxia)**

   Late decelerations in the fetal heart rate are characterized by a pattern where they begin approximately 10 to 30 seconds after the onset of a uterine contraction and end about 10 to 30 seconds after the contraction concludes. These late decelerations are a response to hypoxia, which means that they indicate a compromised oxygen supply to the fetus during uterine contractions. When the uterine contractions temporarily reduce the oxygen flow to the fetus, the fetal heart rate drops, reflecting the fetal distress associated with inadequate oxygenation. Monitoring and recognizing late decelerations are crucial in obstetric care, as they signal a need for prompt assessment and intervention to address the underlying hypoxia and ensure the well-being of the baby.

4. **Answer A (General anesthesia)**

   In Category 1 emergency CS, there is an immediate threat to the life of the mother or fetus. In such life-threatening situations, the primary goal is to perform the caesarean section as rapidly as possible to save lives. General anesthesia is the preferred choice in Category 1 emergencies because it provides a fast and reliable means of inducing unconsciousness and pain relief. General anesthesia can be administered rapidly, ensuring that the surgical procedure can begin without delay. While regional anesthetic techniques are commonly used for caesarean sections, they may take more time to establish and are typically preferred in less urgent situations.

5. **Answer A (True)**

   Relative contraindications for fetal scalp blood pH sampling include intact membranes, infections like HIV and herpes simplex, and fetal coagulopathy. In the case of herpes simplex infection, there may be concerns about potential transmission risks, which could make healthcare providers cautious when considering this procedure in such situations. It is important to assess the specific clinical circumstances and weigh the potential benefits and risks when deciding whether to perform fetal scalp blood pH sampling.

6. **Answer D (Uterine contractions)**

   Late decelerations in the fetal heart rate, as seen in the CTG, are typically associated with conditions that result in hypoxia for the fetus. The list of possible causes mentioned in the scenario includes maternal hypertension, diabetes, preeclampsia, or intrauterine growth retardation. Placental abruption, cord compression, and interruption of gas exchange across the placenta can all lead to late decelerations by reducing oxygen supply to the fetus. However, uterine contractions are not typically a direct cause of late decelerations, as they represent a response to hypoxia rather than a cause. Uterine contractions can lead to transient intermittent hypoxia, but they are not a direct cause of late decelerations.

Recommended literature

1. Morgan and Mikhail's clinical anesthesiology (2022). McGraw Hill Medical. Chapter 41.
2. Caesarean birth NICE guidelines (2021). Available at: https://www.nice.org.uk/guidance/ng192.
3. Omotayo, Rotimi & Akinsowon, OR & Bello, EO & Olumide, Akadiri & Akintan, AL & Omotayo, SE. (2019). Fetal distress, options of anesthesia, and immediate postdelivery outcome at state specialist hospital Akure. Tropical Journal of Obstetrics and Gynaecology. 36. 424.

GESTATIONAL DIABETES

Questions:

1. Which of the following complications is commonly associated with gestational diabetes?

   A. Hypertension

   B. Respiratory distress syndrome

   C. Hyperthyreosis

   D. Malnutrition

2. What is the primary treatment for gestational diabetes?

   A. Insulin

   B. Metformin

   C. Sulfonylureas

   D. Lifestyle modifications

3. Why might gestational diabetes in mothers lead to instrumentally assisted deliveries?

   A. Placental abruption

   B. Oligohidramnios

   C. Perinatal asphyxia

   D. Proportionately larger babies

4. To prevent hyponatremia, what type of intravenous fluid with potassium should be used in the management of gestational diabetes?

   A. 5% glucose in 0.9% saline

   B. Normal saline

   C. Lactated Ringer's solution

   D. Dextrose solution

5. Gestational diabetes most commonly develops in the first trimester.

   A. True

   B. False

6. A 32-year-old pregnant woman, at 41 weeks of gestation, has been admitted to the hospital due to the lack of progress in her labor. The patient has been diagnosed with gestational diabetes earlier in her pregnancy. After a comprehensive evaluation by the medical team, it has been determined that there is a medical indication for a caesarean section (CS). Given the urgency of the situation and the specific circumstances of the patient, it has been decided that the CS will be performed under general anesthesia. What is one of the challenges associated with general anesthesia in diabetic parturients, particularly those with gestational diabetes?

   A. Increased risk of pulmonary edema

   B. Decreased sensitivity to pain

   C. Enhanced response to intubation

   D. Improved counter-regulatory hormone responses

Answers:

1. **Answer A (Hypertension)**

   The most commonly associated complication with gestational diabetes in mothers is hypertension, specifically gestational hypertension and pre-eclampsia. Women with gestational diabetes are at an increased risk of developing high blood pressure during pregnancy, which can progress to pre-eclampsia, posing risks to both the mother and the baby. Additionally, gestational diabetes can lead to a higher likelihood of requiring a caesarean section for delivery, increased chances of experiencing gestational diabetes in future pregnancies, and an elevated risk of developing type 2 diabetes later in life.

2. **Answer D (Lifestyle modifications)**

   Lifestyle changes, including dietary adjustments and physical activity, are often the first-line approach for managing gestational diabetes. These modifications aim to control blood glucose levels and promote a healthy pregnancy outcome without the use of medications or insulin. If lifestyle changes alone do not effectively manage blood glucose levels, then insulin therapy is usually considered the next step in treatment, while options like metformin and sulfonylureas are generally reserved for cases where insulin is not appropriate or effective. The goal is to maintain optimal blood glucose levels during pregnancy to minimize potential risks to both the mother and the baby.

3. **Answer D (Proportionately larger babies)**

   Gestational diabetes in mothers can lead to instrumentally assisted deliveries primarily due to the fact that diabetic mothers often have babies who are proportionately larger than those of non-diabetic mothers. This condition, known as fetal macrosomia, is a common complication associated with gestational diabetes. Larger babies can make the process of vaginal delivery more challenging, leading to a higher likelihood of instrumentally assisted deliveries, such as forceps or vacuum extraction, to safely deliver the baby. These interventions are often employed to avoid potential complications associated with delivering a larger baby, such as shoulder dystocia or birth injury.

4. **Answer A (5% glucose in 0.9% saline)**

   Pregnant individuals with gestational diabetes may require intravenous fluids to maintain their blood glucose levels. 5% glucose in 0.9% saline which combines 0.9% sodium chloride with glucose, is used to provide both hydration and a controlled source of glucose. This solution helps avoid hyponatremia while ensuring that the patient receives the necessary glucose support. Normal saline is a sterile saltwater solution without glucose, which is not suitable for managing gestational diabetes. Lactated Ringer's solution is also devoid of glucose. Dextrose solution contains glucose but lacks the saline component necessary to prevent hyponatremia, making it less ideal for this specific purpose.

5. **Answer B (False)**

   Gestational diabetes mellitus (GDM) typically develops later in pregnancy, often during the second or third trimester. It is a form of diabetes that is first recognized during pregnancy and is characterized by elevated blood sugar levels. While it can sometimes occur earlier, it is more common in the later stages of pregnancy when the body's insulin resistance increases due to hormonal changes. Screening for GDM usually takes place between the 24th and 28th weeks of gestation to detect and manage the condition.

6. **Answer C (Enhanced response to intubation)**

   General anesthesia is often administered to diabetic parturients due to operative urgency or when regional anesthesia is not feasible. In the case of gestational diabetes, there are several challenges associated with general anesthesia. These challenges include an increased hemodynamic response to intubation, which means that diabetic patients, including those with gestational diabetes, tend to exhibit pronounced changes in heart rate, mean arterial pressure, and vascular resistance in response to intubation. Additionally, patients with diabetes, including gestational diabetes, may experience impaired counter-regulatory hormone responses to hypoglycemia during sleep, which further complicates anesthesia management. Other factors to consider in general anesthesia for diabetic parturients include gastroparesis, limited atlantooccipital joint extension, and the potential for stiff joint syndrome affecting the airway and intubation.

Recommended literature

1. Yap Y, Modi A, Lucas N. The peripartum management of diabetes. BJA Educ. 2020;20(1):5-9.

HYSTERECTOMY

Questions:

1. Which type of hysterectomy involves the removal of the uterus, cervix, fallopian tubes, and ovaries?
   A. Total Hysterectomy
   B. Supracervical Hysterectomy
   C. Radical Hysterectomy
   D. Partial Hysterectomy

2. Which surgical technique typically results in the shortest recovery period for patients undergoing a hysterectomy?
   A. Abdominal Hysterectomy
   B. Laparoscopic-Assisted Vaginal Hysterectomy
   C. Total Laparoscopic Hysterectomy
   D. Vaginal Hysterectomy

3. Which of the following complications is NOT commonly associated with hysterectomy?
   A. Heavy bleeding
   B. Infection
   C. Urinary incontinence
   D. Uterine prolapse

4. What is the main advantage of using a laparoscopic surgical technique in a hysterectomy?
   A. Shortest surgery time
   B. Lower risk of bladder or ureter injury
   C. Suitable for patients with cardiopulmonary disease
   D. Lower risk of adhesion formation

5. Supracervical hysterectomy is typically performed to remove uterine cancer.
   A. True
   B. False

6. A 50-year-old woman with no significant comorbidities is presented for a vaginal hysterectomy due to uterine fibroids. She has been experiencing symptoms related to the fibroids, such as heavy menstrual bleeding and pelvic pain. After a thorough evaluation and discussion with her healthcare provider, it was decided that a vaginal hysterectomy is the most appropriate treatment option for her condition. What type of anesthesia is NOT suitable for this type of operation?
   A. General anesthesia with spontaneous breathing
   B. General anesthesia with mechanical ventilation
   C. Neuraxial block with a block height of at least T4
   D. Neuraxial block with a block height of at least T8

Answers:

1. **Answer A (Total Hysterectomy)**

   In a total hysterectomy, the entire uterus is removed, and it may or may not include the cervix. Additionally, the procedure involves the removal of both the fallopian tubes and the ovaries. Therefore, a total hysterectomy encompasses the removal of the uterus, cervix, fallopian tubes, and ovaries. This is a comprehensive surgical procedure often performed for various medical conditions, including gynecological cancers and certain non-cancerous conditions of the uterus.

2. **Answer D (Vaginal Hysterectomy)**

   Vaginal hysterectomy typically results in the shortest recovery period for patients undergoing a hysterectomy. This approach offers the advantage of a shorter surgery time, a quicker postoperative recovery, and a reduced need for pain medication compared to laparoscopic techniques. However, it has limitations related to the size of the uterus and previous surgeries, and it may provide limited access to evaluate the condition of the fallopian tubes and ovaries during the procedure. The choice of hysterectomy technique should be based on the individual patient's specific condition and the surgeon's expertise.

3. **Answer D (Uterine prolapse)**

   Hysterectomy is a surgical procedure that involves the removal of the uterus and may be associated with several potential complications. These complications can include heavy bleeding, infection, urinary incontinence, adhesion formation, bowel obstruction, torn internal stitches, urinary tract injury, vaginal problems, ovarian failure, and early menopause symptoms. However, uterine prolapse is not a complication of hysterectomy; in fact, the procedure is performed to treat uterine prolapse, as it involves the removal of the uterus. Issues related to anesthesia, as well as blood clots (venous thromboembolism or VTE), can also be associated with hysterectomy.

4. **Answer D (Lower risk of adhesion formation)**

   One of the advantages of using laparoscopic techniques in a hysterectomy is the lower risk of adhesion formation. Adhesions are bands of scar tissue that can form after surgery, and laparoscopic procedures typically result in fewer adhesions compared to open abdominal surgeries. Laparoscopic techniques offer several other advantages, including shorter inpatient treatment duration, the possibility to diagnose and treat other pelvic diseases, a quicker return to normal activities, and a reduction in the risk of bleeding, fevers, and infections compared to abdominal techniques. Additionally, it's important to note that laparoscopic surgery requires a high degree of surgical skill, and malignancies can only be removed by this approach if they are intact. Laparoscopic techniques are not typically recommended for patients with significant cardiopulmonary disease due to the challenges they may present.

5. **Answer B (False)**

   Supracervical hysterectomy is not typically performed to remove uterine cancer. Supracervical hysterectomy involves the removal of the upper part of the uterus while preserving the cervix. It is often used to treat conditions such as uterine fibroids, excessive menstrual bleeding, or other non-cancerous uterine conditions. When uterine cancer is present or suspected, a more extensive procedure, such as a total hysterectomy or a radical hysterectomy, is performed to ensure the complete removal of cancerous tissues and prevent the spread of cancer. The choice of procedure depends on the stage and type of uterine cancer and the patient's overall health.

6. **Answer C (Neuraxial block with a block height of at least T4)**

   The most appropriate anesthesia for a vaginal hysterectomy is either general anesthesia with mechanical ventilation or a neuraxial block with a block height of at least T8. A block height of T8 is sufficient for this type of surgery. Neuraxial block with a block height of at least T4 represents a block height that is excessively high and typically associated with abdominal hysterectomy. For vaginal hysterectomy, a block height of T8 is generally considered appropriate. This is because the surgical area for vaginal hysterectomy does not require such a high block level, and T4 would be unnecessarily high for this procedure.

Recommended literature

1. Pollard BJ, Kitchen G. Handbook of Clinical Anaesthesia. 4th ed. Taylor & Francis group; 2018. Chapter 11 Gynaecological surgery, Hobbs A and Craig SK.

MULTIPLE GESTATIONS

Questions:

1. **Which of the following is a sign or symptom of multiple gestation pregnancies?**
   A. Normal weight gain in the first trimester
   B. Lower than usual levels of pregnancy hormones
   C. Larger than usual belly compared to most women at a similar stage of pregnancy
   D. Normal levels of protein alpha-fetoprotein in the mother's blood

2. **Which of the following complications is unique to monochorionic twins?**
   A. Gestational diabetes
   B. Twin-twin transfusion syndrome
   C. Preterm labor
   D. Placental abruption

3. **What is the goal gestational age for twin pregnancies to reduce the risk of complications?**
   A. 32 weeks
   B. 35 weeks
   C. 37 weeks
   D. 40 weeks

4. **What is a risk factor for multiple gestation pregnancies?**
   A. Being under 30 years old
   B. Having a family history of twins
   C. Prenatal vitamins use
   D. Asian rase

5. **Caesarean section is a common method of delivery for most women with multiple gestation pregnancies.**
   A. True
   B. False

6. **A 32-year-old woman at 36 weeks of gestation with twins presents in active labor with contractions and increasing intensity. She has a history of uncomplicated singleton pregnancies. Physical examination reveals the cephalic presentation of the first twin. What is the preferred anesthesia technique for labor analgesia in women with multiple gestations?**
   A. Inhalational Analgesia
   B. Epidural analgesia
   C. Spinal analgesia
   D. Intravenous analgesia

Answers:

1. Answer C (Larger than usual belly compared to most women at a similar stage of pregnancy)

Multiple gestation pregnancies often result in a larger-than-usual belly compared to singleton pregnancies. This is because the uterus must accommodate more than one fetus, leading to increased uterine size. Other signs and symptoms of multiple gestation pregnancies can include exaggerated signs of pregnancy such as extreme nausea, fatigue, and severe vomiting; faster than usual weight gain in the first trimester; sore or very tender breasts; higher than normal levels of pregnancy hormones (human chorionic gonadotrophin); higher than normal levels of protein alpha-fetoprotein in the mother's blood; and the presence of more than one fetal heartbeat.

2. Answer B (Twin-twin transfusion syndrome)

Monochorionic twins share a placenta, which can lead to unique complications such as twin-twin transfusion syndrome (TTTS). TTTS occurs when there is an imbalance in the blood flow between the twins, leading to one twin receiving too much blood (donor) and the other too little (recipient). This can result in serious complications for both twins if not treated promptly. Other possible complications of monochorionic pregnancy include selective fetal growth restriction (sFGR), twin anemia polycythemia sequence (TAPS), and twin reversed arterial perfusion sequence (TRAPS). These complications emphasize the need for close monitoring and specialized care during monochorionic pregnancies to optimize outcomes for both twins.

3. Answer C (37 weeks)

In multiple-gestation pregnancies, the goal is to reach a gestational age of 37 weeks, which is considered full-term for twins. This target gestational age is aimed at reducing the risk of complications that are more common in premature births. Babies born at or after 37 weeks are more likely to have fully developed organs and be of a healthier weight, which can lead to a smoother transition to life outside the womb and a reduced need for neonatal intensive care. Premature birth in multiple gestations is associated with a higher risk of complications such as respiratory distress syndrome, intraventricular hemorrhage, and necrotizing enterocolitis. By reaching 37 weeks, the risk of these complications is significantly reduced, improving the overall outcomes for both babies and mothers.

4. Answer B (Having a family history of twins)

A family history of multiple pregnancies raises the chances of having twins. Other risk factors for multiple gestation pregnancies include older age (women older than 30), high parity (having 1 or more previous pregnancies, especially a multiple pregnancy), and race (African-American women are more likely to have twins than any other race, while Asian and Native Americans have the lowest twinning rates). Additionally, the use of reproductive technologies such as ovulation-stimulating medicines and assisted reproductive technologies can greatly increase the chances of having multiple pregnancies.

5. Answer A (True)

Caesarean section is a common method of delivery for most women with multiple gestation pregnancies. This is often due to the increased risk of complications associated with multiple pregnancies, such as preterm labor, fetal malpresentation, and the need for careful management of the birth process to ensure the safety of both the mother and the babies. Additionally, caesarean delivery may be preferred in cases where there are complications that make vaginal delivery more challenging or risky, such as when the first twin is in breech presentation or monochorionic-monoamniotic twins.

6. Answer B (Epidural analgesia)

Neuraxial labor analgesia, such as epidural analgesia, is the preferred anesthesia technique for labor analgesia in women with multiple gestations. It offers better pain control, and pelvic muscle relaxation, and inhibits early maternal expulsive efforts, which can be beneficial in twin pregnancies. The NICE and ACOG guidelines recommend neuraxial analgesia for women with twin or triplet pregnancies to help facilitate vaginal delivery. While there are potential risks, such as motor block and prolonged labor, these can be managed with proper monitoring and the use of appropriate medications. Overall, neuraxial labor analgesia is considered safe and effective for multiple gestations.

Recommended literature

1. Frölich M.A. (2022). Obstetric anesthesia. Butterworth IV J.F., & Mackey D.C., & Wasnick J.D.(Eds.), Morgan & Mikhail's Clinical Anesthesiology, 7e. McGraw Hill. https://accessanesthesiology.mhmedical.com/content.aspx?bookid=3194&sectionid=266522956
2. Rédai I (2013). Chapter 196. twin pregnancy, breech presentation, trial of labor after caesarean birth: anesthetic considerations for patients attempting vaginal birth. Atchabahian A, & Gupta R(Eds.), The Anesthesia Guide. McGraw Hill. https://accessanesthesiology.mhmedical.com/content.aspx?bookid=572&sectionid=42543788

NON-OBSTETRIC SURGERY

Questions:

1. **What is the most common cause of hypotension in a pregnant patient under anesthesia during non-obstetric surgery?**
   A. Hypovolemia
   B. Decreased cardiac output
   C. Aortocaval compression
   D. Vasopressor overdose

2. **Why is the use of nitrous oxide generally avoided during the first trimester of pregnancy in non-obstetric surgery?**
   A. It causes uterine contractions
   B. It increases the risk of thromboembolic complications
   C. It may inhibit DNA synthesis
   D. It leads to fetal withdrawal syndrome

3. **What is the primary concern when administering local anesthetics to a pregnant patient in late pregnancy during non-obstetric surgery?**
   A. Decreased anesthetic efficacy
   B. Reduced protein binding
   C. Increased fetal sensitivity
   D. Risk of uterine contractions

4. **What effect does pregnancy have on red cell volume, white blood cell count, and coagulation factors?**
   A. Decreased red cell volume, white blood cell count, and coagulation factors
   B. No significant changes in red cell volume, white blood cell count, and coagulation factors
   C. Increased red cell volume, white blood cell count, and coagulation factors
   D. Decreased red cell volume but increased white blood cell count and coagulation factors

5. **Warfarin is preferred for DVT prophylaxis in pregnant patients because it does not cross the placenta and is considered safe for both the mother and the fetus.**
   A. True
   B. False

6. **A patient at 31 weeks of pregnancy recently underwent surgery for acute appendicitis and is now in the postoperative recovery room. As the anesthesiologist, you are considering postoperative analgesia. You have opted for a multimodal analgesic approach and are considering combining acetaminophen with ketorolac. You recognize the importance of choosing medications that are safe for the patient and the developing fetus. When is the use of non-steroidal anti-inflammatory drugs (NSAIDs) generally contraindicated during non-obstetric surgery in pregnant patients?**
   A. First trimester
   B. Second trimester
   C. Third trimester
   D. They are not contraindicated

Answers:

1. **Answer C (Aortocaval compression)**

   Aortocaval compression is the most common cause of hypotension in a pregnant patient under anesthesia during non-obstetric surgery. This compression occurs from the 13th week of pregnancy and results from the enlarged uterus pressing on the abdominal aorta and the inferior vena cava when the patient is in a supine position. This pressure on the major blood vessels impairs venous return to the heart and decreases cardiac output, leading to hypotension.

2. **Answer C (It may inhibit DNA synthesis)**

   The use of nitrous oxide is generally avoided during the first trimester of pregnancy in non-obstetric surgery because it may inhibit DNA synthesis. This inhibition can have adverse effects on the developing fetus, potentially leading to birth defects and other abnormalities. Therefore, it is considered a precautionary measure to avoid nitrous oxide exposure during the critical period of organ formation in the first trimester.

3. **Answer B (Reduced protein binding)**

   When administering local anesthetics to a pregnant patient in late pregnancy during non-obstetric surgery, the primary concern is reduced protein binding. During pregnancy, there is an increase in plasma volume and changes in protein levels, which can lead to reduced protein binding of drugs, including local anesthetics. This alteration in protein binding can result in a higher concentration of free, unbound drugs in the maternal bloodstream, increasing the risk of toxicity.

4. **Answer C (Increased red cell volume, white blood cell count, and coagulation factors)**

   Pregnancy results in increased red cell volume, a heightened white blood cell count, and elevated coagulation factors. These physiological changes are adaptations to meet the increased demands for oxygen and nutrients during pregnancy, enhance the body's immune response, and minimize the risk of excessive bleeding during childbirth.

5. **Answer B (False)**

   Warfarin is generally contraindicated during pregnancy, especially during the first trimester and later stages of pregnancy. This is because warfarin does cross the placenta, and its use during pregnancy is associated with a risk of teratogenic effects in the developing fetus. It can also cause fetal bleeding and other adverse outcomes. Heparin, on the other hand, is typically preferred for deep venous thrombosis (DVT) prophylaxis in pregnant patients because it does not cross the placenta and is considered safer for both the mother and the developing fetus.

6. **Answer C (Third trimester)**

   In the case of the patient at 31 weeks of pregnancy who recently underwent surgery for acute appendicitis and is now in the postoperative recovery room, the use of non-steroidal anti-inflammatory drugs (NSAIDs) like ketorolac should be approached with extreme caution and typically avoided. Specifically, the use of NSAIDs, including ketorolac, is generally contraindicated during the third trimester of pregnancy. This is due to the potential risk of causing premature closure of the fetal ductus arteriosus. The closure of the ductus arteriosus can have serious consequences for the developing fetus, affecting its cardiovascular health. Instead, alternative pain management options should be considered to ensure the safety of both the mother and the unborn child.

Recommended literature

1. Haggerty E, Daly J. Anaesthesia and non-obstetric surgery in pregnancy. BJA Education. 2021;21(2):42-3.
2. Nejdlova M, Johnson T. Anaesthesia for non-obstetric procedures during pregnancy. Continuing Education in Anaesthesia Critical Care & Pain. 2012;12(4):203-6.

PERIPARTUM CARDIAC ARREST

11

CHAPTER

Questions:

1. What is the most appropriate initial treatment for a pregnant patient experiencing a high neuraxial block-induced peripartum cardiac arrest?
   - A. Administer high-dose adrenaline
   - B. Intubate immediately
   - C. Treat hypotension aggressively
   - D. Start chest compressions

2. What is the primary treatment for local anesthetic systemic toxicity (LAST) in a peripartum patient who has experienced a cardiac arrest?
   - A. Administer high-dose epinephrine
   - B. Perform immediate caesarean section
   - C. Give intralipid
   - D. Initiate hyperventilation

3. In the context of peripartum cardiac arrest, what should be the primary goal when managing uterine atony?
   - A. Administer platelet transfusion
   - B. Perform a caesarean section
   - C. Achieve hemostasis
   - D. Stimulate uterine contractions

4. When managing peripartum cardiac arrest in a patient with placenta previa, what is the initial approach if delivery is indicated?
   - A. Administer uterotonics
   - B. Prepare for lower uterine segment atony
   - C. Perform an emergency caesarean section
   - D. Monitor for coagulopathy

5. Peripartum cardiac arrest is a rare event.
   - A. True
   - B. False

6. A 19-week pregnant patient is admitted to the emergency department (ED) due to signs of cardiac arrest. Resuscitation efforts are already underway, and the patient has been intubated. Chest compressions are in progress, and venous access has been established. Volume replacement and adrenaline boluses have been administered to support circulation. Due to the gravid uterus, what is the next step in the management of this patient?
   - A. Wait for spontaneous circulation and then perform a caesarean section
   - B. Perform a caesarean section within 5 minutes for maternal and fetal resuscitation
   - C. Consider a caesarean section for maternal resuscitation, not survival of the infant
   - D. Do not consider a caesarean section

Answers:

1. Answer C (Treat hypotension aggressively)

In the scenario of a pregnant patient experiencing a high neuraxial block-induced peripartum cardiac arrest, the primary concern is usually hypotension resulting from the block. Therefore, the most appropriate initial treatment is to address this hypotension aggressively. This can include measures like administering vasopressors and taking steps to increase the patient's blood pressure to ensure adequate perfusion to vital organs. It's crucial to maintain perfusion and oxygen delivery to both the mother and the fetus in such a critical situation.

2. Answer C (Give intralipid)

In the context of a peripartum patient experiencing a cardiac arrest due to local anesthetic systemic toxicity (LAST), the primary treatment is to give intralipid. Intralipid is a lipid emulsion that acts as a lipid sink, helping to sequester the toxic local anesthetic from the bloodstream. It effectively neutralizes the toxic effects of the local anesthetic by binding to it.

3. Answer D (Stimulate uterine contractions)

Uterine atony is a condition in which the uterus fails to contract effectively after childbirth, leading to postpartum hemorrhage. Stimulating uterine contractions through the administration of uterotonic medications is the initial and crucial step in addressing this condition.

4. Answer C (Perform an emergency caesarean section)

When managing peripartum cardiac arrest in a patient with placenta previa, if delivery is indicated due to the condition, the initial approach is to perform an emergency caesarean section. Placenta previa is a condition where the placenta is low-lying and can obstruct the birth canal, leading to severe bleeding during labor and delivery. In cases where delivery is indicated, and the patient experiences cardiac arrest, a rapid and potentially life-saving intervention is to deliver the baby through a caesarean section.

5. Answer A (True)

Peripartum cardiac arrest is indeed a rare event. It occurs in pregnant women during childbirth or shortly after delivery and is characterized by a sudden cessation of the heart's normal function. The incidence of peripartum cardiac arrest is relatively low compared to other medical emergencies. It is considered a rare but critical medical emergency, and the management of such cases requires a well-coordinated and prepared response due to its infrequent occurrence.

6. Answer D (Do not consider a caesarean section)

In early pregnancy, specifically at < 20 weeks, the size of the gravid uterus is not substantial enough to significantly impair maternal cardiac output. The primary goal remains maternal resuscitation and addressing the underlying cause of the cardiac arrest. The gravid uterus is not the primary concern for cardiac output compromise at this stage of pregnancy. As such, performing a caesarean section is not typically indicated, as it may not provide significant benefits for the mother's resuscitation in this scenario. The focus should be on identifying and addressing the underlying causes of cardiac arrest and optimizing maternal care.

Recommended literature

1. Madden AM, Meng ML. Cardiopulmonary resuscitation in the pregnant patient. BJA Educ. 2020;20(8):252-258.
2. Jeejeebhoy FM, Zelop CM, Lipman S, Carvalho B, Joglar J, Mhyre JM, et al. Cardiac Arrest in Pregnancy. Circulation. 2015;132(18):1747-73.

Obstetrics
PERIPARTUM CARDIOMYOPATHY

11
CHAPTER

Questions:

1. Which of the following is a recognized risk factor for peripartum cardiomyopathy (PPCM)?
   A. Young age
   B. African descent
   C. Nulliparity
   D. Smoking

2. Which symptom is NOT commonly associated with PPCM?
   A. Pedal edema
   B. Paroxysmal nocturnal dyspnea
   C. Dry cough
   D. Syncope

3. What is the first-line pharmacological treatment for PPCM in the postpartum period?
   A. Calcium channel blockers
   B. Angiotensin-converting enzyme (ACE) inhibitors
   C. Hydralazine and nitrates
   D. Loop diuretics

4. Which factor is associated with a good prognosis in PPCM patients?
   A. QRS duration greater than 120 ms
   B. Multiparity
   C. High New York Heart Association (NYHA) class
   D. Left ventricular ejection fraction greater than 30% to 35%

5. Vaginal delivery is contraindicated for patients with cardiomyopathy.
   A. True
   B. False

6. A 42-year-old pregnant patient of African descent, at 37 weeks of pregnancy, with a history of pregnancy-related hypertension, multiparity, multiple gestations, and obesity, presents with signs suggestive of PPCM. Diagnostic tests have confirmed the diagnosis of PPCM. What should be avoided in the pharmacological management of PPCM?
   A. Beta-blockers
   B. Hydralazine and nitrates
   C. Calcium channel blockers
   D. Loop diuretics

Answers:

1. **Answer B (African descent)**

   Peripartum cardiomyopathy (PPCM) is a rare form of heart failure that occurs during late pregnancy or in the early postpartum period. One of the specific risk factors for PPCM is African descent. This means that women of African descent are at a higher risk of developing PPCM compared to other ethnic groups. Other risk factors for PPCM include increasing age, pregnancy-related hypertension, multiparity, multiple gestations, obesity, chronic hypertension, chronic tocolytics use, and cocaine use.

2. **Answer D (Syncope)**

   The symptom not commonly associated with PPCM is syncope. Common symptoms of PPCM include paroxysmal nocturnal dyspnea, pedal edema, orthopnea, dyspnea on exertion, dry cough, palpitations, increase in abdominal girth, lightheadedness, chest pain, jugular venous distention, displaced apical impulse, third heart sound, and mitral regurgitation murmurs. Syncope is not typically a characteristic symptom of PPCM, although it can be associated with other cardiac or non-cardiac conditions.

3. **Answer B (Angiotensin-converting enzyme (ACE) inhibitors)**

   In the postpartum period, the first-line pharmacological treatment for PPCM is angiotensin-converting enzyme (ACE) inhibitors. ACE inhibitors are effective in managing heart failure and are considered the primary choice for treatment. It's important to note that ACE inhibitors are contraindicated during pregnancy, as they can have adverse effects on the developing fetus. Therefore, their use is specifically recommended postpartum to improve cardiac function and alleviate symptoms in PPCM patients. Calcium channel blockers, hydralazine and nitrates, and loop diuretics may also be used in the management of PPCM, but ACE inhibitors are the first-line treatment option in the postpartum period.

4. **Answer D (Left ventricular ejection fraction greater than 30% to 35%)**

   The left ventricular ejection fraction greater than 30% to 35% is associated with a good prognosis in PPCM patients. The ejection fraction is a measure of how well the heart is pumping blood. A higher ejection fraction indicates better heart function. Other factors that are associated with a good prognosis in PPCM patients include a small left ventricular diastolic dimension (less than 5.5cm), absence of troponin elevation, absence of left ventricular thrombus, and being of non-African ethnicity. Conversely, factors associated with a poor prognosis in PPCM patients include a QRS duration greater than 120 ms, delayed diagnosis, a high New York Heart Association (NYHA) class, and multiparity, particularly among women of African descent.

5. **Answer B (False)**

   Vaginal delivery is not universally contraindicated for patients with cardiomyopathy. The decision to opt for a vaginal or caesarean delivery in such cases should be based on a careful evaluation of the patient's condition and a risk-benefit assessment. While there may be situations where a caesarean section is preferred to minimize the physiological stress of labor, the mode of delivery should be determined on a case-by-case basis, considering the severity of cardiomyopathy, the patient's cardiac status, and other relevant factors. This decision is typically made in consultation with a multidisciplinary team, including obstetricians, anesthesiologists, and cardiologists, to ensure the safety of both the mother and the baby.

6. **Answer C (Calcium channel blockers)**

   Calcium channel blockers are generally not preferred in this context due to their potential adverse effects on heart function. These medications are typically avoided in PPCM management because of their negative inotropic properties, which can further impair cardiac contractility and exacerbate the condition. Additionally, aldosterone antagonists like spironolactone are not recommended during pregnancy due to potential adverse effects and should be used with caution in heart failure patients. Instead, other medications such as ACE inhibitors, hydralazine and nitrates, beta-blockers, and loop diuretics may be considered to improve cardiac function and alleviate symptoms, with the choice of therapy guided by the patient's specific clinical status.

Recommended literature

1. Rodriguez Ziccardi M, Siddique MS. Peripartum Cardiomyopathy. [Updated 2022 Jul 19]. In: StatPearls [Internet]. Treasure Island (FL): StatPearls Publishing; 2022 Jan-. Available from: https://www.ncbi.nlm.nih.gov/books/NBK482185/.
2. Honigberg MC, Givertz MM. Peripartum cardiomyopathy. BMJ. 2019;364:k5287. Published 2019 Jan 30. doi:10.1136/bmj.k5287.
3. Thompson L, Hartsilver E. Peripartum cardiomyopathy. WFSA. https://resources.wfsahq.org/atotw/peripartum-cardiomyopathy/#:~:text=Titrated%20neuraxial%20anaesthesia%2C%20by%20incremental,agents%20that%20reduce%20myocardial%20contractility. Published February 24, 2015. Accessed February 13, 2023.

PHYSIOLOGICAL CHANGES DURING PREGNANCY

11

CHAPTER

Questions:

1. Which of the following is NOT a typical physiological change in the cardiovascular system during pregnancy?
   A. Uterine perfusion autoregulation
   B. Increased susceptibility to hypotension
   C. Supine hypotensive syndrome
   D. Expansion of blood volume

2. What physiological change contributes to mild respiratory alkalosis during pregnancy?
   A. Increased tidal volume and respiratory rate
   B. Decreased oxygen consumption
   C. Increased partial pressure of carbon dioxide ($PaCO_2$)
   D. Increased functional residual capacity

3. Which of the following is NOT a hematological change during pregnancy?
   A. Dilutional anemia
   B. Increased risk of thromboembolic complications
   C. Thrombocytopenia and leukopenia
   D. Decreased protein binding of drugs

4. Why do pregnant women have an increased risk of thromboembolic complications?
   A. Increased platelet count
   B. Reduced blood viscosity
   C. Elevated glomerular filtration rate (GFR)
   D. Changes in coagulation factors

5. The thyroid gland undergoes hypertrophy during pregnancy, and the increased production of thyroxine and triiodothyronine is balanced by increased production.
   A. True
   B. False

6. A pregnant patient is rushed to the operating room for a Category 1 emergency caesarean section due to a life-threatening condition that necessitates immediate delivery. The patient is intubated and ventilated to ensure adequate oxygenation and ventilation during the surgery. The anesthesia and surgical teams are working quickly to save both the mother and the baby. Some of the physiological changes during pregnancy may alter or affect anesthetic management; what statement is NOT true?
   A. Venous access is often easier due to engorgement of the venous system
   B. Intubation may be difficult, so adjuncts for difficult intubation should be available
   C. The MAC of volatile anesthetic is slightly reduced
   D. Volatile agents cause uterine contractions

Answers:

1. Answer A (Uterine perfusion not autoregulated)

While other options describe typical physiological changes in the cardiovascular system during pregnancy, such as increased susceptibility to hypotension, the occurrence of supine hypotensive syndrome, and the expansion of blood volume, option A is not accurate as uterine perfusion is not autoregulated during pregnancy. Instead, blood flow to the uterus increases to support fetal growth, and monitoring and management of blood pressure are crucial to ensure adequate uterine perfusion during pregnancy and anesthesia.

2. Answer A (Increased tidal volume and respiratory rate.)

During pregnancy, several physiological changes occur in the respiratory system. One of these changes is an increase in tidal volume and respiratory rate. This increase in ventilation leads to the removal of carbon dioxide from the body at a faster rate than its production, resulting in a slight drop in the partial pressure of carbon dioxide ($PaCO_2$). This drop in $PaCO_2$ leads to mild respiratory alkalosis. The increased respiratory rate and tidal volume are necessary to meet the increased oxygen demands of the mother and the developing fetus. This physiological adaptation helps ensure that both the mother and fetus receive adequate oxygen during pregnancy.

3. Answer C (Thrombocytopenia and leukopenia)

While pregnancy is associated with various hematological changes, including dilutional anemia, an increased risk of thromboembolic complications, and decreased protein binding of drugs, thrombocytopenia, and leukopenia are not typical changes during pregnancy. Instead, pregnancy often leads to an increase in the total concentration of plasma proteins, contributing to a reduction in colloid oncotic pressure, but it does not usually result in low platelet or white blood cell counts.

4. Answer D (Changes in coagulation factors)

Pregnant women have an increased risk of thromboembolic complications primarily due to changes in coagulation factors. Pregnancy is associated with a hypercoagulable state, often referred to as a prothrombotic state. This hypercoagulability is attributed to elevated estrogen levels, which mediate an increase in the synthesis of coagulation factors. As pregnancy progresses, clotting factors such as VII, VIII, X, XII, vWF (von Willebrand factor), and fibrinogen levels markedly increase. These changes in coagulation factors contribute to an increased tendency for blood to clot. The increase in factor VIII, for instance, leads to a shortened activated partial thromboplastin time (aPTT). This hypercoagulable state makes pregnant individuals more susceptible to developing deep vein thrombosis (DVT) and other thromboembolic complications.

5. Answer A (True)

During pregnancy, the thyroid gland undergoes hypertrophy, which means it increases in size. This is a normal physiological change that occurs to support the increased metabolic demands of pregnancy. As the thyroid gland enlarges, it produces and releases more thyroxine (T4) and triiodothyronine (T3), which are the two main thyroid hormones. These hormones play a crucial role in regulating metabolism and ensuring that the pregnant woman's body can meet the needs of both the mother and the developing fetus. The increased production of thyroxine and triiodothyronine is balanced by the increased production of thyroid-binding globulin to help maintain stable levels of the free hormones in the bloodstream. This adaptation ensures that the thyroid hormones are available for various physiological processes during pregnancy.

6. Answer D (Volatile agents cause uterine contractions)

While the other statements accurately describe physiological changes during pregnancy and their impact on anesthetic management, the statement that volatile agents cause uterine contractions is not true. In fact, volatile anesthetic agents, such as inhalation anesthetics, typically cause uterine relaxation rather than contractions. This uterine relaxation can potentially lead to postpartum hemorrhage after the delivery of the fetus. Therefore, it is crucial to monitor uterine tone during surgery and be prepared to manage any uterine atony that may occur as a result of anesthetic agents.

Recommended literature

1. Costantine M. Physiologic and pharmacokinetic changes in pregnancy. Frontiers in Pharmacology. 2014;5.
2. Nejdlova M, Johnson T. Anaesthesia for non-obstetric procedures during pregnancy. Continuing Education in Anaesthesia Critical Care & Pain. 2012;12(4):203-6

PLACENTA ACCRETA

Questions:

1. **What is the primary cause of severe bleeding in patients with placenta accreta?**
   A. Uterine rupture
   B. Thromboembolism
   C. Abnormal placental attachment
   D. Premature birth

2. **Which type of placenta accreta is the most common among cases in the placenta accreta spectrum?**
   A. Placenta increta
   B. Placenta percreta
   C. Placenta accreta
   D. Placenta previa

3. **Which of the following is NOT a recognized risk factor for placenta accreta?**
   A. Placenta previa
   B. Maternal age > 35 years
   C. Oligohydramnios
   D. IVF

4. **Which type of anesthesia is preferred for cases of placenta accreta?**
   A. General anesthesia
   B. Combined spinal-epidural CSE
   C. Spinal anesthesia
   D. Epidural anesthesia

5. **38-40 weeks is the recommended gestational age range for planned delivery in women with suspected placenta accreta.**
   A. True
   B. False

6. **A 36-year-old patient is in her 36th week of pregnancy. During routine prenatal care, she undergoes an ultrasonography examination, which raises concerns about placental abnormalities. The ultrasonography findings indicate a suspected diagnosis of placenta accreta. To confirm the diagnosis, an MRI is performed, which confirms the presence of placenta accreta. What is the recommended approach when placenta accreta is diagnosed antenatally?**
   A. Immediate placental removal
   B. C - section
   C. Caesarean hysterectomy
   D. Vaginal delivery

Answers:

1. **Answer C (Abnormal placental attachment)**

   The primary cause of severe bleeding in patients with placenta accreta is the abnormal attachment of the placenta to the uterine wall. In placenta accreta, the placenta grows too deeply into the uterine wall, and part or all of the placenta remains attached after delivery. This abnormal placental attachment disrupts the normal separation process that occurs during childbirth, leading to a high risk of severe postpartum bleeding. As a result, the placenta cannot be easily detached, and this abnormal attachment is a significant contributor to the hemorrhagic complications associated with placenta accreta. It is important to address this abnormal attachment through appropriate medical and surgical management to minimize the risk of life-threatening bleeding.

2. **Answer C (Placenta accreta)**

   Placenta accreta is the most common type among the cases in the placenta accreta spectrum. Placenta accreta is characterized by placental villi adhering to the myometrium, but the placenta does not pass through the uterine wall and does not impact the uterine muscles. It accounts for the majority of cases within the spectrum. The other two types, placenta increta, and placenta percreta, are less common. Placenta increta involves an invasion of the myometrium without passing through the uterine wall and is seen in approximately 15-18% of cases. Placenta percreta is the most severe type, involving the invasion through the myometrium to the serosa and surrounding organs, which might include the bladder or intestines, and it is found in 5-7% of cases. Placenta previa is a separate condition that involves the abnormal placement of the placenta over or near the cervix and is not part of the placenta accreta spectrum.

3. **Answer C (Oligohydramnios)**

   Placenta accreta is a high-risk pregnancy complication associated with several risk factors. These include a history of previous uterine surgery or caesarean section, placenta position (placenta previa or lower uterine placement), maternal age over 35 years, and multiparity. In vitro fertilization (IVF) is also recognized as a risk factor for placenta accreta. However, oligohydramnios, which refers to a decreased level of amniotic fluid in the uterus, is not typically identified as a direct risk factor for placenta accreta.

4. **Answer A (General anesthesia)**

   General anesthesia is the preferred choice for cases of placenta accreta. This preference is due to several factors, including the extended duration of the surgical procedure, the potential for massive hemorrhage, and the need for additional surgical steps, such as iliac vessel exposure. While neuraxial anesthesia can be safely performed in some cases, general anesthesia is favored when managing placenta accreta because it provides the anesthesiologist with better control over the patient's airway and the ability to rapidly adjust the level of anesthesia as needed during the procedure. This approach ensures the patient's safety and allows for prompt response to potential complications associated with this high-risk condition. Moreover, a multidisciplinary approach involving collaboration among various medical specialists can further enhance patient outcomes when dealing with placenta accreta.

5. **Answer B (False)**

   The recommended gestational age range for planned delivery in women with suspected placenta accreta is not 38-40 weeks. Obstetricians typically plan delivery between 35+0 and 36+6 weeks of gestation for women who are suspected to have placenta accreta. This timing is chosen to reduce the risk of severe bleeding and complications associated with this condition. Additionally, a single course of antenatal glucocorticoids may be administered between 34 and 36 weeks of gestation to promote fetal lung maturation. It's important to note that in cases where there are symptoms of bleeding or preterm labor, the need for delivery may be hastened, and the delivery may occur earlier than the recommended range.

6. **Answer C (Caesarean hysterectomy)**

   When placenta accreta is diagnosed antenatally, the most generally accepted and recommended approach is a caesarean hysterectomy. In this approach, the caesarean section is performed to deliver the fetus, but the placenta is intentionally left in situ after the fetal delivery. Before continuing with the hysterectomy, the uterine wall was closed to minimize bleeding. Attempts at placental removal are associated with significant risks of hemorrhage, making the caesarean hysterectomy approach the preferred choice. Antenatal diagnosis of the placenta accreta spectrum is highly desirable because it allows for optimized outcomes. It enables delivery to occur at a level III or IV maternal care facility before the onset of labor or bleeding, reducing the potential complications associated with this condition.

Recommended literature

1. Reale, S.C., Farber, M.K., 2022. Management of patients with suspected placenta accreta spectrum. BJA Education 22, 43–51.
2. Silver RM, Barbour KD. Placenta accreta spectrum: accreta, increta, and percreta. Obstet Gynecol Clin North Am. 2015;42(2):381-402.

PLACENTA PREVIA

Questions:

1. What is the primary reason for considering a caesarean section in cases of placenta previa?

   A. Maternal age

   B. Fetal distress

   C. High bleeding risk

   D. Uterine rupture risk

2. Which of the following is NOT a standard classification for placenta previa based on placental location?

   A. Marginal

   B. Minor

   C. Complete

   D. Partial

3. What is NOT a maternal complication commonly associated with placenta previa?

   A. Antepartum bleeding

   B. Uterine rupture

   C. Placental abruption

   D. Placenta accreta

4. What factor increases the risk of placenta previa in pregnant women?

   A. Multigravida

   B. Maternal age over 25

   C. Smoking during pregnancy

   D. History of uterine fibroids

5. Placenta previa should be suspected if bleeding occurs around 20 weeks of gestation.

   A. True

   B. False

6. A 32-year-old pregnant woman presents to the obstetric clinic at 36 weeks of gestation. She was previously diagnosed with placenta previa and has been scheduled for a caesarean section. Which mode of anesthesia is recommended for patients with placenta previa?

   A. General anesthesia

   B. Epidural anesthesia

   C. Spinal anesthesia

   D. No consensus on the use of general or regional anesthesia

Answers:

1. Answer C (High bleeding risk)

Placenta previa is a condition where the placenta attaches inside the uterus near or over the cervical opening. In cases of placenta previa, the placenta is positioned so that it can partially or completely cover the cervix. This abnormal placement of the placenta increases the risk of bleeding during labor and delivery. The placenta, in its abnormal location, can easily detach from the uterine wall, leading to significant hemorrhage. To minimize the risk of life-threatening bleeding for both the mother and the baby, a caesarean section is often required.

2. Answer B (Minor)

The standard classifications for placenta previa based on placental location are complete, partial, and marginal. In complete placenta previa, the placenta entirely covers the cervix, blocking the birth canal, while in partial placenta previa, it partially covers the cervix. Marginal placenta previa involves the placenta being positioned at the edge of the cervix, touching but not entirely covering it. Minor is not a recognized classification for placenta previa based on placental location.

3. Answer B (Uterine rupture)

While placenta previa is associated with maternal complications like antepartum bleeding, postpartum hemorrhage, and the risk of placenta accreta due to bleeding and abnormal placentation, it is not commonly associated with uterine rupture. Uterine rupture is a rare but severe complication that can occur during labor, primarily in cases with previous uterine surgery or other uterine abnormalities, whereas placenta previa's main maternal complications are related to bleeding and placental attachment issues.

4. Answer D (History of uterine fibroids)

While there are several risk factors associated with placenta previa, including advanced maternal age, smoking during pregnancy, and previous pregnancies, having a history of uterine fibroids is a notable risk factor. Uterine fibroids can disrupt the normal uterine environment and impact the placental attachment, increasing the likelihood of placenta previa. Other risk factors for placenta previa include previous placenta previa, prior caesarean delivery, myomectomy, or endometrial damage from procedures such as dilation and curettage, being younger than 20 or older than 35, multiparity, and pregnancy with multiples.

5. Answer B (False)

Placenta previa can be suspected if bleeding occurs after 24 weeks of gestation. While it commonly occurs around 32 weeks of gestation, bleeding before 32 weeks is still a significant concern. Placenta previa is characterized by the placenta's abnormal positioning near or over the cervical opening, and if bleeding is encountered at any point after the 24th week of pregnancy, it should raise suspicion of this condition. Therefore, it's important to be vigilant for signs of placenta previa throughout the second and third trimesters of pregnancy.

6. Answer D (No consensus on the use of general or regional anesthesia)

The recommended mode of anesthesia for a patient with placenta previa undergoing a caesarean section remains a matter of debate, and there is no clear consensus. Both general anesthesia and regional anesthesia have their advantages and should be considered based on the individual patient's condition and clinical circumstances. General anesthesia may be preferred in cases of hemodynamic instability, uncorrected hypovolemia, impaired hemostasis, or when there is a risk to the patient's airway, particularly in situations where the patient is semiconscious or unconscious. On the other hand, some prospective randomized trials have suggested that regional anesthesia could offer benefits over general anesthesia for elective caesarean sections in patients with placenta previa. Regional anesthesia has been associated with improved maternal hemodynamics and reduced blood loss due to sympathetic blockade, which lowers arterial pressure and decreases the need for blood transfusion.

Recommended literature

1. Pollard BJ, Kitchen, G. Handbook of Clinical Anaesthesia. Fourth Edition. CRC Press. 2018. 978-1-4987-6289-2.
2. Plaat F, shonfeldd A. 2015. Major obstetric hemorrhage. BJA education. 15;4:190-193.
3. Walfish, M., Neuman, A., Wlody, D., 2009. Maternal haemorrhage. British Journal of Anaesthesia 103, i47–i56.

Obstetrics
PLACENTAL ABRUPTION

Questions:

1. **What is the primary mechanism of placental abruption?**
   A. Placental detachment due to contractions
   B. Cervical dilation
   C. Placental previa
   D. Fetal malposition

2. **Which of the following is NOT a major complication of placental abruption?**
   A. Hemorrhagic shock
   B. Fetal demise
   C. Placental previa
   D. Maternal death

3. **Which of the following is a key diagnostic factor for placental abruption, even though approximately 20% of cases may not exhibit this symptom?**
   A. Uterine tenderness
   B. Rapid contractions
   C. Abdominal pain
   D. Vaginal bleeding

4. **Which of the following maternal factors is a known risk factor for placental abruption?**
   A. Gilbert syndrome
   B. Chronic obstructive pulmonary disease
   C. Cocaine use
   D. Hypotension

5. **Class 1 placental abruption is usually associated with complete or central separation.**
   A. True
   B. False

6. **A patient at 38 weeks of pregnancy presents to the Emergency Department (ED) with complaints of vaginal bleeding, uterine tenderness, rapid contractions, abdominal pain, and fetal heart rate abnormalities. The patient's vital signs reveal maternal tachycardia, orthostatic changes in blood pressure, and evidence of fetal distress. Additionally, a clotting profile alteration with hypofibrinogenemia is noted, and the estimated blood loss is described as a sudden blood loss of over 1500 mL. An ultrasound confirms the diagnosis of partial separation of the placenta. The patient is promptly transported to the operating room for an emergent caesarean section. What statement regarding the best anesthetic plan for abruptio placentae is NOT true?**
   A. General anesthesia with an endotracheal tube
   B. Rapid sequence spinal anesthesia
   C. Ketamine is the agent of choice
   D. Nitrous oxide should not be used

Answers:

1. Answer A (Placental detachment due to contractions)

Placental abruption is characterized by hemorrhage arising from the premature separation of a normally situated placenta. This separation occurs due to contractions that lead to the detachment of the placental bed from the decidua basalis before the delivery of the fetus. The contractions cause the placenta to detach from the uterine wall, leading to the clinical features of placental abruption, such as vaginal bleeding, uterine tenderness, and other signs and symptoms associated with this condition.

2. Answer C (Placental previa)

Major complications of placental abruption encompass severe conditions such as hemorrhagic shock, acute kidney injury, coagulopathy, fetal demise, maternal death, delivering a premature infant, transfusion-associated complications, and the need for a hysterectomy. Placental previa, conversely, is a different obstetric condition characterized by an abnormally located placenta near or covering the cervical opening, and it is distinct from placental abruption, each having its own set of complications.

3. Answer D (Vaginal bleeding)

Vaginal bleeding is a key diagnostic factor for placental abruption. However, it's important to note that approximately 20% of cases of placental abruption may not exhibit this symptom. Therefore, while vaginal bleeding is a crucial diagnostic indicator, the absence of bleeding does not rule out the possibility of placental abruption and other clinical signs and symptoms, such as uterine tenderness, rapid contractions, abdominal pain, and fetal heart rate abnormalities, should also be considered when diagnosing this condition.

4. Answer C (Cocaine use)

Cocaine use is a known risk factor for placental abruption. Placental abruption can be influenced by various maternal and pregnancy-related factors. Other maternal factors that increase the risk of placental abruption include smoking, maternal age over 35 years, and hypertension. Additionally, placental abruption in a prior pregnancy is also a maternal factor that may increase the risk of experiencing it in subsequent pregnancies.

5. Answer B (False)

Class 1 placental abruption is not usually associated with complete or central separation. Classification of 0 or 1 is typically associated with a partial, marginal separation. In contrast, classifications of 2 or 3 are associated with complete or central separation. Therefore, Class 1 placental abruption is more likely to involve a partial separation of the placenta from the uterine wall rather than a complete or central separation.

6. Answer B (Rapid sequence spinal anesthesia)

In cases of abruptio placentae, the best anesthetic plan is typically general anesthesia with an endotracheal tube, even in hemodynamically stable patients. This approach is chosen because there is a high propensity for postpartum hemorrhage in patients with abruptio placentae. Rapid sequence induction should be performed, considering all pregnant patients to have a full stomach to minimize the risk of aspiration. The choice of the induction agent, such as ketamine, strongly depends on the patient's hemodynamic stability, especially in patients presenting with shock. Other induction agents, like etomidate, may also be suitable. However, thiopentone and propofol should be used cautiously due to their potential adverse effects on the circulatory system. For maintenance of anesthesia, a volatile agent is typically added to prevent awareness, with a concentration not exceeding 0.5 MAC, to avoid the risk of uterine atony and postpartum hemorrhage. Nitrous oxide should not be used for maintenance when the indication for caesarean section is fetal distress, as it may not provide sufficient pain relief. In summary, while spinal anesthesia is a valid option for certain obstetric procedures, it is not the preferred choice for abruptio placentae due to the potential for rapid, high-risk blood loss and the need for prompt control of the airway and hemodynamics.

Recommended literature

1. Schmidt P, Skelly CL, Raines DA. Placental Abruption. In: StatPearls. Treasure Island (FL): StatPearls Publishing; April 1, 2022.
2. Walfish, M., Neuman, A., Wlody, D., 2009. Maternal haemorrhage. British Journal of Anaesthesia 103, i47–i56.

Obstetrics
POST-DURAL PUNCTURE HEADACHE (PDPH)

11
CHAPTER

Questions:

1. **What is the primary mechanism of post-dural puncture headache (PDPH)?**
   A. Infection at the dural puncture site
   B. Cerebrospinal fluid leakage through the puncture
   C. Nerve compression in the spinal cord
   D. Blood clot formation in the spinal column

2. **What is the most common age group affected by PDPH?**
   A. Children under 10 years
   B. Adults in their 30s
   C. Teens and early 20s
   D. Elderly individuals

3. **Which of the following equipment-related factors can increase the risk of PDPH?**
   A. Smaller needle gauge
   B. Cutting needle tip design
   C. Longer needle length
   D. Short needle length

4. **How is the diagnosis of PDPH typically made?**
   A. Based on the patient's age and gender
   B. Through imaging radiological guidance
   C. By excluding other potential causes of the headache
   D. By observing neck stiffness and tinnitus

5. **Visual hallucinations are typically associated with PDPH.**
   A. True
   B. False

6. **A 32-year-old pregnant woman at 38 weeks of gestation. The patient is in active labor and requests an epidural for pain relief. She has had a healthy pregnancy with no significant medical issues and has been receiving prenatal care regularly. Her vital signs are within the normal range, and the fetal heart rate tracing is reassuring. While placing the epidural, you notice a "wet tap" where cerebrospinal fluid (CSF) is visible on the epidural needle. What is NOT a recommended strategy for preventing PDPH?**
   A. Bed rest
   B. Prophylactic Epidural Blood Patch
   C. Stylet replacement
   D. Intrathecal catheters

Answers:

1. Answer B (Cerebrospinal fluid leakage through the puncture)

Post-dural puncture headache (PDPH) is primarily caused by cerebrospinal fluid (CSF) leakage through the dural puncture. When a dural puncture occurs, such as during certain medical procedures like epidurals or spinal anesthesia, it can create a small hole or tear in the dura mater. This hole allows CSF to leak out into the surrounding tissues, leading to a decrease in CSF pressure within the spinal canal. This drop in CSF pressure is what results in the characteristic headache associated with PDPH. The loss of CSF can lead to traction on pain-sensitive structures in the brain and surrounding blood vessels, which contributes to the headache. The headache is often described as a severe, positional headache and is usually accompanied by other symptoms such as neck stiffness and, in some cases, subjective hearing symptoms. PDPH typically remits spontaneously within about two weeks as the body gradually replenishes the lost CSF.

2. Answer C (Teens and early 20s)

The most common age group affected by PDPH is teenagers and individuals in their early twenties. PDPH is relatively uncommon in patients under the age of 10 and in older individuals. The peak incidence of PDPH occurs in the teens and early 20s, making this age group the most susceptible to this type of headache after dural puncture procedures. This age-related variation in PDPH incidence is likely due to differences in the properties of the dura mater and the cerebrospinal fluid, as well as the resilience of the tissues in different age groups.

3. Answer B (Cutting needle tip design)

Among the equipment-related factors, the use of a cutting needle tip design can increase the risk of PDPH. Cutting-tip needles have a sharp, beveled edge that can easily penetrate the dura mater, the protective membrane surrounding the spinal cord and brain. This creates a larger hole or tear in the dura, allowing for greater CSF leakage when the needle is withdrawn. The loss of CSF and the subsequent decrease in CSF pressure within the spinal canal are key factors in the development of PDPH. Conversely, noncutting-tip needles are designed to separate rather than cut the dura mater, and they are associated with a lower risk of accidental dural puncture and, by extension, PDPH.

4. Answer C (By excluding other potential causes of the headache)

The typical diagnosis of PDPH is made by excluding other potential causes of the headache. PDPH is characterized by its clinical features, including a delayed onset, symmetric bilateral headache, and sometimes associated symptoms like neck stiffness and tinnitus, particularly with severe headaches. The diagnosis of PDPH is primarily one of exclusion, as other medical conditions can present with similar symptoms.

5. Answer B (False)

Visual hallucinations are not typically associated with PDPH. PDPH is characterized by a headache that is often accompanied by symptoms such as neck stiffness, tinnitus, hypoacusia, photophobia, and nausea. Visual hallucinations are not a common symptom of PDPH. Typically, PDPH presents with various neurological and headache-related symptoms, but visual hallucinations are not among them.

6. Answer A (Bed rest)

Bed rest is not a recommended strategy for preventing PDPH in the context of a "wet tap" during epidural placement. PDPH occurs when CSF leaks from the dural puncture site, leading to a decrease in CSF pressure within the spinal canal. Bed rest has not been shown to be an effective preventative measure for PDPH. The other options listed are relevant strategies for risk management after accidental dural puncture and for preventing PDPH.

Recommended literature

1. Statement on post-dural puncture headache management. American Society of Anesthesiologists (ASA). https://www.asahq.org. Published October 13, 2021. Accessed December 14, 2022.
2. Russell R, Laxton C, Lucas DN, Niewiarowski J, Scrutton M, Stocks G. Treatment of obstetric post-dural puncture headache. Part 2: epidural blood patch. Int J Obstet Anesth. 2019;38:104-118.

POSTPARTUM HEMORRHAGE

11
CHAPTER

Questions:

1. **What is the leading cause of maternal mortality in low-income countries?**
   A. Hypertensive disorders of pregnancy
   B. Postpartum hemorrhage
   C. Placental abruption
   D. Inherited coagulopathy

2. **What is the estimated blood loss (EBL) threshold for diagnosing postpartum hemorrhage (PPH) after a vaginal delivery?**
   A. > 1000 mL
   B. > 500 mL
   C. > 1500 mL
   D. > 2000 mL

3. **What is the primary cause of PPH globally?**
   A. Placental abruption
   B. Atonic uterus
   C. Uterine rupture
   D. Coagulopathy

4. **Which risk factor increases the likelihood of postpartum hemorrhage in women?**
   A. Retained placenta
   B. Small-for-gestational-age fetus
   C. Singleton pregnancy
   D. Lack of uterine fibroids

5. **Air hunger is one of the possible symptoms of postpartum hemorrhage.**
   A. True
   B. False

6. **A 32-year-old woman presents with tachycardia, hypotension, delayed capillary refill, decreased urine output, pallor, lightheadedness, palpitations, and confusion six hours after a vaginal delivery. Her estimated blood loss is approximately 1000 mL, and a pelvic examination reveals a significant vaginal hematoma suspected as the source of bleeding. What is the recommended management for traumatic causes of postpartum hemorrhage, such as hematomas?**
   A. Uterine massage
   B. Administration of uterotonics
   C. Evacuation of hematomas and hemostasis
   D. Methotrexate administration

Answers:

1. **Answer B (Postpartum hemorrhage)**

   Postpartum hemorrhage (PPH) is the abnormal loss of blood within 24 hours after giving birth. In low-income countries, it stands as the primary cause of maternal mortality, making it a significant public health concern. PPH is particularly alarming because it contributes to nearly one-quarter of all maternal deaths globally, highlighting its critical impact on maternal health and survival in these regions. Hypertensive disorders of pregnancy, placental abruption, and inherited coagulopathy are certainly important and can lead to severe complications during pregnancy and childbirth. However, when it comes to maternal mortality in low-income countries, PPH is the most prominent cause due to its potential for rapid and life-threatening blood loss following childbirth.

2. **Answer B (> 500 mL)**

   In the context of postpartum hemorrhage, the estimated blood loss (EBL) refers to the amount of blood loss within 24 hours after giving birth. For a vaginal delivery, an EBL greater than 500 mL is considered indicative of postpartum hemorrhage. This threshold helps healthcare providers identify cases of excessive bleeding and initiate appropriate interventions promptly. It's important to monitor EBL closely to ensure the well-being of the mother and address any signs of PPH.

3. **Answer B (Atonic uterus)**

   The primary cause of PPH globally is an atonic uterus, accounting for approximately 70% of cases. This refers to the loss of uterine tone, leading to ineffective contractions and subsequent excessive bleeding. Other significant causes include issues related to retained or invasive placenta (10%), traumatic injuries like lacerations or hematomas (20%), and coagulopathies (1%).

4. **Answer A (Retained placenta)**

   Retained placenta is a significant risk factor for postpartum hemorrhage. This occurs when the placenta fails to fully detach from the uterine wall after childbirth. This can lead to prolonged bleeding and an increased risk of hemorrhage. Various risk factors can increase the likelihood of PPH in women. These encompass medical or surgical history, including previous PPH, uterine fibroids, and prior Caesarean delivery or uterine instrumentation. Fetal factors such as multifetal gestation, polyhydramnios, and the presence of a large-for-gestational-age or macrosomic fetus also play a role. Maternal issues, including hypertensive disorders of pregnancy, perioperative anemia, and coagulopathies, such as Von Willebrand's Disease or HELLP syndrome, contribute to the risk. Moreover, certain obstetric interventions, like trial of labor after Caesarean delivery and instrumentation during delivery, can heighten the chances of PPH, as can placental or uterine issues like placental abruption, placenta previa, and retained placenta. The management of PPH should consider these factors to ensure timely intervention and prevent complications.

5. **Answer A (True)**

   "Air hunger" is one of the possible symptoms of PPH. PPH can lead to a severe loss of blood, resulting in a reduced oxygen-carrying capacity in the blood, making the affected individual feel a sense of breathlessness or "air hunger." This symptom is often associated with the decreased oxygen supply to the body due to significant blood loss and is a critical sign that healthcare providers monitor when assessing and managing PPH. Other symptoms and signs of PPH include tachycardia, hypotension, delayed capillary refill, decreased urine output, pallor, lightheadedness, palpitations, confusion, syncope, fatigue, and diaphoresis. All these signs and symptoms are crucial in the diagnosis and management of PPH.

6. **Answer C (Evacuation of hematomas and hemostasis)**

   In this scenario, the patient is experiencing postpartum hemorrhage due to a significant vaginal hematoma, which is a traumatic cause. The primary approach to managing this type of PPH involves surgically evacuating the hematoma, which means removing the accumulated blood in the hematoma and then achieving hemostasis. This is a direct and effective intervention for addressing the traumatic cause of postpartum hemorrhage and stabilizing the patient's condition. Uterine massage and administration of uterotonics are more suitable for managing atonic uterus-related PPH.

Recommended literature

1. Watkins EJ, Stem K. Postpartum hemorrhage. JAAPA. 2020;33(4):29-33.
2. Evensen A, Anderson JM, Fontaine P. Postpartum hemorrhage: prevention and treatment. Am Fam Physician. 2017; 95(7): 442-449.
3. 2017. Prevention and Management of Postpartum Haemorrhage. BJOG: An International Journal of Obstetrics & Gynaecology 124, e106-e149.
4. E. Mavrides, S. Allard, E. Chandraharan, P. Collins, L. Green, BJ. Hunt, S. Riris. AJ. Thomason on behalf of the Royal college of obstetricians and gynaecologists. Prevention and management of postpartum haemorrhage. BJOG 2016; 124:e 106-e149
5. Anderson JM, Etches D. Prevention and management of postpartum hemorrhage. Am Fam Physician. 2007;75(6):875-882.
6. WHO recommendations for the prevention and treatment of postpartum haemorrhage.

Obstetrics
PRE-ECLAMPSIA

Questions:

1. **What is the definition of pre-eclampsia?**
   A. New onset hypertension after 10 weeks of gestation
   B. New onset hypertension after 20 weeks of gestation with one or more signs of organ dysfunction
   C. Elevated blood pressure at any time during pregnancy
   D. Elevated blood pressure with proteinuria before 10 weeks of gestation

2. **Which of the following is a symptom of severe pre-eclampsia?**
   A. Mild headache
   B. Blurred vision
   C. Tachypnoea
   D. Thrombocytosis

3. **What is the recommended preventive measure for pre-eclampsia in women with high-risk factors?**
   A. Daily intake of aspirin
   B. Magnesium supplementation
   C. Early delivery of the baby
   D. Labetalol

4. **Which of the following is considered a high-risk factor for pre-eclampsia?**
   A. First pregnancy
   B. Age ≥ 40 years
   C. Pregnancy interval < 5 years
   D. Singleton pregnancy

5. **Labetalol is the first choice medication used for controlling maternal blood pressure in cases of pre-eclampsia.**
   A. True
   B. False

6. **The woman is at 32 weeks of pregnancy and presents with episodes of shaking, confusion, and disorientation. Her blood pressure is elevated at 160/110 mmHg, and she exhibits proteinuria, thrombocytopenia (platelet count of 70,000), elevated liver enzymes (AST, ALT, GGT), and low hemoglobin (90 g/dL). These clinical features are indicative of severe pre-eclampsia with ongoing neurological symptoms, and immediate intervention is crucial. What would be the recommended treatment in this case?**
   A. Magnesium sulfate
   B. Calcium gluconate
   C. Labetalol
   D. Aspirin

Answers:

1. **Answer B (New onset hypertension after 20 weeks of gestation with one or more signs of organ dysfunction)**

   Pre-eclampsia is defined as new onset hypertension with a systolic blood pressure of 140 mmHg or higher, diastolic blood pressure of 90 mmHg or higher, or both, occurring at or after 20 weeks of gestation, accompanied by one or more of the following features: proteinuria (indicated by a spot urinary protein creatinine ratio greater than 30 mg/mmol or a 24-hour urine collection with more than 300 mg of protein) and other maternal organ dysfunction, which may involve acute kidney injury, liver involvement, neurological complications (seizures, severe headaches, visual disturbances, clonus, blindness, altered mental status, or stroke), and hematological complications such as thrombocytopenia, disseminated intravascular coagulation (DIC), and hemolysis.

2. **Answer B (Blurred vision)**

   Blurred vision is a symptom commonly associated with severe pre-eclampsia. Other symptoms of severe pre-eclampsia can include severe headaches, changes in vision (including temporary loss of vision), and other signs of organ dysfunction, such as proteinuria, thrombocytopenia, increased liver enzymes, shortness of breath, abdominal pain, and nausea or vomiting.

3. **Answer A (Daily intake of aspirin)**

   For women with high-risk factors for pre-eclampsia, the recommended preventive measure is daily intake of low-dose aspirin (typically 75-150 mg) from 12 weeks of gestation until 36-37 weeks of gestation. This prophylactic use of aspirin has been shown to be effective in reducing the risk of developing pre-eclampsia in high-risk pregnancies. It is an important strategy to improve maternal and fetal outcomes.

4. **Answer B (Age ≥ 40 years)**

   Among the options provided, age ≥ 40 years is considered a high-risk factor for pre-eclampsia. High-risk factors for pre-eclampsia include various conditions and characteristics, such as hypertensive disease in a previous pregnancy, chronic kidney disease, autoimmune diseases (e.g., antiphospholipid syndrome), and type 1 or type 2 diabetes mellitus. Other high-risk factors include chronic hypertension, advanced maternal age (such as age ≥ 40 years), a pregnancy interval of 10 years or more, a family history of pre-eclampsia, and multiple pregnancies.

5. **Answer A (True)**

   Labetalol is considered one of the first-choice medications used for controlling maternal blood pressure in cases of pre-eclampsia. It is often favored due to its effectiveness in reducing high blood pressure while also being safe for both the mother and the baby. However, the choice of medication and its administration can vary depending on the specific clinical situation, and healthcare providers may consider other antihypertensive agents like nifedipine, hydralazine, or methyldopa based on the patient's individual needs and response to treatment.

6. **Answer A (Magnesium sulfate)**

   Magnesium sulfate is the first-line treatment for controlling convulsions and is the standard of care for managing eclamptic seizures, which can occur in the context of severe pre-eclampsia. In this case, the patient's symptoms of shaking, confusion, and disorientation are suggestive of neurological involvement, which is a critical indication for using magnesium sulfate. A loading dose of 4 to 6 grams of magnesium sulfate should be administered intravenously over 15 to 20 minutes to quickly control seizures. Following the loading dose, a maintenance dose of 2 grams per hour is typically continued. It's important to note that magnesium treatment should be continued for at least 24 hours after the patient's last seizure to prevent the recurrence of convulsions and manage the neurological manifestations associated with severe pre-eclampsia. Magnesium sulfate is a vital component of the management of eclamptic seizures in the setting of pre-eclampsia to ensure the safety of both the mother and the unborn baby.

Recommended literature

1. Goddard, J., Wee, M.Y.K., Vinayakarao, L., 2020. Update on hypertensive disorders in pregnancy. BJA Education 20, 411–416.
2. Leslie, D., Collis, R., 2016. Hypertension in pregnancy. BJA Education 16, 33–37.

PRELABOR RUPTURE OF MEMBRANES (PROM)

11
CHAPTER

Questions:

1. **What is the definition of Prelabor Rupture of Membranes (PROM)?**
   A. Rupture of the amniotic sac during labor
   B. Rupture of the amniotic sac before the onset of labor
   C. Rupture of the amniotic sac after 37 weeks of gestation
   D. Rupture of the amniotic sac before 24 weeks of gestation

2. **Which of the following is NOT a complication of PROM for the mother?**
   A. Placental abruption
   B. Chorioamnionitis
   C. Postpartum endometritis
   D. Cervical cerclage

3. **What is the management approach for PROM if the gestational age is 34 weeks or more and there is evidence of fetal lung maturity?**
   A. Discharge home
   B. Immediate delivery
   C. Antibiotic therapy
   D. Corticosteroid administration

4. **What is the recommended prevention strategy for women with a history of preterm delivery (with or without PROM)?**
   A. Bed rest
   B. Progesterone supplementation
   C. Antibiotic prophylaxis
   D. Corticosteroid administration

5. **Cerebral palsy is a potential complication associated with PROM in the fetal context.**
   A. True
   B. False

6. **A 37-year-old pregnant woman, G3P2 (gravida 3, para 2), at 37 weeks of gestation, presents to the labor and delivery unit with complaints of a gush of fluid from the vagina. She reports that this fluid leakage occurred suddenly and was not associated with pain or contractions. The patient's medical history is unremarkable except for a previous uncomplicated vaginal delivery at term and a history of group B streptococcus (GBS) unknown. She has received regular prenatal care. What statement is NOT true about the management of PROM?**
   A. Expectant management is appropriate in women who are group B streptococcus (GBS) negative or GBS unknown and have no signs of infection or other complications
   B. Induction of labor (IOL) with vaginal prostaglandins is associated with an increased risk of chorioamnionitis and neonatal infection in comparison with an oxytocin induction
   C. Vaginal prostaglandins rather than oxytocin are preferred for the induction of labor in the presence of PROM at term
   D. If the woman has any signs of infection, then advise immediate induction of labor

Answers:

1. **Answer B (Rupture of the amniotic sac before the onset of labor)**

   Prelabor Rupture of Membranes (PROM), previously known as premature rupture of membranes, is defined as the breakage of the amniotic sac before the onset of labor. This can happen at term (after 37 weeks of gestation) or preterm (before 37 weeks of gestation), with the latter being referred to as Preterm PROM (PPROM). It's important to note that PROM occurs before the onset of labor. Approximately 8% of term pregnancies and 30% of preterm pregnancies are affected by PROM, and about 50% of patients with PROM will deliver within one week.

2. **Answer D (Cervical cerclage)**

   Cervical cerclage is not a complication of PROM for the mother. It is a medical procedure used to treat cervical insufficiency, which is a condition where the cervix begins to open too early during pregnancy. Placental abruption, chorioamnionitis, and postpartum endometritis are potential complications that can occur in cases of PROM, affecting the mother's health during or after the episode of PROM.

3. **Answer B (Immediate delivery)**

   When managing PROM and the gestational age is 34 weeks or more with evidence of fetal lung maturity, the recommended management approach is immediate delivery. Evidence of fetal lung maturity suggests that the baby's lungs are sufficiently developed for life outside the uterus, and the risks of complications related to prematurity are reduced. Therefore, immediate delivery is typically considered the best course of action in such cases.

4. **Answer B (Progesterone supplementation)**

   For women with a history of preterm delivery (with or without PROM), the recommended prevention strategy is to take progesterone supplementation. Progesterone supplementation has been shown to be effective in reducing the risk of recurrent preterm birth in women with a history of preterm delivery. It helps in supporting the uterine environment and reducing the likelihood of preterm labor.

5. **Answer A (True)**

   Cerebral palsy is listed as a potential complication associated with PROM in the fetal context. While it's important to note that PROM itself doesn't directly cause cerebral palsy, premature birth, which can be a consequence of PROM, is a known risk factor for cerebral palsy. Babies born prematurely, especially very preterm, have a higher risk of developing cerebral palsy compared to full-term babies. Therefore, while PROM may not directly lead to cerebral palsy, the prematurity associated with PROM can increase the risk of cerebral palsy in affected infants.

6. **Answer C (Vaginal prostaglandins rather than oxytocin are preferred for the induction of labor in the presence of PROM at term)**

   The statement that is not true about the management of Prelabor Rupture of Membranes for this patient is an option which suggests that vaginal prostaglandins are preferred over oxytocin for labor induction in the presence of PROM at term. In fact, it is generally preferred to use oxytocin for induction in such cases, as it provides better control over the process. The other statements are accurate: expectant management is appropriate for GBS-negative or GBS-unknown women with no signs of infection; induction with vaginal prostaglandins is associated with increased risks; and if signs of infection are present, immediate induction is advised. Given the patient's GBS status is unknown and there are no signs of infection, expectant management may be considered. Still, the final decision should be tailored to the patient's individual circumstances and preferences.

Recommended literature

1. Dayal S, Hong PL. Premature Rupture Of Membranes. [Updated 2022 Jul 18]. In: StatPearls [Internet]. Treasure Island (FL): StatPearls Publishing; 2022 Jan. Available from: https://www.ncbi.nlm.nih.gov/books/NBK532888/

Obstetrics
UMBILICAL CORD PROLAPSE

Questions:

1. **What is the primary goal in managing umbilical cord prolapse?**
    A. Administer epidural anesthesia
    B. Avoid cord compression and vasospasm
    C. Perform forceps delivery
    D. Administer tocolytic agents

2. **Which condition is associated with a higher risk of umbilical cord prolapse?**
    A. Maternal age < 20 years
    B. Placenta previa
    C. Post-term pregnancy
    D. High birth weight

3. **What is the recommended position for the patient during umbilical cord prolapse management to aid cord decompression?**
    A. Supine position
    B. Prone position
    C. Knee-chest position
    D. Right lateral position

4. **In umbilical cord prolapse management, what is the primary method used to avoid cord compression?**
    A. Administering tocolytic agents
    B. Manual elevation of the presenting part
    C. Administering intravenous narcotics
    D. Forceps-assisted delivery

5. **Funic reduction is often used as an immediate management approach for umbilical cord prolapse.**
    A. True
    B. False

6. **A 22-year-old patient at 38 weeks of pregnancy, with an otherwise healthy pregnancy, presents with a steady leakage of fluid from the vagina. On examination, there is palpation of a pulsating structure in the vaginal vault, and a visible protrusion is noted from the vaginal introitus. These clinical findings raise concern about the possibility of umbilical cord prolapse, an obstetric emergency. Which parameter should suggest clinical diagnosis immediately for potential cord prolapse?**
    A. Fetal tachycardia
    B. Fetal bradycardia
    C. Late decelerations
    D. Early decelerations

Answers:

1. **Answer B (Avoid cord compression and vasospasm)**

   The primary goal in managing umbilical cord prolapse is to avoid cord compression and vasospasm, which can compromise the blood flow between the placenta and the fetus. This is achieved through a series of steps, including calling for assistance, establishing an intravenous line, continuous fetal monitoring, administering oxygen, and implementing other measures to ensure the safety of both the mother and the baby. In most cases, immediate delivery of the baby via caesarean section is necessary, although instrumental/vaginal delivery may be considered if it is determined to be a quicker option. Various interventions, such as funic decompression, bladder filling, and tocolysis, are employed to relieve cord compression. Keeping the umbilical cord warm and moist is essential to prevent vasospasm and maintain cord integrity. The primary objective is to protect the fetal blood supply and ensure a safe outcome for both the mother and the baby.

2. **Answer B (Placenta previa)**

   Umbilical cord prolapse is a serious obstetric emergency, and certain risk factors can increase the likelihood of its occurrence. Among the listed options, placenta previa is associated with a higher risk of umbilical cord prolapse. Placenta previa occurs when the placenta partially or completely covers the cervix, which can make the cord more vulnerable to descending alongside or past the fetal presenting part. Other risk factors for umbilical cord prolapse include maternal age ≥35 years, premature rupture of membranes, preterm delivery, low birth weight, multiple gestation pregnancies, polyhydramnios, fetal malpresentation (e.g., breech presentation), previous external cephalic version procedures, intrauterine growth restriction, and fetal and cord abnormalities.

3. **Answer C (Knee-chest position)**

   During umbilical cord prolapse management, the recommended position for the patient to aid in cord decompression is the "knee-chest position". It is preferred to have the patient lie on their left side when using the knee-chest position. This position helps alleviate the pressure on the umbilical cord and ensures a more favorable orientation for fetal well-being.

4. **Answer B (Manual elevation of the presenting part)**

   In managing umbilical cord prolapse, the primary method used to avoid cord compression and relieve the pressure on the umbilical cord is the manual elevation of the presenting part. This technique involves using two fingers or a hand in the vagina to physically lift and reposition the fetal presenting part, allowing the umbilical cord to rise above it and decompress. This manual manipulation is crucial in preventing further cord compression and maintaining adequate blood flow between the placenta and the fetus. While other interventions, such as tocolytic agents, may be considered in certain situations, the manual elevation of the presenting part is the immediate and direct method employed to alleviate cord compression during this obstetric emergency.

5. **Answer B (False)**

   Funic reduction is not often used as an immediate management approach for umbilical cord prolapse. It is listed as a rare intervention and is not typically considered a primary method for addressing this obstetric emergency. Instead, the primary management strategies focus on avoiding cord compression and vasospasm, which include measures such as manual elevation of the presenting part, repositioning the patient, and preparing for immediate caesarean section delivery to alleviate the risk to the fetus. Funic reduction, which involves attempting to replace the prolapsed cord into the uterus, is rarely employed due to its technical challenges and potential risks.

6. **Answer B (Fetal bradycardia)**

   In the presented case, the immediate clinical concern is the possibility of umbilical cord prolapse, which is a critical obstetric emergency. One of the key indicators of umbilical cord prolapse is fetal bradycardia. When the umbilical cord descends alongside or past the fetal presenting part, it can become compressed, leading to impaired blood flow between the placenta and the fetus. Fetal bradycardia is a sign of this compromised blood supply and is a strong indicator that immediate intervention is required. The diagnosis of umbilical cord prolapse is primarily clinical, involving the palpation of a pulsating structure in the vaginal vault or a visible protrusion from the vaginal introitus, and it is typically accompanied by fetal bradycardia or severe variable decelerations.

Recommended literature

1. Boushra M, Stone A, Rathbun KM. Umbilical Cord Prolapse. [Updated 2022 Jun 5]. In: StatPearls [Internet]. Treasure Island (FL): StatPearls Publishing; 2022 Jan. Available from: https://www.ncbi.nlm.nih.gov/books/NBK542241/
2. Sayed Ahmed WA, Hamdy MA. Optimal management of umbilical cord prolapse. Int J Womens Health. 2018;10:459-465.

UTERINE INVERSION

11
CHAPTER

Questions:

1. **What is the primary mechanism responsible for uterine inversion during childbirth?**
   A. Mismanagement of the first stage of labor
   B. Mismanagement of the third stage of labor
   C. Maternal hypertension
   D. Umbilical cord prolapse

2. **Which degree of uterine inversion involves the fundus protruding through the cervical os?**
   A. 1st degree (incomplete)
   B. 2nd degree (complete)
   C. 3rd degree (prolapsed)
   D. 4th degree (total)

3. **When does chronic uterine inversion occur in relation to childbirth?**
   A. During labor
   B. Within 24 hours of delivery
   C. More than 24 hours but less than four weeks postpartum
   D. One month or more postpartum

4. **Which factor is not a known risk factor for uterine inversion?**
   A. Short umbilical cord
   B. Fetal macrosomia
   C. Multiple gestations
   D. Maternal age

5. **Uterotonic agents are the first-line therapy in the management of uterine inversion.**
   A. True
   B. False

6. **A 27-year-old nulliparous woman presents to the emergency department 24 hours after delivering her first child. She complains of abdominal pain, a smooth, round mass protruding from her cervix and vagina, urinary retention, and hypotension. After a thorough evaluation, the diagnosis of uterine inversion is confirmed. What is the primary complication associated with uterine inversion?**
   A. Thromboembolism
   B. Maternal hypertension
   C. Major hemorrhage
   D. Vaginal cuff dehiscence

Answers:

1. **Answer B (Mismanagement of the third stage of labor)**

   The primary mechanism responsible for uterine inversion during childbirth is mismanagement of the third stage of labor, particularly through techniques like applying excessive fundal pressure and using excess cord traction when attempting to deliver the placenta. Additionally, natural factors such as uterine weakness, precipitate delivery, and a short umbilical cord can contribute to this condition. Uterine inversion is more common in multiple gestations compared to singleton pregnancies, likely due to increased uterine distention.

2. **Answer B (2nd degree (complete))**

   The degree of uterine inversion that involves the fundus protruding through the cervical os is the 2nd degree (complete). In the other degrees, the 1st degree (incomplete) has the fundus within the endometrial cavity, the 3rd degree (prolapsed) has the fundus protruding to or beyond the introitus, and the 4th degree (total) involves both the uterus and vagina being inverted and protruding outside the body.

3. **Answer D (One month or more postpartum)**

   Chronic uterine inversion is characterized by its occurrence one month or more after childbirth. This temporal classification distinguishes it from acute uterine inversion (within the first 24 hours of delivery) and subacute uterine inversion (occurring more than 24 hours but less than four weeks postpartum).

4. **Answer D (Maternal age)**

   Maternal age is not specifically mentioned among the listed risk factors for uterine inversion. Other factors, such as a short umbilical cord, rapid or prolonged labor, use of uterine relaxants, nulliparity, fetal macrosomia, retained placenta, severe pre-eclampsia, uterine atony, placenta accreta spectrum, and uterine anomalies or tumors (leiomyoma), are recognized as risk factors for uterine inversion. Maternal age is not explicitly associated with an increased risk of uterine inversion.

5. **Answer B (False)**

   Contrary to the statement, uterotonic agents are not the first-line therapy in the management of uterine inversion. Initial interventions should focus on discontinuing uterotonic drugs since uterine relaxation is needed to facilitate the replacement of the uterine fundus. Following the correction of uterine inversion, the subsequent management steps include holding the uterus in place to ensure stability and administering uterotonic drugs to address uterine atony, which is common after the uterus's restoration.

6. **Answer C (Major hemorrhage)**

   The primary complication associated with uterine inversion is major hemorrhage. Uterine inversion can lead to significant blood loss, and if not promptly managed, it can result in severe hemorrhage, shock, and multi-organ damage. In some cases, it may necessitate a hysterectomy to control bleeding. Other potential complications include Sheehan syndrome, but the most immediate and critical concern is the risk of major hemorrhage due to the inversion of the uterine fundus, which can disrupt blood vessels and cause life-threatening bleeding.

Recommended literature

1. Macones G. 2022. Peurperal uterine inversion. Up to date.
2. Wendel MP, Shnaekel KL, Magann EF. Uterine Inversion: A Review of a Life-Threatening Obstetrical Emergency. Obstet Gynecol Surv. 2018;73(7):411-417.
3. Shepherd LJ, Shenassa H, Singh SS. Laparoscopic management of uterine inversion. J Minim Invasive Gynecol. 2010;17(2):255-257.

Obstetrics
UTERINE RUPTURE

11

CHAPTER

Questions:

1. **What is the sign of uterine rupture during labor?**
   A. Vaginal bleeding
   B. Cessation of uterine contractions
   C. Abdominal pain
   D. All of the above

2. **What condition can be ruled out using ultrasound when diagnosing uterine rupture?**
   A. Placenta previa
   B. Uterine inversion
   C. Umbilical cord prolapse
   D. Breech presentation

3. **Which of the following factors increases the risk of uterine rupture during pregnancy and labor?**
   A. Prolonged labor
   B. Attempting vaginal birth after a caesarean section
   C. Cocaine use
   D. Breech presentation

4. **What type of anesthesia is preferred for an emergent C-section in cases of uterine rupture?**
   A. General anesthesia
   B. Regional anesthesia (epidural or spinal)
   C. Intravenous sedation
   D. Local anesthesia

5. **An early deceleration in the fetal heart rate is a common sign of fetal oxygenation compromise in cases of uterine rupture, indicating that the fetus is not receiving sufficient oxygen during labor.**
   A. True
   B. False

6. **The 28-year-old woman in her 36th week of pregnancy with a history of a previous caesarean delivery is showing concerning signs and symptoms, which include vaginal bleeding, abdominal pain, and tenderness. Additionally, the CTG findings are indicative of fetal distress, with late decelerations, reduced variability, and fetal tachycardia. The ultrasound results also reveal an abnormality in the uterine wall, a hematoma next to the hysterotomy scar, and free fluid in the peritoneum, all of which are highly suggestive of uterine rupture. What is the primary management approach for uterine rupture during labor?**
   A. Immediate induction of labor
   B. Administering tocolytic agents
   C. Urgent caesarean delivery
   D. Monitoring fetal heart rate

435

Answers:

1. Answer D (All of the above)

The sign of uterine rupture during labor encompasses a combination of signs and symptoms, including vaginal bleeding, abdominal pain and tenderness, chest pain, pain between the scapulae, or pain upon inspiration, and potentially hypovolemic shock due to significant maternal blood loss. Additionally, uterine rupture can result in signs associated with fetal oxygenation compromise, such as late deceleration in the fetal heart rate, reduced variability, tachycardia, bradycardia, absent fetal heart sounds, cessation of uterine contractions, and, in severe cases, palpation of the fetus outside the uterus, which typically occurs only with a large, complete rupture.

2. Answer A (Placenta previa)

When diagnosing uterine rupture using ultrasound, one condition that can be ruled out is placenta previa. Placenta previa is a separate obstetric complication where the placenta partially or completely covers the cervix. It can lead to bleeding during pregnancy and labor, and it has a distinct appearance on ultrasound. It is important to rule out other conditions, such as placental abruption, spontaneous abortion, or other complications that may present with similar symptoms to uterine rupture, as this helps in proper management and care for the patient.

3. Answer D (Breech presentation)

While a breech presentation itself does NOT inherently increase the risk of uterine rupture, it is important to note that the risk of uterine rupture can escalate when a breech position necessitates external cephalic version (ECV), a procedure in which the healthcare provider tries to manually turn the baby to a head-down position. ECV, as a specific intervention for a breech presentation, poses an increased risk of uterine rupture due to the manipulation and stress on the uterus during the procedure. Recognized risk factors for uterine rupture include a history of uterine surgery, a previous uterine rupture, attempting vaginal birth after a caesarean section (VBAC), cocaine use during pregnancy, conditions that stretch the uterus (such as carrying multiples or having excessive amniotic fluid), a breech position requiring ECV, and prolonged labor.

4. Answer A (General anesthesia)

In cases of an emergent C-section following uterine rupture, general anesthesia is preferred. This is because general anesthesia can be induced quickly, making it the preferred choice when time is of the essence, and there is a need for a rapid onset of anesthesia. Neuraxial anesthesia, such as epidural or spinal anesthesia, takes time to achieve the necessary block level, and it may not be suitable in situations of hemodynamic instability or when there is a severe bleeding diathesis. General anesthesia provides a faster and more controlled way to ensure that the mother is anesthetized for the surgical procedure, especially when there is an urgent need for intervention to address uterine rupture.

5. Answer B (False)

An early deceleration in the fetal heart rate is typically not associated with fetal oxygenation compromise in cases of uterine rupture. Early decelerations are a benign, reassuring pattern, and they are typically caused by head compression during contractions rather than indicating fetal distress. On the other hand, the signs associated with fetal oxygenation are more relevant to fetal distress during uterine rupture. These include late deceleration, reduced variability, tachycardia, or bradycardia. These patterns may suggest that the fetus is not receiving sufficient oxygen, and they are concerning signs that healthcare providers monitor closely during labor and delivery to detect potential complications, such as uterine rupture.

6. Answer C (Urgent caesarean delivery)

Given these findings, the primary management approach for uterine rupture during labor is an urgent caesarean delivery. Uterine rupture is a critical obstetric emergency that requires immediate surgical intervention to rescue both the mother and the baby. This ensures that the fetus is delivered promptly and the uterine wall is repaired to stop further bleeding and minimize the risks associated with uterine rupture. Inducing labor or administering tocolytic agents would not be appropriate in this scenario, as they do not address the urgent nature of uterine rupture. Monitoring fetal heart rate is essential for identifying fetal distress, but in the presence of confirmed uterine rupture, immediate delivery is the standard of care.

Recommended literature

1. Gibbins KJ, Weber T, Holmgren CM, Porter TF, Varner MW, Manuck TA. Maternal and fetal morbidity associated with uterine rupture of the unscarred uterus. Am J Obstet Gynecol. 2015;213(3):382.e1-382.e3826.
2. Plaat F, Shonfeld A. 2015. Major obstetric haemorrhage. BJA Education. 15;4:190-193.
3. Walfish M, Neuman A, Wlody D. 2009. Maternal haemorrhage. BJA:: British Journal of Anaesthesia. 103;1:47-56.
4. Guiliano M, Closset E, Therby D, LeGoueff F, Deruelle P, Subtil D. Signs, symptoms and complications of complete and partial uterine ruptures during pregnancy and delivery. Eur J Obstet Gynecol Reprod Biol. 2014;179:130-134.

PEDIATRICS

Pediatrics

BRONCHOPULMONARY DYSPLASIA

12
CHAPTER

Questions:

1. **What is the primary cause of bronchopulmonary dysplasia (BPD) in premature infants?**
   A. Maternal smoking
   B. Mechanical ventilation
   C. Sepsis
   D. Genetic predisposition

2. **What is a common complication of BPD related to the heart in affected infants?**
   A. Left ventricular hypertrophy
   B. Pulmonary hypertension
   C. Atrial septal defect
   D. Patent foramen ovale

3. **Which of the following is NOT a recommended treatment for BPD in premature infants?**
   A. Diuretics
   B. Bronchodilators
   C. Corticosteroids
   D. Antibiotics

4. **What is the primary pathophysiological process in the development of BPD?**
   A. Alveolar septal injury
   B. Pulmonary vascular resistance reduction
   C. Surfactant production
   D. Increased cardiac output

5. **Antenatal steroid administration is a preventive measure to reduce the risk of BPD in premature infants.**
   A. True
   B. False

6. **A male neonate was born prematurely at 28 weeks of gestation via caesarean section due to non-reassuring fetal status after the onset of labor. In the delivery room, the baby exhibited poor respiratory effort and was subsequently intubated to provide respiratory support. The neonate remained intubated for 15 days, after which he was extubated. Subsequently, the infant was diagnosed with subglottic stenosis and airway granulomas. Additionally, as part of the infant's clinical assessment, a diagnosis of bronchopulmonary dysplasia was made. Which of the following is a feature of BPD diagnosis that indicates severe disease?**
   A. Infant requiring < 30% FiO2
   B. Infant breathing room air
   C. Infant requiring > 30% FiO2 or positive pressure ventilation
   D. Infants with no need for supplemental oxygen

Answers:

1. Answer B (Mechanical ventilation)

Bronchopulmonary dysplasia (BPD) is a chronic lung disease that primarily affects premature infants. It occurs because the alveoli in the lungs are not mature enough to function properly. Infants with immature lungs often require mechanical ventilation and oxygen support in neonatal intensive care units, especially to manage conditions like respiratory distress syndrome. Prolonged mechanical ventilation and oxygen therapy are the main risk factors for developing BPD in these premature infants. While other factors such as maternal smoking, sepsis, and genetic predisposition may contribute to the overall clinical picture, mechanical ventilation is the primary cause of lung damage and the subsequent development of BPD in premature infants.

2. Answer B (Pulmonary hypertension)

Pulmonary hypertension is a common complication associated with BPD. In BPD, chronic lung damage and inflammation lead to changes in the pulmonary vasculature, resulting in increased pulmonary vascular resistance. As a consequence, the pressure within the pulmonary arteries becomes elevated. This condition can strain the right side of the heart, leading to right ventricular dysfunction and, in severe cases, the development of cor pulmonale.

3. Answer D (Antibiotics)

Antibiotics are not a recommended treatment for BPD in premature infants. BPD primarily involves lung-related issues, such as inflammation and structural changes in the airways and alveoli, for which antibiotics are not directly indicated. Instead, treatment typically includes diuretics to reduce fluid accumulation, bronchodilators to alleviate bronchial constriction, and corticosteroids to mitigate inflammation and mucus production. While viral immunization can help prevent infections that exacerbate BPD, antibiotics are not a standard component of BPD management.

4. Answer A (Alveolar septal injury)

The development of BPD is primarily characterized by alveolar septal injury. In premature infants, the immature lungs are particularly vulnerable to various insults, including mechanical ventilation and oxygen exposure. These insults can lead to damage to the delicate alveoli and the septa that separate them. This injury initiates a cascade of inflammatory responses, including the release of proinflammatory cytokines, which ultimately results in impaired lung development, inflammation, and scarring. Alveolar septal injury is a central component of BPD's pathophysiology, leading to the obstructive lung disease and pulmonary vascular remodeling observed in affected infants.

5. Answer A (True)

Antenatal steroid administration is a well-established preventive measure to reduce the risk of BPD in premature infants. This treatment involves giving corticosteroids to expectant mothers who are at risk of preterm delivery. The steroids help accelerate lung maturation in the fetus, improving the baby's lung function and reducing the likelihood of BPD. In addition to antenatal steroid administration, other preventive measures include surfactant therapy to improve lung compliance and function in preterm infants and the use of improved ventilator strategies designed to minimize lung injury in these vulnerable neonates. These interventions collectively aim to reduce the incidence and severity of BPD in premature infants.

6. Answer C (Infant requiring > 30% FiO2 or positive pressure ventilation)

In the context of bronchopulmonary dysplasia diagnosis, the severity of BPD is categorized based on the level of oxygen or ventilatory support needed. An infant is diagnosed with severe BPD when they require > 30% FiO2 or positive pressure ventilation. This indicates a significant degree of respiratory support and impaired lung function, which characterizes severe BPD. Mild BPD is diagnosed when an infant is breathing room air, and moderate BPD is diagnosed when an infant requires < 30% FiO2.

Recommended literature

1. Lauer R, Vadi M, Mason L. Anaesthetic management of the child with co-existing pulmonary disease. BJA. 2012;109(1):i47-i59.

CEREBRAL PALSY

Questions:

1. **What is cerebral palsy primarily attributed to?**
   A. Progressive disturbances in the developing fetal brain
   B. Non-progressive disturbances in the developing fetal or infant brain
   C. Genetic mutations in the infant brain
   D. Hormonal imbalances during infancy

2. **What are some common signs and symptoms of cerebral palsy?**
   A. Excessive drooling and difficulty swallowing
   B. Tremors and jerky involuntary movements
   C. Delayed speech development and learning disability
   D. All of the above

3. **Which of the following factors is a risk factor for congenital cerebral palsy?**
   A. Neonatal seizures
   B. Breech presentation
   C. Fetal alcohol syndrome
   D. All of the above

4. **What is a potential complication of muscle spasticity in cerebral palsy?**
   A. Contracture
   B. Osteoarthritis
   C. Mental health conditions
   D. All of the above

5. **GERD is a common comorbidity associated with cerebral palsy, and it can lead to recurrent chest infections.**
   A. True
   B. False

6. **A 12-year-old child with a diagnosis of cerebral palsy is presented for anesthesia in preparation for a dental procedure. The child exhibits various symptoms related to cerebral palsy, including stiff muscles with normal reflexes, lack of balance and muscle coordination, tremors or jerky involuntary movements, difficulty with sucking, chewing, or eating, excessive drooling, and problems with swallowing. Additionally, the child has experienced delays in reaching motor skills milestones, such as rolling over, sitting, crawling, or walking, as well as challenges with learning, intellectual disability, and delayed growth, resulting in a smaller size than expected for their age. Why is understanding the challenges of airway management important for patients with cerebral palsy?**
   A. Because cerebral palsy primarily affects the respiratory system
   B. Due to the increased risk of aspiration pneumonitis
   C. Because it requires specialized equipment
   D. All of the above

Answers:

1. **Answer B (Non-progressive disturbances in the developing fetal or infant brain)**

   Cerebral palsy (CP) is primarily attributed to non-progressive disturbances that occur in the developing fetal or infant brain. CP is a group of permanent neurodevelopmental disorders that affect an individual's muscle tone, motor functions, movement, and posture. It is the most common motor disability in childhood, and the underlying problems do not worsen over time.

2. **Answer D (All of the above)**

   Common signs and symptoms of CP encompass a range of challenges, including excessive drooling and difficulty swallowing, tremors and jerky involuntary movements, delayed speech development, learning disability, and a host of other issues. These symptoms can affect various aspects of an individual's life, encompassing movement, coordination, speech, eating, development, and intellectual function. CP is a complex neurodevelopmental condition, and the specific manifestations can vary from person to person, but these are some of the common challenges that individuals with CP may face.

3. **Answer D (All of the above)**

   All of the factors listed, namely neonatal seizures, breech presentation, and fetal alcohol syndrome, are risk factors for congenital cerebral palsy. These factors are associated with an increased risk of congenital CP, which occurs during or shortly after birth. Neonatal seizures, breech presentation, and fetal alcohol syndrome are among the fetal and maternal pathogenic factors that can contribute to the development of cerebral palsy in infants.

4. **Answer D (All of the above)**

   Muscle spasticity in cerebral palsy can give rise to various complications. Spasticity can lead to contractures, which result in muscle tissue shortening and may inhibit bone growth, cause joint deformities, or even dislocations like hip dislocation and scoliosis. Additionally, the pressure on joints and abnormal joint alignment caused by muscle spasticity can lead to the early onset of osteoarthritis. Mental health conditions such as depression and behavioral problems can also be exacerbated by the challenges associated with cerebral palsy, including spasticity. Thus, all of the above options are valid complications of muscle spasticity in cerebral palsy.

5. **Answer A (True)**

   GERD, which stands for Gastroesophageal Reflux Disease, is a common comorbidity associated with cerebral palsy. Individuals with cerebral palsy may experience GERD due to factors like swallowing difficulties, esophageal dysmotility, and abnormal lower esophageal sphincter tone. GERD can lead to recurrent chest infections, as the reflux of stomach contents into the esophagus and even the respiratory tract can increase the risk of aspiration pneumonitis and subsequent chronic lung scarring, making individuals more susceptible to chest infections.

6. **Answer B (Due to the increased risk of aspiration pneumonitis)**

   Understanding the challenges of airway management is important for patients with cerebral palsy due to the increased risk of aspiration pneumonitis. Patients with cerebral palsy often experience difficulties with swallowing, chewing, and eating. These challenges can result in the inadvertent entry of food or fluids into the airway during medical procedures, including dental procedures. Aspiration pneumonitis is a significant concern because it can lead to lung inflammation and respiratory complications, potentially compromising the patient's respiratory health. Therefore, a comprehensive understanding of the unique airway management needs of patients with cerebral palsy is essential to minimize the risk of aspiration and ensure the safety and well-being of these individuals during anesthesia.

Recommended literature

1. Prosser DP, Sharma N. Cerebral palsy and anaesthesia. Continuing Education in Anaesthesia Critical Care & Pain. 2010;10(3):72-76.
2. Miller B, Rondeau B. Anesthetic Considerations In Patients With Cerebral Palsy. [Updated 2022 Jun 11]. In: StatPearls [Internet]. Treasure Island (FL): StatPearls Publishing; 2022 Jan. Available from: https://www.ncbi.nlm.nih.gov/books/NBK572057/

CHARGE SYNDROME

Questions:

1. **What is the genetic basis of CHARGE syndrome?**
   A. Autosomal recessive inheritance
   B. X-linked inheritance
   C. Autosomal dominant inheritance
   D. Mitochondrial inheritance

2. **In CHARGE syndrome, what is the NOT common congenital heart disease?**
   A. Tetralogy of Fallot
   B. Ventricular septal defect (VSD)
   C. Patent ductus arteriosus (PDA)
   D. Aortic arch anomalies

3. **What is a common gastrointestinal issue in patients with CHARGE syndrome?**
   A. Celiac disease
   B. Swallowing and feeding problems
   C. Crohn's disease
   D. Gastric ulcers

4. **Which acronym represents the major criteria in CHARGE syndrome?**
   A. 4 C's
   B. HAGER
   C. CHARGE
   D. CHD7

5. **Micrognathia is a potential airway management challenge in pediatric patients with CHARGE syndrome.**
   A. True
   B. False

6. **A 10-month-old patient is presented for surgery to repair a cleft palate. The patient has been diagnosed with CHARGE syndrome and presents with multiple clinical features, including Coloboma of the eye and a ventricular septal defect. What is the recommended approach for anesthetic management in pediatric patients with CHARGE syndrome?**
   A. Rapid sequence induction
   B. Awake fiberoptic intubation
   C. Extubation in the OR
   D. Use of neuromuscular blocking agents

Answers:

1. **Answer C (Autosomal dominant inheritance)**

   CHARGE syndrome is primarily caused by autosomal dominant inheritance, where a mutation in one copy of the CHD7 gene on chromosome 8 is sufficient to cause the syndrome. In the majority of cases, CHARGE syndrome is attributed to mutations in the CHD7 gene, although these mutations often occur de novo, meaning they are not inherited from the parents but arise spontaneously in the affected individual's DNA. In rare instances, patients with CHARGE syndrome may not have a CHD7 gene mutation, or they may have a mutation in another gene in their DNA that leads to the condition.

2. **Answer C (Patent ductus arteriosus (PDA))**

   The patent ductus arteriosus (PDA) is NOT a common congenital heart disease in CHARGE syndrome. In CHARGE syndrome, approximately 75-80% of children have congenital heart defects, with the most common ones being Tetralogy of Fallot (33%), Ventricular septal defect (VSD), AV (atrioventricular) canal defect, and aortic arch anomalies. While PDA is a relatively common congenital heart defect in some conditions, it is not among the most frequently observed heart defects in CHARGE syndrome.

3. **Answer B (Swallowing and feeding problems)**

   While conditions like celiac disease, Crohn's disease, and gastric ulcers are gastrointestinal disorders that can affect individuals, they are not the primary or most commonly associated gastrointestinal issues in CHARGE syndrome. Swallowing and feeding problems are characteristic features of CHARGE syndrome, leading to difficulties in the intake and digestion of food.

4. **Answer A (4 C's)**

   In CHARGE syndrome, the major criteria are often referred to as the "4 C's," which include Choanal atresia, Coloboma, Characteristic ear anomalies, and Cranial nerve anomalies. These major features are key diagnostic indicators for CHARGE syndrome, and patients with all four major characteristics or a combination of three major and three minor characteristics are highly likely to have CHARGE syndrome.

5. **Answer A (True)**

   Micrognathia, which refers to a small or underdeveloped lower jaw, is a potential airway management challenge in pediatric patients with CHARGE syndrome. Patients with CHARGE syndrome may have micrognathia, and this condition can make endotracheal intubation, which is often necessary for anesthesia or airway management, difficult.

6. **Answer A (Rapid sequence induction)**

   The recommended approach for anesthetic management in a 10-month-old pediatric patient with CHARGE syndrome, presenting with Coloboma of the eye and a ventricular septal defect, is rapid sequence induction (RSI). Patients with CHARGE syndrome often have challenging airways and an increased risk of aspiration due to micrognathia and gastroesophageal reflux. RSI provides a swift and secure method for airway management, minimizes the risk of aspiration, ensures hemodynamic stability, and reduces the time between loss of consciousness and securing the airway. This approach is the most appropriate given the patient's clinical characteristics and associated risks.

Recommended literature

1. Houck PJ. CHARGE SYNDROME. In: Houck PJ, Haché M, Sun LS. eds. Handbook of Pediatric Anesthesia. McGraw Hill; 2015. Accessed February 03, 2023. https://accessanesthesiology.mhmedical.com/content.aspx?bookid=1189&sectionid=70364146.
2. Blake KD, Prasad C. CHARGE syndrome. Orphanet J Rare Dis. 2006;1:34.

CLEFT LIP AND PALATE

Questions:

1. **What is the primary mechanism underlying the development of cleft lip and palate?**
   A. Excessive growth of facial tissues
   B. Deficient fusion of facial tissues during development
   C. Abnormal cell proliferation in the facial region
   D. A genetic mutation affecting facial structures

2. **Which of the following is a common complication of cleft palate?**
   A. Frequent tonsil infections
   B. Frequent ear infections
   C. Frequent chest infections
   D. Frequent eye infections

3. **Which of the following is NOT a risk factor for developing cleft lip and palate?**
   A. Smoking during pregnancy
   B. Diabetes
   C. Obesity
   D. Hypertension

4. **What is the primary treatment for cleft lip and palate?**
   A. Speech therapy
   B. Dental care
   C. Corrective surgery
   D. Nutritional supplementation

5. **A cleft palate is always associated with a cleft lip.**
   A. True
   B. False

6. **A 12-month-old baby is scheduled for corrective surgery for a cleft palate. The baby has an opening in the upper lip that may extend into the nose or palate. The cleft palate is incomplete, presenting as a hole in the roof of the mouth, typically known as a cleft soft palate. Which of the following is a consideration for anesthesia in patients with cleft lip and palate?**
   A. Shared airway
   B. Difficult airway
   C. Associated syndromes
   D. All of the above

Answers:

1. **Answer B (Deficient fusion of facial tissues during development)**

   Cleft lip and cleft palate (CLP) are common congenital deformities resulting from the failure of the facial processes to grow or fuse appropriately during early embryologic development (fourth through 12th weeks of gestation). The etiology of CLP is multifactorial and complex and includes both genetic and environmental factors. Orofacial clefting can be classified as nonsyndromic or found as an isolated defect, which occurs in about 85% of cleft lip with or without cleft palate and about 45% of cleft palate alone. Syndromic clefting can be further subdivided as occurring in over 150 chromosomal syndromes, such as van der Woude syndrome and velocardiofacial syndrome; over 300 Mendelian single gene disorders; effects of teratogens, such as alcohol, tobacco smoke, antiepileptic drugs, and organic solvents; and as yet uncategorized syndromes.

2. **Answer B (Frequent ear infections)**

   One of the common complications of cleft palate is frequent ear infections. This is because the opening in the roof of the mouth can affect the Eustachian tube, leading to fluid buildup in the middle ear and an increased risk of infections. Other complications of cleft palate include feeding problems, speech problems, and hearing problems due to the structural abnormalities in the palate.

3. **Answer D (Hypertension)**

   Hypertension is not typically identified as a risk factor for developing cleft lip and palate. However, smoking during pregnancy, diabetes, obesity, and advanced maternal age are all recognized risk factors for these congenital conditions. Certain medications used to treat seizures, among other factors, can also contribute to the risk.

4. **Answer C (Corrective surgery)**

   The primary treatment for cleft lip and palate is corrective surgery, which aims to close the gap in the lip or palate and restore normal function and appearance. This surgery is typically performed in infancy or early childhood. Speech therapy is often required to improve velopharyngeal function and develop normal speech without compensatory articulations. Dental care is also essential to address any dental abnormalities that may arise due to the cleft. Additionally, nutritional supplementation may be necessary to ensure adequate growth and development in affected individuals.

5. **Answer B (False)**

   A cleft palate is an opening or split in the roof of the mouth that occurs when the tissue doesn't fuse during development in the womb. While a cleft palate often includes a split (cleft) in the upper lip (cleft lip), it can occur without affecting the lip. Therefore, it is possible to have a cleft palate without a cleft lip.

6. **Answer D (All of the above)**

   Anesthesia for patients with cleft lip and palate requires careful consideration of several factors. Infants and young pediatric patients are typically involved, which can pose challenges due to their size and age. Associated comorbidities and syndromes, such as those commonly seen with cleft lip and palate, must be taken into account. Nutritional status is important, as these patients may have feeding difficulties. Airway obstruction and the potential for a difficult airway are significant concerns, given the anatomical abnormalities associated with cleft lip and palate. Anesthetic factors such as the use of general anesthesia with a tracheal tube and the management of a shared airway are crucial. Surgical factors, including the timing of the surgery to optimize outcomes, also play a role in the overall management of these patients.

Recommended literature

1. Denning S, Ng E, Wong Riff KWY. Anaesthesia for cleft lip and palate surgery. BJA Education. 2021; 21(10): 384-389.

CONGENITAL DIAPHRAGMATIC HERNIA

12
CHAPTER

Questions:

1. **What is the primary cause of respiratory failure in infants with congenital diaphragmatic hernia (CDH)?**
    A. Pulmonary fibrosis
    B. Pulmonary hypertension and hypoplastic lungs
    C. Right heart failure
    D. Neurological abnormalities

2. **Which antenatal ultrasound parameter is a strong predictor of survival in CDH?**
    A. Fetal heart rate
    B. Fetal weight
    C. Lung-to-head ratio (LHR)
    D. Amniotic fluid index

3. **What is the preferred approach to ventilation in a neonate with CDH during resuscitation?**
    A. Spontaneous ventilation
    B. High-frequency ventilation
    C. Intermittent positive pressure ventilation (IPPV)
    D. Continuous positive airway pressure (CPAP)

4. **What is the primary goal of fluid management in a neonate with CDH?**
    A. Achieve high cardiac output
    B. Maintain low mean arterial pressure (MAP)
    C. Target MAP 45-50 mmHg
    D. Induce hypovolemia

5. **Surgical repair of CDH considered immediately after birth?**
    A. True
    B. False

6. **A neonate with a confirmed diagnosis of congenital diaphragmatic hernia, detected during routine prenatal ultrasound, has been delivered and is experiencing refractory hypoxemia. Given the critical nature of CDH and the immediate care required at delivery, the medical team is faced with the challenge of managing the neonate's respiratory distress. What is NOT the suggested initial intervention for a neonate with CDH experiencing refractory hypoxemia?**
    A. Bag ventilation
    B. Nasal intubation
    C. Administer inhaled nitric oxide (iNO)
    D. Lung protective ventilation

Answers:

1. **Answer B (Pulmonary hypertension and hypoplastic lungs)**

   Infants with congenital diaphragmatic hernia (CDH) primarily experience respiratory failure due to a combination of pulmonary hypertension and pulmonary hypoplasia. The defect in the diaphragm leads to the protrusion of abdominal organs into the thoracic cavity, resulting in decreased lung volume and impaired lung development, termed pulmonary hypoplasia. This, in turn, contributes to inadequate gas exchange. Concurrently, the abnormal anatomy causes increased pulmonary vascular resistance, leading to pulmonary hypertension. The fixed high pulmonary vascular resistance, coupled with decreased vascular cross-sectional area, further compromises respiratory function. The interplay of these factors creates a critical situation for newborns with CDH, emphasizing the pivotal role of pulmonary hypertension and hypoplastic lungs in the development of respiratory failure in this population.

2. **Answer C (Lung-to-head ratio (LHR))**

   CDH is typically identified during routine prenatal ultrasound examinations. The assessment of antenatal ultrasound parameters is crucial for predicting survival in CDH cases. The lung-to-head ratio (LHR) is a strong predictor in this context. LHR is calculated by dividing the fetal lung area (mm2) by the fetal head circumference (mm). The specific LHR values provide valuable prognostic information: LHR > 1.35 is associated with 100% survival, LHR between 1.35 and 0.6 indicates a 61% survival rate, and LHR < 0.6 is correlated with no survival. Additionally, factors such as observed expected LHR (O/E LHR) and the position of the liver further refine survival predictions.

3. **Answer C (Intermittent Positive Pressure Ventilation (IPPV))**

   The preferred approach to ventilation in a neonate with CDH during resuscitation is intermittent positive pressure ventilation (IPPV). The indication for immediate tracheal intubation to facilitate IPPV is critical in CDH cases. CDH creates a challenging respiratory scenario, and tracheal intubation allows for better control over ventilation parameters, including tidal volume and positive end-expiratory pressure (PEEP).

4. **Answer C (Target MAP 45-50 mmHg)**

   The primary goal of fluid management in a neonate with CDH is to maintain a target mean arterial pressure (MAP) between 45-50 mmHg. This specific target is crucial for optimizing perfusion while avoiding excessive fluid administration, which could lead to fluid overload and worsen respiratory compromise in CDH patients. Achieving and maintaining the recommended MAP range helps ensure adequate organ perfusion without putting undue stress on the cardiovascular system. This approach aims to strike a balance between supporting hemodynamic stability and preventing complications associated with excessive fluid administration.

5. **Answer B (False)**

   Surgical repair of CDH is typically considered after stabilization and addressing respiratory issues in the neonate. The immediate postnatal period is focused on resuscitation, ventilation support, and stabilization of the infant, with the surgical intervention scheduled once the patient is deemed clinically stable. This approach allows for a more controlled and optimized perioperative environment, contributing to better outcomes for the neonate with CDH.

6. **Answer A (Bag ventilation)**

   The NOT suggested initial intervention for a neonate with a CDH experiencing refractory hypoxemia is bag ventilation. The recommended approach involves immediate tracheal intubation to facilitate IPPV. Bag ventilation is avoided due to its potential to distend herniated viscera, worsen mediastinal shift, and increase the risk of complications such as pneumothorax. Additionally, barotrauma associated with bag ventilation could further compromise the hypoplastic lungs seen in CDH. Nasal intubation is favored as it aids in fixation and ventilator compliance, providing a safer alternative in the initial resuscitation of neonates with CDH-related respiratory distress.

Recommended literature

1. Leininger K, Chiu K. Anesthetic Considerations In Congenital Diaphragmatic Hernia. [Updated 2022 Nov 15]. In: StatPearls [Internet]. Treasure Island (FL): StatPearls Publishing; 2022 Jan. Available from: https://www.ncbi.nlm.nih.gov/books/NBK572077/.
2. Pollard BJ, Kitchen G. Handbook of Clinical Anaesthesia. 4th ed. Taylor & Francis group; 2018. Chapter 24 Paediatrics, Lomas B.
3. Chandrasekharan PK, Rawat M, Madappa R, Rothstein DH, Lakshminrusimha S. Congenital Diaphragmatic hernia – a review. Matern Health Neonatol Perinatol. 2017;3:6.

CRANIOFACIAL DYSOSTOSIS

Questions:

1. **What is the most common craniofacial dysostosis syndrome?**
   A. Apert syndrome
   B. Pfeiffer syndrome
   C. Crouzon syndrome
   D. Carpenter syndrome

2. **Craniofacial dysostosis syndrome is characterized by premature synostosis of coronal and sagittal sutures leading to facial dysmorphism. What feature is NOT characteristic for this syndrome?**
   A. Hypertelorism
   B. Proptosis
   C. Strabismus
   D. Enoftalmus

3. **In addition to craniofacial abnormalities, what is more likely in individuals with Pfeiffer syndrome?**
   A. Hearing loss
   B. Vision problems
   C. Mental and neurological problems
   D. Dental problems

4. **What is the primary treatment approach for craniofacial dysostosis?**
   A. Medication
   B. Physical therapy
   C. Surgical reconstruction
   D. Speech therapy

5. **Craniofacial dysostosis is a condition caused by an autosomal dominant mutation in the fibroblast growth factor receptor 2 (FGFR2) gene.**
   A. True
   B. False

6. **An 8-year-old, weighing 18 kg, was scheduled for correction of right congenital ptosis. The patient had a known diagnosis of Crouzon syndrome (CS) with evident facial dysmorphism, including dental crowding and a deviated nasal septum to the left. Additionally, the child presented with a history of delayed milestones and short stature. The parents reported symptoms suggestive of obstructive sleep apnea, leading to a prior adenotonsillectomy. What is NOT true about anesthesia for patients with facial dysmorphism?**
   A. Both inhalation and intravenous induction anesthesia are safe to use
   B. Anticipate a difficult airway
   C. Nerve blocks are contraindicated due to malformation
   D. Avoid sedative drugs

Answers:

1. Answer C (Crouzon syndrome)

Crouzon syndrome is the most common craniofacial dysostosis syndrome. This syndrome is characterized by premature fusion of cranial sutures, leading to distinct craniofacial features such as wide-set eyes, bulging eyeballs, crossed eyes, protruding forehead, small beak-shaped nose, underdeveloped jaw, and, in some cases, cleft lip and/or palate. The premature fusion of sutures results in abnormal skull development and head shape.

2. Answer D (Enoftalmus)

Craniofacial dysostosis syndrome, characterized by premature synostosis of coronal and sagittal sutures, results in distinctive facial dysmorphism. Features typical of this syndrome include hypertelorism, proptosis, strabismus, a protruding forehead, a small beak-shaped nose, an underdeveloped jaw, cleft lip and/or palate, an abnormal head shape, and insufficient growth of the midface. However, enophthalmus, the condition where the eyeball is sunken into the eye socket, is not characteristic of this syndrome. The syndrome is more commonly associated with proptosis, where the eyes protrude from the eye sockets.

3. Answer C (Mental and neurological problems)

In addition to craniofacial characteristics typical of Pfeiffer syndrome, such as wide and deviated thumbs or big toes, individuals with Pfeiffer syndrome are more likely to experience mental and neurological problems. While hearing loss, vision problems and dental problems are possible complications in individuals with craniofacial dysostosis syndromes, including Pfeiffer syndrome, mental and neurological problems are specifically highlighted as more likely in the context of Pfeiffer syndrome.

4. Answer C (Surgical reconstruction)

The primary treatment approach for craniofacial dysostosis is surgical reconstruction. Specifically, procedures such as LeFort osteotomies are commonly performed to address the premature fusion of cranial sutures and correct the resulting skull abnormalities. Medication, physical therapy, and speech therapy are not the primary modalities for treating craniofacial dysostosis.

5. Answer A (True)

Craniofacial dysostosis is caused by an autosomal dominant mutation in the fibroblast growth factor receptor 2 (FGFR2) gene. This genetic mutation can be inherited from a parent or occur spontaneously. The FGFR2 gene is located on chromosome 10. This autosomal dominant inheritance pattern means that an individual with the mutation has a 50% chance of passing the condition on to each of their offspring.

6. Answer C (Nerve blocks are contraindicated due to malformation)

While anesthesia for patients with facial dysmorphism, such as in Crouzon syndrome, presents unique challenges, the statement that nerve blocks are contraindicated due to malformation is not accurate. In fact, the use of peripheral nerve blocks can be beneficial in managing these cases. The presented case emphasizes the importance of utilizing peripheral nerve blocks to reduce opioid requirements, ensuring optimal pain management without compromising respiratory function. Both inhalation and intravenous induction anesthesia can be safely used, and anticipating a difficult airway is essential in these scenarios. Additionally, avoiding sedative drugs may be necessary to prevent complications and ensure a smooth anesthetic course.

Recommended literature

1. Pollard BJ, Kitchen, G. Handbook of Clinical Anaesthesia. Fourth Edition. CRC Press. 2018. 978-1-4987-6289-2.
2. Pearson, A., Matava, C.T., 2016. Anaesthetic management for craniosynostosis repair in children. BJA Education 16, 410–416.
3. Posnick JC, Ruiz RL. The craniofacial dysostosis syndromes: current surgical thinking and future directions. Cleft Palate Craniofac J. 2000;37(5):433.

CROUP/ LARYNGOTRACHEOBRONCHITIS

12
CHAPTER

Questions:

1. Which of the following viruses is most commonly associated with the development of croup (laryngotracheobronchitis) in children?
    A. Respiratory Syncytial Virus (RSV)
    B. Influenza Virus
    C. Rhinovirus
    D. Parainfluenza virus

2. What is the hallmark symptom of croup?
    A. Wheezing
    B. Productive cough
    C. Barky or seal-like cough
    D. High-grade fever

3. What is the characteristic radiographic finding associated with croup?
    A. Ground-glass opacities
    B. Butterfly opacities
    C. Steeple sign
    D. Air bronchograms

4. Which clinical parameter is NOT included in the Westley Croup Score for assessing severity?
    A. Level of consciousness
    B. Cyanosis
    C. Oxygen saturation
    D. Air entry

5. Enlarged adenoids are the primary reason for the narrowing of the subglottic region in children.
    A. True
    B. False

6. A 3-year-old child presents with a history of 1-3 days of rhinorrhea, nasal congestion, and fever. The parents note a distinctive barky or seal-like cough, a hoarse voice, and high-pitched inspiratory stridor. Physical examination reveals additional findings of wheezing, crackles, air trapping, and tachypnea. Based on the Westley Croup Score, the severity is categorized as moderate (3 – 7). What is the treatment of choice for croup to reduce airway inflammation and obstruction?
    A. Antibiotics
    B. Nebulized albuterol
    C. Dexamethasone
    D. Antiviral medication

Answers:

1. **Answer D (Parainfluenza virus)**

   Parainfluenza virus is most commonly associated with the development of croup, also known as laryngotracheobronchitis, in children. Parainfluenza virus, particularly types 1 and 2, is a leading cause of viral croup or acute laryngotracheitis. While other viruses such as Respiratory Syncytial Virus (RSV), Influenza Virus (types A and B), Rhinovirus, Enterovirus, and Adenovirus can also cause croup, parainfluenza virus is frequently implicated in the majority of cases.

2. **Answer C (Barky or seal-like cough)**

   The hallmark symptom of croup is a distinctive barky or seal-like cough. This characteristic cough is a key clinical feature that helps differentiate croup from other respiratory conditions. Croup, or laryngotracheobronchitis, involves inflammation of the larynx, trachea, and bronchi. It is a common cause of cough, stridor, and hoarseness in children, often accompanied by fever. The cough in croup is described as "barky" or "seal-like" due to the unique quality of sound it produces. Other associated symptoms include a hoarse voice, high-pitched inspiratory stridor, and, in some cases, wheezing. The onset of symptoms is typically preceded by 1-3 days of rhinorrhea, nasal congestion, and fever. Additionally, signs such as crackles, air trapping, tachypnea, and cyanosis may be observed in more severe cases.

3. **Answer C (Steeple sign)**

   The characteristic radiographic finding associated with croup is the "Steeple sign." The Steeple sign is a term used to describe the appearance of the airway on radiography in children with croup. It represents the glottic and subglottic narrowing of the airway. In radiological images, this narrowing alters the appearance of the tracheal air column, resembling a church steeple or a steeply pitched roof. The Steeple sign is indicative of the characteristic narrowing of the subglottic space, which is the most narrow part of the airway in children. While the Steeple sign can be a helpful diagnostic clue, it's essential to note that the diagnosis of croup is primarily clinical, and radiography is usually not necessary for routine cases.

4. **Answer C (Oxygen saturation)**

   Oxygen saturation is not included in the Westley Croup Score for assessing severity. The Westley Croup Score focuses on clinical parameters such as level of consciousness, cyanosis, stridor, air entry, and retractions to determine the severity of croup. Mild croup is defined by a score of ≤ 2, moderate croup by a score of 3 to 7, severe croup by a score of 8 to 11, and a score of ≥ 12 indicates impending respiratory failure. While oxygen saturation is crucial in assessing respiratory distress, it is not explicitly considered in the Westley Croup Score, which primarily relies on clinical signs.

5. **Answer B (False)**

   Enlarged adenoids are not the primary reason for the narrowing of the subglottic region in children. The primary cause of subglottic narrowing in children with conditions like croup is the inhalation of a virus infecting the nasal and pharyngeal mucosal epithelia. In children, the subglottic space is inherently the most narrow part of the airway. The narrowing occurs due to the inflammation of the mucosa in this region, and it is not related to the size of the adenoids. The inability of the cricoid to expand exacerbates this narrowing. Dynamic obstruction can further occur during crying or agitation, making the subglottic region particularly vulnerable in pediatric airways affected by viral infections like croup.

6. **Answer C (Dexamethasone)**

   The treatment of choice for croup to reduce airway inflammation and obstruction is dexamethasone. Dexamethasone is a glucocorticoid that provides long-lasting and effective treatment by decreasing the swelling of the larynx. It is the most frequently used medication for all types of croup. Dexamethasone typically works within six hours of the first dose, reducing the need for a repeat visit to the emergency department, decreasing the time spent in the emergency department, and potentially decreasing the need for other medications, such as epinephrine. While other therapies, like nebulized epinephrine, may be used for moderate to severe cases, dexamethasone is considered the primary treatment for its long-lasting anti-inflammatory effects. It is important to note that antibiotics, nebulized albuterol, and antiviral medications are not recommended as routine treatments for croup, as croup is typically caused by viruses, and these medications do not effectively treat the underlying viral infection.

Recommended literature

1. Ernest S, Khandhar PB. Laryngotracheobronchitis. [Updated 2022 Jun 27]. In: StatPearls [Internet]. Treasure Island (FL): StatPearls Publishing; 2022 Jan-. Available from: https://www.ncbi.nlm.nih.gov/books/NBK519531/.
2. Smith DK, McDermott AJ, Sullivan JF. Croup: Diagnosis and Management. Am Fam Physician. 2018;97(9):575-580.
3. Maloney E, Meakin GH. Acute stridor in children. Continuing Education in Anaesthesia Critical Care & Pain. 2007;7(6):183-6.

DIGEORGE SYNDROME

Questions:

1. **What genetic anomaly is primarily responsible for DiGeorge Syndrome?**
   A. Trisomy 21
   B. 22q11.2 deletion
   C. Autosomal recessive mutation
   D. 22q13 deletion

2. **What is the classic triad associated with DiGeorge Syndrome, also known as 22q11.2 deletion syndrome?**
   A. Cleft palate, developmental delay, and seizures
   B. Conotruncal cardiac abnormalities, thymic hypoplasia, and hypocalcemia
   C. Velopharyngeal insufficiency, retrognathia, and obstructive sleep apnea
   D. Immunodeficiency, GERD, and recurrent serous otitis media

3. **What is the most common congenital cardiac defect seen in DiGeorge Syndrome?**
   A. Single Ventricle
   B. Double-outlet Right Ventricle
   C. Tetralogy of Fallot
   D. Pulmonary Atresia

4. **Which of the following is NOT associated with dysmorphic facies in 22qDS?**
   A. Low-set ears
   B. Retrognathia
   C. Ocular hypertelorism
   D. Macrognathism

5. **Nasal intubation is the recommended approach to intubation in a patient with DiGeorge Syndrome and a cleft palate.**
   A. True
   B. False

6. **A 12-month-old child with confirmed DiGeorge Syndrome is undergoing cleft palate surgery. The patient develops bleeding during the operation, prompting the need for intervention. What would be your course of action?**
   A. Administration of steroids
   B. Irradiation of blood products
   C. Antibiotic prophylaxis
   D. Administration of cryoprecipitate

Answers:

1. **Answer B (22q11.2 deletion)**

   DiGeorge syndrome, also known as 22q11.2 deletion syndrome, is primarily caused by a heterozygous microdeletion on the long arm of chromosome 22. This deletion leads to the poor development of several body systems. Approximately 90% of cases occur due to a new mutation during early development, while 10% are inherited in an autosomal dominant manner.

2. **Answer B (Conotruncal cardiac abnormalities, thymic hypoplasia, and hypocalcemia)**

   The classic triad associated with DiGeorge Syndrome, also known as 22q11.2 deletion syndrome, comprises conotruncal cardiac abnormalities, thymic hypoplasia leading to cellular-mediated immunodeficiency, and hypocalcemia resulting from the absence of parathyroid glands. This triad, originally described by Dr. Angelo DiGeorge, represents the core features of the syndrome. Individuals with DiGeorge Syndrome may also exhibit a variety of additional features, such as seizures, abnormal facies, palatal dysfunction, feeding problems, congenital gut abnormalities, behavioral disturbances, and developmental delay. However, the combination of congenital heart defects, thymic underdevelopment, and calcium regulation abnormalities remains the hallmark of DiGeorge Syndrome.

3. **Answer C (Tetralogy of Fallot)**

   Conotruncal cardiac defects occur in approximately 80% of patients with DiGeorge Syndrome. Among the various congenital cardiac defects, Tetralogy of Fallot is one of the most common. Tetralogy of Fallot is a complex heart condition characterized by four primary defects: pulmonary stenosis, ventricular septal defect, overriding aorta, and right ventricular hypertrophy. The prevalence of conotruncal cardiac defects, including Tetralogy of Fallot, highlights the significant cardiac involvement in individuals with DiGeorge Syndrome.

4. **Answer D (Macrognathism)**

   Dysmorphic facies associated with 22qDS (DiGeorge Syndrome) include a combination of facial features. The characteristic facial features are hypertelorism, underdeveloped chin, and low-set ears. However, macrognathism, which refers to an unusually large or prominent jaw, is not specifically part of the dysmorphic facies associated with 22qDS. The dysmorphic features play a crucial role in considerations related to airway management, especially in terms of potential difficulties in intubation and the presence of a difficult airway.

5. **Answer B (False)**

   Nasal intubation is not recommended in a patient with DiGeorge Syndrome and a cleft palate. The presence of a cleft palate poses challenges to nasal intubation, and alternative approaches, such as oral intubation, should be considered to minimize complications and ensure effective airway management in individuals with DiGeorge Syndrome and associated anatomical abnormalities.

6. **Answer B (Irradiation of blood products)**

   Given the immunodeficiency risks in DiGeorge Syndrome, particularly T-cell deficiency, it is crucial to prioritize measures that minimize the risk of complications, such as graft-versus-host disease (GVHD). In this case, the appropriate strategy is to choose irradiation of blood products. Irradiation helps prevent GVHD by eliminating viable T lymphocytes in the blood products, which is essential in the context of T-cell deficiency seen in DiGeorge Syndrome. This precautionary measure becomes particularly important during surgical interventions where blood transfusions may be required.

Recommended literature

1. Haché M. DIGEORGE SYNDROME. In: Houck PJ, Haché M, Sun LS. eds. Handbook of Pediatric Anesthesia. McGraw Hill; 2015. Accessed March 06, 2023. https://accessanesthesiology.mhmedical.com/content.aspx?bookid=1189&sectionid=70364073.

DOWN SYNDROME

Questions:

1. **Which of the following cardiac anomalies is most commonly associated with Down syndrome?**
   A. Atrial septal defect (ASD)
   B. Tetralogy of Fallot
   C. Ventricular septal defect (VSD)
   D. Hypoplastic left heart

2. **Which of the following respiratory issues is commonly associated with Down syndrome?**
   A. Asthma
   B. Obstructive sleep apnea
   C. Pneumonia
   D. Pulmonary embolism

3. **In the context of adults with Down syndrome, what is the significance of ligamentous laxity?**
   A. It increases the risk of cardiovascular events
   B. It leads to increased bone density
   C. It is associated with respiratory infections
   D. It can result in atlantoaxial instability

4. **Why is antibiotic prophylaxis recommended in some adults with Down syndrome?**
   A. To treat respiratory infections
   B. To prevent pneumonia
   C. To prevent infective endocarditis
   D. To manage obstructive sleep apnea

5. **Inflammatory bowel disease is a gastrointestinal abnormality often associated with Down syndrome.**
   A. True
   B. False

6. **A 30-year-old patient with confirmed Down syndrome is scheduled for acute appendicitis surgery and is visibly upset, displaying signs of anxiety in the preoperative area. As part of the preoperative management, the healthcare team is considering the administration of anxiolytics to help alleviate the patient's distress. What should be considered when administering anxiolytics to adults with Down syndrome in the preoperative area?**
   A. Use of benzodiazepines is recommended for all patients
   B. Midazolam is contraindicated in adult patients
   C. Administration of anxiolytics may trigger paradoxical reactions
   D. Use opioids as anxiolytics

Answers:

1. Answer C (Ventricular septal defect (VSD))

Individuals with Down syndrome commonly exhibit VSDs among various congenital heart anomalies. A VSD is a condition characterized by an abnormal opening in the wall that separates the two lower chambers of the heart. While other cardiac issues like atrial septal defects, Tetralogy of Fallot, and hypoplastic left heart can also occur in Down syndrome, VSD stands out as the most prevalent cardiac anomaly associated with this genetic condition.

2. Answer B (Obstructive sleep apnea)

Individuals with Down syndrome commonly experience obstructive sleep apnea (OSA), making it a prominent respiratory issue associated with this genetic condition. OSA involves repeated episodes of partial or complete blockage of the upper airway during sleep, leading to disruptions in breathing. While conditions like asthma, pneumonia, and pulmonary embolism can occur in individuals with Down syndrome, OSA is particularly prevalent. The characteristic facial and cranial features of Down syndrome, such as a small and narrowed airway, contribute to the increased susceptibility to OSA.

3. Answer D (It can result in atlantoaxial instability)

In adults with Down syndrome, ligamentous laxity is particularly significant as it can result in atlantoaxial instability, posing challenges during medical procedures such as intubation. This condition involves increased movement between the atlas (C1) and axis (C2) vertebrae in the neck, and the instability can complicate the intubation process. Therefore, healthcare providers need to exercise caution and consider the potential challenges associated with the unique anatomical features of individuals with Down syndrome during intubation procedures to ensure patient safety.

4. Answer C (To prevent infective endocarditis)

Antibiotic prophylaxis is recommended in some adults with Down syndrome to prevent infective endocarditis. If the patient is at risk for infective endocarditis, antibiotic prophylaxis should be used. This preventive measure is particularly important in individuals with Down syndrome who may be susceptible to cardiac issues, and it helps reduce the risk of bacterial infection of the heart valves or endocardium.

5. Answer B (False)

While Down syndrome is associated with certain gastrointestinal abnormalities, including duodenal atresia, it is not commonly linked to inflammatory bowel disease. Duodenal atresia, a condition where there is a blockage in the first part of the small intestine, is indeed more prevalent in individuals with Down syndrome.

6. Answer C (Administration of anxiolytics may trigger paradoxical reactions)

When administering anxiolytics to adults with Down syndrome in the preoperative area, it's essential to consider the potential for paradoxical reactions. Individuals with Down syndrome may react differently to medications, and paradoxical reactions, where the drug has an opposite effect than intended, can occur. Therefore, caution is advised in the use of anxiolytics. While benzodiazepines are commonly used for anxiety, it's not a one-size-fits-all approach, and their use should be carefully evaluated. Midazolam, a benzodiazepine, is not necessarily contraindicated, but its administration should be approached with caution, considering the individual's medical history and potential for adverse reactions. Using opioids as anxiolytics is not a recommended practice, as opioids primarily function as analgesics and may have respiratory depressant effects. Overall, a personalized and careful approach to medication management, considering the unique characteristics of individuals with Down syndrome, is crucial in the preoperative setting.

Recommended literature

1. Meitzner MC, Skurnowicz JA. Anesthetic considerations for patients with Down syndrome. AANA J. 2005;73(2):103-107.

DUCHENNE MUSCULAR DYSTROPHY

12
CHAPTER

Questions:

1. **What is the primary cause of Duchenne muscular dystrophy?**
   A. Autosomal dominant inheritance
   B. Autosomal recessive inheritance
   C. X-linked genetic disorder
   D. Sporadic mutations

2. **Which of the following is a characteristic ECG pattern associated with Duchenne muscular dystrophy?**
   A. T-wave inversion in all leads
   B. Q-waves in the lateral leads, increased ST-segments, poor R-wave progression
   C. Prolonged QT interval
   D. Right bundle branch block

3. **What is the primary role of dystrophin in Duchenne muscular dystrophy?**
   A. Nervous system development
   B. Muscle functioning and repair
   C. Immune system regulation
   D. Hemoglobin synthesis

4. **Which intervention is NOT a part of the symptomatic management of Duchenne muscular dystrophy?**
   A. Corticosteroids
   B. ACE inhibitors
   C. Antibiotics
   D. Physical therapy

5. **Succinylcholine is the neuromuscular agent of choice in individuals with Duchenne muscular dystrophy.**
   A. True
   B. False

6. **A 14-year-old male patient with Duchenne muscular dystrophy (DMD) is scheduled for a tenotomy operation and is planned for general anesthesia. The patient presents with the characteristic symptoms of DMD, including progressive muscle weakness and atrophy. Which of the following is NOT a potential risk during general anesthesia in individuals with Duchenne muscular dystrophy?**
   A. Rhabdomyolysis
   B. Malignant hyperthermia
   C. Hyperkalemia
   D. Hypokalemia

Answers:

1. Answer C (X-linked genetic disorder)

Duchenne muscular dystrophy is primarily caused by a mutation in the gene that encodes for dystrophin. This mutation follows an X-linked genetic inheritance pattern, meaning the defective gene is located on the X chromosome. Since males have only one X chromosome, they are more commonly affected by Duchenne muscular dystrophy than females. Duchenne muscular dystrophy is characterized by progressive muscle weakness and atrophy, affecting not only striated muscles but also smooth and cardiac muscles. It is the most common and severe form among the group of genetically determined primary degenerative myopathies.

2. Answer B (Q-waves in the lateral leads, increased ST-segments, poor R-wave progression)

Duchenne muscular dystrophy (DMD) is associated with a specific ECG pattern, including Q-waves in the lateral leads, increased ST-segments, poor R-wave progression, resting tachycardia, and conduction defects. This particular pattern reflects the cardiac involvement in DMD, which is a multi-systemic condition affecting not only skeletal muscles but also the cardiac muscle. It's important to note that DMD may also present with various other ECG changes, such as sinus tachycardia, reduction of circadian index, decreased heart rate variability, short PR interval, right ventricular hypertrophy, S-T segment depression, and prolonged QTc. Rarely, DMD might be associated with Wolf-Parkinson-White syndrome (WPW syndrome).

3. Answer B (Muscle functioning and repair)

Dystrophin plays a crucial role in the proper functioning and repair of muscles. In DMD, a genetic disorder, there is a mutation in the gene that encodes for dystrophin. Without dystrophin, muscles are unable to function or repair themselves properly. This deficiency leads to progressive muscle weakness and atrophy, which are characteristic features of DMD. While dystrophin is primarily associated with muscle function, it is important to note that DMD is a multi-systemic condition, and the absence of dystrophin can impact various muscle types, including striated, smooth, and cardiac muscles.

4. Answer C (Antibiotics)

The intervention that is NOT a part of the symptomatic management of DMD is Antibiotics. DMD, an incurable genetic disorder, is managed symptomatically to enhance the quality of life for affected individuals. Strategies include corticosteroids for muscle strength preservation, ACE inhibitors and/or beta-blockers to slow cardiomyopathy progression, physical therapy, braces, surgery for orthopedic issues, exercise, tracheostomy, and assisted ventilation for respiratory failure, anticonvulsants for seizure control, and immunosuppressants to delay muscle damage. Antibiotics, while crucial for treating infections that may arise in individuals with DMD, are not considered a routine component of the symptomatic management protocol for the condition.

5. Answer B (False)

Succinylcholine is generally avoided in individuals with DMD. Duchenne muscular dystrophy is characterized by a lack of dystrophin, a protein essential for muscle integrity. Administration of succinylcholine can lead to a rapid release of potassium from muscle cells, causing hyperkalemia. In individuals with DMD, who are already at risk for hyperkalemia due to muscle breakdown, the use of succinylcholine can exacerbate this risk and potentially result in life-threatening complications, such as cardiac arrhythmias. Therefore, alternative neuromuscular agents and careful consideration of the anesthetic plan are essential in individuals with Duchenne muscular dystrophy to minimize the risk of complications during anesthesia.

6. Answer D (Hypokalemia)

The potential risk during general anesthesia in individuals with DMD that is NOT listed is hypokalemia. Patients with DMD are indeed at risk for various complications during anesthesia, including rhabdomyolysis, malignant hyperthermia-like phenomena, and hyperkalemia. The use of succinylcholine, a depolarizing muscle relaxant, can lead to a rapid release of potassium, causing hyperkalemia, and volatile anesthetics may contribute to rhabdomyolysis. However, hypokalemia is not typically associated with DMD during general anesthesia. The emphasis in the anesthetic management of DMD patients lies in avoiding specific triggering agents, closely monitoring for complications related to their underlying muscle pathology, and tailoring the approach to minimize risks associated with the disorder.

Recommended literature

1. Duan, D., Goemans, N., Takeda, S. et al. Duchenne muscular dystrophy. Nat Rev Dis Primers 7, 13 (2021).
2. Pollard BJ, Kitchen, G. Handbook of Clinical Anaesthesia. Fourth Edition. CRC Press. 2018. 978-1-4987-6289-2.
3. Marsh, S., Pittard, A., 2011. Neuromuscular disorders and anaesthesia. Part 2: specific neuromuscular disorders. Continuing Education in Anaesthesia Critical Care & Pain 11, 119–123.
4. Lerman, J., 2011. Perioperative management of the paediatric patient with coexisting neuromuscular disease. British Journal of Anaesthesia 107, i79–i89.
5. Ragoonanan, V., Russell, W., 2010. Anaesthesia for children with neuromuscular disease. Continuing Education in Anaesthesia Critical Care & Pain 10, 143–147.

EPIGLOTTITIS

12
CHAPTER

Questions:

1. **What is the primary cause of epiglottitis?**
   A. Trauma from foreign objects
   B. Chemical burns
   C. Bacterial infection
   D. Viral infection

2. **Which anatomical feature makes the pediatric airway more susceptible to epiglottitis symptoms than adults?**
   A. Smaller epiglottis
   B. More pliant epiglottis
   C. Horizontal trachea
   D. The narrowest part at the glottis

3. **What could be a complication associated with epiglottitis?**
   A. Cellulitis
   B. Pneumothorax
   C. Meningitis
   D. All of the above

4. **What position is commonly observed in patients with epiglottitis due to the difficulty in breathing?**
   A. Supine
   B. Trendelenburg
   C. Tripod position
   D. Left lateral decubitus

5. **MRI is an imaging modality recommended for assessing swelling of the epiglottis in stable, cooperative patients.**
   A. True
   B. False

6. **A 6-year-old patient has been urgently transferred to the Intensive Care Unit (ICU) following intubation in the operating room due to severe hypoxia and respiratory failure caused by epiglottitis. The primary focus now is on antibiotic therapy to address the underlying infection and prevent further complications. Given the critical nature of the condition, choosing the appropriate antibiotic is paramount. Which antibiotic is NOT commonly used in the management of epiglottitis?**
   A. Clindamycin
   B. Ceftriaxone
   C. Ampicillin and sulbactam
   D. Gentamicin

Answers:

1. **Answer C (Bacterial infection)**

   Epiglottitis is primarily caused by bacterial infection. While noninfectious causes such as trauma from foreign objects, inhalation, and chemical burns can contribute, infectious processes are the usual culprits. The infection leads to swelling of the epiglottis and nearby structures, including the arytenoids, aryepiglottic folds, and vallecula. This inflammatory condition is life-threatening, and prompt recognition and management are crucial to prevent complications such as respiratory failure and asphyxia.

2. **Answer B (More pliant epiglottis)**

   The infantile anatomy of the pediatric airway makes it more susceptible to epiglottitis symptoms than adults. The infant epiglottis is comprised of cartilage and is far more pliant than in adults. Additionally, the pediatric airway has a superior and anterior location of the epiglottis, a more oblique angle with the trachea, and the narrowest part is at the subglottis, in contrast to the glottis in adults. These anatomical differences contribute to the increased vulnerability of children to infectious processes that lead to edema and mass increase of the epiglottis. During each inspiration, the edematous epiglottis is pulled over the laryngeal airway, causing symptoms such as respiratory distress, stridor, and difficulty breathing.

3. **Answer D (All of the above)**

   Epiglottitis is associated with a range of serious complications, making it a potentially life-threatening condition. These complications include cellulitis, cervical adenitis, death, empyema, epiglottic abscess, hypoxia, meningitis, pneumonia, pneumothorax, prolonged ventilation, pulmonary edema, respiratory failure, sepsis, septic arthritis, septic shock, tracheostomy, vocal cord granuloma, and Ludwig angina-type submental infection. The diversity of these complications underscores the critical nature of epiglottitis, emphasizing the need for swift diagnosis and appropriate management to prevent severe outcomes.

4. **Answer C (Tripod position)**

   Patients with epiglottitis commonly assume the "tripod position" due to the difficulty in breathing. This physical stance is often adopted by individuals experiencing respiratory distress or breathlessness. In the "tripod position," a person sits or stands leaning forward and supports the upper body with hands on knees or another surface. This posture helps open the airway, facilitating breathing and reducing the work of breathing. Other signs and symptoms associated with epiglottitis include sudden onset, fever, severe sore throat, difficulty swallowing, hypersalivation, stridor, inability to lie flat, voice changes, dysphagia, anxiety, tachypnea, and cyanosis.

5. **Answer B (False)**

   MRI is not the recommended imaging modality for assessing swelling of the epiglottis in suspected cases of epiglottitis, especially in stable, cooperative patients. Instead, a lateral neck radiograph is recommended in such cases to visualize the swelling of the epiglottis. However, it's crucial to be cautious during oropharyngeal exams, as they may lead to loss of the airway. When epiglottitis is suspected, prompt patient transfer to the operating room for airway assessment is essential. The differential diagnosis includes conditions such as laryngotracheobronchitis (croup), airway obstruction from a foreign object, acute angioedema, caustic ingestion, diphtheria, peritonsillar/retropharyngeal abscess.

6. **Answer D (Gentamicin)**

   Gentamicin is not commonly used in the standard antibiotic regimen for epiglottitis. The preferred antibiotics for epiglottic infection include third-generation cephalosporins due to increasing resistance to ampicillin. Specifically, ceftriaxone is often chosen for its broad-spectrum coverage. Options like ampicillin and sulbactam, cefuroxime, cefotaxime, and clindamycin are also considered in certain cases. Therefore, in the management of this 6-year-old patient with severe epiglottitis, gentamicin would not be the first-line choice for antibiotic therapy. Instead, attention should be given to antibiotics with appropriate coverage, such as ceftriaxone.

Recommended literature

1. Guerra AM, Waseem M. Epiglottitis. [Updated 2022 Oct 17]. In: StatPearls [Internet]. Treasure Island (FL): StatPearls Publishing; 2022 Jan-. Available from: https://www.ncbi.nlm.nih.gov/books/NBK430960/.
2. Lichtor JL, Roche Rodriguez M, Aaronson NL, Spock T, Goodman TR, Baum ED. Epiglottitis: It Hasn't Gone Away. Anesthesiology. 2016;124(6):1404-7.

Pediatrics
FONTAN PHYSIOLOGY

Questions:

1. **What type of congenital heart defect is commonly addressed by the Fontan procedure?**
   A. Atrial septal defect
   B. Ventricular septal defect
   C. Dual ventricular physiology
   D. Single ventricle physiology

2. **What are the key selection criteria for performing the Fontan procedure?**
   A. Large pulmonary arteries, high PVR, good LV function, atrial fibrillation
   B. Adequately sized pulmonary arteries, low PVR, good LV function, sinus rhythm
   C. Small pulmonary arteries, high PVR, good LV function, sinus rhythm
   D. Adequately sized pulmonary arteries, low PVR, good LV function, atrial fibrillation

3. **What are the potential complications associated with Fontan physiology?**
   A. Arrhythmias
   B. Protein-losing enteropathy
   C. Thromboembolism
   D. All of the above

4. **What drives blood flow through the pulmonary circulation in Fontan physiology?**
   A. Active pumping by the heart
   B. Atrial pressure
   C. Central venous pressure (CVP)
   D. Difference between CVP and atrial pressure

5. **The Fontan procedure is usually performed in the neonatal period.**
   A. True
   B. False

6. **A 5-year-old child has been diagnosed with functional univentricular physiology, a congenital heart defect characterized by having only one functional ventricle instead of the typical two. The medical team has scheduled her for a hemi-Fontan procedure, a surgical intervention designed to enhance blood flow and optimize cardiac function by redirecting circulation. Recognizing the significance of fluid management in the perioperative care of Fontan physiology, the team is committed to ensuring hemodynamic stability. The paramount objective of fluid management in this context is to carefully guide and maintain an optimal intravascular volume. What is the primary goal of fluid management in Fontan physiology during the perioperative period?**
   A. Maintain low intravascular volume
   B. Guide by CVP or TEE
   C. Limit fluid intake
   D. Minimize vascular capacitance

Answers:

1. Answer D (Single ventricle physiology)

The Fontan procedure is commonly performed for patients born with single ventricle physiology. In this congenital heart defect, there is only one functional ventricle instead of the normal two. The Fontan procedure is a palliative surgical intervention designed to redirect blood flow so that this single ventricle can support both the systemic and pulmonary circulations. It provides a long-term solution for individuals with single ventricle physiology, allowing them to lead as normal a life as possible by improving blood circulation and cardiac function.

2. Answer B (Adequately sized pulmonary arteries, low PVR, good LV function, sinus rhythm)

The key selection criteria for performing the Fontan procedure involve ensuring adequately sized pulmonary arteries, low pulmonary vascular resistance (PVR), good left ventricular (LV) function, and the presence of sinus rhythm. Adequate pulmonary artery size is crucial for proper blood flow, while low PVR facilitates smooth circulation through the pulmonary system. Good LV function contributes to overall cardiac efficiency, and sinus rhythm ensures coordinated atrial and ventricular contractions. These criteria collectively support the success of the Fontan procedure, a palliative surgery designed for patients with single ventricle physiology, allowing for improved blood circulation and cardiac function.

3. Answer D (All of the above)

Fontan physiology is associated with various potential complications, and all the options listed are potential complications. These complications arise due to the altered circulatory dynamics and unique physiology resulting from the Fontan procedure. Arrhythmias can occur due to abnormal blood mixing, and protein-losing enteropathy may develop, leading to abnormal loss of proteins in the gastrointestinal tract. Thromboembolism is also a recognized complication, and it is important to monitor and manage these potential issues in patients with Fontan physiology. Other complications listed include decreased exercise tolerance, ventricular dysfunction, shunts, and developmental deficits, reflecting the complex challenges associated with this palliative surgical approach for patients with single ventricle physiology.

4. Answer D (Difference between CVP and atrial pressure)

In Fontan physiology, the driving force for blood flow through the pulmonary circulation is the difference between central venous pressure (CVP) and atrial pressure. Unlike in a normal circulatory system where the heart actively pumps blood through the lungs, in Fontan physiology, there is no active pumping of blood through the lungs. The Fontan circulation essentially relies on passive flow driven by pressure gradients. Cardiac output in this context is essentially completely dependent on pulmonary blood flow. It is crucial to maintain adequate intravascular volume as hypovolemia is poorly tolerated in Fontan physiology, leading to decreased pulmonary blood flow and cardiac output.

5. Answer B (False)

The Fontan procedure is contraindicated in the neonatal period due to high pulmonary vascular resistance. High pulmonary vascular resistance in neonates makes the Fontan procedure technically challenging and increases the risk of complications. Instead, the Fontan procedure is typically performed as part of a staged approach that facilitates the progressive adaptation of the heart and lungs. The stages include the placement of a systemic-pulmonary shunt, the creation of a superior cavopulmonary connection, and the completion of the Fontan circulation. These stages are usually performed as the patient grows and the pulmonary arteries sufficiently enlarge to allow for a lower pulmonary vascular resistance, typically between 1 and 5 years of age.

6. Answer B (Guide by CVP or TEE)

The primary goal of fluid management in Fontan physiology during the perioperative period is to guide fluid administration based on CVP or transesophageal echocardiography (TEE). TEE is particularly useful in monitoring cardiac function, and it is essential to adapt fluid management to the unique physiology of Fontan circulation. Contrary to conventional approaches, the focus is on maintaining optimal intravascular volume to support cardiac output rather than minimizing volume. Vascular capacitance is increased in Fontan patients, potentially necessitating more fluid than anticipated by traditional formulas.

Recommended literature

1. Jolley M, Colan SD, Rhodes J, DiNardo J. Fontan Physiology Revisited. Anesthesia & Analgesia. 2015;121(1).
2. Nayak S, Booker PD. The Fontan circulation. Continuing Education in Anaesthesia Critical Care & Pain. 2008;8(1):26-30.

FOREIGN BODY ASPIRATION

12

CHAPTER

Questions:

1. **What is the fourth leading cause of death in young children?**
   A. Respiratory infections
   B. Suffocation
   C. Accidents
   D. Congenital anomalies

2. **What is the preferred diagnostic method for identifying inhaled foreign bodies?**
   A. Magnetic Resonance Imaging (MRI)
   B. Chest X-ray
   C. Ultrasound
   D. Bronchoscopy

3. **Why might normal chest radiographs be observed in patients with inhaled foreign bodies?**
   A. The foreign body is radiolucent
   B. Upper airway obstruction
   C. The patient is asymptomatic
   D. All of the above

4. **What is the potential consequence of pushing a foreign body into a mainstem bronchus during airway foreign body management?**
   A. Bronchospasm
   B. Hypotension
   C. Pneumothorax
   D. Complete airway obstruction

5. **Glycopyrrolate is used to dry secretions in airway foreign body management.**
   A. True
   B. False

6. **A 3-year-old child presents with symptoms of coughing, wheezing, dyspnea, choking signs, and cyanosis, indicative of a suspected foreign body aspiration. Due to the severity of symptoms and the potential for lower airway obstruction, an emergency bronchoscopy is scheduled for immediate intervention. In preparing for the bronchoscopy, the anesthesiologist adopts a strategy of maintaining spontaneous ventilation. Why is maintaining spontaneous ventilation a goal in airway foreign body management?**
   A. To prevent bronchospasm
   B. To avoid hyperinflation/barotrauma
   C. To facilitate rigid bronchoscopy
   D. To induce coughing for FB dislodgement

Answers:

1. **Answer B (Suffocation)**

   Inhaled foreign bodies are a common emergency in young children. Due to the high position of the larynx and epiglottis and narrow airways, there is a significant risk of foreign body aspiration in this age group. Loss of concentration during physical activity, eating, or exploring objects by putting them in their mouth can result in sudden symptoms of breathing difficulties. The fourth leading cause of death in young children is suffocation. Inhaled foreign bodies contribute to this category, posing a risk of airway obstruction and respiratory distress.

2. **Answer D (Bronchoscopy)**

   The preferred diagnostic method for identifying inhaled foreign bodies is bronchoscopy. This procedure, involving the insertion of a thin, flexible, or rigid tube with a light and camera through the mouth or nose, allows direct visualization of the airways, making it the most reliable method for both diagnosing and removing foreign bodies.

3. **Answer D (All of the above)**

   Normal chest radiographs may be observed in patients with inhaled foreign bodies for various reasons. Firstly, if the foreign body is radiolucent, meaning it does not absorb X-rays and is not visible on the X-ray film, it may not be detected. Secondly, upper airway obstruction can result in symptoms without significant changes in the chest X-ray. Additionally, some patients may be asymptomatic despite the presence of an inhaled foreign body. The signs and symptoms of foreign body aspiration can vary depending on factors such as the type of foreign body, time after aspiration, and the exact location within the airways. Proximity to the proximal airway tends to result in more severe symptoms. Many aspirated objects are not radiopaque, contributing to normal-appearing chest radiographs. Conversely, normal X-ray results are often associated with upper airway obstruction, while emphysema and infiltration are more commonly seen in distal airway obstruction.

4. **Answer D (Complete airway obstruction)**

   Pushing a foreign body into a mainstem bronchus during airway foreign body management can have serious consequences, with the potential to cause complete airway obstruction. This occurs when the foreign body lodges in a mainstem bronchus, blocking air passage. This can lead to severe respiratory distress, and hypoxemia, and, if not promptly addressed, it poses a life-threatening situation for the patient. While bronchospasm, hypotension, and pneumothorax can be associated with various complications in airway foreign body cases, pushing the foreign body into a mainstem bronchus specifically results in the immediate and critical problem of complete airway obstruction.

5. **Answer A (True)**

   Glycopyrrolate is used to dry secretions in airway foreign body management. This medication, an anticholinergic, reduces salivary and respiratory tract secretions. In the context of airway foreign body procedures, minimizing secretions is important to maintain a clear view of the airway and prevent complications related to excessive mucus or saliva. Glycopyrrolate, along with other medications like dexamethasone, which is used to reduce swelling, is part of the pharmacological strategies employed to optimize conditions for the safe and effective management of airway foreign bodies.

6. **Answer B (To avoid hyperinflation/barotrauma)**

   Maintaining spontaneous ventilation is a crucial goal in the anesthetic management of airway foreign body cases. This strategy aims to prevent hyperinflation and barotrauma associated with positive pressure ventilation, reducing the risk of pushing the foreign body further down the airway and subsequent airway obstruction. This approach allows for the provision of adequate analgesia for the rigid bronchoscopy procedure, ensuring effective pain management without the interference of coughing and mitigating the risk of airway trauma. Collaborative teamwork with the ENT specialist throughout the procedure is emphasized, emphasizing the goal of preventing airway complications and safeguarding the child's respiratory function.

Recommended literature

1. Rose D, Dubensky L. Airway Foreign Bodies. [Updated 2022 Aug 8]. In: StatPearls [Internet]. Treasure Island (FL): StatPearls Publishing; 2022 Jan-. Available from: https://www.ncbi.nlm.nih.gov/books/NBK539756/.
2. Bould MD. Essential notes: the anaesthetic management of an inhaled foreign body in a child. BJA Education. 2019;19(3):66-7.
3. Kendigelen P. The anaesthetic consideration of tracheobronchial foreign body aspiration in children. J Thorac Dis. 2016;8(12):3803-3807.
4. Moehrle NP, Jagannathan N. Management of foreign body aspiration in pediatric and adult patients. In: Berkow LC, Sakles JC, eds. Cases in Emergency Airway Management. Cambridge: Cambridge University Press; 2015:79-88.

GENETIC SYNDROMES: GENERAL CONSIDERATIONS

12
CHAPTER

Questions:

1. **What characterizes genetic syndromes?**
   A. Single phenotypic trait
   B. Multiple identifiable phenotypic traits
   C. Chromosomal abnormalities
   D. Acquired traits

2. **Which syndromes may present challenges related to airway management?**
   A. VACTERL syndrome
   B. Treacher Collins syndrome
   C. Velocardiofacial syndrome
   D. Trisomy 21

3. **What musculoskeletal abnormalities should be assessed in patients with genetic syndromes?**
   A. Limb contractures
   B. Scoliosis
   C. Hip dysplasia
   D. All of the above

4. **In neurocognitive evaluation, what aspects should be considered for patients with genetic syndromes?**
   A. Intelligence
   B. Speech and language development
   C. Neurodevelopmental status
   D. All of the above

5. **Velocardiofacial syndrome may involve both cardiac and craniofacial abnormalities.**
   A. True
   B. False

6. **A 3-year-old child with a confirmed diagnosis of Cerebro-Facio-thoracic dysplasia (CFTD) is scheduled for sedation to undergo an MRI diagnostic procedure. CFTD is a rare genetic disorder characterized by developmental abnormalities affecting the brain, face, and thoracic region. Given the complex nature of CFTD, certain precautions must be taken during sedation to ensure the safety and well-being of the child. What is crucial to preventing spinal nerve injuries in patients with vertebral and rib abnormalities or craniofacial anomalies during anesthesia procedures?**
   A. Rapid intubation
   B. Proper positioning and supportive care
   C. Routine use of muscle relaxants
   D. Increased depth of anesthesia

Answers:

1. **Answer B (Multiple identifiable phenotypic traits)**

Genetic syndromes are characterized by the occurrence of more than one recognizable phenotypic trait in a specific association, and they are caused by a specific genetic defect. This means that individuals with a genetic syndrome exhibit a combination of distinctive physical features or traits that occur together due to an underlying genetic abnormality. The presence of multiple identifiable phenotypic traits is a key defining characteristic of genetic syndromes. It distinguishes them from conditions or traits caused by environmental factors or acquired during an individual's lifetime.

2. **Answer B (Treacher Collins syndrome)**

Treacher-Collins syndrome is a genetic disorder that primarily affects the development of facial bones and tissues. Individuals with Treacher-Collins syndrome often have craniofacial anomalies, including underdeveloped or absent cheekbones, jaw abnormalities, and a downward-slanting palpebral fissure. These facial features can contribute to airway challenges, particularly due to the potential for a smaller or less stable mandible and other anatomical variations in the head and neck region. While other syndromes listed may have associated medical issues, Treacher-Collins syndrome is specifically known for its impact on facial and cranial structures, making airway management a particular consideration in individuals with this syndrome.

3. **Answer D (All of the above)**

Patients with genetic syndromes may present with various musculoskeletal abnormalities that can impact their overall health and quality of life. Limb contractures, scoliosis, and hip dysplasia are among the musculoskeletal issues that healthcare providers should assess in individuals with genetic syndromes. These abnormalities can vary in severity and may be associated with specific syndromes. Regular assessment and monitoring of the musculoskeletal system are important to identify any issues early and implement appropriate interventions or treatments.

4. **Answer D (All of the above)**

In neurocognitive evaluation for patients with genetic syndromes, it is essential to consider multiple aspects, including intelligence, speech and language development, and overall neurodevelopmental status. Assessing intelligence provides insights into cognitive abilities, while evaluating speech and language development is crucial for understanding communication skills, often affected in genetic syndromes. Additionally, a broader assessment of neurodevelopmental status encompasses various neurological aspects, including motor skills and coordination. Considering all these dimensions is integral for a comprehensive understanding of the cognitive profile of individuals with genetic syndromes, facilitating tailored interventions and support as needed.

5. **Answer A (True)**

Velocardiofacial syndrome (VCFS), also known as 22q11.2 deletion syndrome, is characterized by a combination of features, including both cardiac and craniofacial abnormalities. The syndrome is associated with a deletion on the long arm of chromosome 22 and presents a diverse range of manifestations. Cardiac anomalies are common in individuals with VCFS, including conditions like conotruncal heart defects. Craniofacial features often include cleft palate, distinctive facial appearance, and other structural abnormalities. Given the multi-systemic nature of VCFS, individuals may also experience learning disabilities and other health issues.

6. **Answer B (Proper positioning and supportive care)**

Proper positioning and supportive care during anesthesia procedures are crucial in preventing spinal nerve injuries, especially in patients with conditions like CFTD characterized by vertebral and rib abnormalities and craniofacial anomalies. In this case, the child's unique anatomy necessitates careful consideration of head and neck positioning to avoid undue pressure or stress on the spinal column. Proper support and alignment during intubation and the entire procedure duration are essential to minimize the risk of injury.

Recommended literature

1. Mann D, Garcia PJ, Andropoulos DB. Anesthesia for the Patient with a Genetic Syndrome. Gregory's Pediatric Anesthesia2020. p. 1085-105.

Pediatrics

GOLDENHAR SYNDROME

Questions:

1. **What is the primary cause of Goldenhar Syndrome?**
   A. Genetic mutations
   B. Congenital malformation of branchial arches
   C. Environmental factors
   D. Viral infections

2. **Which of the following is a characteristic feature of Goldenhar Syndrome?**
   A. Bilateral microtia
   B. Bilateral mandibular hyperplasia
   C. Absence of vertebral anomalies
   D. Unilateral mandibular hypoplasia

3. **Which organ is NOT commonly affected in Goldenhar Syndrome?**
   A. Heart
   B. Kidneys
   C. Liver
   D. Lungs

4. **What cardiac abnormalities are commonly seen in about a third of Goldenhar Syndrome patients?**
   A. Aortic stenosis
   B. Ventricular septal defect
   C. Tetralogy of Fallot
   D. Patent ductus arteriosus

5. **Second and third branchial arches are primarily affected in Goldenhar Syndrome.**
   A. True
   B. False

6. **A 5-year-old girl diagnosed with Goldenhar Syndrome presented to the hospital for electronic cochlear implantation surgery. Her medical history revealed no prior operations, chronic diseases, or known allergies. Why is the airway considered potentially very difficult in pediatric patients with Goldenhar Syndrome?**
   A. Excessive saliva production
   B. Large tongue size
   C. Mandibular hypoplasia and limited space
   D. Narrow nasal passages

Answers:

1. **Answer B (Congenital malformation of branchial arches)**

    Goldenhar Syndrome, also known as oculo-auriculo-vertebral syndrome or hemifacial microsomia, is primarily caused by congenital malformation of the first and second branchial arches. During embryonic development, these arches give rise to various structures in the head and neck region, including the ear, nose, soft palate, lip, and mandible. In Goldenhar Syndrome, the incomplete development of these branchial arches leads to characteristic features such as mandibular hypoplasia resulting in facial asymmetry, ear and/or eye malformations, and vertebral anomalies.

2. **Answer D (Unilateral mandibular hypoplasia)**

    A characteristic feature of Goldenhar Syndrome is unilateral mandibular hypoplasia. This condition leads to facial asymmetry, as one side of the mandible is underdeveloped or smaller than the other. This asymmetry is a key element of the triad of features seen in Goldenhar Syndrome, along with ear and/or eye malformations and vertebral anomalies.

3. **Answer C (Liver)**

    In Goldenhar Syndrome, the organ that is NOT commonly affected is the liver. Goldenhar Syndrome primarily involves craniofacial and musculoskeletal abnormalities, with a focus on structures derived from the first and second branchial arches. While various organs are affected, including the heart, kidneys, and lungs, the liver is not typically associated with this syndrome. The signs and symptoms of Goldenhar Syndrome encompass a range of features, such as mandibular hypoplasia, eye anomalies (microphthalmia, anophthalmia), ear anomalies (preauricular tags, anotia, microtia), vertebral anomalies (scoliosis, kyphosis), cleft lip/palate, wider than normal mouth, hydrocephalus, congenital heart defects, genitourinary malformations, and partial or complete unilateral lung hypoplasia.

4. **Answer C (Tetralogy of Fallot)**

    In Goldenhar Syndrome, congenital heart disease is present in about a third of patients, with the most common cardiac abnormalities being septal and conotruncal defects. Specifically, Tetralogy of Fallot is one of the most commonly seen congenital heart abnormalities in individuals with Goldenhar Syndrome.

5. **Answer B (False)**

    In Goldenhar Syndrome, the first and second branchial arches are primarily affected. These arches play a crucial role in the development of structures in the head and neck region, including the ear, nose, soft palate, lip, and mandible. Goldenhar Syndrome is characterized by congenital malformation of these first and second branchial arches, resulting in the incomplete development of various facial and cranial structures.

6. **Answer C (Mandibular hypoplasia and limited space)**

    The airway is considered potentially very difficult in pediatric patients with Goldenhar Syndrome due to the characteristic feature of mandibular hypoplasia and limited space. This congenital disorder, affecting the development of the first and second branchial arches, often results in a smaller lower jaw, leading to facial asymmetry. The reduced size of the mandible poses challenges during airway management, particularly with direct laryngoscopy, as there is limited space for visualization and intubation. Alternative techniques such as fiberoptic or video-assisted laryngoscopy are commonly employed in such cases. A multidisciplinary approach involving anesthesia and otolaryngology specialists is crucial for navigating the unique airway anatomy and ensuring the safety of these patients.

Recommended literature

1. Sun YH, Zhu B, Ji BY, Zhang XH. Airway Management in a Child with Goldenhar Syndrome. Chin Med J (Engl). 2017;130(23):2881-2882.
2. Goldenhar Syndrome. In: Bissonnette B, Luginbuehl I, Marciniak B, Dalens BJ. eds. Syndromes: Rapid Recognition and Perioperative Implications. McGraw Hill; 2006. Accessed February 09, 2023. https://accessanesthesiology.mhmedical.com/content.aspx?bookid=852&sectionid=49517623.
3. Kaymak C, Gulhan Y, Ozcan AO, Baltaci B, Unal N, Safak MA, Oguz H. Anaesthetic approach in a case of Goldenhar's syndrome. European Journal of Anaesthesiology. 2022; 19(11):836-838.

MITOCHONDRIAL DISEASE

12
CHAPTER

Questions:

1. **What is the primary function of mitochondria in the cell, and how is it affected in mitochondrial diseases?**
   A. Cell division; enhanced in mitochondrial diseases
   B. Protein synthesis; impaired in mitochondrial diseases
   C. ATP production; affected in mitochondrial diseases
   D. DNA replication; unchanged in mitochondrial diseases

2. **Which diagnostic test is NOT appropriate for identifying genetic defects affecting the mitochondria?**
   A. Muscle biopsy
   B. Brain MRI
   C. Genetic testing
   D. Electroencephalogram

3. **Which of the following is a common neurological feature associated with mitochondrial disease?**
   A. Hypotonia
   B. Hemiparesis
   C. Hyperreflexia
   D. Hemiplegia

4. **Which biochemical analysis result is commonly associated with mitochondrial disease?**
   A. Elevated glucose levels
   B. Elevated lactate levels
   C. Elevated cholesterol levels
   D. Elevated creatinine levels

5. **Cardiomyopathy is a cardiovascular abnormality frequently seen in mitochondrial disease.**
   A. True
   B. False

6. **A 35-year-old male with a known history of mitochondrial disease, presenting with developmental delay, regression, weakness, fatigability, and hypotonia, is scheduled for an emergency operation due to perforated appendicitis. The patient has not undergone sedation or general anesthesia previously. Given the patient's underlying mitochondrial disease, careful consideration of anesthetic medications is crucial. What medication should be avoided, especially during prolonged infusions in patients with mitochondrial disease?**
   A. Dexmedetomidine
   B. Midazolam
   C. Propofol
   D. Ketamine

Answers:

1. Answer C (ATP production; affected in mitochondrial diseases)

Mitochondria play a crucial role as the cell's powerhouse, responsible for producing adenosine triphosphate (ATP), the primary source of cellular energy. In mitochondrial diseases, the function of mitochondria is impaired, leading to a complex multisystem disease of varying severity. The impairment in ATP production is a hallmark of mitochondrial diseases, and this dysfunction can result in various clinical manifestations. The decreased ability to generate ATP affects the energy-dependent processes essential for cell function. Consequently, tissues and organs with high energy demands, such as the nervous system, muscles, and the cardiovascular system, may be particularly impacted.

2. Answer D (Electroencephalogram (EEG))

An EEG is not a primary diagnostic test for identifying genetic defects affecting the mitochondria in the context of mitochondrial diseases. While mitochondrial dysfunction can manifest with neurological symptoms, including seizures, EEG primarily assesses electrical brain activity and is not specific for identifying the underlying genetic mutations associated with mitochondrial disorders. Genetic testing, muscle biopsy revealing characteristic findings, biochemical analysis indicating elevated lactate levels, and brain MRI demonstrating specific patterns are more appropriate diagnostic tools for identifying mitochondrial disease-related genetic defects and associated clinical manifestations.

3. Answer A (Hypotonia)

Mitochondrial diseases often present with a range of neurological features, and one common neurological manifestation associated with mitochondrial disease is hypotonia. Hypotonia refers to reduced muscle tone, leading to floppy or loose muscles. Other neurological features commonly seen in mitochondrial diseases include developmental delay, regression, weakness, fatigability, spasticity, ataxia, and seizure disorders. These symptoms arise due to the impact of mitochondrial dysfunction on energy-dependent processes, affecting various organs and tissues, particularly those with high energy demands, such as the nervous system. While other neurological features listed may also be present, hypotonia is notably recognized as a common clinical manifestation in individuals with mitochondrial disease.

4. Answer B (Elevated lactate levels)

Mitochondrial diseases are commonly associated with elevated lactate levels. Lactate is a byproduct of anaerobic metabolism, and its accumulation suggests impaired mitochondrial function, leading to an inability to efficiently utilize oxygen in cellular respiration. Elevated lactate levels are a key biochemical marker often observed in individuals with mitochondrial disorders. This finding is significant in the diagnosis and management of mitochondrial diseases, reflecting the compromised energy production within cells.

5. Answer A (True)

Mitochondrial diseases often manifest with cardiovascular abnormalities, and cardiomyopathy is a frequently observed condition. Cardiomyopathy refers to a disease of the heart muscle that can lead to structural and functional abnormalities. In the context of mitochondrial diseases, cardiomyopathy can result from the impact of mitochondrial dysfunction on the energy demands of the heart. Additionally, conduction abnormalities in the heart's electrical system are also common in individuals with mitochondrial diseases. These abnormalities can contribute to arrhythmias and other cardiac complications.

6. Answer C (Propofol)

In the context of mitochondrial disease, propofol should be avoided, especially during prolonged infusions. Propofol is unique among parenteral anesthetics in its known impact on mitochondrial metabolism through multiple mechanisms. In vitro studies have demonstrated that propofol can uncouple oxidative phosphorylation and inhibit respiratory complexes I, II, and IV. Importantly, the most potent effect of propofol is its inhibition of the transport of long-chain acylcarnitine esters mediated by acylcarnitine transferase, specifically carnitine palmitoyltransferase 1. This inhibition of acylcarnitine transferase has been implicated in propofol infusion syndrome, a potentially fatal complication associated with long-term propofol infusions used in intensive care. Given these multiple effects on mitochondrial function, it is considered prudent to avoid propofol-based anesthetic techniques, such as continuous infusions or total intravenous anesthesia, in patients with known or suspected mitochondrial disease.

Recommended literature

1. Desai, V. (2021). Mitochondrial disease and anaesthesia : WFSA – resources. Mitochondrial Disease and Anaesthesia. Retrieved February 16, 2023, from https://resources.wfsahq.org/atotw/mitochondrial-disease-and-anaesthesia/.
2. Hsieh VC, Krane EJ, Morgan PG. Mitochondrial Disease and Anesthesia. Journal of Inborn Errors of Metabolism and Screening. 2017;5:2326409817707770.
3. Niezgoda J, Morgan PG. Anesthetic considerations in patients with mitochondrial defects. Paediatr Anaesth. 2013;23(9):785-793.

Pediatrics
MUCOPOLYSACCHARIDOSES

12
CHAPTER

Questions:

1. **What is the primary cause of mucopolysaccharidoses (MPS), except for MPS II?**
   A. Autosomal dominant inheritance
   B. Autosomal recessive inheritance
   C. X-linked recessive inheritance
   D. Multifactorial inheritance

2. **Which enzyme deficiency is associated with MPS I?**
   A. Iduronate-2-sulfatase
   B. N-acetylgalactosamine-4-sulfatase
   C. α-L-iduronidase
   D. Galactose-6-sulfate sulfatase

3. **Which type of MPS primarily affects the central nervous system with symptoms such as dementia, seizures, and language skills impairment?**
   A. MPS II
   B. MPS IV A
   C. MPS III A
   D. MPS VI

4. **Which respiratory complication is commonly associated with MPS?**
   A. Asthma
   B. Obstructive sleep apnea (OSA)
   C. Chronic obstructive pulmonary disease (COPD)
   D. Pulmonary embolism

5. **The airway is the main concern in anesthetic management for MPS patients.**
   A. True
   B. False

6. **A 17-year-old girl with a diagnosis of MPS I is scheduled for corneal graft surgery due to corneal clouding. She presents with characteristic features of MPS I, including small stature and facial and airway characteristics that may pose challenges during anesthetic airway management. Her medical history includes intellectual disability, facial dysmorphism, and a history of recurrent respiratory infections. What is the suggested approach for airway management in MPS patients?**
   A. Rapid sequence induction with endotracheal intubation
   B. Awake fiberoptic intubation
   C. Spontaneous breathing without intubation
   D. Use of supraglottic airway devices

Answers:

1. Answer B (Autosomal recessive inheritance)

Mucopolysaccharidoses (MPS) are primarily caused by autosomal recessive inheritance, where an individual must inherit two copies of the defective gene (one from each parent) to manifest the disorder. This is the general pattern for most types of MPS. However, an exception exists for MPS II, which is inherited as an X-linked recessive disorder. In X-linked recessive inheritance, the defective gene is located on the X chromosome, and the disorder is more commonly expressed in males. The deficiency of specific lysosomal enzymes in MPS leads to the accumulation of glycosaminoglycans in various tissues, resulting in clinical manifestations. This includes hypertrophy of adenoids, tonsils, tongue, and laryngopharynx, contributing to airway and other systemic complications.

2. Answer C (α-L-iduronidase)

In MPS I, the accumulation of heparan sulfate and dermatan sulfate occurs due to the insufficient activity of α-L-iduronidase. This deficiency results from mutations in the IDUA gene located on chromosome 4p16.3. Clinical manifestations of MPS I include intellectual disability, facial dysmorphism, dwarfism, cardiomegaly, valvular disease, obstructive sleep apnea (OSA), and hepatosplenomegaly.

3. Answer C (MPS III A)

Mucopolysaccharidosis type III A (MPS III A), also known as Sanfilippo syndrome type A, primarily affects the central nervous system. In MPS III A, the enzyme heparan N-sulfatase is deficient, which is encoded by the SGSH gene located on chromosome 17q25.3. This deficiency leads to the accumulation of heparan sulfate and results in neurological symptoms such as dementia, seizures, language skills impairment, deafness, blindness, enlarged tonsils, adenoids, and respiratory infections.

4. Answer B (Obstructive sleep apnea (OSA))

Individuals with MPS often experience upper airway obstruction due to the accumulation of glycosaminoglycans in tissues, leading to hypertrophy of adenoids, tonsils, and tongue. This, in turn, can contribute to obstructive sleep apnea. Other respiratory complications mentioned in the context of MPS include restrictive lung disease, breathing at closing capacity, recurrent pulmonary infections, pectus excavatum, kyphoscoliosis, and a narrow trachea.

5. Answer A (True)

MPS are multisystem diseases, but the airway is a major focus of attention during anesthesia. Approximately 53% of MPS patients are reported to have difficult intubation, and 23% experience failed intubation. The characteristic facial and airway features in individuals with MPS, such as hypertrophy of adenoids, tonsils, macroglossia, and other upper airway abnormalities, can present challenges during intubation and ventilation.

6. Answer B (Awake fiberoptic intubation)

The suggested approach for airway management in a 17-year-old girl with MPS I undergoing corneal graft surgery is awake fiberoptic intubation. Given the characteristic features of MPS I, including small stature, macroglossia, and potential airway challenges, awake fiberoptic intubation provides a controlled and gradual method to secure the airway while maintaining spontaneous breathing. This approach minimizes the risk of complications associated with difficult intubations and allows for better visualization of the airway structures. Additionally, it ensures patient comfort and communication, which is crucial, especially in the presence of intellectual disability.

Recommended literature

1. Clark BM, Sprung J, Weingarten TN, Warner ME. Anesthesia for patients with mucopolysaccharidoses: Comprehensive review of the literature with emphasis on airway management. Bosn J Basic Med Sci. 2018;18(1):1-7.
2. Walker R, Belani KG, Braunlin EA, et al. Anaesthesia and airway management in mucopolysaccharidosis. J Inherit Metab Dis. 2013;36(2):211-219.

NECROTIZING ENTEROCOLITIS

Questions:

1. **What is the most common gastrointestinal emergency in Neonatal Intensive Care Units (NICUs)?**
   A. Hirschsprung's disease
   B. Necrotizing enterocolitis (NEC)
   C. Intussusception
   D. Malrotation

2. **In NEC, what stage is characterized by mild systemic signs with absent bowel sounds, abdominal tenderness, dilated loops of intestines, metabolic acidosis, and thrombocytopenia?**
   A. Stage I
   B. Stage II
   C. Stage III
   D. Stage IV

3. **What are the main risk factors for developing necrotizing enterocolitis?**
   A. Low birth weight
   B. Enteral feedings
   C. Cyanotic heart disease
   D. All of the above

4. **What is the priority intervention for necrotizing enterocolitis?**
   A. Immediate surgical intervention
   B. Packed red blood cell transfusion
   C. Place nasogastric tube
   D. Enteral nutrition

5. **Breast milk is considered a preventive measure against NEC.**
   A. True
   B. False

6. **A 32-week premature infant is admitted to the NICU with a diagnosis of Necrotizing Enterocolitis. The infant presents with abdominal pain and distention, changes in heart rate, blood pressure, and breathing, diarrhea with bloody stool, increased gastric residuals, vomiting of bile, lethargy, feeding intolerance, failure to thrive, hyperglycemia, temperature instability, gross abdominal distension, peritonitis, and pneumoperitoneum. The clinical presentation indicates an advanced stage of NEC, necessitating surgical intervention. Preoperative optimization is initiated to address critical considerations and improve the infant's overall condition before surgery. What is NOT a critical consideration to optimize in premature infants with NEC?**
   A. Hypoxia
   B. Sepsis, hypovolemia
   C. DIC, thrombocytopenia
   D. Metabolic alkalosis

Answers:

1. **Answer B (Necrotizing enterocolitis (NEC))**

   NEC is a life-threatening intestinal disease that primarily affects premature or very low birth-weight infants. It is highlighted as the most common gastrointestinal (GI) emergency in Neonatal Intensive Care Units (NICUs). The condition can lead to severe consequences, including long-term disability in preterm infants. The pathophysiology of NEC involves inflammation of the intestine, bacterial invasion, cellular damage, and necrosis of the colon and intestine. As NEC progresses, it can lead to intestinal perforation, causing peritonitis, sepsis, and ultimately death. The mortality rate associated with NEC can be as high as 30%.

2. **Answer B (Stage II)**

   In NEC, the stages are classified according to Bell's staging system. Stage II is characterized by mild systemic signs, including absent bowel sounds, abdominal tenderness, dilated loops of intestines, metabolic acidosis, and thrombocytopenia. This stage signifies definite disease with additional gastrointestinal signs and specific radiological findings, such as pneumatosis intestinalis, along with abnormal laboratory investigations. Stage I involves suspected disease with mild systemic and gastrointestinal signs, while Stage III represents advanced disease with severe systemic illness, gross abdominal distension, peritonitis, pneumoperitoneum, and additional laboratory abnormalities. Overall, the staging system aids in the assessment and management of NEC, guiding appropriate interventions based on the severity of clinical and diagnostic features in affected premature or very low birth-weight infants.

3. **Answer D (All of the above)**

   The main risk factors for developing NEC include prematurity, low birth weight, birth asphyxia, hypoxemia, enteral feedings, cyanotic heart disease, patent ductus arteriosus, exchange transfusion, and prolonged rupture of membranes. Premature infants, particularly those with low birth weight, are at a higher risk of developing NEC due to the immaturity of their gastrointestinal system. Enteral feedings, especially in the context of preterm infants, can contribute to the development of NEC. Additionally, cyanotic heart disease, patent ductus arteriosus, and other cardiovascular issues can further increase susceptibility. Prolonged rupture of membranes and other perinatal factors also contribute to the overall risk. Therefore, the correct answer is All of the above, as these factors collectively contribute to the predisposition and occurrence of NEC in neonates.

4. **Answer C (Place nasogastric tube)**

   The priority intervention for NEC is to place a nasogastric tube to decompress the stomach. This intervention is crucial in the medical management of NEC and aims to relieve pressure within the gastrointestinal tract, reducing the risk of complications such as intestinal perforation. Stopping enteral nutrition and decompressing the stomach with a nasogastric tube are key components of the initial approach to NEC. Medical management, which includes fluid resuscitation, antibiotics, and blood transfusions (packed red blood cells and platelets), is the primary strategy and will avoid surgery in approximately 85% of cases. Immediate surgical intervention is reserved for cases with complications such as perforation, obstruction, peritonitis, or worsening clinical status.

5. **Answer A (True)**

   Breast milk is considered a preventive measure against NEC. Numerous studies have shown that feeding premature infants with breast milk reduces the risk of developing NEC compared to formula feeding. Breast milk contains essential nutrients, antibodies, and growth factors contributing to the maturation and protection of the immature gastrointestinal system in preterm infants. It also contains beneficial factors that promote the growth of a healthy gut microbiome. The protective effects of breast milk against NEC highlight the importance of breastfeeding, especially in the NICU setting, where preterm infants are at an increased risk of developing this serious gastrointestinal condition.

6. **Answer D (Metabolic alkalosis)**

   In a premature infant diagnosed with advanced NEC, necessitating surgical intervention, the critical considerations for preoperative optimization include addressing hypoxia, managing sepsis and hypovolemia, and addressing coagulation abnormalities such as disseminated intravascular coagulation (DIC) and thrombocytopenia. However, metabolic alkalosis is not a primary concern in this context. The clinical presentation of NEC is typically associated with metabolic acidosis, stemming from compromised tissue perfusion and necrosis of the intestines. Therefore, correcting metabolic acidosis and ensuring adequate respiratory support, fluid resuscitation, and coagulation management are key priorities to optimize the infant's overall condition before surgery and improve outcomes.

Recommended literature

1. Houck PJ. Chapter 175. Necrotizing Enterocolitis. In: Atchabahian A, Gupta R. eds. The Anesthesia Guide. McGraw Hill; 2013. Accessed February 13, 2023. https://accessanesthesiology.mhmedical.com/content.aspx?bookid=572&sectionid=42543766
2. Sodhi P, Fiset P. Necrotizing enterocolitis. Continuing Education in Anaesthesia Critical Care & Pain. 2012;12(1):1-4.

OMPHALOCELE AND GASTROSCHISIS

12

CHAPTER

Questions:

1. **What is the difference between omphalocele and gastroschisis?**
   A. The presence of a sac covering the herniated intestines
   B. Location of the abdominal wall defect
   C. Association with genetic syndromes
   D. All of the above

2. **Why is early delivery beneficial in cases of gastroschisis?**
   A. To reduce the risk of underdevelopment of the lungs
   B. To limit bowel damage from exposure to amniotic fluid
   C. To prevent aspiration
   D. To facilitate easier surgical closure

3. **What is the primary difference between omphalocele minor and omphalocele major?**
   A. Association with genetic syndromes
   B. The presence of a sac covering the herniated intestines
   C. Involvement of the liver
   D. Location of the defect

4. **What is the recommended initial post-delivery care for neonates with abdominal wall defects?**
   A. Immediate surgical closure
   B. Bowel decompression using a nasogastric tube
   C. Early feeding
   D. Induce therapeutic hypothermia

5. **Neonates are highly susceptible to dehydration, making fluid resuscitation essential before the repair of the abdominal wall defect.**
   A. True
   B. False

6. **The neonate was delivered at 37 weeks of gestation, and prenatal ultrasound showed herniation of abdominal contents from a defect lateral to the umbilicus on the right side. The patient was promptly taken for urgent surgical intervention to close the abdominal wall defect. The neonate was admitted to the Neonatal Intensive Care Unit (NICU) postoperatively. What is a potential postoperative complication associated with closure of abdominal wall defects?**
   A. Hypertension
   B. Gastroesophageal reflux
   C. Abdominal compartment syndrome
   D. Short bowel syndrome

Answers:

1. **Answer D (All of the above)**

   The main differences between omphalocele and gastroschisis lie in the presence of a sac covering the herniated intestines, the location of the abdominal wall defect, and the association with genetic syndromes. Omphalocele is characterized by a herniation through the middle of the abdominal wall at the umbilicus, with the intestines covered by a thin sac formed from an outpouching of the peritoneum. It commonly occurs with other congenital defects, chromosome abnormalities, and genetic syndromes. In contrast, gastroschisis involves a defect lateral to the umbilicus, usually right-sided, and the protruding organs are not covered by a sac, leading to direct contact with amniotic fluid and inflammation. Gastroschisis is rarely associated with other congenital defects, chromosome abnormalities, or genetic syndromes.

2. **Answer B (To limit bowel damage from exposure to amniotic fluid)**

   Early delivery in cases of gastroschisis is beneficial to limit bowel damage from exposure to amniotic fluid. Gastroschisis is characterized by herniation of abdominal contents without a covering sac, exposing the intestines directly to amniotic fluid in the uterus. Prolonged exposure to amniotic fluid can lead to inflammation and damage to the exposed bowel. Delivering the baby early, around 37 weeks gestation, helps mitigate this risk and allows for timely surgical intervention to address the abdominal wall defect and protect the exposed organs. This strategy aims to minimize complications and improve the overall outcome for neonates with gastroschisis.

3. **Answer C (Involvement of the liver)**

   The primary difference between omphalocele minor and omphalocele major lies in the involvement of the liver. Omphalocele minor is characterized by a minor herniation into the umbilical cord, typically with a small 5-8 cm defect. In contrast, omphalocele major includes a larger defect that encompasses the liver. The presence of the liver in the herniated contents distinguishes the omphalocele major from the minor form. Additionally, omphalocele major is associated with poorly developed abdominal and pulmonary structures.

4. **Answer B (Bowel decompression using a nasogastric tube)**

   The recommended initial post-delivery care for neonates with abdominal wall defects involves several key measures to address the unique challenges associated with these conditions. Bowel decompression using a nasogastric tube is one crucial aspect of this care. The purpose of the nasogastric tube is to alleviate pressure on the intestines, assist in preventing aspiration, and promote the reduction of abdominal distension. Other essential components of the initial post-delivery care include fluid resuscitation to address any potential dehydration, temperature regulation to prevent heat loss, and careful inspection of the herniated bowel or viscera. Immediate surgical closure may be required, but it is not the initial step in post-delivery care, and the decision depends on the specific circumstances of the abdominal wall defect.

5. **Answer A (True)**

   Neonates with abdominal wall defects, such as omphalocele or gastroschisis, are highly susceptible to dehydration. These conditions can lead to fluid loss and electrolyte imbalances, posing a risk to the newborn's overall well-being. Therefore, fluid resuscitation is an essential aspect of the initial post-delivery care for neonates with abdominal wall defects. Administering fluids helps to address dehydration, maintain adequate hydration, and support the neonate's physiological stability before any surgical intervention to repair the abdominal wall defect. Ensuring proper fluid balance is crucial for optimizing outcomes and minimizing complications in these vulnerable newborns.

6. **Answer C (Abdominal compartment syndrome)**

   The potential postoperative complication associated with the closure of abdominal wall defects, especially in neonates, is abdominal compartment syndrome (ACS). Abdominal compartment syndrome occurs when there is increased pressure within the abdominal cavity. This increased pressure can compromise blood flow to organs, leading to multiorgan dysfunction. Closure of the abdominal wall defect may contribute to elevated intra-abdominal pressure, particularly in neonates with limited abdominal space. Monitoring for signs of abdominal compartment syndrome is crucial in the postoperative period. This may include increased abdominal distension, respiratory distress, and cardiovascular instability. Timely recognition and intervention, which may involve reopening the abdominal incision or other measures to reduce intra-abdominal pressure, are essential to prevent severe complications associated with abdominal compartment syndrome.

Recommended literature

1. Saraiya NR. GASTROSCHISIS AND OMPHALOCELE. In: Houck PJ, Haché M, Sun LS. eds. Handbook of Pediatric Anesthesia. McGraw Hill; 2015. Accessed February 14, 2023. https://accessanesthesiology.mhmedical.com/content.aspx?bookid=1189&sectionid=70363342.
2. Poddar R, Hartley L. Exomphalos and gastroschisis. Continuing Education in Anaesthesia Critical Care & Pain. 2009;9(2):48-51.
3. Wouters K, Walker I. Neonatal anaesthesia 2: Anaesthesia for neonates with abdominal wall defects. WFSA. August 28, 2008. Accessed February 14, 2023. https://resources.wfsahq.org/atotw/neonatal-anaesthesia-2-anaesthesia-for-neonates-with-abdominal-wall-defects/.

PATENT DUCTUS ARTERIOSUS

12
CHAPTER

Questions:

1. What is the primary hemodynamic consequence of patent ductus arteriosus (PDA)?
   A. Right-to-left shunt
   B. Left-to-right shunt
   C. Bidirectional shunt
   D. Obstruction of blood flow

2. Which of the following is a common sign of patent ductus arteriosus in infants?
   A. Bradycardia
   B. Cyanosis
   C. Sweating during feeding
   D. Hypertension

3. Why is nitrous oxide avoided during the anesthetic management of a patient with PDA?
   A. Causes pulmonary edema
   B. Increases left-to-right shunt
   C. Increases right-to-left shunt
   D. Promotes bronchopulmonary dysplasia

4. Which medication is commonly used in premature babies with PDA for closure of the ductus arteriosus?
   A. Nitroglycerin
   B. Indomethacin
   C. Furosemide
   D. Atropine

5. Eisenmenger syndrome is a complication of untreated PDA, leading to right-to-left shunting and cyanosis.
   A. True
   B. False

6. A 6-month-old premature neonate, born at 32 weeks of gestation, presents with symptoms indicative of PDA, including shortness of breath, sweating during feeding, fatigue, feeding difficulties, and a detected heart murmur. Diagnostic assessments confirm the presence of PDA, necessitating a scheduled catheter procedure for closure. The anesthetic plan involves the use of muscle relaxation during the procedure. Why should succinylcholine be avoided in patients with PDA?
   A. Causes pulmonary edema
   B. Induces hypothermia
   C. Leads to bronchopulmonary dysplasia
   D. Results in contracture of the ductus arteriosus

Answers:

1. **Answer B (Left-to-right shunt)**

   Patent ductus arteriosus (PDA) is characterized by a persistent opening between the aorta and pulmonary artery. In a normal heart, the ductus arteriosus allows most of the blood from the right ventricle to bypass the non-functioning fetal lungs by connecting the trunk of the pulmonary artery to the proximal descending aorta. After birth, this ductus arteriosus is expected to close. However, in PDA, it fails to close, resulting in a left-to-right shunt. In a left-to-right shunt, oxygenated blood from the left heart flows back to the lungs. This occurs because of the pressure difference between the aorta (higher pressure) and the pulmonary artery. The consequence is abnormal circulation, where oxygen-rich blood recirculates to the lungs instead of being distributed to the systemic circulation, potentially leading to various signs, symptoms, and complications associated with PDA.

2. **Answer C (Sweating during feeding)**

   One of the common signs of PDA in infants is sweating during feeding. This occurs due to increased work of breathing and cardiac effort during feeding, as the left-to-right shunt characteristic of PDA leads to abnormal blood flow patterns. The persistence of the ductus arteriosus causes oxygenated blood from the left heart to flow back to the lungs instead of being distributed to the systemic circulation. While other signs and symptoms, such as rapid breathing, shortness of breath, fatigue, feeding difficulties, failure to thrive, tachycardia, and the presence of a heart murmur, can also be associated with PDA, sweating during feeding is particularly noteworthy as it reflects the impact of the abnormal circulation on the infant's cardiovascular and respiratory systems during this specific activity.

3. **Answer B (Increases left-to-right shunt)**

   Nitrous oxide is avoided during the anesthetic management of a patient with PDA because it can increase the left-to-right shunt. In PDA, there is a persistent opening between the aorta and pulmonary artery, allowing oxygenated blood from the left heart to flow back to the lungs. Nitrous oxide can elevate pulmonary vascular resistance, exacerbating the left-to-right shunt by increasing blood flow through the pulmonary circuit. The avoidance of nitrous oxide is particularly important in the context of pulmonary hypertension, as it can further disrupt the delicate balance of blood flow and exacerbate the abnormal circulation associated with PDA. Therefore, in patients with PDA, anesthetic management aims to maintain hemodynamic stability and avoid factors that could worsen the shunting of blood between the systemic and pulmonary circulations.

4. **Answer B (Indomethacin)**

   Indomethacin, a nonsteroidal anti-inflammatory drug (NSAID), is commonly used in premature babies for the closure of the ductus arteriosus associated with PDA. NSAIDs, including indomethacin, effectively promote the closure of the ductus arteriosus by inhibiting prostaglandin synthesis, which plays a role in maintaining the patency of the ductus arteriosus. It's important to note that NSAIDs are used in premature babies, and they are not typically used for the closure of PDA in full-term babies, children, or adults. Other treatment options for PDA include surgery (catheter procedure or open-heart surgery), depending on the severity and clinical presentation.

5. **Answer A (True)**

   Eisenmenger syndrome is a complication of untreated or poorly managed congenital heart defects, including PDA. In Eisenmenger syndrome, there is a reversal of the shunt, leading to right-to-left shunting of blood. This occurs due to elevated pulmonary vascular resistance, which causes blood to flow from the right side of the heart to the left side, bypassing the lungs. The right-to-left shunting results in cyanosis, as deoxygenated blood is circulated systemically. This condition typically develops over time and is associated with progressive pulmonary vascular disease.

6. **Answer D (Results in contracture of the ductus arteriosus)**

   In patients with PDA, succinylcholine should be avoided because it can result in the contracture of the ductus arteriosus. Succinylcholine is a depolarizing neuromuscular blocking agent that causes a transient but intense muscle contraction. In the context of PDA, administration of succinylcholine can lead to a sudden contraction of the smooth muscle in the ductus arteriosus, potentially exacerbating the left-to-right shunt and complicating the cardiovascular dynamics. To achieve muscle relaxation during the catheter procedure for PDA closure in the 6-month-old premature neonate, an alternative neuromuscular blocking agent, vecuronium (0.1 mg/kg IV), should be chosen.

Recommended literature

1. Kritzmire SM, Boyer TJ, Singh P. Anesthesia For Patients With Patent Ductus Arteriosus. [Updated 2022 Aug 9]. In: StatPearls [Internet]. Treasure Island (FL): StatPearls Publishing; 2022 Jan. Available from: https://www.ncbi.nlm.nih.gov/books/NBK572063/

PEDIATRIC ANXIETY

Questions:

1. What is the most stressful procedure for pediatric patients during the perioperative period?
   A. Postoperative recovery
   B. Preoperative assessment
   C. Anesthetic induction
   D. Surgical procedure

2. Which factor is NOT associated with an increased risk of preoperative anxiety in children?
   A. Age over 6-years
   B. Temperament
   C. Limited time for preoperative preparation
   D. Multiple previous hospital admissions

3. What is a cautionary consideration for using Clonidine as a sedative premedication in pediatric patients?
   A. Hypertension
   B. Age over 6 years
   C. Grade 1 heart block
   D. Use of opioids

4. In which age group does separation anxiety typically develop?
   A. Less than 6 months
   B. 6-8 months
   C. 8-12 months
   D. More than 12 months

5. Midazolam administered intranasally (IN) at a dose of 0.3 mg/kg is associated with a stinging sensation.
   A. True
   B. False

6. A 3-year-old patient is scheduled for surgery and is currently in the preoperative preparation phase. The child has a history of multiple hospital admissions, and the parents express significant anxiety, recounting previous experiences where the child required substantial rescue analgesia, encountered postoperative nausea and vomiting (PONV), and exhibited shivering after operations. Which drug is a potential option for sedative premedication with the added benefits of reduced need for rescue analgesia, emergence agitation, PONV, and shivering?
   A. Midazolam
   B. Lorazepam
   C. Ketamine
   D. Clonidine

Answers:

1. Answer C (Anesthetic induction)

Hospitalization and surgery can induce stress and anxiety in pediatric patients. Specifically, children experience the induction of anesthesia as the most stressful procedure during the entire perioperative period. Intense levels of anxiety during anesthetic induction are linked to various adverse outcomes, including a higher risk of pain (resulting in increased opioid requirements), poor recovery, and emergence delirium. Preoperative anxiety is not only a momentary concern; it is associated with psychological problems and negative behavioral changes in the two weeks following surgery. These changes may manifest as apathy, separation anxiety, sleeping disturbances, enuresis, and aggression toward authority figures.

2. Answer A (Age over 6-years)

The factor not associated with an increased risk of preoperative anxiety in children is age over 6 years. The identified risk factors for preoperative anxiety include age under 4 years, specific temperaments such as being shy, inhibited, dependent, or withdrawn, limited time for preoperative preparation, anxious parents, previous negative experiences with anesthesia or hospitalization, and multiple previous hospital admissions. Separation anxiety typically develops at 6-8 months old, and children under 6 months can be soothed by a surrogate, like a nurse or a physician. Therefore, younger age, temperament, and past experiences are recognized as significant predictors of preoperative anxiety in pediatric patients, emphasizing the need for tailored approaches in the anesthetic plan.

3. Answer A (Hypertension)

When considering the use of Clonidine as a sedative premedication in pediatric patients, a cautionary consideration is hypertension. Clonidine, an alpha-2 agonist, offers added benefits, including a reduced need for rescue analgesia, decreased emergence agitation, postoperative nausea and vomiting (PONV), and shivering. However, caution is advised in patients with specific medical conditions, such as grade 2 or 3 heart block, hypertension, cardiovascular disease, instability, or those on digoxin.

4. Answer B (6-8 months)

Separation anxiety typically develops at 6-8 months old. During this developmental stage, infants form strong attachments to their primary caregivers, and the fear of separation becomes more pronounced. This period is characterized by heightened distress when separated from familiar individuals, and it is a normal part of emotional development.

5. Answer A (True)

Intranasal administration of Midazolam at the specified dose is known to cause a stinging sensation. Healthcare professionals must be aware of potential side effects and sensations associated with medications to ensure optimal patient care and comfort.

6. Answer D (Clonidine)

In this case, where a 3-year-old patient with a history of multiple hospital admissions is scheduled for surgery, and the parents express concerns about rescue analgesia, PONV, and shivering, Clonidine emerges as a potential option for sedative premedication. Administered orally at a dose of 3-4 mcg/kg, Clonidine is an alpha-2 agonist with added benefits, including a reduced need for rescue analgesia, diminished emergence agitation, and addressing issues such as PONV and shivering. Given the child's history of heightened responses to previous surgeries, Clonidine's ability to provide sedation while simultaneously addressing concerns related to analgesia, emergence agitation, and complications like PONV and shivering makes it a suitable choice.

Recommended literature

1. Eijlers R, Staals LM, Legerstee JS, et al. Predicting Intense Levels of Child Anxiety During Anesthesia Induction at Hospital Arrival. J Clin Psychol Med Settings. 2021;28(2):313-322.
2. Heikal S, Stuart G. Anxiolytic premedication for children. BJA Educ. 2020;20(7):220-225.
3. Dave NM. Premedication and Induction of Anaesthesia in paediatric patients. Indian J Anaesth. 2019;63(9):713-720.

PEDIATRIC PATIENT

Questions:

1. **Why is the neonatal airway described as funnel-shaped?**
   A. Enlarged nasal passages
   B. Prominent occiput
   C. Narrowest at the cricoid cartilage
   D. Presence of a U-shaped epiglottis

2. **What is the significance of sinus arrhythmia in children?**
   A. Indicates cardiac pathology
   B. Normal physiological variation
   C. Associated with bradycardia
   D. Requires immediate intervention

3. **Why is the administration of vitamin K at birth recommended for newborns?**
   A. Enhances liver function
   B. Prevents hypoglycemia
   C. Stimulates hemoglobin synthesis
   D. Prevents hemorrhagic disease

4. **What is the primary factor contributing to neonates' increased susceptibility to bradycardia during anesthesia?**
   A. Low cardiac output
   B. Vagal parasympathetic tone
   C. Thin-walled myocardium
   D. Sinus arrhythmia

5. **Rib cage movement is the primary ventilation mechanism in neonates and infants.**
   A. True
   B. False

6. **A term neonate is delivered via a caesarean section, and upon assessment, the heart rate is around 90 beats per minute (bpm). What is the first recommended treatment for this patient?**
   A. No treatment required
   B. Providing oxygen and ventilation
   C. External cardiac compression
   D. Administering atropine

Answers:

1. **Answer C (Narrowest at the cricoid cartilage)**

   The neonatal airway is described as funnel-shaped because the narrowest portion of the airway is located at the level of the cricoid cartilage. This is in contrast to the adult airway, which is described as cylindrical, with the narrowest portion being the glottis. The funnel shape of the neonatal airway has implications for airway management and intubation in pediatric patients, emphasizing the need for careful consideration and skill in navigating the unique anatomy of the pediatric airway during anesthesia procedures.

2. **Answer B (Normal physiological variation)**

   Sinus arrhythmia in children is a normal physiological variation. Unlike in adults, where irregular heart rhythms may indicate cardiac pathology, sinus arrhythmia is commonly observed in the pediatric population and is considered a normal variation. Sinus arrhythmia refers to the variation in heart rate that naturally occurs during the respiratory cycle, with the heart rate increasing during inspiration and decreasing during expiration. This phenomenon is a result of the influence of the autonomic nervous system on the heart.

3. **Answer D (Prevents hemorrhagic disease)**

   The administration of vitamin K at birth is recommended for newborns to prevent hemorrhagic disease. In the early months of life, newborns have deficient levels of vitamin K-dependent clotting factors, including factors II, VII, IX, and X, as well as impaired platelet function. These factors are crucial for the normal blood clotting process. Vitamin K is essential for the synthesis of these clotting factors in the liver. The administration of vitamin K at birth helps prevent the risk of hemorrhagic disease in newborns by ensuring the prompt and adequate production of clotting factors.

4. **Answer B (Vagal parasympathetic tone)**

   The primary factor contributing to neonates' increased susceptibility to bradycardia during anesthesia is the predominance of vagal parasympathetic tone. Neonates and infants have a higher level of vagal tone compared to sympathetic tone, making them more prone to bradycardia. Bradycardia, or a slower heart rate, is associated with an increased vagal influence on the heart. This can occur during anesthesia due to various factors, including stimulation of the vagus nerve, hypoxia, or other events that trigger the parasympathetic nervous system.

5. **Answer B (False)**

   The primary ventilation mechanism in neonates and infants is not rib cage but diaphragmatic movement. Unlike adults who rely on the "bucket handle" action of the ribs to increase tidal volume, neonates and infants have horizontal ribs that limit this type of movement. Neonates and infants predominantly use diaphragmatic ventilation, where the diaphragm contracts and moves downward, creating negative pressure in the chest and allowing air to flow into the lungs.

6. **Answer B (Providing oxygen and ventilation)**

   In the case of a term neonate delivered via caesarean section with a heart rate of around 90 beats per minute (bpm), the first recommended treatment is providing oxygen and ventilation. Bradycardia in neonates, especially when associated with hypoxia, should be addressed promptly by optimizing oxygenation and ventilation. The initial response to neonatal bradycardia focuses on ensuring adequate oxygen supply to meet the infant's metabolic demands and supporting effective ventilation. Oxygen therapy and positive-pressure ventilation, if required, aim to correct hypoxia, which is often a primary contributor to bradycardia in neonates.

Recommended literature

1. Macfarlane F. Paediatric anatomy and physiology and the basics of paediatric anaesthesia. December 16, 2005. Accessed February 2, 2023. https://resources.wfsahq.org/atotw/paediatric-anatomy-and-physiology-and-the-basics-of-paediatric-anaesthesia/

Pediatrics
PIERRE-ROBIN SEQUENCE

12
CHAPTER

Questions:

1. **What is the primary anatomical feature characterizing the Pierre-Robin Sequence (PRS)?**
   - A. Microcephaly
   - B. Micrognathia
   - C. Marfanoid appearance
   - D. Craniofacial clefting

2. **Which syndrome is NOT commonly associated with PRS?**
   - A. Stickler syndrome
   - B. Fetal Alcohol Syndrome (FAS)
   - C. Down syndrome
   - D. Velocardiofacial (DiGeorge) syndrome

3. **What is the primary cause of upper airway obstruction in PRS?**
   - A. Microcephaly
   - B. Glossoptosis
   - C. High-arched palate
   - D. Craniofacial clefting

4. **Which syndrome associated with PRS may exhibit ventricular septal defects and cognitive developmental delay?**
   - A. Stickler Syndrome
   - B. Treacher-Collins Syndrome
   - C. Velocardiofacial (DiGeorge) Syndrome
   - D. Fetal Alcohol Syndrome

5. **Tongue-lip adhesion is the initial treatment of choice for airway compromise in PRS patients.**
   - A. True
   - B. False

6. **A 2-year-old patient with PRS underwent mandibular distraction osteogenesis and has been in the Pediatric Intensive Care Unit (PICU) for two days. The patient is still intubated, and the medical team is considering extubation. What is a potential postoperative complication in PRS related to airway collapse?**
   - A. Negative pressure pulmonary edema
   - B. Surgical site infection
   - C. Gastroesophageal reflux
   - D. Cleft palate repair failure

Answers:

1. **Answer B (Micrognathia)**

    Pierre-Robin Sequence (PRS) is primarily characterized by micrognathia, which refers to mandibular hypoplasia or underdevelopment. This condition leads to glossoptosis, the posterior displacement or retraction of the tongue. The interplay of these features results in upper airway obstruction, causing breathing difficulties. While PRS can manifest as an isolated mandibular abnormality, it is often associated with other congenital disorders or syndromes, such as fetal alcohol syndrome, Stickler syndrome, Treacher-Collins syndrome, and velocardiofacial syndrome.

2. **Answer C (Down syndrome)**

    Down syndrome is not commonly associated with PRS. PRS, characterized by micrognathia leading to glossoptosis and upper airway obstruction, is more frequently linked with syndromes such as Fetal Alcohol Syndrome, Stickler Syndrome, Treacher-Collins Syndrome, and Velocardiofacial (DiGeorge) Syndrome.

3. **Answer B (Glossoptosis)**

    The primary cause of upper airway obstruction in the PRS is glossoptosis, which refers to the posterior displacement or retraction of the tongue. In PRS, micrognathia leads to glossoptosis, resulting in the tongue falling toward the throat. This anatomical phenomenon causes breathing problems due to upper airway obstruction. While other features such as a high-arched palate and craniofacial clefting may be present in PRS, it is the glossoptosis that directly contributes to respiratory distress and upper airway obstruction in affected individuals.

4. **Answer D (Fetal Alcohol Syndrome)**

    The syndrome associated with PRS that may exhibit ventricular septal defects and cognitive developmental delay is Fetal Alcohol Syndrome (FAS). FAS is characterized by various abnormalities, including microcephaly, maxillary hypoplasia, micrognathia, short neck, ventricular septal defects, cognitive developmental delay, and hyperactivity. Ventricular septal defects indicate structural heart abnormalities and cognitive developmental delay is a common feature of Fetal Alcohol Syndrome. The anesthetic considerations for patients with FAS include potential difficulty in ventilation and intubation, the need for preoperative echocardiography, and consideration of subacute bacterial endocarditis prophylaxis, given the risk of congenital heart defects.

5. **Answer B (False)**

    Historically, tongue-lip adhesion was indeed considered the initial treatment of choice for airway compromise in PRS patients when the tongue was large and posteriorly placed, leading to respiratory compromise. However, the current treatment of choice is mandibular distraction osteogenesis (MDO). MDO involves gradually lengthening the mandible, providing more space for the tongue, and alleviating airway obstruction. This procedure can be performed from the neonatal period up to the teenage years. Placing the child in a prone position may be attempted initially to relieve obstruction. The shift towards MDO has reduced the reliance on tongue-lip adhesion as the primary intervention for PRS-related airway compromise.

6. **Answer A (Negative pressure pulmonary edema)**

    The risk of acute postoperative airway obstruction is heightened in PRS, leading to negative intrathoracic pressure during inspiration and subsequent pulmonary edema. Vigilance is essential to prevent hypoxia and potentially fatal outcomes. PRS patients, susceptible to respiratory complications, require careful postoperative management, including periodic release of the mouth retractor to minimize the risk of tongue edema. Emphasizing nonopioid analgesics, reducing opioid doses, and continuous monitoring with pulse oximetry are integral components of postoperative care to promptly identify and address any respiratory challenges.

Recommended literature

1. Hegde N, Singh A. Anesthetic Consideration In Pierre-Robin Sequence. [Updated 2022 Jul 26]. In: StatPearls [Internet]. Treasure Island (FL): StatPearls Publishing; 2022 Jan. Available from: https://www.ncbi.nlm.nih.gov/books/NBK576442/
2. Cladis F, Kumar A, Grunwaldt L, Otteson T, Ford M, Losee JE. Pierre Robin Sequence: a perioperative review. Anesth Analg. 2014;119(2):400-412.

PREMATURE INFANT

Questions:

1. **What is the definition of prematurity?**
   A. Live birth before 32 weeks of gestational age
   B. Live birth before 37 weeks of gestational age
   C. Live birth before 28 weeks of gestational age
   D. Live birth before 40 weeks of gestational age

2. **Which respiratory condition is common in premature infants due to insufficient surfactant production until 35 weeks?**
   A. Bronchopulmonary dysplasia
   B. Respiratory distress syndrome
   C. Chronic obstructive pulmonary disease
   D. Cystic fibrosis

3. **Why are premature infants prone to hypothermia?**
   A. Low body surface area (BSA)
   B. Incomplete suppression of hepatic glucose production
   C. Altered thermoregulation and limited subcutaneous fat
   D. Hyperactive sweat glands

4. **What is a known risk factor for premature delivery?**
   A. Singleton pregnancy
   B. Smoking
   C. An interval of over 6 months between pregnancies
   D. Late prenatal care initiation

5. **Postoperative apnea monitoring for 24-48 hours after surgery (unless the infant is > 50-60 weeks postmenstrual age) is recommended for premature infants.**
   A. True
   B. False

6. **A premature infant weighing 1.42 kg at birth is presented for surgery due to intestinal atresia. The infant has been closely monitored in the neonatal intensive care unit (NICU) since birth. The small size and weight of the infant present unique challenges in anesthesia and surgical care. What is the primary goal of anesthesia in premature infants during surgery?**
   A. Achieve deep anesthesia quickly
   B. Monitor and titrate to the desired effect
   C. Rapidly reverse neuromuscular blockade
   D. Rapid extubation post-surgery

Answers:

1. **Answer B (Live birth before 37 weeks of gestational age)**

   Prematurity is defined as a live birth occurring before 37 weeks of gestational age. It is further classified into moderate to late preterm (32-37 weeks), very preterm (28-32 weeks), and extremely preterm (less than 28 weeks). This classification is crucial for assessing the degree of prematurity and understanding the associated risks. Premature infants often face anatomical, physiological, and pharmacological challenges due to incomplete development of vital organs and systems.

2. **Answer B (Respiratory distress syndrome)**

   Premature infants commonly experience respiratory distress syndrome (RDS) due to insufficient surfactant production until approximately 35 weeks of gestational age. Surfactant is a substance that prevents the collapse of the alveoli in the lungs, facilitating proper breathing. In premature infants, the underdeveloped lungs often lack sufficient surfactant, leading to difficulties in maintaining adequate respiratory function. This condition is characterized by rapid desaturation, as the lungs struggle to inflate properly, resulting in persistent pulmonary hypertension and an increased risk of postoperative apnea. While bronchopulmonary dysplasia is another respiratory condition associated with prematurity, RDS specifically correlates with the insufficient production of surfactant in premature infants.

3. **Answer C (Altered thermoregulation and limited subcutaneous fat)**

   Premature infants are prone to hypothermia due to altered thermoregulation and limited subcutaneous fat. Unlike full-term infants, premature babies have underdeveloped mechanisms to regulate their body temperature. They possess a higher surface area-to-body mass ratio, making them more susceptible to heat loss. Additionally, their limited subcutaneous fat serves as inadequate insulation. Premature infants lack the necessary physiological adaptations to maintain body warmth, leading to challenges in temperature regulation. It is crucial to provide external support, such as incubators or warmers, to help these infants maintain normothermia and reduce the risk of hypothermia-related complications.

4. **Answer B (Smoking)**

   Smoking and drug use are recognized risk factors that can significantly increase the likelihood of delivering a baby before completing a full-term pregnancy. Other risk factors include a previous premature birth, multiple pregnancies (e.g., twins, triplets), problems with the uterus, cervix, or placenta, and chronic conditions such as hypertension and diabetes. It's important to note that while these risk factors contribute to the overall understanding of premature delivery, many women who experience premature birth may not have identifiable risk factors, emphasizing the complexity of this issue.

5. **Answer A (True)**

   Postoperative apnea monitoring for 24-48 hours after surgery is recommended for premature infants unless the infant is > 50-60 weeks postmenstrual age and has no other risk factors for apnea. Postoperative apnea monitoring is crucial to detect and manage any apneic episodes that may occur after surgery, allowing timely intervention if needed. However, as infants mature and reach a certain postmenstrual age, the risk of apnea decreases, and monitoring may be adjusted accordingly based on individual clinical assessments and the absence of risk factors.

6. **Answer B (Monitor and titrate to desired effect)**

   Premature infants, especially those with low birth weight, pose unique challenges in anesthesia and surgical care. Anesthetic considerations for premature infants are grounded in their physiological immaturity, potential congenital disorders, and heightened sensitivity to anesthetic drugs. The primary goal of anesthesia in this pediatric patient population is to monitor and titrate anesthetics to the desired effect while carefully assessing and managing the cardiorespiratory status. Achieving an appropriate depth of anesthesia is crucial to facilitate the surgery while avoiding complications, and this goal aligns with the overarching principle that the benefits of adequate anesthesia and analgesia must outweigh the risks of cardiorespiratory depression. Rapidly reversing neuromuscular blockade may be necessary in certain situations, but the emphasis is on titrating anesthesia for optimal surgical conditions and patient safety.

Recommended literature

1. Macrae J, Ng E, Whyte H. Anaesthesia for premature infants. BJa Education. 2021;21(9):355-363.
2. Taneja B, Srivastava V, Saxena KN. Physiological and anaesthetic considerations for the preterm neonate undergoing surgery. J Neonatal Surg. 2012;1(1):14.

PYLORIC STENOSIS

12
CHAPTER

Questions:

1. **Which age range is typically associated with the onset of pyloric stenosis symptoms?**
   A. Birth to 1 week
   B. 2 to 12 weeks
   C. 3 to 6 months
   D. 1 to 2 years

2. **What are the signs and symptoms of pyloric stenosis?**
   A. Persistent hunger
   B. Stomach contractions
   C. Weight problems
   D. All of the above

3. **What is the primary electrolyte abnormality associated with pyloric stenosis?**
   A. Hypernatremia
   B. Hypochloremia
   C. Hyperkalemia
   D. Hypermagnesemia

4. **What is the primary complication associated with persistent vomiting in pyloric stenosis?**
   A. Respiratory distress syndrome
   B. Dehydration and hypovolemia
   C. Gastroesophageal reflux disease
   D. Cardiac arrhythmias

5. **Bottle feeding is a risk factor associated with pyloric stenosis.**
   A. True
   B. False

6. **A 6-week-old infant is presented for surgery to address pyloric stenosis. The infant's clinical history includes projectile vomiting after feedings, dehydration, and failure to thrive. Additionally, there are signs of metabolic alkalosis and electrolyte abnormalities, specifically hypochloremia, hyponatremia, and hypokalemia. What is the primary goal of preoperative management in pyloric stenosis?**
   A. Immediate surgery
   B. Correction of dehydration and electrolyte abnormalities
   C. Symptomatic relief
   D. Weight gain

Answers:

1. Answer B (2 to 12 weeks)

Pyloric stenosis, or infantile hypertrophic pyloric stenosis, is a condition characterized by abnormal thickening of the pylorus muscles in the stomach, resulting in gastric outlet obstruction. Typically, symptoms of pyloric stenosis are observed between 2 and 12 weeks of age. During this period, patients commonly present with projectile vomiting after feedings, dehydration, and failure to thrive.

2. Answer D (All of the above)

The signs and symptoms of pyloric stenosis typically manifest within 3-5 weeks after birth and encompass a combination of clinical features. Infants with pyloric stenosis commonly experience bile-free projectile vomiting after each feeding, which is a distinctive characteristic of the condition. Persistent hunger is observed as infants struggle to feed effectively due to gastric outlet obstruction. Stomach contractions, manifested as visible peristalsis in the left upper quadrant from left to right, indicate hypertrophy and hyperplasia of the pyloric muscles. Changes in bowel movements may also occur. Additionally, weight problems, such as failure to thrive and inadequate weight gain, contribute to the clinical presentation of pyloric stenosis.

3. Answer B (Hypochloremia)

The primary electrolyte abnormality associated with pyloric stenosis is hypochloremia. Vomiting in pyloric stenosis leads to the loss of gastric hydrochloric acid, resulting in decreased chloride levels. This condition, along with hyponatremia and hypokalemia, is part of the electrolyte disturbances caused by persistent vomiting. It is essential to correct these electrolyte imbalances preoperatively before general anesthesia and surgery.

4. Answer B (Dehydration and hypovolemia)

The primary complications associated with persistent vomiting in pyloric stenosis are dehydration and hypovolemia. Vomiting leads to a loss of fluids and electrolytes, causing dehydration and a decrease in blood volume. Hypovolemia can result, leading to various systemic issues. To address this complication, preoperative management focuses on correcting dehydration and hypochloremic alkalosis through the administration of IV fluids.

5. Answer A (True)

Bottle feeding is identified as a risk factor associated with pyloric stenosis. Among the various risk factors listed, which include first-born male children, preterm birth, caesarean section, family history, smoking during pregnancy, early antibiotic use (e.g., erythromycin to treat whooping cough), and being White and Hispanic children, bottle feeding is highlighted as a factor that may contribute to the development of pyloric stenosis. While not all infants who are bottle-fed will develop pyloric stenosis, it is considered one of the factors that may increase the risk of this condition.

6. Answer B (Correction of dehydration and electrolyte abnormalities)

The primary goal of preoperative management in pyloric stenosis is the correction of dehydration and electrolyte abnormalities. In this case, the infant needs stabilization before surgery, and the focus is on correcting dehydration and hypochloremic alkalosis with intravenous fluids. The danger associated with pyloric stenosis arises from dehydration and electrolyte disturbances rather than the underlying problem. Correcting these imbalances is typically accomplished within 24-48 hours before surgery, ensuring the infant is more stable for the surgical intervention. Immediate surgery is not the primary goal, as stabilization through fluid and electrolyte correction is essential for safe perioperative management. Symptomatic relief and weight gain are important but are secondary to the immediate correction of electrolyte imbalances to ensure the infant's well-being during surgery and recovery.

Recommended literature

1. Craig R, Deeley A. Anaesthesia for pyloromyotomy. BJA Educ. 2018;18(6):173-177.
2. Pollard BJ, Kitchen G. Handbook of Clinical Anaesthesia. 4th ed. Taylor & Francis group; 2018. Chapter 24 Paediatrics, Lomas B.
3. Houck PJ. PYLORIC STENOSIS. In: Houck PJ, Haché M, Sun LS. eds. Handbook of Pediatric Anesthesia. McGraw Hill; 2015. Accessed February 14, 2023. https://accessanesthesiology.mhmedical.com/content.aspx?bookid=1189&sectionid=70363285

Questions:

1. What is the recommended Cobb angle threshold for surgical intervention in scoliosis?

    A. 30°–35°

    B. 40°–45°

    C. 45°–50°

    D. 50°–55°

2. Which type of scoliosis is often associated with conditions such as Goldenhar syndrome or spina bifida?

    A. Idiopathic scoliosis

    B. Neuromuscular scoliosis

    C. Congenital scoliosis

    D. Myopathic scoliosis

3. What is the main factor contributing to increased intraoperative blood loss in neuromuscular scoliosis compared to idiopathic scoliosis?

    A. Anesthesia techniques

    B. Surgical complexity

    C. Patient age

    D. Type of scoliosis

4. What is the primary indication for using serial full-body casting in the non-operative management of scoliosis?

    A. Adult scoliosis

    B. Adolescent scoliosis

    C. Infantile scoliosis

    D. Neuromuscular scoliosis

5. MRI is the primary diagnostic method for visualizing the curvature of the spine in scoliosis.

    A. True

    B. False

6. A 20-year-old female with a history of scoliosis is presented for surgery due to worsening deformity and axial back pain. Preoperative investigations were unremarkable, indicating no significant comorbidities or abnormalities. The surgical procedure involved the insertion of pedicle screws, and an hour and 15 minutes into the procedure, a critical event occurred. The end-tidal carbon dioxide (ETCO2) suddenly dropped from 31 to 19 and then to 0 within a few seconds, the HR suddenly dropped to 0, and BP was 28/28 mmHg. SpO2 dropped abruptly from 100% to 86%. The surgery was promptly stopped, and the patient was turned supine. Cardiopulmonary resuscitation (CPR) was initiated immediately, and return of spontaneous circulation (ROSC) was achieved after 10 minutes. What is a potential complication associated with the prone position during scoliosis surgery?

    A. Venous air embolism

    B. Intraoperative cardiac arrest

    C. Postoperative respiratory failure

    D. Venous thromboembolism

Answers:

1. Answer C (45°–50°)

The recommended Cobb angle threshold for surgical intervention in scoliosis is typically set at greater than 45°–50°. The Cobb angle, measured from a standing anteroposterior radiograph of the spine, represents the angle formed by lines drawn parallel to the endplates of the most tilted vertebrae in the curve. Surgical treatment is advised when the Cobb angle exceeds this range, as higher degrees of curvature are associated with an increased risk of pulmonary and cardiovascular dysfunction. This threshold provides a guideline for determining the appropriateness of surgical intervention to correct the spinal curvature and mitigate potential complications. However, the decision ultimately considers individual patient factors and overall health.

2. Answer C (Congenital scoliosis)

Scoliosis, characterized by lateral curvature of the spine, vertebral body rotation, and angulation of the rib, can be classified as either structural or non-structural. Congenital scoliosis may present at any age and results from either a failure of vertebral segmentation (a bar) or failure of formation (a hemivertebra). It is noteworthy that congenital scoliosis is frequently part of a more generalized condition, such as Goldenhar syndrome or spina bifida, and may be accompanied by abnormalities in renal, cardiac, respiratory, or neurological systems. This type of scoliosis is distinct from acquired scoliosis, which is mainly idiopathic. Infantile onset idiopathic scoliosis, occurring before the age of 8 years, carries a serious prognosis and, if left untreated, may lead to cardiopulmonary failure in middle age.

3. Answer D (Type of scoliosis)

The main factor contributing to increased intraoperative blood loss in neuromuscular scoliosis compared to idiopathic scoliosis is the type of scoliosis. Neuromuscular scoliosis has been associated with higher intraoperative blood loss compared to idiopathic scoliosis. This increased blood loss is likely attributed to the underlying neuromuscular conditions affecting the patient, such as cerebral palsy, spinal cord injury, or spinal muscular atrophy, which can lead to altered vascular dynamics and increased bleeding tendencies. While factors like anesthesia techniques, surgical complexity, and patient age can influence blood loss to some extent, the fundamental contributor in this context is the specific type of scoliosis.

4. Answer C (Infantile scoliosis)

The primary indication for using serial full-body casting in the non-operative management of scoliosis is infantile scoliosis. This method involves the application of successive casts to gradually correct the spinal curvature. Notably, the casting process requires general anesthesia and is typically performed every 2-3 months. This approach is particularly effective in managing infantile scoliosis by allowing continuous correction of the developing spine. Other types of scoliosis, such as adolescent or neuromuscular scoliosis, may require different non-operative interventions based on their specific characteristics and underlying causes.

5. Answer B (False)

The primary diagnostic method for visualizing the curvature of the spine in scoliosis is an X-ray, not an MRI. While both imaging modalities are valuable in healthcare, X-rays are the preferred initial tool for diagnosing scoliosis. X-rays provide detailed images of the bony structures, allowing for accurate assessment of the spinal curvature and measurement of the Cobb angle, which is essential in determining the severity of scoliosis. Clinical examinations, including physical and neurological assessments, complement imaging in the overall diagnostic process.

6. Answer A (Venous air embolism)

A potential complication associated with the prone position during scoliosis surgery is Venous air embolism (VAE). The patient's sudden drop in end-tidal carbon dioxide (ETCO2), bradycardia, hypotension, and a drop in oxygen saturation is indicative of a severe event such as a venous air embolism. The prone position, especially when the operative site is above the level of the heart, can increase the risk of venous entrainment of air. Studies have highlighted that the prone surgical position, along with gravity gradients, can lead to air entry into the venous circulation. This air can then progress to the right ventricle and pulmonary artery, causing symptoms resembling a pulmonary embolism. The prompt recognition of symptoms and collaboration between orthopedic surgeons, anesthesiologists, and surgical nurses is crucial for early diagnosis and intervention to save the patient's life in such critical situations.

Recommended literature

1. Yao FS, Hemmings HC, Malhotra V, Fong J. 2021. Yao & Artusio's Anesthesiology: Problem-Oriented Patient Management. Chapter 58 – scoliosis (9th edition). Wolters Kluwer Health/Lippincott Williams & Wilkins.
2. Pollard BJ, Kitchen, G. Handbook of Clinical Anaesthesia. Fourth Edition. CRC Press. 2018. 978-1-4987-6289-2.
3. Gadsden, J., & Jones, D. (2011). Anesthesiology Oral Board Flash Cards. McGraw-Hill Education.
4. Gambrall MA. Anesthetic implications for surgical correction of scoliosis. AANA J. 2007;75(4):277-285.

STATUS EPILEPTICUS IN PEDIATRIC PATIENTS

12
CHAPTER

Questions:

1. **What is the primary defining criterion for status epilepticus?**
   A. Presence of convulsive movements
   B. Continuous seizure activity for more than 30 minutes
   C. Two or more sequential seizures with full recovery of consciousness
   D. Two or more sequential seizures without full recovery of consciousness between seizures

2. **Which of the following is NOT an etiological factor for status epilepticus in children?**
   A. Metabolic Abnormalities
   B. Systemic infection
   C. Smoking
   D. Low concentration of anti-epileptic drugs

3. **Which compensatory mechanism is NOT associated with the first stage of status epilepticus?**
   A. Massive catecholamine release
   B. Hypertension
   C. Raised cardiac output
   D. Decreased central venous pressure

4. **Which of the following is NOT a potential complication of status epilepticus?**
   A. Hypoxia
   B. Hypernatremia
   C. Cerebral edema
   D. Rhabdomyolysis

5. **Status epilepticus can present as non-convulsive, characterized by prolonged seizure activity identifiable through epileptiform discharges on EEG, and it may also involve changes in behavior or cognition in certain patients.**
   A. True
   B. False

6. **A 9-year-old boy has been brought to the emergency department with signs of unresponsiveness and tonic-clonic movements of the extremities. The clinical presentation raises concerns about the possibility of status epilepticus, with the seizure activity having persisted for approximately 15 minutes. Given the situation's urgency, prompt and effective pharmacological intervention is imperative. In the management of status epilepticus, what is the primary pharmacological intervention in the initial stages?**
   A. Thiopental
   B. Midazolam
   C. Phenytoin
   D. Benzodiazepines

Answers:

1. Answer D (Two or more sequential seizures without full recovery of consciousness between seizures)

Status epilepticus is defined as either continuous seizure activity lasting more than 30 minutes or two or more sequential seizures without full recovery of consciousness between seizures. This means that if a patient experiences either continuous seizures for more than 30 minutes or has two or more seizures without regaining consciousness between them, it meets the criteria for status epilepticus.

2. Answer C (Smoking)

Smoking is not identified as an etiological factor for status epilepticus in children among the provided options. The listed factors include acute causes such as stroke, metabolic abnormalities, hypoxia, systemic infection, anoxia, trauma, traumatic brain injury, drug overdose, CNS infection, and CNS hemorrhage. Chronic factors encompass inheritance tendency, low concentration of anti-epileptic drugs, structural changes to the brain due to trauma or space-occupying lesions like tumors or strokes, and idiopathic cases where the exact cause is unknown.

3. Answer D (Decreased central venous pressure)

In the first stage of status epilepticus, compensatory mechanisms are activated to address the increased cerebral metabolism, blood flow, and glucose concentration. The compensatory mechanisms associated with this stage include massive catecholamine release, raised cardiac output, hypertension, and increased central venous pressure. These responses aim to maintain adequate perfusion to the brain and other vital organs. However, the decreased central venous pressure is not typically associated with the compensatory mechanisms in the initial stage of status epilepticus.

4. Answer B (Hypernatremia)

The potential complications of status epilepticus are outlined after the failure of compensatory mechanisms, typically occurring after 30-60 minutes. The complications include hypoxia, hypoglycemia, increased intracranial pressure, cerebral edema, hyponatremia, potassium imbalance, evolving metabolic acidosis, consumptive coagulopathy, rhabdomyolysis, and multi-organ failure. However, "hypernatremia" is not one of the potential complications associated with the failure of compensatory mechanisms in the context of status epilepticus.

5. Answer A (True)

Status epilepticus can manifest as non-convulsive, characterized by prolonged seizure activity observed through epileptiform discharges on an EEG. In this form, patients may experience alterations in behavior or cognition without the overt tonic, clonic, or tonic-clonic movements seen in convulsive presentations. This diverse range of manifestations highlights the importance of recognizing both convulsive and non-convulsive forms of status epilepticus for accurate diagnosis and appropriate management.

6. Answer D (Benzodiazepines)

In the acute management of status epilepticus, intravenous benzodiazepines are considered the primary pharmacological intervention in the initial stages. This preference is based on their ability to provide rapid seizure control. It is important to note that, when possible, intravenous administration is the preferred route. However, various formulations, including buccal, intranasal, intramuscular, and rectal, are available for administration if intravenous access cannot be rapidly established.

Recommended literature

1. Glauser T, Shinnar S, Gloss D, et al. Evidence-Based Guideline: Treatment of Convulsive Status Epilepticus in Children and Adults: Report of the Guideline Committee of the American Epilepsy Society. Epilepsy Curr. 2016;16(1):48-61.
2. Betjemann JP, Lowenstein DH. Status epilepticus in adults. Lancet Neurol. 2015;14(6):615-624.
3. Perks A, Cheema S, Mohanraj R. Anaesthesia and epilepsy. BJA: British Journal of Anaesthesia. 2012;108(4):562-71.
4. Barakat, A.R., Mallory, S., 2011. Anaesthesia and childhood epilepsy. Continuing Education in Anaesthesia Critical Care & Pain 11, 93-98.

Pediatrics
STRABISMUS SURGERY

Questions:

1. **What is the most common ophthalmic surgery in pediatric patients?**
   A. Cataract surgery
   B. Retinal detachment surgery
   C. Glaucoma surgery
   D. Strabismus surgery

2. **What is the primary purpose of strabismus surgery?**
   A. Improve cosmetic appearance
   B. Correct refractive errors
   C. Adjust extraocular muscles to correct eye misalignment
   D. Treat amblyopia

3. **Which of the following is a risk factor for strabismus?**
   A. High maternal age
   B. Smoking during pregnancy
   C. Gestational diabetes
   D. Bottle-feeding

4. **What is a common issue with the airway during strabismus surgery related to the microscope's position?**
   A. Difficult intubation
   B. Inability to ventilate
   C. Restricted access
   D. Aspiration risk

5. **Infantile strabismus needs early surgery before the child reaches the age of 1 year for the best visual outcome.**
   A. True
   B. False

6. **A 6-year-old patient is scheduled for strabismus surgery due to presenting with complaints of diplopia, loss of stereopsis, headache, discomfort while reading, fatigue, amblyopia, and psychosocial issues affecting normal eye contact. The surgical intervention aims to correct the misalignment of the eyes. Which reflex should an anesthesiologist be aware of during strabismus surgery?**
   A. Gag reflex
   B. Corneal reflex
   C. Oculocardiac reflex
   D. Pupillary reflex

Answers:

1. **Answer D (Strabismus surgery)**

   Strabismus surgery is the most common ophthalmic surgery in pediatric patients. Strabismus, the misalignment of the eyes, occurs in 3-5% of children worldwide. The surgical intervention involves adjustments to the extraocular muscles to correct the misalignment.

2. **Answer C (Adjust extraocular muscles to correct eye misalignment)**

   The primary purpose of strabismus surgery is to adjust the extraocular muscles to correct the misalignment of the eyes. Strabismus surgery involves various procedures such as tightening, lengthening, transposing, or shortening the eye muscles to achieve proper alignment. Strabismus itself results from an imbalance in extraocular muscle function, leading to the transmission of two different images (one from each eye) to the brain. This misalignment results in a loss of visual depth. In children, the brain may suppress the image from the weaker eye, contributing to amblyopia, characterized by decreased vision in an otherwise healthy eye, commonly known as a "lazy eye."

3. **Answer B (Smoking during pregnancy)**

   Strabismus has several associated risk factors, and smoking during pregnancy is one of them. Other risk factors include premature birth, low birth weight, family history of strabismus, Down syndrome, cerebral palsy, and syndromes with craniofacial dysostosis.

4. **Answer C (Restricted access)**

   A common issue with the airway during strabismus surgery, related to the microscope's position, is restricted access. The microscope's position may make the airway less accessible for the anesthesiologist, posing a challenge during the surgical procedure. The anesthesia team must be aware of this potential issue and plan accordingly to ensure proper airway management and patient safety during strabismus surgery.

5. **Answer A (True)**

   Infantile strabismus needs early surgery, ideally between 6-12 months, for the best visual outcome. The prognosis is considered good if the correction is performed as early as possible. Early intervention is crucial to prevent complications such as amblyopia, which can result from the brain suppressing the image from the weaker eye due to the misalignment. Therefore, timely correction through surgery is recommended to optimize visual development in children with infantile strabismus.

6. **Answer C (Oculocardiac reflex)**

   The anesthesiologist should be particularly aware of the oculocardiac reflex (OCR) during strabismus surgery. The OCR is most commonly triggered by traction of the extraocular muscles, making strabismus surgery a procedure with a high risk for the development of this reflex. The OCR is characterized by a decrease in heart rate by greater than 20% following pressure on the eye, and it is mediated by the connection between the ophthalmic branch of the trigeminal nerve and the vagus nerve. In strabismus surgery, manipulation of the eye muscles can activate the OCR, leading to bradycardia, arrhythmias, or, in extreme cases, cardiac arrest. Given the reported high incidence of OCR during pediatric ophthalmologic surgery, especially strabismus surgery, it is crucial for the anesthesiologist to monitor and manage this reflex to ensure the safety of the patient during the procedure.

Recommended literature

1. Lewis H, James I. Update on anaesthesia for paediatric ophthalmic surgery. BJA Educ. 2021;21(1):32-38.
2. Chua AW, Chua MJ, Leung H, Kam PC. Anaesthetic considerations for strabismus surgery in children and adults. Anaesthesia and Intensive Care. 2020;48(4):277-288.
3. Pollard BJ, Kitchen G. Handbook of Clinical Anaesthesia. 4th ed. Taylor & Francis group; 2018. Chapter 18 Ophthalmic surgery, Slater RM.

Pediatric
TETRALOGY OF FALLOT

Questions:

1. **What is the primary pathophysiological mechanism responsible for cyanosis in Tetralogy of Fallot?**
   A. Left-to-right shunt
   B. Right-to-left shunt
   C. Pulmonary artery dilation
   D. Aortic valve stenosis

2. **Which of the following is NOT a component of Tetralogy of Fallot?**
   A. Ventricular septal defect (VSD)
   B. Pulmonary stenosis
   C. Atrial septal defect (ASD)
   D. Right ventricular hypertrophy

3. **What is the primary goal during the management of tet spells in a patient with Tetralogy of Fallot?**
   A. Increase systemic vascular resistance
   B. Reduce oxygen saturation
   C. Induce permissive hypercapnia
   D. Decrease cardiac output

4. **When does surgical repair of Tetralogy of Fallot typically take place?**
   A. At birth
   B. During adolescence
   C. In the first year following birth
   D. At age 10

5. **Infundibular muscle spasm is the primary cause of tet spells in Tetralogy of Fallot.**
   A. True
   B. False

6. **A 6-month-old infant diagnosed with Tetralogy of Fallot (TOF) undergoes ventricular septal defect repair. Post-induction, the infant develops tet spells, presenting with cyanosis and a drop in peripheral saturation. Following the management protocol, the anesthesia team administers 100% oxygen, checks the endotracheal tube position, deepens anesthesia with a morphine bolus, provides a fluid bolus, and initiates vasopressor therapy (phenylephrine) and β-blockers (propranolol). Which position might be adopted to temporarily reverse the right-to-left shunt?**
   A. Supine position
   B. Head-down position
   C. Knee-to-chest flexion position
   D. Left lateral decubitus position

Answers:

1. Answer B (Right-to-left shunt)

The primary pathophysiological mechanism responsible for cyanosis in the Tetralogy of Fallot is a right-to-left shunt. This occurs due to the combination of a non-restrictive ventricular septal defect (VSD) and pulmonary stenosis. The VSD allows the mixing of oxygenated and deoxygenated blood, while pulmonary stenosis results in decreased blood flow to the lungs. As a result, deoxygenated blood is preferentially directed to the systemic circulation, causing cyanosis, particularly during situations of increased oxygen demand.

2. Answer C (Atrial septal defect (ASD))

TOF is characterized by a combination of a VSD, pulmonary stenosis, right ventricular hypertrophy, and an overriding aorta. The VSD allows the mixing of oxygenated and deoxygenated blood; pulmonary stenosis leads to decreased blood flow to the lungs, right ventricular hypertrophy results from an increased workload, and the overriding aorta is positioned above the VSD. The presence of an ASD is not typically part of the classic tetralogy. However, it's important to note that combining TOF with an ASD or patent foramen ovale would result in a more complex condition known as the "pentalogy of Fallot".

3. Answer A (Increase systemic vascular resistance)

The primary goal during the management of tet spells in a patient with Tetralogy of Fallot (TOF) is to increase systemic vascular resistance. Tet spells, characterized by acute hypoxia, are triggered by events leading to decreased oxygen saturation or reduced systemic vascular resistance, resulting in an increased right-to-left shunt through the VSD. Interventions aim to improve oxygenation, enhance cardiac output, and reduce infundibular spasm to manage tet spells. Increasing systemic vascular resistance helps counteract the right-to-left shunt, mitigating hypoxia and improving overall hemodynamics in patients with TOF.

4. Answer C (In the first year following birth)

Surgical repair of TOF typically takes place in the first year following birth, usually around 3-6 months of age. The surgical procedure involves patch closure of the VSD to separate the pulmonary and systemic circulation. Additionally, there is an enlargement of the right ventricular outflow tract (RVOT) to relieve right ventricular outflow tract obstruction (RVOTO). This intervention aims to address the anatomical abnormalities associated with TOF, allowing for improved blood flow and oxygenation. Early surgical intervention is crucial for improving long-term outcomes and preventing complications in individuals with TOF.

5. Answer A (True)

Infundibular muscle spasm, particularly during distress or increased oxygen demand, results in dynamic RVOTO. This dynamic obstruction, when added to any fixed RVOTO, increases the right-to-left shunt fraction through the VSD. The culmination of these factors leads to profound hypoxemia during episodes commonly known as 'cyanotic spells' or tet spells. Managing these spells involves interventions to alleviate infundibular spasms, increase systemic vascular resistance, and enhance oxygenation to prevent life-threatening complications associated with severe hypoxemia.

6. Answer C (Knee-to-Chest Flexion Position)

In managing tet spells during anesthesia in TOF, adopting the knee-to-chest flexion position is crucial to temporarily reverse the right-to-left shunt. This position increases systemic vascular resistance, reduces the infundibular spasm, and enhances oxygenation, aligning with the established goals of managing tet spells. The comprehensive approach, including administration of 100% oxygen, checking endotracheal tube position, deepening anesthesia with a morphine bolus, providing a fluid bolus, and initiating vasopressor therapy (phenylephrine) and β-blockers (propranolol), collectively addresses the underlying causes of TOF-related cyanotic spells. The knee-to-chest flexion position plays a pivotal role in optimizing hemodynamics and ensuring the infant's safety during VSD repair.

Recommended literature

1. Wilson R, Ross O, Griksaitis MJ. Tetralogy of Fallot. BJA Educ. 2019;19(11):362-369.
2. Pollard BJ, Kitchen G. Handbook of Clinical Anaesthesia. 4th ed. Taylor & Francis group; 2018. Chapter 2 Cardiovascular system, Tully RP and Turner R.

Pediatric
TONSILLECTOMY

12
CHAPTER

Questions:

1. **What is the most common indication for tonsillectomy in children?**
   A. Recurrent otitis media
   B. Chronic tonsillitis
   C. Upper airway obstruction
   D. Adenoid hypertrophy

2. **Which of the following is NOT an absolute indication for tonsillectomy?**
   A. Peritonsillar abscess unresponsive to medical management
   B. Recurrent tonsillitis with febrile convulsions
   C. > 5 episodes of tonsillitis in one year
   D. Upper airway obstruction and dysphagia

3. **What is NOT a relative contraindication for tonsillectomy?**
   A. Anemia
   B. Symptoms < 1 year
   C. Bleeding diathesis
   D. Acute infection

4. **What is a potential complication of post-tonsillectomy bleeding that may occur in the recovery or hours later?**
   A. Pulmonary edema
   B. Mandibular Dislocation
   C. Cardiac arrhythmia
   D. Aspiration

5. **The use of a laryngeal mask airway (LMA) is contraindicated for airway management in tonsillectomy.**
   A. True
   B. False

6. **The patient, one day post-tonsillectomy, presents with signs of bleeding, demonstrating a critical need for immediate attention. The patient is hypovolemic and requires fluid resuscitation before any further intervention. A rapid sequence induction plan is initiated to ensure quick and secure intubation, which is crucial for protecting the airway during induction. What position should be preferred during induction in a patient with post-tonsillectomy bleeding?**
   A. Left lateral position
   B. Supine position
   C. Head-up tilt
   D. Head-down tilt

Answers:

1. Answer C (Upper airway obstruction)

Tonsillectomy is commonly performed in children with upper airway obstruction, which can manifest as symptoms like nasal obstruction, obstructive sleep apnea (OSA), and dysphagia. The most common indication for tonsillectomy in children is upper airway obstruction, accounting for a significant percentage of cases (66%). This is often due to the enlargement of the palatine tonsils, leading to symptoms that affect breathing, swallowing, and overall airway function. While recurrent infections (such as chronic tonsillitis) are also indications for tonsillectomy, they are not as prevalent as upper airway obstruction in the pediatric population.

2. Answer C (> 5 episodes of tonsillitis in one year)

The absolute indications for tonsillectomy include upper airway obstruction, dysphagia, OSA, peritonsillar abscess unresponsive to medical management, recurrent tonsillitis with associated febrile convulsions, and the need for biopsy to confirm tissue pathology. While recurrent tonsillitis indicates tonsillectomy, having more than five episodes in one year is not an absolute indication. It is considered a relative indication, indicating that the decision for tonsillectomy in such cases may depend on factors such as the severity of symptoms, impact on the patient's quality of life, and response to medical treatment.

3. Answer B (Symptoms < 1 year)

While bleeding diathesis, acute infection, anemia, and significant anesthetic risk are contraindications for tonsillectomy, symptoms lasting less than one year are not considered contraindications. The decision for tonsillectomy is typically influenced by factors such as the severity and impact of symptoms on the patient's health rather than the specific duration of symptoms.

4. Answer D (Aspiration)

A potential complication of post-tonsillectomy bleeding that may occur in the recovery or hours later is aspiration. Post-tonsillectomy bleeding is a serious complication characterized by the potential for bleeding from the tonsillar bed. The patient may be hypovolemic, necessitating fluid resuscitation before induction, and there is a risk of aspiration due to a potentially full stomach with blood. Additionally, blood in the airway and edema from recent intubation can contribute to a potentially difficult airway during this critical period. Aspiration is a significant concern as it can lead to respiratory compromise and further complications.

5. Answer B (False)

The use of the LMA is considered a safe and effective option for airway management during tonsillectomy and adenoidectomy. There are potential advantages associated with the LMA, including a reduction in operating room time compared to endotracheal tube (ETT) use. The LMA is particularly favored in ear, nose, and throat (ENT) procedures due to its lack of tracheal stimulation, leading to a lower incidence of coughing on emergence. While there may be specific cases where the LMA is not suitable, it is generally well-tolerated and offers benefits in terms of patient outcomes during tonsillectomy.

6. Answer D (Head-down tilt)

The preferred position during induction in a patient with post-tonsillectomy bleeding is a head-down tilt. This position facilitates the drainage of blood away from the larynx, helping to maintain a clearer airway. Given the risk of aspiration and the need to manage bleeding effectively, a head-down tilt is crucial during the induction phase. Additionally, it is emphasized that extubation should only be performed when the patient is fully awake, in the head-down, left lateral position. This approach ensures a smoother recovery and reduces the potential for postoperative complications.

Recommended literature

1. Pollard BJ, Kitchen G. Handbook of Clinical Anaesthesia. 4th ed. Taylor & Francis group; 2018. Chapter 19 ENT Surgery, MacNab R, Bexon K, Clegg S, Hutchinson A.
2. Davies K. Anaesthesia for tonsillectomy. WFSA. April 2, 2007. Accessed February 10, 2023. https://resources.wfsahq.org/atotw/anaesthesia-for-tonsillectomy/

TRACHEOESOPHAGEAL FISTULA

12
CHAPTER

Questions:

1. **Which congenital malformation is commonly associated with Tracheoesophageal Fistula?**
   A. Diaphragmatic hernia
   B. Intestinal atresia
   C. Esophageal atresia (EA)
   D. Cardiac septal defect

2. **Which congenital anomaly is NOT commonly associated with TEF and EA?**
   A. Tetralogy of Fallot
   B. Spina bifida
   C. Renal agenesis
   D. Gastroschisis

3. **When is surgical correction typically performed for TEF/EA to minimize the risk of complications?**
   A. Within 24 hours of birth
   B. Within 1 week of birth
   C. Within 6 months of birth
   D. Within 1 year of birth

4. **Which of the following is NOT a potential complication after surgical correction of TEF/EA?**
   A. Asthma-like symptoms
   B. Esophageal strictures
   C. Polyphagia
   D. Damage to the laryngeal nerve

5. **In the context of Tracheoesophageal fistula repair, the technique for tracheal intubation involves the insertion of the endotracheal tube (ETT) deep endobronchial, followed by a gradual withdrawal until the ETT is positioned just above the carina.**
   A. True
   B. False

6. **A 12-hour-old infant is presented for the repair of TEF associated with EA. The upper portion of the esophagus culminates in a blind pouch, while the lower part is aberrantly connected to the trachea via a TEF. When is muscle relaxant administered during Tracheoesophageal fistula repair?**
   A. Before induction
   B. After the ligation of the fistula
   C. During bronchoscopic evaluation
   D. Throughout the procedure

Answers:

1. Answer C (Esophageal atresia (EA))

A tracheoesophageal fistula (TEF) is defined as an abnormal connection (fistula) between the esophagus and trachea. TEF commonly occurs with EA, a related congenital malformation. EA is characterized by an abnormal connection between the esophagus and stomach, where the esophagus ends in a blind-ended pouch instead of connecting normally to the stomach. This condition can occur with or without the presence of a fistula.

2. Answer D (Gastroschisis)

Tracheoesophageal malformations are frequently associated with various congenital anomalies, with approximately 70% of affected infants exhibiting at least one additional malformation. The commonly associated anomalies include cardiovascular (35%), genitourinary (25%), gastrointestinal (25%), musculoskeletal (15%), and central nervous system (7%). Cardiac anomalies such as ventricular septal defect, patent ductus arteriosus, tetralogy of Fallot, atrial septal defect, and right-sided aortic arch are prevalent. Genitourinary anomalies encompass renal agenesis or dysplasia, horseshoe kidney, polycystic kidney, ureteral and urethral malformations, and hypospadias. However, gastroschisis, an abdominal wall defect where the intestines protrude through an opening near the umbilical cord, is not commonly associated with tracheoesophageal malformations.

3. Answer A (Within 24 hours of birth)

Surgical correction for TEF and EA involves the resection of any fistula and the anastomosis of any discontinuous segments of the esophagus. The correct timing for surgical correction is typically within 24 hours of birth. Early intervention is essential to prevent complications related to the abnormal connection between the trachea and esophagus, such as aspiration of oral or gastric contents into the respiratory system.

4. Answer C (Polyphagia)

Polyphagia, characterized by excessive hunger or increased appetite, is not a typical complication following the surgical correction of TEF and EA. Common complications after TEF/EA surgery include anastomotic leaks, esophageal strictures, damage to the laryngeal nerve, recurrence of the fistula, gastroesophageal reflux disease (GERD), dysphagia, asthma-like symptoms, recurrent chest infections, and tracheomalacia. These complications arise due to the delicate nature of the surgical repair and the inherent challenges in restoring normal esophageal continuity.

5. Answer A (True)

Correct placement of the endotracheal tube (ETT) is essential to prevent complications. This technique, commonly employed, entails inserting the ETT deep endobronchial and gradually withdrawing it until it is positioned just above the carina. Bilateral equal breath sounds are confirmed through chest auscultation. Additionally, the ETT is rotated to ensure the bevel faces anteriorly, away from the posteriorly located fistula. This positioning ensures that the tip of the ETT occludes the fistula. Confirmation of correct placement can be done through auscultation or bronchoscopic evaluation.

6. Answer B (After the ligation of the fistula)

Muscle relaxants are administered during TEF repair after the ligation of the fistula. The correct placement of the ETT below the level of the fistula is critical for proper ventilation and is achieved during the induction process. Spontaneous respiration is maintained during induction with inhalational anesthetic agents to prevent gastric insufflations from positive pressure ventilation. Muscle relaxants are introduced only after the ligation of the fistula, ensuring that the ETT remains in the correct position and minimizing the risk of complications associated with incorrect placement.

Recommended literature

1. Pollard BJ, Kitchen G. Handbook of Clinical Anaesthesia. 4th ed. Taylor & Francis group; 2018. Chapter 24 Paediatrics, Lomas B.
2. Choumanovai I, Sanusii A, Evansii F. Anaesthetic management of tracheo-oesophageal fistula/ oesophageal atresia. WFSA. October 17, 2017. Accessed February 16, 2023. https://resources.wfsahq.org/atotw/anaesthetic-management-of-tracheo-oesophageal-fistula-oesophageal-atresia/
3. Saraiya NR. TRACHEOESOPHAGEAL FISTULA. In: Houck PJ, Haché M, Sun LS. eds. Handbook of Pediatric Anesthesia. McGraw Hill; 2015. Accessed February 16, 2023. https://accessanesthesiology.mhmedical.com/content.aspx?bookid=1189&sectionid=70363324

TREACHER COLLINS SYNDROME

Questions:

1. **What is the primary genetic mechanism underlying Treacher Collins syndrome (TCS)?**
   A. Autosomal recessive inheritance
   B. De novo mutation (60%)
   C. X-linked inheritance
   D. Maternal mitochondrial DNA mutation

2. **Which of the following is a main feature of Treacher Collins syndrome affecting the eyes?**
   A. Proptosis
   B. Hypertelorism
   C. Myopia
   D. Nystagmus

3. **Which of the following is NOT an intraoral feature commonly seen in TCS?**
   A. Anterior open bite
   B. Steep occlusal plane
   C. Supernumerary teeth
   D. Eroded tooth enamel

4. **In Treacher Collins syndrome, what type of hearing loss is commonly associated with abnormalities in the auditory canal and middle ear?**
   A. Sensorineural hearing loss
   B. Conductive hearing loss
   C. Mixed hearing loss
   D. Central hearing loss

5. **Direct laryngoscopy may become more difficult with increasing age in TCS patients.**
   A. True
   B. False

6. **A 17-year-old woman is presented for orthognathic surgery. An extraoral examination reveals a narrow face with mandibular and zygomatic hypoplasia, along with an antimongoloid slant of the eyes. Mandibular hypoplasia has caused the upper dentition to appear protruded. Malar hypoplasia results in a 'sunk-in' appearance temporally, causing the nose to appear very prominent. The patient's eyes are remarkable, showing a partial absence of lower eyelashes and coloboma of the lower lateral eyelid. External ear malformation in the form of a rudimentary pinna is present bilaterally. What is TCS primarily known for in the context of anesthesia management?**
   A. Difficult intubation
   B. Cardiovascular abnormalities
   C. Gastrointestinal complications
   D. Musculoskeletal deformities

Answers:

1. Answer B (De novo mutation (60%))

Treacher Collins syndrome (TCS) is primarily caused by de novo mutations, which means that the genetic alteration occurs spontaneously and is not inherited from either parent. Approximately 60% of cases result from de novo mutations, while the remaining 40% can be inherited. The syndrome is associated with mutations in specific genes, including TCOF1, POLR1B, POLR1C, and POLR1D. These genes play a crucial role in craniofacial development, and mutations in them contribute to the characteristic features and anomalies observed in TCS.

2. Answer B (Hypertelorism)

Hypertelorism refers to an increased distance between the eyes, and is a characteristic feature of TCS affecting the eyes. Other eye-related features in Treacher Collins syndrome include antimongloid slant of palpebrae, coloboma of the lower eyelid, hypoplasia of lower eyelids with partial absence of cilia, and hypoplasia of lateral canthi.

3. Answer D (Eroded tooth enamel)

Eroded tooth enamel, or dental erosion, is not typically associated with TCS. Intraoral features commonly seen in Treacher Collins syndrome include cleft palate, anterior open bite, steep occlusal plane, supernumerary teeth, T-shaped teeth, enamel opacity/hypoplasia, microdontia, tooth agenesis, and ectopic eruption/rotation of teeth. While dental anomalies such as enamel opacity/hypoplasia may be present, erosion of tooth enamel is not a characteristic feature of this syndrome. The focus of dental abnormalities in Treacher Collins syndrome is often on developmental and structural issues rather than erosion.

4. Answer B (Conductive hearing loss)

Abnormalities of the external ear, auditory canal, and malformed middle ear ossicles in Treacher Collins syndrome contribute to conductive hearing loss. Conductive hearing loss occurs when there is a problem conducting sound waves through the outer or middle ear. In TCS, these abnormalities can interfere with the normal transmission of sound to the inner ear, resulting in conductive hearing loss. This type of hearing loss is distinct from sensorineural hearing loss, which involves damage to the inner ear or auditory nerve, and mixed hearing loss, which is a combination of both conductive and sensorineural components.

5. Answer A (True)

Direct laryngoscopy may become more difficult with increasing age in TCS patients. This difficulty can be attributed to the progressive nature of craniofacial abnormalities associated with TCS. As individuals with TCS age, there may be increased rigidity and deformities in the facial and airway structures, making direct laryngoscopy more challenging. The changes in the anatomy of the head and neck region over time can pose obstacles during airway management procedures, including laryngoscopy.

6. Answer A (Difficult intubation)

TCS is primarily known for difficult airway management, specifically difficult intubation, due to the craniofacial abnormalities associated with the syndrome. In this case, the patient exhibits characteristic features of TCS, including mandibular and zygomatic hypoplasia, an antimongoloid slant of the eyes, malar hypoplasia, and external ear malformation with a rudimentary pinna. The mandibular and zygomatic hypoplasia can lead to retrognathia and a narrow face, resulting in a limited oral opening, making direct laryngoscopy challenging. Patients with TCS often have unique facial features requiring careful planning and consideration during anesthesia management. While cardiovascular abnormalities, gastrointestinal complications, and musculoskeletal deformities can be associated with TCS, the primary concern during anesthesia in these patients is often related to securing a patent airway.

Recommended literature

1. Hosking J, Zoanetti D, Carlyle A, Anderson P, Costi D. Anesthesia for Treacher Collins syndrome: a review of airway management in 240 pediatric cases. Paediatr Anaesth. 2012;22(8):752-758.
2. Goel L, Bennur SK, Jambhale S. Treacher-collins syndrome-a challenge for anaesthesiologists. Indian J Anaesth. 2009;53(4):496-500.

Pediatric
UPPER RESPIRATORY TRACT INFECTION

12
CHAPTER

Questions:

1. **What is a significant independent risk factor for adverse respiratory events in children with active upper respiratory tract infections (URTIs)?**
   A. Age over 5 years
   B. Absence of parental confirmation of a cold
   C. Absence of copious secretions
   D. History of asthma or atopy

2. **In which category of URTIs would a child present with a green runny nose, productive cough, and mucopurulent secretion?**
   A. Mild URTIs
   B. Moderate URTIs
   C. Severe URTIs
   D. No URTI symptoms

3. **What is the recommended induction agent to minimize adverse respiratory events in children with URTIs?**
   A. Ketamine
   B. Propofol
   C. Sevoflurane
   D. Thiopental

4. **What is the role of IV lidocaine in the anesthetic management of URTIs?**
   A. Induction agent
   B. Bronchodilator
   C. Reduction of laryngospasm reflex
   D. Maintenance agent

5. **In the context of upper respiratory tract infections in children, it is advisable to avoid tracheal intubation, especially in those younger than 5 years.**
   A. True
   B. False

6. **A 4-year-old boy is scheduled for urgent surgery due to an elbow fracture. However, upon examination, the child presents with symptoms indicative of a severe upper respiratory tract infection. These symptoms include a green runny nose, productive cough, mucopurulent secretion, nasal congestion, fever exceeding 38°C, severe sore or scratchy throat, pulmonary involvement in the lower respiratory tract, wheezing, and lethargy. What is the most effective combination for minimizing bronchoconstriction during intubation in children with URTIs?**
   A. β2-agonist alone
   B. Inhaled corticosteroid alone
   C. Combining β2-agonist with inhaled corticosteroid
   D. IV lidocaine

Answers:

1. **Answer D (History of asthma or atopy)**

    A history of asthma or atopy is identified as a significant independent risk factor for adverse respiratory events in children with active upper respiratory tract infections (URTIs). This risk factor is part of a broader list that includes intubation, prematurity (< 37 weeks), age less than 1 year, passive smoking, airway surgery, presence of copious secretions, nasal congestion, parental confirmation "my child has a cold," snoring, and the use of an endotracheal tube (ETT). Additionally, it's essential to note that airway hyperreactivity persists for up to 6-8 weeks following a URTI, emphasizing the extended period during which children may be at an increased risk of perioperative respiratory complications.

2. **Answer C (Severe URTIs)**

    In the categorization of URTIs based on medical history and physical examination, a child presenting with a green runny nose, productive cough, and mucopurulent secretion falls into the category of Severe URTIs. The characteristics of severe URTIs include not only a green runny nose and productive cough but also additional symptoms such as nasal congestion, fever (> 38°C), severe sore or scratchy throat, pulmonary involvement, wheezing, and lethargy.

3. **Answer B (Propofol)**

    Minimizing adverse respiratory events is crucial during anesthesia for children with URTIs, as these events may include complications such as coughing, laryngospasm, bronchospasm, and airway obstruction. Propofol, as an intravenous induction agent, has been associated with fewer respiratory complications compared to inhalation agents like sevoflurane in this specific context.

4. **Answer C (Reduction of laryngospasm reflex)**

    The role of IV lidocaine in the anesthetic management of URTIs is primarily the reduction of the laryngospasm reflex. When administered intravenously, lidocaine has a local anesthetic effect that can help suppress the laryngospasm reflex, which may be triggered by irritation during intubation or other airway manipulations. Specifically, IV lidocaine may help reduce the laryngospasm reflex during anesthesia for children with URTIs. This can contribute to a smoother induction process and decrease the risk of complications related to airway reactivity.

5. **Answer A (True)**

    It is recommended to avoid tracheal intubation, particularly in children under 5 years of age, when managing upper respiratory tract infections. This precaution is taken to minimize airway irritation and reduce the risk of adverse respiratory events during anesthesia in this specific age group. Opting for alternatives such as a laryngeal mask airway or facemask is considered a safer approach in children with URTIs, aligning to provide optimal care while mitigating potential complications.

6. **Answer C (Combining β2-agonist with inhaled corticosteroid)**

    In managing a 4-year-old boy with a severe URTI scheduled for urgent surgery due to an elbow fracture, the most effective combination for minimizing bronchoconstriction during intubation is combining β2-agonist with inhaled corticosteroid. Administering this combination as preoperative bronchodilators 10-30 minutes before surgery has been shown to effectively reduce bronchoconstriction and perioperative respiratory events compared to using an inhaled β2-agonist alone. Given the severity of the URTI, it is essential to consider several strategies to minimize respiratory complications, such as avoiding tracheal intubation, especially in children under 5 years. Instead, a laryngeal mask airway or facemask is preferred. Additionally, utilizing IV lidocaine can help reduce the laryngospasm reflex, and opting for propofol over sevoflurane as the induction agent is associated with fewer adverse respiratory events. Maintenance of anesthesia, whether intravenous or inhalation techniques, should ensure an adequate depth, and airway suctioning should only be performed under deep anesthesia. Humidifiers may also aid in clearing secretions and preventing bronchial mucus plugging, contributing to a comprehensive approach to mitigating respiratory complications in this challenging case.

Recommended literature

1. Lema GF, Berhe YW, Gebrezgi AH, Getu AA. Evidence-based perioperative management of a child with upper respiratory tract infections (URTIs) undergoing elective surgery; A systematic review. International Journal of Surgery Open. 2018;12:17-24.
2. Regli A, Becke K, von Ungern-Sternberg BS. An update on the perioperative management of children with upper respiratory tract infections. Curr Opin Anaesthesiol. 2017;30(3):362-367.
3. Tait AR, Malviya S. Anesthesia for the child with an upper respiratory tract infection: still a dilemma?. Anesth Analg. 2005;100(1):59-65.

VACTERL

Questions:

1. **What is the primary diagnostic criterion for VACTERL association?**
   A. Presence of limb defects
   B. Identification of tracheoesophageal fistula
   C. Presence of at least three malformations
   D. Cardiovascular anomalies

2. **When is VACTERL association diagnosed?**
   A. At birth
   B. During the first year of life
   C. In adolescence
   D. As a diagnosis of exclusion

3. **What is the primary consideration in the anesthetic management of a pediatric patient with VACTERL undergoing surgery?**
   A. Cardiovascular assessment
   B. Identification of limb defects
   C. Evaluation for a difficult airway
   D. Monitoring for renal anomalies

4. **What is the significance of a single umbilical artery?**
   A. It can be found in unaffected individuals.
   B. It is always seen in VACTERL syndrome
   C. It may indicate Tetralogy of Fallot (TOF)
   D. It is associated with tracheoesophageal fistula (TEF)

5. **Polycystic kidneys are a typical renal anomaly associated with VACTERL syndrome.**
   A. True
   B. False

6. **A neonate with VACTERL syndrome, presenting with anal atresia and tracheoesophageal fistula, is scheduled for surgical correction. The patient is at a high risk of aspiration due to the TEF, necessitating careful anesthetic management to mitigate this risk. Why is succinylcholine use a concern during anesthesia for VACTERL patients?**
   A. Increased risk of arrhythmias
   B. Potential for renal failure
   C. Risk of hyperkalemia
   D. Induction of difficult airway

Answers:

1. **Answer C (Presence of at least three malformations)**

   VACTERL association is diagnosed based on the presence of at least three congenital malformations, and one of these must be tracheoesophageal fistula (TEF). The acronym VACTERL itself represents the various organ systems affected: Vertebral anomalies (V), Anorectal malformations (A), Cardiovascular anomalies (C), Tracheoesophageal fistula (TEF), Esophageal atresia (EA), Renal anomalies (R), and Limb defects (L). The diagnostic criteria emphasize the multifactorial nature of VACTERL association and the need for a combination of specific malformations for the diagnosis. This approach helps distinguish VACTERL association from other overlapping conditions and contributes to its status as a diagnosis of exclusion.

2. **Answer D (As a diagnosis of exclusion)**

   VACTERL association is diagnosed as a diagnosis of exclusion. Not all malformations associated with VACTERL are always present, and the diagnosis is made when at least three malformations, including TEF, are identified. Importantly, there must be no clinical or laboratory-based evidence for the presence of one of the many similar overlapping conditions. This approach ensures that the diagnosis is specific to VACTERL association, distinguishing it from other conditions with similar presentations.

3. **Answer C (Evaluation for a difficult airway)**

   The primary consideration in the anesthetic management of a pediatric patient with VACTERL undergoing surgery is the evaluation of a difficult airway. This is because patients with VACTERL syndrome, especially those with TEF, may have associated anomalies affecting the airway. Identifying potential airway difficulties is crucial for planning and implementing a safe anesthetic induction and maintaining adequate ventilation during surgery. While cardiovascular assessment, monitoring for renal anomalies, and identification of limb defects are all important aspects of the overall anesthetic management, the potential for a difficult airway takes precedence due to the nature of the syndrome.

4. **Answer A (It can be found in unaffected individuals)**

   A single umbilical artery (SUA) is a variation in umbilical cord anatomy where only one umbilical artery is present instead of the typical two arteries. While SUA may be associated with an increased risk of chromosomal abnormalities, it can also be found as an isolated finding and does not always indicate a congenital syndrome or anomaly. The umbilical cord typically contains two arteries and one vein. The vein carries oxygenated blood from the placenta to the fetus, and the arteries carry deoxygenated blood and waste products from the fetus to the placenta. SUA can occur due to primary agenesis or secondary atrophy of one of the arteries, resulting in a single umbilical artery. The significance of SUA lies in its association with aneuploidy and other congenital anomalies, including those seen in VACTERL syndrome. However, it is crucial to recognize that SUA can also be found in otherwise unaffected individuals. Therefore, while SUA may prompt further investigation and monitoring, it does not always indicate a specific congenital syndrome or pathology.

5. **Answer B (False)**

   Polycystic kidneys are not a typical renal anomaly associated with VACTERL syndrome. Renal anomalies in VACTERL syndrome often include conditions such as horseshoe kidneys, cystic, aplastic, dysplastic, or ectopic kidneys, hydronephrosis, unilateral/bilateral agenesis, pyelonephritis, and nephrolithiasis. These anomalies contribute to urological problems, such as severe reflux or obstruction of urine outflow from both kidneys, observed in 50-80% of cases.

6. **Answer C (Risk of hyperkalemia)**

   In the context of VACTERL syndrome, succinylcholine use is a concern primarily due to the associated risk of hyperkalemia. Succinylcholine, a depolarizing neuromuscular blocking agent, can lead to an acute increase in serum potassium levels. Hyperkalemia poses a significant threat, particularly in neonates with VACTERL syndrome, as it may lead to severe arrhythmias and cardiac arrest. Therefore, the avoidance or careful use of succinylcholine is crucial in the anesthetic management of VACTERL patients to minimize the risk of hyperkalemia and associated complications during induction.

Recommended literature

1. Aycan IO. Turgut H, Yildirim ZB, Kavak GO. Anesthetic management in VACTERL syndrome. J Clin Exp Invest. 2014;5(1):103-105.

PSYCHIATRIC DISORDERS

ELECTROCONVULSIVE THERAPY (ECT)

13
CHAPTER

Questions:

1. **What is the primary reason for administering general anesthesia during Electroconvulsive Therapy (ECT)?**
   A. To induce a deep sleep
   B. To prevent seizures
   C. To protect against cardiovascular effects
   D. To reduce cerebral oxygen consumption

2. **What physiological effect might contribute to the occurrence of myocardial ischemia and infarction during ECT?**
   A. Decreased blood flow
   B. Increased myocardial oxygen consumption
   C. Bradycardia
   D. Systolic arterial pressure decrease

3. **In which condition is ECT considered a safe and effective treatment?**
   A. Neurodevelopmental disorders
   B. Anxiety disorders
   C. Medication-resistant depression
   D. Bipolar disorder

4. **Which physiological effect occurs in the cerebral system during ECT?**
   A. Decreased intracranial pressure
   B. Reduced cerebral blood flow
   C. Increased cerebral oxygen consumption
   D. Prevention of transient ischemic deficits

5. **The electrodes for electroconvulsive therapy can either be attached on both sides of the head, typically bitemporal, for bilateral ECT or on the dominant hemisphere for unilateral ECT.**
   A. True
   B. False

6. **A 55-year-old woman recently underwent ECT due to medication-resistant depression. Following the ECT sessions, she presents with symptoms indicative of the postictal period. She is notably disoriented, exhibiting difficulty in maintaining attention. What is the potential postictal effect of ECT?**
   A. Extreme paranoia
   B. Delusions
   C. Short-term memory impairment
   D. Suicide ideation

Answers:

1. **Answer C (To protect against cardiovascular effects)**

   General anesthesia is administered during Electroconvulsive Therapy (ECT) primarily to protect against cardiovascular effects associated with the procedure. ECT can induce bradycardia, hypotension, and possibly asystole, making it crucial to provide a controlled and protective environment. In the context of ECT, the administration of anesthesia serves to manage hemodynamic changes and prevent related complications. It is essential to strike a balance, as the anesthesia level should be sufficient to control cardiovascular responses without suppressing the seizure activity, which is the therapeutic goal of ECT.

2. **Answer B (Increased myocardial oxygen consumption)**

   During ECT, the physiological effect that might contribute to the occurrence of myocardial ischemia and infarction is the increased myocardial oxygen consumption. ECT induces bradycardia, hypotension, and possibly asystole, and it can lead to a significant increase in systolic arterial pressure. However, the critical factor in the context of myocardial ischemia is the increased demand for oxygen by the myocardium. This increased oxygen demand, coupled with the possibility of reduced oxygen supply, can contribute to myocardial ischemia and infarction.

3. **Answer C (Medication-resistant depression)**

   ECT is considered a safe and effective treatment, particularly in cases of severe medication-resistant depression. When individuals do not respond to other forms of treatment, such as medications, ECT becomes a viable option. Furthermore, ECT can be beneficial in a range of psychiatric conditions, including severe mania, catatonia, agitation, and aggression in people with dementia and schizophrenia.

4. **Answer C (Increased cerebral oxygen consumption)**

   During ECT, the physiological effect that occurs in the cerebral system is increased cerebral oxygen consumption. ECT leads to an intentional seizure, and this process involves an increase in cerebral oxygen consumption. The overall cerebral effects during ECT include not only increased cerebral oxygen consumption but also an increase in cerebral blood flow and intracranial pressure. However, these effects are balanced with potential risks, as seen in reports of transient ischemic deficits, intracranial hemorrhage, cortical blindness, prolonged seizures, and status epilepticus.

5. **Answer A (True)**

   The electrodes for ECT can be positioned in two main configurations: bitemporal, where electrodes are attached on both sides of the head, typically used for bilateral ECT, and unilateral, where electrodes are placed on the dominant hemisphere. This versatility in electrode placement allows clinicians to tailor the treatment to individual patient needs, with bilateral ECT often chosen for its efficacy in severe cases and unilateral ECT employed to minimize cognitive side effects. The selection between the two configurations depends on factors such as the nature and severity of the psychiatric condition being treated, aiming to optimize therapeutic benefits while managing potential adverse effects.

6. **Answer C (Short-term memory impairment)**

   The potential postictal effect of ECT in this case is short-term memory impairment. Disorientation and impaired attention are commonly observed during the immediate postictal period, and these symptoms align with the expected cognitive effects of ECT. The short-term memory impairment described in the scenario is consistent with the recognized cognitive side effects of the treatment. While this impairment is generally temporary, it underscores the importance of close monitoring and supportive care during the postictal phase.

Recommended literature

1. Pollard BJ, Kitchen, G. Handbook of Clinical Anaesthesia. Fourth Edition. CRC Press. 2018. 978-1-4987-6289-2.
2. Uppa VI, Dourish J, Macfarlane A. Anaesthesia for electroconvulsive therapy. Continuing Education in Anaesthesia Critical Care & Pain. 2010. 10;(6); 192-196.

MONOAMINE OXIDASE INHIBITORS (MAOI)

13
CHAPTER

Questions:

1. **Which neurotransmitters experience increased availability due to the inhibition of MAO Type A by MAOIs?**
   A. Dopamine and acetylcholine
   B. Serotonin and norepinephrine
   C. GABA and glutamate
   D. Endorphins and enkephalins

2. **What psychiatric conditions are effectively treated with MAOIs?**
   A. Schizophrenia
   B. Autism
   C. Panic disorder, atypical depression, and anxiety disorder
   D. Attention-deficit/hyperactivity disorder (ADHD)

3. **In the context of MAOIs, what may lead to a hypertensive crisis?**
   A. Serotonin depletion
   B. Tyramine accumulation
   C. GABAergic inhibition
   D. Dopamine accumulation

4. **What neuromuscular blocking drug should be avoided with MAOI?**
   A. Atracurium
   B. Rocuronium
   C. Pancuronium
   D. Vecuronium

5. **Ephedrine is the drug of choice for the treatment of hypotension caused by spinal anesthesia in patients on MAOIs.**
   A. True
   B. False

6. **A 35-year-old woman, treated for depression with 45 mg daily of the MAOI phenelzine throughout her pregnancy, is presenting for vaginal delivery and requests labor analgesia. What type of labor analgesia should be avoided?**
   A. Remifentanil
   B. Epidural bupivacaine
   C. Meperidine
   D. Entonox

Answers:

1. Answer B (Serotonin and norepinephrine)

Monoamine oxidase inhibitors (MAOIs) inhibit the activity of monoamine oxidase enzymes A and B. In this context, MAO type A has a preference for norepinephrine and serotonin. Therefore, when MAO Type A is inhibited by MAOIs, the breakdown of norepinephrine and serotonin is prevented, leading to increased availability of these neurotransmitters in the synaptic cleft.

2. Answer C (Panic disorder, atypical depression, and anxiety disorder)

MAOIs, or Monoamine Oxidase Inhibitors, are effective antidepressants used in the treatment of various psychiatric conditions. Specifically, they have shown efficacy in managing panic disorder, atypical depression, anxiety disorder, depression, bulimia, post-traumatic stress disorder, borderline personality disorder, obsessive-compulsive disorder, and bipolar depression. These drugs work by inhibiting the breakdown of monoamine neurotransmitters such as serotonin and norepinephrine, thereby increasing their availability in the synaptic cleft. While MAOIs are beneficial for the aforementioned conditions, they are not typically indicated for schizophrenia, autism, or attention-deficit/hyperactivity disorder (ADHD).

3. Answer B (Tyramine accumulation)

In the context of MAOIs, a hypertensive crisis may result from tyramine accumulation. MAOIs prevent the breakdown of tyramine, which is naturally present in the body as well as in certain foods, drinks, and medications. When individuals on MAOIs consume tyramine-containing foods or drinks, it can lead to high serum tyramine levels. In humans, the interaction between MAOIs and foods high in tyramine can result in a hypertensive crisis. This occurs because tyramine, when not degraded due to MAOI inhibition, displaces stored monoamines such as dopamine, norepinephrine, and epinephrine from synaptic vesicles. This displacement, coupled with the release of norepinephrine, poses a risk of hypertensive crisis. Foods containing tyramine include smoked or processed meats, pickled or fermented foods, and certain sauces, such as soy sauce and fish sauce.

4. Answer C (Pancuronium)

Pancuronium, a non-depolarizing neuromuscular blocking drug with vagolytic effects, should be avoided with MAOIs. Particularly if resting tachycardia is noted, the use of vagolytics like pancuronium can exacerbate the cardiovascular effects associated with MAOIs. MAOIs, by inhibiting the breakdown of monoamine neurotransmitters, can have various effects on the autonomic nervous system, including potential increases in heart rate. Vagolytic drugs, like pancuronium, may have enhanced effects in the presence of MAOIs, leading to further cardiovascular complications.

5. Answer B (False)

Indirect-acting vasopressors, including ephedrine and pseudoephedrine, should be avoided in patients taking MAOIs due to the potential risk of inducing a hypertensive crisis. The use of these agents is contraindicated in such patients. Ephedrine, in particular, may lead to the release of large amounts of stored presynaptic neurotransmitters, including norepinephrine, potentially causing a hypertensive crisis.

6. Answer C (Meperidine)

In the context of the patient being treated with the MAOI phenelzine, labor analgesia with meperidine should be avoided. Meperidine, also known as pethidine or Demerol, is a phenylpiperidine opioid recognized as a weak serotonin reuptake inhibitor (SRI). Patients on MAOIs, like phenelzine, should avoid analgesics known to be weak SRIs, including meperidine, to prevent potential adverse effects and interactions. The use of meperidine in patients on MAOIs may lead to serotonin syndrome, a potentially serious condition. Remifentanil, epidural bupivacaine analgesia, and Entonox are not known to have the same documented interactions with MAOIs as meperidine. The choice of labor analgesia should be carefully considered based on the patient's medical history, and alternative options should be explored to ensure safety during delivery.

Recommended literature

1. Peck T, Wong A, Norman E. 2010. Anaesthetic implications of psychoactive drugs. Continuing Education in Anaesthesia Critical Care & Pain.10;(6); 177-181.

NEUROLEPTIC MALIGNANT SYNDROME

13

CHAPTER

Questions:

1. **What is the primary mechanism underlying the development of Neuroleptic Malignant Syndrome (NMS)?**
   A. Increased serotonin levels
   B. Dopaminergic transmission blockade
   C. Cholinergic hyperactivity
   D. GABAergic inhibition

2. **What mnemonic is used to remember the clinical manifestations of NMS?**
   A. SMILES
   B. FEVERS
   C. HASTE
   D. RAPID

3. **Which brain region is primarily responsible for the production of rigidity in NMS?**
   A. Hippocampus
   B. Nigrostriatum
   C. Thalamus
   D. Amygdala

4. **Which of the following is a risk factor for NMS?**
   A. Fatigue
   B. Sedation
   C. Dehydration
   D. Relaxation

5. **NMS usually develops within the first 2 weeks of treatment with neuroleptic or antipsychotic agents.**
   A. True
   B. False

6. **A 35-year-old woman presents with a myriad of symptoms, including muscle cramps, tremors, fever, sweating, unstable blood pressure, stupor, muscular rigidity, autonomic dysfunction, confusion, agitation, delirium, and tachycardia. Notably, she underwent strabismus surgery a week ago, and Droperidol was administered for the prevention of postoperative nausea and vomiting (PONV). Given the constellation of symptoms and the recent use of Droperidol, neuroleptic malignant syndrome is suspected. Which of the following is NOT a major criterion for diagnosing NMS?**
   A. High fever
   B. Muscular rigidity
   C. Elevated serum creatine kinase
   D. Tachycardia

Answers:

1. **Answer B (Dopaminergic transmission blockade)**

   The primary mechanism underlying the development of Neuroleptic Malignant Syndrome (NMS) is the blockade of dopaminergic transmission. Specifically, antipsychotics, which include neuroleptic medications, exert their effects through dopamine D2 receptor antagonism. This blockade occurs in key brain areas, including the hypothalamus, nigrostriatal pathways, and the spinal cord. It's important to note that NMS is a rare but potentially life-threatening condition associated with the use of neuroleptic or antipsychotic agents.

2. **Answer B (FEVERS)**

   The mnemonic used to remember the clinical manifestations of NMS is "FEVERS." Each letter represents a significant symptom: Fever, Encephalopathy, Vital signs unstable, Elevated labs, Rigidity, and Sweating. This mnemonic is a concise and effective way to recall the key clinical features associated with NMS, aiding in the prompt recognition and management of this rare but potentially life-threatening neurological condition caused by adverse reactions to neuroleptic or antipsychotic agents.

3. **Answer B (Nigrostriatum)**

   The brain region primarily responsible for the production of rigidity in NMS is the Nigrostriatum. NMS is characterized by an acute blockade of dopaminergic transmission in specific brain regions, including the Nigrostriatum. The dopaminergic transmission blockade in the Nigrostriatum leads to the development of muscle rigidity, which is one of the hallmark clinical manifestations of NMS. Other regions affected by this blockade include the Hypothalamus, responsible for hyperthermia, and the Corticolimbic system, contributing to an altered mental state.

4. **Answer C (Dehydration)**

   NMS is a rare but serious condition associated with the use of neuroleptic or antipsychotic medications, and certain factors increase the susceptibility to its development. Dehydration, along with agitation, catatonia, and the use of specific medications such as typical neuroleptics (e.g., haloperidol, chlorpromazine), atypical neuroleptics (e.g., olanzapine, clozapine, risperidone), and anti-dopaminergic antiemetics (e.g., droperidol), can contribute to the occurrence of NMS. Additionally, the withdrawal of dopaminergic agents like levodopa and amantadine is recognized as a risk factor.

5. **Answer A (True)**

   NMS typically develops within the first 2 weeks of treatment with neuroleptic or antipsychotic agents. While most cases manifest within the initial two weeks, NMS can potentially occur at any point during the course of treatment or even after discontinuation of the medication.

6. **Answer D (Tachycardia)**

   The major criteria for NMS are high fever, muscular rigidity, and elevated serum creatine kinase. While tachycardia is a significant clinical manifestation, it falls under the category of minor criteria, along with raised blood pressure, tachypnea, altered consciousness level, and sweating. The patient, in this case, exhibits several major criteria, including high fever, muscular rigidity, and the possibility of elevated serum creatine kinase. These findings, in conjunction with the administration of Droperidol and the recent strabismus surgery, raise strong suspicion for NMS.

Recommended literature

1. Bartakke, A., Corredor, C., Van Rensburg, A., 2020. Serotonin syndrome in the perioperative period. BJA Education 20, 10–17.
2. Pollard BJ, Kitchen, G. Handbook of Clinical Anaesthesia. Fourth Edition. CRC Press. 2018. 978-1-4987-6289-2.
3. Adnet, P., Lestavel, P., Krivosic-Horber, R., 2000. Neuroleptic malignant syndrome. British Journal of Anaesthesia 85, 129–135.

Psychiatric disorders
SEROTONIN SYNDROME

Questions:

1. **What is the primary mechanism underlying serotonin syndrome (SS)?**
   A. Cholinergic overstimulation
   B. Excessive serotoninergic activity
   C. Dopaminergic hyperactivity
   D. GABAergic inhibition

2. **Which medication is commonly associated with the development of serotonin syndrome?**
   A. Aspirin
   B. Hlorpromazine
   C. Sertraline
   D. Droperidol

3. **What is the mnemonic used to remember key symptoms of serotonin syndrome?**
   A. SAD PERSONS
   B. MAD HOT
   C. ABCDE
   D. FAST HUG

4. **Which of the following medications is a serotonin antagonist commonly used in the management of serotonin syndrome?**
   A. Diazepam
   B. Cyproheptadine
   C. Bromocriptine
   D. Dantrolene

5. **Hyperthermia is the distinguishing clinical feature between serotonin syndrome and neuroleptic malignant syndrome.**
   A. True
   B. False

6. **A 33-year-old woman, post laparoscopic ovarian cancer surgery, presented with symptoms including shivering, diaphoresis, hypomania, hypervigilance, hypertension, hyperreflexia, myoclonus, and severe hyperthermia (> 40°C) with seizures. The patient is currently receiving an analgesic infusion of Metamizole, Tramadol, and Metoclopramide. Given the clinical picture and the potential for serotonin syndrome, suspicion is directed towards Metoclopramide and Tramadol as potential triggers. What is the initial step in the management of serotonin syndrome?**
   A. Administer cyproheptadine
   B. Administer benzodiazepines
   C. Discontinue the triggering agent
   D. Administer noradrenaline

Answers:

1. **Answer B (Excessive serotoninergic activity)**

   The primary mechanism underlying serotonin syndrome (SS) is excessive serotoninergic activity in the central nervous system (CNS). SS is typically triggered by the use of medications that increase serotonin levels, either through increased production or decreased metabolism. Serotonin, a neurotransmitter, plays a crucial role in mood regulation, among other functions. When there is an excess of serotonin, it can lead to overstimulation of serotonin receptors, causing a range of symptoms from mild to severe.

2. **Answer C (Sertraline)**

   Sertraline belongs to the class of medications known as Selective Serotonin Reuptake Inhibitors (SSRIs), which are widely used for the treatment of depression, anxiety disorders, and other psychiatric conditions. SSRIs, including sertraline, increase serotonin levels in the synaptic cleft by inhibiting its reuptake, thereby enhancing serotoninergic activity. SS can occur when there is an excessive accumulation of serotonin due to various factors, such as the use of multiple serotonergic medications, drug interactions, or intentional overdose. Symptoms of serotonin syndrome range from mild to severe and can include hyperthermia, altered mental status, autonomic dysfunction, neuromuscular abnormalities, and more.

3. **Answer B (MAD HOT)**

   The mnemonic used to remember key symptoms of serotonin syndrome is MAD HOT, representing Myoclonus, Autonomic instability, Delirium, Diarrhea, and Hot (fever). This acronym helps recall the diverse clinical features associated with serotonin syndrome, a potentially life-threatening condition resulting from excessive serotoninergic activity in the central nervous system.

4. **Answer B (Cyproheptadine)**

   Cyproheptadine is a serotonin antagonist commonly used in the management of serotonin syndrome. As an H1 receptor antagonist and a 5-HT2A receptor antagonist, cyproheptadine helps mitigate the excessive serotonergic activity associated with serotonin syndrome. It has been identified as a specific antidote for serotonin syndrome and is often employed to counteract the effects of elevated serotonin levels. The recommended dose for cyproheptadine in the context of serotonin syndrome is 12 mg initially, followed by 2 mg every 2 hours or 4-8 mg every 6 hours, depending on the severity of symptoms.

5. **Answer B (False)**

   Hyperthermia is a shared clinical feature between serotonin syndrome and neuroleptic malignant syndrome (NMS), and therefore, it is not a distinguishing feature. Both conditions can manifest with elevated body temperature. In serotonin syndrome, hyperthermia is commonly observed, especially in more severe cases. Neuroleptic malignant syndrome, which is associated with the use of dopamine antagonists, also presents with hyperthermia. Other distinguishing features should be considered to differentiate between the two syndromes. For example, serotonin syndrome is characterized by symptoms such as clonus, hyperreflexia, and hyperactive bowel sounds. In contrast, neuroleptic malignant syndrome is associated with features like bradykinesia and the absence of clonus or hyperreflexia.

6. **Answer C (Discontinue the triggering agent)**

   The initial and crucial step in the management of serotonin syndrome is to discontinue the triggering agent, which, in this case, includes Metoclopramide and Tramadol. Stopping the medications responsible for excessive serotonergic activity is essential to prevent further serotonin accumulation. Following this, supportive care should be initiated, including intravenous fluids for hydration and measures to address hyperthermia. Benzodiazepines can be administered to manage agitation and neuromuscular symptoms, while the serotonin antagonist cyproheptadine may be considered to counteract excessive serotonergic effects. Continuous monitoring of vital signs and close observation of seizure activity is crucial. Individual responses to treatment may vary, and severe cases may necessitate intensive care and specialist consultation. Early recognition and intervention are pivotal for optimizing outcomes in serotonin syndrome.

Recommended literature

1. Bartakke, A., Corredor, C., Van Rensburg, A., 2020. Serotonin syndrome in the perioperative period. BJA Education 20, 10–17.
2. Francescangeli, J., Karamchandani, K., Powell, M., Bonavia, A., 2019. The Serotonin Syndrome: From Molecular Mechanisms to Clinical Practice. International Journal of Molecular Sciences 20, 2288.
3. Chinniah, S., French, J.L.H., Levy, D.M., 2008. Serotonin and anaesthesia. Continuing Education in Anaesthesia Critical Care & Pain 8, 43–45.

RARE CO-EXISTING DISEASES

AMYLOIDOSIS

14
CHAPTER

Questions:

1. **What is the hallmark feature of amyloidosis?**
   A. Intracellular deposition of protein aggregates
   B. Extracellular deposition of insoluble protein aggregates
   C. Nuclear fragmentation in affected tissues
   D. Hyperplasia of affected organs

2. **What is a major consideration when using anticoagulants in patients with amyloidosis?**
   A. Increased efficacy due to protein deposition
   B. Controversial use due to bleeding risk
   C. Enhanced anticoagulant effects in neurological dysfunction
   D. Anticoagulants do not affect amyloidosis patients

3. **What is the recommended approach for managing AL (light chain) amyloidosis?**
   A. Symptomatic treatment
   B. Chemotherapy
   C. Renal transplant
   D. Immunization

4. **What is a cautionary consideration when using depolarizing neuromuscular blocking agents in amyloidosis patients?**
   A. Reduced action with anticholinesterase inhibitors
   B. Increased risk of hemorrhage
   C. Hyperkalaemic response in neurological dysfunction
   D. Aminoglycosides augment resistance to activity

5. **Airway difficulties are a major anesthetic consideration associated with patients with amyloidosis.**
   A. True
   B. False

6. **The 55-year-old male patient presents with a complex medical history, including systemic amyloidosis, a condition characterized by the extracellular deposition of insoluble protein aggregates. The patient has a history of myocardial infarction, hypothyroidism, and controlled hypertension on medications. The planned procedure is tongue volume reduction surgery. Why is caution advised with halogenated volatile agents in amyloidosis patients?**
   A. They do not affect amyloid deposition
   B. They increase b-amyloid deposition in animal models
   C. They cause hyperkalemic responses
   D. They antagonize the effects of anticholinesterase inhibitors

Answers:

1. **Answer B (Extracellular deposition of insoluble protein aggregates)**

   Amyloidosis is characterized by the extracellular deposition of insoluble protein aggregates. This hallmark feature involves the accumulation of precursor proteins, produced through various mechanisms, as insoluble fibrils. These deposits disrupt tissue architecture, leading to organ dysfunction. Amyloidosis can manifest as an inherited or acquired disorder, and it may be localized or systemic. It can occur independently or in association with conditions such as dialysis-dependent renal failure, chronic infection, or inflammation. The definitive diagnosis of amyloidosis is based on the histological demonstration of amyloid deposits in affected tissues. The presence of these deposits, primarily extracellular, distinguishes amyloidosis from other pathological conditions involving intracellular protein aggregates or nuclear fragmentation.

2. **Answer B (Controversial use due to bleeding risk)**

   The use of anticoagulants in patients with amyloidosis is contentious if a bleeding risk is evident. Amyloidosis is characterized by the extracellular deposition of insoluble protein aggregates, leading to disruption of tissue architecture and organ dysfunction. The involvement of various organ systems, such as the cardiovascular and hematological systems, can result in complications like microvascular fragility, platelet dysfunction, impaired fibrin formation, clotting factor deficiencies, and an increased risk of hemorrhage.

3. **Answer B (Chemotherapy)**

   The recommended approach for managing AL (Light chain) amyloidosis is chemotherapy. AL amyloidosis is characterized by the deposition of light chain proteins derived from plasma cells. This subtype is associated with various complications, including airway difficulties, cardiomyopathy, arrhythmias, renal failure, hepatic failure, bleeding, autonomic/peripheral neuropathy, and endocrine organ dysfunction. The deposition of these light chain proteins as insoluble fibrils leads to disruption of tissue architecture and organ dysfunction. Symptomatic treatment is often initiated to address specific complications and manage symptoms associated with AL amyloidosis. However, chemotherapy plays a crucial role in targeting the underlying plasma cell dyscrasia, reducing the production of abnormal light chains, and slowing down the progression of the disease.

4. **Answer C (Hyperkalaemic response in neurological dysfunction)**

   When using depolarizing neuromuscular blocking agents in patients with amyloidosis, a cautionary consideration is the potential for a hyperkalaemic response in neurological dysfunction. Amyloidosis can affect the neurological system, leading to autonomic and peripheral neuropathy. In the context of neuromuscular blockade, depolarizing agents such as succinylcholine may induce a hyperkalaemic response, particularly in patients with neurological dysfunction associated with amyloidosis. This hyperkalaemic response can be attributed to the release of potassium from depolarized muscle cells. Therefore, careful monitoring and consideration of alternative neuromuscular blocking agents may be warranted in amyloidosis patients, especially those with neurological involvement.

5. **Answer A (True)**

   Airway difficulties are major anesthetic considerations associated with patients with amyloidosis. Amyloidosis, characterized by the extracellular deposition of insoluble protein aggregates, can involve various organ systems, leading to various complications. In the context of anesthesia, patients with amyloidosis may present with challenges related to the airway. The potential involvement of the respiratory system, including airway difficulties, necessitates careful planning and consideration of appropriate airway management techniques during anesthesia to ensure patient safety.

6. **Answer B (They increase b-amyloid deposition in animal models)**

   Caution is advised with halogenated volatile agents in patients with systemic amyloidosis as these agents have been shown to increase β-amyloid deposition in animal models. Given the unique nature of each amyloidosis case, anesthesia must be individualized, and alternative approaches such as Total Intravenous Anesthesia (TIVA) may be preferred to minimize exposure to volatile agents. Regional anesthesia techniques, used alone or in combination with sedation or general anesthesia, offer advantages such as superior analgesia and stress response attenuation, potentially avoiding risks associated with airway management. Additionally, the potential for amyloid-associated bleeding should be considered when opting for the regional blockade, alongside standard risks associated with this technique.

Recommended literature

1. Wani Z, Harkawat DK, Sharma M. Amyloidosis and Anesthesia. Anesth Essays Res. 2017;11(1):233-237.
2. Fleming I, Dubrey S, Williams B. 2012. Amyloidosis and anaesthesia, Continuing Education in Anaesthesia Critical Care & Pain.12;(2);72-77.

GLYCOGEN STORAGE DISORDERS

14
CHAPTER

Questions:

1. **What is the primary reason for the risk of hypoglycemia in individuals with glycogen storage disorders (GSD)?**
   A. Increased insulin production
   B. Inability to metabolize glycogen to glucose
   C. Elevated blood glucose levels
   D. Excessive glycogen breakdown

2. **What is the most common type of GSD?**
   A. Type II (Pompe disease)
   B. Type I (von Gierke disease)
   C. Type V (McArdle disease)
   D. Type III (Cori disease)

3. **Which of the following is NOT a common feature associated with GSD?**
   A. Acidosis
   B. Hyperglycemia
   C. Cardiac dysfunction
   D. Hepatic dysfunction

4. **What is the primary metabolic consequence of glycogen storage disorders that contributes to acidosis during fasting periods?**
   A. Hyperglycemia
   B. Hypolipidemia
   C. Protein metabolism
   D. Glycogen breakdown

5. **Administering a higher dose of suxamethonium in patients with GSD is recommended.**
   A. True
   B. False

6. **A patient with a known diagnosis of Type I Glycogen Storage Disorder (von Gierke disease) is scheduled for surgery due to bowel obstruction. The patient presents with hypotension, and as part of the initial management, fluid loading is initiated. Why is it important to avoid lactate-containing solutions in individuals with GSD during surgery?**
   A. Lactate interferes with glucose metabolism
   B. Lactate contributes to acidosis
   C. Lactate inhibits hepatic glycogen synthesis
   D. Lactate increases insulin resistance

Answers:

1. **Answer B (Inability to metabolize glycogen to glucose)**

   Individuals with glycogen storage disorders (GSD) have an increased risk of hypoglycemia primarily due to the inability to metabolize glycogen to glucose. GSD is characterized by inherited disorders caused by abnormalities in enzymes that regulate glycogen synthesis and breakdown. Glycogen serves as a critical source of fuel, especially in skeletal muscles during exercise, and hepatic glycogen helps maintain plasma glucose levels during fasting. In individuals with GSD, the deficiency in enzymes involved in glycogen breakdown hinders the conversion of stored glycogen into glucose. As a result, these individuals face challenges in maintaining glucose homeostasis, leading to an increased risk of hypoglycemia. Attempts to regulate glucose levels may inadvertently result in muscle degradation, as amino acids are used as an alternative substrate, further complicating the metabolic balance in these individuals. The primary concern is the failure to mobilize glycogen stores efficiently to meet the body's glucose needs, resulting in a hypoglycemic state.

2. **Answer B (Type I (von Gierke disease))**

   The most common type of GSD is Type I, also known as von Gierke disease. Type I GSD is characterized by an autosomal recessive inheritance pattern, and it occurs at an incidence of approximately 1 in 100,000 to 200,000 births. Type I GSD primarily affects the liver (and renal tissue). Clinically, individuals with von Gierke disease present with a spectrum of symptoms, including hypoglycemia, lactic acidosis, ketosis, hepatomegaly, truncal obesity, short stature, hypertriglyceridemia, hyperuricemia, gout, platelet dysfunction, and renal dysfunction. Despite the complexity of symptoms, individuals with Type I GSD generally have a good prognosis with supportive treatment.

3. **Answer B (Hyperglycemia)**

   GSDs are characterized by three common features: acidosis due to fat and protein metabolism, risk of hypoglycemia resulting from the failure to metabolize glycogen to glucose, and cardiac and hepatic dysfunction stemming from the destruction of normal tissue by accumulated glycogen. The primary metabolic challenge in GSD lies in the impaired breakdown of glycogen, leading to a heightened risk of hypoglycemia and the associated clinical manifestations.

4. **Answer C (Protein metabolism)**

   The primary metabolic consequence of glycogen storage disorders that contributes to acidosis during fasting periods is protein metabolism. Individuals with GSD experience challenges in glycogen breakdown, leading to the reliance on alternative energy sources such as fats and proteins. During fasting, when glycogen cannot be efficiently utilized, there is an increased reliance on protein metabolism. This process produces ketones and results in the accumulation of acidic byproducts, leading to metabolic acidosis.

5. **Answer B (False)**

   Administering a higher dose of suxamethonium in patients with GSD is not recommended due to the associated risks of rhabdomyolysis and hyperkalemia. Suxamethonium, a depolarizing neuromuscular blocking agent, may lead to complications in individuals with GSD, particularly due to the risk of rhabdomyolysis, and hyperkalemia. These risks are associated with suxamethonium use in individuals with muscle disorders, and caution should be exercised to avoid potential complications.

6. **Answer B (Lactate contributes to acidosis)**

   It is crucial to avoid lactate-containing solutions in individuals with Type I Glycogen Storage Disorder (von Gierke disease) during surgery because lactate contributes to acidosis. Individuals with GSD cannot efficiently convert lactate to glycogen, and the accumulation of lactate can exacerbate metabolic acidosis, posing additional challenges during the perioperative period. In von Gierke disease, there is a deficiency in glucose-6-phosphatase, a key enzyme in gluconeogenesis and glycogenolysis, leading to impaired glucose homeostasis. As a result, lactate, a byproduct of metabolism, cannot be effectively converted to glycogen, contributing to the risk of acidosis.

Recommended literature

1. Yeoh C, Teng H, Jackson J, et al. Metabolic Disorders and Anesthesia. Curr Anesthesiol Rep. 2019;9(3):340-359.
2. Pollard BJ, Kitchen, G. Handbook of Clinical Anaesthesia. Fourth Edition. CRC Press. 2018. 978-1-4987-6289-2.
3. Grant S, Nargis A. 2011. Perioperative care of children with inherited metabolic disorders. Continuing Education in Anaesthesia Critical Care & Pain.11:2;62-68.

Rare co-existing diseases

HEREDITARY ANGIOEDEMA (C1 ESTERASE DEFICIENCY)

Questions:

1. **What is the primary cause of hereditary angioedema (HAE)?**
   A. Excessive histamine release
   B. Impaired production of C1 esterase inhibitor
   C. Overactivation of the kallikrein-kinin system
   D. Hyperactivation of the coagulation cascade

2. **What is the primary function of C1 esterase inhibitor (C1-INH) in the complement system?**
   A. Activating C1
   B. Inhibiting C2
   C. Preventing autoactivation of C1
   D. Enhancing C3 activation

3. **Which of the following is NOT considered a trigger for hereditary angioedema attacks?**
   A. Physical exercise
   B. Alcohol consumption
   C. ACE-inhibitors
   D. Corticosteroids

4. **What is the recommended approach for prophylaxis in HAE?**
   A. Loratadine
   B. Danazol
   C. Prednisone
   D. Ibuprofen

5. **The onset of symptoms in hereditary angioedema may be delayed 60 minutes to 36 hours after the trigger exposure.**
   A. True
   B. False

6. **A 6-year-old girl weighing 15 kg is admitted for dental rehabilitation due to multiple dental caries. She has a known diagnosis of C1-INH deficiency, a hereditary disorder resulting in angioedema without urticaria. After induction of anesthesia for dental rehabilitation, the patient experiences facial swelling, with progressive swelling noted on the right side of the neck. Given her medical history of C1-INH deficiency, the clinical picture strongly suggests an acute attack of hereditary angioedema. C1INHRP (C1 esterase inhibitor replacement protein) and Androgens (danazol) are not available. What therapy may be considered for the treatment of acute attacks of hereditary angioedema in this case?**
   A. Steroids
   B. Epinephrine
   C. Antihistamines
   D. Fresh Frozen Plasma (FFP)

Answers:

1. **Answer B (Impaired production of C1 esterase inhibitor)**

   The primary cause of hereditary angioedema (HAE) is the impaired production (Type 1) or poor function (Type 2) of C1 esterase inhibitor. This crucial protein prevents the autoactivation of C1 in the complement system. This deficiency or dysfunction leads to the release of vasoactive mediators, resulting in increased vascular permeability and edema formation. HAE is a hereditary disorder with a prevalence of approximately 1:50,000 and occurs due to autosomal dominant deficiency or dysfunction of the C1 esterase inhibitor.

2. **Answer C (Preventing autoactivation of C1)**

   C1 esterase inhibitor (C1-INH) plays a crucial role in the complement system by preventing the autoactivation of C1, which is the first factor of the classical pathway. The lack of C1-INH leads to uncontrolled complement activation, resulting in the release of vasoactive and chemotactic peptides. This uncontrolled activation causes increased vascular permeability, vasodilatation, and contraction of vascular smooth muscle, ultimately leading to the characteristic features of hereditary angioedema. These features include acute, localized, non-pitting, non-pruritic, non-erythematous, and demarcated angioedema. The swelling typically lasts for 2–5 days before resolving spontaneously. HAE is a lifelong condition, with the first attack often occurring before the age of 15, and symptoms tend to decrease with increasing age.

3. **Answer D (Corticosteroids)**

   Corticosteroids are not listed as triggers for hereditary angioedema attacks. HAE attacks can be precipitated by various triggers, including dental treatment, surgery, trauma, stress (mental or physical), exercise, infection, alcohol consumption, anesthesia, menstruation, as well as certain agents like ACE inhibitors and estrogens.

4. **Answer B (Danazol)**

   The recommended approach for prophylaxis in hereditary angioedema includes the use of androgens, with danazol being a common choice. If C1 esterase inhibitor replacement protein (C1INHRP) is not available, androgens such as danazol are administered. The dosage typically ranges from 2.5 to 10 mg/kg per day, up to a maximum of 600 mg/day. The prophylactic treatment is initiated five days before a surgical procedure and extended for five days afterward.

5. **Answer A (True)**

   In HAE, the onset of symptoms can be delayed, and manifestations may occur within a timeframe ranging from 60 minutes to as long as 36 hours after exposure to a trigger. This delayed onset underscores the importance of postoperative monitoring for individuals with HAE, especially after potential triggering events such as surgical procedures.

6. **Answer D (FFP (Fresh Frozen Plasma))**

   Given the unavailability of C1INHRP (C1 esterase inhibitor replacement protein) and androgens (danazol), the recommended therapy for the treatment of acute attacks of hereditary angioedema in this case would be FFP. FFP contains a functional C1 esterase inhibitor, and its infusion can effectively replace the deficient enzyme, mitigating the symptoms associated with the acute HAE attack. It's important to note that other options, such as steroids, epinephrine, and antihistamines, are not considered helpful in the treatment of acute HAE events.

Recommended literature

1. Williams AH, Craig TJ. Perioperative management for patients with hereditary angioedema. Allergy Rhinol (Providence). 2015;6(1):50-55.
2. Hoyer C, Hill MR, Kaminski ER. 2012. An overview of differential diagnosis and clinical management. Continuing Education in Anaesthesia Critical Care & Pain. 1:6;307–311.

HEREDITARY HEMORRHAGIC TELANGIECTASIAS

14
CHAPTER

Questions:

1. **What is the primary underlying cause of complications in individuals with Hereditary Hemorrhagic Telangiectasias (HHT)?**
   A. Increased blood viscosity
   B. Arterial hypertension
   C. Abnormal connections between arteries and veins
   D. Impaired coagulation cascade

2. **Which of the following is a common location affected by arteriovenous malformations (AVMs) in individuals with HHT?**
   A. Kidneys
   B. Heart
   C. Lungs
   D. Pancreas

3. **What is the significance of the "Curaçao criteria" in the diagnosis of HHT?**
   A. Assessing genetic predisposition
   B. Identifying risk factors for complications
   C. Diagnosing associated anesthetic considerations
   D. Establishing diagnostic criteria based on symptoms and family history

4. **What is a common manifestation of telangiectasias in HHT?**
   A. Joint pain
   B. Skin rash
   C. Red or purple spots under the skin
   D. Muscle weakness

5. **Spinal MRI is recommended before neuraxial anesthesia in HHT patients.**
   A. True
   B. False

6. **A 25-year-old male is scheduled for acute appendicitis surgery. He had the triad of recurrent epistaxis, family history, and telangiectasia and had been diagnosed with HHT. What is a potential intraoperative concern during procedures involving HHT patients with telangiectasias?**
   A. Risk of paradoxical emboli
   B. Hemodynamic instability
   C. Development of chronic anemia
   D. Difficulty in airway manipulation

Answers:

1. Answer C (Abnormal connections between arteries and veins)

The primary underlying cause of complications in individuals with Hereditary Hemorrhagic Telangiectasias (HHT) is the development of abnormal connections, known as arteriovenous malformations (AVMs), between arteries and veins. HHT, also called Osler-Weber-Rendu disease, is an autosomal dominant genetic disorder. These abnormal connections, or AVMs, can occur in various organs, such as the nose, lungs, brain, and liver. These AVMs lead to disruptions in normal blood flow. They are more prone to hemorrhage, contributing to the characteristic symptoms and complications associated with HHT, including nosebleeds, anemia, and the risk of bleeding in different organs. The increased fragility of these abnormal vessels and the potential for bleeding are key factors underlying the clinical manifestations and complications seen in individuals with HHT.

2. Answer C (Lungs)

The most common locations affected by arteriovenous malformations in individuals with HHT include the nose, lungs, brain, and liver. It's important to note that the term "visceral AVM" refers to AVMs in internal organs, and in the context of HHT, the lungs are one of the visceral organs commonly affected. These AVMs in the lungs can lead to various complications, including the risk of bleeding and other respiratory symptoms.

3. Answer D (Establishing diagnostic criteria based on symptoms and family history)

The "Curaçao criteria" hold significance in the diagnosis of HHT by providing a comprehensive set of criteria based on symptoms and family history. To establish a diagnosis of HHT, individuals are required to meet at least three of the four criteria, which include spontaneous recurrent epistaxis, the presence of multiple telangiectasias in typical locations, the confirmation of visceral arteriovenous malformation in organs such as the lung, liver, brain, or spine, and having a first-degree family member with HHT.

4. Answer C (Red or purple spots under the skin)

A common manifestation of telangiectasias in HHT is the appearance of red or purple spots just underneath the skin. These abnormal blood vessels, known as telangiectasias, can be visible on various parts of the body. In individuals with HHT, these red or purple spots often form on fingertip pads, the lips, and the lining of the nose or the gut. This visible manifestation is one of the clinical features of HHT, alongside other symptoms such as recurrent nosebleeds, iron deficiency anemia, shortness of breath, headaches, seizures, and abnormal artery-vein connections within the brain, lungs, and liver.

5. Answer A (True)

Spinal MRI is recommended before neuraxial anesthesia in HHT patients to rule out the presence of spinal arteriovenous malformations. Neuraxial anesthesia involves procedures such as epidural or spinal anesthesia, and in HHT patients, there is a risk of spinal AVMs. These AVMs may pose a risk of epidural hematoma formation, leading to potential paralysis.

6. Answer D (Difficulty in airway manipulation)

In patients with a diagnosis of HHT, a potential intraoperative concern is the difficulty in airway manipulation. The most common occurrence of telangiectasias in HHT patients is in the oral cavity and nasopharyngeal passages. Therefore, bleeding from the oropharynx becomes a primary concern during airway manipulation. Rupture of a known or unknown arteriovenous malformation during direct laryngoscopy and the passage of the endotracheal tube (ETT) may lead to bleeding, causing obstruction of the view of the vocal cords and potentially resulting in a difficult airway situation. To optimize conditions and minimize the risk of trauma, the anesthesiologist should employ measures such as gentle direct laryngoscopy, lubrication of the ETT, consideration of a smaller size ETT if appropriate, and the use of soft and gentle suction. These precautions are essential to prevent bleeding-related complications and ensure safe airway management for patients with HHT and telangiectasias.

Recommended literature

1. Robinson, D., Rogers, B., Kapoor, R., Swan, J., Speas, G., Gutmann, R., 2014. Anesthetic Considerations for a Patient With Hereditary Hemorrhagic Telangiectasia (Osler-Weber–Rendu Syndrome) Undergoing a Five-Box Thoracoscopic Maze Procedure for Atrial Fibrillation. Journal of Investigative Medicine High Impact Case Reports 2, 232470961455366.

HIV AND AIDS

Questions:

1. What characterizes Chronic or Clinical Latent HIV Infection (Stage 2)?
   A. Flu-like symptoms
   B. Asymptomatic HIV infection
   C. Severe opportunistic infections
   D. High viral load

2. What is the NOT primary factor determining progression to AIDS in individuals with HIV?
   A. High viral load
   B. CD4 cell count below 200 cells/mm3
   C. Opportunistic infections
   D. Antiretroviral therapy resistance

3. Which of the following is NOT a major opportunistic pathogen in HIV/AIDS?
   A. Cryptococcus neoformans
   B. MRSA
   C. Cytomegalovirus
   D. Pneumocystis carinii

4. What is the role of Highly Active Antiretroviral Therapy (HAART) in HIV management?
   A. Cure HIV
   B. Reduce viral load
   C. Treat opportunistic infections
   D. Enhance immune response

5. Elective caesarean section in HIV-positive mothers is recommended to reduce the incidence of mother-to-child transmission of HIV.
   A. True
   B. False

6. A 45-year-old woman, known to be HIV positive, is scheduled for hip replacement surgery due to osteoarthritis. She has been compliant with her antiretroviral therapy (ART) regimen, consisting of a triple-drug combination of zidovudine, didanosine, and nevirapine. Her recent viral load is well controlled, and her CD4 cell count is within normal limits. The choice of regional anesthesia has been made, taking into account the patient's HIV status and the planned surgical procedure. Preoperative considerations include assessing potential side effects related to the antiretroviral medications. Which of the following is NOT a potential side effect of antiretroviral therapy that an anesthesiologist should consider?
   A. Insulin resistance
   B. Renal failure
   C. Peripheral neuropathy
   D. Gastroesophageal reflux disease (GERD)

Answers:

1. Answer B (Asymptomatic HIV infection)

Chronic or Clinical Latent HIV Infection (stage 2) is characterized by asymptomatic HIV infection or clinical latency, where the virus remains active and continues to reproduce, even though patients may not exhibit any symptoms. Despite the absence of apparent signs, individuals in this stage can still transmit HIV to others. The intake of HIV treatment during this phase is crucial, as it can effectively prevent the development of the more severe Stage 3 (AIDS). However, if left untreated or inadequately managed, the HIV viral load may increase towards the end of this stage, leading to progression into AIDS, marked by a significantly compromised immune system and the potential onset of opportunistic infections or other serious illnesses.

2. Answer D (Antiretroviral therapy resistance)

The primary factor determining progression to AIDS in individuals with HIV is not antiretroviral therapy resistance. The progression to AIDS is chiefly influenced by factors such as a high viral load, a CD4 cell count below 200 cells/mm3, and the development of opportunistic infections or other serious illnesses. A high viral load signifies increased viral replication and potential immune system damage, while a CD4 cell count below 200 cells/mm3 indicates severe immunosuppression. Opportunistic infections or serious illnesses, regardless of CD4 count, are additional criteria for defining the transition to AIDS. Although antiretroviral therapy resistance is a significant consideration in HIV management, it is not the primary determinant of progression to AIDS.

3. Answer B (MRSA (Methicillin-resistant Staphylococcus aureus))

Among the options provided, MRSA (Methicillin-resistant Staphylococcus aureus) is NOT a major opportunistic pathogen in HIV/AIDS. Opportunistic infections in individuals with HIV/AIDS are primarily caused by specific pathogens that take advantage of the compromised immune system. The major opportunistic pathogens in HIV/AIDS include various protozoa, fungi and yeasts, viruses, and bacteria. MRSA, a bacterial strain resistant to certain antibiotics, is not traditionally considered a major opportunistic pathogen in the context of HIV/AIDS.

4. Answer B (Reduce of viral load)

The primary role of Highly Active Antiretroviral Therapy (HAART) in HIV management is to reduce the viral load in individuals infected with the virus. While HAART does not represent a cure for HIV, it is instrumental in slowing the progression of the disease. HAART involves administering a combination or cocktail of antiretroviral agents, typically including a non-nucleoside reverse transcriptase inhibitor (NNRTI) and two nucleoside analog reverse transcriptase inhibitors (NRTIs). This combination aims to suppress the replication of HIV, leading to a reduction in the viral load circulating in the bloodstream.

5. Answer A (True)

In the context of pregnancy considerations for HIV-positive mothers, the use of Antiretroviral Therapy (AZT) helps decrease perinatal transmission. Elective caesarean section is recommended as it may further reduce the risk of transmission, especially when the viral load is elevated (above 1000 copies/mL). It is important to note that all HIV-positive mothers should be offered this option. Still, vaginal delivery may also be considered, particularly if the viral load is below the specified threshold. Additionally, regional anesthesia is considered acceptable during labor or caesarean section, with careful documentation of peripheral neuropathy, coagulation status, and adherence to strict sterile techniques with gown usage.

6. Answer D (Gastroesophageal reflux disease (GERD))

Gastroesophageal reflux disease is generally not considered a significant side effect of antiretroviral therapy (ART). However, when assessing HIV-positive patients for surgery, anesthesiologists should be attentive to potential side effects associated with ART. These may include insulin resistance affecting glucose metabolism, the risk of renal failure, the development of peripheral neuropathy, drug interactions mediated by p450 activation, the rare occurrence of lactic acidosis, and the impact on lipid metabolism leading to dyslipidemia.

Recommended literature

1. Leelanukrom R. Anaesthetic considerations of the HIV-infected patients. Curr Opin Anaesthesiol. 2009;22(3):412-418.
2. Wilson, S. 2009 HIV and anaesthesia. Updtae in anaesthesia.
3. Prout J, Agarwal B. 2005. Anaesthesia and critical care for patients with HIV infection. Continuing Education in Anaesthesia Critical Care & Pain. 5;5:153-156.

HUNTINGTON'S DISEASE

Questions:

1. **What is the primary genetic inheritance pattern of Huntington's Disease (HD)?**
   A. Autosomal recessive
   B. X-linked recessive
   C. Autosomal dominant
   D. Y-linked

2. **What is the primary consequence of the increased production of the mutant protein Huntington in HD?**
   A. Increased cell proliferation
   B. Nerve cell degeneration
   C. Enhanced neurotransmitter release
   D. Improved cognitive function

3. **What are the common clinical features associated with Huntington's Disease?**
   A. Tremors, euphoria, and hyperactivity
   B. Choreaform movements, depression, and dementia
   C. Muscle stiffness, anxiety, and hallucinations
   D. Ataxia, irritability, and seizures

4. **What is a potential preoperative sedation option to control choreiform movements in patients with Huntington's disease?**
   A. Midazolam
   B. Propofol
   C. Haloperidol
   D. Ketamine

5. **Succinylcholine is contraindicated in individuals with Huntington's Disease.**
   A. True
   B. False

6. **A 50-year-old male, weighing 50 kg, with a history of Huntington's chorea diagnosed at the age of 40, was admitted for an emergency laparoscopic hernia repair. On physical examination, the patient exhibited choreic movements in all limbs, swallowing dysfunction, and excessive oral secretions. What types of anesthetic medications are generally considered okay for use in individuals with Huntington's Disease?**
   A. Inhalational anesthetics only
   B. Intravenous anesthetics only
   C. Both inhalational and intravenous anesthetics
   D. Regional anesthetics only

Answers:

1. **Answer C (Autosomal dominant)**

Huntington's Disease (HD) is an autosomal dominant genetic disorder. This means that the mutated gene responsible for HD is located on an autosome, and an individual needs only one copy of the mutated gene from either parent to inherit the disease. In the context of autosomal dominant inheritance, a person with an affected parent has a 50% chance of inheriting the mutated gene.

2. **Answer B (Nerve cell degeneration)**

The mutated gene associated with HD leads to an overproduction of the mutant protein Huntington. This protein, in turn, initiates a cascade of events that ultimately result in the degeneration and loss of nerve cells in various brain regions. As a result of nerve cell degeneration, individuals with HD experience a range of symptoms, including uncontrollable dance-like movements (chorea) and abnormal body postures. Beyond motor symptoms, HD affects other aspects of neurological function, leading to problems with behavior, emotion, thinking, and personality.

3. **Answer B (Choreaform movements, depression, and dementia)**

Huntington's Disease is characterized by a range of motor and non-motor symptoms that progressively worsen over time. The most prominent motor symptom is chorea, which refers to uncontrollable dance-like movements of the limbs and body. These movements are a hallmark feature of HD and contribute to the characteristic presentation of the disease. In addition to chorea, individuals with HD often experience a spectrum of non-motor symptoms, including depression and dementia. The comprehensive list of symptoms associated with HD encompasses difficulty concentrating, memory lapses, stumbling and clumsiness, irritability, hallucinations, paranoia, psychosis, problems with swallowing, speaking, and breathing, muscle problems such as rigidity or dystonia, slow or unusual eye movements, impaired gait, posture, and balance. As the disease progresses, full-time nursing care is often needed in the later stages.

4. **Answer C (Haloperidol)**

Haloperidol is a potential preoperative sedation option to control choreiform movements in patients with Huntington's disease. The use of butyrophenones, such as haloperidol, can be beneficial in managing the characteristic dance-like movements (chorea) associated with Huntington's disease. Haloperidol is an antipsychotic medication that acts on the central nervous system, helping to regulate dopamine levels. In the context of Huntington's disease, where chorea is a prominent motor symptom, haloperidol's neuroleptic properties can aid in reducing these involuntary movements.

5. **Answer B (False)**

Succinylcholine is not contraindicated in individuals with Huntington's Disease, but caution is advised. Succinylcholine is generally considered acceptable in HD patients undergoing anesthesia; however, there are considerations regarding its duration of action. In individuals with Huntington's Disease, the duration of succinylcholine may be prolonged due to decreased plasma cholinesterase activity. This can result in a slower metabolism and elimination of succinylcholine from the body.

6. **Answer C (Both inhalational and intravenous anesthetics)**

Both inhalational and intravenous anesthetics are generally considered appropriate for use in individuals with Huntington's Disease. While all IV anesthetics are deemed acceptable with caution due to potential slower recovery, inhalational anesthetics provide controlled and reversible anesthesia, especially useful for longer procedures. Neuraxial/regional anesthesia is also considered acceptable, but pre-existing deficits, such as choreic movements and swallowing dysfunction, need to be documented. In the case of a 50-year-old male with Huntington's chorea undergoing an emergency laparoscopic hernia repair, a combination of inhalational and intravenous agents may be employed, with careful monitoring and adjustments to ensure a safe and effective anesthetic outcome. Close collaboration between the anesthesia and surgical teams is crucial for tailored perioperative care.

Recommended literature

1. Batra A, Sahni N, Mete UK. Anesthetic management of a patient with Huntington's chorea undergoing robot-assisted nephron-sparing surgery. Indian J Anaesth. 2016;60(11):866-867.
2. Kang JM, Chung JY, Han JH, Kim YS, Lee BJ, Yi JW. Anesthetic management of a patient with Huntington's chorea -A case report-. Korean J Anesthesiol. 2013;64(3):262-264.

NEUROFIBROMATOSIS

14

CHAPTER

Questions:

1. **What is the primary genetic basis of neurofibromatosis (NF)?**
   A. Autosomal recessive
   B. Autosomal dominant
   C. X-linked recessive
   D. X-linked dominant

2. **What are the common signs of Neurofibromatosis 1 (NF1)?**
   A. Hearing loss, ringing in ears, poor balance
   B. Cafe au lait spots, freckling, Lisch nodules
   C. Soft, pea-sized bumps (neurofibromas), slow-growing acoustic neuromas
   D. Schwannomas cause pain and numbness

3. **What is a potential respiratory complication associated with neurofibromatosis?**
   A. Asthma
   B. Restrictive lung disease
   C. Chronic obstructive pulmonary disease (COPD)
   D. Pulmonary embolism

4. **What is NOT the treatment modality commonly used for the management of tumors in neurofibromatosis?**
   A. Immunotherapy
   B. Chemotherapy
   C. Radiotherapy
   D. Surgical removal

5. **Hypertension is the cardiovascular manifestation commonly associated with neurofibromatosis.**
   A. True
   B. False

6. **A 44-year-old male with a confirmed diagnosis of neurofibromatosis presents with a broken ankle requiring immediate surgical intervention. Notably, he has a coexisting neurofibroma on the tongue, posing potential challenges during anesthesia management. What conflict might arise in the context of neuraxial anesthesia in a patient with neurofibromatosis?**
   A. Neuraxial vs Cardiomyopathy
   B. Increased ICP vs Neuraxial
   C. Neuraxial vs Pheochromocytoma
   D. Spinal neuromas vs Difficult airway

Answers:

1. Answer B (Autosomal dominant)

Neurofibromatosis (NF) is a group of genetic disorders characterized by the formation of tumors on nerve tissue. These tumors can develop in various locations, including the brain, spinal cord, and nerves. The primary genetic basis of neurofibromatosis is autosomal dominant inheritance. This means that the disorder is caused by a genetic mutation in oncogenes located on autosomal chromosomes. In autosomal dominant inheritance, an individual with one affected parent has a 50% chance of inheriting the mutated gene and, consequently, developing the disorder.

2. Answer B (Cafe au lait spots, freckling, Lisch nodules)

Various signs and symptoms characterize neurofibromatosis 1 (NF1). The common signs of NF1 include cafe au lait spots (flat, light brown spots on the skin), freckling in the armpits or groin area, and tiny bumps on the eye's iris known as Lisch nodules. Other features associated with NF1 include soft, pea-sized bumps on or under the skin (neurofibromas), bone deformities, and the potential development of a tumor on the optic nerve known as optic glioma. Individuals with NF1 may also experience learning disabilities, have a larger-than-average head size, and exhibit short stature. NF2 is characterized by the development of benign, slow-growing acoustic neuromas, leading to gradual hearing loss, ear ringing, poor balance, and headaches.

3. Answer B (Restrictive lung disease)

A potential respiratory complication associated with neurofibromatosis is restrictive lung disease. In individuals with neurofibromatosis, kyphoscoliosis, a curvature of the spine involving lateral and rotational deformities, is a common manifestation, affecting approximately 25% of individuals. Kyphoscoliosis can lead to a restrictive pattern of lung disease. Additionally, there is a potential for pulmonary fibrosis from parenchymal tumors associated with neurofibromatosis. Pulmonary fibrosis can further contribute to restrictive lung disease. Other respiratory complications include the potential for pulmonary hypertension and right ventricular (RV) failure. Furthermore, a mediastinal neurofibroma may present with cardiopulmonary complaints, adding to the respiratory challenges associated with neurofibromatosis.

4. Answer A (Immunotherapy)

The treatment modalities commonly employed for managing tumors in neurofibromatosis include surgical removal, chemotherapy, and radiotherapy. Surgical removal is a primary and often essential approach for accessible tumors. At the same time, chemotherapy is considered for cases where systemic treatment is necessary or when tumors are challenging to reach surgically. Radiotherapy is another effective method, particularly when surgery is not feasible. However, immunotherapy is not currently identified as a standard treatment for neurofibromatosis-associated tumors.

5. Answer A (True)

Hypertension is a cardiovascular manifestation commonly associated with neurofibromatosis. Hypertension is usually essential, but secondary causes are considered, with renal artery stenosis (RAS) being more common than pheochromocytoma. Therefore, hypertension is a recognized cardiovascular consideration in neurofibromatosis, and its prevalence is often associated with the underlying characteristics of the condition. Other cardiovascular manifestations include dysrhythmias, idiopathic cardiomyopathy, and the presence of a tumor in the right ventricular outflow tract.

6. Answer B (Increased ICP vs Neuraxial)

In patients with neurofibromatosis undergoing neuraxial anesthesia, a significant conflict arises regarding the potential elevation of intracranial pressure (ICP). Neurofibromatosis is linked to the formation of tumors, encompassing both spinal neurofibromas and intracranial tumors, potentially leading to elevated intracranial pressure. Neuraxial anesthesia procedures, such as epidural or spinal anesthesia, can impact cerebrospinal fluid dynamics and potentially exacerbate elevated ICP. Therefore, careful consideration and imaging (MRI or CT) of the spine are crucial before planning any regional anesthesia technique to rule out increased intracranial pressure. While considerations such as difficult airway, spinal neuromas, and the selection between general and neuraxial anesthesia are pertinent in the context of neurofibromatosis, the specific focus on the potential conflict between increased intracranial pressure and the use of neuraxial anesthesia underscores the critical need for a comprehensive preoperative assessment and meticulous decision-making to uphold patient safety.

Recommended literature

1. Fox CJ, Tomajian S, Kaye AJ, Russo S, Abadie JV, Kaye AD. Perioperative management of neurofibromatosis type 1. Ochsner J. 2012;12(2):111-121.
2. Griffiths, S., Durbridge, J.A., 2011. Anaesthetic implications of neurological disease in pregnancy. Continuing Education in Anaesthesia Critical Care & Pain 11, 157–161.
3. Hirsch NP, Murphy A, Radcliffe JJ. Neurofibromatosis: clinical presentations and anaesthetic implications. Br J Anaesth. 2001;86(4):555-564.

PERIODIC PARALYSIS

14
CHAPTER

Questions:

1. **Which of the following triggers is NOT specific to Hyperkalemic Periodic Paralysis (hyperPP)?**
   A. Strenuous exercise
   B. Metabolic alkalosis
   C. Hypothermia
   D. Potassium infusion

2. **What is the primary factor leading to muscle weakness in Hypokalemic Periodic Paralysis (HypoPP)?**
   A. Low serum potassium levels
   B. Defective calcium channels
   C. Sodium channel dysfunction
   D. High levels of thyroid hormone

3. **Which form of periodic paralysis is associated with facial features such as a broad forehead, widely spaced eyes, low-set ears, and a small chin?**
   A. Hypokalemic Periodic Paralysis (HypoPP)
   B. Hyperkalemic Periodic Paralysis (HyperPP)
   C. Thyrotoxic Periodic Paralysis
   D. Andersen-Tawil Syndrome

4. **Which form of periodic paralysis may spare the diaphragm during paralysis attacks?**
   A. Hyperkalemic Periodic Paralysis
   B. Hypokalemic Periodic Paralysis
   C. Andersen-Tawil Syndrome
   D. Thyrotoxic Periodic Paralysis

5. **Hypothermia should be avoided in patients with Hypokalemic Periodic Paralysis.**
   A. True
   B. False

6. **A 41-year-old male with a history of HyperPP, asthma, and hypertension undergoes laparoscopic sigmoid resection following failed conservative management. Preoperative assessments, including normal ECG and laboratory values, reveal serum potassium at 4.3 mEq/L and glucose at 82 mg/dL. The patient is prescribed a high carbohydrate diet and acetazolamide. What is the recommended anesthetic consideration for patients with periodic paralysis during surgery?**
   A. High-dose non-depolarizing neuromuscular blocking agents
   B. Succinylcholine for rapid induction
   C. Continuous monitoring with a Twitch monitor
   D. Prophylactic administration of loop diuretics

Answers:

1. **Answer B (Metabolic alkalosis)**

   Hyperkalemic Periodic Paralysis is typically provoked by factors that elevate serum potassium levels, including strenuous exercise, stress, cold, potassium infusion, metabolic acidosis, and hypothermia. In contrast, metabolic alkalosis, characterized by increased blood pH, is not commonly associated with the onset of Hyperkalemic Periodic Paralysis.

2. **Answer A (Low serum potassium levels)**

   The primary factor leading to muscle weakness in Hypokalemic Periodic Paralysis (HypoPP) is low serum potassium levels. During acute attacks of HypoPP, there is a decrease in serum potassium levels, leading to potassium leakage into muscle cells from the bloodstream. This can be triggered by factors such as strenuous exercise, high carbohydrate meals, stress, cold temperatures, and infusion of glucose and insulin. The resulting potassium imbalance disrupts normal muscle cell function, causing temporary paralysis, typically affecting the limbs and trunk but sparing the diaphragm. Chronic muscle weakness tends to develop in most patients with HypoPP as they age.

3. **Answer D (Andersen-Tawil Syndrome)**

   Individuals with Andersen-Tawil Syndrome often exhibit distinctive facial characteristics such as a broad forehead, widely spaced eyes, low-set ears, and a small chin. This syndrome is a rare autosomal dominant condition caused by a genetic defect that results in defective calcium channels. It is characterized not only by facial features but also by periodic paralysis, cardiac abnormalities, and other features. Triggers for attacks in Andersen-Tawil Syndrome include exercise, stress, and certain foods. It is more prevalent in men, particularly those of Asian backgrounds.

4. **Answer B (Hypokalemic Periodic Paralysis)**

   During acute attacks of Hypokalemic Periodic Paralysis, the paralysis typically affects the limbs and trunk but spares the diaphragm. Chronic muscle weakness tends to develop in most patients with Hypokalemic Periodic Paralysis as they age. Hypokalemic Periodic Paralysis is characterized by attacks of muscle weakness associated with low serum potassium levels. The diaphragm's sparing during attacks is crucial for differentiating it from other forms of periodic paralysis where respiratory muscles may be affected.

5. **Answer B (False)**

   Hypothermia is not a specific trigger for HypoPP. The triggers for HypoPP include factors such as strenuous exercise, glucose/insulin infusion, and ingestion of carbohydrates and sodium-rich food, but hypothermia is not listed as a trigger.

6. **Answer C (Continuous monitoring with a Twitch monitor)**

   For a patient with a history of Hyperkalemic Periodic Paralysis (HyperPP), the primary consideration during surgery involves minimizing the risk of triggering paralysis attacks and closely monitoring neuromuscular function. Continuous monitoring with a twitch monitor is recommended for patients with periodic paralysis. This monitoring allows precise assessment of the patient's response to neuromuscular blocking agents (NMBA), helping to avoid excessive blockade and potential complications. Patients with periodic paralysis, including HyperPP, may be sensitive to NDMRs, and using a reduced dose is advisable. Additionally, avoiding succinylcholine, as it can trigger hyperkalemia, is essential in patients with HyperPP. The patient's prescribed acetazolamide aims to reduce the frequency and severity of paralysis attacks by addressing the underlying ion channel dysfunction. Frequent electrolyte monitoring, especially potassium levels, is crucial to promptly address any fluctuations that may arise during the perioperative period.

Recommended literature

1. Marsh, S., Pittard, A., 2011. Neuromuscular disorders and anaesthesia. Part 2: specific neuromuscular disorders. Continuing Education in Anaesthesia Critical Care & Pain 11, 119–123.

Rare co-existing diseases
SARCOIDOSIS

Questions:

1. **What is the primary mechanism believed to be involved in the development of sarcoidosis?**
   A. Genetic mutations
   B. Autoimmune reaction
   C. Allergic response
   D. Abnormal immune reaction to triggers

2. **Which organ is less commonly affected but can lead to potentially fatal complications in sarcoidosis?**
   A. Lungs
   B. Liver
   C. Skin
   D. Heart

3. **What is a common site of sarcoid infiltration in the upper airway that may cause vocal cord palsy?**
   A. Trachea
   B. Epiglottis
   C. Larynx
   D. Tongue

4. **What diagnostic method is typically used to confirm the diagnosis of sarcoidosis?**
   A. Blood tests
   B. Imaging studies
   C. Biopsy
   D. Echocardiography

5. **In addition to vocal cord palsy, bronchoconstriction is the most common next airway-related complication that may be encountered during intubation in sarcoidosis patients.**
   A. True
   B. False

6. **A 54-year-old lady with a history of sarcoidosis presented for a mastectomy due to carcinoma of the breast. Two years ago, she began experiencing difficulty breathing, even during routine conversations. A cervical lymph node biopsy revealed sarcoidosis as the underlying cause of her respiratory symptoms. Following the diagnosis, she was initiated on a course of oral steroids, resulting in significant improvement in her symptoms over a year. What is NOT a goal of anesthetic considerations for sarcoidosis patients?**
   A. Anticipate potentially difficult airway
   B. Anticipate exacerbation of cor pulmonale
   C. Anticipate the use of high-dose opioids
   D. Anticipate hypercalcemia

Answers:

1. **Answer D (Abnormal immune reaction to triggers)**

   Sarcoidosis is characterized as an idiopathic multisystem granulomatous disorder that typically occurs in the age group of 20-40 years, with a slight preponderance in females. The exact etiology of sarcoidosis remains unknown; however, it is thought to arise from an exaggerated cell-mediated immune response. This immune response can have both inherited and acquired components. The pathogenesis of sarcoidosis is complex and involves the formation of noncaseating granulomas in affected organs. While the specific trigger for the abnormal immune reaction is unidentified, it is believed to be a response to certain environmental factors, such as infections or exposure to chemicals. The granulomas represent an accumulation of inflammatory cells and are a hallmark feature of sarcoidosis.

2. **Answer D (Heart)**

   The lungs and lymph nodes are the most commonly affected organs in sarcoidosis. However, less commonly affected organs include the eyes, skin, liver, and brain. Although less common, cardiac involvement is particularly significant as it can lead to potentially fatal complications. Symptoms of cardiac involvement in sarcoidosis include chest pain, dyspnea, syncope, fatigue, arrhythmias, palpitations, and edema.

3. **Answer C (Larynx)**

   Sarcoidosis can involve the upper airway, with the supraglottic region being a common site of sarcoid infiltration. This infiltration can result in complications such as vocal cord palsy. Patients with laryngeal sarcoidosis may present with symptoms such as hoarseness of voice, dyspnea, wheezing, and stridor. The potential for vocal cord palsy and other upper airway issues in sarcoidosis patients emphasizes the importance of anticipating a potentially difficult airway during intubation.

4. **Answer C (Biopsy)**

   The characteristic feature of sarcoidosis is the presence of noncaseating granulomas in the involved organs. These granulomas are collections of inflammatory cells and are a hallmark finding in sarcoidosis. While blood tests and imaging studies such as MRI and echocardiography can provide valuable information, a definitive diagnosis is often achieved by examining tissue obtained by biopsy. This allows for a detailed analysis of the cellular composition of the granulomas and helps distinguish sarcoidosis from other conditions with similar clinical presentations.

5. **Answer B (False)**

   While vocal cord palsy and bronchoconstriction are potential airway-related complications in sarcoidosis patients, the most common next complication is tracheal stenosis. In cases of supraglottic region involvement, which is common in sarcoidosis, tracheal stenosis can be encountered during intubation.

6. **Answer C (Anticipate use of high-dose opioids)**

   The primary goal that is not typically considered in anesthetic considerations for sarcoidosis patients is the anticipation of using high-dose opioids. The essential goals include anticipating a potentially difficult airway due to possible upper airway involvement, managing potential cardiomyopathy and Automatic Implantable Cardioverter-Defibrillator (AICD) presence, tailoring an appropriate ventilatory strategy for restrictive lung disease, avoiding exacerbation of cor pulmonale and pulmonary hypertension, considering stress dose steroids in patients on chronic steroid therapy, and being prepared to manage potential complications such as prolonged neuromuscular blockade, hypercalcemia, and arrhythmias. While opioids may be used based on individual patient and surgical factors, it is not a primary goal in the comprehensive approach to anesthetic management in sarcoidosis patients.

Recommended literature

1. Pollard BJ, Kitchen, G. Handbook of Clinical Anaesthesia. Fourth Edition. CRC Press. 2018. 978-1-4987-6289-2.
2. Sanders, D., Rowland, R., Howell, T., 2016. Sarcoidosis and anaesthesia. BJA Education 16, 173–177.

RENAL DISEASES

Renal diseases
ACUTE KIDNEY INJURY (AKI)

15
CHAPTER

Questions:

1. **Which of the following is NOT a cause of pre-renal acute kidney injury (AKI)?**
   A. Bleeding
   B. Sepsis
   C. Intrinsic renal disease
   D. Dehydration

2. **Intrinsic renal AKI can result from which of the following conditions?**
   A. Bleeding
   B. Prostatic hypertrophy
   C. Sepsis
   D. Dehydration

3. **What is the primary characteristic of post-renal AKI?**
   A. Inadequate perfusion
   B. Obstructive uropathy
   C. Vasodilatory hypotension
   D. Locally impaired renal circulation

4. **What electrolyte disturbance is commonly associated with AKI?**
   A. Hypernatremia
   B. Hypocalcemia
   C. Hyperkalemia
   D. Hypomagnesemia

5. **Succinylcholine administration is contraindicated in patients with AKI.**
   A. True
   B. False

6. **A 62-year-old patient presents to the Emergency Department with abdominal pain, distension, and vomiting. The patient appears dehydrated and reports a decrease in urine output. Clinical examination reveals signs of ileus, and laboratory results show metabolic acidosis, increased serum creatinine concentration, elevated blood urea nitrogen (BUN), and electrolyte disturbances with an elevated potassium level. The concentrated urine output raises concern for oliguria. Given the suspicion of mesenteric thrombosis as a potential cause of bowel obstruction, an emergency contrast-enhanced CT scan is indicated to evaluate the blood supply to the intestines and rule out vascular compromise. Which strategy is recommended for preventing contrast dye-induced acute kidney injury?**
   A. Contrast dye is contraindicated
   B. Limiting sodium bicarbonate
   C. Withholding other nephrotoxic agents
   D. Encouraging fluid overload

Answers:

1. Answer C (Intrinsic renal disease)

Pre-renal acute kidney injury (AKI) is primarily characterized by reduced renal perfusion, leading to impaired kidney function. Bleeding and dehydration contribute to hypovolemia, a common cause of pre-renal AKI. Sepsis induces vasodilatory hypotension, further compromising renal blood flow. However, intrinsic renal diseases, such as glomerulonephritis or interstitial nephritis, fall under a distinct category of AKI that involves direct damage to the renal parenchyma. Intrinsic renal diseases are not considered causes of pre-renal AKI, as they do not primarily involve factors external to the kidneys affecting blood flow.

2. Answer C (Sepsis)

Intrinsic renal acute kidney injury occurs when conditions directly impact the renal parenchyma, and sepsis, characterized by systemic inflammation, is one such cause. The inflammatory response and associated hemodynamic changes in sepsis contribute to acute tubular injury, impairing renal function. Bleeding is more aligned with pre-renal AKI, while prostatic hypertrophy is linked to post-renal AKI due to urine flow obstruction. Dehydration is commonly associated with pre-renal AKI. Moreover, intrinsic renal AKI can result from various other conditions, including acute tubular injury due to systemic inflammation, major surgery, or prolonged ischemia; exposure to nephrotoxins like aminoglycosides or radiological contrast; pigment nephropathy (e.g., rhabdomyolysis or hemolysis); metabolic syndromes (e.g., hypercalcemia or hyperuricemia); and autoimmune/inflammatory conditions like glomerulonephritis, vasculitis, thrombotic microangiopathies, or interstitial nephritis.

3. Answer B (Obstructive uropathy)

Post-renal acute kidney injury is characterized by obstruction of the urinary flow downstream from the kidneys, leading to impaired urine excretion. The primary characteristic of post-renal AKI is obstructive uropathy, where the normal urine flow is hindered. This obstruction can occur at various points along the urinary tract. The prostatic hypertrophy, nephrolithiasis, retroperitoneal fibrosis, pelvic masses, and bladder tumors all represent potential causes of obstruction contributing to post-renal AKI. In these cases, the urine flow is obstructed, leading to increased pressure within the urinary system, which can subsequently impact renal function.

4. Answer C (Hyperkalemia)

AKI, or acute kidney injury, often leads to dysregulation of volume status, metabolic acidosis, and electrolytes. Hyperkalemia is a common complication associated with AKI. When the injury involves the late distal nephron and extends into the collecting duct, it can cause direct injury to cells responsible for potassium (K+) secretion. As a result, impaired renal excretion of potassium leads to elevated serum potassium levels. Hyperkalemia is a potentially life-threatening condition characterized by a serum potassium concentration exceeding 5.5 mmol/L. It can arise from various causes, and in the context of AKI, compromised renal function contributes to the inability to regulate potassium levels properly.

5. Answer A (True)

Succinylcholine administration is contraindicated in patients with acute kidney injury. This is due to the risk of hyperkalemia associated with succinylcholine use, especially in patients with renal dysfunction. Succinylcholine is a depolarizing neuromuscular blocking agent that can trigger a rapid release of potassium from muscle cells, leading to an increase in serum potassium levels. In patients with AKI, impaired renal function limits the ability to excrete excess potassium efficiently, making them more susceptible to succinylcholine-induced hyperkalemia.

6. Answer C (Withholding other nephrotoxic agents)

In patients at risk for renal impairment, it is crucial to avoid additional insults to the kidneys. Contrast dye-induced AKI can be mitigated by avoiding concomitant administration of other nephrotoxic substances, such as nonsteroidal anti-inflammatory drugs (NSAIDs) and aminoglycoside antibiotics. The pathophysiology of contrast dye-induced AKI involves a combination of hypoxic and toxic damage, as well as endothelial dysfunction. Therefore, careful management of risk factors and the avoidance of nephrotoxic agents are crucial to mitigate the potential adverse effects of contrast dye on renal function.

Recommended literature

1. Gumbert SD, Kork F, Jackson ML, et al. Perioperative Acute Kidney Injury. Anesthesiology. 2020;132(1):180-204.
2. Pollard BJ, Kitchen, G. Handbook of Clinical Anaesthesia. Fourth Edition. CRC Press. 2018. 978-1-4987-6289-2.
3. Goren O, Matot I. Perioperative acute kidney injury. Br J Anaesth. 2015;115 Suppl 2:ii3-ii14.
4. Gross JL, Prowle JR. Perioperative acute kidney injury, BJA Education, Volume 15, Issue 4, 2015, Pages 213-218.

CHRONIC KIDNEY DISEASE

15
CHAPTER

Questions:

1. **What is the primary cause of chronic kidney disease (CKD)?**
   A. Hypertension and Heart disease/failure
   B. Hypertension and High cholesterol
   C. Hypertension and Diabetes
   D. Hypertension and use of NSAIDs

2. **What is NOT a potential respiratory complication of CKD?**
   A. Pleural effusion
   B. Pulmonary edema
   C. Chronic obstructive pulmonary disease
   D. Respiratory infection

3. **Which electrolyte disturbance is common in CKD?**
   A. Hypernatremia
   B. Hyperglycemia
   C. Hyperkalemia
   D. Hypercalcemia

4. **How can decreased renal function in CKD affect the administration of anesthetic drugs?**
   A. It shortens the duration of drug effects
   B. It does not affect anesthetic drug metabolism
   C. It prolongs the duration of drug effects
   D. It increases drug sensitivity

5. **Gastroparesis and risk of aspiration is a potential complication of CKD.**
   A. True
   B. False

6. **A patient with CKD stage 5 is in the recovery room following emergency surgery for a perforated gastric ulcer. The patient complains of severe pain. Considering the patient's renal status, an appropriate approach to pain management is crucial to avoid complications associated with reduced renal function. Which drug class should be used with caution in CKD patients?**
   A. Oxycodone
   B. Morphine
   C. Tramadol
   D. Codeine phosphate

Answers:

1. Answer C (Hypertension and Diabetes)

The primary cause of chronic kidney disease (CKD) is often a combination of factors, but diabetes and high blood pressure stand out as the most common culprits. Among the provided options, hypertension and diabetes contribute significantly to the development and progression of CKD. Hypertension can lead to damage in the small blood vessels of the kidneys, impairing their function over time. Similarly, diabetes, especially if not well-controlled, can result in kidney damage. Other factors, such as high cholesterol, kidney infections, glomerulonephritis, polycystic kidney disease, heart disease or failure, and prolonged use of certain medications like lithium or NSAIDs, can also play a role in CKD. However, managing diabetes and hypertension is crucial in preventing and addressing CKD.

2. Answer C (Chronic obstructive pulmonary disease)

CKD primarily affects the renal system, leading to complications such as pulmonary edema, pleural effusion, and respiratory infections. Pulmonary edema may occur due to fluid retention and electrolyte imbalances associated with CKD, resulting in congestion in the lungs. Pleural effusion can develop as a consequence of fluid overload and impaired kidney function. Respiratory infections may be more common in CKD patients due to compromised immune function. While CKD can impact various systems, it is not a direct cause of chronic obstructive pulmonary disease, which is primarily associated with long-term exposure to irritating gases or particulate matter, often seen in conditions like smoking.

3. Answer C (Hyperkalemia)

CKD can lead to dysregulation of volume status, acid-base balance, and electrolytes. In particular, impaired kidney function in CKD can result in potassium retention, leading to elevated potassium levels in the blood, known as hyperkalemia. This electrolyte imbalance can have significant implications for cardiac function and overall patient health. Monitoring and managing potassium levels are essential components of the care for individuals with CKD to prevent complications associated with hyperkalemia.

4. Answer C (It prolongs the duration of drug effects)

Altered pharmacokinetics due to decreased elimination, acidosis, and hypoalbuminemia in chronic kidney disease can lead to a prolonged duration of anesthetic drug effects. In CKD, impaired renal function affects the clearance of drugs from the body, potentially resulting in increased drug concentrations and prolonged action. The combination of reduced elimination, acidosis, and lower levels of albumin in the blood can contribute to these altered pharmacokinetics, emphasizing the need for careful consideration and adjustment of anesthesia dosages in patients with CKD to avoid complications related to prolonged drug effects.

5. Answer A (True)

Gastroparesis and the associated risk of aspiration are potential complications of chronic kidney disease. Gastroparesis in CKD is characterized by abnormalities in the autonomic nervous system, smooth muscle cells, and enteric neurons. The pathophysiology of gastroparesis in CKD remains undefined, and diagnostic procedures such as upper endoscopy and gastric emptying scintigraphy, along with alternative methods like wireless capsule motility, antroduodenal manometry, and breath testing, are utilized for its diagnosis. Despite conflicting results in studies attempting to delineate gastric emptying time in both pre-dialysis and maintenance dialysis CKD patients, the risk of delayed gastric emptying in CKD patients remains a concern during anesthesia.

6. Answer B (Morphine)

Short-term or initial management of severe pain in a CKD patient post-surgery should consider avoiding morphine due to the risk of active metabolite accumulation in patients with reduced renal function. Oxycodone can be considered a reasonable first-line strong opioid; however, it is partly renally excreted, necessitating dose reduction in patients with severe renal impairment. Regular monitoring of opioid side effects is crucial. Oxycodone is significantly cleared by hemodialysis, indicating the potential need for additional dosing after dialysis. An alternative for parenteral analgesia in CKD patients is alfentanil, which is not significantly renally excreted and can be a suitable option.

Recommended literature

1. Domi R, Huti G, Sula H, et al. From Pre-Existing Renal Failure to Perioperative Renal Protection: The Anesthesiologist's Dilemmas. Anesth Pain Med. 2016;6(3):e32386. Published 2016 May 14.
2. Sladen RN. Chronic kidney disease: the silent enemy?. Anesth Analg. 2011;112(6):1277-1279.

HEMOLYTIC UREMIC SYNDROME

15

CHAPTER

Questions:

1. **What is the most common cause of Hemolytic Uremic Syndrome (HUS) in children, leading to the typical form of the disease?**
   A. Salmonella infection
   B. E. coli infection
   C. Streptococcus pneumoniae infection
   D. Shigella infection

2. **What is the primary symptom preceding Typical HUS by 4-6 days?**
   A. Hematuria
   B. Hemorrhagic gastritis
   C. Diarrhea
   D. Severe hypertension

3. **In atypical HUS, dysregulation of which complement pathway is a significant contributing factor?**
   A. Classical complement pathway
   B. Lectin complement pathway
   C. Alternative complement pathway
   D. Terminal complement pathway

4. **What is a common manifestation in the cardiovascular system in HUS?**
   A. Deep vein thrombosis
   B. Myocarditis
   C. Atherosclerosis
   D. Cardiac arrhythmias

5. **Antibiotics are the first-line treatment for managing HUS.**
   A. True
   B. False

6. **A 3-year-old child is brought to the Emergency Department after a day of diarrhea, presenting with a variety of signs and symptoms. The child complains of abdominal pain, cramping, and bloating. Notably, the diarrhea is bloody, accompanied by fever and vomiting. Upon examination, the child appears pale, exhibiting a loss of pink color in the cheeks and inside the lower eyelids. The child seems extremely fatigued, experiences shortness of breath, and has unexplained bruises, easy bruising, and unusual bleeding. Given these symptoms, a differential diagnosis of HUS is being considered. What biochemical evidence is NOT associated with Acute Kidney Injury (AKI) in HUS?**
   A. Thrombocytopenia
   B. Elevated creatinine
   C. Elevated direct bilirubin
   D. Elevated lactate dehydrogenase

Answers:

1. **Answer B (E. coli infection)**

   Hemolytic Uremic Syndrome (HUS) is characterized by a triad of renal failure, hemolytic anemia, and thrombocytopenia, making it the most common cause of renal failure in infancy and childhood. The most common cause of HUS, specifically the typical form of the disease, is infection with a specific type of E. coli, particularly Shiga toxin-producing E. coli (O157:H7). While other pathogens such as Streptococcus pneumoniae, Shigella, and Salmonella can also cause HUS, the specific type of E. coli mentioned, particularly O157:H7, is the primary and most common cause.

2. **Answer C (Diarrhea)**

   The primary symptom preceding HUS by 4-6 days is diarrhea. Most HUS cases occur after infectious diarrhea due to a specific type of E. coli, particularly Shiga toxin-producing E. coli (O157:H7). The first symptoms of infection can emerge between 1 to 10 days later, but usually after 3 to 4 days.

3. **Answer C (Alternative complement pathway)**

   In Atypical HUS, dysregulation of the alternative complement pathway is a significant contributing factor. Moreover, the involvement of mutations in specific components of the alternative complement pathway, such as factor H, factor I, CD46/MCP, factor B, and C3, further supports the importance of the alternative complement pathway in the development of Atypical HUS. The alternative complement pathway is unique in its continuous low-level hydrolysis of C3 in the plasma, leading to the formation of C3b. Dysregulation in this pathway can result in an aberrant immune response and contribute to the multisystemic manifestations observed in Atypical HUS.

4. **Answer B (Myocarditis)**

   A common manifestation in the cardiovascular system in HUS is myocarditis. HUS can affect the cardiovascular system and lead to conditions such as myocarditis, congestive heart failure, and severe hypertension. Myocarditis can have significant implications for cardiac function and may contribute to the overall morbidity in individuals with HUS.

5. **Answer B (False)**

   Antibiotics are not the first-line treatment for managing HUS. The recommended initial interventions for HUS include supportive measures such as fluid resuscitation, treatment of hyperkalemia, and dialysis. Pharmacological interventions involve controlling hypertension with standard antihypertensive agents, along with the use of steroids, blood transfusion, and plasmapheresis. While antibiotics may be considered in specific cases, particularly if HUS is triggered by a bacterial infection, they are not the primary focus of treatment, and the emphasis is on addressing complications and the underlying pathophysiology through the outlined supportive and pharmacological measures.

6. **Answer C (Elevated direct bilirubin)**

   In the assessment of a patient exhibiting symptoms suggestive of HUS, the presence of elevated direct bilirubin stands out as a biochemical marker less commonly associated with Acute Kidney Injury (AKI) in HUS. A Complete Blood Count typically reveals anemia (Hb < 10 g/dl) and thrombocytopenia, consistent findings in HUS cases. Additionally, a Comprehensive Metabolic Panel may unveil elevated creatinine, indirect bilirubin, and lactate dehydrogenase, all indicative of renal dysfunction and hemolysis—hallmark features of HUS. It is crucial to note that while elevated direct bilirubin suggests liver dysfunction or obstruction, it does not serve as a direct marker for AKI in the context of HUS. Immediate attention to these biochemical indicators and a comprehensive diagnostic approach is imperative for accurate diagnosis, assessment of potential multi-organ involvement, and the initiation of appropriate management strategies for HUS.

Recommended literature

1. Pollard BJ, Kitchen, G. Handbook of Clinical Anaesthesia. Fourth Edition. CRC Press. 2018. 978-1-4987-6289-2.
2. Noris M, Remuzzi G. Hemolytic uremic syndrome. J Am Soc Nephrol. 2005;16(4):1035-1050.

NEPHRECTOMY

15
CHAPTER

Questions:

1. **What is the primary indication for performing a radical nephrectomy?**
   A. Shrunken kidney
   B. Renal cell carcinoma
   C. Chronic infection
   D. Trauma

2. **What is the primary reason for performing a nephrectomy in cases of hydronephrosis?**
   A. Chronic infection
   B. Urinary fistula
   C. Severe urinary tract obstruction
   D. Shrunken kidney

3. **Which surgical approach is associated with less postoperative pain and quicker recovery in nephrectomy?**
   A. Thoracoabdominal incision
   B. Anterior subcostal incision
   C. Laparoscopic approach
   D. Dorsal incision

4. **What is a potential complication following nephrectomy that may present with symptoms such as dyspnea and chest pain?**
   A. Hemorrhage
   B. Pneumothorax
   C. Myocardial infarction
   D. Pancreatitis

5. **Thoracic epidural analgesia (TEA) is considered the gold standard for open nephrectomy.**
   A. True
   B. False

6. **A 58-year-old male with a confirmed diagnosis of renal cell carcinoma (RCC) in the left kidney is scheduled for an open nephrectomy. The surgical team plans to utilize a lateral position and flank incision for optimal access. To manage postoperative pain effectively, an epidural catheter is inserted between the T7 and T8 vertebrae. What dermatomes require regional anesthesia blockade after an open nephrectomy using a flank incision?**
   A. T9–T11
   B. T7–T9
   C. T6–T8
   D. T12–L2

Answers:

1. Answer B (Renal cell carcinoma)

Radical nephrectomy is the preferred surgical option for patients with neoplastic disease, particularly renal cell carcinoma (RCC). In a radical nephrectomy, the entire kidney, part of the ureter, the renal fascia, the adrenal gland, and regional lymph nodes are removed. This extensive procedure is undertaken in cases with malignant involvement of the kidney. RCC is the most common type of renal malignancy, and radical nephrectomy is often recommended for patients with this form of kidney cancer.

2. Answer C (Severe urinary tract obstruction)

Hydronephrosis refers to the swelling or enlargement of the kidney due to the accumulation of urine caused by obstruction of the urine flow. If the obstruction is severe and not amenable to other forms of intervention, nephrectomy may be considered to relieve the obstruction and prevent further damage to the affected kidney.

3. Answer C (Laparoscopic approach)

The surgical approach associated with less postoperative pain and quicker recovery in nephrectomy is the laparoscopic approach. This minimally invasive technique allows surgeons to perform nephrectomy through small incisions using a camera and specialized instruments. The laparoscopic approach is known for reduced postoperative pain, shorter hospital stays, and quicker recovery compared to traditional open approaches.

4. Answer B (Pneumothorax)

Pneumothorax is a potential complication following nephrectomy that may present with symptoms such as dyspnea and chest pain. It occurs when air leaks into the space between the lung and the chest wall, leading to lung collapse. This can cause respiratory symptoms, including difficulty breathing (dyspnea) and chest pain.

5. Answer A (True)

Thoracic epidural analgesia (TEA) is considered the gold standard for analgesia in major abdominal surgery, including open nephrectomy. In the context of open nephrectomy, which is associated with a significant degree of acute pain, TEA is widely used to manage postoperative pain. The administration of analgesia through TEA helps improve patient comfort and facilitates early mobilization and recovery.

6. Answer A (T9–T11)

For an open nephrectomy using a flank incision, the relevant dermatomes that require regional anesthesia blockade are T9–T11. The epidural catheter inserted between the T7 and T8 vertebrae aims to cover this specific area, ensuring effective pain relief for the patient in the postoperative period. Regional anesthesia techniques, such as low thoracic epidural analgesia, play a crucial role in managing the acute pain associated with open nephrectomy.

Recommended literature

1. Pollard BJ, Kitchen, G. Handbook of Clinical Anaesthesia. Fourth Edition. CRC Press. 2018. 978-1-4987-6289-2.
2. Chapman, E., Pichel, A., 2016. Anaesthesia for nephrectomy. BJA Education 16, 98–101.

Renal diseases
NEPHROTIC SYNDROME

Questions:

1. Which of the following is a primary cause of nephrotic syndrome characterized by glomerular injury?
   A. Diabetes mellitus
   B. Focal segmental glomerulosclerosis
   C. Amyloidosis
   D. Systemic lupus erythematosus

2. What is the primary mechanism leading to proteinuria in nephrotic syndrome?
   A. Increased tubular reabsorption
   B. Decreased glomerular permeability
   C. Increased plasma oncotic pressure
   D. Defect in the glomerular barrier

3. Which of the following is NOT a secondary cause of nephrotic syndrome?
   A. Sarcoidosis
   B. Multiple myeloma
   C. HIV
   D. Hyperthyroidism

4. What is the primary reason for the development of peripheral edema in nephrotic syndrome?
   A. Elevated plasma oncotic pressure
   B. Sodium and water retention
   C. Decreased glomerular permeability
   D. Hypovolemia

5. Captopril is associated with the development of nephrotic syndrome.
   A. True
   B. False

6. A 33-year-old female presents to the hospital with a history of severe headaches and increased episodes of visual blurring over the past week. On examination, puffy eyelids and swelling in the legs are noted. Laboratory investigations reveal significant proteinuria with a 24-hour urine collection showing 8 grams of protein and foamy urine. Albuminuria is elevated at 30 mg/dL (normal < 10 mg/dL). A renal biopsy is performed, confirming the diagnosis of Minimal-change disease (nephropathy) and establishing the presence of nephrotic syndrome. What is the recommended first-line treatment for nephrotic syndrome?
   A. Diuretics
   B. ACE inhibitors and angiotensin-receptor blockers
   C. Cyclophosphamide
   D. Corticosteroids

Answers:

1. **Answer B (Focal segmental glomerulosclerosis)**

   Focal segmental glomerulosclerosis (FSGS) is the primary cause of nephrotic syndrome characterized by glomerular injury. This condition, along with other primary causes such as minimal-change disease (nephropathy), membranous glomerulonephritis, membranoproliferative glomerulonephritis, and hereditary nephropathies, contributes to the manifestation of nephrotic syndrome. FSGS specifically involves damage to the glomeruli, leading to symptoms like proteinuria, low blood albumin levels, high blood lipids, and edema.

2. **Answer D (Defect in the glomerular barrier)**

   The primary mechanism leading to proteinuria in nephrotic syndrome is a defect in the glomerular barrier. This defect increases glomerular permeability, allowing proteins, including albumin, to pass into the urine. As a consequence of proteinuria, there is a decrease in plasma oncotic pressure, leading to the retention of sodium and water. This retention contributes to peripheral edema, ascites, pleural effusions, and hypovolemia. While most cases of nephrotic syndrome spontaneously remit without treatment, hypertension is a common occurrence, and renal failure is rare. However, patients may develop renal failure along with secondary complications such as arterial and venous thromboembolism and infections.

3. **Answer D (Hyperthyroidism)**

   Among the provided options, hyperthyroidism is not a secondary cause of nephrotic syndrome. The secondary causes of nephrotic syndrome encompass various conditions such as diabetes mellitus, systemic lupus erythematosus, sarcoidosis, amyloidosis, paraproteinemias, viral infections (e.g., hepatitis B, hepatitis C, HIV), pre-eclampsia, Sjögren's syndrome, multiple myeloma, vasculitis, cancer, and certain medications like penicillin and captopril.

4. **Answer B (Sodium and water retention)**

   The primary reason for the development of peripheral edema in nephrotic syndrome is sodium and water retention. The defect in the glomerular barrier leads to an increased glomerular permeability, resulting in proteinuria and albuminuria. This, in turn, causes a decrease in plasma oncotic pressure. The reduction in oncotic pressure triggers the retention of sodium and water, leading to peripheral edema, ascites, pleural effusions, and hypovolemia.

5. **Answer A (True)**

   Captopril, an angiotensin-converting enzyme (ACE) inhibitor, has been associated with the development of proteinuria and, more rarely, nephrotic syndrome. The risk of these side effects appears to be higher when captopril is used at higher doses, especially in individuals with pre-existing renal impairment. While nephrotic syndrome is a rare side effect, healthcare providers need to monitor patients taking captopril for signs of proteinuria and kidney function.

6. **Answer D (Corticosteroids)**

   Corticosteroids, specifically prednisone, are considered the cornerstone and first-line treatment for inducing remission in nephrotic syndrome, including cases of Minimal-change disease. They act by reducing inflammation and immune system activity. In situations where patients are steroid-resistant or show inadequate response, backup options include cyclophosphamide or cyclosporine. These immunosuppressive agents can be employed as alternative treatments. While diuretics are useful for managing edema, and angiotensin-converting enzyme inhibitors and angiotensin II receptor blockers are employed to reduce proteinuria, they are not the primary agents for inducing remission in nephrotic syndrome.

Recommended literature

1. Pollard BJ, Kitchen, G. Handbook of Clinical Anaesthesia. Fourth Edition. CRC Press. 2018. 978-1-4987-6289-2.
2. Vishnu D, Tempe D, Arora K, Virmani S, Chander J, Agarwal S.(2012). Anesthetic management of a child with nephrotic syndrome undergoing open heart surgery. Report of a rare case. Annals of cardiac anaesthesia. 15. 305-8.

Renal diseases
RENAL TRANSPLANT

Questions:

1. Which of the following is the most common cause of ESRD requiring renal transplantation?
   A. Glomerulonephritis
   B. Polycystic kidney disease
   C. Diabetes mellitus
   D. Pyelonephritis

2. Which postoperative complication is NOT commonly associated with renal transplantation?
   A. Myocardial infarction
   B. Hepatitis
   C. Pneumonia
   D. Diabetes insipidus

3. What is the recommended use of non-steroidal anti-inflammatory drugs (NSAIDs) in the postoperative care of renal transplant recipients?
   A. NSAIDs are recommended for pain relief
   B. NSAIDs are contraindicated
   C. NSAIDs should be used to prevent graft rejection
   D. NSAIDs are preferred for their anti-inflammatory properties

4. Which electrolyte imbalance is least commonly observed in renal transplant recipients?
   A. Hypermagnesemia
   B. Hyperkalemia
   C. Hypocalcemia
   D. Hypophosphatemia

5. The right kidney is typically chosen for donation from a living donor.
   A. True
   B. False

6. A 20-year-old female patient with chronic renal failure underwent renal transplantation under total intravenous anesthesia. Immediate urine production after unclamping the iliac vessels and reperfusion of the graft was observed, but during the closure of the surgical wound, there was a decrease in urine output. To rule out any obstruction, the urinary catheter was irrigated. Additionally, loop diuretics and mannitol were administered to enhance urine production. What is the role of mannitol in the context of renal transplantation?
   A. Inducing osmotic diuresis
   B. Stabilizing blood pressure
   C. Enhancing calcium absorption
   D. Blocking Na/K channels in the ascending limb of Henle

549

Answers:

1. **Answer C (Diabetes mellitus)**

Diabetes mellitus (DM) is the most common cause of End-Stage Renal Disease (ESRD) requiring renal transplantation. It is a leading contributor to the development of chronic kidney disease, ultimately progressing to ESRD. Following DM, other common causes of ESRD include glomerulonephritis, polycystic kidney disease, pyelonephritis, hypertension, and autoimmune disorders. These conditions can lead to irreversible damage to the kidneys, necessitating renal transplantation as a treatment option for those with ESRD.

2. **Answer D (Diabetes insipidus)**

While renal transplantation is associated with various complications, such as pulmonary embolism, hepatitis, myocardial infarction, arrhythmias, pneumonia, atelectasis, urinary tract infection, wound infections, and splenic lacerations, diabetes insipidus is not a typical complication. Diabetes insipidus is more commonly related to dysfunction of the posterior pituitary gland or the hypothalamus, and its occurrence in the context of renal transplantation is rare.

3. **Answer B (NSAIDs are contraindicated)**

Postoperative pain after renal transplantation is typically mild to moderate. While NSAIDs are commonly used for pain relief in many surgical scenarios, they are not recommended for renal transplant recipients. NSAIDs inhibit the synthesis of prostaglandins, which play a crucial role in renal blood flow and the autoregulation of glomerular filtration rate. As a result, the use of NSAIDs in this context is considered absolutely contraindicated to avoid potential negative effects on renal function. Alternative pain management strategies, such as epidural analgesia, patient-controlled analgesia with opioids, and regional nerve blocks, have been successfully employed for postoperative pain control in renal transplant recipients.

4. **Answer A (Hypermagnesemia)**

While renal transplant recipients often experience disruptions in electrolyte balance, including hyperkalemia, hypocalcemia, and hypophosphatemia, hypermagnesemia is relatively infrequent. Electrolyte imbalances, particularly disruptions in calcium and phosphate levels, are common due to tubular dysfunction caused by rejection episodes and the toxic effects of calcineurin inhibitors (CNIs) like cyclosporine or tacrolimus. The incidence of hyperkalemia is 5-40% in patients treated with CNIs, while hypomagnesemia is a common early complication. Serum phosphate levels often decline in the immediate posttransplant period, and phosphate substitution may be necessary when levels fall below 0.5 mm/L. Hypercalcemia, primarily due to persistent hyperparathyroidism, is also a common disorder in the chronic posttransplant phase.

5. **Answer B (False)**

The left kidney is typically chosen for donation from a living donor due to its longer renal vein. This anatomical consideration makes the surgical procedure and vascular anastomosis more manageable.

6. **Answer A (Inducing osmotic diuresis)**

Immediate urine production is a positive sign, but a decrease in urine output during the later stages of the surgical procedure raises concerns about potential mechanical impingement on the graft, vessels, or ureter. To address this, the urinary catheter is irrigated to ensure patency. Loop diuretics, mannitol, and occasionally dopamine can be employed to enhance urine production. In this context, mannitol plays a crucial role by inducing osmotic diuresis. Mannitol not only increases urine output but also provides a protective effect on the tubular cells of the transplanted kidney, guarding against ischemic injury. Loop diuretics act by blocking the Na/K channels in the thin ascending limb of Henle. While low-dose dopamine is sometimes used to stimulate DA1 dopaminergic receptors, its efficacy in a newly transplanted, denervated kidney is debated, as these kidneys may not respond to dopamine as normal kidneys do.

Recommended literature

1. Pollard BJ, Kitchen, G. Handbook of Clinical Anaesthesia. Fourth Edition. CRC Press. 2018. 978-1-4987-6289-2.
2. Mayhew D, Ridgway d, Hunter JM. 2016. Update on the intraoperative management of adult cadaveric renal transplantation. BJA education. 16;2:53-57.
3. O'Brien, B., Koertzen, M., 2012. Anaesthesia for living donor renal transplant nephrectomy. Continuing Education in Anaesthesia Critical Care & Pain 12, 317-321.
4. Rabey P. 2001. Anesthesia for renal transplantation. BJA CEPD Reviews. 1;1:24-17.

Renal diseases
TURP AND TURP SYNDROME

15
CHAPTER

Questions:

1. **What is the primary purpose of Transurethral Resection of the Prostate (TURP)?**
   A. Treatment of Chronic Pelvic Pain Syndrome
   B. Management of urinary incontinence
   C. Resolution of retrograde ejaculation
   D. Treatment of Benign Prostatic Hyperplasia (BPH)

2. **Which complication is a potential consequence of TURP syndrome?**
   A. Peripheral neuropathy
   B. Respiratory alkalosis
   C. Disseminated intravascular coagulation
   D. Hypernatremia

3. **What is a significant risk factor for TURP syndrome during the procedure?**
   A. Duration of the resection (< 1 hour)
   B. The small size of opened venous sinuses
   C. Hypotonic intravenous fluids
   D. Use of regional anesthesia

4. **Which electrolyte imbalance is commonly associated with TURP syndrome?**
   A. Hypokalemia
   B. Hypocalcemia
   C. Hypomagnesemia
   D. Hyponatremia

5. **Staging resections for large prostates helps prevent prolonged operative times and reduces the risk of TURP syndrome.**
   A. True
   B. False

6. **A 70-year-old patient scheduled for TURP surgery under spinal anesthesia in the lithotomy position presents with concerning symptoms after 60 minutes of the operation. The patient is confused with a reduced Glasgow Coma Scale score, hypertensive, and on auscultation, both lungs reveal reduced breath sounds and coarse crackles. Urgent laboratory tests show hyponatremia (Na 110 mmol/L) and hyperkalemia (K 6.1 mmol/L), raising suspicion of TURP syndrome. What is NOT the primary treatment for TURP syndrome?**
   A. Stop the procedure as soon as possible
   B. Administration of hypertonic fluids
   C. Diuretics
   D. Anticoagulant medications

Answers:

1. Answer D (Treatment of Benign Prostatic Hyperplasia (BPH))

BPH is a common condition, affecting over 40% of men aged over 60 years. When symptoms of BPH become resistant to medical management, TURP is often considered as the second-line treatment. TURP involves the surgical removal of prostate tissue to alleviate symptoms associated with BPH, such as urinary obstruction and difficulty in urination. It is not primarily indicated for the treatment of Chronic Pelvic Pain Syndrome, management of urinary incontinence, or resolution of retrograde ejaculation.

2. Answer C (Disseminated intravascular coagulation)

A potential consequence of TURP (Transurethral Resection of the Prostate) syndrome is Disseminated Intravascular Coagulation (DIC). TURP syndrome is a rare but serious complication of the TURP procedure, where absorption of irrigation fluid, such as glycine, can lead to electrolyte imbalances, fluid overload, and various systemic complications. Disseminated Intravascular Coagulation is characterized by widespread activation of the clotting cascade, leading to bleeding and clotting throughout the body. It can result in serious complications, including multi-organ failure. The diagnosis of TURP syndrome is often based on clinical manifestations such as confusion, reduced Glasgow Coma Scale score, hyponatremia, hyperkalemia, glycine toxicity, intravascular hemolysis, and, as mentioned, Disseminated Intravascular Coagulation.

3. Answer C (Hypotonic intravenous fluids)

A significant risk factor for TURP syndrome during the procedure is the use of hypotonic intravenous fluids. TURP syndrome is a rare but potentially life-threatening complication characterized by the absorption of irrigation fluid, such as glycine, leading to electrolyte imbalances and systemic complications. Hypotonic intravenous fluids, if used excessively, can contribute to the development of hyponatremia, a common feature of TURP syndrome. Other risk factors for TURP syndrome include the size of the opened venous sinuses, the amount of irrigation fluid used, the duration of the resection (especially if exceeding 1 hour), and the possibility of bladder perforation during the procedure.

4. Answer D (Hyponatremia)

Hyponatremia is commonly associated with TURP syndrome. The symptoms of TURP syndrome result from hyponatremia, defined as a serum sodium concentration less than 120 mmol/L. While hyponatremia is a common electrolyte imbalance in TURP syndrome, hyperkalemia (K > 6.0 mmol/L) is also a possible consequence. The excessive absorption of irrigation fluid, often containing glycine, can lead to dilutional hyponatremia and electrolyte imbalances, affecting the overall homeostasis of sodium and potassium levels.

5. Answer A (True)

Staging resections for large prostates is a true and effective strategy in preventing prolonged operative times and reducing the risk of TURP syndrome. This approach involves dividing the procedure into multiple stages, allowing for better control of the surgery and mitigating the potential complications associated with extended operative times, including the rare but serious TURP syndrome.

6. Answer D (Anticoagulant medications)

TURP syndrome is characterized by the absorption of irrigation fluid leading to electrolyte imbalances, and its management primarily involves stopping the procedure, providing oxygenation, and addressing complications. The correct approach includes stopping the ongoing surgery, providing oxygenation and circulatory support, administering hypertonic fluids to manage fluid overload, and using diuretics to treat fluid overload. Anticoagulant medications are not indicated in the primary treatment; instead, interventions focus on correcting electrolyte imbalances, managing hemodynamic instability, and addressing complications such as disseminated intravascular coagulation, seizures, nausea, and vomiting.

Recommended literature

1. Pollard BJ, Kitchen, G. Handbook of Clinical Anaesthesia. Fourth Edition. CRC Press. 2018. 978-1-4987-6289-2.
2. Nakahira, J., Sawai, T., Fujiwara, A., Minami, T., 2014. Transurethral resection syndrome in elderly patients: a retrospective observational study. BMC Anesthesiology 14, 30.
3. Demirel I, Ozer AB, Bayar MK, Erhan OL. TURP syndrome and severe hyponatremia under general anaesthesia. BMJ Case Rep. 2012;2012:bcr-2012-006899.
4. O'Donnell AM, Foo I. 2009. Anaesthesia for transurethral resection of the prostate. Continuing Education in Anaesthesia Critical Care & Pain. 9;3:92-96.

RESPIRATORY & THORACICS

ANTERIOR MEDIASTINAL MASS

16
CHAPTER

Questions:

1. **Which structure borders the anterior mediastinal space superiorly?**

   A. Sternum

   B. Middle mediastinum

   C. Thoracic inlet

   D. Diaphragm

2. **What are the most frequent causes of Anterior Mediastinal Masses (AMMs)?**

   A. Aneurysms

   B. Lymphoma, thymoma, germ cell tumors

   C. Small cell carcinoma

   D. Myxoma

3. **What is NOT a common symptom associated with anterior mediastinal masses?**

   A. Chest discomfort

   B. Stridor

   C. Excess phlegm or sputum

   D. Rhonchi

4. **Which syndrome may be associated with anterior mediastinal masses and presents with symptoms such as dyspnea and headache?**

   A. Horner's syndrome

   B. Superior vena cava syndrome

   C. Cushing's syndrome

   D. Lambert-Eaton syndrome

5. **Coughing while in a supine position is a red flag in the anesthesia management of Anterior Mediastinal Mass.**

   A. True

   B. False

6. **A 24-year-old female presented with a six-month history of recurrent cough, chest pain, and a sensation of heaviness over the upper chest. No hemoptysis was reported, and she had no significant medical history, being a nonsmoker and nonalcoholic. Physical examination revealed mild anemia, and when lying flat, she experienced dyspnea and pre-syncope. A contrast-enhanced CT scan of the chest unveiled a large, smoothly marginated lesion in the anterior mediastinum with calcification and necrosis, resulting in more than 50% tracheobronchial obstruction. Given the findings, the patient was scheduled for a left-sided thoracotomy. Considering the risk associated with anesthesia induction in the presence of an anterior mediastinal mass, which technique might be employed to secure the airway?**

   A. Awake fiberoptic intubation

   B. Rapid sequence induction

   C. Jet ventilation

   D. Laryngeal mask airway (LMA) insertion

Answers:

1. **Answer C (Thoracic Inlet)**

   Distinct anatomical boundaries within the thoracic cavity define the anterior mediastinal space. It is bordered anteriorly by the sternum, posteriorly by the middle mediastinum housing the heart and great vessels, superiorly by the thoracic inlet, and inferiorly by the diaphragm. The thoracic inlet, also known as the superior thoracic aperture, serves as the upper boundary of the anterior mediastinal space. This anatomical structure is a critical opening at the top of the thoracic cavity, surrounded by a bony ring. The thoracic inlet is formed by the first thoracic vertebra (T1) posteriorly, the first pair of ribs laterally, creating lateral C-shaped curves from posterior to anterior, and the costal cartilage of the first rib along with the superior border of the manubrium anteriorly.

2. **Answer B (Lymphoma, thymoma, germ cell tumors)**

   Mediastinal masses, in general, encompass a diverse group of tumors, both benign and malignant. mediastinal masses. The most frequent causes of Anterior Mediastinal Masses (AMMs) include lymphoma, thymoma, germ cell tumors, metastatic lesions, bronchogenic masses, and thyroid masses. The classic mnemonic for remembering the common causes is the "4 Ts": thymoma, teratoma, "terrible" lymphoma, and thyroid.

3. **Answer C (Excess phlegm or sputum)**

   Anterior mediastinal masses can present with various symptoms, including systemic syndromes and localized pathology. Common symptoms associated with these masses include dyspnea, noisy breathing, nonspecific cough, chest discomfort, tachypnea, stridor, rhonchi, decreased breath sounds, and headache, depending on the specific pathology and involvement of adjacent structures. Excess phlegm or sputum is not typically highlighted as a common symptom associated with anterior mediastinal masses.

4. **Answer B (Superior vena cava syndrome)**

   Superior vena cava syndrome (SVCS) is associated with anterior mediastinal masses and manifests with symptoms such as dyspnea and headache. The superior vena cava is a major vein that returns blood from the head, neck, arms, and chest to the heart. SVCS occurs when there is pressure on the superior vena cava, leading to impaired blood flow and increased pressure in the veins. This results in shortness of breath, a feeling of fullness in the head or ears, swelling of the face, neck, upper body, and arms, coughing, hoarseness, chest pain, difficulty swallowing, and headache.

5. **Answer A (True)**

   Coughing while in a supine position is a critical red flag in the anesthesia management of Anterior Mediastinal Mass (AMM). This symptom indicates potential airway compromise, necessitating careful preoperative risk stratification. Patients are categorized into three risk levels: low risk for those asymptomatic or mildly symptomatic without significant radiographic evidence of compression, intermediate risk for individuals with mild to moderate postural symptoms and tracheal compression below 50%, and high risk for those with severe postural symptoms, stridor, cyanosis, tracheal compression exceeding 50%, or tracheal compression associated with bronchial compression, pericardial effusion, or SCVS.

6. **Answer A (Awake fiberoptic intubation)**

   Given the high risk associated with anterior mediastinal masses and the potential for tracheobronchial obstruction exceeding 50%, a cautious approach to general anesthesia is crucial. Maintaining spontaneous ventilation and keeping the patient awake during endotracheal tube (ETT) placement distal to the obstruction are essential to prevent airway compromise. Therefore, the preferred technique during anesthesia induction in this scenario is awake fiberoptic intubation. This approach allows careful airway management without triggering airway reflexes and exacerbating compression. Avoiding positive pressure ventilation and muscle paralysis, if possible, further mitigates the risk of complications associated with anterior mediastinal masses.

Recommended literature

1. Almeida PT, Heller D. Anterior Mediastinal Mass. [Updated 2022 Sep 26]. In: StatPearls [Internet]. Treasure Island (FL): StatPearls Publishing; 2022 Jan-. Available from: https://www.ncbi.nlm.nih.gov/books/NBK546608/
2. McLeod M, Dobbie M. Anterior mediastinal masses in children. BJA Education. 2019;19(1):21-6.
3. Ku, Chih Min. "Anesthesia for patients with mediastinal masses." Principles and Practice of Anesthesia for Thoracic Surgery. Springer New York, 2011. 201-210.

ASTHMA

Questions:

1. **Which of the following is a characteristic feature of asthma symptoms?**
   A. Constant chest tightness
   B. Gradual onset in children
   C. Absence of cough
   D. Variable respiratory symptoms

2. **What is the recommended initial treatment for acute asthma exacerbation?**
   A. Long-acting β2-agonists
   B. Ipratropium bromide
   C. Oral corticosteroids
   D. Short-acting β2-agonists

3. **What is NOT the recommended approach to control ventilation in severe asthma exacerbation?**
   A. Higher respiratory rates
   B. I:E ratio 1:3
   C. Tidal volume 6-8 cc/kg
   D. Permissive hypercapnia

4. **What medication, in addition to direct beta-adrenoceptor mediated bronchodilatation, may have beneficial effects in asthma, such as alpha-receptor mediated reduction in microvascular leakage and oedema, and inhibition of bronchoconstrictor neural pathways?**
   A. Ipratropium
   B. Ketamine
   C. Salbutamol
   D. Epinephrine

5. **Magnesium is recommended for life-threatening asthma exacerbation.**
   A. True
   B. False

6. **A 45-year-old woman with a known history of asthma for the last 5 years presents for a hysterectomy due to uterine fibroids. She manages her asthma with a salbutamol inhaler as needed. After induction of general anesthesia and intubation, wheezing is noted, accompanied by a drop in oxygen saturation. Immediate intervention involves the administration of 100% oxygen, manual ventilation, and cessation of any ongoing interventions. A thorough assessment is performed, including lung auscultation, to ensure bilateral breath sounds and proper positioning of the endotracheal tube (ETT). The goal is to rule out potential mechanical problems, such as ETT obstruction, kinking, mainstem intubation, or ventilatory malfunction. Upon confirming bronchospasm, the depth of anesthesia should be deepened. When bronchospasm is confirmed, which anesthetic drug should be avoided in suspected bronchospasm?**
   A. Propofol
   B. Ketamine
   C. Sevoflurane
   D. Morphine

Answers:

1. Answer D (Variable respiratory symptoms)

Variable respiratory symptoms, including wheezing, shortness of breath, chest tightness, and cough characterize asthma. These symptoms can vary in intensity and frequency, and they may be absent between asthma attacks. It's important to note that asthma is associated with variable airflow limitation, often linked to airway inflammation and remodeling. During asymptomatic periods, lung function tests may appear normal, highlighting the intermittent nature of asthma symptoms.

2. Answer D (Short-acting β2-agonists)

The recommended initial treatment for acute asthma exacerbation is to give short-acting β2-agonists (SABAs) to resolve acute symptoms. These medications are effective in rapidly relieving bronchoconstriction and improving airflow. The use of SABAs is crucial in the early management of acute symptoms, and they can be administered every 15 to 20 minutes for the first hour to achieve prompt relief. It's important to note that while other components, such as ipratropium bromide and systemic corticosteroids, play vital roles in the overall management of asthma exacerbations, the initial intervention, particularly for symptom resolution, is the administration of short-acting β2-agonists.

3. Answer A (Higher respiratory rates)

In the context of intubation and ventilation during severe asthma exacerbation, the recommended approach includes using permissive hypercapnia, low respiratory rates (starting at 10-12 breaths/minute but may need lower rates), and prolonged expiratory time (e.g., I:E ratios 1:3, 1:4, or even 1:5). Additionally, maintaining a tidal volume of 6-8cc/kg is part of the ventilation strategy. The objective is to optimize ventilation while minimizing the risk of dynamic hyperinflation.

4. Answer D (Epinephrine)

Epinephrine, in addition to its direct beta-adrenoceptor-mediated bronchodilatory effects, may have beneficial effects on asthma. These include alpha-receptor-mediated reduction in microvascular leakage and edema, as well as inhibition of bronchoconstrictor neural pathways. The theoretical advantages conferred by alpha-agonist activity do not result in additional bronchodilation but may prevent a fall in PaO_2 due to ventilation-perfusion mismatching. Recent asthma guidelines recommend using subcutaneous epinephrine at 0.3-0.5 mg every 20 minutes for three doses. Epinephrine is also available for oral inhalation as an aerosol and is used as needed to control asthma symptoms.

5. Answer A (True)

Magnesium sulfate is recommended for life-threatening asthma exacerbation. The correct dosage is 2g IV over 20 minutes. Magnesium has bronchodilatory effects and can be particularly beneficial in severe cases of asthma exacerbation where standard therapies may not be sufficient. The use of magnesium aims to improve bronchial smooth muscle relaxation and reduce airway hyperresponsiveness.

6. Answer D (Morphine)

In suspected bronchospasm during anesthesia, the anesthetic drug that should be avoided is morphine due to its potential to release histamine, which can exacerbate bronchoconstriction. Additionally, other medications to avoid in this context include thiopental, a barbiturate used for induction, and atracurium, a neuromuscular blocking agent, both known to release histamine. Instead, it is recommended to opt for anesthetics that promote bronchodilation, such as ketamine, propofol, and volatile anesthetics, like sevoflurane, to mitigate the risk of worsening bronchospasm during anesthesia. Among the options presented, sevoflurane is likely the best choice.

Recommended literature

1. Papi A, Brightling C, Pedersen SE, Reddel HK. Asthma. Lancet. 2018;391(10122):783-800.
2. Castillo JR, Peters SP, Busse WW. Asthma Exacerbations: Pathogenesis, Prevention, and Treatment. J Allergy Clin Immunol Pract. 2017;5(4):918-927.
3. Woods BD, Sladen RN. Perioperative considerations for the patient with asthma and bronchospasm. BJA. 2009;103(1):i57-i65.

BRONCHIECTASIS

Questions:

1. What genetic disorder may result in abnormal ciliary motility, contributing to bronchiectasis?

   A. Down syndrome

   B. Turner syndrome

   C. Kartagener syndrome

   D. Marfan syndrome

2. Which of the following conditions is LEAST likely to contribute to the development of bronchiectasis?

   A. Cystic fibrosis

   B. Pneumothorax

   C. Tuberculosis

   D. Hypogammaglobulinemia

3. What is the primary purpose of chest physiotherapy in bronchiectasis patients?

   A. Reduction of airway inflammation

   B. Promotion of bronchodilation

   C. Assistance in sputum clearance

   D. Prevention of atelectasis

4. Why is early antibiotic intervention crucial in bronchiectasis management?

   A. To treat the underlying cause

   B. To prevent acute exacerbations

   C. To induce bronchodilation

   D. To improve oxygenation

5. Amyloidosis is a possible complication associated with bronchiectasis.

   A. True

   B. False

6. A 30-year-old male with a known case of severe bilateral bronchiectasis, bullous emphysema, and bilateral fibrothorax, diagnosed at the age of 27, was admitted to the respiratory ICU. The patient presented with symptoms of respiratory distress, including agitation requiring sedation, hypotension (systolic blood pressure < 70 mmHg), tachycardia, and fatigue. Physical examination revealed signs of pulmonary cachexia, tachypnea (30 breaths/min), cyanosis, weak cough with purulent sputum, and diffuse subcrepitant bilateral rales. Arterial blood gas analysis indicated severe hypoxia and hypercapnia, with pH 7.36, $PaCO_2$ of 58 mmHg, PaO_2 of 48 mmHg, and HCO_3- of 38.1 mmol/L. Due to the severity of the respiratory distress, the patient has been intubated and is receiving mechanical ventilation. Which intervention must be used with caution during ventilation in bronchiectasis to prevent barotrauma and hyperinflation?

   A. Use of high tidal volumes

   B. Prolonged inspiratory times

   C. Positive end-expiratory pressure (PEEP)

   D. Rapid changes in ventilation settings

Answers:

1. Answer C (Kartagener syndrome)

Kartagener's syndrome is a rare genetic disorder characterized by abnormal ciliary motility. It is an autosomal recessive condition that presents with a triad of situs inversus, chronic sinusitis, and bronchiectasis. The primary issue in Kartagener's syndrome is the defective movement of cilia, which is particularly relevant in the context of bronchiectasis. The compromised ability of cilia to clear mucus from the airways contributes to the development of bronchiectasis in affected individuals.

2. Answer B (Pneumothorax)

Bronchiectasis is characterized by chronic and irreversible dilation of the bronchi, often due to recurrent infections and inflammation. While pneumothorax can cause lung collapse and present symptoms similar to bronchiectasis, it is not a direct cause of the bronchial dilation seen in bronchiectasis. Cystic fibrosis, tuberculosis, smoking, COPD, asthma, childhood pneumonia, bronchial cartilage deficiency, abnormal ciliary motility (Kartagener's), hypogammaglobulinemia, immunodeficiency, inhaled foreign body, and tumors are conditions known to contribute to the development of bronchiectasis due to various mechanisms such as infections, structural abnormalities, or immune system dysfunction.

3. Answer C (Assistance in sputum clearance)

Chest physiotherapy, often performed with percussion and postural drainage, aims to help clear excessive sputum, a prevalent feature in bronchiectasis. The dilation and damage to the bronchi in bronchiectasis lead to increased production and retention of mucus, contributing to the risk of complications such as recurrent infections and airway obstruction. By employing techniques like percussion and postural drainage, chest physiotherapy assists in mobilizing and clearing the accumulated sputum from the airways, promoting effective airway clearance. This is crucial in preventing complications associated with bronchiectasis and maintaining respiratory function.

4. Answer B (To prevent acute exacerbations)

Early antibiotic intervention is crucial in managing bronchiectasis primarily because it helps prevent acute exacerbations. Bronchiectasis patients are prone to recurrent respiratory infections, and these acute episodes can lead to a worsening of symptoms, increased sputum production, and further lung damage. By administering antibiotics early, healthcare providers aim to suppress bacterial infections promptly, reducing the likelihood of exacerbations. This proactive approach helps maintain respiratory stability, preventing the progression of bronchiectasis-related complications and preserving lung function.

5. Answer A (True)

Amyloidosis is a rare complication associated with bronchiectasis. Historically, in the pre-antibiotic era, cases of amyloidosis and metastatic abscesses were reported in individuals with bronchiectasis. However, with the advent of antibiotics and advancements in medical care, these complications have become rare in contemporary medical practice. Amyloidosis involves the deposition of abnormal proteins called amyloids in various tissues and organs, and its association with bronchiectasis is now uncommon. Today, effective management of respiratory infections and improved healthcare practices have significantly reduced the occurrence of amyloidosis as a complication in bronchiectasis patients.

6. Answer C (Positive end-expiratory pressure (PEEP))

In bronchiectasis patients, especially those with severe respiratory compromise, careful ventilation strategies are crucial to avoid complications such as barotrauma and hyperinflation. Excessive positive end-expiratory pressure can lead to dynamic hyperinflation, potentially worsening the patient's condition. Therefore, it is essential to use PEEP cautiously during ventilation in bronchiectasis patients. For this patient, we propose implementing an initial ventilation strategy using assist control volume-limited ventilation, with tidal volumes set at 6 ml/kg predicted body weight. The respiratory rate and positive end-expiratory pressure settings will be carefully adjusted to optimize ventilation parameters. As the patient's condition improves, we plan to transition to pressure support ventilation with a pressure setting of 15 cmH$_2$O, ensuring a controlled respiratory rate below 30/min. Additionally, to enhance respiratory care, we will introduce auxiliary measures, including the use of heat and moisture exchangers to maintain optimal airway conditions, inline suctioning for effective secretion management, and the delivery of bronchodilators through the ventilator circuit to address bronchoconstriction. To guide the sedation and weaning process, a protocol directed by nursing and respiratory therapists will be implemented. This protocol will include daily spontaneous awakening and breathing trials aimed at optimizing patient comfort and facilitating a smooth transition towards weaning from mechanical ventilation.

Recommended literature

1. Pollard BJ, Kitchen, G. Handbook of Clinical Anaesthesia. Fourth Edition. CRC Press. 2018. 978-1-4987-6289-2.
2. Chalmers, J.D., Chang, A.B., Chotirmall, S.H. et al. Bronchiectasis. Nat Rev Dis Primers 4, 45 (2018).

BRONCHOPLEURAL FISTULA

16
CHAPTER

Questions:

1. **What is the most common cause of bronchopleural fistula (BPF)?**
   A. Persistent spontaneous pneumothorax
   B. Tuberculosis
   C. Lung cancer surgery
   D. Infection

2. **Which of the following is a characteristic symptom of acute BPF?**
   A. Wasting
   B. Dyspnea
   C. Malaise
   D. Fibrosis of the pleural space

3. **How is a bronchopleural fistula usually diagnosed?**
   A. Blood tests
   B. Physical examination
   C. CT scan
   D. Chest X-ray

4. **Why is a double-lumen endotracheal tube (ETT) preferred over a bronchial blocker in bronchopleural fistula cases?**
   A. Cost-effectiveness
   B. Easier insertion
   C. Support for suctioning
   D. Minimized bronchial irritation

5. **A bronchopulmonary fistula occurs most often within 24 hours after surgery after lung surgery.**
   A. True
   B. False

6. **A 55-year-old male patient was referred to the thoracic department following lung cancer surgery complicated by a bronchopleural fistula and pneumonia. The patient underwent a lobectomy for lung adenocarcinoma three weeks ago. He presented with worsening dyspnea, persistent cough with purulent expectoration, and a chest CT confirming the presence of a bronchopleural fistula. Antibiotic treatment failed to improve his condition, necessitating surgical intervention. What considerations balance the need for lung isolation during anesthesia?**
   A. Patient age and gender
   B. Possible full stomach
   C. Past medical history
   D. Allergies and sensitivities

Answers:

1. Answer C (Lung cancer surgery)

The most common cause of bronchopleural fistula (BPF) is lung cancer surgery, particularly after lung resection procedures. This complication can also arise from various other factors, including the breakdown of suture/staple lines following lung resection, rupture of a cavity, erosion of the bronchial wall by infection or neoplasm, penetrating trauma, pulmonary infarction, persistent spontaneous pneumothorax, and treatments such as chemotherapy or radiotherapy. Iatrogenic factors may also contribute to the development of BPF.

2. Answer B (Dyspnea)

Acute BPF is associated with specific signs and symptoms, and dyspnea is a key characteristic. Other symptoms of acute BPF include hypotension, subcutaneous emphysema, cough with expectoration of purulent fluid, tracheal or mediastinal shift, persistent air leak, and reduction or disappearance of pleural effusion on chest radiograph. Dyspnea is a common manifestation reflecting the urgency and severity of the condition.

3. Answer C (CT scan)

While a chest X-ray is considered the basic imaging modality for diagnosing bronchopleural fistula, a CT scan is often the preferred and more comprehensive test. A CT scan is particularly helpful in visualizing the site of the rupture and providing detailed information about the condition. Additionally, bronchoscopy allows direct visualization of the bronchial and pleural structures. The "fallen lung" sign on the chest X-ray, along with features such as atelectatic lung, inadequate lung expansion, and a massive air leak, highly suggest bronchial rupture. The combination of these diagnostic approaches aids in the accurate and timely identification of bronchopleural fistula.

4. Answer C (Support for suctioning)

A double-lumen endotracheal tube (DLT) is preferred in cases of bronchopleural fistula due to its ability to provide comprehensive support. Unlike a bronchial blocker, a DLT allows for suctioning, optimal ventilation, and effectively isolating the affected lung. This versatility is crucial in managing bronchopleural fistula cases, where maintaining clear airways, effective suctioning, and ensuring optimal ventilation are essential components of anesthetic management.

5. Answer B (False)

A bronchopulmonary fistula does not typically occur within 24 hours after lung surgery. It occurs most often one to two weeks after lung surgery. Clinicians should be aware of this delayed occurrence during the postoperative period, emphasizing the need for vigilant monitoring and early recognition of potential complications.

6. Answer B (Possible full stomach)

In managing a patient with a bronchopleural fistula following lung cancer surgery, considerations for lung isolation during anesthesia are crucial for preventing pathophysiological complications. These considerations are balanced with factors such as a possible full stomach, difficult airway, hemodynamic instability, limited functional reserve, and the need for rapid sequence induction (RSI). A spectrum of techniques for lung isolation was evaluated, ranging from regional anesthesia to awake fibreoptic intubation involving a single lumen endotracheal tube (ETT) with or without a bronchial blocker, double lumen ETT administration before the onset of general anesthesia (GA) and even asleep intubation with spontaneous ventilation preceding isolation. A double-lumen ETT was preferred over a bronchial blocker to support suctioning, provide optimal ventilation, and ensure effective isolation.

Recommended literature

1. Salik I, Vashisht R, Abramowicz AE. Bronchopleural Fistula. [Updated 2022 May 8]. In: StatPearls [Internet]. Treasure Island (FL): StatPearls Publishing; 2022 Jan-. Available from: https://www.ncbi.nlm.nih.gov/books/NBK534765/
2. Kiyota Y, Topulos GP, Hartigan PM. Bronchopleural fistula. In: Aglio LS, Lekowski RW, Urman RD, eds. Essential Clinical Anesthesia Review: Keywords, Questions and Answers for the Boards. Cambridge: Cambridge University Press; 2015:518-519.
3. Pollard BJ, Kitchen, G. Handbook of Clinical Anaesthesia. Fourth Edition. CRC Press. 2018. 978-1-4987-6289-2.

BULLOUS LUNG DISEASE

16
CHAPTER

Questions:

1. **What is the defining characteristic of a bulla in the context of bullous lung disease?**
   A. Layers of the visceral pleura are < 1 cm in diameter
   B. Air-filled space within the lung parenchyma
   C. Collections that have an epithelial or fibrous lining
   D. Tents in the lung parenchyma that usually arise from blunt trauma

2. **What is NOT the primary diagnostic tool for evaluating bullous lung disease?**
   A. Chest X-ray
   B. CT scan
   C. Magnetic Resonance Imaging (MRI)
   D. Pulmonary function test

3. **Which syndrome is NOT associated with the development of bullous lung disease?**
   A. Marfan syndrome
   B. Loeys-Dietz syndrome
   C. Ehlers-Danlos syndrome
   D. Turner syndrome

4. **What is the primary consequence of bullae not participating in gas exchange?**
   A. Respiratory alkalosis
   B. Hypoxia
   C. Increased lung compliance
   D. Hypocapnia

5. **The term giant bulla is used for bullae that occupy at least 30 percent of a hemithorax.**
   A. True
   B. False

6. **A 61-year-old man without significant past medical history presented with worsening shortness of breath for 2 days duration. Three months prior to presentation, he was hospitalized for acute hypoxemic respiratory failure due to COVID-19 pneumonia. On this current presentation, he was hypoxemic, and a repeat CT scan of the chest showed extensive bullous lung disease throughout the right lung with mediastinal shift, not reported on prior imaging. Intubating the patient and initiating positive-pressure ventilation is being contemplated. What complication may arise from the use of positive pressure in patients with bullous lung disease?**
   A. Pulmonary fibrosis
   B. Hyperinflation and rupture
   C. Pleural effusion
   D. Atelectasis

Answers:

1. Answer B (Air-filled space within the lung parenchyma)

A bulla is specifically characterized as a permanent, air-filled space within the lung parenchyma, with a minimum size of 1 cm and featuring a thin or poorly defined wall. It is crucial to highlight that bullae are situated within the lung tissue, distinguishing them from blebs, which are air-filled collections within the layers of the visceral pleura and are typically smaller, measuring <1 cm in diameter. Additionally, other air-filled spaces in the lung, such as cysts and cavities, exhibit distinct characteristics. Pneumatoceles, described as temporary tents in the lung parenchyma, typically result from blunt trauma or over-distension.

2. Answer C (Magnetic Resonance Imaging (MRI))

The primary diagnostic tools for evaluating bullous lung disease include chest X-ray, CT scan, arterial blood gas analysis, and pulmonary function tests. Chest X-ray serves as an initial screening tool, while CT scans provide detailed imaging for assessing the size and characteristics of bullae. Arterial blood gas analysis helps evaluate respiratory status, and pulmonary function tests aid in assessing lung function. Notably, MRI is not a primary diagnostic tool for bullous lung disease in the provided text, making it the correct answer among the options given.

3. Answer D (Turner syndrome)

Among the given options, Turner syndrome is not associated with the development of bullous lung disease. Turner syndrome, affecting only females, is characterized by the absence or partial absence of one X chromosome and is known for various medical and developmental issues, including short height, ovarian failure, and heart defects. In contrast, Marfan syndrome, Loeys-Dietz syndrome, and Ehlers-Danlos syndrome are associated with the development of bullous lung disease. The other etiological factors for bullous lung disease encompass conditions such as cigarette or marijuana smoking, HIV infection, intravenous drug use, and alpha-1 antitrypsin deficiency.

4. Answer B (Hypoxia)

Bullae, air-filled spaces within the lung parenchyma that do not contribute to the exchange of gases, lead to decreased functional lung tissue. This results in reduced blood oxygenation, causing hypoxia. The inefficient gas exchange, in turn, contributes to symptoms like dyspnea.

5. Answer A (True)

The term "giant bulla" is used for bullae that occupy at least 30 percent of a hemithorax. This designation helps convey the significant size and impact of these bullae on the lung and thoracic cavity. It is an important criterion in describing the extent of bullous involvement in the lung parenchyma, emphasizing the considerable space occupied by these bullae within the hemithorax.

6. Answer B (Hyperinflation and rupture)

Bullae, which are air-filled spaces within the lung parenchyma, grow in size over time. When positive pressure is applied, as in mechanical ventilation, the intra-bulla pressure can rise relative to the surrounding lung regions. This poses a concomitant risk of hyperinflation and rupture of the bullae. Bulla rupture in bullous lung disease can be life-threatening due to the potential development of a tension pneumothorax, leading to hemodynamic collapse. Additionally, rupture may result in a bronchopleural fistula, causing inadequate ventilation. Therefore, the use of positive pressure ventilation in patients with extensive bullous lung disease requires careful consideration due to the associated risk of hyperinflation and rupture, potentially leading to serious complications.

Recommended literature

1. Saini V, Assu SM, Bhatia N, Sethi S. Abdominal surgery in a patient with bullous emphysema: Anesthetic concerns. J Anaesthesiol Clin Pharmacol. 2019;35(3):414-415.
2. Goldberg, C., Carey, K., 2013. Bullous Lung Disease. Western Journal of Emergency Medicine 14, 450–451.
3. Johnson MK, Smith RP, Morrison D, et alLarge lung bullae in marijuana smokersThorax 2000;55:340-342.

CHRONIC OBSTRUCTIVE PULMONARY DISEASE

16
CHAPTER

Questions:

1. What is the primary factor in the pathophysiology of chronic obstructive pulmonary disease (COPD) that leads to chronic dyspnea and airway obstruction?
   A. Bullae formation
   B. Bronchospasm
   C. Chronic hypoxemia/hypercarbia
   D. Emphysema

2. What should be considered in the preoperative assessment of COPD patients over 40 years old with a significant smoking history?
   A. Electrocardiogram (ECG)
   B. Chest X-ray
   C. Spirometry
   D. All of the above

3. What is the primary cause of inflammation in chronic obstructive pulmonary disease?
   A. Allergies
   B. Infection
   C. Cigarette smoke
   D. Occupational exposure

4. Which of the following is NOT a physiological change associated with COPD?
   A. Metabolic alkalosis
   B. Chronic hypoxemia
   C. Obstructive physiology
   D. Bullous disease

5. Serum albumin level < 35 mg/L is a strong predictor of postoperative pulmonary complications in patients with COPD.
   A. True
   B. False

6. A 52-year-old obese woman with chronic obstructive pulmonary disease Gold III and a history of acute myocardial infarction (AMI) was scheduled for laparoscopic cholecystectomy; the patient is intubated and mechanically ventilated. What is the recommended approach for ventilation during surgery to prevent dynamic hyperinflation in COPD patients?
   A. High peak pressure, high tidal volume
   B. Low tidal volume, rapid rate
   C. Long I:E, low peak pressure, low tidal volume, slow rate, permissive hypercapnia
   D. Normal I:E ratio, low tidal volume, hyperventilation

Answers:

1. **Answer D (Emphysema)**

The cardinal pathophysiological determinant of chronic dyspnea and airway obstruction in COPD is emphysema. This condition, coexisting with chronic obstructive bronchitis, involves the destruction of lung parenchyma, resulting in the loss of elastic recoil and alveolar septa. This intricate process enhances the likelihood of airway collapse, leading to lung hyperinflation, airflow limitation, and persistent air trapping. Emphysema significantly contributes to the overarching airflow restriction that characterizes COPD, thereby playing a pivotal role in the manifestation of chronic dyspnea and persistent airway obstruction observed in affected individuals.

2. **Answer D (All of the above)**

In the preoperative assessment of COPD patients over 40 years old with a significant smoking history, it is crucial to consider Electrocardiogram (ECG), Chest X-ray, and Spirometry. Chest X-ray aids in excluding active infection and detecting occult malignancies, with extensive bullous disease indicating potential pneumothorax risk. ECG helps reveal right heart disease, and echocardiography may be considered based on ECG findings. Spirometry is pivotal in clarifying the diagnosis and assessing COPD severity, contributing to comprehensive risk stratification for optimal perioperative management.

3. **Answer C (Cigarette smoke)**

COPD is characterized by airflow limitation resulting from an inflammatory response to inhaled toxins, with tobacco smoke being the most significant contributor. Other noxious stimuli include air pollution from burning carbon-based fuels or biomass and occupational exposure to chemical fumes or fine particulate matter. While individual risk factors like a history of lung infections, genetics, maternal exposure, asthma, premature birth, and socioeconomic factors can contribute, tobacco smoke remains the predominant and most common cause of the inflammatory process leading to COPD. Alpha-1 antitrypsin deficiency and certain occupational exposures are mentioned as less common causes in nonsmokers.

4. **Answer A (Metabolic alkalosis)**

Several changes are associated with COPD, including bronchospasm, mucous plugging, obstructive physiology, bullous disease, pneumothorax, pulmonary tamponade, and chronic hypoxemia/hypercarbia. Metabolic alkalosis, however, is not a typical feature of COPD. COPD is more commonly associated with respiratory chronic retention of carbon dioxide.

5. **Answer A (True)**

A serum albumin level below 35 mg/L is recognized as a strong predictor of postoperative pulmonary complications in patients with COPD. This marker is indicative of nutritional status and overall health. When the serum albumin level is below this threshold, it suggests potential nutritional deficiencies and increased vulnerability to postoperative complications. Therefore, providing preoperative nutritional supplementation becomes crucial to optimize the nutritional status of COPD patients, potentially reducing the risk of postoperative pulmonary complications.

6. **Answer C (Long I:E, low peak pressure, low tidal volume, slow rate, permissive hypercapnia)**

This strategy aims to prevent dynamic hyperinflation and barotrauma common in COPD patients. Lengthening the inspiratory to expiratory ratio provides more time for expiration, reducing air trapping while maintaining low peak pressure and tidal volume safeguards against excessive lung inflation. A slow respiratory rate complements these measures, allowing permissive hypercapnia within acceptable limits to avoid excessive respiratory efforts. This lung protective ventilation, combined with measures to promptly treat bronchospasm and provide positive end-expiratory pressure, ensures comprehensive management and minimizes the risk of complications associated with COPD during surgery.

Recommended literature

1. Christenson SA, Smith BM, Bafadhel M, Putcha N. Chronic obstructive pulmonary disease. Lancet. 2022;399(10342):2227-2242.
2. National Institute for Health and Care Excellence. (2018) Chronic Obstructive Pulmonary Disease in over 16s: diagnosis and management (NICE guideline 115) available at https://www.nice.org.uk/guidance/ng115.
3. Lumb AB, Biercamp C. Chronic obstructive pulmonary disease and anaesthesia. Continuing Education in Anaesthesia, Critical Care & Pain. 2014;14:1-5.

CYSTIC FIBROSIS

16
CHAPTER

Questions:

1. **What is considered the most common lethal genetic disease in Caucasians?**
   A. Huntington's disease
   B. Duchenne muscular dystrophy
   C. Cystic fibrosis
   D. Hemochromatosis

2. **What is the primary respiratory manifestation of cystic fibrosis?**
   A. Bullae formation
   B. Chronic bronchitis
   C. Bronchospasm
   D. Patchy atelectasis

3. **Which non-respiratory component of cystic fibrosis is associated with the highest mortality?**
   A. Meconium ileus
   B. Liver disease
   C. Nasal polyposis
   D. Absence of vas deferens

4. **What is the gold standard for the diagnosis of cystic fibrosis?**
   A. Chest radiograph
   B. Genetic testing
   C. Sweat testing
   D. Pulmonary function test

5. **The absence of vas deferens is commonly seen in men with cystic fibrosis.**
   A. True
   B. False

6. **A 28-year-old woman with a confirmed diagnosis of cystic fibrosis (CF) is scheduled for cholecystectomy due to non-functioning gallbladders. Her clinical profile includes an FEV1 of 0.79L (24% predicted), and she presents with several co-morbidities, such as pancreatic insufficiency, impaired glucose tolerance, as well as osteopenia. Additionally, she relies on long-term oxygen therapy, nocturnal bi-level positive airway pressure (BiPAP), and has central venous access (Port-A-Cath) and a percutaneous endoscopic gastrostomy (PEG tube) in situ. Which therapeutic approach is a key anesthetic consideration for preparing this patient with cystic fibrosis for elective surgery?**
   A. Antibiotics
   B. Enteral supplementation
   C. Gene therapy
   D. Physical therapy and inhaled bronchodilators

Answers:

1. Answer C (Cystic fibrosis)

Cystic fibrosis is an autosomal recessive genetic disorder that predominantly affects Caucasians. It is characterized by mutations in the CFTR gene, which lead to the production of thick and sticky mucus and impact various organ systems. While Huntington's disease, Duchenne muscular dystrophy, and hemochromatosis are also genetic disorders, cystic fibrosis is specifically recognized as the most common lethal genetic disease in Caucasians.

2. Answer D (Patchy atelectasis)

Cystic fibrosis (CF) is characterized by viscid mucous secretions and impaired mucociliary clearance, leading to the development of patchy atelectasis, airway inflammation, and chronic hypoxia. The thick mucus traps bacterial microbes, fostering biofilm formation and bacterial proliferation, initiating a cycle of inflammation and infection primarily mediated by neutrophils. CF patients commonly experience chronic colonization of the airways with pathogens, including Pseudomonas aeruginosa, Staphylococcus aureus, Haemophilus influenzae, Stenotrophomonas maltophilia, Burkholderia cepacia, and Aspergillus. As the disease progresses, airway obstruction ensues, resulting in air trapping and the development of bronchiectasis. The respiratory course in CF may involve a relapse-remit pattern or a steady decline in lung function, leading to complications such as cor pulmonale, respiratory failure, and increased mortality.

3. Answer B (Liver disease)

Cystic fibrosis is a complex multisystem disorder where, despite the predominant impact on the respiratory system, non-respiratory manifestations play a substantial role in shaping morbidity and mortality. Liver disease in CF is primarily attributed to the obstruction of bile ductules by abnormal mucoid secretions, leading to the development of focal biliary cirrhosis. In more severe cases, this condition may progress to portal hypertension and multinodular biliary cirrhosis, amplifying its non-respiratory impact on overall health outcomes. This liver involvement stands as a noteworthy contributor to morbidity and mortality in individuals with CF. Additionally, CF-related diabetes mellitus (CFRD) is a prevalent complication, particularly in those with pancreatic insufficiency. The incidence of CFRD is associated with worse lung function, compromised nutrition, frequent hospitalization, and elevated mortality rates when compared to CF patients without diabetes.

4. Answer C (Sweat testing)

The gold standard for diagnosing cystic fibrosis involves laboratory evidence, and sweat testing is a crucial diagnostic tool. This test, performed from 2 weeks of age, includes transdermal administration of pilocarpine to stimulate sweating, followed by analyzing electrolyte concentration in the sweat. This method has been a longstanding and reliable approach. Genetic testing, another diagnostic option, can confirm diagnoses, and it may be performed antenatally by amniocentesis or chorionic villus sampling. Newborn screening (NBS) is also conducted in many regions, analyzing immunoreactive trypsinogen levels, but it has a high false-positive rate. The accurate diagnosis of cystic fibrosis often involves a combination of these diagnostic modalities.

5. Answer A (True)

In men with cystic fibrosis, the absence of vas deferens is a common manifestation, affecting approximately 98% of individuals. This congenital bilateral absence of the vas deferens leads to primary infertility in affected men. Interestingly, in some cases, this absence of vas deferens may be the only clinical manifestation of the disease in this subgroup of individuals with CF. On the other hand, women with CF typically have abnormally viscid cervical secretions, which can impede the passage of sperm, resulting in primary infertility. However, despite these challenges, successful pregnancies can be achieved through assisted reproductive technologies such as in vitro fertilization.

6. Answer D (Physical therapy and inhaled bronchodilators)

In the preoperative phase, optimizing CF patients for surgery involves a thorough medication review, intensified daily physiotherapy, and administering nebulized drugs as close to surgery as possible. Key anesthetic considerations encompass providing airway clearance therapies (ACTs) and inhaled airway clearance agents on the morning of surgery. Utilizing warm, humidified gases and bronchodilators enhances airway clearance. Employing multimodal analgesia and avoiding atelectasis are pivotal components of the anesthetic approach to optimize respiratory function during and after surgery, recognizing the importance of the patient's unique CF-related challenges.

Recommended literature

1. Fitzgerald M, Ryan D. Cystic fibrosis and anaesthesia. Continuing Education in Anaesthesia Critical Care & Pain. 2011;11(6):204-9.
2. Huffmyer JL, Littlewood KE, Nemergut EC. Perioperative Management of the Adult with Cystic Fibrosis. Anesthesia & Analgesia. 2009;109(6).

ESOPHAGECTOMY

16
CHAPTER

Questions:

1. Which surgical approach involves a laparotomy and a right thoracotomy?
   A. Transhiatal
   B. Ivor Lewis
   C. Three-hole
   D. Laparoscopic/thoracoscopic

2. Which of the following is NOT a risk factor for esophageal adenocarcinoma?
   A. Smoking
   B. Gastro-oesophageal reflux
   C. Poor oral hygiene
   D. Alcohol consumption

3. What is a significant risk factor for squamous cell carcinoma of the esophagus?
   A. Caucasian is more common than Asian or African
   B. Barrett's esophagus
   C. Salted vegetables
   D. Low dietary intake of fruits and vegetables

4. How can smaller anastomotic leaks post-esophagectomy be managed?
   A. Surgical exploration
   B. Revision surgery
   C. High protein enteral feed
   D. Prokinetics

5. Adequate analgesia is a strategy to minimize the risk of respiratory complications post-esophagectomy.
   A. True
   B. False

6. A 70-year-old Caucasian male with a long history of smoking has been diagnosed with adenocarcinoma of the esophagus. Given the nature of his condition, he is scheduled for an esophagectomy. Understanding the high risk associated with respiratory complications post-esophagectomy, the medical team is keen on implementing strategies to minimize such risks. One key approach they are considering is the use of adequate analgesia to ensure postoperative pain control. Which of the following is the first choice for analgesia to minimize the risk of respiratory complications post-esophagectomy?
   A. Paravertebral block or catheter
   B. Intravenous opioids
   C. Patient-controlled analgesia
   D. Thoracic epidural

Answers:

1. Answer B (Ivor Lewis)

In the Ivor Lewis esophagectomy, the surgical approach involves a laparotomy and a right thoracotomy. During this procedure, the esophageal tumor is removed through an abdominal laparotomy and a right thoracotomy. This approach allows for the resection of the esophageal tumor and the creation of the esophagogastric anastomosis, where the remaining esophagus is reconnected to the stomach. The anastomosis is typically located in the upper chest. The Ivor Lewis approach provides access to both the abdominal and thoracic cavities, facilitating the removal of the tumor and reconstruction of the digestive tract.

2. Answer C (Poor oral hygiene)

Poor oral hygiene is not a recognized risk factor for esophageal adenocarcinoma. Established risk factors for adenocarcinoma include gastro-oesophageal reflux, smoking, obesity, and Barrett's esophagus. In contrast, poor oral hygiene, along with alcohol and smoking, is associated with an increased risk of squamous cell carcinoma, a different histological type of esophageal cancer.

3. Answer C (Salted vegetables)

Salted vegetables are a significant risk factor for squamous cell carcinoma of the esophagus. Other risk factors for squamous cell carcinoma include smoking, alcohol consumption (particularly when there is synergism with smoking), and poor oral hygiene. Additionally, dietary habits such as consuming salted vegetables and preserved fish are associated with an increased risk. Other factors, such as low socioeconomic status, male gender, and specific medical conditions like achalasia, caustic injury, and nutritional deficiencies, are also linked to an elevated risk of squamous cell carcinoma.

4. Answer C (High protein enteral feed)

Smaller anastomotic leaks post-esophagectomy can be managed through conservative measures. This includes keeping the patient nil by mouth, providing high protein enteral feed or total parenteral nutrition, administering antibiotics, implementing chest physiotherapy, conducting radiologically guided drainage collection, and performing serial contrast studies. These conservative approaches aim to support the patient's nutritional status, facilitate healing, and manage the leak without the need for surgical exploration or revision surgery, which are typically reserved for major anastomotic leaks. Monitoring the patient closely and adjusting the management plan based on their clinical response is crucial in optimizing outcomes and preventing further complications.

5. Answer A (True)

Adequate analgesia is a strategy employed to minimize the risk of respiratory complications post-esophagectomy. Effective pain management after surgery is crucial in preventing respiratory issues such as pneumonia and atelectasis. In addition to analgesia, other measures mentioned in the context include the reversal of muscular block, maintaining normothermia, chest physiotherapy, and ensuring hemodynamic stability. By addressing pain appropriately, the patient is more likely to engage in activities such as deep breathing and coughing, which are essential for maintaining optimal respiratory function and reducing the risk of postoperative complications.

6. Answer D (Thoracic epidural)

Preemptive thoracic epidural analgesia is the first-choice approach to minimize the risk of respiratory complications post-esophagectomy. Epidural analgesia (EA) has been suggested to reduce postoperative pneumonia and prevent chronic postsurgical pain (CPSP) compared to opioid-based systemic analgesia. It is considered the gold standard for pain management in esophagectomy procedures. However, if a contraindication or limitation arises, options like Paravertebral block or catheter can be suitable alternatives. Patient-controlled analgesia may be considered if regional techniques are contraindicated or prove ineffective, ensuring that the patient's pain is well-managed to promote optimal respiratory function and overall recovery.

Recommended literature

1. Howells P, Bieker M, Yeung J. Oesophageal cancer and the anaesthetist. BJA Education. 2017;17(2):68-73.
2. Veelo DP, Geerts BF. Anaesthesia during oesophagectomy. J Thorac Dis. 2017;9(Suppl 8):S705-S712. doi:10.21037/jtd.2017.03.153.

LUNG CANCER

Questions:

1. **What is the most common form of lung cancer, accounting for approximately 80% of cases?**
   A. Small-cell lung cancer (SCLC)
   B. Adenocarcinoma
   C. Squamous cell carcinoma
   D. Large-cell carcinoma

2. **Which route is NOT involved in the spread of lung cancer?**
   A. Lymphatic
   B. Hematological
   C. Neurological
   D. Per continuitatem

3. **Which lung cancer type is known for spreading faster and being more challenging to treat?**
   A. Adenocarcinoma
   B. Squamous cell carcinoma
   C. Large-cell carcinoma
   D. Small-cell lung cancer

4. **In the context of lung cancer, what does TNM stand for?**
   A. Tumor, Nodule, Metastasis
   B. Trachea, Nodes, Mass
   C. Thorax, Nodes, Malignancy
   D. Tissue, Nerve, Metabolic

5. **Lung cancer commonly metastasizes to the brain, bone, liver, and adrenal glands.**
   A. True
   B. False

6. **A 55-year-old female patient and a long-time smoker presented with right-sided chest pain that had developed two weeks prior. A nodule was discovered in the right upper lobe just seven days later. The patient had no previous history of chronic diseases. A chest computed tomography (CT) scan revealed a circular-like nodule approximately 1.8 cm × 1.6 cm in the anterior segment of the right upper lobe. A bronchoscopy was performed, and the pathologic diagnosis confirmed invasive adenocarcinoma. The preoperative diagnosis was lung cancer of the right upper lobe, staged as T1aN0M0. The plan is to proceed with one-lung ventilation (OLV) during surgery. Which anesthesia technique interferes with hypoxic pulmonary vasoconstriction (HPV) during one-lung ventilation?**
   A. Inhalation of volatile agents
   B. Thoracic epidural analgesia
   C. Inhaled nitric oxide
   D. Propofol-based total intravenous anesthesia (TIVA)

Answers:

1. Answer B (Adenocarcinoma)

Adenocarcinoma is the most common form of lung cancer, contributing to approximately 80% of cases. This type of lung cancer usually originates in the peripheral lung tissue and is more common in non-smokers. The other common types, squamous cell carcinoma and large-cell carcinoma, also fall under the category of non-small-cell lung cancer (NSCLC), together constituting the majority of lung cancer cases. Small-cell lung cancer (SCLC) is less common but is known for its aggressive nature, faster spread, and challenges in treatment. Lung cancer is the leading cause of cancer mortality worldwide, affecting both men and women, and often originates in the bronchi, bronchioles, or alveoli.

2. Answer C (Neurological)

Lung cancer can spread (metastasize) through various routes. It commonly metastasizes through the lymphatic system, where cancerous cells invade nearby lymph nodes and travel to other parts of the body. This is known as distant metastasis. Additionally, lung cancer can spread through the bloodstream (hematological spread), allowing cancer cells to reach distant organs. Another mode of spread is per continuitatem, involving the invasion of cancerous cells into surrounding healthy tissues.

3. Answer D (Small-cell lung cancer)

Small-cell lung cancer is characterized by its aggressive behavior, rapid progression, and heightened difficulty in treatment compared to non-small-cell lung cancer. SCLC, less prevalent but more challenging, is often linked to a prolonged history of tobacco smoking. It is known for its propensity to spread swiftly, making it a formidable adversary in terms of therapeutic intervention. The two primary subtypes of SCLC are small cell carcinoma, the more common form, and combined small cell carcinoma, constituting a small percentage and representing a combination of non-small-cell and small-cell lung cancer cells. This aggressive nature and swift dissemination contribute to the reputation of SCLC as a formidable and challenging lung cancer type to manage effectively.

4. Answer A (Tumor, Nodule, Metastasis)

TNM stands for Tumor, Node, Metastasis. TNM is a widely used staging system for various cancers, including lung cancer. It provides a standardized way to describe the extent of the disease by assessing the size and extent of the primary tumor (T), the involvement of regional lymph nodes (N), and the presence of distant metastasis (M). This staging system helps healthcare professionals determine the appropriate treatment and prognosis for individuals diagnosed with lung cancer.

5. Answer A (True)

Lung cancer commonly metastasizes to various distant sites, including the brain, bone, liver, and adrenal glands. The spread of lung cancer can occur through both the lymphatic and hematological routes. Distal metastasis to these organs is not uncommon, and the presence of metastases in these sites can significantly impact the prognosis and treatment approach for individuals with lung cancer.

6. Answer A (Inhalation of volatile agents)

OLV is employed to collapse and isolate the operative lung, optimizing surgical exposure, but it can lead to a significant shunt affecting gas exchange. Hypoxic pulmonary vasoconstriction (HPV) is a crucial compensatory mechanism during OLV, reducing blood flow to the poorly ventilated operative lung and improving the ventilation/perfusion (V/Q) mismatch. Inhalation of volatile agents, particularly sevoflurane, is common in general anesthesia; however, when administered at concentrations exceeding one minimum alveolar concentration (MAC), these agents can interfere with HPV.

Recommended literature

1. Hackett, S., Jones, R., Kapila, R., 2019. Anaesthesia for pneumonectomy. BJA Education 19, 297–304. .
2. Pollard BJ, Kitchen, G. Handbook of Clinical Anaesthesia. Fourth Edition. CRC Press. 2018. 978-1-4987-6289-2.

Respiratory & Thoracics
MASSIVE HEMOPTYSIS

16
CHAPTER

Questions:

1. **Which of the following statements best describes hemoptysis?**
   A. The expectoration of blood originating from the upper respiratory tract
   B. The expectoration of blood originating from the lower respiratory tract
   C. The presence of blood in the saliva
   D. The coughing up of blood clots

2. **Which diagnostic tool is most appropriate for identifying the site of bleeding in a patient with massive hemoptysis?**
   A. Magnetic resonance imaging (MRI)
   B. Chest radiography
   C. Computed tomography (CT)
   D. Fiberoptic bronchoscopy

3. **In the management of massive hemoptysis, what is the recommended positioning to optimize airway protection?**
   A. Trendelenburg position
   B. Bleeding side up
   C. Bleeding side down
   D. Supine position

4. **In the context of massive hemoptysis, what is the role of CPAP to the bleeding lung?**
   A. Enhancing oxygenation to the non-bleeding lung
   B. Tamponade effect on the bleeding site
   C. Prevention of contralateral contamination
   D. Facilitating bronchial artery embolization

5. **In 90% of cases, the source of the massive hemoptysis is the bronchial circulation.**
   A. True
   B. False

6. **A 35 year-old woman with a long history of Systemic lupus erythematosus (SLE) was admitted to the hospital with a complaint of massive hemoptysis. Over the preceding 3 months, the patient had been experiencing frequent coughing episodes. Chest radiography revealed opacities in the left lung. The diagnostic process estimated blood loss exceeding 1000 mL, necessitating blood transfusion and fluid replacement. What is the appropriate intervention for a patient with massive hemoptysis and known bleeding side?**
   A. Bleeding side-up positioning
   B. Awake intubation
   C. Contralateral isolation and single-lung ventilation
   D. Trendelenburg position

Answers:

1. **Answer B (The expectoration of blood originating from the lower respiratory tract)**

   Hemoptysis is the expectoration of blood originating from the lower respiratory tract. It represents a medical emergency, and while there is no universally agreed-upon definition of massive hemoptysis, it is generally recognized as volumes ranging from 100 mL to 1000 mL within 24 hours. Life-threatening hemoptysis occurs with any volume of blood that could obstruct the airway or cause significant hemodynamic compromise, necessitating prompt management. Hemoptysis involves the discharge of blood or blood-stained mucus through the mouth from the bronchi, larynx, trachea, or lungs, and it does not necessarily involve coughing.

2. **Answer D (Fiberoptic bronchoscopy)**

   Fiberoptic bronchoscopy is a key and immediate diagnostic modality in evaluating hemoptysis, allowing direct visualization of the airways and identification of the bleeding source. It can be performed at the bedside and provides valuable information about the location, extent, and nature of the bleeding. If oxygenation remains inadequate or brisk bleeding persists, a transfer to the operating room for rigid bronchoscopy may be considered. Rigid bronchoscopy, although more invasive, allows for better suctioning of clots and facilitates therapeutic interventions. Additionally, further investigation with CT can complement the information obtained from fiberoptic bronchoscopy and aid in planning subsequent angiography if needed.

3. **Answer C (Bleeding side down)**

   This position is crucial for minimizing the risk of contralateral contamination and asphyxia by allowing blood to pool away from the unaffected lung. Placing the bleeding side down facilitates the selective intubation of the bronchus supplying the bleeding lung, aiding in the control of hemorrhage. The management approach involves prioritizing the ABCs (Airway, Breathing, Circulation), followed by interventions such as intubation with rigid bronchoscopy, contralateral lung isolation, and volume resuscitation. Additionally, a multidisciplinary team involving interventional radiology, intensive care unit, interventional pulmonology, anesthesiology, and surgery may be called upon for further management, including lung resection if necessary.

4. **Answer B (Tamponade effect on the bleeding site)**

   Applying CPAP to the bleeding lung can contribute to tamponading the bleeding site, exerting positive pressure that may help control hemorrhage. This is part of the overall strategy to optimize oxygenation and ventilation to both lungs, with the bleeding lung positioned down after selective bronchial intubation. CPAP can provide a tamponade effect, potentially aiding in reducing bleeding and stabilizing the patient. This approach is particularly important in the emergency management of massive hemoptysis, where rapid interventions are necessary to prevent airway compromise and hemodynamic instability.

5. **Answer A (True)**

   In 90% of cases, the source of massive hemoptysis is the bronchial circulation. This means that bleeding originates from the bronchial arteries, which supply the bronchial tree at systemic pressure rather than the low-pressure pulmonary circulation. Chronic inflammatory conditions, abnormal anatomical variations, bronchial-systemic connections, pulmonary arteriovenous malformations, and other conditions affecting the bronchial circulation can predispose individuals to massive hemoptysis.

6. **Answer C (Contralateral isolation and single-lung ventilation)**

   Given the patient's history of Systemic lupus erythematosus and the occurrence of massive hemoptysis, the appropriate intervention for a patient with a known bleeding side is contralateral isolation and single-lung ventilation. This approach involves isolating the non-bleeding lung to prevent contamination and optimize oxygenation to the unaffected side. In this scenario, the patient should be positioned with the bleeding side down to minimize the risk of aspiration into the contralateral lung. Intubation is necessary, and a single-lumen endotracheal tube can be initially used for suction and bronchial toilet. Subsequently, contralateral isolation can be achieved, and single-lung ventilation can be initiated to isolate the affected lung during further management, which may include interventions such as bronchoscopy, nebulized adrenaline, and transfer to a high dependency or intensive care unit.

Recommended literature

1. Radchenko C, Alraiyes AH, Shojaee S. A systematic approach to the management of massive hemoptysis. J Thorac Dis. 2017;9(Suppl 10):S1069-S1086.
2. Thomas, A. and Lynch, G. (2011) Management Of Massive Haemoptysis, WFSA. Available at: https://resources.wfsahq.org/atotw/management-of-massive-haemoptysis/ (Accessed: January 23, 2023).

MEDIASTINOSCOPY

16

CHAPTER

Questions:

1. **What is the primary purpose of mediastinoscopy?**
   A. Treatment of lung cancer
   B. Biopsy of mediastinal masses
   C. Removal of anterior mediastinal masses
   D. Evaluation of pleural effusion

2. **What is the recommended approach for the majority of mediastinoscopies?**
   A. Thoracic approach
   B. Abdominal approach
   C. Cervical approach
   D. Axillary approach

3. **Which of the following is an absolute contraindication for mediastinoscopy?**
   A. Thoracic aortic aneurysm
   B. Previous recurrent laryngeal nerve injury
   C. Severe tracheal deviation
   D. SVC syndrome

4. **Which condition may present as a mediastinal mass in the middle mediastinum?**
   A. Thymic tumor
   B. Germ cell tumors
   C. Esophageal cancer
   D. Mesenchymal tumor

5. **Phrenic nerve paralysis is one of the major complications of mediastinoscopy.**
   A. True
   B. False

6. **A 58-year-old female presents with suspected mesenchymal tumors in the middle mediastinum. A diagnostic mediastinoscopy with a biopsy is recommended to confirm the diagnosis and guide further management. What is the recommended postoperative analgesia after mediastinoscopy?**
   A. Intramuscular opioids
   B. Superficial cervical plexus block
   C. Short-acting opioids
   D. Epidural analgesia

Answers:

1. **Answer B (Biopsy of mediastinal masses)**

   Mediastinoscopy is a highly sensitive and specific diagnostic procedure for lung cancer staging. While it is employed in evaluating lymph node involvement in lung carcinoma, its primary purpose is the biopsy of mediastinal masses. Additionally, it is used to diagnose diseases presenting with mediastinal lymphadenopathy.

2. **Answer C (Cervical approach)**

   The recommended approach for the majority of mediastinoscopies is the cervical approach. This involves entering the mediastinum through a 3 cm incision in the suprasternal notch. A dissection is made between the left innominate vein and the sternum, creating a tunnel in the fascial layers. Subsequently, the mediastinoscope is inserted anterior to the aortic arch. This approach allows access to the mediastinum for diagnostic purposes, such as biopsy of mediastinal masses and staging of lung cancer, with relatively less invasiveness than other approaches.

3. **Answer B (Previous recurrent laryngeal nerve injury)**

   An absolute contraindication for mediastinoscopy is a previous recurrent laryngeal nerve injury, as it poses a heightened risk for complications during the procedure. Other absolute contraindications include the presence of an anterior mediastinal mass, an inoperable tumor, extremely debilitated patients, a history of previous mediastinoscopy, and an ascending aortic aneurysm. Additionally, there are relative contraindications such as thoracic inlet obstruction, SVC syndrome, severe tracheal deviation, a history of radiation therapy to the chest, cerebrovascular disease, severe cervical spine disease with limited neck extension, and thoracic aortic aneurysm.

4. **Answer D (Mesenchymal tumor)**

   Mesenchymal tumors, neoplasms arising from mesenchymal tissues, including connective tissues such as muscles, blood vessels, and other supportive tissues, may present as mediastinal masses in the middle mediastinum. Understanding the potential origin and location of different tumors within the mediastinum is crucial for accurate diagnosis and appropriate management.

5. **Answer A (True)**

   Phrenic nerve paralysis is one of the major complications of mediastinoscopy. The phrenic nerve innervates the diaphragm, and its paralysis can impair diaphragmatic function, leading to respiratory compromise. Among the other listed complications, major hemorrhage, stroke, air embolism, pneumothorax, reflex arrhythmias, recurrent laryngeal nerve palsy, esophageal tear, tracheobronchial laceration, and thoracic duct injury are also noted as potential complications associated with mediastinoscopy

6. **Answer B (Superficial cervical plexus block)**

   Following a diagnostic mediastinoscopy with biopsy for suspected mesenchymal tumors, the optimal postoperative analgesia strategy involves a combination of techniques for multimodal pain control. Specifically, a superficial cervical plexus block is recommended to target pain in the cervical and upper thoracic regions affected during the procedure. This approach aligns with the concept of multimodal analgesia, complemented by local infiltration of the wound and administration of oral or intravenous paracetamol and NSAIDs. While intramuscular opioids and short-acting opioids can be considered, the emphasis is on utilizing more targeted and regional techniques to enhance pain relief and minimize systemic side effects. Epidural analgesia, although effective, may not be routinely recommended due to its invasiveness.

Recommended literature

1. McNally PA, Arthur ME. Mediastinoscopy. [Updated 2022 Sep 12]. In: StatPearls [Internet]. Treasure Island (FL): StatPearls Publishing; 2022 Jan-. Available from: https://www.ncbi.nlm.nih.gov/books/NBK534863/.
2. Ahmed-Nusrath A, Swanevelder J. Anaesthesia for mediastinoscopy. Continuing Education in Anaesthesia Critical Care & Pain. 2007;7(1):6-9.

OBSTRUCTIVE SLEEP APNEA

16
CHAPTER

Questions:

1. **Which of the following is NOT a consequence of obstructive sleep apnea (OSA)?**
   A. Depression
   B. Testicular and ovarian dysfunction
   C. Decreased adrenocorticotropic hormone concentration
   D. Pulmonary hypertension

2. **Which of the following is a predisposing factor for obstructive sleep apnea?**
   A. Prinzmetal angina
   B. Female gender
   C. Low physical activity
   D. Neck circumference < 40 cm

3. **What is the preferred treatment for obese patients with OSA?**
   A. CPAP therapy
   B. Surgical uvula-palate-pharyngoplasty
   C. Weight loss
   D. Mandibular advancement devices

4. **What is the role of continuous positive airway pressure (CPAP) therapy in OSA?**
   A. It is a preferred treatment for obese patients with OSA
   B. It may reduce the risk of cardiac and cerebrovascular events
   C. It is used to promote weight loss
   D. It is a surgical procedure for OSA

5. **Surgical uvula-palate-pharyngoplasty is a surgical treatment option for OSA.**
   A. True
   B. False

6. **A 50-year-old male with a BMI of 50 presents for laparoscopic cholecystectomy surgery. He has a history of alcohol abuse, smoking, low physical activity, and unemployment. His neck circumference is greater than 40 cm, and he has been using continuous positive airway pressure during the night for the last 5 years due to obstructive sleep apnea. How should patients with OSA be managed in the perioperative period?**
   A. Sedation should be avoided unless the patient is properly monitored
   B. CPAP treatment should be discontinued during hospital admission
   C. Intubation should be performed without consideration of the patient's OSA status
   D. Locoregional techniques should be avoided

Answers:

1. Answer C (Decreased adrenocorticotropic hormone concentration)

Obstructive sleep apnea (OSA) is associated with various medical consequences, including neurocognitive issues like an increased risk of cerebrovascular accidents with poorer outcomes, psychosocial problems, decreased cognitive function, and depression. Endocrine effects include impaired glucose tolerance, dyslipidemia, and increased adrenocorticotropic hormone and cortisol concentrations, but not decreased ACTH concentration. OSA also has cardiovascular implications, such as hypertension, brady and tachyarrhythmias, pulmonary hypertension, congestive heart failure, and myocardial infarction.

2. Answer C (Low physical activity)

While Prinzmetal angina is a condition that can be triggered by obstructive sleep apnea, it is not a predisposing factor for OSA itself. Predisposing factors for OSA include obesity, age 40-70, male gender, alcohol abuse, smoking, pregnancy, low physical activity, unemployment, neck circumference > 40 cm, tonsillar and adenoidal hypertrophy, craniofacial abnormalities (e.g., Pierre Robin, Down's syndrome), and neuromuscular disease. Low physical activity can contribute to OSA by affecting muscle tone and overall health, making it a predisposing factor for the condition.

3. Answer C (Weight loss)

Weight loss is the preferred treatment for obese patients with obstructive sleep apnea. Losing weight can significantly reduce the severity of OSA symptoms, such as daytime sleepiness, irritability, and other neuropsychiatric dysfunctions. It can also improve cardiovascular health, high blood pressure, insulin resistance, type 2 diabetes, and overall quality of life. Even a modest weight loss of 10-15% can reduce the severity of OSA by 50% in moderately obese patients. However, it's important to note that while weight loss can provide meaningful improvements in OSA, it usually does not lead to a complete cure, and additional therapies may be needed for some patients.

4. Answer B (It may reduce the risk of cardiac and cerebrovascular events)

Continuous positive airway pressure (CPAP) therapy is a common treatment for obstructive sleep apnea. It involves wearing a mask over the nose or mouth during sleep, which delivers a continuous flow of air to keep the airway open. CPAP therapy is effective in reducing the symptoms of OSA, such as daytime sleepiness and fatigue, and improving quality of life. Additionally, CPAP therapy may reduce the risk of cardiac and cerebrovascular events, particularly in non-obese patients. This effect is thought to be due to the positive effects of CPAP on reducing the frequency and severity of apnea episodes, which can lead to improved cardiovascular function and reduced risk of complications.

5. Answer A (True)

Surgical uvula-palate-pharyngoplasty is a surgical treatment option for obstructive sleep apnea. It involves removing excess tissue from the uvula, palate, and pharynx to widen the airway and reduce obstruction during sleep. However, it is important to note that surgical interventions like uvula-palate-pharyngoplasty and supportive airway devices promoting mandibular advancement can be offered to selected patients. However, they generally have lower efficacy than weight loss and continuous positive airway pressure therapy. Therefore, these surgical options are typically considered when other treatments have not been effective or are not feasible for the patient.

6. Answer A (Sedation should be avoided unless the patient is properly monitored)

Patients with obstructive sleep apnea should be carefully managed in the perioperative period to reduce the risk of complications. Sedation should be avoided unless the patient is properly monitored, as OSA is associated with an increased risk of airway obstruction and respiratory depression. CPAP treatment should be continued during hospital admission and in the recovery room to maintain airway patency and oxygenation. Intubation should be performed with consideration of the patient's OSA status, as OSA is associated with difficult intubation. Locoregional techniques should be considered where possible to minimize the need for sedation and intubation. Preoperative assessment should include an evaluation for conditions associated with OSA, such as obesity, alcohol abuse, smoking, and a large neck circumference.

Recommended literature

1. Martinez G, Faber P. Obstructive sleep apnoea. Continuing Education in Anaesthesia Critical Care & Pain. 2011;11(1):5-8.

PNEUMONECTOMY

16
CHAPTER

Questions:

1. **When is extrapleural pneumonectomy considered?**
   A. Tuberculosis
   B. Mesothelioma
   C. Traumatic lung injury
   D. Chronic obstructive pulmonary disease (COPD)

2. **What is the primary purpose of completion pneumonectomy?**
   A. Removal of residual lung tissue after previous surgery
   B. Excision of lung and carina
   C. Treatment of chronic obstructive pulmonary disease
   D. Removal of lung affected by tuberculosis

3. **What is the primary reason for avoiding placing the patient on the operative side in the dependent position after a pneumonectomy?**
   A. Prevention of bronchopleural fistula
   B. Risk of myocardial ischemia
   C. Avoidance of acute lung injury
   D. Risk of cardiac herniation

4. **What is the primary postoperative concern after pneumonectomy?**
   A. Atrial fibrillation
   B. Hypovolemia
   C. Respiratory alkalosis
   D. Hyperthermia

5. **Thoracic epidural and paravertebral anesthesia are considered the anesthesia of choice for postoperative analgesia after pneumonectomy.**
   A. True
   B. False

6. **A 55-year-old male has been admitted to the Intensive Care Unit (ICU) following a standard pneumonectomy for Bronchial carcinoma. The surgical procedure involved the removal of the affected lung as part of the treatment plan for the bronchial carcinoma. What is the primary purpose of fluid restriction in the first 24 hours post-pneumonectomy?**
   A. Preventing bronchopleural fistula
   B. Minimizing the risk of myocardial infarction
   C. Reducing the likelihood of acute lung injury
   D. Preventing pulmonary embolism

Answers:

1. Answer B (Mesothelioma)

Extrapleural pneumonectomy is a radical surgical procedure that is considered in selected cases, and one of its primary indications is mesothelioma. Mesothelioma is a type of cancer that affects the mesothelial cells lining the pleura, pericardium, and peritoneum. Extrapleural pneumonectomy involves the excision of not only the affected lung but also the ipsilateral pleura, hemidiaphragm, and hemopericardium, with subsequent patch reconstruction. This aggressive surgical approach is often employed in cases where mesothelioma has invaded these structures and necessitates a comprehensive resection.

2. Answer A (Removal of residual lung tissue after previous surgery)

Completion pneumonectomy (CP) is a surgical procedure performed to remove the remaining lung tissue after an ipsilateral partial pulmonary resection, whether the initial surgery was for malignant or non-malignant causes. The primary purpose of completion pneumonectomy is to address situations where there is a need to excise the residual lung tissue left after a prior surgery. In the context of non-small cell lung cancer (NSCLC), completion pneumonectomy may be performed due to factors such as local recurrence or the presence of a second primary cancer. Completion pneumonectomy can also be considered for non-malignant causes, including early bronchopleural fistula (BPF), lobar torsion, or anastomotic dehiscence after sleeve lobectomy. It is associated with higher morbidity and mortality compared to standard pneumonectomy, emphasizing the complexity and potential challenges of this surgical procedure.

3. Answer D (Risk of cardiac herniation)

The primary reason for avoiding placing the patient on the operative side in the dependent position after a pneumonectomy is to minimize the risk of cardiac herniation. Placing the patient in this position can lead to a pressure difference between the two hemithoraces, particularly if there is a pericardial defect. This pressure difference may result in the heart being extruded through the defect, leading to cardiac herniation. Cardiac herniation is a serious and potentially life-threatening complication after pneumonectomy. The pathophysiology varies based on whether it's a right or left pneumonectomy. In the case of a right pneumonectomy, impaired venous return can result in obstructive shock, leading to symptoms such as tachycardia, increased central venous pressure (CVP), hypotension, and shock. On the other hand, left pneumonectomy can cause myocardial compression, leading to myocardial ischemia, arrhythmias, and left ventricular outflow tract (LVOT) obstruction.

4. Answer A (Atrial fibrillation)

The primary postoperative concern after pneumonectomy is atrial fibrillation. Atrial fibrillation is a common cardiac arrhythmia that can occur after thoracic surgeries, including pneumonectomy. The loss of a lung can lead to changes in hemodynamics, and surgical manipulation during the procedure can contribute to the development of atrial fibrillation. Postoperative atrial fibrillation can be of concern due to its potential impact on cardiac output and the risk of thromboembolic events. Monitoring for arrhythmias, especially atrial fibrillation, is crucial in the immediate postoperative period. Patients may require close observation, and interventions such as antiarrhythmic medications or anticoagulation may be considered based on the clinical context.

5. Answer A (True)

Thoracic epidural and paravertebral anesthesia are indeed considered the anesthesia of choice for postoperative analgesia after pneumonectomy. These techniques involve the administration of local anesthetics to the thoracic epidural space or the paravertebral space, targeting specific dermatomes in the thoracic region. The choice between thoracic epidural and paravertebral anesthesia depends on various factors, including the surgeon's preference, patient characteristics, and institutional practices. Both methods provide effective pain relief in the chest and upper abdominal regions, which are typically affected after pneumonectomy.

6. Answer C (Reducing the likelihood of acute lung injury)

The primary purpose of fluid restriction in the first 24 hours post-pneumonectomy, specifically limiting intake to less than 20cc/kg, is to reduce the likelihood of acute lung injury. The controlled restriction of fluids is a crucial component of perioperative management aimed at maintaining an optimal balance to prevent excessive fluid accumulation in both intravascular and extravascular spaces. This meticulous approach is particularly significant in the context of pneumonectomy, where alterations in fluid dynamics may occur. By implementing strict fluid restrictions, the medical team aims to minimize the risk of complications and facilitate a smoother recovery process for the patient.

Recommended literature

1. Beshara M, Bora V. Pneumonectomy. [Updated 2022 Sep 18]. In: StatPearls [Internet]. Treasure Island (FL): StatPearls Publishing; 2022 Jan-. Available from: https://www.ncbi.nlm.nih.gov/books/NBK555969/
2. Hackett S, Jones R, Kapila R. Anaesthesia for pneumonectomy. BJA Educ. 2019;19(9):297-304.
3. Lederman D, Easwar J, Feldman J, Shapiro V. Anesthetic considerations for lung resection: preoperative assessment, intraoperative challenges and postoperative analgesia. Ann Transl Med. 2019;7(15):356.

PNEUMONIA

Questions:

1. **What is the most common cause of pneumonia in adults?**
   A. Mycoplasma pneumoniae
   B. Streptococcus pneumoniae
   C. Influenza virus
   D. Aspiration of gastric contents

2. **Pneumonia involves inflammation of the alveoli in one or both lungs and may be classified by where it was acquired. What is NOT part of this classification?**
   A. Healthcare-associated pneumonia
   B. Lobar pneumonia
   C. Hospital-acquired pneumonia
   D. Community-acquired pneumonia

3. **What symptom is NOT a common characteristic of bacterial pneumonia in adults?**
   A. Abdominal pain
   B. Dry cough
   C. High fever (up to 40.5°C)
   D. Confusion or altered mental state

4. **What is NOT the recommended preventive measure for pneumonia in adults with chronic diseases such as asthma or COPD?**
   A. Regular exercise
   B. Smoking cessation
   C. Pneumococcal vaccination
   D. Annual chest X-rays

5. **Severe community-acquired pneumonia requires prompt broad-spectrum antibiotics within one hour of consideration of diagnosis.**
   A. True
   B. False

6. **A 65-year-old man presents at the Anesthesia Preoperative Evaluation Clinic for preparation before inguinal hernia repair. He reports a history of severe lobar pneumonia seven days ago, for which he is currently on CEFTRIAXONE antibiotics. While he mentions feeling better, he still experiences a lingering cough, lack of energy, and shortness of breath during slight exertion. The scheduled operation is set for the next day. How should you proceed with the surgery for this patient?**
   A. Proceed to operation without restriction
   B. Proceed to operation, but regional anesthesia is the only option
   C. Postpone surgery at least two weeks after the pneumonia resolves
   D. Postpone surgery until two chest X-rays show no signs of pneumonia

Answers:

1. Answer B (Streptococcus pneumoniae)

The most common type of bacterial pneumonia in adults is pneumococcal pneumoniae, which is caused by the bacterium Streptococcus pneumoniae. This bacterium normally resides in the upper respiratory tract but can cause infection when it invades the lungs. Pneumococcal pneumonia is a significant health concern, infecting over 900,000 Americans each year.

2. Answer B (Lobar pneumonia)

A pneumonia infection is classified based on its acquisition setting, which includes community-acquired, hospital-acquired, healthcare-associated, or aspiration pneumonia. Lobar pneumonia, while describing a specific pattern of lung involvement, is not part of the primary classification based on how pneumonia is acquired.

3. Answer A (Dry cough)

Common symptoms of bacterial pneumonia in adults include a high fever (up to 40.5°C), cough with yellow, green, or bloody mucus, tiredness, rapid breathing, shortness of breath, rapid heart rate, sweating or chills, chest pain, and/or abdominal pain, especially with coughing or deep breathing. However, a dry cough is not typically a common characteristic of bacterial pneumonia.

4. Answer D (Annual chest X-rays)

The recommended preventive measures for pneumonia in adults with chronic diseases such as asthma or COPD include regular exercise, smoking cessation, and vaccination, specifically pneumococcal vaccine, flu vaccine, and COVID-19 vaccine. However, annual chest X-rays are not a standard preventive measure for pneumonia in this context. Chest X-rays are typically used for diagnostic purposes rather than as a routine preventive screening tool.

5. Answer A (True)

Severe community-acquired pneumonia (CAP) necessitates prompt initiation of broad-spectrum antibiotics within one hour of considering the diagnosis based on current available evidence. Early administration of appropriate antibiotics, typically at the emergency department, is recommended within this timeframe, taking into account local epidemiology and resistance patterns. In areas endemic for tuberculosis (TB), combination therapy with macrolides is preferred over fluoroquinolones. Additionally, in regions where melioidosis is endemic, empiric coverage for melioidosis is recommended. However, empiric anti-pseudomonal or MRSA therapy is not recommended in patients without risk factors for multi-drug resistant pathogens, especially in areas with low incidence of healthcare-associated pneumonia (HCAP) organisms or those not meeting HCAP criteria.

6. Answer C (Postpone surgery at least two weeks after the pneumonia resolves)

Given the patient's recent history of severe lobar pneumonia and ongoing symptoms, it is prudent to postpone the surgery until the pneumonia has fully resolved. No concrete recommendations exist for the management of pneumonia in surgical patients, but elective surgery is generally advised to be delayed until the infection has completely resolved. Preoperative pneumonia has been shown to significantly increase the risk of postoperative morbidity and mortality across various surgical settings and patient populations. Therefore, a cautious approach is recommended, allowing for a recovery period of at least two weeks to four weeks after complete symptom resolution.

Recommended literature

1. Morgan, A., Glossop, A., 2016. Severe community-acquired pneumonia. BJA Education 16, 167–172.
2. Sadashivaiah, JB., Carr, B., 2009. Severe community-acquired pneumonia. Continuing Eduction in Anaesthesia Critical Care & Pain. 9;3:87–91.

POST-LUNG TRANSPLANT PATIENT

Questions:

1. Which of the following is NOT an indication of lung transplantation?
   A. Chronic Obstructive Pulmonary Disease (COPD)
   B. Pulmonary Fibrosis
   C. Lung carcinoma
   D. Pulmonary Hypertension

2. What is the typical recovery period for a post-lung transplant patient?
   A. 1-2 weeks
   B. 3-6 months
   C. 9-12 months
   D. Over a year

3. What is the recommended position for endotracheal cuff placement in post-lung transplant patients?
   A. Just below the vocal cords
   B. Mid-trachea
   C. Above the vocal cords
   D. In the mainstem bronchus

4. Why is early extubation preferred in post-lung transplant patients?
   A. Minimizes the risk of infection
   B. Improves oxygen saturation
   C. Reduces the risk of rejection
   D. Enhances fluid balance

5. Transdermal buprenorphine and methadone are considered safe and efficacious analgesic options for post-lung transplant patients, even in the presence of renal dysfunction.
   A. True
   B. False

6. A 33-year-old male is currently in the operating room undergoing a lung transplant procedure due to severe pulmonary hypertension. The surgical intervention aims to alleviate his respiratory distress and improve overall pulmonary function. Adequate access to intravenous (IV) lines for fluid administration and monitoring is pivotal in ensuring a successful and safe procedure. Where is the preferred location for placing a central line in post-lung transplant patients?
   A. Subclavian vein
   B. Femoral vein
   C. Internal jugular vein
   D. According to anesthesiologist preferences

Answers:

1. **Answer C (Lung carcinoma)**

   Lung carcinoma (lung cancer) is not considered an indication for lung transplantation. The primary indications for lung transplantation include chronic obstructive pulmonary disease (COPD) with emphysema, pulmonary fibrosis, cystic fibrosis, pulmonary hypertension, and alpha-1-antitrypsin deficiency. Lung transplantation is generally reserved for non-malignant, end-stage lung diseases where conventional treatments have proven ineffective, and its focus is on providing a new, functional lung to individuals with irreversible respiratory conditions. Patients with lung cancer typically pursue alternative treatments such as surgery, chemotherapy, or radiation therapy.

2. **Answer B (3-6 months)**

   Post-lung transplant patients undergo a surgical procedure to replace one or both diseased or failing lungs with healthy lungs from a deceased donor, sometimes along with a donor's heart. The recovery period for a post-lung transplant patient typically spans 3 to 6 months. During this time, individuals gradually regain strength, and various aspects of their health are closely monitored. It's important to consider the increased risk of infection or rejection of the transplanted lungs during the recovery phase. This duration allows for the healing of surgical incisions, adaptation to the new organ, and the implementation of immunosuppressive therapy to prevent rejection. The 3-6 month timeframe represents a general guideline, and individual recovery experiences may vary.

3. **Answer A (Just below the vocal cords)**

   In post-lung transplant patients, the recommended position for endotracheal cuff placement is just below the vocal cords. This positioning is advised to avoid trauma to the trachea or bronchial anastomosis, as precise placement minimizes the risk of injury. The use of a fibreoptic laryngoscope is considered, which aids in visualizing the airway structures and ensures accurate cuff placement. This approach is crucial in maintaining the integrity of the newly transplanted lungs and reducing the potential for complications related to the airway.

4. **Answer A (Minimizes the risk of infection)**

   Early extubation is preferred in post-lung transplant patients primarily because it minimizes the risk of infection. Prolonged intubation can increase the likelihood of respiratory infections, a significant concern in individuals with compromised respiratory function, such as those who have undergone lung transplantation. Early removal of the endotracheal tube reduces the duration of exposure to potential sources of infection, contributing to a lower risk of respiratory complications. While early extubation may have additional benefits, such as improved oxygen saturation and enhanced fluid balance, the primary emphasis is on infection prevention in the vulnerable post-transplant period.

5. **Answer A (True)**

   Transdermal buprenorphine and methadone are considered safe and effective analgesic agents in post-lung transplant patients, even in the presence of renal dysfunction. This is highlighted in the context of administering adequate analgesia, where caution is advised with opioids due to their potential for central nervous system (CNS) and respiratory depression. Parenteral paracetamol is recommended as an effective analgesic agent. Importantly, nonsteroidal anti-inflammatory drugs (NSAIDs) should be avoided in post-lung transplant patients due to the associated risk of adverse reactions, particularly considering their potential impact on renal function.

6. **Answer C (Internal jugular vein)**

   In the ongoing lung transplant procedure for a 33-year-old male with severe pulmonary hypertension, the preferred location for placing a central line is the internal jugular vein. This decision is rooted in the objective of minimizing the risk of pneumothorax, a critical consideration in post-lung transplant patients with compromised respiratory function. Placing the central line in the antecubital fossa or internal jugular vein facilitates effective fluid administration and continuous monitoring during the procedure. Simultaneously, femoral lines are intentionally avoided due to their association with an increased risk of infection, considering the patient's immunocompromised state and the stringent infection control measures required in the surgical setting.

Recommended literature

1. Brusich, K.T., Acan, I., 2018. Anesthetic Considerations in Transplant Recipients for Nontransplant Surgery. doi:10.5772/intechopen.74329.
2. Seo M, Kim WJ, Choi IC. Anesthesia for non-pulmonary surgical intervention following lung transplantation: two cases report. Korean J Anesthesiol. 2014;66(4):322-326.
3. Haddow, G.R., 1997. Anaesthesia for patients after lung transplantation. Canadian Journal of Anesthesia/Journal canadien d'anesthésie 44, 182-197.

PULMONARY EMBOLISM

16
CHAPTER

Questions:

1. **What is the primary cause of death in severe pulmonary embolism (PE)?**
   A. Ventilation/perfusion mismatch
   B. Right ventricular failure
   C. Low cardiac output
   D. Hypoxemia

2. **Which of the following conditions is categorized as a strong risk factor for venous thromboembolism (VTE)?**
   A. Blood transfusion
   B. Congestive heart failure
   C. Fracture of the lower limb
   D. Pregnancy

3. **What is the gold standard for diagnosing PE?**
   A. Chest X-ray
   B. D-dimer level
   C. Ventilation / perfusion scintigraphy
   D. Computed Tomographic Pulmonary Angiography (CTPA)

4. **What diagnostic score helps determine whether further investigations for PE are warranted?**
   A. Pulmonary Embolism Severity Index (PESI)
   B. D-dimer test
   C. Pulmonary Embolism Rule-Out Criteria (PERC)
   D. Computed Tomographic Pulmonary Angiography (CTPA)

5. **LMWHs are preferred over unfractionated heparin (UFH) for initial anticoagulation in PE.**
   A. True
   B. False

6. **A 70-year-old woman with a history of hypertension and atrial fibrillation presented with a chief complaint of "chest tightness." An electrocardiogram (ECG) revealed atrial fibrillation (AF), with a possible S1Q3T3 pattern, and D-dimer levels were elevated at 2000 µg/l. Computed tomographic pulmonary angiography confirmed the presence of pulmonary thromboembolism (PTE), revealing thrombi in the main stems and branches within the bilateral pulmonary arteries. During diagnostic testing, the patient experienced a sudden loss of consciousness, accompanied by a temporary drop in blood pressure. Given the critical nature of the situation, the decision was made to proceed with intubation and mechanical ventilation to ensure adequate oxygenation and ventilation. What is NOT a recommended consideration during intubation and ventilation in PE management?**
   A. Avoid high intrathoracic pressures
   B. Encourage hypercarbia to assess pulmonary vascular resistance
   C. Ensure pre-induction arterial line/central line
   D. Avoid intubation if possible

Answers:

1. Answer B (Right Ventricular Failure)

In severe pulmonary embolism (PE), the primary cause of death is often attributed to acute right ventricular (RV) failure. Pulmonary embolism involves the obstruction of pulmonary blood vessels, leading to increased pulmonary vascular resistance and strain on the right side of the heart. The RV, responsible for pumping blood to the lungs, faces acute pressure overload due to the obstructed pulmonary vasculature. As a result, right ventricular failure ensues, causing a cascade of hemodynamic compromise. This can lead to a decrease in cardiac output, inadequate perfusion to vital organs, and, ultimately, life-threatening conditions such as cardiogenic shock, pulseless electrical activity (PEA) arrest, or cardiac collapse.

2. Answer C (Fracture of the Lower Limb)

Fracture of the lower limb is categorized as a strong risk factor for venous thromboembolism (VTE), indicating a significant association with the development of blood clots. The classification of risk factors is based on odds ratios (OR), with strong risk factors having an OR greater than 10. Other conditions listed as strong risk factors include hip or knee replacement, major trauma, myocardial infarction within the last three months, previous VTE, and spinal cord injury. Recognizing these strong risk factors is crucial in clinical practice to identify individuals who may require targeted VTE prevention strategies, such as anticoagulation or mechanical prophylaxis, to mitigate the risk of thromboembolic events.

3. Answer D (Computed Tomographic Pulmonary Angiography (CTPA))

CTPA is considered the gold standard for diagnosing PE. It provides detailed imaging of the pulmonary arteries, allowing visualization of blood clots and vessel obstruction. Unlike chest X-rays, which may not directly visualize the emboli, CTPA offers high sensitivity and specificity in detecting PE. Regarding D-dimer levels, while they have a high negative predictive value, meaning that a normal D-dimer level makes acute PE or deep vein thrombosis (DVT) unlikely, they are not reliable as a confirmatory test due to a low positive predictive value.

4. Answer C (Pulmonary Embolism Rule-Out Criteria (PERC))

The diagnostic score that helps determine whether further investigations for pulmonary embolism are warranted is the Pulmonary Embolism Rule-Out Criteria (PERC). PERC is a set of criteria used to rule out the likelihood of PE in patients with low pretest probability and low clinical suspicion. The eight variables in PERC include age greater than or equal to 50 years, heart rate greater than or equal to 100 beats per minute, arterial oxygen saturation (SaO2) on room air less than 95%, history of venous thromboembolism, recent trauma or surgery within the last 28 days, unilateral leg swelling, hemoptysis, and oral hormone use. If none of the eight variables is positive and there is a less than 15% pretest probability that the patient has a pulmonary embolism, a PE workup can be ruled out using PERC. The PERC evaluation is considered positive if any one of the eight criteria is met.

5. Answer A (True)

Low-molecular-weight heparin (LMWH) is preferred over unfractionated heparin (UFH) for initial anticoagulation in patients with a high or intermediate clinical probability of pulmonary embolism. LMWH, along with fondaparinux, has several advantages, including subcutaneous administration, predictable anticoagulant response, and less need for monitoring compared to UFH. It is important to note that UFH may still be considered in specific situations, such as patients with overt hemodynamic instability or renal impairment (glomerular filtration rate ≤ G4). The choice of anticoagulant should be individualized based on the patient's clinical characteristics, risk factors, and contraindications. The preference for LMWH is generally due to its convenience and favorable pharmacokinetic profile.

6. Answer B (Encourage hypercarbia to assess pulmonary vascular resistance)

In the context of pulmonary embolism, it is crucial to avoid encouraging hypercarbia during intubation and ventilation. Encouraging hypercarbia can increase pulmonary vascular resistance, exacerbating the hemodynamic compromise in patients with PE. The correct approach is to avoid intubation if possible due to the very high risk of cardiac collapse. However, if intubation becomes necessary, recommended considerations include ensuring pre-induction arterial line/central line placement if possible, having vasopressors in-line, using a titrated induction with avoidance of hypoxemia and hypercarbia (utilizing bag-mask ventilation once the patient stops breathing), and avoiding high intrathoracic pressures, hypercarbia, and hypoxemia.

Recommended literature

1. Konstantinides SV, Meyer G, Becattini C, et al. 2019 ESC Guidelines for the diagnosis and management of acute pulmonary embolism developed in collaboration with the European Respiratory Society (ERS). Eur Heart J. 2020;41(4):543-603.

RESTRICTIVE LUNG DISEASE

Questions:

1. **What is the hallmark feature of restrictive lung disease on pulmonary function tests?**
   A. Decreased FEV1
   B. Increased FVC
   C. Decreased FEV1/FVC ratio
   D. Increased total lung capacity

2. **Which of the following diseases is NOT considered a cause of intrinsic restrictive lung disease?**
   A. Rheumatoid arthritis
   B. Asbestosis
   C. Pectus carinatum
   D. Sarcoidosis

3. **What is a common symptom of restrictive lung disease in the postoperative period?**
   A. Hyperthermia
   B. Bradycardia
   C. Hypertension
   D. Exertional dyspnea

4. **Which medication is associated with the development of restrictive lung disease?**
   A. Albuterol
   B. Amiodarone
   C. Prednisone
   D. Ipratropium

5. **Idiopathic pulmonary fibrosis (IPF) is the most common type of pulmonary fibrosis.**
   A. True
   B. False

6. **A 44-year-old male with a known history of idiopathic pulmonary fibrosis presents to the Emergency Department with a sudden onset of progressive exertional dyspnea, cough, shortness of breath, wheezing, and chest pain. The patient had been relatively stable with his IPF for many years until this acute presentation. Chest radiography reveals bilateral mixed alveolar-interstitial infiltrates, and CT scanning confirms the presence of ground-glass opacities and consolidation. What is the primary treatment approach for managing acute exacerbations of idiopathic pulmonary fibrosis?**
   A. Antibiotics
   B. Diuretics
   C. Immunotherapy
   D. Steroids

Answers:

1. Answer C (Decreased FEV1/FVC ratio)

In restrictive lung disease, reduced lung compliance leads to a decrease in both forced vital capacity (FVC) and forced expiratory volume in one second (FEV1). However, as the decline in FVC is more pronounced, the FEV1/FVC ratio is elevated (> 80%). This contrasts with obstructive lung diseases, where the FEV1/FVC ratio is typically reduced due to airway obstruction.

2. Answer C (Pectus carinatum)

Intrinsic factors leading to restrictive lung diseases primarily affect the lungs themselves, and while conditions like rheumatoid arthritis and asbestosis are intrinsic causes, pectus carinatum is a nonmuscular disease affecting the chest wall, categorizing it as an extrinsic factor. In contrast, intrinsic conditions encompass a range of disorders, such as sarcoidosis, which involves inflammation in the lungs, contributing to restrictive lung pathology.

3. Answer D (Exertional dyspnea)

Exertional dyspnea is a common symptom associated with restrictive lung disease, characterized by a decreased lung volume and increased work of breathing. In the postoperative period, this symptom may be exacerbated due to factors such as reduced lung compliance, atelectasis, or respiratory muscle weakness. This symptom can be attributed to factors like impaired lung expansion, altered chest wall mechanics, or postoperative pain inhibiting deep breathing and coughing. Early mobilization, adequate pain management, and respiratory support can help alleviate postoperative symptoms in patients with restrictive lung disease.

4. Answer B (Amiodarone)

Amiodarone, frequently employed as an antiarrhythmic agent, has been associated with pulmonary toxicity, culminating in fibrotic alterations in lung tissue and the development of restrictive lung disease. This adverse effect may present with symptoms such as dyspnea and cough. Additionally, other medications linked to pulmonary toxicity and consequential fibrotic changes in lung tissue, leading to restrictive lung disease, include Bleomycin and Methotrexate.

5. Answer A (True)

Idiopathic pulmonary fibrosis (IPF) is the most common type of pulmonary fibrosis. The term "idiopathic" signifies that the cause of this specific form of pulmonary fibrosis is unknown. Approximately 50,000 new cases of IPF are diagnosed each year, with most patients first experiencing symptoms between the ages of 50 and 70 years old. IPF is characterized by scarring (fibrosis) of the lungs, leading to stiffness and difficulty breathing. The irreversible and progressive nature of lung damage in IPF means that the condition tends to worsen over time. While there is no cure, certain medications may slow down the progression in some cases. In severe instances, a lung transplant might be recommended as a treatment option.

6. Answer D (Steroids)

Acute exacerbation in patients with IPF is a recognized and unpredictable complication that manifests as a sudden worsening of dyspnea. Despite the challenges in management and limited efficacy, high-dose systemic corticosteroids, such as prednisone 1 mg/kg per day orally to methylprednisolone 1 gram per day intravenously for three days, followed by a taper, are typically employed. The treatment strategy is adjusted based on the severity of the disease and the patient's response to therapy.

Recommended literature

1. Vyas, Varsha & Gehdoo, Raghbirsingh & Hazari, Shruti & Hirpara, Parthkumar & Kaur, Mankeerat & Vashwani, Jayshree. (2021). Anesthesia Management in a Case of Restrictive Lung Disease. Journal of Research & Innovation in Anesthesia. 6. 49-50. 10.5005/jp-journals-10049-0104.
2. Pollard BJ, Kitchen, G. Handbook of Clinical Anaesthesia. Fourth Edition. CRC Press. 2018. 978-1-4987-6289-2.
3. Mangera Z, Panesar G, Makker H. Practical approach to management of respiratory complications in neurological disorders. Int J Gen Med. 2012;5:255-263.

SMOKING

16
CHAPTER

Questions:

1. **What is the primary cause of preventable illness and premature death mentioned?**
   A. Obesity
   B. Alcohol consumption
   C. Cigarette smoking
   D. Sedentary lifestyle

2. **What is the recommended time frame for ideally stopping smoking before surgery to maximize the benefits?**
   A. 24 hours
   B. 4 weeks
   C. 8 weeks
   D. 12 weeks

3. **Which of the following is NOT listed as a possible intraoperative complication associated with smoking?**
   A. Reintubation after planned extubation
   B. Pulmonary edema
   C. Deep wound infection
   D. Aspiration

4. **Which of the following is listed as an associated disease linked to cigarette smoking?**
   A. Chronic obstructive lung disease
   B. Reduced fertility
   C. Diabetes mellitus
   D. All of the above

5. **Cigarette smoking is associated with an increased risk of perioperative respiratory complications, including atelectasis and hypoxemia.**
   A. True
   B. False

6. **A 66-year-old male is scheduled for gastric bypass surgery. He has been a long-time smoker, and his medical history includes cardiac issues. Given his age and smoking history, it is essential to thoroughly assess the potential consequences of cigarette smoking on both his respiratory and cardiovascular systems. What cardiovascular effect is associated with nicotine?**
   A. Bradycardia
   B. Tachycardia
   C. Hypotension
   D. Decreased myocardial contractility

Answers:

1. **Answer C (Cigarette smoking)**

   Cigarette smoking is identified as one of the primary causes of preventable illness and premature death. This conclusion emphasizes the significant impact of cigarette smoking on public health. Quitting smoking before surgery is highlighted as a crucial step in reducing the incidence of postoperative complications, underlining the importance of addressing smoking as a modifiable risk factor for adverse health outcomes. The longer the period of cessation before surgery, the greater the benefit, further emphasizing the detrimental effects of cigarette smoking and the potential for positive health outcomes with smoking cessation.

2. **Answer C (8 weeks)**

   The optimal period for achieving maximum benefits by discontinuing smoking before surgery is ideally set at 8 weeks. This timeframe is linked to enhanced advantages, particularly in terms of minimizing the risk of perioperative complications. Ceasing smoking 8 weeks before the surgery presents an ideal scenario, providing ample time for individuals to undergo positive physiological changes. In instances where an 8-week cessation period may not be achievable, a minimum recommendation is to halt smoking at least 24 hours before the scheduled surgery. This proactive measure is designed to counteract the immediate effects of nicotine and carboxyhemoglobin (COHb).

3. **Answer C (Deep wound infection)**

   In the context of smoking-related complications during surgery, the intraoperative issues encompass respiratory challenges such as reintubation, laryngospasm, bronchospasm, aspiration, hypoventilation, and hypoxemia, along with the occurrence of pulmonary edema. Deep wound infection, however, is categorized as a postoperative complication rather than an intraoperative concern associated with smoking.

4. **Answer D (All of the above)**

   Smoking is a major risk factor for a spectrum of diseases with notable respiratory implications, including lung cancer, COPD, and asthma. Additionally, it contributes to heart disease, stroke, reproductive issues, premature and low birth-weight babies, diabetes, blindness, and various types of cancer, emphasizing the extensive health hazards associated with smoking.

5. **Answer A (True)**

   Cigarette smoking is associated with an increased risk of perioperative respiratory complications, including atelectasis and hypoxemia. Smoking can contribute to airway inflammation, impaired mucociliary clearance, and increased mucus production, all of which can lead to respiratory complications during the perioperative period. The higher risk of atelectasis and hypoxemia is consistent with the adverse effects of smoking on respiratory function, emphasizing the importance of addressing smoking as a modifiable risk factor in the preoperative period.

6. **Answer B (Tachycardia)**

   Nicotine increases heart rate, myocardial contractility, and blood pressure. These effects are primarily attributed to the stimulation of sympathetic neurotransmission. Nicotine stimulates catecholamine release by activating nicotine acetylcholine receptors located on peripheral postganglionic sympathetic nerve endings and the adrenal medulla. The activation of nicotinic acetylcholine receptors leads to a conformational change in the central pore, resulting in the influx of sodium and calcium ions. This, in turn, stimulates the release of catecholamines, contributing to increased heart rate and heightened cardiovascular activity.

Recommended literature

1. Carrick MA, Robson JM, Thomas C. Smoking and anaesthesia. BJA Educ. 2019;19(1):1-6.

THYMECTOMY

16

CHAPTER

Questions:

1. **What is the primary characteristic of myasthenia gravis (MG)?**
   A. Muscle hypertrophy
   B. Weakness and fatigability of skeletal muscles
   C. Increased acetylcholine receptors
   D. Acetylcholine imbalance

2. **What is the most common indication for thymectomy?**
   A. Thymic carcinoma
   B. Myasthenia gravis
   C. Thymic cysts
   D. Ectopic parathyroid glands

3. **Which technique is NOT considered a standard approach in thymectomy?**
   A. Median Sternotomy
   B. Video-Assisted Thoracoscopic Surgery (VATS)
   C. Robotic Surgery
   D. Lateral Thoracotomy

4. **In the preoperative evaluation, what symptoms should be monitored in a patient undergoing thymectomy?**
   A. Hypertension
   B. Dysphagia
   C. Gastrointestinal bleeding
   D. Acetylcholine level

5. **The myasthenic crisis should be differentiated from the cholinergic crisis with the edrophonium test.**
   A. True
   B. False

6. **A 57-year-old female with a known history of myasthenia gravis is scheduled for an extended thymectomy using Video-Assisted Thoracoscopic Surgery (VATS). The surgical team has decided to use neuromuscular blocking drugs (NMBs) for both intubation and the operation. How do patients with myasthenia gravis typically respond to neuromuscular blocking drugs?**
   A. Sensitive to succinylcholine
   B. Resistant to nondepolarizing muscle relaxants
   C. Sensitive to both succinylcholine and nondepolarizing muscle relaxants
   D. Resistant to succinylcholine and sensitive to nondepolarizing muscle relaxants

Answers:

1. Answer B (Weakness and fatigability of skeletal muscles)

Myasthenia Gravis (MG) is an autoimmune disease characterized by weakness and fatigability of skeletal muscles, which improves following rest. This weakness and fatigability can be localized to specific muscle groups or generalized. In MG, there is a decrease in the number of postsynaptic acetylcholine receptors at the neuromuscular junction. This reduction in receptors diminishes the capacity of the neuromuscular end-plate to transmit the nerve signal. When stimulated, acetylcholine is released presynaptically, but in MG, the number of activated postsynaptic receptors may be insufficient to trigger a muscle action potential. This deficiency, coupled with the decline in acetylcholine release with repeated stimulation, leads to the characteristic fatigability observed in individuals with MG.

2. Answer B (Myasthenia gravis)

Thymectomy is primarily performed for the treatment of myasthenia gravis. In myasthenia gravis, the thymus can enlarge, and thymectomy is considered a standard therapeutic approach for managing the disease. Thymectomy has been shown to be beneficial in improving symptoms and, in some cases, achieving remission in individuals with myasthenia gravis. While other conditions like thymic carcinoma, thymic cysts, and ectopic parathyroid glands may also be indications for thymectomy, myasthenia gravis remains the most common reason for the surgical removal of the thymus gland.

3. Answer D (Lateral Thoracotomy)

Thymectomy, the resection of the thymus gland, is commonly performed using median sternotomy, video-assisted thoracoscopic surgery (VATS), and robotic surgery. While the choice of technique may vary based on factors such as patient condition and surgeon preference, lateral thoracotomy is not among the standard approaches for thymectomy.

4. Answer B (Dysphagia)

Bulbar symptoms such as dysphagia, dysarthria, dysphonia, and dyspnea are crucial to assess in the preoperative evaluation of a patient undergoing thymectomy. Thymectomy is commonly performed for conditions like myasthenia gravis, where bulbar symptoms may be prominent. Monitoring these symptoms helps in understanding the patient's baseline neuromuscular status and assists in planning the perioperative management.

5. Answer A (True)

The myasthenic crisis and cholinergic crisis can both present with weakness, but their management differs. The edrophonium test is used to differentiate between these two conditions. In a myasthenic crisis, which is characterized by insufficient neuromuscular transmission, the administration of edrophonium, an acetylcholinesterase inhibitor, can temporarily improve muscle strength. On the contrary, in a cholinergic crisis, additional edrophonium administration can worsen symptoms due to further acetylcholine accumulation.

6. Answer D (Resistant to succinylcholine and sensitive to nondepolarizing muscle relaxants)

Patients with myasthenia gravis typically exhibit resistance to succinylcholine, a depolarizing neuromuscular blocking agent. Instead, they are sensitive to nondepolarizing muscle relaxants, such as Rocuronium or Vecuronium. Patients with MG exhibit unpredictable sensitivity to nondepolarizing muscle relaxants, and the response may vary among individuals. The best strategy in MG patients is to avoid muscle relaxants whenever possible. However, in situations where neuromuscular blockade is deemed necessary, the use of a small dose of Rocuronium, closely monitored, is considered a safer alternative. Reversal agents like sugammadex should be readily available to promptly reverse the effects and minimize the risk of prolonged paralysis.

Recommended literature

1. Bennett B, Rentea RM. Thymectomy. [Updated 2022 Jul 25]. In: StatPearls [Internet]. Treasure Island (FL): StatPearls Publishing; 2022 Jan-. Available from: https://www.ncbi.nlm.nih.gov/books/NBK564302/
2. Daum P, Smelt J, Ibrahim IR. Perioperative management of myasthenia gravis. BJA Education. 2021;21(11):414-9.

Respiratory & Thoracics

TRANSFUSION-RELATED ACUTE LUNG INJURY (TRALI)

Questions:

1. **Which of the following is a leading cause of death associated with blood transfusions?**
   - A. Anaphylactic shock
   - B. Septic transfusion reaction
   - C. Transfusion-related circulatory overload
   - D. Transfusion-related acute lung injury (TRALI)

2. **What are the characteristic features of TRALI?**
   - A. Gradual onset of cardiogenic pulmonary edema
   - B. Slow progression of hypoxia with minimal fever
   - C. Sudden onset of non-cardiogenic pulmonary edema
   - D. Asymptomatic presentation with a normal chest radiograph

3. **What is the primary mechanism by which TRALI causes pulmonary edema?**
   - A. Direct cardiogenic dysfunction
   - B. Activation of neutrophils leading to capillary leakage
   - C. Excessive fluid overload
   - D. Anaphylactic reaction

4. **What is emphasized as a crucial step in reducing TRALI cases?**
   - A. Administration of prophylactic corticosteroids
   - B. Minimizing the number of blood transfusions
   - C. Using blood products with high plasma contents
   - D. Immediate treatment with vasopressors

5. **TRALI is frequently observed and tends to be more severe when associated with transfusions of packed red cells.**
   - A. True
   - B. False

6. **The patient, a 43-year-old woman, underwent emergency transurethral hemostasis for bladder hemorrhage characterized by hematuria and a low hemoglobin concentration of 3.2 g/dL. During the operation, two units of red blood cells (RBC) were transfused. Post-operation, upon extubation, the patient exhibited low oxygen saturation (90%) despite receiving 6 liters per minute of oxygen. She complained of dyspnea, and a chest X-ray revealed bilateral diffuse pulmonary edema indicative of hypoxemia (80%). What is the most appropriate initial step in managing a suspected case of TRALI during a transfusion?**
   - A. Administering diuretics
   - B. Initiating broad-spectrum antibiotics
   - C. High dose of corticosteroids
   - D. Stopping the transfusion

Answers:

1. **Answer D (Transfusion-related acute lung injury (TRALI))**

Transfusion-related acute lung injury is identified as the leading cause of death associated with blood transfusions. TRALI is characterized by acute, noncardiogenic pulmonary edema leading to hypoxia, and it occurs during or after a transfusion. This condition is particularly serious as it can result in severe respiratory distress and is documented as the primary cause of death related to transfusions by the U.S. Food and Drug Administration (FDA).

2. **Answer C (Sudden onset of non-cardiogenic pulmonary edema)**

Transfusion-related acute lung injury is characterized by the sudden onset of non-cardiogenic pulmonary edema. This condition is associated with marked systemic hypovolemia and hypotension, often occurring during or within a few hours of a blood transfusion. Symptoms include acute dyspnea, fever, hypotension, and tachycardia. The chest radiograph typically shows features consistent with acute respiratory distress syndrome (ARDS), and there may be copious frothy yellow or pink fluid in the trachea. Laboratory findings may include unexpected haemoconcentration and a sudden fall in serum albumin. While peripheral blood neutropenia has been reported, neutrophilia is more common, and monocytopenia may also be observed. The diagnosis of TRALI relies on excluding other causes of pulmonary edema or ARDS.

3. **Answer B (Activation of neutrophils leading to capillary leakage)**

TRALI primarily induces pulmonary edema through the activation of neutrophils leading to capillary leakage, as per the two-hit hypothesis in its pathophysiology. The first hit involves the priming of neutrophils due to various factors, while the second hit occurs when antibodies or proinflammatory factors in the transfusion product activate these primed neutrophils. This activation results in localized inflammation, damaging lung tissue and pulmonary blood vessels, ultimately causing non-cardiogenic pulmonary edema and respiratory distress. The absence of signs of circulatory overload distinguishes TRALI from other transfusion reactions. Reporting TRALI cases is essential for identifying potential donors causing similar reactions and implementing preventive measures.

4. **Answer B (Minimizing the number of blood transfusions)**

A crucial step in reducing TRALI cases is minimizing the number of blood transfusions. Avoiding unnecessary transfusions, particularly of plasma and platelets, is emphasized as a preventive measure. Additionally, using pooled plasma preparations rather than standard single-donor Fresh Frozen Plasma (FFP) can help prevent TRALI because relevant antibodies are diluted in pooled plasma. The increased use of optimal additive red cells, which contain less plasma, is also highlighted as a strategy to reduce the clinical incidence and severity of TRALI resulting from red cell transfusions.

5. **Answer B (False)**

While TRALI is most commonly seen and appears to be more severe with products containing larger amounts of plasma, such as whole blood or fresh frozen plasma, it can still occur after the transfusion of packed red cells. TRALI is associated with 1 in 5–10,000 units of plasma-containing products transfused. Although there are no published cases of TRALI specifically implicating packed red cells, it is highlighted that TRALI may occur with optimal additive red cells if the antibody titer in the remaining plasma is high enough.

6. **Answer D (Stopping the transfusion)**

The most appropriate initial step in managing a suspected case of TRALI during a transfusion is to stop the transfusion immediately. TRALI is a serious transfusion reaction associated with acute noncardiogenic pulmonary edema, and discontinuing the transfusion is crucial to prevent further exposure to potential triggers of TRALI. Supportive measures such as additional oxygen, restrictive tidal volume ventilation, and judicious use of diuretics may be considered in managing symptoms. Recognizing and promptly addressing TRALI is essential, as there is currently no specific treatment for this condition, and management revolves around mitigating respiratory distress and preventing further complications.

Recommended literature

1. Cho MS, Modi P, Sharma S. Transfusion-related Acute Lung Injury. [Updated 2022 Jul 25]. In: StatPearls [Internet]. Treasure Island (FL): StatPearls Publishing; 2022 Jan-. Available from: https://www.ncbi.nlm.nih.gov/books/NBK507846/
2. Vlaar AP, Juffermans NP. Transfusion-related acute lung injury: a clinical review. Lancet. 2013;382(9896):984-994.

SKIN & MUSCULOSKELETAL DISORDERS

ACHONDROPLASIA

17
CHAPTER

Questions:

1. **What is the primary genetic mechanism underlying achondroplasia?**
   A. Environmental exposure during pregnancy
   B. Spontaneous mutation in FGFR3
   C. X-linked recessive mutation
   D. Autosomal recessive inheritance

2. **Which of the following facial features is characteristic of achondroplasia?**
   A. Small forehead
   B. Microglossia
   C. Flattened nasal bridge
   D. Small mandible

3. **What is the primary cause of long-bone shortening in achondroplasia?**
   A. Abnormal osteoblast function
   B. Cartilage overgrowth
   C. Premature ossification in epiphyseal growth plates
   D. Excessive growth hormone production

4. **Which deformity is a result of mucopolysaccharide deposition in achondroplasia?**
   A. Maxillary hypoplasia
   B. Rib hypoplasia
   C. Sternal prominence
   D. Narrowed nasal passages

5. **Spinal stenosis is one of the most common serious problems that people with achondroplasia may develop.**
   A. True
   B. False

6. **A 30-year-old morbidly obese male with a history of achondroplasia, hypertension, and a left-sided perirectal abscess is scheduled for emergent incision and drainage. Preoperative evaluation reveals challenges, including a Mallampati IV airway, short neck, small maxillary overbite, and mild scoliotic cervical spine with atlantoaxial instability. Lumbar spine CT shows shortening of lumbar vertebral bodies and spinal stenosis. Which of the following techniques may be employed in managing difficult airways in achondroplasia?**
   A. Rapid sequence induction
   B. Laryngeal mask airway (LMA) insertion
   C. Awake fiberoptic intubation
   D. Cricothyrotomy

Answers:

1. Answer B (Spontaneous mutation in FGFR3)

Achondroplasia is a genetic disorder with an autosomal dominant pattern of inheritance. The primary genetic mechanism involves a spontaneous mutation in the fibroblast growth factor receptor 3 (FGFR3) gene. This mutation leads to the inhibition of cartilage formation, causing premature ossification in the epiphyseal growth plates and concurrent restriction of growth. Individuals with achondroplasia, despite having a normal life expectancy, fail to achieve a height of 148 cm by adulthood.

2. Answer C (Flattened nasal bridge)

Achondroplasia is characterized by several facial deformities, including macrocephaly with a prominent forehead, macroglossia, short maxilla, large mandible, midfacial hypoplasia with a flattened nasal bridge, and a small mouth. These features contribute to the distinct facial appearance observed in individuals affected by this genetic disorder.

3. Answer C (Premature ossification in epiphyseal growth plates)

The primary cause of long-bone shortening in achondroplasia is premature ossification in the epiphyseal growth plates. This occurs due to a mutation in the FGFR3 gene, leading to the inhibition of cartilage formation. Cartilage normally serves as a template for bone growth in the long bones of the arms and legs. However, in achondroplasia, there is premature conversion of cartilage to bone (ossification) in the epiphyseal growth plates, resulting in restricted growth of these long bones. This process contributes to the characteristic short stature observed in individuals with achondroplasia. The shortening is particularly evident in the proximal upper and lower extremities, contributing to the overall disproportionate dwarfism seen in this condition.

4. Answer D (Narrowed nasal passages)

Mucopolysaccharide deposition in achondroplasia primarily affects the nasal passages, leading to narrowed nasal passages. This deposition contributes to airway deformities observed in individuals with achondroplasia, causing potential difficulties in breathing. The accumulation of mucopolysaccharides can result in obstructed nasal passages, which, in turn, may contribute to respiratory challenges and potential complications such as obstructive sleep apnea. While other structures, such as the trachea and pharynx, may also be affected, narrowed nasal passages are a direct consequence of mucopolysaccharide deposition in achondroplasia.

5. Answer A (True)

Spinal stenosis is one of the most common serious problems that people with achondroplasia may develop. In achondroplasia, abnormal growth of the vertebrae can lead to the formation of the spinal canal with less room. This abnormal spinal anatomy can result in spinal stenosis, a condition where the spinal canal narrows, causing compression of the spinal cord. Spinal stenosis in individuals with achondroplasia can lead to various complications, including cauda equina syndrome, nerve root compression, thoracolumbar spinal cord compression, or high cervical cord compression secondary to stenosis of the foramen magnum (although this is rare). These complications may result in neurological symptoms and require careful management and monitoring.

6. Answer C (Awake fiberoptic intubation)

Given the complex challenges identified in the preoperative evaluation of the morbidly obese male with achondroplasia, including a Mallampati IV airway, short neck, small maxillary overbite, and cervical spine instability, the preferred technique for managing difficult airways is awake fiberoptic intubation. This approach is particularly indicated in alert and hemodynamically stable patients, allowing for careful and controlled airway management prior to induction of anesthesia. The anesthetic challenges associated with achondroplasia, such as potential difficulty in airway management and altered respiratory mechanics, necessitate a tailored approach. Awake fiberoptic intubation offers the advantage of securing the airway while avoiding complications associated with induction in the presence of a difficult airway. In situations where awake fiberoptic intubation is contraindicated, a comprehensive anesthesia contingency plan, including video-assisted laryngoscopy, rescue supraglottic airways, or elective surgical airways, should be in place to address and mitigate any anticipated dilemmas in this challenging case.

Recommended literature

1. Kim JH, Woodruff BC, Girshin M. Anesthetic Considerations in Patients With Achondroplasia. Cureus. 2021;13(6):e15832. Published 2021 Jun 22.
2. Spiegel JE, Hellman M. Achondroplasia: Implications and Management Strategies in Anesthesia. December 23, 2015. Accessed January 24, 2023. https://anesthesiaexperts.com/uncategorized/achondroplasia-implications-management-strategies-anesthesia/.

ANKYLOSING SPONDYLITIS

17
CHAPTER

Questions:

1. What is the primary manifestation of ankylosing spondylitis (AS) in the spine over time?

   A. Lumbar lordosis

   B. Kyphosis

   C. Scoliosis

   D. Bamboo spine

2. Which of the following is an extra-articular manifestation of ankylosing spondylitis?

   A. GERD

   B. Renal calculi

   C. Raynaud phenomenon

   D. Eye inflammation

3. What is a respiratory manifestation of ankylosing spondylitis?

   A. Asthma

   B. Obstructive lung disease

   C. Restrictive lung disease

   D. Pulmonary embolism

4. What is the recommended approach for neuraxial anesthesia in ankylosing spondylitis patients?

   A. Midline approach

   B. Caudal approach

   C. Paramedian approach

   D. Oblique approach

5. Aortic insufficiency is the common cardiovascular abnormality associated with ankylosing spondylitis.

   A. True

   B. False

6. A 29-year-old male with a known case of severe ankylosing spondylitis, symptomatic for the last 6 years, was listed for total hip replacement. The patient presented with a classical bamboo spine and exhibited no mobility in the cervical or thoracolumbar spine. The patient's airway posed a significant challenge due to the lack of any extension of the cervical spine and a mouth opening of about 2.5 cm. Lumbar punctures were attempted at different spinal levels using both median and paramedian approaches by two experienced anesthesiologists, but they were unsuccessful. Consequently, the decision was made to proceed with general anesthesia and tracheal intubation. Which method is considered the safest option for tracheal intubation in AS patients?

   A. Rapid sequence induction

   B. Video laryngoscopy

   C. Awake fiberoptic intubation

   D. Retrograde intubation

Answers:

1. Answer D (Bamboo spine)

Ankylosing spondylitis (AS) primarily affects the spine and sacroiliac joints. Over time, the characteristic manifestation is the development of a "bamboo spine." This term is used to describe the fusion and rigidity of the spine, resembling the appearance of a bamboo stalk. The chronic inflammatory arthritis associated with AS leads to the fusion of vertebrae, resulting in decreased joint mobility and an eventual rigid, fused spine. This process is a hallmark feature of ankylosing spondylitis and is represented by the term "bamboo spine".

2. Answer D (Eye inflammation)

An extra-articular manifestation of ankylosing spondylitis is eye inflammation, which can manifest as iritis or uveitis. Patients with ankylosing spondylitis may experience inflammation of the eye, leading to symptoms such as eye pain, lacrimation, and photophobia. This ocular involvement is a significant extra-articular manifestation associated with ankylosing spondylitis and can impact the health of the eyes.

3. Answer C (Restrictive lung disease)

Ankylosing spondylitis can lead to respiratory manifestations, and one of them is restrictive lung disease. The restrictive lung disease in AS is a consequence of both parenchymal fibrosis and chest wall musculoskeletal disease. As the disease progresses, the fusion and rigidity of the spine (bamboo spine) can affect the chest wall's ability to expand during breathing, contributing to restrictive lung disease.

4. Answer C (Paramedian approach)

In patients with ankylosing spondylitis, regional and neuraxial anesthesia can be challenging due to factors such as poor positioning, axial spine fusion, obliteration of the epidural space, and underlying radiculopathies/neuropathic pain. There is also a higher risk of epidural hematoma, as indicated by the American Society of Regional Anesthesia and Pain Medicine (ASRA). Considering these challenges, the recommended approach for neuraxial anesthesia in ankylosing spondylitis patients is often the paramedian approach. The paramedian approach may offer better success in these patients, as it allows for better access in the presence of spinal fusion and other anatomical changes associated with AS.

5. Answer A (True)

Aortic insufficiency is one of the cardiovascular abnormalities associated with ankylosing spondylitis. In AS, the inflammation can affect the aorta and its valves, leading to aortic insufficiency. Other cardiovascular manifestations mentioned in the context of AS include myocarditis, conduction defects, cardiomegaly, cardiomyopathy, and pericardial effusion. It's essential to note that the prevalence of specific cardiovascular manifestations can vary among individuals with AS.

6. Answer C (Awake fiberoptic intubation)

In the challenging case of a 29-year-old male with severe ankylosing spondylitis and limited cervical spine mobility scheduled for total hip replacement, the safest option for tracheal intubation is awake fiberoptic intubation (AFOI). Given the rigid and immobile spine characteristic of AS, AFOI allows for direct visualization of the airway, minimizing the risk of injury and ensuring a controlled intubation process. The awake approach maintains protective airway reflexes and patient comfort. While supraglottic airway devices can be alternatives, the choice of AFOI prioritizes safety in navigating the challenges posed by AS, aligning with the principles of minimizing cervical spine manipulation during airway management in AS patients.

Recommended literature

1. Pahwa D, Chhabra A, Arora MK. Anaesthetic management of patients with ankylosing spondylitis. Trends in Anaesthesia and Critical Care. 2013;3(1):19-24.
2. Woodward LJ, Kam PC. Ankylosing spondylitis: recent developments and anaesthetic implications. Anaesthesia. 2009;64(5):540-548.

EHLERS-DANLOS SYNDROME

Questions:

1. **What is the most common subtype of Ehlers-Danlos Syndrome?**
   A. Classic
   B. Hypermobile
   C. Vascular
   D. Kyphoscoliotic

2. **Which manifestation is NOT typically associated with the classic subtype of Ehlers-Danlos Syndrome?**
   A. Joint hypermobility
   B. Muscle hypotonia
   C. Widened atrophic scars
   D. Sagging, redundant skin

3. **What is a significant cardiovascular consideration in patients with Ehlers-Danlos Syndrome?**
   A. Hypertension
   B. Mitral regurgitation
   C. Aortic stenosis
   D. Coronary artery disease

4. **What is a significant risk during obstetrical anesthesia in Ehlers-Danlos Syndrome patients, especially in the presence of the vascular subtype?**
   A. Placental abruption
   B. Uterine rupture
   C. Preeclampsia
   D. Thromboembolism

5. **Ambulatory surgery is a preferred option for patients with Ehlers-Danlos Syndrome.**
   A. True
   B. False

6. **A 20-year-old woman, BMI 39 (morbid obesity), with a history of seizures, Barrett's esophagus, and joint hypermobility, is scheduled for elective caesarean delivery at 39 weeks of gestation. She is being evaluated for Ehlers-Danlos Syndrome-Hypermobile Type (EDS-HT), and her family history is positive for a sister with EDS-HT. What statement is NOT true about the recommended approach to anesthesia in obstetrical cases involving patients with Ehlers-Danlos Syndrome, considering the potential complications?**
   A. Neuraxial anesthesia is preferred
   B. Succinylcholine should be used for RSI
   C. General anesthesia is preferred
   D. The use of nitrous oxide is safe

Answers:

1. Answer B (Hypermobile)

Ehlers-Danlos Syndrome (EDS) is classified into 13 subtypes, each characterized by distinct clinical features and genetic implications. Among these subtypes, Hypermobile EDS is the most common. This subtype is associated with joint hypermobility, skin hyperextensibility, and other clinical manifestations. The other subtypes include Classical, Classical-like, Cardiac-valvular, Vascular, Arthrochalasia, Dermatosparaxis, Kyphoscoliotic, Brittle Cornea syndrome, Spondylodysplastic, Musculocontractural, Myopathic, and Periodontal EDS.

2. Answer D (Sagging, redundant skin)

The classic subtype of Ehlers-Danlos Syndrome is characterized by specific manifestations, and sagging, redundant skin is NOT typically associated with this subtype. The key features of the classic subtype include skin hyperextensibility, widened atrophic scars, and joint hypermobility. Smooth, velvety skin, molluscoid pseudotumors, and subcutaneous spheroids are also part of the classic subtype. Muscle hypotonia, motor delay, easy bruising, complications of joint hypermobility, manifestations of tissue extensibility and fragility, surgical complications, and positive family history are additional characteristics associated with the classic subtype.

3. Answer B (Mitral regurgitation)

A significant cardiovascular consideration in patients with EDS is mitral regurgitation. Mitral regurgitation is characterized by the backward flow of blood into the left atrium due to improper closure of the mitral valve. In individuals with EDS, particularly the vascular type and cardiac-valvular EDS, there can be severe progressive problems with the aortic and mitral valves, leading to conditions like mitral regurgitation. The cardiovascular manifestations in EDS also include proximal aortic dilatation and conduction abnormalities. While the vascular type of EDS carries a risk of arterial rupture at a young age, and cardiac-valvular EDS is associated with severe progressive problems of the aortic and mitral valves, hypermobile EDS may present with milder dilation of the aortic root and conditions like postural tachycardia syndrome.

4. Answer B (Uterine rupture)

A significant risk during obstetrical anesthesia in EDS patients, especially in the presence of the vascular subtype, is uterine rupture. Patients with EDS, particularly the vascular subtype, are at high risk of complications during pregnancy, including preterm labor, uterine rupture, and hemorrhage. The vascular subtype of EDS is associated with arterial fragility, which increases the risk of vascular complications, including uterine rupture. Due to these heightened risks, recommendations for patients with the vascular subtype may include termination of pregnancy or caesarean section before 32 weeks to mitigate the potential complications.

5. Answer B (False)

Ambulatory surgery is generally avoided in patients with EDS due to the potential for complications associated with this connective tissue disorder. EDS is characterized by joint hypermobility, skin fragility, and vascular issues, making patients more prone to complications during surgical procedures. It is advised to avoid ambulatory surgery in EDS patients, and healthcare providers should be aware of typical EDS-related emergency situations. These may include difficult airway status, increased bleeding risks, and the potential for organ rupture, especially in specific subtypes of EDS.

6. Answer A (Neuraxial anesthesia is preferred)

While neuraxial anesthesia can be used, it is not preferred in obstetrical cases involving patients with Ehlers-Danlos Syndrome. The correct approach is often general anesthesia due to the relative contraindication of neuraxial anesthesia, especially in patients with joint hypermobility and EDS. General anesthesia provides a more controlled environment, reducing the risks associated with potential complications during the caesarean delivery. There are no specific guidelines or indications favoring particular general anesthetic techniques for patients with Ehlers-Danlos Syndrome-Hypermobile Type (EDS-HT). The assumption is that volatile anesthetics, nitrous oxide, total intravenous anesthesia, depolarizing agents, and non-depolarizing agents are all considered safe and effective unless an additional contraindication exists.

Recommended literature

1. Malfait F, Francomano C, Byers P, et al. The 2017 international classification of the Ehlers-Danlos syndromes. Am J Med Genet C Semin Med Genet. 2017;175(1):8-26.
2. Wiesmann T, Castori M, Malfait F, Wulf H. Recommendations for anesthesia and perioperative management in patients with Ehlers-Danlos syndrome(s). Orphanet J Rare Dis. 2014;9(109).

MARFAN'S SYNDROME

17

CHAPTER

Questions:

1. **What is the role of prophylactic beta-blockers in Marfan syndrome?**
   A. Preventing retinal detachment
   B. Reduce the risk of aortic dilatation
   C. Reduce the risk of spontaneous pneumothorax
   D. Improve joint hypermobility

2. **What is the primary cardiovascular complication associated with Marfan's Syndrome?**
   A. Coronary artery disease
   B. Aortic dissection
   C. Pulmonary embolism
   D. Myocardial infarction

3. **Which of the following is a common ocular manifestation of Marfan's Syndrome?**
   A. Cataract
   B. Retinal detachment
   C. Macular degeneration
   D. Conjunctivitis

4. **What is the main consideration for neuraxial anesthesia in patients with Marfan's Syndrome?**
   A. Increased risk of epidural hematoma
   B. Dural ectasia
   C. Predisposition to spinal cord compression
   D. Elevated intracranial pressure

5. **Monthly echocardiography is recommended during pregnancy in patients with Marfan's Syndrome.**
   A. True
   B. False

6. **A 20-year-old parturient with Marfan's Syndrome, presented for her first pregnancy. Prior to conception, she had a documented history of aortic root dilation measuring 4.34 cm. Throughout her pregnancy, she was closely monitored by both her obstetrician and cardiologist. Serial transthoracic echocardiograms (TTEs) were performed to assess the cardiovascular status. At term, the TTE revealed an increase in aortic root dilation to 4.42 cm, along with mild mitral valve regurgitation. Importantly, there was no evidence of aortic dissection, and the severity of mitral valve regurgitation remained stable. In obstetric anesthesia, when might a caesarean section (CS) be recommended for a patient with Marfan's Syndrome?**
   A. Aorta diameter < 4 cm
   B. Aorta diameter > 4.5 cm
   C. No special considerations
   D. Marfan syndrome is an indication for CS

Answers:

1. Answer B (Reduce the risk of aortic dilatation)

Prophylactic beta-blockers play a pivotal role in Marfan syndrome by reducing the risk of aortic dilatation. This is achieved through mechanisms such as a decrease in the rate of pressure increase in the aorta and a lower heart rate, resulting in fewer systolic impulses. Beta-blockers are considered standard care in adults with Marfan syndrome, aiming to mitigate stress on the aortic wall and subsequently lower the risk of aortic dissection. Despite their established use, gaps in knowledge persist regarding their impact on the rate of aortic root dilatation, clinical outcomes, and the optimal timing for initiation. Additionally, alternative medications such as calcium channel blockers or ACE inhibitors may be considered if beta-blockers are contraindicated or not well-tolerated.

2. Answer B (Aortic dissection)

The primary cardiovascular complication associated with Marfan's Syndrome is aortic dissection. Individuals with Marfan syndrome are at an increased risk of cardiovascular abnormalities, including aortic root dilatation, aneurysm formation, and aortic regurgitation. Aortic dissection, the tearing of the inner layer of the aorta, is a severe and potentially life-threatening complication. The weakened connective tissue in Marfan syndrome predisposes individuals to aortic dissection, making it a critical concern.

3. Answer B (Retinal detachment)

A common ocular manifestation of Marfan's Syndrome is retinal detachment. Individuals with Marfan syndrome may experience various ocular abnormalities, including lens dislocation, myopia, and retinal detachment. The connective tissue weakness in Marfan syndrome can affect the structural integrity of the eye, leading to retinal detachment, a serious condition where the retina separates from the back of the eye.

4. Answer B (Dural ectasia)

The main consideration for neuraxial anesthesia in patients with Marfan's Syndrome is the presence of dural ectasia. Dural ectasia refers to the ballooning or widening of the dural sac, particularly in the lower lumbar and sacral regions. In individuals with Marfan syndrome, dural ectasia poses a higher risk for a failed epidural, dural puncture, and post-dural puncture headache during neuraxial anesthesia. The condition may lead to difficulties in achieving successful spinal anesthesia due to the altered anatomy and increased volume of cerebrospinal fluid (CSF) in the lumbar theca. Consideration of imaging studies such as CT or MRI may be necessary to assess the extent of dural ectasia and guide anesthesia management in these patients.

5. Answer A (True)

Monthly echocardiography is recommended during pregnancy in patients with Marfan's Syndrome. This practice is essential for monitoring aortic dimensions and assessing the risk of complications associated with aortic involvement, such as aortic dilatation or dissection. The goal is to manage the pregnancy in a way that minimizes risks related to the connective tissue abnormalities characteristic of Marfan's Syndrome, particularly those affecting the aorta.

6. Answer B (Aorta diameter > 4.5 cm)

For patients with Marfan's Syndrome, the decision on the mode of delivery, including the consideration of a caesarean section, is influenced by cardiovascular parameters. Guidelines generally recommend no special considerations and vaginal delivery if there are no symptoms and the aorta diameter is less than 4 cm. However, in the presence of aortic root dilation and aortic regurgitation, a multidisciplinary approach involving cardiology, cardiac surgery, and obstetrics is recommended. The recommendation for a caesarean section is often considered when the aorta diameter exceeds 4.5 cm, as this poses an increased risk of complications. The decision is individualized based on the patient's specific cardiovascular status, and the input from multiple specialties ensures a comprehensive and tailored approach to the delivery method, prioritizing the safety of both the mother and the baby.

Recommended literature

1. Araújo MR, Marques C, Freitas S, Santa-Bárbara R, Alves J, Xavier C. Marfan Syndrome: new diagnostic criteria, same anesthesia care? Case report and review. Braz J Anesthesiol. 2016;66(4):408-413.
2. Castellano JM, Silvay G, Castillo JG. Marfan Syndrome: Clinical, Surgical, and Anesthetic Considerations. Seminars in Cardiothoracic and Vascular Anesthesia. 2014;18(3):260-271.
3. Allyn J, Guglielminotti J, Omnes S, Guezouli L, Egan M, Jondeau G, Longrois D, Montravers P. Marfan's Syndrome During Pregnancy: Anesthetic Management of Delivery in 16 Consecutive Patients. Anesthesia & Analgesia. 2013;116(2): 392-398.
4. Marfan Syndrome. In: Bissonnette B, Luginbuehl I, Marciniak B, Dalens BJ. eds. Syndromes: Rapid Recognition and Perioperative Implications. McGraw Hill; 2006. Accessed January 26, 2023.

OSTEOGENESIS IMPERFECTA

17
CHAPTER

Questions:

1. **What is the underlying mechanism of Osteogenesis Imperfecta (OI)?**
   A. Lack of vitamin D
   B. Connective tissue disorder
   C. Excessive calcium absorption
   D. Autoimmune response

2. **What musculoskeletal abnormalities are commonly associated with Osteogenesis Imperfecta?**
   A. Genu varum
   B. Kyphoscoliosis and pectus excavatum
   C. Anterior pelvic tilt
   D. Lateral meniscal tear

3. **What is the primary focus of the treatment in OI?**
   A. Eliminating genetic mutations
   B. Managing symptoms
   C. Stem cell therapy
   D. Immunosuppressive therapy

4. **What is a specific anesthetic concern in patients with Osteogenesis imperfecta?**
   A. Hyperthermia
   B. Platelet dysfunction
   C. Dental damage
   D. All of the above

5. **The use of blood pressure cuffs be approached cautiously in Osteogenesis Imperfecta OI patients.**
   A. True
   B. False

6. **A 15-year-old girl with a known diagnosis of OI type I came in for surgery to remove her appendix due to acute appendicitis. She had experienced multiple fractures before and had successfully undergone three surgeries under general anesthesia in the past for similar issues. The girl, who is 103 cm tall, weighs 49 kg, has blue sclera, fragile bones, hearing loss, and kyphoscoliosis, faced special challenges because of her health condition. The medical team decided to go ahead with rapid sequence induction (RSI) for anesthesia since she had eaten a full meal an hour before the surgery. Why is succinylcholine use a potential issue in Osteogenesis Imperfecta patients?**
   A. Risk of hyperthermia
   B. Bone fractures
   C. Allergic reactions
   D. Risk of hyperkalemia

Answers:

1. Answer B (Connective tissue disorder)

Osteogenesis Imperfecta (OI), also known as brittle bone disease, is a genetic disorder that manifests at birth, characterized by bones that are exceptionally fragile and prone to breaking easily. The underlying mechanism of OI is primarily a connective tissue disorder, specifically caused by a deficiency or poor formation of type I collagen. Type I collagen is a crucial component of bone, skin, tendons, and other connective tissues. In OI, mutations in the COL1A1 and COL1A2 genes, which are responsible for encoding the alpha chains of type I collagen, are observed in more than 90% of cases. These mutations disrupt the normal structure and function of type I collagen, leading to the characteristic features of fragile bones in individuals with OI. The inheritance pattern of OI is autosomal dominant, meaning that a mutation in one copy of the gene from either parent is sufficient to cause the disorder. However, de novo mutations, where the mutation occurs spontaneously in the affected individual and is not inherited from either parent, can also give rise to OI.

2. Answer B (Kyphoscoliosis and pectus excavatum)

Musculoskeletal abnormalities commonly associated with OI include kyphoscoliosis, characterized by a combined curvature of the spine in both the sagittal and frontal planes and pectus excavatum, a condition involving a sunken or depressed appearance of the chest due to abnormal shaping of the sternum and rib cage. These deformities contribute to the overall clinical presentation of OI, along with skeletal fragility, impacting mobility and posing challenges for individuals with this genetic disorder.

3. Answer B (Managing symptoms)

The primary focus of the treatment in OI is on managing symptoms and increasing bone strength to prevent deformities and fractures. Treatment strategies include maintaining a healthy lifestyle through regular exercise, consuming a balanced diet sufficient in vitamin D and calcium, and avoiding smoking. Additionally, bisphosphonate medicines are commonly used to increase bone density, and acute care of fractures is essential. Orthopedic treatment, such as bracing and splinting, may be employed, and rod surgery may be considered. Physical and occupational therapy are crucial components of the treatment plan to enhance mobility and function. The use of assistive devices, such as leg braces and wheelchairs, may be recommended based on the severity of symptoms. Oral and dental care is also emphasized to address associated dental issues, such as dentinogenesis imperfecta.

4. Answer D (All of the above)

Patients with OI present various anesthetic concerns, encompassing hyperthermia, platelet dysfunction, and dental damage. OI, an autosomal dominant connective tissue disorder, manifests with extremely brittle bones, posing challenges during anesthesia. Difficulties include a fragile cervical spine, making airway management intricate, and susceptibility to fractures, necessitating careful patient positioning. Platelet dysfunction increases the risk of bleeding during procedures, emphasizing the need for meticulous hemostasis. Additionally, dental damage concerns arise during oropharyngeal instrumentation. Although OI patients are prone to hyperthermia, it is crucial to differentiate it from malignant hyperthermia (MH) risk. Anesthesia in OI requires comprehensive consideration of these factors to ensure safe and effective perioperative care.

5. Answer A (True)

Individuals with OI have an increased risk of fractures due to the fragility of their bones. Blood pressure cuffs, if applied with excessive force or improperly, may pose a hazard by causing fractures. Therefore, it is crucial for healthcare professionals, including those administering anesthesia, to exercise caution and use appropriately sized and applied blood pressure cuffs to minimize the risk of injury to the patient's fragile bones.

6. Answer B (Bone fractures)

Succinylcholine use is a potential issue in OI patients due to the risk of bone fractures. Succinylcholine, a type of muscle relaxant, can cause involuntary muscle contractions known as fasciculations. In individuals with OI, who already have fragile bones, succinylcholine-induced fasciculations may lead to fractures. Given the increased susceptibility of OI patients to fractures, it is recommended to use Rocuronium, a non-depolarizing muscle relaxant, for induction as an alternative to succinylcholine. The unique challenges presented by OI necessitate careful anesthetic management to ensure patient safety and minimize complications related to the underlying musculoskeletal fragility.

Recommended literature

1. Wang H, Huang X, Wu A, Li Q. Management of anesthesia in a patient with osteogenesis imperfecta and multiple fractures: a case report and review of the literature. Journal of International Medical Research. 2021;49(6).
2. Gupta D, Purohit A. Anesthetic management in a patient with osteogenesis imperfecta for rush nail removal in femur. Anesth Essays Res. 2016;10(3):677-679.
3. Frost EAM. Osteogenesis imperfecta and anesthetic implications. October 21, 2019. Accessed January 27, 2023. https://anesthesiaexperts.com/uncategorized/16596/#:~:text=In%20OI%2C%20the%20need%20for,or%20chipping%20of%20damaged%20teeth

PSORIASIS

Questions:

1. **What is the most common type of psoriasis?**
   A. Nail psoriasis
   B. Guttate psoriasis
   C. Plaque psoriasis
   D. Inverse psoriasis

2. **What is NOT a risk factor associated with developing psoriasis?**
   A. Smoking
   B. Alcohol
   C. Obesity
   D. Age

3. **Which medication is LEAST commonly associated with triggering or exacerbating psoriasis symptoms?**
   A. Beta-blockers
   B. Chloroquine
   C. Lithium
   D. Loop diuretics

4. **What phenomenon is described as triggering psoriatic changes at the site of skin injury?**
   A. Koebner's phenomenon
   B. Guttate phenomenon
   C. Inverse phenomenon
   D. Plaque phenomenon

5. **Nitrous oxide is a preferred component in inhalation anesthesia for patients with psoriasis.**
   A. True
   B. False

6. **A 24-year-old female patient, diagnosed with Plaque psoriasis for the past 10 years, is in the recovery room following a caesarean section performed under spinal anesthesia with isobaric levobupivacaine 0.5% (2.6 mL), Fentanyl 25 mcg, and Morphine 150 mcg. The procedure went uneventfully; however, the patient is now complaining of severe pruritus, making her extremely uncomfortable. What is the next treatment?**
   A. Naloxone
   B. Antihistamines
   C. Corticosteroids
   D. Epinephrine

Answers:

1. **Answer C (Plaque psoriasis)**

   The most common type of psoriasis is plaque psoriasis, also known as psoriasis vulgaris, representing approximately 85-90% of cases. It manifests as raised, red patches covered by silvery-white scales, typically appearing symmetrically on the scalp, trunk, and limbs, especially the elbows and knees. Other types include nail psoriasis, affecting fingernails and toenails; guttate psoriasis, primarily seen in young adults and triggered by bacterial infections; inverse psoriasis, affecting skin folds; pustular psoriasis, characterized by pus-filled blisters; and erythrodermic psoriasis, the least common type involving widespread inflammation and exfoliation of the skin. Each type presents distinct features, contributing to the diverse clinical spectrum of psoriasis.

2. **Answer D (Age)**

   Age is not considered a risk factor associated with developing psoriasis. Psoriasis is influenced by a combination of genetic and environmental factors, and while it can occur at any age, it often manifests in early adulthood. The identified risk factors include genetic predisposition (HLA-Cw6) and a family history of psoriasis. Smoking, alcohol consumption, obesity, infections (such as streptococcal pharyngitis and HIV), certain drugs (like β blockers and lithium), stress, and weather conditions are recognized triggers or exacerbating factors. However, age itself is not a standalone risk factor for the onset or development of psoriasis.

3. **Answer D (Loop diuretics)**

   While studies on drug-related psoriasis may not be exhaustive, certain medications have traditionally shown stronger associations, including beta-blockers, lithium, and synthetic antimalarials like chloroquine. Loop diuretics, on the other hand, are less commonly reported as agents associated with drug-provoked psoriasis.

4. **Answer A (Koebner's phenomenon)**

   The phenomenon referred to as Koebner's phenomenon involves the manifestation of psoriatic skin changes, specifically at sites of skin injury or trauma. Named after the dermatologist Heinrich Koebner, this phenomenon is characterized by the appearance of psoriatic lesions in areas where the skin has been physically damaged, including those resulting from external stimuli like cuts, scratches, surgical incisions, and even pressure from medical instruments such as blood pressure cuffs. The Koebner response underscores the reactive nature of psoriasis, highlighting how various external factors, including medical interventions, can influence the development and exacerbation of psoriatic lesions.

5. **Answer B (False)**

   Nitrous oxide is not a preferred component in inhalation anesthesia for patients with psoriasis. Studies have indicated that nitrous oxide may potentiate the cytotoxic effects of methotrexate on proliferating cells. As methotrexate is a commonly used drug for the treatment of psoriasis, the interaction with nitrous oxide could be detrimental. Therefore, it is recommended to avoid the use of nitrous oxide before or during methotrexate administration in patients with psoriasis.

6. **Answer A (Naloxone)**

   The patient's complaint of severe pruritus after a caesarean section under spinal anesthesia suggests opioid-induced pruritus, a challenging issue in the context of psoriasis. Considering the patient's history of Plaque psoriasis, which involves skin inflammation and hypersensitivity, managing pruritus becomes crucial. Naloxone, an opioid receptor antagonist, is effective against opioid-induced pruritus. However, given the refractory nature of pruritus in psoriasis and its poor response to conventional treatments, combining Naloxone with Propofol, a sedative with anti-pruritic properties, can provide a more comprehensive approach. Propofol has been shown to alleviate pruritus effectively. Therefore, the recommended course of action is administering Naloxone in combination with Propofol to address the opioid-induced pruritus more comprehensively and provide relief to the patient with psoriasis.

Recommended literature

1. Pollard BJ, Kitchen G. Handbook of Clinical Anaesthesia. 4th ed. Taylor & Francis group; 2018. Chapter 9 Connective tissue, Lomas JP.

Skin & Musculoskeletal disorders
RHABDOMYOLYSIS

Questions:

1. **What is the gold standard for laboratory diagnosis in suspected cases of rhabdomyolysis?**
   A. Troponin levels
   B. Myoglobin levels
   C. Creatine kinase (CK) levels
   D. Lactate dehydrogenase levels

2. **Which drug class, widely prescribed for cardiovascular disease, has been associated with the risk of drug-induced myalgia and rhabdomyolysis?**
   A. Beta-blockers
   B. Angiotensin-converting enzyme (ACE) inhibitors
   C. Statins
   D. Calcium Channel Blockers

3. **What is the effect of myoglobin on renal blood flow during rhabdomyolysis?**
   A. Increased blood flow
   B. No effect on blood flow
   C. Renal vasoconstriction
   D. Renal vasodilation

4. **Which electrolyte imbalance is NOT commonly reported in rhabdomyolysis with associated acute kidney injury (AKI)?**
   A. Hypercalcemia
   B. Hyperphosphatemia
   C. Hyperuricemia
   D. Hyperkalemia

5. **Ketamine has been identified as a potential trigger for the initiation of rhabdomyolysis.**
   A. True
   B. False

6. **A 9-year-old, 40 kg female underwent an elective tonsillectomy, receiving 80 mg of intravenous propofol, 50 µg of intravenous fentanyl for induction, and succinylcholine for intubation. The operation proceeded without complications. However, 24 hours postoperatively, the patient exhibited poor urine output, passing only a small amount of "tea-colored" urine. She complained of proximal muscle weakness in all four limbs with associated tenderness, necessitating assistance for mobilization. Urgent blood tests revealed a creatinine kinase of 22,679 units/L and potassium levels of 6 mEq/L. Rhabdomyolysis is suspected based on the clinical presentation and blood test results. What is the recommended resuscitation strategy to prevent acute tubular necrosis (ATN) in rhabdomyolysis?**
   A. Administer hypertonic saline
   B. Administer isotonic IV fluids
   C. Administer diuretics immediately
   D. Limit fluid intake to prevent volume overload

Answers:

1. Answer C (Creatine kinase (CK) levels)

The gold standard for laboratory diagnosis in suspected cases of rhabdomyolysis is creatine kinase levels. A blood test showing CK levels greater than 5000 U/L is indicative of rhabdomyolysis. While myoglobin levels peak before increases in CK, myoglobin is rapidly metabolized outside of the kidney, making CK a more reliable marker for this condition. The diagnosis of rhabdomyolysis requires a high index of suspicion, thorough history, and physical examination, especially in patients with known risk factors such as trauma, sepsis, muscular disease, or immobilization. CK, with a half-life of 1.5 days, is considered the gold standard, and a concentration exceeding 5000 IU/L is closely associated with kidney damage development. In contrast, myoglobin concentrations normalize within 6-8 hours post-injury, making it less sensitive for diagnosis. Plasma myoglobin is less reliable due to its short half-life, leading to false-negative tests, and urine myoglobin may show erythrocyte positivity on urine dipstick due to the ortho-toluidine portion reacting with myoglobin.

2. Answer C (Statins)

The link between statins, specifically 3-hydroxymethyl-3-methylglutaryl coenzyme A reductase inhibitors, and myalgia/rhabdomyolysis has been extensively investigated since the 1980s. While statins are the most prescribed drugs globally for their cardiovascular benefits, they carry a real risk of myopathy. The U.S. Food and Drug Administration (FDA) has issued warnings about statins, citing potential side effects, including myopathy and rhabdomyolysis. Incidence rates of myopathic events in patients taking statins vary, with randomized controlled trials estimating it at 1.5%-5.0%, while rates in clinical practice range from 0.3%-33%. Risk factors for statin-induced rhabdomyolysis include high dosages, advanced age, female sex, renal or hepatic insufficiency, and diabetes mellitus. Despite the high incidence of general muscle toxicity, rhabdomyolysis secondary to statin use is extremely rare, and the mortality risk is considered outweighed by the reduction in all-cause mortality seen with statin use. Various statins exhibit different rates of rhabdomyolysis, with the lowest rates for pravastatin and the highest for rosuvastatin. The overall occurrence of fatal rhabdomyolysis with statins is low, and cerivastatin, a statin pulled from the market in 2001, had notably high rates of fatal rhabdomyolysis.

3. Answer C (Renal vasoconstriction)

Myoglobin, released from damaged muscle cells, contributes to renal vasoconstriction by scavenging nitrous oxide. Additionally, myoglobin interacts with the Tamm-Horsfall protein in the renal tubules, forming brown granular casts that can lead to tubular obstruction. This process is favored when the urine is acidic. The heme group of myoglobin may contribute to lipid peroxidation. In the context of rhabdomyolysis, renal blood flow is further reduced by factors such as hypovolemia, activation of the renin-angiotensin-aldosterone system (RAAS), and other vascular mediators. The combination of these mechanisms contributes to renal vasoconstriction during rhabdomyolysis.

4. Answer A (Hypercalcemia)

Rhabdomyolysis, characterized by muscle injury and the release of breakdown products into the bloodstream, often leads to complications such as hyperkalemia, hyperphosphatemia, hypocalcemia, and anion-gap metabolic acidosis. Rapid development of hyperkalemia, hyperuricemia, and hyperphosphatemia is observed in these cases. The muscle injury results in intracellular sodium and calcium influx, leading to cell swelling, disruption of structures, and myofibrillar contraction. Reperfusion amplifies the damage, causing the release of various substances into the bloodstream and contributing to electrolyte imbalances. While hypocalcemia is initially observed, hypercalcemia is not a commonly reported complication in rhabdomyolysis.

5. Answer A (True)

No anesthetic agent is without risk, and rhabdomyolysis has been reported with various anesthetics, including nontriggering ones, barbiturates, benzodiazepines, propofol, ketamine, and fasting. Ketamine hydrochloride, commonly used in the operating room for procedural sedation, is an analog of phencyclidine and is believed to induce agitation and prolonged muscular activity, potentially leading to the development of rhabdomyolysis. A case study by Weiner et al. observed clinical rhabdomyolysis in 2 out of 20 patients aged 15-40 who presented to the emergency room after ketamine abuse.

6. Answer B (Administer isotonic IV fluids)

Rhabdomyolysis from non-traumatic causes is managed similarly. Adequate and appropriate fluid resuscitation with normal isotonic saline should be provided depending on the underlying cause of rhabdomyolysis. The management involves removing the offending agent at the time of diagnosis and titrating IV fluids to maintain a urine output of 200 to 300 mL/h. Serial monitoring of CPK levels daily is essential to document downtrend levels. CPK levels exceeding 5,000 IU/L have an increased risk of developing acute kidney injury (AKI). In patients with CPK levels less than 5,000 IU/L, extensive volume fluid resuscitation is discouraged, as they are less likely to develop AKI. Forceful alkaline diuresis can be considered in severe cases where CPK exceeds 30,000 IU/L in the absence of oliguria, anuria, and AKI. Loop diuretics may be considered in the setting of volume overload resulting from aggressive fluid resuscitation. Patients who remain oliguric or anuric, despite aggressive fluid resuscitation and develop AKI should be considered for hemodialysis. The role of dialysis in myoglobin removal is not well established.

Recommended literature

1. Floridis, J., Barbour, R., 2022. Postoperative weakness and anesthetic-associated rhabdomyolysis in a pediatric patient: a case report and review of the literature. Journal of Medical Case Reports 16.
2. Pollard BJ, Kitchen, G. Handbook of Clinical Anaesthesia. Fourth Edition. CRC Press. 2018. 978-1-4987-6289-2.
3. Torres PA, Helmstetter JA, Kaye AM, Kaye AD. Rhabdomyolysis: pathogenesis, diagnosis, and treatment. Ochsner J. 2015;15(1):58-69.
4. Williams J, Thrope C. 2014. Rhabdomyolysis. Continuing Education in Anaesthesia Critical Care & Pain. 14;4:163-166.
5. Hunter JD, Greggg K, Damani S. 2006. Rhabdomyolysis. Continuing Education in Anaesthesia Critical Care. 6;4:141-143.

Skin & Musculoskeletal disorders
RHEUMATOID ARTHRITIS

Questions:

1. **Which joints are typically affected first in early rheumatoid arthritis (RA)?**
   A. Knees
   B. Hips
   C. Hands
   D. Shoulders

2. **Which of the following is a risk factor for developing rheumatoid arthritis?**
   A. Male gender
   B. Underweight
   C. Young age
   D. Smoking

3. **Which of the following is NOT an extra-articular manifestation of rheumatoid arthritis?**
   A. Carpal tunnel syndrome
   B. Kerato-conjunctivitis
   C. Colitis ulcerosa
   D. Valvular heart disease

4. **During surgery, how should conventional disease-modifying anti-rheumatic drugs (DMARDs) be managed in a patient with RA?**
   A. Continue as usual
   B. Administer an increased dose
   C. Withhold before surgery, schedule at the end of the dosing cycle
   D. Administer only after surgery

5. **Morning stiffness is a common symptom of RA.**
   A. True
   B. False

6. **A 55-year-old woman presents with a confirmed diagnosis of rheumatoid arthritis. She is scheduled for laparoscopic chole-cystectomy due to gallbladder issues. She has been managing her RA with oral methotrexate at a weekly dose of 10 milligrams and has been on a regimen of 10 milligrams of prednisone every other day for several months. The medical team has decided to continue methotrexate during the perioperative period, as it is a conventional disease-modifying anti-rheumatic drug. However, there is a question about the management of prednisone (Nizon), a corticosteroid, during the surgery. What is the recommended approach for managing corticosteroids during major surgery in a patient with RA?**
   A. Usual daily dose
   B. No corticosteroids needed
   C. Usual daily dose plus hydrocortisone 50 mg i.v. before incision + hydrocortisone 25 mg i.v. every 8 hrs for 1 day + usual daily dose
   D. Usual daily dose plus hydrocortisone 100 mg i.v. before incision + continuous i.v. infusion of hydrocortisone 200 mg for > 1 day

Answers:

1. **Answer C (Hands)**

Rheumatoid arthritis (RA) is a chronic autoimmune inflammatory disorder that primarily affects the synovial joints, leading to symmetrical erosive polyarthropathy. In the early stages of RA, smaller joints are typically affected first, with a predilection for the joints of the hands and feet. As RA progresses, the symptoms may spread to involve larger joints such as the wrists, knees, ankles, elbows, hips, and shoulders. This pattern of joint involvement is a key feature in the diagnosis of rheumatoid arthritis. Additionally, RA is characterized by periods of increased disease activity (flares) that alternate with periods of relative remission. It is important to note that RA can also have systemic manifestations, affecting other organs in more than 15–25% of cases.

2. **Answer D (Smoking)**

RA is a chronic autoimmune inflammatory disorder primarily affecting synovial joints, characterized by symmetrical erosive polyarthropathy. In the early stages, RA typically involves smaller joints, particularly those in the hands and feet, with progression to larger joints as the disease advances. The risk factors for developing RA include female gender, family history, increasing age, smoking, and overweight. Among the options provided, smoking is a recognized risk factor for the development of RA.

3. **Answer C (Colitis ulcerosa)**

Extra-articular manifestations in RA involve organs or systems outside the joints. Carpal tunnel syndrome represents a neurological manifestation, kerato-conjunctivitis is an ocular manifestation, and valvular heart disease falls under cardiovascular manifestations associated with RA. Colitis ulcerosa, however, is an inflammatory bowel disease affecting the colon and rectum, and it is not considered an extra-articular manifestation of RA. The extra-articular manifestations of RA encompass various organ systems, including the nervous, ocular, cardiovascular, respiratory, hematological, hepatic, renal, and cutaneous systems, as well as musculoskeletal manifestations.

4. **Answer A (Continue as usual)**

During surgery in a patient with rheumatoid arthritis, conventional disease-modifying anti-rheumatic drugs (DMARDs) such as methotrexate, leflunomide, hydroxychloroquine, and sulfasalazine are generally recommended to be continued as usual. These medications play a crucial role in managing RA by slowing down the progression of the disease and reducing symptoms. Discontinuing them abruptly may lead to disease flares, compromising the patient's condition. It is important to maintain the continuity of these medications to ensure optimal control of RA during the perioperative period. However, the management of other DMARDs, such as biologic DMARDs and targeted synthetic DMARDs, may involve withholding before surgery and scheduling at the end of the dosing cycle to minimize the risk of infections and complications.

5. **Answer A (True)**

Morning stiffness is a common and characteristic symptom of rheumatoid arthritis. Individuals with RA often experience joint stiffness that is more pronounced in the mornings and after periods of inactivity. This stiffness can affect multiple joints and may last for at least 30 minutes to several hours. The morning stiffness associated with RA is a key clinical feature used in the diagnosis of the condition. It reflects the inflammatory nature of RA, where the joints become more rigid after periods of rest.

6. **Answer C (Usual daily dose plus hydrocortisone 50 mg i.v. before incision + hydrocortisone 25 mg i.v. every 8 hrs for 1 day + usual daily dose)**

Patients on long-term glucocorticoid therapy, such as prednisone, require perioperative glucocorticoid coverage to manage the surgical stress response. The recommended approach involves continuing the patient's usual daily dose of prednisone and supplementing with additional hydrocortisone intravenously before incision and in the postoperative period. This strategy helps prevent complications such as infection and wound-healing issues associated with glucocorticoid use. The specific dosage may vary depending on the complexity of the surgery, with more extensive procedures requiring higher doses. The medical team should closely monitor blood glucose levels and blood pressure during the perioperative period. Additionally, avoiding nitrous oxide in patients on methotrexate is advised to prevent folate depletion. Strict aseptic technique and appropriate antibiotic prophylaxis are crucial for patients on glucocorticoids or DMARDs to minimize the risk of infection.

Recommended literature

1. Kim HR, Kim SH. Perioperative and anesthetic management of patients with rheumatoid arthritis. Korean J Intern Med. 2022;37(4):732-739.
2. Samanta R, Shoukrey K, Griffiths R. Rheumatoid arthritis and anaesthesia. Anaesthesia. 2011;66(12):1146-1159.

Skin & Musculoskeletal disorders
SCLERODERMA

17

CHAPTER

Questions:

1. **What is the characteristic feature of systemic sclerosis (SSc) that leads to skin hardening and tightening?**
   A. Hyperpigmentation
   B. Abnormal collagen synthesis
   C. Telangiectasis
   D. Muscle atrophy

2. **Which cardiovascular manifestation is commonly associated with SSc?**
   A. Hypotension
   B. Raynaud's phenomenon
   C. Bradycardia
   D. Deep vein thrombosis

3. **Which pulmonary manifestation is associated with SSc and can cause chest pain?**
   A. Asthma
   B. Chronic obstructive pulmonary disease (COPD)
   C. Interstitial lung disease (ILD)
   D. Pulmonary embolism (PE)

4. **What medication is recommended for the prevention of new digital ulcers in patients with SSc?**
   A. Triptans
   B. Calcium channel blockers
   C. Cyclophosphamide
   D. Phosphodiesterase-5-inhibitors

5. **Radial arterial line placement is mandatory for monitoring hemodynamic complications in scleroderma patients.**
   A. True
   B. False

6. **A 61-year-old woman with a 10-year history of SSc is scheduled for inner fixation of her acetabular fracture. Complications associated with her SSc history include interstitial pneumonia due to pulmonary fibrosis, Raynaud phenomenon, gastroesophageal reflux disease (GERD), and a remote history of pericardial effusion. The decision is made to proceed with general anesthesia. Which factor is NOT a significant risk for a difficult airway in SSc patients during anesthesia?**
   A. Microstomia
   B. Enlarged tongue
   C. Reduced neck mobility
   D. Oral telangiectasia

Answers:

1. Answer B (Abnormal collagen synthesis)

Systemic sclerosis (SSc) is a systemic, immune-mediated disease characterized by abnormal cutaneous and organ-based fibrosis. In SSc, there is damage to small blood vessels, activation of T lymphocytes, and the production of altered connective tissue. The excessive production of collagen leads to fibrosis, causing the skin to become thickened and tight. This abnormal collagen synthesis is a key mechanism underlying the pathophysiology of SSc. This fibrotic process extends beyond the skin, affecting various organs and resulting in progressive end-organ dysfunction.

2. Answer B (Raynaud's phenomenon)

Raynaud's phenomenon is a common cardiovascular manifestation associated with systemic sclerosis. It is characterized by vasospasm in response to cold or stress, leading to reduced blood flow to the fingers and toes. The presence of Raynaud's phenomenon is a hallmark feature of SSc and often precedes other systemic manifestations.

3. Answer C (Interstitial lung disease (ILD))

In systemic sclerosis, interstitial lung disease is a pulmonary manifestation associated with progressive dyspnea and chest pain. ILD involves inflammation and scarring of the lung tissue, leading to restrictive lung disease. The chest pain observed in individuals with SSc is predominantly linked to the impact of ILD. Additionally, other pulmonary manifestations associated with SSc encompass pulmonary fibrosis, pulmonary hypertension, and cor pulmonale.

4. Answer D (Phosphodiesterase-5-inhibitors)

Digital ulcers are part of the spectrum of SSc-related digital vasculopathy, with severe Raynaud's phenomenon often progressing to digital ulceration in approximately 50% of patients. The recommended medication for the prevention of new digital ulcers (DUs) in patients with systemic sclerosis is phosphodiesterase-5-inhibitors (PDE5i). Specifically, medications like sildenafil and tadalafil fall into this category. In addition to PDE5 inhibitors, alternative therapeutic options include iloprost, an intravenous prostanoid, and bosentan, an endothelin-1 (ET-1) receptor antagonist. Iloprost supplements the prostacyclin pathway, while bosentan blocks the ET-1 pathway. Current clinical practice involves the use of these medications to manage and prevent digital ulcers in SSc patients. Ongoing research explores combination treatments, such as iloprost plus endothelin antagonists or endothelin antagonists plus PDE5i, aiming to enhance the efficacy of preventive strategies.

5. Answer B (False)

While radial arterial lines are commonly used for monitoring hemodynamic status, their placement in scleroderma patients may pose risks. Raynaud's phenomenon, prevalent in scleroderma, can make radial arterial lines contraindicated due to the potential triggering of critical ischemic events. Experience suggests that the decision to place radial arterial lines in scleroderma patients should be carefully considered, weighing the potential risks. Alternative monitoring options should be explored to ensure patient safety.

6. Answer B (Enlarged tongue)

In SSc patients, factors contributing to a potentially difficult airway during anesthesia include microstomia, limited cervical extension, and bleeding nasal/oral telangiectasia. Microstomia refers to a reduced mouth opening, which may pose challenges during intubation. Limited cervical extension can make proper visualization of the airway difficult. Bleeding nasal/oral telangiectasia increases the risk of bleeding complications during airway management. However, an enlarged tongue is not typically associated with SSc and is not a significant risk factor for a difficult airway in this patient population.

Recommended literature

1. Carr ZJ, Klick J, McDowell BJ, Charchaflieh JG, Karamchandani K. An Update on Systemic Sclerosis and its Perioperative Management. Curr Anesthesiol Rep. 2020;10:512-521.

SJOGREN'S SYNDROME

Questions:

1. **What is the hallmark symptom of Sjogren's syndrome?**
   A. Joint pain
   B. Dry eyes
   C. Vaginal dryness
   D. Chronic dry cough

2. **Which environmental factor is NOT associated with Sjogren's syndrome?**
   A. Epstein-Barr virus
   B. Hepatitis C
   C. Human T-cell leukemia virus type 1
   D. Influenza virus

3. **What is a potential complication of Sjogren's syndrome related to vision?**
   A. Glaucoma
   B. Cataracts
   C. Corneal damage
   D. Vitreous Detachment

4. **What medication is used to decrease eye inflammation in Sjogren's syndrome?**
   A. Pilocarpine
   B. Hydroxychloroquine
   C. NSAIDs
   D. Cyclosporine

5. **Pilocarpine is effective in the treatment of Sjögren's syndrome.**
   A. True
   B. False

6. **A 45-year-old female presents for a laparoscopically assisted vaginal hysterectomy under general anesthesia. The patient has a past medical history significant for primary Sjogren's syndrome (SS), gastroesophageal reflux disease, and chronic gastritis. She reports symptoms consistent with Sjogren's syndrome, including dry eyes, dry mouth, arthralgia, fatigue, and occasional Raynaud's phenomenon. Her systemic medications include pilocarpine 5 mg six times per day for the management of dry mouth, hydroxychloroquine 200 mg twice per day, and pantoprazole sodium 40 mg for gastroesophageal reflux disease. Additionally, she uses ibuprofen two to three 200-mg tablets every four hours as needed for arthralgia. Which drug should be avoided during anesthesia in Sjogren's syndrome?**
   A. Norepinephrine
   B. Glycopyrrolate
   C. Epinephrine
   D. Dobutamine

Answers:

1. **Answer B (Dry eyes)**

Sjogren's syndrome, marked by autoimmune dysfunction and destruction of exocrine glands like lacrimal and salivary glands, manifests primarily with the hallmark symptoms of dry eyes and dry mouth. Beyond these, individuals with Sjogren's syndrome may experience a spectrum of additional signs and symptoms, encompassing joint pain, swelling, and stiffness, as well as skin rashes or dry skin, vaginal dryness, chronic dry cough, prolonged fatigue, and thyroid problems. Importantly, this autoimmune condition often coexists with other immune system disorders, including rheumatoid arthritis, systemic lupus erythematosus, and multiple sclerosis, necessitating a comprehensive understanding for effective diagnosis and management.

2. **Answer D (Influenza virus)**

Sjogren's syndrome is associated with various environmental factors, including viruses. The environmental factors linked to Sjogren's syndrome are Epstein-Barr virus, hepatitis C, and human T-cell leukemia virus type 1. These viruses have been implicated in the development or exacerbation of the autoimmune response seen in Sjogren's syndrome. Influenza virus is not typically linked to Sjogren's syndrome. Additionally, hormonal factors such as estrogen and prolactin are implicated as environmental contributors to the development of the syndrome.

3. **Answer C (Corneal damage)**

A potential complication of Sjogren's syndrome related to vision is corneal damage. This includes issues such as light sensitivity, blurred vision, and, in severe cases, corneal damage. Sjogren's syndrome-associated dry eye is a progressive condition that not only causes symptoms of ocular discomfort but also leads to visual dysfunction. Moreover, the impact of Sjogren's syndrome on vision extends beyond dry eyes. The syndrome can contribute to complications such as corneal melt/perforation, uveitis, scleritis, retinal vasculitis, and optic neuritis.

4. **Answer D (Cyclosporine)**

The medication used to decrease eye inflammation in Sjogren's syndrome is Cyclosporine. Cyclosporine, available as prescription eyedrops (e.g., Restasis), is recommended for individuals with moderate to severe dry eyes associated with Sjogren's syndrome. The goal of using Cyclosporine is to alleviate eye inflammation and improve the overall condition of dry eyes. Additionally, another option mentioned in the information is Lifitegrast (Xiidra), another prescription eyedrop, which can also be recommended for the management of moderate to severe dry eyes.

5. **Answer A (True)**

Pilocarpine tablets are used specifically to address dryness of the mouth and throat resulting from a reduction in saliva production, which can occur in conditions like Sjogren's syndrome. This medication is recognized for its efficacy in managing Sjögren's syndrome-induced dry mouth and dry eyes. It's important to note that while pilocarpine is effective, it may not be as tolerable as another medication called cevimeline. Despite differences in tolerability, both pilocarpine and cevimeline are recommended for the treatment of dry mouth associated with Sjögren's syndrome, as outlined in clinical guidelines.

6. **Answer B (Glycopyrrolate)**

In patients with Sjogren's syndrome, it is advisable to avoid drugs with parasympatholytic or anticholinergic effects during anesthesia, as they can exacerbate the decrease in gland secretions. This includes medications like atropine, diphenhydramine, glycopyrrolate, and promethazine. A preference for regional anesthesia is observed due to the drying effects of anesthetic gases in general anesthesia, which can lead to decreased tear production. In instances where general anesthesia is unavoidable, the addition of a humidifier to the rebreathing system helps mitigate the potential drying impact of anesthetic gases. This comprehensive approach aims to optimize perioperative care, recognizing the unique challenges associated with Sjogren's syndrome and anesthesia.

Recommended literature

1. Sjögren Syndrome. In: Bissonnette B, Luginbuehl I, Marciniak B, Dalens BJ. eds. Syndromes: Rapid Recognition and Perioperative Implications. McGraw Hill; 2006. Accessed February 20, 2023. https://accessanesthesiology.mhmedical.com/content.aspx?bookid=852&sectionid=49518220.

Skin & Musculoskeletal disorders
STEVENS-JOHNSON SYNDROME

17

CHAPTER

Questions:

1. Which of the following is NOT a characteristic sign or symptom of Stevens-Johnson syndrome?
   A. Fever
   B. Erythematous macules with purpuric, necrotic centers
   C. Blisters on the skin and mucous membranes
   D. Yellow discoloration of the eyes

2. What is the main mechanism underlying the development of Stevens-Johnson syndrome?
   A. Immediate-type hypersensitivity reaction
   B. Delayed-type hypersensitivity reaction
   C. Type I hypersensitivity reaction
   D. Autoimmune disorder

3. Which of the following is NOT a common cause of Stevens-Johnson syndrome?
   A. Antibiotics
   B. Antiepileptic drugs
   C. Antifungal medications
   D. Anti-gout medications

4. What is the preferred method for fluid management in the acute phase of Stevens-Johnson Syndrome?
   A. Administering fluids based on body weight
   B. Using the Parkland formula
   C. Administering hypotonic fluids
   D. Limiting fluid intake to prevent fluid overload

5. Ketamine is recommended for induction in patients with Stevens-Johnson syndrome.
   A. True
   B. False

6. A 14-year-old child presents to the Emergency Department (ED) with a history of epileptic seizures. The patient has been previously treated with Perampanel 2 mg. Upon examination, the child is noted to have peeling of the skin around the eyes, neck, anterior torso, and upper and lower extremities. Additionally, blisters are observed on the skin and mucous membranes of the mouth, nose, eyes, and genitals. The child reports unexplained widespread skin pain. Stevens-Johnson syndrome (SJS) is suspected. Which of the following precautions is NOT recommended during the anesthetic management of patients with Stevens-Johnson syndrome?
   A. Minimize handling and transfer of patients
   B. Avoid manipulation and trauma to the oral mucosa
   C. Induce hypothermia for better wound healing
   D. Adhere to strict aseptic precautions

Answers:

1. **Answer D (Yellow discoloration of the eyes)**

   Stevens-Johnson syndrome (SJS) is characterized by a variety of signs and symptoms involving the skin and mucous membranes. Common features include fever, sore mouth and throat, fatigue, burning or red eyes, widespread skin pain, a spreading rash that is typically red or purple, blisters on the skin and mucous membranes of the mouth, nose, eyes, and genitals, and shedding of skin within days after blisters form. While fever, sore mouth and throat, fatigue, burning or red eyes, skin pain, spreading rash, and blisters on the skin and mucous membranes are all characteristic signs and symptoms of Stevens-Johnson syndrome, yellow discoloration of the eyes is not typically associated with this condition. Yellow discoloration of the eyes (jaundice) is more commonly seen in conditions affecting the liver, such as hepatitis or liver failure, and is not a characteristic feature of SJS.

2. **Answer B (Delayed-type hypersensitivity reaction)**

   SJS is primarily characterized by a delayed-type hypersensitivity reaction. This means that the condition typically develops over time rather than immediately after exposure to certain medications or infections. In the case of SJS, exposure to SJS-inducing drugs or their metabolites stimulates cytotoxic T cells (CD8+ T cells) or T helper cells (CD4+ T cells), leading to an autoimmune response. This delayed hypersensitivity reaction results in the characteristic manifestations of SJS, including diffuse erythematous macules with purpuric, necrotic centers, overlying blisters, progression to skin sloughing, widespread superficial ulcers, and loss of the epidermal barrier. This process can ultimately lead to fluid and protein loss, fluid and electrolyte imbalances, and hypoproteinemia.

3. **Answer C (Antifungal medications)**

   SJS can be triggered by various medications and infections, but antifungal medications are not commonly associated with causing this condition. Common causes of Stevens-Johnson syndrome include antibiotics, antiepileptic drugs, anti-gout medications, nevirapine, and certain pain relievers such as acetaminophen, ibuprofen, and naproxen sodium. These medications have been identified as potential triggers for SJS due to their propensity to induce hypersensitivity reactions in susceptible individuals.

4. **Answer B (Using the Parkland formula)**

   In the acute phase of SJS, fluid management is an essential component of supportive care. The preferred method for fluid management during this phase is to use the Parkland formula. The Parkland formula is a widely accepted guideline for fluid resuscitation in burn patients, and it is also applicable to patients with SJS during the acute phase. This formula calculates the volume of fluid required for resuscitation based on the patient's body surface area and the extent of injury.

5. **Answer A (True)**

   Ketamine is recommended for induction in patients with Stevens-Johnson syndrome due to its ability to provide better cardiovascular stability, particularly in hypotensive patients. This recommendation is supported by evidence suggesting that induction with ketamine or etomidate could offer better hemodynamic stability compared to other induction agents such as propofol or thiopental. In the context of SJS, where patients may experience fluid and electrolyte imbalances, cardiovascular stability during induction is crucial. Ketamine's sympathomimetic properties make it a suitable choice for induction in hypotensive patients with SJS, as it can help maintain blood pressure and heart rate.

6. **Answer C (Induce hypothermia for better wound healing)**

   Inducing hypothermia is not recommended during the anesthetic management of patients with SJS; instead, maintaining normothermia is preferred. Various precautions, including minimizing patient handling, avoiding trauma to the oral mucosa, and adhering to strict aseptic precautions, are crucial to prevent exacerbation of symptoms and complications in patients suspected of having SJS. Additionally, to optimize patient outcomes, comprehensive supportive care measures should be implemented, such as fluid replacement, wound care, eye care, temperature management, and medication administration. Induction with agents like etomidate or ketamine may provide better hemodynamic stability than propofol or thiopental, while non-depolarizing muscle relaxants are preferred to avoid hyperkalemia. In the operating room, maintaining normothermia and providing warm intravenous fluids are essential for preventing hypothermia and optimizing patient care.

Recommended literature

1. Ramsali MV, Puduchira KG, Maganti SP, Vankaylapatti SD, Pasupuleti S, Kulkarni D. Anesthetic management and outcomes of patients with Steven-Johnson Syndrome-A retrospective review study. J Anaesthesiol Clin Pharmacol. 2021;37(1):119-123.
2. Kwass WK, Chow J. Anesthetic Management in Stevens-Johnson syndrome: Case Report. Integr Anesthesiol. 2019;2(1):001-004.

SYSTEMIC LUPUS ERYTHEMATOSUS

17
CHAPTER

Questions:

1. **Which of the following is a characteristic symptom of systemic lupus erythematosus (SLE)?**
   A. Persistent cough
   B. Fatigue
   C. Epigastric pain
   D. Hematuria

2. **What is the primary mechanism underlying the pathophysiology of SLE?**
   A. Deficiency of complement proteins
   B. Overproduction of interleukins
   C. Dysregulation of the immune system
   D. Decreased activity of B-cells

3. **Which laboratory test is NOT useful for assessing disease activity in patients with SLE?**
   A. Erythrocyte sedimentation rate (ESR)
   B. C-reactive protein
   C. Anti-double-stranded DNA (anti-dsDNA) antibodies
   D. Coagulation studies

4. **What is the NOT recommended pharmacological treatment for patients with SLE?**
   A. Aspirin
   B. Acetaminophen
   C. Hydroxychloroquine
   D. Prednisone

5. **Anemia is a common hematological complication of SLE.**
   A. True
   B. False

6. **A 40-year-old female with a history of systemic lupus erythematosus and thrombocytopenia presents for a scheduled vaginal hysterectomy. She reports experiencing breathlessness on mild exertion and displays a characteristic malar rash. Laboratory tests reveal thrombocytopenia, consistent with her medical history. Currently, she is on hydroxychloroquine and prednisolone therapy, which has been continued until the morning of surgery. Which of the following statements regarding the management of SLE patients undergoing surgery is accurate?**
   A. NSAIDs are contraindicated due to their potential to exacerbate renal dysfunction
   B. Steroids should be abruptly discontinued perioperatively to prevent adrenal suppression
   C. Immunosuppressants should be continued perioperatively to maintain disease control
   D. Hydroxychloroquine is not considered a potent immunosuppressant and is, therefore, typically used in elective surgeries

Answers:

1. Answer B (Fatigue)

Fatigue is a characteristic symptom of systemic lupus erythematosus (SLE). Other common symptoms of SLE include fever, joint pain, stiffness, and swelling, butterfly-shaped rash on the face, skin lesions exacerbated by sun exposure, Raynaud's phenomenon, shortness of breath, chest pain, dry eyes, photosensitivity, headaches, confusion, memory loss, hair loss, mouth ulcers, and swollen lymph nodes. While cough, epigastric pain, and hematuria can occur in some individuals with SLE, they are not as characteristic or common as fatigue.

2. Answer C (Dysregulation of the immune system)

The primary mechanism underlying the pathophysiology of systemic lupus erythematosus is dysregulation of the immune system. In individuals with SLE, there is aberrant activation of various components of the immune system, including dendritic cells, B-cells, and T-cells. This dysregulation leads to the production of autoantibodies and auto-reactive T-cells, which form immune complexes and target self-tissues, resulting in tissue damage and inflammation throughout the body. While deficiencies in complement proteins, overproduction of interleukins, and decreased activity of B-cells may contribute to the pathogenesis of SLE, dysregulation of the immune system is the central and most fundamental mechanism driving the development and progression of the disease.

3. Answer D (Coagulation studies)

Coagulation studies, such as prothrombin time (PT) and activated partial thromboplastin time (aPTT), are not typically used for assessing disease activity in patients with systemic lupus erythematosus. While abnormalities in coagulation parameters may occur in some individuals with SLE, they are not specific markers of disease activity. Instead, coagulation studies are primarily utilized to evaluate the risk of thrombosis or bleeding complications in patients with SLE, particularly those with antiphospholipid syndrome (APS) or lupus anticoagulant. On the other hand, erythrocyte sedimentation rate (ESR), C-reactive protein (CRP), and anti-double-stranded DNA (anti-dsDNA) antibodies are commonly used laboratory tests for assessing disease activity in SLE. Elevated ESR and CRP levels indicate inflammation, which may reflect disease activity in SLE. Anti-dsDNA antibodies are specific markers of SLE, and their levels often correlate with disease flares.

4. Answer B (Acetaminophen)

Acetaminophen is not a recommended pharmacological treatment for systemic lupus erythematosus, as it does not address the underlying autoimmune processes or inflammation associated with the condition. Instead, aspirin and nonsteroidal anti-inflammatory drugs (NSAIDs) are commonly used for managing symptoms of arthritis in SLE and their antiplatelet effects in antiphospholipid syndrome, while hydroxychloroquine is prescribed for various manifestations of SLE and to reduce the frequency of disease flares. Prednisone and other corticosteroids, on the other hand, are mainstays of SLE treatment, effectively suppressing inflammation and modulating the immune response across a range of SLE manifestations. Therefore, while acetaminophen may provide symptomatic relief for pain and fever, it is not considered a primary pharmacological treatment for SLE.

5. Answer A (True)

Hematologic abnormalities, including anemia, are common in systemic lupus erythematosus. Anemia can occur due to various mechanisms in SLE, including chronic inflammation, autoimmune hemolysis, or bone marrow suppression from medications. Therefore, anemia is considered a common hematological complication of SLE. Additionally, leukopenia, thrombocytopenia, lymphadenopathy, and splenomegaly are also recognized hematologic manifestations of SLE, further underscoring the hematologic involvement commonly seen in this autoimmune disease.

6. Answer D (Hydroxychloroquine is not considered a potent immunosuppressant and is therefore typically used in elective surgeries)

Hydroxychloroquine, an antimalarial drug commonly used in the treatment of SLE, is not considered a potent immunosuppressant. Studies have shown that continuation of hydroxychloroquine perioperatively does not significantly increase the risk of infection or wound healing complications. Furthermore, its toxicity profile is relatively low, and patients are typically able to recover quickly after surgery, even with continued use of the medication. Therefore, it is typically safe to continue hydroxychloroquine perioperatively, especially in elective surgeries like vaginal hysterectomy. Conversely, options A, B, and C are not accurate in this context: NSAIDs are typically avoided due to their potential to exacerbate renal dysfunction in patients with SLE; abruptly discontinuing steroids perioperatively can lead to adrenal suppression; and while immunosuppressants like azathioprine may need interruption perioperatively due to potential interactions with anesthesia, hydroxychloroquine is generally considered safe to continue.

Recommended literature

1. Erez BM. Systemic Lupus Erythematosus: A Review for Anesthesiologists. Anesthesia & Analgesia. 2010;111(3):665-676.

Skin & Musculoskeletal disorders
WEGENER'S GRANULOMATOSIS

17
CHAPTER

Questions:

1. Which of the following is a characteristic feature of Wegener's granulomatosis?
    A. Periorbital edema
    B. Gingival hyperplasia
    C. Saddle nose deformity
    D. Clubbing of fingers

2. Which of the following organs is NOT commonly affected by Wegener's granulomatosis?
    A. Kidneys
    B. Liver
    C. Lungs
    D. Upper respiratory tract

3. Which treatment regimen is typically used to induce remission in severe cases of Wegener's granulomatosis?
    A. High-dose aspirin therapy
    B. Nonsteroidal anti-inflammatory drugs (NSAIDs)
    C. Immunosuppressants with corticosteroids
    D. Antibiotics

4. Which complication is NOT associated with Wegener's granulomatosis?
    A. Hearing loss
    B. Skin scarring
    C. Hypertension
    D. Deep vein thrombosis

5. Hydroxychloroquine is commonly used for maintenance therapy in Wegener's granulomatosis.
    A. True
    B. False

6. A 67-year-old female patient with a longstanding diagnosis of Wegener's granulomatosis (WG) is admitted for urgent foot amputation due to necrosis in the left foot toes. The patient has been under the care of rheumatology for 5 years. On physical examination, petechiae are noted on the bilateral upper and lower extremities, and the patient presents with inspiratory rales. Additionally, she reports symptoms of bloody sputum, cough, and hearing loss. Posteroanterior chest radiography reveals bilateral cavities and nodularity suggestive of pulmonary involvement. What is NOT part of the preoperative management of patients with Wegener's disease?
    A. Indirect laryngoscopy
    B. Chest x-ray, chest CECT, and renal function profile
    C. Corticosteroid coverage
    D. Echocardiogram

Answers:

1. **Answer C (Saddle nose deformity)**

   This deformity, marked by a loss of height in the bridge of the nose, results from the destruction of nasal cartilage due to the inflammatory process associated with the disease. As Wegener's granulomatosis primarily affects the upper respiratory tract, including the nose and sinuses, the weakening and collapse of nasal cartilage lead to a distinctive saddle-like appearance. This feature is highly characteristic and often diagnostic of the condition, distinguishing it from other diseases.

2. **Answer B (Liver)**

   Wegener's granulomatosis primarily involves the upper and lower respiratory tract, kidneys, and sometimes other organs such as the eyes and joints. Liver involvement is not typically a prominent feature of the disease. Instead, Wegener's granulomatosis is characterized by necrotizing granulomas in the respiratory tract, small- to medium-sized vessel vasculitis, and glomerulonephritis. Nearly all patients with Wegener's granulomatosis experience involvement of the upper respiratory tract, particularly the nose and sinuses, which can lead to symptoms such as nasal drainage, sinus infections, and nosebleeds.

3. **Answer C (Immunosuppressants with corticosteroids)**

   In severe cases, remission induction typically involves a combination of immunosuppressants such as rituximab or cyclophosphamide, along with high-dose corticosteroids like prednisone. This aggressive therapy aims to suppress the autoimmune response and reduce inflammation. Additionally, plasmapheresis may be utilized if the kidneys are involved to remove circulating autoantibodies and inflammatory mediators. After remission is achieved, the steroid dose is tapered slowly, and the focus shifts to maintaining remission and preventing disease flares. This often involves transitioning to less toxic immunosuppressants like rituximab, methotrexate, azathioprine, leflunomide, or mycophenolate.

4. **Answer C (Hypertension)**

   Wegener's granulomatosis primarily affects the respiratory tract, kidneys, and other organs through vasculitis and granuloma formation. Complications commonly associated with Wegener's granulomatosis include hearing loss due to middle or inner ear involvement, skin scarring from cutaneous manifestations, chronic kidney disease secondary to glomerulonephritis, and a loss of height in the bridge of the nose (saddle nose deformity) caused by weakened cartilage. Additionally, patients with Wegener's granulomatosis may be at an increased risk of deep vein thrombosis due to systemic inflammation and endothelial damage. However, hypertension is not a typical complication of Wegener's granulomatosis.

5. **Answer B (False)**

   Hydroxychloroquine is not commonly used for maintenance therapy in Wegener's granulomatosis. Maintenance therapy in Wegener's granulomatosis typically involves the use of less toxic immunosuppressants such as azathioprine (AZA), methotrexate (MTX), or mycophenolate mofetil (MMF) after achieving remission. These medications help to prevent disease relapses and maintain a remission state. Hydroxychloroquine is not included in the standard maintenance therapy regimen for Wegener's granulomatosis, as it is not considered as effective as other immunosuppressants in controlling the disease. Instead, hydroxychloroquine is commonly used in the treatment of other autoimmune diseases, such as systemic lupus erythematosus and rheumatoid arthritis.

6. **Answer D (Echocardiogram)**

   The preoperative management of patients with Wegener's granulomatosis (WG) involves several key components to optimize perioperative care. Indirect laryngoscopy is crucial to assess the involvement of the upper airway. At the same time, a comprehensive examination of the lungs and kidneys, including chest X-ray, chest CT scan, and renal function profile, helps evaluate the extent of disease involvement. Administration of IV hydrocortisone ensures adequate corticosteroid coverage to prevent adrenal insufficiency during the perioperative period. However, routine cardiac testing such as echocardiography or stress testing is typically not performed preoperatively in patients with WG unless specific cardiac symptoms or concerns are present, as cardiovascular manifestations are not commonly associated with WG.

Recommended literature

1. Sharma J, Lal J, Gehlaut P, Amanpreet, Dhawan G, Yadav A. Wegener's Granulomatosis and Anaesthetic Implications: A Case Report. Int J Med Res Prof. 2018; 4(1): 479-81.
2. Frost EAM. Wegener's Granulomatosis, PHACE Syndrome: Rarities With Anesthetic Implications. December 20, 2018. Accessed January 26, 2023. https://anesthesiaexperts.com/uncategorized/wegeners-granulomatosis-phace-syndrome-rarities-anesthetic-implications/.

ANESTHETIC TECHNIQUES

BLIND NASAL INTUBATION

18

CHAPTER

Questions:

1. **What is the primary indication for awake (with or without sedation) blind nasal intubation?**
   A. Unstable blood pressure
   B. Known difficult intubation
   C. Allergy to local anesthetic
   D. History of gastrointestinal bleeding

2. **Which of the following is an absolute contraindication to blind nasal intubation?**
   A. The base of the skull fracture
   B. Risk of impending airway obstruction
   C. Patient refusal or inability to cooperate
   D. Coagulopathy

3. **Which maneuvers are NOT recommended to facilitate successful blind nasal intubation?**
   A. Head extension
   B. Inflate the cuff with 15 mL of air to direct the tip anteriorly
   C. Cricoid pressure
   D. Laryngeal mask airway insertion

4. **What is the appropriate action if breath sounds are heard through the tube but unable to advance further during blind nasal intubation?**
   A. Withdraw the tube 2 cm
   B. Rotate the tube to the midline
   C. Inflate the cuff with 15 mL of air
   D. Advance the tube further forcefully

5. **During nasotracheal intubation, it is essential to orient the bevel of the tube towards the nasal septum for optimal passage.**
   A. True
   B. False

6. **An 18-year-old female patient presents for elective Bilateral Temporomandibular Joint Reconstruction surgery due to bilateral temporomandibular ankylosis, which has resulted in limited mouth opening. Given the anticipation of a difficult airway, the decision is made to proceed with nasal intubation. During the procedure, after placing the tube through the right nostril, it advances smoothly with the loss of breath sounds, no cough, and the larynx is elevated. Where is the most likely position of the tube?**
   A. Trachea
   B. Anterior
   C. Left/right piriform fossa
   D. Esophagus

Answers:

1. **Answer B (Known difficult intubation)**

   Blind nasal intubation is primarily indicated in patients with known difficult intubation or those who have previously undergone nasal intubation. It is also indicated in cases of anticipated difficult intubation, after failed intubation attempts in an unanticipated difficult airway, and when there are known or suspected difficulties with mask ventilation. Additionally, blind nasal intubation is recommended in patients with an unstable C-spine. Blind nasal intubation, historically used in anesthetized patients, has been adapted for awake patients, with or without sedation. While fiber-optic intubation has become the preferred method in many cases, blind nasal intubation remains relevant, particularly when fiber-optic equipment is unavailable or when fiber-optic intubation attempts have failed. It is particularly useful in patients with difficult airways or structural abnormalities affecting the mouth.

2. **Answer C (Patient refusal or inability to cooperate)**

   An absolute contraindication to blind nasal intubation is a condition that prohibits the procedure from being performed due to potential risks or lack of feasibility. In this context, patient refusal or inability to cooperate falls under this category. If a patient refuses or is unable to cooperate with the procedure, blind nasal intubation cannot be safely and effectively performed. Cooperation from the patient is crucial for successful intubation and to minimize potential complications. While the other options listed (A) Base of skull fracture, (B) Risk of impending airway obstruction, and (D) Coagulopathy are contraindications to blind nasal intubation, they are considered relative contraindications. Relative contraindications imply that the procedure may still be feasible under certain circumstances or with appropriate precautions but may carry increased risks or require special considerations.

3. **Answer D (Laryngeal mask airway insertion)**

   While head extension, cricoid pressure, and inflating the cuff with 15 mL of air to direct the tip anteriorly are recommended maneuvers to aid intubation based on clinical findings, the insertion of a laryngeal mask airway (LMA) is not part of the standard approach for blind nasal intubation. LMAs are typically utilized as rescue airway devices in difficult ventilation or intubation scenarios but are not integral to the technique of blind nasal intubation.

4. **Answer A (Withdraw the tube 2 cm)**

   When encountering this clinical finding, it indicates that the tube may be incorrectly positioned anteriorly. Withdrawing the tube 2 cm allows for reevaluation of the tube placement and potentially repositioning it to ensure proper advancement into the trachea. Additionally, reducing neck extension or externally manipulating the larynx may help facilitate tube advancement in subsequent attempts.

5. **Answer A (True)**

   During nasotracheal intubation, it is essential to orient the bevel of the tube towards the nasal septum for optimal passage through the nasopharynx. This orientation helps guide the tube along the natural curvature of the nasal cavity, reducing the risk of trauma and improving the likelihood of successful intubation; after reaching the nasopharynx turning the tube 1/4 turn is recommended to facilitate passage and forcing the tube should be avoided to prevent injury. If encountering resistance, alternative approaches, such as directing the tube toward the occipital protuberance may be attempted, and gentle manipulation can aid in easing passage. Once the tube reaches the oropharynx, further manipulation with instruments like Magill's forceps and laryngoscope is performed to facilitate its movement into the trachea.

6. **Answer D (Esophagus)**

   Given the clinical findings of a smooth advancement of the tube with the absence of breath sounds, no cough, and an elevated larynx, the most probable location of the tube is the esophagus rather than the trachea. In such a scenario, it is crucial to withdraw the tube until breath sounds return. Subsequently, specific maneuvers should be attempted to facilitate proper intubation into the trachea. These maneuvers may include head extension, cricoid pressure application, and inflating the cuff with 15 mL of air to direct the tip anteriorly. Advancing the tube slowly while ensuring that breath sounds are retained at the laryngeal inlet confirms correct placement into the trachea.

Recommended literature

1. Pollard BJ, Kitchen, G. Handbook of Clinical Anaesthesia. Fourth Edition. CRC Press. 2018. 978-1-4987-6289-2.

CLOSED CIRCLE ANESTHESIA

Questions:

1. **What is the primary purpose of closed-circle anesthesia?**
   A. To maximize the flow of fresh gas to the patient
   B. To minimize waste and environmental impact of inhalational anesthetic agents
   C. To increase the concentration of inspired oxygen
   D. To ensure rapid elimination of exhaled carbon dioxide

2. **Which of the following is NOT an advantage of closed-circle anesthesia?**
   A. Economy of gases and inhalational agents
   B. Humidification of inspired gases
   C. Reduced atmospheric pollution
   D. Accumulation of unwanted gases

3. **What is the main concern associated with uneven filling of the CO2 absorber canister in closed-circle anesthesia?**
   A. Increased risk of compound A formation
   B. Reduced efficiency due to the channeling of gases
   C. Accumulation of unwanted gases
   D. Sticking of unidirectional valves

4. **Which component of the closed-circle anesthesia system helps prevent the sticking of unidirectional valves due to water vapor condensation?**
   A. CO2 absorber
   B. Reservoir bag
   C. APL valve
   D. Hydrophobic filter

5. **The CO2 absorber in closed-circle anesthesia removes carbon dioxide from exhaled gases, allowing for the rebreathing of exhaled gases after CO2 absorption.**
   A. True
   B. False

6. **A 53-year-old male is undergoing an open right hemicolectomy procedure due to a diagnosed colon tumor. The surgery is being conducted under general anesthesia, and the patient is intubated and ventilated. The anesthesia machine is set to deliver a tidal volume of 400 mL and a respiratory rate of 14 breaths per minute, with a fresh gas flow of 0.5 L/min and an oxygen concentration of 40%. Approximately one hour into the operation, the anesthesia team notices a sudden drop in the minute volume, accompanied by a decrease in airway peak pressure. Subsequently, the machine emits a fresh gas alarm, and the reservoir bag collapses. What intervention will solve this problem?**
   A. Turn the alarm off
   B. Decrease TV and increase respiratory rate
   C. Increase oxygen concentration
   D. Increase the fresh gas flow to 4 L/min

Answers:

1. **Answer B (To minimize waste and environmental impact of inhalational anesthetic agents)**

   Closed-circle anesthesia, also known as closed-circuit anesthesia, primarily aims to minimize the waste and environmental impact of inhalational anesthetic agents. This technique operates by maintaining a constant anesthetic state through the addition of gases and vapors to the breathing circuit at a rate that matches the patient's body redistribution or elimination. By using a closed-circle system, the inhalational anesthetic agents are efficiently utilized, as they are continuously recycled within the system rather than being released into the environment or wasted. This approach significantly reduces the amount of anesthetic agents required for anesthesia procedures, thereby minimizing environmental impact and reducing overall cost.

2. **Answer D (Accumulation of unwanted gases)**

   Accumulation of unwanted gases is not an advantage of closed-circle anesthesia. In fact, it is listed as a potential disadvantage, albeit less of a problem with modern systems. Closed-circle anesthesia primarily offers several advantages, including the economy of gases and inhalational agents, by efficiently recycling them within the system, leading to cost savings and sustainable resource utilization. Additionally, closed-circle anesthesia systems typically incorporate mechanisms for humidifying inspired gases, improving patient comfort and reducing the risk of airway irritation. Moreover, by minimizing the release of inhalational agents into the environment, closed-circle anesthesia helps reduce atmospheric pollution, contributing to environmental sustainability and reducing the ecological footprint of anesthesia practice.

3. **Answer B (Reduced efficiency due to the channeling of gases)**

   Uneven filling of the CO_2 absorber canister in closed-circle anesthesia can lead to reduced efficiency due to the channeling of gases. This uneven distribution of soda lime within the absorber canister can result in pathways forming where gases pass through without being effectively absorbed. As a consequence, the gases may not undergo proper filtration, leading to a decrease in the effectiveness of CO_2 removal from the breathing circuit. This scenario compromises patient safety by potentially exposing them to higher levels of carbon dioxide during anesthesia. Therefore, maintaining proper and uniform filling of the CO_2 absorber canister is essential to ensure efficient removal of CO_2 from the closed circle anesthesia system, thereby promoting patient safety and optimal anesthesia delivery.

4. **Answer D (Hydrophobic filter)**

   A hydrophobic filter is the component of the closed circle anesthesia system that helps prevent the sticking of unidirectional valves due to water vapor condensation. Placing a hydrophobic filter at the end of the expiratory limb, before the CO_2 absorber, serves to prevent moisture from accumulating within the system and causing the valves to stick. This filter acts as a barrier, allowing only gases to pass through while repelling any moisture or liquid that may be present in the exhaled gases. By effectively managing water vapor condensation, the hydrophobic filter helps maintain the proper functioning of the unidirectional valves, ensuring smooth and uninterrupted gas flow within the closed-circle anesthesia system.

5. **Answer A (True)**

   The CO_2 absorber in closed-circle anesthesia removes carbon dioxide from exhaled gases, allowing for the rebreathing of exhaled gases after CO_2 absorption. This component chemically removes and binds exhaled carbon dioxide from the breathing circulation system, typically using soda lime mainly consisting of calcium hydroxide ($Ca(OH)_2$). As CO_2 is absorbed, heat and moisture are generated, which helps condition the breathing gas in the circuit system. The absorber is inserted into the inhalational limb of the breathing system, allowing the rebreathed portion of exhaled air to flow through it. This process helps maintain appropriate gas composition and conditions within the closed-circle anesthesia system, facilitating efficient and safe anesthesia delivery.

6. **Answer D (Increase the fresh gas flow to 4 L/min)**

   The sudden drop in minute volume, airway peak pressure, and the collapse of the reservoir bag indicate a problem with the delivery of gas to the patient's airway. This could be due to a leak in the breathing system, resulting in inadequate ventilation. Increasing the fresh gas flow to 4 L/min (1 liter of oxygen, 3 liters of air) would help to fill the breathing system and compensate for any leaks. This step ensures that the patient receives an adequate supply of oxygen and anesthetic gases, maintaining proper ventilation during the surgery. Additionally, the anesthesia team should also conduct a thorough check for any leaks in the system, including inspecting the hose system and bag valve mask and ensuring the CO_2 absorber is correctly secured. If a leak cannot be repaired, increasing the fresh gas flow further and switching to low-flow anesthesia may be necessary to maintain adequate ventilation. Monitoring the filling/volume of gas in the reservoir is essential to ensure the patient's safety and to prevent the development of a hypoxic gas mixture.

Recommended literature

1. Pollard BJ, Kitchen, G. Handbook of Clinical Anaesthesia. Fourth Edition. CRC Press. 2018. 978-1-4987-6289-2.
2. Herbert L, Magee P. Circle systems and low-flow anaesthesia. BJA Education. 2017;17(9):301-5.

Anesthetic techniques
FIBEROPTIC INTUBATION

Questions:

1. **What is the gold standard for managing known difficult intubation or anticipated difficult airways?**

   A. Blind nasal intubation

   B. Direct laryngoscopy

   C. Fiberoptic intubation

   D. Video laryngoscopy

2. **Which of the following is NOT a relative contraindication to fiberoptic intubation?**

   A. Lack of trained personnel

   B. Risk of impending airway obstruction

   C. Coagulopathy or bleeding in the airway

   D. Allergy to opioids

3. **Which route provides a more direct path to the larynx during fiberoptic intubation?**

   A. Transnasal route

   B. Transoral route

   C. Oropharyngeal route

   D. Subglottic route

4. **What is recommended regarding the size of the endotracheal tube (ETT) for transnasal fiberoptic intubation?**

   A. Use a larger ETT for better visualization

   B. Use the same size ETT as for transoral intubation

   C. Use a smaller ETT such as size 5 or 6

   D. Use a larger ETT for obese patients

5. **Sedation may be contraindicated in morbidly obese patients with sleep apnea undergoing transoral fiberoptic intubation.**

   A. True

   B. False

6. **A 55-year-old male presents to the operating room (OR) for a laparoscopic hernia repair surgery. He has a known history of difficult intubation and has undergone previous awake fiberoptic intubation successfully. During the procedure, the anesthesia team successfully places the fiberoptic scope past the vocal cords and visualizes the carina. However, when attempting to advance the endotracheal tube, they encounter resistance as the tube becomes stuck at the level of the arytenoids. Which maneuver is recommended when encountering resistance during transoral fiberoptic intubation, with the endotracheal tube stuck at the level of the arytenoids?**

   A. Rotate the tube 90 degrees

   B. Withdraw the tube and try a larger size

   C. Advance the tube forcefully

   D. Spray more lidocaine

Answers:

1. **Answer C (Fiberoptic intubation)**

   Fiberoptic intubation is considered the gold standard for managing known difficult intubation or anticipated difficult airways. This technique can be performed in awake patients, with or without sedation, or in anesthetized patients. Awake fiberoptic intubation is particularly advantageous in cases of anticipated difficult airways because it allows for direct visualization of the airway structures without the need for muscle relaxation, which may compromise airway patency. Additionally, awake fiberoptic intubation provides the opportunity for patient cooperation, reducing the risk of airway complications and ensuring a smoother intubation process.

2. **Answer D (Allergy to opioid)**

   Relative contraindications to fiberoptic intubation include lack of trained personnel, risk of impending airway obstruction, coagulopathy or bleeding in the airway, and allergy to local anesthetic. Lack of trained personnel refers to the necessity of skilled individuals for the safe and effective performance of the procedure, while the risk of impending airway obstruction and coagulopathy or bleeding in the airway poses challenges during intubation. Allergy to local anesthetic may necessitate alternative strategies. However, allergy to opioids, while relevant in anesthesia management, is not directly related to fiberoptic intubation as a contraindication for this specific procedure.

3. **Answer A (Transnasal route)**

   The transnasal route provides a very direct path to the larynx for the scope and endotracheal tube (ETT) after the turn at the nasopharynx is made. This route allows for easier navigation toward the trachea while following the nasopharyngeal route. In contrast, the transoral route, although used for elective intubations in the operating room, requires additional topical anesthesia to the oropharynx and larynx, often supplemented by sedation. Awake intubation via the oral route may be less comfortable and more stimulating compared to the nasal route. Navigating the bronchoscope around the curve at the base of the tongue requires an extremely sharp turn at the oropharynx, making it more challenging to find the larynx.

4. **Answer C (Use a smaller ETT such as size 5 or 6)**

   For transnasal fiberoptic intubation, it is recommended to use a smaller endotracheal tube, such as a size 5 or 6. This recommendation is based on the consideration of the size of the nasal airway. Using a smaller ETT allows for easier passage through the nasal cavity and reduces the risk of trauma or discomfort to the patient. Additionally, a smaller tube may facilitate better maneuverability and visualization during the intubation process.

5. **Answer A (True)**

   Sedation may be contraindicated in morbidly obese patients with sleep apnea undergoing transoral fiberoptic intubation. The transoral route, commonly used for elective intubations in the operating room, typically requires additional topical anesthesia to the oropharynx and larynx, often supplemented by sedation. However, sedation in morbidly obese patients with sleep apnea can pose risks such as respiratory depression, airway obstruction, and worsening of sleep apnea symptoms. Additionally, awake intubation via the oral route may be less comfortable and more stimulating compared to the nasal route, potentially exacerbating these risks. Therefore, in such cases, opting for awake, unsedated fiberoptic intubation via the transnasal route may be preferred to minimize complications and ensure patient safety.

6. **Answer A (Rotate the tube 90 degrees)**

   When the endotracheal tube is stuck at the level of the arytenoids during transoral fiberoptic intubation, the recommended action is to rotate the tube 90 degrees. This maneuver helps the tube to roll off the arytenoid and facilitates its passage into the trachea. It is important to ensure that the tube moves smoothly and without resistance to avoid trauma or injury to the airway structures. Once the tube is successfully advanced beyond the obstruction, further confirmation of its placement should be performed, such as visualization of the carina and confirmation of bilateral breath sounds. This approach minimizes complications and ensures successful intubation in patients with a history of difficult airways undergoing fiberoptic intubation.

Recommended literature

1. Pollard BJ, Kitchen, G. Handbook of Clinical Anaesthesia. Fourth Edition. CRC Press. 2018. 978-1-4987-6289-2.
2. Collins SR, Blank RS. Fiberoptic intubation: an overview and update. Respir Care. 2014;59(6):865-880.

Anesthetic techniques
ONE-LUNG ANESTHESIA

18
CHAPTER

Questions:

1. **Which of the following best describes one-lung anesthesia?**
   A. Alternate ventilation of both lungs
   B. Collapsing both lungs for surgical exposure
   C. Complete functional separation of the lungs
   D. Administering anesthesia to only one lung

2. **What is a primary indication for one-lung anesthesia?**
   A. Bilateral lung ventilation dependency
   B. Intraluminal airway masses
   C. Severe hypoxia
   D. Facilitation of surgical exposure in thoracic surgeries

3. **Which technique excels for a rapid transition between one-lung ventilation and two-lung ventilation?**
   A. Bronchial blockers
   B. Uncut tracheal tube
   C. Papworth BiVent tube
   D. Double lumen tube (DLT)

4. **Which complication is commonly encountered during one-lung anesthesia?**
   A. Hypocarbia
   B. Hypertension
   C. Hypoxemia
   D. Bradycardia

5. **Intraluminal airway masses are a contraindication for one-lung anesthesia.**
   A. True
   B. False

6. **A 66-year-old male presents to the hospital for a right lung lobectomy due to lung cancer. The patient undergoes right lung lobectomy under general anesthesia, with lung isolation achieved using a double lumen tube. The correct position of the DLT is confirmed with a fiberoptic bronchoscope, and adequate ventilation is confirmed before the start of the surgical procedure. One hour after the initiation of the surgical procedure, the patient develops hypoxemia, with a decrease in oxygen saturation below 90%. What is NOT a suggested management approach for hypoxemia during one-lung anesthesia?**
   A. Increase inspired oxygen
   B. Positive end-expiratory pressure 5-10 cm H_2O to the dependent lung
   C. Improve oxygenation by reducing cardiac output
   D. Continuous positive airway pressure 5-10 cm H_2O with 100% oxygen to the non-ventilated lung

Answers:

1. **Answer C (Complete functional separation of the lungs)**

   One-lung anesthesia involves the complete functional separation of the lungs. This process entails ventilating one lung while collapsing the other. While this technique facilitates certain types of surgery, such as thoracic procedures, it also presents significant physiological disadvantages due to the altered ventilation-perfusion ratio and potential for hypoxemia. Therefore, the primary objective of one-lung anesthesia is to achieve complete functional separation of the lungs to optimize surgical conditions while managing the associated physiological challenges.

2. **Answer D (Facilitation of surgical exposure in thoracic surgeries)**

   One of the primary indications for one-lung anesthesia is the facilitation of surgical exposure in thoracic surgeries. This technique allows surgeons better access to the thoracic cavity, enabling procedures such as pneumonectomy, lobectomy, thoracoscopy, esophageal surgery, thoracic aneurysm repair, and thoracic spinal surgery. By collapsing one lung while ventilating the other, surgeons can operate more effectively within the confined space of the chest cavity. Additionally, one-lung anesthesia helps to minimize contamination or spillage of infectious material from the contralateral lung and aids in controlling ventilation distribution in the presence of specific conditions such as bronchopleural fistula or giant unilateral cyst/bulla.

3. **Answer D (Double lumen tube (DLT))**

   The double-lumen tube (DLT) is the technique that allows for a rapid transition between one-lung ventilation and two-lung ventilation. It is the most commonly used technique for achieving lung isolation during thoracic surgeries. The DLT has two lumens, one for each lung, allowing for selective ventilation. By adjusting the position of the tube, an anesthesiologist can easily switch between ventilating both lungs simultaneously and isolating one lung for surgical procedures. This flexibility makes the DLT an essential tool in managing ventilation during thoracic surgeries where one-lung ventilation is required.

4. **Answer C (Hypoxemia)**

   Hypoxemia is one of the most important complications encountered during one-lung anesthesia. Factors contributing to hypoxemia during one-lung anesthesia include ventilation-perfusion mismatch, shunting of blood away from the ventilated lung, and reduced functional residual capacity of the collapsed lung. The anesthesia team must closely monitor oxygen levels and take appropriate measures to prevent and manage hypoxemia during one-lung anesthesia to ensure patient safety and optimal surgical conditions.

5. **Answer A (True)**

   Intraluminal airway masses are a contraindication for one-lung anesthesia. This is because these masses can obstruct airflow within the airways, potentially leading to further complications during the process of lung isolation and ventilation. Other contraindications include patients dependent on bilateral ventilation, hemodynamic instability, severe hypoxia, severe COPD, severe pulmonary hypertension, and known or suspected difficult intubation. The anesthesia team should carefully consider these contraindications when evaluating a patient's suitability for one-lung anesthesia to ensure patient safety and optimal outcomes.

6. **Answer C (Improve oxygenation by reducing cardiac output)**

   During one-lung anesthesia, maintaining adequate cardiac output is essential for tissue perfusion and oxygen delivery, making reducing cardiac output an inappropriate management approach for hypoxemia. Instead, suggested strategies include increasing inspired oxygen to 100%, applying positive end-expiratory pressure (PEEP) to the dependent lung to prevent atelectasis, and providing continuous positive airway pressure (CPAP) with 100% oxygen to the non-ventilated lung. Other interventions, such as checking the tube's position with a fiberoptic bronchoscope, ensuring adequate blood pressure and cardiac output, abandoning one-lung ventilation if hypoxemia persists, and early clamping of the appropriate pulmonary artery may be necessary in severe cases of hypoxemia.

Recommended literature

1. Mehrotra M, Jain A. Single Lung Ventilation. [Updated 2022 Jul 25]. In: StatPearls [Internet]. Treasure Island (FL): StatPearls Publishing; 2022 Jan-. Available from: https://www.ncbi.nlm.nih.gov/books/NBK538314/
2. Ashok V, Francis J. A practical approach to adult one-lung ventilation. BJA Educ. 2018;18(3):69-74.
3. Pollard BJ, Kitchen, G. Handbook of Clinical Anaesthesia. Fourth Edition. CRC Press. 2018. 978-1-4987-6289-2.

PREOPERATIVE FASTING

18
CHAPTER

Questions:

1. Which of the following factors is associated with increased gastric emptying?

    A. Sitting position

    B. Large duodenal volume

    C. Secretion of cholecystokinin

    D. Opioid administration

2. What is the recommended fasting time for clear liquids in healthy adults before procedures requiring general anesthesia?

    A. 4 hours

    B. 3 hours

    C. 2 hours

    D. 1 hour

3. Which of the following is NOT a recommended clear liquid for preoperative fasting?

    A. Water

    B. Black coffee

    C. Milk

    D. Juice without pulp

4. Which pharmacological agent is NOT associated with increased gastric emptying?

    A. Metoclopramide

    B. Erythromycin

    C. Domperidone

    D. Antimuscarinics

5. Hyperthyroidism is associated with decreased gastric emptying.

    A. True

    B. False

6. A 44-year-old obese patient with a BMI of 44 presents to the emergency department with symptoms suggestive of acute appendicitis. Given the urgency of the situation and the unclear information regarding preoperative fasting, the anesthesia team decides to use gastric ultrasound to estimate the gastric content and guide perioperative management. What is the recommended patient position for obtaining optimal sonographic views of the gastric antrum?

    A. Prone position

    B. Sitting position

    C. Supine position

    D. Right lateral decubitus position

Answers:

1. **Answer A (Sitting position)**

   Gastric emptying is influenced by various factors, including body position, gastric volume, and hormonal regulation. The sitting position, particularly for non-caloric liquids, promotes gastric emptying by leveraging gravity to assist in moving gastric contents more efficiently into the duodenum compared to other positions, like lying down. In contrast, factors such as large duodenal volume, secretion of cholecystokinin, and opioid administration typically slow gastric emptying, either by limiting the capacity of the duodenum or by inhibiting gastrointestinal motility and responsiveness.

2. **Answer C (2 hours)**

   Adults are advised to fast for a minimum of 2 hours for clear liquids. This recommendation aims to reduce the risk of pulmonary aspiration during anesthesia by ensuring that the stomach is relatively empty, thus minimizing the potential for regurgitation and aspiration of gastric contents into the lungs during surgery. While shorter fasting times may be acceptable for clear liquids compared to solid foods, it's crucial to follow the specific fasting recommendations provided by healthcare professionals to ensure patient safety during anesthesia.

3. **Answer C (Milk)**

   While water, black coffee, and juice without pulp are generally considered safe clear liquids for preoperative fasting until 2 hours before general anesthesia, milk is not recommended. Milk contains proteins and fats that can delay gastric emptying compared to other clear liquids. Therefore, protein-containing clear liquids like milk should be avoided before elective procedures requiring general anesthesia, regional anesthesia, or procedural sedation up to 6 hours before the procedure.

4. **Answer D (Antimuscarinics)**

   Pharmacological agents associated with increased gastric emptying include metoclopramide, domperidone, and erythromycin. Metoclopramide and domperidone exert prokinetic effects by antagonizing dopamine receptors in the gastrointestinal tract, thereby enhancing gastric emptying. Erythromycin, primarily known as an antibiotic, also stimulates gastrointestinal motility by acting as a motilin receptor agonist. Conversely, antimuscarinic agents, such as anticholinergics, work by blocking the action of acetylcholine at muscarinic receptors, leading to the inhibition of gastrointestinal motility and gastric emptying. Therefore, antimuscarinics are not associated with increased gastric emptying but rather have the opposite effect, slowing down gastric motility.

5. **Answer B (False)**

   Hyperthyroidism is associated with increased gastric emptying. Thyroid hormones, particularly triiodothyronine (T3), have been shown to enhance gastrointestinal motility, leading to accelerated gastric emptying. Therefore, hyperthyroidism, characterized by elevated levels of circulating thyroid hormones, can contribute to increased gastric emptying. Conversely, conditions such as hypothyroidism, characterized by decreased thyroid hormone levels, are associated with decreased gastric emptying. Other factors that can decrease gastric emptying include pain, anxiety and stress, trauma, pregnancy, alcohol ingestion, diabetes, pyloric stenosis, intestinal obstruction, and vagotomy.

6. **Answer D (Right lateral decubitus position)**

   Gastric ultrasound is valuable in various patient populations, including obese individuals, pregnant patients, and pediatric patients, among others. When performing gastric ultrasound, the aim is to accurately visualize the gastric antrum and assess its contents. Typically, an empty gastric antrum appears small, flat, and collapsed on ultrasound, with thick walls and no visible content. To achieve optimal sonographic views and facilitate accurate measurement of gastric volume, imaging the gastric antrum in both the supine and right lateral decubitus (RLD) positions is recommended. However, for obtaining the best possible visualization of the gastric antrum, particularly for accurate measurement of gastric volume, the right lateral decubitus position is preferred. This positioning encourages gravitational drainage of gastric content to the dependent antrum and enhances the sensitivity of ultrasound in detecting smaller volumes. Consequently, the right lateral decubitus position is the recommended patient position for obtaining optimal sonographic views of the gastric antrum, especially in urgent scenarios such as this case of acute appendicitis.

Recommended literature

1. Girish P. Joshi, Basem B. Abdelmalak, Wade A. Weigel, Monica W. Harbell, Catherine I. Kuo, Sulpicio G. Soriano, Paul A. Stricker, Tommie Tipton, Mark D. Grant, Anne M. Marbella, Madhulika Agarkar, Jaime F. Blanck, Karen B. Domino; 2023 American Society of Anesthesiologists Practice Guidelines for Preoperative Fasting: Carbohydrate-containing Clear Liquids with or without Protein, Chewing Gum, and Pediatric Fasting Duration—A Modular Update of the 2017 American Society of Anesthesiologists Practice Guidelines for Preoperative Fasting. Anesthesiology 2023; 138:132-151.
2. Fawcett, W.J., Thomas, M., 2019. Pre-operative fasting in adults and children: clinical practice and guidelines. Anaesthesia 74, 83–88.
3. Pollard BJ, Kitchen, G. Handbook of Clinical Anaesthesia. Fourth Edition. CRC Press. 2018. 978-1-4987-6289-2.
4. Mesbah, A., Thomas, M., 2017. Preoperative fasting in children. BJA Education 17, 346–350.
5. Wilson, G.R., Dorrington, K.L., 2017. Starvation before surgery: is our practice based on evidence?. BJA Education 17, 275–282.
6. Coté CJ. Preoperative preparation and premedication. Br J Anaesth. 1999;83(1):16-28.

Anesthetic techniques
PROLONGED ANESTHESIA

18
CHAPTER

Questions:

1. Which of the following complications is associated with prolonged immobility during anesthesia?

   A. Increased risk of myocardial infarction

   B. Compartment syndrome

   C. Corneal damage

   D. Postoperative shivering

2. Prolonged exposure to nitrous oxide can result in which of the following conditions?

   A. Acute vitamin C deficiency

   B. Megaloblastic anemia

   C. Hypokalemia

   D. Microcytic anemia

3. What effect can prolonged anesthesia have on renal function?

   A. Increased urine output

   B. Water and salt retention

   C. Decreased serum creatinine levels

   D. Enhanced glomerular filtration rate

4. What complication is associated with inadvertent perioperative hypothermia?

   A. Increased wound infection

   B. Impaired immune function

   C. Malignant arrhythmias

   D. All of the above

5. Prolonged anesthesia can decrease carbohydrate metabolism, leading to intraoperative hyperglycemia.

   A. True

   B. False

6. During the six-hour laparoscopic surgery for severe endometriosis, a 33-year-old female is positioned in the Trendelenburg position and kept under general anesthesia. As the surgery progresses, the anesthesia team monitors the patient closely for any signs of respiratory compromise due to the prolonged duration of anesthesia and the positioning. Which of the following is a potential consequence of prolonged anesthesia on gas exchange and respiratory mechanics?

   A. Hypocarbia

   B. Increased lung compliance

   C. Hypoxemia

   D. Pneumothorax

637

Answers:

1. Answer B (Compartment syndrome)

Prolonged immobility during anesthesia can lead to several complications, including an increased risk of deep vein thrombosis, nerve damage, pressure sores, bilateral compartment syndrome, rhabdomyolysis, and corneal damage if the eyes are left open. Compartment syndrome is a serious condition that occurs when increased pressure within a muscle compartment compromises the blood supply to the muscles and nerves within that compartment.

2. Answer B (Megaloblastic anemia)

Prolonged exposure to nitrous oxide can result in acute vitamin B12 deficiency, which can lead to megaloblastic anemia and neurological deficits. Nitrous oxide inactivates vitamin B12 by converting it to an inactive form, impairs the function of enzymes dependent on vitamin B12 for proper function. This can lead to megaloblastic anemia, characterized by the production of large, immature red blood cells. Nitrous oxide does not directly cause acute vitamin C deficiency, hypokalemia, or microcytic anemia.

3. Answer B (Water and salt retention)

Prolonged anesthesia can have various effects on renal function. Anesthetic agents can interfere with the normal regulation of water and electrolyte balance in the body, leading to water and salt retention. This can increase extracellular fluid volume and may contribute to the development of edema and hypertension.

4. Answer D (All of the above)

Inadvertent perioperative hypothermia can lead to several complications, including increased wound infection due to impaired wound healing and decreased immune function. It can also contribute to surgical bleeding by impairing platelet function and clotting cascade enzymes. Hypothermia increases the risk of malignant arrhythmias by affecting the electrical conduction system of the heart. Additionally, hypothermia can increase the incidence of myocardial ischemia and infarction by causing vasoconstriction and increasing myocardial oxygen demand. Finally, patients may experience postoperative shivering as a result of hypothermia.

5. Answer A (True)

Prolonged anesthesia can decrease carbohydrate metabolism, leading to intraoperative hyperglycemia. The stress of surgery and anesthesia disrupts the finely regulated balance between hepatic glucose production and glucose utilization in peripheral tissues, causing an increase in the secretion of counterregulatory hormones such as catecholamines, cortisol, glucagon, and growth hormone. This results in excessive release of inflammatory cytokines, including tumor necrosis factor-α, interleukin-6, and interleukin-1β. Cortisol increases hepatic glucose production, stimulates protein catabolism, and promotes gluconeogenesis, leading to elevated blood glucose levels. Catecholamines increase glucagon secretion and inhibit insulin release by pancreatic β-cells. Additionally, the increase in stress hormones leads to enhanced lipolysis and high free fatty acid (FFA) concentrations, which inhibit insulin-stimulated glucose uptake and limit glucose transport activity in skeletal muscle. TNF-α interferes with the synthesis and/or translocation of the glucose transporter GLUT-4, further reducing glucose uptake in peripheral tissues, ultimately resulting in an altered state of insulin action and intraoperative hyperglycemia.

6. Answer C (Hypoxemia)

During prolonged anesthesia, especially in the Trendelenburg position, patients are at risk of developing impaired gas exchange and respiratory mechanics, leading to conditions like hypoxemia and hypercarbia. These issues can arise due to the slow development of dependent atelectasis, where parts of the lungs collapse due to decreased ventilation. To prevent atelectasis, it's crucial to implement strategies such as using appropriate levels of positive end-expiratory pressure (PEEP) to keep the airways open and performing lung recruitment maneuvers to maintain lung volume. Additionally, employing lung protective ventilation strategies, such as limiting tidal volumes and avoiding excessive airway pressures, can help prevent lung injury and further improve gas exchange during prolonged anesthesia. These measures help to optimize gas exchange and respiratory function, reducing the risk of complications during and after surgery.

Recommended literature

1. Pollard BJ, Kitchen, G. Handbook of Clinical Anaesthesia. Fourth Edition. CRC Press. 2018. 978-1-4987-6289-2.
2. Cheng H, Clymer JW, Po-Han Chen B, et al. Prolonged operative duration is associated with complications: a systematic review and meta-analysis. J Surg Res. 2018;229:134-144.

Anesthetic techniques
TOTAL INTRAVENOUS ANESTHESIA (TIVA)

Questions:

1. **Which of the following is the best indication for Total Intravenous Anesthesia (TIVA)?**
   A. History of mild postoperative nausea and vomiting
   B. Patients with depleted intravascular volumes
   C. History of perioperative awareness
   D. Malignant hyperthermia susceptibility

2. **Which intravenous agent is the hypnotic agent of choice for TIVA for short operative procedures?**
   A. Ketamine
   B. Midazolam
   C. Propofol
   D. Etomidate

3. **What is a recommended practice when maintaining general anesthesia with propofol infusion?**
   A. Use manual dosing for better control
   B. Use a target-controlled infusion (TCI)
   C. Administer a fixed infusion rate throughout
   D. Use a bolus infusion only

4. **Which of the following is an advantage of TIVA?**
   A. Ability to assess actual blood levels accurately
   B. Low risk of accidental awareness
   C. Variability in patient response
   D. More predictable onset and stability of maintenance

5. **Opioids reduce the propofol dose required to produce loss of consciousness and to obtund movement and hemodynamic responses to noxious stimuli.**
   A. True
   B. False

6. **A 60-year-old patient with Charcot-Marie-Tooth disease is scheduled for elective cholecystectomy. Due to the possible connection between this disease and malignant hyperthermia, the decision is made to proceed with TIVA. Which of the following is NOT a safety measure for TIVA?**
   A. Using a processed EEG monitor
   B. Ensuring the cannula is visible or accessible
   C. Using an anti-reflux valve on the infusion set
   D. Mixing propofol and remifentanil in the same syringe for simplicity

Answers:

1. Answer D (Malignant hyperthermia susceptibility)

Total Intravenous Anesthesia (TIVA) is indicated for various clinical situations where the use of volatile anesthetics may not be suitable or may pose risks. Malignant hyperthermia susceptibility is an indication for TIVA because volatile anesthetics can trigger a potentially fatal reaction in these patients. TIVA can be used as an alternative to volatile anesthetics in these cases to avoid this risk. Other indications for TIVA include patients with long QT syndrome, a history of severe postoperative nausea and vomiting (PONV), surgery requiring neurophysiological monitoring, anesthesia in non-theatre environments, transfer of anesthetized patients between different locations, sedation in intensive care, tubeless ENT procedures and rigid bronchoscopy, thoracic surgery, intracranial surgery, and procedures requiring sedation (e.g., endoscopy, cardioversion).

2. Answer C (Propofol)

Propofol is the preferred hypnotic agent for TIVA for short operative procedures. It has several advantages, including rapid onset and offset of action, smooth induction and emergence, and minimal accumulation with prolonged infusion. Propofol can be titrated easily to achieve the desired level of sedation or anesthesia. In TIVA, propofol can be administered using target-controlled infusion (TCI), which allows for easy control and rapid change of the target propofol concentration based on the patient's response and the surgical stimulus. This helps to maintain a stable level of anesthesia throughout the procedure. For long procedures and in the ICU, midazolam is also an agent of choice for TIVA.

3. Answer B (Use a target-controlled infusion (TCI))

When maintaining general anesthesia with a propofol infusion, it is recommended to use a target-controlled infusion. TCI allows for precise control of the propofol concentration in the patient's plasma or 'brain' (effect-site). This method involves a TCI pump that is programmed with pharmacokinetic models for propofol. The anesthesia team selects the appropriate model based on the patient's characteristics (such as body weight and age) and inputs the target concentration. The pump then calculates the initial bolus and subsequent infusion rates to achieve and maintain the desired propofol concentration. Using TCI provides several advantages, including easy control and rapid adjustment of the target propofol concentration, leading to smoother anesthesia maintenance. It also allows for individualized dosing based on patient factors, which can improve the overall safety and efficacy of anesthesia.

4. Answer D (More predictable onset and stability of maintenance)

One of the advantages of TIVA is the more predictable onset and stability of maintenance compared to other forms of anesthesia. TIVA allows for precise control of the anesthetic drug concentration in the patient's body, leading to a smoother and more controlled anesthesia experience. This can result in more stable anesthesia levels throughout the procedure, reducing the risk of under or overdosing and providing a more consistent depth of anesthesia. TIVA also offers other advantages, such as faster recovery with fewer complications, the elimination of potential risks associated with volatile anesthetics, and the avoidance of drugs like nitrous oxide, which can have specific effects on the body. While TIVA has several advantages, it also has some disadvantages, including variability in patient response, the need for dedicated IV access, and a potential risk of accidental awareness. Despite these drawbacks, TIVA remains a valuable technique for anesthesia management, particularly in situations where other forms of anesthesia may not be suitable.

5. Answer A (True)

Opioids can reduce the propofol dose required to produce loss of consciousness and to obtund movement and hemodynamic responses to noxious stimuli. This is because opioids provide analgesia, which complements the hypnotic effects of propofol. Propofol itself does not have analgesic properties, so when opioids are used in conjunction with propofol, they can enhance the overall anesthetic effect, allowing for lower doses of propofol to be used. Short-acting opioids such as alfentanil and remifentanil are commonly used in TIVA to provide analgesia. These opioids can be titrated to achieve the desired level of analgesia, allowing for a more tailored and balanced anesthesia regimen.

6. Answer D (Mixing propofol and remifentanil in the same syringe for simplicity)

This practice is not a recommended safety measure for TIVA due to the risk of dosing errors and compromised patient safety. Safety measures for TIVA include ensuring the cannula is visible and accessible, checking the pump setup regularly, ensuring the drug concentration matches the programmed concentration, using anti-reflux and anti-siphon valves, and using a processed EEG monitor when a neuromuscular blocker is used. Mixing drugs in the same syringe can lead to inaccuracies in dosing and should be avoided to maintain control over the anesthesia regimen.

Recommended literature
1. Nimmo AF, Absalom AR, Bagshaw O, Biswas A, Cook TM, Costello A, et al. Guidelines for the safe practice of total intravenous anaesthesia (TIVA). Anaesthesia. 2019;74(2):211-24.
2. Pollard BJ, Kitchen, G. Handbook of Clinical Anaesthesia. Fourth Edition. CRC Press. 2018. 978-1-4987-6289-2.
3. Al-Rifai Z, Mulvey D. (2016). Principles of total intravenous anaesthesia: Basic pharmacokinetics and model descriptions. BJA Educ 16(3): 92-7.

Anesthetic techniques
VIDEOLARYNGOSCOPY

Questions:

1. Which of the following statements regarding videolaryngoscopy (VL) is true?
   A. VL requires a direct line of sight to visualize airway structures
   B. VL utilizes indirect laryngoscopy via a camera
   C. VL requires significant cervical manipulation
   D. VL is associated with higher rates of stress response

2. What is NOT the primary advantage of videolaryngoscopy over direct laryngoscopy?
   A. Easier to learn and maintain the skill
   B. Improved glottic visualization
   C. Higher first-pass success rate
   D. Helps in development/maintenance of direct laryngoscopy skill set

3. Which of the following is NOT a potential complication of videolaryngoscopy?
   A. Palatal perforation
   B. Dental or oropharyngeal soft tissue trauma during tube insertion
   C. Hypoxia during the intubation attempt
   D. Increased risk of PONV

4. What is a contraindication for videolaryngoscopy?
   A. Restricted mouth opening that blocks tube insertion
   B. Apnea or impending respiratory arrest
   C. Elective anesthesia
   D. Need for prolonged mechanical ventilation

5. CCL is a useful mnemonic aid used for preparing for videolaryngoscopy.
   A. True
   B. False

6. A resident with limited experience in videolaryngoscopy is in charge of anesthesia for a laparoscopic appendectomy. The patient has a Mallampati score of 3, indicating a possible difficult intubation. The resident is considering using VL for airway management and intubation. Which statement regarding the learning curve of VL is true?
   A. Novices require more intubations to achieve proficiency with VL than with direct laryngoscopy
   B. VL has a longer learning curve compared to direct laryngoscopy
   C. Inexperienced operators needed only a few intubations to achieve proficiency with VL
   D. VL is difficult to master, even for experienced anesthesiologists

Answers:

1. **Answer B (VL utilizes indirect laryngoscopy via a camera)**

   Unlike direct laryngoscopy (DL), which requires a direct line of sight to align airway axes, videolaryngoscopy (VL) uses a camera to visualize airway structures indirectly. This indirect visualization improves glottic visualization and reduces the need for significant cervical manipulation, which is often required with DL. VL also requires less force and is associated with lower rates of stress response compared to DL.

2. **Answer D (Helps in development/maintenance of DL skill set)**

   While it is true that VL offers advantages such as improved glottic visualization, higher first-pass success rates, and easier learning and maintenance of the skill compared to direct laryngoscopy, the primary advantage of VL is not to help in the development or maintenance of the DL skill set. Instead, VL provides a different approach to visualizing the airway that does not require aligning the airway axes for a line of sight, which can be challenging with DL. This unique advantage of indirect visualization contributes significantly to the effectiveness and safety of airway management with VL.

3. **Answer D (Increased risk of PONV (Postoperative nausea and vomiting))**

   Videolaryngoscopy is associated with several potential complications, including palatal perforation, palatopharyngeal arch tear, injury to tonsillar pillars, dental or oropharyngeal soft tissue trauma during tube insertion, vomiting and aspiration during tube insertion, incorrect tube placement (e.g., esophageal intubation), and hypoxia during the intubation attempt. However, an increased risk of postoperative nausea and vomiting is not typically considered a direct complication of VL. PONV is more commonly associated with factors such as anesthesia, surgery, and patient characteristics rather than the specific airway management technique used.

4. **Answer A (Restricted mouth opening that blocks tube insertion)**

   While videolaryngoscopy is a valuable tool for airway management in many situations, it may be contraindicated in cases where there is a restricted mouth opening that blocks tube insertion. This limitation can prevent the effective use of a videolaryngoscope to visualize the airway and guide the endotracheal tube placement. In such cases, alternative airway management techniques may be necessary. Other contraindications for videolaryngoscopy include an impassable upper airway obstruction, the presence of blood or emesis in the airway, the need for foreign body removal, and consciousness or the presence of a gag reflex.

5. **Answer A (True)**

   The mnemonic "CCL" is indeed a useful aid for preparing for videolaryngoscopy. It helps ensure that the necessary steps are taken to prepare for the procedure, including choosing the right tube, checking the endotracheal tube cuff, lubricating the stylet and tube, and loading the stylet appropriately.

6. **Answer C (Inexperienced operators needed only a few intubations to achieve proficiency with VL)**

   Videolaryngoscopy has a faster learning curve compared to DL, regardless of whether the operator is a novice or an experienced laryngoscopist. Novices trained with VL achieved a 69% endotracheal intubation (ETI) success rate, while anesthesiologists achieved a 99.6% ETI success rate on their first use of the videolaryngoscope. This indicates that inexperienced operators needed only a few (less than ten) intubations to achieve proficiency with VL.

Recommended literature

1. Asai T, Jagannathan N. Videolaryngoscopy Is Extremely Valuable, But Should It Be the Standard for Tracheal Intubation?. Anesth Analg. 2023;136(4):679–682.
2. Prekker ME, Driver BE, Trent SA, et al. Video versus Direct Laryngoscopy for Tracheal Intubation of Critically Ill Adults [published online ahead of print, 2023 Jun 16]. N Engl J Med. 2023;10.1056/NEJMoa2301601.
3. Hansel, J., Rogers, A.M., Lewis, S.R., Cook, T.M., Smith, A.F., 2022. Videolaryngoscopy versus direct laryngoscopy for adults undergoing tracheal intubation: a Cochrane systematic review and meta-analysis update. British Journal of Anaesthesia 129, 612–623.
4. Goranović, T., 2021. Videolaryngoscopy, the Current Role in Airway Management. https://doi.org/10.5772/intechopen.93490
5. Pollard BJ, Kitchen, G. Handbook of Clinical Anaesthesia. Fourth Edition. CRC Press. 2018. 978-1-4987-6289-2.
6. Chemsian R, Bhananker S, Ramaiah R. Videolaryngoscopy. Int J Crit Illn Inj Sci. 2014;4(1):35–41.

TOXICITIES

BETA-BLOCKER OVERDOSE

Questions:

1. Beta-blockers are employed in the treatment of various medical conditions. Among the provided options, which condition is NOT typically addressed using beta-blockers?
    A. Hypothyroidism
    B. Migraine
    C. Anxiety
    D. Hemangiomas

2. Which of the following symptoms is NOT associated with beta-blocker overdose?
    A. Atrioventricular Nodal Reentry Tachycardia
    B. Blurred vision
    C. Confusion
    D. Hyperkalemia

3. Which beta-blocker is associated with the risk of Torsades de pointes?
    A. Metoprolol
    B. Atenolol
    C. Propranolol
    D. Sotalol

4. In the context of beta-blocker overdose, metabolic acidosis is commonly associated with which electrolyte imbalance?
    A. Hyperkalemia
    B. Hypoglycemia
    C. Hyponatremia
    D. Hypomagnesemia

5. Patients with no history of asthma can potentially experience life-threatening bronchospasm as a complication of beta-blocker therapy.
    A. True
    B. False

6. A 55-year-old male patient is brought to the emergency department with altered mental status and severe hypotension. The patient's family reports that he has a history of hypertension and has been prescribed beta blockers for his condition. On examination, the patient's blood pressure is 100/50 mmHg, heart rate is 40 beats per minute, and he appears confused. His ECG shows bradycardia and conduction disturbances. The family mentions that they suspect he might have taken more of his prescribed medications accidentally. What would be the first-line therapeutic approach for managing bradycardia and hypotension linked to beta-blocker overdose?
    A. Fluid therapy 20 mL/kg
    B. Epinephrine 50-100 mcg/min
    C. Insulin 1 U/kg/hr insulin + 1g/kg/hr glucose
    D. Atropine 0,01-0,03 mg/kg IV

Answers:

1. **Answer A (Hypothyroidism)**

Beta-blockers are employed in the management of an array of cardiovascular conditions, including angina, heart failure, atrial fibrillation, heart attack, and high blood pressure. They are also used to prevent migraines and treat hyperthyroidism. Additionally, beta-blockers are utilized for managing anxiety conditions, tremors, and glaucoma. Notably, beta-blockers have shown effectiveness in treating hemangiomas in children.

2. **Answer A (Atrioventricular Nodal Reentry Tachycardia)**

Beta-blocker overdose is typically not associated with Atrioventricular Nodal Reentry Tachycardia (AVNRT). However, it can lead to a diverse range of symptoms spanning different physiological systems. Respiratory effects may include bronchospasm, while the visual system might experience symptoms like blurred or double vision. Cardiovascular manifestations can encompass hypotension, bradycardia, AV block, and even heart failure. Metabolic imbalances like hypoglycemia and hyperkalemia are possible, and within the nervous system, symptoms range from weakness and nervousness to drowsiness, confusion, seizures, fever, stupor, and coma. The severity and presentation of these symptoms depend on factors like the specific beta-blocker ingested and the amount consumed, underscoring the need for prompt medical attention to address these wide-ranging effects.

3. **Answer D (Sotalol)**

Among the listed beta-blockers, sotalol stands out as having an association with the risk of Torsades de pointes (TdP), a potentially dangerous arrhythmia characterized by a distinctive twisting pattern on electrocardiograms (ECGs). Sotalol's dual nature as a beta-blocker and class III antiarrhythmic agent contributes to the prolongation of QT intervals on ECGs, creating a vulnerable period where TdP can emerge. Therefore, when sotalol is prescribed, careful monitoring of the QT interval is essential to detect any QT prolongation and to take appropriate measures to prevent the occurrence of Torsades de pointes).

4. **Answer A (Hyperkalemia)**

In the context of beta-blocker overdose, metabolic acidosis is commonly associated with hyperkalemia, which refers to elevated levels of potassium in the bloodstream. Beta-blockers can lead to a decrease in the activity of the sodium-potassium pump in cellular membranes. This reduction in pump activity impairs the uptake of potassium into cells, resulting in an accumulation of potassium in the blood. The elevated levels of potassium can disrupt the acid-base balance in the body and contribute to metabolic acidosis.

5. **Answer A (True)**

Despite having no previous history of asthma, a patient can still develop severe bronchospasm as a potential complication of beta-blocker therapy. Beta-blockers, particularly non-selective ones, can antagonize beta-2 receptors in the bronchial smooth muscles, leading to their constriction and resulting in bronchospasm. This can be dangerous, especially in patients with underlying respiratory conditions, and underscores the importance of careful evaluation and monitoring when prescribing beta-blockers, even to individuals without a history of asthma.

6. **Answer A (Fluid therapy 20 mL/kg)**

Administering 20 mL/kg of isotonic intravenous fluids and positioning the patient in the Trendelenburg position is the first-line approach for managing hypotension associated with beta-blocker overdose. If the patient does not respond adequately to this initial intervention, further therapeutic options may be considered, including inotropes, vasopressors, glucagon, gastric decontamination, benzodiazepines for seizures, hemodialysis, cardiac pacing, high-dose insulin, intravenous calcium, and extracorporeal membrane oxygenation (ECMO). These interventions can address the complex cardiovascular effects of beta-blocker overdose and help stabilize the patient's condition effectively.

Recommended literature

1. Shepherd G. Treatment of poisoning caused by beta-adrenergic and calcium-channel blockers. Am J Health Syst Pharm. 2006;63(19):1828-1835.

CALCIUM CHANNEL BLOCKER TOXICITY

19
CHAPTER

Questions:

1. **What is the predominant site of action of calcium channel blockers (CCBs)?**
   A. Sinoatrial node (SA) and atrioventricular node (AV)
   B. Atria and ventricles
   C. Purkinje fibers
   D. Bundle of His

2. **What is a common symptom of CCB toxicity?**
   A. Metabolic alkalosis
   B. Tachycardia
   C. Hyperkalemia
   D. Hypotension

3. **Which of the following ECG findings is associated with CCB toxicity?**
   A. Atrial fibrillation
   B. Shortened QT interval
   C. Bradycardia
   D. Ventricular tachycardia

4. **How soon after ingestion do symptoms of CCB overdose typically occur?**
   A. Immediately
   B. Within 1 hour
   C. Within 6 hours
   D. After 24 hours

5. **Hyperglycemia is a common finding in patients with calcium channel blocker toxicity.**
   A. True
   B. False

6. **A 45-year-old male is brought to the emergency department (ED) by ambulance after ingesting an unknown quantity of verapamil tablets approximately 8 hours ago. The patient is conscious but appears lethargic and confused. He complains of dizziness, fatigue, nausea, vomiting, and difficulty breathing. On examination, his vital signs reveal hypotension (blood pressure 80/50 mmHg), bradycardia (heart rate 45 bpm), and hyperglycemia (blood glucose 200 mg/dL). Arterial blood gas analysis shows metabolic acidosis. What is the management for calcium channel blocker toxicity in this patient?**
   A. Sodium bicarbonate
   B. Glucagon
   C. Insulin and glucose
   D. All of the above

Answers:

1. Answer A (Sinoatrial node (SA) and atrioventricular node (AV))

Calcium channel blockers (CCBs) target the L-type voltage-gated calcium channels, which are predominantly found in the SA node and AV node. These channels play a crucial role in depolarization of the SA node and impulse propagation through the AV node, influencing heart rate and conduction. By blocking these channels, CCBs can slow down heart rate and reduce conduction velocity, making them effective in treating conditions such as hypertension, supraventricular tachycardia, and angina.

2. Answer D (Hypotension)

Hypotension is a common symptom of calcium channel blocker toxicity. CCBs block calcium channels in vascular smooth muscle, leading to vasodilation and a decrease in blood pressure. This can result in symptoms such as dizziness, lightheadedness, and even shock in severe cases. Other common symptoms of CCB toxicity include bradycardia, altered mental status, metabolic acidosis, and pulmonary edema.

3. Answer C (Bradycardia)

Bradycardia is a common ECG finding associated with CCB toxicity. CCBs can block calcium channels in the heart's conduction system, leading to a slowing of the heart rate. Other ECG findings that may be seen in CCB toxicity include QT prolongation, bundle branch block, first-degree atrioventricular block, junctional rhythms, and sinus tachycardia (with dihydropyridine CCBs).

4. Answer C (Within 6 hours)

Symptoms of calcium channel blocker overdose typically occur within six hours after ingestion. However, it's important to note that some formulations of CCBs, particularly extended-release formulations, can have delayed onset of symptoms, which may not manifest until after 24 hours. Therefore, patients should be monitored closely for an extended period, even if symptoms do not appear immediately.

5. Answer A (True)

Hyperglycemia is a common finding in patients with calcium channel blocker toxicity. CCBs inhibit insulin release from pancreatic beta cells, leading to elevated blood glucose levels. Additionally, CCBs interfere with calcium-stimulated mitochondrial action and glucose catabolism, contributing to hyperglycemia. Hyperglycemia is a useful clinical marker for the severity of CCB poisoning and should be monitored and managed accordingly.

6. Answer D (All of the above)

The management for calcium channel blocker toxicity in this patient should include all of the above options. Given the patient's presentation with hypotension, bradycardia, hyperglycemia, and metabolic acidosis, these interventions are aimed at stabilizing hemodynamics, reversing the effects of CCB overdose, and managing associated metabolic abnormalities. Sodium bicarbonate can help correct the metabolic acidosis and may improve cardiovascular function. Glucagon can be effective in reversing the cardiovascular effects of CCB overdose, particularly in cases of severe bradycardia or hypotension. Insulin and glucose therapy can help improve tissue perfusion and counteract the hypoinsulinemia and hyperglycemia seen in CCB toxicity. Additionally, supportive measures such as airway and ventilator support, gut decontamination if appropriate, and fluid resuscitation should be initiated. Monitoring for complications such as pulmonary edema is also important.

Recommended literature

1. Alshaya, O.A., Alhamed, A., Althewaibi, S., Fetyani, I., Alshehri, S., Alnashmi, F., Alharbi, S., Alrashed, M., Alqifari, S.F., Alshaya, A.I., 2022. Calcium Channel Blocker Toxicity: A Practical Approach. Journal of Multidisciplinary Healthcare Volume 15, 1851–1862.
2. Jackson, R., Bellamy, M., 2015. Antihypertensive drugs. BJA Education 15, 280–285.
3. St-Onge M, Dubé PA, Gosselin S, et al. Treatment for calcium channel blocker poisoning: a systematic review. Clin Toxicol (Phila). 2014;52(9):926-944.
4. Kerns W 2nd. Management of beta-adrenergic blocker and calcium channel antagonist toxicity. Emerg Med Clin North Am. 2007;25(2):309-viii.

CARBON MONOXIDE POISONING

19
CHAPTER

Questions:

1. **Which of the following is a mechanism of carbon monoxide (CO) intoxication?**

   A. Increased oxygen delivery to tissues

   B. Competitive inhibition of cytochrome oxidase

   C. Decreased hemoglobin affinity for oxygen

   D. Stimulation of the respiratory center in the brain

2. **Which of the following is NOT a common symptom of carbon monoxide poisoning?**

   A. Headache

   B. Nausea

   C. Confusion

   D. Muscle weakness

3. **What is the effect of carbon monoxide on the oxygen dissociation curve?**

   A. Shift to the right, enhancing oxygen unloading

   B. Shift to the left, impeding oxygen unloading

   C. No effect on the curve

   D. Increases the curve slope

4. **How is carbon monoxide poisoning diagnosed?**

   A. Standard SpO2 measurement

   B. ECG findings of ischemia

   C. HbCO level measurement

   D. Clinically significant alkalosis

5. **Diagnosis of carbon monoxide poisoning is confirmed by low SpO2 level.**

   A. True

   B. False

6. **A 60-year-old woman with a medical history of depression, anxiety, and prior suicide attempts is brought to the emergency department by ambulance after being found unconscious in an enclosed garage with the car engine running. On arrival, she is confused and has an altered mental status. Her heart rate is 130 beats per minute, and her blood pressure is 85/50 mm Hg. An initial arterial blood gas analysis reveals a pH of 7.30, Pco2 of 34 mm Hg, Po2 of 390 mm Hg, bicarbonate of 17 mEq/L, and a carboxyhemoglobin level of 24.0%. What is the recommended initial treatment for a patient with suspected carbon monoxide poisoning?**

   A. High-flow normobaric oxygen therapy

   B. Administration of hydroxocobalamin

   C. Intravenous fluids

   D. Hyperbaric oxygen therapy

Answers:

1. **Answer B (Competitive inhibition of cytochrome oxidase)**

   Carbon monoxide (CO) intoxication primarily occurs through the competitive inhibition of cytochrome oxidase, a key mitochondrial enzyme involved in cellular respiration. CO binds to cytochrome oxidase with high affinity, impairing its ability to utilize oxygen for cellular energy production. This mechanism leads to tissue hypoxia despite normal or even elevated levels of oxygen in the blood. Additionally, CO also binds to hemoglobin, reducing its oxygen-carrying capacity and further contributing to tissue hypoxia. CO poisoning causes impaired oxygen delivery and utilization as well as the generation of reactive oxygen species. It diffuses rapidly across the pulmonary capillary membrane and is eliminated based on the degree of oxygenation and minute ventilation.

2. **Answer D (Muscle weakness)**

   Muscle weakness is not commonly reported as a symptom of carbon monoxide poisoning. The most common symptoms of CO poisoning include headache, nausea, confusion, dizziness, and drowsiness. Other less common symptoms may include vomiting, cough/choking, shortness of breath, syncope, and throat or eye irritation. Muscle weakness is not typically listed among the common symptoms of CO poisoning. It's important to note that the clinical presentation of CO poisoning can vary widely, and symptoms may depend on factors such as the level and duration of exposure, individual susceptibility, and comorbid conditions.

3. **Answer B (Shift to the left, impeding oxygen unloading)**

   Carbon monoxide binds to hemoglobin with approximately 240 times the affinity of oxygen, forming carboxyhemoglobin (COHb). This binding induces an allosteric change that greatly diminishes the ability of the other three oxygen-binding sites in hemoglobin to release oxygen to peripheral tissues. As a result, CO causes a leftward shift in the oxygen dissociation curve, which means that hemoglobin holds onto oxygen more tightly and is less able to release it to tissues. This shift impedes oxygen unloading, contributing to tissue hypoxia in CO poisoning.

4. **Answer C (HbCO level measurement)**

   The diagnosis of CO poisoning is made by measuring the level of carboxyhemoglobin in the blood. This is typically done using co-oximetry, which can accurately measure COHb levels in venous blood samples. Elevated COHb levels confirm exposure to CO, although the level may not precisely indicate the severity of poisoning. In patients with symptoms such as loss of consciousness, altered mental status, or cardiac ischemia, any abnormally elevated COHb level should be considered indicative of severe poisoning, regardless of the specific level.

5. **Answer B (False)**

   Standard pulse oximetry (SpO2) cannot be used to diagnose or confirm carbon monoxide poisoning. This is because SpO2 measures the oxygen saturation of hemoglobin, but it cannot distinguish between oxygenated hemoglobin (O2Hb) and carboxyhemoglobin. In CO poisoning, the presence of COHb can lead to a falsely normal or even elevated SpO2 reading, despite the patient being hypoxic. Therefore, SpO2 is not a reliable indicator of CO poisoning, and the diagnosis must be confirmed by measuring the level of COHb in the blood using co-oximetry.

6. **Answer A (High-flow normobaric oxygen therapy)**

   In the management of suspected carbon monoxide poisoning, the primary goal is to rapidly eliminate CO from the body and restore tissue oxygenation. The recommended initial treatment is high-flow normobaric oxygen therapy. This involves administering 100 percent oxygen via a nonrebreathing face mask to displace CO from hemoglobin and reduce carboxyhemoglobin levels. This treatment is crucial as CO binds to hemoglobin with a higher affinity than oxygen, leading to tissue hypoxia. Additionally, supportive care and monitoring for complications such as neurological sequelae and cardiac dysfunction are essential. In severe cases, hyperbaric oxygen therapy may be considered to further enhance CO elimination.

Recommended literature

1. Chenoweth JA, Albertson TE, Greer MR. Carbon Monoxide Poisoning. Crit Care Clin. 2021;37(3):657-672.
2. Horncastle, E., Lumb, A.B., 2019. Hyperoxia in anaesthesia and intensive care. BJA Education 19, 176-182.
3. Gill, P., Martin, R.V., 2015. Smoke inhalation injury. BJA Education 15, 143-148.

COCAINE INTOXICATION

Questions:

1. **What is the primary mechanism of action of cocaine?**
   A. Direct activation of opioid receptors
   B. Indirect sympathomimetic effect
   C. Inhibition of acetylcholinesterase
   D. Blockade of NMDA receptors

2. **What is the main danger in an overdose of cocaine?**
   A. Central nervous system depression
   B. Respiratory depression
   C. Cardiovascular complications
   D. Renal failure

3. **Which of the following is a common cardiovascular complication of cocaine intoxication?**
   A. Hypotension
   B. Bradycardia
   C. Acute coronary syndrome
   D. Shortened QT interval

4. **What is the antidote for cocaine intoxication?**
   A. Flumazenil
   B. Naloxone
   C. Physostigmine
   D. There is no specific antidote

5. **Miosis is a common peripheral sympathomimetic effect of cocaine.**
   A. True
   B. False

6. **A 28-year-old male is brought to the emergency department by paramedics after being found in a state of agitation and aggression in a public area. According to witnesses, he had been exhibiting bizarre behavior, including talking to himself and appearing paranoid. The patient is known to have a history of cocaine use and was reportedly intoxicated with cocaine approximately 2 hours before the presentation. On examination, the patient is tachycardic with a heart rate of 130 beats per minute and hypertensive with a blood pressure of 160/90 mmHg. He is diaphoretic and has mydriasis (dilated pupils). He appears restless and is experiencing myoclonic movements. He is also exhibiting signs of euphoria alternating with anxiety, dysphoria, and agitation. There are no signs of trauma or other obvious injuries. What is the first-line treatment for this patient?**
   A. Midazolam
   B. Fluid treatment
   C. Dantrolene
   D. Beta-blocker

Answers:

1. Answer B (Indirect sympathomimetic effect)

The primary mechanism of action of cocaine is its indirect sympathomimetic effect, leading to increased levels of catecholamines such as dopamine, norepinephrine, and epinephrine. This effect results in rapid euphoria, a sensation of power, and tirelessness upon intranasal or intravenous administration. At higher doses, cocaine can cause agitation, insomnia, hallucinations, and seizures. These effects are mediated by the increase in catecholamines acting at central receptors, with peripheral effects of sympathetic stimulation, including increased heart rate and blood pressure, also prominent. Overall, cocaine intoxication refers to the subjective, desired, and adverse effects of cocaine on the mind and behavior of users, primarily driven by its indirect sympathomimetic actions.

2. Answer C (Cardiovascular complications)

The main danger in an overdose of cocaine is the risk of severe cardiovascular complications. Cocaine can cause various cardiovascular effects, including tachycardia, hypertension, arrhythmias, and acute coronary syndromes (vasospastic and/or thrombotic). These complications can lead to serious consequences such as myocardial infarction, stroke, or sudden cardiac death. Therefore, the primary concern in managing a cocaine overdose is addressing these cardiovascular complications.

3. Answer C (Acute coronary syndrome)

Acute coronary syndrome (ACS) is a common cardiovascular complication of cocaine intoxication. Cocaine can cause vasospasm or thrombosis in coronary arteries, leading to ACS, which includes conditions such as unstable angina, non-ST-segment elevation myocardial infarction (NSTEMI), and ST-segment elevation myocardial infarction (STEMI). Other cardiovascular complications of cocaine intoxication include tachycardia, hypertension, arrhythmias, cardiac conduction abnormalities, QT prolongation, and aortic dissection.

4. Answer D (There is no specific antidote)

There is currently no specific antidote for cocaine intoxication. Management of cocaine intoxication is primarily supportive and symptomatic. This may include interventions to manage cardiovascular complications, such as arrhythmias or hypertension, as well as addressing neurological symptoms like seizures or agitation. Additionally, supportive care may involve measures to manage hyperthermia and monitor for other potential complications of cocaine intoxication. While medications such as benzodiazepines may be used to manage symptoms, there is no specific medication that can reverse the effects of cocaine itself.

5. Answer B (False)

Miosis, or constriction of the pupil, is not a common peripheral sympathomimetic effect of cocaine. Instead, cocaine typically causes mydriasis, or dilation of the pupil, as part of its sympathomimetic actions. Mydriasis, along with other effects such as sweating and tremors, is more commonly observed in individuals experiencing cocaine intoxication. Miosis, on the other hand, is often associated with opioid use rather than cocaine use.

6. Answer A (Midazolam)

Given the patient's presentation of agitation and aggression, the first-line treatment would be to sedate him with a benzodiazepine such as midazolam. A wild, combative patient intoxicated with cocaine may be sedated with lorazepam or midazolam, both of which can be adequately absorbed via the intramuscular route if intravenous access is unobtainable. Midazolam is particularly attractive because its short duration of effect more closely matches the toxicodynamics of cocaine and is, therefore, less likely to produce oversedation when cocaine has worn off. It is reasonable to start with 1–2 mg doses of midazolam (or 5–10 mg doses of diazepam) intravenously with repeat dosing every 3–5 min until sedation occurs. When intravenous access has not yet been achieved, either midazolam (5–10 mg) or lorazepam (2–4 mg) intramuscularly may be acceptable. Diazepam should not be given intramuscularly because of erratic absorption.

Recommended literature

1. Kramers C. et al. Toxicologische behandel informatie: Cocaine, 2020, accessed 25/01/2023, https://toxicologie.org/cocaine.
2. Nicholson Roberts, T., Thompson, J.P., 2013. Illegal substances in anaesthetic and intensive care practices. Continuing Education in Anaesthesia Critical Care & Pain 13, 42–46.
3. Jenkins BJ. 2002. Drug abusers and anaesthesia, BJA CEPD Reviews. 2;1:15-19.

Toxicities
CYANIDE POISONING

19
CHAPTER

Questions:

1. **What is the mechanism of cyanide poisoning?**
   A. Inhibition of acetylcholinesterase
   B. Inhibition of oxidative phosphorylation
   C. Stimulation of NMDA receptors
   D. Activation of potassium channels

2. **How does cyanide poisoning affect the cellular metabolism?**
   A. Increases ATP production
   B. Inhibits ATP production
   C. Enhances oxygen delivery to cells
   D. Activates anaerobic respiration

3. **What is the smell often associated with cyanide poisoning?**
   A. Fishy odor
   B. Garlic odor
   C. Bitter almond odor
   D. Rotten egg odor

4. **How can cyanide poisoning be diagnosed?**
   A. Measurement of methemoglobin level
   B. Measurement of carboxyhemoglobin level
   C. Elevated anion gap acidosis
   D. All of the above

5. **Carbon monoxide inhalation is a differential diagnosis in cases of suspected cyanide poisoning.**
   A. True
   B. False

6. **A 4-year-old boy presents to the emergency department (ED) with vomiting and sudden unconsciousness after ingesting approximately 15-20 apricot kernels. He became unconscious 30 minutes after ingestion and remained so until arrival at the hospital. On examination, he is comatose with a Glasgow Coma Scale (GCS) score of 8, tachycardic, and tachypneic. Arterial blood gas analysis shows metabolic acidosis and lactic acidosis. The anion gap is increased. Based on the history and clinical findings, he is diagnosed with acute cyanide poisoning. What is the most appropriate next step in management?**
   A. Start intravenous fluids
   B. Administer hydroxocobalamin
   C. Perform endotracheal intubation
   D. Monitor for signs of respiratory distress

Answers:

1. Answer B (Inhibition of oxidative phosphorylation)

Cyanide poisoning occurs due to the inhibition of oxidative phosphorylation. Cyanide binds to the enzyme cytochrome C oxidase (also known as complex IV) in the mitochondrial electron transport chain, blocking the transfer of electrons to oxygen. This prevents the formation of ATP, which is essential for cellular energy production. As a result, cellular respiration is halted, leading to cellular hypoxia and the depletion of ATP. The toxicity of cyanide is primarily linked to the cessation of aerobic cell metabolism, which can have serious consequences, especially in organs with high oxygen demand, such as the brain and heart.

2. Answer B (Inhibits ATP production)

Cyanide poisoning inhibits ATP production in cells. Cyanide binds to the enzyme cytochrome C oxidase in the mitochondria, which is crucial for the final step in the electron transport chain that produces ATP. By binding to this enzyme, cyanide blocks the transport of electrons and prevents the synthesis of ATP. This leads to cellular hypoxia and a depletion of ATP, disrupting cellular metabolism and eventually causing metabolic acidosis.

3. Answer C (Bitter almond odor)

Cyanide poisoning is often associated with a bitter almond odor, although not everyone can detect it. This odor is due to the presence of hydrogen cyanide, which has a characteristic smell resembling bitter almonds. However, it's important to note that not all cases of cyanide poisoning may present with this odor, and relying solely on odor for diagnosis is not reliable.

4. Answer D (All of the above)

Cyanide poisoning can be diagnosed using a combination of clinical presentation and laboratory tests. Measurement of methemoglobin and carboxyhemoglobin levels can help in the diagnosis, as both can be elevated in cyanide poisoning. Additionally, cyanide poisoning often presents with metabolic acidosis characterized by an elevated anion gap. Other laboratory findings may include elevated lactate levels (> 7 mmol/L) and a reduced arteriovenous oxygen gradient. Combining these findings with a history of cyanide exposure or characteristic symptoms can help confirm the diagnosis of cyanide poisoning.

5. Answer A (True)

Carbon monoxide inhalation is a significant consideration in cases of suspected cyanide poisoning. Both cyanide and carbon monoxide poisoning can present with similar symptoms, such as altered mental status, hypotension, and lactic acidosis. However, there are key differences between the two conditions. Patients with carbon monoxide poisoning typically improve when removed from the smoke-filled area and given 100% oxygen. Seizures are common in cyanide poisoning but rare in carbon monoxide poisoning. Additionally, carbon monoxide does not affect the pupils, while cyanide poisoning causes pupillary dilation. Other possible differential diagnoses for patients presenting with similar symptoms include ingestions of tricyclic antidepressants, isoniazid, organophosphates, and salicylates.

6. Answer B (Administer hydroxocobalamin)

Hydroxocobalamin is an effective antidote for cyanide poisoning. It works by binding to cyanide to form cyanocobalamin, which is nontoxic and can be excreted in the urine. Hydroxocobalamin does not induce methemoglobinemia, unlike some other antidotes, and has fewer side effects. It is considered the first choice of therapy for cyanide poisoning if available. In the management of acute cyanide poisoning, the initial step involves supportive care, including stabilizing vital signs (ABCs) and establishing intravenous access. Gastric decontamination with activated charcoal should be performed within the first 1 to 4 hours after ingestion. Oxygen therapy is crucial to compete with cyanide for cytochrome oxidase binding sites and to reactivate mitochondrial enzymes. The specific antidote, such as hydroxocobalamin, should be administered as soon as possible to bind and neutralize cyanide. Other antidotes like dicobalt edetate have potential adverse effects and limited use in pediatric patients.

Recommended literature

1. Gill, P., Martin, R.V., 2015. Smoke inhalation injury. BJA Education 15, 143–148.
2. Huzar TF, George T, Cross JM. Carbon monoxide and cyanide toxicity: etiology, pathophysiology, and treatment in inhalation injury. Expert Rev Respir Med. 2013;7(2):159-170.

DIGOXIN TOXICITY

Questions:

1. **What is the primary mechanism of action of digoxin toxicity?**
    A. Inhibition of sodium-potassium ATPase
    B. Inhibition of calcium channels
    C. Activation of beta receptors
    D. Inhibition of sodium channels

2. **Which of the following is NOT a common symptom of acute digoxin toxicity?**
    A. Nausea
    B. Bradycardia
    C. Hyperkalemia
    D. Hypercalcemia

3. **Which of the following is a risk factor for digoxin toxicity?**
    A. High magnesium levels
    B. Low calcium levels
    C. High potassium levels
    D. Low potassium levels

4. **Which of the following is a characteristic ECG finding in digoxin toxicity?**
    A. ST elevation
    B. Ventricular fibrillation
    C. Normal sinus rhythm
    D. Downsloping ST depression

5. **Hyperkalemia is characteristic of digoxin toxicity.**
    A. True
    B. False

6. A 22-year-old man was admitted to the coronary care unit through the emergency department with complaints of abdominal pain, reduced urine output, loss of appetite, weight loss, and constipation for the past week. His medical history included acyanotic congenital heart disease and congestive cardiac failure (Class IV). On examination, the patient was found to be in atrial fibrillation (AF) with a pulse rate of 40 beats per minute (irregular). His jugular venous pressure (JVP) was elevated up to the angle of the mandible, and the "A" wave was absent. He also had pedal edema up to the knee and facial puffiness. His ECG showed AF with ventricular bigeminy and complete heart block, suggestive of digoxin toxicity. Laboratory tests revealed a sodium level of 115 mmol/L (normal range: 136–145 mmol/L) and potassium level of 6.12 mmol/L (normal range: 3.5–5 mmol/L). Serum digoxin concentration was not available. What is the treatment for severe digoxin toxicity?
    A. Calcium supplementation
    B. Magnesium sulfate
    C. Digibind
    D. Atropine

Answers:

1. **Answer A (Inhibition of sodium-potassium ATPase)**

   Digoxin inhibits the sodium-potassium ATPase pump, which is the primary mechanism of action in digoxin toxicity. This inhibition leads to an increase in intracellular sodium, which leads to increased intracellular calcium due to reduced calcium expulsion through the sodium-calcium exchanger. The increased intracellular calcium levels contribute to increased inotropy of the heart. Additionally, digoxin increases parasympathetic (vagal) tone, which reduces conduction through the atrioventricular (AV) node.

2. **Answer D (Hypercalcemia)**

   Hypercalcemia is not a common symptom of acute digoxin toxicity. Acute digoxin toxicity is more commonly associated with gastrointestinal symptoms such as nausea, vomiting, and diarrhea, as well as cardiovascular symptoms such as tachyarrhythmias (e.g., atrial fibrillation with AV block, ventricular tachycardia), bradyarrhythmias, hypotension, and shock. Central nervous system symptoms such as lethargy and confusion can also occur. Hyperkalemia, not hypercalcemia, is a metabolic symptom of acute digoxin toxicity.

3. **Answer D (Low potassium levels)**

   Low potassium levels are a well-known risk factor for digoxin toxicity. Hypokalemia can potentiate the effects of digoxin on cardiac tissue, leading to an increased risk of toxicity. Other risk factors for digoxin toxicity include low magnesium levels and high calcium levels.

4. **Answer D (Downsloping ST depression)**

   A characteristic ECG finding in digoxin toxicity is downsloping ST depression with a characteristic "reverse tick" or "Salvador Dali sagging" appearance. This is often accompanied by other ECG changes, such as flattened, inverted, or biphasic T waves and a shortened QT interval. It's important to note that the presence of these ECG changes alone is not a marker of digoxin toxicity; it simply indicates that the patient is taking digoxin.

5. **Answer A (True)**

   Hyperkalemia is characteristic of digoxin toxicity. Digoxin inhibits the sodium-potassium ATPase pump, leading to an increase in intracellular sodium and a subsequent increase in intracellular calcium. This can lead to potassium efflux, which can result in hyperkalemia. Hyperkalemia is a common metabolic symptom of digoxin toxicity.

6. **Answer C (Digibind)**

   The treatment for severe digoxin toxicity is Digibind (Digoxin Immune Fab). Digibind is indicated for the treatment of potentially life-threatening digoxin intoxication. Manifestations of life-threatening toxicity include severe ventricular arrhythmias such as ventricular tachycardia or ventricular fibrillation, or progressive bradyarrhythmias such as severe sinus bradycardia or second or third-degree heart block not responsive to atropine. Digitalis-induced progressive elevation of the serum potassium concentration also suggests imminent cardiac arrest. If the potassium concentration exceeds 5 mEq/L in the setting of severe digitalis intoxication, therapy with Digibind is indicated. Digibind acts by binding to digoxin in the blood, forming a complex that is then excreted by the kidneys. This reduces free digoxin concentration in the bloodstream, thereby reversing its toxic effects. Digibind should be administered promptly in cases of severe digoxin toxicity to prevent life-threatening complications.

Recommended literature

1. Pincus M. Management of digoxin toxicity. Aust Prescr. 2016;39(1):18-20.
2. Levine M, O'Connor A. Digitalis (cardiac glycoside) poisoning. UpToDate. 2016.
3. Kotzé, A., Howell, S.J., 2008. Heart failure: pathophysiology, risk assessment, community management and anaesthesia. Continuing Education in Anaesthesia Critical Care & Pain 8, 161-166.

HEROIN OR OPIOID TOXICITY

19
CHAPTER

Questions:

1. Which of the following is a common sign of heroin or opioid toxicity?
   A. Hypertension
   B. Pinpoint pupils
   C. Hyperactivity
   D. Tachypnea

2. What is the first-line treatment for opioid overdose?
   A. Naloxone
   B. Buprenorphine
   C. Methadone
   D. Naltrexone

3. What is the average half-life of heroin in the blood after intravenous administration?
   A. 30 minutes
   B. 3 hours
   C. 3 minutes
   D. 30 seconds

4. Which medication is commonly used to treat opiate withdrawal symptoms?
   A. Morphine
   B. Naloxone
   C. Methadone
   D. Fentanyl

5. Intravascular heroin use can lead to the growth of infectious material on heart valves, requiring surgical intervention such as valve replacement.
   A. True
   B. False

6. The patient is a 28-year-old male, a long-term heroin addict, who presents to the emergency department (ED) with altered mental status and respiratory depression. On examination, he is found to have shallow breathing, extremely small pupils (pinpoint pupils), delirium, disorientation, hypotension, weak pulse, and bluish-colored nails and lips, consistent with opioid toxicity. Given his presentation, intravenous naloxone is administered. What is the primary goal of naloxone administration in opioid toxicity?
   A. To reverse respiratory depression
   B. To induce analgesia
   C. To increase heart rate
   D. To prevent seizures

Answers:

1. **Answer B (Pinpoint pupils)**

   Pinpoint pupils, or miosis, are a hallmark sign of heroin or opioid toxicity. Other common signs include respiratory depression (shallow or slow breathing), CNS depression (such as drowsiness, confusion, and delirium), and physical symptoms like dry mouth and muscle spasms. Hypertension, hyperactivity, and tachypnea are not typical features of opioid toxicity. This constellation of symptoms reflects the central nervous system and respiratory depression caused by opioid effects on the brainstem respiratory centers, and autonomic nervous system.

2. **Answer A (Naloxone)**

   Naloxone is a pure competitive antagonist of opiate receptors and has no agonistic activity. The drug is relatively safe and can be administered intravenously, intramuscularly, subcutaneously, or via the endotracheal tube. Recently, the FDA approved an intranasal formula, which is showing promise, especially in patients who do not have intravenous access. Whether naloxone is administered via the endotracheal tube or intravenously, the onset of action is within minutes. A second dose can be administered every 2 to 3 minutes. With subcutaneous or intramuscular injection, the onset may be delayed for 3 to 10 minutes. As soon as the patient is alert and awake, the dose of naloxone should be discontinued. For patients overdosed on diphenoxylate, methadone, butorphanol, nalbuphine, and pentazocine, higher doses of naloxone are required.

3. **Answer C (3 minutes)**

   The average half-life of heroin in the blood after intravenous administration is approximately 3 minutes. This short half-life contributes to the need for frequent administration in individuals using heroin to maintain its effects. Heroin is rapidly metabolized into morphine in the body, leading to its potent opioid effects. Tolerance to heroin's effects typically develops over time, necessitating higher doses to achieve the desired effects. Heroin's peak levels are reached around 5 minutes after intranasal or intravenous use, with intravenous administration having about two to three times the effect of a similar dose of morphine.

4. **Answer C (Methadone)**

   Methadone is a long-acting opioid that helps reduce withdrawal symptoms and cravings in individuals recovering from opiate addiction. It works by binding to the same opioid receptors in the brain as other opiates, such as heroin or morphine, but it does so more gradually, helping to stabilize brain function and reduce withdrawal symptoms. Methadone maintenance therapy is a well-established treatment for opioid dependence, allowing individuals to function normally while reducing the risk of relapse and overdose.

5. **Answer A (True)**

   Intravascular heroin use can lead to infective endocarditis, particularly in cases where contaminated needles introduce infectious material into the bloodstream. This condition can result in the growth of infectious material on heart valves, necessitating surgical intervention such as valve replacement. This is a serious complication of intravenous drug use and highlights the importance of sterile injection practices to prevent such infections. Additionally, intravascular heroin use is associated with a range of other complications, including the transmission of infectious diseases such as HIV, hepatitis B, and hepatitis C, as well as the risk of skin infections, compartment syndrome, and septic emboli.

6. **Answer A (To reverse respiratory depression)**

   The primary goal of administering naloxone in opioid toxicity is to rapidly reverse respiratory depression, a critical complication of opioid overdose that can lead to respiratory arrest and death. Whether administered via the endotracheal tube or intravenously, naloxone's onset of action is within minutes, making it an effective emergency intervention. A second dose can be given every 2 to 3 minutes as needed. In cases of overdose involving specific opioids like diphenoxylate, methadone, butorphanol, nalbuphine, and pentazocine, higher doses of naloxone may be required. Naloxone's immediate action helps restore normal breathing patterns and prevent respiratory failure, ultimately improving the patient's chances of recovery.

Recommended literature

1. World Health Organization. 2021. Opioid overdose. https://www.who.int/news-room/fact-sheets/detail/opioid-overdose.
2. Volkow ND, Jones EB, Einstein EB, Wargo EM. Prevention and Treatment of Opioid Misuse and Addiction: A Review. JAMA Psychiatry. 2019;76(2):208-216.
3. Simpson, G., Jackson, M., 2017. Perioperative management of opioid-tolerant patients. BJA Education 17, 124–128.
4. Nicholson Roberts, T., Thompson, J.P., 2013. Illegal substances in anaesthetic and intensive care practices. Continuing Education in Anaesthesia Critical Care & Pain 13, 42–46.
5. Boyer EW. Management of opioid analgesic overdose. N Engl J Med. 2012;367(2):146-155.

LITHIUM TOXICITY

Questions:

1. **What is the proposed MOA of lithium?**
   A. Inhibition of serotonin release
   B. Stimulation of alpha-adrenergic stimulation
   C. Inhibition of adenylate cyclase and G proteins
   D. Inhibition of dopamine receptors

2. **What is the most appropriate method for removing lithium in a patient with severe poisoning?**
   A. Activated charcoal
   B. Gastric lavage
   C. Hemodialysis
   D. Whole-bowel irrigation

3. **Which of the following drugs is NOT associated with an increased risk of lithium toxicity?**
   A. NSAIDs
   B. Calcium channel blockers
   C. ACE inhibitors
   D. Opioids

4. **Which of the following is a cardiovascular effect associated with lithium toxicity?**
   A. QT shortening
   B. Sinus node dysfunction
   C. ST elevation
   D. T wave inversion

5. **Lithium prolongs both depolarizing and non-depolarizing blockade.**
   A. True
   B. False

6. **A 45-year-old male presents to the emergency department with altered mental status and decreased oral intake for the past two days. The patient appears anxious and disoriented to time and place. On neurological examination, the patient exhibits resting tremors, increased tone, and hyperreflexia. The patient's medical history is significant for manic depressive psychosis, for which he has been taking lithium. Which of the following is NOT a recommended diagnostic test for lithium toxicity?**
   A. Serum lithium level
   B. Coagulation studies
   C. Renal function tests
   D. Thyroid-stimulating hormone

Answers:

1. Answer C (Inhibition of adenylate cyclase and G proteins)

The proposed mechanism of action (MOA) of lithium involves inhibiting adenylate cyclase and G proteins, which reduces cyclic adenosine monophosphate (cAMP) levels and alters cellular signaling pathways. This action is thought to contribute to lithium's mood-stabilizing effects by reducing neuronal responsiveness to neurotransmitters. Additionally, lithium can deplete brain inositol, further impacting neurotransmitter signaling. It also stimulates serotonin release from the hippocampus and affects ion transport and cell membrane potential similar to potassium and sodium. These multifaceted effects on neurotransmission and cellular signaling likely underlie lithium's therapeutic actions in bipolar disorder, but the exact MOA remains incompletely understood.

2. Answer C (Hemodialysis)

Hemodialysis is considered the most effective method for removing lithium in cases of severe poisoning. This is particularly true if the patient is demonstrating signs and symptoms of severe lithium poisoning or is experiencing renal failure. Hemodialysis is preferred due to lithium's small volume of distribution and marginal protein binding, which make it more effectively removed by this method compared to others. Peritoneal dialysis can be considered if hemodialysis facilities are not available, but it is generally not as effective as hemodialysis for lithium removal.

3. Answer D (Opioids)

Among the listed options, opioids are not typically associated with an increased risk of lithium toxicity. However, the other options can increase the risk of lithium toxicity when co-ingested. NSAIDs (Nonsteroidal anti-inflammatory drugs) such as indomethacin and selective COX-2 inhibitors, as well as medications like acetaminophen, metronidazole, calcium channel blockers, ACE inhibitors, and diuretics, can all impact lithium levels through various mechanisms. For example, NSAIDs can reduce lithium clearance by affecting renal function, while calcium channel blockers and ACE inhibitors can also impact lithium excretion.

4. Answer B (Sinus node dysfunction)

Sinus node dysfunction is a cardiovascular effect associated with lithium toxicity. Other cardiovascular effects include T wave flattening, QT prolongation, intraventricular conduction defects, and U waves. QT shortening and ST elevation are not typically associated with lithium toxicity. T wave inversion may occur in some cases of lithium toxicity, but it is not as specific as the other listed cardiovascular effects.

5. Answer A (True)

Lithium has been reported to prolong both depolarizing and non-depolarizing neuromuscular blockade. This effect can be clinically significant, particularly in patients undergoing general anesthesia who are also on lithium therapy. It is recommended to perform neuromuscular monitoring in these patients when using neuromuscular blocking agents to ensure appropriate reversal. Additionally, patients on lithium undergoing general anesthesia should be monitored closely for conduction defects and ST changes on ECG, as lithium can affect cardiac conduction.

6. Answer B (Coagulation studies)

While important for assessing bleeding risks and clotting disorders, coagulation studies are not typically included in the recommended diagnostic workup for lithium toxicity. The key diagnostic tests for lithium toxicity include cardiac monitoring, electrocardiogram, assessment of oxygenation, monitoring of urine output, serum electrolytes, calcium, renal function, glucose, serum lithium level, and thyroid-stimulating hormone. Both therapeutic lithium usage and intoxication can be accompanied by leukocytosis. Furthermore, interference by the carbonate anion after lithium carbonate acute ingestion in the calculation of anion gap might lead to a low anion gap. If the initial diagnosis is unclear, brain imaging may be required.

Recommended literature

1. Gitlin, M., 2016. Lithium side effects and toxicity: prevalence and management strategies. International Journal of Bipolar Disorders 4.
2. Flood S, Bodenham A. 2010. Lithium: mimicry, mania, and muscle relaxants. Continuing Education in Anaesthesia Critical Care & Pain. 10;3:77-80.

MAOI TOXICITY

Questions:

1. Which of the following is NOT a mechanism by which MAOIs can lead to toxicity?
   A. Inhibition of monoamine neurotransmitter breakdown
   B. Increased synthesis of monoamines
   C. Decreased reuptake of monoamines
   D. Increased metabolism of monoamines

2. Which of the following is a common presenting symptom of MAOI toxicity?
   A. Dry skin
   B. Bradycardia
   C. Hypotension
   D. Agitation

3. Which of the following is NOT a way in which MAOI toxicity can occur?
   A. Drug-food interaction with tyramine-containing foods
   B. Overdose of MAOIs
   C. Drug-drug interaction with NSAIDs
   D. Combining MAOIs with agents that increase the synthesis or release of monoamines

4. What should be considered in the anesthetic management of a patient with MAOI toxicity?
   A. Use of indirect sympathomimetics
   B. Caution with direct sympathomimetics
   C. Avoidance of benzodiazepines
   D. Use Lidocaine with epinephrine

5. Protamine sulfate is a recommended antidote for MAOI toxicity.
   A. True
   B. False

6. A 45-year-old male with a history of depression is brought to the emergency department (ED) by ambulance due to agitation and altered mental status. According to the patient's family, he has been taking antidepressant medications, including amitriptyline and phenelzine, for the past few months. On arrival, the patient is diaphoretic, tachycardic, and hyperthermic, with a temperature of 39.5°C. He is also tachypneic and hypertensive. Additionally, the patient vomits and exhibits signs of dysrhythmias on the monitor. The ED team suspects that the patient's symptoms may be related to the antidepressant drugs he is taking. What is NOT a characteristic feature of MAOI toxicity compared to other hyperthermic toxidromes?
   A. Diaphoresis
   B. Ocular clonus
   C. Muscle rigidity
   D. Ping-pong gaze

Answers:

1. Answer D (Increased metabolism of monoamines)

MAOIs prevent the breakdown of monoamine neurotransmitters, leading to increased levels of serotonin, norepinephrine, dopamine, and other monoamines. This increased availability of monoamines is a key mechanism of action of MAOIs. Therefore, increased metabolism of monoamines is not a mechanism by which MAOIs can lead to toxicity; rather, it is their inhibition of monoamine breakdown that can lead to toxicity symptoms such as tachycardia, hyperthermia, myoclonus, hypertension, and agitation.

2. Answer D (Agitation)

MAOI toxicity commonly presents with agitation, along with other symptoms such as diaphoresis, tachycardia, and mild temperature elevation. Agitation is one of the mild signs of MAOI toxicity, which can progress to more severe symptoms if not promptly recognized and treated. Other signs and symptoms of MAOI toxicity include altered mental status, tachypnea, vomiting, dysrhythmias, hypertension, severe hyperthermia, seizures, central nervous system (CNS) depression, coma, cardiorespiratory depression, muscle rigidity, and myoclonus.

3. Answer C (Drug-drug interaction with NSAIDs)

MAOI toxicity can occur through three main mechanisms: drug-food interaction with tyramine-containing foods, overdose of MAOIs, and drug-drug interactions. When MAOIs are combined with other agents that increase the synthesis, release, or effect of monoamines or decrease the metabolism or reuptake of monoamines, it can lead to toxicity. Examples of such agents include dextromethorphan, linezolid, methylene blue, selective serotonin reuptake inhibitors (SSRIs), serotoninergic agents, and tramadol. NSAIDs are not typically implicated in MAOI toxicity.

4. Answer B (Caution with direct sympathomimetics)

When managing a patient with MAOI toxicity, several considerations are important. There is a risk of developing serotonin syndrome if the patient is also receiving other serotonergic agents, so this should be taken into account. Additionally, there is a risk of hypertensive crisis, so agents that can increase blood pressure should be used cautiously. It is advisable to avoid indirect sympathomimetics and be cautious with direct sympathomimetics. Cocaine should be avoided due to its potential to exacerbate adrenergic effects. The use of benzodiazepines is not contraindicated in the management of MAOI toxicity and can be used as needed. Lidocaine with epinephrine can be used cautiously, but the epinephrine component should be used judiciously due to the risk of exacerbating adrenergic symptoms.

5. Answer B (False)

Protamine sulfate is not a recommended antidote for MAOI toxicity. There is no specific antidote available for MAOI toxicity. Treatment is primarily supportive and focused on managing symptoms and complications. Activated charcoal may be used to reduce absorption in cases of overdose, and other supportive measures, such as benzodiazepines for agitation and hyperthermia, as well as cooling measures for hyperthermia, may be employed. Monitoring and management of cardiovascular and neurological symptoms are also crucial in the management of MAOI toxicity.

6. Answer C (Muscle rigidity)

Muscle rigidity can be seen in MAOI toxicities as well as in other hyperthermic toxidromes, but diaphoresis, ocular clonus, and a "ping-pong" gaze are more commonly associated with MAOI toxicities. These signs, along with the patient's history of taking amitriptyline and phenelzine, are more indicative of MAOI toxicity. NMS, on the other hand, typically presents with severe muscle rigidity, altered mental status, hyperthermia, and autonomic dysfunction. Given the patient's presentation, MAOI toxicity should be strongly considered, and appropriate management, including supportive care and discontinuation of the offending agents, should be initiated.

Recommended literature

1. Bartakke, A., Corredor, C., Van Rensburg, A., 2020. Serotonin syndrome in the perioperative period. BJA Education 20, 10–17.
2. Peck T, Wong A, Norman E. 2010. Anaesthetic implications of psychoactive drugs. Continuing Education in Anaesthesia Critical Care & Pain.10;(6); 177-181.
3. Gillman, P.K., 2005. Monoamine oxidase inhibitors, opioid analgesics and serotonin toxicity. British Journal of Anaesthesia 95, 434–441.

MDMA (ECSTASY) TOXICITY

19

CHAPTER

Questions:

1. What is the mechanism of action of MDMA (ectasy)?
   A. GABA agonist
   B. Serotonin, dopamine, and norepinephrine reuptake inhibitor
   C. NMDA receptor antagonist
   D. Muscarinic antagonist

2. Which of the following is a typical effect of MDMA intoxication?
   A. Bradycardia
   B. Hypothermia
   C. Decreased reflexes
   D. Feelings of euphoria

3. What is a risk factor for developing MDMA toxicity?
   A. Sedentary lifestyle
   B. Mixing MDMA with alcohol or other drugs
   C. Low ambient temperature
   D. Older age

4. Which of the following is a life-threatening side effect of MDMA toxicity?
   A. Blood Clots
   B. Stevens-Johnson Syndrome
   C. Hyperpyrexia > 41.5°C
   D. Priapism

5. Serotonin syndrome is a neurological complication of MDMA toxicity.
   A. True
   B. False

6. A 29-year-old male presents to the emergency department with a sudden onset of generalized seizures. His friends report that he had ingested 2 ecstasy tablets with 750 mL of spirits approximately 2 hours prior to presentation. The seizures started approximately 30 minutes before arrival. On examination, his core temperature is 41°C, systolic blood pressure is 76 mmHg, heart rate is 160 beats per minute, and respiratory rate is 28 per minute. The patient appears mottled, cyanosed, and cool peripherally with labored respirations. He has generalized muscular rigidity and a Glasgow coma score of 3. Which of the following is NOT a recommended treatment for MDMA toxicity?
   A. Benzodiazepines
   B. Dantrolen
   C. Ice packs
   D. Acetaminophen

Answers:

1. Answer B (Serotonin, dopamine, and norepinephrine reuptake inhibitor)

MDMA is a potent releaser and/or reuptake inhibitor of presynaptic serotonin (5-HT), dopamine (DA), and norepinephrine (NE). These actions result from the interaction of MDMA with the membrane transporters involved in neurotransmitter reuptake and vesicular storage systems. This mechanism leads to increased levels of these neurotransmitters in the synaptic cleft, contributing to the characteristic effects of MDMA, such as euphoria, wakefulness, intimacy, excitement, and a loss of inhibitions. It is important to note that while MDMA may initially increase neurotransmitter levels, chronic or high-dose use can lead to depletion and long-term changes in neurotransmitter function, which may contribute to the potential for neurotoxicity and mood disturbances associated with MDMA use.

2. Answer D (Feelings of euphoria)

MDMA (ecstasy) intoxication typically leads to feelings of euphoria. Users often experience heightened sensory perception, increased energy, emotional warmth, and a distorted sense of time. These effects are due to the drug's ability to increase the release of serotonin, dopamine, and norepinephrine in the brain, leading to altered mood and perception. It is important to note that while these effects are commonly reported, MDMA use can also lead to serious health risks, including hyperthermia, dehydration, and serotonin syndrome.

3. Answer B (Mixing MDMA with alcohol or other drugs)

One of the risk factors for developing MDMA toxicity is mixing MDMA with alcohol or other drugs. This combination can increase the risk of adverse effects and overdose. Other risk factors include ingesting several doses at once or in a short period, vigorous physical activity, and using MDMA in a hot environment. These factors can contribute to dehydration, hyperthermia, and other serious complications associated with MDMA use.

4. Answer C (Hyperpyrexia > 41.5°C)

Hyperpyrexia, or extremely high fever, is a life-threatening side effect of MDMA toxicity. It can lead to severe complications such as organ damage and central nervous system dysfunction. Other potentially life-threatening complications of MDMA toxicity include rhabdomyolysis, serotonin syndrome, acute liver failure, and hyponatremia with cerebral edema. These complications underscore the importance of recognizing and promptly treating MDMA toxicity.

5. Answer A (True)

Serotonin syndrome is a neurological complication of MDMA toxicity. MDMA increases serotonin levels in the brain, and at high doses, it can lead to a severe form of serotonin syndrome characterized by hyperthermia, muscle rigidity, autonomic instability, and altered mental status. This severe form of serotonin syndrome can be life-threatening and requires prompt medical attention.

6. Answer D (Acetaminophen)

Acetaminophen (paracetamol) should not be used in the management of MDMA toxicity, as it can worsen already compromised liver function. MDMA toxicity is primarily managed with supportive care and symptomatic treatment. Benzodiazepines are used to manage seizures and agitation, while dantrolene is indicated for the treatment of hyperthermia and muscle rigidity. Ice packs can be used for external cooling to help reduce core body temperature. However, caution should be exercised to avoid inducing shivering, which can increase metabolic heat production.

Recommended literature

1. Davies N, English W, Grundlingh J. MDMA toxicity: management of acute and life-threatening presentations. Br J Nurs. 2018;27(11):616-622.
2. Nicholson Roberts, T., Thompson, J.P., 2013. Illegal substances in anaesthetic and intensive care practices. Continuing Education in Anaesthesia Critical Care & Pain 13, 42–46.
3. Hall, A.P., Henry, J.A., 2006. Acute toxic effects of 'Ecstasy' (MDMA) and related compounds: overview of pathophysiology and clinical management. British Journal of Anaesthesia 96, 678–685.

Toxicities
METHAMPHETAMINE TOXICITY

19
CHAPTER

Questions:

1. **How does methamphetamine affect the central nervous system (CNS)?**
   A. By inhibiting neurotransmitter release
   B. By blocking dopamine receptors
   C. By enhancing the release of monoamine neurotransmitters
   D. By increasing GABAergic activity

2. **What cardiovascular effects are commonly associated with methamphetamine use?**
   A. Bradycardia and hypotension
   B. Tachycardia and hypertension
   C. Irregular heart rhythms and heart block
   D. Cardiomyopathy and endocarditis

3. **What is NOT the potential consequence of severe methamphetamine toxicity?**
   A. Ischemic stroke
   B. Renal failure
   C. Respiratory depression
   D. Intracranial hemorrhage

4. **How does methamphetamine differ from cocaine in terms of its pharmacokinetics?**
   A. Methamphetamine has a shorter duration of action than cocaine
   B. Methamphetamine has a longer half-life than cocaine
   C. Methamphetamine is metabolized by the same enzymes as cocaine
   D. Methamphetamine is excreted primarily in urine, while cocaine is excreted in feces

5. **"Meth mouth" is a term used to describe the severe dental problems, including tooth decay and loss, associated with methamphetamine use.**
   A. True
   B. False

6. **A 32-year-old man is brought to the emergency department by ambulance after being found agitated and confused in a public park. On arrival, he is diaphoretic, tachypneic, and agitated. His heart rate is 140 beats per minute, blood pressure is 160/100 mmHg, and temperature is 105.5°F (40.8°C). The patient appears disoriented and is unable to provide coherent answers to questions. The patient is accompanied by friends who report that he has a history of methamphetamine use. There is no history of recent illness or trauma. What is the initial management approach for a patient with suspected methamphetamine toxicity?**
   A. Administer activated charcoal
   B. Perform gastric lavage
   C. Administer naloxone
   D. Provide supportive care

Answers:

1. **Answer C (By enhancing the release of monoamine neurotransmitters)**

   Methamphetamine affects the central nervous system (CNS) by enhancing the release of monoamine neurotransmitters such as dopamine, serotonin, and norepinephrine within central and peripheral nerve endings. Additionally, it blocks the reuptake of dopamine, similar to cocaine. These actions lead to increased levels of these neurotransmitters in the synaptic cleft, resulting in the characteristic euphoric effects of methamphetamine in the CNS. The drug's sympathomimetic effects, such as tachycardia and hypertension, are also a result of these actions on the neurotransmitter systems.

2. **Answer B (Tachycardia and hypertension)**

   Methamphetamine use is associated with tachycardia and hypertension. These cardiovascular effects are commonly observed in both acute and chronic methamphetamine users. The drug's stimulant effects on the sympathetic nervous system lead to increased heart rate and blood pressure, which can have serious implications for cardiovascular health. Additionally, methamphetamine abuse can result in atrial and ventricular dysrhythmias, chest pain from cardiac ischemia and infarction, and even acute congestive heart failure exacerbation in some cases. These other cardiovascular effects are also possible but less common.

3. **Answer C (Respiratory depression)**

   Respiratory depression is not a typical consequence of severe methamphetamine toxicity. Methamphetamine is a stimulant that typically increases respiratory rate rather than causing depression. However, other potential consequences of severe methamphetamine toxicity include ischemic stroke, renal failure, intracranial hemorrhage, seizures, coma, heart failure, arrhythmias, delusional behavior, extreme paranoia, major mood swings, severe insomnia, dental problems (such as "meth mouth"), repeated infections, severe weight loss, and abscesses or boils.

4. **Answer B (Methamphetamine has a longer half-life than cocaine)**

   Methamphetamine has a longer half-life than cocaine, meaning it remains in the body for a longer period of time. While cocaine is quickly metabolized and removed from the body, methamphetamine has a longer duration of action, and a larger percentage of the drug remains unchanged. This difference in pharmacokinetics contributes to the longer-lasting stimulant effects of methamphetamine compared to cocaine. Additionally, methamphetamine and cocaine are metabolized by different enzymes, with methamphetamine primarily metabolized by the liver enzyme CYP2D6, while cocaine is metabolized by the enzyme carboxylesterase.

5. **Answer A (True)**

   Methamphetamine use is associated with severe dental problems, often referred to as "meth mouth." These dental problems include tooth decay, tooth loss, and other oral health issues. Several factors contribute to the development of meth mouth, including the acidic content of the drug, poor oral hygiene practices, teeth grinding, and dry mouth caused by methamphetamine use. These factors can lead to rapid and severe dental deterioration, often requiring extensive dental treatment.

6. **Answer D (Provide supportive care)**

   The initial management approach for a patient with suspected methamphetamine toxicity is to provide supportive care. This includes ensuring adequate oxygenation and ventilation, monitoring vital signs closely, and addressing dehydration and hyperthermia with intravenous fluids. Benzodiazepines are the first-line treatment for managing agitation and can be used in combination with antipsychotics if needed. Cooling measures should be initiated to address hyperthermia, and close monitoring for complications such as rhabdomyolysis and acute kidney injury is essential. There is no role for activated charcoal or gastric lavage in the management of methamphetamine toxicity, and naloxone is not indicated unless there is a suspicion of concomitant opioid use.

Recommended literature

1. Richards JR, Laurin EG. Methamphetamine Toxicity. In: StatPearls. Treasure Island (FL): StatPearls Publishing; October 10, 2022
2. Dignam, G., Bigham, C., 2017. Novel psychoactive substances: a practical approach to dealing with toxicity from legal highs. BJA Education 17, 172–177.

Toxicities

METHANOL AND ETHYLENE GLYCOL POISONING

19

CHAPTER

Questions:

1. **What is the main toxic metabolite of methanol?**
   A. Glycolic acid
   B. Glycolaldehyde
   C. Oxalic acid
   D. Formic acid

2. **Which enzyme is responsible for the metabolism of methanol and ethylene glycol to their toxic metabolites?**
   A. Alcohol dehydrogenase (ADH)
   B. Aldehyde dehydrogenase (ALDH)
   C. Cytochrome P450
   D. Glutathione-S-transferase

3. **Which of the following is a characteristic feature of methanol poisoning?**
   A. Hypercalcemia
   B. Hypoglycemia
   C. Visual disturbances
   D. Respiratory alkalosis

4. **How does oxalic acid contribute to organ dysfunction in ethylene glycol poisoning?**
   A. By inhibiting ATP synthesis
   B. By forming insoluble crystals with calcium
   C. By directly damaging cell membranes
   D. By increasing oxidative stress

5. **Activated charcoal and gastric lavage are the first line in the treatment of toxic alcohol intoxication.**
   A. True
   B. False

6. **A 59-year-old female presents to the emergency department after consuming alcohol. She is disoriented and complaining of severe abdominal pain. Her vital signs are stable, but she appears confused and agitated. Upon examination, the patient is found to have severe metabolic acidosis and some visual impairment. Due to limitations in laboratory testing and time constraints, a clinical suspicion of methanol intoxication is made, and treatment is initiated accordingly. Which antidote is used in the treatment of methanol poisoning?**
   A. Naloxone
   B. Flumazenil
   C. Fomepizole
   D. N-acetylcysteine

Answers:

1. Answer D (Formic acid)

Formic acid is the main toxic metabolite of methanol metabolism. In the body, methanol is metabolized by alcohol dehydrogenase to formaldehyde, which is further metabolized to formic acid. Formic acid is highly toxic and is responsible for many of the toxic effects seen in methanol poisoning. Formic acid is directly toxic to the retina and can cause visual disturbances and even blindness. Additionally, formic acid inhibits mitochondrial cytochrome oxidase, which deranges ATP synthesis and leads to cellular dysfunction. These effects can contribute to the serious complications of methanol poisoning, including metabolic acidosis, central nervous system depression, and organ damage.

2. Answer A (Alcohol dehydrogenase (ADH))

Alcohol dehydrogenase is the hepatic enzyme responsible for metabolizing methanol and ethylene glycol (EG) to their toxic metabolites. In the case of methanol, ADH converts methanol to formaldehyde, which is further metabolized to formic acid. In the case of ethylene glycol, ADH converts ethylene glycol to glycolaldehyde, which is further metabolized to glycolic acid and then to oxalic acid. These toxic metabolites are responsible for many of the adverse effects seen in methanol and ethylene glycol poisoning.

3. Answer C (Visual disturbances)

Visual disturbances are a characteristic feature of methanol poisoning. Methanol is metabolized to formic acid, which is directly toxic to the retina and can cause visual disturbances and even blindness. Other early symptoms of methanol poisoning include mild euphoria, drunkenness, headache, lethargy, and confusion. As the poisoning progresses, more severe symptoms such as metabolic acidosis, Kussmaul breathing, and eventually blindness, coma, cardiovascular shock, respiratory failure, and death can occur. Hypercalcemia, hypoglycemia, and respiratory alkalosis are not typical features of methanol poisoning.

4. Answer B (By forming insoluble crystals with calcium)

Oxalic acid, the main toxic metabolite of ethylene glycol metabolism, binds to calcium, forming insoluble calcium oxalate crystals. These crystals can deposit in various tissues and organs, leading to organ dysfunction. In the case of ethylene glycol poisoning, this can result in hypocalcemia and crystal deposition, contributing to renal damage and other complications. Oxalic acid does not directly inhibit ATP synthesis, damage cell membranes, or increase oxidative stress.

5. Answer B (False)

Activated charcoal and gastric lavage have no place in the treatment of toxic alcohol intoxication. These measures are not effective in removing alcohols such as methanol and ethylene glycol from the body. Instead, treatment focuses on supportive care, correcting metabolic abnormalities, and administering specific antidotes such as fomepizole or ethanol to inhibit the metabolism of methanol and ethylene glycol, respectively.

6. Answer C (Fomepizole)

Fomepizole and ethanol are effective antidotes against methanol toxicity. Fomepizole is preferred due to its advantages over ethanol, including easier dosing and fewer adverse effects. The management of methanol poisoning includes standard supportive care, correction of metabolic acidosis, administration of folinic acid, and provision of an antidote to inhibit the metabolism of methanol to formate. Selective hemodialysis may also be required to correct severe metabolic abnormalities and enhance methanol and formate elimination. Fomepizole or ethanol should be administered as soon as possible once the patient has been admitted to a medical care facility. For patients presenting with ophthalmologic abnormalities or significant acidosis, intravenous sodium bicarbonate should be administered to correct acidosis. The further generation of toxic metabolites should be blocked by the administration of fomepizole or ethanol, and formic acid metabolism should be enhanced by the administration of intravenous folinic acid.

Recommended literature

1. Rietjens SJ at al. Ethylene glycol or methanol intoxication: which antidote should be used, fomepizole or ethanol? Neth J Med. 2014 Feb;72(2):73-9. PMID: 24659589
2. Grouls R. et al. Toxicologie behandel informatie: Methanol, 2022, accessed 25/01/2023 https://toxicologie.org/methanol

Toxicities

OPIOID TOLERANCE OR
METHADON-USING PATIENTS

Questions:

1. **Which of the following best describes opioid tolerance?**
   A. Increased responsiveness to an opioid agonist
   B. Reduced responsiveness to an opioid agonist
   C. No change in responsiveness to an opioid agonist
   D. A state of euphoria induced by opioids

2. **Which opioid is used in addiction medicine to suppress opioid withdrawal and craving?**
   A. Fentanyl
   B. Morphine
   C. Oxycodone
   D. Buprenorphine

3. **Which of the following is NOT an adverse effect of methadone?**
   A. Heart failure
   B. Renal failure
   C. Liver failure
   D. Respiratory failure

4. **Which opioid is both a µ-agonist and an NMDA-antagonist?**
   A. Morphine
   B. Buprenorphine
   C. Fentanyl
   D. Oxycodone

5. **Buprenorphine is a synthetic opioid agonist used for chronic pain and opioid dependence due to its partial agonist activity.**
   A. True
   B. False

6. **A 45-year-old man with a history of chronic low back pain due to degenerative disc disease presents for elective surgery to treat chronic appendicitis. He has been managed on oxycodone 30 mg twice daily for the past year for his back pain. Which statement is true regarding opioid tolerance and opioid-dependent patients?**
   A. Opioid-dependent patients have a reduced pain threshold
   B. Addiction relapse cannot occur with the use of opioids for analgesia
   C. Maintenance opioids like methadone provide analgesia
   D. Respiratory and CNS depression are likely with additional opioid use

Answers:

1. Answer B (Reduced responsiveness to an opioid agonist)

Opioid tolerance is a process characterized by neuroadaptations that result in reduced drug effects. Specifically, opioid tolerance is characterized by reduced responsiveness to an opioid agonist such as morphine. This reduced responsiveness is usually manifested by the need to use increasing doses to achieve the desired effect. Opioid tolerance is a common occurrence in individuals taking high doses of opioids for extended periods. It is important to note that addiction to opioids is common among recreational opioid users (such as heroin users), but relatively rare in chronic pain patients. Additionally, successful approaches to pharmacotherapy of opioid addiction often rely on the substitution of short-acting agonists such as heroin with oral administration of long-acting high-efficacy agonists such as methadone or partial agonists like buprenorphine.

2. Answer D (Buprenorphine)

Buprenorphine is an opioid used in addiction medicine to suppress opioid withdrawal and craving. It is a partial agonist at μ-receptors and an antagonist at κ- and δ-receptors. This unique pharmacological profile allows buprenorphine to reduce withdrawal symptoms and cravings without producing the same level of euphoria or respiratory depression as full agonists like morphine or oxycodone. Buprenorphine is typically used in addiction medicine to help individuals manage opioid withdrawal symptoms and reduce the risk of relapse.

3. Answer C (Liver failure)

Methadone therapy has not been linked to serum enzyme elevations or idiosyncratic acute, clinically apparent liver injury. However, chronic hepatitis B and C are common among persons on methadone maintenance. There is no evidence that methadone maintenance worsens the course of chronic viral hepatitis. Heart failure, renal failure, and respiratory failure are all potential adverse effects of methadone. Methadone can have direct and indirect effects on the kidney, including rhabdomyolysis leading to acute kidney injury, volumetric changes, renal lipidosis and amyloidosis, kidney growth during pregnancy, and kidney transplant rejection. Methadone may also cause QT prolongation and torsades de pointes, which can lead to potentially fatal arrhythmias. Additionally, methadone accumulation can lead to sedation, respiratory depression, respiratory arrest, and death.

4. Answer B (Buprenorphine)

Buprenorphine is both a μ-opioid receptor agonist and an antagonist at the NMDA receptor. It acts as a partial agonist at μ-receptors, meaning it activates these receptors but to a lesser extent than full agonists like morphine. It also acts as an antagonist at κ- and δ-receptors. The NMDA receptor antagonism is thought to contribute to its analgesic effects and may play a role in reducing opioid tolerance and dependence.

5. Answer A (True)

Buprenorphine is a synthetic opioid developed in the late 1960s and is used to treat pain and opioid use disorder. This drug is a synthetic analog of thebaine—an alkaloid compound derived from the poppy flower. Buprenorphine is categorized as a Schedule III drug, which means it has a moderate-to-low potential for physical dependence or a high potential for psychological dependence. Buprenorphine is approved by the U.S. Food and Drug Administration (FDA) to treat acute and chronic pain and opioid dependence. Buprenorphine relieves pain similar to morphine and other opiates. It is more potent and has a longer duration of action than morphine. It is well absorbed following most routes of administration, including the sublingual route, and produces rapid analgesia. Buprenorphine hydrochloride is also an effective maintenance drug in the treatment of opioid dependence and is rapidly replacing methadone in this use.

6. Answer A (Opioid-dependent patients have a reduced pain threshold)

Opioid-dependent patients often experience hyperalgesia and a reduced pain threshold, which can contribute to the need for higher doses of opioids for pain relief. This phenomenon is known as opioid-induced hyperalgesia. It is important to differentiate between physical dependence and addiction; physical dependence is a physiological adaptation to chronic opioid exposure, while addiction is a complex behavioral disorder characterized by compulsive drug use despite harmful consequences. Opioid maintenance therapy, such as methadone or buprenorphine, is used to treat opioid addiction and does not provide analgesia in the same way that opioids do for pain management.

Recommended literature

1. Srivastava, D., Hill, S., Carty, S., Rockett, M., Bastable, R., Knaggs, R., Lambert, D., Levy, N., Hughes, J., Wilkinson, P., 2021. Surgery and opioids: evidence-based expert consensus guidelines on the perioperative use of opioids in the United Kingdom. British Journal of Anaesthesia 126, 1208–1216.
2. Sritapan Y, Clifford S, Bautista A. Perioperative Management of Patients on Buprenorphine and Methadone: A Narrative Review. Balkan Med J. 2020;37(5):247-252.
3. Simpson, G., Jackson, M., 2017. Perioperative management of opioid-tolerant patients. BJA Education 17, 124–128.
4. Rajan, J., Scott-Warren, J., 2016. The clinical use of methadone in cancer and chronic pain medicine. BJA Education 16, 102–106.
5. Morgan MM, Christie MJ. Analysis of opioid efficacy, tolerance, addiction and dependence from cell culture to human. Br J Pharmacol. 2011;164(4):1322-1334.

Toxicities

ORGANOPHOSPHATES TOXICITY

19
CHAPTER

Questions:

1. **Which of the following is the primary mechanism of action of organophosphates in causing toxicity?**
   A. Inhibition of sodium channels
   B. Inhibition of acetylcholinesterase (AChE)
   C. Activation of NMDA receptors
   D. Inhibition of monoamine oxidase

2. **Why should succinylcholine be avoided during intubation in patients with organophosphate toxicity?**
   A. It can cause bronchospasm
   B. It can cause prolonged paralysis
   C. It can cause seizures
   D. It can cause hyperkalemia

3. **Which of the following is NOT a muscarinic effect of organophosphate poisoning?**
   A. Diarrhea
   B. Miosis
   C. Bronchodilation
   D. Salivation

4. **Which medication is an antidote for organophosphate toxicity by reactivating acetylcholinesterase?**
   A. Atropine
   B. Pralidoxime
   C. Naloxone
   D. Physostigmine

5. **Measurement of AChE in red blood cells can help confirm organophosphate toxicity.**
   A. True
   B. False

6. **A 19-year-old female presents to the emergency room with nausea, vomiting, increased salivation, chills, progressive sweating, breathing difficulties, and dizziness. She reports drinking organophosphate insecticide two hours before admission. Clinical examination reveals a mean arterial blood pressure of 150/90 mmHg, a pulse rate of 50 beats per minute, an oxygen saturation level of 89% in room air, and a respiratory rate of 22 breaths per minute. Pupils are pinpoint bilaterally with absent Doll's eye movement. There is a garlic-like odor present. Gastric lavage was performed upon admission, and atropine 2 mg IV was ordinated. What is the goal of atropine therapy in organophosphate poisoning?**
   A. To improve neuromuscular junction function
   B. To reverse the effects of acetylcholinesterase inhibition
   C. To compete with acetylcholine at the muscarinic receptors
   D. To reverse miosis

Answers:

1. **Answer B (Inhibition of acetylcholinesterase (AChE))**

   The primary mechanism of action of organophosphates in causing toxicity is the inhibition of acetylcholinesterase, an essential enzyme in the breakdown of acetylcholine (ACh) in the synaptic cleft. This inhibition leads to the accumulation of ACh, which results in overstimulation of both nicotinic and muscarinic receptors in the nervous system. Organophosphates, often found in insecticides, can lead to toxicity through inhalation, ingestion, or dermal contact, with symptoms appearing within minutes and potentially persisting for weeks. This toxicity most commonly affects individuals working in agriculture and farmers, and it stimulates both the sympathetic and parasympathetic nervous systems, leading to a range of symptoms.

2. **Answer B (It can cause prolonged paralysis)**

   In patients with organophosphate toxicity, airway control is crucial, and intubation may be necessary due to complications such as bronchospasm, seizures, or bronchorrhea. However, succinylcholine should be avoided during intubation in these patients because it cannot be metabolized and can lead to prolonged paralysis. Organophosphates inhibit acetylcholinesterase, which is necessary for the breakdown of succinylcholine, resulting in its prolonged effects. Therefore, alternative agents should be used for intubation in patients with organophosphate toxicity to avoid this complication.

3. **Answer C (Bronchodilation)**

   Organophosphate poisoning is characterized by the inhibition of cholinesterase activity, leading to an accumulation of acetylcholine and subsequent muscarinic effects. These effects include salivation, lacrimation, urination, diarrhea, emesis, bronchorrhea, bronchospasm, bradycardia, and miosis. However, bronchodilation is not typically associated with muscarinic effects and is, therefore, not a symptom of organophosphate poisoning. Instead, bronchospasm, which causes airway constriction, is a more common manifestation of muscarinic effects in organophosphate poisoning.

4. **Answer B (Pralidoxime)**

   Chronic alcohol abuse can lead to a lowered threshold for paracetamol-induced liver damage. Chronic alcohol consumption can Pralidoxime (2-PAM) is an antidote for organophosphate toxicity that works by reactivating acetylcholinesterase that has been inhibited by organophosphates. It binds to the phosphorylated AChE and restores its enzymatic activity, helping to break down excess acetylcholine and reduce the effects of organophosphate poisoning. It is important to administer pralidoxime before the onset of "aging," which is the irreversible binding of the organophosphate to AChE. The effectiveness of pralidoxime in treating organophosphate poisoning is subject to some controversy. However, it is still recommended for use in conjunction with atropine, which helps to counteract the muscarinic effects of organophosphates.

5. **Answer A (True)**

   Measurement of acetylcholinesterase in red blood cells can help confirm organophosphate toxicity. Organophosphates inhibit AChE activity, leading to the accumulation of acetylcholine and subsequent clinical effects. A decreased AChE activity in red blood cells can indicate exposure to organophosphates. However, diagnosis of organophosphate toxicity is primarily based on clinical suspicion, as patients may present with a range of symptoms related to cholinergic excess. Other diagnostic tests, such as complete blood count, serum glucose levels, troponin levels, liver and renal function tests, arterial blood gas analysis, and electrocardiography (ECG), may also be performed to assess the severity of toxicity and guide treatment. Some organophosphates may have a distinct garlic or petroleum odor, which can aid in the diagnosis if a history of exposure is present.

6. **Answer C (To compete with acetylcholine at the muscarinic receptors)**

   Atropine is the primary treatment for organophosphate poisoning, as it competes with acetylcholine at the muscarinic receptors. This helps to counteract the excessive stimulation caused by the accumulation of acetylcholine due to the inhibition of acetylcholinesterase by organophosphates. Atropine is administered intravenously (IV) with an initial dose of 2 to 5 mg for adults. The goal is to achieve atropinization, which is characterized by the appearance of anticholinergic signs and symptoms, including dry skin and mucosa, decreased bowel sounds, tachycardia, no bronchospasm, reduced secretions, and mydriasis. In severe cases, large doses of atropine may be required, and close monitoring for the development of neuromuscular junction dysfunction and respiratory failure is essential.

Recommended literature

1. Ward C, Sair M. 2010. Oral poisoning: an update. Continuing Education in Anaesthesia Critical Care & Pain. 10;1: 6–11.
2. Geoghegan, J., Tong, J.L., 2006. Chemical warfare agents. Continuing Education in Anaesthesia Critical Care & Pain 6, 230–234.

PARACETAMOL OVERDOSE

Questions:

1. Which of the following is the most common cause of acute liver failure in the Western world?

   A. Ibuprofen

   B. Aspirin

   C. Paracetamol

   D. Morphine

2. What is the primary mechanism of hepatotoxicity in paracetamol overdose?

   A. Glutathione depletion

   B. Oxidative stress

   C. Endoplasmic reticulum stress

   D. Mitochondrial dysfunction

3. What is the threshold dose of paracetamol (acetaminophen) that can cause liver damage?

   A. $\geq$ 50 mg/kg

   B. $\geq$ 100 mg/kg

   C. $\geq$ 150 mg/kg

   D. $\geq$ 200 mg/kg

4. Which of the following can lead to a lowered threshold for paracetamol-induced liver damage?

   A. Chronic ibuprofen use

   B. Chronic alcohol abuse

   C. Chronic aspirin consumption

   D. Chronic caffeine intake

5. Acute liver failure may be seen 4-8 hours after ingestion of a potentially fatal dose of paracetamol.

   A. True

   B. False

6. A 16-year-old female presents to the emergency department after ingesting 50 g of acetaminophen (paracetamol) as a self-harm attempt. She is found drowsy but arousable, with several episodes of vomiting. Her blood chemistry and transaminase levels are within normal limits, but her acetaminophen concentration is 400 mcg/mL, measured 6 hours post-ingestion. She is given 50 g activated charcoal and started on antidote therapy. What is the antidote of choice for paracetamol overdose?

   A. Vitamin K

   B. N-acetylcysteine

   C. Flumazenil

   D. Sodium bicarbonate

673

Answers:

1. **Answer C (Paracetamol)**

   Taking too much acetaminophen (known as paracetamol outside the United States) is the most common cause of acute liver failure in the Western world. Acute liver failure (ALF) is a rare but serious clinical syndrome, with an annual incidence of less than 10 cases per million population in developed countries. In the United States, approximately 2,000 cases of ALF are diagnosed each year. Acute liver failure primarily affects younger individuals and is associated with high morbidity and mortality rates. Geographically, acute liver failure is more common in developing countries due to the higher incidence of infectious hepatitis in these regions. However, regardless of geographic location, acetaminophen overdose remains a leading cause of acute liver failure, emphasizing the importance of awareness and appropriate use of this medication.

2. **Answer A (Glutathione depletion)**

   In paracetamol overdose, the primary mechanism of hepatotoxicity is glutathione depletion. In therapeutic doses, paracetamol is primarily metabolized by conjugation to inactive metabolites. However, in overdose, a minor route of metabolism involving oxidation by cytochrome P450 enzymes leads to the production of N-acetyl-p-benzoquinoneimine (NAPQI). NAPQI normally binds to glutathione, forming a non toxic conjugate. In cases of overdose, excessive NAPQI formation depletes hepatic glutathione stores. This depletion allows NAPQI to bind to hepatic cellular proteins, resulting in cellular injury and hepatotoxicity. Additionally, hepatotoxicity may occur with doses within the therapeutic range in cases of glutathione deficiency, inadequate nutrition, or due to P450 enzyme induction by chronic alcohol excess or concomitant use of other medications.

3. **Answer C ($\geq$ 150 mg/kg)**

   A dose of $\geq$ 150 mg/kg of paracetamol (acetaminophen) can cause liver damage. It's important to note that this threshold might be lower in people with chronic alcohol abuse or anorexia. Ingestion of as little as 150 mg/kg (75 mg/kg in high-risk patients) is potentially fatal. For obese patients weighing over 110 kg, the toxic dose in mg/kg should be calculated using 110 kg rather than their actual weight.

4. **Answer B (Chronic alcohol abuse)**

   Chronic alcohol abuse can lead to a lowered threshold for paracetamol-induced liver damage. Chronic alcohol consumption can induce hepatic enzyme activity, particularly the cytochrome P450 enzymes, which are involved in the metabolism of paracetamol. This increased enzyme activity can lead to enhanced production of the toxic metabolite N-acetyl-p-benzoquinoneimine (NAPQI) from paracetamol, contributing to liver damage. Additionally, chronic alcohol abuse can deplete hepatic glutathione stores, further increasing the risk of paracetamol-induced hepatotoxicity.

5. **Answer B (False)**

   Acute liver failure is not typically seen 4-8 hours after ingestion of a potentially fatal dose of paracetamol. In the early stages, patients may be asymptomatic or experience mild symptoms such as nausea, vomiting, and anorexia. Acute liver failure is more likely to occur at 24-36 hours post-ingestion, with symptoms such as confusion, encephalopathy, and jaundice developing over 36-72 hours. The peak of hepatocellular necrosis, a key feature of liver damage in paracetamol overdose, typically occurs 3-4 days after ingestion.

6. **Answer B (N-acetylcysteine)**

   The antidote of choice for paracetamol (acetaminophen) overdose is N-acetylcysteine (NAC). Paracetamol overdose can lead to the production of the toxic metabolite NAPQI when the liver metabolizes it. NAPQI can deplete hepatic stores of glutathione, leading to oxidative stress and hepatocellular damage. NAC works by replenishing glutathione stores, which helps to detoxify NAPQI and reduce liver injury. The timing of NAC administration is crucial, with maximal benefit seen when it is started within 8 hours of ingestion. NAC can still be effective if started later, but the efficacy decreases with time. Therefore, it is important to initiate NAC therapy as soon as possible in cases of paracetamol overdose. In addition to NAC, other treatments for paracetamol overdose may include activated charcoal to reduce absorption of the drug and supportive care to manage symptoms and complications. Regular monitoring of liver function tests, acetaminophen concentrations, and clinical status is essential to guide further management and ensure optimal patient outcomes.

Recommended literature

1. NHS Greater Glasgow and Clyde Area Drug and Therapeutics Committee. (2022). Paracetamol Overdose Protocol and Shortened N-acetylcysteine (NAC) Administration Chart. Adult paracetamol overdose protocol and shortened N-acetylcysteine (NAC) administration chart (904). H ttps://clinicalguidelines.nhsggc. org.uk/emergency-department/substance-related/adult-paracetamol-overdose-protocol-and-shortened-n-acetylcysteine-nac-administration-chart-904/
2. Pettie JM, Caparrotta TM, Hunter RW, et al. Safety and Efficacy of the SNAP 12-hour Acetylcysteine Regimen for the Treatment of Paracetamol Overdose. Clinical medicine. 2019;11:11-17.
3. Sharma CV, Mehta V. 2014. Paracetamol: mechanisms and updates, Continuing Education in Anaesthesia Critical Care & Pain, 14;4:153–158.

SALICYLATE TOXICITY

Questions:

1. Which of the following is a characteristic feature of salicylate toxicity?

    A. Hyponatremia

    B. Hypokalemia

    C. Hypercalcemia

    D. Hyperglycemia

2. What is the classic triad of mild salicylate toxicity?

    A. Hypertension, diaphoresis, tachycardia

    B. Nausea, vomiting, tinnitus

    C. Bradycardia, confusion, hypotension

    D. Hyperpnea, fever, restlessness

3. How does salicylate toxicity lead to respiratory alkalosis?

    A. Stimulation of the respiratory center

    B. Inhibition of the respiratory center

    C. Direct damage to the lungs

    D. Blockade of COX-1

4. Which of the following is NOT a complication of severe salicylate toxicity?

    A. Pulmonary edema

    B. Cerebral edema

    C. Rhabdomyolysis

    D. Hepatic failure

5. Activated charcoal is the first-line treatment for acute salicylate toxicity.

    A. True

    B. False

6. A 61-year-old woman presented to the emergency department after awakening with left-sided weakness. She complained of nausea, vomiting, and tinnitus. Following her arrival, she became acutely confused and complained of shortness of breath and blurred vision. On direct questioning, she gave a history of excessive use of salicylate for a headache a few hours before. Her initial serum salicylate level was significantly increased at 78.1 mg/dL (upper therapeutic limit, 19.9 mg/dL.) What is NOT the recommended management for salicylate toxicity?

    A. Activated charcoal

    B. Sodium bicarbonate

    C. Hyperventilation to correct acidosis

    D. Fluid resuscitation

Answers:

1. **Answer B (Hypokalemia)**

   The characteristic feature of salicylate toxicity is hypokalemia. Salicylate toxicity progresses through phases, with hyperventilation and respiratory alkalosis occurring initially, followed by paradoxical aciduria and renal potassium wasting, leading to hypokalemia. Other electrolyte abnormalities, such as hypocalcemia and hypophosphatemia, may also be present. Early symptoms include nausea, vomiting, diaphoresis, and tinnitus, while as toxicity advances, symptoms such as agitation, delirium, hallucinations, convulsions, lethargy, stupor, and hyperthermia may manifest, especially in young children.

2. **Answer B (Nausea, vomiting, tinnitus)**

   The classic triad of mild salicylate toxicity consists of nausea, vomiting, and tinnitus. These symptoms are among the earliest signs and symptoms of salicylate toxicity, along with other early manifestations such as vertigo, hyperventilation, tachycardia, and hyperactivity. As toxicity progresses, more severe symptoms such as agitation, delirium, hallucinations, convulsions, lethargy, and stupor may occur. Hyperthermia is also an indication of severe toxicity, particularly in young children. Therefore, recognizing the classic triad of symptoms is important in the early identification and management of salicylate toxicity.

3. **Answer A (Stimulation of the respiratory center)**

   Salicylate toxicity leads to respiratory alkalosis primarily due to the stimulation of the respiratory center in the brain. This stimulation increases the rate and depth of breathing, leading to hyperventilation. Hyperventilation, in turn, decreases the partial pressure of carbon dioxide ($PaCO_2$) in the blood, resulting in respiratory alkalosis.

4. **Answer D (Hepatic failure)**

   While hepatic failure can occur as a complication of severe toxicity from other substances, it is not a direct complication of salicylate toxicity. Salicylate toxicity primarily affects the respiratory and metabolic systems, leading to respiratory alkalosis, metabolic acidosis, and potentially severe complications such as pulmonary and cerebral edema, rhabdomyolysis, and cardiovascular collapse.

5. **Answer A (True)**

   Activated charcoal is the first-line treatment for acute salicylate toxicity. It decreases the absorption of salicylates in the gastrointestinal tract and thus reduces serum levels. However, it is not effective in cases of chronic salicylism. Gastric lavage may be considered in cases of acute ingestion of enteric-coated aspirin, but its use should be avoided if there is a risk of aspiration. Whole bowel irrigation has not been shown to be beneficial and may even increase the absorption of salicylates.

6. **Answer C (Hyperventilation to correct acidosis)**

   While hyperventilation is a characteristic feature of salicylate toxicity due to its stimulation of the respiratory center, it is not a recommended management strategy to correct acidosis. Instead, the primary treatment for salicylate toxicity includes fluid resuscitation with D5 and 3 amps of sodium bicarbonate, which helps correct the metabolic acidosis. Sodium bicarbonate administration is a cornerstone in managing salicylate toxicity as it helps to correct metabolic acidosis and enhances renal excretion of salicylates by alkalinizing the urine. Activated charcoal may be used to decrease the absorption of salicylates, especially if the ingestion was recent. However, its effectiveness in improving outcomes is unclear. Gastric lavage and whole bowel irrigation are generally not recommended due to the risks of aspiration and the potential for worsening toxicity. In severe cases of salicylate toxicity with significant acidosis, hemodialysis may be necessary to enhance the elimination of salicylates and correct acid-base disturbances. Hemodialysis is indicated in cases of severe acidosis (pH < 7.2), renal failure, pulmonary edema, altered mental status, or persistent salicylate levels above 100 mg/dL despite supportive care measures.

Recommended literature

1. Palmer BF, Clegg DJ. Salicylate Toxicity. N Engl J Med. 2020;382(26):2544-2555.

Toxicities
TCA TOXICITY

Questions:

1. Which of the following is NOT a mechanism of action of tricyclic antidepressants (TCAs)?

   A. Inhibition of presynaptic norepinephrine reuptake

   B. Inhibition of acetylcholinesterase

   C. Antimuscarinic effects

   D. Antihistaminergic effects

2. Which of the following TCAs carries the highest risk of toxicity?

   A. Amitriptyline

   B. Imipramine

   C. Nortriptyline

   D. Doxepin

3. Which of the following is NOT a sign or symptom of TCA toxicity?

   A. Mydriasis

   B. Sinus bradycardia

   C. Dry mouth

   D. Blurred vision

4. Which ECG finding is characteristic of TCA toxicity and predisposes to broad complex tachyarrhythmias?

   A. U Wave

   B. ST-elevation

   C. Large terminal R wave in aVR

   D. Tall T waves

5. Intralipid emulsion is a treatment option for TCA toxicity.

   A. True

   B. False

6. A 56-year-old woman is found unconscious at home with an empty bottle of amitriptyline nearby. Emergency medical services arrive, and she is transferred to the emergency department (ED). On initial assessment in the ED, her Glasgow Coma Scale (GCS) is 8, initial blood pressure is 100/60 mmHg, and an electrocardiogram (ECG) indicates a broad complex tachyarrhythmia (ventricular tachycardia) at approximately 160/min. Arterial blood gas (ABG) analysis reveals mixed acidosis with both respiratory depression and an increase in lactate levels. Which of the following antiarrhythmic agents is NOT contraindicated in this patient?

   A. Procainamide

   B. Flecainide

   C. Amiodarone

   D. Lidocaine

Answers:

1. **Answer B (Inhibition of acetylcholinesterase)**

Tricyclic antidepressants (TCAs) primarily work by inhibiting the reuptake of norepinephrine and serotonin, leading to increased levels of these neurotransmitters in the synaptic cleft. This action is thought to be the primary mechanism behind their antidepressant effects. Additionally, TCAs have antimuscarinic effects, contributing to side effects such as dry mouth, blurred vision, and constipation. They also have antihistaminergic effects, which can cause sedation. However, TCAs do not inhibit acetylcholinesterase; instead, they exert their anticholinergic effects by blocking muscarinic receptors.

2. **Answer A (Amitriptyline)**

Amitriptyline has a higher risk of toxicity compared to other TCAs, likely due to its stronger anticholinergic and cardiotoxic effects. The lethal dose of amitriptyline can vary, but serious toxicity is seen with doses between 10 and 30 mg/kg in adults. It is reported that ingestion of more than 1 g of TCA or a blood level of 1,000 mg/l predicts a high risk of mortality.

3. **Answer B (Sinus bradycardia)**

TCA toxicity can present with a range of signs and symptoms, including anticholinergic effects such as mydriasis, dry mouth, and blurred vision. Cardiovascular effects can include sinus tachycardia, not bradycardia. Other symptoms can include constipation, urinary retention, changes in mental status, agitation, seizures, and coma.

4. **Answer C (Large terminal R wave in aVR)**

TCA toxicity can manifest on an electrocardiogram (ECG) with characteristic findings such as QRS prolongation, PR/QT prolongation, and a large terminal R wave in aVR. This large terminal R wave in aVR indicates sodium channel blockade and is a high-risk marker for developing broad complex tachyarrhythmias, such as ventricular tachycardia (VT).

5. **Answer A (True)**

Intralipid emulsion treatment should be considered in hemodynamically unstable patients with overdoses of lipophilic TCAs. TCAs are highly protein-bound with an extensive volume of distribution, and enhanced elimination with dialysis and hemoperfusion is not effective. Therefore, using intralipid emulsion can help sequester the lipophilic TCAs and reduce their effects, making it a viable treatment option for TCA toxicity.

6. **Answer D (Lidocaine)**

In managing TCA toxicity, it is crucial to avoid certain antiarrhythmic agents that can exacerbate cardiac conduction abnormalities. Agents like Type 1A (e.g., procainamide), Type 1C (e.g., flecainide), and Type 3 (e.g., amiodarone) should be avoided due to their potential to prolong the QT interval and increase the risk of arrhythmias, mirroring the effects of TCAs. In contrast, lidocaine, a Class 1B antiarrhythmic, is considered safe in TCA toxicity. Lidocaine acts by blocking sodium channels, stabilizing the myocardial cell membrane, and reducing automaticity while slowing conduction. The recommended dose of lidocaine is 1-1.5 mg/kg. In this context, cardioversion is unlikely to succeed due to the arrhythmia induced by TCA toxicity.

Recommended literature

1. Lott C, Truhlář A, Alfonzo A, et al. European Resuscitation Council Guidelines 2021: Cardiac arrest in special circumstances [published correction appears in Resuscitation. 2021 Oct;167:91-92]. Resuscitation. 2021;161:152-219.
2. Peck, T., Wong, A., Norman, E., 2010. Anaesthetic implications of psychoactive drugs. Continuing Education in Anaesthesia Critical Care & Pain 10, 177-181.
3. Kerr GW, McGuffie AC, Wilkie S. Tricyclic antidepressant overdose: a review. Emerg Med J. 2001;18(4):236-241. doi:10.1136/emj.18.4.236

VASCULAR DISORDERS

ABDOMINAL AORTIC ANEURYSM

Questions:

1. Which of the following is a risk factor for the development of abdominal aortic aneurysm (AAA)?
   A. Female gender
   B. African American race
   C. History of deep vein thrombosis (DVT)
   D. Smoking

2. What is the most common etiology of AAA?
   A. Cystic medial necrosis
   B. Atherosclerosis
   C. Trauma
   D. Connective tissue disorders

3. Which medication is commonly started preoperatively for AAA repair to reduce cardiovascular risk?
   A. Diuretics
   B. ACE inhibitors
   C. Statins
   D. NSAIDs

4. Which of the following is a characteristic feature of EVAR (Endovascular Aneurysm Repair)?
   A. Insertion of a stent graft through a large incision in the abdomen
   B. Requires full systemic anticoagulation
   C. Utilizes small incisions in the groin for stent graft insertion
   D. Associated with higher rates of postoperative infections

5. Graft migration is the most common postoperative complication following EVAR.
   A. True
   B. False

6. A 74-year-old man presents for open AAA repair. He has a medical history of hypertension, dyslipidemia, and a long-standing smoking habit. Abdominal computed tomography (CT) reveals an infrarenal abdominal aortic aneurysm measuring 5.5 cm. The patient is scheduled for elective surgery due to the size of the aneurysm and the risk of rupture. Which analgesic technique provides superior pain control, reduces the duration of tracheal intubation and mechanical ventilation, and decreases the overall incidence of cardiovascular complications, acute respiratory failure, gastrointestinal complications, and renal insufficiency after abdominal aortic surgery?
   A. Epidural analgesia
   B. Intravenous opioid patient-controlled analgesia (PCA)
   C. Bilateral paravertebral blocks (PVB)
   D. Wound infiltration of local anesthetics

Answers:

1. Answer D (Smoking)

Smoking is a significant risk factor for the development of abdominal aortic aneurysms (AAA). Other risk factors for AAA include age over 60 years, male gender, family history of AAA, hyperlipidemia, hypertension, chronic obstructive pulmonary disease (COPD), diabetes, Caucasian race, sedentary lifestyle, coronary artery disease, and peripheral vascular disease.

2. Answer B (Atherosclerosis)

The most common etiology of AAA is atherosclerosis. Atherosclerosis is a progressive condition characterized by the buildup of plaque inside arteries, including the aorta. Over time, this plaque can lead to the weakening and dilation of the arterial wall, contributing to the formation of an aneurysm. Aneurysms develop when the force of blood flowing through the artery causes a weakened section of the arterial wall to balloon outwards. In the case of AAA, this occurs in the abdominal segment of the aorta. Atherosclerosis contributes to this process by causing arterial walls to become stiff and less elastic, making them more susceptible to dilation and aneurysm formation. While atherosclerosis is the primary cause of AAA, other less common etiologies include cystic medial necrosis, connective tissue disorders (such as Marfan syndrome and Ehlers-Danlos syndrome type IV), trauma, arteritis (inflammation of the arteries, including giant cell arteritis and Takayasu's disease), and infections (such as syphilis, salmonella, and mycotic infections).

3. Answer C (Statins)

Statins are commonly started preoperatively for AAA repair to reduce cardiovascular risk. This is because patients with AAA often have atherosclerosis and are at increased risk for cardiovascular events. Statins help stabilize atherosclerotic plaques and reduce the risk of perioperative cardiovascular complications. Additionally, patients undergoing AAA repair are often started on antiplatelet medications to further reduce the risk of cardiovascular events. Diuretics and ACE inhibitors may be considered in some patients based on their cardiovascular risk profile, but they are not specifically stated for cardiovascular risk reduction in the context of AAA repair. NSAIDs are generally avoided preoperatively due to their potential to increase the risk of bleeding.

4. Answer C (Utilizes small incisions in the groin for stent graft insertion)

In the EVAR procedure, a stent graft is inserted into the aneurysm through small incisions in the groin. This minimally invasive approach is a key characteristic of EVAR, as it avoids the need for a large abdominal incision. The stent graft is guided into place using fluoroscopic imaging, and once positioned correctly, it is expanded to seal off the aneurysm and reinforce the weakened aortic wall. This approach offers several advantages over traditional open repair, including reduced operative time, less postoperative pain, shorter hospital stays, and faster recovery times.

5. Answer B (False)

Graft migration is a potential complication of EVAR, but it is not the most common. The most common complications following EVAR are endoleak, graft infection, arterial rupture, limb thrombosis, and ischemia of vital organs. These complications are often related to technical aspects of endograft placement, such as vascular injury, endoleak from inadequate fixation or sealing of the graft, stent fractures, component separations, and endograft collapse.

6. Answer A (Epidural analgesia)

Intravenous opioid patient-controlled analgesia (PCA) with hydromorphone or morphine is the standard method of pain relief after abdominal aortic surgery, to which other methods are compared. However, epidural analgesia has been shown to provide superior pain control, reduce the duration of tracheal intubation and mechanical ventilation by 20%, and decrease the overall incidence of cardiovascular complications, acute respiratory failure, gastrointestinal complications, and renal insufficiency. Patients presenting for AAA resection often have associated thromboembolic and cardiovascular disease and may take antiplatelet agents and anticoagulants. Therefore, medication and preoperative coagulation studies should be reviewed before insertion of epidural catheters. Lower thoracic epidural catheters are typically used in AAA surgery. Typically, epidural analgesia is continued for 3-5 days. Epidural analgesia is especially useful in patients with chronic obstructive pulmonary disease, as it decreases the duration of mechanical ventilation and the incidence of pulmonary complications. Bilateral paravertebral blocks (PVB) offer an alternate effective method of pain relief with infrequent neurologic and hemodynamic effects. In conclusion, epidural analgesia is the preferred analgesic technique for open AAA repair due to its superior pain control and potential for reducing postoperative complications.

Recommended literature

1. Kothandan H, Haw Chieh GL, Khan SA, Karthekeyan RB, Sharad SS. Anesthetic considerations for endovascular abdominal aortic aneurysm repair. Ann Card Anaesth. 2016;19(1):132–141.
2. Al-Hashimi M, Thompson J. Anaesthesia for elective open abdominal aortic aneurysm repair, Continuing Education in Anaesthesia Critical Care & Pain, Volume 13, Issue 6, December 2013, Pages 208–212.
3. Gelzinis TA, Subramaniam K. Anesthesia for Open Abdominal Aortic Aneurysm Repair. Anesthesia and Perioperative Care for Aortic Surgery. 2010;301–327.
4. Nataraj V, Mortimer AJ. Endovascular abdominal aortic aneurysm repair, Continuing Education in Anaesthesia Critical Care & Pain, Volume 4, Issue 3, June 2004, Pages 91–94.

CAROTID ENDARTERECTOMY

Questions:

1. What is NOT the primary goal of carotid endarterectomy (CEA)?
   A. To improve blood flow to the brain
   B. To reduce the risk of stroke or transient ischemic attack
   C. To remove plaque from the carotid artery
   D. To prevent myocardial infarction

2. Which of the following is NOT a potential direct complication of CEA?
   A. Stroke or transient ischemic attack
   B. Myocardial infarction
   C. Cranial nerve injury
   D. Pneumothorax

3. Which of the following is a potential complication of CEA related to the cardiovascular system?
   A. Hyperperfusion syndrome
   B. Infection
   C. Labile blood pressure
   D. Seizures

4. Which anesthesia technique can be utilized for CEA?
   A. Superficial cervical plexus block
   B. Cervical epidural
   C. General anesthesia
   D. All of the above

5. Hematoma formation following CEA can lead to swelling and potential airway obstruction.
   A. True
   B. False

6. A 70-year-old male with a history of hypertension, hyperlipidemia, and smoking is scheduled for a carotid endarterectomy. His current medications include Enalapril 10 mg, Nebivolol 5 mg, Atorvastatin 20 mg, and Aspirin 75 mg. Which of the following medications should be stopped on the day of surgery for a patient undergoing carotid endarterectomy?
   A. ACE inhibitors
   B. Beta-blockers
   C. Statins
   D. Aspirin

Answers:

1. Answer D (To prevent myocardial infarction)

Carotid endarterectomy (CEA) is a surgical procedure performed to remove plaque buildup in the common carotid and internal carotid arteries to improve blood flow. The primary goal of CEA is to reduce the risk of stroke or transient ischemic attack (TIA) by removing the plaque that can lead to blockage or clot formation in the carotid artery. By improving blood flow to the brain, CEA significantly reduces the risk of stroke or TIA. While improving blood flow and reducing the risk of stroke are primary goals of CEA, preventing myocardial infarction is not a primary goal of this procedure. The focus of CEA is on the carotid arteries and their impact on cerebral circulation rather than on the coronary arteries and the risk of myocardial infarction.

2. Answer D (Pneumothorax)

CEA is a surgical procedure performed to remove plaque buildup in the carotid arteries to reduce the risk of stroke or (TIA). While CEA is associated with several potential complications, pneumothorax is not typically one of them. Common complications of CEA include stroke or TIA, myocardial infarction, cranial nerve injury, swelling and bleeding around the incision site, intracerebral hemorrhage, seizures, repeated or new blockage of the carotid artery, infection, high blood pressure, irregular heartbeat, and blocked airway from swelling or bleeding in the neck.

3. Answer C (Labile blood pressure)

CEA is a surgical procedure performed to remove plaque buildup in the carotid arteries to reduce the risk of stroke or TIA. Labile blood pressure, including hypertension and hypotension, can occur as a complication of CEA. Changes in blood pressure can be a result of various factors related to the surgery, carotid sinus manipulation, changes in vascular tone, or the release of vasoactive substances.

4. Answer D (All of the above)

CEA can be performed using various anesthesia techniques, including superficial cervical plexus block, cervical epidural, and general anesthesia. The choice of anesthesia technique depends on factors such as patient preference, surgeon preference, and the patient's medical condition. Superficial cervical plexus block can provide anesthesia to the surgical site and may be used as the primary anesthetic technique for CEA in some cases. Cervical epidural anesthesia can also be used to provide anesthesia and analgesia for CEA. General anesthesia is another option for CEA and may be preferred in some cases to ensure the patient is unconscious and pain-free during the procedure. General anesthesia can also allow for controlled ventilation, which may be beneficial in patients with significant comorbidities or who require careful hemodynamic management. The choice of anesthesia technique for CEA should be made based on the individual patient's needs and the preferences of the surgical team. Each technique has its advantages and potential complications, so the decision should be made after careful consideration of the risks and benefits of each option.

5. Answer A (True)

Hematoma formation following CEA can lead to swelling and potential airway obstruction. If the hematoma is large or expanding, it can compress the airway and lead to obstruction, which can be life-threatening. Therefore, careful monitoring for signs of hematoma formation and prompt intervention, if necessary, is important in the postoperative management of patients undergoing CEA.

6. Answer A (ACE inhibitors))

Patients undergoing CEA who are chronically treated with angiotensin-converting enzyme inhibitors (ACEIs) (Enalapril) may develop hypotension after induction of general anesthesia. It is recommended to cease ACE inhibitor therapy at least 10 hours before surgery to reduce the risk of intraoperative hypotension. This precaution is important as some patients may be resistant to therapeutic doses of vasopressors, which can pose serious concerns for hemodynamic management during surgery.

Recommended literature

1. Zdrehuş C. Anaesthesia for carotid endarterectomy – general or loco-regional?. Rom J Anaesth Intensive Care. 2015;22(1):17-24.
2. Howell SJ. Carotid endarterectomy, BJA: British Journal of Anaesthesia, Volume 99, Issue 1, July 2007, Pages 119-131.

Made in United States
Orlando, FL
25 January 2025

57765642R00376